W9-CHL-510

In this table we see historical data for the various components of nominal GDP. These are given in the first four columns. We then show the rest of the national income accounts going from GDP to NDP to NI to PI to DPI. The last column gives real GDP.

Year	The Sum of These Expenditures: Personal Consumption Expenditures	Gross Private Domestic Investment	Government Purchases of Goods and Services	Net Exports	Equals: Gross Domestic Product	Less: Depreciation	Equals: Net Domestic Product	Plus: Net U.S. Income Earned Abroad	Less: Indirect Business Taxes, Transfers, Adjustments	Equals: National Income	Less: Undistributed Corporate Profits	Social Security Taxes	Corporate Income Taxes	Plus: Transfer Payments and Net Interest Earnings	Equals: Personal Income	Less: Personal Income Taxes and Nontax Payments	Equals: Disposable Personal Income	Real GDP (2005 dollars)
1985	2720.3	736.2	879.0	-115.2	4220.3	506.7	3713.6	26.5	16.7	3723.4	133.4	281.4	99.4	317.5	3526.7	417.4	3109.3	6839.7
1986	2899.7	746.5	949.3	-132.7	4462.8	531.1	3931.7	17.8	47.2	3902.3	103.7	303.4	109.7	336.9	3722.4	437.3	3285.1	7076.0
1987	3100.2	785.0	999.5	-145.2	4739.5	561.9	4177.6	17.9	21.8	4173.7	126.1	323.1	130.4	353.3	3947.4	489.1	3458.3	7316.0
1988	3353.6	821.6	1039.0	-110.4	5103.8	597.6	4506.2	23.6	-19.6	4549.4	161.1	361.5	141.6	368.5	4253.7	505.0	3748.7	7618.0
1989	3598.5	874.9	1099.1	-88.2	5484.4	644.3	4840.1	26.2	39.7	4826.6	122.6	385.2	146.1	415.1	4587.8	566.1	4021.7	7887.8
1990	3839.9	861.0	1180.2	-78.0	5803.1	682.5	5120.6	34.8	66.3	5089.1	123.3	410.1	145.4	468.3	4878.6	592.8	4285.8	8034.8
1991	3986.1	802.9	1234.4	-27.5	5995.9	725.9	5270.0	30.4	72.5	5227.9	131.9	430.2	138.6	523.8	5051.0	586.7	4464.3	8022.3
1992	4235.3	864.8	1271.0	-33.2	6337.9	751.9	5586.0	29.7	102.9	5512.8	142.7	455.0	148.7	595.6	5362.0	610.6	4751.4	8288.7
1993	4477.9	953.4	1291.2	-65.0	6657.5	776.4	5881.1	31.9	139.6	5773.4	168.1	477.7	171.0	601.9	5558.5	646.6	4911.9	8511.0
1994	4743.3	1097.1	1325.5	-93.6	7072.3	833.7	6238.6	26.2	142.5	6122.3	171.8	508.2	193.7	593.9	5842.5	690.7	5151.8	8853.5
1995	4975.8	1144.0	1369.2	-91.4	7397.6	878.4	6519.2	35.8	101.1	6453.9	223.8	532.8	218.7	673.7	6152.3	744.1	5408.2	9075.0
1996	5256.8	1240.3	1416.0	-96.2	7816.9	918.1	6898.8	35.0	93.7	6840.1	256.9	555.2	231.7	724.3	6520.6	832.1	5688.5	9411.0
1997	5547.4	1389.8	1468.7	-101.6	8304.3	974.4	7329.9	33.0	70.7	7292.2	287.9	587.2	246.1	744.1	6915.1	926.3	5988.8	9834.9
1998	5879.5	1509.1	1518.3	-159.9	8747.0	1030.2	7716.8	21.3	-14.7	7752.8	201.7	624.2	248.3	744.4	7423.0	1027.1	6395.9	10245.6
1999	6342.8	1641.5	1631.3	-262.1	9353.5	1101.3	8252.2	33.8	-72.0	8358.0	255.3	661.4	258.6	728.1	7910.8	1107.5	6803.3	10779.8
2000	6830.4	1772.2	1731.0	-382.1	9951.5	1187.8	8763.7	39.0	-136.2	8938.9	174.8	691.7	265.2	752.2	8559.4	1232.2	7327.2	11226.0
2001	7148.8	1661.9	1846.4	-371.0	10286.1	1281.5	9004.6	43.6	-137.0	9185.2	192.3	717.5	204.1	812.0	8883.3	1234.8	7648.5	11347.2
2002	7439.2	1647.0	1983.3	-427.2	10642.3	1292.0	9350.3	30.7	-27.5	9408.5	294.5	734.3	192.6	873.0	9060.1	1050.4	8009.7	11553.0
2003	7804.0	1729.7	2112.6	-504.1	11142.2	1336.5	9805.7	68.1	33.6	9840.2	325.1	758.9	243.3	865.2	9378.1	1000.3	8377.8	11840.7
2004	8285.1	1968.6	2232.8	-618.7	11867.8	1436.1	10431.7	53.7	-48.6	10534.0	384.4	805.2	307.4	900.2	9937.2	1047.8	8889.4	12263.8
2005	8819.0	2172.2	2369.9	-722.7	12638.4	1609.5	11028.9	68.5	-176.4	11273.8	456.9	850.0	413.7	932.7	10485.9	1208.6	9277.3	12638.4
2006	9322.7	2327.2	2518.4	-769.4	13398.9	1615.2	11783.7	58.0	-189.5	12031.2	497.5	902.4	468.9	1105.7	11268.1	1352.4	9915.7	12976.2
2007	9826.4	2288.5	2676.5	-713.8	14077.6	1720.5	12357.1	64.4	-26.7	12448.2	403.4	942.3	450.4	1242.0	11894.1	1491.0	10403.1	13254.1
2008	10129.9	2136.1	2883.2	-707.8	14441.4	1998.9	12442.5	66.8	-126.0	12635.2	324.9	924.8	440.6	1293.9	12238.8	1432.4	10806.4	13312.2
2009[a]	9912.8	1420.9	3440.1	-390.4	14383.4	2219.0	12164.4	67.2	231.5	12000.1	350.9	942.1	449.2	1654.1	11912.0	1057.4	10854.6	13096.8
2010[a]	10008.9	1433.2	3489.9	-404.2	14527.8	2243.1	12284.7	66.3	148.4	12202.6	380.8	946.3	451.3	1569.5	11993.7	1117.3	10876.4	13223.8

[a] author's estimates

*Note: Some rows may not add up due to rounding errors.

MACROECONOMIC PRINCIPLES

Nominal versus Real Interest Rate

$$i_n = i_r + \text{expected rate of inflation}$$

where i_n = nominal rate of interest
i_r = real rate of interest

Marginal versus Average Tax Rates

$$\text{Marginal tax rate} = \frac{\text{change in taxes due}}{\text{change in taxable income}}$$

$$\text{Average tax rate} = \frac{\text{total taxes due}}{\text{total taxable income}}$$

GDP—The Expenditure and Income Approaches

$$\text{GDP} = C + I + G + X$$

where C = consumption expenditures
I = investment expenditures
G = government expenditures
X = net exports

$$\text{GDP} = \text{wages} + \text{rent} + \text{interest} + \text{profits}$$

Say's Law

Supply creates its own demand, or *desired* aggregate expenditures will equal *actual* aggregate expenditures.

Saving, Consumption, and Investment

$$\text{Consumption} + \text{saving} = \text{disposable income}$$

$$\text{Saving} = \text{disposable income} - \text{consumption}$$

Average and Marginal Propensities

$$\text{APC} = \frac{\text{real consumption}}{\text{real disposable income}}$$

$$\text{APS} = \frac{\text{real saving}}{\text{real disposable income}}$$

$$\text{MPC} = \frac{\text{change in real consumption}}{\text{change in real disposable income}}$$

$$\text{MPS} = \frac{\text{change in real saving}}{\text{change in real disposable income}}$$

The Multiplier Formula

$$\text{Multiplier} = \frac{1}{\text{MPS}} = \frac{1}{1 - \text{MPC}}$$

$$\text{Multiplier} \times \begin{array}{c}\text{change in} \\ \text{autonomous} \\ \text{spending}\end{array} = \begin{array}{c}\text{change in} \\ \text{equilibrium level} \\ \text{of national income}\end{array}$$

Relationship Between Bond Prices and Interest Rates

The market price of existing (old) bonds is inversely related to "the" rate of interest prevailing in the economy.

Government Spending and Taxation Multipliers

$$M_g = \frac{1}{\text{MPS}}$$

$$M_t = -\text{MPC} \times \frac{1}{\text{MPS}}$$

Economics Today

Fifteenth Edition
UPDATED EDITION

Roger LeRoy Miller

Institute for University Studies, Arlington, Texas

Addison-Wesley

Boston   Columbus   Indianapolis   New York   San Francisco   Upper Saddle River
Amsterdam   Cape Town   Dubai   London   Madrid   Milan   Munich   Paris   Montreal   Toronto
Delhi   Mexico City   Sao Paulo   Sydney   Hong Kong   Seoul   Singapore   Taipei   Tokyo

The Pearson Series in Economics

Abel/Bernanke/Croushore
Macroeconomics*

Bade/Parkin
Foundations of Economics*

Bierman/Fernandez
*Game Theory with Economic
Applications*

Blanchard
Macroeconomics

Blau/Ferber/Winkler
*The Economics of Women,
Men and Work*

**Boardman/Greenberg/Vining/
Weimer**
Cost-Benefit Analysis

Boyer
*Principles of Transportation
Economics*

Branson
*Macroeconomic Theory
and Policy*

Brock/Adams
*The Structure of American
Industry*

Bruce
*Public Finance and the
American Economy*

Carlton/Perloff
*Modern Industrial
Organization*

Case/Fair/Oster
Principles of Economics*

Caves/Frankel/Jones
*World Trade and Payments:
An Introduction*

Chapman
*Environmental Economics:
Theory, Application,
and Policy*

Cooter/Ulen
Law & Economics

Downs
*An Economic Theory of
Democracy*

Ehrenberg/Smith
Modern Labor Economics

Ekelund/Ressler/Tollison
Economics*

Farnham
Economics for Managers

Folland/Goodman/Stano
*The Economics of Health
and Health Care*

Fort
Sports Economics

Froyen
Macroeconomics

Fusfeld
The Age of the Economist

Gerber
International Economics

Gordon
Macroeconomics

Greene
Econometric Analysis

Gregory
Essentials of Economics

Gregory/Stuart
*Russian and Soviet Economic
Performance and Structure*

Hartwick/Olewiler
*The Economics of Natural
Resource Use*

Heilbroner/Milberg
*The Making of the Economic
Society*

Heyne/Boettke/Prychitko
*The Economic Way
of Thinking*

Hoffman/Averett
*Women and the Economy:
Family, Work, and Pay*

Holt
*Markets, Games and
Strategic Behavior*

Hubbard
*Money, the Financial System,
and the Economy*

Hubbard/OBrien
Economics*

Hughes/Cain
American Economic History

Husted/Melvin
International Economics

Jehle/Reny
*Advanced Microeconomic
Theory*

Johnson-Lans
A Health Economics Primer

Keat/Young
Managerial Economics

Klein
*Mathematical Methods
for Economics*

Krugman/Obstfeld
*International Economics:
Theory & Policy**

Laidler
The Demand for Money

Leeds/von Allmen
The Economics of Sports

Leeds/von Allmen/Schiming
Economics*

Lipsey/Ragan/Storer
*Economics**

Lynn
*Economic Development:
Theory and Practice for a
Divided World*

Melvin
*International Money and
Finance*

Miller
*Economics Today**

*Understanding Modern
Economics*

Miller/Benjamin
*The Economics of Macro
Issues*

Miller/Benjamin/North
*The Economics of Public
Issues*

Mills/Hamilton
Urban Economics

Mishkin
*The Economics of Money,
Banking, and Financial
Markets**

*The Economics of Money,
Banking, and Financial
Markets, Business School
Edition**

Murray
*Econometrics: A Modern
Introduction*

Nafziger
*The Economics of
Developing Countries*

O'Sullivan/Sheffrin/Perez
*Economics: Principles,
Applications and Tools**

Parkin
*Economics**

Perloff
*Microeconomics**

*Microeconomics:
Theory and Applications
with Calculus*

**Perman/Common/
McGilvray/Ma**
*Natural Resources and
Environmental Economics*

Phelps
Health Economics

Pindyck/Rubinfeld
*Microeconomics**

**Riddell/Shackelford/Stamos/
Schneider**
*Economics: A Tool for
Critically Understanding
Society*

Ritter/Silber/Udell
*Principles of Money,
Banking & Financial Markets**

Roberts
*The Choice: A Fable of Free
Trade and Protection*

Rohlf
*Introduction to Economic
Reasoning*

Ruffin/Gregory
Principles of Economics

Sargent
*Rational Expectations and
Inflation*

Sawyer/Sprinkle
International Economics

Scherer
*Industry Structure, Strategy,
and Public Policy*

Schiller
*The Economics of Poverty
and Discrimination*

Sherman
Market Regulation

Silberberg
*Principles of
Microeconomics*

Stock/Watson
*Introduction to
Econometrics*

*Introduction to
Econometrics,*

Brief Edition

Studenmund
*Using Econometrics:
A Practical Guide*

Tietenberg/Lewis
*Environmental and Natural
Resource Economics*

*Environmental Economics
and Policy*

Todaro/Smith
Economic Development

Waldman
Microeconomics

Waldman/Jensen
*Industrial Organization:
Theory and Practice*

Weil
Economic Growth

Williamson
Macroeconomics

Dedication

To Richard Wolf
Your kindness and support for all of my family have known no bounds.
You truly are one of the world's good guys. — R. L. M.

Editorial Director: Sally Yagan
Editor in Chief: Donna Battista
Acquisitions Editor: Noel Kamm Seibert
Editorial Assistant: Carolyn Terbush
Managing Editor: Nancy H. Fenton
Senior Production Supervisor: Kathryn Dinovo
Supplements Production Coordinator: Alison Eusden
Rights and Permissions Advisor: Michael Joyce
Manager, Visual Research: Beth Brenzel
Manager, Rights and Permissions: Zina Arabia

Director of Media: Susan Schoenberg
Senior Media Producer: Melissa Honig
Content Leads, MyEconLab: Douglas Ruby and Noel Lotz
Director of Marketing: Kate Valentine
AVP/Executive Marketing Manager: Lori DeShazo
Marketing Assistant: Justin Jacob
Senior Manufacturing Buyer: Carol Melville
Cover Designer: Christina Gleason
Text Designer: Geri Davis, The Davis Group, Inc.
Production Coordinator: Orr Book Services
Compositor: Nesbitt Graphics, Inc.
Art Studio: ElectraGraphics, Inc.

Photo credits appear on page C-1, which constitutes a continuation of the copyright page.

Library of Congress Cataloging-in-Publication Data
Miller, Roger LeRoy.
  Economics today / Roger LeRoy Miller. -- 15th ed.
      p. cm. -- (The Addison-Wesley series in economics)
  Includes index.
  ISBN 978-0-321-57131-1 (main volume; chapters 1-34) -- ISBN 978-0-321-59453-2
      (macro view; chapters 1-19 and 33-34) -- ISBN 978-0-321-59452-5 (micro view;
      chapters 1-6 and 20-34)
  1. Economics. 2. Microeconomics. 3. Macroeconomics. I. Title.

HB171.5.M642 2010
330--dc22

                                                                    2008049775

4 5 6 7 8 9 10—CRK—13 12 11

Addison-Wesley
is an imprint of

PEARSON

www.pearsonhighered.com

ISBN-13: 978-0-13-213946-5
ISBN-10: 0-13-213946-4

Brief Contents

Contents

Part Seven   Labor Resources and the Environment

One-Semester Course Outline

Preface

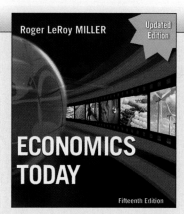

Economics is More Relevant than Ever

One might say that for economists, these are exciting times. Since I wrote the latest edition of *Economics Today*, the U.S. has entered into what everyone is calling the Great Recession. So much has changed in the American economy and indeed worldwide that I felt compelled to offer an updated version of my text.

I have always championed the notion that the way to motivate students to learn more about economics is to present them with current and relevant examples. What better way to do so than to include some of the major changes that have happened to our economy in the last several years. Some of my colleagues contend that they have an increasingly difficult time getting their students interested in economics because the concepts and theories seem so abstract. Today, there is nothing abstract about an unemployment rate hovering around 10 percent—such a historically high rate of unemployment is going to affect your students' job possibilities when they graduate. As another example, what has occurred in the housing market can serve as a lesson to young people today about what happens when certain policies lead to an over expansion in home financing.

> *Students learn most effectively when they can apply the concepts to their everyday lives.*

> *This Updated Edition presents coverage of the most recent economic events and changes.*

Those of you who have been using the current edition of *Economics Today* know that I added a new feature in every chapter called *You Are There*. I have updated a number of these features to make sure they cover some very current events. For example, in Chapter 13, I ask the students to contemplate whether temporary tax cuts have smaller effects on total planned spending than do long-lasting tax reductions. In Chapter 14, I have students look at why the U.S. government has to reassure Asian owners of U.S. government debt that they have nothing to worry about (let's hope!). Other chapters have new *You Are There* features such as Chapter 15—"Is It Time for the Federal Reserve to Issue Its Own Bonds?" and Chapter 17—"The Fed Finds That the Harder It Works to Push Down Treasury Bond Rates, the More They Rise."

Of course, because this is an updated edition, all of the changes that I made to the previous edition remain. In particular, I have retained the emphasis on assessment, given its importance on so many college campuses. Students will continue to utilize the quick quizzes, and you will still be able to use the Clicker/Personal Response System questions. MyEconLab continues to be the gold standard for online course management and tutorial systems that allow for self-assessment.

The Great Recession has brought with it more institutional changes put into place at a faster pace than perhaps any time since the 1930s. What better time to use the real world to show the relevance of our discipline?

—Roger LeRoy Miller

New to This Updated Edition

This **Updated Edition** of *Economics Today* seeks to enable students to recognize the relevance of economics principles in their daily lives, with the aim to helping students to see the advantages of studying and learning key economic concepts. Of course, I have focused on the dramatic changes that have occurred since the Great Recession began not long ago.

Issues associated with the financial crunch and Great Recession feature prominently in this *UPDATED* edition along with other important changes. They include:

- Federal government **bailout policy as it affects the automobile sector** in Chapter 5; specifically, why *General Motors Has Become "Government Motors."*
- How state governments have reacted to their increased deficits (in Chapter 5) by increasing **marginal tax rates,** specifically with what are being called "millionaire taxes."
- Chapter 7 considers how economists **distinguish depressions from recessions.**
- Chapter 11 discusses the altered relationship between **oil prices and economic activity in the late 2000s.**
- Chapter 13 delves into reasons why **the 2009 "Fiscal Stimulus Package"** had a muted impact on the U.S. economy, as well as how the states created **direct fiscal offsets to increased federal spending**.
- Chapter 14 evaluates the **massive expansion of the federal budget deficit** and asks the question, "What will happen to the share of GDP going to government?"
- I look at **Federal Reserve Interest-Rate-Based Policymaking in the Midst of a Banking Meltdown and Severe Economic Downturn.** This edition includes expanded discussions of the Fed's operation of its **interest-rate-based monetary policy** procedure during the crisis.
- Chapter 15 explains the roles of Fed policymaking and deposit insurance during the **financial panic of the late 2000s.**
- Chapter 16 evaluates the effect of the huge **run-up in excess reserves** on the money multiplier.
- Chapter 17 analyzes implications of the **sudden plunge in the income velocity of money.**
- Chapter 18 considers policy implications of the **New Keynesian theory** in the face of a **jump in unemployment.** I look at the eventual threat of stagflation.
- In Chapter 33, I look at how **protectionist history** seems to be repeating itself.
- In Chapter 34, I examine the implications of a **weakening dollar** and whether Middle Eastern oil producers want to switch to another currency for pricing petroleum.

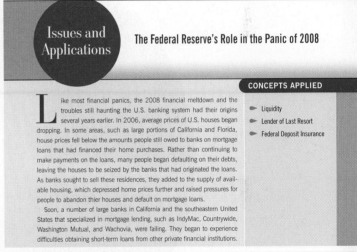

Issues and Applications

The Federal Reserve's Role in the Panic of 2008

CONCEPTS APPLIED
- Liquidity
- Lender of Last Resort
- Federal Deposit Insurance

Like most financial panics, the 2008 financial meltdown and the troubles still haunting the U.S. banking system had their origins several years earlier. In 2006, average prices of U.S. houses began dropping. In some areas, such as large portions of California and Florida, house prices fell below the amounts people still owed to banks on mortgage loans that had financed their home purchases. Rather than continuing to make payments on the loans, many people began defaulting on their debts, leaving the houses to be seized by the banks that had originated the loans. As banks sought to sell these residences, they added to the supply of available housing, which depressed home prices further and raised pressures for people to abandon thier houses and default on mortgage loans.

Soon, a number of large banks in California and the southeastern United States that specialized in mortgage lending, such as IndyMac, Countrywide, Washington Mutual, and Wachovia, were failing. They began to experience difficulties obtaining short-term loans from other private financial institutions.

Making the Connection— from the Classroom to the Real World

Today's students need to connect and apply economic theory to their diverse interests and lives. *Economics Today* speaks to students of all backgrounds, providing relentlessly current examples that effectively demonstrate economic principles. For the 15th edition, **95 percent** of the examples were new. In this updated edition, there are **42** new or revised examples.

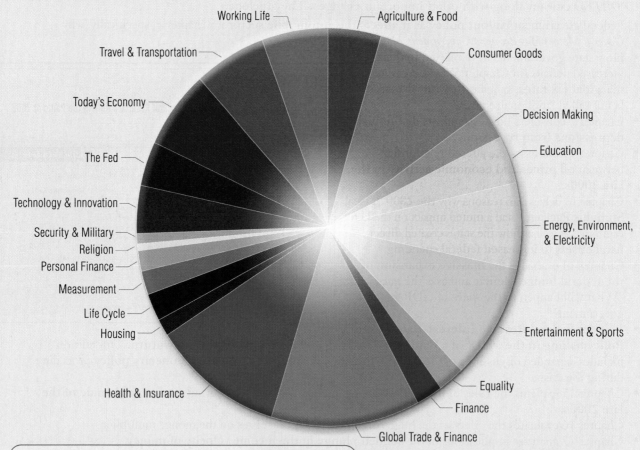

Working Life — Agriculture & Food

Travel & Transportation — Consumer Goods

Today's Economy — Decision Making

The Fed — Education

Technology & Innovation —

Security & Military — Energy, Environment, & Electricity

Religion —

Personal Finance —

Measurement —

Life Cycle — Entertainment & Sports

Housing —

Health & Insurance — Equality

Finance

Global Trade & Finance

Domestic topics and events are presented through thought-provoking discussions, such as:

- Why Are Men Confronting Higher Unemployment Than Women?
- Zero-Priced Seats at Graduation Ceremonies Become Hot Items
- Explaining the Rising U.S. "Saving Rate"

EXAMPLE
Cash-Squeezed Small Businesses Resort to Barter

In the midst of the Great Recession of the late 2000s, many small businesses found that customer payments were trickling in slowly. In addition, small businesses had difficulty obtaining loans from banks hit hard by financial troubles of their own. Consequently, a number of small firms found themselves strapped for cash.

Indeed, so many small businesses in the United States were low on cash that they resorted to bartering goods and services. For instance, a small accounting firm might provide its services to a small advertising agency in exchange for advertising services. In many cases, small businesses also allowed customers pinched for cash and behind on paying their bills to provide goods and services instead. A company with past-due bills from a sandwich shop, for example, might accept payment from the shop in the form of catered lunches. Estimates indicate that during 2008 and 2009, small U.S. companies conducted barter transactions worth nearly $25 billion.

FOR CRITICAL ANALYSIS
Why do you suppose that during the recession, many small businesses utilized the services of "barter companies" that specialize in matching parties interested in barter transactions— typically in exchange for fees paid in cash?

Important policy questions help students see how they can evaluate public debates, such as:

- Incentives Coax Senior Citizens from Behind the Wheel
- The U.S. Military Confronts a Trade-Off
- Why It Can Pay to Form a Partnership Instead of a Corporation

POLICY EXAMPLE

"Millionaire" Taxes Become the New Government Fad

In the mid-2000s, California established a 1 percent income tax *surcharge*—a special additional tax—on incomes of millionaires, defined as people earning more than $1 million per year. Shortly thereafter, New Jersey created its own "millionaire" tax by establishing a new top tax bracket with a tax rate 2.6 percentage points higher than the previous top rate. New Jersey, however, decided that "millionaires" were people earning more than $500,000 per year. A few years later, New York government officials also decided to impose a "millionaire" tax surcharge, but they defined a "millionaire" as someone earning $300,000 per year. By the late 2000s, the idea of a federal "millionaire" tax surcharge was catching on in Washington, D.C. Members of the U.S. House of Representatives introduced bills that would apply a range of "millionaire" tax surcharges to annual incomes above $280,000.

FOR CRITICAL ANALYSIS

Does imposing special "millionaire" taxes make an income tax system more or less progressive?

INTERNATIONAL EXAMPLE

In Germany, Fractional Reserve Banking Moves to the Auto Showroom

Even as auto sales slumped in Germany in 2008 and 2009, savers began withdrawing funds from traditional depository institutions and placing them on deposit with the banking arms of auto manufacturers. Between November 2008 and March 2009, for instance, deposits at Volkswagen's banking subsidiary increased by more than 70 percent, and deposits at Mercedes-Benz Bank increased by more than 100 percent. The automakers promptly funneled the portion of

INTERNATIONAL POLICY EXAMPLE

Why the British Government Must Pay More Interest on Its Debt

Bonds issued by the British government receive the highest risk ratings, meaning that risk-assessment services have viewed as almost zero the likelihood of even a partial default on these obligations. Since the spring of 2009, however, a key bond-rating agency, Standard & Poor's (S&P) Rating Service, has placed British bonds in what it calls the "negative" category among highest-rated bonds. When it put United Kingdom bonds in this classification, S&P indicated that it would be watching carefully for an increased risk that the British government might be unable to fully meet its future debt responsibilities. The highest-rated bonds that receive negative ratings from S&P commonly are downgraded to a lower category within a couple of years. Thus, S&P's action signaled a likelihood of a future downgrade in its ratings of British government bonds.

The negative rating had an immediate effect on the interest rate that the British government was required to offer to induce individuals and companies to continue buying its bonds. Within minutes, this interest rate rose five one-hundredths of a percentage point above the previous level. Thus, since the spring of 2009, the British government has had to pay almost $500,000 more in interest for each additional $1 billion that it has borrowed.

FOR CRITICAL ANALYSIS

Why do you suppose that individuals and companies require a higher interest payment to induce them to lend to governments that present higher risks of default on their debt obligations?

Global and international policy examples emphasize the continued importance of international perspectives and policy decisions, including:

- In a Global Economy, World Saving Equals World Investment
- A French Handbag Manufacturer Opts for Multitasking
- "Struggling to Boost Government Spending in Peru—and in the United States
- EU Governments Get Serious About Emissions—Or Do They?

Information technology is presented in relevant e-commerce examples, such as:

- The New Online Dating Incentive: Health Insurance
- Digital Imaging Boosts the Supply of Dentistry Services
- Help, I'm Shopping, and I Can't Stop!

E-COMMERCE EXAMPLE

Failure to Hit the Print Icon May Yield a New Leading Indicator

During the most significant business downturn since World War II, economic analysts of the late 2000s noticed that another downturn was in progress. Sales of printer cartridges by Hewlett-Packard and other producers of printing consumables, which had displayed positive annual growth rates for years, started to decline just before the recession began. Furthermore, sales dropped even more just before the recession picked up steam in the first and second quarters of 2009. Now some forecasters have added sales of printer cartridges to their list of potential leading indicators. Current choices by businesses and individuals to print fewer pages, the forecasters theorize, may reflect decisions to produce fewer goods and services in the future.

FOR CRITICAL ANALYSIS

Can you suggest a rationale for why reductions in printed pages could suggest that firms may be about to cut back on production of new goods and services

Helping Students Focus and Think Critically

New and revised pedagogical tools in each chapter engage students and help them focus on the central ideas in economics today.

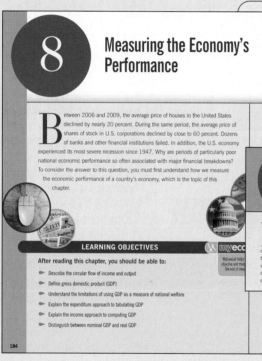

8 Measuring the Economy's Performance

Between 2006 and 2009, the average price of houses in the United States declined by nearly 20 percent. During the same period, the average price of shares of stock in U.S. corporations declined by close to 60 percent. Dozens of banks and other financial institutions failed. In addition, the U.S. economy experienced its most severe recession since 1947. Why are periods of particularly poor national economic performance so often associated with major financial breakdowns? To consider the answer to this question, you must first understand how we measure the economic performance of a country's economy, which is the topic of this chapter.

LEARNING OBJECTIVES

After reading this chapter, you should be able to:

- Describe the circular flow of income and output
- Define gross domestic product (GDP)
- Understand the limitations of using GDP as a measure of national welfare
- Explain the expenditure approach to tabulating GDP
- Explain the income approach to computing GDP
- Distinguish between nominal GDP and real GDP

184

Chapter Openers tie to the **Issues and Applications** feature at the end of each chapter.
The current applications in the book—all new to this edition—get students' attention right at the beginning of the chapter, then follow through at the end of the chapter with an Issues and Applications feature that presents a more in-depth discussion of the issue.

Issues and Applications — Financial Crises and National Economic Performance

In 2009, the International Monetary Fund (IMF) declared that the global economy was experiencing a recession. More than 90 percent of the world's nations, the IMF concluded, were undergoing economic downturns, and most forecasters predicted at best a slight probability of turnarounds within the next year or two. Leading the way toward negative world real GDP growth were the United States and Europe, which were seeking to recover from a financial crisis that had contributed to sharp declines in production of final goods and services.

CONCEPTS APPLIED
- Real GDP
- Investment
- Durable Consumer Goods

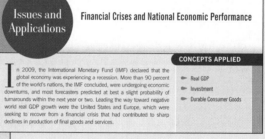

Some food items, such as canned beans and packaged macaroni and cheese, are inferior goods, so higher incomes have reduced consumption of these and similar foods. The vast majority of food items, however, are normal goods. Hence, the substantial rise in individual incomes has tended to raise the demand for foods as well as for other normal goods, such as personal computers and video games.

A Double-Whammy Effect on Food Consumption

Thus, two key factors have contributed to greater food consumption: the lower relative price of food and higher incomes. Increases in incomes have boosted demands for most food items, and declines in the relative prices have induced people to buy even more foods. Hence, people have been consuming more food and, with it, more calories. Without additional exercise, they have also been gaining more weight.

Test your understanding of this chapter by going online to **MyEconLab**.
In the Study Plan for this chapter, select Section N: News.

Each Issues and Applications concludes by encouraging students to visit **MyEconLab** for additional news coverage of this topic. Critical Analysis questions, Web Resources, and a Suggested Research Project give students opportunities for in-depth discussion and exploration of the application. Suggested answers to critical analysis questions appear in the *Instructor's Manual*.

For Critical Analysis

1. If the demands for most food items have been rising as incomes have increased, what must have happened to the supplies of most food items to account for the declining relative price of food?

2. What factors might have accounted for the changes in food supplies discussed in Question 1? (Hint: What *ceteris paribus* conditions affect the position of a supply curve?)

Web Resources

1. For a review of the worldwide trend toward higher body masses, go to www.econtoday.com/chapter03.

2. To learn about various ways states and the federal government are trying to combat childhood obesity,

click on the link to the National Center for Chronic Disease Prevention and Health Promotion, available at www.econtoday.com/chapter03.

Research Project

One way that the federal government seeks to assist low-income people is by issuing them food stamps, which they can use to purchase food items. Some observers have suggested that the government's food stamp program contributes to the higher obesity rates observed among low-income people as compared with rates observed among middle- and high-income individuals. Evaluate this argument. (Hint: Many of the least-expensive food items are often the highest-fat foods containing the most calories per unit of food.)

Quick Quizzes encourage students' interaction with the text, providing them the opportunity to quickly judge their understanding of a section through fill-in-the-blank concept checks. Answers to Quick Quizzes at the end of each chapter provide immediate feedback. To further test their understanding of the concepts covered, students are encouraged to go to **MyEconLab**.

QUICK QUIZ See page 50 for the answers. Review concepts from this section in MyEconLab.

_____ is the situation in which human wants always exceed what can be produced with the limited resources and time that nature makes available.

We use scarce resources, such as _____, _____ and _____ capital, and _____, to produce economic goods—goods that are desired but are not directly obtainable from nature to the extent demanded or desired at a zero price.

_____ are unlimited; they include all material desires and all nonmaterial desires, such as love, affection, power, and prestige.

The concept of _____ is difficult to define objectively for every person; consequently, we simply consider every person's wants to be unlimited. In a world of **scarcity**, satisfaction of one want necessarily means non-satisfaction of one or more other wants.

How does marginal utility derived from a music download influence the quantity of music downloads consumed?

Critical Thinking Captions
New to this edition, margin photos illustrate key concepts underlying current issues. Captions pose critical thinking questions to engage students' analyses of the topic. Suggested answers to all captions appear on the Companion Web site at www.econtoday.com.

INTERNATIONAL EXAMPLE
Evidence of a More Unequal Distribution of Income in China

In addition to using Lorenz curves to measure the degree of income inequality, economists sometimes calculate an index measure of inequality known as the Gini coefficient, which has a value varying between 0 and 1. A Gini-coefficient value of 0 represents complete equality of income, and a value of 1 represents complete income inequality in which one person receives all income. In the late 1970s, the value of the Gini coefficient for China was 0.15,

indicating considerable income equality. Today, it is estimated to be closer to 0.60, indicating that income in China has become much more unequal during the past three decades.

FOR CRITICAL ANALYSIS
Based on the change in value of the Gini coefficient since the late 1970s, has the Lorenz curve for China likely become more or less outward bowed?

For Critical Analysis questions
At the end of each boxed example, students are asked to "think like economists" as they answer For Critical Analysis questions. These probing questions are effective tools for sharpening students' analytical skills. Suggested answers to all questions are found in the *Instructor's Manual*.

ECONOMICS ON THE NET

Looking at the Unemployment and Inflation Data This chapter reviewed key concepts relating to unemployment and inflation. In this application, you get a chance to examine U.S. unemployment and inflation data on your own.

Title: Bureau of Labor Statistics: Employment and Unemployment

Navigation: Use the link at www.econtoday.com/chapter07 to visit the "Employment & Unemployment" page of the Bureau of Labor Statistics (BLS). Click on *Labor Force Statistics from the Current Population Survey.*

Application Perform the indicated operations, and answer the following questions.

1. Click checkmarks in the boxes for Civilian Labor Force Level, Employment Level, and Unemployment Level. Retrieve the data, and click a checkmark next to "include graphs." Can you identify periods of sharp cyclical swings? Do they show up in data for the labor force, employment, or unemployment?

2. Are cyclical factors important?

For Group Study and Analysis Divide the class into groups, and assign a price index to each group. Ask each group to take a look at the index for All Years at the link to the BLS statistics on inflation at www.econtoday.com/chapter07. Have each group identify periods during which their index accelerated or decelerated (or even fell). Do the indexes ever provide opposing implications about inflation and deflation?

Economics on the Net activities are designed to build student research skills and reinforce key concepts. The activities guide students to a Web site and provide structured assignments for both individual and group work.

myeconlab (continued)

WHAT YOU SHOULD KNOW		WHERE TO GO TO PRACTICE
Relative Prices versus Money Prices When determining the quantity of a good to purchase, people respond to changes in its relative price, which is the price of the good in terms of other goods. If the price of a unit of health care services rises by 50 percent next year while at the same time all other prices, including your wages, also increase by 50 percent, then the relative price of the health care services has not changed. Thus, in a world of generally rising prices, you have to compare the price of one good with the general level of prices of other goods in order to decide whether the relative price of that one good has gone up, gone down, or stayed the same.	relative price, 53 money price, 53	• **MyEconLab** Study Plan 3.1 • Video: The Difference Between Relative and Absolute Prices and the Importance of Looking at Only Relative Prices
A Change in Quantity Demanded versus a Change in Demand The demand schedule shows the relationship between various possible prices and respective quantities purchased per unit of time. Graphically, the demand schedule is a downward-sloping demand curve. A change in the price of the good generates a change in the quantity demanded, which is a movement along the demand curve. Factors other than the price of the good that affect the amount demanded are (1) income, (2) tastes and preferences, (3) the prices of related goods, (4) expectations, and (5) market size (the number of potential buyers). Whenever any of these *ceteris paribus* conditions of demand changes, there is a change in the demand for the good, and the demand curve shifts to a new position.	demand curve, 56 market demand, 56 *ceteris paribus* conditions, 59 normal goods, 59 inferior goods, 59 substitutes, 60 complements, 60 KEY FIGURE Figure 3-2, 56 Figure 3-4, 58 Figure 3-5, 62	• **MyEconLab** Study Plans 3.2, 3.3 • Video: The Importance of Distinguishing Between a Shift in a Demand Curve and a Move Along the Demand Curve • Animated Figures 3-2, 3-4, 3-5 • ABC News Video: What Drives the Market: Supply and Demand
The Law of Supply According to the law of supply, sellers will produce and offer for sale more units of a good at a higher price, and they will produce and offer for sale fewer units of the good at a lower price.	supply, 62 law of supply, 63	• **MyEconLab** Study Plan 3.4
A Change in Quantity Supplied versus a Change in Supply The supply schedule shows the relationship between various possible prices and respective quantities produced and sold per unit of time. On a graph, the supply schedule is a supply curve that slopes upward. A change in the price of the good generates a change in the quantity supplied, which is a movement along the supply curve. Factors other than the price of the good that affect the amount supplied are (1) input prices, (2) technology and productivity, (3) taxes and subsidies, (4) price expectations, and (5) the number of sellers. Whenever any of these *ceteris paribus* conditions changes, there is a change in the supply of the good, and the supply curve shifts to a new position.	supply curve, 64 subsidy, 68 KEY FIGURES Figure 3-6, 64 Figure 3-7, 65 Figure 3-9, 67	• **MyEconLab** Study Plans 3.5, 3.6 • Video: The Importance of Distinguishing Between a Change in Supply versus a Change in Quantity Supplied • Animated Figures 3-6, 3-7, 3-9

The **end-of-chapter summary** makes *Economics Today* an efficient study tool by integrating chapter contents with online learning resources available in **MyEconLab**. A thorough summary of the key concepts—What You Should Know—is directly linked with the text and online resources—Where to Go to Practice.

A variety of end-of-chapter problems offer students opportunities to test their knowledge and review chapter concepts. These problem sets have been heavily revised for this edition. Answers for all odd-numbered questions are provided in the back of the text, and **all** questions are assignable in **MyEconLab**.

Economic Concepts in Today's News

Economics Today strives to bring the latest news and current events into the classroom, keeping students engaged and interested.

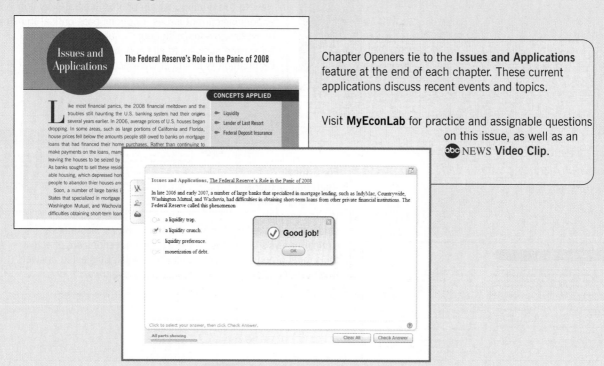

Chapter Openers tie to the **Issues and Applications** feature at the end of each chapter. These current applications discuss recent events and topics.

Visit **MyEconLab** for practice and assignable questions on this issue, as well as an abc NEWS **Video Clip**.

Each week, new microeconomic and macroeconomic current events are updated in **MyEconLab**'s **Weekly News** feature. Discussion questions, also posted weekly, test students' knowledge of the issues and ask them to apply the economic concepts.

You Are There

New to this edition, margin notes lead students to the You Are There feature at the conclusion of the text of each chapter. This feature, which depicts events involving **actual people confronting specific concepts** covered in the text, helps students see the relevance of those concepts in daily life. Topics include:

- An Invention Becomes a Market Innovation—By Accident
- In a Cold Twist, a Millionaire Bequeaths His Wealth to Himself
- Why Pouring Vegetable Oil into a Car Is Illegal in Illinois

---

INTERNATIONAL POLICY EXAMPLE (cont.)

coordinated with regional governments. Abiding by these rules severely limited the Peruvian national government's spending discretion.

Shortly after Barack Obama assumed the U.S. presidency in January 2009, he convinced the U.S. Congress to authorize new spending aimed at heading off a worsening recession. Five months later, the federal government had managed to dispense only about $31 billion, or just over 10 percent, of $300 billion in planned expenditures on roads, waterways, and schools. As

WHEN THERE IS AN INFLATIONARY GAP The entire process of Figure 13-1 can be reversed, as shown in panel (b). There, we shock has left the economy at point E_1, at which an inflationary section of *SRAS* and AD_1. Real GDP cannot be sustained at $15 because this exceeds long-run aggregate supply, which in real the government recognizes this and reduces its spending (pu fiscal policy), this action reduces aggregate demand from *AD* will fall to E_2 on the *LRAS*, where real GDP per year is $15 tr will fall from 130 to 120.

Changes in Taxes

The spending decisions of firms, individuals, and other countries' residents depend on the taxes levied on them. Individuals in their role as consumers look to their disposable (after-tax) income when determining their desired rates of consumption. Firms look at their after-tax profits when deciding on the levels of investment to undertake. Foreign residents look at the tax-inclusive cost of goods when deciding whether to buy in the United States or elsewhere. Therefore, holding all other things constant, a rise in taxes causes a reduction in aggregate demand because it reduces consumption, investment, or net exports.

WHEN THE CURRENT SHORT-RUN EQUILIBRIUM IS TO THE RIGHT OF *LRAS*
Assume that aggregate demand is AD_1 in panel (a) of Figure 13-2 on the following page. It intersects *SRAS* at E_1, which yields real GDP greater than *LRAS*. In this situation, an increase in taxes shifts the aggregate demand curve inward to the left. For argument's sake, assume that it intersects *SRAS* at E_2, or exactly where *LRAS* intersects AD_2. In this situation, the level of real GDP falls from $15.5 trillion per year to $15 trillion per year. The price level falls from 120 to 100.

WHEN THE CURRENT SHORT-RUN EQUILIBRIUM IS TO THE LEFT OF *LRAS*
Look at panel (b) in Figure 13-2. AD_1 intersects *SRAS* at E_1, with real GDP at $14.5 trillion, less than the *LRAS* of $15 trillion. In this situation, a decrease in taxes shifts the aggregate demand curve outward to the right. At AD_2, equilibrium is established at E_2, with the price level at 120 and equilibrium real GDP at $15 trillion per year.

> **You Are There**
> To contemplate whether temporary tax cuts have smaller effects on total planned spending than long-lasting tax reductions, take a look at **Assessing the Effects of a Temporary Tax Rebate**, on page 331.

You Are There — Assessing the Effects of a Temporary Tax Rebate

It is January 2009, and economists with the U.S. Treasury are considering a proposed income tax rebate program. Under the proposal, the U.S. government will provide a partial reimbursement of income taxes of as much as $300 for individuals who earned less than $75,000 and up to $600 for two-earner households that had incomes below $150,000. The rebate is to apply only to taxes paid in 2008.

The Treasury economists estimate that 130 million U.S. households will qualify for the tax rebates. Nevertheless, many of the economists are pessimistic about how much one-time tax rebates are likely to boost aggregate consumption. A similar rebate program the previous year contributed to a short-lived increase in aggregate disposable income of nearly $500 billion during the spring of 2008, but aggregate consumption did not rise. The one-time rebates did not have long-term effects on disposable incomes, so most people

receiving them either saved the funds or used them to pay off some of their debts. Thus, the previous year's tax rebates did not boost the circular flow of spending. A large majority of the economists at the meeting agree that a repeat of this outcome is likely if rebates are issued again this year.

CRITICAL ANALYSIS QUESTIONS

1. Congress did indeed authorize 2008 tax rebates to be issued in the spring of 2009, and personal saving jumped by as much as 6 percent while personal consumption barely changed. Does this outcome support the Treasury economists' prediction? Explain briefly.

2. Why do you suppose that people are less likely to increase their consumption spending in response to a one-time tax cut than to a permanent reduction?

Economics Videos featuring abc NEWS

A series of videos covering core economic concepts including ABC News footage and commentary by economists can be found in **MyEconLab**. New **assessment questions** have been added for optional instructor assignment.

Videos in this series include:

- *Coca Cola in India,* which examines international trade, incentives, causation, and externalities.
- *The Ripple Effects of Oil Prices,* which discusses equilibrium and inflation.
- *Big Government: Who Is Going to Pay the Bill?* which discusses concepts such as taxes, budget, GDP, and fiscal policy.

MyEconLab now offers RSS feed for up-to-the-minute coverage of economic news. Please see page **xxxi** for additional news and issues options.

Where Students Go to Practice

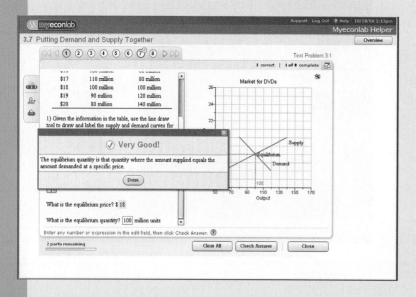

myeconlab is the premier student and instructor tool, integrating lessons from the text into a powerful online learning and teaching resource.

New in MyEconLab for *Economics Today*

3-1. Suppose that in a recent market period, the following relationship existed between the price of prerecorded movie DVDs and the quantity supplied and quantity demanded.

Price	Quantity Demanded	Quantity Supplied
$19	100 million	40 million
$20	90 million	60 million
$21	80 million	80 million
$22	70 million	100 million
$23	60 million	120 million

Graph the supply and demand curves for movie DVDs given the information in the table. What are the equilibrium price and quantity? If the industry price is $20, is there a shortage or surplus of DVDs? How much is the shortage or surplus?

- **100% of all end-of-chapter problems** are now assignable.

- For most chapters, **additional, instructor-only questions** are available to provide a larger pool of assignable options. A selection of these questions is algorithmic for additional learning opportunity. Instructors can also always choose from end-of-chapter problems, select test bank problems, or create their own exercises.

- Each chapter includes **questions for the Issues and Applications feature** found in the text, along with a related abc NEWS **Video Clip** and critical thinking questions. Selected questions in this section are visible for student practice and others are instructor-only for assignable options.

Students control their learning through a variety of features unique to MyEconLab.

- **Sample Tests,** two for every chapter, ask students to test their understanding of the concepts. The powerful graphing application allows students to draw graphs themselves, and **MyEconLab** evaluates and grades them automatically.

- **Personalized Study Plans** analyze students' performance on Sample Tests, identify areas where they need further study, and offer additional exercises to reinforce learning. Tutorial instruction provides targeted learning aids and step-by-step explanations.

- **An integrated eText** allows access to the textbook on any computer.

- **Learning aids** such as animated graphs with audio explanations for each step, video clips of author Roger LeRoy Miller reviewing key points in every chapter, and glossary flashcards allow review of important terms.

Students can get additional help and resources.

- **Weekly News updates** feature new micro and macro current events. Discussion questions posted online each week by Andrew J. Dane of Angelo State University test students' knowledge of relevant issues and their ability to apply economic concepts. Instructor answer keys are available. The Weekly News is now **archived for easy searching and reference.**

- **Economic Videos featuring ABC News** provide students with a glimpse of economics behind the news. Each video presents an issue using ABC News footage and includes commentary by economists.

- **Research Navigator** develops students' research skills by offering exclusive access to databases of *The New York Times*, the *Financial Times*, and peer-reviewed journals. This is available with **MyEconLab in CourseCompass.**

Instructors save time and gain flexibility.

- Instructors can design their own quizzes, tests, or homework assignments from the significant bank of questions or assign pre-loaded Sample Tests. All problems in **MyEconLab** are directly correlated to the text.

- **MyEconLab** automatically grades tests, quizzes, or homework—including graphing questions—and tracks the results in an online gradebook.

- For more information about **MyEconLab,** or to request an Instructor Access code, visit www.myeconlab.com.

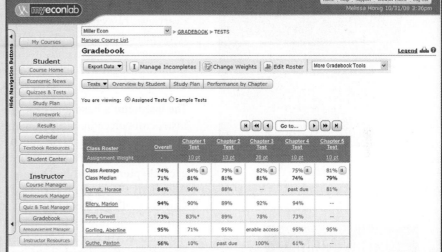

Supplemental Resources

Student and instructor materials provide tools for success.

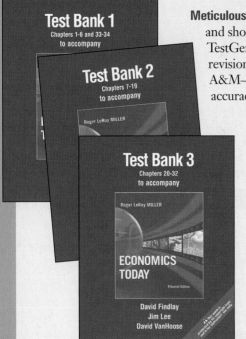

Meticulously Revised and Updated! Test Banks 1, 2, and 3 offer over 10,000 multiple choice and short answer questions, all of which are available in computerized format in the TestGen software. A selection of questions is also in **MyEconLab**. The significant revision process by authors David Findlay of Colby College and Jim Lee of Texas A&M–Corpus Christi and reviewer David VanHoose of Baylor University ensures the accuracy of problems and solutions in these heavily revised and updated test banks.

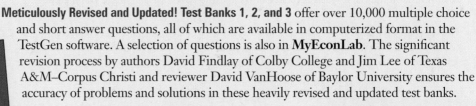

The Instructor's Manual, prepared by Andrew J. Dane of Angelo State University and reviewed by Victoria L. Figiel of Troy University, offers instructors materials to make the course successful. Features include lecture-ready examples; chapter overviews, objectives, and outlines; points to emphasize; answers to all critical analysis questions; answers to end-of-chapter problems; suggested answers to *You Are There* questions; and selected references.

The Instructor's Resource Disk offers instructors electronic supplements conveniently packaged on a CD-ROM. **PowerPoint lecture presentations** for each chapter, revised by Dennis Kovach of the Community College of Allegheny County and reviewed by Pete Mavrokordatos of Tarrant County College, include graphs from the text and outline key terms, concepts, and figures from the text. The entire **Instructor's Manual** is included as Microsoft Word files, and all three **Computerized Test Banks** are offered with TestGen software for simple test preparation.

Updated Powerpoints for this edition were revised by Jim Lee and are available for download online at the Instructor's Resource Center.

Clicker PowerPoint Slides allow professors to instantly quiz students in class and receive immediate feedback through Clicker Response System technology.

The Instructor Resource Center puts supplements right at instructors' fingertips. By registering for the Instructor Resource Center, instructors can download supplements directly from the Internet. Visit www.pearsonhighered.com/irc to register.

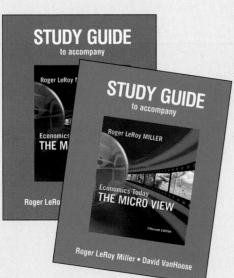

The Study Guide offers the practice and review students need to excel. Written by Roger LeRoy Miller and updated by David VanHoose, the study guide has been thoroughly revised to take into account changes to the Fifteenth Edition.

PearsonChoices

A variety of options for students and instructors provide convenience and flexibility.

Student Value Edition is created for the student who wants a more flexible portable text. Students who use this three-hole punched version of *Economics Today* can take only what they need to class, incorporate their own notes, and save money. This version is packaged with a laminated study card and comes with access to MyEconLab.

The CourseSmart eTextbook for the text is available through www.coursesmart.com. CourseSmart goes beyond traditional expectations providing instant, online access to the textbooks and course materials you need at a lower cost to students. And, even as students save money, you can save time and hassle with a digital textbook that allows you to search the most relevant content at the very moment you need it. Whether it's evaluating textbooks or creating lecture notes to help students with difficult concepts, CourseSmart can make life a little easier. See how when you visit www.coursesmart.com/instructors.

Standalone Access to MyEconLab and the Complete eText may be purchased online at www.myeconlab.com or through the campus bookstore. This access to MyEconLab includes online access to the complete, searchable eText.

MyEconLab access may be purchased online at www.myeconlab.com. Students gain full access to MyEconLab's assessment and learning resources. Partial access to the eText is included, which links practice problems to relevant sections of the text.

Print Upgrade from within MyEconLab may be purchased at any point following students' online purchase of MyEconLab.

Pearson Custom Business Resources offers instructors the option of building their own book by selecting just the chapters they want and ordering them to fit their syllabus. Professors can also select chapters of the accompanying Study Guide as well as readings from Miller/Benjamin/North's *Economics of Public Issues* and Miller/Benjamin's *The Economics of Macro Issues*. For more information, please contact your local Pearson sales representative.

Economist.com provides your students with the premier online source of news analysis, insight, and opinion on current economic events. When packaged with the text, students receive a low-cost subscription to Economist.com for three months, including the complete text of the current issue and access to searchable archives. Professors receive a complimentary one-year subscription to Economist.com.

The *Financial Times* features international news and analysis from journalists in more than 50 countries. For a small charge, a 15-week student subscription to the *Financial Times* can be included with the text. Professors will receive a complimentary one-year print subscription, as well as access to the online edition at FT.com.

Acknowledgments

I am the most fortunate of economics textbook writers, for I receive the benefit of literally hundreds of suggestions from those of you who use *Economics Today*. I continue to be fully appreciative of the constructive criticisms that you offer. There are some professors who have been asked by my publisher to participate in a more detailed reviewing process of this edition. I list them below. I hope that each one of you so listed accepts my sincere appreciation for the fine work that you have done.

Ali A. Ataiifar, *Delaware County Community College*
Emil Berendt, *Siena Heights University*
John Bockino, *Suffolk County Community College*
Patrick M. Crowley, *Texas A&M University–Corpus Christi*
Diana Denison, *Red Rocks Community College*
Victoria L. Figiel, *Troy University*
Timothy S. Fuerst, *Bowling Green State University*
Peter A. Groothuis, *Appalachian State University*
Michael J. Haupert, *University of Wisconsin–La Crosse*
George Hughes, *University of Hartford*
Nancy Jianakoplos, *Colorado State University*
Brian Kench, *University of Tampa*

Dennis Lee Kovach, *Community College of Allegheny County–North Campus*
Dan Marburger, *Arkansas State University*
Pete Mavrokordatos, *Tarrant County College*
William H. Moon, *Georgia Perimeter College–Lawrenceville*
Ronald M. Nate, *Brigham Young University–Idaho*
Joan Osborne, *Palo Alto College*
Leila J. Pratt, *University of Tennessee at Chattanooga*
Basel Saleh, *Radford University*
Phil Smith, *Georgia Perimeter College*
Sharmila Vishwasrao, *Florida Atlantic University*
Ethel Weeks, *Nassau Community College*
George K. Zestos, *Christopher Newport University*

I also thank the reviewers of previous editions:

Rebecca Abraham
Cinda J. Adams
Esmond Adams
John Adams
Bill Adamson
Carlos Aguilar
John R. Aidem
John W. Allen
Mohammed Akacem
E. G. Aksoy
M. C. Alderfer
John Allen
Ann Al-Yasiri
Charles Anderson
Leslie J. Anderson
Fatma W. Antar
Rebecca Arnold,
Mohammad Ashraf
Aliakbar Ataiifar
Leonard Atencio
John M. Atkins
Glen W. Atkinson
Thomas R. Atkinson
James Q. Aylesworth
John Baffoe-Bonnie
Kevin Baird
Charley Ballard
Maurice B. Ballabon
G. Jeffrey Barbour
Daniel Barszcz
Robin L. Bartlett
Kari Battaglia
Robert Becker
Charles Beem
Glen Beeson
Bruce W. Bellner
Daniel K. Benjamin
Charles Berry
Abraham Bertisch
John Bethune

R.A. Blewett
Scott Bloom
M. L. Bodnar
Mary Bone
Karl Bonnhi
Thomas W. Bonsor
John M. Booth
Wesley F. Booth
Thomas Borcherding
Melvin Borland
Tom Boston
Barry Boyer
Maryanna Boynton
Ronald Brandolini
Fenton L. Broadhead
Elba Brown
William Brown
Michael Bull
Maureen Burton
Conrad P. Caligaris
Kevin Carey
James Carlson
Robert Carlsson
Dancy R. Carr
Scott Carson
Doris Cash
Thomas H. Cate
Richard J. Cebula
Catherine Chanbers
K. Merry Chambers
Richard Chapman
Ronald Cherry
Young Back Choi
Marc Chopin
Carol Cies
Joy L. Clark
Curtis Clarke
Gary Clayton
Marsha Clayton
Dale O. Cloninger

Warren L. Coats
Ed Coen
Pat Conroy
James Cox
Stephen R. Cox
Eleanor D. Craig
Peggy Crane
Jerry Crawford
Joanna Cruse
John P. Cullity
Will Cummings
Thomas Curtis
Margaret M. Dalton
Andrew J. Dane
Mahmoud Davoudi
Diana Denison
Edward Dennis
Julia G. Derrick
Carol Dimamro
William Dougherty
Barry Duman
Diane Dumont
Floyd Durham
G. B. Duwaji
James A. Dyal
Ishita Edwards
Robert P. Edwards
Alan E. Ellis
Mike Ellis
Steffany Ellis
Frank Emerson
Carl Enomoto
Zaki Eusfzai
Sandy Evans
John L. Ewing-Smith
Frank Falero
Frank Fato
Abdollah Ferdowsi
Grant Ferguson
Mitchell Fisher

David Fletcher
James Foley
John Foreman
Diana Fortier
Ralph G. Fowler
Arthur Friedberg
Peter Frost
Tom Fullerton
E. Gabriel
James Gale
Byron Gangnes
Steve Gardner
Peter C. Garlick
Neil Garston
Alexander Garvin
Joe Garwood
Doug Gehrke
J. P. Gilbert
Otis Gilley
Frank Glesber
Jack Goddard
Michael G. Goode
Allen C. Goodman
Richard J. Gosselin
Paul Graf
Anthony J. Greco
Edward Greenberg
Gary Greene
Philip J. Grossman
Nicholas Grunt
William Gunther
Kwabena Gyimah-
  Brempong
Demos Hadjiyanis
Martin D. Haney
Mehdi Haririan
Ray Harvey
E. L. Hazlett
Sanford B. Helman
William Henderson

John Hensel
Robert Herman
Gus W. Herring
Charles Hill
John M. Hill
Morton Hirsch
Benjamin Hitchner
Charles W. Hockert
R. Bradley Hoppes
James Horner
Grover Howard
Nancy Howe-Ford
Yu-Mong Hsiao
Yu Hsing
James Hubert
Joseph W. Hunt Jr.
Scott Hunt
John Ifediora
R. Jack Inch
Christopher Inya
Tomotaka Ishimine
E. E. Jarvis
Parvis Jenab
Allan Jenkins
Mark Jensen
S. D. Jevremovic
J. Paul Jewell
Frederick Johnson
David Jones
Lamar B. Jones
Paul A. Joray
Daniel A. Joseph
Craig Justice
M. James Kahiga
Septimus Kai Kai
Devajyoti Kataky
Timothy R. Keely
Ziad Keilany
Norman F. Keiser
Randall G. Kesselring

Alan Kessler
E. D. Key
Saleem Khan
M. Barbara Killen
Bruce Kimzey
Philip G. King
Terrence Kinal
E. R. Kittrell
David Klingman
Charles Knapp
Jerry Knarr
Faik Koray
Janet Koscianski
Marie Kratochvil
Peter Kressler
Paul J. Kubik
Michael Kupilik
Larry Landrum
Margaret Landman
Richard LaNear
Keith Langford
Theresa Laughlin
Anthony T. Lee
Loren Lee
Bozena Leven
Donald Lien
George Lieu
Stephen E. Lile
Lawrence W. Lovick
Marty Ludlum
G. Dirk Mateer
Robert McAuliffe
James C. McBrearty
Howard J. McBride
Bruce McClung
John McDowell
E. S. McKuskey
James J. McLain
John L. Madden
Mary Lou Madden

John Marangos
Glen Marston
John M. Martin
Paul J. Mascotti
James D. Mason
Paul M. Mason
Tom Mathew
Warren Matthews
Warren T. Matthews
Akbar Marvasti
G. Hartley Mellish
Mike Melvin
Diego Mendez-Carbajo
Dan C. Messerschmidt
Michael Metzger
Herbert C. Milikien
Joel C. Millonzi
Glenn Milner
Daniel Mizak
Khan Mohabbat
Thomas Molloy
Margaret D. Moore
William E. Morgan
Stephen Morrell
Irving Morrissett
James W. Moser
Thaddeaus Mounkurai
Martin F. Murray
Densel L. Myers
George L. Nagy
Solomon Namala

Jerome Neadly
James E. Needham
Claron Nelson
Douglas Nettleton
William Nook
Gerald T. O'Boyle
Greg Okoro
Richard E. O'Neill
Lucian T. Orlowski
Diane S. Osborne
Melissa A. Osborne
James O'Toole
Jan Palmer
Zuohong Pan
Gerald Parker
Ginger Parker
Randall E. Parker
Kenneth Parzych
Norm Paul
Wesley Payne
Raymond A. Pepin
Martin M. Perline
Timothy Perri
Jerry Petr
Bruce Pietrykowski
Maurice Pfannesteil
James Phillips
Raymond J. Phillips
I. James Pickl
Dennis Placone
Mannie Poen

William L. Polvent
Robert Posatko
Greg Pratt
Reneé Prim
Robert W. Pulsinelli
Rod D. Raehsler
Kambriz Raffiee
Sandra Rahman
Jaishankar Raman
John Rapp
Richard Rawlins
Gautam Raychaudhuri
Ron Reddall
Mitchell Redlo
Charles Reichhelu
Robert S. Rippey
Charles Roberts
Ray C. Roberts
Richard Romano
Judy Roobian-Mohr
Duane Rosa
Richard Rosenberg
Larry Ross
Barbara Ross-Pfeiffer
Philip Rothman
John Roufagalas
Stephen Rubb
Henry Ryder
Patricia Sanderson
Thomas N. Schaap
William A. Schaeffer

William Schaniel
David Schauer
A. C. Schlenker
David Schlow
Scott J. Schroeder
William Scott
Dan Segebarth
Paul Seidenstat
Swapan Sen
Augustus Shackelford
Richard Sherman Jr.
Liang-rong Shiau
David Shorow
Vishwa Shukla
R. J. Sidwell
David E. Sisk
Alden Smith
Garvin Smith
Howard F. Smith
Lynn A. Smith
Phil Smith
Steve Smith
William Doyle Smith
Lee Spector
George Spiva
Richard L. Sprinkle
Alan Stafford
Amanda Stallings-Wood
Herbert F. Steeper
Diane L. Stehman
Columbus Stephens

William Stine
Allen D. Stone
Osman Suliman
J. M. Sullivan
Rebecca Summary
Joseph L. Swaffar
Thomas Swanke
Frank D. Taylor
Daniel Teferra
Lea Templer
Gary Theige
Dave Thiessen
Robert P. Thomas
Deborah Thorsen
Richard Trieff
George Troxler
William T. Trulove
William N. Trumbull
Arianne K. Turner
Kay Unger
Anthony Uremovic
John Vahaly
Jim Van Beek
David VanHoose
Lee J. Van Scyoc
Roy Van Til
Craig Walker
Robert F. Wallace
Henry C. Wallich
Milledge Weathers
Roger E. Wehr

Robert G. Welch
Terence West
James Wetzel
Wylie Whalthall
James H. Wheeler
Everett E. White
Michael D. White
Mark A. Wilkening
Raburn M. Williams
James Willis
George Wilson
Travis Wilson
Mark Wohar
Ken Woodward
Tim Wulf
Peter R. Wyman
Whitney Yamamura
Donald Yankovic
Alex Yguado
Paul Young
Shik Young
Mohammed Zaheer
Ed Zajicek
Sourushe Zandvakili
Paul Zarembka
William J. Zimmer Jr.

Revising *Economics Today* this time around was one of the biggest challenges I've faced with this textbook, given that changes in the economy within the United States and the world were so rapid. I believe that I was up to the task, but only because I had help along the way from not only the reviewers mentioned above, but my fantastic editorial team at Addison-Wesley. I was pushed hard by two unrelenting members of that team: Noel Seibert, my editor, and Julie Lindstrom, my developmental editor. In addition to managing this major project, they came up with numerous ideas "on the fly," which they suggested I incorporate into this new edition. Furthermore, all of us were dependent on Courtney Schinke, the assistant editor on this project. Courtney was great at coordination and making sure all aspects of the project moved along quickly. For this Updated Edition, I also thank Carolyn Terbush, the Editorial Assistant on this project.

On the production side of this revision, I was again fortunate enough to have as my production supervisor Kathryn Dinovo at Addison-Wesley. The designer, Geri Davis, succeeded in creating a new look that still kept the traditional feel of this text. As always, I benefited from the years of experience of John Orr of Orr Book Services. He has always faced the daunting task of putting this book together in a minimum amount of time—and he does it extremely well. I appreciate the fabulous copyediting and proofing services that Pat Lewis again provided. For this edition on the print supplements side, Marianne Groth and Alison Eusden did the job in a singularly professional matter, guaranteeing revised error-free ancillaries. I would also like to thank Roxanne McCarley, Lori DeShazo, and Justin Jacob for continued marketing and promotional efforts.

As you can imagine, more emphasis for each edition has been placed on online and other media materials. Melissa Honig and Susan Schoenberg worked overtime to make sure that MyEconLab was fully functional and without bugs. I also was lucky to have the services of Douglas Ruby and Noel Lotz who helped develop new content for MyEconLab.

This time around, I had some extremely talented colleagues who created a fully revised supplements package. Jim Lee of Texas A&M–Corpus Christi and David Findlay of Colby College authored the three test banks, and David VanHoose of Baylor University ensured they were error-free. He also continued to create not only accurate, but useful study guides. Similarly, Andrew J. Dane of Angelo State University has kept the *Instructor's Manual* in sync with the latest revisions, while Dennis Kovach of the Community College of Allegheny County provided the PowerPoint presentations. I would also like to thank the superb eagle-eyed professors who reviewed the text for accuracy: Victoria L. Figiel from Troy University, Ethel Weeks from Nassau Community College, Pete Mavrokordatos from Tarrant County College, and Leila J. Pratt from the University of Tennessee at Chattanooga.

Finally, there are two individuals I must thank for their work above and beyond the call of duty. The first is Professor Dan Benjamin of Clemson University, who continues to act as my "super reviewer" and "super proofreader." He again helped make this edition the best ever. Finally, Sue Jasin, my long-time assistant, could probably teach a course in economics after all of the typing and retyping of various drafts of this revision.

I welcome comments and ideas from professors and students alike and hope you enjoy the new edition of *Economics Today*.

R. L. M.

The Nature of Economics

J ust a few years ago, a passenger on a commuter train in Mumbai, India (formerly known as Bombay), rarely had difficulty finding an empty seat even during peak commuting hours. Today, a Mumbai commuter train's passenger car built to hold a maximum of 200 people often carries as many as 550 passengers—some of whom hang out of the doors of the car or even cling to its exterior. Falls from train cars and other accidents are common events. As a consequence, at least 3,000 people are killed each year in the Mumbai commuter-rail system, and many more experience injuries. Why is Mumbai's rail system so overloaded? Why do people risk life and limb to ride the city's overcrowded trains? This chapter will equip you to contemplate the answers to these questions.

LEARNING OBJECTIVES

myeconlab

MyEconLab helps you master each objective and study more efficiently. See end of chapter for details.

After reading this chapter, you should be able to:

- ➤ Discuss the difference between microeconomics and macroeconomics
- ➤ Evaluate the role that rational self-interest plays in economic analysis
- ➤ Explain why economics is a science
- ➤ Distinguish between positive and normative economics

Did you know that economics is one of the fastest-growing college majors? During the past 10 years, the number of students majoring in economics at U.S. colleges and universities has increased by nearly 40 percent. Certainly, a key factor motivating many students to opt for extensive study of economics is that they find the subject fascinating. Nevertheless, another important factor is self-interest. The fact that economics majors typically land higher-paying jobs than other majors—for instance, at least 10 percent more than business management majors and 75 percent more than psychology majors—provides a strong incentive to consider majoring in economics.

In this chapter, you will learn why contemplating the nature of self-interested responses to **incentives** is the starting point for analyzing choices people make in all walks of life. After all, how much time you devote to studying economics in this introductory course depends in part on the incentives established by your instructor's grading system. As you will see, self-interest and incentives are the underpinnings for all the decisions you and others around you make each day.

Incentives
Rewards for engaging in a particular activity.

The Power of Economic Analysis

Simply knowing that self-interest and incentives are central to any decision-making process is not sufficient for predicting the choices that people will actually make. You also have to develop a framework that will allow you to analyze solutions to each economic problem—whether you are trying to decide how much to study, which courses to take, whether to finish school, or whether the U.S. government should provide more grants to universities or raise taxes. The framework that you will learn in this text is the *economic way of thinking*.

This framework gives you power—the power to reach informed judgments about what is happening in the world. You can, of course, live your life without the power of economic analysis as part of your analytical framework. Indeed, most people do. But economists believe that economic analysis can help you make better decisions concerning your career, your education, financing your home, and other important matters. In the business world, the power of economic analysis can help you increase your competitive edge as an employee or as the owner of a business. As a voter, for the rest of your life you will be asked to make judgments about policies that are advocated by political parties. Many of these policies will deal with questions related to international economics, such as whether the U.S. government should encourage or discourage immigration, prevent foreign residents and firms from investing in port facilities or domestic banks, or restrict other countries from selling their goods here.

Finally, just as taking an art, music, or literature appreciation class increases the pleasure you receive when you view paintings, listen to concerts, or read novels, taking an economics course will increase your understanding and pleasure when watching the news on TV or reading articles in the newspaper or on the Internet.

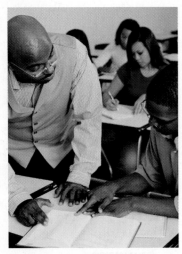

What determines how much time you decide to devote to studying one particular subject?

Defining Economics

Economics
The study of how people allocate their limited resources to satisfy their unlimited wants.

Economics is part of the social sciences and as such seeks explanations of real events. All social sciences analyze human behavior, as opposed to the physical sciences, which generally analyze the behavior of electrons, atoms, and other nonhuman phenomena.

Economics is the study of how people allocate their limited resources in an attempt to satisfy their unlimited wants. As such, economics is the study of how people make choices.

To understand this definition fully, two other words need explaining: *resources* and *wants*. **Resources** are things that have value and, more specifically, are used to produce goods and services that satisfy people's wants. **Wants** are all of the items that people would purchase if they had unlimited income.

Whenever an individual, a business, or a nation faces alternatives, a choice must be made, and economics helps us study how those choices are made. For example, you have to choose how to spend your limited income. You also have to choose how to spend your limited time. You may have to choose how much of your company's limited funds to spend on advertising and how much to spend on new-product research. In economics, we examine situations in which individuals choose how to do things, when to do things, and with whom to do them. Ultimately, the purpose of economics is to explain choices.

Resources
Things used to produce goods and services to satisfy people's wants.

Wants
What people would buy if their incomes were unlimited.

Microeconomics versus Macroeconomics

Economics is typically divided into two types of analysis: **microeconomics** and **macroeconomics**.

Microeconomics is the part of economic analysis that studies decision making undertaken by individuals (or households) and by firms. It is like looking through a microscope to focus on the small parts of our economy.

Macroeconomics is the part of economic analysis that studies the behavior of the economy as a whole. It deals with economywide phenomena such as changes in unemployment, in the general price level, and in national income.

Microeconomics
The study of decision making undertaken by individuals (or households) and by firms.

Macroeconomics
The study of the behavior of the economy as a whole, including such economywide phenomena as changes in unemployment, the general price level, and national income.

Microeconomic analysis, for example, is concerned with the effects of changes in the price of gasoline relative to that of other energy sources. It examines the effects of new taxes on a specific product or industry. If price controls were reinstituted in the United States, how individual firms and consumers would react to them would be in the realm of microeconomics. The effects of higher wages brought about by an effective union strike would also be analyzed using the tools of microeconomics.

In contrast, issues such as the rate of inflation, the amount of economywide unemployment, and the yearly growth in the output of goods and services in the nation all fall into the realm of macroeconomic analysis. In other words, macroeconomics deals with **aggregates,** or totals—such as total output in an economy.

Be aware, however, of the blending of microeconomics and macroeconomics in modern economic theory. Modern economists are increasingly using microeconomic analysis—the study of decision making by individuals and by firms—as the basis of macroeconomic analysis. They do this because even though macroeconomic analysis focuses on aggregates, those aggregates are the result of choices made by individuals and firms.

Aggregates
Total amounts or quantities; aggregate demand, for example, is total planned expenditures throughout a nation.

The Economic Person: Rational Self-Interest

Economists assume that individuals act *as if* motivated by self-interest and respond predictably to opportunities for gain. This central insight of economics was first clearly articulated by Adam Smith in 1776. Smith wrote in his most famous book, *An Inquiry into the Nature and Causes of the Wealth of Nations*, that "it is not from the benevolence of the butcher, the brewer, or the baker that we expect our dinner, but from their regard to their own interest." Thus, the typical person about whom economists make behavioral predictions is assumed to act *as though* motivated by self-interest. Because monetary benefits and costs of actions are often the most easily measured, economists make behavioral predictions about individuals' responses to opportunities to increase their wealth, measured in money terms.

Is it possible to apply the theory of rational self-interest to help in explaining regular church attendance?

EXAMPLE
Earthly Rewards of Religiosity

Undoubtedly, most people who attend church regularly do so because they feel an innate desire to participate actively in their chosen religious faith. Nevertheless, habitual church attendance has concrete rewards as well, in the form of more education, a lower chance of divorce, and even higher income. A 10 percent increase in church attendance boosts a typical individual's income by nearly 1 percent.

Why might churchgoing lead to higher income? One possible explanation is that attending church helps people establish trust within a social network and find more business opportunities. Another is that church membership provides a type of insurance that helps people recover emotionally and even financially following life setbacks such as illnesses or job losses. Finally, religious faith may reduce personal stresses, thereby making churchgoers more productive and employable. Thus, there are several channels by which greater church involvement can contribute to higher incomes.

FOR CRITICAL ANALYSIS
How might the fact that many churches sponsor schools help to boost incomes of families that maintain their church memberships over a generation or more? (Hint: People who are better educated possess more skills and hence are more employable.)

The Rationality Assumption

Rationality assumption
The assumption that people do not intentionally make decisions that would leave them worse off.

The **rationality assumption** of economics, simply stated, is as follows:

We assume that individuals do not intentionally make decisions that would leave them worse off.

The distinction here is between what people may think—the realm of psychology and psychiatry and perhaps sociology—and what they do. Economics does *not* involve itself in analyzing individual or group thought processes. Economics looks at what people actually do in life with their limited resources. It does little good to criticize the rationality assumption by stating, "Nobody thinks that way" or "I never think that way" or "How unrealistic! That's as irrational as anyone can get!"

Take the example of driving. When you consider passing another car on a two-lane highway with oncoming traffic, you have to make very quick decisions: You must estimate the speed of the car that you are going to pass, the speed of the oncoming cars, the distance between your car and the oncoming cars, and your car's potential rate of acceleration. If we were to apply a model to your behavior, we would use the rules of calculus. In actual fact, you and most other drivers in such a situation do not actually think of using the rules of calculus, but to predict your behavior, we could make the prediction *as if* you understood those rules.

How might regular church attendance lead to higher income?

How can magnetic resonance imaging (MRI) scans aid in assessing the rationality assumption?

EXAMPLE
"Neuroeconomics" Evaluates Rational Choice

Neuroeconomics is a field of study aimed at determining how the human brain makes choices. Researchers in neuroeconomics have found that three parts of the brain typically interact in decision making. The *nucleus accumbens* processes emotions regarding the desirability of an item, and the *insular cortex* responds to the potential for a monetary loss associated with paying for the item. The *prefrontal cortex* handles rational calculation.

MRI scans reveal that when a person's brain is evaluating a purchase, the prefrontal cortex synthesizes conflicting positive feelings in the nucleus accumbens and negative emotions associated with payment in the insular cortex. Thus, there is evidence that the human brain naturally attempts to factor in reasoned calculations aimed at making a choice consistent with the "best" overall outcome. This conclusion, of course, supports the rationality assumption.

FOR CRITICAL ANALYSIS
Why might a person rationally pass up a choice that would yield a significant immediate gain in favor of a choice that would yield a series of smaller future gains? (Hint: The sum of many small numbers can exceed a single large number.)

Responding to Incentives

If it can be assumed that individuals never intentionally make decisions that would leave them worse off, then almost by definition they will respond to changes in incentives. Indeed, much of human behavior can be explained in terms of how individuals respond to changing incentives over time.

Schoolchildren are motivated to do better by a variety of incentive systems, ranging from gold stars and certificates of achievement when they are young, to better grades with accompanying promises of a "better life" as they get older. Of course, negative incentives affect our behavior, too. Penalties, punishments, and other forms of negative incentives can raise the cost of engaging in various activities.

What do you suppose is now a commonplace incentive at online dating sites?

You Are There

To contemplate how tax changes can provide incentives for people to alter their choices, consider **Herding Alpacas Toward a Tax Break,** on pages 11 and 12.

E-COMMERCE EXAMPLE
The New Online Dating Incentive: Health Insurance

"I'm looking for a woman who knows what she wants and isn't afraid to ask for it—one with a nice smile and a healthy attitude who is open and honest . . . and health insurance wouldn't hurt, either." So reads an ad at an online dating site. Another ad states: "Are you strong, smart and sophisticated, confident and kind, without being too uppity and conceited? Do you make at least $75,000 a year and have health insurance?" One ad is particularly straightforward: "My ideal man will have health insurance."

These ads reflect a growing trend at online dating sites. Alongside a winning personality, good looks, and other traditional attributes, another incentive that may induce an individual to agree to a date is a potential dating partner's access to health insurance.

FOR CRITICAL ANALYSIS
How might efforts by many U.S. companies to drastically reduce health insurance benefits influence the incentive effects of health insurance at online dating services?

Defining Self-Interest

Self-interest does not always mean increasing one's wealth measured in dollars and cents. We assume that individuals seek many goals, not just increased wealth measured in monetary terms. Thus, the self-interest part of our economic-person assumption includes goals relating to prestige, friendship, love, power, helping others, creating works of art, and many other matters. We can also think in terms of enlightened self-interest, whereby individuals, in the pursuit of what makes them better off, also achieve the betterment of others around them. In brief, individuals are assumed to want the ability to further their goals by making decisions about how things around them are used. The head of a charitable organization usually will not turn down an additional contribution, because accepting the funds yields control over how they are used, even though it is for other people's benefit.

Thus, self-interest does not rule out doing charitable acts. Giving gifts to relatives can be considered a form of charity that is nonetheless in the self-interest of the giver. But how efficient is such gift giving?

EXAMPLE
The Perceived Value of Gifts

Every holiday season, aunts, uncles, grandparents, mothers, and fathers give gifts to their college-aged loved ones. Joel Waldfogel, an economist at Yale University, surveyed several thousand college students after Christmas to find out the value of holiday gifts. He found that recorded music and outerwear (coats and jackets) had a perceived intrinsic value about equal to their actual cash equivalent. By the time he got down the list to socks, underwear, and cosmetics, the students' valuation was only about 85 percent of the cash value of the gift. He found out that aunts, uncles, and grandparents gave the "worst" gifts and friends, siblings, and parents gave the "best."

FOR CRITICAL ANALYSIS
What argument could you use against the idea of substituting cash or gift cards for physical gifts?

QUICK QUIZ
See page 17 for the answers. Review concepts from this section in MyEconLab.

Economics is a social science that involves the study of how individuals choose among alternatives to satisfy their _____, which are what people would buy if their incomes were _____.

_____, the study of the decision-making processes of individuals (or households) and firms, and _____, the study of the performance of the economy as a whole, are the two main branches into which the study of economics is divided.

In economics, we assume that people do not intentionally make decisions that will leave them worse off. This is known as the _____ assumption.

_____ is not confined to material well-being but also involves any action that makes a person feel better off, such as having more friends, love, power, or affection or providing more help to others.

Economics as a Science

Economics is a social science that employs the same kinds of methods used in other sciences, such as biology, physics, and chemistry. Like these other sciences, economics uses models, or theories. Economic **models,** or **theories,** are simplified representations of the real world that we use to help us understand, explain, and predict economic phenomena in the real world. There are, of course, differences between sciences. The social sciences—especially economics—make little use of laboratory experiments in which changes in variables are studied under controlled conditions. Rather, social scientists, and especially economists, usually have to test their models, or theories, by examining what has already happened in the real world.

Models, or **theories**
Simplified representations of the real world used as the basis for predictions or explanations.

Models and Realism

At the outset it must be emphasized that no model in *any* science, and therefore no economic model, is complete in the sense that it captures *every* detail or interrelationship that exists. Indeed, a model, by definition, is an abstraction from reality. It is conceptually impossible to construct a perfectly complete realistic model. For example, in physics we cannot account for every molecule and its position and certainly not for every atom and subatomic particle. Not only is such a model impossibly expensive to build, but working with it would be impossibly complex.

The nature of scientific model building is that the model should capture only the *essential* relationships that are sufficient to analyze the particular problem or answer the particular question with which we are concerned. *An economic model cannot be faulted as unrealistic simply because it does not represent every detail of the real world.* A map of a city that shows only major streets is not faulty if, in fact, all you need to know is how to pass through the city using major streets. As long as a model is able to shed light on the *central* issue at hand or forces at work, it may be useful.

A map is the quintessential model. It is always a simplified representation. It is always unrealistic. But it is also useful in making predictions about the world. If the model—the map—predicts that when you take Campus Avenue to the north, you always run into the campus, that is a prediction. If a simple model can explain observed behavior in repeated settings just as well as a complex model, the simple model has some value and is probably easier to use.

Assumptions

Every model, or theory, must be based on a set of assumptions. Assumptions define the array of circumstances in which our model is most likely to be applicable. When some people predicted that sailing ships would fall off the edge of the earth, they used the *assumption* that the earth was flat. Columbus did not accept the implications of such a model because he did not accept its assumptions. He assumed that the world was round. The real-world test of his own model refuted the flat-earth model. Indirectly, then, it was a test of the assumption of the flat-earth model.

Is it possible to use our knowledge about assumptions to understand why driving directions sometimes contain very few details?

EXAMPLE
Getting Directions

Assumptions are a shorthand for reality. Imagine that you have decided to drive from your home in San Diego to downtown San Francisco. Because you have never driven this route, you decide to use a travel-planner device such as global-positioning-system equipment.

When you ask for directions, the electronic travel planner could give you a set of detailed maps that shows each city through which you will travel—Oceanside, San Clemente, Irvine, Anaheim, Los Angeles, Bakersfield, Modesto, and so on—and then, opening each map, show you exactly how the freeway threads through each of these cities. You would get a nearly complete description of reality because the AAA travel planner will not have used many simplifying assumptions. It

is more likely, however, that the travel planner will simply say, "Get on Interstate 5 going north. Stay on it for about 500 miles. Follow the signs for San Francisco. After crossing the toll bridge, take any exit marked 'Downtown.'" By omitting all of the trivial details, the travel planner has told you all that you really need and want to know. The models you will be using in this text are similar to the simplified directions on how to drive from San Diego to San Francisco—they focus on what is relevant to the problem at hand and omit what is not.

FOR CRITICAL ANALYSIS
In what way do small talk and gossip represent the use of simplifying assumptions?

THE *CERERIS PARIBUS* ASSUMPTION: ALL OTHER THINGS BEING EQUAL
Everything in the world seems to relate in some way to everything else in the world. It would be impossible to isolate the effects of changes in one variable on another variable if we always had to worry about the many other variables that might also enter the analysis. Similar to other sciences, economics uses the ***ceteris paribus* assumption.** *Ceteris paribus* means "other things constant" or "other things equal."

Ceteris paribus [KAY-ter-us PEAR-uh-bus] assumption
The assumption that nothing changes except the factor or factors being studied.

Consider an example taken from economics. One of the most important determinants of how much of a particular product a family buys is how expensive that product is relative to other products. We know that in addition to relative prices, other factors influence decisions about making purchases. Some of them have to do with income, others with tastes, and yet others with custom and religious beliefs. Whatever these other factors are, we hold them constant when we look at the relationship between changes in prices and changes in how much of a given product people will purchase.

Deciding on the Usefulness of a Model

We generally do not attempt to determine the usefulness, or "goodness," of a model merely by evaluating how realistic its assumptions are. Rather, we consider a model "good" if it yields usable predictions that are supported by real-world observations. In other words, can we use the model to predict what will happen in the world around us? Does the model provide useful implications about how things happen in our world?

Once we have determined that the model does predict real-world phenomena, the scientific approach to the analysis of the world around us requires that we consider evidence. Evidence is used to test the usefulness of a model. This is why we call economics an **empirical** science. *Empirical* means that evidence (data) is looked at to see whether we are right. Economists are often engaged in empirically testing their models.

Empirical
Relying on real-world data in evaluating the usefulness of a model.

How can empirical data help in combating terrorism?

POLICY EXAMPLE
How Empirical Evidence Aids in Thwarting Terrorism

Since 1968, there have been more than 13,000 incidents of "transnational" terrorism, or violent attacks in nations where the attackers do not reside. These data suggest predictable cycles in terrorist attacks. When terrorists launch a complex large-scale operation, such as an attack aimed at the destruction of high-rise buildings, public pressure to thwart such attacks remains high for a long time afterwards. Consequently, government countermeasures also remain in place for a lengthy period. Knowing this, terrorists lie low and begin long-term planning for a future large-scale attack. Thus, there are predictably long lulls between large-scale attacks. In contrast, public pressure to prevent simple small-scale attacks, such as bus bombings, wanes more quickly. Government prevention efforts also dissipate more rapidly, thereby tempting terrorists to launch more small-scale attacks. Thus, there tend to be predictably short pauses between smaller-scale attacks.

Recognition of empirical regularities in terrorism has assisted governments in predicting terrorism upsurges. Governments can utilize these predictions to determine how to allocate their antiterrorism resources more effectively.

FOR CRITICAL ANALYSIS
Why do you suppose that when making predictions to help thwart terrorism, economists typically assume that terrorists behave rationally?

Models of Behavior, Not Thought Processes

Take special note of the fact that economists' models do not relate to the way people *think*; they relate to the way people *act*, to what they do in life with their limited resources. Normally, the economist does not attempt to predict how people will think about a particular topic, such as a higher price of oil products, accelerated inflation, or higher taxes. Rather, the task at hand is to predict how people will behave, which may be quite different from what they *say* they will do (much to the consternation of poll takers and market researchers). The people involved in examining thought processes are psychologists and psychiatrists, not typically economists.

Behavioral Economics and Bounded Rationality

In recent years, some economists have proposed paying more attention to psychologists and psychiatrists. They have suggested an alternative approach to economic analysis. Their approach, which is known as **behavioral economics,** examines consumer behavior in the face of psychological limitations and complications that may interfere with rational decision making.

Behavioral economics
An approach to the study of consumer behavior that emphasizes psychological limitations and complications that potentially interfere with rational decision making.

BOUNDED RATIONALITY Proponents of behavioral economics suggest that traditional economic models assume that people exhibit three "unrealistic" characteristics:

1. *Unbounded selfishness.* People are interested only in their own satisfaction.
2. *Unbounded willpower.* Their choices are always consistent with their long-term goals.
3. *Unbounded rationality.* They are able to consider every relevant choice.

Instead, advocates of behavioral economics have proposed replacing the rationality assumption with the assumption of **bounded rationality,** which assumes that people cannot examine and think through every possible choice they confront. As a consequence, behavioral economists suggest, people cannot always pursue their long-term

Bounded rationality
The hypothesis that people are *nearly*, but not fully, rational, so that they cannot examine every possible choice available to them but instead use simple rules of thumb to sort among the alternatives that happen to occur to them.

personal interests. From time to time, they must also rely on other people and take into account other people's interests as well as their own.

RULES OF THUMB   A key behavioral implication of the bounded rationality assumption is that people should use so-called *rules of thumb*: Because every possible choice cannot be considered, an individual will tend to fall back on methods of making decisions that are simpler than trying to sort through every possibility.

A problem confronting advocates of behavioral economics is that people who *appear* to use rules of thumb may in fact behave *as if* they are fully rational. For instance, if a person faces persistently predictable ranges of choices for a time, the individual may rationally settle into repetitive behaviors that an outside observer might conclude to be consistent with a rule of thumb. The bounded rationality assumption indicates that the person should continue to rely on a rule of thumb even if there is a major change in the environment that the individual faces. Time and time again, however, economists find that people respond to altered circumstances by fundamentally changing their behaviors. Economists also generally observe that people make decisions that are consistent with their own self-interest and long-term objectives.

BEHAVIORAL ECONOMICS: A WORK IN PROGRESS   It remains to be seen whether the application of the assumption of bounded rationality proposed by behavioral economists will truly alter the manner in which economists construct models intended to better predict human decision making. So far, proponents of behavioral economics have not conclusively demonstrated that paying closer attention to psychological thought processes can improve economic predictions.

As a consequence, the bulk of economic analysis continues to rely on the rationality assumption as the basis for constructing economic models. As you will learn in Chapter 20, advocates of behavioral economics continue to explore ways in which psychological elements might improve analysis of decision making by individual consumers.

Positive versus Normative Economics

Economics uses *positive analysis*, a value-free approach to inquiry. No subjective or moral judgments enter into the analysis. Positive analysis relates to statements such as "If A, then B." For example, "If the price of gasoline goes up relative to all other prices, then the amount of it that people buy will fall." That is a positive economic statement. It is a statement of *what is*. It is not a statement of anyone's value judgment or subjective feelings.

Distinguishing Between Positive and Normative Economics

For many problems analyzed in the "hard" sciences such as physics and chemistry, the analyses are considered to be virtually value-free. After all, how can someone's values enter into a theory of molecular behavior? But economists face a different problem. They deal with the behavior of individuals, not molecules. That makes it more difficult to stick to what we consider to be value-free or **positive economics** without reference to our feelings.

When our values are interjected into the analysis, we enter the realm of **normative economics,** involving *normative analysis*. A positive economic statement is "If the price of gas rises, people will buy less." If we add to that analysis the statement "so we

Positive economics
Analysis that is *strictly* limited to making either purely descriptive statements or scientific predictions; for example, "If A, then B." A statement of *what is*.

Normative economics
Analysis involving value judgments about economic policies; relates to whether things are good or bad. A statement of *what ought to be*.

should not allow the price to go up," we have entered the realm of normative economics—we have expressed a value judgment. In fact, any time you see the word *should*, you will know that values are entering into the discussion. Just remember that positive statements are concerned with *what is*, whereas normative statements are concerned with *what ought to be*.

Each of us has a desire for different things. That means that we have different values. When we express a value judgment, we are simply saying what we prefer, like, or desire. Because individual values are diverse, we expect—and indeed observe—people expressing widely varying value judgments about how the world ought to be.

A Warning: Recognize Normative Analysis

It is easy to define positive economics. It is quite another matter to catch all unlabeled normative statements in a textbook, even though an author goes over the manuscript many times before it is printed. Therefore, do not get the impression that a textbook author will be able to keep all personal values out of the book. They will slip through. In fact, the very choice of which topics to include in an introductory textbook involves normative economics. There is no value-free way to decide which topics to use in a textbook. The author's values ultimately make a difference when choices have to be made. But from your own standpoint, you might want to be able to recognize when you are engaging in normative as opposed to positive economic analysis. Reading this text will help equip you for that task.

What might motivate U.S. residents to breed more llamas?

QUICK QUIZ   *See page 17 for the answers. Review concepts from this section in MyEconLab.*

A _____, or _____, uses assumptions and is by nature a simplification of the real world. The usefulness of a _____ can be evaluated by bringing empirical evidence to bear on its predictions.

Most models use the _____ _____ assumption that all other things are held constant, or equal.

_____ economics emphasizes psychological constraints and complexities that potentially interfere with rational

decision making. This approach utilizes the _____ _____ hypothesis that people are not quite rational, because they cannot study every possible alternative but instead use simple rules of thumb to decide among choices.

_____ economics is value-free and relates to statements that can be refuted, such as "If A, then B."
_____ economics involves people's values and typically uses the word *should*.

You Are There   ▶ Herding Alpacas Toward a Tax Break

Recently, Claudia Weiner, a teacher in Ventura, California, was looking for a way to shelter a portion of household income from federal taxation. She found that in 2003, Congress passed the Jobs and Growth Tax Relief Reconciliation Act, which authorizes a 100 percent tax deduction for an asset purchased by a small business. One asset that qualifies

under the law is an alpaca, a small, long-necked South American llama that yields fleece prized by some clothing designers.

Weiner learned that raising several alpacas requires only about an acre of land and a direct annual expense of about $300. On any property designated as an "alpaca farm,"

You Are There (cont.)

tax-deductible expenses include purchases of food, water, fences, land upkeep, and under some circumstances even additions to homes.

Weiner and her husband ultimately decided to reclassify their home as an alpaca farm, which they call "As You Like It Alpacas." By responding in this way to the tax incentive Congress created, she and her husband joined nearly 2,500 new entrants into the U.S. alpaca-farming industry, which increased to about 4,500 farms. Few of these alpaca farmers have earned significant profits from selling alpaca fleece. Many of them, however, have succeeded in reducing the total taxes they must pay to the federal government each year.

CRITICAL ANALYSIS QUESTIONS

1. *How would a steep decline in the price of alpaca fleece, the main product of alpaca farmers, likely affect the incentive to raise alpacas?*

2. *Unless Congress takes action to renew the 2003 legislation, it will no longer be in force beginning in 2010. How might this affect the incentive to be an alpaca farmer?*

Risking Life and Limb on Mumbai Commuter Trains

Issues and Applications

CONCEPTS APPLIED

- Incentives
- Self-Interest
- Rationality Assumption

Every day, the commuter-rail network in Mumbai, India, carries more than 32,000 passengers per mile, a passenger rate 175 percent greater than the rail system was originally designed to transport. During peak hours, Mumbai rail commuters push their way across platforms and pack themselves into what they call the "super-dense crush load" of a typical passenger car— about 350 more passengers than the intended capacity of 200.

On a typical day, two or three people are killed when the surging crowd causes them to lose their footing on the platform and tumble onto the tracks. Two or three others die when they lose their grips on exterior handholds of passenger cars and fall from moving trains. Occasionally, someone is killed when he sticks his head out an open window or door to gasp for fresh air at an inopportune time, such as when the train is passing a pole near the tracks. Others die when they rush to catch a train and dart across the tracks in front of a locomotive. All told, 13 people on average are killed each working day in what media commentators have called the world's most dangerous train commute.

Incentives to Cram onto Mumbai Commuter Trains

Why do 6 million people per day wish to travel via Mumbai's commuter-rail system? To answer this question, we must consider the incentives faced by the 18 million residents of the Mumbai metropolitan area.

India's economy is growing rapidly. Most of the nation's highest-paying jobs are within its cities. Large numbers of people seeking to fill these positions are relocating from rural areas to the outskirts of metropolitan areas such as Mumbai. The government does not permit private autos to enter Mumbai's downtown interior, and taxi service into that area is sparse and relatively expensive. Reaching the central city from the city's outer edges by bus can take several hours, whereas commuter trains transit the same distance in 60 minutes or less. Furthermore, India's government, which operates the nation's rail systems, sets fares—typically little more than 25 cents for a one-hour ride—well below the levels that private operators would charge.

Self-Interest, Rationality, and Super-Dense Crush Loads

Clearly, higher-paying employment inside the city, lack of substitute transportation of equal quality, and low ticket prices are all strong positive incentives for the residents of Mumbai to choose rail transport. These incentives help to explain why so many self-interested people continue to brave the Mumbai rail commute.

At the same time, though, the discomfort of being packed into passenger cars or perhaps even having to hang to the outside of the cars is certainly a negative incentive to train travel in Mumbai. So is the average daily toll of 13 people killed in accidents. This overall death toll, however, implies an average daily death *rate* of about 2 per million passengers. The injury rate in the Mumbai commuter-rail system is somewhat higher than the death rate. Nevertheless, the overall chance of experiencing an injury to life or limb on a given day is still less than 1 out of 200,000.

Under the rationality assumption, people do not intentionally make decisions that make themselves worse off. Someone who resides on the outskirts of Mumbai typically can double her annual income by commuting into the city. In most cases, taking a commuter train to her place of employment is her only reasonable option, and the price of this mode of transport is very low. She must weigh these positive incentives against the disincentives of a cramped commute and a relatively low individual likelihood of injury or death. On net, a resident on the outer edge of Mumbai is unlikely to perceive the decision to make the "world's most dangerous commute" as inconsistent with her own self-interest. Thus, each working day she and 6 million others are likely to continue to traverse Mumbai's 813-mile commuter-rail system.

Test your understanding of this chapter by going online to **MyEconLab**.
In the Study Plan for this chapter, select Section N: News.

For Critical Analysis

1. Under Indian law, the family of a commuter killed in an accident is entitled to a government death benefit. Why do you suppose that India's government imposes fines on people caught crossing tracks or riding on top of trains?

2. What do you think would happen to Mumbai's average daily rail passenger totals if a private company were to manage the system and charge higher fares?

Web Resources

1. For a description of the Mumbai passenger rail system, go to www.econtoday.com/chapter01.

2. Read an Indian court's directions for trying to reduce Mumbai's rail death toll at www.econtoday.com/chapter01.

Research Project

Suppose that you have been appointed to a commission that the Indian government has charged with making recommendations about how to reduce the death toll on Mumbai's commuter-rail system. The Indian government states that it already plans to lay 113 miles of new track, thereby extending the Mumbai rail network by 13 percent. It also plans to add 147 more trains, which will increase the number of passenger cars by more than 70 percent. Based on what you have learned about incentives, self-interest, and rational behavior, what other recommendations do you have for the Indian government?

myeconlab

Here is what you should know after reading this chapter. **MyEconLab** will help you identify what you know, and where to go when you need to practice.

WHAT YOU SHOULD KNOW

WHERE TO GO TO PRACTICE

Microeconomics versus Macroeconomics In general, economics is the study of how individuals make choices to satisfy wants. Economics is usually divided into microeconomics, which is the study of decision making by individual households and individual firms, and macroeconomics, which is the study of nationwide phenomena, such as inflation and unemployment.

incentives, 2
economics, 2
resources, 3
wants, 3
microeconomics, 3
macroeconomics, 3
aggregates, 3

- **MyEconLab** Study Plans 1.1, 1.2, 1.3
- Audio introduction to Chapter 1
- Video: The Difference Between Microeconomics and Macroeconomics

Self-Interest in Economic Analysis Rational self-interest is the assumption that people never intentionally make decisions that would leave them worse off. Instead, they are motivated mainly by their self-interest, which can relate to monetary and nonmonetary goals, such as love, prestige, and helping others.

rationality assumption, 4

- **MyEconLab** Study Plan 1.4
- Video: The Economic Person: Rational Self-Interest

Economics as a Science Economic models, or theories, are simplified representations of the real world. Economic models are never completely realistic because by definition they are simplifications using assumptions that are not directly testable. Nevertheless, economists can subject the predictions of economic theories to empirical tests in which real-world data are used to decide whether or not to reject the predictions.

models, or theories, 7
ceteris paribus
   assumption, 8
empirical, 8
behavioral economics, 9
bounded rationality, 9

- **MyEconLab** Study Plan 1.5
- ABC News Video: Coca-Cola in India

(continued)

 (continued)

WHAT YOU SHOULD KNOW		WHERE TO GO TO PRACTICE
Positive and Normative Economics Positive economics deals with *what is*, whereas normative economics deals with *what ought to be*. Positive economic statements are of the "if . . . then" variety; they are descriptive and predictive. In contrast, statements embodying values are within the realm of normative economics, or how people think things ought to be.	positive economics, 10 normative economics, 10	• **MyEconLab** Study Plan 1.6 • Video: Difference Between Normative and Positive Economics

Log in to MyEconLab, take a chapter test, and get a personalized Study Plan that tells you which concepts you understand and which ones you need to review. From there, MyEconLab will give you further practice, tutorials, animations, videos, and guided solutions.
Log in to www.myeconlab.com

PROBLEMS

All problems are assignable in  *. Answers to odd-numbered problems appear at the back of the book.*

1-1. Define economics. Explain briefly how the economic way of thinking—in terms of rational, self-interested people responding to incentives—relates to each of the following situations.

   a. A student deciding whether to purchase a textbook for a particular class

   b. Government officials seeking more funding for mass transit through higher taxes

   c. A municipality taxing hotel guests to obtain funding for a new sports stadium

1-2. Some people claim that the "economic way of thinking" does not apply to issues such as health care. Explain how economics does apply to this issue by developing a "model" of an individual's choices.

1-3. Does the phrase "unlimited wants and limited resources" apply to both a low-income household and a middle-income household? Can the same phrase be applied to a very high-income household?

1-4. In a single sentence, contrast microeconomics and macroeconomics. Next, categorize each of the following issues as either a microeconomic issue, a macroeconomic issue, or not an economic issue.

   a. The national unemployment rate

   b. The decision of a worker to work overtime or not

   c. A family's choice to have a baby

   d. The rate of growth of the money supply

   e. The national government's budget deficit

   f. A student's allocation of study time across two subjects

1-5. One of your classmates, Sally, is a hardworking student, serious about her classes, and conscientious about her grades. Sally is also involved, however, in volunteer activities and an extracurricular sport. Is Sally displaying rational behavior? Based on what you read in this chapter, construct an argument supporting the conclusion that she is.

1-6. Recently, a bank was trying to decide what fee to charge for "expedited payments"—payments that the bank would transmit extra speedily to enable customers to avoid late fees on cable TV bills, electric bills, and the like. To try to determine what fee customers were willing to pay for expedited payments, the bank conducted a survey. It was able to determine that many of the people surveyed already paid fees for expedited payment services that *exceeded* the maximum fees that they said they were willing to pay. How does the bank's finding relate to economists' traditional focus on what people do, rather than what they *say* they will do?

1-7. Explain, in your own words, the rationality assumption, and contrast it with the assumption of bounded rationality proposed by adherents of behavioral economics.

1-8. Why does the assumption of bounded rationality suggest that people might use rules of thumb to guide their decision making instead of considering every possible choice available to them?

1-9. Under what circumstances might people appear to use rules of thumb, as suggested by the assumption of bounded rationality, even though they really were behaving in a manner suggested by the rationality assumption?

1-10. Which of the following predictions appears to follow from a model based on the assumption that rational, self-interested individuals respond to incentives?

   a. For every 10 exam points Myrna must earn in order to pass her economics course and meet her graduation requirements, she will study one additional hour for her economics test next week.

   b. A coin toss will best predict Leonardo's decision about whether to purchase an expensive business suit or an inexpensive casual outfit to wear next week when he interviews for a high-paying job he is seeking.

   c. Celeste, who uses earnings from her regularly scheduled hours of part-time work to pay for her room and board at college, will decide to buy a newly released DVD this week only if she is able to work two additional hours.

1-11. Consider two models for estimating, in advance of an election, the shares of votes that will go to rival candidates. According to one model, pollsters' surveys of a randomly chosen set of registered voters before an election can be used to forecast the percentage of votes that each candidate will receive. This first model relies on the assumption that unpaid survey respondents will give truthful responses about how they will vote and that they will actually cast a ballot in the

election. The other model uses prices of financial assets (legally binding IOUs) issued by the Iowa Electronic Markets, operated by the University of Iowa, to predict electoral outcomes. The final payments received by owners of these assets, which can be bought or sold during the weeks and days preceding an election, depend on the shares of votes the candidates actually end up receiving. This second model assumes that owners of these assets wish to earn the highest possible returns, and it indicates that the market prices of these assets provide an indication of the percentage of votes that each candidate will actually receive on the day of the election.

   a. Which of these two models for forecasting electoral results is more firmly based on the rationality assumption of economics?

   b. How would an economist evaluate which is the better model for forecasting electoral outcomes?

1-12. Write a sentence contrasting positive and normative economic analysis.

1-13. Based on your answer to Problem 1–12, categorize each of the following conclusions as being the result of positive analysis or normative analysis.

   a. A higher minimum wage will reduce employment opportunities for minimum wage workers.

   b. Increasing the earnings of minimum wage employees is desirable, and raising the minimum wage is the best way to accomplish this.

   c. Everyone should enjoy open access to health care.

   d. Heath care subsidies will increase the consumption of health care.

1-14. Consider the following statements, based on a positive economic analysis that assumes that all other things remain constant. For each, list one other thing that might change and thus offset the outcome stated.

   a. Increased demand for laptop computers will drive up their price.

   b. Falling gasoline prices will result in additional vacation travel.

   c. A reduction of income tax rates will result in more people working.

ECONOMICS ON THE NET

The Usefulness of Studying Economics This application helps you see how accomplished people benefited from their study of economics. It also explores ways in which these people feel others of all walks of life can gain from learning more about the economics field.

Title: How Taking an Economics Course Can Lead to Becoming an Economist

Navigation: Go to **www.econtoday.com/chapter01** to visit the Federal Reserve Bank of Minneapolis publication, *The Region*. Select the last article of the issue, "Economists in *The Region* on Their Student Experiences and the Need for Economic Literacy."

Application Read the interviews of the six economists, and answer the following questions.

1. Based on your reading, which economists do you think other economists regard as influential? What educational institutions do you think are the most influential in economics?

2. Which economists do you think were attracted to microeconomics and which to macroeconomics?

For Group Study and Analysis Divide the class into three groups, and assign the groups the Blinder, Yellen, and Rivlin interviews. Have each group use the content of its assigned interview to develop a statement explaining why the study of economics is important, regardless of a student's chosen major.

ANSWERS TO QUICK QUIZZES

p. 6: (i) wants . . . unlimited; (ii) Microeconomics . . . macroeconomics; (iii) rationality; (iv) Self-interest
p. 11: (i) model . . . theory . . . model; (ii) *ceteris paribus*; (iii) Behavioral . . . bounded rationality; (iv) Positive . . . Normative

Reading and Working with Graphs

Independent variable
A variable whose value is determined independently of, or outside, the equation under study.

Dependent variable
A variable whose value changes according to changes in the value of one or more independent variables.

A graph is a visual representation of the relationship between variables. In this appendix, we'll deal with just two variables: an **independent variable,** which can change in value freely, and a **dependent variable,** which changes only as a result of changes in the value of the independent variable. For example, even if nothing else is changing in your life, your weight depends on your intake of calories. The independent variable is caloric intake, and the dependent variable is weight.

A table is a list of numerical values showing the relationship between two (or more) variables. Any table can be converted into a graph, which is a visual representation of that list. Once you understand how a table can be converted to a graph, you will understand what graphs are and how to construct and use them.

Consider a practical example. A conservationist may try to convince you that driving at lower highway speeds will help you conserve gas. Table A-1 shows the relationship between speed—the independent variable—and the distance you can go on a gallon of gas at that speed—the dependent variable. This table does show a pattern. As the data in the first column get larger in value, the data in the second column get smaller.

Now let's take a look at the different ways in which variables can be related.

Direct and Inverse Relationships

Two variables can be related in different ways, some simple, others more complex. For example, a person's weight and height are often related. If we measured the height and weight of thousands of people, we would surely find that taller people tend to weigh more than shorter people. That is, we would discover that there is a **direct relationship** between height and weight. By this we simply mean that an *increase* in one variable is usually associated with an *increase* in the related variable. This can easily be seen in panel (a) of Figure A-1.

TABLE A-1

Gas Mileage as a Function of Driving Speed

Miles per Hour	Miles per Gallon
45	25
50	24
55	23
60	21
65	19
70	16
75	13

Direct relationship
A relationship between two variables that is positive, meaning that an increase in one variable is associated with an increase in the other and a decrease in one variable is associated with a decrease in the other.

FIGURE A-1

Direct and Inverse Relationships

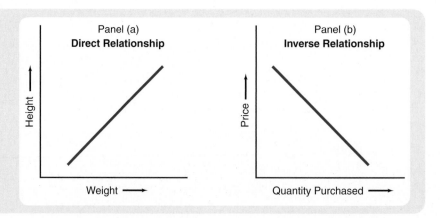

Let's look at another simple way in which two variables can be related. Much evidence indicates that as the price of a specific commodity rises, the amount purchased decreases—there is an **inverse relationship** between the variable's price per unit and quantity purchased. Such a relationship indicates that for higher and higher prices, smaller and smaller quantities will be purchased. We see this relationship in panel (b) of Figure A-1.

Inverse relationship
A relationship between two variables that is negative, meaning that an increase in one variable is associated with a decrease in the other and a decrease in one variable is associated with an increase in the other.

Constructing a Graph

Let us now examine how to construct a graph to illustrate a relationship between two variables.

A Number Line

The first step is to become familiar with what is called a **number line.** One is shown in Figure A-2. You should know two things about it:

Number line
A line that can be divided into segments of equal length, each associated with a number.

1. The points on the line divide the line into equal segments.
2. The numbers associated with the points on the line increase in value from left to right; saying it the other way around, the numbers decrease in value from right to left. However you say it, what you're describing is formally called an *ordered set of points*.

On the number line, we have shown the line segments—that is, the distance from 0 to 10 or the distance between 30 and 40. They all appear to be equal and, indeed, are each equal to $\frac{1}{2}$ inch. When we use a distance to represent a quantity, such as barrels of oil, graphically, we are *scaling* the number line. In the example shown, the distance between 0 and 10 might represent 10 barrels of oil, or the distance from 0 to 40 might represent 40 barrels. Of course, the scale may differ on different number lines. For example, a distance of 1 inch could represent 10 units on one number line but 5,000 units on another. Notice that on our number line, points to the left of 0 correspond to negative numbers and points to the right of 0 correspond to positive numbers.

Of course, we can also construct a vertical number line. Consider the one in Figure A-3 on the next page. As we move up this vertical number line, the numbers increase in value; conversely, as we descend, they decrease in value. Below 0 the numbers are negative, and above 0 the numbers are positive. And as on the horizontal number line, all the line segments are equal. This line is divided into segments such that the distance between −2 and −1 is the same as the distance between 0 and 1.

Combining Vertical and Horizontal Number Lines

By drawing the horizontal and vertical lines on the same sheet of paper, we are able to express the relationships between variables graphically. We do this in Figure A-4 on the next page. We draw them (1) so that they intersect at each other's 0 point and (2) so that they are perpendicular to each other. The result is a set of coordinate axes, where each line is called an *axis*. When we have two axes, they span a *plane*.

FIGURE A-2

Horizontal Number Line

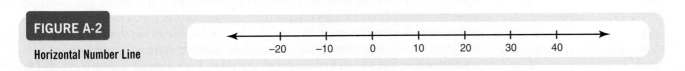

Vertical Number Line

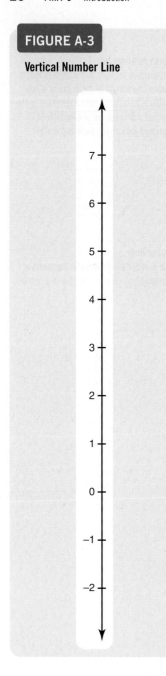

A Set of Coordinate Axes

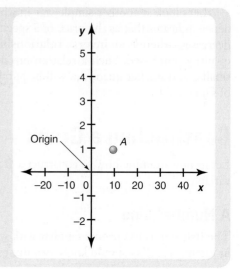

For one number line, you need only one number to specify any point on the line; equivalently, when you see a point on the line, you know that it represents one number or one value. With a coordinate value system, you need two numbers to specify a single point in the plane; when you see a single point on a graph, you know that it represents two numbers or two values.

The basic things that you should know about a coordinate number system are that the vertical number line is referred to as the **y axis,** the horizontal number line is referred to as the **x axis,** and the point of intersection of the two lines is referred to as the **origin.**

Any point such as A in Figure A-4 represents two numbers—a value of x and a value of y. But we know more than that: We also know that point A represents a positive value of y because it is above the x axis, and we know that it represents a positive value of x because it is to the right of the y axis.

Point A represents a "paired observation" of the variables x and y; in particular, in Figure A-4, A represents an observation of the pair of values $x = 10$ and $y = 1$. Every point in the coordinate system corresponds to a paired observation of x and y, which can be simply written (x, y)—the x value is always specified first and then the y value. When we give the values associated with the position of point A in the coordinate number system, we are in effect giving the coordinates of that point. A's coordinates are $x = 10$, $y = 1$, or $(10, 1)$.

Graphing Numbers in a Table

Consider Table A-2. Column 1 shows different prices for T-shirts, and column 2 gives the number of T-shirts purchased per week at these prices. Notice the pattern of these numbers. As the price of T-shirts falls, the number of T-shirts purchased per week increases. Therefore, an inverse relationship exists between these two variables, and as soon as we represent it on a graph, you will be able to see the relationship. We can graph this relationship using a coordinate number system—a vertical and horizontal number line for each of these two variables. Such a graph is shown in panel (b) of Figure A-5.

y axis
The vertical axis in a graph.

x axis
The horizontal axis in a graph.

Origin
The intersection of the y axis and the x axis in a graph.

In economics, it is conventional to put dollar values on the y axis and quantities on the horizontal axis. We therefore construct a vertical number line for price and a horizontal number line, the x axis, for quantity of T-shirts purchased per week. The resulting coordinate system allows the plotting of each of the paired observation points; in panel (a), we repeat Table A-2, with a column added expressing these points in paired-data (x, y) form. For example, point J is the paired observation (30, 9). It indicates that when the price of a T-shirt is $9, 30 will be purchased per week.

If it were possible to sell parts of a T-shirt ($\frac{1}{2}$ or $\frac{1}{20}$ of a shirt), we would have observations at every possible price. That is, we would be able to connect our paired observations, represented as lettered points. Let's assume that we can make T-shirts perfectly divisible so that the linear relationship shown in Figure A-5 also holds for fractions of dollars and T-shirts. We would then have a line that connects these points, as shown in the graph in Figure A-6 on the following page.

In short, we have now represented the data from the table in the form of a graph. Note that an inverse relationship between two variables shows up on a graph as a line or curve that slopes *downward* from left to right. (You might as well get used to the idea that economists call a straight line a "curve" even though it may not curve at all. Economists' data frequently turn out to be curves, so they refer to everything represented graphically, even straight lines, as curves.)

The Slope of a Line (A Linear Curve)

An important property of a curve represented on a graph is its *slope*. Consider Figure A-7 on page 22, which represents the quantities of shoes per week that a seller is willing to offer at different prices. Note that in panel (a) of Figure A-7, as in Figure A-5, we have expressed the coordinates of the points in parentheses in paired-data form.

TABLE A-2

T-Shirts Purchased

(1) Price of T-Shirts	(2) Number of T-Shirts Purchased per Week
$10	20
9	30
8	40
7	50
6	60
5	70

FIGURE A-5

Graphing the Relationship Between T-Shirts Purchased and Price

Panel (a)

Price per T-Shirt	T-Shirts Purchased per Week	Point on Graph
$10	20	I (20, 10)
9	30	J (30, 9)
8	40	K (40, 8)
7	50	L (50, 7)
6	60	M (60, 6)
5	70	N (70, 5)

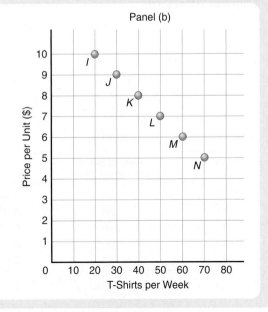

Panel (b)

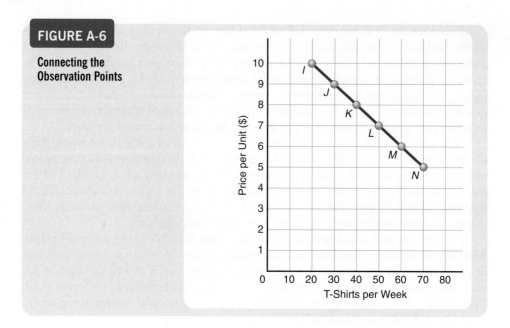

FIGURE A-6

Connecting the Observation Points

Slope

The change in the *y* value divided by the corresponding change in the *x* value of a curve; the "incline" of the curve.

The **slope** of a line is defined as the change in the *y* values divided by the corresponding change in the *x* values as we move along the line. Let's move from point *E* to point *D* in panel (b) of Figure A-7. As we move, we note that the change in the *y* values, which is the change in price, is +$20, because we have moved from a price of $20 to a price of $40 per pair. As we move from *E* to *D*, the change in the *x* values is +80; the number of pairs of shoes willingly offered per week rises from 80 to 160 pairs.

FIGURE A-7

A Positively Sloped Curve

Panel (a)

Price per Pair	Pairs of Shoes Offered per Week	Point on Graph
$100	400	A (400, 100)
80	320	B (320, 80)
60	240	C (240, 60)
40	160	D (160, 40)
20	80	E (80, 20)

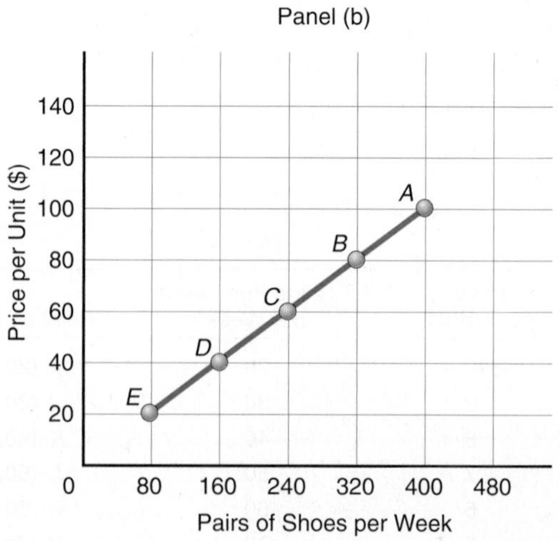

Panel (b)

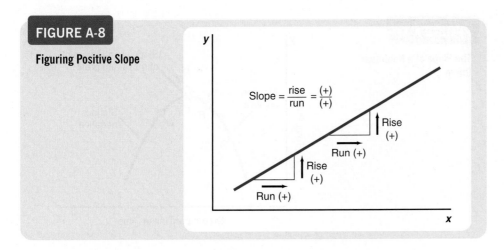

FIGURE A-8

Figuring Positive Slope

The slope, calculated as a change in the *y* values divided by the change in the *x* values, is therefore

$$\frac{20}{80} = \frac{1}{4}$$

It may be helpful for you to think of slope as a "rise" (movement in the vertical direction) over a "run" (movement in the horizontal direction). We show this abstractly in Figure A-8. The slope is the amount of rise divided by the amount of run. In the example in Figure A-8, and of course in Figure A-7, the amount of rise is positive and so is the amount of run. That's because it's a direct relationship. We show an inverse relationship in Figure A-9. The slope is still equal to the rise divided by the run, but in this case the rise and the run have opposite signs because the curve slopes downward. That means that the slope is negative and that we are dealing with an inverse relationship.

Now let's calculate the slope for a different part of the curve in panel (b) of Figure A-7. We will find the slope as we move from point *B* to point *A*. Again, we note that the slope, or rise over run, from *B* to *A* equals

$$\frac{20}{80} = \frac{1}{4}$$

A specific property of a straight line is that its slope is the same between any two points; in other words, the slope is constant at all points on a straight line in a graph.

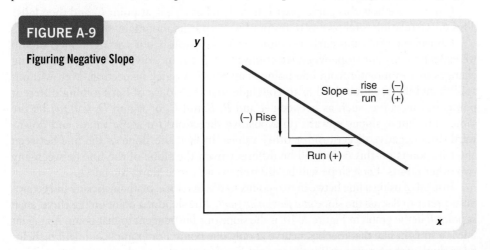

FIGURE A-9

Figuring Negative Slope

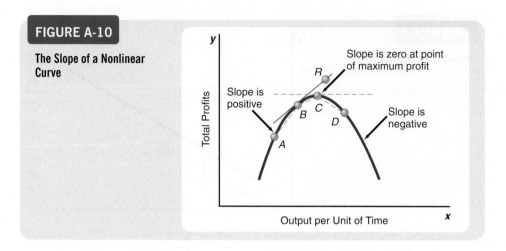

FIGURE A-10

The Slope of a Nonlinear Curve

We conclude that for our example in Figure A-7 on page 22, the relationship between the price of a pair of shoes and the number of pairs of shoes willingly offered per week is *linear*, which simply means "in a straight line," and our calculations indicate a constant slope. Moreover, we calculate a direct relationship between these two variables, which turns out to be an upward-sloping (from left to right) curve. Upward-sloping curves have positive slopes—in this case, the slope is $+\frac{1}{4}$.

We know that an inverse relationship between two variables shows up as a downward-sloping curve—rise over run will be negative because the rise and run have opposite signs, as shown in Figure A-9 on the previous page. When we see a negative slope, we know that increases in one variable are associated with decreases in the other. Therefore, we say that downward-sloping curves have negative slopes. Can you verify that the slope of the graph representing the relationship between T-shirt prices and the quantity of T-shirts purchased per week in Figure A-6 on page 22 is $-\frac{1}{10}$?

Slopes of Nonlinear Curves

The graph presented in Figure A-10 indicates a *nonlinear* relationship between two variables, total profits and output per unit of time. Inspection of this graph indicates that at first, increases in output lead to increases in total profits; that is, total profits rise as output increases. But beyond some output level, further increases in output cause decreases in total profits.

Can you see how this curve rises at first, reaches a peak at point C, and then falls? This curve relating total profits to output levels appears mountain-shaped.

Considering that this curve is nonlinear (it is obviously not a straight line), should we expect a constant slope when we compute changes in y divided by corresponding changes in x in moving from one point to another? A quick inspection, even without specific numbers, should lead us to conclude that the slopes of lines joining different points in this curve, such as between A and B, B and C, or C and D, will *not* be the same. The curve slopes upward (in a positive direction) for some values and downward (in a negative direction) for other values. In fact, the slope of the line between any two points on this curve will be different from the slope of the line between any two other points. Each slope will be different as we move along the curve.

Instead of using a line between two points to discuss slope, mathematicians and economists prefer to discuss the slope *at a particular point*. The slope at a point on the curve, such as point B in the graph in Figure A-10, is the slope of a line tangent to that point. A tangent line is a straight line that touches a curve at only one point. For example, it might be helpful to think of the tangent at B as the straight line that just "kisses" the curve at point B.

To calculate the slope of a tangent line, you need to have some additional information besides the two values of the point of tangency. For example, in Figure A-10, if we knew that the point *R* also lay on the tangent line and we knew the two values of that point, we could calculate the slope of the tangent line. We could calculate rise over run between points *B* and *R*, and the result would be the slope of the line tangent to the one point *B* on the curve.

myeconlab

Here is what you should know after reading this appendix. **MyEconLab** will help you identify what you know, and where to go when you need to practice.

WHAT YOU SHOULD KNOW

WHERE TO GO TO PRACTICE

Direct and Inverse Relationships In a direct relationship, a dependent variable changes in the same direction as the change in the independent variable. In an inverse relationship, the dependent variable changes in the opposite direction of the change in the independent variable.

independent variable, 18
dependent variable, 18
direct relationship, 18
inverse relationship, 19

- **MyEconLab** Study Plan 1.7

Constructing a Graph When we draw a graph showing the relationship between two economic variables, we are holding all other things constant (the Latin term for which is *ceteris paribus*).

number line, 19
y axis, 20
x axis, 20
origin, 20

- **MyEconLab** Study Plan 1.8

Graphing Numbers We obtain a set of coordinates by putting vertical and horizontal number lines together. The vertical line is called the *y* axis; the horizontal line, the *x* axis.

- **MyEconLab** Study Plan 1.9

The Slope of a Linear Curve The slope of any linear (straight-line) curve is the change in the *y* values divided by the corresponding change in the *x* values as we move along the line. Otherwise stated, the slope is calculated as the amount of rise over the amount of run, where rise is movement in the vertical direction and run is movement in the horizontal direction.

slope, 22

KEY FIGURES
Figure A-8, 23
Figure A-9, 23

- **MyEconLab** Study Plan 1.10
- Animated Figures A-8, A-9

The Slope of a Nonlinear Curve The slope of a nonlinear curve changes; it is positive when the curve is rising and negative when the curve is falling. At a maximum or minimum point, the slope of the nonlinear curve is zero.

KEY FIGURE
Figure A-10, 24

- **MyEconLab** Study Plan 1.10
- Animated Figure A-10

Log in to MyEconLab, take an appendix test, and get a personalized Study Plan that tells you which concepts you understand and which ones you need to review. From there, MyEconLab will give you further practice, tutorials, animations, videos, and guided solutions.
Log in to www.myeconlab.com

PROBLEMS

All problems are assignable in Xmyeconlab . *Answers to odd-numbered problems appear at the back of the book.*

A-1. Explain which is the independent variable and which is the dependent variable for each of the following examples.

   a. Once you determine the price of a notebook at the college bookstore, you will decide how many notebooks to buy.

   b. You will decide how many credit hours to register for this semester once the university tells you how many work-study hours you will be assigned.

   c. You anticipate earning a higher grade on your next economics exam because you studied more hours in the weeks preceding the exam.

A-2. For each of the following items, state whether a direct or an inverse relationship is likely to exist.

   a. The number of hours you study for an exam and your exam score

   b. The price of pizza and the quantity purchased

   c. The number of games the university basketball team won last year and the number of season tickets sold this year

A-3. Review Figure A-4 on page 20, and then state whether each of the following paired observations is on, above, or below the x axis and on, to the left of, or to the right of the y axis.

   a. $(-10, 4)$

   b. $(20, -2)$

   c. $(10, 0)$

A-4. State whether each of the following functions specifies a direct or an inverse relationship.

   a. $y = 5x$

   b. $y = 10 - 2x$

   c. $y = 3 + x$

   d. $y = -3x$

A-5. Given the function $y = 5x$, complete the following schedule and plot the curve.

y	x
	−4
	−2
	0
	2
	4

A-6. Given the function $y = 8 - 2x$, complete the following schedule and plot the curve.

y	x
	−4
	−2
	0
	2
	4

A-7. Calculate the slope of the function you graphed in Problem A-5.

A-8. Calculate the slope of the function you graphed in Problem A-6.

Scarcity and the World of Trade-Offs

T he employer of seven former college athletes requires them to practice five days per week. Each day, they lift weights to maintain their muscle strength, and they sprint through obstacle courses to reduce their reaction time. To improve their footwork and hand speed, they watch videos of previous performances. They consider themselves to be professional athletes, but thousands of people with the opportunity to observe them at work pay little heed to their exertions. These seven individuals constitute a pit crew at a motor speedway. Each crew member performs a very specific task, and the crew's tasks are organized so as to attain maximum output from their combined resources. These aspects of the activities of a speedway pit crew conform to key economic concepts that are the subject of this chapter.

LEARNING OBJECTIVES

MyEconLab helps you master each objective and study more efficiently. See end of chapter for details.

After reading this chapter, you should be able to:

- Evaluate whether even affluent people face the problem of scarcity

- Understand why economics considers individuals' "wants" but not their "needs"

- Explain why the scarcity problem induces individuals to consider opportunity costs

- Discuss why obtaining increasing increments of any particular good typically entails giving up more and more units of other goods

- Explain why society faces a trade-off between consumption goods and capital goods

- Distinguish between absolute and comparative advantage

? Did you know that there are more than 105 million parking spaces in the United States? Although parking spaces vary in size, the typical space is about 19 feet long and 8 feet wide and takes up an area of about 152 square feet. Consequently, U.S. parking spaces occupy almost 16 billion square feet of space, or almost 575 square miles.

All of this land devoted to parking spaces could, of course, be allocated to numerous alternative uses, such as housing developments, office buildings, city parks, and green spaces. These alternative uses of land now occupied by parking spaces could yield benefits to numerous members of society. Because this land does not yield these benefits, the allocation of land to parking spaces entails costs. Land, like all other resources, is scarce.

Scarcity

Whenever individuals or communities cannot obtain everything they desire simultaneously, they must make choices. Choices occur because of *scarcity*. **Scarcity** is the most basic concept in all of economics. Scarcity means that we do not ever have enough of everything, including time, to satisfy our *every* desire. Scarcity exists because human wants always exceed what can be produced with the limited resources and time that nature makes available.

Scarcity
A situation in which the ingredients for producing the things that people desire are insufficient to satisfy all wants at a zero price.

What Scarcity Is Not

Scarcity is not a shortage. After a hurricane hits and cuts off supplies to a community, TV newscasts often show people standing in line to get minimum amounts of cooking fuel and food. A news commentator might say that the line is caused by the "scarcity" of these products. But cooking fuel and food are always scarce—we cannot obtain all that we want at a zero price. Therefore, do not confuse the concept of scarcity, which is general and all-encompassing, with the concept of shortages as evidenced by people waiting in line to obtain a particular product.

Scarcity is not the same thing as poverty. Scarcity occurs among the poor and among the rich. Even the richest person on earth faces scarcity. For instance, even the world's richest person has only limited time available. Low income levels do not create more scarcity. High income levels do not create less scarcity.

Scarcity is a fact of life, like gravity. And just as physicists did not invent gravity, economists did not invent scarcity—it existed well before the first economist ever lived. It has existed at all times in the past and will exist at all times in the future.

What underlying fact about parking spaces would motivate someone to buy a small car?

Scarcity and Resources

Scarcity exists because resources are insufficient to satisfy our every desire. Resources are the inputs used in the production of the things that we want. **Production** can be defined as virtually any activity that results in the conversion of resources into products that can be used in consumption. Production includes delivering things from one part of the country to another. It includes taking ice from an ice tray to put it in your soft-drink glass. The resources used in production are called *factors of production*, and some economists use the terms *resources* and *factors of production* interchangeably. The total quantity of all resources that an economy has at any one time determines what that economy can produce.

Factors of production can be classified in many ways. Here is one such classification:

Production
Any activity that results in the conversion of resources into products that can be used in consumption.

1. *Land.* **Land** encompasses all the nonhuman gifts of nature, including timber, water, fish, minerals, and the original fertility of land. It is often called the *natural resource*.

Land
The natural resources that are available from nature. Land as a resource includes location, original fertility and mineral deposits, topography, climate, water, and vegetation.

2. *Labor.* **Labor** is the *human resource*, which includes productive contributions made by individuals who work, such as Web page designers, ballet dancers, and professional football players.

3. *Physical capital.* **Physical capital** consists of the factories and equipment used in production. It also includes improvements to natural resources, such as irrigation ditches.

4. *Human capital.* **Human capital** is the economic characterization of the education and training of workers. How much the nation produces depends not only on how many hours people work but also on how productive they are, and that in turn depends in part on education and training. To become more educated, individuals have to devote time and resources, just as a business has to devote resources if it wants to increase its physical capital. Whenever a worker's skills increase, human capital has been improved.

5. *Entrepreneurship.* **Entrepreneurship** (actually a subdivision of labor) is the component of human resources that performs the functions of organizing, managing, and assembling the other factors of production to create and operate business ventures. Entrepreneurship also encompasses taking risks that involve the possibility of losing large sums of wealth on new ventures. It includes new methods of doing common things and generally experimenting with any type of new thinking that could lead to making more income. Without entrepreneurship, virtually no business organization could operate.

Why do you suppose that the U.S. Navy wants its top officers to develop entrepreneurial skills?

Labor
Productive contributions of humans who work.

Physical capital
All manufactured resources, including buildings, equipment, machines, and improvements to land that are used for production.

Human capital
The accumulated training and education of workers.

Entrepreneurship
The component of human resources that performs the functions of raising capital, organizing, managing, and assembling other factors of production, making basic business policy decisions, and taking risks.

POLICY EXAMPLE
Schooling Admirals in Entrepreneurship

The U.S. Navy regularly sends officers back to school for graduate courses in areas such as nuclear engineering and foreign policy analysis. In recent years, however, admirals are as likely to find themselves enrolling in graduate business courses with titles such as "Using Effects-Based Thinking" and "Organizational Innovation." The Secretary of the Navy has decided that top officers should know as much about supply-chain management, management delegation, and organizational behavior as they know about seaborne aviation and submarine technology. Acquainting admirals with entrepreneurial skills, those heading the Navy have concluded, will lead to wiser allocation and utilization of military resources.

FOR CRITICAL ANALYSIS
In what ways is a military organization such as the U.S. Navy like a business?

Goods versus Economic Goods

Goods are defined as all things from which individuals derive satisfaction or happiness. Goods therefore include air to breathe and the beauty of a sunset as well as food, cars, and iPods.

Economic goods are a subset of all goods—they are scarce goods, about which we must constantly make decisions regarding their best use. By definition, the desired quantity of an economic good exceeds the amount that is available at a zero price. Virtually every example we use in economics concerns economic goods—cars, DVD players,

Goods
All things from which individuals derive satisfaction or happiness.

Economic goods
Goods that are scarce, for which the quantity demanded exceeds the quantity supplied at a zero price.

computers, socks, baseball bats, and corn. Weeds are a good example of *bads*—goods for which the desired quantity is much *less* than what nature provides at a zero price.

Sometimes you will see references to "goods and services." **Services** are tasks that are performed for someone else, such as laundry, Internet access, hospital care, restaurant meal preparation, car polishing, psychological counseling, and teaching. One way of looking at services is to think of them as *intangible goods*.

Wants and Needs

Wants are not the same as needs. Indeed, from the economist's point of view, the term *needs* is objectively undefinable. When someone says, "I need some new clothes," there is no way to know whether that person is stating a vague wish, a want, or a life-saving requirement. If the individual making the statement were dying of exposure in a northern country during the winter, we might argue that indeed the person does need clothes—perhaps not new ones, but at least some articles of warm clothing. Typically, however, the term *need* is used very casually in conversation. What people mean, usually, is that they desire something that they do not currently have.

Humans have unlimited wants. Just imagine that every single material want that you might have was satisfied. You could have all of the clothes, cars, houses, DVDs, yachts, and other items that you want. Does that mean that nothing else could add to your total level of happiness? Undoubtedly, you might continue to think of new goods and services that you could obtain, particularly as they came to market. You would also still be lacking in fulfilling all of your wants for compassion, friendship, love, affection, prestige, musical abilities, sports abilities, and so on.

In reality, every individual has competing wants but cannot satisfy all of them, given limited resources. This is the reality of scarcity. Each person must therefore make choices. Whenever a choice is made to produce or buy something, something else that is also desired is not produced or not purchased. In other words, in a world of scarcity, every want that ends up being satisfied causes one or more other wants to remain unsatisfied or to be forfeited.

Services
Mental or physical labor or help purchased by consumers. Examples are the assistance of physicians, lawyers, dentists, repair personnel, housecleaners, educators, retailers, and wholesalers; items purchased or used by consumers that do not have physical characteristics.

Would you classify a flat-screen TV as a want or a need? What is the difference?

QUICK QUIZ See page 50 for the answers. Review concepts from this section in MyEconLab.

_____ is the situation in which human wants always exceed what can be produced with the limited resources and time that nature makes available.

We use scarce resources, such as _____, _____, _____ and _____ capital, and _____, to produce economic goods—goods that are desired but are not directly obtainable from nature to the extent demanded or desired at a zero price.

_____ are unlimited; they include all material desires and all nonmaterial desires, such as love, affection, power, and prestige.

The concept of _____ is difficult to define objectively for every person; consequently, we simply consider every person's wants to be unlimited. In a world of **scarcity,** satisfaction of one want necessarily means nonsatisfaction of one or more other wants.

Scarcity, Choice, and Opportunity Cost

The natural fact of scarcity implies that we must make choices. One of the most important results of this fact is that every choice made means that some opportunity must be sacrificed. Every choice involves giving up an opportunity to produce or consume something else.

Valuing Forgone Alternatives

Consider a practical example. Every choice you make to study economics for one more hour requires that you give up the opportunity to engage in any of the following activities: study more of another subject, listen to music, sleep, browse at a local store, read a novel, or work out at the gym. The most highly valued of these opportunities is forgone if you choose to study economics an additional hour.

Because there were so many alternatives from which to choose, how could you determine the value of what you gave up to engage in that extra hour of studying economics? First of all, no one else can tell you the answer because only *you* can put a value on the alternatives forgone. Only you know the value of another hour of sleep or of an hour looking for the latest digital music downloads—whatever one activity *you* would have chosen if you had not opted to study economics for that hour. That means that only you can determine the highest-valued, next-best alternative that you had to sacrifice in order to study economics one more hour. Only you can determine the value of the next-best alternative.

What is your next-highest alternative when you study an extra hour?

Opportunity cost
The highest-valued, next-best alternative that must be sacrificed to obtain something or to satisfy a want.

Opportunity Cost

The value of the next-best alternative is called **opportunity cost.** The opportunity cost of any action is the value of what is given up—the next-highest-ranked alternative—because a choice was made. When you study one more hour, there may be many alternatives available for the use of that hour, but assume that you can do only one other thing in that hour—your next-highest-ranked alternative. What is important is the choice that you would have made if you hadn't studied one more hour. Your opportunity cost is the *next-highest-ranked* alternative, not *all* alternatives.

In economics, cost is always a forgone opportunity.

One way to think about opportunity cost is to understand that when you choose to do something, you lose something else. What you lose is being able to engage in your next-highest-valued alternative. The cost of your chosen alternative is what you lose, which is by definition your next-highest-valued alternative. This is your opportunity cost.

What is the opportunity cost of precisely synchronizing the world's clocks?

INTERNATIONAL EXAMPLE
The Significant Opportunity Cost of a Second of Time

The tug of the moon's gravity slows the earth's rotation, so the length of a day on earth is always increasing a tiny bit. At intervals averaging about 18 months, astronomers notify a United Nations group charged with regulating global timekeeping that the world's day has gained another second. Telecommunications companies, satellite operators, and governments then add an extra, "leap" second to the planet's atomic clocks.

Many computers, however, are not equipped with software that can handle the 61-second minute that results when a leap second is added. Particularly vulnerable are programs that manage the global positioning systems (GPS) utilized by surveyors, engineers, surgeons, and navigators, among others. The last time a leap second was added, GPS breakdowns created snafus that temporarily idled equipment and workers on every continent.

The U.S. government has proposed adding a "leap minute" every century instead of leap seconds every 18 months. In this way, the world's economies might avoid a significant opportunity cost—that is, forgoing productive activities—in order to keep the earth's time precisely synchronized with its rotation.

INTERNATIONAL EXAMPLE (cont.)

FOR CRITICAL ANALYSIS
If leap seconds are not added, astronomical observatories would have to devote some of their budgets to paying $10,000 to $500,000 per facility for telescope realignments *to take into account the extra seconds not appearing on clocks. Why do astronomers argue that they would bear opportunity costs if the U.S. government's "leap minute" proposal is adopted?*

The World of Trade-Offs

Whenever you engage in any activity using any resource, even time, you are *trading off* the use of that resource for one or more alternative uses. The extent of the trade-off is represented by the opportunity cost. The opportunity cost of studying economics has already been mentioned—it is the value of the next-best alternative. When you think of any alternative, you are thinking of trade-offs.

Let's consider a hypothetical example of a trade-off between the results of spending time studying economics and mathematics. For the sake of this argument, we will assume that additional time studying either economics or mathematics will lead to a higher grade in the subject to which additional study time is allocated. One of the best ways to examine this trade-off is with a graph. (If you would like a refresher on graphical techniques, study Appendix A at the end of Chapter 1 before going on.)

Graphical Analysis

In Figure 2-1, the expected grade in mathematics is measured on the vertical axis of the graph, and the expected grade in economics is measured on the horizontal axis. We simplify the world and assume that you have a maximum of 12 hours per week to spend studying these two subjects and that if you spend all 12 hours on economics, you will get an A in the course. You will, however, fail mathematics. Conversely, if you spend all of your 12 hours studying mathematics, you will get an A in that subject, but you will flunk economics. Here the trade-off is a special case: one to one. A one-to-one trade-off means that the opportunity cost of receiving one grade higher in economics (for example, improving from a C to a B) is one grade lower in mathematics (falling from a C to a D).

The Production Possibilities Curve (PPC)

The graph in Figure 2-1 illustrates the relationship between the possible results that can be produced in each of two activities, depending on how much time you choose to devote to each activity. This graph shows a representation of a **production possibilities curve (PPC).**

Production possibilities curve (PPC)
A curve representing all possible combinations of maximum outputs that could be produced assuming a fixed amount of productive resources of a given quality.

Consider that you are producing a grade in economics when you study economics and a grade in mathematics when you study mathematics. Then the line that goes from A on one axis to A on the other axis therefore becomes a production possibilities curve. It is defined as the maximum quantity of one good or service that can be produced, given that a specific quantity of another is produced. It is a curve that shows the possibilities available for increasing the output of one good or service by reducing the amount of another. In the example in Figure 2-1, your time for studying was limited to 12 hours per week. The two possible outputs were your grade in mathematics and your grade in economics. The particular production possibilities curve presented in Figure 2-1 is a graphical representation of the opportunity cost of studying one more hour in one subject. It is a *straight-line production possibilities curve*, which is a spe-

FIGURE 2-1

Production Possibilities Curve for Grades in Mathematics and Economics (Trade-Offs)

We assume that only 12 hours can be spent per week on studying. If the student is at point *x*, equal time (6 hours a week) is spent on both courses, and equal grades of C will be received. If a higher grade in economics is desired, the student may go to point *y*, thereby receiving a B in economics but a D in mathematics. At point *y*, 3 hours are spent on mathematics and 9 hours on economics.

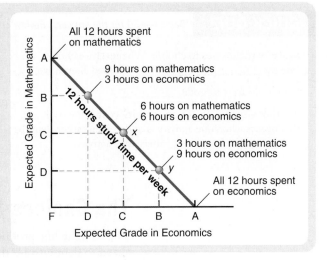

cial case. (The more general case will be discussed next.) If you decide to be at point *x* in Figure 2-1, you will devote 6 hours of study time to mathematics and 6 hours to economics. The expected grade in each course will be a C. If you are more interested in getting a B in economics, you will go to point *y* on the production possibilities curve, spending only 3 hours on mathematics but 9 hours on economics. Your expected grade in mathematics will then drop from a C to a D.

Note that these trade-offs between expected grades in mathematics and economics are the result of *holding constant* total study time as well as all other factors that might influence your ability to learn, such as computerized study aids. Quite clearly, if you were able to spend more total time studying, it would be possible to have higher grades in both economics and mathematics. In that case, however, we would no longer be on the specific production possibilities curve illustrated in Figure 2-1. We would have to draw a new curve, farther to the right, to show the greater total study time and a different set of possible trade-offs.

What trade-off have the U.S. armed forces recently confronted as a result of the continuing military operations in Iraq and Afghanistan?

POLICY EXAMPLE
The U.S. Military Confronts a Trade-Off

Recently, U.S. military leaders decided to allocate an extra $1 billion in resources to expanding ground operations by troops in Iraq and Afghanistan. Given their available resources, the U.S. armed forces could undertake this expansion of troop operations only by forgoing the allocation of $1 billion in resources to a program known as Transformational Satellite Communications, or TSAT. The TSAT program would have involved development of space-based lasers and satellite-based Internet connections to facilitate ultrafast and highly secure data and video transmissions among military

planes, ships, and troops. Thus, for the U.S. armed forces, the opportunity cost of maintaining troop levels in Iraq and Afghanistan was the forgone production of better military communications networks.

FOR CRITICAL ANALYSIS

How could Congress and taxpayers have made it possible for the U.S. armed forces to maintain their Iraq and Afghanistan operations without forgoing the allocation of resources to the TSAT program?

QUICK QUIZ   *See page 50 for the answers. Review concepts from this section in MyEconLab.*

Scarcity requires us to choose. Whenever we choose, we lose the _____-_____-valued alternative.

Cost is always a forgone _____.

Another way to look at **opportunity cost** is the trade-off that occurs when one activity is undertaken rather than the _____-_____ alternative activity.

A _____ _____ curve graphically shows the trade-off that occurs when more of one output is obtained at the sacrifice of another. This curve is a graphical representation of, among other things, opportunity cost.

The Choices Society Faces

The straight-line production possibilities curve presented in Figure 2-1 can be generalized to demonstrate the related concepts of scarcity, choice, and trade-offs that our entire nation faces. As you will see, the production possibilities curve is a simple but powerful economic model because it can demonstrate these related concepts.

A Two-Good Example

The example we will use is the choice between the production of computer servers and high-definition televisions (HDTVs). We assume for the moment that these are the only two goods that can be produced in the nation.

Panel (a) of Figure 2-2 gives the various combinations of servers and HDTVs that are possible. If all resources are devoted to server production, 50 million per year can be produced. If all resources are devoted to production of HDTVs, 60 million per year can be produced. In between are various possible combinations.

Production Trade-Offs

The nation's production combinations are plotted as points *A, B, C, D, E, F,* and *G* in panel (b) of Figure 2-2. If these points are connected with a smooth curve, the nation's production possibilities curve (PPC) is shown, demonstrating the trade-off between the production of servers and HDTVs. These trade-offs occur *on* the PPC.

Notice the major difference in the shape of the production possibilities curves in Figure 2-1 on the previous page and Figure 2-2 on the facing page. In Figure 2-1, there is a constant trade-off between grades in economics and in mathematics. In Figure 2-2, the trade-off between production of computer servers and HDTV production is not constant, and therefore the PPC is a *bowed* curve. To understand why the production possibilities curve for a society is typically bowed outward, you must understand the assumptions underlying the PPC.

Go to www.econtoday.com/chapter02 for one perspective, offered by the National Center for Policy Analysis, on whether society's production decisions should be publicly or privately coordinated.

Assumptions Underlying the Production Possibilities Curve

When we draw the curve that is shown in Figure 2-2, we make the following assumptions:

1. Resources are fully employed.
2. Production takes place over a specific time period—for example, one year.
3. The resource inputs, in both quantity and quality, used to produce computer servers or HDTVs are fixed over this time period.
4. Technology does not change over this time period.

FIGURE 2-2

Society's Trade-Off Between Computer Servers and HDTVs

The production of computer servers and HDTVs is measured in millions of units per year. The various combinations are given in panel (a) and plotted in panel (b). Connecting the points A–G with a relatively smooth line gives society's production possibilities curve for servers and HDTVs. Point R lies outside the production possibilities curve and is therefore unattainable at the point in time for which the graph is drawn. Point S lies inside the production possibilities curve and therefore entails unemployed or underemployed resources.

Panel (a)

Combination	Servers (millions per year)	HDTVs (millions per year)
A	50.0	0
B	48.0	10
C	45.0	20
D	40.0	30
E	33.0	40
F	22.5	50
G	0.0	60

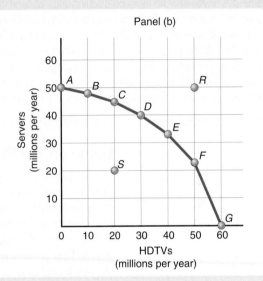

Panel (b)

Technology is defined as society's pool of applied knowledge concerning how goods and services can be produced by managers, workers, engineers, scientists, and artisans, using land, physical and human capital, and entrepreneurship. You can think of technology as the formula or recipe used to combine factors of production. (When better formulas are developed, more production can be obtained from the same amount of resources.) The level of technology sets the limit on the amount and types of goods and services that we can derive from any given amount of resources. The production possibilities curve is drawn under the assumption that we use the best technology that we currently have available and that this technology doesn't change over the time period under study.

The land available to a town with established borders is an example of a fixed resource that is fully employed and used with available technology along a production possibilities curve. Why do you suppose that deciding how to allocate a fixed amount of land recently posed "grave" problems for a town in France?

Technology
Society's pool of applied knowledge concerning how goods and services can be produced.

INTERNATIONAL EXAMPLE
Making Death Illegal—At Least, Inside City Limits

Le Lavandou, France, a Riviera community known for breathtaking views of a rocky coastline along a clear-blue section of the Mediterranean Sea, recently drew international ridicule when it passed a law that appeared aimed at regulating death. Specifically, the law stated, "It is forbidden without a cemetery plot to die on the territory of the commune."

Of course, it is not possible for a law to prevent someone from dying inside a town. The purpose of the law was to indicate a permissible choice along a production possibilities curve. Land is a scarce resource with many alternative uses, so trade-offs involving different productive uses of land arise everywhere on the planet where people establish communities. Le Lavandou is no exception. The town's cemetery filled up, and the townspeople had to decide whether to allocate more land to cemetery plots, thereby providing a service for deceased individuals and for their family and friends, or to continue allocating remaining land resources to the production of other goods and services. The point of the legal requirement was to emphasize that the town had decided not to incur an opportunity cost by allocating more space to cemetery plots.

Nonetheless, it was still true that someone who happened to die in Le Lavandou without first buying an existing cemetery plot was technically breaking the law.

FOR CRITICAL ANALYSIS
What is likely to happen to the opportunity cost of cemetery space as the world's population continues to increase and spread over available land resources?

Being off the Production Possibilities Curve

Look again at panel (b) of Figure 2-2 on the previous page. Point *R* lies *outside* the production possibilities curve and is *impossible* to achieve during the time period assumed. By definition, the PPC indicates the *maximum* quantity of one good, given the quantity produced of the other good.

It is possible, however, to be at point *S* in Figure 2-2. That point lies beneath the production possibilities curve. If the nation is at point *S*, it means that its resources are not being fully utilized. This occurs, for example, during periods of relatively high unemployment. Point *S* and all such points inside the PPC are always attainable but imply unemployed or underemployed resources.

Efficiency

The production possibilities curve can be used to define the notion of efficiency. Whenever the economy is operating on the PPC, at points such as *A*, *B*, *C*, or *D*, we say that its production is efficient. Points such as *S* in Figure 2-2, which lie beneath the PPC, are said to represent production situations that are not efficient.

Efficiency
The case in which a given level of inputs is used to produce the maximum output possible. Alternatively, the situation in which a given output is produced at minimum cost.

Efficiency can mean many things to many people. Even in economics, there are different types of efficiency. Here we are discussing *productive efficiency*. An economy is productively efficient whenever it is producing the maximum output with given technology and resources.

A simple commonsense definition of efficiency is getting the most out of what we have. Clearly, we are not getting the most out of what we have if we are at point *S* in panel (b) of Figure 2-2. We can move from point *S* to, say, point *C*, thereby increasing the total quantity of servers produced without any decrease in the total quantity of HDTVs produced. Alternatively, we can move from point *S* to point *E*, for example, and have both more servers and more HDTVs. Point *S* is called an **inefficient point**, which is defined as any point below the production possibilities curve.

Inefficient point
Any point below the production possibilities curve, at which the use of resources is not generating the maximum possible output.

The Law of Increasing Relative Cost

In the example in Figure 2-1 on page 33, the trade-off between a grade in mathematics and a grade in economics was one to one. The trade-off ratio was constant. That is, the production possibilities curve was a straight line. The curve in Figure 2-2 is a more general case. We have re-created the curve in Figure 2-2 as Figure 2-3. Each combination, *A* through *G*, of computer servers and HDTVs is represented on the production

FIGURE 2-3

The Law of Increasing Relative Cost

Consider equal increments of production of HDTVs, as measured on the horizontal axis. All of the horizontal arrows—*aB*, *bC*, and so on—are of equal length (10 million). In contrast, the length of each vertical arrow—*Aa*, *Bb*, and so on—increases as we move down the production possibilities curve. Hence, the opportunity cost of going from 50 million HDTVs per year to 60 million (*Ff*) is much greater than going from zero units to 10 million (*Aa*). The opportunity cost of each additional equal increase in production of HDTVs rises.

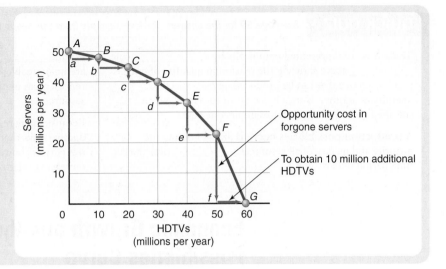

possibilities curve. Starting with the production of zero HDTVs, the nation can produce 50 million servers with its available resources and technology.

INCREASING RELATIVE COSTS   When we increase production of HDTVs from zero to 10 million per year, the nation has to give up in servers an amount shown by that first vertical arrow, *Aa*. From panel (a) of Figure 2-2 on page 35 you can see that this is 2 million per year (50 million minus 48 million). Again, if we increase production of HDTVs by another 10 million units per year, we go from *B* to *C*. In order to do so, the nation has to give up the vertical distance *Bb*, or 3 million servers per year. By the time we go from 50 million to 60 million HDTVs, to obtain that 10 million increase, we have to forgo the vertical distance *Ff*, or 22.5 million servers. In other words, we see that the opportunity cost of the last 10 million HDTVs has increased to 22.5 million servers, compared to 2 million servers for the same increase in HDTVs when we started with none at all being produced.

What we are observing is called the **law of increasing relative cost.** When society takes more resources and applies them to the production of any specific good, the opportunity cost increases for each additional unit produced.

EXPLAINING THE LAW OF INCREASING RELATIVE COST   The reason that as a nation we face the law of increasing relative cost (shown as a production possibilities curve that is bowed outward) is that certain resources are better suited for producing some goods than they are for other goods. Generally, resources are not *perfectly* adaptable for alternative uses. When increasing the output of a particular good, producers must use less suitable resources than those already used in order to produce the additional output. Hence, the cost of producing the additional units increases.

With respect to our hypothetical example here, at first the computing specialists at server firms would shift over to producing HDTVs. After a while, though, networking technicians, workers who normally design servers, and others would be asked to help design and manufacture HDTV components. Clearly, they would be less effective at making HDTVs than the people who previously specialized in this task.

In general, *the more specialized the resources, the more bowed the production possibilities curve.* At the other extreme, if all resources are equally suitable for server production or production of HDTVs, the curves in Figures 2-2 and 2-3 would approach the straight line shown in our first example in Figure 2-1 on page 33.

Law of increasing relative cost
The fact that the opportunity cost of additional units of a good generally increases as society attempts to produce more of that good. This accounts for the bowed-out shape of the production possibilities curve.

Trade-offs are represented graphically by a _____ _____ curve showing the maximum quantity of one good or service that can be produced, given a specific quantity of another, from a given set of resources over a specified period of time—for example, one year.

A **production possibilities curve** is drawn holding the quantity and quality of all resources _____ over the time period under study.

Points _____ the **production possibilities curve** are unattainable; points _____ are attainable but represent an inefficient use or underuse of available resources.

Because many resources are better suited for certain productive tasks than for others, society's production possibilities curve is bowed _____, reflecting the law of increasing relative cost.

Economic Growth and the Production Possibilities Curve

At any particular point in time, a society cannot be outside the production possibilities curve. *Over time*, however, it is possible to have more of everything. This occurs through economic growth. (An important reason for economic growth, capital accumulation, is discussed next. A more complete discussion of why economic growth occurs appears in Chapter 9.) Figure 2-4 shows the production possibilities curve for computer servers and HDTVs shifting outward. The two additional curves shown represent new choices open to an economy that has experienced economic growth. Such economic growth occurs because of many things, including increases in the number of workers and productive investment in equipment.

Scarcity still exists, however, no matter how much economic growth there is. At any point in time, we will always be on some production possibilities curve; thus, we will always face trade-offs. The more we have of one thing, the less we can have of others.

If a nation experiences economic growth, the production possibilities curve between servers and HDTVs will move outward, as shown in Figure 2-4. This takes time and does not occur automatically. One reason it will occur involves the choice about how much to consume today.

FIGURE 2-4

Economic Growth Allows for More of Everything

If the nation experiences economic growth, the production possibilities curve between computer servers and HDTVs will move out as shown. This takes time, however, and it does not occur automatically. This means, therefore, that we can have more of both computer servers and HDTVs only after a period of time during which we have experienced economic growth.

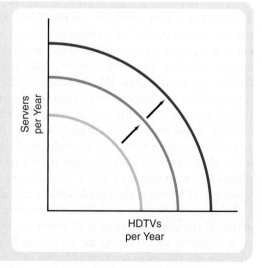

The Trade-Off Between the Present and the Future

The production possibilities curve and economic growth can be combined to examine the trade-off between present **consumption** and future consumption. When we consume today, we are using up what we call consumption or consumer goods—food and clothes, for example.

Consumption
The use of goods and services for personal satisfaction.

Why We Make Capital Goods

Why would we be willing to use productive resources to make things—capital goods—that we cannot consume directly? For one thing, capital goods enable us to produce larger quantities of consumer goods or to produce them less expensively than we otherwise could. Before fish are "produced" for the market, equipment such as fishing boats, nets, and poles is produced first. Imagine how expensive it would be to obtain fish for market without using these capital goods. Catching fish with one's hands is not an easy task. The cost per fish would be very high if capital goods weren't used.

Forgoing Current Consumption

Whenever we use productive resources to make capital goods, we are implicitly forgoing current consumption. We are waiting for some time in the future to consume the rewards that will be reaped from the use of capital goods. In effect, when we forgo current consumption to invest in capital goods, we are engaging in an economic activity that is forward-looking—we do not get instant utility or satisfaction from our activity.

The Trade-Off Between Consumption Goods and Capital Goods

To have more consumer goods in the future, we must accept fewer consumer goods today, because resources must be used in producing capital goods instead of consumer goods. In other words, an opportunity cost is involved. Every time we make a choice of more goods today, we incur an opportunity cost of fewer goods tomorrow, and every time we make a choice of more goods in the future, we incur an opportunity cost of fewer goods today. With the resources that we don't use to produce consumer goods for today, we invest in capital goods that will produce more consumer goods for us later. The trade-off is shown in Figure 2-5 on the following page. On the left in panel (a), you can see this trade-off depicted as a production possibilities curve between capital goods and consumption goods.

Assume that we are willing to give up $1 trillion worth of consumption today. We will be at point *A* in the left-hand diagram of panel (a). This will allow the economy to grow. We will have more future consumption because we invested in more capital goods today. In the right-hand diagram of panel (a), we see two goods represented, food and entertainment. The production possibilities curve will move outward if we collectively decide to restrict consumption now and invest in capital goods.

In panel (b), we show the results of our willingness to forgo even more current consumption. We move to point *C* in the left-hand side, where we have many fewer consumer goods today but produce many more capital goods. This leads to more future growth in this simplified model, and thus the production possibilities curve in the right-hand side of panel (b) shifts outward more than it did in the right-hand side of panel (a). In other words, the more we give up today, the more we can have tomorrow, provided, of course, that the capital goods are productive in future periods.

Capital Goods and Growth

In panel (a), the nation chooses not to consume $1 trillion, so it invests that amount in capital goods. As a result, more of all goods may be produced in the future, as shown in the right-hand diagram in panel (a). In panel (b), society chooses even more capital goods (point *C*). The result is that the production possibilities curve (PPC) moves even more to the right on the right-hand diagram in panel (b).

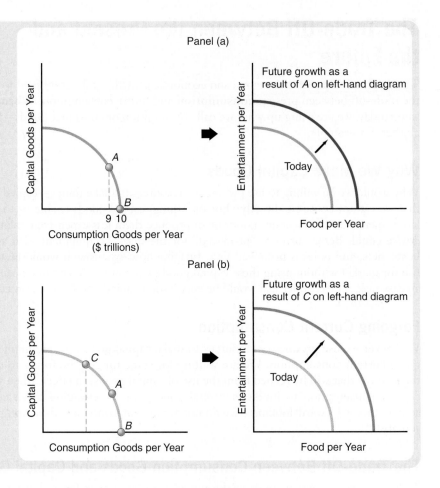

Panel (a)

Panel (b)

_____ goods are goods that will later be used to produce consumer goods.

A trade-off is involved between current consumption and capital goods or, alternatively, between current consumption and future consumption. The _____ we invest in capital goods today, the greater the amount of consumer goods we can produce in the future and the _____ the amount of consumer goods we can produce today.

Specialization and Greater Productivity

Specialization

The organization of economic activity so that what each person (or region) consumes is not identical to what that person (or region) produces. An individual may specialize, for example, in law or medicine. A nation may specialize in the production of coffee, computers, or digital cameras.

Specialization involves working at a relatively well-defined, limited endeavor, such as accounting or teaching. It involves the organization of economic activity among different individuals and regions. Most individuals do specialize. For example, you could change the oil in your car if you wanted to. Typically, though, you take your car to a garage and let the mechanic change the oil. You benefit by letting the garage mechanic specialize in changing the oil and in doing other repairs on your car. The specialist normally will get the job finished sooner than you could and has the proper equipment to make the job go more smoothly. Specialization usually leads to greater productivity, not only for each individual but also for the nation.

Comparative Advantage

Specialization occurs because different individuals experience different costs when they engage in the same activities. Some individuals can accurately solve mathematical problems at lower cost than others who might try to solve the same problems. Thus, those who solve math problems at lower cost sacrifice production of fewer alternative items. Some people can develop more high-quality computer programs than others while giving up less production of other items, such as clean houses and neatly manicured yards.

Comparative advantage is the ability to perform an activity *at a lower opportunity cost*. You have a comparative advantage in one activity whenever you have a lower opportunity cost of performing that activity. Comparative advantage is always a *relative* concept. You may be able to change the oil in your car; you might even be able to change it faster than the local mechanic. But if the opportunity cost you face by changing the oil exceeds the mechanic's opportunity cost, the mechanic has a comparative advantage in changing the oil. The mechanic faces a lower opportunity cost for that activity.

You may be convinced that everybody can do more of everything than you can during the same period of time and using the same resources. In this extreme situation, do you still have a comparative advantage? The answer is yes. You do not have to be a mathematical genius to figure this out. The market tells you so very clearly by offering you the highest income for the job for which you have a comparative advantage. Stated differently, to find your comparative advantage, simply find the job that maximizes your income.

Comparative advantage
The ability to produce a good or service at a lower opportunity cost compared to other producers.

Absolute Advantage

Suppose that, conversely, you have a job at a firm and are convinced that you have the ability to do every job in that company at a lower cost than everyone else who works there. You might be able to keyboard documents into a computer faster than any of the other employees, file documents in order in a file cabinet faster than any of the file clerks, and wash windows faster than any of the window washers. Indeed, you might even be able to manage the firm in less time just as effectively as the current company president—and in less time than you would have to spend in any alternative function.

If all of these self-perceptions were really true, then you would have an **absolute advantage** in all of these endeavors. In other words, if you were to spend a given amount of time in any one of them, you could produce more than anyone else in the company. Nonetheless, you would not spend your time doing these other activities. Why not? Because your advantage in undertaking the president's managerial duties is even greater. Therefore, you would find yourself specializing in that particular task even though you have an *absolute* advantage in all these other tasks. Indeed, absolute advantage is irrelevant in predicting how you will allocate your time. Only *comparative advantage* matters in determining how you will allocate your time.

The coaches of sports teams often have to determine the comparative advantage of an individual player who has an absolute advantage in every aspect of the sport in question. Babe Ruth, who could hit more home runs and pitch more strikeouts per game than other players on the Boston Red Sox, was a pitcher on that professional baseball team. After he was traded to the New York Yankees, the owner and the manager decided to make him an outfielder, even though he could also hurl more strikeouts per game than other Yankees. They wanted "The Babe" to concentrate on his hitting because a home-run king would bring in more fans than a good pitcher would. Babe Ruth had an absolute advantage in both aspects of the game of baseball, but his

Absolute advantage
The ability to produce more units of a good or service using a given quantity of labor or resource inputs. Equivalently, the ability to produce the same quantity of a good or service using fewer units of labor or resource inputs.

comparative advantage was clearly in hitting homers rather than in practicing and developing his pitching game.

The opportunity cost of buying groceries is higher for some people than for others. How has this given entrepreneurs an opportunity to profit from taking grocery orders online?

E-COMMERCE EXAMPLE
A Comparative Advantage in Grocery Shopping

Traveling to a grocery store, grabbing a shopping cart, and searching through the store's aisles for items are time-consuming activities. Individuals who want a very particular grocery item, such as steak or salmon marinated with specific spices or herbs, may have to devote considerable time going to several grocery stores.

Increasingly, people are concluding that grocery shopping is a next-best alternative. These individuals allocate their time to other activities, such as earning more income, and pay others to shop for items on their grocery lists. FreshDirect is a company that takes online grocery orders from finicky eaters in New York City. Each year FreshDirect's trucks fulfill 2 million grocery orders for $200 million worth of food by transporting 60 million items packed into 8 million boxes. The Web-based company has a comparative advantage in tracking down gourmet steaks, salmon, and a wide variety of other grocery items, so it specializes in this activity.

FOR CRITICAL ANALYSIS
Why do you suppose that people who frequently consume hard-to-find gourmet foods are among FreshDirect's most regular customers?

You Are There

For an example of how the concepts of comparative advantage and specialization can matter in a realistic business context, read **Specializing in Providing Baggage-Free Business Trips,** on page 44.

Scarcity, Self-Interest, and Specialization

In Chapter 1, you learned about the assumption of rational self-interest. To repeat, for the purposes of our analyses we assume that individuals are rational in that they will do what is in their own self-interest. They will not consciously carry out actions that will make them worse off. In this chapter, you learned that scarcity requires people to make choices. We *assume* that they make choices based on their self-interest. When they make these choices, they attempt to maximize benefits net of opportunity cost. In so doing, individuals choose their comparative advantage and end up specializing.

The Division of Labor

Division of labor
The segregation of resources into different specific tasks; for example, one automobile worker puts on bumpers, another doors, and so on.

In any firm that includes specialized human and nonhuman resources, there is a **division of labor** among those resources. The best-known example comes from Adam Smith, who in *The Wealth of Nations* illustrated the benefits of a division of labor in the making of pins, as depicted in the following example:

> One man draws out the wire, another straightens it, a third cuts it, a fourth points it, a fifth grinds it at the top for receiving the head; to make the head requires two or three distinct operations; to put it on is a peculiar business, to whiten the pins is another; it is even a trade by itself to put them into the paper.

Making pins this way allowed 10 workers without very much skill to make almost 48,000 pins "of a middling size" in a day. One worker, toiling alone, could have made perhaps 20 pins a day; therefore, 10 workers could have produced 200. Division of labor allowed for an increase in the daily output of the pin factory from 200 to 48,000! (Smith did not attribute all of the gain to the division of labor but credited also the use of machinery and the fact that less time was spent shifting from task to task.)

What we are discussing here involves a division of the resource called labor into different uses of labor. The different uses of labor are organized in such a way as to increase the amount of output possible from the fixed resources available. We can therefore talk about an organized division of labor within a firm leading to increased output.

Comparative Advantage and Trade Among Nations

This automobile assembly line is a good example of what concept in economics?

Most of our analysis of absolute advantage, comparative advantage, and specialization has dealt with individuals. Nevertheless, it is equally applicable to nations.

Trade Among Regions

Consider the United States. The Plains states have a comparative advantage in the production of grains and other agricultural goods. Relative to the Plains states, the states to the east tend to specialize in industrialized production, such as automobiles. Not surprisingly, grains are shipped from the Plains states to the eastern states, and automobiles are shipped in the reverse direction. Such specialization and trade allow for higher incomes and standards of living.

If both the Plains states and the eastern states were separate nations, the same analysis would still hold, but we would call it international trade. Indeed, the European Union (EU) is comparable to the United States in area and population, but instead of one nation, the EU has 27. What U.S. residents call *interstate* trade, Europeans call *international* trade. There is no difference, however, in the economic results—both yield greater economic efficiency and higher average incomes.

International Aspects of Trade

Political problems that normally do not occur within a particular nation often arise between nations. For example, if California avocado growers develop a cheaper method of producing a tastier avocado than growers in southern Florida use, the Florida growers will lose out. They cannot do much about the situation except try to lower their own costs of production or improve their product.

If avocado growers in Mexico, however, develop a cheaper method of producing better-tasting avocados, both California and Florida growers can (and likely will) try to raise political barriers that will prevent Mexican avocado growers from freely selling their product in the United States. U.S. avocado growers will use such arguments as "unfair" competition and loss of U.S. jobs. Certainly, avocado-growing jobs may decline in the United States, but there is no reason to believe that U.S. jobs will decline overall. Instead, former U.S. avocado workers will move into alternative employment—something that 1 million people do every *week* in the United States. If the argument of U.S. avocado growers had any validity, every time a region in the United States developed a better way to produce a product manufactured somewhere else in the country, U.S. employment would decline. That has never happened and never will.

Go to www.econtoday.com/chapter02 to find out from the World Trade Organization how much international trade takes place. Under "Resources," click on "Trade statistics" and then click on "International Trade Statistics" for the most recent year.

When nations specialize where they have a comparative advantage and then trade with the rest of the world, the average standard of living in the world rises. In effect, international trade allows the world to move from inside the global production possibilities curve toward the curve itself, thereby improving worldwide economic efficiency. Thus, all countries that engage in trade can benefit from comparative advantage, just as regions in the United States benefit from interregional trade.

QUICK QUIZ | *See page 50 for the answers. Review concepts from this section in MyEconLab.*

With a given set of resources, specialization results in _____ output; in other words, there are gains to specilization in terms of greater material well-being.

Individuals and nations specialize in their areas of _____ advantage in order to reap the gains of specialization.

Comparative advantages are found by determining which activities have the _____ opportunity cost—that is,

which activities yield the highest return for the time and resources used.

A _____ of labor occurs when different workers are assigned different tasks. Together, the workers produce a desired product.

You Are There ◀ Specializing in Providing Baggage-Free Business Trips

When Steve Zilinek was working as an investment adviser, he noticed something about traveling businesspeople. Although many of these individuals possess considerable financial resources, they must expend another key resource when they travel—namely, time that they could otherwise devote to other activities. Zilinek estimated that packing bags, waiting at airport check-in, security, and baggage stations, and laundering clothing takes about three hours per trip—time that otherwise could be devoted to alternative pursuits.

Zilinek decided that he might have a comparative advantage in providing baggage services to frequent travelers. He founded FlyLite, a company that specializes in storing, caring for, and shipping all the items that individuals desire to have with them on business trips, such as clothing and toiletries. FlyLite's customers send the items they regularly take on business trips to the company, which places them in storage. Before a trip, a client fills out and submits a Web form indicating which items she will require at her destination. FlyLite then arranges for the items to be shipped to her hotel. When her business trip concludes, the customer sends the items back to FlyLite, which dry cleans the clothing and then re-stores all items until her next trip. For FlyLite's clients, paying about $100 per trip for its services is the next-best alternative to devoting three hours to handling baggage on their own.

CRITICAL ANALYSIS QUESTIONS

1. *What is the approximate minimum opportunity cost of three hours of time per trip for the typical FlyLite customer?*

2. *How do you suppose that an increase in the average amount of time that people must spend dealing with baggage at airports affects the number of people utilizing FlyLite's services?*

Issues and Applications

Specialization and Division of Labor at the Speedway

The driver wheels his high-performance racecar around the track at speeds up to 200 miles per hour. After the next turn, he decelerates down a side track to a pre-assigned location. As soon as his car comes to a halt, seven individuals rapidly converge around it: front- and rear-tire carriers, front- and rear-tire changers, an individual who jacks up the car, and two others carrying 11-gallon cans of fuel. These seven people together produce a combined service without which no auto race could long continue: the motor speedway "pit stop."

Achieving Speedy Production of Auto Services

Racing a car around an oval track at high speeds for a few hours consumes two key resources. The most obvious resource is the high-performance fuel required to keep racecar engine components spinning at thousands of revolutions per second. Another resource is tire tread, which must remain above a minimum threshold if the driver is to be able to safely accelerate, decelerate, and round turns.

Thus, the purpose of a pit stop is to refuel and change tires. From the moment that auto racing was born, racecar drivers began wrestling with how best to perform and organize these services. Obviously, at various points during a race, one person could perform the required tasks of pouring fuel, jacking up the racecar, and changing its four tires. Using a single person would never do, however, because in an auto race, speed is truly the name of the game. Racers recognized that several people could refuel a car and change its tires much faster than one person, and the idea of the speedway pit crew was born.

Division of Labor in the Pit

In gauging the production of pit services at a motor speedway, the fundamental unit of measurement is the rate at which refueling and tire-changing services are performed per unit of time. The involvement of several people is required to perform these services most rapidly. Hence, motor speedway pit crews have a natural division of labor: refueling, jacking up the car, carrying and changing front and rear tires.

After years of trial and error, racecar drivers settled on pit crews of seven members each. They found that given the technology involved in the provision of pit services, this division of labor yields the fastest rate of production.

Specialization Breeds Production Improvements in the Pits

Attaining the speediest possible pit stop requires each pit crew member's function to be highly specialized. Today, the person who jacks up a racecar aims to haul a 25-pound aluminum jack from the car's right side to the left within 3.8 seconds. Tire changers do their best to get five lug nuts off a car's wheel within 1.2 seconds. Tire carriers aim to raise 60-pound tires from the pavement to mounted positions on the car within 0.7 second. While five crew members carry out these activities with the car's body and wheels, the two crew members responsible for refueling are punching the necks of fuel cans into tank openings.

Twenty years ago, pit crews were doing well to complete a pit stop in fewer than 30 seconds. Today, a pit crew that takes more than 16 seconds to complete a stop is regarded as having failed to deliver a timely service to the driver. Thus, two decades of careful attention to division of labor and specialization have reduced by nearly 50 percent the time that a racecar driver typically spends obtaining pit services instead of racing in pursuit of prize money.

Test your understanding of this chapter by going online to **MyEconLab**.
In the Study Plan for this chapter, select Section N: News.

For Critical Analysis

1. Why do you suppose that having more than seven members tends to reduce a pit crew's service output per unit of time? (Hint: In a service pit area at a racetrack, there is limited physical space beside or beneath a racecar.)

2. Why do you suppose that there is a school, called 5 Off 5 On, that trains individuals in the fine art of rapidly removing and replacing the five lug nuts that attach tires to the wheels of racecars?

Web Resources

1. For information about a pit crew training program provided by the National Association for Stock Car Auto Racing (NASCAR), go to www.econtoday.com/chapter02.

2. To learn more about characteristics that NASCAR teams desire in their pit crew members, go to www.econtoday .com/chapter02.

Research Project

Compare the above description of the activities of a speedway pit crew with those of pin makers as described by Adam Smith (see page 42). In addition, compare the division of labor in the provision of pit services and eighteenth-century pin making to the division of labor in the production of educational services at your college or university (or, if you prefer, another production process with which you are familiar). Is the division of labor a fundamental aspect of production of goods and services?

---

myeconlab Here is what you should know after reading this chapter. **MyEconLab** will help you identify what you know, and where to go when you need to practice.

WHAT YOU SHOULD KNOW		WHERE TO GO TO PRACTICE
The Problem of Scarcity, Even for the Affluent Scarcity is very different from poverty. No one can obtain all one desires from nature without sacrifice. Thus, even the richest people face scarcity because they have to make choices among alternatives. Despite their high levels of income or wealth, affluent people, like everyone else, want more than they can have (in terms of goods, power, prestige, and so on).	scarcity, 28 production, 28 land, 28 labor, 29 physical capital, 29 human capital, 29 entrepreneurship, 29 goods, 29 economic goods, 29 services, 30	• **MyEconLab** Study Plan 2.1 • Audio introduction to Chapter 2 • Video: Scarcity, Resources, and Production

(continued)

 (continued)

WHAT YOU SHOULD KNOW		WHERE TO GO TO PRACTICE
Why Economists Consider Individuals' Wants but Not Their "Needs" Goods are all things from which individuals derive satisfaction. Economic goods are those for which the desired quantity exceeds the amount that is directly available from nature at a zero price. To economists, the term *need* is undefinable, whereas humans have unlimited *wants*, which are defined as the goods and services on which we place a positive value.		• **MyEconLab** Study Plan 2.2
Why Scarcity Leads People to Evaluate Opportunity Costs Opportunity cost is the highest-valued alternative that one must give up to obtain an item. The trade-offs that we face as individuals and as a society can be represented by a production possibilities curve (PPC), and moving from one point on a PPC to another entails incurring an opportunity cost. Along a PPC, all currently available resources and technology are being used, so obtaining more of one good requires shifting resources to production of that good and away from production of another. That is, there is an opportunity cost of allocating scarce resources toward producing one good instead of another good.	opportunity cost, 31 production possibilities curve (PPC), 32 KEY FIGURE Figure 2-1, 33	• **MyEconLab** Study Plans 2.3, 2.4 • Animated Figure 2-1 • ABC News Video: Incentives for Perfect Attendance
Why Obtaining Increasing Increments of a Good Requires Giving Up More and More Units of Other Goods Typically, resources are specialized. Thus, when society allocates additional resources to producing more units of a good, it must increasingly employ resources that would be better suited for producing other goods. As a result, the law of increasing relative cost holds. Each additional unit of a good can be obtained only by giving up more and more of other goods, which means that the production possibilities curve is bowed outward.	technology, 35 efficiency, 36 inefficient point, 36 law of increasing relative cost, 37 KEY FIGURES Figure 2-3, 37 Figure 2-4, 38	• **MyEconLab** Study Plan 2.5 • Animated Figures 2-3, 2-4
The Trade-Off Between Consumption Goods and Capital Goods If we allocate more resources to producing capital goods today, then, other things being equal, the economy will grow faster than it would have otherwise. Thus, the production possibilities curve will shift outward by a larger amount in the future, which means that we can have more consumption goods in the future. The trade-off, however, is that producing more capital goods today entails giving up consumption goods today.	consumption, 39	• **MyEconLab** Study Plans 2.6, 2.7

(continued)

 *(continued)*

WHAT YOU SHOULD KNOW		WHERE TO GO TO PRACTICE
Absolute Advantage versus Comparative Advantage A person has an absolute advantage if she can produce more of a good than someone else who uses the same amount of resources. An individual can gain from specializing in producing a good if she has a comparative advantage in producing that good, meaning that she can produce the good at a lower opportunity cost than someone else. By specializing in producing the good for which she has a comparative advantage, she assures herself of reaping gains from specialization in the form of a higher income.	specialization, 40 comparative advantage, 41 absolute advantage, 41 division of labor, 42	• **MyEconLab** Study Plans 2.8, 2.9 • Video: Absolute versus Comparative Advantage

Log in to MyEconLab, take a chapter test, and get a personalized Study Plan that tells you which concepts you understand and which ones you need to review. From there, MyEconLab will give you further practice, tutorials, animations, videos, and guided solutions. Log in to www.myeconlab.com

PROBLEMS

All problems are assignable in myeconlab . *Answers to odd-numbered problems appear at the back of the book.*

2-1. Define opportunity cost. What is your opportunity cost of attending a class at 11:00 A.M.? How does it differ from your opportunity cost of attending a class at 8:00 A.M.?

2-2. If you receive a ticket to a concert at no charge, what, if anything, is your opportunity cost of attending the concert? How does your opportunity cost change if miserable weather on the night of the concert requires you to leave much earlier for the concert hall and greatly extends the time it takes to get home afterward?

2-3. Recently, a woman named Mary Krawiec attended an auction in Troy, New York. At the auction, a bank was seeking to sell a foreclosed property: a large Victorian house suffering from years of neglect in a neighborhood in which many properties had been on the market for years yet remained unsold. Her $10 offer was the highest bid in the auction, and she handed over a $10 bill for a title to ownership. Once she acquired the house, however, she became responsible for all taxes on the property and for an overdue water bill of $2,000. In addition, to make the house habitable, she and her husband devoted months of time and unpaid labor to renovating the property. In the process, they incurred explicit expenses totaling $65,000.

Why do you suppose that the bank was willing to sell the house to Ms. Krawiec for only $10? (Hint: Contemplate the bank's expected gain, net of all explicit and opportunity costs, if it had attempted to make the house habitable.)

2-4. The following table illustrates the points a student can earn on examinations in economics and biology if the student uses all available hours for study.

Economics	Biology
100	40
90	50
80	60
70	70
60	80
50	90
40	100

Plot this student's production possibilities curve. Does the PPC illustrate the law of increasing relative cost?

2-5. Based on the information provided in Problem 2-4, what is the opportunity cost to this student of allocating enough additional study time on economics to move her grade up from a 90 to a 100?

2-6. Consider a change in the table in Problem 2-4. The student's set of opportunities is now as follows:

Economics	Biology
100	40
90	60
80	75
70	85
60	93
50	98
40	100

Does the PPC illustrate the law of increasing relative cost? What is the opportunity cost to this student for the additional amount of study time on economics required to move her grade from 60 to 70? From 90 to 100?

2-7. Construct a production possibilities curve for a nation facing increasing opportunity costs for producing food and video games. Show how the PPC changes given the following events.

   a. A new and better fertilizer is invented.

   b. Immigration occurs, and immigrants' labor can be employed in both the agricultural sector and the video game sector.

   c. A new programming language is invented that is less costly to code and is more memory-efficient, enabling the use of smaller game cartridges.

   d. A heat wave and drought result in a 10 percent decrease in usable farmland.

Consider the following diagram when answering Problems 2-8, 2-9, and 2-10.

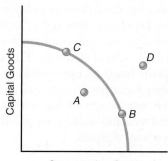

2-8. During a debate on the floor of the U.S. Senate, Senator Creighton states, "Our nation should not devote so many of its fully employed resources to producing capital goods because we already are not producing enough consumption goods for our citizens." Compared with the other labeled points on the diagram, which one could be con-

sistent with the *current* production combination choice that Senator Creighton believes the nation has made?

2-9. In response to Senator Creighton's statement reported in Problem 2-8, Senator Long replies, "We must remain at our current production combination if we want to be able to produce more consumption goods in the future." Of the labeled points on the diagram, which one could depict the *future* production combination Senator Long has in mind?

2-10. Senator Borman interjects the following comment after the statements by Senators Creighton and Long reported in Problems 2-8 and 2-9: "In fact, both of my esteemed colleagues are wrong, because an unacceptably large portion of our nation's resources is currently unemployed." Of the labeled points on the diagram, which one is consistent with Senator Borman's position?

2-11. A nation's residents can allocate their scarce resources either to producing consumption goods or to producing human capital—that is, providing themselves with training and education. The following table displays the production possibilities for this nation:

Production Combination	Units of Consumption Goods	Units of Human Capital
A	0	100
B	10	97
C	20	90
D	30	75
E	40	55
F	50	30
G	60	0

   a. Suppose that the nation's residents currently produce combination A. What is the opportunity cost of increasing production of consumption goods by 10 units? By 60 units?

   b. Does the law of increasing relative cost hold true for this nation? Why or why not?

2-12. Like physical capital, human capital produced in the present can be applied to the production of future goods and services. Consider the table in Problem 2-11, and suppose that the nation's residents are trying to choose between combination C and combination F. Other things being equal, will the future production possibilities curve for this nation be located farther outward if the nation chooses combination F instead of combination C? Explain.

2-13. You can wash, fold, and iron a basket of laundry in two hours and prepare a meal in one hour. Your roommate can wash, fold, and iron a basket of laundry in three hours and prepare a meal in one hour. Who has the absolute advantage in laundry, and who has an absolute advantage in meal preparation? Who has the comparative advantage in laundry, and who has a comparative advantage in meal preparation?

2-14. Based on the information in Problem 2-13, should you and your roommate specialize in a particular task? Why? And if so, who should specialize in which task? Show how much labor time you save if you choose to "trade" an appropriate task with your roommate as opposed to doing it yourself.

2-15. Using only the concept of comparative advantage, evaluate this statement: "A professor with a Ph.D. in physics should never mow his or her own lawn, because this would fail to take into account the professor's comparative advantage."

2-16. Country A and country B produce the same consumption goods and capital goods and currently have *identical* production possibilities curves. They also have the same resources at present, and they have access to the same technology.

    a. At present, does either country have a comparative advantage in producing capital goods? Consumption goods?

    b. Currently, country A has chosen to produce more consumption goods, compared with country B. Other things being equal, which country will experience the larger outward shift of its PPC during the next year?

ECONOMICS ON THE NET

Opportunity Cost and Labor Force Participation Many students choose to forgo full-time employment to concentrate on their studies, thereby incurring a sizable opportunity cost. This application explores the nature of this opportunity cost.

Title: College Enrollment and Work Activity of High School Graduates

Navigation: Go to **www.econtoday.com/chapter02** to visit the Bureau of Labor Statistics (BLS) home page. Select A–Z Index and then click on *Educational attainment (Statistics)*. Finally, under the heading "Economic News Releases," click on "Annual," and then click on *College Enrollment and Work Activity of High School Graduates*.

Application Read the abbreviated report on college enrollment and work activity of high school graduates. Then answer the following questions.

1. Based on the article, explain who the BLS considers to be in the labor force and who it does not view as part of the labor force.

2. What is the difference in labor force participation rates between high school students entering four-year universities and those entering two-year universities? Using the concept of opportunity cost, explain the difference.

3. What is the difference in labor force participation rates between part-time college students and full-time college students? Using the concept of opportunity cost, explain the difference.

For Group Study and Analysis Read the last paragraph of the article. Then divide the class into two groups. The first group should explain, based on the concept of opportunity cost, the difference in labor force participation rates between youths not in school but with a high school diploma and youths not in school and without a high school diploma. The second group should explain, based on opportunity cost, the difference in labor force participation rates between men and women not in school but with a high school diploma and men and women not in school and without a high school diploma.

ANSWERS TO QUICK QUIZZES

p. 30: (i) Scarcity; (ii) land . . . labor . . . physical . . . human . . . entrepreneurship; (iii) Wants; (iv) need

p. 34: (i) next-highest; (ii) opportunity; (iii) next-best; (iv) production possibilities

p. 38: (i) production possibilities; (ii) fixed; (iii) outside . . . inside; (iv) outward

p. 40: (i) Capital; (ii) more . . . smaller

p. 44: (i) higher; (ii) comparative; (iii) lowest; (iv) division

Demand and Supply

Three decades ago, about 45 percent of U.S. residents were classified as "overweight." Today, estimates indicate that as many as 67 percent of U.S. residents fall into this category. About 31 percent of the U.S. population is classified as extremely overweight, or obese, which is more than double the percentage of 30 years ago. One explanation for higher body weights is that people are exercising less, and thus the calories they consume are being transformed into body mass instead of energy. Another is that people are simply choosing to consume more food than in years past. Determining why individuals are opting to eat more requires an understanding, which you will develop by reading this chapter, of how two key factors—price and income—influence desired consumption of an item such as food.

LEARNING OBJECTIVES

MyEconLab helps you master each objective and study more efficiently. See end of chapter for details.

After reading this chapter, you should be able to:

➤ Explain the law of demand

➤ Discuss the difference between money prices and relative prices

➤ Distinguish between changes in demand and changes in quantity demanded

➤ Explain the law of supply

➤ Distinguish between changes in supply and changes in quantity supplied

➤ Understand how the interaction of the demand for and supply of a commodity determines the market price of the commodity and the equilibrium quantity of the commodity that is produced and consumed

? DID YOU KNOW THAT no new oil refineries—facilities that refine crude oil into transportation fuels such as gasoline—have been built in the United States since 1976? Recently, however, Hyperion, a Dallas-based company, announced its intention to build a new refinery at Elk Point, South Dakota, which would refine about 400,000 barrels of heavy Canadian crude oil per day. Hyperion indicated that the key factor motivating its decision was a significant, sustained increase in the U.S. price of gasoline during the preceding years.

If we use the economist's primary set of tools, *demand* and *supply,* we can develop a better understanding of why we sometimes observe relatively large increases in the price of gasoline. We can also better understand why a persistent increase in the price of gasoline ultimately induces an increase in gasoline production. Demand and supply are two ways of categorizing the influences on the prices of goods that you buy and the quantities available. Indeed, demand and supply characterize much economic analysis of the world around us.

As you will see throughout this text, the operation of the forces of demand and supply takes place in *markets*. A **market** is an abstract concept summarizing all of the arrangements individuals have for exchanging with one another. Goods and services are sold in markets, such as the automobile market, the health care market, and the market for Internet DSL services. Workers offer their services in the labor market. Companies, or firms, buy workers' labor services in the labor market. Firms also buy other inputs in order to produce the goods and services that you buy as a consumer. Firms purchase machines, buildings, and land. These markets are in operation at all times. One of the most important activities in these markets is the determination of the prices of all of the inputs and outputs that are bought and sold in our complicated economy. To understand the determination of prices, you first need to look at the law of demand.

Market
All of the arrangements that individuals have for exchanging with one another. Thus, for example, we can speak of the labor market, the automobile market, and the credit market.

Demand
A schedule showing how much of a good or service people will purchase at any price during a specified time period, other things being constant.

Law of demand
The observation that there is a negative, or inverse, relationship between the price of any good or service and the quantity demanded, holding other factors constant.

Demand

Demand has a special meaning in economics. It refers to the quantities of specific goods or services that individuals, taken singly or as a group, will purchase at various possible prices, other things being constant. We can therefore talk about the demand for microprocessor chips, french fries, multifunction printer-copiers, children, and criminal activities.

The Law of Demand

Associated with the concept of demand is the **law of demand,** which can be stated as follows:

> *When the price of a good goes up, people buy less of it, other things being equal. When the price of a good goes down, people buy more of it, other things being equal.*

The law of demand tells us that the quantity demanded of any commodity is inversely related to its price, other things being equal. In an inverse relationship, one variable moves up in value when the other moves down. The law of demand states that a change in price causes a change in the quantity demanded in the *opposite* direction.

Notice that we tacked on to the end of the law of demand the statement "other things being equal." We referred to this in Chapter 1 as the *ceteris paribus* assumption. It means, for example, that when we predict that people will buy fewer DVD players if their price goes up, we are holding constant the price of all other goods in the economy as well as people's incomes. Implicitly, therefore, if we are assuming that no other

How does the law of demand affect how much gas people buy?

prices change when we examine the price behavior of DVD players, we are looking at the *relative* price of DVD players.

The law of demand is supported by millions of observations of people's behavior in the marketplace. Theoretically, it can be derived from an economic model based on rational behavior, as was discussed in Chapter 1. Basically, if nothing else changes and the price of a good falls, the lower price induces us to buy more over a certain period of time because we can enjoy additional net gains that were unavailable at the higher price. If you examine your own behavior, you will see that it generally follows the law of demand.

Relative Prices versus Money Prices

The **relative price** of any commodity is its price in terms of another commodity. The price that you pay in dollars and cents for any good or service at any point in time is called its **money price.** You might hear from your grandparents, "My first new car cost only fifteen hundred dollars." The implication, of course, is that the price of cars today is outrageously high because the average new car may cost $32,000. But that is not an accurate comparison. What was the price of the average house during that same year? Perhaps it was only $12,000. By comparison, then, given that the average price of houses today is close to $270,000, the price of a new car today doesn't sound so far out of line, does it?

How much have both the price of attending college and the relative price of textbooks increased in recent years?

Relative price
The money price of one commodity divided by the money price of another commodity; the number of units of one commodity that must be sacrificed to purchase one unit of another commodity.

Money price
The price that we observe today, expressed in today's dollars; also called the *absolute* or *nominal price*.

EXAMPLE
College Students Face Higher Relative Prices

If you feel that you are paying relatively high prices for your college training, you are correct. During the past 20 years, average tuition and fees at U.S. colleges and universities have increased by 67 percent more than the average prices of other goods and services. The price of an average college textbook has risen about 60 percent compared with the average prices of other items. Thus, the relative prices of college enrollment and reading materials have increased substantially.

FOR CRITICAL ANALYSIS
In the past two decades, has the average price of attending college increased or decreased relative to the average price of a textbook?

The point is that money prices during different time periods don't tell you much. You have to calculate relative prices. Consider an example of the price of 4-gigabyte flash memory drives versus the price of 4 gigabytes of rewritable DVDs from last year and this year. In Table 3-1 on page 54, we show the money prices of flash memory drives and rewritable DVDs for two years during which they have both gone down. That means that in today's dollars we have to pay out less for both flash memory drives and rewritable DVDs. If we look, though, at the relative prices of flash memory drives and rewritable DVDs, we find that last year, 4-gigabyte flash memory drives were four times as expensive as 4-gigabytes of rewritable DVDs, whereas this year they are only three and a half times as expensive. Conversely, if we compare rewritable DVDs to flash memory drives, last year the price of rewritable DVDs was 25 percent of the price of flash memory drives, but today the price of flash memory drives is about

TABLE 3-1

Money Price versus Relative Price

The money prices of both 4-gigabyte flash memory drives and 4 gigabytes of rewritable DVDs have fallen. But the relative price of rewritable DVDs has risen (or conversely, the relative price of flash memory drives has fallen).

	Money Price		Relative Price	
	Price Last Year	Price This Year	Price Last Year	Price This Year
4-Gigabyte flash memory drives	$20	$14	$\frac{\$20}{\$5} = 4.0$	$\frac{\$14}{\$4} = 3.50$
4 Gigabytes of rewritable DVDs	$5	$4	$\frac{\$5}{\$20} = 0.25$	$\frac{\$4}{\$14} = 0.29$

29 percent of the price of flash memory drives. In the one-year period, although both prices have declined in money terms, the relative price of rewritable DVDs has risen relative to that of flash memory drives.

Sometimes relative price changes occur because the quality of a product improves, thereby bringing about a decrease in the item's effective *price per constant-quality unit*. The price of an item may decrease simply because producers have reduced the item's quality. Thus, when evaluating the effects of price changes, we must always compare *price per constant-quality unit*.

For many Web surfers, speed defines quality. What difference does it make when the speed of Internet access is taken into account in comparisons of monthly prices for Internet broadband access?

E-COMMERCE EXAMPLE
Adjusting the Price of Broadband Service for Quality

In most U.S. locales, basic broadband Internet service is priced at about $15 per month. This appears to compare favorably with most locations in France, where the price of basic broadband Internet access is about $36 per month.

U.S. providers, however, typically offer broadband speeds of less than 0.77 megabit per second, implying a speed-adjusted price as high as $20 per megabit in most U.S. locales. In contrast, French service providers offer speeds as high as 20 megabits per second, yielding a speed-adjusted price as low as $1.80 per megabit. Thus, the U.S. speed-adjusted price is nearly 10 times higher than the French price.

FOR CRITICAL ANALYSIS
In some U.S. locales, broadband access service with a speed of 20 megabits per second is now available at a price of about $50 per month. How does this price compare with the speed-adjusted price in France?

QUICK QUIZ   *See page 81 for the answers. Review concepts from this section in MyEconLab.*

The **law of demand** posits a(n) _____ relationship between the quantity demanded of a good and its price, other things being equal.

The law of _____ applies when other things, such as income and the prices of all other goods and services, are held constant.

The Demand Schedule

Let's take a hypothetical demand situation to see how the inverse relationship between the price and the quantity demanded looks (holding other things equal). We will consider the quantity of 256-megabyte secure digital cards (also known as "SD cards," used in cameras and other digital devices) demanded *per year*. Without stating the *time dimension*, we could not make sense out of this demand relationship because the numbers would be different if we were talking about the quantity demanded per month or the quantity demanded per decade.

In addition to implicitly or explicitly stating a time dimension for a demand relationship, we are also implicitly referring to *constant-quality units* of the good or service in question. Prices are always expressed in constant-quality units in order to avoid the problem of comparing commodities that are in fact not truly comparable.

In panel (a) of Figure 3-1, we see that if the price is $1 apiece, 50 secure digital (SD) cards will be bought each year by our representative individual, but if the price is $5 apiece, only 10 SD cards will be bought each year. This reflects the law of demand. Panel (a) is also called simply demand, or a *demand schedule*, because it gives a schedule of alternative quantities demanded per year at different possible prices.

The Demand Curve

Tables expressing relationships between two variables can be represented in graphical terms. To do this, we need only construct a graph that has the price per constant-quality secure digital card on the vertical axis and the quantity measured in constant-quality SD

FIGURE 3-1

The Individual Demand Schedule and the Individual Demand Curve

In panel (a), we show combinations *A* through *E* of the quantities of secure digital (SD) cards demanded, measured in constant-quality units at prices ranging from $5 down to $1 apiece. These combinations are points on the demand schedule. In panel (b), we plot combinations *A* through *E* on a grid. The result is the individual demand curve for SD cards.

Panel (a)

Combination	Price per Constant-Quality Secure Digital Card	Quantity of Constant-Quality Secure Digital Cards per Year
A	$5	10
B	4	20
C	3	30
D	2	40
E	1	50

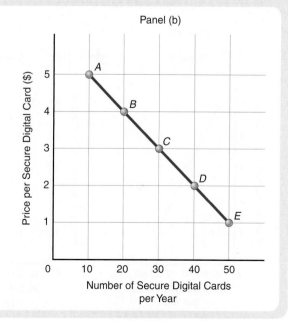

cards per year on the horizontal axis. All we have to do is take combinations *A* through *E* from panel (a) of Figure 3-1 and plot those points in panel (b). Now we connect the points with a smooth line, and *voilà*, we have a **demand curve.** It is downward sloping (from left to right) to indicate the inverse relationship between the price of SD cards and the quantity demanded per year. Our presentation of demand schedules and curves applies equally well to all commodities, including dental floss, bagels, textbooks, credit, and labor. Remember, the demand curve is simply a graphical representation of the law of demand.

Demand curve

A graphical representation of the demand schedule; a negatively sloped line showing the inverse relationship between the price and the quantity demanded (other things being equal).

Individual versus Market Demand Curves

The demand schedule shown in panel (a) of Figure 3-1 on the previous page and the resulting demand curve shown in panel (b) are both given for an individual. As we shall see, the determination of price in the marketplace depends on, among other things, the

Market demand

The demand of all consumers in the marketplace for a particular good or service. The summation at each price of the quantity demanded by each individual.

FIGURE 3-2

The Horizontal Summation of Two Demand Curves

Panel (a) shows how to sum the demand schedule for one buyer with that of another buyer. In column 2 is the quantity demanded by buyer 1, taken from panel (a) of Figure 3-1 on page 55. Column 4 is the sum of columns 2 and 3.

We plot the demand curve for buyer 1 in panel (b) and the demand curve for buyer 2 in panel (c). When we add those two demand curves horizontally, we get the market demand curve for two buyers, shown in panel (d).

Panel (a)

(1) Price per Secure Digital Card	(2) Buyer 1's Quantity Demanded	(3) Buyer 2's Quantity Demanded	(4) = (2) + (3) Combined Quantity Demanded per Year
$5	10	10	20
4	20	20	40
3	30	40	70
2	40	50	90
1	50	60	110

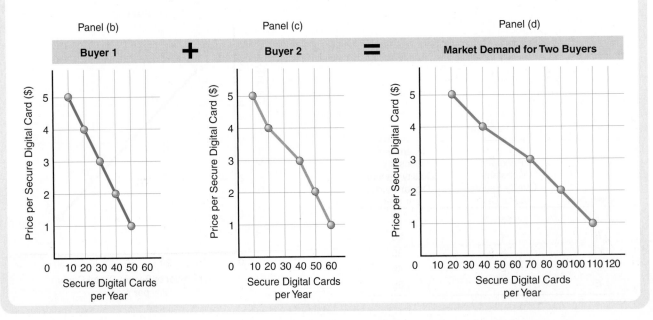

Panel (b) — Buyer 1

Panel (c) — Buyer 2

Panel (d) — Market Demand for Two Buyers

market demand for a particular commodity. The way in which we measure a market demand schedule and derive a market demand curve for secure digital cards or any other good or service is by summing (at each price) the individual quantities demanded by all buyers in the market. Suppose that the market demand for SD cards consists of only two buyers: buyer 1, for whom we've already shown the demand schedule, and buyer 2, whose demand schedule is displayed in column 3 of panel (a) of Figure 3-2 on the facing page. Column 1 shows the price, and column 2 shows the quantity demanded by buyer 1 at each price. These data are taken directly from Figure 3-1 on page 55. In column 3, we show the quantity demanded by buyer 2. Column 4 shows the total quantity demanded at each price, which is obtained by simply adding columns 2 and 3. Graphically, in panel (d) of Figure 3-2, we add the demand curves of buyer 1 [panel (b)] and buyer 2 [panel (c)] to derive the market demand curve.

There are, of course, numerous potential consumers of SD cards. We'll simply assume that the summation of all of the consumers in the market results in a demand schedule, given in panel (a) of Figure 3-3, and a demand curve, given in panel (b). The quantity demanded is now measured in millions of units per year. Remember, panel (b) in Figure 3-3 shows the market demand curve for the millions of users of SD cards. The "market" demand curve that we derived in Figure 3-2 was undertaken assuming that there were only two buyers in the entire market. That's why we assume that the "market" demand curve for two buyers in panel (d) of Figure 3-2 is not a smooth line, whereas the true market demand curve in panel (b) of Figure 3-3 is a smooth line with no kinks.

FIGURE 3-3

The Market Demand Schedule for Secure Digital Cards

In panel (a), we add up the existing demand schedules for secure digital cards. In panel (b), we plot the quantities from panel (a) on a grid; connecting them produces the market demand curve for secure digital cards.

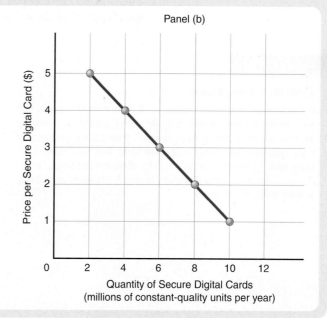

Panel (a)

Price per Constant-Quality Secure Digital Card	Total Quantity Demanded of Constant-Quality Secure Digital Cards per Year (millions)
$5	2
4	4
3	6
2	8
1	10

QUICK QUIZ *See page 81 for the answers. Review concepts from this section in MyEconLab.*

We measure the **demand schedule** in terms of a time dimension and in _____-quality units.

The _____ _____ curve is derived by summing the quantity demanded by individuals at each price. Graphically, we add the individual demand curves horizontally to derive the total, or market, demand curve.

Shifts in Demand

Assume that the federal government gives every student registered in a college, university, or technical school in the United States a laptop computer with a slot for secure digital cards. The demand curve presented in panel (b) of Figure 3-3 on the preceding page would no longer be an accurate representation of total market demand for SD cards. What we have to do is shift the curve outward, or to the right, to represent the rise in demand that would result from this program. There will now be an increase in the number of SD cards demanded at *each and every possible price*. The demand curve shown in Figure 3-4 will shift from D_1 to D_2. Take any price, say, $3 per SD card. Originally, before the federal government giveaway of laptop computers, the amount demanded at $3 was 6 million SD cards per year. After the government giveaway of laptop computers, however, the new amount demanded at the $3 price is 10 million SD cards per year. What we have seen is a shift in the demand for SD cards.

Under different circumstances, the shift can also go in the opposite direction. What if colleges uniformly prohibited the use of laptop computers by any of their students? Such a regulation would cause a shift inward—to the left—of the demand curve for SD cards. In Figure 3-4, the demand curve would shift to D_3; the number demanded would now be less at each and every possible price.

The Other Determinants of Demand

The demand curve in panel (b) of Figure 3-3 is drawn with other things held constant, specifically all of the other factors that determine how many SD cards will be bought.

FIGURE 3-4

A Shift in the Demand Curve

If some factor other than price changes, we can show its effect by moving the entire demand curve, say, from D_1 to D_2. We have assumed in our example that this move was precipitated by the government's giving a laptop computer to every registered college student in the United States. Thus, at *all* prices, a larger number of secure digital cards would be demanded than before. Curve D_3 represents reduced demand compared to curve D_1, caused by a prohibition of laptop computers on campus.

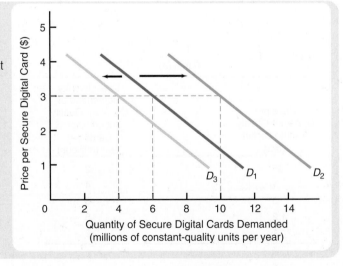

There are many such determinants. We refer to these determinants as *ceteris paribus* **conditions,** and they include consumers' income; tastes and preferences; the prices of related goods; expectations regarding future prices and future incomes; and market size (number of potential buyers). Let's examine each of these determinants more closely.

INCOME   For most goods, an increase in income will lead to an increase in demand. That is, an increase in income will lead to a rightward shift in the position of the demand curve from, say, D_1 to D_2 in Figure 3-4. You can avoid confusion about shifts in curves by always relating a rise in demand to a rightward shift in the demand curve and a fall in demand to a leftward shift in the demand curve. Goods for which the demand rises when consumer income rises are called **normal goods.** Most goods, such as shoes, computers, and flash memory drives, are "normal goods." For some goods, however, demand *falls* as income rises. These are called **inferior goods.** Beans might be an example. As households get richer, they tend to purchase fewer and fewer beans and purchase more and more meat. (The terms *normal* and *inferior* are merely part of the economist's lexicon; no value judgments are associated with them.)

Remember, a shift to the left in the demand curve represents a decrease in demand, and a shift to the right represents an increase in demand.

TASTES AND PREFERENCES   A change in consumer tastes in favor of a good can shift its demand curve outward to the right. When Pokémon trading cards became the rage, the demand curve for them shifted outward to the right; when the rage died out, the demand curve shifted inward to the left. Fashions depend to a large extent on people's tastes and preferences. Economists have little to say about the determination of tastes; that is, they don't have any "good" theories of taste determination or why people buy one brand of product rather than others. Advertisers, however, have various theories that they use to try to make consumers prefer their products over those of competitors.

How has "Web buzz" influenced preferences regarding remote-controlled toy helicopters and hence the demand for these items?

Ceteris paribus conditions
Determinants of the relationship between price and quantity that are unchanged along a curve; changes in these factors cause the curve to shift.

Normal goods
Goods for which demand rises as income rises. Most goods are normal goods.

Inferior goods
Goods for which demand falls as income rises.

E-COMMERCE EXAMPLE
Video Bloggers Generate a Takeoff in Toy Helicopter Demand

During the past couple of years, video bloggers on YouTube and Internet viral-network participants have directed Web viewers to creative videos of remote-controlled toy helicopters in action. Kids of all ages, including adults rediscovering the "child within," have been captivated by videos of toy helicopters rumbling above rough terrain, gliding over lakes, and being chased by housecats. Many have decided that they wish to have one of the toys to control on their own. As a consequence, the number of toy helicopters demanded at prevailing prices has risen by hundreds of thousands of units per year. The demand curve for remote-controlled toy helicopters has shifted outward and to the right.

FOR CRITICAL ANALYSIS
What do you suppose has happened in recent years to the demand for toy helicopters that are incapable of flying under their own power via remote control?

PRICES OF RELATED GOODS: SUBSTITUTES AND COMPLEMENTS   Demand schedules are always drawn with the prices of all other commodities held constant. That is to say, when deriving a given demand curve, we assume that only the price of the good under study changes. For example, when we draw the demand curve for butter, we assume that the price of margarine is held constant. When we draw the demand curve for home cinema speakers, we assume that the price of surround-sound amplifiers is held constant. When we refer to *related goods*, we are talking about goods for which demand is interdependent. If a change in the price of one good shifts the demand for another good, those two goods have interdependent demands. There are two types of demand interdependencies: those in which goods are *substitutes* and those in which goods are *complements*. We can define and distinguish between substitutes and complements in terms of how the change in price of one commodity affects the demand for its related commodity.

Substitutes

Two goods are substitutes when a change in the price of one causes a shift in demand for the other in the same direction as the price change.

Butter and margarine are **substitutes.** Either can be consumed to satisfy the same basic want. Let's assume that both products originally cost $2 per pound. If the price of butter remains the same and the price of margarine falls from $2 per pound to $1 per pound, people will buy more margarine and less butter. The demand curve for butter shifts inward to the left. If, conversely, the price of margarine rises from $2 per pound to $3 per pound, people will buy more butter and less margarine. The demand curve for butter shifts outward to the right. In other words, an increase in the price of margarine will lead to an increase in the demand for butter, and an increase in the price of butter will lead to an increase in the demand for margarine. For substitutes, a change in the price of a substitute will cause a change in demand *in the same direction*.

How do you suppose that laboratory techniques that replicate natural geologic processes are contributing to a decrease in the demand for diamonds extracted from the earth's interior?

EXAMPLE
Diamonds May Not Really Be Forever

The day that sellers of diamonds have long dreaded has arrived. Several professionals who have each spent more than 700 hours in classrooms to become certified experts on precious stones examine three gems. The first gem is a real diamond, created by natural geologic processes beneath the earth's surface. The second is cubic zirconia, a fake diamond commonly used in costume jewelry. The third is something new—a "synthetic" diamond. It is a gem-quality diamond produced in a laboratory by machines that exert pressures 58,000 times that of the earth's at temperatures exceeding 2,300 degrees Fahrenheit. The jewelry experts readily distinguish cubic zirconia from the true diamond. But when they view the synthetic diamond, they cannot tell that it is not a real diamond until they examine it under a microscope and spot its inscribed serial number. Yet the experts have already pronounced the synthetic gem the highest quality of the three.

A number of U.S. jewelry retailers are utilizing synthetic diamonds, which are available at lower prices than real diamonds. At the same time, they are purchasing fewer real diamonds. Thus, the availability of the lower-priced substitute gems is reducing the demand for true gems.

FOR CRITICAL ANALYSIS
In what direction has the demand curve for real diamonds shifted as lower-priced synthetic diamonds have become available?

Complements

Two goods are complements when a change in the price of one causes an opposite shift in the demand for the other.

For **complements,** goods typically consumed together, the situation is reversed. Consider desktop computers and printers. We draw the demand curve for printers with the price of desktop computers held constant. If the price per constant-quality unit of computers decreases from, say, $700 to $500, that will encourage more people to purchase computer peripheral devices. They will now buy more printers, at any given printer price, than before. The demand curve for printers will shift outward to the right. If, by contrast, the price of desktop computers increases from $550 to $750, fewer people will purchase computer peripheral devices. The demand curve for printers will shift inward to the left. To summarize, a decrease in the price of computers leads to an increase in the demand for printers. An increase in the price of computers leads to a decrease in the demand for printers. Thus, for complements, a change in the price of a product will cause a change in demand *in the opposite direction* for the other good.

EXPECTATIONS Consumers' expectations regarding future prices and future incomes will prompt them to buy more or less of a particular good without a change in its current money price. For example, consumers getting wind of a scheduled 100 percent increase in the price of secure digital cards next month will buy more of them today at today's prices. Today's demand curve for SD cards will shift from D_1 to D_2 in Figure 3-4 on page 58. The opposite would occur if a decrease in the price of SD cards were scheduled for next month (from D_1 to D_3).

Expectations of a rise in income may cause consumers to want to purchase more of everything today at today's prices. Again, such a change in expectations of higher future income will cause a shift in the demand curve from D_1 to D_2 in Figure 3-4.

Finally, expectations that goods will not be available at any price will induce consumers to stock up now, increasing current demand.

MARKET SIZE (NUMBER OF POTENTIAL BUYERS) An increase in the number of potential buyers (holding buyers' incomes constant) at any given price shifts the market demand curve outward. Conversely, a reduction in the number of potential buyers at any given price shifts the market demand curve inward.

Changes in Demand versus Changes in Quantity Demanded

We have made repeated references to demand and to quantity demanded. It is important to realize that there is a difference between a *change in demand* and a *change in quantity demanded*.

Demand refers to a schedule of planned rates of purchase and depends on a great many *ceteris paribus* conditions, such as incomes, expectations, and the prices of substitutes or complements. Whenever there is a change in a *ceteris paribus* condition, there will be a change in demand—a shift in the entire demand curve to the right or to the left.

A quantity demanded is a specific quantity at a specific price, represented by a single point on a demand curve. When price changes, quantity demanded changes according to the law of demand, and there will be a movement from one point to another along the same demand curve. Look at Figure 3-5 on the following page. At a price of $3 per secure digital card, 6 million SD cards per year are demanded. If the price falls to $1, quantity demanded increases to 10 million per year. This movement occurs because the current market price for the product changes. In Figure 3-5, you can see the arrow pointing down the given demand curve *D*.

When you think of demand, think of the entire curve. Quantity demanded, in contrast, is represented by a single point on the demand curve.

*A change or shift in demand is a movement of the entire curve. The **only** thing that can cause the entire curve to move is a change in a determinant **other than** its own price.*

If the price of iPods goes down, what will happen to the demand for amplified speaker systems for iPods?

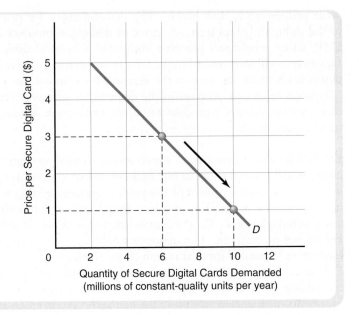

FIGURE 3-5

Movement Along a Given Demand Curve

A change in price changes the quantity of a good demanded. This can be represented as movement along a given demand schedule. If, in our example, the price of secure digital cards falls from $3 to $1 apiece, the quantity demanded will increase from 6 million to 10 million units per year.

In economic analysis, we cannot emphasize too much the following distinction that must constantly be made:

A change in a good's own price leads to a change in quantity demanded for any given demand curve, other things held constant. This is a movement along *the curve.*

A change in any of the ceteris paribus *conditions for demand leads to a change in demand. This causes a* **shift** *of the curve.*

QUICK QUIZ   *See page 81 for the answers. Review concepts from this section in MyEconLab.*

Demand curves are drawn with determinants other than the price of the good held constant. These other determinants, called *ceteris paribus* **conditions,** are (1) _____; (2) _____; (3) _____; (4) _____; and (5) _____ at any given price. If any one of these determinants changes, the demand curve will shift to the right or to the left.

A change in demand comes about only because of a change in the _____ _____ conditions of demand. This change in demand is a shift in the demand curve to the left or to the right.

A change in the quantity demanded comes about when there is a change in the price of the good (other things held constant). Such a change in quantity demanded involves _____ _____ a given demand curve.

The Law of Supply

Supply
A schedule showing the relationship between price and quantity supplied for a specified period of time, other things being equal.

The other side of the basic model in economics involves the quantities of goods and services that firms will offer for sale to the market. The **supply** of any good or service is the amount that firms will produce and offer for sale under certain conditions during a specified time period. The relationship between price and quantity supplied, called the **law of supply,** can be summarized as follows:

> *At higher prices, a larger quantity will generally be supplied than at lower prices, all other things held constant. At lower prices, a smaller quantity will generally be supplied than at higher prices, all other things held constant.*

There is generally a direct relationship between price and quantity supplied. For supply, as the price rises, the quantity supplied rises; as price falls, the quantity supplied also falls. Producers are normally willing to produce and sell more of their product at a higher price than at a lower price, other things being constant. At $5 per secure digital card, manufacturers would almost certainly be willing to supply a larger quantity than at $1 per SD card, assuming, of course, that no other prices in the economy had changed.

As with the law of demand, millions of instances in the real world have given us confidence in the law of supply. On a theoretical level, the law of supply is based on a model in which producers and sellers seek to make the most gain possible from their activities. For example, as a manufacturer attempts to produce more and more SD cards over the same time period, it will eventually have to hire more workers, pay overtime wages (which are higher), and overutilize its machines. Only if offered a higher price per SD card will the manufacturer be willing to incur these higher costs. That is why the law of supply implies a direct relationship between price and quantity supplied.

How do you suppose that producers of minerals responded when prices of minerals rose during the 2000s?

Law of supply
The observation that the higher the price of a good, the more of that good sellers will make available over a specified time period, other things being equal.

EXAMPLE
Mining Production's Direct Response to Higher Prices for Minerals

Prices of minerals have jumped significantly during the 2000s. For instance, the price of uranium oxide, a mineral used as a key ingredient in fuel for nuclear power plants, has risen from just over $7 per pound in 2001 to more than $40 per pound today. Prices of other minerals, including nickel, zinc, copper, iron ore, and gold, have climbed as well. In response, mining companies have unveiled plans to carve out more mines. For instance, global minerals-producing firms such as BHP Billiton, Anglo American PLC, and OAO

Rusal have indicated that they intend to nearly double their mining production by 2011.

FOR CRITICAL ANALYSIS
Some observers of markets for minerals suggest that prices of minerals may decline during the 2010s. Other things being equal, how would you expect mining production to respond if this prediction holds true?

The Supply Schedule

Just as we were able to construct a demand schedule, we can construct a *supply schedule,* which is a table relating prices to the quantity supplied at each price. A supply schedule can also be referred to simply as *supply.* It is a set of planned production rates that depends on the price of the product. We show the individual supply schedule for a hypothetical producer in panel (a) of Figure 3-6 on the next page. At a price of $1 per secure digital card, for example, this producer will supply 20,000 SD cards per year. At a price of $5 per SD card, this producer will supply 55,000 SD cards per year.

FIGURE 3-6

The Individual Producer's Supply Schedule and Supply Curve for Secure Digital Cards

Panel (a) shows that at higher prices, a hypothetical supplier will be willing to provide a greater quantity of secure digital cards. We plot the various price-quantity combinations in panel (a) on the grid in panel (b). When we connect these points, we create the individual supply curve for SD cards. It is positively sloped.

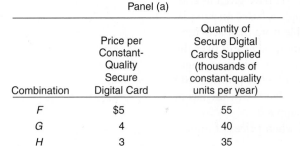

Panel (a)

Combination	Price per Constant-Quality Secure Digital Card	Quantity of Secure Digital Cards Supplied (thousands of constant-quality units per year)
F	$5	55
G	4	40
H	3	35
I	2	25
J	1	20

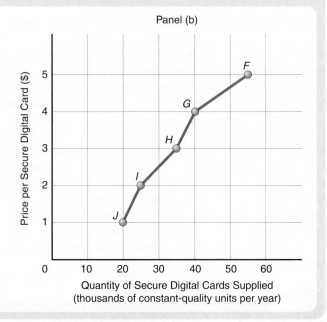

Panel (b)

The Supply Curve

Supply curve
The graphical representation of the supply schedule; a line (curve) showing the supply schedule, which generally slopes upward (has a positive slope), other things being equal.

We can convert the supply schedule from panel (a) of Figure 3-6 into a **supply curve,** just as we earlier created a demand curve in Figure 3-1 on page 55. All we do is take the price-quantity combinations from panel (a) of Figure 3-6 and plot them in panel (b). We have labeled these combinations *F* through *J.* Connecting these points, we obtain an upward-sloping curve that shows the typically direct relationship between price and quantity supplied. Again, we have to remember that we are talking about quantity supplied *per year*, measured in constant-quality units.

The Market Supply Curve

Just as we summed the individual demand curves to obtain the market demand curve, we sum the individual producers' supply curves to obtain the market supply curve. Look at Figure 3-7, in which we horizontally sum two typical supply curves for manufacturers of SD cards. Supplier 1's data are taken from Figure 3-6. Supplier 2 is added. The numbers are presented in panel (a). The graphical representation of supplier 1 is in panel (b), of supplier 2 in panel (c), and of the summation in panel (d). The result, then, is the supply curve for SD cards, for suppliers 1 and 2. We assume that there are more suppliers of SD cards, however. The total market supply schedule and total market supply curve for SD cards are represented in Figure 3-8 on page 66, with the curve in panel (b) obtained by adding all of the supply curves such as those shown in panels (b) and (c) of Figure 3-7. Notice the difference between the market supply curve with only two suppliers in Figure 3-7 and the one with many suppliers—the entire true market—in panel (b) of Figure 3-8. (For simplicity, we assume that the true total market supply curve is a straight line.)

You Are There

To learn how the law of supply applies to the production of specialized insects, read **Beetle Factories Respond to Higher Demand for Weed-Eating Bugs,** on page 75.

PRICE EXPECTATIONS A change in the expectation of a future relative price of a product can affect a producer's current willingness to supply, just as price expectations affect a consumer's current willingness to purchase. For example, suppliers of SD cards may withhold from the market part of their current supply if they anticipate higher prices in the future. The current amount supplied at each and every price will decrease.

How is one company profiting from helping producers form expectations of the weather's influence on the prices of various items?

EXAMPLE
Keeping Price Expectations Updated with Forecasts of Forecasts

The prices of certain products often vary with the weather. The price of oranges, for instance, climbs whenever a cold snap grips Florida. Prices of natural gas drop when springlike weather settles into place during winter months. Consequently, forming accurate expectations of future prices of such items requires forecasting the weather.

The propensity for meteorologists to constantly revise weather forecasts complicates the process of forming expectations about future prices of products such as oranges or natural gas. To assist those producers who wish to continually update expectations about future prices of such products, WSI, the company that owns the Weather Channel, offers a new service. At a price of $90,000 per year, it sells subscriptions to its prediction about the daily weather forecast provided by the National Oceanic and Atmospheric Administration (NOAA). Each day, one hour before NOAA meteorologists issue a weather forecast for the next several days, WSI provides its subscribers with a prediction of how the NOAA's forecast will change from its forecast the previous day. Then subscribing firms can use WSI's forecast of the NOAAs forecast to adjust their own expectations of the weather's likely effects on prices in the following days.

FOR CRITICAL ANALYSIS
If an item's price typically increases on days with good weather and decreases on days with bad weather, how would a producer of the item adjust today's output in light of an expectation of improved weather during the next few days?

NUMBER OF FIRMS IN THE INDUSTRY In the short run, when firms can change only the number of employees they use, we hold the number of firms in the industry constant. In the long run, the number of firms may change. If the number of firms increases, supply will increase, and the supply curve will shift outward to the right. If the number of firms decreases, supply will decrease, and the supply curve will shift inward to the left.

Changes in Supply versus Changes in Quantity Supplied

We cannot overstress the importance of distinguishing between a movement along the supply curve—which occurs only when the price changes for a given supply curve—and a shift in the supply curve—which occurs only with changes in *ceteris paribus* conditions. A change in the price of the good in question always (and only) brings about a change in the quantity supplied along a given supply curve. We move to a different point on the existing supply curve. This is specifically called a *change in quantity supplied*. When price changes, quantity supplied changes—there is a movement from one point to another along the same supply curve.

When you think of *supply*, think of the entire curve. Quantity supplied is represented by a single point on the supply curve.

Why are these people waiting in line for the new iPhone?

*A change, or shift, in supply is a movement of the entire curve. The **only** thing that can cause the entire curve to move is a change in one of the **ceteris paribus** conditions.*

Consequently,

*A change in price leads to a change in the quantity supplied, other things being constant. This is a movement **along** the curve.*

*A change in any **ceteris paribus** condition for supply leads to a change in supply. This causes a **shift of the curve.***

QUICK QUIZ   *See page 81 for the answers. Review concepts from this section in MyEconLab.*

If the price changes, we _____ _____ a curve—there is a change in quantity demanded or supplied. If some other determinant changes, we _____ a curve—there is a change in demand or supply.

The **supply curve** is drawn with other things held constant. If these *ceteris paribus* conditions of supply change, the supply curve will shift. The major *ceteris paribus* conditions are (1) _____, (2) _____, (3) _____, (4) _____, and (5) _____.

Putting Demand and Supply Together

In the sections on demand and supply, we tried to confine each discussion to demand or supply only. But you have probably already realized that we can't view the world just from the demand side or just from the supply side. There is interaction between the two. In this section, we will discuss how they interact and how that interaction determines the prices that prevail in our economy and other economies in which the forces of demand and supply are allowed to work.

Let's first combine the demand and supply schedules and then combine the curves.

Demand and Supply Schedules Combined

Go to www.econtoday.com/chapter03 to see how the U.S. Department of Agriculture seeks to estimate demand and supply conditions for major agricultural products.

Let's place panel (a) from Figure 3-3 (the market demand schedule) on page 57 and panel (a) from Figure 3-8 (the market supply schedule) on page 66 together in panel (a) of Figure 3-10. Column 1 shows the price; column 2, the quantity supplied per year at any given price; and column 3, the quantity demanded. Column 4 is the difference between columns 2 and 3, or the difference between the quantity supplied and the quantity demanded. In column 5, we label those differences as either excess quantity supplied (called a *surplus*, which we shall discuss shortly) or excess quantity demanded (commonly known as a *shortage*, also discussed shortly). For example, at a price of $1, only 2 million secure digital cards would be supplied, but the quantity demanded would be 10 million. The difference would be −8 million, which we label excess quantity demanded (a shortage). At the other end, a price of $5 would elicit 10 million in quantity supplied, but quantity demanded would drop to 2 million, leaving a difference of +8 million units, which we call excess quantity supplied (a surplus).

Now, do you notice something special about the price of $3? At that price, both the quantity supplied and the quantity demanded per year are 6 million. The difference then is zero. There is neither excess quantity demanded (shortage) nor excess quantity

FIGURE 3-10

Putting Demand and Supply Together

In panel (a), we see that at the price of $3, the quantity supplied and the quantity demanded are equal, resulting in neither an excess quantity demanded nor an excess quantity supplied. We call this price the equilibrium, or market clearing, price. In panel (b), the intersection of the supply and demand curves is at *E*, at a price of $3 and a quantity of 6 million per year. At point *E*, there is neither an excess quantity demanded nor an excess quantity supplied. At a price of $1, the quantity supplied will be only 2 million per year,

but the quantity demanded will be 10 million. The difference is excess quantity demanded at a price of $1. The price will rise, so we will move from point *A* up the supply curve and from point *B* up the demand curve to point *E*. At the other extreme, a price of $5 elicits a quantity supplied of 10 million but a quantity demanded of only 2 million. The difference is excess quantity supplied at a price of $5. The price will fall, so we will move down the demand curve and the supply curve to the equilibrium price, $3 per SD card.

Panel (a)

(1) Price per Constant-Quality Secure Digital Card	(2) Quantity Supplied (secure digital cards per year)	(3) Quantity Demanded (secure digital cards per year)	(4) Difference (2) − (3) (secure digital cards per year)	(5) Condition
$5	10 million	2 million	8 million	Excess quantity supplied (surplus)
4	8 million	4 million	4 million	Excess quantity supplied (surplus)
3	6 million	6 million	0	Market clearing price—equilibrium (no surplus, no shortage)
2	4 million	8 million	−4 million	Excess quantity demanded (shortage)
1	2 million	10 million	−8 million	Excess quantity demanded (shortage)

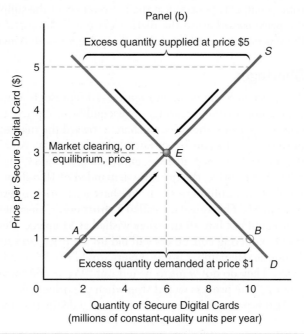

Panel (b)

supplied (surplus). Hence the price of $3 is very special. It is called the **market clearing price**—it clears the market of all excess quantities demanded or supplied. There are no willing consumers who want to pay $3 per SD card but are turned away by sellers, and there are no willing suppliers who want to sell SD cards at $3 who cannot sell all they want at that price. Another term for the market clearing price is the **equilibrium price,** the price at which there is no tendency for change. Consumers are able to get all they want at that price, and suppliers are able to sell all they want at that price.

Equilibrium

We can define **equilibrium** in general as a point at which quantity demanded equals quantity supplied at a particular price. There tends to be no movement of the price or the quantity away from this point unless demand or supply changes. Any movement away from this point will set into motion forces that will cause movement back to it. Therefore, equilibrium is a stable point. Any point that is not an equilibrium is unstable and will not persist.

The equilibrium point occurs where the supply and demand curves intersect. The equilibrium price is given on the vertical axis directly to the left of where the supply and demand curves cross. The equilibrium quantity is given on the horizontal axis directly underneath the intersection of the demand and supply curves.

Panel (b) in Figure 3-3 and panel (b) in Figure 3-8 are combined as panel (b) in Figure 3-10 on the previous page. The demand curve is labeled D, the supply curve S. We have labeled the intersection of the supply curve with the demand curve as point E, for equilibrium. That corresponds to a market clearing price of $3, at which both the quantity supplied and the quantity demanded are 6 million units per year. There is neither excess quantity supplied nor excess quantity demanded. Point E, the equilibrium point, always occurs at the intersection of the supply and demand curves. This is the price *toward which* the market price will automatically tend to gravitate, because there is no outcome better than this price for both consumers and producers.

Shortages

The price of $3 depicted in Figure 3-10 represents a situation of equilibrium. If there were a non-market-clearing, or disequilibrium, price, this would put into play forces that would cause the price to change toward the market clearing price at which equilibrium would again be sustained. Look again at panel (b) in Figure 3-10. Suppose that instead of being at the equilibrium price of $3, for some reason the market price is $1. At this price, the quantity demanded of 10 million per year exceeds the quantity supplied of 2 million per year. We have a situation of excess quantity demanded at the price of $1. This is usually called a **shortage.** Consumers of SD cards would find that they could not buy all that they wished at $1 apiece. But forces will cause the price to rise: Competing consumers will bid up the price, and suppliers will increase output in response. (Remember, some buyers would pay $5 or more rather than do without SD cards. They do not want to be left out.) We would move from points A and B toward point E. The process would stop when the price again reached $3 per SD card.

At this point, it is important to recall a distinction made in Chapter 2:

Shortages and scarcity are not the same thing.

A shortage is a situation in which the quantity demanded exceeds the quantity supplied at a price that is somehow kept *below* the market clearing price. Our definition of scarcity was much more general and all-encompassing: a situation in which the resources available for producing output are insufficient to satisfy all wants. Any choice necessarily costs an opportunity, and the opportunity is lost. Hence, we will always live in a world of scarcity because we must constantly make choices, but we do not necessarily have to live in a world of shortages.

In what field is there currently a significant shortage of skilled workers?

EXAMPLE
In Nursing, Quantity Demanded Exceeds Quantity Supplied

At present, there are about 2.6 million positions filled or available for nurses at hospitals, physicians' offices, and other health care facilities across the land. Only about 2.2 million nurses are employed, however. Thus, at this time there is an excess quantity demanded—that is, a shortage—of nurses that is equal to approximately 0.4 million (at current wage rates, of course).

FOR CRITICAL ANALYSIS
What do you predict is likely to happen to the average hourly price of nurses' services—the average wage rate earned by nurses—within the next few years?

Surpluses

Now let's repeat the experiment with the market price at $5 rather than at the market clearing price of $3. Clearly, the quantity supplied will exceed the quantity demanded at that price. The result will be an excess quantity supplied at $5 per unit. This excess quantity supplied is often called a **surplus.** Given the curves in panel (b) in Figure 3-10 on page 71, however, there will be forces pushing the price back down toward $3 per SD card: Competing suppliers will cut prices and reduce output, and consumers will purchase more at these new lower prices. If the two forces of supply and demand are unrestricted, they will bring the price back to $3 per SD card.

Shortages and surpluses are resolved in unfettered markets—markets in which price changes are free to occur. The forces that resolve them are those of competition: In the case of shortages, consumers competing for a limited quantity supplied drive up the price; in the case of surpluses, sellers compete for the limited quantity demanded, thus driving prices down to equilibrium. The equilibrium price is the only stable price, and the (unrestricted) market price tends to gravitate toward it.

What happens when the price is set below the equilibrium price? Here come the scalpers.

Surplus
A situation in which quantity supplied is greater than quantity demanded at a price above the market clearing price.

POLICY EXAMPLE
Should Shortages in the Ticket Market Be Solved by Scalpers?

If you have ever tried to get tickets to a playoff game in sports, a popular Broadway play, or a superstar's rap concert, you know about "shortages." The standard Super Bowl ticket situation is shown in Figure 3-11 on the next page. At the face-value price of Super Bowl tickets ($800), the quantity demanded (175,000) greatly exceeds the quantity supplied

POLICY EXAMPLE (cont.)

(80,000). Because shortages last only as long as prices and quantities do not change, markets tend to exhibit a movement out of this disequilibrium toward equilibrium. Obviously, the quantity of Super Bowl tickets cannot change, but the price can go as high as $6,000.

Enter the scalper. This colorful term is used because when you purchase a ticket that is being resold at a price higher than face value, the seller is skimming an extra profit off the top ("taking your scalp"). If an event sells out and people who wished to purchase tickets at current prices were unable to do so, ticket prices by definition were lower than market clearing prices. People without tickets may be willing to buy high-priced tickets because they place a greater value on the entertainment event than the face value of the ticket. Without scalpers, those individuals would not be able to attend the event. In the case of the Super Bowl, various forms of scalping occur nationwide. Tickets for a seat on the 50-yard line have been sold for as much as $6,000 apiece. In front of every Super Bowl arena, you can find ticket scalpers hawking their wares.

In most states, scalping is illegal. In Pennsylvania, convicted scalpers are either fined $5,000 or sentenced to two years behind bars. For an economist, such legislation seems strange. As one New York ticket broker said, "I look at scalping like working as a stockbroker, buying low and selling high. If people are willing to pay me the money, what kind of problem is that?"

FOR CRITICAL ANALYSIS
What happens to ticket scalpers who are still holding tickets after an event has started?

FIGURE 3-11

Shortages of Super Bowl Tickets

The quantity of tickets for a Super Bowl game is fixed at 80,000. At the price per ticket of $800, the quantity demanded is 175,000. Consequently, there is an excess quantity demanded at the below-market clearing price. In this example, prices can go as high as $6,000 in the scalpers' market.

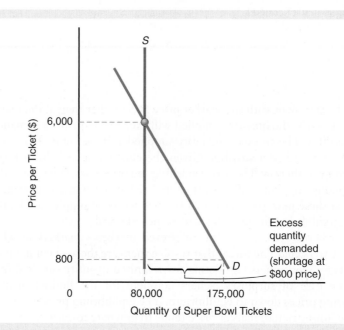

QUICK QUIZ
See page 81 for the answers. Review concepts from this section in MyEconLab.

The market clearing price occurs at the _____ of the market demand curve and the market supply curve. It is also called the _____ price, the price from which there is no tendency to change unless there is a change in demand or supply.

Whenever the price is _____ than the equilibrium price, there is an excess quantity supplied (a **surplus**).

Whenever the price is _____ than the equilibrium price, there is an excess quantity demanded (a **shortage**).

You Are There

Beetle Factories Respond to Higher Demand for Weed-Eating Bugs

Dan Palmer, production chief at the Phillip Alampi Beneficial Insect Rearing Laboratory in New Jersey, is struggling to handle new orders for one of the lab's products: *Galerucella,* which are brown beetles smaller than ladybugs. In the past, his lab mainly received daily orders for the beetles from private landowners and municipal governments in New Jersey, but now he is receiving numerous out-of-state orders as well.

The *Galerucella* beetles eat purple loosestrife, a weed imported from Europe 200 years ago that has spread throughout much of the United States and Canada. During the 1980s, environmentalists discovered that purple loosestrife chokes out native American flora and fills in spaces around lakes where wildlife such as ducks and turtles otherwise would thrive. Numerous landowners are now striving to halt and, if possible, reverse the spread of purple loosestrife. Weed-eating beetles such as *Galerucella* are increasingly regarded as a fundamental part of this effort—hence, the growing volume of orders placed for the beetles bred at labs such as Palmer's.

Dan Palmer contemplates the stack of orders that have arrived today. He concludes that the 12 people in his lab cannot possibly breed beetles in sufficient volumes to meet all his new orders. To increase daily beetle output, the lab must expand its staff, but to do that, it requires higher revenues and therefore must receive a higher price for each unit of beetles it ships. Otherwise, some of the orders that have been received today and that are likely to arrive in the days and weeks to come must go unfilled. He knows that the same situation exists at other labs that produce *Galerucella* and other weed-eating beetles. At current prices, these labs are simply unable to produce as many beetles as landowners would like to purchase.

CRITICAL ANALYSIS QUESTIONS

1. If the price of weed-eating beetles remains unchanged in the face of the recent rise in demand for these insects, what situation will exist in the market for the beetles?

2. If the price of the beetles increases, will there be a movement along the market supply curve, or will the market supply curve shift?

Issues and Applications

Why Are People Eating More?

Being overweight or obese predisposes an individual to ailments such as arthritis, diabetes, heart disease, high blood pressure, respiratory problems, and strokes. Nevertheless, about two-thirds of the U.S. population is overweight. Nearly half of these people are classified as obese.

CONCEPTS APPLIED

- Relative Price
- Law of Demand
- Normal Good

Undoubtedly, a generally more sedentary lifestyle helps to explain the increase in the body mass of the average U.S. resident. Panel (a) of Figure 3-12 suggests, however, that increased calorie consumption has contributed as well. Why are people ingesting so many more calories? To answer this question, one needs to look no further than two fundamental developments: (1) a falling relative price of food that has increased the quantity of food demanded and (2) rising incomes that have contributed to a higher demand for food.

FIGURE 3-12

U.S. Calorie Consumption and the Relative Price of Food

Panel (a) shows that the average U.S. resident's daily calorie consumption has surged since the late 1970s. Panel (b) shows that the price of food relative to the average price of all other items has declined since the 1970s.
Sources: U.S. Department of Agriculture; U.S. Department of Labor.

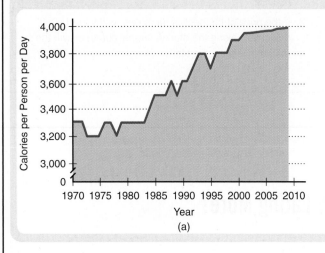

(a)

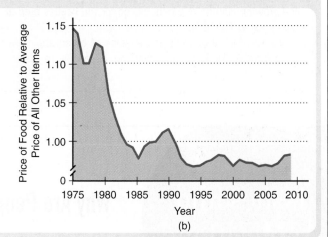

(b)

Moving Along the Food Demand Curve: Falling Relative Prices

Panel (b) of Figure 3-12 displays an index measure of the price of food relative to the average price of all other goods and services. This relative price measure indicates that the relative price of food has declined by almost 0.5 percent per year, which over the past three decades translates into an overall drop exceeding 17 percent.

The law of demand states that a decline in the relative price of an item leads to an increase in the quantity demanded of that item. With other things being equal, therefore, the significant decline in the relative price of food boosted desired food consumption. Hence, one reason that people today buy and eat more food is simply that food is cheaper than it used to be.

A Shift in the Food Demand Curve: Higher Incomes

Of course, other things have not remained unchanged since the mid-1970s. A key factor that has changed is incomes. The average inflation-adjusted income of a U.S. resident has increased by about 2 percent per year since the mid-1970s. The overall rise during the period has been more than 100 percent.

Some food items, such as canned beans and packaged macaroni and cheese, are inferior goods, so higher incomes have reduced consumption of these and similar foods. The vast majority of food items, however, are normal goods. Hence, the substantial rise in individual incomes has tended to raise the demand for foods as well as for other normal goods, such as personal computers and video games.

A Double-Whammy Effect on Food Consumption

Thus, two key factors have contributed to greater food consumption: the lower relative price of food and higher incomes. Increases in incomes have boosted demands for most food items, and declines in the relative prices have induced people to buy even more foods. Hence, people have been consuming more food and, with it, more calories. Without additional exercise, they have also been gaining more weight.

Test your understanding of this chapter by going online to **MyEconLab**.
In the Study Plan for this chapter, select Section N: News.

For Critical Analysis

1. If the demands for most food items have been rising as incomes have increased, what must have happened to the supplies of most food items to account for the declining relative price of food?

2. What factors might have accounted for the changes in food supplies discussed in Question 1? (Hint: What *ceteris paribus* conditions affect the position of a supply curve?)

Web Resources

1. For a review of the worldwide trend toward higher body masses, go to www.econtoday.com/chapter03.

2. To learn about various ways states and the federal government are trying to combat childhood obesity,

click on the link to the National Center for Chronic Disease Prevention and Health Promotion, available at www.econtoday.com/chapter03.

Research Project

One way that the federal government seeks to assist low-income people is by issuing them food stamps, which they can use to purchase food items. Some observers have suggested that the government's food stamp program contributes to the higher obesity rates observed among low-income people as compared with rates observed among middle- and high-income individuals. Evaluate this argument. (Hint: Many of the least-expensive food items are often the highest-fat foods containing the most calories per unit of food.)

Here is what you should know after reading this chapter. **MyEconLab** will help you identify what you know, and where to go when you need to practice.

WHAT YOU SHOULD KNOW		WHERE TO GO TO PRACTICE
The Law of Demand According to the law of demand, other things being equal, individuals will purchase fewer units of a good at a higher price, and they will purchase more units of a good at a lower price.	market, 52 demand, 52 law of demand, 52	• **MyEconLab** Study Plan 3.1 • Audio introduction to Chapter 3

(continued)

 *(continued)*

WHAT YOU SHOULD KNOW		WHERE TO GO TO PRACTICE

Relative Prices versus Money Prices When determining the quantity of a good to purchase, people respond to changes in its relative price, which is the price of the good in terms of other goods. If the price of a unit of health care services rises by 50 percent next year while at the same time all other prices, including your wages, also increase by 50 percent, then the relative price of the health care services has not changed. Thus, in a world of generally rising prices, you have to compare the price of one good with the general level of prices of other goods in order to decide whether the relative price of that one good has gone up, gone down, or stayed the same.

relative price, 53
money price, 53

- **MyEconLab** Study Plan 3.1
- Video: The Difference Between Relative and Absolute Prices and the Importance of Looking at Only Relative Prices

A Change in Quantity Demanded versus a Change in Demand The demand schedule shows the relationship between various possible prices and respective quantities purchased per unit of time. Graphically, the demand schedule is a downward-sloping demand curve. A change in the price of the good generates a change in the quantity demanded, which is a movement along the demand curve. Factors other than the price of the good that affect the amount demanded are (1) income, (2) tastes and preferences, (3) the prices of related goods, (4) expectations, and (5) market size (the number of potential buyers). Whenever any of these *ceteris paribus* conditions of demand changes, there is a change in the demand for the good, and the demand curve shifts to a new position.

demand curve, 56
market demand, 56
ceteris paribus
  conditions, 59
normal goods, 59
inferior goods, 59
substitutes, 60
complements, 60
KEY FIGURE
Figure 3-2, 56
Figure 3-4, 58
Figure 3-5, 62

- **MyEconLab** Study Plans 3.2, 3.3
- Video: The Importance of Distinguishing Between a Shift in a Demand Curve and a Move Along the Demand Curve
- Animated Figures 3-2, 3-4, 3-5
- ABC News Video: What Drives the Market: Supply and Demand

The Law of Supply According to the law of supply, sellers will produce and offer for sale more units of a good at a higher price, and they will produce and offer for sale fewer units of the good at a lower price.

supply, 62
law of supply, 63

- **MyEconLab** Study Plan 3.4

A Change in Quantity Supplied versus a Change in Supply The supply schedule shows the relationship between various possible prices and respective quantities produced and sold per unit of time. On a graph, the supply schedule is a supply curve that slopes upward. A change in the price of the good generates a change in the quantity supplied, which is a movement along the supply curve. Factors other than the price of the good that affect the amount supplied are (1) input prices, (2) technology and productivity, (3) taxes and subsidies, (4) price expectations, and (5) the number of sellers. Whenever any of these *ceteris paribus* conditions changes, there is a change in the supply of the good, and the supply curve shifts to a new position.

supply curve, 64
subsidy, 68
KEY FIGURES
Figure 3-6, 64
Figure 3-7, 65
Figure 3-9, 67

- **MyEconLab** Study Plans 3.5, 3.6
- Video: The Importance of Distinguishing Between a Change in Supply versus a Change in Quantity Supplied
- Animated Figures 3-6, 3-7, 3-9

 *(continued)*

WHAT YOU SHOULD KNOW

Determining the Market Price and the Equilibrium Quantity
The equilibrium price of a good and the equilibrium quantity of the good that is produced and sold are determined by the intersection of the demand and supply curves. At this intersection point, the quantity demanded by buyers of the good just equals the quantity supplied by sellers. At the equilibrium price at this point of intersection, the plans of buyers and sellers mesh exactly. Hence, there is neither an excess quantity of the good supplied (surplus) nor an excess quantity of the good demanded (shortage) at this equilibrium point.

market clearing, or
  equilibrium, price, 72
equilibrium, 72
shortage, 72
surplus, 73

KEY FIGURE
Figure 3-11, 74

WHERE TO GO TO PRACTICE

- **MyEconLab** Study Plan 3.7
- Animated Figure 3-11
- ABC News Video: The Ripple Effects of Oil Prices

Log in to MyEconLab, take a chapter test, and get a personalized Study Plan that tells you which concepts you understand and which ones you need to review. From there, MyEconLab will give you further practice, tutorials, animations, videos, and guided solutions.
Log in to www.myeconlab.com

PROBLEMS

All problems are assignable in myeconlab. *Answers to odd-numbered problems appear at the back of the book.*

3-1. Suppose that in a recent market period, the following relationship existed between the price of prerecorded movie DVDs and the quantity supplied and quantity demanded.

Price	Quantity Demanded	Quantity Supplied
$19	100 million	40 million
$20	90 million	60 million
$21	80 million	80 million
$22	70 million	100 million
$23	60 million	120 million

Graph the supply and demand curves for movie DVDs given the information in the table. What are the equilibrium price and quantity? If the industry price is $20, is there a shortage or surplus of DVDs? How much is the shortage or surplus?

3-2. Suppose that in a later market period, the quantities supplied in the table in Problem 3-1 are unchanged. The quantity demanded, however, has increased by 30 million at each price. Construct the resulting demand curve in the illustration you made for Problem 3-1. Is this an increase or a decrease in demand? What are the new equilibrium quantity and the new market price? Give two examples of changes in *ceteris paribus* conditions that might cause such a change.

3-3. Consider the market for DSL high-speed Internet access service, which is a normal good. Explain whether the following events would cause an increase or a decrease in demand or an increase or a decrease in the quantity demanded.

a. Firms providing cable (an alternative to DSL) Internet access services reduce their prices.

b. Firms providing DSL high-speed Internet access services reduce their prices.

c. There is a decrease in the incomes earned by consumers of DSL high-speed Internet access services.

d. Consumers of DSL high-speed Internet access services anticipate a decline in the future price of these services.

3-4. In the market for flash memory drives (a normal good), explain whether the following events would cause an increase or a decrease in demand or an increase or a decrease in the quantity demanded. Also explain what happens to the equilibrium quantity and the market clearing price.

a. There are increases in the prices of storage racks and boxes for flash memory drives.

b. There is a decrease in the price of computer drives that read the information contained on flash memory drives.

c. There is a dramatic increase in the price of secure digital cards that, like flash memory drives, can be used to store digital data.

d. A booming economy increases the income of the typical buyer of flash memory drives.

e. Consumers of flash memory drives anticipate that the price of this good will decline in the future.

3-5. Give an example of a complement and a substitute in consumption for each of the following items.

a. Bacon

b. Tennis racquets

c. Coffee

d. Automobiles

3-6. At the beginning of the 2000s, the United States imposed high import taxes on a number of European goods due to a trade dispute. One of these goods was Roquefort cheese. Show how this tax affects the market for Roquefort cheese in the United States, shifting the appropriate curve and indicating a new equilibrium quantity and market price.

3-7. Consider the following diagram of a market for one-bedroom rental apartments in a college community.

a. At a rental rate of $1,000 per month, is there an excess quantity supplied, or is there an excess quantity demanded? What is the amount of the excess quantity supplied or demanded?

b. If the present rental rate of one-bedroom apartments is $1,000 per month, through what mechanism will the rental rate adjust to the equilibrium rental rate of $800?

c. At a rental rate of $600 per month, is there an excess quantity supplied, or is there an excess quantity demanded? What is the amount of the excess quantity supplied or demanded?

d. If the present rental rate of one-bedroom apartments is $600 per month, through what mechanism will the rental rate adjust to the equilibrium rental rate of $800?

3-8. Consider the market for economics textbooks. Explain whether the following events would cause an increase or a decrease in supply or an increase or a decrease in the quantity supplied.

a. The market price of paper increases.

b. The market price of economics textbooks increases.

c. The number of publishers of economics textbooks increases.

d. Publishers expect that the market price of economics textbooks will increase next month.

3-9. Consider the market for laptop computers. Explain whether the following events would cause an increase or a decrease in supply or an increase or a decrease in the quantity supplied. Illustrate each, and show what would happen to the equilibrium quantity and the market price.

a. The price of memory chips used in laptop computers declines.

b. The price of machinery used to produce laptop computers increases.

c. The number of manufacturers of laptop computers increases.

d. There is a decrease in the demand for laptop computers.

3-10. The U.S. government offers significant per-unit subsidy payments to U.S. sugar growers. Describe the effects of the introduction of such subsidies on the market for sugar and the market for artificial sweeteners. Explain whether the demand curve or the supply curve shifts in each market, and if so, in which direction. Also explain what happens to the equilibrium quantity and the market price in each market.

3-11. Platinum's white luster has made the rare metal the chic look in engagement rings and wedding bands. Recently, however, the price of palladium, a more abundant metal with virtually identical characteristics, has declined considerably. Explain the likely effects that the drop in the price of palladium will have on the market for platinum.

3-12. Ethanol is a motor fuel manufactured from corn, barley, or wheat, and it can be used to power the engines of many autos and trucks. Suppose that the government decides to provide a large per-unit subsidy to ethanol producers. Explain the effects in the markets for the following items:

a. Corn

b. Gasoline

c. Automobiles

3-13. If the price of processor chips used in manufacturing personal computers decreases, what will happen in the market for personal computers? How will the equilibrium price and equilibrium quantity of personal computers change?

3-14. Assume that the cost of aluminum used by soft-drink companies increases. Which of the following correctly describes the resulting effects in the market for soft drinks distributed in aluminum cans? (More than one statement may be correct.)

a. The demand for soft drinks decreases.

b. The quantity of soft drinks demanded decreases.

c. The supply of soft drinks decreases.

d. The quantity of soft drinks supplied decreases.

ECONOMICS ON THE NET

The U.S. Nursing Shortage For some years media stories have discussed a shortage of qualified nurses in the United States. This application explores some of the factors that have caused the quantity of newly trained nurses demanded to tend to exceed the quantity of newly trained nurses supplied.

Title: Nursing Shortage Resource Web Link

Navigation: Go to the Nursing Shortage Resource Web Link at **www.econtoday.com/chapter03**, and click on *Enrollment Increase Insufficient to Meet the Projected Increase in Demand for New Nurses.*

Application Read the discussion, and answer the following questions.

1. What has happened to the demand for new nurses in the United States? What has happened to the supply of new nurses? Why has the result been a shortage?

2. If there is a free market for the skills of new nurses, what can you predict is likely to happen to the wage rate earned by individuals who have just completed their nursing training?

For Group Study and Analysis Discuss the pros and cons of high schools and colleges trying to factor predictions about future wages into student career counseling. How might this potentially benefit students? What problems might high schools and colleges face in trying to assist students in evaluating the future earnings prospects of various jobs?

ANSWERS TO QUICK QUIZZES

p. 54: (i) inverse; (ii) demand

p. 58: (i) constant; (ii) market demand

p. 62: (i) income . . . tastes and preferences . . . prices of related goods . . . expectations about future prices and incomes . . . market size (the number of potential buyers in the market); (ii) *ceteris paribus*; (iii) movement along

p. 65: (i) direct; (ii) supply; (iii) market supply

p. 70: (i) move along . . . shift; (ii) input prices . . . technology and productivity . . . taxes and subsidies . . . expectations of future relative prices . . . the number of firms in the industry

p. 74: (i) intersection . . . equilibrium; (ii) greater; (iii) less

4

Extensions of Demand and Supply Analysis

bout 100,000 U.S. residents possessing a malfunctioning organ, such as a liver, heart, or lung, are on waiting lists for transplants from deceased or living donors. A majority of the people waiting for organ transplants are individuals who are suffering from kidney failure. As they wait for donations of compatible kidneys, most people with failed kidneys must undergo years of dialysis, which is an artificial means of cleaning their bloodstreams of harmful toxins. Many never receive a kidney transplant, and a number of these individuals die each year. Why do people suffering from kidney failure have to wait for years to obtain transplants? Why are so many individuals never able to obtain transplants? By the end of this chapter, you will understand the answer to these questions.

LEARNING OBJECTIVES

myeconlab

MyEconLab helps you master each objective and study more efficiently. See end of chapter for details.

After reading this chapter, you should be able to:

➤ Discuss the essential features of the price system

➤ Evaluate the effects of changes in demand and supply on the market price and equilibrium quantity

➤ Understand the rationing function of prices

➤ Explain the effects of price ceilings

➤ Explain the effects of price floors

➤ Describe various types of government-imposed quantity restrictions on markets

? DID YOU KNOW THAT when the owner of a Wisconsin gasoline station recently offered a 2-cent-per-gallon price discount to senior citizens, the state's Department of Agriculture, Trade, and Consumer Protection objected? The state government agency informed the station owner that the price he had offered senior citizens was too low. Under state law, the station owner could not offer to sell gasoline to anyone at a price below a permissible minimum price, or price *floor*.

What effects can a price floor have on production and consumption of a good or service? As you will learn in this chapter, we can use the supply and demand analysis developed in Chapter 3 to answer this question. You will find that when a government sets a price floor above the equilibrium price, the result will be a surplus, in which quantity supplied remains above quantity demanded. Similarly, you will learn about how we can use supply and demand analysis to examine the "surplus" of various agricultural products, the "shortage" of apartments in certain cities, and many other phenomena. All of these examples are part of our economy, which we characterize as a *price system*.

The Price System and Markets

In a **price system,** otherwise known as a *market system*, relative prices are constantly changing to reflect changes in supply and demand for different commodities. The prices of those commodities are the signals to everyone within the system as to what is relatively scarce and what is relatively abundant. In this sense, prices provide information.

Indeed, it is the *signaling* aspect of the price system that provides the information to buyers and sellers about what should be bought and what should be produced. In a price system, there is a clear-cut chain of events in which any changes in demand and supply cause changes in prices that in turn affect the opportunities that businesses and individuals have for profit and personal gain. Such changes influence our use of resources.

Price system
An economic system in which relative prices are constantly changing to reflect changes in supply and demand for different commodities. The prices of those commodities are signals to everyone within the system as to what is relatively scarce and what is relatively abundant.

Exchange and Markets

The price system features **voluntary exchange,** acts of trading between individuals that make both parties to the trade subjectively better off. The **terms of exchange**—the prices we pay for the desired items—are determined by the interaction of the forces underlying supply and demand. In our economy, exchanges take place voluntarily in markets. A market encompasses the exchange arrangements of both buyers and sellers that underlie the forces of supply and demand. Indeed, one definition of a market is that it is a low-cost institution for facilitating exchange. A market increases incomes by helping resources move to their highest-valued uses.

Voluntary exchange
An act of trading, done on an elective basis, in which both parties to the trade expect to be better off after the exchange.

Terms of exchange
The conditions under which trading takes place. Usually, the terms of exchange are equal to the price at which a good is traded.

Transaction Costs

Individuals turn to markets because markets reduce the cost of exchanges. These costs are sometimes referred to as **transaction costs,** which are broadly defined as the costs associated with finding out exactly what is being transacted as well as the cost of enforcing contracts. If you were Robinson Crusoe and lived alone on an island, you would never incur a transaction cost. For everyone else, transaction costs are just as real as the costs of production. Today, high-speed computers have allowed us to reduce transaction costs by increasing our ability to process information and keep records.

How have real-time dating services via cellphone reduced the transaction costs of searching for a date?

Transaction costs
All of the costs associated with exchange, including the informational costs of finding out the price and quality, service record, and durability of a product, plus the cost of contracting and enforcing that contract.

E-COMMERCE EXAMPLE
Cellphone Services Reduce the Transaction Costs of Dating

Internet matchmaking is moving to a new level. Singles can now find potential dating partners in nearby locales via cellphone. Web dating services such as MeetMoi permit a registered user to indicate that she is available for text messaging within a ZIP code or at a nearby street address. The dating service's computer system then identifies other members who have indicated they are looking for a date in the specified area and sends back profiles matching the user's criteria. Match.com offers a cellphone service utilizing global-positioning-system technology to help users locate a nearby match. At another service, Zogo, a person can use a cellphone Web browser to view a list of potential matches. If the individual requests a phone conversation, a phone connection is initiated immediately if the requested party approves a text message request forwarded by Zogo. In these and other ways, Internet and telecommunication technologies continue to reduce the transaction costs of finding a date near you.

FOR CRITICAL ANALYSIS
How do you suppose that computer technology makes it possible for MeetMoi to charge only 99 cents for 10 anonymous text messages to potential dating partners who otherwise might take weeks of effort for a customer to identify on her own?

In what way does Costco reduce transaction costs?

Consider some simple examples of transaction costs. A club warehouse such as Sam's Club or Costco reduces the transaction costs of having to go to numerous specialty stores to obtain the items you desire. Financial institutions, such as commercial banks, have reduced the transaction costs of directing funds from savers to borrowers. In general, the more organized the market, the lower the transaction costs. Among those who constantly attempt to lower transaction costs are the much maligned middlemen.

The Role of Middlemen

As long as there are costs of bringing together buyers and sellers, there will be an incentive for intermediaries, normally called middlemen, to lower those costs. This means that middlemen specialize in lowering transaction costs. Whenever producers do not sell their products directly to the final consumer, by definition, one or more middlemen are involved. Farmers typically sell their output to distributors, who are usually called wholesalers, who then sell those products to retailers such as supermarkets.

As videos flood the Internet, are there profitable opportunities for middlemen?

E-COMMERCE EXAMPLE
Helping People Keep Up with the Flood of Online Videos

As video postings stream onto the Internet, consumers interested in seeing everything from the latest clip from *Saturday Night Live* to a professional baseball game that may alter league standings can find assistance from MeeVee. The company's Web service allows a user to store a list of interests as keywords or category listings. The service rummages through the Internet in search of relevant videos, which it automatically forwards to the client's hard drive, digital video recorder, or cellphone. MeeVee also notifies clients of future television shows or online broadcasts. Clients receive the services at no charge from MeeVee, which profits from deals with advertisers and revenue sharing with providers of pay-per-view video content.

FOR CRITICAL ANALYSIS
What would happen to the demand for the services of online video middlemen such as MeeVee if low-priced software enabling searches for video offerings via cellphones or home computers became available for purchase?

Changes in Demand and Supply

A key function of middlemen is to reduce transaction costs of buyers and sellers in markets for goods and services, and it is in markets that we see the results of changes in demand and supply. Market equilibrium can change whenever there is a *shock* caused by a change in a *ceteris paribus* condition for demand or supply. A shock to the supply and demand system can be represented by a shift in the supply curve, a shift in the demand curve, or a shift in both curves. Any shock to the system will result in a new set of supply and demand relationships and a new equilibrium. Forces will come into play to move the system from the old price-quantity equilibrium (now a disequilibrium situation) to the new equilibrium, where the new demand and supply curves intersect.

Effects of Changes in Either Demand or Supply

In many situations, it is possible to predict what will happen to both equilibrium price and equilibrium quantity when demand or supply changes. Specifically, whenever one curve is stable while the other curve shifts, we can tell what will happen to both price and quantity. Consider the possibilities in Figure 4-1. In panel (a), the supply curve remains unchanged, but demand increases from D_1 to D_2. Note that the results are an increase in the market clearing price from P_1 to P_2 and an increase in the equilibrium quantity from Q_1 to Q_2.

FIGURE 4-1

Shifts in Demand and in Supply: Determinate Results

In panel (a), the supply curve is unchanged at S. The demand curve shifts outward from D_1 to D_2. The equilibrium price and quantity rise from P_1, Q_1 to P_2, Q_2, respectively. In panel (b), again the supply curve is unchanged at S. The demand curve shifts inward to the left, showing a decrease in demand from D_1 to D_3. Both equilibrium price and equilibrium quantity fall. In panel (c), the demand curve now remains unchanged at D. The supply curve shifts from S_1 to S_2. The equilibrium price falls from P_1 to P_2. The equilibrium quantity increases, however, from Q_1 to Q_2. In panel (d), the demand curve is unchanged at D. Supply decreases as shown by a leftward shift of the supply curve from S_1 to S_3. The market clearing price increases from P_1 to P_3. The equilibrium quantity falls from Q_1 to Q_3.

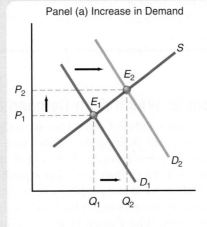

Panel (a) Increase in Demand

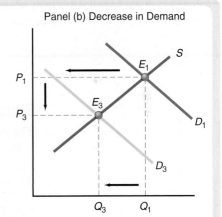

Panel (b) Decrease in Demand

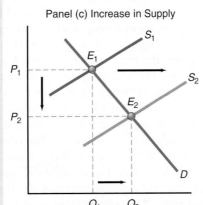

Panel (c) Increase in Supply

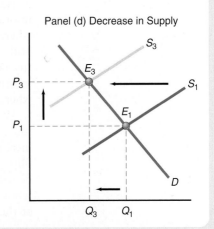

Panel (d) Decrease in Supply

In panel (b) on the previous page, there is a decrease in demand from D_1 to D_3. This results in a decrease in both the equilibrium price of the good and the equilibrium quantity. Panels (c) and (d) show the effects of a shift in the supply curve while the demand curve is unchanged. In panel (c), the supply curve has shifted rightward. The equilibrium price of the product falls; the equilibrium quantity increases. In panel (d), supply has shifted leftward—there has been a supply decrease. The product's equilibrium price increases, and the equilibrium quantity decreases.

Why has the demand for decades-old music recently risen and pushed up the prices of hit songs from the past?

EXAMPLE
The Rising Price of Using Old Songs as Video Background Music

As video content pours onto televisions, cellphones, and computers, producers of videos are scrambling for background music. Indeed, an increasing number of video creators are producing videos carefully synchronized with music, in some cases with videos scripted to fit storylines in song lyrics. The result has been a significant increase in the demand for background music, often purchased for these specific uses from catalogs of long-retired or deceased songwriters. As more producers seek to include hit songs from the past in their video productions, the prices of the rights to use the songs have increased, too. Nearly forgotten songs once available for a few hundred dollars now cost as much as $50,000.

FOR CRITICAL ANALYSIS
What do you suppose has happened to the market clearing price of copyrighted songs newly written for use as background music for video productions?

Situations in Which Both Demand and Supply Shift

The examples in Figure 4-1 show a theoretically determinate outcome of a shift either in the demand curve, holding the supply curve constant, or in the supply curve, holding the demand curve constant. When both the supply and demand curves change, the outcome is indeterminate for either equilibrium price or equilibrium quantity.

When both demand and supply increase, the equilibrium quantity unambiguously rises, because the increase in demand and the increase in supply *both* tend to generate a rise in quantity. The change in the equilibrium price is uncertain without more information, because the increase in demand tends to increase the equilibrium price, whereas the increase in supply tends to decrease the equilibrium price. Decreases in both demand and supply tend to generate a fall in quantity, so the equilibrium quantity falls. Again, the effect on the equilibrium price is uncertain without additional information, because a decrease in demand tends to reduce the equilibrium price, whereas a decrease in supply tends to increase the equilibrium price.

We can be certain that when demand decreases and supply increases at the same time, the equilibrium price will fall, because *both* the decrease in demand and the increase in supply tend to push down the equilibrium price. The change in the equilibrium quantity is uncertain without more information, because the decrease in demand tends to reduce the equilibrium quantity, whereas the increase in supply tends to increase the equilibrium quantity. If demand increases and supply decreases at the same time, both occurrences tend to push up the equilibrium price, so the equilibrium price definitely rises. The change in the equilibrium quantity cannot be determined without more information, because the increase in demand tends to raise the equilibrium quantity, whereas the decrease in supply tends to reduce the equilibrium quantity.

Why is one of the most common physical elements in the universe selling at a higher price here on planet Earth?

EXAMPLE
A Hot Market for a Cooling Element

The element helium is utilized by manufacturers of electronic components because its inert nature helps prevent other gases or impurities from lodging on microchips. In addition, helium readily absorbs heat, so it is very useful for cooling hot substances. Indeed, it can be used to cool metals to such low temperatures that they become superconductors. Even though helium is the second-most-abundant element in the known universe, on our world it is primarily found as a trace component of natural gas. Helium is extracted from natural gas by cooling it to the point at which component gases other than helium liquefy, leaving only helium gas.

The expanding range of industrial applications of helium has led to a rapidly expanding demand for the element. Thus, there has been a rightward shift in the demand curve

for helium, as shown in Figure 4-2. At the same time, however, breakdowns in aging equipment at natural gas fields in locales such as Qatar and Algeria have resulted in significant cutbacks in helium production. Thus, there has been a leftward shift in the helium supply curve. On net, the equilibrium quantity of helium produced and consumed has risen slightly, and the market clearing price of helium has also increased. Indeed, since early 2007 the world price of helium has risen by more than 20 percent.

FOR CRITICAL ANALYSIS

How do you suppose that the recent completion of a number of many new Asian factories that utilize helium as an input will affect the global price of helium?

FIGURE 4-2

The Effects of a Simultaneous Decrease in Helium Supply and Increase in Helium Demand

In the mid-2000s, various factors contributed to a reduction in the global supply of helium, depicted by the leftward shift in the helium supply curve from S_1 to S_2. At the same time, there was an increase in the demand for helium, as shown by the shift in the helium demand curve from D_1 to D_2. On net, the equilibrium quantity of helium produced and consumed rose slightly, from 100 million cubic feet per year at point E_1 to 110 million cubic feet per year at point E_2, and the equilibrium price of helium increased from about $0.04 per cubic foot to about $0.05 per cubic foot.

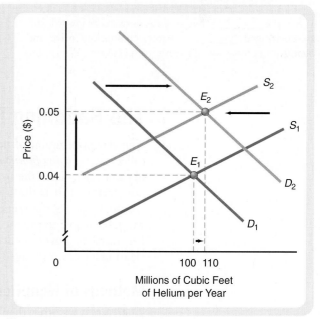

Price Flexibility and Adjustment Speed

We have used as an illustration for our analysis a market in which prices are quite flexible. Some markets are indeed like that. In others, however, price flexibility may take the form of subtle adjustments such as hidden payments or quality changes. For example, although the published price of bouquets of flowers may stay the same, the freshness of the flowers may change, meaning that the price per constant-quality unit changes. The published price of French bread might stay the same, but the quality could go up or down, perhaps through use of a different recipe, thereby changing the price per constant-quality unit. There are many ways to implicitly change prices without actually changing the published price for a *nominal* unit of a product or service.

We must also note that markets do not always return to equilibrium immediately. There may be a significant adjustment time. A shock to the economy in the form of an oil embargo, a drought, or a long strike will not be absorbed overnight. This means that even in unfettered market situations, in which there are no restrictions on changes in prices and quantities, temporary excess quantities supplied or excess quantities demanded may appear. Our analysis simply indicates what the market clearing price and equilibrium quantity ultimately will be, given a demand curve and a supply curve. Nowhere in the analysis is there any indication of the speed with which a market will get to a new equilibrium after a shock. The price may even temporarily overshoot the new equilibrium level. Remember this warning when we examine changes in demand and in supply due to changes in their *ceteris paribus* conditions.

QUICK QUIZ   *See page 106 for the answers. Review concepts from this section in MyEconLab.*

The _____ of _____ in a voluntary exchange are determined by the interaction of the forces underlying demand and supply. These forces take place in markets, which tend to minimize _____ costs.

When the _____ curve shifts outward or inward with an unchanged _____ curve, equilibrium price and quantity increase or decrease, respectively. When the

_____ curve shifts outward or inward given an unchanged _____ curve, equilibrium price moves in the direction opposite to equilibrium quantity.

When there is a shift in demand or supply, the new equilibrium price is not obtained _____. Adjustment takes _____.

The Rationing Function of Prices

The synchronization of decisions by buyers and sellers that leads to equilibrium is called the *rationing function of prices*. Prices are indicators of relative scarcity. An equilibrium price clears the market. The plans of buyers and sellers, given the price, are not frustrated. It is the free interaction of buyers and sellers that sets the price that eventually clears the market. Price, in effect, rations a good to demanders who are willing and able to pay the highest price. Whenever the rationing function of prices is frustrated by government-enforced price ceilings that set prices below the market clearing level, a prolonged shortage results.

Methods of Nonprice Rationing

There are ways other than price to ration goods. *First come, first served* is one method. *Political power* is another. *Physical force* is yet another. Cultural, religious, and physical differences have been and are used as rationing devices throughout the world.

RATIONING BY WAITING Consider first come, first served as a rationing device. We call this *rationing by queues*, where *queue* means "line." Whoever is willing to wait in line the longest obtains the good that is being sold at less than the market clearing price. All who wait in line are paying a higher *total* price than the money price paid for the good. Personal time has an opportunity cost. To calculate the total price of the good, we must add up the money price plus the opportunity cost of the time spent waiting.

Rationing by waiting may occur in situations in which entrepreneurs are free to change prices to equate quantity demanded with quantity supplied but choose not to do so. This results in queues of potential buyers. It may seem that the price in the market is being held below equilibrium by some noncompetitive force. That is not true, however. Such queuing may arise in a free market when the demand for a good is subject to large or unpredictable fluctuations, and the additional costs to firms (and ultimately to consumers) of constantly changing prices or of holding sufficient inventories or providing sufficient excess capacity to cover peak demands are greater than the costs to consumers of waiting for the good. Common examples are waiting in line to purchase a fast-food lunch and queuing to purchase a movie ticket a few minutes before the next show.

RATIONING BY RANDOM ASSIGNMENT OR COUPONS *Random assignment* is another way to ration goods. You may have been involved in a rationing-by-random-assignment scheme in college if you were assigned a housing unit. Sometimes rationing by random assignment is used to fill slots in popular classes.

Rationing by *coupons* has also been used, particularly during wartime. In the United States during World War II, families were allotted coupons that allowed them to purchase specified quantities of rationed goods, such as meat and gasoline. To purchase such goods, they had to pay a specified price *and* give up a coupon.

What are some alternative rationing methods to the ususal rationing-by-random-assignment schemes used for college housing units?

The Essential Role of Rationing

In a world of scarcity, there is, by definition, competition for what is scarce. After all, any resources that are not scarce can be had by everyone at a zero price in as large a quantity as everyone wants, such as air to burn in internal combustion engines. Once scarcity arises, there has to be some method to ration the available resources, goods, and services. The price system is one form of rationing; the others that we mentioned are alternatives. Economists cannot say which system of rationing is "best." They can, however, say that rationing via the price system leads to the most efficient use of available resources. This means that generally in a freely functioning price system, all of the gains from mutually beneficial trade will be captured.

How is it that a number of summer internships for college students are now being rationed by the price system?

EXAMPLE
Summer Internships for Sale

Traditionally, college students have obtained summer internships with prestigious companies in two ways. One way is to apply for an internship administered through a school program and wait for university administrators to ration available internships to the students they deem most meritorious. Another is to apply to the companies directly and hope to be rated among the most desirable candidates.

In recent years, however, college students and their families have discovered a third method of securing a summer internship with a top firm: buy one at an auction. An increasing

EXAMPLE (cont.)

number of companies are now donating summer internships to charities, which raise funds by auctioning the internships to parents of college students looking for ways to obtain marketable experience for their children. Thus, a growing percentage of available summer college internships with highly regarded companies are now rationed by a freely functioning price system.

FOR CRITICAL ANALYSIS
How do you suppose that the auction price of a summer internship with investment bank Morgan Stanley would compare with the auction price of a summer internship with a small community bank?

QUICK QUIZ See page 106 for the answers. Review concepts from this section in MyEconLab.

Prices in a market economy perform a rationing function because they reflect relative scarcity, allowing the market to clear. Other ways to ration goods include _____, _____ _____; _____ _____; _____ _____; _____

_____; and _____.

Even when businesspeople can change prices, some rationing by waiting may occur. Such _____ arises when there are large changes in demand coupled with high costs of satisfying those changes immediately.

The Policy of Government-Imposed Price Controls

Price controls
Government-mandated minimum or maximum prices that may be charged for goods and services.

Price ceiling
A legal maximum price that may be charged for a particular good or service.

Price floor
A legal minimum price below which a good or service may not be sold. Legal minimum wages are an example.

Nonprice rationing devices
All methods used to ration scarce goods that are price-controlled. Whenever the price system is not allowed to work, nonprice rationing devices will evolve to ration the affected goods and services.

The rationing function of prices is prevented when governments impose price controls. **Price controls** often involve setting a **price ceiling**—the maximum price that may be allowed in an exchange. The world has had a long history of price ceilings applied to product prices, wages, rents, and interest rates. Occasionally, a government will set a **price floor**—a minimum price below which a good or service may not be sold. Price floors have most often been applied to wages and agricultural products. Let's first consider price ceilings.

Price Ceilings and Black Markets

As long as a price ceiling is below the market clearing price, imposing a price ceiling creates a shortage, as can be seen in Figure 4-3. At any price below the market clearing, or equilibrium, price of $1,000, there will always be a larger quantity demanded than quantity supplied—a shortage, as you will recall from Chapter 3. Normally, whenever quantity demanded exceeds quantity supplied—that is, when a shortage exists—there is a tendency for the price to rise to its equilibrium level. But with a price ceiling, this tendency cannot be fully realized because everyone is forbidden to trade at the equilibrium price.

The result is fewer exchanges and **nonprice rationing devices.** Figure 4-3 illustrates the situation for portable electricity generators after a natural disaster: the equilibrium quantity of portable generators demanded and supplied (or traded) would be 10,000 units, and the market clearing price would be $1,000 per generator. But, if the government essentially imposes a price ceiling by requiring the price of portable

FIGURE 4-3

Black Markets

The demand curve is *D*. The supply curve is *S*. The equilibrium price is $1,000. The government, however, steps in and imposes a maximum price of $600. At that lower price, the quantity demanded will be 15,000, but the quantity supplied will be only 5,000. There is a "shortage." The implicit price (including time costs) tends to rise to $1,400. If black markets arise, as they generally will, the equilibrium black market price will end up somewhere between $600 and $1,400. The actual quantity transacted will be between 5,000 and 10,000.

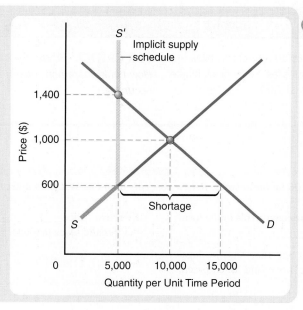

You Are There

To consider the problems faced by government-sponsored public schools confronting salary scales that effectively create a ceiling on teachers' wages, read **Finding a Spanish Instructor in the Midst of a Teacher Shortage,** on page 99.

generators to remain at the predisaster level, which the government determines was a price of $600, the equilibrium quantity offered is only 5,000. Because frustrated consumers will be able to purchase only 5,000 units, there is a shortage. The most obvious nonprice rationing device to help clear the market is queuing, or physical lines, which we have already discussed. To avoid physical lines, waiting lists may be established.

Typically, an effective price ceiling leads to a **black market.** A black market is a market in which the price-controlled good is sold at an illegally high price through various methods. For example, if the price of gasoline is controlled at lower than the market clearing price, drivers who wish to fill up their cars may offer the gas station attendant a cash payment on the side (as happened in the United States in the 1970s and in China and India in the mid-2000s during price controls on gasoline). If the price of beef is controlled at below its market clearing price, a customer who offers the butcher good tickets to an upcoming football game may be allocated otherwise unavailable beef. Indeed, the true implicit price of a price-controlled good or service can be increased in an infinite number of ways, limited only by the imagination. (Black markets also occur when goods are made illegal.)

In what black market have long-distance runners been known to participate?

Black market

A market in which goods are traded at prices above their legal maximum prices or in which illegal goods are sold.

INTERNATIONAL EXAMPLE
The Global Black Market for Marathon Entry Numbers

The world's top marathons are held in Amsterdam, Berlin, Boston, Chicago, Honolulu, London, New York, Paris, Rotterdam, and Stockholm. When runners register for a marathon in one of these cities, they receive "bibs," or officially authorized paper numbers, which must be worn on their shirts during the event. Marathon organizers typically set registration fees between $80 and $120, well below the equilibrium price. As a result, every year there are shortages of bibs. Even though most marathon organizers say that they ban the reselling of bibs, each year hundreds of individuals who have no intention of participating in marathons register to run, obtain bibs, and put them up for sale on Web auction sites. Some black market bibs have fetched prices as high as $1,000.

FOR CRITICAL ANALYSIS

How could marathon organizers prevent bib shortages from occurring?

QUICK QUIZ   *See page 106 for the answers. Review concepts from this section in MyEconLab.*

Governments sometimes impose **price controls** in the form of price _____ and price _____.

An effective price _____ is one that sets the legal price below the market clearing price and is enforced.

Effective price _____ lead to nonprice rationing devices and black markets.

The Policy of Controlling Rents

Rent control
Price ceilings on rents.

More than 200 U.S. cities and towns, including Berkeley, California, and New York City, operate under some kind of rent control. **Rent control** is a system under which the local government tells building owners how much they can charge their tenants for rent. In the United States, rent controls date back to at least World War II. The objective of rent control is to keep rents below levels that would be observed in a freely competitive market.

The Functions of Rental Prices

In any housing market, rental prices serve three functions: (1) to promote the efficient maintenance of existing housing and stimulate the construction of new housing, (2) to allocate existing scarce housing among competing claimants, and (3) to ration the use of existing housing by current demanders. Rent controls interfere with all of these functions.

RENT CONTROLS AND CONSTRUCTION Rent controls discourage the construction of new rental units. Rents are the most important long-term determinant of profitability, and rent controls artificially depress them. Consider some examples. In a recent year in Dallas, Texas, with a 16 percent rental vacancy rate but no rent control laws, 11,000 new rental housing units were built. In the same year in San Francisco, California, only 2,000 units were built, despite a mere 1.6 percent vacancy rate. The major difference? San Francisco has had stringent rent control laws. In New York City, until changes in the law in 1997 and 2003, the only rental units being built were luxury units, which were exempt from controls.

EFFECTS ON THE EXISTING SUPPLY OF HOUSING When rental rates are held below equilibrium levels, property owners cannot recover the cost of maintenance, repairs, and capital improvements through higher rents. Hence, they curtail these activities. In the extreme situation, taxes, utilities, and the expenses of basic repairs exceed rental receipts. The result is abandoned buildings from Santa Monica, California, to New York City. Some owners have resorted to arson, hoping to collect the insurance on their empty buildings before the city claims them for back taxes.

RATIONING THE CURRENT USE OF HOUSING Rent controls also affect the current use of housing because they restrict tenant mobility. Consider a family whose children have gone off to college. That family might want to live in a smaller apartment. But in a rent-controlled environment, giving up a rent-controlled unit can entail a substantial cost. In most rent-controlled cities, rents can be adjusted only when a tenant leaves. That means that a move from a long-occupied rent-controlled apartment to a smaller apartment can involve a hefty rent hike. In New York, this artificial preservation of the status quo came to be known as "housing gridlock."

Attempts to Evade Rent Controls

The distortions produced by rent controls lead to efforts by both property owners and tenants to evade the rules. This leads to the growth of expensive government bureaucracies whose job it is to make sure that rent controls aren't evaded. In New York City, because rent on an apartment can be raised only if the tenant leaves, property owners have had an incentive to make life unpleasant for tenants in order to drive them out or to evict them on the slightest pretext. The city has responded by making evictions extremely costly for property owners. Eviction requires a tedious and expensive judicial proceeding. Tenants, for their part, routinely try to sublet all or part of their rent-controlled apartments at fees substantially above the rent they pay to the owner. Both the city and the property owners try to prohibit subletting and often end up in the city's housing courts—an entire judicial system developed to deal with disputes involving rent-controlled apartments. The overflow and appeals from the city's housing courts sometimes clog the rest of New York's judicial system.

How have universities' policies of providing students' family members with tickets to graduation ceremonies at no charge provided some students with a profit incentive?

Go to www.econtoday.com/chapter04 to learn more about New York City's rent controls from Tenant.net.

EXAMPLE
Zero-Priced Seats at Graduation Ceremonies Become Hot Items

Whenever you purchase a ticket to a concert or sporting event, you are effectively renting from the owner of the concert hall or sports center the space where you will sit during the time of the scheduled event. Likewise, a ticket to a college graduation ceremony grants the bearer the right to utilize space owned by the college for the duration of that particular occasion.

Colleges typically extend a few tickets at no charge to each graduating student to pass along for use by family members who wish to attend the student's graduation ceremony. Some students have more loved ones who would like to attend their graduation ceremonies than their allotments of no-charge tickets. Other students do not even wish to

attend their own graduation ceremonies, let alone ask family members to attend. The latter students recognize, however, that some students are willing to pay positive prices for access to seats for loved ones lacking tickets. Many colleges threaten to discipline students who sell their graduation seating tickets, but to no avail. Each year at colleges across the nation, tickets to graduation ceremonies sell at prices ranging from as low as $5 per ticket to as high as $100 per ticket.

FOR CRITICAL ANALYSIS
Does anyone "lose out" as a result of black market exchanges of tickets to college graduation ceremonies?

Who Gains and Who Loses from Rent Controls?

The big losers from rent controls are clearly property owners. But there is another group of losers—low-income individuals, especially single mothers, trying to find their first apartment. Some observers now believe that rent controls have worsened the problem of homelessness in cities such as New York.

Often, owners of rent-controlled apartments charge "key money" before allowing a new tenant to move in. This is a large up-front cash payment, usually illegal but demanded nonetheless—just one aspect of the black market in rent-controlled apartments. Poor individuals have insufficient income to pay the hefty key money payment, nor can they assure the owner that their rent will be on time or even paid each month. Because controlled rents are usually below market clearing levels, apartment owners have little incentive to take any risk on low-income individuals as tenants. This is particularly true when a prospective tenant's chief source of income is a welfare check. Indeed, a large number of the litigants in the New York housing courts are welfare mothers who have missed their rent payments due to emergency expenses or delayed welfare checks. Their appeals often end in evictions and a new home in a temporary public shelter—or on the streets.

Who benefits from rent control? Ample evidence indicates that upper-income professionals benefit the most. These people can use their mastery of the bureaucracy and their large network of friends and connections to exploit the rent control system. Consider that in New York, actresses Mia Farrow and Cicely Tyson live in rent-controlled apartments, paying well below market rates. So do the former director of the Metropolitan Museum of Art and singer and children's book author Carly Simon.

QUICK QUIZ *See page 106 for the answers. Review concepts from this section in MyEconLab.*

_____ prices perform three functions: (1) allocating existing scarce housing among competing claimants, (2) promoting efficient maintenance of existing houses and stimulating new housing construction, and (3) rationing the use of existing houses by current demanders.

Effective rent _____ impede the functioning of rental prices. Construction of new rental units is discouraged. Rent _____ decrease spending on maintenance of existing ones and also lead to "housing gridlock."

There are numerous ways to evade rent controls; _____ _____ is one.

Price Floors in Agriculture

Another way that government can affect markets is by imposing price floors or price supports. In the United States, price supports are most often associated with agricultural products.

Price Supports

During the Great Depression, the federal government swung into action to help farmers. In 1933, it established a system of price supports for many agricultural products. Since then, there have been price supports for wheat, feed grains, cotton, rice, soybeans, sorghum, and dairy products, among other foodstuffs. The nature of the supports is quite simple: The government simply chooses a *support price* for an agricultural product

FIGURE 4-4

Agricultural Price Supports

Free market equilibrium occurs at *E*, with an equilibrium price of $250 per ton and an equilibrium quantity of 1.4 million tons. When the government sets a support price at $350 per ton, the quantity demanded is 1.0 million tons, and the quantity supplied is 2.2 million tons. The difference is the surplus, which the government buys. Farmers' income from consumers equals $350 × 1.0 million = $350 million. Farmers' additional income from taxpayers equals $350 × (2.2 million − 1.0 million) = $420 million.

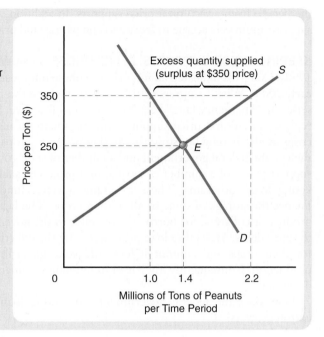

and then acts to ensure that the price of the product never falls below the support level. Figure 4-4 shows the market demand for and supply of peanuts. Without a price-support program, competitive forces would yield an equilibrium price of $250 per ton and an equilibrium quantity of 1.4 million tons per year. Clearly, if the government were to set the support price at or below $250 per ton, the quantity of peanuts demanded would equal the quantity of peanuts supplied at point *E*, because farmers could sell all they wanted at the market clearing price of $250 per ton.

But what happens when the government sets the support price *above* the market clearing price, at $350 per ton? At a support price of $350 per ton, the quantity demanded is only 1.0 million tons, but the quantity supplied is 2.2 million tons. The 1.2-million-ton difference between them is called the *excess quantity supplied*, or *surplus*. As simple as this program seems, its existence creates a fundamental question: How can the government agency charged with administering the price-support program prevent market forces from pushing the actual price down to $250 per ton?

If production exceeds the amount that consumers want to buy at the support price, what happens to the surplus? Quite simply, if the price-support program is to work, the government has to buy the surplus—the 1.2-million-ton difference. As a practical matter, the government acquires the 1.2-million-ton surplus indirectly through a government agency. The government either stores the surplus or sells it to foreign countries at a greatly reduced price (or gives it away free of charge) under the Food for Peace program.

Who Benefits from Agricultural Price Supports?

Although agricultural price supports have traditionally been promoted as a way to guarantee decent earnings for low-income farmers, most of the benefits have in fact gone to the owners of very large farms. Price-support payments are made on a per-bushel basis, not on a per-farm basis. Thus, traditionally, the larger the farm, the bigger

If this wheat farmer is guaranteed a high price, will he grow more or less wheat?

the benefit from agricultural price supports. In addition, *all* of the benefits from price supports ultimately accrue to *landowners* on whose land price-supported crops grow.

KEEPING PRICE SUPPORTS ALIVE UNDER A NEW NAME   Back in the early 1990s, Congress indicated an intention to phase out most agricultural subsidies by the early 2000s. What Congress actually *did* throughout the 1990s, however, was to pass a series of "emergency laws" keeping farm subsidies alive. Some of these laws aimed to replace agricultural price supports with payments to many farmers for growing no crops at all, thereby boosting the market prices of crops by reducing supply. Nevertheless, the federal government and a number of state governments have continued to support prices of a number of agricultural products, such as peanuts, through "marketing loan" programs. These programs advance funds to farmers to help them finance the storage of some or all of their crops. The farmers can then use the stored produce as collateral for borrowing or sell it to the government and use the proceeds to repay debts. Marketing loan programs raise the effective price that farmers receive for their crops and commit federal and state governments to purchasing surplus production. Consequently, they lead to outcomes similar to traditional price-support programs.

How does the federal government's marketing loan program operate for U.S. cotton growers?

POLICY EXAMPLE
King Cotton Receives Royal Government Subsidies

Every year, before a U.S. cotton farmer plants a crop, the federal government extends a direct payment, based on the average size of the farmer's past planting, which the farmer uses to help finance the coming year's planting expenses. After the crop is planted, the farmer can borrow from the government, using the newly sown cotton as collateral. If the world price of cotton falls below a price floor of 65 cents per pound, the grower receives a payment from the government—effectively compensating the farmer for surplus cotton the farmer has planted—equal to 13 cents per pound. The world price of cotton has been less than 65 cents per pound for some time, so the government funds the production of surplus cotton in this manner every year. If the world price of cotton falls below 52 cents per pound, farmers turn their cotton over to the govern-

ment, which sells the cotton at the world price and absorbs the loan losses. In this way, the government effectively buys increased surpluses of cotton caused by unexpected drops in cotton prices well below the 65 cent price floor.

All told, total payments to cotton growers by the federal government amount to more than $3 billion per year. The entire U.S. cotton crop typically generates revenues to farmers of about $5 billion per year. Thus, the government usually provides at least 50 percent of all revenues received by cotton producers.

FOR CRITICAL ANALYSIS
What would happen to cotton farmers' revenues if the government raised the price floor?

The Main Beneficiaries of Agricultural Subsidies

In 2002, Congress enacted the Farm Security Act, which has perpetuated marketing loan programs and other subsidy and price-support arrangements for such farm products as wheat, corn, rice, peanuts, and soybeans. All told, the more than $9 billion in U.S. government payments for these and other products amounts to about 25 percent of the annual market value of all U.S. farm production.

The government seeks to cap the annual subsidy payment that an individual farmer can receive at $360,000 per year, but some farmers are able to garner higher annual amounts by exploiting regulatory loopholes. The greatest share of total agricultural subsidies goes to the owners of the largest farming operations. At present, 10 percent of U.S. farmers receive more than 70 percent of agricultural subsidies.

The 2007 Food, Security, and Bioenergy Act expanded on the 2002 legislation by giving farmers raising a number of crops a choice between federal subsidy programs. On the one hand, farmers can opt to participate in traditional programs involving a mix of direct payments and marketing loan programs. On the other hand, farmers can choose a program offering guaranteed revenues. If market clearing crop prices end up higher than those associated with the government's revenue guarantee, farmers sell their crops at the higher prices instead of collecting government subsidies. But if equilibrium crop prices end up below a level consistent with the government guarantee, farmers receive direct subsidies to bring their total revenues up to the guaranteed level.

Price Floors in the Labor Market

The **minimum wage** is the lowest hourly wage rate that firms may legally pay their workers. Proponents favor higher minimum wages to ensure low-income workers a "decent" standard of living. Opponents counter that higher minimum wages cause increased unemployment, particularly among unskilled minority teenagers.

Minimum wage
A wage floor, legislated by government, setting the lowest hourly rate that firms may legally pay workers.

Minimum Wages in the United States

The federal minimum wage started in 1938 at 25 cents an hour, about 40 percent of the average manufacturing wage at the time. Typically, its level has stayed at about 40 to 50 percent of average manufacturing wages. After holding the minimum wage at $5.15 per hour from 1997 to 2007, Congress enacted a series of phased increases in the hourly minimum wage, effective on July 24 of each year, to $5.85 in 2007, $6.55 in 2008, and $7.25 in 2009.

Many states and cities have their own minimum wage laws that exceed the federal minimum. A number of municipalities refer to their minimum wage rules as "living wage" laws. Governments of these municipalities seek to set minimum wages consistent with living standards they deem to be socially acceptable—that is, overall wage income judged to be sufficient to purchase basic items such as housing and food.

Go to www.econtoday.com/chapter04 for information from the U.S. Department of Labor about recent developments concerning the federal minimum wage.

Economic Effects of a Minimum Wage

What happens when the government establishes a floor on wages? The effects can be seen in Figure 4-5 on the next page. We start off in equilibrium with the equilibrium wage rate of W_e and the equilibrium quantity of labor equal to Q_e. A minimum wage, W_m, higher than W_e, is imposed. At W_m, the quantity demanded for labor is reduced to Q_d, and some workers now become unemployed. Some workers will become unemployed as a result of the minimum wage, but others will move to sectors where minimum wage laws do not apply; wages will be pushed down in these uncovered sectors.

Note that the reduction in employment from Q_e to Q_d, or the distance from B to A, is less than the excess quantity of labor supplied at wage rate W_m. This excess quantity supplied is the distance between A and C, or the distance between Q_d and Q_s. The reason the reduction in employment is smaller than the excess quantity of labor supplied at the minimum wage is that the excess quantity of labor supplied also includes the *additional* workers who would like to work more hours at the new, higher minimum wage.

FIGURE 4-5

The Effect of Minimum Wages

The market clearing wage rate is W_e. The market clearing quantity of employment is Q_e, determined by the intersection of supply and demand at point E. A minimum wage equal to W_m is established. The quantity of labor demanded is reduced to Q_d. The reduction in employment from Q_e to Q_d is equal to the distance between B and A. That distance is smaller than the excess quantity of labor supplied at wage rate W_m. The distance between B and C is the increase in the quantity of labor supplied that results from the higher minimum wage rate.

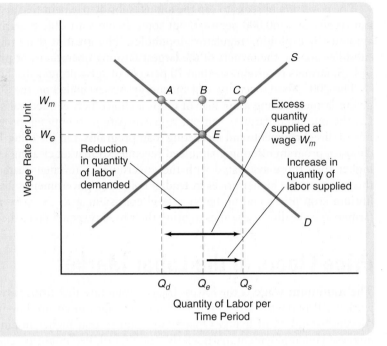

In the long run (a time period that is long enough to allow for full adjustment by workers and firms), some of the reduction in the quantity of labor demanded will result from a reduction in the number of firms, and some will result from changes in the number of workers employed by each firm. Economists estimate that a 10 percent increase in the minimum wage relative to the average prices of goods and services decreases total employment of those affected by 1 to 2 percent.

We can conclude from application of demand and supply analysis that a minimum wage established above the equilibrium wage rate typically has two fundamental effects. On the one hand, it boosts the wage earnings of those people who obtain employment. On the other hand, the minimum wage results in unemployment for other individuals. Thus, demand and supply analysis implies that the minimum wage makes some people better off while making others much worse off.

Quantity Restrictions

Governments can impose quantity restrictions on a market. The most obvious restriction is an outright ban on the ownership or trading of a good. It is currently illegal to buy and sell human organs. It is also currently illegal to buy and sell certain psychoactive drugs such as cocaine, heroin, and marijuana. In some states, it is illegal to start a new hospital without obtaining a license for a particular number of beds to be offered to patients. This licensing requirement effectively limits the quantity of hospital beds in some states. From 1933 to 1973, it was illegal for U.S. citizens to own gold except for manufacturing, medicinal, or jewelry purposes.

Some of the most common quantity restrictions exist in the area of international trade. The U.S. government, as well as many foreign governments, imposes import quotas on a variety of goods. An **import quota** is a supply restriction that prohibits

Import quota

A physical supply restriction on imports of a particular good, such as sugar. Foreign exporters are unable to sell in the United States more than the quantity specified in the import quota.

the importation of more than a specified quantity of a particular good in a one-year period. The United States has had import quotas on tobacco, sugar, and immigrant labor. For many years, there were import quotas on oil coming into the United States. There are also "voluntary" import quotas on certain goods. For instance, in 2005 the Chinese government agreed to "voluntarily" restrict the amount of textile products China sends to the United States and the European Union.

QUICK QUIZ   *See page 106 for the answers. Review concepts from this section in MyEconLab.*

With a price-_____ system, the government sets a minimum price at which, say, qualifying farm products can be sold. Any farmers who cannot sell at that price in the market can "sell" their surplus to the government. The only way a price-_____ system can survive is for the government or some other entity to buy up the excess quantity supplied at the support price.

When a _____ is placed on wages at a rate that is above market equilibrium, the result is an excess quantity of labor supplied at that minimum wage.

Quantity restrictions may take the form of _____ _____, which are limits on the quantity of specific foreign goods that can be brought into the United States for resale purposes.

You Are There ➤ Finding a Spanish Instructor in the Midst of a Teacher Shortage

This year, average starting salaries for all college graduates have increased 5 percent. But the good news for college graduates only magnifies the problem faced by Jill Rogers, superintendent of schools in Martinsville, Illinois.

Like most public school superintendents across the land, Rogers must deal with what promises to be a wave of retirements by experienced teachers who entered the profession in the 1960s and 1970s. As schools scramble to replace these teachers, the demand for new teachers in sciences and languages is rising rapidly. On this late summer day, finding a Spanish teacher is the challenge that Rogers confronts. Classes begin in a week, and so far she has been unable to hire a qualified person to fill an open position. The source of her difficulty is a dollar figure—$28,352, the maximum permissible salary for an inexperienced teacher mandated under the government-sponsored school system's salary scale. As the day begins, Rogers is among the hundreds of public school superintendents nationwide trying to hire Spanish teachers at a salary at least $3,000 below the market clearing salary for new liberal arts graduates.

Fortunately, good news arrives before the end of the day. Rogers finally has landed a Spanish teacher. The new hire is a native Spanish-speaking woman from Argentina. She lacks teaching credentials, so Rogers quickly arranges for her to begin an accelerated teaching certification program at a local university. Rogers realizes that her school district is now among the fortunate few that will manage to hire a new Spanish teacher this year.

CRITICAL ANALYSIS QUESTIONS

1. Average nonteaching salaries for college graduates in the sciences are almost $20,000 higher than those for graduates in languages and other liberal arts fields. Given that teachers in all fields are paid similar salaries, how does this help to explain why the shortage of public school science teachers is particularly acute?

2. During the coming years, barring changes in public school salary structures, what is likely to happen to shortages of teachers in various fields as more experienced teachers retire?

Effects of the $0 Price Ceiling in the Market for Kidneys

CONCEPTS APPLIED

- Price Ceilings
- Nonprice Rationing Devices
- Black Markets

At any given moment, about 76,000 U.S. residents are waiting for kidneys for transplant from donors. Even though so many people suffering from kidney failure would like to obtain a transplant, there are only about 16,000 kidney transplants per year. Most people with two healthy kidneys could get by with only one without shortening their lives. In principle, almost any willing individual with a compatible kidney could provide it to someone on the kidney-transplant waiting list who has the same blood type. Nevertheless, nearly all transplanted kidneys obtained from living donors are donated by relatives or friends of the recipients. There are two key reasons for this. One is that relatives are more likely to have compatible kidneys. Another is that a person who cares about a recipient is more likely to be willing to incur the explicit and implicit costs associated with donating a kidney at the legal price ceiling of $0.

The Predictable Result of a $0 Price Ceiling: A Shortage

In the United States and most other nations, it is illegal to pay someone to provide an organ for transplantation. Hence, the only price at which an organ can be obtained is $0. Effectively, this is a price ceiling for organs such as kidneys.

Figure 4-6 provides a graphical representation of the market for kidneys for transplant. The quantity of kidneys demanded at the ceiling price of $0, at the point at which the demand curve touches the horizontal axis, is about 76,000. For most goods and services, a positive price is required to induce a positive quantity supplied, so supply curves usually touch the vertical axis. In the market for kidneys for transplantation, however, some people

are willing to provide kidneys at the legal price of $0, as evidenced by the fact that donors now provide an average of about 16,000 kidneys per year at this price. Thus, there is an excess quantity demanded equal to about 60,000 kidneys per year—that is, 60,000 people suffering from kidney failure and languishing on the transplant list.

Predictable Consequences of a Kidney Shortage

Because elimination of the kidney shortage through the price system is illegal, nonprice rationing devices are the main focus of efforts to direct available kidneys to people with failed kidneys. Most medical centers utilize three key criteria. First, the donor kidney must be compatible with the recipient's blood type and other

FIGURE 4-6

The Shortage of Kidneys for Transplantation at a Ceiling Price of $0

If kidneys for transplantation could be exchanged at an unregulated price, the equilibrium price would be equal to P_1, and the equilibrium quantity of transplants per year would be Q_1. At present, however, payments for organ transplants are illegal. Hence, there is a ceiling price of $0. At this price, about 16,000 kidneys for transplantation are supplied by donors each year. Approximately 76,000 kidneys for transplantation are demanded by people suffering from failed kidneys. Thus, there is a shortage of kidneys for transplantation equal to about 60,000 per year.

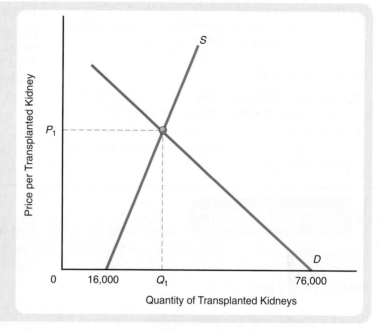

physical requirements. Second, a living donor must have a documented relationship—as a family member or friend—with a specially designated recipient. Third, if there is no clear relationship between a donor and a potential recipient, transplants take place strictly on a first-come, first-served basis.

For people with failed kidneys who are far down on the waiting list, the only legal option is to continue waiting. An illegal option is the black market. At fees starting at about $150,000, so-called organ brokers offer to locate a donor willing to provide a compatible kidney and a surgeon willing to perform a transplant (but often only for an additional fee). An estimated 6,000 kidney transplants worldwide are arranged by black market brokers.

Kidney Exchanges?

Economists have come up with a legal approach that may help reduce the size of the kidney shortage: organized "kidney exchanges" involving loved ones of people awaiting transplants. For instance, if a father with blood type A cannot donate a kidney to his daughter with blood type B, he may be amenable to donating a kidney to a young man with blood type A, whose sister with blood type B in turn donates a kidney to the father's daughter. Several medical centers are already utilizing kidney-exchange programs aimed at increasing the number of lifesaving transplants.

Test your understanding of this chapter by going online to **MyEconLab**.
In the Study Plan for this chapter, select Section N: News.

For Critical Analysis

1. Given normally shaped demand and supply curves, why does the maximum possible shortage of a good or service exist at a ceiling price of $0?

2. In recent years, an increasing number of medical facilities have struggled to prevent surgery patients from contracting infections caused by drug-resistant bacteria.

How do you suppose that the shortage of kidneys for transplantation would be affected if potential kidney donors become more fearful of such infections?

Web Resources

1. Read a description of the New England Program for Kidney Exchange at www.econtoday.com/chapter04.

2. To learn about the system of organized kidney exchange utilized by Johns Hopkins Medicine, go to www.econtoday.com/chapter04.

Research Project

Abstracting from normative issues relating to morals or ethics, what positive economic prediction can you make about the likely effect of legalized payments for transplanted kidneys on the size of the kidney shortage? Refer to Figure 4-6 on the previous page in explaining your answer.

 myeconlab Here is what you should know after reading this chapter. **MyEconLab** will help you identify what you know, and where to go when you need to practice.

WHAT YOU SHOULD KNOW		WHERE TO GO TO PRACTICE
Essential Features of the Price System The price system, otherwise called the market system, allows prices to respond to changes in supply and demand for different commodities. Consumers' and business managers' decisions on resource use depend on what happens to prices. In the price system, exchange takes place in markets. The terms of exchange are communicated by prices in the marketplace, where middlemen reduce transaction costs by bringing buyers and sellers together.	price system, 83 voluntary exchange, 83 terms of exchange, 83 transaction costs, 83	• **MyEconLab** Study Plan 4.1 • Audio introduction to Chapter 4
How Changes in Demand and Supply Affect the Market Price and Equilibrium Quantity With a given supply curve, an increase in demand causes a rise in the market price and an increase in the equilibrium quantity, and a decrease in demand induces a fall in the market price and a decline in the equilibrium quantity. With a given demand curve, an increase in supply causes a fall in the market price and an increase in the equilibrium quantity, and a decrease in supply causes a rise in the market price and a decline in the equilibrium quantity. When both demand and supply shift at the same time, indeterminate results may occur. We must know the direction and degree of each shift in order to predict the change in the market price and the equilibrium quantity.	**KEY FIGURE** Figure 4-1, 85	• **MyEconLab** Study Plan 4.2 • Animated Figure 4-1 • ABC News Video: What Drives the Market: Supply and Demand
The Rationing Function of Prices In the market system, prices perform a rationing function—they ration scarce goods and services. Other ways of rationing include first come, first served; political power; physical force; random assignment; and coupons.		• **MyEconLab** Study Plan 4.3 • Video: Price Flexibility, the Essential Role of Rationing via Price and Alternative Rationing Systems

(continued)

 *(continued)*

WHAT YOU SHOULD KNOW

		WHERE TO GO TO PRACTICE

The Effects of Price Ceilings Government-imposed price controls that require prices to be no higher than a certain level are price ceilings. If a government sets a price ceiling below the market price, then at the ceiling price the quantity of the good demanded will exceed the quantity supplied. There will be a shortage of the good at the ceiling price. For instance, rent controls place a ceiling on permitted rental prices and create shortages in housing markets. Price ceilings can lead to nonprice rationing devices and black markets.

price controls, 90
price ceiling, 90
price floor, 90
nonprice rationing
  devices, 90
black market, 91
rent control, 92

KEY FIGURE
Figure 4-3, 91

- **MyEconLab** Study Plans 4.4, 4.5
- Animated Figure 4-3

The Effects of Price Floors Government-mandated price controls that require prices to be no lower than a certain level are price floors. If a government sets a price floor above the market price, then at the floor price the quantity of the good supplied will exceed the quantity demanded. There will be a surplus of the good at the floor price. For instance, minimum wage laws that establish a price floor in the labor market and government price-support policies that set price floors in markets for agricultural goods often generate surpluses in these markets.

minimum wage, 97

KEY FIGURES
Figure 4-4, 95
Figure 4-5, 98

- **MyEconLab** Study Plans 4.6, 4.7
- Video: Minimum Wages
- Animated Figures 4-4, 4-5

Government-Imposed Restrictions on Market Quantities Quantity restrictions can take the form of outright government bans on the sale of certain goods, such as human organs or various psychoactive drugs. They can also arise from licensing requirements that limit the number of producers and thereby restrict the amount supplied of a good or service. Another example is an import quota, which limits the number of units of a foreign-produced good that can legally be sold domestically.

import quota, 98

- **MyEconLab** Study Plan 4.8

Log in to MyEconLab, take a chapter test, and get a personalized Study Plan that tells you which concepts you understand and which ones you need to review. From there, MyEconLab will give you further practice, tutorials, animations, videos, and guided solutions.
Log in to www.myeconlab.com

PROBLEMS

All problems are assignable in *. Answers to odd-numbered problems appear at the back of the book.*

4-1. In recent years, technological improvements have greatly reduced the costs of producing music CDs, and a number of new firms have entered the music CD industry. At the same time, prices of substitutes for music CDs, such as Internet downloads and music DVDs, have declined considerably. Construct a supply and demand diagram of the market for music CDs. Illustrate the impacts of these developments, and evaluate the effects on the market price and equilibrium quantity.

4-2. Advances in research and development in the pharmaceutical industry have enabled manufacturers to identify potential cures more quickly and therefore at lower cost. At the same time, the aging of our society has increased the demand for new drugs. Construct a supply and demand diagram of the market for pharmaceutical drugs. Illustrate the impacts of these developments, and evaluate the effects on the market price and the equilibrium quantity.

4-3. The following table depicts the quantity demanded and quantity supplied of studio apartments in a small college town.

Monthly Rent	Quantity Demanded	Quantity Supplied
$600	3,000	1,600
$650	2,500	1,800
$700	2,000	2,000
$750	1,500	2,200
$800	1,000	2,400

What are the market price and equilibrium quantity of apartments in this town? If this town imposes a rent control of $650 per month, how many studio apartments will be rented?

4-4. The U.S. government imposes a price floor for U.S. sugar that is above the market clearing price. Illustrate the U.S. sugar market with the price floor in place. Discuss the effects of the price floor on conditions in the market for sugar in the United States.

4-5. The Canadian sugar industry has complained that U.S. sugar manufacturers "dump" sugar surpluses in the Canadian market. U.S. chocolate manufacturers have also complained about the high U.S. price of sugar. Explain how the imposition of a price floor for U.S. sugar, as described in Problem 4-4, affects each of these markets. What are the changes in equilibrium quantities and market prices due to the price floor?

4-6. Suppose that the U.S. government places a ceiling on the price of Internet access.

a. Show why there is a shortage of Internet access at the legal price.

b. Suppose that a black market for Internet providers arises, with Internet service providers developing hidden connections. Illustrate the black market for Internet access, including the implicit supply schedule, the legal price, the black market supply and demand, and the highest feasible black market price.

4-7. The table below illustrates the demand and supply schedules for seats on air flights between two cities:

Price	Quantity Demanded	Quantity Supplied
$200	2,000	1,200
$300	1,800	1,400
$400	1,600	1,600
$500	1,400	1,800
$600	1,200	2,000

What are the market price and equilibrium quantity in this market? Now suppose that federal authorities limit the number of flights between the two cities to ensure that no more than 1,200 passengers can be flown. Evaluate the effects of this quota if price adjusts. (Hint: How much are the 1,200 passengers willing to pay for their flights?)

4-8. The consequences of decriminalizing illegal drugs have long been debated. Some claim that legalization will lower the price of these drugs and reduce related crime. Others claim that more people will use these drugs. Suppose that some of these drugs are legalized so that anyone may sell them and use them. Now consider the two claims—that price will fall and quantity demanded will increase. Based on positive economic analysis, are these claims sound?

4-9. In recent years, the government of Pakistan has established a support price for wheat of about $0.20 per kilogram of wheat. At this price, consumers are willing to purchase 10 billion kilograms of wheat per year, while Pakistani farmers are willing to grow and harvest 18 billion kilograms of wheat per year. The government purchases and stores all surplus wheat.

a. What are annual consumer expenditures on the Pakistani wheat crop?

b. What are annual government expenditures on the Pakistani wheat crop?

c. How much, in total, do Pakistani wheat farmers receive for the wheat they produce?

4-10. Consider the information in Problem 4-9 and your answers to that question. Suppose that the market clearing price of Pakistani wheat in the absence of price supports is equal to $0.10 per kilogram. At this price, the quantity of wheat demanded is 12 billion kilograms. Under the government wheat price-support program, how much more is spent each year on wheat harvested in Pakistan than otherwise would have been spent in an unregulated market for Pakistani wheat?

4-11. Consider the diagram below, which depicts the labor market in a city that has adopted a "living wage law" requiring employers to pay a minimum wage rate of $9 per hour. Answer the questions that follow.

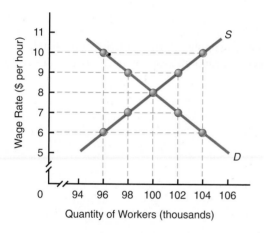

a. What condition exists in this city's labor market at the present minimum wage of $9 per hour? How many people are unemployed at this wage?

b. A city councilwoman has proposed amending the living wage law. She suggests reducing the minimum wage to $6 per hour. Assuming that the labor demand and supply curves were to remain in their present positions, how many people would be unemployed at a $6 minimum wage?

c. A councilman has offered a counterproposal. In his view, the current minimum wage is too low and should be increased to $10 per hour. Assuming that the labor demand and supply curves remain in their present positions, how

many people would be unemployed at a $10 minimum wage?

4-12. Suppose that owners of high-rise office buildings are the main employers of custodial workers in a city. The city has decided to impose rent controls, and it has established a rent ceiling below the previous equilibrium rental rate for offices throughout the city.

a. How will the quantity of offices the building owners lease change?

b. How will the market wage and equilibrium quantity of labor services provided by custodial workers be affected by the imposition of rent controls?

4-13. In 2007, the government of a nation established a price support for wheat. The government's support price has been above the equilibrium price each year since, and the government has purchased all wheat over and above the amounts that consumers have bought at the support price. Every year since 2007, there has been an increase in the number of wheat producers in the market. No other factors affecting the market for wheat have changed. Predict what has happened every year since 2007 to each of the following:

a. Amount of wheat supplied by wheat producers

b. Amount of wheat demanded by wheat consumers

c. Amount of wheat purchased by the government

4-14. In advance of the recent increase in the U.S. minimum wage rate, the government of the state of Arizona decided to boost its own minimum wage by $1.60 per hour. This pushed the wage rate earned by Arizona teenagers above the equilibrium wage rate in the teen labor market. What is the predicted effect of this action by Arizona's government on each of the following?

a. The quantity of labor supplied by Arizona teenagers

b. The quantity of labor demanded by employers of Arizona teenagers

c. The number of unemployed Arizona teenagers

ECONOMICS ON THE NET

The Floor on Milk Prices At various times, the U.S. government has established price floors for milk. This application gives you an opportunity to apply what you have learned in this chapter to this real-world issue.

Title: Northeast Dairy Compact Commission

Navigation: Go to **www.econtoday.com/chapter04** to visit the Web site of the Northeast Dairy Compact Commission.

Application Read the contents and answer these questions.

1. Based on the government-set price control concepts discussed in Chapter 4, explain the Northeast Dairy Compact that was once in place in the northeastern United States.

2. Draw a diagram illustrating the supply of and demand for milk in the Northeast Dairy Compact and the supply of and demand for milk outside the Northeast Dairy Compact. Illustrate how the compact affected the quantities demanded and supplied for participants in the compact. In addition, show how this affected the market for milk produced by those producers outside the dairy compact.

3. Economists have found that while the Northeast Dairy Compact functioned, midwestern dairy farmers lost their dominance of milk production and sales. In light of your answer to Question 2, explain how this occurred.

For Group Discussion and Analysis Discuss the impact of congressional failure to reauthorize the compact based on your above answers. Identify which arguments in your debate are based on positive economic analysis and which are normative arguments.

ANSWERS TO QUICK QUIZZES

p. 88: (i) terms . . . exchange . . . transaction; (ii) demand . . . supply . . . supply . . . demand; (iii) immediately . . . time
p. 90: (i) first come, first served . . . political power . . . physical force . . . random assignment . . . coupons; (ii) queuing
p. 92: (i) ceilings . . . floors; (ii) ceiling . . . controls
p. 94: (i) Rental; (ii) controls . . . controls; (iii) key money
p. 99: (i) support . . . support; (ii) floor; (iii) import quotas

Public Spending and Public Choice

5

Recently, the U.S. government decided that General Motors (GM) deserved tens of billions of taxpayer dollars in government support. The federal government funneled funds to GM to meet payrolls and to construct new plants even as the company was in the midst of bankruptcy proceedings. In addition, agencies of the government worked to boost the demand for GM vehicles. Two agencies, the U.S. Treasury and the Federal Reserve, bailed out GMAC, the partly GM-owned financial company that extends credit that many GM customers use to buy the firm's vehicles. Another agency, the National Highway Traffic Safety Administration, managed a program offering cash payments to people trading in old cars for new vehicles, including those produced by GM. In this chapter, you will learn about rationales for and implications of the U.S. government's financial support for GM.

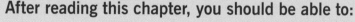

LEARNING OBJECTIVES

After reading this chapter, you should be able to:

- Explain how market failures such as externalities might justify economic functions of government

- Distinguish between private goods and public goods and explain the nature of the free-rider problem

- Describe political functions of government that entail its involvement in the economy

- Analyze how Medicare affects the incentives to consume medical services

- Explain why increases in government spending on public education have not been associated with improvements in measures of student performance

- Discuss the central elements of the theory of public choice

? DID YOU KNOW THAT the U.S. government has a roughly 30 percent ownership share in Citigroup, a New York–based banking organization that ranks among the world's largest financial institutions? The federal government so far has purchased in excess of $200 billion of ownership shares in Citigroup and more than 600 other financial companies. Among other things, these financial firms have utilized the government's funds to repay debts, purchase other banks, and make profitable investments. Critics have argued that the banks instead should have directed the taxpayer dollars to loans to consumers and businesses even if such lending might have been less profitable for the banks. As you will learn in this chapter, the incentives and institutional arrangements that condition the behavior of private firms and governments differ in some fundamental respects. One key distinction is that while firms function within the price system, a key rationale for the operations of government is to perform functions that the price system does not do well.

What a Price System Can and Cannot Do

Throughout the book so far, we have alluded to the advantages of a price system. High on the list is economic efficiency. In its ideal form, a price system allows all resources to move from lower-valued uses to higher-valued uses via voluntary exchange, by which mutually advantageous trades take place. In a price system, consumers are sovereign; that is to say, they have the individual freedom to decide what they wish to purchase. Politicians and even business managers do not ultimately decide what is produced; consumers decide. Some proponents of the price system argue that this is its most important characteristic. Competition among sellers protects consumers from coercion by one seller, and sellers are protected from coercion by one consumer because other consumers are available.

Sometimes, though, the price system does not generate these results, and too few or too many resources go to specific economic activities. Such situations are called **market failures.** Market failures prevent the price system from attaining economic efficiency and individual freedom. Market failures offer one of the strongest arguments in favor of certain economic functions of government, which we now examine.

Market failure
A situation in which the market economy leads to too few or too many resources going to a specific economic activity.

Correcting for Externalities

In a pure market system, competition generates economic efficiency only when individuals know and must bear the true opportunity cost of their actions. In some circumstances, the price that someone actually pays for a resource, good, or service is higher or lower than the opportunity cost that all of society pays for that same resource, good, or service.

Externalities

Consider a hypothetical world in which there is no government regulation against pollution. You are living in a town that until now has had clean air. A steel mill moves into town. It produces steel and has paid for the inputs—land, labor, capital, and entrepreneurship. The price the mill charges for the steel reflects, in this example, only the costs that it incurs. In the course of production, however, the mill utilizes one input—clean air—by simply using it. This is indeed an input because in making steel, the furnaces emit smoke. The steel mill doesn't have to pay the cost of dirtying the air. Rather, it is the people in the community who incur that cost in the form of dirtier clothes, dirtier cars and houses, and more respiratory illnesses. The effect is similar to

What externality is this family attempting to avoid?

what would happen if the steel mill could take coal or oil or workers' services without paying for them. There is an **externality,** an external cost. Some of the costs associated with the production of the steel have "spilled over" to affect **third parties,** parties other than the buyer and the seller of the steel.

A fundamental reason that air pollution creates external costs is that the air belongs to everyone and hence to no one in particular. Lack of clearly assigned **property rights,** or the rights of an owner to use and exchange property, prevents market prices from reflecting all the costs created by activities that generate spillovers onto third parties.

Why do some observers contend that negative externalities are associated with the growing use of digital billboards?

Externality
A consequence of an economic activity that spills over to affect third parties. Pollution is an externality.

Third parties
Parties who are not directly involved in a given activity or transaction.

Property rights
The rights of an owner to use and to exchange property.

EXAMPLE
Billboards That Catch Drivers' Eyes, Sometimes for Too Long

Outdoor advertising is now the second-fastest-growing form of advertising after Internet ads. Increasingly, advertisers are returning to old-fashioned roadside billboards. Not all billboards are so old-fashioned, however. Of the 500,000 billboards lining U.S. highways and city streets, approximately 2,000 are digital billboards. The number of digital billboards is likely to grow considerably in coming years, because the $500,000 cost of installing a digital billboard is more than outweighed by the ability to sell advertising space to multiple advertisers simultaneously.

For years, critics have regarded old-fashioned billboards as a form of visual pollution blocking views of scenery. In 1965, the federal Highway Beautification Act called for a reduction in the number of billboards but failed to provide sufficient funds to pay owners to remove them. Now, critics

deride billboards for more than just blocking scenic views. They suggest that the bright, eye-catching digital billboards are diverting drivers' eyes from roadways and causing accidents. The digital billboards' bright messages distract drivers, they argue, and thereby create a negative externality by making the roads less safe for drivers and for their passengers and occupants of other cars as well.

FOR CRITICAL ANALYSIS
Why might an owner of a digital billboard respond that assignment of property rights already solves the negative externality "problem" alleged by critics? (Hint: In most states, drivers must obtain liability insurance, and laws typically hold drivers solely responsible for accidents resulting from their being distracted while driving.)

External Costs in Graphical Form

To consider how market prices fail to take into account external costs in situations in which third-party spillovers exist without a clear assignment of property rights, look at panel (a) in Figure 5-1 on the following page. Here we show the demand curve for steel as D. The supply curve is S_1. The supply curve includes only the costs that the firms have to pay. Equilibrium occurs at point E, with a price of $500 per ton and a quantity equal to 110 million tons per year. But producing steel also involves externalities—the external costs that you and your neighbors pay in the form of dirtier clothes, cars, and houses and increased respiratory disease due to the air pollution emitted from the steel mill. In this case, the producers of steel use clean air without having to pay for it. Let's include these external costs in our graph to find out what the full cost of steel production would really be if property rights to the air around the steel mill could generate payments for "owners" of that air. We do this by imagining that steel producers have to pay the "owners" of the air for the input—clean air—that the producers previously used at a zero price.

FIGURE 5-1

External Costs and Benefits

In panel (a), we show a situation in which the production of steel generates external costs. If the steel mills ignore pollution, at equilibrium the quantity of steel will be 110 million tons. If the steel mills had to pay for the external costs that are caused by the mills' production but are currently borne by nearby residents, the supply curve would shift the vertical distance A–E_1, to S_2. If consumers of steel were forced to pay a price that reflected the spillover costs, the quantity demanded would fall to 100 million tons. In panel (b), we show a situation in which inoculations against communicable diseases generate external benefits to those individuals who may not be inoculated but who will benefit because epidemics will not occur. If each individual ignores the external benefit of inoculations, the market clearing quantity will be 150 million. If external benefits were taken into account by purchasers of inoculations, however, the demand curve would shift to D_2. The new equilibrium quantity would be 200 million inoculations, and the price of an inoculation would rise from $10 to $15.

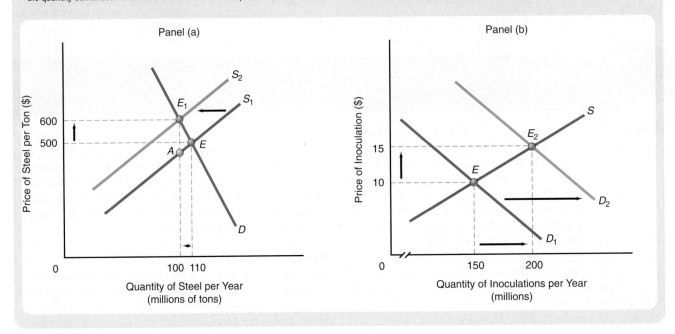

Panel (a)

Panel (b)

Recall from Chapter 3 that an increase in input prices shifts the supply curve up and to the left. Thus, in panel (a) of the figure, the supply curve shifts from S_1 to S_2. External costs equal the vertical distance between A and E_1. In this example, if steel firms had to take into account these external costs, the equilibrium quantity would fall to 100 million tons per year, and the price would rise to $600 per ton. Equilibrium would shift from E to E_1. In contrast, if the price of steel does not account for external costs, third parties bear those costs—represented by the distance between A and E_1—in the form of dirtier clothes, houses, and cars and increased respiratory illnesses.

External Benefits in Graphical Form

Externalities can also be positive. To demonstrate external benefits in graphical form, we will use the example of inoculations against communicable disease. In panel (b) of Figure 5-1, we show the demand curve as D_1 (without taking account of any external benefits) and the supply curve as S. The equilibrium price is $10 per inoculation, and the equilibrium quantity is 150 million inoculations.

We assume, however, that inoculations against communicable diseases generate external benefits to individuals who may not be inoculated but will benefit nevertheless because epidemics will not break out. If such external benefits were taken into account by those who purchase inoculations, the demand curve would shift from D_1 to D_2.

As a consequence of this shift in demand at point E_2, the new equilibrium quantity would be 200 million inoculations, and the new equilibrium price would be $15 per inoculation. If people who consider getting inoculations fail to take external benefits into account, this society is not devoting enough resources to inoculations against communicable diseases.

Resource Misallocations of Externalities

When there are external costs, the market will tend to *overallocate* resources to the production of the good or service in question, for those goods or services are implicitly priced deceptively low. In the steel example, too many resources will be allocated to steel production, because the steel mill owners and managers are not required to take account of the external cost that steel production is imposing on the rest of society. In essence, the full cost of production is not borne by the owners and managers, so the price they charge the public for steel is lower than it would otherwise be. And, of course, the lower price means that buyers are willing and able to buy more. More steel is produced and consumed than if the sellers were to bear external costs.

In contrast, when there are external benefits, the price is too low to induce suppliers to allocate resources to the production of that good or service (because the demand, which fails to reflect the external benefits, is relatively too low). Thus, the market *underallocates* resources to producing the good or service. Hence, in a market system, too many of the goods that generate external costs are produced, and too few of the goods that generate external benefits are produced.

How the Government Can Correct Negative Externalities

In theory, the government can take action to try to correct situations in which a lack of property rights allows third-party spillovers to create an externality. In the case of negative externalities, at least two avenues are open to the government: special taxes and legislative regulation or prohibition.

SPECIAL TAXES In our example of the steel mill, the externality problem arises because using the air for waste disposal is costless to the firm but not to society. The government could attempt to tax the steel mill commensurate with the cost to third parties from smoke in the air. This, in effect, would be a pollution tax or an **effluent fee.** The ultimate effect would be to reduce the supply of steel and raise the price to consumers, ideally making the price equal to the full cost of production to society.

REGULATION Alternatively, to correct a negative externality arising from steel production, the government could specify a maximum allowable rate of pollution. This regulation would require that the steel mill install pollution abatement equipment at its facilities, reduce its rate of output, or some combination of the two. Note that the government's job would not be simple, for it would have to determine the appropriate level of pollution, which would require extensive knowledge of both the benefits and the costs of pollution control.

How the Government Can Correct Positive Externalities

What can the government do when the production of one good spills *benefits* over to third parties? It has several policy options: financing the production of the good or producing the good itself, subsidies (negative taxes), and regulation.

How do inoculations generate positive externalities?

Effluent fee
A charge to a polluter that gives the right to discharge into the air or water a certain amount of pollution; also called a *pollution tax.*

Go to **www.econtoday.com/chapter05** to learn more about how the Environmental Protection Agency uses regulations to try to protect the environment.

GOVERNMENT FINANCING AND PRODUCTION If the positive externalities seem extremely large, the government has the option of financing the desired additional production facilities so that the "right" amount of the good will be produced. Again consider inoculations against communicable diseases. The government could—and often does—finance campaigns to inoculate the population. It could (and does) even produce and operate inoculation centers where inoculations are given at no charge.

SUBSIDIES A subsidy is a negative tax; it is a payment made either to a business or to a consumer when the business produces or the consumer buys a good or a service. To generate more inoculations against communicable diseases, the government could subsidize everyone who obtains an inoculation by directly reimbursing those inoculated or by making payments to private firms that provide inoculations. Subsidies reduce the net price to consumers, thereby causing a larger quantity to be demanded.

How are governments seeking to help society capture the external benefits of transportation services that keep elderly drivers off the roads?

POLICY EXAMPLE
Incentives Coax Senior Citizens from Behind the Wheel

Many people continue driving even after their skills and senses falter. Drivers age 75 and older have higher crash rates per mile traveled than all age groups except 16- and 18-year-olds. Drivers age 85 and older are at fault in accidents more than twice as often as younger drivers. Members of the baby boom generation are already reaching the age of 65, when driving capabilities begin to falter, and many more will reach this age during the coming two decades. The Insurance Institute for Highway Safety estimates that if current U.S. population trends continue, by 2030 these drivers will account for 16 percent of all auto accidents and 25 percent of all fatal crashes.

Governments are already working to make roadways safer by providing incentives for aging baby boomers to park their cars and choose alternative modes of transportation. Many state governments are easing regulations that impede efforts by private firms to offer elderly people transportation. Some municipal governments, such as those in Atlanta and Oklahoma City, are providing vouchers that help cover most of the price of public transportation. A few cities, such as Portland, Maine, are supporting efforts by nonprofit organizations to provide transportation services to seniors. One Portland-supported nonprofit organization even accepts car trade-ins from seniors in return for credit toward future transportation services. Thus, governments are promoting alternative modes of transportation for seniors in an effort to attain the external benefit of getting more elderly residents out from behind the wheel.

FOR CRITICAL ANALYSIS
How do government subsidies for alternative modes of transportation affect seniors' demands for these alternative transportation services?

REGULATION In some cases involving positive externalities, the government can require by law that individuals in the society undertake a certain action. For example, regulations require that all school-age children be inoculated before entering public and private schools. Some people believe that a basic school education itself generates positive externalities. Perhaps as a result of this belief, we have regulations—laws—that require all school-age children to be enrolled in a public or private school.

QUICK QUIZ   *See page 133 for the answers. Review concepts from this section in MyEconLab.*

External _____ lead to an overallocation of resources to the specific economic activity. Two possible ways of correcting these spillovers are _____ and _____.

External _____ result in an underallocation of resources to the specific activity. Three possible government

corrections are _____ the production of the activity, _____ private firms or consumers to engage in the activity, and _____.

The Other Economic Functions of Government

Besides correcting for externalities, the government performs many other economic functions that affect the way exchange is carried out. In contrast, the political functions of government have to do with deciding how income should be redistributed among households and selecting which goods and services have special merits and should therefore be treated differently. The economic and political functions of government can and do overlap.

Let's look at four more economic functions of government.

Providing a Legal System

The courts and the police may not at first seem like economic functions of government. Their activities nonetheless have important consequences for economic activities in any country. You and I enter into contracts constantly, whether they be oral or written, expressed or implied. When we believe that we have been wronged, we seek redress of our grievances through our legal institutions. Moreover, consider the legal system that is necessary for the smooth functioning of our economic system. Our system has defined quite explicitly the legal status of businesses, the rights of private ownership, and a method of enforcing contracts. All relationships among consumers and businesses are governed by the legal rules of the game. In its judicial function, then, the government serves as the referee for settling disputes in the economic arena. In this role, the government often imposes penalties for violations of legal rules.

Much of our legal system is involved with defining and protecting property rights. One might say that property rights are really the rules of our economic game. When property rights are well defined, owners of property have an incentive to use that property efficiently. Any mistakes in their decisions about the use of property have negative consequences that the owners suffer. Furthermore, when property rights are well defined, owners of property have an incentive to maintain that property so that if they ever desire to sell it, it will fetch a better price.

Promoting Competition

Many people believe that the only way to attain economic efficiency is through competition. One of the roles of government is to serve as the protector of a competitive economic system. Congress and the various state governments have passed **antitrust legislation.** Such legislation makes illegal certain (but not all) economic activities that might restrain trade—that is, that might prevent free competition among actual and potential rival firms in the marketplace. The avowed aim of

Antitrust legislation
Laws that restrict the formation of monopolies and regulate certain anticompetitive business practices.

Monopoly
A firm that can determine the market price of a good. In the extreme case, a monopoly is the only seller of a good or service.

antitrust legislation is to reduce the power of **monopolies**—firms that can determine the market price of the goods they sell. A large number of antitrust laws have been passed that prohibit specific anticompetitive actions. Both the Antitrust Division of the Department of Justice and the Federal Trade Commission attempt to enforce these antitrust laws. Various state judicial agencies also expend efforts at maintaining competition.

Providing Public Goods

The goods used in our examples up to this point have been **private goods.** When I eat a cheeseburger, you cannot eat the same one. So you and I are rivals for that cheeseburger, just as much as contenders for the title of world champion are. When I use a DVD player, you cannot play some other disc at the same time. When I use the services of an auto mechanic, that person cannot work at the same time for you. That is the distinguishing feature of private goods—their use is exclusive to the people who purchase or rent them. The **principle of rival consumption** applies to all private goods by definition. Rival consumption is easy to understand. Either you use a private good or I use it.

Private goods
Goods that can be consumed by only one individual at a time. Private goods are subject to the principle of rival consumption.

Principle of rival consumption
The recognition that individuals are rivals in consuming private goods because one person's consumption reduces the amount available for others to consume.

There is an entire class of goods that are not private goods. These are called **public goods.** The principle of rival consumption does not apply to them. They can be consumed *jointly* by many individuals simultaneously, and no one can be excluded from consuming these goods even if they fail to pay to do so. National defense, police protection, and the legal system are examples of public goods.

Public goods
Goods for which the principle of rival consumption does not apply; they can be jointly consumed by many individuals simultaneously at no additional cost and with no reduction in quality or quantity. Also no one who fails to help pay for the good can be denied the benefit of the good.

CHARACTERISTICS OF PUBLIC GOODS Two fundamental characteristics of public goods set them apart from all other goods:

1. *Public goods can be used by more and more people at no additional opportunity cost and without depriving others of any of the services of the goods.* Once funds have been spent on national defense, the defense protection you receive does not reduce the amount of protection bestowed on anyone else. The opportunity cost of your receiving national defense once it is in place is zero because once national defense is in place to protect you, it also protects others.

2. *It is difficult to design a collection system for a public good on the basis of how much individuals use it.* Nonpayers can often utilize a public good without incurring any monetary cost, because the cost of excluding them from using the good is so high. Those who provide the public good find that it is not cost-effective to prevent nonpayers from utilizing it. For instance, taxpayers who pay to provide national defense typically do not incur the costs that would be entailed in excluding nonpayers from benefiting from national defense.

One of the problems of public goods is that the private sector has a difficult, if not impossible, time providing them. Individuals in the private sector have little or no incentive to offer public goods. It is difficult for them to make a profit doing so, because nonpayers cannot be excluded. Consequently, true public goods must necessarily be provided by government. Note, though, that economists do not categorize something as a public good simply because the government provides it.

When it comes to public goods, what's new about "dot-nu" on the Internet?

E-COMMERCE EXAMPLE
Is the "Nu" Internet Domain a Public Good?

With its closest neighbor, Tonga, more than 350 miles distant, the South Pacific island nation of Niue (pronounced "new-ay") is among the earth's most remote locales. Nevertheless, a key national objective is to be one of the most Web-connected countries on the planet. Niue's residents were the first to possess nationwide wireless Internet access; hence, Niue's self-proclaimed nickname—the "WiFi nation." Complete wireless access is provided by a private company based in Medfield, Massachusetts. In return, Niue's government has granted to that company most legal rights to the Internet domain name "dot-nu." Of course, "nu" sounds like "new" in English, and in Swedish "nu" happens to mean "now." Thus, firms in English-speaking nations and in Sweden have been rushing to purchase Web addresses with the "nu" domain name.

Now many residents are objecting to this arrangement. If the Niue government had retained control over Web addresses within the "nu" domain, they contend, the nation could have reaped benefits, such as a steady stream of registration fees that more and more of its residents could have received at no additional opportunity cost. Furthermore, they argue, none of Niue's residents could have been denied such benefits, even if they had not paid for them. Hence, critics of the deal with the U.S. company suggest that residents of Niue have been cheated out of control over what ought to be a public good—at least, by their logic.

FOR CRITICAL ANALYSIS
Is the "nu" domain on the Internet really a public good? (Hint: Is the "nu" domain name currently subject to the principle of rival consumption? Does possession of only one of the two characteristics of a public good mean that an item is a public good?)

FREE RIDERS The nature of public goods leads to the **free-rider problem,** a situation in which some individuals take advantage of the fact that others will assume the burden of paying for public goods such as national defense. Suppose that citizens were taxed directly in proportion to how much they tell an interviewer that they value national defense. Some people who actually value national defense will probably tell interviewers that it has no value to them—they don't want any of it. Such people are trying to be free riders. We may all want to be free riders if we believe that someone else will provide the commodity in question that we actually value.

The free-rider problem often arises in connection with sharing the burden of international defense. A country may choose to belong to a multilateral defense organization, such as the North Atlantic Treaty Organization (NATO), but then consistently attempt to avoid contributing funds to the organization. The nation knows it would be defended by others in NATO if it were attacked but would rather not pay for such defense. In short, it seeks a free ride.

Free-rider problem
A problem that arises when individuals presume that others will pay for public goods so that, individually, they can escape paying for their portion without causing a reduction in production.

Ensuring Economywide Stability

Our economy sometimes faces the problems of undesired unemployment and rising prices. The government, especially the federal government, has made an attempt to solve these problems by trying to stabilize the economy by smoothing out the ups and downs in overall business activity. The notion that the federal government should undertake actions to stabilize business activity is a relatively new idea in the United States, encouraged by high unemployment rates during the Great Depression of the 1930s and subsequent theories about possible ways that government could reduce unemployment. In 1946, Congress passed the Full-Employment Act, a landmark law concerning government responsibility for economic performance. It established three goals for government stabilization policy: full employment, price stability, and economic growth. These goals have provided the justification for many government economic programs during the post–World War II period.

QUICK QUIZ *See page 133 for the answers. Review concepts from this section in MyEconLab.*

The economic activities of government include (1) correcting for _____, (2) providing a _____ _____, (3) promoting _____, (4) producing _____ goods, and (5) ensuring _____ _____.

The principle of _____ _____ does not apply to public goods as it does to private goods.

Public goods have two characteristics: (1) Once they are produced, there is no additional _____ _____ when additional consumers use them, because your use of a public good does not deprive others of its simultaneous use; and (2) consumers cannot conveniently be _____ on the basis of use.

The Political Functions of Government

At least two functions of government are political or normative functions rather than economic ones like those discussed in the first part of this chapter. These two areas are (1) the provision and regulation of government-sponsored and government-inhibited goods and (2) income redistribution.

Government-Sponsored and Government-Inhibited Goods

Government-sponsored good
A good that has been deemed socially desirable through the political process. Museums are an example.

Through political processes, governments often determine that certain goods possess special merit and seek to promote their production and consumption. A **government-sponsored good** is defined as any good that the political process has deemed socially desirable. (Note that nothing inherent in any particular good makes it a government-sponsored good. The designation is entirely subjective.) Examples of government-sponsored goods in our society are sports stadiums, museums, ballets, plays, and concerts. In these areas, the government's role is the provision of these goods to the people in society who would not otherwise purchase them at market clearing prices or who would not purchase an amount of them judged to be sufficient. This provision may take the form of government production and distribution of the goods. It can also take the form of reimbursement for spending on government-sponsored goods or subsidies to producers or consumers for part of the goods' costs. Governments do indeed subsidize such goods as professional sports, concerts, ballets, museums, and plays. In most cases, those goods would not be so numerous without subsidization.

Government-inhibited good
A good that has been deemed socially undesirable through the political process. Heroin is an example.

Government-inhibited goods are the opposite of government-sponsored goods. They are goods that, through the political process, have been deemed socially undesirable. Heroin, cigarettes, gambling, and cocaine are examples. The government exercises its role with respect to these goods by taxing, regulating, or prohibiting their manufacture, sale, and use. Governments justify the relatively high taxes on alcohol and tobacco by declaring that they are socially undesirable. The best-known example of governmental exercise of power in this area is the stance against certain psychoactive drugs. Most psychoactives (except nicotine, caffeine, and alcohol) are either expressly prohibited, as is the case for heroin, cocaine, and opium, or heavily regulated, as in the case of prescription psychoactives.

This drug bust represents what type of government activity?

What item is a government-inhibited good in the United States but a government-sponsored good in China?

INTERNATIONAL POLICY EXAMPLE
China's Government Struggles with How to Regard Tobacco

About 36 percent of all adults in China smoke, whereas only 21 percent of adults in the United States do. An estimated 10 percent of Chinese middle school students smoke, which is nearly double the U.S. rate. All told, the number of smokers in China—about 350 million—exceeds the entire U.S. population.

For China's government, the good news is that it owns the nation's cigarette manufacturing company, China National Tobacco Corporation. The government plows earnings from the firm's tobacco sales into a variety of activities, including constructing highways, hydroelectric dams, and railroads. The bad news is that all the smoking that the China National Tobacco Corporation has promoted in advertising campaigns is creating an epidemic of diseases, including lung cancer,

emphysema, and oral cancer. At present, more than 1 million Chinese residents die of tobacco-related diseases each year. The rate of growth of smoking is so high that this death toll is projected to more than double by 2025.

Consequently, even as the Chinese government sponsors tobacco production, the government's Center for Disease Control and Prevention has declared tobacco use to be the nation's biggest public health problem. China's government has regarded cigarettes as a government-sponsored good for 50 years. Now it is beginning to reconsider this designation.

FOR CRITICAL ANALYSIS
Who stands to lose if China's government ends tobacco's status as a government-sponsored good?

Income Redistribution

Another relatively recent political function of government has been the explicit redistribution of income. This redistribution uses two systems: the progressive income tax (described in Chapter 6) and transfer payments. **Transfer payments** are payments made to individuals for which no services or goods are rendered in return. The two primary money transfer payments in our system are Social Security old-age and disability benefits and unemployment insurance benefits. Income redistribution also includes a large amount of income **transfers in kind,** rather than money transfers. Some income transfers in kind are food stamps, Medicare and Medicaid, government health care services, and subsidized public housing.

The government has also engaged in other activities as a form of redistribution of income. For example, the provision of public education is at least in part an attempt to redistribute income by making sure that the poor have access to education.

Transfer payments
Money payments made by governments to individuals for which no services or goods are rendered in return. Examples are Social Security old-age and disability benefits and unemployment insurance benefits.

Transfers in kind
Payments that are in the form of actual goods and services, such as food stamps, subsidized public housing, and medical care, and for which no goods or services are rendered in return.

| QUICK QUIZ | *See page 133 for the answers. Review concepts from this section in MyEconLab.* |

Political, or normative, activities of the government include the provision and regulation of _____-_____ and _____-_____ goods and _____ redistribution.

Government-sponsored and government-inhibited goods do not have any inherent characteristics that qualify them as such; rather, collectively, through the _____ process,

we make judgments about which goods and services are "good" for society and which are "bad."

Income redistribution can be carried out by a system of progressive taxation, coupled with _____ payments, which can be made in money or in kind, such as food stamps and Medicare.

Public Spending and Transfer Programs

The size of the public sector can be measured in many different ways. One way is to count the number of public employees. Another is to look at total government outlays. Government outlays include all government expenditures on employees, rent, electricity, and the like. In addition, total government outlays include transfer payments, such as welfare and Social Security. In Figure 5-2, you see that government outlays prior to World War I did not exceed 10 percent of annual national income. There was a spike during World War I, a general increase during the Great Depression, and then a huge spike during World War II. After World War II, government outlays as a percentage of total national income rose steadily before dropping in the 1990s, rising again in the early 2000s, and then jumping sharply in the late 2000s.

How do federal and state governments allocate their spending? A typical federal government budget is shown in panel (a) of Figure 5-3. The three largest categories are Medicare and other health-related spending, Social Security and other income-security programs, and national defense, which together constitute 78.4 percent of the total federal budget.

The makeup of state and local expenditures is quite different. As panel (b) shows, education is the biggest category, accounting for 34.2 percent of all expenditures.

Publicly Subsidized Health Care: Medicare

Figure 5-3 shows that health-related spending is a significant portion of total government expenditures. Certainly, medical expenses are a major concern for many elderly people. Since 1965, that concern has been reflected in the existence of the Medicare program, which pays hospital and physicians' bills for U.S. residents over the age of 65 (and for those younger than 65 in some instances). In return for paying a tax on their earnings while in the workforce (currently set at 2.9 percent of wages and salaries), retirees are assured that the majority of their hospital and physicians' bills will be paid for with public monies.

Go to www.econtoday.com/chapter05 to visit the U.S. government's official Medicare Web site.

FIGURE 5-2

Total Government Outlays over Time

Total government outlays (federal, state, and local combined) remained small until the 1930s, except during World War I. After World War II, government outlays did not fall back to their historical average and recently have risen back close to their World War II levels.

Sources: Facts and Figures on Government Finance, various issues; Economic Indicators, various issues.

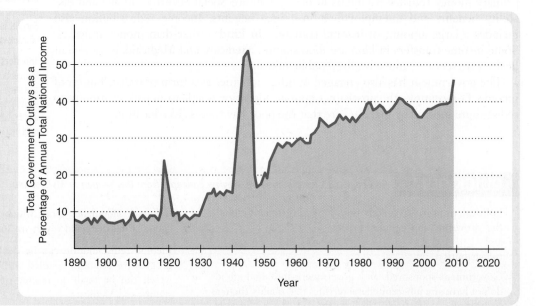

FIGURE 5-3

Federal Government Spending Compared to State and Local Spending

The federal government's spending habits are quite different from those of the states and cities. In panel (a), you can see that the most important categories in the federal budget are Medicare and other health-related spending, Social Security and other income-security programs, and national defense, which make up 78.4 percent. In panel (b), the most important category at the state and local level is education, which makes up 34.2 percent. "Other" includes expenditures in such areas as waste treatment, garbage collection, mosquito abatement, and the judicial system.

Sources: Budget of the United States government; government finances.

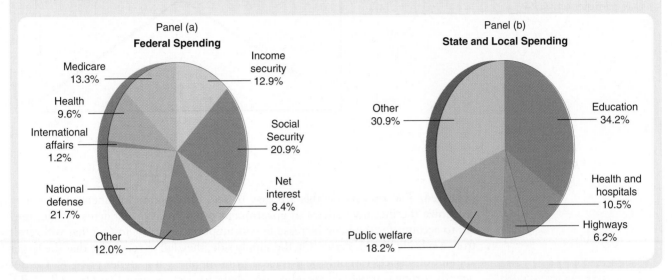

Panel (a)
Federal Spending

Medicare 13.3%
Income security 12.9%
Health 9.6%
Social Security 20.9%
International affairs 1.2%
Net interest 8.4%
National defense 21.7%
Other 12.0%

Panel (b)
State and Local Spending

Other 30.9%
Education 34.2%
Health and hospitals 10.5%
Highways 6.2%
Public welfare 18.2%

THE SIMPLE ECONOMICS OF MEDICARE To understand how, in less than 40 years, Medicare became the second-biggest domestic government spending program in existence, a bit of economics is in order. Consider Figure 5-4 on the following page, which shows the demand for and supply of medical care.

The initial equilibrium price is P_0 and equilibrium quantity is Q_0. Perhaps because the government believes that Q_0 is not enough medical care for these consumers, suppose that the government begins paying a subsidy that eventually is set at M for each unit of medical care consumed. This will simultaneously tend to raise the price per unit of care received by providers (physicians, hospitals, and the like) and lower the perceived price per unit that consumers see when they make decisions about how much medical care to consume. As presented in the figure, the price received by providers rises to P_s, while the price paid by consumers falls to P_d. As a result, consumers of medical care want to purchase Q_m units, and suppliers are quite happy to provide it for them.

MEDICARE INCENTIVES AT WORK We can now understand the problems that plague the Medicare system today. First, one of the things that people observed during the 20 years after the founding of Medicare was a huge upsurge in physicians' incomes and medical school applications, the spread of private for-profit hospitals, and the rapid proliferation of new medical tests and procedures. All of this was being encouraged by the rise in the price of medical services from P_0 to P_s, which encouraged entry into this market.

Second, government expenditures on Medicare have routinely turned out to be far in excess of the expenditures forecast at the time the program was put in place or was

How has the existence of Medicare changed seniors' consumption of medical services?

FIGURE 5-4

The Economic Effects of Medicare Subsidies

When the government pays a per-unit subsidy M for medical care, consumers pay the price of services P_d for the quantity of services Q_m. Providers receive the price P_s for supplying this quantity. Originally, the federal government projected that its total spending on Medicare would equal an amount such as the area $Q_0 \times (P_0 - P_d)$. Because actual consumption equals Q_m, however, the government's total expenditures equal $Q_m \times M$.

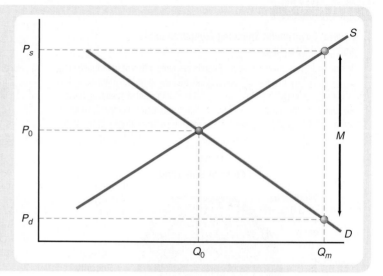

expanded. The reasons for this are easy to see. Bureaucratic planners often fail to recognize the incentive effects of government programs. On the demand side, they fail to account for the huge increase in consumption (from Q_0 to Q_m) that will result from a subsidy like Medicare. On the supply side, they fail to recognize that the larger amount of services can only be extracted from suppliers at a higher price, P_s. Consequently, original projected spending on Medicare was an area like $Q_0 \times (P_0 - P_d)$, because original plans for the program only contemplated consumption of Q_0 and assumed that the subsidy would have to be only $P_0 - P_d$ per unit. In fact, consumption rises to Q_m, and the additional cost per unit of service rises to P_s, implying an increase in the per-unit subsidy to M. Hence, actual expenditures turn out to be the far larger number $Q_m \times M$. Every expansion of the program, including the 2004 broadening of Medicare to cover obesity as a new illness eligible for coverage and the extension of Medicare to cover patients' prescription drug expenses beginning in 2006, has followed the same pattern.

Third, total spending on medical services soars, consuming far more income than initially expected. Originally, total spending on medical services was $P_0 \times Q_0$. In the presence of Medicare, spending rises to $P_s \times Q_m$.

HEALTH CARE SUBSIDIES CONTINUE TO GROW Just how fast are Medicare subsidies growing? Medicare's cost has risen from 0.7 percent of U.S. national income in 1970 to more than 2.8 percent today, which amounts to nearly $400 billion per year. Because Medicare spending is growing much faster than total employer and employee contributions, future spending guarantees far outstrip the taxes to be collected in the future to pay for the system. (The current Medicare tax rate is 2.9 percent on all earnings, with 1.45 percent paid by the employee and 1.45 percent paid by the employer.) Today, unfunded guarantees of Medicare spending in the future are estimated at more than $25 trillion (in today's dollars).

These amounts fail to reflect the costs of another federal health program called Medicaid. The Medicaid program is structured similarly to Medicare, in that the government also pays per-unit subsidies for health care to qualifying patients. Medicaid, however, provides subsidies only to people who qualify because they have lower incomes. At present, about 50 million people, or about one out of every six U.S. residents, qualify for Medicaid coverage. Medicaid is administered by state governments, but the federal government pays about 57 percent of the program's total cost from general tax revenues. The current cost of the program is more than $400 billion per year. In recent years, Medicaid spending has grown even faster than expenditures on Medicare, rising by more than 75 percent since 2000 alone. Of course, in recent years the U.S. Congress has been contemplating expanding the rate of growth of government health care spending, which already has been growing at an average pace of 8 percent per year.

How have government health care subsidy programs such as Medicare contributed to a preference by physicians for expensive face-to-face communications with patients instead of less costly phone and e-mail consultations?

POLICY EXAMPLE
If the Government Doesn't Pay for It, Physicians Don't Do It

Lawyers, accountants, and most other professionals regard telephone and e-mail as indispensable tools for communicating with clients. In contrast, phone consultations with physicians are very rare, and only 2 percent of patients have regular e-mail contact with their physicians. Medicare pays for about 7,500 specific health-care-related services, including face-to-face visits with physicians. The program does not, however, recompense physicians for time they devote to telephone or e-mail consultations with patients. Hence, Medicare gives physicians incentives to schedule appointments with patients in their offices but provides no incentives to utilize modes of communication that would be more efficient in a number of situations. Physicians, in turn, have responded to these incentives by scheduling steady streams of office visits with patients and avoiding phone calls and e-mail communications.

FOR CRITICAL ANALYSIS
Who pays for the fact that Medicare's payment rules promote higher-priced, face-to-face physician-patient communications instead of lower-priced, remote communications?

Economic Issues of Public Education

In the United States, government involvement in health care is a relatively recent phenomenon. In contrast, state and local governments have assumed primary responsibility for public education for many years. Currently, these governments spend more than $700 billion on education—more than 4 percent of total U.S. national income. State and local sales, excise, property, and income taxes finance the bulk of these expenditures. In addition, each year the federal government provides tens of billions of dollars of support for public education through grants and other transfers to state and local governments.

THE NOW-FAMILIAR ECONOMICS OF PUBLIC EDUCATION State and local governments around the United States have developed a variety of complex mechanisms for funding public education. What all public education programs have in common, however, is the provision of educational services to primary, secondary, and college students at prices well below those that would otherwise prevail in the marketplace for these services.

So how do state and local governments accomplish this? The answer is that they operate public education programs that share some of the features of government-subsidized health care programs such as Medicare. Analogously to Figure 5-4, public schools provide educational services at a price below the market price. They are willing to produce the quantity of educational services demanded at this below-market price as long as they receive a sufficiently high per-unit subsidy from state and local governments.

THE INCENTIVE PROBLEMS OF PUBLIC EDUCATION Since the 1960s, various measures of the performance of U.S. primary and secondary students have failed to increase even as public spending on education has risen. Some measures of student performance have even declined.

Many economists argue that the incentive effects that have naturally arisen with higher government subsidies for public education help to explain this lack of improvement in student performance. A higher per-pupil subsidy creates a difference between the relatively high per-unit costs to schools of providing the amount of educational services that parents and students are willing to purchase and the relatively lower valuations of those services. As a consequence, some schools have provided services, such as after-school babysitting and various social services, that have contributed relatively little to student learning.

A factor that complicates efforts to assess the effects of education subsidies is that the public schools often face little or no competition from unsubsidized providers of educational services. In addition, public schools rarely compete against each other. In most locales, therefore, parents who are unhappy with the quality of services provided at the subsidized price cannot transfer their child to a different public school.

Have subsidies intended to promote public schools' Internet connectivity improved student learning outcomes?

> ### You Are There
>
> To contemplate the operation of a college as a private business, read **Aiming to Prevent Cost from Exceeding Value per Dollar in Higher Education,** on page 126.

E-COMMERCE EXAMPLE
The Minuscule Payoff from Public School Internet Subsidies

Among other things, the U.S. Telecommunications Act of 1996 created a program known as E-Rate, which provides subsidies to public schools for use in connecting classrooms to the Web. Under the E-Rate program, about $2 billion per year goes to subsidize between 20 and 90 percent of recipient schools' Internet-related telecommunications spending, depending on the schools' qualifying characteristics. On average, the E-Rate subsidy amounts to about $100 per pupil.

Although the immediate objective of this subsidy was to ensure that more students would have access to the Internet, E-Rate's creators also predicted that the program would improve student learning. Nevertheless, studies of student performances in two of the most populous states, Texas and

California, find no concrete evidence that the program has improved outcomes. A decade after E-Rate was established, performances on standardized tests were virtually unchanged, as were student enrollments in advanced courses. High school dropout and graduation rates also remained the same. The E-Rate program has boosted Web access in the nation's public schools, but there is little evidence that more Internet connectivity has improved learning.

FOR CRITICAL ANALYSIS
Why might the $100-per-student E-Rate subsidy provide a minuscule learning payoff for students who already have Internet access at home?

QUICK QUIZ   See page 133 for the answers. Review concepts from this section in MyEconLab.

Medicare subsidizes the consumption of medical care by the elderly, thus increasing the amount of such care consumed. People tend to purchase large amounts of _____-value, _____-cost services in publicly funded health care programs such as Medicare, because they do not directly bear the full cost of their decisions.

Basic economic analysis indicates that higher subsidies for public education have widened the differential between parents' and students' relatively _____ per-unit valuations of the educational services of public schools and the _____ costs that schools incur in providing those services.

Collective Decision Making: The Theory of Public Choice

Governments consist of individuals. No government actually thinks and acts; rather, government actions are the result of decision making by individuals in their roles as elected representatives, appointed officials, and salaried bureaucrats. Therefore, to understand how government works, we must examine the incentives of the people in government as well as those who would like to be in government—avowed or would-be candidates for elective or appointed positions—and special-interest lobbyists attempting to get government to do something. At issue is the analysis of **collective decision making.** Collective decision making involves the actions of voters, politicians, political parties, interest groups, and many other groups and individuals. The analysis of collective decision making is usually called the **theory of public choice.** It has been given this name because it involves hypotheses about how choices are made in the public sector, as opposed to the private sector. The foundation of public-choice theory is the assumption that individuals will act within the political process to maximize their *individual* (not collective) well-being. In that sense, the theory is similar to our analysis of the market economy, in which we also assume that individuals act as though they are motivated by self-interest.

> **Collective decision making**
> How voters, politicians, and other interested parties act and how these actions influence nonmarket decisions.

> **Theory of public choice**
> The study of collective decision making.

To understand public-choice theory, it is necessary to point out other similarities between the private market sector and the public, or government, sector; then we will look at the differences.

Similarities in Market and Public-Sector Decision Making

In addition to the assumption of self-interest being the motivating force in both sectors, there are other similarities.

OPPORTUNITY COST Everything that is spent by all levels of government plus everything that is spent by the private sector must add up to the total income available at any point in time. Hence, every government action has an opportunity cost, just as in the market sector.

COMPETITION Although we typically think of competition as a private-market phenomenon, it is also present in collective action. Given the scarcity constraint government faces, bureaucrats, appointed officials, and elected representatives will always be in competition for available government funds. Furthermore, the individuals within any government agency or institution will act as individuals do in the private sector: They will try to obtain higher wages, better working conditions, and higher job-level classifications. We assume that they will compete and act in their own interest, not society's.

SIMILARITY OF INDIVIDUALS Contrary to popular belief, the types of individuals working in the private sector and working in the public sector are not inherently different. The difference, as we shall see, is that the individuals in government face a different **incentive structure** than those in the private sector. For example, the costs and benefits of being efficient or inefficient differ in the private and public sectors.

One approach to predicting government bureaucratic behavior is to ask what incentives bureaucrats face. Take the United States Postal Service (USPS) as an example. The bureaucrats running that government corporation are human beings with

> **Incentive structure**
> The system of rewards and punishments individuals face with respect to their own actions.

IQs not dissimilar to those possessed by workers in similar positions at Microsoft or American Airlines. Yet the USPS does not function like either of these companies. The difference can be explained in terms of the incentives provided for managers in the two types of institutions. When the bureaucratic managers and workers at Microsoft make incorrect decisions, work slowly, produce shoddy products, and are generally "inefficient," the profitability of the company declines. The owners—millions of shareholders—express their displeasure by selling some of their shares of company stock. The market value, as tracked on the stock exchange, falls. This induces owners of shares of stock to pressure managers to pursue strategies more likely to boost revenues and reduce costs.

But what about the USPS? If a manager, a worker, or a bureaucrat in the USPS gives shoddy service, the organization's owners—the taxpayers—have no straightforward mechanism for expressing their dissatisfaction. Despite the postal service's status as a "government corporation," taxpayers as shareholders do not really own shares of stock in the organization that they can sell.

Thus, to understand purported inefficiency in the government bureaucracy, we need to examine incentives and institutional arrangements—not people and personalities.

Differences Between Market and Collective Decision Making

There are probably more dissimilarities between the market sector and the public sector than there are similarities.

Government, or political, goods
Goods (and services) provided by the public sector; they can be either private or public goods.

GOVERNMENT GOODS AND SERVICES AT ZERO PRICE The majority of goods that governments produce are furnished to the ultimate consumers without payment required. **Government, or political, goods** can be either private or public goods. The fact that they are furnished to the ultimate consumer free of charge does *not* mean that the cost to society of those goods is zero, however. It only means that the price *charged* is zero. The full opportunity cost to society is the value of the resources used in the production of goods produced and provided by the government.

For example, none of us pays directly for each unit of consumption of defense or police protection. Rather, we pay for all these items indirectly through the taxes that support our governments—federal, state, and local. This special feature of government can be looked at in a different way. There is no longer a one-to-one relationship between consumption of government-provided goods and services and payment for these items. Indeed, most taxpayers will find that their tax bill is the same whether or not they consume government-provided goods.

USE OF FORCE All governments can resort to using force in their regulation of economic affairs. For example, governments can use *expropriation*, which means that if you refuse to pay your taxes, your bank account and other assets may be seized by the Internal Revenue Service. In fact, you have no choice in the matter of paying taxes to governments. Collectively, we decide the total size of government through the political process, but individually, we cannot determine how much service we pay for during any one year.

VOTING VERSUS SPENDING In the private market sector, a dollar voting system is in effect. This dollar voting system is not equivalent to the voting system in the public sector. There are at least three differences:

1. In a political system, one person gets one vote, whereas in the market system, each dollar a person spends counts separately.

2. The political system is run by **majority rule,** whereas the market system is run by **proportional rule.**

3. The spending of dollars can indicate intensity of want, whereas because of the all-or-nothing nature of political voting, a vote cannot.

Ultimately, the main distinction between political votes and dollar votes is that political outcomes may differ from economic outcomes. Remember that economic efficiency is a situation in which, given the prevailing distribution of income, consumers obtain the economic goods they want. There is no corresponding situation when political voting determines economic outcomes. Thus, a political voting process is unlikely to lead to the same decisions that a dollar voting process would yield in the marketplace.

Indeed, consider the dilemma every voter faces. Usually, a voter is not asked to decide on a single issue (although this happens); rather, a voter is asked to choose among candidates who present a large number of issues and state a position on each of them. Just consider the average U.S. senator, who has to vote on several thousand different issues during a six-year term. When you vote for that senator, you are voting for a person who must make thousands of decisions during the next six years.

How are economic outcomes in the world oil market affected by governmental involvement in extraction and distribution?

Majority rule
A collective decision-making system in which group decisions are made on the basis of more than 50 percent of the vote. In other words, whatever more than half of the electorate votes for, the entire electorate has to accept.

Proportional rule
A decision-making system in which actions are based on the proportion of the "votes" cast and are in proportion to them. In a market system, if 10 percent of the "dollar votes" are cast for blue cars, 10 percent of automobile output will be blue cars.

INTERNATIONAL EXAMPLE
Why a Synonym for "Big Oil" Is "Big Government"

Politicians and pundits commonly blame "big oil"—their shorthand for private oil companies—for higher oil prices. In fact, one factor contributing to the upward creep of inflation-adjusted oil prices is that an ever-greater share of oil is produced under government direction. In the early days of oil production, private firms produced the bulk of the world's oil. In contrast, today private companies such as Chevron, British Petroleum, ConocoPhillips, and ExxonMobil directly manage oil production from only 5 percent of the world's known reserves. Governments and government-owned companies coordinate production from the remaining 95 percent of reserves. To the extent that political factors influence governmentally managed oil production, output and price outcomes differ from those that privately directed production would have produced. Indeed, there is evidence that government-coordinated oil extraction and distribution is more costly than private oil production. These higher costs, in turn, lead to depressed oil output and higher oil prices.

FOR CRITICAL ANALYSIS
Why might dictators in totalitarian regimes make different oil production choices than private companies would have made?

QUICK QUIZ   *See page 133 for the answers. Review concepts from this section in MyEconLab.*

The theory of _____ _____ examines how voters, politicians, and other parties collectively reach decisions in the public sector of the economy.

As in private markets, _____ _____ and _____ have incentive effects that influence public-sector decision making. In contrast to private market situations, however, there is not a one-to-one relationship between consumption of a publicly provided good and the payment for that good.

You Are There

Aiming to Prevent Cost from Exceeding Value per Dollar in Higher Education

In 2001, Graham Doxey, Scott McKinley, and Marlow Einelund pooled their resources to start a new business: a private computer engineering college called Neumont University. Salt Lake City–based Neumont, which has operated since 2004, has no summer breaks. Instead, it offers students a year-round curriculum with a daily class schedule that stretches from 8 AM to 5 PM, thereby enabling students to graduate after two years instead of four years. Unlike a traditional university with a sprawling—and costly-to-maintain—campus, Neumont is housed in a glass-and-steel executive office building. Rather than residing in dorms, fraternities, or sororities on a campus quad, students live in nearby apartments.

These are not, however, the most dramatic differences between Neumont and other U.S. institutions of higher learning. Neumont's single goal is to provide students with training geared to meet the desires of employers. In contrast to students in computer engineering programs at most other universities, Neumont's students spend 30 percent of their time on theory and 70 percent on applications—essentially a reversal of the percentages in traditional programs. Most Neumont students obtain professional certification as well as a bachelor's degree, which makes them both more employable and highly valued. Consequently, virtually all Neumont graduates obtain jobs, and most earn starting salaries 20 percent above the average for computer science graduates. In essence, Neumont seeks to ensure that the per-dollar cost of higher education is not higher than the per-dollar valuation that its graduates place on the tuition bills they pay for their education.

CRITICAL ANALYSIS QUESTIONS

1. Why might a university that is operated as a private firm be more likely than a traditional university to produce educational services at a cost per dollar that does not exceed students' per-dollar valuation of those services?

2. How could the entry of a number of other business-oriented universities such as Neumont induce traditional universities to alter their modes of operation?

General Motors Becomes "Government Motors"

Issues and Applications

CONCEPTS APPLIED

- Government-Sponsored Good
- Proportional Rule
- Majority Rule

The 1908 founding of General Motors (GM) ultimately brought together the Buick, Cadillac, Chevrolet, Oldsmobile, and Pontiac vehicle lines and the ignition system and spark plugs of Champion. The company's share of total sales of U.S.-made vehicles grew steadily and surpassed 50 percent by the mid-1950s. By the end of the 1970s, the company was the largest private employer in the United States. In 1980, however, the company's vehicle sales plunged by 26 percent. GM never regained its previous status among U.S. firms, despite developing a new Saturn subsidiary and acquiring Saab and Hummer. Indeed, in several years during the 1980s and 1990s, the firm experienced losses as its sales declined further. By the 2000s, it was a seriously weakened company.

Between 2007 and 2008, overall U.S. purchases of motor vehicles dropped by nearly 20 percent, but GM's sales declined by an even larger percentage. By December 2008, company officials were in Washington, D.C., seeking government assistance.

Enter the U.S. Government

Initially, GM requested and received a "bridge loan" of about $13 billion from the U.S. Treasury. After GM's sales dropped more than 20 percent during the first three months of 2009, however, the company could not continue operations without additional government assistance. Indeed, the U.S. Treasury became a majority stakeholder in GM. In March 2009, U.S. President Barack Obama replaced the company's chief executive officer—who was not fired but continued to receive government-financed payments. On June 1, 2009, the company entered a government-organized bankruptcy proceeding and emerged a month later 70 percent owned by the U.S. government. Thus, GM vehicles became a government-sponsored good whose production was subsidized by U.S. taxpayers.

By 2010, GM had received federal subsidies amounting to more than $60 billion. These included about $54 billion in funds to keep the company operating and more than $6 billion for the government's assumption of pension debts owed by GM to retired employees

Subsidizing the Consumption of GM Vehicles

Even as GM was receiving government subsidies to continue manufacturing its vehicles, government agencies were hard at work spending an additional $13 billion on giving consumers more incentives to buy cars and trucks. In December 2008, the Federal Reserve approved GMAC's emergency application to become a "bank," which qualified the company to receive direct Federal Reserve loans. The Federal Reserve also began purchasing some of GMAC's debts, and the U.S. Treasury provided GMAC with direct cash injections.

These actions enabled GMAC to continue to provide credit to buyers of GM vehicles.

In addition, Congress authorized the National Highway Traffic Safety Administration to oversee distribution of tax-funded vouchers worth up to $4,500 apiece to people trading in "clunkers"—older, fuel-inefficient cars and trucks—for new vehicles. GM also benefited from this consumption-subsidization program during the summer of 2009.

Proportional Rule versus Majority Rule at GM

In response to continued proportional-rule "voting" by consumers not to buy many of its products, GM sought to sell its Saab, Saturn, and Hummer subsidiaries. GM also announced its intention to end ties to more than 2,400 vehicle dealerships.

Then the company discovered that its new primary owner, the U.S. government, is driven by majority-rule voting. The U.S. House of Representatives voted to require GM to reinstate a number of dealerships. The U.S. Senate did not join the House vote, but GM quietly began reconsidering the status of some of the dealerships. GM also agreed to government demands to begin manufacturing a more fuel-efficient compact car, which required building a new plant. The company opted not to base the location of the plant on cost considerations governed by the proportional rule of the market. Instead, GM based its choice on "community impact" and "carbon footprint" as revealed by unemployment rates and carbon emissions in different locales—characteristics determined by the majority rule of government.

Test your understanding of this chapter by going online to **MyEconLab**.
In the Study Plan for this chapter, select Section N: News.

For Critical Analysis

1. Who is ultimately paying all of the subsidies required to maintain GM's production of cars and trucks and to give consumers an incentive to buy its vehicles?

2. Why do you suppose that most economists predict that managing GM based on government-based majority rule instead of market-based proportional rule is likely to make the company less responsive to market forces?

Web Resources

1. For a timeline of the history of General Motors and of its emergence as a government-sponsored institution, go to www.econtoday.com/chapter05.

2. To learn more about GM's plan to "reinvent" itself as a government-sponsored institution, go to www.econtoday .com/chapter05.

Research Project

Are the vehicles produced by General Motors private goods or public goods? Support your reasoning by evaluating whether GM's products possess the fundamental characteristics that distinguish the two types of goods.

---

myeconlab Here is what you should know after reading this chapter. **MyEconLab** will help you identify what you know, and where to go when you need to practice.

WHAT YOU SHOULD KNOW

How Market Failures Such as Externalities Might Justify Economic Functions of Government A market failure is a situation in which an unhindered free market gives rise to too many or too few resources being directed to a specific form of economic activity. One market failure is an externality, which is a spillover effect on third parties not directly involved in producing or purchasing a good or service. In the case of a negative externality, firms do not pay for the costs arising from spillover effects that their production of a good imposes on others, so they produce too much of the good in question. Government may be able to improve the situation by restricting production or by imposing fees on producers. In the case of a positive externality, buyers fail to take into account the benefits that their consumption of a good yields to others, so they purchase too little of the good. Government may be able to induce more consumption of the good by regulating the market or subsidizing consumption. It can also provide a legal system to adjudicate disagreements about property rights, conduct antitrust policies to discourage monopoly and promote competition, provide public goods, and engage in policies designed to promote economic stability.

market failure, 108
externality, 109
third parties, 109
property rights, 109
effluent fee, 111
antitrust legislation, 113
monopoly, 114

KEY FIGURE
Figure 5-1, 110

WHERE TO GO TO PRACTICE

- **MyEconLab** Study Plans 5.1, 5.2
- Audio introduction to Chapter 5
- Animated Figure 5-1

(continued)

 *(continued)*

WHAT YOU SHOULD KNOW		**WHERE TO GO TO PRACTICE**
Private Goods versus Public Goods and the Free-Rider Problem Private goods are subject to the principle of rival consumption, meaning that one person's consumption of such a good reduces the amount available for another person to consume. This is not so for public goods, which can be consumed by many people simultaneously at no additional opportunity cost and with no reduction in the quality or quantity of the good. In addition, no individual can be excluded from the benefits of a public good even if that person fails to help pay for it. This leads to the free-rider problem, which occurs when a person who thinks that others will pay for a public good seeks to avoid contributing to financing its production.	private goods, 114 principle of rival consumption, 114 public goods, 114 free-rider problem, 115	• **MyEconLab** Study Plan 5.3 • Video: Private Goods and Public Goods
Political Functions of Government That Lead to Its Involvement in the Economy Through the political process, government may determine that certain goods are deemed socially desirable and seek to promote their production and consumption. These are called government-sponsored goods. The government may also seek to restrict or even ban the production and sale of other goods that have been deemed socially undesirable through the political process, called government-inhibited goods. In addition, the political process may determine that income redistribution is socially desirable, and governments may become involved in supervising transfer payments or in-kind transfers in the form of nonmoney payments.	government-sponsored good, 116 government-inhibited good, 116 transfer payments, 117 transfers in kind, 117	• **MyEconLab** Study Plan 5.4
The Effect of Medicare on the Incentives to Consume Medical Services Medicare subsidizes the consumption of medical services by the elderly. As a result, the quantity consumed is higher, as is the price sellers receive per unit of those services. Medicare also encourages people to consume medical services that are very low in per-unit value relative to the cost of providing them. Medicare thereby places a substantial tax burden on other sectors of the economy.	KEY FIGURES Figure 5-2, 118 Figure 5-4, 120	• **MyEconLab** Study Plan 5.5 • Video: Medicare • Animated Figures 5-2, 5-4
Why Bigger Subsidies for Public Schools Do Not Necessarily Translate into Improved Student Performance When governments subsidize public schools, the last unit of educational services provided by public schools costs more than its valuation by parents and students. Thus, public schools provide services in excess of those best suited to promoting student learning. This helps explain why overall U.S. student performance has stagnated even as per-pupil subsidies have increased.		• **MyEconLab** Study Plan 5.5

 *(continued)*

WHAT YOU SHOULD KNOW

WHERE TO GO TO PRACTICE

Central Elements of the Theory of Public Choice The theory of public choice applies to collective decision making, or the process through which voters and politicians interact to influence nonmarket choices. Public-choice theory emphasizes the incentive structures, or system of rewards or punishments, that affect the provision of government goods by the public sector. This theory points out that certain aspects of public-sector decision making, such as scarcity and competition, are similar to those that affect private-sector choices. Others, however, such as legal coercion and majority-rule decision making, differ from those involved in the market system.

collective decision
   making, 123
theory of public choice,
   123
incentive structure, 123
government, or political,
   goods, 124
majority rule, 125
proportional rule, 125

- **MyEconLab** Study
  Plan 5.6

Log in to MyEconLab, take a chapter test, and get a personalized Study Plan that tells you which concepts you understand and which ones you need to review. From there, MyEconLab will give you further practice, tutorials, animations, videos, and guided solutions.
Log in to www.myeconlab.com

PROBLEMS

All problems are assignable in . *Answers to odd-numbered problems appear at the back of the book.*

5-1. Many people who do not smoke cigars are bothered by the odor of cigar smoke. In the absence of any government involvement in the market for cigars, will too many or too few cigars be produced and consumed? From society's point of view, will the market price of cigars be too high or too low?

5-2. Suppose that repeated application of a pesticide used on orange trees causes harmful contamination of groundwater. The pesticide is applied annually in virtually all of the orange groves throughout the world. Most orange growers regard the pesticide as a key input in their production of oranges.

   a. Use a diagram of the market for the pesticide to illustrate the implications of a failure of orange producers' costs to reflect the social costs of groundwater contamination.

   b. Use your diagram from part (a) to explain a government policy that might be effective in achieving the amount of orange production that fully reflects all social costs.

5-3. Now draw a diagram of the market for oranges. Explain how the government policy you discussed in part (b) of Problem 5-2 is likely to affect the market price and equilibrium quantity in the orange market. In what sense do consumers of oranges now "pay" for dealing with the spillover costs of pesticide production?

5-4. Suppose that the U.S. government determines that cigarette smoking creates social costs not reflected in the current market price and equilibrium quantity of cigarettes. A study has recommended that the government can correct for the externality effect of cigarette consumption by paying farmers *not* to plant tobacco used to manufacture cigarettes. It also recommends raising the funds to make these payments by increasing taxes on cigarettes. Assuming that the government is correct that cigarette smoking creates external costs, evaluate whether the study's recommended policies might help correct this negative externality.

5-5. The government of a major city in the United States has determined that mass transit, such as bus lines, helps alleviate traffic congestion, thereby benefiting both individual auto commuters and companies that desire to move products and factors of production speedily along streets and highways. Nevertheless, even though several private bus lines are in service, commuters in the city are failing to take the social benefits of the use of mass transit into account.

   a. Discuss, in the context of demand-supply analysis, the essential implications of commuters' failure to take into account the social benefits associated with bus ridership.

   b. Explain a government policy that might be effective in achieving the socially efficient use of bus services.

5-6. Draw a diagram of the market for automobiles, which are a substitute for buses. Explain how the government policy you discussed in part (b) of Problem 5-5 is likely to affect the market price and equilibrium quantity in the auto market. How are auto consumers affected by this policy to attain the spillover benefits of bus transit?

5-7. Displayed in the next column are conditions in the market for residential Internet access in a small U.S. state. The government of this state has determined that access to the Internet improves the learning skills of children, which it has concluded is an external benefit of Internet access. The government has also concluded that if these external benefits were to be taken into account, 3 million residences would have Internet access. Suppose that the state government's judgments about the benefits of Internet access are correct and that it wishes to offer a per-unit subsidy just sufficient to increase total Internet access to 3 million residences. What per-unit subsidy should it offer? Use the diagram to explain how providing this subsidy would affect conditions in the state's market for residential Internet access.

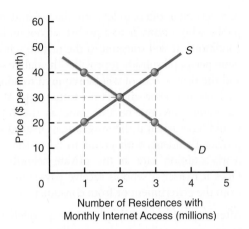

Number of Residences with Monthly Internet Access (millions)

5-8. The French government recently allocated the equivalent of more than $120 million in public funds to *Quaero* (Latin for "I search"), an Internet search engine analogous to Google or Yahoo. Does an Internet search engine satisfy the key characteristics of a public good? Why or why not? Based on your answer, is a publicly funded Internet search engine a public good or a government-sponsored good?

5-9. To promote increased use of port facilities in a major coastal city, a state government has decided to construct a state-of-the-art lighthouse at a projected cost of $10 million. The state proposes to pay half this cost and asks the city to raise the additional funds. Rather than raise its $5 million in funds via an increase in city taxes and fees, however, the city's government asks major businesses in and near the port area to contribute voluntarily to the project. Discuss key problems that the city is likely to face in raising the funds.

5-10. Governments of country A and country B spend the same amount each year. Spending on functions relating to dealing with market externalities and public goods accounts for 25 percent of government expenditures in country A but makes up 75 percent of government expenditures in country B. Funding to provide government-sponsored goods and efforts to restrict the production of government-inhibited goods account for 75 percent of government expenditures in country A but only 25 percent of government expenditures in country B. Which country's government is more heavily involved in the economy through economic functions of government as opposed to political functions? Explain.

5-11. A government offers to let a number of students at a public school transfer to a private school under two conditions: It will transmit to the private school the same per-pupil subsidy it provides the public school, and the private school will be required to admit the students at a below-market net tuition rate. Will the economic outcome be the same as the one that would have arisen if the government instead simply provided students with grants to cover the current market tuition rate at the private school? (Hint: Does it matter if schools receive payments directly from the government or from consumers?)

5-12. After a government implements a voucher program, granting funds that families can spend at schools of their choice, numerous students in public schools switch to private schools. Parents' and students' valuations of the services provided at both private and public schools adjust to equality with the true market price of educational services. Is anyone likely to lose out nonetheless? If so, who?

5-13. Suppose that the current price of a DVD drive is $100 and that people are buying 1 million drives per year. In order to improve computer literacy, the government decides to begin subsidizing the purchase of new DVD drives. The government believes that the appropriate price is $60 per drive, so the program offers to send people cash for the difference between $60 and whatever the people pay for each drive they buy.

   a. If no consumers change their DVD-drive-buying behavior, how much will this program cost the taxpayers?

   b. Will the subsidy cause people to buy more, fewer, or the same number of drives? Explain.

   c. Suppose that people end up buying 1.5 million drives once the program is in place. If the market price of drives does not change, how much will this program cost the taxpayers?

   d. Under the assumption that the program causes people to buy 1.5 million drives and also causes the market price of drives to rise to $120, how much will this program cost the taxpayers?

5-14. Scans of internal organs using magnetic resonance imaging (MRI) devices are often covered by subsidized health insurance programs such as Medicare. Consider the following table illustrating hypothetical quantities of individual MRI testing procedures demanded and supplied at various prices, and then answer the questions that follow.

Price	Quantity Demanded	Quantity Supplied
$100	100,000	40,000
$300	90,000	60,000
$500	80,000	80,000
$700	70,000	100,000
$900	60,000	120,000

   a. In the absence of a government-subsidized health plan, what is the equilibrium price of MRI tests? What is the amount of society's total spending on MRI tests?

   b. Suppose that the government establishes a health plan guaranteeing that all qualified participants can purchase MRI tests at an effective price (that is, out-of-pocket cost) to the individual of $100 per test. How many MRI tests will people consume?

   c. What is the per-unit price that induces producers to provide the amount of MRI tests demanded at the government-guaranteed price of $100? What is society's total spending on MRI tests?

   d. Under the government's coverage of MRI tests, what is the per-unit subsidy it provides? What is the total subsidy that the government pays to support MRI testing at its guaranteed price?

5-15. Suppose that, as part of an expansion of its State Care health system, a state government decides to offer a $50 subsidy to all people who, according to their physicians, should have their own blood pressure monitoring devices. Prior to this governmental decision, the market clearing price of blood pressure monitors in this state was $50, and the equilibrium quantity purchased was 20,000 per year.

   a. After the government expands its State Care plan, people in this state desire to purchase 40,000 devices each year. Manufacturers of blood pressure monitors are willing to provide 40,000 devices at a price of $60 per device. What out-of-pocket price does each consumer pay for a blood pressure monitor?

   b. What is the dollar amount of the increase in total expenditures on blood pressure monitors in this state following the expansion in the State Care program?

   c. Following the expansion of the State Care program, what *percentage* of total expenditures on blood pressure monitors is paid by the government? What percentage of total expenditures is paid by consumers of these devices?

5-16. A government agency is contemplating launching an effort to expand the scope of its activities. One rationale for doing so is that another government agency might make the same effort and, if successful, receive larger budget allocations in future years. Another rationale for expanding the agency's activities is that this will make the jobs of its workers more interesting, which may help the agency attract better-qualified employees. Nevertheless,

to broaden its legal mandate, the agency will have to convince more than half of the House of Representatives and the Senate to approve a formal proposal to expand its activities. In addition, to expand its activities, the agency must have the authority to force private companies it does not currently regulate to be officially licensed by agency personnel. Identify which aspects of this problem are similar to those faced by firms that operate in private markets and which aspects are specific to the public sector.

ECONOMICS ON THE NET

Putting Tax Dollars to Work   In this application, you will learn about how the U.S. government allocates its expenditures. This will enable you to conduct an evaluation of the current functions of the federal government.

Title: Historical Tables: Budget of the United States Government

Navigation: Go to **www.econtoday.com/chapter05** to visit the home page of the U.S. Government Printing Office. Select the most recent budget available, and then click on *Historical Tables.*

Application   After the document downloads, examine Section 3, Federal Government Outlays by Function, and in particular Table 3.1, Outlays by Superfunction and Function. Then answer the following questions.

1. What government functions have been capturing growing shares of government spending in recent years? Which of these do you believe are related to the problem of addressing externalities, providing

public goods, or dealing with other market failures? Which appear to be related to political functions instead of economic functions?

2. Which government functions are receiving declining shares of total spending? Are any of these related to the problem of addressing externalities, providing public goods, or dealing with other market failures? Are any related to political functions instead of economic functions?

For Group Study and Analysis   Assign groups to the following overall categories of government functions: national defense, health, income security, and Social Security. Have each group prepare a brief report concerning long-term and recent trends in government spending on its category. Each group should take a stand on whether specific spending on items in its category is likely to relate to resolving market failures, public funding of government-sponsored goods, regulating the sale of government-inhibited goods, and so on.

ANSWERS TO QUICK QUIZZES

p. 113: (i) costs . . . taxation . . . regulation; (ii) benefits . . . financing . . . subsidizing . . . regulation

p. 116: (i) externalities . . . legal system . . . competition . . . public . . . economywide stability; (ii) rival consumption; (iii) opportunity cost . . . charged

p. 117: (i) government-sponsored . . . government-inhibited . . . income; (ii) political; (iii) transfer

p. 122: (i) low . . . high; (ii) low . . . higher

p. 125: (i) public choice; (ii) opportunity cost . . . competition

6

Funding the Public Sector

Ever since the U.S. federal income tax was established in 1913, there has been disagreement about how much income tax rates should differ across households based on their incomes. In recent years, various U.S. politicians and pundits have called for boosts in tax rates for higher-income individuals and cuts in tax rates for middle- and lower-income individuals. "The rich should pay their fair share" and "The middle class deserves a break" are typical rallying cries you may have encountered in media reports. Are tax rates currently low for higher-income households relative to those faced by lower-income households? To evaluate this question, you must understand more about the structure of tax systems, which is one issue that governments confront in paying for their operations.

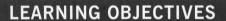

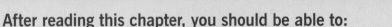

LEARNING OBJECTIVES

After reading this chapter, you should be able to:

- Distinguish between average tax rates and marginal tax rates

- Explain the structure of the U.S. income tax system

- Understand the key factors influencing the relationship between tax rates and the tax revenues governments collect

- Explain how the taxes governments levy on purchases of goods and services affect market prices and equilibrium quantities

- Understand how the Social Security system works and explain the nature of the problems it poses for today's students

? DID YOU KNOW THAT since 1986, Congress has added 14,000 amendments containing 3 million words to U.S. tax laws? In addition, Congress has added 6 million words to regulations designed to implement all these amendments.

To obtain the funds required to finance their operations, governments collect taxes from many different sources—hence, the multitude of words written into a variety of legal statutes governing taxation. State and local governments assess sales taxes, property taxes, income taxes, hotel occupancy taxes, and electricity, gasoline, water, and sewage taxes. At the federal level, there are income taxes, Social Security taxes, Medicare taxes, and so-called excise taxes. When a person dies, state and federal governments also collect estate and inheritance taxes. Clearly, governments give considerable attention to their roles as tax collectors.

Paying for the Public Sector

There are three sources of funding available to governments. One source is explicit fees, called user *charges*, for government services. The second and main source of government funding is taxes. Nevertheless, sometimes federal, state, and local governments spend more than they collect in taxes. To do this, they must rely on a third source of financing, which is borrowing. During a specific interval, the **government budget constraint** expresses the key limitation on public expenditures. It states that the sum of public spending on goods, services, and transfer payments during a given period cannot exceed the sum of user charges, tax revenues, and borrowed funds.

A government cannot borrow unlimited amounts, however. After all, a government, like an individual or a firm, can convince others to lend it funds only if it can provide evidence that it will repay its debts. A government must ultimately rely on taxation and user charges, the sources of its own current and future revenues, to repay its debts. Over the long run, therefore, taxes and user charges are any government's *fundamental* sources of revenues. This long-term constraint indicates that the total amount that a government plans to spend and transfer today and into the future cannot exceed the total taxes and user charges that it currently earns and can reasonably anticipate collecting in future years. Taxation dwarfs user charges as a source of government resources, so let's begin by looking at taxation from a government's perspective.

How did California recently satisfy its government budget constraint when state government spending exceeded tax revenues and user charges?

Government budget constraint
The limit on government spending and transfers imposed by the fact that every dollar the government spends, transfers, or uses to repay borrowed funds must ultimately be provided by the user charges and taxes it collects.

POLICY EXAMPLE
California Makes Payments with IOUs Instead of Cash

During the Great Depression, hundreds of cash-strapped U.S. businesses and municipalities paid their creditors with IOUs instead of U.S. dollars. Most of the IOUs issued during the 1930s looked like paper currency or checks, but some issuers were more creative and printed their IOUs on fish-skin parchment, strips of leather, or metal plates. The town of Tenino, Washington, printed its IOUs on spruce wedges, and an Oregon tire company even printed IOUs on scraps of old tires.

In 2009, the state of California began issuing its own IOUs when its indebtedness exceeded its capacity to make payments.

California's IOUs, officially known as "registered warrants," are pale green and resemble ordinary government-issue checks. California's registered warrants are not checks, however. They are borrowings against future tax receipts, issued in a time of emergency to enable the state of California to satisfy its government budget constraint.

FOR CRITICAL ANALYSIS
Why do you suppose that California offered to pay an annual interest rate of 3.75 percent to holders of its registered warrants?

Systems of Taxation

In light of the government budget constraint, a major concern of any government is how to collect taxes. Jean-Baptiste Colbert, the seventeenth-century French finance minister, said the art of taxation was in "plucking the goose so as to obtain the largest amount of feathers with the least possible amount of hissing." In the United States, governments have designed a variety of methods of plucking the private-sector goose.

The Tax Base and the Tax Rate

Tax base
The value of goods, services, wealth, or incomes subject to taxation.

Tax rate
The proportion of a tax base that must be paid to a government as taxes.

To collect a tax, a government typically establishes a **tax base**, which is the value of goods, services, wealth, or incomes subject to taxation. Then it assesses a **tax rate**, which is the proportion of the tax base that must be paid to the government as taxes.

Federal, state, and local governments have established a number of tax bases and tax rates. How does a "dual-bracket" tax system with two different tax bases function?

POLICY EXAMPLE
The Same Tax Rate, but Different Tax Bases for Different People

Like municipalities in most states, city and county governments in Florida collect property taxes by applying a tax rate to assessed valuations of structures and surrounding properties. Unlike most states, Florida permits municipalities to establish a "dual-bracket" property tax system, meaning that municipalities can set the taxable values of properties at lower levels for permanent residents than for seasonal residents. To determine the property taxes owed, a municipality multiplies the differently assessed property values by the same property tax rate.

In some Florida communities, assessed values of properties owned by seasonal residents are up to 10 times higher than assessed values of virtually identical properties that permanent residents own on the same streets. Thus, the property taxes paid by seasonal residents are as much as 10 times higher than those paid by permanent residents.

FOR CRITICAL ANALYSIS
Why do you suppose that democratically elected municipal governments in Florida choose to value properties of permanent residents lower than properties of seasonal residents for purposes of establishing tax bases for property tax payments? (Hint: Seasonal residents typically register to vote in the cities and counties in which they reside most of the year.)

As we discuss shortly, for the federal government and many state governments, incomes are key tax bases. Therefore, to discuss tax rates and the structure of taxation systems in more detail, let's focus for now on income taxation.

Marginal and Average Tax Rates

If somebody says, "I pay 28 percent in taxes," you cannot really tell what that person means unless you know whether he or she is referring to average taxes paid or the tax rate on the last dollars earned. The latter concept refers to the **marginal tax rate**, where the word *marginal* means "incremental."

The marginal tax rate is expressed as follows:

Marginal tax rate
The change in the tax payment divided by the change in income, or the percentage of additional dollars that must be paid in taxes. The marginal tax rate is applied to the highest tax bracket of taxable income reached.

$$\text{Marginal tax rate} = \frac{\text{change in taxes due}}{\text{change in taxable income}}$$

It is important to understand that the marginal tax rate applies only to the income in the highest **tax bracket** reached, where a tax bracket is defined as a specified range of taxable income to which a specific and unique marginal tax rate is applied.

The marginal tax rate is not the same thing as the **average tax rate,** which is defined as follows:

$$\text{Average tax rate} = \frac{\text{total taxes due}}{\text{total taxable income}}$$

Taxation Systems

No matter how governments raise revenues—from income taxes, sales taxes, or other taxes—all of those taxes fit into one of three types of taxation systems: proportional, progressive, or regressive, according to the relationship between the tax rate and income. To determine whether a tax system is proportional, progressive, or regressive, we simply ask, What is the relationship between the average tax rate and the marginal tax rate?

PROPORTIONAL TAXATION **Proportional taxation** means that regardless of an individual's income, taxes comprise exactly the same proportion. In a proportional taxation system, the marginal tax rate is always equal to the average tax rate. If every dollar is taxed at 20 percent, then the average tax rate is 20 percent, and so is the marginal tax rate.

Under a proportional system of taxation, taxpayers at all income levels end up paying the same *percentage* of their income in taxes. With a proportional tax rate of 20 percent, an individual with an income of $10,000 pays $2,000 in taxes, while an individual making $100,000 pays $20,000. Thus, the identical 20 percent rate is levied on both taxpayers.

PROGRESSIVE TAXATION Under **progressive taxation,** as a person's taxable income increases, the percentage of income paid in taxes increases. In a progressive system, the marginal tax rate is above the average tax rate. If you are taxed 5 percent on the first $10,000 you earn, 10 percent on the next $10,000 you earn, and 30 percent on the last $10,000 you earn, you face a progressive income tax system. Your marginal tax rate is always above your average tax rate.

REGRESSIVE TAXATION With **regressive taxation,** a smaller percentage of taxable income is taken in taxes as taxable income increases. The marginal rate is *below* the average rate. As income increases, the marginal tax rate falls, and so does the average tax rate. The U.S. Social Security tax is regressive. Once the legislative maximum taxable wage base is reached, no further Social Security taxes are paid. Consider a simplified hypothetical example: Suppose that every dollar up to $100,000 is taxed at 10 percent. After $100,000 there is no Social Security tax. Someone making $200,000 still pays only $10,000 in Social Security taxes. That person's average Social Security tax is 5 percent. The person making $100,000, by contrast, effectively pays 10 percent. The person making $1 million faces an average Social Security tax rate of only 1 percent in our simplified example.

What particular form of income tax has been catching on with some state governments and the U.S. Congress?

Tax bracket
A specified interval of income to which a specific and unique marginal tax rate is applied.

Average tax rate
The total tax payment divided by total income. It is the proportion of total income paid in taxes.

You Are There

To contemplate how marginal income tax rates can affect a person's job decisions, read **For This Physician, the Tax Rate Is Too High to Justify Working,** on pages 151 and 152.

Proportional taxation
A tax system in which, regardless of an individual's income, the tax bill comprises exactly the same proportion.

Progressive taxation
A tax system in which, as income increases, a higher percentage of the additional income is paid as taxes. The marginal tax rate exceeds the average tax rate as income rises.

Regressive taxation
A tax system in which as more dollars are earned, the percentage of tax paid on them falls. The marginal tax rate is less than the average tax rate as income rises.

POLICY EXAMPLE
"Millionaire" Taxes Become the New Government Fad

In the mid-2000s, California established a 1 percent income tax *surcharge*—a special additional tax—on incomes of millionaires, defined as people earning more than $1 million per year. Shortly thereafter, New Jersey created its own "millionaire" tax by establishing a new top tax bracket with a tax rate 2.6 percentage points higher than the previous top rate. New Jersey, however, decided that "millionaires" were people earning more than $500,000 per year. A few years later, New York government officials also decided to impose a "millionaire" tax surcharge, but they defined a "millionaire" as someone earning $300,000 per year. By the late 2000s, the idea of a federal "millionaire" tax surcharge was catching on in Washington, D.C. Members of the U.S. House of Representatives introduced bills that would apply a range of "millionaire" tax surcharges to annual incomes above $280,000.

FOR CRITICAL ANALYSIS
Does imposing special "millionaire" taxes make an income tax system more or less progressive?

QUICK QUIZ See page 158 for the answers. Review concepts from this section in MyEconLab.

Governments collect taxes by applying a tax _____ to a tax _____, which refers to the value of goods, services, wealth, or incomes. Income tax rates are applied to tax brackets, which are ranges of income over which the tax rate is constant.

The _____ tax rate is the total tax payment divided by total income, and the _____ tax rate is the change in the tax payment divided by the change in income.

Tax systems can be _____, _____, or _____, depending on whether the marginal tax rate is the same as, greater than, or less than the average tax rate as income rises.

The Most Important Federal Taxes

What types of taxes do federal, state, and local governments collect? The two pie diagrams in Figure 6-1 show the percentages of receipts from various taxes obtained by the federal government and by state and local governments. For the federal government, key taxes are individual income taxes, corporate income taxes, Social Security taxes, and excise taxes on items such as gasoline and alcoholic beverages. For state and local governments, sales taxes, property taxes, and personal and corporate income taxes are the main types of taxes.

The Federal Personal Income Tax

The most important tax in the U.S. economy is the federal personal income tax, which, as Figure 6-1 indicates, accounts for about 46.6 percent of all federal revenues. All U.S. citizens, resident aliens, and most others who earn income in the United States are required to pay federal income taxes on all taxable income, including income earned abroad.

The rates that are paid rise as income increases, as can be seen in Table 6-1 on page 140. Marginal income tax rates at the federal level have ranged from as low as 1 percent after the 1913 passage of the Sixteenth Amendment, which made the individual continue to receive a net amount of $3.35 per gallon to induce them to supply 180,000 gallons each week, so they must now receive $3.75 per gallon to supply that weekly quantity. Likewise, gasoline producers now will be willing to supply 200,000 gallons each week only if they receive $0.40 more per gallon, or a total amount of $3.85 per gallon.

As you can see, imposing the combined $0.40 per gallon excise taxes on gasoline shifts the supply curve vertically by exactly that amount to S_2 in panel (a). Thus, the effect of levying excise taxes on gasoline is to shift the supply curve vertically by the total per-unit taxes levied on gasoline sales. Hence, there is a decrease in supply. (In the case of an *ad valorem* sales tax, the supply curve would shift vertically by a proportionate amount equal to the tax rate.)

How Taxes Affect the Market Price and Equilibrium Quantity

Panel (b) of Figure 6-4 shows how imposing $0.40 per gallon in excise taxes affects the market price of gasoline and the equilibrium quantity of gasoline produced and sold. In the absence of excise taxes, the market supply curve S_1 crosses the demand curve D at a market price of $3.45 per gallon. At this market price, the equilibrium quantity of gasoline is 200,000 gallons of gasoline per week.

The excise tax levy of $0.40 per gallon shifts the supply curve to S_2. At the original $3.45 per gallon price, there is now an excess quantity of gasoline demanded, so the market price of gasoline rises to $3.75 per gallon. At this market price, the equilibrium quantity of gasoline produced and consumed each week is 180,000 gallons.

What factors determine how much the equilibrium quantity of a good or service declines in response to taxation? The answer to this question depends on how responsive quantities demanded and supplied are to changes in price.

Who Pays the Tax?

In our example, imposing excise taxes of $0.40 per gallon of gasoline causes the market price to rise to $3.75 per gallon from $3.45 per gallon. Thus, the price that each consumer pays is $0.30 per gallon higher. Consumers pay three-fourths of the excise tax levied on each gallon of gasoline produced and sold.

Gasoline producers must pay the rest of the tax. Their profits decline by $0.10 per gallon because costs have increased by $0.40 per gallon while consumers pay $0.30 more per gallon.

In the gasoline market, as in other markets for products subject to excise taxes and other taxes on sales, the shapes of the market demand and supply curves determine who pays most of a tax. The reason is that the shapes of these curves reflect the responsiveness to price changes of the quantity demanded by consumers and of the quantity supplied by producers.

In the example illustrated in Figure 6-4, the fact that consumers pay most of the excise taxes levied on gasoline reflects a relatively low responsiveness of quantity demanded by consumers to a change in the price of gasoline. Consumers pay most of the excise taxes on each gallon produced and sold because in this example the amount of gasoline they desire to purchase is relatively (but not completely) unresponsive to a change in the market price induced by excise taxes. We will revisit the issue of who pays excise taxes in Chapter 20.

If a state government increases the tax on a pack of cigarettes, who pays the tax?

When the government levies a tax on sales of a particular product, firms must receive a higher price to continue supplying the same quantity as before, so the supply curve shifts _____. If the tax is a unit excise tax, the supply curve shifts _____ by the amount of the tax.

Imposing a tax on sales of an item _____ the equilibrium quantity produced and consumed and _____ the market price.

When a government assesses a unit excise tax, the market price of the good or service typically rises by an amount _____ than the per-unit tax. Hence, consumers pay a portion of the tax, and firms pay the remainder.

Financing Social Security

In Chapter 5, you learned about Medicare, which is one of two major federal transfer programs. The other is Social Security, the federal system that transfers portions of the incomes of working-age people to elderly and disabled individuals. If current laws are maintained, Medicare's share of total national income will double over the next 20 years, as will the number of "very old" people—those over 85 and most in need of care. When Social Security is also taken into account, probably *half* of all federal government spending will go to the elderly by 2025. In a nutshell, senior citizens are the beneficiaries of an expensive and rapidly growing share of all federal spending.

Good Times for the First Retirees

The Social Security system was founded in 1935, as the United States was recovering from the Great Depression. The decision was made to establish Social Security as a means of guaranteeing a minimum level of pension benefits to all residents. Today, many people regard Social Security as a kind of "social compact"—a national promise to successive generations that they will receive support in their old age.

BIG PAYOFFS FOR THE EARLIEST RECIPIENTS The first Social Security taxes (called "contributions") were collected in 1937, but it was not until 1940 that the first retirement benefits were paid. Ida May Fuller was the first person to receive a regular Social Security pension. She had paid a total of $25 in **Social Security contributions** before she retired. By the time she died in 1975 at age 100, she had received benefits totaling $23,000. Although Fuller perhaps did better than most, for the average retiree of 1940, the Social Security system was still more generous than any private investment plan anyone is likely to devise: After adjusting for inflation, the implicit **rate of return** on their contributions was an astounding 135 percent. (Roughly speaking, every $100 of combined employer and employee contributions yielded $135 *per year* during each and every year of that person's retirement. This is also called the **inflation-adjusted return**.)

Ever since the early days of Social Security, however, the implicit rate of return has decreased. Nonetheless, Social Security was an excellent deal for most retirees during the twentieth century. Figure 6-5 shows the implicit rate of return for people retiring in different years.

Given that the inflation-adjusted long-term rate of return on the stock market is about 7 to 9 percent, it is clear that for retirees, Social Security was a good deal until

Social Security contributions
The mandatory taxes paid out of workers' wages and salaries.

Rate of return
The proportional annual benefit that results from making an investment.

Inflation-adjusted return
A rate of return that is measured in terms of real goods and services; that is, after the effects of inflation have been factored out.

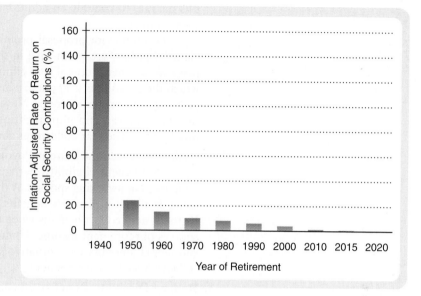

FIGURE 6-5

Private Rates of Return on Social Security Contributions, by Year of Retirement

The rate of return on Social Security contributions has steadily declined.

Sources: Social Security Administration and author's estimates.

at least 1970. In fact, because Social Security benefits are a lot less risky than stocks, Social Security actually remained a pretty good "investment" for many people until around 1990.

SLOWING GROWTH IN WORKERS' CONTRIBUTIONS Social Security has managed to pay such high returns because at each point in time, current retirees are paid benefits out of the contributions of individuals who are currently working. (The contributions of today's retirees were long ago used to pay the benefits of previous retirees.) As long as Social Security was pulling in growing numbers of workers, either through a burgeoning workforce or by expanding its coverage of individuals in the workforce, the impressive rates of return during the early years of the program were possible.

But as birthrates declined beginning in the mid-1960s and the post–World War II baby boom generation began to reach retirement age, membership growth slowed, and the rate of return fell. Moreover, because the early participants received more than they contributed, it follows that if the number of participants stops growing, later participants must receive less—and that ultimately means a *negative* rate of return. And for today's college students—indeed for most people now under the age of 50 or so—that negative rate of return is what lies ahead, unless reforms are implemented.

What Will It Take to Salvage Social Security?

The United States now finds itself with a social compact—the Social Security system—that entails a flow of promised benefits that could exceed the inflow of taxes sometime between 2010 and 2015. What, if anything, might be done about this? There are five relevant options to consider.

1. **Raise Taxes**. The history of Social Security has been one of steadily increasing tax rates applied to an ever-larger portion of workers' wages. In 1935, a Social Security payroll tax rate of 2 percent was applied to the first $3,000 of an individual's earnings (more than $40,000 in today's dollars). Now the Social Security payroll tax rate is 10.4 percentage points higher, and the government applies

Go to **www.econtoday.com/chapter06** to learn more about Social Security at the official Web site of the Social Security Administration.

this tax rate to roughly an additional $65,000 of a worker's wages measured in today's dollars.

One prominent proposal promises an $80 billion increase in contributions via a 2.2 percentage-point hike in the payroll tax rate, to an overall rate of 14.6 percent. Another proposal is to eliminate the current cap on the level of wages to which the payroll tax is applied, which would also generate about $80 billion per year in additional tax revenues. Nevertheless, even a combined policy of eliminating the wage cap and implementing a 2.2 percentage-point tax increase would not, by itself, keep tax collections above benefit payments over the long run.

2. **Reduce Retirement Benefit Payouts**. Proposals are on the table to increase the age of full benefit eligibility, perhaps to as high as 70. Another option is to cut benefits to nonworking spouses. A third proposal is to impose "means testing" on some or all Social Security benefits. As things stand now, all individuals covered by the system collect benefits when they retire, regardless of their assets or other sources of retirement income. Under a system of means testing, individuals with substantial amounts of alternative sources of retirement income would receive reduced Social Security benefits.

3. **Reduce Disability Benefits**. In addition to old-age pension payments, the U.S. Social Security system also offers benefits to people with various types of disabilities. In 1984, Congress greatly liberalized the definition of "disability" for purposes of qualifying for these benefits, and the result has been a near doubling of disability beneficiaries, from 2.6 million to more than 5 million today. One way to help shore up Social Security's financial situation would be to tighten requirements for this program or perhaps separate it from the Social Security system.

4. **Reform Immigration Policies**. Many experts believe that significant changes in U.S. immigration laws could offer the best hope of dealing with the tax burdens and workforce shrinkage of the future. Currently, however, more than 90 percent of new immigrants are admitted on the basis of a selection system unchanged since 1952. This system ties immigration rights to family preference. That is why most people admitted to the United States happen to be the spouses, children, or siblings of earlier immigrants. Unless Congress makes skills or training that are highly valued in the U.S. workplace a criterion in the U.S. immigration preference system, new immigrants are unlikely to contribute significant payments to Social Security, because their incomes will remain relatively low. Without reforms, it is unlikely that immigration will relieve much of the pressure building due to our aging population.

5. **Find a Way to Increase Social Security's Implicit Rate of Return**. As noted earlier, a major current problem for Social Security is a low implicit rate of return. Looking into the future, however, the situation appears even worse. As Figure 6-6 indicates, implicit rates of return for the system will be *negative* by 2020.

The long-term inflation-adjusted return available in the stock market has been 7 to 9 percent since the 1930s. It is not surprising, therefore, that some observers have advocated that the Social Security system purchase stocks rather than Treasury bonds with the current excess of payroll taxes over current benefit payments. (Because this would necessitate the Treasury's borrowing more from the public, this amounts to having the government borrow from the public for purposes of investing in the stock market.)

Although the added returns on stock investments could help stave off tax increases or benefit cuts, there are a few potential problems with this proposal. Despite the stock market's higher long-term returns, the inherent uncertainty of those returns is not entirely

FIGURE 6-6

Projected Social Security Rates of Return for Future Retirees

Whereas workers who paid into Social Security in earlier years got a good deal, those who are now paying in and those who will pay in the future are facing low or negative implicit rates of return.

Sources: Social Security Administration and author's estimates.

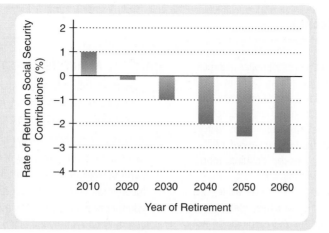

consistent with the function of Social Security as a source of *guaranteed* retirement income. Another issue is which stocks would be purchased. Political pressure to invest in companies that happened to be politically popular and to refrain from investing in those that were unpopular, regardless of their returns, would reduce the expected returns from the government's stock portfolio—possibly even below the returns on Treasury bonds.

QUICK QUIZ   See page 158 for the answers. Review concepts from this section in MyEconLab.

Social Security and Medicare payments are using up a large and _____ portion of the federal budget. Because of a shrinking number of workers available to support each retiree, the per capita expense for future workers to fund these programs will _____ rapidly unless reforms are made.

During the early years of the Social Security system, taxes were _____ relative to benefits, resulting in a

_____ implicit rate of return for retirees. As taxes have risen relative to benefits, the implicit rate of return on Social Security has _____ steadily.

There are only five options—or combinations of these five options—for preserving the current social compact: _____ taxes, _____ retirement benefit payouts, _____ disability benefits, reform _____ policies, or _____ Social Security's rate of return.

You Are There   For This Physician, the Tax Rate Is Too High to Justify Working

John McGoldrick and his wife are physicians living in Brunswick, Maine. Their combined income puts them among higher-income U.S. households. Thus, every dollar that John earns over and above his wife's income is normally taxed at an effective top marginal income tax rate of 51.1 percent (including Medicare, Social Security, and state taxes). Today,

though, John has completed a tax worksheet indicating that the couple also owes the *alternative minimum tax (AMT)*. Congress created the AMT in 1969 to prevent very-high-income taxpayers from using numerous special deductions and credits to reduce their tax liabilities. When Congress created the AMT, however, it failed to take inflation into account.

You Are There (cont.)

Since 1969, inflation has pushed up current-dollar incomes. Hence, current-dollar incomes that were "very high" in 1969 are just "high" or even "middle" today. In addition, since then Congress has added numerous deductions and exemptions intended to benefit middle-income taxpayers. Both factors have had the effect of imposing the AMT on more households, including the McGoldricks', thereby pushing John's effective marginal income tax rate even higher.

John realizes that after he and his wife pay all federal taxes including the AMT, state and local taxes, malpractice insurance premiums, and the like, his net earnings do not cover expenses he and his wife incur for child care. The time has come, he decides, to quit his job as an emergency room physician and care for their children himself.

CRITICAL ANALYSIS QUESTIONS

1. How does John McGoldrick know that his effective marginal income tax rate for his year of labor has turned out to be higher than 51.1 percent?

2. Why does the AMT's existence make it difficult for someone contemplating employment or more hours of wage-earning work in her current job to assess her marginal income tax rate? (Hint: Individuals often do not know whether they face the AMT in a given year until after the year-end when they calculate their federal tax liability.)

Progressive Income Taxation in the United States

Issues and Applications

CONCEPTS APPLIED

➤ Progressive Taxation

➤ Tax Rate

➤ Average Tax Rate

On a regular basis, a number of members of the U.S. Congress propose decreasing income tax rates for middle- and lower-income households and increasing income tax rates for higher-income households. They argue that the federal income tax system places a disproportionate burden on middle- and lower-income households and that higher-income taxpayers do not pay "their fair share" of income taxes.

Just how progressive is the *current* U.S. income tax system? One way to evaluate this question is to look at the tax rates—percentages of incomes transmitted to the federal government as income taxes—that apply to different income groups. Another is to compare different income groups' shares of income to their shares of total tax payments.

FIGURE 6-7

Average Tax Rates and Shares of U.S. Federal Income Taxes for Different Income Groups

As panel (a) shows, average tax rates increase for groups with higher incomes. In addition, panel (b) indicates that among those who pay federal income taxes, lower-income taxpayers account for a much smaller portion of payments than higher-income taxpayers. These patterns indicate that the U.S. federal income tax system is progressive.

Source: Internal Revenue Service.

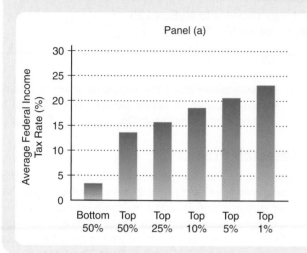

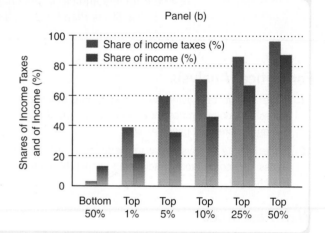

Average Tax Rates for Different Income Groups

Figure 6-7 above displays the average federal income tax rates paid by various income groups in the United States. As you can see in panel (a), the average tax rate for all taxpayers in the lower half of the income distribution of taxpayers is about 3 percent. The average tax rate paid by those in the top half of income earners paying taxes is more than 10 percentage points higher.

Also shown in panel (a) are the average tax rates for those in the top 25, 10, 5, and 1 percent of income earners. The tax rate rises as incomes increase, so the U.S. income tax system is clearly progressive throughout the upper range of incomes.

The Distribution of Federal Income Tax Payments

Naturally, even if lower-income individuals faced the same income tax rates as higher-income individuals, the former group would pay a smaller share of total income taxes because they earn lower incomes. In a progressive income tax system, however, lower-income individuals also pay lower tax rates than those assessed against incomes of higher earners. Thus, under progressive taxation lower-income people typically pay a very small share of total tax payments.

Panel (b) of Figure 6-7 verifies that this is currently true in the United States. Taxpayers among the bottom 50 percent of income earners, who earn about 14 percent of all income, account for less than 4 percent of federal income taxes. Thus, the share of taxes paid by the lowest-income individuals is considerably less than their share of total income. Furthermore, panel (b) shows that the bulk of income tax payments is concentrated among the highest-income taxpayers. The top 10 percent of taxpaying income earners, who earn just about 45 percent of all income, pay almost 66 percent of federal income taxes. Those among the top 1 percent earn about 20 percent of all income but account for more than 38 percent of the government's total receipts.

In summary, U.S. income tax rates increase as incomes rise. Consequently, the highest-income taxpayers pay considerably larger shares of the nation's overall income tax bill than lower-income taxpayers.

The highest-income taxpayers also pay proportionately higher shares of taxes than their own shares of total income. Clearly, the United States has a progressive tax system.

Test your understanding of this chapter by going online to **MyEconLab**.
In the Study Plan for this chapter, select Section N: News.

For Critical Analysis

1. If the income tax system were made more progressive across all income groups, how would panel (a) of Figure 6-7 on the previous page change?

2. If the income tax system were made more progressive across all income groups, how would panel (b) of Figure 6-7 change?

Web Resources

1. To see the latest Internal Revenue Service statistics on U.S. income tax rates paid by different income groups, go to www.econtoday.com/chapter06.

2. For information about the increasing share of income earners who owe no federal income taxes at all, go to www.econtoday.com/chapter06.

Research Project

Figure 6-7 on the facing page includes data only for U.S. income earners who actually paid taxes. Each year, a slightly larger portion—currently about one-third—of income earners in the United States owes zero federal income taxes. Other things being equal, does this trend tend to make the U.S. tax system more progressive? Explain. (Hint: Recall that by definition, 50 percent of all income earners are below the middle-income level.)

Here is what you should know after reading this chapter. **MyEconLab** will help you identify what you know, and where to go when you need to practice.

WHAT YOU SHOULD KNOW

WHERE TO GO TO PRACTICE

Average Tax Rates versus Marginal Tax Rates The average tax rate is the ratio of total tax payments to total income. In contrast, the marginal tax rate is the change in tax payments induced by a change in total taxable income. Thus, the marginal tax rate applies to the last dollar that a person earns.

government budget
 constraint, 135
tax base, 136
tax rate, 136
marginal tax rate, 136
tax bracket, 137
average tax rate, 137
proportional taxation,
 137
progressive taxation, 137
regressive taxation, 137

- **MyEconLab** Study Plans 6.1, 6.2
- Audio introduction to Chapter 6
- Video: Types of Tax Systems
- ABC News Video: Big Government: Who Is Going to Pay the Bill?

(continued)

WHAT YOU SHOULD KNOW		WHERE TO GO TO PRACTICE

The U.S. Income Tax System The U.S. income tax system assesses taxes against both personal and business income. It is designed to be a progressive tax system, in which the marginal tax rate increases as income rises, so that the marginal tax rate exceeds the average tax rate. This contrasts with a regressive tax system, in which higher-income people pay lower marginal tax rates, resulting in a marginal tax rate that is less than the average tax rate. The marginal tax rate equals the average tax rate only under proportional taxation, in which the marginal tax rate does not vary with income.

capital gain, 140
capital loss, 140
retained earnings, 140
tax incidence, 141

- **MyEconLab** Study Plan 6.3
- Video: The Corporate Income Tax

The Relationship Between Tax Rates and Tax Revenues Static tax analysis assumes that the tax base does not respond significantly to an increase in the tax rate, so it seems to imply that a tax rate hike must always boost a government's total tax collections. Dynamic tax analysis reveals, however, that increases in tax rates cause the tax base to decline. Thus, there is a tax rate that maximizes the government's tax revenues. If the government pushes the tax rate higher, tax collections decline.

sales taxes, 142
ad valorem taxation, 142
static tax analysis, 142
dynamic tax analysis, 143

KEY FIGURE
Figure 6-3, 145

- **MyEconLab** Study Plan 6.4
- Animated Figure 6-3

How Taxes on Purchases of Goods and Services Affect Market Prices and Quantities When a government imposes a per-unit tax on a good or service, a seller is willing to supply any given quantity only if the seller receives a price that is higher by exactly the amount of the tax. Hence, the supply curve shifts vertically by the amount of the tax per unit. In a market with typically shaped demand and supply curves, this results in a fall in the equilibrium quantity and an increase in the market price. To the extent that the market price rises, consumers pay a portion of the tax on each unit they buy. Sellers pay the remainder in lower profits.

excise tax, 146
unit tax, 146

KEY FIGURE
Figure 6-4, 146

- **MyEconLab** Study Plan 6.5
- Animated Figure 6-4

How Social Security Works and Why It Poses Problems for Today's Students Since its inception, Social Security benefits have been paid out of taxes. Because of the growing mismatch between elderly and younger citizens, future scheduled benefits vastly exceed future scheduled taxes, so some combination of higher taxes and lower benefits will have to be implemented to maintain the current system. The situation might also be eased a bit if more skilled workers were permitted to immigrate and if Social Security contributions were invested in the stock market, where they could earn higher rates of return.

Social Security contributions, 148
rate of return, 148
inflation-adjusted return, 148

KEY FIGURE
Figure 6-6, 151

- **MyEconLab** Study Plan 6.6
- Animated Figure 6-6

Log in to MyEconLab, take a chapter test, and get a personalized Study Plan that tells you which concepts you understand and which ones you need to review. From there, MyEconLab will give you further practice, tutorials, animations, videos, and guided solutions. Log in to www.myeconlab.com

PROBLEMS

All problems are assignable in [X] myeconlab . *Answers to odd-numbered problems appear at the back of the book.*

6-1. A senior citizen gets a part-time job at a fast-food restaurant. She earns $8 per hour for each hour she works, and she works exactly 25 hours per week. Thus, her total pretax weekly income is $200. Her total income tax assessment each week is $40, but she has determined that she is assessed $3 in taxes for the final hour she works each week.

 a. What is this person's average tax rate each week?

 b. What is the marginal tax rate for the last hour she works each week?

6-2. For purposes of assessing income taxes, there are three official income levels for workers in a small country: high, medium, and low. For the last hour on the job during a 40-hour workweek, a high-income worker pays a marginal income tax rate of 15 percent, a medium-income worker pays a marginal tax rate of 20 percent, and a low-income worker is assessed a 25 percent marginal income tax rate. Based only on this information, does this nation's income tax system appear to be progressive, proportional, or regressive?

6-3. Suppose that a state has increased its sales tax rate every other year since 2001. Assume that the state collected all sales taxes that residents legally owed. The following table summarizes its experience. What were total taxable sales in this state during each year displayed in the table?

Year	Sales Tax Rate	Sales Tax Collections
2001	0.03 (3 percent)	$9.0 million
2003	0.04 (4 percent)	$14.0 million
2005	0.05 (5 percent)	$20.0 million
2007	0.06 (6 percent)	$24.0 million
2009	0.07 (7 percent)	$29.4 million

6-4. The sales tax rate applied to all purchases within a state was 0.04 (4 percent) throughout 2008 but increased to 0.05 (5 percent) during all of 2009. The state government collected all taxes due, but its tax revenues were equal to $40 million each year. What happened to the sales tax base between 2008 and 2009? What could account for this result?

6-5. A city government imposes a proportional income tax on all people who earn income within its city limits. In 2008, the city's income tax rate was 0.05 (5 percent), and it collected $20 million in income taxes. In 2009, it raised the income tax rate to 0.06 (6 percent), and its income tax collections declined to $19.2 million. What happened to the city's income tax base between 2008 and 2009? How could this have occurred?

6-6. An obscure subsidiary of Microsoft Corporation, Ireland-based Round Island One Limited, has only about 1,000 employees. Nevertheless, Microsoft has gradually been shifting more income-generating activities to Ireland, which has a lower corporate tax rate than nations such as the United States and the United Kingdom. In one year alone, shifting more of its operations to Ireland allowed Microsoft to reduce its worldwide corporate income tax rate by 6 percentage points. What has happened to Ireland's tax base as a result? What has happened to tax bases in nations such as the United States and the United Kingdom?

6-7. The British government recently imposed a unit excise tax of about $154 per ticket on airline tickets applying to flights to or from London airports. In answering the following questions, assume normally shaped demand and supply curves.

 a. Use an appropriate diagram to predict effects of the ticket tax on the market clearing price of London airline tickets and on the equilibrium number of flights into and out of London.

 b. What do you predict is likely to happen to the equilibrium price of tickets for air flights into and out of cities that are in close proximity to London but are not subject to the new ticket tax? Explain your reasoning.

6-8. To raise funds aimed at providing more support for public schools, a state government has just imposed a unit excise tax equal to $4 for each monthly unit of telephone services sold by each telephone company operating in the state. The diagram on the next page depicts the positions of the demand and supply curves for telephone services *before* the unit excise tax was imposed. Use this diagram to determine the position of the new market supply curve now that the tax hike has gone into effect.

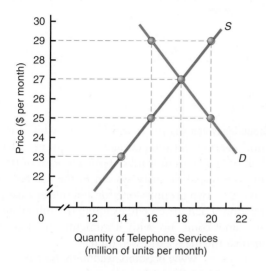

a. Does imposing the $4-per-month unit excise tax cause the market price of telephone services to rise by $4 per month? Why or why not?

b. What portion of the $4-per-month unit excise tax is paid by consumers? What portion is paid by providers of telephone services?

6-9. Suppose that the federal government imposes a unit excise tax of $2 per month on the monthly rates that Internet service providers charge for providing DSL high-speed Internet access to households and businesses. Draw a diagram of normally shaped market demand and supply curves for DSL Internet access services. Use this diagram to predict how the Internet service tax is likely to affect the market price and market quantity.

6-10. Consider the $2-per-month tax on DSL Internet access in Problem 6-9. Suppose that in the market for DSL Internet access services provided to households, the market price increases by $2 per month after the unit excise tax is imposed. If the market supply curve slopes upward, what can you say about the shape of the market demand curve over the relevant ranges of prices and quantities? Who pays the excise tax in this market?

6-11. Consider once more the DSL Internet access tax of $2 per month discussed in Problem 6-9. Suppose that in the market for DSL Internet access services provided to businesses, the market price does not change after the unit excise tax is imposed. If the market supply curve slopes upward, what can you say about the shape of the market demand curve over the relevant ranges of prices and quantities? Who pays the excise tax in this market?

6-12. The following information applies to the market for a particular item in the *absence* of a unit excise tax:

Price ($ per unit)	Quantity Supplied	Quantity Demanded
4	50	200
5	75	175
6	100	150
7	125	125
8	150	100
9	175	75

a. According to the information above, in the *absence* of a unit excise tax, what is the market price? What is the equilibrium quantity?

b. Suppose that the government decides to subject producers of this item to a unit excise tax equal to $2 per unit sold. What is the new market price? What is the new equilibrium quantity?

c. What portion of the tax is paid by producers? What portion of the tax is paid by consumers?

6-13. In the following situations, what is the rate of return on the investment? (Hint: In each case, what is the percentage by which next year's benefit exceeds—or falls short of—this year's cost?)

a. You invest $100 today and receive in return $150 exactly one year from now.

b. You invest $100 today and receive in return $80 exactly one year from now.

6-14. Suppose that the following Social Security reform became law: All current Social Security recipients will continue to receive their benefits, but no increase will be made other than cost-of-living adjustments; U.S. citizens between age 40 and retirement not yet receiving Social Security can opt to continue with the current system; those who opt out can place what they would have contributed to Social Security into one or more government-approved investments; and those under 40 must place their contributions into one or more government-approved investments.

Now answer the following questions:

a. Who will be in favor of this reform and why?

b. Who will be against this reform and why?

c. What might happen to stock market indexes?

d. What additional risk is involved for those who end up in the private system?

e. What additional benefits are possible for the people in the private system?

f. Which firms in the investment industry might not be approved by the federal government and why?

ECONOMICS ON THE NET

Social Security Privatization There are many proposals for reforming Social Security, but only one fundamentally alters the nature of the current system: privatization. The purpose of this exercise is to learn more about what would happen if Social Security were privatized.

Title: Social Security Privatization

Navigation: Go to **www.econtoday.com/chapter06** to learn about Social Security privatization. Click on *FAQ on Social Security* in the left-hand column.

Application For each of the three entries noted here, read the entry and answer the question.

1. Click on *Is there really a Social Security crisis?* According to this article, when will the system begin to experience difficulties? Why?

2. Click on *What about raising the tax cap?* What does this article contend are the likely consequences of applying the Social Security payroll tax to more of a person's income? Why?

3. Click on *What about personal accounts in addition to Social Security?* Why does this article argue that simply adding personal accounts will not solve Social Security's problems?

For Group Study and Analysis It will be worthwhile for those not nearing retirement age to examine what the "older" generation thinks about the idea of privatizing the Social Security system in the United States. So create two groups—one for and one against privatization. Each group will examine the following Web site and come up with arguments in favor of or against the ideas expressed on it.

Go to **www.econtoday.com/chapter06** to read a proposal for Social Security reform. Accept or rebut the proposal, depending on the side to which you have been assigned. Be prepared to defend your reasons with more than just your feelings. At a minimum, be prepared to present arguments that are logical, if not entirely backed by facts.

Taking into account the characteristics of your group as a whole, is it likely to be made better off or worse off if Social Security is privatized? Should your decision to support or oppose privatization be based solely on how it affects you personally? Or should your decision take into account how it might affect others in your group?

ANSWERS TO QUICK QUIZZES

p. 138: (i) rate . . . base; (ii) average . . . marginal; (iii) proportional . . . progressive . . . regressive

p. 142: (i) income . . . sales . . . property; (ii) double; (iii) Social Security . . . Medicare . . . unemployment

p. 145: (i) static; (ii) dynamic . . . static; (iii) fall . . . decline

p. 148: (i) vertically . . . vertically; (ii) reduces . . . raises; (iii) less

p. 151: (i) rising . . . grow; (ii) low . . . high . . . decreased; (iii) raise . . . reduce . . . reduce . . . immigration . . . increase

The Macroeconomy: Unemployment, Inflation, and Deflation

7

*T*he *Economist* magazine tabulates what it calls the "R-word index," which is the number of times the print media use the word *recession*, meaning an economic downturn. Use of this word rose considerably in 2006 and 2007. By the end of 2008, an official determination had been made that the U.S. economy entered a recession beginning in December 2007. As the recession dragged on, however, *The Economist* and other media outlets began to consider whether another word might be worth tracking. That word was *depression*. What distinguishes an economic depression from a more run-of-the-mill recession? In this chapter, you will contemplate the answer to this question.

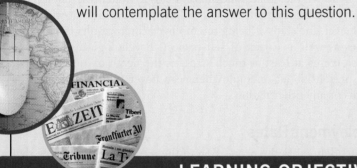

LEARNING OBJECTIVES

myeconlab

After reading this chapter, you should be able to:

- Explain how the U.S. government calculates the official unemployment rate
- Discuss the types of unemployment
- Describe how price indexes are calculated and define the key types of price indexes
- Distinguish between nominal and real interest rates
- Evaluate who loses and who gains from inflation
- Understand key features of business fluctuations

? DID YOU KNOW THAT small businesses—defined as companies that employ fewer than 500 people—provide jobs to more than half of all people holding private-sector positions in the United States? Indeed, small businesses accounted for more than 60 percent of all net new private-sector jobs created between 1998 and 2007. Thus, the fact that small businesses were hit particularly hard by the economic downturn in 2008 through 2010 does much to explain why nearly 7 million U.S. residents lost their jobs during those years. As these companies' fortunes sagged, so did their willingness to provide gainful employment to millions of U.S. workers.

Trying to understand and forecast unemployment and the overall performance of the national economy is a central objective of macroeconomics. This branch of economics seeks to explain and predict movements in the average level of prices, unemployment, and the total production of goods and services. This chapter introduces you to these key issues of macroeconomics.

Unemployment

Unemployment

The total number of adults (aged 16 years or older) who are willing and able to work and who are actively looking for work but have not found a job.

Unemployment is normally defined as the number of adults who are actively looking for work but do not have a job. Unemployment creates a cost to the entire economy in terms of lost output. One estimate indicates that at the beginning of the 2000s, when the unemployment rate rose by 2 percentage points and firms were operating below 80 percent of their capacity, the amount of output that the economy lost due to idle resources was roughly 2 percent of the total production throughout the United States. (In other words, we were somewhere inside the production possibilities curve that we talked about in Chapter 2.) That was the equivalent of more than an inflation-adjusted $200 billion of schools, houses, restaurant meals, cars, and movies that *could have been* produced. It is no wonder that policymakers closely watch the unemployment figures published by the Department of Labor's Bureau of Labor Statistics.

On a more personal level, the state of being unemployed often results in hardship and failed opportunities as well as a lack of self-respect. Psychological researchers believe that being fired creates at least as much stress as the death of a close friend. The numbers that we present about unemployment can never fully convey its true cost to the people of this or any other nation.

Historical Unemployment Rates

The unemployment rate, defined as the proportion of the measured **labor force** that is unemployed, hit a low of 1.2 percent of the labor force at the end of World War II, after having reached 25 percent during the Great Depression in the 1930s. You can see in Figure 7-1 what has happened to the unemployment rate in the United States since 1890. The highest level ever was reached in the Great Depression, but the unemployment rate was also high during the Panic of 1893.

Labor force

Individuals aged 16 years or older who either have jobs or who are looking and available for jobs; the number of employed plus the number of unemployed.

Employment, Unemployment, and the Labor Force

Figure 7-2 presents the population of individuals 16 years of age or older broken into three segments: (1) employed, (2) unemployed, and (3) not in the civilian labor force (a category that includes homemakers, full-time students, military personnel, persons in institutions, and retired persons). The employed and the unemployed, added together, make up the labor force. In 2009, the labor force amounted to 139.9 million + 15.2 million = 155.1 million people. To calculate the unemployment rate, we simply divide the number of unemployed by the number of people in the labor force and multiply by 100: 15.2 million/155.1 million × 100 = 9.8 percent.

What is the reason why large retailers, such at Wal-Mart and Costco, offer relatively low prices for their products, thereby keeping the overall inflation rate lower than it would be otherwise?

FIGURE 7-1

More Than a Century of Unemployment

The U.S. unemployment rate dropped below 2 percent during World Wars I and II but exceeded 25 percent during the Great Depression. During the Great Recession following 2007, the unemployment rate rose above 10 percent.

Source: U.S. Department of Labor, Bureau of Labor Statistics.

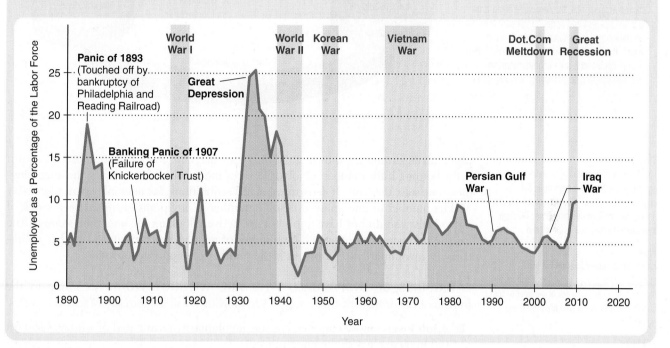

FIGURE 7-2

Adult Population

The population aged 16 and older can be broken down into three groups: people who are employed, those who are unemployed, and those not in the labor force.

Source: U.S. Department of Labor, Bureau of Labor Statistics.

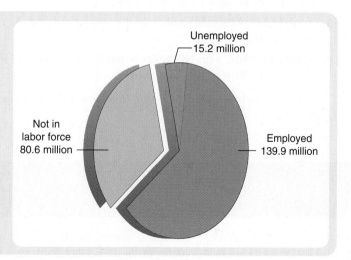

The Arithmetic Determination of Unemployment

Because there is a transition between employment and unemployment at any point in time—people are leaving jobs and others are finding jobs—there is a simple relationship between the employed and the unemployed, as can be seen in Figure 7-3 on the following

FIGURE 7-3

The Logic of the Unemployment Rate

Individuals who depart jobs but remain in the labor force are subtracted from the employed and added to the unemployed. When the unemployed acquire jobs, they are subtracted from the unemployed and added to the employed. In an unchanged labor force, if both flows are equal, the unemployment rate is stable. If more people depart jobs than acquire them, the unemployment rate increases, and vice versa.

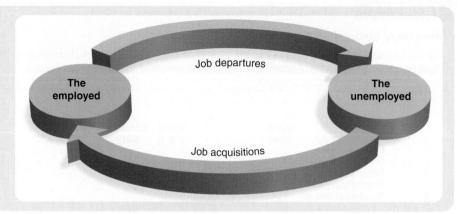

Stock

The quantity of something, measured at a given point in time—for example, an inventory of goods or a bank account. Stocks are defined independently of time, although they are assessed at a point in time.

Flow

A quantity measured per unit of time; something that occurs over time, such as the income you make per week or per year or the number of individuals who are fired every month.

Job loser

An individual in the labor force whose employment was involuntarily terminated.

Reentrant

An individual who used to work full-time but left the labor force and has now reentered it looking for a job.

Job leaver

An individual in the labor force who quits voluntarily.

page. Job departures are shown at the top of the diagram, and job acquisitions are shown at the bottom. If the numbers of job departures and acquisitions are equal, the unemployment rate stays the same. If departures exceed acquisitions, the unemployment rate rises.

The number of unemployed is some number at any point in time. It is a **stock** of individuals who do not have a job but are actively looking for one. The same is true for the number of employed. The number of people departing jobs, whether voluntarily or involuntarily, is a **flow,** as is the number of people acquiring jobs.

CATEGORIES OF INDIVIDUALS WHO ARE WITHOUT WORK According to the Bureau of Labor Statistics, an unemployed individual will fall into any of four categories:

1. A **job loser,** whose employment was involuntarily terminated or who was laid off (40 to 60 percent of the unemployed)
2. A **reentrant,** who worked a full-time job before but has been out of the labor force (20 to 30 percent of the unemployed)
3. A **job leaver,** who voluntarily ended employment (less than 10 to around 15 percent of the unemployed)
4. A **new entrant,** who has never worked a full-time job for two weeks or longer (10 to 15 percent of the unemployed)

Why are elderly people accounting for a larger share of unemployed workers in the United States?

EXAMPLE
There Is No Upper Age Limit on Unemployment

In the late 1990s, individuals aged 65 or older comprised less than 12 percent of the U.S. labor force, and people aged 75 or older made up less than 5 percent. During subsequent years, a larger share of workers opted to stay in the labor force as they aged. In addition, some older individuals who previously had left the labor force

decided to reenter. By the late 2000s, nearly 17 percent of people in the U.S. labor force were 65 or older, and more than 7 percent were 75 or older.

A consequence of this shift toward more elderly people in the labor force is that the recent downswing in U.S. economic activity has resulted in a larger proportion of unemployed elderly

EXAMPLE (cont.)

people. Whereas the unemployment rate among people 65 and older averaged less than 3 percent between the late 1990s and early 2000s, today this rate is 7 percent. The unemployment rate for people aged 75 and older has jumped from just above 2 percent to nearly 5 percent.

FOR CRITICAL ANALYSIS

Do you suppose that most of the elderly people who have recently become unemployed are classified as job leavers or job losers?

DURATION OF UNEMPLOYMENT If you are out of a job for a week, your situation is typically much less serious than if you are out of a job for, say, 14 weeks. An increase in the duration of unemployment can increase the unemployment rate because workers stay unemployed longer, thereby creating a greater number of them at any given time. The most recent information on duration of unemployment paints the following picture: more than a third of those who become unemployed acquire a new job by the end of one month, approximately one-third more acquire a job by the end of two months, and only about a sixth are still unemployed after six months. Since the mid-1960s, the average annual duration of unemployment for all the unemployed has varied between 10 and 20 weeks. The overall average duration for the past 25 years has been about 15 weeks.

When overall business activity goes into a downturn, the duration of unemployment tends to rise, thereby accounting for much of the increase in the estimated unemployment rate. In a sense, then, it is the increase in the *duration* of unemployment during a downturn in national economic activity that generates the bad news that concerns policymakers in Washington, D.C. Furthermore, the individuals who stay unemployed longer than six months are the ones who create pressure on Congress to "do something." What Congress does, typically, is extend and supplement unemployment benefits.

THE DISCOURAGED WORKER PHENOMENON Critics of the published unemployment rate calculated by the federal government believe that it fails to reflect the true numbers of **discouraged workers** and "hidden unemployed." Though there is no agreed-on method to measure discouraged workers, the Department of Labor defines them as people who have dropped out of the labor force and are no longer looking for a job because they believe that the job market has little to offer them. To what extent do we want to include in the measured labor force individuals who voluntarily choose not to look for work or those who take only a few minutes a day to scan the want ads and then decide that there are no jobs?

Some economists argue that people who work part-time but are willing to work full-time should be classified as "semihidden" unemployed. Estimates range as high as 6 million workers at any one time. Offsetting this factor, though, is *overemployment*. An individual working 50 or 60 hours a week is still counted as only one full-time worker. Some people hold two or three jobs.

LABOR FORCE PARTICIPATION The way in which we define unemployment and membership in the labor force will affect the **labor force participation rate.** It is defined as the proportion of noninstitutionalized (i.e., not in prisons, mental institutions, etc.) working-age individuals who are employed or seeking employment.

New entrant
An individual who has never held a full-time job lasting two weeks or longer but is now seeking employment.

You Are There

To learn about how Denmark's government keeps the nation's unemployment level low, read **Staying Employed in Denmark —at the Taxpayers' Expense,** on pages 176 and 177.

Discouraged workers
Individuals who have stopped looking for a job because they are convinced that they will not find a suitable one.

Labor force participation rate
The percentage of noninstitutionalized working-age individuals who are employed or seeking employment.

The U.S. labor force participation rate has risen somewhat over time, from 60 percent in 1950 to about 66 percent today. The gender composition of the U.S. labor force has changed considerably during this time. In 1950, more than 83 percent of men and fewer than 35 percent of women participated in the U.S. labor force. Today, fewer than 75 percent of men and more than 60 percent of women are U.S. labor force participants.

QUICK QUIZ See page 183 for the answers. Review concepts from this section in MyEconLab.

_____ persons are adults who are willing and able to work and are actively looking for a job but have not found one. The unemployment rate is computed by dividing the number of unemployed by the total _____ _____, which is equal to those who are employed plus those who are unemployed.

The unemployed are classified as _____ _____, _____, _____ _____, and _____ _____ to the labor force. The flow of people departing jobs and people acquiring jobs determines the stock of the unemployed as well as the stock of the employed.

The duration of unemployment affects the unemployment rate. If the duration of unemployment increases, the measured unemployment rate will _____, even though the number of unemployed workers may remain the same.

Whereas overall labor force participation has risen only modestly since World War II, there has been a major increase in _____ labor force participation.

The Major Types of Unemployment

Unemployment has been categorized into four basic types: frictional, structural, cyclical, and seasonal.

Frictional Unemployment

Of the more than 155 million people in the labor force, more than 50 million will either change jobs or take new jobs during the year. In the process, in excess of 22 million persons will report themselves unemployed at one time or another. This continuous flow of individuals from job to job and in and out of employment is called **frictional unemployment.** There will always be some frictional unemployment as resources are redirected in the economy, because job-hunting costs are never zero, and workers never have full information about available jobs. To eliminate frictional unemployment, we would have to prevent workers from leaving their present jobs until they had already lined up other jobs at which they would start working immediately. And we would have to guarantee first-time job seekers a job *before* they started looking.

Frictional unemployment
Unemployment due to the fact that workers must search for appropriate job offers. This takes time, and so they remain temporarily unemployed.

Structural Unemployment

Structural changes in our economy cause some workers to become unemployed for very long periods of time because they cannot find jobs that use their particular skills. This is called **structural unemployment.** Structural unemployment is not caused by general business fluctuations, although business fluctuations may affect it. And unlike frictional unemployment, structural unemployment is not related to the movement of workers from low-paying to high-paying jobs.

At one time, economists thought about structural unemployment only from the perspective of workers. The concept applied to workers who did not have the ability, training, and skills necessary to obtain available jobs. Today, it still encompasses these

Structural unemployment
Unemployment resulting from a poor match of workers' abilities and skills with current requirements of employers.

workers. In addition, however, economists increasingly look at structural unemployment from the viewpoint of employers, many of whom face government mandates requiring them to take such steps as providing funds for social insurance programs for their employees and announcing plant closings months or even years in advance. There is now considerable evidence that government labor market policies influence how many positions businesses wish to create, thereby affecting structural unemployment. In the United States, many businesses appear to have adjusted to these policies by hiring more "temporary workers" or establishing short-term contracts with "private consultants." Such measures may have reduced the extent of U.S. structural unemployment in recent years.

Cyclical Unemployment

Cyclical unemployment is related to business fluctuations. It is defined as unemployment associated with changes in business conditions—primarily recessions and depressions. The way to lessen cyclical unemployment would be to reduce the intensity, duration, and frequency of downturns of business activity. Economic policymakers attempt, through their policies, to reduce cyclical unemployment by keeping business activity on an even keel.

Why has the recent drop in U.S. business activity pushed up the male unemployment rate faster than the female unemployment rate?

Cyclical unemployment
Unemployment resulting from business recessions that occur when aggregate (total) demand is insufficient to create full employment.

EXAMPLE
Why Men Are Confronting Higher Unemployment Than Women

When U.S. business activity fell after 2007, the unemployment rates soared for both men and women. The differential between the male and female unemployment rates also increased, to 2.5 percentage points—the largest differential since the government began systemically collecting unemployment data in 1940.

The explanation for the widening gap between male and female unemployment rates is straightforward. Two of the industries making significant contributions to the job-loss count during the Great Recession were construction and manufacturing, which employ disproportionate numbers of male workers. The only industries to show a net increase in job growth were health care and education, which have much higher concentrations of female workers.

FOR CRITICAL ANALYSIS
Why do you suppose that during the recent downturn, unemployment rose faster among unskilled workers than among skilled workers? (Hint: Why might struggling employers choose to lay off unskilled workers before skilled workers?)

Seasonal Unemployment

Seasonal unemployment comes and goes with seasons of the year in which the demand for particular jobs rises and falls. In northern states, construction workers can often work only during the warmer months; they are seasonally unemployed during the winter. Summer resort workers can usually get jobs in resorts only during the summer season. They, too, become seasonally unemployed during the winter; the opposite is true for ski resort workers.

Seasonal unemployment
Unemployment resulting from the seasonal pattern of work in specific industries. It is usually due to seasonal fluctuations in demand or to changing weather conditions that render work difficult, if not impossible, as in the agriculture, construction, and tourist industries.

When this employee in a summer tourist area is laid off in the winter, she becomes part of what type of unemployment?

The unemployment rate that the Bureau of Labor Statistics releases each month is "seasonally adjusted." This means that the reported unemployment rate has been adjusted to remove the effects of variations in seasonal unemployment. Thus, the unemployment rate that the media dutifully announce reflects only the sum of frictional unemployment, structural unemployment, and cyclical unemployment.

Full Employment and the Natural Rate of Unemployment

Does full employment mean that everybody has a job? Certainly not, for not everyone is looking for a job—full-time students and full-time homemakers, for example, are not. Is it always possible for everyone who is looking for a job to find one? No, because transaction costs in the labor market are not zero. Transaction costs are those associated with any activity whose goal is to enter into, carry out, or terminate contracts. In the labor market, these costs involve time spent looking for a job, being interviewed, negotiating the terms of employment, and the like.

Full Employment

Full employment

An arbitrary level of unemployment that corresponds to "normal" friction in the labor market. In 1986, a 6.5 percent rate of unemployment was considered full employment. Since the 1990s, it has been assumed to be around 5 percent.

We will always have some frictional unemployment as individuals move in and out of the labor force, seek higher-paying jobs, and move to different parts of the country. **Full employment** is therefore a concept implying some sort of balance or equilibrium in an ever-shifting labor market. Of course, this general notion of full employment must somehow be put into numbers so that economists and others can determine whether the economy has reached the full-employment point.

The Natural Rate of Unemployment

Natural rate of unemployment

The rate of unemployment that is estimated to prevail in long-run macroeconomic equilibrium, when all workers and employers have fully adjusted to any changes in the economy.

To try to assess when a situation of balance has been attained in the labor market, economists estimate the **natural rate of unemployment,** the rate that is expected to prevail in the long run once all workers and employers have fully adjusted to any changes in the economy. If correctly estimated, the natural rate of unemployment should not include cyclical unemployment. When seasonally adjusted, the natural unemployment rate should include only frictional and structural unemployment.

A long-standing difficulty, however, has been a lack of agreement about how to estimate the natural unemployment rate. From the mid-1980s to the early 1990s, the President's Council of Economic Advisers (CEA) consistently estimated that the natural unemployment rate in the United States was about 6.5 percent. Even into the 2000s, Federal Reserve staff economists, employing an approach to estimating the natural rate of unemployment that was intended to improve on the CEA's traditional method, arrived at a natural rate just over 6 percent. When the measured unemployment rate fell to 4 percent in 2000, however, economists began to rethink their approach to estimating the natural unemployment rate. This led some to alter their estimation methods to take into account such factors as greater rivalry among domestic businesses and increased international competition, which at that time led to an estimated natural rate of unemployment of roughly 5 percent. We shall return to the concept of the natural unemployment rate in Chapter 10.

Inflation and Deflation

During World War II, you could buy bread for 8 to 10 cents a loaf and have milk delivered fresh to your door for about 25 cents a half gallon. The average price of a new car was less than $700, and the average house cost less than $3,000. Today, bread, milk, cars, and houses all cost more—a lot more. Prices are about 14 times what they were in 1940. Clearly, this country has experienced quite a bit of *inflation* since then. We define **inflation** as an upward movement in the average level of prices. The opposite of inflation is **deflation,** defined as a downward movement in the average level of prices. Notice that these definitions depend on the *average* level of prices. This means that even during a period of inflation, some prices can be falling if other prices are rising at a faster rate. The prices of electronic equipment have dropped dramatically since the 1960s, even though there has been general inflation.

To discuss what has happened to prices here and in other countries, we have to know how to measure inflation.

Inflation
A sustained increase in the average of all prices of goods and services in an economy.

Deflation
A sustained decrease in the average of all prices of goods and services in an economy.

Inflation and the Purchasing Power of Money

The value of a dollar does not stay constant when there is inflation. The value of money is usually talked about in terms of **purchasing power.** A dollar's purchasing power is the real goods and services that it can buy. Consequently, another way of defining inflation is as a decline in the purchasing power of money. The faster the rate of inflation, the greater the rate of decline in the purchasing power of money.

One way to think about inflation and the purchasing power of money is to discuss dollar values in terms of *nominal* versus *real* values. The nominal value of anything is simply its price expressed in today's dollars. In contrast, the real value of anything is its value expressed in purchasing power, which varies with the overall price level. Let's say that you received a $100 bill from your grandparents this year. One year from now, the nominal value of that bill will still be $100. The real value will depend on what the purchasing power of money is after one year's worth of inflation. Obviously, if there is inflation during the year, the real value of that $100 bill will have diminished. For example, if you keep the $100 bill in your pocket for a year during which the rate of inflation is 3 percent, at the end of the year you will have to come up with $3 more to buy the same amount of goods and services that the $100 bill can purchase today.

Purchasing power
The value of money for buying goods and services. If your money income stays the same but the price of one good that you are buying goes up, your effective purchasing power falls, and vice versa.

Measuring the Rate of Inflation

How can we measure the rate of inflation? This is a thorny problem for government statisticians. It is easy to determine how much the price of an individual commodity has risen: If last year a light bulb cost 50 cents and this year it costs 75 cents, there has

If the price of women's shoes falls, can there still be inflation?

Price index
The cost of today's market basket of goods expressed as a percentage of the cost of the same market basket during a base year.

Base year
The year that is chosen as the point of reference for comparison of prices in other years.

been a 50 percent rise in the price of that light bulb over a one-year period. We can express the change in the individual light bulb price in one of several ways: The price has gone up 25 cents; the price is one and a half (1.5) times as high; the price has risen by 50 percent. An *index number* of this price rise is simply the second way (1.5) multiplied by 100, meaning that the index today would stand at 150. We multiply by 100 to eliminate decimals because it is easier to think in terms of percentage changes using whole numbers. This is the standard convention adopted for convenience in dealing with index numbers or price levels.

Computing a Price Index

The measurement problem becomes more complicated when it involves a large number of goods, especially if some prices have risen faster than others and some have even fallen. What we have to do is pick a representative bundle, a so-called market basket, of goods and compare the cost of that market basket of goods over time. When we do this, we obtain a **price index,** which is defined as the cost of a market basket of goods today, expressed as a percentage of the cost of that identical market basket of goods in some starting year, known as the **base year.**

$$\text{Price index} = \frac{\text{cost of market basket today}}{\text{cost of market basket in base year}} \times 100$$

In the base year, the price index will always be 100, because the year in the numerator and in the denominator of the fraction is the same; therefore, the fraction equals 1, and when we multiply it by 100, we get 100. A simple numerical example is given in Table 7-1. In the table, there are only two goods in the market basket—corn and computers. The *quantities* in the basket are the same in the base year, 2001, and the current year, 2011. Only the *prices* change. Such a *fixed-quantity* price index is the easiest to compute because the statistician need only look at prices of goods and services sold every year rather than observing how much of these goods and services consumers actually purchase each year.

What caused the rate of change in the average price of the typical consumer's market basket to turn negative for the first time in more than 50 years?

INTERNATIONAL EXAMPLE
Explaining a Drop in the Price Index for the U.S. Market Basket

Between March 2008 and March 2009, the average price of the market basket of goods and services purchased by a typical U.S. consumer decreased. Hence, a typical U.S. resident observed a full year of deflation for the first time since 1955.

Economists noted, however, that during the same period, the average price of a market basket of goods and services *excluding* food and energy-related products *increased* slightly. A number of these goods—in particular, oil—are imported from abroad. Indeed, economists determined that if the price of imported foreign oil had remained unchanged,

the average price of the U.S. market basket of goods and services would not have declined. Thus, the crucial element leading to the first annual U.S. deflation in more than five decades was a fall in the price of imported oil.

FOR CRITICAL ANALYSIS
If we were to use March 2008 as the base period for constructing a price index for food and energy-related products and another index for all other goods and services, would the values of the indexes for March 2008 be larger or smaller than the values for March 2009?

TABLE 7-1

Calculating a Price Index for a Two-Good Market Basket

In this simplified example, there are only two goods—corn and computers. The quantities and base-year prices are given in columns 2 and 3. The cost of the 2001 market basket, calculated in column 4, comes to $1,400. The 2011 prices are given in column 5. The cost of the market basket in 2011, calculated in column 6, is $1,650. The price index for 2011 compared with 2001 is 117.86.

(1) Commodity	(2) Market Basket Quantity	(3) 2001 Price per Unit	(4) Cost of Market Basket in 2001	(5) 2011 Price per Unit	(6) Cost of Market Basket in 2011
Corn	100 bushels	$ 4	$ 400	$ 8	$ 800
Computers	2	500	1,000	425	850
Totals			**$1,400**		**$1,650**

$$\text{Price index} = \frac{\text{cost of market basket in 2011}}{\text{cost of market basket in base year 2001}} \times 100 = \frac{\$1,650}{\$1,400} \times 100 = \textbf{117.86}$$

REAL-WORLD PRICE INDEXES Government statisticians calculate a number of price indexes. The most often quoted are the **Consumer Price Index (CPI)**, the **Producer Price Index (PPI)**, the **GDP deflator**, and the **Personal Consumption Expenditure (PCE) Index.** The CPI attempts to measure changes only in the level of prices of goods and services purchased by consumers. The PPI attempts to show what has happened to the average price of goods and services produced and sold by a typical firm. (There are also *wholesale price indexes* that track the price level for commodities that firms purchase from other firms.) The GDP deflator is the most general indicator of inflation because it measures changes in the level of prices of all new goods and services produced in the economy. The PCE Index measures average prices using weights from surveys of consumer spending.

THE CPI The Bureau of Labor Statistics (BLS) has the task of identifying a market basket of goods and services of the typical consumer. Today, the BLS uses the time period 1982–1984 as its base of market prices. It intends to change the base to 1993–1995 but has yet to do so. It has, though, updated the expenditure weights for its market basket of goods to reflect consumer spending patterns in 2001–2002. All CPI numbers since February 1998 reflect the new expenditure weights.

Economists have known for years that the way the BLS measures changes in the CPI is flawed. Specifically, the BLS has been unable to account for the way consumers substitute less expensive items for higher-priced items. The reason is that the CPI is a fixed-quantity price index, meaning that the BLS implicitly ignores changes in consumption patterns that occur between years in which it revises the index. Until recently, the BLS also has been unable to take quality changes into account as they occur. Now, though, it is subtracting from certain list prices estimated effects of qualitative improvements and adding to other list prices to account for deteriorations in quality. An additional flaw is that the CPI usually ignores successful new products until long after they have been introduced. Despite these flaws, the CPI is widely followed because its level is calculated and published monthly.

Why may efforts by the BLS to insulate the CPI from seasonal factors actually be adding to seasonal variations in the measurement of CPI inflation?

Consumer Price Index (CPI)

A statistical measure of a weighted average of prices of a specified set of goods and services purchased by typical consumers in urban areas.

Producer Price Index (PPI)

A statistical measure of a weighted average of prices of goods and services that firms produce and sell.

GDP deflator

A price index measuring the changes in prices of all new goods and services produced in the economy.

Personal Consumption Expenditure (PCE) Index

A statistical measure of average prices that uses annually updated weights based on surveys of consumer spending.

POLICY EXAMPLE
Have Seasonal Adjustments to the CPI Caused Seasonal Inflation?

The agency that calculates the CPI, the Bureau of Labor Statistics (BLS), seeks to prevent the CPI from being influenced by price movements that occur seasonally and hence are not related to any underlying economic trend. For example, gasoline prices usually rise in late spring as people begin driving more and then decline in the autumn months as people cut back on driving. To account for this, the BLS adjusts the gasoline component of the CPI downward in the spring and upward in the fall. The BLS designs these seasonal adjustments to cancel out exactly over a full year. In addition, the BLS makes "intervention" adjustments whenever a world event, such as a terrorist attack or a regional war flare-up, causes prices of gasoline and other items to vary in ways that the BLS deems to be unrelated to underlying economic trends.

Nevertheless, in nearly every year since 2000 that inflation has occurred, the estimated CPI inflation rate for the first few months of each year has been noticeably higher than the estimated CPI inflation rate in later months. Some economists suggest that world events are occurring in seasonal inflation cycles and that the BLS is *overreacting* in ways that actually *add* to seasonal cycles. Hence, BLS interventions to keep seasonal effects from contaminating the CPI may actually be contributing to seasonal fluctuations in CPI inflation rates.

FOR CRITICAL ANALYSIS
Why do you think that policymakers desire to prevent seasonal factors from showing up in macroeconomic data?

THE PPI There are a number of Producer Price Indexes, including one for foodstuffs, another for intermediate goods (goods used in the production of other goods), and one for finished goods. Most of the producer prices included are in mining, manufacturing, and agriculture. The PPIs can be considered general-purpose indexes for nonretail markets.

Although in the long run the various PPIs and the CPI generally show the same rate of inflation, that is not the case in the short run. Most often the PPIs increase before the CPI because it takes time for producer price increases to show up in the prices that consumers pay for final products. Often changes in the PPIs are watched closely as a hint that inflation is going to increase or decrease.

Go to www.econtoday.com/chapter07 to obtain information about inflation and unemployment in other countries from the International Monetary Fund. Click on "World Economic Outlook Databases."

THE GDP DEFLATOR The broadest price index reported in the United States is the GDP deflator, where GDP stands for gross domestic product, or annual total national income. Unlike the CPI and the PPIs, the GDP deflator is *not* based on a fixed market basket of goods and services. The basket is allowed to change with people's consumption and investment patterns. In this sense, the changes in the GDP deflator reflect both price changes and the public's market responses to those price changes. Why? Because new expenditure patterns are allowed to show up in the GDP deflator as people respond to changing prices.

THE PCE INDEX Another price index that takes into account changing expenditure patterns is the Personal Consumption Expenditure (PCE) Index. The Bureau of Economic Analysis, an agency of the U.S. Department of Commerce, uses continuously updated annual surveys of consumer purchases to construct the weights for the PCE Index. Thus, an advantage of the PCE Index is that weights in the index are updated every year. The Federal Reserve has used the rate of change in the PCE Index as its primary inflation indicator because Fed officials believe that the updated weights in the PCE Index make it more accurate than the CPI as a measure of consumer price changes. Nevertheless, the CPI remains the most widely reported price index, and the U.S. government continues to use the CPI to adjust the value of Social Security benefits to account for inflation.

HISTORICAL CHANGES IN THE CPI Between World War II and the early 1980s, the Consumer Price Index showed a fairly dramatic trend upward. Figure 7-4 shows the annual rate of change in the CPI since 1860. Prior to World War II, there were numerous periods of deflation interspersed with periods of inflation. Persistent year-in and year-out inflation seems to be a post–World War II phenomenon, at least in this country. As far back as before the American Revolution, prices used to rise during war periods but then would fall back toward prewar levels afterward. This occurred

---

FIGURE 7-4

Inflation and Deflation in U.S. History

For 80 years after the Civil War, the United States experienced alternating inflation and deflation. Here we show them as reflected by changes in the Consumer Price Index. Since World War II, the periods of inflation have not been followed by periods of deflation. Even during peacetime, the price index has continued to rise. The shaded areas represent wartime.

Source: U.S. Department of Labor, Bureau of Labor Statistics.

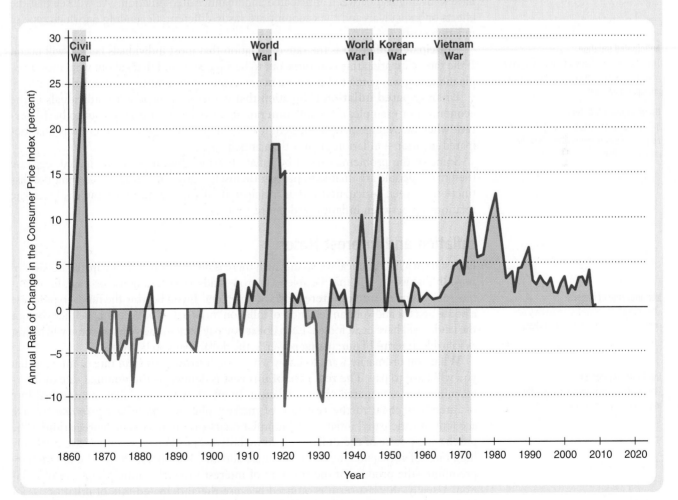

after the Revolutionary War, the War of 1812, the Civil War, and to a lesser extent World War I. Consequently, the overall price level in 1940 wasn't much different from 150 years earlier.

QUICK QUIZ See page 183 for the answers. Review concepts from this section in MyEconLab.

Once we pick a market basket of goods, we can construct a **price index** that compares the cost of that market basket today with the cost of the same market basket in a _____ year.

The _____ _____ **Index** is the most often used price index in the United States. The Producer Price Index (PPI) is also widely mentioned.

The _____ _____ measures what is happening to the average price level of *all* new, domestically produced final goods and services in our economy.

The _____ _____ _____ **Index** uses annually updated weights from consumer spending surveys to measure average prices faced by consumers.

Anticipated versus Unanticipated Inflation

To determine who is hurt by inflation and what the effects of inflation are in general, we have to distinguish between anticipated and unanticipated inflation. We will see that the effects on individuals and the economy are vastly different, depending on which type of inflation exists.

Anticipated inflation is the rate of inflation that most individuals believe will occur. If the rate of inflation this year turns out to be 5 percent, and that's about what most people thought it was going to be, we are in a situation of fully anticipated inflation.

Unanticipated inflation is inflation that comes as a surprise to individuals in the economy. For example, if the inflation rate in a particular year turns out to be 10 percent when on average people thought it was going to be 3 percent, there was unanticipated inflation—inflation greater than anticipated.

Some of the problems caused by inflation arise when it is unanticipated, because then many people are unable to protect themselves from its ravages. Keeping the distinction between anticipated and unanticipated inflation in mind, we can easily see the relationship between inflation and interest rates.

Inflation and Interest Rates

Let's start in a hypothetical world in which there is no inflation and anticipated inflation is zero. In that world, you may be able to borrow funds—to buy a house or a car, for example—at a **nominal rate of interest** of, say, 6 percent. If you borrow the funds to purchase a house or a car and your anticipation of inflation turns out to be accurate, neither you nor the lender will have been fooled. Each dollar you pay back in the years to come will be just as valuable in terms of purchasing power as the dollar that you borrowed.

What you ordinarily want to know when you borrow is the *real* rate of interest that you will have to pay. The **real rate of interest** is defined as the nominal rate of interest minus the anticipated rate of inflation. In effect, we can say that the nominal rate of interest is equal to the real rate of interest plus an *inflationary premium* to take account of anticipated inflation. That inflationary premium covers depreciation in the purchasing power of the dollars repaid by borrowers. (Whenever there are relatively high rates of anticipated inflation, we must add an additional factor to the inflationary premium—the product of the real rate of interest times the anticipated rate of inflation. Usually, this last term is omitted because the anticipated rate of inflation is not high enough to make much of a difference.)

Anticipated inflation
The inflation rate that we believe will occur; when it does, we are in a situation of fully anticipated inflation.

Unanticipated inflation
Inflation at a rate that comes as a surprise, either higher or lower than the rate anticipated.

Nominal rate of interest
The market rate of interest observed on contracts expressed in today's dollars.

Real rate of interest
The nominal rate of interest minus the anticipated rate of inflation.

Does Inflation Necessarily Hurt Everyone?

Most people think that inflation is bad. After all, inflation means higher prices, and when we have to pay higher prices, are we not necessarily worse off? The truth is that inflation affects different people differently. Its effects also depend on whether it is anticipated or unanticipated.

UNANTICIPATED INFLATION: CREDITORS LOSE AND DEBTORS GAIN In most situations, unanticipated inflation benefits borrowers because the nominal interest rate they are being charged does not fully compensate creditors for the inflation that actually occurred. In other words, the lender did not anticipate inflation correctly. Whenever inflation rates are underestimated for the life of a loan, creditors lose and debtors gain. Periods of considerable unanticipated (higher than anticipated) inflation occurred in the late 1960s and all of the 1970s. During those years, creditors lost and debtors gained.

PROTECTING AGAINST INFLATION Lenders attempt to protect themselves against inflation by raising nominal interest rates to reflect anticipated inflation. Adjustable-rate mortgages in fact do just that: The interest rate varies according to what happens to interest rates in the economy. Workers can protect themselves from inflation by obtaining **cost-of-living adjustments (COLAs),** which are automatic increases in wage rates to take account of increases in the price level.

> **Cost-of-living adjustments (COLAs)**
> Clauses in contracts that allow for increases in specified nominal values to take account of changes in the cost of living.

To the extent that you hold non-interest-bearing cash, you will lose because of inflation. If you have put $100 in a mattress and the inflation rate is 5 percent for the year, you will have lost 5 percent of the purchasing power of that $100. If you have your funds in a non-interest-bearing checking account, you will suffer the same fate. Individuals attempt to reduce the cost of holding cash by putting it into interest-bearing accounts, a wide variety of which often pay nominal rates of interest that reflect anticipated inflation.

THE RESOURCE COST OF INFLATION Some economists believe that the main cost of inflation is the opportunity cost of resources used to protect against distortions that inflation introduces as firms attempt to plan for the long run. Individuals have to spend time and resources to figure out ways to adjust their behavior in case inflation is different from what it has been in the past. That may mean spending a longer time working out more complicated contracts for employment, for purchases of goods in the future, and for purchases of raw materials.

Inflation requires that price lists be changed. This is called the **repricing,** or **menu, cost of inflation.** The higher the rate of inflation, the higher the repricing cost of inflation, because prices must be changed more often within a given period of time.

> **Repricing,** or **menu, cost of inflation**
> The cost associated with recalculating prices and printing new price lists when there is inflation.

QUICK QUIZ *See page 183 for the answers. Review concepts from this section in MyEconLab.*

Whenever inflation is _____ than anticipated, creditors lose and debtors gain. Whenever the rate of inflation is _____ than anticipated, creditors gain and debtors lose.

Holders of cash lose during periods of inflation because the _____ _____ of their cash depreciates at the rate of inflation.

Households and businesses spend resources in attempting to protect themselves against the prospect of inflation, thus imposing a _____ cost on the economy.

Changing Inflation and Unemployment: Business Fluctuations

Business fluctuations
The ups and downs in business activity throughout the economy.

Expansion
A business fluctuation in which the pace of national economic activity is speeding up.

Contraction
A business fluctuation during which the pace of national economic activity is slowing down.

Recession
A period of time during which the rate of growth of business activity is consistently less than its long-term trend or is negative.

Depression
An extremely severe recession.

Some years unemployment goes up, and some years it goes down. Some years there is a lot of inflation, and other years there isn't. We have fluctuations in all aspects of our macroeconomy. The ups and downs in economywide economic activity are sometimes called **business fluctuations.** When business fluctuations are positive, they are called **expansions**—speedups in the pace of national economic activity. The opposite of an expansion is a **contraction,** which is a slowdown in the pace of national economic activity. The top of an expansion is usually called its *peak*, and the bottom of a contraction is usually called its *trough*. Business fluctuations used to be called *business cycles*, but that term no longer seems appropriate because *cycle* implies regular or automatic recurrence, and we have never had automatic recurrent fluctuations in general business and economic activity. What we have had are contractions and expansions that vary greatly in length. For example, the 10 post–World War II expansions have averaged 57 months, but three of those exceeded 90 months, and two lasted less than 25 months.

If the contractionary phase of business fluctuations becomes severe enough, we call it a **recession.** An extremely severe recession is called a **depression.** Typically, at the beginning of a recession, interest rates rise and as the recession gets worse, they fall. In addition, people's incomes start to fall, and the duration of unemployment increases so that the unemployment rate increases. In times of expansion, the opposite occurs.

In Figure 7-5, you see that typical business fluctuations occur around a growth trend in overall national business activity shown as a straight upward-sloping line. Starting out at a peak, the economy goes into a contraction (recession). Then an expansion starts that moves up to its peak, higher than the last one, and the sequence starts over again.

FIGURE 7-5

The Idealized Course of Business Fluctuations

A hypothetical business cycle would go from peak to trough and back again in a regular cycle. Real-world business cycles are not as regular as this hypothetical cycle.

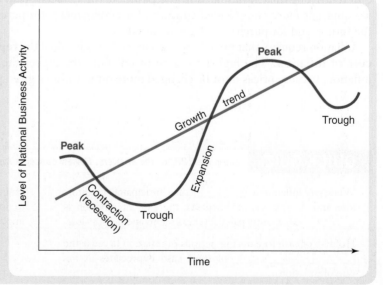

A Historical Picture of Business Activity in the United States

Figure 7-6 traces changes in U.S. business activity from 1880 to the present. Note that the long-term trend line is shown as horizontal, so all changes in business activity focus around that trend line. Major changes in business activity in the United States occurred during the Great Depression, World War II, and, most recently, the Great Recession of the late 2000s. Note that none of the actual business fluctuations in Figure 7-6 exactly mirror the idealized course of a business fluctuation shown in Figure 7-5.

Go to **www.econtoday.com/chapter07** to learn about how economists at the National Bureau of Economic Research formally determine when a recession started.

Explaining Business Fluctuations: External Shocks

As you might imagine, because changes in national business activity affect everyone, economists for decades have attempted to understand and explain business fluctuations. For years, one of the most obvious explanations has been external events that tend to disrupt the economy. In many of the graphs in this chapter, you have seen that World War II was a critical point in this nation's economic history. A war is certainly an external shock—something that originates outside our economy.

To try to help account for shocks to economic activity that may induce business fluctuations and thereby make fluctuations easier to predict, the U.S. Department of Commerce and private firms and organizations tabulate indexes (weighted averages) of **leading indicators.** These are events that economists have noticed typically occur *before* changes in business activity. For example, economic downturns often follow such events

Leading indicators

Events that have been found to occur before changes in business activity.

FIGURE 7-6

National Business Activity, 1880 to the Present

Variations around the trend of U.S. business activity have been frequent since 1880.

Sources: *American Business Activity from 1790 to Today,* 67th ed., AmeriTrust Co., January 1996, plus author's estimates.

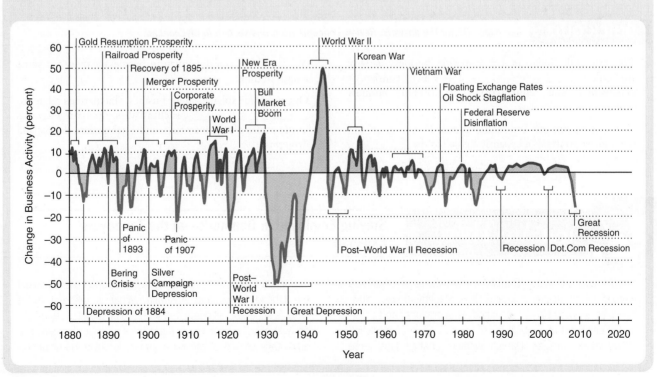

as a reduction in the average workweek, an increase in unemployment insurance claims, a decrease in the prices of raw materials, or a drop in the quantity of money in circulation.

To better understand the role of shocks in influencing business fluctuations, we need a theory of why national economic activity changes. The remainder of the macro chapters in this book develop the models that will help you understand the ups and downs of our business fluctuations.

Why are a few forecasters contemplating using sales of printer cartridges as a leading indicator of business fluctuations?

E-COMMERCE EXAMPLE
Failure to Hit the Print Icon May Yield a New Leading Indicator

During the most significant business downturn since World War II, economic analysts of the late 2000s noticed that another downturn was in progress. Sales of printer cartridges by Hewlett-Packard and other producers of printing consumables, which had displayed positive annual growth rates for years, started to decline just before the recession began. Furthermore, sales dropped even more just before the recession picked up steam in the first and second quarters of 2009. Now some forecasters have added sales of printer cartridges to their list of potential leading indicators. Current choices by businesses and individuals to print fewer pages, the forecasters theorize, may reflect decisions to produce fewer goods and services in the future.

FOR CRITICAL ANALYSIS

Can you suggest a rationale for why reductions in printed pages could suggest that firms may be about to cut back on production of new goods and services

QUICK QUIZ   *See page 183 for the answers. Review concepts from this section in MyEconLab.*

The ups and downs in economywide business activity are called _____ _____, which consist of **expansions** and **contractions** in overall business activity.

The lowest point of a contraction is called the _____; the highest point of an expansion is called the _____.

A _____ is a downturn in business activity for some length of time.

One possible explanation for business fluctuations relates to _____ _____, such as wars, dramatic increases in the prices of raw materials, and earthquakes, floods, and droughts.

You Are There ▸ Staying Employed in Denmark—at the Taxpayers' Expense

For just over 10 years, Danish resident Susanne Olsen has worked as an unskilled laborer in a slaughterhouse. Now, however, the company has halted its operations, and Olsen finds herself out of a job. It is not unusual to be unemployed in Denmark. Indeed, Danish workers change jobs more frequently than workers in any other developed nation except the United States and Australia. What is different about Olsen's situation, as compared with the circumstances a U.S. or Australian worker would encounter, is that she can take advantage of one of the most generous government unem-

You Are There   (cont.)

ployment programs on the planet. Now the Danish government's Public Employment Service has placed Olsen in a position as an apprentice golf landscaper. Her wages will be subsidized by the Danish government for the next four years. Many of her former slaughterhouse co-workers likewise have begun government-subsidized jobs with new employers.

Olsen knows that subsidizing jobs for all recent Danish job losers, including Olsen and her former co-workers, is very costly to taxpayers. In fact, the government spends about 4.4 percent of annual national income to support newly unemployed workers and subsidize their retraining. On average, therefore, every Danish resident contributes the

equivalent of about $1,600 per year in taxes that the government uses to subsidize recent job losers.

CRITICAL ANALYSIS QUESTIONS

1. What are the likely effects of Denmark's retraining subsidy program on the nation's average duration of unemployment?

2. Danish residents who are simply between jobs are not eligible for subsidies from the government, so does the retraining program have any effect on the nation's level of frictional unemployment?

Issues and Applications

What Is an Economic Depression?

CONCEPTS APPLIED

- Contraction
- Recession
- Depression

When the U.S. economy contracted in late 2007 and then slipped into a much deeper recession in 2008 through 2010, many people began to wonder if a downslide into an economic depression might be under way. Economists agree that a depression is an extremely severe recession, but they do not agree on how to define "extremely severe." Some define a depression in terms of long-lasting decreases in the inflation-adjusted value of the flow in the nation's output of goods and services. Others define a depression as an enduring spell of high unemployment.

A Production-Focused Definition of a Depression

The most common definition of an economic depression is a peak-to-trough drop of at least 10 percent in the production of goods and services that persists at least three years. Figure 7-7 on the next page displays nations that, based on these criteria, have experienced peacetime depressions during the past century.

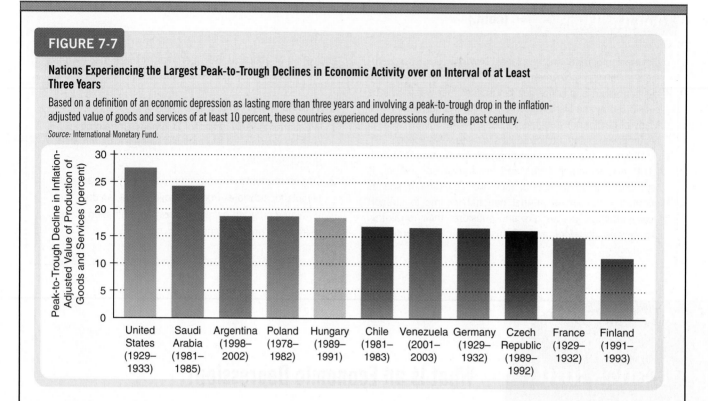

FIGURE 7-7

Nations Experiencing the Largest Peak-to-Trough Declines in Economic Activity over on Interval of at Least Three Years

Based on a definition of an economic depression as lasting more than three years and involving a peak-to-trough drop in the inflation-adjusted value of goods and services of at least 10 percent, these countries experienced depressions during the past century.

Source: International Monetary Fund.

Absent from the list are some very sharp contractions that fail to satisfy the three-year criterion, such as the 13 percent drop in U.S. output of goods and services between 1937 and 1938. Missing as well are Japan's series of downturns in the 1990s and the U.S. Great Recession of the late 2000s, which also fail to meet the minimum-three-year criterion for defining an economic depression.

Defining a Depression in Terms of the Unemployment Rate

Some economists define a depression in terms of its impact on jobs. Thus, an alternative definition of a depression is a period of stagnant or declining production in which the unemployment rate remains above 10 percent for at least three years. According to this definition, the United States unambiguously experienced a depression over the entire period stretching from 1930 to World War II (see Figure 7-1 on page 161). In contrast, the nation did not experience a depression in the early 1980s, when the unemployment rate reached 10 percent for only a few months.

Some define a depression using an unemployment rate that the U.S. Bureau of Labor Statistics calls *U6*. The numerator of U6 sums all people who are unemployed, people who are employed part-time but are seeking full-time work, and those who are "marginally attached" to the labor force—meaning that they are not currently in the labor force but were within the past 12 months. The denominator is the sum of the labor force and those who are "marginally attached." Again, using the definition of a depression as a three-year period in which the U6 unemployment rate exceeds 15 percent, the United States was in a depression during the entire decade from 1930 to World War II.

Under either unemployment-based depression definition, the United States may have entered a depression in 2008 or 2009, when the standard unemployment rate reached 10 percent and U6 topped 16 percent. Whether the nation experiences an unemployment-based depression depends on how long high unemployment lasts.

Test your understanding of this chapter by going online to **MyEconLab**.
In the Study Plan for this chapter, select Section N: News.

For Critical Analysis

1. In light of the fact that a rise in the unemployment rate often follows a decline in inflation-adjusted production of goods and services, why might starting dates of depressions differ under the alternative definitions?

2. Would you anticipate that the U6 unemployment rate is usually higher or lower than the standard unemployment rate? Explain your reasoning.

Web Resources

1. To compare different unemployment rate measures computed by the U.S. Bureau of Labor Statistics, go to www.econtoday.com/chapter07.

2. To view the official dates for U.S. business fluctuations determined by the National Bureau of Economic Research, go to www.econtoday.com/chapter07.

Research Project

Sometimes countries have experienced what some economists call "jobless recoveries," during which the unemployment rate remains high even as the inflation-adjusted value of the production of goods and services rises following the trough of a business cycle. Discuss why this might lead to depression periods being of different lengths depending on whether a depression is defined as a production decrease during at least a three-year downturn or as a high unemployment rate persisting longer than three years. Why might it be possible for a nation to experience a depression based on one of the definitions but not the other?

Here is what you should know after reading this chapter. **MyEconLab** will help you identify what you know, and where to go when you need to practice.

WHAT YOU SHOULD KNOW

How the U.S. Government Calculates the Official Unemployment Rate The total number of workers who are officially unemployed consists of noninstitutionalized people aged 16 or older who are willing and able to work and who are actively looking for work but have not found a job. To calculate the unemployment rate, the government determines what percentage this quantity is of the labor force, which consists of all noninstitutionalized people aged 16 years or older who either have jobs or are available for and actively seeking employment. Thus, the official unemployment rate does not include discouraged workers who have stopped looking for work because they are convinced that they will not find suitable employment. These individuals are not included in the labor force.

unemployment, 160
labor force, 160
stock, 162
flow, 162
job loser, 162
reentrant, 162
job leaver, 162
new entrant, 163
discouraged workers, 163
labor force participation
  rate, 163

KEY FIGURE
Figure 7-3, 162

WHERE TO GO TO PRACTICE

- **MyEconLab** Study Plan 7.1
- Audio introduction to Chapter 7
- Animated Figure 7-3
- ABC News Video: The Ripple Effect of Oil Prices

(*continued*)

 *(continued)*

WHAT YOU SHOULD KNOW		WHERE TO GO TO PRACTICE
The Types of Unemployment Workers who are temporarily unemployed because they are searching for appropriate job offers are frictionally unemployed. The structurally unemployed lack the skills currently required by prospective employers. People unemployed due to business contractions are said to be cyclically unemployed. And certain workers find themselves seasonally unemployed because of the seasonal patterns of occupations within specific industries. The natural unemployment rate is the seasonally adjusted rate of unemployment including only those who are frictionally and structurally unemployed during a given interval.	frictional unemployment, 164 structural unemployment, 164 cyclical unemployment, 165 seasonal unemployment, 165 full employment, 166 natural rate of unemployment, 166	• **MyEconLab** Study Plans 7.2, 7.3 • Video: Major Types of Unemployment
How Price Indexes Are Calculated and Key Price Indexes To calculate any price index, economists multiply 100 times the ratio of the cost of a market basket of goods and services in the current year to the cost of the same market basket in a base year. The market basket used to compute the Consumer Price Index (CPI) is a weighted set of goods and services purchased by a typical consumer in urban areas. The Producer Price Index (PPI) is a weighted average of prices of goods sold by a typical firm. The GDP deflator measures changes in the overall level of prices of all goods produced in the economy during a given interval. The Personal Consumption Expenditure (PCE) Index is a statistical measure of average prices using weights from annual surveys of consumer spending.	inflation, 167 deflation, 167 purchasing power, 167 price index, 168 base year, 168 Consumer Price Index (CPI), 169 Producer Price Index (PPI), 169 GDP deflator, 169 Personal Consumption Expenditure (PCE) Index, 169 KEY FIGURE Figure 7-4, 171	• **MyEconLab** Study Plan 7.4 • Video: Measuring the Rate of Inflation • Video: Inflation and Interest Rates • Animated Figure 7-4
Nominal Interest Rate versus Real Interest Rate The nominal interest rate is the market rate of interest applying to contracts expressed in current dollars. The real interest rate is net of inflation that borrowers and lenders anticipate will erode the value of nominal interest payments during the period that a loan is repaid. Hence, the real interest rate equals the nominal interest rate minus the expected inflation rate.	anticipated inflation, 172 unanticipated inflation, 172 nominal rate of interest, 172 real rate of interest, 172	• **MyEconLab** Study Plan 7.5
Losers and Gainers from Inflation Creditors lose as a result of unanticipated inflation that comes as a surprise after they have made a loan, because the real value of the interest payments they receive will turn out to be lower than they had expected. Borrowers gain when unanticipated inflation occurs, because the real value of their interest and principal payments declines. Key costs of inflation are the expenses that people incur to protect themselves against inflation, costs of altering business plans because of unexpected changes in prices, and menu costs arising from expenses incurred in repricing goods and services.	cost-of-living adjustments (COLAs), 173 repricing, or menu, cost of inflation, 173	• **MyEconLab** Study Plan 7.5

(continued)

 *(continued)*

WHAT YOU SHOULD KNOW

| | WHERE TO GO TO PRACTICE |

Key Features of Business Fluctuations Business fluctuations are increases and decreases in business activity. A positive fluctuation is an expansion, which is an upward movement in business activity from a trough, or low point, to a peak, or high point. A negative fluctuation is a contraction, which is a drop in the pace of business activity from a previous peak to a new trough.

business fluctuations, 174
expansion, 174
contraction, 174
recession, 174
depression, 174
leading indicators, 175

KEY FIGURE
Figure 7-6, 175

WHERE TO GO TO PRACTICE

- **MyEconLab** Study Plan 7.6
- Animated Figure 7-6

Log in to MyEconLab, take a chapter test, and get a personalized Study Plan that tells you which concepts you understand and which ones you need to review. From there, MyEconLab will give you further practice, tutorials, animations, videos, and guided solutions.
Log in to www.myeconlab.com

PROBLEMS

All problems are assignable in **myeconlab** *. Answers to odd-numbered problems appear at the back of the book.*

7-1. Suppose that you are given the following information:

Total population	300.0 million
Adult, noninstitutionalized, nonmilitary population	200.0 million
Unemployment	7.5 million

   a. If the labor force participation rate is 70 percent, what is the labor force?

   b. How many workers are employed?

   c. What is the unemployment rate?

7-2. Suppose that you are given the following information:

Labor force	206.2 million
Adults in the military	1.5 million
Nonadult population	48.0 million
Employed adults	196.2 million
Institutionalized adults	3.5 million
Nonmilitary, noninstitutionalized adults not in labor force	40.8 million

   a. What is the total population?

   b. How many people are unemployed, and what is the unemployment rate?

   c. What is the labor force participation rate?

7-3. Suppose that the U.S. adult population is 224 million, the number employed is 156 million, and the number unemployed is 8 million.

   a. What is the unemployment rate?

   b. Suppose that there is a difference of 60 million between the adult population and the combined total of people who are employed and unemployed. How do we classify these 60 million people? Based on these figures, what is the U.S. labor force participation rate?

7-4. During the course of a year, the labor force consists of the same 1,000 people. Employers have chosen not to hire 20 of these people in the face of government regulations making it to costly to employ them. Hence, they remain unemployed throughout the year. At the same time, every month during the year, 30 different people become unemployed, and 30 other different people who were unemployed find jobs. There is no seasonal employment.

a. What is the frictional unemployment rate?

b. What is the unemployment rate?

c. Suppose that a system of unemployment compensation is established. Each month, 30 new people (not including the 20 that employers have chosen not to employ) continue to become unemployed, but each monthly group of newly unemployed now takes two months to find a job. After this change, what is the frictional unemployment rate?

d. After the change discussed in part (c), what is the unemployment rate?

7-5. Suppose that a nation has a labor force of 100 people. In January, Amy, Barbara, Carine, and Denise are unemployed; in February, those four find jobs, but Evan, Francesco, George, and Horatio become unemployed. Suppose further that every month, the previous four who were unemployed find jobs and four different people become unemployed. Throughout the year, however, the same three people—Ito, Jack, and Kelley—continually remain unemployed because firms facing government regulations view them as too costly to employ.

a. What is this nation's frictional unemployment rate?

b. What is its structural unemployment rate?

c. What is its unemployment rate?

7-6. In a country with a labor force of 200, a different group of 10 people becomes unemployed each month, but becomes employed once again a month later. No others outside these groups are unemployed.

a. What is this country's unemployment rate?

b. What is the average duration of unemployment?

c. Suppose that establishment of a system of unemployment compensation increases to two months the interval that it takes each group of job losers to become employed each month. Nevertheless, a different group of 10 people still becomes unemployed each month. Now what is the average duration of unemployment?

d. Following the change discussed in part (c), what is the country's unemployment rate?

7-7. A nation's frictional unemployment rate is 1 percent. Seasonal unemployment does not exist in this country. Its cyclical rate of unemployment is 3 percent, and its structural unemployment rate is 4 percent. What is this nation's overall rate of unemployment? What is its natural rate of unemployment?

7-8. In 2008, the cost of a market basket of goods was $2,000. In 2010, the cost of the same market basket of goods was $2,100. Use the price index formula to calculate the price index for 2010 if 2008 is the base year.

7-9. Consider the following price indexes: 90 in 2009, 100 in 2010, 110 in 2011, 121 in 2012, and 150 in 2013. Answer the following questions.

a. What is the base year?

b. What is the inflation rate from 2010 to 2011?

c. What is the inflation rate from 2011 to 2012?

d. If the cost of a market basket in 2010 is $2,000, what is the cost of the same basket of goods and services in 2009? In 2013?

7-10. The real interest rate is 4 percent, and the nominal interest rate is 6 percent. What is the anticipated rate of inflation?

7-11. Currently, the price index used to calculate the inflation rate is equal to 90. The general expectation throughout the economy is that next year its value will be 99. The current nominal interest rate is 12 percent. What is the real interest rate?

7-12. At present, the nominal interest rate is 7 percent, and the expected inflation rate is 5 percent. The current year is the base year for the price index used to calculate inflation.

a. What is the real interest rate?

b. What is the anticipated value of the price index next year?

7-13. Suppose that in 2013 there is a sudden, unanticipated burst of inflation. Consider the situations faced by the following individuals. Who gains and who loses?

a. A homeowner whose wages will keep pace with inflation in 2013 but whose monthly mortgage payments to a savings bank will remain fixed

b. An apartment landlord who has guaranteed to his tenants that their monthly rent payments during 2013 will be the same as they were during 2012

c. A banker who made an auto loan that the auto buyer will repay at a fixed rate of interest during 2013

d. A retired individual who earns a pension with fixed monthly payments from her past employer during 2013

7-14. Consider the diagram in the next column. The line represents the economy's growth trend, and the curve represents the economy's actual course of business fluctuations. For each part at the right, provide the letter label from the portion of the curve that corresponds to the associated term.

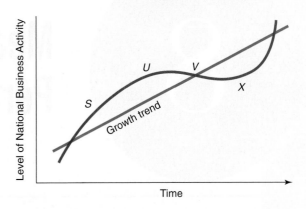

a. Contraction

b. Peak

c. Trough

d. Expansion

ECONOMICS ON THE NET

Looking at the Unemployment and Inflation Data This chapter reviewed key concepts relating to unemployment and inflation. In this application, you get a chance to examine U.S. unemployment and inflation data on your own.

Title: Bureau of Labor Statistics: Employment and Unemployment

Navigation: Use the link at **www.econtoday.com/chapter07** to visit the "Employment & Unemployment" page of the Bureau of Labor Statistics (BLS). Click on *Labor Force Statistics from the Current Population Survey.*

Application Perform the indicated operations, and answer the following questions.

1. Click checkmarks in the boxes for Civilian Labor Force Level, Employment Level, and Unemployment Level. Retrieve the data, and click a checkmark next to "include graphs." Can you identify periods of sharp cyclical swings? Do they show up in data for the labor force, employment, or unemployment?

2. Are cyclical factors important?

For Group Study and Analysis Divide the class into groups, and assign a price index to each group. Ask each group to take a look at the index for All Years at the link to the BLS statistics on inflation at **www.econtoday.com/chapter07.** Have each group identify periods during which their index accelerated or decelerated (or even fell). Do the indexes ever provide opposing implications about inflation and deflation?

ANSWERS TO QUICK QUIZZES

p. 164: (i) Unemployed . . . labor force; (ii) job losers . . . reentrants . . . job leavers . . . new entrants; (iii) increase; (iv) female

p. 167: (i) Frictional . . . Structural; (ii) natural

p. 172: (i) base; (ii) Consumer Price; (iii) GDP deflator; (iv) Personal Consumption Expenditure

p. 173: (i) greater . . . less; (ii) purchasing power; (iii) resource

p. 176: (i) business fluctuations; (ii) trough . . . peak; (iii) recession; (iv) external shocks

8 Measuring the Economy's Performance

Between 2006 and 2009, the average price of houses in the United States declined by nearly 20 percent. During the same period, the average price of shares of stock in U.S. corporations declined by close to 60 percent. Dozens of banks and other financial institutions failed. In addition, the U.S. economy experienced its most severe recession since 1947. Why are periods of particularly poor national economic performance so often associated with major financial breakdowns? To consider the answer to this question, you must first understand how we measure the economic performance of a country's economy, which is the topic of this chapter.

LEARNING OBJECTIVES

MyEconLab helps you master each objective and study more efficiently. See end of chapter for details.

After reading this chapter, you should be able to:

- Describe the circular flow of income and output
- Define gross domestic product (GDP)
- Understand the limitations of using GDP as a measure of national welfare
- Explain the expenditure approach to tabulating GDP
- Explain the income approach to computing GDP
- Distinguish between nominal GDP and real GDP

? DID YOU KNOW THAT during the past half-century, manufactured goods' share of total U.S. output of goods and services has declined by more than one-half? The value of manufactured goods as a percentage of *gross domestic product,* the government's key measure of overall annual economic activity, has fallen from about 28 percent in 1955 to less than 12 percent today.

The government conducts what has become known as **national income accounting** in an effort to measure the nation's overall economic performance over time. How this is done is the main focus of this chapter. But first we need to look at the flow of income within an economy, for it is the flow of goods and services from businesses to consumers and of payments from consumers to businesses that constitutes economic activity.

National income accounting
A measurement system used to estimate national income and its components; one approach to measuring an economy's aggregate performance.

The Simple Circular Flow

The concept of a circular flow of income (ignoring taxes) involves two principles:

1. In every economic exchange, the seller receives exactly the same amount that the buyer spends.
2. Goods and services flow in one direction and money payments flow in the other.

In the simple economy shown in Figure 8-1 on the following page, there are only businesses and households. It is assumed that businesses sell their *entire* output in the current period to households and that households spend their *entire* income in the current period on consumer products. Households receive their income by selling the use of whatever factors of production they own, such as labor services.

Profits Explained

We have indicated in Figure 8-1 that profit is a cost of production. You might be under the impression that profits are not part of the cost of producing goods and services, but profits are indeed a part of this cost because entrepreneurs must be rewarded for providing their services or they won't provide them. Their reward, if any, is profit. The reward—the profit—is included in the cost of the factors of production. If there were no expectations of profit, entrepreneurs would not incur the risk associated with the organization of productive activities. That is why we consider profits a cost of doing business.

Total Income or Total Output

The arrow that goes from businesses to households at the bottom of Figure 8-1 is labeled "Total income." What would be a good definition of **total income?** If you answered "the total of all individuals' income," you would be right. But all income is actually a payment for something, whether it be wages paid for labor services, rent paid for the use of land, interest paid for the use of capital, or profits paid to entrepreneurs. It is the amount paid to the resource suppliers. Therefore, total income is also defined as the annual *cost* of producing the entire output of **final goods and services.**

The arrow going from households to businesses at the top of the figure represents the dollar value of output in the economy. This is equal to the total monetary value of all final goods and services for this simple economy. In essence, it represents the total business receipts from the sale of all final goods and services produced by businesses and consumed by households. Business receipts are the opposite side of household expenditures. When households purchase goods and services, those payments become a *business receipt.* Every transaction, therefore, simultaneously involves an expenditure and a receipt.

Total income
The yearly amount earned by the nation's resources (factors of production). Total income therefore includes wages, rent, interest payments, and profits that are received by workers, landowners, capital owners, and entrepreneurs, respectively.

Final goods and services
Goods and services that are at their final stage of production and will not be transformed into yet other goods or services. For example, wheat ordinarily is not considered a final good because it is usually used to make a final good, bread.

FIGURE 8-1

The Circular Flow of Income and Product

Businesses provide final goods and services to households (upper clockwise loop), who in turn pay for them (upper counterclockwise loop). Payments flow in a counterclockwise direction and can be thought of as a circular flow. The dollar value of output is identical to total income because profits are defined as being equal to total business receipts minus business outlays for wages, rents, and interest. Households provide factor services to businesses and receive income (lower loops).

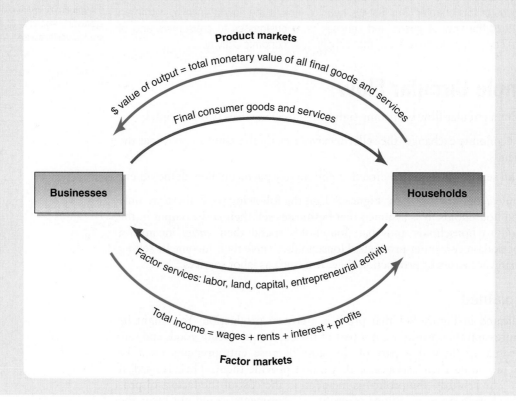

PRODUCT MARKETS Transactions in which households buy goods take place in the product markets—that's where households are the buyers and businesses are the sellers of consumer goods. *Product market* transactions are represented in the upper loops in Figure 8-1. Note that consumer goods and services flow to household demanders, while money flows in the opposite direction to business suppliers.

FACTOR MARKETS *Factor market* transactions are represented by the lower loops in Figure 8-1. In the factor market, households are the sellers; they sell resources such as labor, land, capital, and entrepreneurial ability. Businesses are the buyers in factor markets; business expenditures represent receipts or, more simply, income for households. Also, in the lower loops of Figure 8-1, factor services flow from households to businesses, while the money paid for these services flows in the opposite direction from businesses to households. Observe also the flow of money (counterclockwise) from households to businesses and back again from businesses to households: It is an endless circular flow.

Why the Dollar Value of Total Output Must Equal Total Income

Total income represents the income received by households in payment for the production of goods and services. Why must total income be identical to the dollar value of total output? First, as Figure 8-1 shows, spending by one group is income to another. Second, it is a matter of simple accounting and the economic definition of profit as a cost of production. Profit is defined as what is *left over* from total business receipts after all other costs—wages, rents, interest—have been paid. If the dollar value of total output is $1,000 and the total of wages, rent, and interest for producing that output is $900, profit is $100. Profit is always the *residual* item that makes total income equal to the dollar value of total output.

QUICK QUIZ	*See page 212 for the answers. Review concepts from this section in MyEconLab.*

In the circular flow model of income and output, households sell _____ services to businesses that pay for those services. The receipt of payments is total _____. Businesses sell goods and services to households that pay for them.	The dollar value of total output is equal to the total monetary value of all _____ goods and services produced. The dollar value of final output must always equal total income; the variable that adjusts to make this so is known as _____.

National Income Accounting

We have already mentioned that policymakers require information about the state of the national economy. Economists use historical statistical records on the performance of the national economy in testing their theories about how the economy really works. Thus, national income accounting is important. Let's start with the most commonly presented statistic on the national economy.

Gross Domestic Product (GDP)

Gross domestic product (GDP) represents the total market value of the nation's annual final product, or output, produced by factors of production located within national borders. We therefore formally define GDP as the total market value of all final goods and services produced in an economy during a year. We are referring here to the value of a *flow of production*. A nation produces at a certain rate, just as you receive income at a certain rate. Your income flow might be at a rate of $20,000 per year or $100,000 per year. Suppose you are told that someone earns $5,000. Would you consider this a good salary? There is no way to answer that question unless you know whether the person is earning $5,000 per month or per week or per day. Thus, you have to specify a time period for all flows. Income received is a flow. You must contrast this with, for example, your total accumulated savings, which are a stock measured at a point in time, not over time. Implicit in just about everything we deal with in this chapter is a time period—usually one year. All the measures of domestic product and income are specified as *rates* measured in dollars per year.

Gross domestic product (GDP)
The total market value of all final goods and services produced during a year by factors of production located within a nation's borders.

Stress on Final Output

Intermediate goods
Goods used up entirely in the production of final goods.

GDP does not count **intermediate goods** (goods used up entirely in the production of final goods) because to do so would be to count them twice. For example, even though grain that a farmer produces may be that farmer's final product, it is not the final product for the nation. It is sold to make bread. Bread is the final product.

We can use a numerical example to clarify this point further. Our example will involve determining the value added at each stage of production. **Value added** is the amount of dollar value contributed to a product at each stage of its production. In Table 8-1, we see the difference between total value of all sales and value added in the production of a donut. We also see that the sum of the values added is equal to the sale price to the final consumer. It is the 45 cents that is used to measure GDP, not the 96 cents. If we used the 96 cents, we would be double counting from stages 2 through 5, for each intermediate good would be counted at least twice—once when it was produced and again when the good it was used in making was sold. Such double counting would grossly exaggerate GDP.

Value added
The dollar value of an industry's sales minus the value of intermediate goods (for example, raw materials and parts) used in production.

TABLE 8-1

Sales Value and Value Added at Each Stage of Donut Production

(1) Stage of Production	(2) Dollar Value of Sales	(3) Value Added
Stage 1: Fertilizer and seed	$.03	$.03
Stage 2: Growing	.06	.03
Stage 3: Milling	.12	.06
Stage 4: Baking	.30	.18
Stage 5: Retailing	.45	.15
Total dollar value of all sales $.96		Total value added $.45

Stage 1: A farmer purchases 3 cents' worth of fertilizer and seed, which are used as factors of production in growing wheat.

Stage 2: The farmer grows the wheat, harvests it, and sells it to a miller for 6 cents. Thus, we see that the farmer has added 3 cents' worth of value. Those 3 cents represent income over and above expenses incurred by the farmer.

Stage 3: The miller purchases the wheat for 6 cents and adds 6 cents as the value added; that is, there is 6 cents for the miller as income. The miller sells the ground wheat flour to a donut-baking company.

Stage 4: The donut-baking company buys the flour for 12 cents and adds 18 cents as the value added. It then sells the donut to the final retailer.

Stage 5: The donut retailer sells donuts at 45 cents apiece, thus creating an additional value of 15 cents.

We see that the total value of the transactions involved in the production of one donut is 96 cents, but the total value added is 45 cents, which is exactly equal to the retail price. The total value added is equal to the sum of all income payments.

Exclusion of Financial Transactions, Transfer Payments, and Secondhand Goods

Remember that GDP is the measure of the dollar value of all final goods and services produced in one year. Many more transactions occur that have nothing to do with final goods and services produced. There are financial transactions, transfers of the ownership of preexisting goods, and other transactions that should not and do not get included in our measure of GDP.

FINANCIAL TRANSACTIONS There are three general categories of purely financial transactions: (1) the buying and selling of securities, (2) government transfer payments, and (3) private transfer payments.

Securities. When you purchase shares of existing stock in Microsoft Corporation, someone else has sold it to you. In essence, there was merely a *transfer* of ownership rights. You paid $100 to obtain the stock. Someone else received the $100 and gave up the stock. No producing activity was consummated at that time, unless a broker received a fee for performing the transaction, in which case only the fee is part of GDP. The $100 transaction is not included when we measure GDP.

Government Transfer Payments. Transfer payments are payments for which no productive services are concurrently provided in exchange. The most obvious government transfer payments are Social Security benefits, veterans' payments, and unemployment compensation. The recipients make no contribution to current production in return for such transfer payments (although they may have contributed in the past to be eligible to receive them). Government transfer payments are not included in GDP.

Private Transfer Payments. Are you receiving funds from your parents in order to attend school? Has a wealthy relative ever given you a gift of cash? If so, you have been the recipient of a private transfer payment. This is merely a transfer of funds from one individual to another. As such, it does not constitute productive activity and is not included in GDP.

TRANSFER OF SECONDHAND GOODS If I sell you my two-year-old laptop computer, no current production is involved. I transfer to you the ownership of a computer that was produced years ago; in exchange, you transfer to me $350. The original purchase price of the computer was included in GDP in the year I purchased it. To include the price again when I sell it to you would be counting the value of the computer a second time.

OTHER EXCLUDED TRANSACTIONS Many other transactions are not included in GDP for practical reasons:

- Household production—housecleaning, child care, and other tasks performed by people in their *own* households and for which they are not paid through the marketplace
- Otherwise legal underground transactions—those that are legal but not reported and hence not taxed, such as paying housekeepers in cash that is not declared as income
- Illegal underground activities—these include prostitution, illegal gambling, and the sale of illicit drugs

Go to www.econtoday.com/chapter08 for the most up-to-date U.S. economic data at the Web site of the Bureau of Economic Analysis.

When this student bought her used computer, did that transaction add to the value of the nation's final goods and services?

You Are There

To contemplate gender differences in the performance of productive activities not included as part of gross domestic product, read **Housework's Exclusion from GDP Is Not Gender Neutral,** on pages 204 and 205.

What price did the Greek government pay for attempting to account for illegal activities in its GDP tabulations?

INTERNATIONAL POLICY EXAMPLE
Greece Pays a Price for Broadening Its GDP Definition

The government of Greece recently announced that its official tabulation of GDP would now include the total estimated value of production in black market industries, such as illegal gambling and prostitution. Consequently, the Greek government revised upward by about 25 percent its official GDP figures for every year since 2000. This change in GDP measurement came at a price, however. The European Union (EU), of which Greece is a member nation, makes regular payments to governments of the lowest-income EU mem-

bers. As a result of the big jump in its annual GDP figures, Greece was no longer officially as "poor" in the eyes of the EU, which reduced its annual payments to the Greek government by almost $600 million.

FOR CRITICAL ANALYSIS
Why do you suppose that economists now have a harder time comparing Greek GDP to the levels of GDP in other nations, such as the United States?

Recognizing the Limitations of GDP

Like any statistical measure, gross domestic product is a concept that can be both well used and misused. Economists find it especially valuable as an overall indicator of a nation's economic performance. But it is important to realize that GDP has significant weaknesses. Because it includes only the value of goods and services traded in markets, it excludes *nonmarket* production, such as the household services of homemakers discussed earlier. This can cause some problems in comparing the GDP of an industrialized country with the GDP of a highly agrarian nation in which nonmarket production is relatively more important. It also causes problems if nations have different definitions of legal versus illegal activities. For instance, a nation with legalized gambling will count the value of gambling services, which has a reported market value as a legal activity. But in a country where gambling is illegal, individuals who provide such services will not report the market value of gambling activities, and so they will not be counted in that country's GDP. This can complicate comparing GDP in the nation where gambling is legal with GDP in the country that prohibits gambling.

Furthermore, although GDP is often used as a benchmark measure for standard-of-living calculations, it is not necessarily a good measure of the well-being of a nation. No measured figure of total national annual income can take account of changes in the degree of labor market discrimination, declines or improvements in personal safety, or the quantity or quality of leisure time. Measured GDP also says little about our environmental quality of life. As the now-defunct Soviet Union illustrated to the world, the large-scale production of such items as minerals, electricity, and irrigation for farming can have negative effects on the environment: deforestation from strip mining, air and soil pollution from particulate emissions or nuclear accidents at power plants, and erosion of the natural balance between water and salt in bodies of water such as the Aral Sea. Other nations, such as China and India, have also experienced greater pollution problems as their levels of GDP have increased. Hence, it is important to recognize the following point:

GDP is a measure of the value of production in terms of market prices and an indicator of economic activity. It is not a measure of a nation's overall welfare.

Nonetheless, GDP is a relatively accurate and useful measure to map *changes* in the economy's domestic economic activity. Understanding GDP is thus important for recognizing changes in economic activity over time.

QUICK QUIZ   *See page 212 for the answers. Review concepts from this section in MyEconLab.*

_____ _____ _____ is the total market value of final goods and services produced in an economy during a one-year period by factors of production within the nation's borders. It represents the dollar value of the flow of final production over a one-year period.

To avoid double counting, we look only at final goods and services produced or, equivalently, at _____ _____ .

In measuring GDP, we must _____ (1) purely financial transactions, such as the buying and selling of securities; (2) government transfer payments and private transfer payments; and (3) the transfer of secondhand goods.

Many other transactions are excluded from measured _____, among them household services rendered by homemakers, underground economy transactions, and illegal economic activities, even though many of these result in the production of final goods and services.

GDP is a useful measure for tracking changes in the _____ _____ of overall economic activity over time, but it is not a measure of the well-being of a nation's residents because it fails to account for nonmarket transactions, the amount and quality of leisure time, environmental or safety issues, labor market discrimination, and other factors that influence general welfare.

Two Main Methods of Measuring GDP

The definition of GDP is the total value of all final goods and services produced during a year. How, exactly, do we go about actually computing this number?

The circular flow diagram presented in Figure 8-1 on page 186 gave us a shortcut method for calculating GDP. We can look at the *flow of expenditures*, which consists of consumption, investment, government purchases of goods and services, and net expenditures in the foreign sector (net exports). In this **expenditure approach** to measuring GDP, we add the dollar value of all final goods and services. We could also use the *flow of income*, looking at the income received by everybody producing goods and services. In this **income approach,** we add the income received by all factors of production.

Deriving GDP by the Expenditure Approach

To derive GDP using the expenditure approach, we must look at each of the separate components of expenditures and then add them together. These components are consumption expenditures, investment, government expenditures, and net exports.

CONSUMPTION EXPENDITURES How do we spend our income? As households or as individuals, we spend our income through consumption expenditure (*C*), which falls into three categories: **durable consumer goods, nondurable consumer goods,** and **services.** Durable goods are *arbitrarily* defined as items that last more than three years; they include automobiles, furniture, and household appliances. Nondurable goods are all the rest, such as food and gasoline. Services are intangible commodities: medical care, education, and the like.

Housing expenditures constitute a major proportion of anybody's annual expenditures. Rental payments on apartments are automatically included in consumption expenditure estimates. People who own their homes, however, do not make rental payments. Consequently, government statisticians estimate what is called the *implicit rental value* of

Expenditure approach
Computing GDP by adding up the dollar value at current market prices of all final goods and services.

Income approach
Measuring GDP by adding up all components of national income, including wages, interest, rent, and profits.

Durable consumer goods
Consumer goods that have a life span of more than three years.

Nondurable consumer goods
Consumer goods that are used up within three years.

Services
Mental or physical labor or help purchased by consumers. Examples are the assistance of physicians, lawyers, dentists, repair personnel, housecleaners, educators, retailers, and wholesalers; things purchased or used by consumers that do not have physical characteristics.

existing owner-occupied homes. It is roughly equal to the amount of rent you would have to pay if you did not own the home but were renting it from someone else.

GROSS PRIVATE DOMESTIC INVESTMENT We now turn our attention to **gross private domestic investment** (*I*) undertaken by businesses. When economists refer to investment, they are referring to additions to productive capacity. **Investment** may be thought of as an activity that uses resources today in such a way that they allow for greater production in the future and hence greater consumption in the future. When a business buys new equipment or puts up a new factory, it is investing; it is increasing its capacity to produce in the future.

In estimating gross private domestic investment, government statisticians also add consumer expenditures on *new* residential structures because new housing represents an addition to our future productive capacity in the sense that a new house can generate housing services in the future.

The layperson's notion of investment often relates to the purchase of stocks and bonds. For our purposes, such transactions simply represent the *transfer of ownership* of assets called stocks and bonds. Thus, you must keep in mind the fact that in economics, investment refers *only* to *additions* to productive capacity, not to transfers of assets.

FIXED VERSUS INVENTORY INVESTMENT In our analysis, we will consider the basic components of investment. We have already mentioned the first one, which involves a firm's buying equipment or putting up a new factory. These are called **producer durables, or capital goods.** A producer durable, or a capital good, is simply a good that is purchased not to be consumed in its current form but to be used to make other goods and services. The purchase of equipment and factories—capital goods—is called **fixed investment.**

The other type of investment has to do with the change in inventories of raw materials and finished goods. Firms do not immediately sell off all their products to consumers. Some of this final product is usually held in inventory waiting to be sold. Firms hold inventories to meet future expected orders for their products. When a firm increases its inventories of finished products, it is engaging in **inventory investment.** Inventories consist of all finished goods on hand, goods in process, and raw materials.

The reason that we can think of a change in inventories as being a type of investment is that an increase in such inventories provides for future increased consumption possibilities. When inventory investment is zero, the firm is neither adding to nor subtracting from the total stock of goods or raw materials on hand. Thus, if the firm keeps the same amount of inventories throughout the year, inventory *investment* has been zero.

GOVERNMENT EXPENDITURES In addition to personal consumption expenditures, there are government purchases of goods and services (*G*). The government buys goods and services from private firms and pays wages and salaries to government employees. Generally, we value goods and services at the prices at which they are sold. But many government goods and services are not sold in the market. Therefore, we cannot use their market value when computing GDP. The value of these goods is considered equal to their *cost*. For example, the value of a newly built road is considered equal to its construction cost and is included in the GDP for the year it was built.

NET EXPORTS (FOREIGN EXPENDITURES) To get an accurate representation of gross domestic product, we must include the foreign sector. As U.S. residents, we purchase foreign goods called *imports*. The goods that foreign residents purchase from us are our *exports*. To determine the *net* expenditures from the foreign sector, we subtract the value of imports from the value of exports to get net exports (*X*) for a year:

$$\text{Net exports } (X) = \text{total exports} - \text{total imports}$$

Gross private domestic investment
The creation of capital goods, such as factories and machines, that can yield production and hence consumption in the future. Also included in this definition are changes in business inventories and repairs made to machines or buildings.

Investment
Any use of today's resources to expand tomorrow's production or consumption.

Producer durables, or capital goods
Durable goods having an expected service life of more than three years that are used by businesses to produce other goods and services.

Fixed investment
Purchases by businesses of newly produced producer durables, or capital goods, such as production machinery and office equipment.

Inventory investment
Changes in the stocks of finished goods and goods in process, as well as changes in the raw materials that businesses keep on hand. Whenever inventories are decreasing, inventory investment is negative; whenever they are increasing, inventory investment is positive.

How are the expenditures on this recently built factory classified?

To understand why we subtract imports rather than ignoring them altogether, recall that we want to estimate *domestic* output, so we have to subtract U.S. expenditures on the goods produced in other nations.

Presenting the Expenditure Approach

We have just defined the components of GDP using the expenditure approach. When we add them all together, we get a definition for GDP, which is as follows:

$$GDP = C + I + G + X$$

where
C = consumption expenditures
I = investment expenditures
G = government expenditures
X = net exports

THE HISTORICAL PICTURE To get an idea of the relationship among C, I, G, and X, look at Figure 8-2 on the next page, which shows GDP, personal consumption expenditures, government purchases, and gross private domestic investment plus net exports since 1929. When we add up the expenditures of the household, business, government, and foreign sectors, we get GDP.

How does the Easter holiday's position in the calendar influence measured changes in Mexican GDP?

INTERNATIONAL EXAMPLE
How Easter Complicates Measuring Mexican GDP Growth

The Christian holiday Easter, which is a major holiday throughout Mexico, takes place on the first Sunday after the first full moon following the initial day of spring. In some years, Easter occurs before March 31 and hence during the first three-month period, or *quarter,* of the year. In other years, however, Easter falls after March 31 and hence during the second quarter.

Most Mexican companies halt operations and suspend sales for several days around the Easter holiday. This practice significantly depresses GDP during the affected quarter and influences percentage changes in GDP measured between quarters. Year-to-year measures of Mexican GDP growth are also affected. For instance, consider what happens when Easter happens to fall within the first quarter one year but the

second quarter of the following year. The percentage change in GDP between the first quarters of the two years is artificially lower as a result, but the percentage change in GDP between the second quarters of the two years is biased upward. Economists must always keep these Easter effects in mind when tracking Mexico's GDP from quarter to quarter or from year to year.

FOR CRITICAL ANALYSIS

How do you suppose that the Christmas holiday in the last week of December influences percentage changes in U.S. GDP from the third quarter to the fourth within a year and from the fourth quarter to the first quarter of the next year?

DEPRECIATION AND NET DOMESTIC PRODUCT We have used the terms *gross domestic product* and *gross private domestic investment* without really indicating what *gross* means. The dictionary defines it as "without deductions," the opposite of *net.* Deductions for what? you might ask. The deductions are for something we call **depreciation.** In the course of a year, machines and structures wear out or are used up in the production of domestic product. For example, houses deteriorate as they are occupied, and machines

Depreciation
Reduction in the value of capital goods over a one-year period due to physical wear and tear and also to obsolescence; also called *capital consumption allowance.*

FIGURE 8-2

GDP and Its Components

Here we see a display of gross domestic product, personal consumption expenditures, government purchases, and gross private domestic investment plus net exports for the years since 1929. Note that the scale of the vertical axis changes as we move up the axis. During the Great Depression of the 1930s, gross private domestic investment *plus* net exports was negative because we were investing very little at that time. During the 2000s, gross private domestic investment initially declined and then recovered slowly until the Great Recession when it turned sharply downward. Net exports also became increasingly negative. Hence, the sum of these two items has declined since 2007.

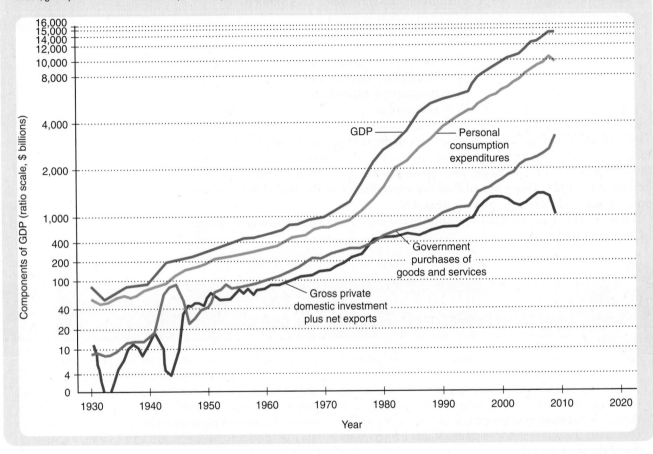

Net domestic product (NDP)
GDP minus depreciation.

Capital consumption allowance
Another name for depreciation, the amount that businesses would have to save in order to take care of deteriorating machines and other equipment.

need repairs or they will fall apart and stop working. Most capital, or durable, goods depreciate.

An estimate of the amount that capital goods have depreciated during the year is subtracted from gross domestic product to arrive at a figure called **net domestic product (NDP),** which we define as follows:

$$NDP = GDP - depreciation$$

Depreciation is also called **capital consumption allowance** because it is the amount of the capital stock that has been consumed over a one-year period. In essence, it equals the amount a business would have to put aside to repair and replace deteriorating machines. Because we know that

$$GDP = C + I + G + X$$

we know that the formula for NDP is

$$NDP = C + I + G + X - depreciation$$

You Are There (cont.)

GDP. Thus, to the extent that parents may accidentally be requiring daughters to do more housework than sons, they may be perpetuating a tendency for women to direct more of their time to activities that do not contribute to measured GDP.

CRITICAL ANALYSIS QUESTIONS

1. What would happen to the level of GDP if economists could find a feasible way of assigning dollar values to nonmarket housework when computing GDP?

2. Why is it difficult for economists to assign values to nonmarket housework?

Issues and Applications

Financial Crises and National Economic Performance

CONCEPTS APPLIED

- Real GDP
- Investment
- Durable Consumer Goods

In 2009, the International Monetary Fund (IMF) declared that the global economy was experiencing a recession. More than 90 percent of the world's nations, the IMF concluded, were undergoing economic downturns, and most forecasters predicted at best a slight probability of turnarounds within the next year or two. Leading the way toward negative world real GDP growth were the United States and Europe, which were seeking to recover from a financial crisis that had contributed to sharp declines in production of final goods and services.

Why a Financial Crisis Generates a Reduction in Real GDP

Typically, a financial crisis involves a sudden decline in prices of key components of a nation's stock of wealth, such as houses and shares of stock in companies. Such price declines reduce the values of assets held by banks and other financial institutions. Financial firms react by reducing flows of credit to businesses desiring to undertake investment spending on new capital goods and to households wishing to engage in investment in housing and purchases of durable consumer goods.

Total expenditures on final goods and services decrease as businesses and consumers respond to reduced flows of credit from financial firms by reducing their investment and consumption spending. As a consequence, real GDP begins to fall, often rapidly and sharply, which—with a stable population—also results in lower per capita real GDP. If banks and other financial institutions remain unable to extend credit for some time, then the decreases in per capita real GDP can last for a number of months or perhaps even years.

FIGURE 8-5

Average Total Percentage Changes in House Prices, Stock Prices, and Per Capita Real GDP in Recessions Associated with Financial Crises

Recessions associated with financial crises during the past several decades typically entail significant average total percentage declines in house prices, in stock prices, and in per capita real GDP.

Source: Kenneth Rogoff and Carmen Reinhart, "The Aftermath of Financial Crisis," Working Paper, Harvard University and the University of Maryland, 2009.

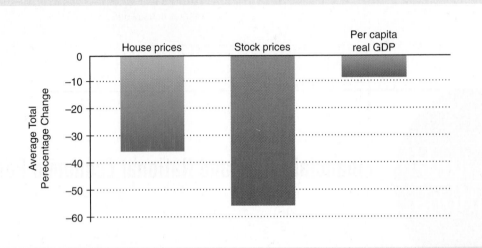

Financial Crises and Economic Performance: Evidence from Previous Events

How severe are the real GDP effects of financial crises? To try to answer this question, Kenneth Rogoff of Harvard University and Carmen Reinhart of the University of Maryland have examined a number of financial crises that occurred during the past several decades. Computing the average effects of all these events, they found that house prices declined, on average, for a period of five years, for a total decrease in price of about 36 percent, as shown in Figure 8-5 above. Stock prices fell, on average, for about three and a half years, for a total decrease of close to 56 percent. On average, the associated total downturn in per capita real GDP exceeded 9 percent and persisted for nearly two years.

A financial crisis can sometimes have a particularly severe and long-lasting effect on an economy's performance. Based on a separate study of a larger set of past financial crises, Robert Barro and José Ursúa of Harvard University have estimated the probabilities of a financial crisis generating significant and long-duration decreases in real GDP. They estimate a one in nine chance of a total multi-year real GDP decrease of 10 percent as a consequence of any given financial crisis. The probability of a multiyear total real GDP decline exceeding 25 percent, they conclude, is 3 percent (about 1 chance out of 30).

Test your understanding of this chapter by going online to **MyEconLab**.
In the Study Plan for this chapter, select Section N: News.

For Critical Analysis

1. Why do you suppose that difficulties that businesses and households experience in obtaining credit during a financial crisis can contribute to long-duration declines in real GDP and in per capita real GDP?

2. If the U.S. population were to rise as real GDP was falling, would the population increase add to or reduce the resulting fall in per capita real GDP?

Web Resources

1. For a look at Rogoff and Reinhart's study of the relationship between financial crises and economic performance, go to www.econtoday.com/chapter08.

2. To read a summary by Robert Barro of estimated probabilities of a major economic downturn resulting from a financial crisis, go to www.econtoday.com/chapter08.

Research Project

During the first full year of the most recent U.S. economic downturn, the total decline in real GDP was nearly 4 percent. Suppose that the U.S. economy experienced this same annual percentage drop in real GDP each year during a continuing recession. Suppose also that the U.S. population remained constant throughout the recession. Why would the total percentage decline in per capita real GDP resulting from a downturn lasting three years be greater than the total percentage decline in per capita real GDP generated by a two-year downturn? In light of your answer, why is the duration of a recession a key determinant of its ultimate effect on per capita real GDP?

Here is what you should know after reading this chapter. **MyEconLab** will help you identify what you know, and where to go when you need to practice.

WHAT YOU SHOULD KNOW

		WHERE TO GO TO PRACTICE
The Circular Flow of Income and Output The circular flow of income and output captures two key principles: (1) In every transaction, the seller receives exactly the same amount that the buyer spends; and (2) goods and services flow in one direction, and money payments flow in the other direction. In the circular flow, households ultimately purchase the nation's total output of final goods and services. They make these purchases using income—wages, rents, interest, and profits—earned from selling labor, land, capital, and entrepreneurial services, respectively. Hence, the values of total income and total output must be the same in the circular flow.	national income accounting, 185 total income, 185 final goods and services, 185 **KEY FIGURE** Figure 8-1, 186	• **MyEconLab** Study Plan 8.1 • Audio introduction to Chapter 8 • Animated Figure 8-1 • ABC News Video: Economic Growth: How Much, How Fast?
Gross Domestic Product (GDP) A nation's gross domestic product is the total market value of its final output of goods and services produced within a given year using factors of production located within the nation's borders. Because GDP measures the value of a flow of production during a year in terms of market prices, it is not a measure of a nation's wealth.	gross domestic product (GDP), 187 intermediate goods, 188 value added, 188	• **MyEconLab** Study Plan 8.2
The Limitations of Using GDP as a Measure of National Welfare Gross domestic product is a useful measure for tracking year-to-year changes in the value of a nation's overall economic activity in terms of market prices. But it excludes nonmarket transactions that may contribute to or detract from general welfare. It also fails to account for factors such as labor market discrimination, personal safety, environmental quality, and the amount and quality of leisure time. That is why GDP is not a perfect measure of national well-being.		• **MyEconLab** Study Plan 8.2 • Video: What GDP Excludes

(continued)

 *(continued)*

WHAT YOU SHOULD KNOW		WHERE TO GO TO PRACTICE
The Expenditure Approach to Tabulating GDP To calculate GDP using the expenditure approach, we sum consumption spending, investment expenditures, government spending, and net export expenditures. Thus, we add up the total amount spent on newly produced goods and services during the year to obtain the dollar value of the output produced and purchased during the year.	expenditure approach, 191 income approach, 191 durable consumer goods, 191 nondurable consumer goods, 191 services, 191 gross private domestic investment, 192 investment, 192 producer durables, or capital goods, 192 fixed investment, 192 inventory investment, 192 depreciation, 193 net domestic product (NDP), 194 capital consumption allowance, 194 net investment, 195 KEY FIGURE Figure 8-2, 194	• **MyEconLab** Study Plan 8.3 • Video: Investment and GDP • Animated Figure 8-2
The Income Approach to Computing GDP To tabulate GDP using the income approach, we add total wages and salaries, rental income, interest income, profits, and nonincome expense items—indirect business taxes and depreciation—to obtain gross domestic income, which is equivalent to gross domestic product. Thus, the total value of all income earnings (equivalent to total factor costs) equals GDP.	gross domestic income (GDI), 195 indirect business taxes, 196 nonincome expense items, 196 national income (NI), 197 personal income (PI), 199 disposable personal income (DPI), 199	• **MyEconLab** Study Plans 8.3, 8.4 • Video: Investment and GDP
Distinguishing Between Nominal GDP and Real GDP Nominal GDP is the value of newly produced output during the current year measured at current market prices. Real GDP adjusts the value of current output into constant dollars by correcting for changes in the overall level of prices from year to year. To calculate real GDP, we divide nominal GDP by the price index (the GDP deflator) and multiply by 100.	nominal values, 200 real values, 200 constant dollars, 200 foreign exchange rate, 203 purchasing power parity, 203 KEY FIGURE Figure 8-4, 202	• **MyEconLab** Study Plans 8.5, 8.6 • Animated Figure 8-4

PROBLEMS

All problems are assignable in X myeconlab *. Answers to odd-numbered problems appear at the back of the book.*

8-1. Each year after a regular spring cleaning, Juanita spruces up her home a little by retexturing and repainting the walls of one room in her house. In a given year, she spends $25 on magazines to get ideas about wall textures and paint shades, $45 on newly produced texturing materials and tools, $35 on new paintbrushes and other painting equipment, and $175 on newly produced paint. Normally, she preps the walls, a service that a professional wall-texturing specialist would charge $200 to do, and applies two coats of paint, a service that a painter would charge $350 to do, on her own.

  a. When she purchases her usual set of materials and does all the work on her home by herself in a given spring, how much does Juanita's annual spring texturing and painting activity contribute to GDP?

  b. Suppose that Juanita hurt her back this year and is recovering from surgery. Her surgeon has instructed her not to do any texturing work, but he has given her the go-ahead to paint a room as long as she is cautious. Thus, she buys all the equipment required to both texture and paint a room. She hires someone else to do the texturing work but does the painting herself. How much would her spring painting activity add to GDP?

  c. As a follow-up to part (b), suppose that as soon as Juanita bends down to dip her brush into the paint, she realizes that painting will be too hard on her back after all. She decides to hire someone else to do all the work using the materials she has already purchased. In this case, how much will her spring painting activity contribute to GDP?

8-2. Each year, Johan typically does all his own landscaping and yard work. He spends $200 per year on mulch for his flower beds, $225 per year on flowers and plants, $50 on fertilizer for his lawn, and $245 on gasoline and lawn mower maintenance. The lawn and garden store where he obtains his mulch and fertilizer charges other customers $500 for the service of spreading that much mulch in flower beds and $50 for the service of distributing fertilizer over a yard the size of Johan's. Paying a professional yard care service to mow his lawn would require an expenditure of $1,200 per year, but in that case Johan would not have to buy gasoline or maintain his own lawn mower.

  a. In a normal year, how much does Johan's landscaping and yard work contribute to GDP?

  b. Suppose that Johan has developed allergy problems this year and will have to reduce the amount of his yard work. He can wear a mask while running his lawn mower, so he will keep mowing his yard, but he will pay the lawn and garden center to spread mulch and distribute fertilizer. How much will all the work on Johan's yard contribute to GDP this year?

  c. As a follow-up to part (b), at the end of the year, Johan realizes that his allergies are growing worse and that he will have to arrange for all his landscaping and yard work to be done by someone else next year. How much will he contribute to GDP next year?

8-3. Consider the following hypothetical data for the U.S. economy in 2012 (all amounts are in trillions of dollars).

Consumption	11.0
Indirect business taxes	.8
Depreciation	1.3
Government spending	2.8
Imports	2.7
Gross private domestic investment	3.0
Exports	2.5

  a. Based on the data, what is GDP? NDP? NI?

  b. Suppose that in 2013, exports fall to $2.3 trillion, imports rise to $2.85 trillion, and gross private domestic investment falls to $2.25 trillion. What will GDP be in 2013, assuming that other values do not change between 2012 and 2013?

8-4. Look back at Table 8-3 on page 201, which explains how to calculate real GDP in terms of 2005 constant dollars. Change the base year to 2000. Recalculate the price index, and then recalculate real GDP—that is, express column 4 of Table 8-3 in terms of 2000 dollars instead of 2005 dollars.

8-5. Consider the following hypothetical data for the U.S. economy in 2012 (in trillions of dollars), and assume that there are no statistical discrepancies or other adjustments.

Profit	2.8
Indirect business taxes and transfers	.8
Rent	.7
Interest	.8
Wages	8.2
Depreciation	1.3
Consumption	11.0
Exports	1.5
Government transfer payments	2.0
Personal income taxes and nontax payments	1.7
Imports	1.7
Corporate taxes and retained earnings	.5
Social Security contributions	2.0
Government spending	1.8

  a. What is gross domestic income? GDP?

  b. What is gross private domestic investment?

  c. What is personal income? Personal disposable income?

8-6. Which of the following are production activities that are included in GDP? Which are not?

  a. Mr. King performs the service of painting his own house instead of paying someone else to do it.

  b. Mr. King paints houses for a living.

  c. Mrs. King earns income from parents by taking baby photos in her home photography studio.

  d. Mrs. King takes photos of planets and stars as part of her astronomy hobby.

  e. E*Trade charges fees to process Internet orders for stock trades.

  f. Mr. Ho spends $10,000 on shares of stock via an Internet trade order and pays a $10 brokerage fee.

  g. Mrs. Ho receives a Social Security payment.

  h. Ms. Hernandez makes a $300 payment for an Internet-based course on stock trading.

  i. Mr. Langham sells a used laptop computer to his neighbor.

8-7. Explain what happens to contributions to GDP in each of the following situations.

  a. A woman who makes a living charging for investment advice on her Internet Web site marries one of her clients, to whom she now provides advice at no charge.

  b. A tennis player wins two top professional tournaments as an unpaid amateur, meaning the tournament sponsor does not have to pay out his share of prize money.

  c. A company that had been selling used firearms illegally finally gets around to obtaining an operating license and performing background checks as specified by law prior to each gun sale.

8-8. Explain what happens to the official measure of GDP in each of the following situations.

  a. Air quality improves significantly throughout the United States, but there are no effects on aggregate production or on market prices of final goods and services.

  b. The U.S. government spends considerably less on antipollution efforts this year than it did in recent years.

  c. The quality of cancer treatments increases, so patients undergo fewer treatments, which hospitals continue to provide at the same price per treatment as before.

8-9. Which of the following activities of a computer manufacturer during the current year are included in this year's measure of GDP?

  a. The manufacturer purchases a chip in June, uses it as a component in a computer in August, and sells the computer to a customer in November.

  b. A retail outlet of the company sells a computer manufactured during the current year.

  c. A marketing arm of the company receives fee income during the current year when a buyer of one of its computers elects to use the computer manufacturer as her Internet service provider.

8-10. A number of economists contend that official measures of U.S. gross private investment expenditures are understated. Answer parts (a) and (b) below to determine just how understated these economists believe that officially measured investment spending may be.

a. Household spending on education, such as college tuition expenditures, is counted as consumption spending. Some economists suggest that these expenditures, which amount to 6 percent of GDP, should be counted as investment spending instead. Based on this 6 percent estimate and the GDP computations detailed in Figure 8-3 on page 198, how many billions of dollars would shift from consumption to investment if this suggestion was adopted?

b. Some economists argue that intangible forms of investment—business research spending, educational expenses for employees, and the like—should be included in the official measure of gross private domestic investment. These expenditures, which amount to about 12 percent of GDP, currently are treated as business input expenses and are not included in GDP. Based on this 12 percent estimate and the GDP computations detailed in Figure 8-3 on page 198, how much higher would gross private domestic investment be if intangible investment expenditures were counted as investment spending?

c. Based on your answers to parts (a) and (b), what is the total amount that gross private domestic investment may be understated, according to economists who argue that household education spending and business intangible investments should be added? How much may GDP be understated?

8-11. Consider the following table for the economy of a nation whose residents produce five final goods.

| | 2009 | | 2013 | |
Good	Price	Quantity	Price	Quantity
Shampoo	$ 2	15	$ 4	20
DVD drives	200	10	250	10
Books	40	5	50	4
Milk	3	10	4	3
Candy	1	40	2	20

Assuming a 2009 base year:

a. What is nominal GDP for 2009 and 2013?

b. What is real GDP for 2009 and 2013?

8-12. Consider the following table for the economy of a nation whose residents produce four final goods.

| | 2011 | | 2012 | |
Good	Price	Quantity	Price	Quantity
Computers	$1,000	10	$800	15
Bananas	6	3,000	11	1,000
Televisions	100	500	150	300
Cookies	1	10,000	2	10,000

Assuming a 2012 base year:

a. What is nominal GDP for 2011 and 2012?

b. What is real GDP for 2011 and 2012?

8-13. In the table for Problem 8-12, if 2012 is the base year, what is the price index for 2011? (Round decimal fractions to the nearest tenth.)

8-14. Suppose that early in a year, a hurricane hits a town in Florida and destroys a substantial number of homes. A portion of this stock of housing, which had a market value of $100 million (not including the market value of the land), was uninsured. The owners of the residences spent a total of $5 million during the rest of the year to pay salvage companies to help them save remaining belongings. A small percentage of uninsured owners had sufficient resources to spend a total of $15 million during the year to pay construction companies to rebuild their homes. Some were able to devote their own time, the opportunity cost of which was valued at $3 million, to work on rebuilding their homes. The remaining people, however, chose to sell their land at its market value and abandon the remains of their houses. What was the combined effect of these transactions on GDP for this year? (Hint: Which transactions took place in the markets for *final* goods and services?) In what ways, if any, does the effect on GDP reflect a loss in welfare for these individuals?

8-15. Suppose that in 2013, geologists discover large reserves of oil under the tundra in Alaska. These reserves have a market value estimated at $50 billion at current oil prices. Oil companies spend $1 billion to hire workers and move and position equipment to begin exploratory pumping during that same year. In the process of loading some of the oil onto tankers at a port, one company accidentally spills some of the oil into a bay and by the end of the year pays $1 billion to other companies to clean it up. The oil spill kills thousands of birds, seals, and other wildlife. What was the combined effect of these events on GDP for this year? (Hint: Which transactions took place in the markets for *final* goods and services?) In what ways, if any, does the effect on GDP reflect a loss in national welfare?

8-16. Consider the diagram in the next column, and answer the following questions.

    a. What is the base year? Explain

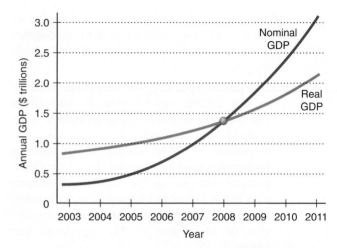

b. Has this country experienced inflation or deflation since the base year? How can you tell?

ECONOMICS ON THE NET

Tracking the Components of Gross Domestic Product One way to keep tabs on the components of GDP is via the FRED database at the Web site of the Federal Reserve Bank of St. Louis.

Title: Gross Domestic Product and Components

Navigation: Use the link at **www.econtoday.com/chapter08** to visit the home page of the Federal Reserve Bank of St. Louis. Click on *Gross Domestic Product (GDP) and Components*.

Application

1. Click on *GDP/GNP*, and then click a checkmark next to *GDP (Gross Domestic Product)*. Write down nominal GDP data for the past 10 quarters.

2. Back up to *GDPCA (Real Gross Domestic Product) Dollars*. Write down the amounts for the past 10 quarters. Use the formula on page 200 to calculate the price level for each quarter. Has the price level decreased or increased in recent quarters?

For Group Study and Analysis Divide the class into "consumption," "investment," "government sector," and "foreign sector" groups. Have each group evaluate the contribution of each category of spending to GDP and to its quarter-to-quarter volatility. Reconvene the class, and discuss the factors that appear to create the most variability in GDP.

ANSWERS TO QUICK QUIZZES

p. 187: (i) factor . . . income; (ii) final; (iii) profit
p. 191: (i) Gross domestic product; (ii) value added; (iii) exclude; (iv) GDP; (v) market value
p. 195: (i) expenditure . . . durables . . . nondurables . . . services; (ii) capacity . . . inventories; (iii) market; (iv) depreciation
p. 197: (i) wages . . . interest . . . rent . . . profits; (ii) indirect business taxes . . . depreciation
p. 199: (i) national income; (ii) personal income; (iii) income taxes
p. 202: (i) 100 . . . 110; (ii) population
p. 204: (i) exchange rate; (ii) exchange rate; (iii) cost . . . living

Global Economic Growth and Development

What do Australia, Bulgaria, Germany, and Japan all have in common? The answer is that they are among more than 20 nations throughout the world that now offer significant financial incentives for women to bear children. These nations' efforts to boost birthrates are aimed both at halting current population declines and at generating net population increases over the longer term. In all these nations, the ultimate objective of giving women incentives to have more babies is to provide a stronger foundation for future *economic growth*. In this chapter, you will learn about the measurement of economic growth, the importance of growth rates, and the key factors that determine economic growth.

LEARNING OBJECTIVES

MyEconLab helps you master each objective and study more efficiently. See end of chapter for details.

After reading this chapter, you should be able to:

- Define economic growth
- Recognize the importance of economic growth rates
- Explain why productivity increases are crucial for maintaining economic growth
- Describe the fundamental determinants of economic growth
- Understand the basis of new growth theory
- Discuss the fundamental factors that contribute to a nation's economic development

? DID YOU KNOW THAT only one European nation, Luxembourg, has per capita real GDP—real GDP divided by the population—higher than the U.S. per capita real GDP? Luxembourg's per capita real GDP is nearly 50 percent greater than overall U.S. per capita real GDP, which puts its residents' incomes on a par with those of the U.S. states of Connecticut and Delaware. In Belgium, France, Germany, and Italy, however, per capita real GDP is only slightly higher than in the U.S. states of Arkansas and Montana, where per capita real GDP is less than 75 percent of the overall U.S. level. In fact, per capita real GDP in these four European nations is only about 14 percent higher than in Mississippi and West Virginia, the U.S. states with the lowest per capita real GDP.

A few decades ago, per capita real GDP in Arkansas, Mississippi, Montana, and West Virginia was far below the levels in Belgium, France, Germany, and Italy. Then, up to the Great Recession of the late 2000s, per capita real GDP grew more rapidly in the four U.S. states than in the four European nations. Thus, the four U.S. states experienced a higher rate of *economic growth,* which is the topic of this chapter.

How Do We Define Economic Growth?

Recall from Chapter 2 that we can show economic growth graphically as an outward shift of a production possibilities curve, as is seen in Figure 9-1. If there is economic growth between 2011 and 2035, the production possibilities curve will shift outward toward the red curve. The distance that it shifts represents the amount of economic growth, defined as the increase in the productive capacity of a nation. Although it is possible to come up with a measure of a nation's increased productive capacity, it would not be easy. Therefore, we turn to a more readily obtainable definition of economic growth.

Most people have a general idea of what economic growth means. When a nation grows economically, its citizens must be better off in at least some ways, usually in terms of their material well-being. Typically, though, we do not measure the well-being of any nation solely in terms of its total output of real goods and services or in terms of real GDP without making some adjustments. After all, India

How does spending on this new research and development facility add to economic growth in the future?

FIGURE 9-1

Economic Growth

If there is growth between 2011 and 2035, the production possibilities curve for the entire economy will shift outward from the blue line labeled 2011 to the red line labeled 2035. The distance that it shifts represents an increase in the productive capacity of the nation.

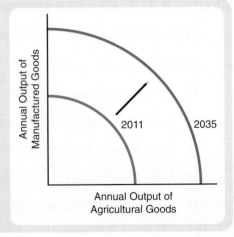

has a real GDP more than 15 times as large as that of Denmark. The population in India, though, is about 200 times greater than that of Denmark. Consequently, we view India as a relatively poor country and Denmark as a relatively rich country. Thus, when we measure economic growth, we must adjust for population growth. Our formal definition becomes this: **Economic growth** occurs when there are increases in *per capita* real GDP, measured by the rate of change in per capita real GDP per year. Figure 9-2 presents the historical record of real GDP per person in the United States.

Economic growth
Increases in per capita real GDP measured by its rate of change per year.

Problems in Definition

Our definition of economic growth says nothing about the *distribution* of output and income. A nation might grow very rapidly in terms of increases in per capita real output, while its poor people remain poor or become even poorer. Therefore, in assessing the economic growth record of any nation, we must be careful to pinpoint which income groups have benefited the most from such growth. How much does economic growth differ across countries?

FIGURE 9-2

The Historical Record of U.S. Economic Growth

The graph traces per capita real GDP in the United States since 1900. Data are given in 2005 dollars.

Source: U.S. Department of Commerce.

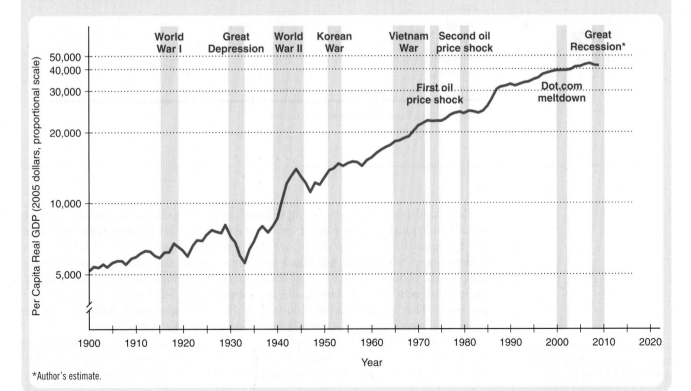

*Author's estimate.

INTERNATIONAL EXAMPLE
Growth Rates Around the World

Table 9-1 shows the average annual rate of growth of real GDP per person in selected countries since 1970. During this time period, the United States has been positioned about midway in the pack. Thus, even though we are one of the world's richest countries, our rate of economic growth has been in the middle range. The reason that U.S. per capita real GDP has remained higher than per capita real GDP in most other nations is that, despite the late-2000s downturn, U.S. growth has been sustained over many decades. This is something that most other countries have so far been unable to accomplish.

FOR CRITICAL ANALYSIS
"The largest change is from zero to one." Does this statement have anything to do with relative growth rates in poorer versus richer countries?

TABLE 9-1

Per Capita Real GDP Growth Rates in Various Countries

Country	Average Annual Rate of Growth of Real GDP Per Capita, 1970–2009 (%)
Sweden	1.7
France	1.8
Germany	1.8
United States	1.9
Canada	2.0
Brazil	2.1
Japan	2.1
Turkey	2.1
India	3.2
Indonesia	4.1
Malaysia	4.7
China	7.2

Sources: World Bank, International Monetary Fund, and author's estimates.

Real standards of living can go up without any positive economic growth. This can occur if individuals are, on average, enjoying more leisure by working fewer hours but producing as much as they did before. For example, if per capita real GDP in the United States remained at $45,000 a year for a decade, we could not automatically jump to the conclusion that U.S. residents were, on average, no better off. What if, during that same 10-year period, average hours worked fell from 37 per week to 33 per week? That would mean that during the 10 years under study, individuals in the labor force were "earning" 4 more hours of leisure a week.

Nothing so extreme as this example has occurred in this country, but something similar has. Average hours worked per week fell steadily until the 1960s, when they leveled off. That means that during much of the history of this country, the increase

Go to www.econtoday.com/chapter09 to get the latest figures and estimates on economic growth throughout the world.

in per capita real GDP *understated* the actual economic growth that we were experiencing because we were enjoying more and more leisure as time passed.

Why are economists reexamining officially reported rates of economic growth in China and India?

POLICY EXAMPLE
Are Growth Rates in China and India Overstated?

No one doubts that per capita real GDP has been growing very rapidly in China and India in recent years. Nevertheless, preliminary evidence from an ongoing World Bank study suggests that errors in measuring prices used to adjust GDP figures for China and India may have led to overstatements in their per capita real GDP for a number of years. New estimates indicate that per capita real GDP in China may be as much as 40 percent lower than the figures listed in World Bank reports. In India, per capita real GDP could be up to 38 percent lower.

Consequently, per capita real GDP in these two nations has not grown at the officially reported rates. As you read this page, economists are undoubtedly in the process of recalculating recent economic growth rates in China, India, and a number of other nations.

FOR CRITICAL ANALYSIS
Why must economists recalculate a nation's annual rates of economic growth after revising annual estimates of per capita real GDP for that country?

Is Economic Growth Bad?

Some commentators on our current economic situation believe that the definition of economic growth ignores its negative effects. Some psychologists even contend that economic growth makes us worse off. They say that the more the economy grows, the more "needs" are created so that we feel worse off as we become richer. Our expectations are rising faster than reality, so we presumably always suffer from a sense of disappointment. Also, economists' measurement of economic growth does not take into account the spiritual and cultural aspects of the good life. As with all activities, both costs and benefits are associated with growth. You can see some of those listed in Table 9-2.

Any measure of economic growth that we use will be imperfect. Nonetheless, the measures that we do have allow us to make comparisons across countries and over

What phenomenon now allows a larger percentage of Indian citizens to purchase expensive clothes?

TABLE 9-2		
Costs and Benefits of Economic Growth	Benefits	Costs
	Reduction in illiteracy	Environmental pollution
	Reduction in poverty	Breakdown of the family
	Improved health	Isolation and alienation
	Longer lives	Urban congestion
	Political stability	

TABLE 9-3

One Dollar Compounded Annually at Different Interest Rates

Here we show the value of a dollar at the end of a specified period during which it has been compounded annually at a specified interest rate. For example, if you took $1 today and invested it at 5 percent per year, it would yield $1.05 at the end of one year. At the end of 10 years, it would equal $1.63, and at the end of 50 years, it would equal $11.50.

	Interest Rate						
Number of Years	3%	4%	5%	6%	8%	10%	20%
1	1.03	1.04	1.05	1.06	1.08	1.10	1.20
2	1.06	1.08	1.10	1.12	1.17	1.21	1.44
3	1.09	1.12	1.16	1.19	1.26	1.33	1.73
4	1.13	1.17	1.22	1.26	1.36	1.46	2.07
5	1.16	1.22	1.28	1.34	1.47	1.61	2.49
6	1.19	1.27	1.34	1.41	1.59	1.77	2.99
7	1.23	1.32	1.41	1.50	1.71	1.94	3.58
8	1.27	1.37	1.48	1.59	1.85	2.14	4.30
9	1.30	1.42	1.55	1.68	2.00	2.35	5.16
10	1.34	1.48	1.63	1.79	2.16	2.59	6.19
20	1.81	2.19	2.65	3.20	4.66	6.72	38.30
30	2.43	3.24	4.32	5.74	10.00	17.40	237.00
40	3.26	4.80	7.04	10.30	21.70	45.30	1,470.00
50	4.38	7.11	11.50	18.40	46.90	117.00	9,100.00

time and, if used judiciously, can enable us to gain important insights. Per capita real GDP, used so often, is not always an accurate measure of economic well-being, but it is a serviceable measure of productive activity.

The Importance of Growth Rates

Notice in Table 9-1 on page 216 that the growth rates in real per capita income for most countries differ very little—generally by only a few percentage points. You might want to know why such small differences in growth rates are important. What does it matter if we grow at 3 percent rather than at 4 percent per year? The answer is that in the long run, it matters a lot.

A small difference in the rate of economic growth does not matter very much for next year or the year after. For the more distant future, however, it makes considerable difference. The power of *compounding* is impressive. Let's see what happens with three different annual rates of growth: 3 percent, 4 percent, and 5 percent. We start with $1 trillion per year of U.S. GDP at some time in the past. We then compound this $1 trillion, or allow it to grow at these three different growth rates. The difference is huge. In 50 years, $1 trillion per year becomes $4.38 trillion per year if compounded at 3 percent per year. Just one percentage point more in the growth rate, 4 percent, results in a real GDP of $7.11 trillion per year in 50 years, almost double the previous amount. Two percentage points' difference in the growth rate—5 percent per year—results in a real GDP of $11.5 trillion per year in 50 years, or nearly three times as much. Obviously, very small differences in annual growth rates result in great differences in cumulative economic growth. That is why nations are concerned if the growth rate falls even a little in absolute percentage terms.

Thus, when we talk about growth rates, we are talking about compounding. In Table 9-3, we show how $1 compounded annually grows at different interest rates. We see in the 3 percent column that $1 in 50 years grows to $4.38. We merely multiplied $1 trillion times 4.38 to get the growth figure in our earlier example. In the 5 percent column, $1 grows to $11.50 after 50 years. Again, we multiplied $1 trillion times 11.50 to get the growth figure for 5 percent in the preceding example.

How do economists measure the pace of world economic growth?

INTERNATIONAL EXAMPLE
Measuring Global Economic Growth

Calculating aggregate world per capita real GDP is complicated by the fact that prices of goods and services are measured in terms of various nations' currencies, such as the dollar, the euro, and the yen. To measure global GDP, economists commonly start by converting the value of every country's GDP into U.S. dollars, which is accomplished by multiplying the country's GDP by the exchange rate of the dollar for its currency. Then they adjust for the fact that price levels vary across countries relative to the United States. Next, they develop worldwide GDP deflators to adjust the resulting global GDP measure for inflation, thereby computing a measure of world *real* GDP. Dividing world real GDP by the estimated world population yields world per capita real GDP. Finally, by computing annual percentage changes in world per capita real GDP, economists measure global economic growth.

Between 1870 and 1913, world per capita real GDP increased at an average annual rate of only 1.3 percent per year. Prior to the current century, the highest average global economic growth rate ever recorded was 2.9 percent, which occurred during the period 1950–1973. Between 2000 and 2007, world per capita real GDP grew at an average annual rate of 3.2 percent. Since the onset of the Great Recession in 2008, however, the rate of global economic growth has slowed to only slightly above zero.

FOR CRITICAL ANALYSIS
Based on Table 9-3, if the rate of global economic growth had remained unchanged at 3.2 percent per year from 2008 through 2010, by what total percentage would world per capita real GDP have grown by the end of 2010?

THE RULE OF 70 Table 9-3 indicates that how quickly the level of a nation's per capita real GDP increases depends on the rate of economic growth. A formula called the **rule of 70** provides a shorthand way to calculate approximately how long it will take a country to experience a significant increase in per capita real GDP. According to the rule of 70, the approximate number of years necessary for a nation's per capita real GDP to increase by 100 percent—that is, to *double*—is equal to 70 divided by the average rate of economic growth. Thus, at an annual growth rate of 10 percent, per capita real GDP should double in about 7 years. As you can see in Table 9-3, at a 10 percent growth rate, in 7 years per capita real GDP would rise by a factor of 1.94, which is very close to 2, or very nearly the doubling predicted by the rule of 70. At an annual growth rate of 8 percent, the rule of 70 predicts that nearly 9 years will be required for a nation's per capita real GDP to double. Table 9-3 verifies that this prediction is correct. Indeed, the table shows that after 9 years an exact doubling will occur at a growth rate of 8 percent.

The rule of 70 implies that at lower rates of economic growth, much more time must pass before per capita real GDP will double. At a 3 percent growth rate, just over 23 (70/3) years must pass before per capita real income doubles. At a rate of growth of only 1 percent per year, 70 (70/1) years must pass. This means that if a nation's average rate of economic growth is 1 percent instead of 3 percent, 47 more years—about two generations—must pass for per capita real GDP to double. Clearly, the rule of 70 verifies that even very slight differences in economic growth rates are important.

Rule of 70
A rule stating that the approximate number of years required for per capita real GDP to double is equal to 70 divided by the average rate of economic growth.

Economic growth can be defined as the increase in _____ _____ real GDP, measured by its rate of change per year.

The _____ of economic growth are reductions in illiteracy, poverty, and illness and increases in life spans and political stability. The _____ of economic growth

may include environmental pollution, alienation, and urban congestion.

Small percentage-point differences in growth rates lead to _____ differences in per capita real GDP over time. These differences can be seen by examining a compound interest table such as the one in Table 9-3 on page 218.

Productivity Increases: The Heart of Economic Growth

Let's say that you are required to type 10 term papers and homework assignments a year. You have a computer, but you do not know how to touch-type. You end up spending an average of two hours per typing job. The next summer, you buy a touch-typing tutorial to use on your computer and spend a few minutes a day improving your speed. The following term, you spend only one hour per typing assignment, thereby saving 10 hours a semester. You have become more productive. This concept of productivity summarizes your ability (and everyone else's) to produce the same output with fewer inputs. Thus, **labor productivity** is normally measured by dividing the total real domestic output (real GDP) by the number of workers or the number of labor hours. By definition, labor productivity increases whenever average output produced per worker during a specified time period increases.

Would both U.S. labor productivity and per capita real GDP be higher if U.S. students learned more about mathematics and the physical sciences?

Labor productivity
Total real domestic output (real GDP) divided by the number of workers (output per worker).

EXAMPLE
Are Weak Math and Science Skills Affecting Our Productivity and Economic Growth?

In the early 1990s, the U.S. government announced an objective of improving learning outcomes in mathematics and the physical sciences in U.S. elementary and secondary schools. Improved understanding of these subjects, the government determined, would enable more graduates to perform at higher levels in jobs in information technology and other fields requiring strong math and science backgrounds. The results, the government suggested, would be increases in labor productivity and, hence, the rate of economic growth.

Since then, however, objective measures of student learning in mathematics and the sciences have shown little overall

improvement. Indeed, some measures have indicated drops in math and science skills of U.S. high school graduates that have retarded growth in labor productivity. Some studies have found evidence suggesting that today's per capita real GDP is as much as 5 percent lower than it would have been if the government's math and science goals had been attained.

FOR CRITICAL ANALYSIS
How do you suppose that possession of stronger skills in mathematics and physical sciences could translate into higher labor productivity?

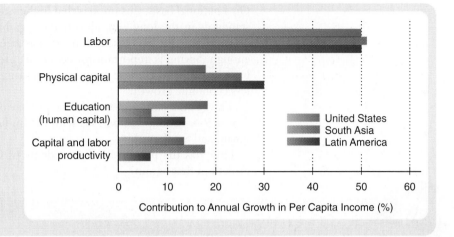

FIGURE 9-3

Factors Accounting for Economic Growth in Selected Regions

In the United States, South Asia, and Latin America, growth in labor resources is the main contributor to economic growth.

Source: International Monetary Fund.

Clearly, there is a relationship between economic growth and increases in labor productivity. If you divide all resources into just capital and labor, economic growth can be defined simply as the cumulative contribution to per capita GDP growth of three components: the rate of growth of capital, the rate of growth of labor, and the rate of growth of capital and labor productivity. If everything else remains constant, improvements in labor productivity ultimately lead to economic growth and higher living standards.

Figure 9-3 displays estimates of the relative contributions of the growth of labor and capital and the growth of labor and capital productivity to economic growth in the United States, nations in South Asia, and Latin American countries. The growth of labor resources, through associated increases in labor force participation, has contributed to the expansion of output that has accounted for at least half of economic growth in all three regions. Total capital is the sum of physical capital, such as tools and machines, and human capital, which is the amount of knowledge acquired from research and education. Figure 9-3 shows the separate contributions of the growth of these forms of capital, which together have accounted for roughly a third of the growth rate of per capita incomes in the United States, South Asia, and Latin America. In these three parts of the world, growth in overall capital and labor productivity has contributed the remaining 7 to 18 percent.

Go to **www.econtoday.com/chapter09** for information about the latest trends in U.S. labor productivity.

Saving: A Fundamental Determinant of Economic Growth

Economic growth does not occur in a vacuum. It is not some predetermined fate of a nation. Rather, economic growth depends on certain fundamental factors. One of the most important factors that affects the rate of economic growth and hence long-term living standards is the rate of saving.

A basic proposition in economics is that if you want more tomorrow, you have to consume less today.

To have more consumption in the future, you have to consume less today and save the difference between your consumption and your income.

On a national basis, this implies that higher saving rates eventually mean higher living standards in the long run, all other things held constant. Although the U.S. saving rate has recently increased, concern has been growing that we still are not saving enough. Saving is important for economic growth because without saving, we cannot have investment. If there is no investment in our capital stock, there would be much less economic growth.

The relationship between the rate of saving and per capita real GDP is shown in Figure 9-4. Among the nations with the highest rates of saving are China, Germany, Japan, and Saudi Arabia.

How has the propensity for residents of China to save helped to fuel economic growth in that nation?

INTERNATIONAL EXAMPLE
Saving and Growth in China

Since the late 1980s, residents of China have consistently directed at least 35 percent of their real GDP to saving. Indeed, since 2001 saving in China has exceeded 40 percent of real GDP, and currently this percentage hovers near 50 percent. The bulk of this saving has been channeled into investment in capital. Today, investment spending accounts for more than 44 percent of that nation's total expenditures on final goods and services. These consistently high rates of saving and capital investment in China help to explain why the nation's economy maintains an annual rate of growth of per capita real GDP of about 10 percent.

FOR CRITICAL ANALYSIS
Why do you suppose that economists who predict that consumption's share of real GDP in China is likely to increase in future years also project an eventual falloff in the nation's rate of economic growth?

FIGURE 9-4

Relationship Between Rate of Saving and Per Capita Real GDP

This diagram shows the relationship between per capita real GDP and the rate of saving expressed as the average share of annual real GDP saved.

Source: World Bank.

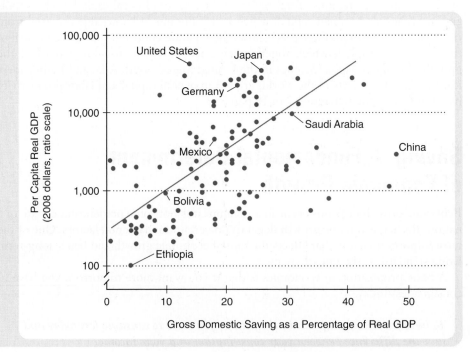

QUICK QUIZ *See page 238 for the answers. Review concepts from this section in MyEconLab.*

Economic growth is numerically equal to the rate of growth of _____ plus the rate of growth of _____ plus the rate of growth in the productivity of _____ and of _____. Improvements in labor productivity, all other things being equal, lead to greater economic growth and higher living standards.

One fundamental determinant of the rate of growth is the rate of _____. To have more consumption in the future, we have to _____ rather than consume. In general, countries that have had higher rates of _____ have had higher rates of growth in per capita real GDP.

New Growth Theory and the Determinants of Growth

A simple arithmetic definition of economic growth has already been given. The per capita growth rates of capital and labor plus the per capita growth rate of their productivity constitute the rate of economic growth. Economists have had good data on the growth of the physical capital stock in the United States as well as on the labor force. But when you add those two growth rates together, you still do not get the total economic growth rate in the United States. The difference has to be due to improvements in productivity. Economists typically labeled this "improvements in technology," and that was that. More recently, proponents of what is now called **new growth theory** argue that technology cannot simply be looked at as an outside factor without explanation. Technology must be understood in terms of what drives it. What are the forces that make productivity grow in the United States and elsewhere?

New growth theory
A theory of economic growth that examines the factors that determine why technology, research, innovation, and the like are undertaken and how they interact.

Growth in Technology

Consider some startling statistics about the growth in technology. Microprocessor speeds may increase from 4,000 megahertz to 10,000 megahertz by the year 2015. By that same year, the size of the thinnest circuit line within a transistor may decrease by 90 percent. The typical memory capacity (RAM) of computers will jump from 2 gigabytes, or about 32 times the equivalent text in the Internal Revenue Code, to more than 300 gigabytes. Recent developments in phase-change memory technologies and in new techniques for storing bits of data on molecules and even individual atoms promise even greater expansions of computer memory capacities. Predictions are that computers may become as powerful as the human brain by 2020.

Technology: A Separate Factor of Production

We now recognize that technology must be viewed as a separate factor of production that is sensitive to rewards. Otherwise stated, one of the major foundations of new growth theory is this:

> *When the rewards are greater, more technological advances will occur.*

Let's consider several aspects of technology here, the first one being research and development.

Research and Development

A certain amount of technological advance results from research and development (R&D) activities that have as their goal the development of specific new materials, new products, and new machines. How much spending a nation devotes to R&D can have an impact on its long-term economic growth. Part of how much a nation spends depends on what businesses decide is worth spending. That in turn depends on their expected rewards from successful R&D. If your company develops a new way to produce computer memory chips, how much will it be rewarded? The answer depends on what you can charge others to use the new technique.

Patent

A government protection that gives an inventor the exclusive right to make, use, or sell an invention for a limited period of time (currently, 20 years).

PATENTS To protect new techniques developed through R&D, we have a system of **patents,** in which the federal government gives the patent holder the exclusive right to make, use, and sell an invention for a period of 20 years. One can argue that this special protection given to owners of patents increases expenditures on R&D and therefore adds to long-term economic growth. Figure 9-5 shows that U.S. patent grants fell during the 1970s, increased steadily after 1982, surged from 1995 until 2001, and increased again during the past few years.

POSITIVE EXTERNALITIES AND R&D As we discussed in Chapter 5, positive externalities are benefits from an activity that are not enjoyed by the instigator of the activity. In the case of R&D spending, a certain amount of the benefits go to other companies that do not have to pay for them. In particular, according to economists David Coe of the International Monetary Fund and Elhanan Helpman of Tel Aviv University, about a quarter of the global productivity gains of R&D investment in the top seven industrialized countries goes to other nations. For every 1 percent rise in the stock of R&D in the United States alone, for example, productivity in the rest of the world increases by about 0.25 percent. One country's R&D expenditures benefit other countries because they are able to import capital goods—computers, telecommunications networks—from technologically advanced countries and then use them as inputs in making their own industries more efficient. In addition, countries that import high-tech goods are able to imitate the technology.

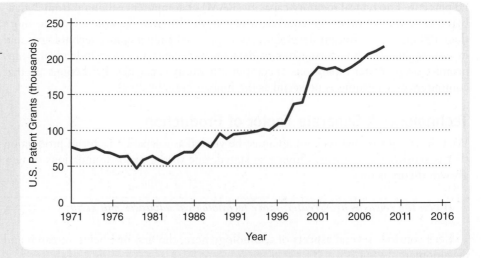

FIGURE 9-5

U.S. Patent Grants

The U.S. Patent and Trademark Office gradually began awarding more patent grants between the early 1980s and the mid-1990s. Since 1995, the number of patents granted each year has risen in most years.

Source: U.S. Patent and Trademark Office.

The Open Economy and Economic Growth

People who study economic growth today emphasize the importance of the openness of the economy. Free trade encourages a more rapid spread of technology and industrial ideas. Moreover, open economies may experience higher rates of economic growth because their own industries have access to a bigger market. When trade barriers are erected in the form of tariffs and the like, domestic industries become isolated from global technological progress. This occurred for many years in Communist countries and in most developing countries in Africa, Latin America, and elsewhere. Figure 9-6 on the following page shows the relationship between economic growth and openness as measured by the level of tariff barriers.

How have relative per capita incomes in Latin America and Asia changed since most Latin American countries opted for much higher trade barriers?

INTERNATIONAL EXAMPLE
A Story of Different Choices Regarding Trade—and Economic Growth

In 1950, per capita real GDP in Latin America exceeded the Asian level by 75 percent. Today, Latin America's per capita real GDP is almost 20 percent *less* than Asia's per capita real GDP. One factor that contributed to the Asian turnaround relative to Latin America stands out sharply: much greater Asian openness to international trade. Since the late 1950s, a number of Asian nations, including Hong Kong, Japan, and Singapore, have adopted low trade barriers. In contrast, the majority of Latin American countries have maintained some of the highest trade barriers in the world. For nearly 60 years, trade barriers in nations such as Argentina, Brazil, and Chile have been up to 100 times greater than those in Asia. Hence, residents of most Latin American countries have been denied the benefits of economic growth resulting from openness to trade that have been experienced by many Asian residents.

FOR CRITICAL ANALYSIS
In light of the evidence that low trade barriers promote economic growth, why do you suppose that some people in every nation favor high barriers to trade?

Innovation and Knowledge

We tend to think of technological progress as, say, the invention of the transistor. But invention means nothing by itself; **innovation** is required. Innovation involves the transformation of something new, such as an invention, into something that benefits the economy either by lowering production costs or by providing new goods and services. Indeed, the new growth theorists believe that real wealth creation comes from innovation and that invention is but a facet of innovation.

Historically, technologies have moved relatively slowly from invention to innovation to widespread use, and the dispersion of new technology remains for the most part slow and uncertain. The inventor of the transistor thought it might be used to make better hearing aids. At the time it was invented, the *New York Times*'s sole reference to it was in a small weekly column called "News of Radio." When the laser was invented, no one really knew what it could be used for. It was initially used to help in navigation, measurement, and chemical research. Today, it is used in the reproduction of music, printing, surgery, telecommunications, and optical data transmittal and storage. Tomorrow, who knows?

Innovation
Transforming an invention into something that is useful to humans.

You Are There

To contemplate a real-world example of how an innovation can take place slowly and even unexpectedly, consider **An Invention Becomes a Market Innovation—by Accident,** on page 233.

FIGURE 9-6

The Relationship Between Economic Growth and Tariff Barriers to International Trade

Nations with low tariff barriers are relatively open to international trade and have tended to have higher average annual rates of real GDP per capita growth since 1965.

Source: World Bank.

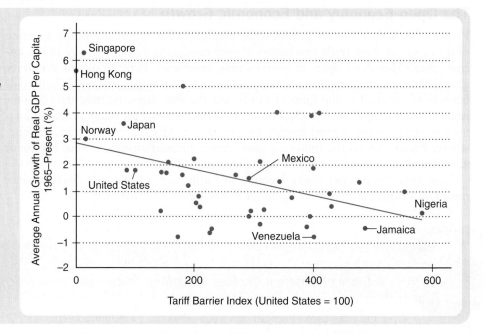

Typically, thousands of raw ideas emerge each year at a large firm's R&D laboratories. Only a few hundred of these ideas develop into formal proposals for new processes or products. Of these proposals, the business selects perhaps a few dozen that it deems suitable for further study to explore their feasibility. After careful scrutiny, the firm concludes that only a handful of these ideas are inventions worthy of being integrated into actual production processes or launched as novel products. The firm is fortunate if one or two ultimately become successful marketplace innovations.

The Importance of Ideas and Knowledge

Economist Paul Romer has added at least one important factor that determines the rate of economic growth. He contends that production and manufacturing knowledge is just as important as the other determinants and perhaps even more so. He considers knowledge a factor of production that, like capital, has to be paid for by forgoing current consumption. Economies must therefore invest in knowledge just as they invest in machines. Because past investment in capital may make it more profitable to acquire more knowledge, there may be an investment-knowledge cycle in which investment spurs knowledge and knowledge spurs investment. A once-and-for-all increase in a country's rate of investment may permanently raise that country's growth rate. (According to traditional theory, a once-and-for-all increase in the rate of saving and therefore in the rate of investment simply leads to a new steady-state standard of living, not one that continues to increase.)

Another way of looking at knowledge is that it is a store of ideas. According to Romer, ideas are what drive economic growth. We have become, in fact, an idea economy. Consider Microsoft Corporation. A relatively small percentage of that company's labor force is involved in actually building products. Rather, a majority of Microsoft employees are attempting to discover new ideas that can be translated into

Does the existence of a Segway involve an invention or an innovation?

computer code that can then be turned into products. The major conclusion that Romer and other new growth theorists draw is this:

Economic growth can continue as long as we keep coming up with new ideas.

The Importance of Human Capital

Knowledge, ideas, and productivity are all tied together. One of the threads is the quality of the labor force. Increases in the productivity of the labor force are a function of increases in human capital, the fourth factor of production discussed in Chapter 2. Recall that human capital consists of the knowledge and skills that people in the workforce acquire through education, on-the-job training, and self-teaching. To increase your own human capital, you have to invest by forgoing income-earning activities while you attend school. Society also has to invest in the form of teachers and education.

According to the new growth theorists, human capital is at least as important as physical capital, particularly when trying to explain international differences in living standards. It is therefore not surprising that one of the most effective ways that developing countries can become developed is by investing in secondary schooling.

One can argue that policy changes that increase human capital will lead to more technological improvements. One of the reasons that concerned citizens, policymakers, and politicians are looking for a change in the U.S. schooling system is that our educational system seems to be falling behind those of other countries. This lag is greatest in science and mathematics—precisely the areas required for developing better technology.

QUICK QUIZ   See page 238 for the answers. Review concepts from this section in MyEconLab.

_____ _____ theory argues that the greater the rewards, the more rapid the pace of technology. And greater rewards spur research and development.

The openness of a nation's economy to international _____ seems to correlate with its rate of economic growth.

Invention and innovation are not the same thing. _____ are useless until _____ transforms them into goods and services that people find valuable.

According to _____ _____ theory, economic growth can continue as long as we keep coming up with new ideas.

Increases in _____ capital can lead to greater rates of economic growth. These come about by increased education, on-the-job training, and self-teaching.

Immigration, Property Rights, and Growth

New theories of economic growth have also shed light on two additional factors that play important roles in influencing a nation's rate of growth of per capita real GDP: immigration and property rights.

Population and Immigration as They Affect Economic Growth

There are several ways to view population growth as it affects economic growth. On the one hand, population growth can result in a larger labor force and increases in human capital, which contribute to economic growth. On the other hand, population growth can be seen as a drain on the economy because for any given amount of GDP, more population means lower per capita GDP. According to MIT economist Michael Kremer, the first of these effects is historically more important. His conclusion is that population growth drives technological progress, which then increases economic growth. The theory is simple: If there are 50 percent more people in the United States, there will be 50 percent more geniuses. And with 50 percent more people, the rewards for creativity are commensurately greater. Otherwise stated, the larger the potential market, the greater the incentive to become ingenious.

A larger market also provides an incentive for well-trained people to immigrate, which undoubtedly helps explain why the United States attracts a disproportionate number of top scientists from around the globe.

Does immigration help spur economic growth? Yes, according to the late economist Julian Simon, who pointed out that "every time our system allows in one more immigrant, on average, the economic welfare of American citizens goes up. . . . Additional immigrants, both the legal and the illegal, raise the standard of living of U.S. natives and have little or no negative impact on any occupational or income class." He further argued that immigrants do not displace natives from jobs but rather create jobs through their purchases and by starting new businesses. Immigrants' earning and spending simply expand the economy.

Not all researchers agree with Simon, and few studies have tested the theories he and Kremer have advanced. This area is currently the focus of much research.

Property Rights and Entrepreneurship

If you were in a country where bank accounts and businesses were periodically expropriated by the government, how willing would you be to leave your financial assets in a savings account or to invest in a business? Certainly, you would be less willing than if such actions never occurred. In general, the more securely private property rights (see page 109) are assigned, the more capital accumulation there will be. People will be willing to invest their savings in endeavors that will increase their wealth in future years. This requires that property rights in their wealth be sanctioned and enforced by the government. In fact, some economic historians have attempted to show that it was the development of well-defined private property rights and legal structures that allowed Western Europe to increase its growth rate after many centuries of stagnation. The ability and certainty with which they can reap the gains from investing also determine the extent to which business owners in other countries will invest capital in developing countries. The threat of loss of property rights that hangs over some developing nations probably stands in the way of foreign investments that would allow these nations to develop more rapidly.

The legal structure of a nation is closely tied to the degree with which its citizens use their own entrepreneurial skills. In Chapter 2, we identified entrepreneurship as the fifth factor of production. Entrepreneurs are the risk takers who seek out new ways to do things and create new products. To the extent that entrepreneurs are allowed to capture the rewards from their entrepreneurial activities, they will seek to engage in those activities. In countries where such rewards cannot be captured because of a lack of property rights, there will be less entrepreneurship. Typically, this results in fewer investments and a lower rate of growth. We shall examine the implications this has for policymakers in Chapter 18.

QUICK QUIZ   *See page 238 for the answers. Review concepts from this section in MyEconLab.*

While some economists argue that population growth reduces _____ growth, others contend that the opposite is true. The latter economists consequently believe that immigration should be encouraged rather than discouraged.

Well-defined and protected _____ rights are important for fostering entrepreneurship. In the absence of well-defined _____ rights, individuals have less incentive to take risks, and economic growth rates suffer.

Economic Development

How did developed countries travel paths of growth from extreme poverty to relative riches? That is the essential issue of **development economics,** which is the study of why some countries grow and develop and others do not and of policies that might help developing economies get richer. It is not enough simply to say that people in different countries are different and that is why some countries are rich and some countries are poor. Economists do not deny that different cultures have different work ethics, but they are unwilling to accept such a pat and fatalistic answer.

Development economics
The study of factors that contribute to the economic growth of a country.

Look at any world map. About four-fifths of the countries you will see on the map are considered relatively poor. The goal of economists who study development is to help the more than 4 billion people today with low living standards join the more than 2 billion people who have at least moderately high living standards.

Putting World Poverty into Perspective

Most U.S. residents cannot even begin to understand the reality of poverty in the world today. At least one-half, if not two-thirds, of the world's population lives at subsistence level, with just enough to eat for survival. Indeed, the World Bank estimates that nearly 20 percent of the world's people live on less than $1.50 per day. The official poverty line in the United States is set above the average income of at least half the human beings on the planet. This is not to say that we should ignore domestic problems with the poor and homeless simply because they are living better than many people elsewhere in the world. Rather, it is necessary for us to maintain an appropriate perspective on what are considered problems for this country relative to what are considered problems elsewhere.

The Relationship Between Population Growth and Economic Development

The world's population is growing at the rate of about 2.3 people a second. That amounts to 198,720 a day or 72.5 million a year. Today, there are nearly 7 billion people on earth. By 2050, according to the United Nations, the world's population will be close to leveling off at around 9.1 billion. Panel (a) of Figure 9-7 on page 230 shows population growth. Panel (b) emphasizes an implication of panel (a), which is that virtually all the growth in population is occurring in developing nations. Many developed countries are expected to lose population over the next several decades.

Ever since the Reverend Thomas Robert Malthus wrote *An Essay on the Principle of Population* in 1798, excessive population growth has been a concern. Modern-day Malthusians are able to generate great enthusiasm for the concept that population growth is bad. Over and over, media pundits and a number of scientists tell us that rapid population growth threatens economic development and the quality of life.

FIGURE 9-7

Expected Growth in World Population by 2050

Panel (a) displays the percentages of the world's population residing in the various continents by 2050 and shows projected population growth for these continents and for selected nations. It indicates that Asia and Africa are expected to gain the most in population by the year 2050. Panel (b) indicates that population will increase in developing countries before beginning to level off around 2050, whereas industrially advanced nations will grow very little in population in the first half of this century.

Source: United Nations.

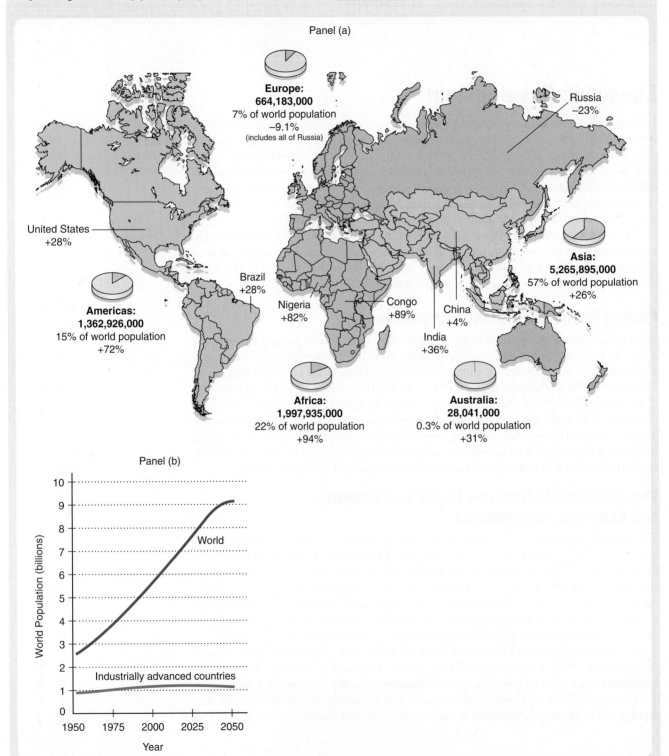

MALTHUS WAS PROVED WRONG Malthus predicted that population would outstrip food supplies. This prediction has never been supported by the facts, according to economist Nicholas Eberstadt of the Harvard Center for Population Studies. As the world's population has grown, so has the world's food supply, measured by calories per person. Furthermore, the price of food, corrected for inflation, has generally been falling for more than a century. That means that the supply of food has been expanding faster than the rise in demand caused by increased population.

GROWTH LEADS TO SMALLER FAMILIES Furthermore, economists have found that as nations become richer, average family size declines. Otherwise stated, the more economic development occurs, the slower the population growth rate becomes. This has certainly been true in Western Europe and in the former Soviet Union, where populations in some countries are actually declining. Predictions of birthrates in developing countries have often turned out to be overstated if those countries experience rapid economic growth. This was the case in Chile, Hong Kong, Mexico, and Taiwan. Recent research on population and economic development has revealed that social and economic modernization has been accompanied by a decline in childbearing significant enough that it might be called a fertility revolution. Modernization reduces infant mortality, which in turn reduces the incentive for couples to have many children to make sure that a certain number survive to adulthood. Modernization also lowers the demand for children for a variety of reasons, not the least being that couples in more developed countries do not need to rely on their children to take care of them in old age.

The Stages of Development: Agriculture to Industry to Services

If we analyze the development of modern rich nations, we find that they went through three stages. First is the agricultural stage, when most of the population is involved in agriculture. Then comes the manufacturing stage, when much of the population becomes involved in the industrialized sector of the economy. And finally there is a shift toward services. That is exactly what happened in the United States: The so-called tertiary, or service, sector of the economy continues to grow, whereas the manufacturing sector (and its share of employment) is declining in relative importance.

Of particular significance, however, is the requirement for early specialization in a nation's comparative advantage (see Chapter 2). The doctrine of comparative advantage is particularly appropriate for the developing countries of the world. If trading is allowed among nations, a country is best off if it produces what it has a comparative advantage in producing and imports the rest (for more details, see Chapter 33). This means that many developing countries should continue to specialize in agricultural production or in labor-intensive manufactured goods.

Keys to Economic Development

One theory of development states that for a country to develop, it must have a large natural resource base. This theory goes on to assert that much of the world is running out of natural resources, thereby limiting economic growth and development. Only the narrowest definition of a natural resource, however, could lead to such an opinion. In broader terms, a natural resource is something occurring in nature that we can use for our own purposes. As emphasized by new growth theory, natural resources therefore include human capital—education and experience. Also, the natural resources that we could define several hundred years ago did not, for example, include hydroelectric power—no one knew that such a natural resource existed or how to bring it into existence.

Natural resources by themselves are not a prerequisite for or a guarantee of economic development, as demonstrated by Japan's extensive development despite a lack

Go to **www.econtoday.com/chapter09** to contemplate whether there may be a relationship between inequality and a nation's growth and to visit the home page of the World Bank's Thematic Group on Inequality, Poverty, and Socioeconomic Performance.

of domestic oil resources and by Brazil's slow pace of development in spite of a vast array of natural resources. Resources must be transformed into something usable for either investment or consumption.

Economists have found that four factors seem to be highly related to the pace of economic development:

1. *Establishing a system of property rights.* As noted earlier, if you were in a country where bank accounts and businesses were periodically expropriated by the government, you would be reluctant to leave some of your wealth in a savings account or to invest in a business. Expropriation of private property rarely takes place in developed countries. It has occurred in numerous developing countries, however. For example, private property was once nationalized in Chile and still is for the most part in Cuba. Economists have found that other things being equal, the more secure private property rights are, the more private capital accumulation and economic growth there will be.

2. *Developing an educated population.* Both theoretically and empirically, we know that a more educated workforce aids economic development because it allows individuals to build on the ideas of others. Thus, developing countries can advance more rapidly if they increase investments in education. Or, stated in the negative, economic development is difficult to sustain if a nation allows a sizable portion of its population to remain uneducated. Education allows impoverished young people to acquire skills that enable them to avoid poverty as adults.

3. *Letting "creative destruction" run its course.* The twentieth-century Harvard economist Joseph Schumpeter championed the concept of "creative destruction," through which new businesses ultimately create new jobs and economic growth after first destroying old jobs, old companies, and old industries. Such change is painful and costly, but it is necessary for economic advancement. Nowhere is this more important than in developing countries, where the principle is often ignored. Many governments in developing nations have had a history of supporting current companies and industries by discouraging new technologies and new companies from entering the marketplace. The process of creative destruction has not been allowed to work its magic in these countries.

4. *Limiting protectionism.* Open economies experience faster economic development than economies closed to international trade. Trade encourages individuals and businesses to discover ways to specialize so that they can become more productive and earn higher incomes. Increased productivity and subsequent increases in economic growth are the results. Thus, having fewer trade barriers promotes faster economic development.

Go to www.econtoday.com/chapter09 to link to a World Trade Organization explanation of how free trade promotes greater economic growth and higher employment.

QUICK QUIZ   *See page 238 for the answers. Review concepts from this section in MyEconLab.*

Although many people believe that population growth hinders economic development, there is little evidence to support that notion. What is clear is that economic development tends to lead to a reduction in the rate of _____ growth.

Historically, there are three stages of economic development: the _____ stage, the _____ stage, and the _____-_____ stage, when a large part of the workforce is employed in providing services.

Although one theory of economic development holds that a sizable natural resource base is the key to a nation's development, this fails to account for the importance of the human element: The _____ _____ must be capable of using a country's natural resources.

Fundamental factors contributing to the pace of economic development are a well-defined system of _____ _____, training and _____, allowing new generations of companies and industries to _____ older generations, and promoting an open economy by allowing _____ _____.

You Are There An Invention Becomes a Market Innovation—by Accident

Several years ago, Richard Bracke was working as a bodyguard and chef. He happened to meet Robert Cotton and Mark Zickel, who were making hammocks and marketing them on the Web site of Amazon.com. The three men agreed that portable audio products were likely to become popular, and they began developing flat-panel speakers for use with laptop computers. Together, they formed a company called Sonic Impact Technologies, based in San Diego.

In 2003, the three businessmen learned about a small amplifier utilizing a tiny microchip. They decided to power it with two AA batteries and sell it for $39 as a child's beach plaything called the T-Amp. A couple of years later, sales suddenly took off. Adults, it turned out, were buying T-Amps at the $39 price as fast as the company could get them to stores. Some adult customers reported that they were connecting the "toy" amplifiers to $6,000 CD players and

$18,000 speakers. Purely by accident, the T-Amp had become a major innovation in the stereo-amplifier market.

Today, Sonic Impact Technologies sells a line of products that includes speakers for iPods, mini-subwoofers and portable speakers for stereo systems, and speaker bags and cases. Nevertheless, the T-Amp remains a major product, undoubtedly still purchased for use by some children but mainly by adults.

CRITICAL ANALYSIS QUESTIONS

1. How does the experience of Sonic Impact Technologies provide support for the view that invention is only one facet of innovation?

2. How does the T-Amp story bolster the argument that technologies often move relatively slowly from initial invention to widespread use?

Issues and Applications

Governments Get Serious About "Child Support"

CONCEPTS APPLIED

▸ Economic Growth
▸ Labor Productivity
▸ Immigration and Growth

In the United States and the United Kingdom, the current birthrate of slightly less than 2.0 children per woman is just below the level of 2.1 children per woman that would be necessary to maintain the current populations of those countries. In a number of other nations, such as Canada, Estonia, Germany, Italy, Japan, and South Korea, the birthrate has dropped below 1.5 children per woman. Consequently, the populations of these nations are tending to *shrink*—leading their governments to worry that prospects for economic growth likewise are dwindling.

Government-Funded Incentives to Have Babies

In an effort to reverse population downturns, the governments of more than 20 countries are offering compensation to women who bear children. For instance, new mothers receive lump-sum payments in Italy (about $1,500), Australia (just under $4,000), and Russia ($9,200). The French government promises the mother of a third child about $1,125 per month for the child's first year. South Korea's government provides fertility treatments for women seeking to have children, tax breaks and grants to help cover child care, and extra grants for those women who choose to bear several children.

Some national governments offer explicit wage compensation to women who have babies. The Bulgarian government offers 315 days of compensation equal to 90 percent of the average market wage rate, and under many circumstances, the stipend can be extended to two years. Estonia's government pays mothers 100 percent of the average market wage for 15 months, and Lithuania offers 100 percent wage compensation for 6 months followed by a payment of 85 percent of the market wage rate for another 6 months. In Germany, even fathers receive wage compensation for up to two months.

Can the Baby-Subsidy Fad Regenerate Labor Growth?

Both the number of hours that a nation's residents work and the average units of output they produce per hour determine the country's overall labor productivity. Thus, in the long run, increasing population growth could pay off in higher economic growth in countries where governments are rushing to offer child-bearing inducements.

During a single decade or so, however, more babies will not translate into larger, more productive workforces.

Countries with shrinking populations that are seeking to maintain or boost labor growth—and, hence, economic growth rates—in the near term must consider additional options.

Other Options: Human Capital Development and Immigration

For governments of nations with shrinking native-born populations, one alternative way to boost overall labor productivity is to adopt policies that promote greater individual productivity—higher output per existing worker. For instance, in France, Germany, and other European nations with declining populations, national governments have taken tentative steps toward reversing policies that have had the effect of reducing output per worker. Governments in these and other nations have also boosted subsidies aimed at increasing human capital investments. Many subsidies have been aimed explicitly at forms of education, on-the-job training, and self-teaching most likely to yield immediate productivity payoffs.

Another near-term alternative is to boost national labor forces through immigration. Governments of European nations have permitted more immigrants from Africa and the Middle East, where women on average bear about five children. The Japanese, South Korean, and Taiwanese governments have also loosened restrictions on immigration from the rest of Asia, where women bear an average of about three children each.

Over the next decade, policies aimed at raising labor productivity via investments in human capital and greater openness to immigration are more likely than baby subsidies to boost economic growth in nations with shrinking populations. Indeed, it remains to be seen whether offering incentives to women to have more children in order to raise native-born populations will succeed in reenergizing economic growth.

Test your understanding of this chapter by going online to **MyEconLab.**
In the Study Plan for this chapter, select Section N: News.

For Critical Analysis

1. Why is steady population growth, by itself, unable to assure steadily increasing overall economic growth?

2. Why is it at least possible that in some cases allowing more immigration will not necessarily boost economic growth? (Hint: Recall that economic growth is measured as the rate of change in real GDP *per capita.*)

Web Resources

1. For a discussion of recent shifts in global population growth, go to www.econtoday.com/chapter09.

2. To learn about why population growth in much of Eastern Europe has been negative in recent years, go to www.econtoday.com/chapter09.

Research Project

Suppose that you have been appointed to a commission charged with recommending policies for promoting economic growth in a nation experiencing a shrinking native-born population, lagging labor productivity, and stagnant growth in per capita real GDP. Develop a list of three policies, and rank them on the basis of their likely success in boosting long-run economic growth. Briefly defend your ranking.

 Here is what you should know after reading this chapter. **MyEconLab** will help you identify what you know, and where to go when you need to practice.

WHAT YOU SHOULD KNOW		WHERE TO GO TO PRACTICE
Economic Growth The rate of economic growth is the annual rate of change in per capita real GDP. This measure of the rate of growth of a nation's economy takes into account both its growth in overall production of goods and services and the growth rate of its population. It is an average measure that does not account for possible changes in the distribution of income or various welfare costs or benefits that may accompany growth of the economy.	economic growth, 215 **KEY FIGURES** Figure 9-1, 214 Figure 9-2, 215	• **MyEconLab** Study Plan 9.1 • Audio introduction to Chapter 9 • Animated Figures 9-1, 9-2 • ABC News Video: Economic Growth: How Much, How Fast?
Why Economic Growth Rates Are Important Over long intervals, relatively small differences in the rate of economic growth can accumulate to produce large disparities in per capita incomes. The reason is that like accumulations of interest, economic growth compounds over time. Thus, if a nation's rate of per capita real GDP growth rises by 3 percentage points per year, it will have a level of per capita real GDP that is more than four times higher after 50 years. But a country with a per capita real GDP growth rate 4 percentage points higher per year ends up with per capita real GDP more than seven times higher.	rule of 70, 219	• **MyEconLab** Study Plan 9.1 • Video: Growth Rates and Compound Interest
Why Productivity Increases Are Crucial for Maintaining Economic Growth For a nation with a relatively stable population and a steady rate of capital accumulation, productivity growth emerges as a fundamental factor influencing near-term changes in economic growth. Higher productivity growth unambiguously contributes to greater annual increases in a nation's per capita real GDP.	labor productivity, 220	• **MyEconLab** Study Plan 9.2

(continued)

 *(continued)*

WHAT YOU SHOULD KNOW	WHERE TO GO TO PRACTICE
The Key Determinants of Economic Growth The fundamental factors contributing to economic growth are growth in a nation's pool of labor, growth of its capital stock, and growth in the productivity of its capital and labor. A key determinant of capital accumulation is a nation's saving rate. Higher saving rates contribute to greater investment and hence increased capital accumulation and economic growth.	• **MyEconLab** Study Plan 9.3 • Video: Saving and Economic Growth
New Growth Theory This is a theory that examines why individuals and businesses conduct research into inventing and developing new technologies and how this process interacts with the rate of economic growth. This theory emphasizes how rewards to technological innovation contribute to higher economic growth rates. A key implication of the theory is that ideas and knowledge are crucial elements of the growth process. new growth theory, 223 patent, 224 innovation, 225 KEY FIGURES Figure 9-5, 224 Figure 9-6, 226	• **MyEconLab** Study Plan 9.4 • Video: The Importance of Human Capital • Animated Figures 9-5, 9-6
Fundamental Factors That Contribute to a Nation's Economic Development Key features shared by nations that attain higher levels of economic development are protection of property rights, significant opportunities for their residents to obtain training and education, policies that permit new companies and industries to replace older ones, and the avoidance of protectionist barriers that hinder international trade. development economics, 229 KEY FIGURE Figure 9-7, 230	• **MyEconLab** Study Plans 9.5, 9.6 • Animated Figure 9-7

Log in to MyEconLab, take a chapter test, and get a personalized Study Plan that tells you which concepts you understand and which ones you need to review. From there, MyEconLab will give you further practice, tutorials, animations, videos, and guided solutions. Log in to www.myeconlab.com

PROBLEMS

All problems are assignable in (X) myeconlab *. Answers to odd-numbered problems appear at the back of the book.*

9-1. The graph shows a production possibilities curve for 2012 and two potential production possibilities curves for 2013, denoted 2013$_A$ and 2013$_B$.

    a. Which of the labeled points corresponds to maximum feasible 2012 production that is more likely to be associated with the curve denoted 2013$_A$?

    b. Which of the labeled points corresponds to maximum feasible 2012 production that is more likely to be associated with the curve denoted 2013$_B$?

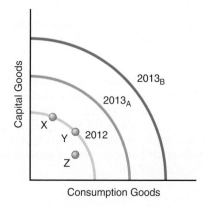

9-2. A nation's capital goods wear out over time, so a portion of its capital goods become unusable every year. Last year, its residents decided to produce no capital goods. It has experienced no growth in its population or in the amounts of other productive resources during the past year. In addition, the nation's technology and resource productivity have remained unchanged during the past year. Will the nation's economic growth rate for the current year be negative, zero, or positive?

9-3. In the situation described in Problem 9-2, suppose that educational improvements during the past year enable the people of this nation to repair all capital goods so that they continue to function as well as new. All other factors are unchanged, however. In light of this single change to the conditions faced in this nation, will the nation's economic growth rate for the current year be negative, zero, or positive?

9-4. Consider the following data. What is the per capita real GDP in each of these countries?

Country	Population (millions)	Real GDP ($ billions)
A	10	55
B	20	60
C	5	70

9-5. Suppose that during the next 10 years, real GDP triples and population doubles in each of the nations in Problem 9-4. What will per capita real GDP be in each country after 10 years have passed?

9-6. Consider the following table displaying annual growth rates for nations X, Y, and Z, each of which entered 2009 with real per capita GDP equal to $20,000:

Country	Annual Growth Rate (%)			
	2009	2010	2011	2012
X	7	1	3	4
Y	4	5	7	9
Z	5	4	3	2

a. Which nation most likely experienced a sizable earthquake in late 2009 that destroyed a significant portion of its stock of capital goods,

but was followed by speedy investments in rebuilding the nation's capital stock? What is this nation's per capita real GDP at the end of 2012, rounded to the nearest dollar?

b. Which nation most likely adopted policies in 2009 that encouraged a gradual shift in production from capital goods to consumption goods? What is this nation's per capita real GDP at the end of 2012, rounded to the nearest dollar?

c. Which nation most likely adopted policies in 2009 that encouraged a quick shift in production from consumption goods to capital goods? What is this nation's per capita real GDP at the end of 2012, rounded to the nearest dollar?

9-7. Per capita real GDP grows at a rate of 3 percent in country F and at a rate of 6 percent in country G. Both begin with equal levels of per capita real GDP. Use Table 9-3 on page 218 to determine how much higher per capita real GDP will be in country G after 20 years. How much higher will real GDP be in country G after 40 years?

9-8. Per capita real GDP in country L is three times as high as in country M. The economic growth rate in country M, however, is 8 percent, while country L's economy grows at a rate of 5 percent. Use Table 9-3 on page 218 to determine approximately how many years will pass before per capita real GDP in country M surpasses per capita real GDP in country L.

9-9. Per capita real GDP in country S is only half as great as per capita real GDP in country T. Country T's rate of economic growth is 4 percent. The government of country S, however, enacts policies that achieve a growth rate of 20 percent. Use Table 9-3 on page 218 to determine how long country S must maintain this growth rate before its per capita real GDP surpasses that of country T.

9-10. In 2010, a nation's population was 10 million. Its nominal GDP was $40 billion, and its price index was 100. In 2011, its population had increased to 12 million, its nominal GDP had risen to $57.6 billion, and its price index had increased to 120. What was this nation's economic growth rate during the year?

9-11. Between the start of 2010 and the start of 2011, a country's economic growth rate was 4 percent. Its population did not change during the year, nor did its price level. What was the rate of increase of the country's nominal GDP during this one-year interval?

9-12. In 2010, a nation's population was 10 million, its real GDP was $1.21 billion, and its GDP deflator had a value of 121. By 2011, its population had increased to 12 million, its real GDP had risen to $1.5 billion, and its GDP deflator had a value of 125. What was the percentage change in per capita real GDP between 2010 and 2011?

9-13. A nation's per capita real GDP was $2,000 in 2009, and the nation's population was 5 million in that year. Between 2009 and 2010, the inflation rate in this country was 5 percent, and the nation's annual rate of economic growth was 10 percent. Its population remained unchanged. What was per capita real GDP in 2010? What was the *level* of real GDP in 2010?

9-14. Brazil has a population of about 190 million, with about 140 million over the age of 15. Of these, an estimated 25 percent, or 35 million people, are functionally illiterate. The typical literate individual reads only about two nonacademic books per year, which is less than half the number read by the typical literate U.S. or European resident. Answer the following questions solely from the perspective of new growth theory:

a. Discuss the implications of Brazil's literacy and reading rates for its growth prospects in light of the key tenets of new growth theory.

b. What types of policies might Brazil implement to improve its growth prospects? Explain.

ECONOMICS ON THE NET

Multifactor Productivity and Its Growth Growth in productivity is a key factor determining a nation's overall economic growth.

Title: Bureau of Labor Statistics: Multifactor Productivity Trends

Navigation: Use the link at **www.econtoday.com/chapter09** to visit the multifactor productivity home page of the Bureau of Labor Statistics.

Application Read the summary, and answer the following questions.

1. What does multifactor productivity measure? Based on your reading of this chapter, how does multifactor productivity relate to the determination of economic growth?

2. Click on *Multifactor Productivity Trends in Manufacturing*, and then click on *Manufacturing Industries: Multifactor Productivity Trends*. According to these data, which industries have exhibited the greatest productivity growth in recent years?

For Group Study and Analysis Divide the class into three groups to examine multifactor productivity data for the private business sector, the private nonfarm business sector, and the manufacturing sector. Have each group identify periods when multifactor productivity growth was particularly fast or slow. Then compare notes. Does it appear to make a big difference which sector one looks at when evaluating periods of greatest and least growth in multifactor productivity?

ANSWERS TO QUICK QUIZZES

p. 220: (i) per capita; (ii) benefits . . . costs; (iii) large

p. 223: (i) capital . . . labor . . . capital . . . labor; (ii) saving . . . save . . . saving

p. 227: (i) New growth; (ii) trade; (iii) Inventions . . . innovation; (iv) new growth; (v) human

p. 229: (i) economic; (ii) property . . . property

p. 232: (i) population; (ii) agricultural . . . manufacturing . . . service-sector; (iii) labor force; (iv) property rights . . . education . . . replace . . . international trade

Real GDP and the Price Level in the Long Run

10

From the 1930s until the early 1960s, the annual rate of U.S. real GDP growth steadily increased, but it generally trended downward in the 1970s and 1980s. During the 1990s, annual real GDP growth recovered somewhat. Nevertheless, during the 2000s there has been yet another decline. What factors determine variations in real GDP growth rates over long periods of time? How are long-run changes in the rate of real GDP growth related to rates of change in the level of prices—that is, the inflation rate? In this chapter, you will learn the answers to these questions.

LEARNING OBJECTIVES

After reading this chapter, you should be able to:

- Understand the concept of long-run aggregate supply
- Describe the effect of economic growth on the long-run aggregate supply curve
- Explain why the aggregate demand curve slopes downward and list key factors that cause this curve to shift
- Discuss the meaning of long-run equilibrium for the economy as a whole
- Evaluate why economic growth can cause deflation
- Evaluate likely reasons for persistent inflation in recent decades

MyEconLab helps you master each objective and study more efficiently. See end of chapter for details.

DID YOU KNOW THAT between 1920 and 1929—the period known in the United States as the "Roaring Twenties"—the U.S. price level declined? Between 1920 and 1922, the price level fell at an average annual rate of 8.2 percent. From 1923 to 1926, however, the level of prices rose at an annual rate of about 1.4 percent. Then, from 1927 to 1929, the price level fell once more, at an average annual rate of decline equal to 1.1 percent. In the meantime, the average prices of shares of stock in U.S. corporations more than doubled, and real GDP increased.

Why did the United States experience periods of deflation even as the nation experienced economic growth during the 1920s? Why did deflation continue even when economic growth turned negative in the 1930s, a time we now call the Great Depression? To answer these questions, you must learn about factors that influence the long-run stability of the price level.

Output Growth and the Long-Run Aggregate Supply Curve

In Chapter 2, we showed the derivation of the production possibilities curve (PPC). At any point in time, the economy can be inside or on the PPC but never outside it. Along the PPC, a country's resources are fully employed in the production of goods and services, and the sum total of the inflation-adjusted value of all final goods and services produced is the nation's real GDP. Economists refer to the total of all planned production for the entire economy as the **aggregate supply** of real output.

Aggregate supply
The total of all planned production for the economy.

Long-run aggregate supply curve
A vertical line representing the real output of goods and services after full adjustment has occurred. It can also be viewed as representing the real GDP of the economy under conditions of full employment—the full-employment level of real GDP.

The Long-Run Aggregate Supply Curve

Put yourself in a world in which nothing has been changing, year in and year out. The price level has not changed. Technology has not changed. The prices of inputs that firms must purchase have not changed. Labor productivity has not changed. All resources are fully employed, so the economy operates on its production possibilities curve, such as the one depicted in panel (a) of Figure 10-1. This is a world that is fully adjusted and in which people have all the information they are ever going to have about that world. The **long-run aggregate supply curve** (*LRAS*) in this world is some amount of real GDP—say,

---

FIGURE 10-1

The Production Possibilities Curve and the Economy's Long-Run Aggregate Supply Curve

At a point in time, a nation's base of resources and its technological capabilities define the position of its production possibilities curve (PPC), as shown in panel (a). This defines the real GDP that the nation can produce when resources are fully employed, which determines the position of the long-run aggregate supply curve (*LRAS*) displayed in panel (b). Because people have complete information and input prices adjust fully in the long run, the *LRAS* is vertical.

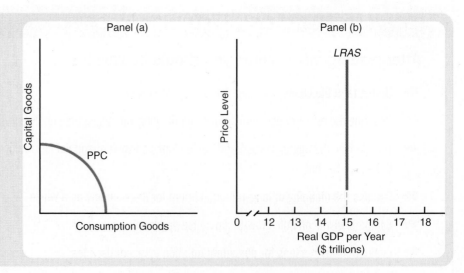

$15 trillion of real GDP—which is the value of the flow of production of final goods and services measured in **base-year dollars.** We can represent long-run aggregate supply by a vertical line at $15 trillion of real GDP. This is what you see in panel (b) of the figure. That curve, labeled *LRAS*, is a vertical line determined by technology and **endowments,** or resources that exist in our economy. It is the full-information and full-adjustment level of real output of goods and services. It is the level of real GDP that will continue being produced year after year, forever, if nothing changes.

Another way of viewing the *LRAS* is to think of it as the full-employment level of real GDP. When the economy reaches full employment along its production possibilities curve, no further adjustments will occur unless a change occurs in the other variables that we are assuming constant and stable. Some economists suggest that the *LRAS* occurs at the level of real GDP consistent with the natural rate of unemployment, the unemployment rate that occurs in an economy with full adjustment in the long run. As we discussed in Chapter 7, many economists like to think of the natural rate of unemployment as consisting of frictional and structural unemployment.

To understand why the *LRAS* is vertical, think about the long run, which is a sufficiently long period that all factors of production and prices, including wages and other input prices, can change. A change in the level of prices of goods and services has no effect on real GDP per year in the long run, because higher prices will be accompanied by comparable changes in input prices. Suppliers will therefore have no incentive to increase or decrease their production of goods and services. Remember that in the long run, everybody has full information, and there is full adjustment to price level changes. (Of course, this is not necessarily true in the short run, as we shall discuss in Chapter 11.)

Base-year dollars
The value of a current sum expressed in terms of prices in a base year.

Endowments
The various resources in an economy, including both physical resources and such human resources as ingenuity and management skills.

Go to **www.econtoday.com/chapter10** to find out how fast wages are adjusting. Click on "Employment Costs," and then on "Employment Cost Index."

Economic Growth and Long-Run Aggregate Supply

In Chapter 9, you learned about the determinants of the growth in per capita real GDP: the annual growth rate of labor, the rate of year-to-year capital accumulation, and the rate of growth of the productivity of labor and capital. As time goes by, population gradually increases, and labor force participation rates may even rise. The capital stock typically grows as businesses add such capital equipment as new information-technology hardware. Furthermore, technology improves. Thus, the economy's production possibilities increase, and the production possibilities curve shifts outward, as shown in panel (a) of Figure 10-2.

FIGURE 10-2

The Long-Run Aggregate Supply Curve and Shifts in It

In panel (a), we repeat a diagram that we used in Chapter 2, on page 38, to show the meaning of economic growth. Over time, the production possibilities curve shifts outward. In panel (b), we demonstrate the same principle by showing the long-run aggregate supply curve as initially a vertical line at $14.3 trillion of real GDP per year. As our productive abilities increase, the *LRAS* moves outward to *LRAS*$_{2011}$ at $15 trillion.

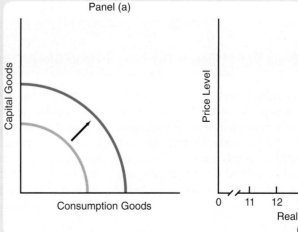

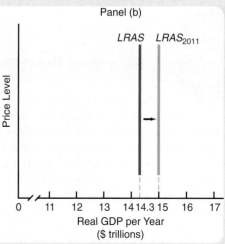

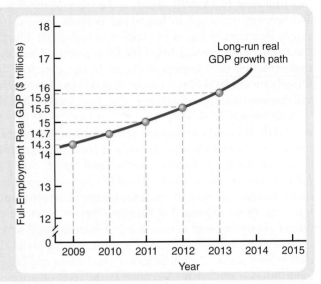

FIGURE 10-3

A Sample Long-Run Growth Path for Real GDP

Year-to-year shifts in the long-run aggregate supply curve yield a long-run trend path for real GDP growth. In this example, from 2011 onward, real GDP grows by a steady 3 percent per year.

The result is economic growth: Aggregate real GDP and per capita real GDP increase. This means that in a growing economy such as ours, the *LRAS* will shift outward to the right, as in panel (b). We have drawn the *LRAS* for the year 2011 to the right of our original *LRAS* of $14.3 trillion of real GDP. We assume that between now and 2011, real GDP increases to $15 trillion, to give us the position of the $LRAS_{2011}$ curve. Thus, it is to the right of today's *LRAS* curve.

We may conclude that in a growing economy, the *LRAS* shifts ever farther to the right over time. If the *LRAS* happened to shift rightward at a constant pace, real GDP would increase at a steady annual rate. As shown in Figure 10-3, this means that real GDP would increase along a long-run, or *trend*, path that is an upward-sloping line. Thus, if the *LRAS* shifts rightward from $14.3 trillion to $15 trillion between now and 2011 and then increases at a steady 3 percent annual rate every year thereafter, in 2012 long-run real GDP will equal $15.5 trillion, in 2013 it will equal $15.9 trillion, and so on.

How is a net outflow of skilled workers threatening to make Germany's long-run real GDP growth path less steeply sloped?

INTERNATIONAL EXAMPLE
Will a "Brain Drain" Flatten Germany's Trend Growth Path?

When a nation loses some of its best-educated workers, it experiences a *brain drain*. A nation undergoing a brain drain experiences an outflow of human capital and hence loses a portion of a key productive resource. As a result, the nation's economic growth slows. Its long-run aggregate supply curve shifts rightward at a slower pace, and its long-run real GDP growth path becomes less steeply sloped.

Germany has been experiencing a brain drain since the early 2000s. In recent years, nearly 150,000 residents, including numerous engineers, physicians, and university professors, have departed from Germany annually. Their departures have left the nation with more than 20,000 open jobs in engineering, 5,000 unfilled positions for physicians, and hundreds of vacant academic posts. An insufficient number of German residents are choosing to be trained in these fields,

---

INTERNATIONAL EXAMPLE (cont.)

and immigration rules hinder efforts by engineers, physicians, and professors from other countries to move to Germany. Consequently, a net outflow of human capital appears likely to continue. If so, we can predict that Germany's economic growth will probably continue to slow, and a shallower long-run real GDP growth path is likely to result.

FOR CRITICAL ANALYSIS
How is a declining birthrate in Germany likely to affect the nation's long-run real GDP growth path?

QUICK QUIZ   *See page 260 for the answers. Review concepts from this section in MyEconLab.*

The **long-run aggregate supply curve,** *LRAS,* is a _____ line determined by amounts of available resources such as labor and capital and by technology and resource productivity. The position of the *LRAS* gives the full-information and full-adjustment level of real GDP.

The _____ rate of unemployment occurs at the long-run level of real GDP given by the position of the *LRAS.*

If labor or capital increases from year to year or if the productivity of either of these resources rises from one year to the next, the *LRAS* shifts _____. In a growing economy, therefore, real GDP gradually _____ over time.

Total Expenditures and Aggregate Demand

In equilibrium, individuals, businesses, and governments purchase all the goods and services produced, valued in trillions of real dollars. As explained in Chapters 7 and 8, GDP is the dollar value of total expenditures on domestically produced final goods and services. Because all expenditures are made by individuals, firms, or governments, the total value of these expenditures must be what these market participants decide it shall be.

The decisions of individuals, managers of firms, and government officials determine the annual dollar value of total expenditures. You can certainly see this in your role as an individual. You decide what the total dollar amount of your expenditures will be in a year. You decide how much you want to spend and how much you want to save. Thus, if we want to know what determines the total value of GDP, the answer is clear: the spending decisions of individuals like you; firms; and local, state, and national governments. In an open economy, we must also include foreign individuals, firms, and governments (foreign residents, for short) that decide to spend their money income in the United States.

Simply stating that the dollar value of total expenditures in this country depends on what individuals, firms, governments, and foreign residents decide to do really doesn't tell us much, though. Two important issues remain:

1. What determines the total amount that individuals, firms, governments, and foreign residents want to spend?

2. What determines the equilibrium price level and the rate of inflation (or deflation)?

The *LRAS* tells us only about the economy's long-run real GDP. To answer these additional questions, we must consider another important concept. This is **aggregate demand,** which is the total of all *planned* real expenditures in the economy.

Because there is a net outflow of graduates and researchers from German universities like this one, what can you predict about Germany's long-run GDP growth path?

Aggregate demand
The total of all planned expenditures in the entire economy.

The Aggregate Demand Curve

The **aggregate demand curve**, *AD*, gives the various quantities of all final commodities demanded at various price levels, all other things held constant. Recall the components of GDP that you studied in Chapter 8: consumption spending, investment expenditures, government purchases, and net foreign demand for domestic production. They are all components of aggregate demand. Throughout this chapter and the next, whenever you see the aggregate demand curve, realize that it is a shorthand way of talking about the components of GDP that are measured by government statisticians when they calculate total economic activity each year. In Chapter 12, you will look more closely at the relationship between these components and, in particular, at how consumption spending depends on income.

The aggregate demand curve gives the total amount, measured in base-year dollars, of *real* domestic final goods and services that will be purchased at each price level—everything produced for final use by households, businesses, the government, and foreign residents. It includes iPhones, socks, shoes, medical and legal services, computers, and millions of other goods and services that people buy each year.

A graphical representation of the aggregate demand curve is seen in Figure 10-4. On the horizontal axis, real GDP is measured. For our measure of the price level, we use the GDP price deflator on the vertical axis. The aggregate demand curve is labeled *AD*. If the GDP deflator is 110, aggregate quantity demanded is $15 trillion per year (point *A*). At the price level 115, it is $14 trillion per year (point *B*). At the price level 120, it is $13 trillion per year (point *C*). The higher the price level, the lower the total real amount of final goods and services demanded in the economy, everything else remaining constant, as shown by the arrow along *AD* in Figure 10-4. Conversely, the lower the price level, the higher the total real GDP demanded by the economy, everything else staying constant.

Let's take the year 2009. Estimates based on U.S. Department of Commerce preliminary statistics reveal the following information:

- Nominal GDP was estimated to be $14,383.4 billion.
- The price level as measured by the GDP deflator was about 109.8 (base year is 2005, for which the index equals 100).
- Real GDP (output) was approximately $13,096.8 billion in 2005 dollars.

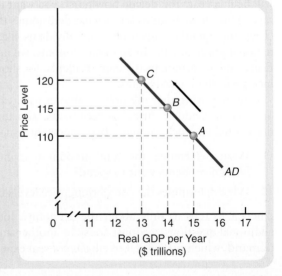

FIGURE 10-4

The Aggregate Demand Curve

The aggregate demand curve, *AD*, slopes downward. If the price level is 110, we will be at point *A* with $15 trillion of real GDP demanded per year. As the price level increases to 115 and to 120, we move up the aggregate demand curve to points *B* and *C*.

What can we say about 2009? Given the dollar cost of buying goods and services and all of the other factors that go into spending decisions by individuals, firms, governments, and foreign residents, the total amount of planned spending on final goods and services by firms, individuals, governments, and foreign residents was $12,841.7 billion in 2009 (in terms of 2005 dollars).

What Happens When the Price Level Rises?

What if the price level in the economy rose to 160 tomorrow? What would happen to the amount of real goods and services that individuals, firms, governments, and foreigners wish to purchase in the United States? We know from Chapter 3 that when the price of one good or service rises, the quantity of it demanded will fall. But here we are talking about the *price level*—the average price of *all* goods and services in the economy. The answer is still that the total quantities of real goods and services demanded would fall, but the reasons are different. When the price of one good or service goes up, the consumer substitutes other goods and services. For the entire economy, when the price level goes up, the consumer doesn't simply substitute one good for another, for now we are dealing with the demand for *all* goods and services in the nation. There are *economywide* reasons that cause the aggregate demand curve to slope downward. They involve at least three distinct forces: the *real-balance effect*, the *interest rate effect*, and the *open economy effect*.

THE REAL-BALANCE EFFECT A rise in the price level will have an effect on spending. Individuals, firms, governments, and foreign residents carry out transactions using money, a portion of which consists of currency and coins that you have in your pocket (or stashed away) right now. Because people use money to purchase goods and services, the amount of money that people have influences the amount of goods and services they want to buy. For example, if you find a $100 bill on the sidewalk, the amount of money you have will rise. Given your now greater level of money, or cash, balances—currency in this case—you will almost surely increase your spending on goods and services. Similarly, if your pocket is picked while you are at the mall, your desired spending would be affected. For example, if your wallet had $150 in it when it was stolen, the reduction in your cash balances—in this case, currency—would no doubt cause you to reduce your planned expenditures. You would ultimately buy fewer goods and services.

This response is sometimes called the **real-balance effect** (or *wealth effect*) because it relates to the real value of your cash balances. While your *nominal* cash balances may remain the same, any change in the price level will cause a change in the *real* value of those cash balances—hence the real-balance effect on total planned expenditures.

When you think of the real-balance effect, just think of what happens to your real wealth if you have, say, a $100 bill hidden under your mattress. If the price level increases by 5 percent, the purchasing power of that $100 bill drops by 5 percent, so you have become less wealthy. You will reduce your purchases of all goods and services by some small amount.

THE INTEREST RATE EFFECT There is a more subtle but equally important effect on your desire to spend. A higher price level leaves people with too few money balances. Hence, they try to borrow more (or lend less) to replenish their cash. This drives up interest rates. Higher interest rates raise borrowing costs for consumers and businesses. They will borrow less and consequently spend less. The fact that a higher price level pushes up interest rates and thereby reduces borrowing and spending is known as the **interest rate effect.**

Real-balance effect
The change in expenditures resulting from a change in the real value of money balances when the price level changes, all other things held constant; also called the *wealth effect*.

Interest rate effect
One of the reasons that the aggregate demand curve slopes downward: Higher price levels increase the interest rate, which in turn causes businesses and consumers to reduce desired spending due to the higher cost of borrowing.

Higher interest rates make it more costly for people to finance purchases of houses and cars. Higher interest rates also make it less profitable for firms to install new equipment and to erect new office buildings. Whether we are talking about individuals or firms, a rise in the price level will cause higher interest rates, which in turn reduce the amount of goods and services that people are willing to purchase. Therefore, an increase in the price level will tend to reduce total planned expenditures. (The opposite occurs if the price level declines.)

THE OPEN ECONOMY EFFECT: THE SUBSTITUTION OF FOREIGN GOODS   Recall from Chapter 8 that GDP includes net exports—the difference between exports and imports. In an open economy, we buy imports from other countries and ultimately pay for them through the foreign exchange market. The same is true for foreign residents who purchase our goods (exports). Given any set of exchange rates between the U.S. dollar and other currencies, an increase in the price level in the United States makes U.S. goods more expensive relative to foreign goods. Foreign residents have downward-sloping demand curves for U.S. goods. When the relative price of U.S. goods goes up, foreign residents buy fewer U.S. goods and more of their own. At home, relatively cheaper prices for foreign goods cause U.S. residents to want to buy more foreign goods instead of domestically produced goods. Thus, when the domestic price level rises, the result is a fall in exports and a rise in imports. That means that a price level increase tends to reduce net exports, thereby reducing the amount of real goods and services purchased in the United States. This is known as the **open economy effect.**

Open economy effect
One of the reasons that the aggregate demand curve slopes downward: Higher price levels result in foreign residents desiring to buy fewer U.S.-made goods, while U.S. residents now desire more foreign-made goods, thereby reducing net exports. This is equivalent to a reduction in the amount of real goods and services purchased in the United States.

What Happens When the Price Level Falls?

What about the reverse? Suppose now that the GDP deflator falls to 100 from an initial level of 120. You should be able to trace the three effects on desired purchases of goods and services. Specifically, how do the real-balance, interest rate, and open economy effects cause people to want to buy more? You should come to the conclusion that the lower the price level, the greater the total planned spending on goods and services.

The aggregate demand curve, *AD*, shows the quantity of aggregate output that will be demanded at alternative price levels. It is downward sloping, just like the demand curve for individual goods. The higher the price level, the lower the real amount of total planned expenditures, and vice versa.

Demand for All Goods and Services versus Demand for a Single Good or Service

Even though the aggregate demand curve, *AD*, in Figure 10-4 on page 244 looks similar to the one for individual demand, *D*, for a single good or service that you encountered in Chapters 3 and 4, the two are not the same. When we derive the aggregate demand curve, we are looking at the entire economic system. The aggregate demand curve, *AD*, differs from an individual demand curve, *D*, because we are looking at total planned expenditures on *all* goods and services when we construct *AD*.

Shifts in the Aggregate Demand Curve

In Chapter 3, you learned that any time a nonprice determinant of demand changes, the demand curve will shift inward to the left or outward to the right. The same analysis holds for the aggregate demand curve, except we are now talking about the non-price-level determinants of aggregate demand. So, when we ask the question, "What determines the position of the aggregate demand curve?" the fundamental proposition is as follows:

> *Any non-price-level change that increases aggregate spending (on domestic goods) shifts **AD** to the right. Any non-price-level change that decreases aggregate spending (on domestic goods) shifts **AD** to the left.*

The list of potential determinants of the position of the aggregate demand curve is long. Some of the most important "curve shifters" for aggregate demand are presented in Table 10-1.

TABLE 10-1

Determinants of Aggregate Demand

Aggregate demand consists of the demand for domestically produced consumption goods, investment goods, government purchases, and net exports. Consequently, any change in total planned spending on any one of these components of real GDP will cause a change in aggregate demand. Some possibilities are listed here.

Changes That Cause an Increase in Aggregate Demand	Changes That Cause a Decrease in Aggregate Demand
An increase in the amount of money in circulation	A decrease in the amount of money in circulation
Increased security about jobs and future income	Decreased security about jobs and future income
Improvements in economic conditions in other countries	Declines in economic conditions in other countries
A reduction in real interest rates (nominal interest rates corrected for inflation) not due to price level changes	A rise in real interest rates (nominal interest rates corrected for inflation) not due to price level changes
Tax decreases	Tax increases
A drop in the foreign exchange value of the dollar	A rise in the foreign exchange value of the dollar

QUICK QUIZ   *See page 260 for the answers. Review concepts from this section in MyEconLab.*

Aggregate demand is the total of all planned _____ in the economy, and **aggregate supply** is the total of all planned _____ in the economy. The aggregate demand curve shows the various quantities of total planned _____ on final goods and services at various price levels; it is downward sloping.

There are three reasons why the aggregate demand curve is downward sloping: the _____ - _____ effect, the _____ _____ effect, and the _____ _____ effect.

The _____ - _____ effect occurs because price level changes alter the real value of cash balances, thereby causing people to desire to spend more or less, depending on whether the price level decreases or increases.

The _____ _____ effect is caused by interest rate changes that mimic price level changes. At higher interest rates, people seek to buy _____ houses and cars, and at lower interest rates, they seek to buy _____ .

The **open economy effect** occurs because of a shift away from expenditures on _____ goods and a shift toward expenditures on _____ goods when the domestic price level increases.

Long-Run Equilibrium and the Price Level

As noted in Chapter 3, equilibrium occurs where the demand and supply curves intersect. The same is true for the economy as a whole, as shown in Figure 10-5: The equilibrium price level occurs at the point where the aggregate demand curve (AD) crosses the long-run aggregate supply curve (LRAS). At this equilibrium price level of 120, the total of all planned real expenditures for the entire economy is equal to actual real GDP produced by firms after all adjustments have taken place. Thus, the equilibrium depicted in Figure 10-5 is the economy's *long-run equilibrium.*

The Long-Run Equilibrium Price Level

Note in Figure 10-5 that if the price level were to increase to 140, actual real GDP would exceed total planned real expenditures. Inventories of unsold goods would begin to accumulate, and firms would stand ready to offer more services than people wish to purchase. As a result, the price level would tend to fall.

In contrast, if the price level were 100, then total planned real expenditures by individuals, businesses, and the government would exceed actual real GDP. Inventories of unsold goods would begin to be depleted. The price level would rise toward 120, and higher prices would encourage firms to expand production and replenish inventories of goods available for sale.

The Effects of Economic Growth on the Price Level

We now have a basic theory of how real GDP and the price level are determined in the long run when all of a nation's resources can change over time and all input prices can adjust fully to changes in the overall level of prices of goods and services that firms produce. Let's begin by evaluating the effects of economic growth on the nation's price level.

ECONOMIC GROWTH AND SECULAR DEFLATION Take a look at panel (a) of Figure 10-6, which shows what happens, other things being equal, when the LRAS shifts rightward over time. If the economy were to grow steadily during, say, a 10-year

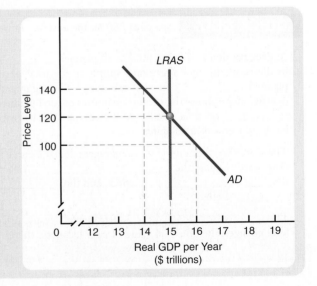

FIGURE 10-5

Long-Run Economywide Equilibrium

For the economy as a whole, long-run equilibrium occurs at the price level where the aggregate demand curve crosses the long-run aggregate supply curve. At this long-run equilibrium price level, which is 120 in the diagram, total planned real expenditures equal real GDP at full employment, which in our example is a real GDP of $15 trillion.

FIGURE 10-6

Secular Deflation versus Long-Run Price Stability in a Growing Economy

Panel (a) illustrates what happens when economic growth occurs without a corresponding increase in aggregate demand. The result is a decline in the price level over time, known as *secular deflation.* Panel (b) shows that, in principle, secular deflation can be eliminated if the aggregate demand curve shifts rightward at the same pace that the long-run aggregate supply curve shifts to the right.

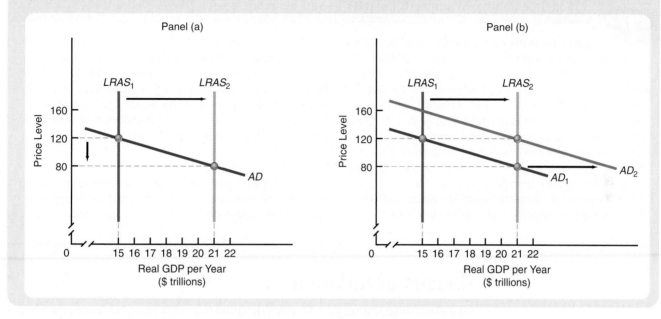

interval, the long-run aggregate supply schedule would shift to the right, from $LRAS_1$ to $LRAS_2$. In panel (a), this results in a downward movement along the aggregate demand schedule. The equilibrium price level falls, from 120 to 80.

Thus, if all factors that affect total planned real expenditures are unchanged, so that the aggregate demand curve does not noticeably move during the 10-year period of real GDP growth, the growing economy in the example would experience deflation. This is known as **secular deflation,** or a persistently declining price level resulting from economic growth in the presence of relatively unchanged aggregate demand.

SECULAR DEFLATION IN THE UNITED STATES In the United States, between 1872 and 1894, the price of bricks fell by 50 percent, the price of sugar by 67 percent, the price of wheat by 69 percent, the price of nails by 70 percent, and the price of copper by nearly 75 percent. Founders of a late-nineteenth-century political movement called *populism* offered a proposal for ending deflation: They wanted the government to issue new money backed by silver. As noted in Table 10-1 on page 247, an increase in the quantity of money in circulation causes the aggregate demand curve to shift to the right. It is clear from panel (b) of Figure 10-6 that the increase in the quantity of money would indeed have pushed the price level back upward, because the *AD* curve would shift from AD_1 to AD_2.

Nevertheless, money growth remained low for several more years. Not until the early twentieth century would the United States put an end to secular deflation, namely, by creating a new monetary system.

Secular deflation

A persistent decline in prices resulting from economic growth in the presence of stable aggregate demand.

Go to **www.econtoday.com/chapter10** to learn about how the price level has changed during recent years. Then click on "Gross Domestic Product and Components" (for GDP deflators) or "Consumer Price Indexes."

In what country is a warming climate boosting the pace at which the long-run aggregate supply curve is shifting rightward?

INTERNATIONAL EXAMPLE
For Greenland, a Warming Climate Is Good Economic News

Greenland is the world's largest island by surface area, but its population is only about 60,000. The island nation is located at the meeting point of the Atlantic and Arctic oceans. Greenland owes its name to the fact that when it was discovered in the thirteenth century, the Medieval Warm Period was in progress, so birch trees, grass, and willows lined its shores. Global temperatures declined slightly in later centuries, and today more than 80 percent of the country is covered with ice. During the past 30 years, however, the nation's average temperature has risen by 2.7 degrees Fahrenheit. Some climatologists project that Greenland's average temperature could rise by more than 10 addi-

tional degrees by the end of this century. Warmer days allow farmers to take advantage of the extended sunlight and raise more crops and animals, and fishermen have begun catching large numbers of warm-water cod that previously had been absent from the region. Thus, the general warming trend has boosted Greenland's productive capabilities and shifted its long-run aggregate supply curve rightward.

FOR CRITICAL ANALYSIS
If growth of aggregate demand in Greenland were to fail to keep pace with the climate-induced increase in long-run aggregate supply, what would happen to the nation's price level?

Causes of Inflation

Of course, so far during your lifetime, deflation has not been a problem in the United States. Instead, what you have experienced is inflation. Figure 10-7 shows annual U.S. inflation rates for the past few decades. Clearly, inflation rates have been variable. The other obvious fact, however, is that inflation rates have been consistently *positive*. The price level in the United States has *risen* almost every year. For today's United States, secular deflation has not been a big political issue. If anything, it is secular *inflation* that has plagued the nation.

FIGURE 10-7

Inflation Rates in the United States

Annual U.S. inflation rates rose considerably during the 1970s but declined to lower levels after the 1980s. The inflation rate has declined significantly in recent years after creeping upward during the early and middle 2000s.

Sources: Economic Report of the President; Economic Indicators, various issues.

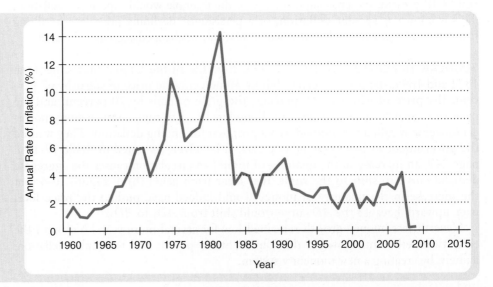

Supply-Side Inflation?

What causes such persistent inflation? The model of aggregate demand and long-run aggregate supply provides two possible explanations for inflation. One potential rationale is depicted in panel (a) of Figure 10-8. This panel shows a rise in the price level caused by a *decline in long-run aggregate supply*. Hence, one possible reason for persistent inflation would be continual reductions in economywide production.

A leftward shift in the aggregate supply schedule could be caused by several factors, such as reductions in labor force participation, higher marginal tax rates on wages, or the provision of government benefits that give households incentives *not* to supply labor services to firms. Tax rates and government benefits have increased during recent decades, but so has the U.S. population. The significant overall rise in real GDP that has taken place during the past few decades tells us that population growth and productivity gains undoubtedly have dominated other factors. In fact, the aggregate supply schedule has actually shifted *rightward*, not leftward, over time. Consequently, this supply-side explanation for persistent inflation *cannot* be the correct explanation.

Demand-Side Inflation

This leaves only one other explanation for the persistent inflation that the United States has experienced in recent decades. This explanation is depicted in panel (b) of Figure 10-8. If aggregate demand increases for a given level of long-run aggregate supply, the price level must increase. The reason is that at an initial price level such as 120, people desire to purchase more goods and services than firms are willing and able to produce given currently available resources and technology. As a result, the rise in

How has global warming changed the position of Greenland's long-run aggregate supply curve?

You Are There

To contemplate what life is like in a country experiencing a very high rate of inflation, read **Another Day's Battle with Inflation in Zimbabwe**, on pages 253 and 254.

FIGURE 10-8

Explaining Persistent Inflation

As shown in panel (a), it is possible for a decline in long-run aggregate supply to cause a rise in the price level. Long-run aggregate supply *increases* in a growing economy, however, so this cannot explain the observation of persistent U.S. inflation. Panel (b) provides the actual explanation of persistent inflation in the United States and most other nations today, which is that increases in aggregate demand push up the long-run equilibrium price level. Thus, it is possible to explain persistent inflation if the aggregate demand curve shifts rightward at a faster pace than the long-run aggregate supply curve.

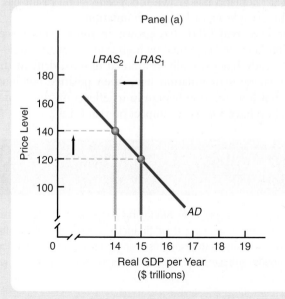

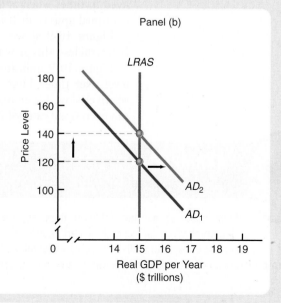

FIGURE 10-9

Real GDP and the Price Level in the United States, 1970 to the Present

This figure shows the points where aggregate demand and aggregate supply have intersected each year from 1970 to the present. The United States has experienced economic growth over this period, but not without inflation.

Sources: Economic Report of the President; Economic Indicators, various issues; author's estimates.

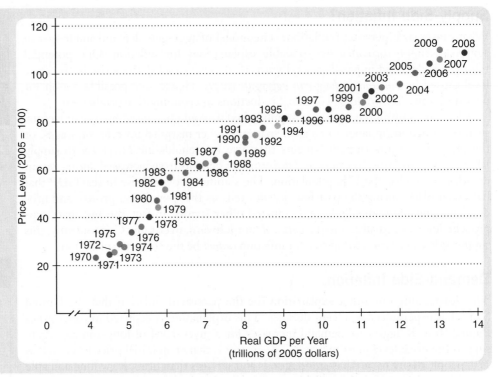

aggregate demand leads only to a general rise in the price level, such as the increase to a value of 140 depicted in the figure.

From a long-run perspective, we are left with only one possibility: Persistent inflation in a growing economy is possible only if the aggregate demand curve shifts rightward over time at a faster pace than the rightward progression of the long-run aggregate supply curve. Thus, in contrast to the experience of people who lived in the latter portion of the nineteenth century, when aggregate demand grew too slowly relative to aggregate supply to maintain price stability, your grandparents, parents, and you have lived in times when aggregate demand has grown too *speedily*. The result has been a continual upward drift in the price level, or long-term inflation.

Figure 10-9 shows that U.S. real GDP has grown in most years since 1970. Nevertheless, this growth has been accompanied by higher prices every single year.

Figure 10-9 indicates a steady but generally restrained upward drift in the price level over time. Thus, annual rates of inflation have been positive but have been relatively low. Is persistent but low inflation benign in its effects on the economy, or can even small rates of inflation have a negative impact on real GDP?

EXAMPLE
Does Sustained Low Inflation Depress Real GDP?

Economists agree that inflation imposes two fundamental types of costs that can reduce real GDP. First, because unexpected inflation reduces real rates of return on financial assets, people have an incentive to divert resources away from producing goods and services to more carefully managing their financial assets. Second, inflation hinders efforts to distinguish temporary variations in prices of goods and services from permanent price changes, which

EXAMPLE (cont.)

complicates firms' efforts to determine profitable rates of production of goods and services.

These resource costs of inflation are naturally larger at higher inflation rates. Most studies show that negative effects on real GDP are most significant at annual inflation rates above 15 percent. They also indicate that even low sustained inflation can depress real GDP. Nevertheless, most research has concluded that the currently low rates of inflation reduce U.S. real GDP by no more than $500 million per year—when total real GDP is about $13 *trillion* per year.

Some recent estimates, however, take into account a third cost of inflation. Several forms of taxation, such as the federal government's alternative minimum tax, are not indexed to

inflation. Thus, sustained low inflation eventually pushes more and more people into higher tax brackets. As their marginal tax rates increase, people cut back on productive activities. Estimates that take into account this supplemental effect of inflation suggest that each additional percentage point of annual inflation depresses annual real GDP by as much as 0.5 to 1.0 percent, which amounts to as much as tens of *billions* of base-year dollars per year.

FOR CRITICAL ANALYSIS
What does the government have to gain from failing to index its taxes to inflation?

QUICK QUIZ
See page 260 for the answers. Review concepts from this section in MyEconLab.

When the economy is in long-run equilibrium, the price level adjusts to equate total planned real _____ by individuals, businesses, and the government with total planned _____ by firms.

Economic growth causes the long-run aggregate supply schedule to shift _____ over time. If the position of the aggregate demand curve does not change, the long-run

equilibrium price level tends to _____, and there is **secular deflation.**

Because the U.S. economy has grown in recent decades, the persistent inflation during those years has been caused by the aggregate demand curve shifting _____ at a faster pace than the long-run aggregate supply curve.

 You Are There **Another Day's Battle with Inflation in Zimbabwe**

Ayina Musoni and her daughter and two grandchildren share a house in Harare, Zimbabwe, with three lodgers who pay weekly rent totaling 3 million Zimbabwean dollars. In light of her high costs of equipping the house with basic items, she is raising the rent she charges her lodgers. At the grocery this morning, she had to pay nearly 150,000 Zimbabwean dollars to purchase one roll of toilet paper. Thus, one two-ply sheet of toilet paper cost almost 500 Zimbabwean dollars, which is the value of the lowest-denomination currency note now issued in Zimbabwe. Musoni anticipates that within three months the price will be about twice as high, because Zimbabwe's price level has been doubling four times per year. At this time, the nation's inflation rate is nearly 1,000 percent per year.

To an economist, one key factor contributing to Zimbabwe's bout with inflation is apparent from just a glance at people as they shop. Instead of carrying wallets or purses, shoppers carry bags of cash. There is so much paper money in circulation that instead of making transactions using individual currency bills, people deal in currency "bricks"—stacks of 10 million Zimbabwean dollars. And Zimbabwe's government continues to churn out more money into circulation, thereby generating still more inflation.

During her morning trip to the grocery, Musoni noticed that her cash bag was beginning to run low on "bricks." She sighs as she contemplates the lengthy line she will face at the cash machine at her bank this afternoon. It takes a long

You Are There (cont.)

time for the machine to discharge the daily maximum of 250,000 Zimbabwean dollars that she is allowed to withdraw from her bank account.

CRITICAL ANALYSIS QUESTIONS

1. In Zimbabwe, which curve has been shifting rapidly rightward—the *AD* curve or the *LRAS* curve?

2. Can the rapid pace at which new money is being placed into circulation in Zimbabwe indirectly help to explain why the nation's real GDP has also been steadily declining in recent years? (Hint: Can people produce as many goods and services while waiting in lines to obtain cash?)

Is U.S. Long-Run Real GDP Growth Declining?

Issues and Applications

CONCEPTS APPLIED

- Aggregate Supply
- Long-Run Aggregate Supply
- Long-Run Aggregate Supply Curve

Since the 1930s, U.S. real GDP has increased in all but a few years. This implies that the long-run growth path for real GDP has sloped upward. The steepness of the nation's long-run real GDP growth path depends on the pace at which the total of all planned production for the economy, or aggregate supply, rises under conditions of full employment. To gauge the speed of growth of long-run aggregate supply, economists and policymakers utilize a concept known as *potential real GDP,* which is a concrete measure of the position of the long-run aggregate supply curve. The rate at which potential real GDP increases each year, or the potential annual rate of real GDP growth, indicates how fast the long-run aggregate supply curve shifts rightward over time.

Estimated U.S. Potential Real GDP Growth Rates

To estimate the potential annual rate of real GDP growth, economists must develop projections of long-run growth paths for three key factors: the capital stock, labor employment, and productivity of labor and capital. Based on such projections, most economists agree that potential real GDP growth in the United States rose from about 3.5 percent per year during the 1930s and 1940s to just above 4 percent in the early 1960s. This upsurge in growth followed an unprecedented wave of innovations—the development and use of new products and novel production techniques—that came on the heels of major inventions during the 1930s and 1940s. As a consequence, U.S. long-run aggregate supply increased during the 1950s and 1960s.

Most estimates indicate that from the early 1960s to the early 1990s, potential annual rates of growth of real GDP steadily declined to somewhere between 2.8 and 2.9 percent. The main factors driving this decline were a reduction in the long-run rate of growth in investment and a diminished long-run rate of productivity growth.

Of course, between the 1980s and 1990s, rapid innovations in the utilization of computer and communications technologies occurred. To some extent, these developments may help explain why the estimated annual rate of potential U.S. real GDP growth rose sharply during the 1990s, to around 3.1 or 3.2 percent. Indeed, during those years some economists suggested that long-run growth of capital investment and long-run productivity growth might eventually rise closer to the levels observed in the 1950s and 1960s. A few observers even suggested that the United States might be on the cusp of a "golden age" of growth.

Lower Potential Real GDP Growth in the 2000s

Since 2000, however, estimated potential annual rates of U.S. real GDP growth have been steadily declining once again. Long-run productivity growth appears to have held steady. Long-run growth in measured capital investment has tapered off, however, and returned to the levels observed during the 1980s.

In addition, a new factor has pushed down potential real GDP growth during the 2000s. The U.S. labor force participation rate has trended downward, reducing the growth of labor employment. According to most estimates, the current potential real GDP growth rate is between 2 and 2.5 percent—the lowest for the United States since the 1920s. Thus, these estimates indicate that the U.S. long-run aggregate supply curve is currently shifting rightward at the slowest pace in more than 80 years.

Test your understanding of this chapter by going online to **MyEconLab.**
In the Study Plan for this chapter, select Section N: News.

For Critical Analysis

1. If the rate at which the long-run aggregate supply curve shifts rightward decreases but aggregate demand continues increasing at the same rate, what must happen to the rate of change in the long-run equilibrium price level?

2. Could your answer to Question 1 assist in explaining why the average annual U.S. inflation rate has been higher in the 2000s than in the 1990s? Why or why not?

Web Resources

1. To learn how the U.S. Congressional Budget Office estimates potential U.S. real GDP growth, go to www .econtoday.com/chapter10.

2. For a discussion of the difficulties economists confront in estimating the potential growth of real GDP, use the link available at www.econtoday.com/chapter10.

Research Project

Explain how it might be possible for the estimated annual rate of U.S. potential real GDP growth to increase even if projections indicate that the growth of labor employment and productivity growth are both likely to decline over time. In what sense is it true that estimates of U.S. potential real GDP growth are based on other estimates?

Here is what you should know after reading this chapter. **MyEconLab** will help you identify what you know, and where to go when you need to practice.

WHAT YOU SHOULD KNOW		WHERE TO GO TO PRACTICE
Long-Run Aggregate Supply The long-run aggregate supply curve is vertical at the amount of real GDP that firms plan to produce when they have full information and when complete adjustment of input prices to any changes in output prices has taken place. This is the full-employment level of real GDP, or the economywide output level at which the natural rate of unemployment—the sum of frictional and structural unemployment as a percentage of the labor force—occurs.	aggregate supply, 240 long-run aggregate supply curve, 240 base-year dollars, 241 endowments, 241 **KEY FIGURE** Figure 10-1, 240	• **MyEconLab** Study Plan 10.1 • Audio introduction to Chapter 10 • Video: The Long-Run Aggregate Supply Curve • Animated Figure 10-1
Economic Growth and the Long-Run Aggregate Supply Curve Economic growth is an expansion of a country's production possibilities. Thus, the production possibilities curve shifts rightward when the economy grows, and so does the nation's long-run aggregate supply curve. In a growing economy, the changes in full-employment real GDP defined by the shifting long-run aggregate supply curve define the nation's long-run, or trend, growth path.	**KEY FIGURES** Figure 10-2, 241 Figure 10-3, 242	• **MyEconLab** Study Plan 10.1 • Video: The Long-Run Aggregate Supply Curve • Animated Figures 10-2, 10-3
Why the Aggregate Demand Curve Slopes Downward and Factors That Cause It to Shift A rise in the price level reduces the real value of cash balances in the hands of the public, which induces people to cut back on planned spending. This is the real-balance effect. In addition, higher interest rates typically accompany increases in the price level, and this interest rate effect induces people to cut back on borrowing and, consequently, spending. Finally, a rise in the price level at home causes domestic goods to be more expensive relative to foreign goods, so there is a fall in exports and a rise in imports, both of which cause domestic planned expenditures to fall. These three factors together account for the downward slope of the aggregate demand curve. A shift in the aggregate demand curve results from a change in total planned real expenditures at any given price level.	aggregate demand, 243 aggregate demand curve, 244 real-balance effect, 245 interest rate effect, 245 open economy effect, 246 **KEY FIGURE** Figure 10-4, 244	• **MyEconLab** Study Plans 10.2, 10.3 • Video: The Aggregate Demand Curve and What Happens When the Price Level Rises • Video: Shifts in the Aggregate Demand Curve • Animated Figure 10-4

(continued)

 *(continued)*

WHAT YOU SHOULD KNOW		**WHERE TO GO TO PRACTICE**
Long-Run Equilibrium for the Economy In a long-run economywide equilibrium, the price level adjusts until total planned real expenditures equal actual real GDP. Thus, the long-run equilibrium price level is determined at the point where the aggregate demand curve intersects the long-run aggregate supply curve. If the price level is below its long-run equilibrium value, total planned real expenditures exceed actual real GDP, and the level of prices of goods and services will rise back toward the long-run equilibrium price level. In contrast, if the price level is above its long-run equilibrium value, actual real GDP is greater than total planned real expenditures, and the price level declines in the direction of the long-run equilibrium price level.	KEY FIGURE Figure 10-5, 248	• **MyEconLab** Study Plan 10.4 • Animated Figure 10-5
Why Economic Growth Can Cause Deflation If the aggregate demand curve is stationary during a period of economic growth, the long-run aggregate supply curve shifts rightward along the aggregate demand curve. The long-run equilibrium price level falls, so there is deflation. Historically, economic growth has in this way generated secular deflation, or relatively long periods of declining prices.	secular deflation, 249 KEY FIGURE Figure 10-6, 249	• **MyEconLab** Study Plan 10.4 • Animated Figure 10-6
Likely Reasons for Recent Persistent Inflation One event that can induce inflation is a decline in long-run aggregate supply, because this causes the long-run aggregate supply curve to shift leftward. In a growing economy, however, the long-run aggregate supply curve generally shifts rightward. This indicates that a much more likely cause of persistent inflation is a pace of aggregate demand growth that exceeds the pace at which long-run aggregate supply increases.	KEY FIGURES Figure 10-7, 250 Figure 10-8, 251	• **MyEconLab** Study Plan 10.5 • Animated Figures 10-7, 10-8

Log in to MyEconLab, take a chapter test, and get a personalized Study Plan that tells you which concepts you understand and which ones you need to review. From there, MyEconLab will give you further practice, tutorials, animations, videos, and guided solutions.
Log in to www.myeconlab.com

PROBLEMS

All problems are assignable in 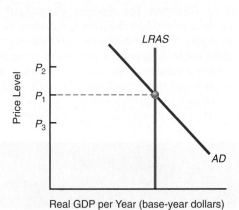 myeconlab. *Answers to odd-numbered problems appear at the back of the book.*

10-1. Many economists view the natural rate of unemployment as the level observed when real GDP is given by the position of the long-run aggregate supply curve. How can there be positive unemployment in this situation?

10-2. Suppose that the long-run aggregate supply curve is positioned at a real GDP level of $15 trillion in base-year dollars, and the long-run equilibrium price level (in index number form) is 115. What is the full-employment level of *nominal* GDP?

10-3. Continuing from Problem 10-2, suppose that the full-employment level of *nominal* GDP in the following year rises to $17.7 trillion. The long-run equilibrium price level, however, remains unchanged. By how much (in real dollars) has the long-run aggregate supply curve shifted to the right in the following year? By how much, if any, has the aggregate demand curve shifted to the right? (Hint: The equilibrium price level can stay the same only if *LRAS* and *AD* shift rightward by the same amount.)

10-4. Suppose that the position of a nation's long-run aggregate supply curve has not changed, but its long-run equilibrium price level has increased. Which of the following factors might account for this event?

a. A rise in the value of the domestic currency relative to other world currencies

b. An increase in the quantity of money in circulation

c. An increase in the labor force participation rate

d. A decrease in taxes

e. A rise in real incomes of countries that are key trading partners of this nation

f. Increased long-run economic growth

10-5. Suppose that during a given year, the quantity of U.S. real GDP that can be produced in the long run rises from $14.9 trillion to $15.0 trillion, measured in base-year dollars. During the year, no change occurs in the various factors that influence aggregate demand. What will happen to the U.S. long-run equilibrium price level during this particular year?

10-6. Assume that the position of a nation's aggregate demand curve has not changed, but the long-run equilibrium price level has declined. Other things being equal, which of the following factors might account for this event?

a. An increase in labor productivity

b. A decrease in the capital stock

c. A decrease in the quantity of money in circulation

d. The discovery of new mineral resources used to produce various goods

e. A technological improvement

10-7. Suppose that there is a sudden rise in the price level. What will happen to economywide planned spending on purchases of goods and services? Why?

10-8. Assume that the economy is in long-run equilibrium with complete information and that input prices adjust rapidly to changes in the prices of goods and services. If there is a sudden rise in the price level induced by an increase in aggregate demand, what happens to real GDP?

10-9. Consider the accompanying diagram when answering the questions that follow.

Real GDP per Year (base-year dollars)

a. Suppose that the current price level is P_2. Explain why the price level will decline toward P_1.

b. Suppose that the current price level is P_3. Explain why the price level will rise toward P_1.

10-10. Explain whether each of the following events would cause a movement along or a shift in the position of the *LRAS* curve, other things being equal. In each case, explain the direction of the movement along the curve or shift in its position.

a. Last year, businesses invested in new capital equipment, so this year the nation's capital stock is higher than it was last year.

b. There has been an 8 percent increase in the quantity of money in circulation that has shifted the *AD* curve.

c. A hurricane of unprecedented strength has damaged oil rigs, factories, and ports all along the nation's coast.

d. Inflation has occurred during the past year as a result of rightward shifts of the *AD* curve.

10-11. Explain whether each of the following events would cause a movement along or a shift in the position of the *AD* curve, other things being equal. In each case, explain the direction of the movement along the curve or shift in its position.

a. Deflation has occurred during the past year.

b. Real GDP levels of all the nation's major trading partners have declined.

c. There has been a decline in the foreign exchange value of the nation's currency.

d. The price level has increased this year.

10-12. This year, a nation's long-run equilibrium real GDP and price level both increased. Which of the following combinations of factors might simultaneously account for *both* occurrences?

a. An isolated earthquake at the beginning of the year destroyed part of the nation's capital stock, and the nation's government significantly reduced its purchases of goods and services.

b. There was a minor technological improvement at the end of the previous year, and the quantity of money in circulation rose significantly during the year.

c. Labor productivity increased somewhat throughout the year, and consumers significantly increased their total planned purchases of goods and services.

d. The capital stock increased somewhat during the year, and the quantity of money in circulation declined considerably.

10-13. Explain how, if at all, each of the following events would affect equilibrium real GDP and the long-run equilibrium price level.

a. A reduction in the quantity of money in circulation

b. An income tax rebate (the return of previously paid taxes) from the government to house-

holds, which they can apply only to purchases of goods and services

c. A technological improvement

d. A decrease in the value of the home currency in terms of the currencies of other nations

10-14. For each question below, suppose that the economy *begins* at the long-run equilibrium point *A*. Identify which of the other points on the diagram—points *B*, *C*, *D*, or *E*—could represent a *new* long-run equilibrium after the described events take place and move the economy away from point *A*.

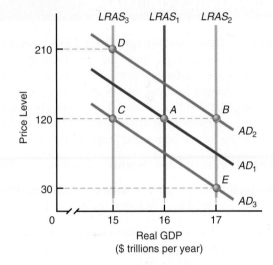

a. Significant productivity improvements occur, and the quantity of money in circulation increases.

b. No new capital investment takes place, and a fraction of the existing capital stock depreciates and becomes unusable. At the same time, the government imposes a large tax increase on the nation's households.

c. More efficient techniques for producing goods and services are adopted throughout the economy at the same time that the government reduces its spending on goods and services.

10-15. In Ciudad Barrios, El Salvador, the latest payments from relatives working in the United States have finally arrived. When the credit unions open for business, up to 150 people are already waiting in line. After receiving the funds their relatives have transmitted to these institutions, customers go off to outdoor markets to stock up on food or clothing or to appliance stores to purchase new stereos or televisions. Similar scenes occur throughout the developing world, as each year migrants working in higher-income, developed nations send around $200 billion of their earnings back to their relatives in less developed nations. Evidence indicates that the relatives, such as those in Ciudad Barrios, typically spend nearly all of the funds on current consumption.

a. Based on the information supplied, are developing countries' income inflows transmitted by migrant workers primarily affecting their economies' long-run aggregate supply curves or aggregate demand curves?

b. How are equilibrium price levels in nations that are recipients of large inflows of funds from migrants likely to be affected? Explain your reasoning.

ECONOMICS ON THE NET

Wages, Productivity, and Aggregate Supply How much firms pay their employees and the productivity of those employees influence firms' total planned production, so changes in these factors affect the position of the aggregate supply curve. This application gives you the opportunity to examine recent trends in measures of the overall wages and productivity of workers.

Title: Bureau of Labor Statistics: Economy at a Glance

Navigation: Use the link at **www.econtoday.com/chapter10** to visit the Bureau of Labor Statistics (BLS) Web site.

Application Perform the indicated operations, and answer the following questions.

1. Click on *Employment Costs*, and then click on *Employment Cost Index—NAICS Basis.* Choose the first data series in the list. What are the recent trends in wages and salaries and in benefits? In the long run, how should these trends be related to movements in the overall price level?

2. Back up to the home page, and click on *Productivity and Costs* and then on *PDF* next to "Economic News

Releases: Productivity and Costs." How has labor productivity behaved recently? What does this imply for the long-run aggregate supply curve?

3. Back up to U.S. Economy at a Glance, and now click on *National Employment* and then on *PDF* next to "Economic News Releases: Employment Situation Summary." Does it appear that the U.S. economy is currently in a long-run growth equilibrium?

For Group Study and Analysis

1. Divide the class into aggregate demand and long-run aggregate supply groups. Have each group search the Internet for data on factors that influence its assigned curve. For which factors do data appear to be most readily available? For which factors are data more sparse or more subject to measurement problems?

2. The BLS home page displays a map of the United States. Assign regions of the nation to different groups, and have each group develop a short report about current and future prospects for economic growth within its assigned region. What similarities exist across regions? What regional differences are there?

ANSWERS TO QUICK QUIZZES

p. 243: (i) vertical; (ii) natural; (iii) rightward . . . increases
p. 247: (i) expenditures . . . production . . . spending; (ii) real-balance . . . interest rate . . . open economy; (iii) real-balance; (iv) interest rate . . . fewer . . . more; (v) domestic . . . foreign
p. 253: (i) expenditures . . . production; (ii) rightward . . . decline; (iii) rightward

Classical and Keynesian Macro Analyses

11

Like a rerun of a bad TV show, the same basic pattern has repeated five times in recent U.S. history: 1973–1974, 1979–1980, 1990, 2000–2001, and, apparently, 2007. First, world oil prices jump. Then companies scale back production plans. Finally, the price level rises even as real GDP drops. Within a few weeks, the word *recession* is in the air, and within a few more months, a committee of economists at the National Bureau of Economic Research announces that a recession is actually under way. Why have oil price increases so often preceded recessions? Do recessions necessarily follow a run-up in the world price of oil? Before you can answer these questions, you must learn about how changes in the price of oil and other key inputs can exert short-run effects on real GDP and the price level.

LEARNING OBJECTIVES

myeconlab

MyEconLab helps you master each objective and study more efficiently. See end of chapter for details.

After reading this chapter, you should be able to:

➤ Discuss the central assumptions of the classical model

➤ Describe the short-run determination of equilibrium real GDP and the price level in the classical model

➤ Explain circumstances under which the short-run aggregate supply curve may be either horizontal or upward sloping

➤ Understand what factors cause shifts in the short-run and long-run aggregate supply curves

➤ Evaluate the effects of aggregate demand and supply shocks on equilibrium real GDP in the short run

➤ Determine the causes of short-run variations in the inflation rate

? DID YOU KNOW THAT the price of a bottle containing 6.5 ounces of Coca-Cola remained unchanged at 5 cents from 1886 to 1959? The prices of many other goods and services changed at least slightly during that 73-year period, and since then the prices of most items, including Coca-Cola, have generally moved in an upward direction. Nevertheless, prices of final goods and services have not always adjusted immediately in response to changes in aggregate demand. Consequently, one approach to understanding the determination of real GDP and the price level emphasizes *incomplete* adjustment in the prices of many goods and services. The simplest version of this approach was first developed by a twentieth-century economist named John Maynard Keynes (pronounced like *canes*). It assumes that in the short run, prices of most goods and services are nearly as rigid as the price of Coca-Cola from 1886 to 1959. Although the modern version of the Keynesian approach allows for greater flexibility of prices in the short run, incomplete price adjustment still remains a key feature of the modern Keynesian approach.

The Keynesian approach does not retain the long-run assumption, which you encountered in Chapter 10, of fully adjusting prices. Economists who preceded Keynes employed this assumption in creating an approach to understanding variations in real GDP and the price level that Keynes called the *classical model.* Like Keynes, we shall begin our study of variations in real GDP and the price level by considering the earlier, classical approach.

The Classical Model

The classical model, which traces its origins to the 1770s, was the first systematic attempt to explain the determinants of the price level and the national levels of real GDP, employment, consumption, saving, and investment. Classical economists—Adam Smith, J. B. Say, David Ricardo, John Stuart Mill, Thomas Malthus, A. C. Pigou, and others—wrote from the 1770s to the 1930s. They assumed, among other things, that all wages and prices were flexible and that competitive markets existed throughout the economy.

Say's Law

Every time you produce something for which you receive income, you generate the income necessary to make expenditures on other goods and services. That means that an economy producing $15 trillion of real GDP, measured in base-year dollars, simultaneously produces the income with which these goods and services can be purchased. As an accounting identity, *actual* aggregate output always equals *actual* aggregate income. Classical economists took this accounting identity one step further by arguing that total national supply creates its own national demand. They asserted what has become known as **Say's law:**

> *Supply creates its own demand; hence, it follows that* desired *expenditures will equal* actual *expenditures.*

What does Say's law really mean? It states that the very process of producing specific goods (supply) is proof that other goods are desired (demand). People produce more goods than they want for their own use only if they seek to trade them for other goods. Someone offers to supply something only because he or she has a demand for something else. The implication of this, according to Say, is that no general glut, or overproduction, is possible in a market economy. From this reasoning, it seems to follow that full employment of labor and other resources would be the normal state of affairs in such an economy.

Say's law
A dictum of economist J. B. Say that supply creates its own demand; producing goods and services generates the means and the willingness to purchase other goods and services.

FIGURE 11-1

Say's Law and the Circular Flow

Here we show the circular flow of income and output. The very act of supplying a certain level of goods and services necessarily equals the level of goods and services demanded, in Say's simplified world.

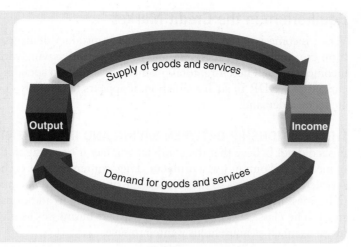

Say acknowledged that an oversupply of some goods might occur in particular markets. He argued that such surpluses would simply cause prices to fall, thereby decreasing production as the economy adjusted. The opposite would occur in markets in which shortages temporarily appeared.

All this seems reasonable enough in a simple barter economy in which households produce most of the goods they want and trade for the rest. This is shown in Figure 11-1, where there is a simple circular flow. But what about a more sophisticated economy in which people work for others and money is used instead of barter? Can these complications create the possibility of unemployment? And does the fact that laborers receive money income, some of which can be saved, lead to unemployment? No, said the classical economists to these last two questions. They based their reasoning on a number of key assumptions.

Assumptions of the Classical Model

The classical model makes four major assumptions:

1. *Pure competition exists.* No single buyer or seller of a commodity or an input can affect its price.

2. *Wages and prices are flexible.* The assumption of pure competition leads to the notion that prices, wages, interest rates, and the like are free to move to whatever level supply and demand dictate (as the economy adjusts). Although no *individual* buyer can set a price, the community of buyers or sellers can cause prices to rise or to fall to an equilibrium level.

3. *People are motivated by self-interest.* Businesses want to maximize their profits, and households want to maximize their economic well-being.

4. *People cannot be fooled by money illusion.* Buyers and sellers react to changes in relative prices. That is to say, they do not suffer from **money illusion.** For example, workers will not be fooled into thinking that a doubling of wages makes them better off if the price level has also doubled during the same time period.

Money illusion

Reacting to changes in money prices rather than relative prices. If a worker whose wages double when the price level also doubles thinks he or she is better off, that worker is suffering from money illusion.

The classical economists concluded, after taking account of the four major assumptions, that the role of government in the economy should be minimal. If pure competition prevails, if all prices and wages are flexible, and if people are self-interested and do not experience money illusion, then any problems in the macroeconomy will be temporary. The market will correct itself.

According to the classical model, what will happen to the prices of these canned goods if aggregate demand increases?

Go to www.econtoday.com/chapter11 to link to Federal Reserve data on U.S. interest rates.

Equilibrium in the Credit Market

When income is saved, it is not reflected in product demand. It is a type of *leakage* from the circular flow of income and output because saving withdraws funds from the income stream. Therefore, total planned consumption spending *can* fall short of total current real GDP. In such a situation, it appears that supply does not necessarily create its own demand.

THE RELATIONSHIP BETWEEN SAVING AND INVESTMENT The classical economists did not believe that the complicating factor of saving in the circular flow model of income and output was a problem. They contended that each dollar saved would be invested by businesses so that the leakage of saving would be matched by the injection of business investment. *Investment* here refers only to additions to the nation's capital stock. The classical economists believed that businesses as a group would intend to invest as much as households wanted to save.

THE EQUILIBRIUM INTEREST RATE Equilibrium between the saving plans of consumers and the investment plans of businesses comes about, in the classical economists' model, through the working of the credit market. In the credit market, the *price* of credit is the interest rate. At equilibrium, the price of credit—the interest rate—ensures that the amount of credit demanded equals the amount of credit supplied. Planned investment just equals planned saving, so there is no reason to be concerned about the leakage of saving. This is illustrated graphically in Figure 11-2.

In the figure, the vertical axis measures the rate of interest in percentage terms, and the horizontal axis measures amounts of desired saving and desired investment per unit time period. The desired saving curve is really a supply curve of saving. It shows that people wish to save more at higher interest rates than at lower interest rates.

In contrast, the higher the rate of interest, the less profitable it is to invest and the lower is the level of desired investment. Thus, the desired investment curve slopes downward. In this simplified model, the equilibrium rate of interest is 5 percent, and the equilibrium quantity of saving and investment is $2 trillion per year.

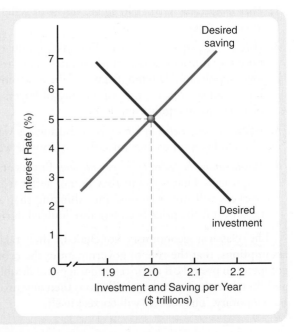

FIGURE 11-2

Equating Desired Saving and Investment in the Classical Model

The schedule showing planned investment is labeled "Desired investment." The desired saving curve is shown as an upward-sloping supply curve of saving. The equilibrating force here is, of course, the interest rate. At higher interest rates, people desire to save more. But at higher interest rates, businesses wish to engage in less investment because it is less profitable to invest. In this model, at an interest rate of 5 percent, planned investment just equals planned saving, which is $2 trillion per year.

How does globalization of the world economy help to explain why saving and investment are not necessarily equalized within an individual nation's borders?

INTERNATIONAL EXAMPLE
In a Global Economy, World Saving Equals World Investment

In the classical model, saving equals investment when the interest rate is at an equilibrium value. At a given time when full adjustment to equilibrium may not yet have occurred, however, saving will not equal investment.

Nevertheless, even in full equilibrium, saving and investment may not always be equal *within* individual countries. In our increasingly globalized economy, saving and investment flow across national borders. Thus, the classical model implies that if the entire world economy is considered, the world interest rate should adjust until world saving equals world investment.

Take a look at Figure 11-3, which displays investment and saving as shares of world GDP for both industrialized nations and so-called emerging nations whose economies are gradually becoming more industrialized. Notice the pattern of the curves in the two panels: During periods in which investment exceeds saving in one group, saving exceeds investment in the other group. Since 1998, for example, investment has

exceeded saving in the industrialized nations in panel (a), while saving has exceeded investment in the emerging nations in panel (b). This indicates that some saving in the emerging nations during this period flowed to the industrialized nations to help finance investment in those countries. Indeed, in most years, the sums of investment and saving as percentages of world GDP for the two groups are equal. For example, in 2009, saving for both groups of nations summed to an estimated 20.4 percent of world GDP, and investment for both groups added up to an estimated 20.4 percent of world GDP. Hence, world saving was equal to world investment in that year, as predicted by the classical model for the global economy.

FOR CRITICAL ANALYSIS

Why does the classical model predict that world saving should end up being equal to world investment even if no funds flow across nations' borders? (Hint: Interest rate.)

FIGURE 11-3

Saving and Investment in Industrialized and Emerging Nations Since 1970

Saving and investment as percentages of world GDP since 1970 are shown for industrialized nations in panel (a) and for emerging nations in panel (b).

Source: International Monetary Fund.

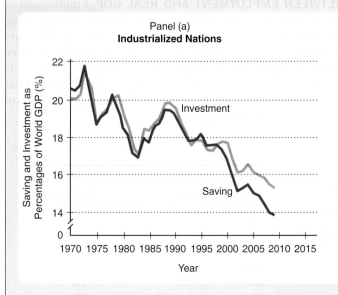

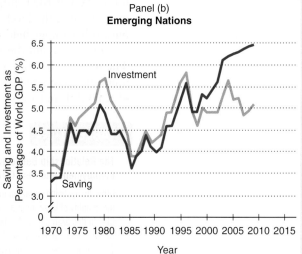

Go to www.econtoday.com/chapter11 for Federal Reserve Bank of New York data showing how the dollar's value is changing relative to other currencies.

(10 billion) cubic feet of natural gas from suppliers in Nigeria. Suppose that the price of Nigerian natural gas, quoted in Nigerian naira, is 0.910 naira per million cubic feet. At a rate of exchange of 130 naira per dollar, this means that the U.S. dollar price is $0.0070 per million cubic feet (0.910 naira divided by 130 naira per dollar equals $0.0070), so that 10 billion cubic feet of Nigerian natural gas imports cost U.S. distributors $70 million. If the U.S. dollar weakens against the Nigerian naira, so that a dollar purchases only 120 naira, then the U.S. dollar price rises to $0.0076 per million cubic feet (0.910 naira divided by 120 naira per dollar equals $0.0076). As a consequence, the U.S. dollar price of 10 billion cubic feet of Nigerian natural gas imports increases to $76 million.

Thus, a general weakening of the dollar against the naira and other world currencies will lead to a shift inward to the left in the short-run aggregate supply curve as shown in panel (a) of Figure 11-15. In that simplified model, equilibrium real GDP would fall, and the price level would rise. Employment would also tend to decrease.

HOW A WEAKER DOLLAR AFFECTS AGGREGATE DEMAND A weaker dollar has another effect that we must consider. Foreign residents will find that U.S.-made goods are now less expensive, expressed in their own currency. Suppose that as a result of the dollar's weakening, the dollar, which previously could buy 0.70 euros, can now buy only 0.67 euros. Before the dollar weakened, a U.S.-produced $10 compact disc cost a French resident 7.00 euros at the exchange rate of 0.70 euro per $1. After the dollar weakens and the exchange rate changes to 0.67 euro per $1, that same $10 CD will cost 6.70 euros. Conversely, U.S. residents will find that the weaker dollar

FIGURE 11-15

The Two Effects of a Weaker Dollar

When the dollar decreases in value in the international currency market, there are two effects. The first is higher prices for imported inputs, causing a shift inward to the left in the short-run aggregate supply schedule from $SRAS_1$ to $SRAS_2$ in panel (a). Equilibrium tends to move from E_1 to E_2 at a higher price level and a lower equilibrium real GDP per year. Second, a weaker dollar can also affect the aggregate demand curve because it will lead to more net exports and cause AD_1 to rise to AD_2 in panel (b). Due to this effect, equilibrium will move from E_1 to E_2 at a higher price level and a higher equilibrium real GDP per year. On balance, the combined effects of the increase in aggregate demand and decrease in aggregate supply will be to push up the price level, but real GDP may rise or fall.

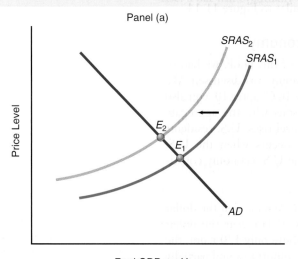

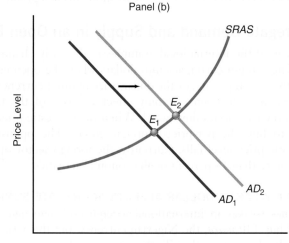

Panel (a)

Panel (b)

makes imported goods more expensive. The result for U.S. residents is more exports and fewer imports, or higher net exports (exports minus imports). If net exports rise, employment in export industries will rise: This is represented in panel (b) of Figure 11-15 on the facing page. After the dollar becomes weaker, the aggregate demand curve shifts outward from AD_1 to AD_2. The result is a tendency for equilibrium real GDP and the price level to rise and for unemployment to decrease.

THE NET EFFECTS ON INFLATION AND REAL GDP. We have learned, then, that a weaker dollar *simultaneously* leads to a decrease in SRAS and an increase in AD. In such situations, the equilibrium price level definitely rises. A weaker dollar contributes to inflation.

The effect of a weaker dollar on real GDP depends on which curve—AD or SRAS—shifts more. If the aggregate demand curve shifts more than the short-run aggregate supply curve, equilibrium real GDP will rise. Conversely, if the aggregate supply curve shifts more than the aggregate demand curve, equilibrium real GDP will fall.

You should be able to redo this entire analysis for a stronger dollar.

What happens to the quantity demanded of American-made dresses when the dollar becomes weaker?

QUICK QUIZ | *See page 286 for the answers. Review concepts from this section in MyEconLab.*

_____-run equilibrium occurs at the intersection of the aggregate demand curve, *AD*, and the short-run aggregate supply curve, *SRAS*. _____-run equilibrium occurs at the intersection of *AD* and the long-run aggregate supply curve, *LRAS*. Any unanticipated shifts in aggregate demand or supply are called aggregate demand _____ or aggregate supply _____.

When aggregate demand decreases while aggregate supply is stable, a _____ gap can occur, defined as the difference between the equilibrium level of real GDP and how much the economy could be producing if it were operating on its *LRAS*. An increase in aggregate demand leads to an _____ gap.

With stable aggregate supply, an abrupt outward shift in *AD* may lead to what is called _____-_____ inflation. With stable aggregate demand, an abrupt shift inward in *SRAS* may lead to what is called _____-_____ inflation.

A _____ dollar will raise the cost of imported inputs, thereby causing *SRAS* to shift inward to the left. At the same time, a _____ dollar will also lead to higher net exports, causing the aggregate demand curve to shift outward. The equilibrium price level definitely rises, but the net effect on equilibrium real GDP depends on which shift is larger.

You Are There ► Putting More Weight on Stability Than Growth in Denmark

Dalum Papir A/S is almost halfway through its second century as a Danish paper manufacturer. Years ago, the firm was one of many paper companies, but now it constitutes one-half of Denmark's two-firm paper industry. The company utilizes highly energy-efficient techniques to manufacture glossy paper from recycled materials for magazines. Dalum Papir has had little choice but to conserve energy. Government taxation has boosted energy prices more than 45 percent above the U.S. level. In addition, like other Danish

firms, Dalum Papir must meet government-mandated standards for energy conservation.

Ever since the 1970s, when a worldwide spike in oil prices set off a prolonged recession, Denmark's government has sought to shield the nation's economy from future aggregate supply shocks induced by jumps in energy prices. Toward that end, it has enacted high energy taxes and tough regulatory conservation measures. A consequence is that Danish oil consumption per $1 million of real GDP has

You Are There (cont.)

declined by more than 30 percent—to 120 tons of oil per $1 million of real GDP—over the last 30 years. Indeed, Denmark's *total* oil consumption has remained unchanged since the late 1970s. Thus, consistent with the government's intent, whenever oil prices suddenly shoot up, Denmark's economy tends to experience smaller aggregate supply shocks than it did in years past.

As the experience of Dalum Papir and the dwindling Danish paper industry illustrates, however, the government's quest for aggregate supply stability has come at the cost of growth in production of goods and services. Since the late 1970s, Denmark's real GDP has doubled, whereas U.S. real GDP has *quadrupled*. During that period, total U.S. oil consumption has increased by more than 40 percent, yet because U.S. real GDP has increased fourfold, U.S. oil consumption per $1 million of real GDP has fallen

by more than 25 percent—almost as much as the percentage decline in Danish oil consumption per $1 million in real GDP. Thus, although the Danish economy is less susceptible than the U.S. economy to aggregate supply shocks, Denmark's aggregate supply is growing at about half the pace at which U.S. aggregate supply is expanding.

CRITICAL ANALYSIS QUESTIONS

1. Why do unexpected variations in energy prices generate aggregate supply shocks, while sudden changes in total planned expenditures do not?

2. Other things being equal, why might we expect the Danish price level to be more stable over time than the U.S. price level?

Higher Oil Prices and (Usually) U.S. Recessionary Gaps

Issues and Applications

CONCEPTS APPLIED

- Aggregate Supply Shock
- Short-Run Aggregate Supply Curve
- Recessionary Gap

During the past four decades, sudden increases in oil prices have been associated with onsets of recessions. The U.S. economy recently has been more resilient to oil price hikes, but the latest oil price increase contributed to a slowdown.

A Recurring History of Oil Price Jumps and Recessions

Figure 11-16 displays the real, inflation-adjusted price per barrel of oil since 1970 in blue. The figure also shows rates of growth in a measure of real consumption expenditures in orange. The shaded intervals indicate

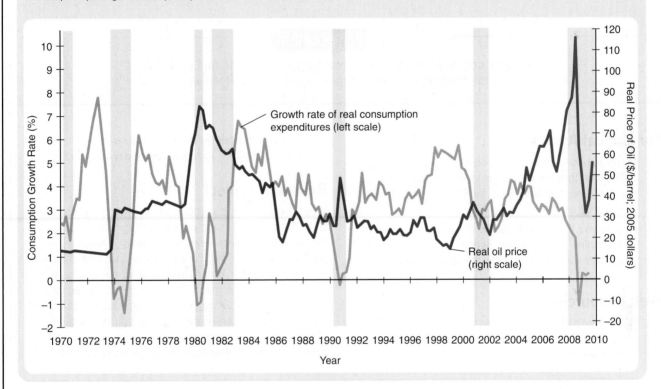

FIGURE 11-16

Real Oil Prices and Year-to-Year Growth in U.S. Personal Consumption Expenditures Since 1970

Real oil prices rose in advance of or coincided with five of the past seven recession periods (indicated by shaded intervals). In the late 2000s, the real price of oil rose considerably. Then both the rate of growth of U.S. real consumption spending and real oil prices plummeted.

Sources: Federal Reserve Bank of St. Louis, Bureau of Economic Analysis, National Bureau of Economic Research.

U.S. recession periods. As you can see, the price of oil increased noticeably in late 1973 and early 1974. The result was an aggregate supply shock. The U.S. aggregate supply curve shifted leftward, generating a recessionary gap. Real expenditures on goods and services declined, as indicated in the figure by the negative rate of change in real consumption expenditures. The economy experienced a recession that lasted just over a year before concluding in early 1975.

Analogous patterns, in which an oil price increase was followed in succession by an aggregate supply shock, a recessionary gap, a consumption spending decline, and a recession, repeated in 1979–1980, 1990, 2000–2001, and post-2007. Out of the past seven recessions, only two

(1970 and 1981–1982) were not linked to oil price increases and resulting aggregate supply shocks.

An Oil Price Run-Up, but Not the Usual Pattern

As Figure 11-16 indicates, the real price of oil trended significantly higher from late 2001 until late 2008. This rise in inflation-adjusted oil prices certainly generated an aggregate supply shock, and real consumption expenditure growth became negative in late 2008. The Great Recession of the late 2000s had begun. Throughout 2009 the rate of growth of consumption spending barely returned to a positive range.

In contrast to the U.S. experience with rising oil prices in the late 1970s, however, in 2008 the inflation-adjusted price of oil plummeted at the same time that the rate of growth of consumption became negative. Economists agree that there were two reasons for this unusual pattern. First, the fall in consumption in 2008 included a decline in oil consumption that contributed to lower oil prices. Second, the initial run-up in oil prices was followed by another major shock: a vast financial crisis that contributed further to the drop in oil consumption and lower oil prices. Because the financial crisis came so soon after the oil price run-up, it is hard to tell how much higher oil prices added to the Great Recession. Undoubtedly, economists will spend the next few years trying to sort out the effects of the two shocks on consumption spending.

Test your understanding of this chapter by going online to **MyEconLab.**
In the Study Plan for this chapter, select Section N: News.

For Critical Analysis

1. Would the comparison of the oil price increases of the 2000s with those of the 1970s be affected by choosing, say, 1975 as the base year for inflation adjustment? Why or why not?

2. Why do you think that it can be difficult for economists to determine the separate effects of two aggregate shocks that take place at nearly the same time?

Web Resources

1. To see how nominal and inflation-adjusted oil prices have varied since the end of World War II, go to www.econtoday.com/chapter11.

2. For a very detailed discussion of historical and current factors affecting oil prices, go to www.econtoday.com/chapter11.

Research Project

When we consider the effects of oil price increases on the short-run aggregate supply curve, equilibrium real GDP, and the equilibrium price level, we usually engage in *ceteris paribus* reasoning. That is, we assume that everything else, including any other factor affecting short-run aggregate supply and aggregate demand, is unchanged. Evaluate why our analysis of effects of aggregate supply shocks, particularly during the run-up of inflation-adjusted oil prices during the 2000s, may be incomplete or misleading if we forget that more than one condition can change at the same time.

Here is what you should know after reading this chapter. **MyEconLab** will help you identify what you know, and where to go when you need to practice.

WHAT YOU SHOULD KNOW		WHERE TO GO TO PRACTICE
Central Assumptions of the Classical Model The classical model makes four key assumptions: (1) pure competition prevails, so no individual buyer or seller of a good or service or of a factor of production can affect its price; (2) wages and prices are completely flexible; (3) people are motivated by self-interest; and (4) buyers and sellers do not experience money illusion, meaning that they respond only to changes in relative prices.	Say's law, 262 money illusion, 263	• **MyEconLab** Study Plan 11.1 • Audio introduction to Chapter 11 • Video: Say's Law

(continued)

 *(continued)*

WHAT YOU SHOULD KNOW		WHERE TO GO TO PRACTICE

Short-Run Determination of Equilibrium Real GDP and the Price Level in the Classical Model Under the four assumptions of the classical model, the short-run aggregate supply curve is vertical at full-employment real GDP and thus corresponds to the long-run aggregate supply curve. So, even in the short run, real GDP cannot increase in the absence of changes in factors of production, such as labor, capital, and technology, which induce longer-term economic growth. Given the position of the classical aggregate supply curve, movements in the equilibrium price level are generated by variations in the position of the aggregate demand curve.

KEY FIGURES
Figure 11-2, 264
Figure 11-4, 266
Figure 11-5, 267
Figure 11-6, 268

- **MyEconLab** Study Plan 11.1
- Audio introduction to Chapter 11
- Animated Figures 11-2, 11-4, 11-5, 11-6

Circumstances Under Which the Short-Run Aggregate Supply Curve May Be Horizontal or Upward Sloping If product prices and wages and other input prices are "sticky," perhaps because of labor and other contracts, the short-run aggregate supply schedule can be horizontal over much of its range. This is the Keynesian short-run aggregate supply curve. More generally, however, to the extent that there is incomplete adjustment of prices in the short run, the short-run aggregate supply curve slopes upward.

Keynesian short-run aggregate supply curve, 269
short-run aggregate supply curve, 271

KEY FIGURES
Figure 11-7, 269
Figure 11-9, 271

- **MyEconLab** Study Plans 11.2, 11.3
- Video: The Short-Run Aggregate Supply Curve
- Animated Figures 11-7, 11-9

Factors That Induce Shifts in the Short-Run and Long-Run Aggregate Supply Curves Both the long-run aggregate supply curve and the short-run aggregate supply curve shift in response to changes in the availability of labor or capital or to changes in technology and productivity. Because output prices may adjust only partially to changing input prices in the short run, however, a widespread change in the prices of factors of production, such as an economywide change in wages, can cause a shift in the short-run aggregate supply curve without affecting the long-run aggregate supply curve.

KEY TABLE
Table 11-2, 274

KEY FIGURES
Figure 11-10, 273
Figure 11-11, 273

- **MyEconLab** Study Plan 11.4
- Animated Figures 11-10, 11-11

Effects of Aggregate Demand and Supply Shocks on Equilibrium Real GDP in the Short Run An aggregate demand shock that causes the aggregate demand curve to shift leftward pushes equilibrium real GDP below full-employment real GDP in the short run, so there is a recessionary gap. An aggregate demand shock that induces a rightward shift in the aggregate demand curve results in an inflationary gap, in which short-run equilibrium real GDP exceeds full-employment real GDP.

aggregate demand shock, 275
aggregate supply shock, 275
recessionary gap, 275
inflationary gap, 276

KEY FIGURES
Figure 11-12, 275
Figure 11-13, 276

- **MyEconLab** Study Plan 11.5
- Video: Shifts in the Short-Run Aggregate Supply Curve
- Animated Figures 11-12, 11-13

(continued)

 *(continued)*

WHAT YOU SHOULD KNOW

WHERE TO GO TO PRACTICE

Causes of Short-Run Variations in the Inflation Rate In the short run, demand-pull inflation can occur when the aggregate demand curve shifts rightward along an upward-sloping short-run aggregate supply curve. Cost-push inflation can arise in the short run when the short-run aggregate supply curve shifts leftward along the aggregate demand curve. A weakening of the dollar shifts the short-run aggregate supply curve leftward and the aggregate demand curve rightward, which causes inflation but has uncertain effects on real GDP.

demand-pull inflation, 276
cost-push inflation, 277

KEY FIGURE
Figure 11-14, 277

• **MyEconLab** Study Plan 11.6
• Animated Figure 11-14

Log in to MyEconLab, take a chapter test, and get a personalized Study Plan that tells you which concepts you understand and which ones you need to review. From there, MyEconLab will give you further practice, tutorials, animations, videos, and guided solutions.
Log in to www.myeconlab.com

PROBLEMS

All problems are assignable in **myeconlab** . *Answers to odd-numbered problems appear at the back of the book.*

11-1. Consider a country whose economic structure matches the assumptions of the classical model. After reading a recent best-seller documenting a growing population of low-income elderly people who were ill-prepared for retirement, most residents of this country decide to increase their saving at any given interest rate. Explain whether or how this could affect the following:

   a. The current equilibrium interest rate

   b. Current equilibrium real GDP

   c. Current equilibrium employment

   d. Current equilibrium investment

   e. Future equilibrium real GDP (see Chapter 9)

11-2. Consider a country with an economic structure consistent with the assumptions of the classical model. Suppose that businesses in this nation suddenly anticipate higher future profitability from investments they undertake today. Explain whether or how this could affect the following:

   a. The current equilibrium interest rate

   b. Current equilibrium real GDP

   c. Current equilibrium employment

   d. Current equilibrium saving

   e. Future equilibrium real GDP (see Chapter 9)

11-3. "There is *absolutely no distinction* between the classical model and the model of long-run equilibrium discussed in Chapter 10." Is this statement true or false? Support your answer.

11-4. A nation in which the classical model applies experiences a decline in the quantity of money in circulation. Use an appropriate aggregate demand and aggregate supply diagram to explain what happens to equilibrium real GDP and to the equilibrium price level.

11-5. Suppose that the classical model is appropriate for a country that has suddenly experienced an influx of immigrants who possess a wide variety of employable skills and who have reputations for saving relatively large portions of their incomes, compared with native-born residents, at any given interest rate. Evaluate the effects of this event on the following:

   a. Current equilibrium employment

   b. Current equilibrium real GDP

   c. The current equilibrium interest rate

  d. Current equilibrium investment

  e. Future equilibrium real GDP (See Chapter 9)

11-6. Suppose that the Keynesian short-run aggregate supply curve is applicable for a nation's economy. Use appropriate diagrams to assist in answering the following questions:

  a. What are two factors that can cause the nation's real GDP to increase in the short run?

  b. What are two factors that can cause the nation's real GDP to increase in the long run?

11-7. What determines how much real GDP responds to changes in the price level along the short-run aggregate supply curve?

11-8. At a point along the short-run aggregate supply curve that is to the right of the point where it crosses the long-run aggregate supply curve, what must be true of the unemployment rate relative to the long-run, full-employment rate of unemployment? Why?

11-9. Suppose that the stock market crashes in an economy with an upward-sloping short-run aggregate supply curve, and consumer and business confidence plummets. What are the short-run effects on equilibrium real GDP and the equilibrium price level?

11-10. Suppose that there is a temporary, but significant, increase in oil prices in an economy with an upward-sloping *SRAS* curve. If policymakers wish to prevent the equilibrium price level from changing in response to the oil price increase, should they increase or decrease the quantity of money in circulation? Why?

11-11. As in Problem 11-10, suppose that there is a temporary, but significant, increase in oil prices in an economy with an upward-sloping *SRAS* curve. In this case, however, suppose that policymakers wish to prevent equilibrium real GDP from changing in response to the oil price increase. Should they increase or decrease the quantity of money in circulation? Why?

11-12. Based on your answers to Problems 11-10 and 11-11, can policymakers stabilize *both* the price level *and* real GDP simultaneously in response to a short-lived but sudden rise in oil prices? Explain briefly.

11-13. For each question that follows, suppose that the economy *begins* at the short-run equilibrium point *A*. Identify which of the other points on the diagram—

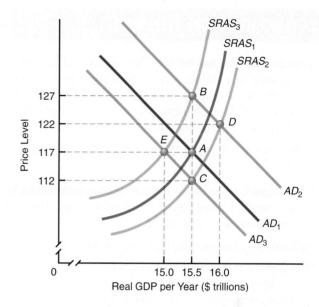

point *B*, *C*, *D*, or *E*—could represent a *new* short-run equilibrium after the described events take place and move the economy away from point *A*. Briefly explain your answers.

  a. Most workers in this nation's economy are union members, and unions have successfully negotiated large wage boosts. At the same time, economic conditions suddenly worsen abroad, reducing real GDP and disposable income in other nations of the world.

  b. A major hurricane has caused short-term halts in production at many firms and created major bottlenecks in the distribution of goods and services that had been produced prior to the storm. At the same time, the nation's central bank has significantly pushed up the rate of growth of the nation's money supply.

  c. A strengthening of the value of this nation's currency in terms of other countries' currencies affects both the *SRAS* curve and the *AD* curve.

11-14. Consider an open economy in which the aggregate supply curve slopes upward in the short run. Firms in this nation do not import raw materials or any other productive inputs from abroad, but foreign residents purchase many of the nation's goods and services. What is the most likely short-run effect on this nation's economy if there is a significant downturn in economic activity in other nations around the world?

ECONOMICS ON THE NET

Money, the Price Level, and Real GDP The classical and Keynesian theories have differing predictions about how changes in the money supply should affect the price level and real GDP. Here you get to look at data on growth in the money supply, the price level, and real GDP.

Title: Federal Reserve Bank of St. Louis Monetary Trends

Navigation: Use the link at **www.econtoday.com/chapter11** to visit the Federal Reserve Bank of St. Louis. Click on *Gross Domestic Product and M2*.

Application Read the article; then answer these questions.

1. Classical theory indicates that, *ceteris paribus*, changes in the price level should be closely related to changes in aggregate demand induced by variations in the quantity of money. Click on *Gross Domestic Product and M2*, and take a look at the charts labeled "Gross Domestic Product Price Index" and "M2." (M2 is a measure of the quantity of money in circulation.) Are

annual percentage changes in these variables closely related?

2. Keynesian theory predicts that, *ceteris paribus*, changes in GDP and the quantity of money should be directly related. Take a look at the charts labeled "Real Gross Domestic Product" and "M2." Are annual percentage changes in these variables closely related?

For Group Study and Analysis Both classical and Keynesian theories of relationships among real GDP, the price level, and the quantity of money hinge on specific assumptions. Have class groups search through the FRED database (accessible at **www.econtoday.com/chapter11**) to evaluate factors that provide support for either theory's predictions. Which approach appears to receive greater support from recent data? Does this necessarily imply that this is the "true theory"? Why or why not?

ANSWERS TO QUICK QUIZZES

p. 268: (i) supply . . . demand; (ii) pure competition . . . wages . . . prices . . . self-interest . . . money illusion; (iii) saving . . . investment; (iv) wage rate; (v) vertical . . . price level
p. 274: (i) demand; (ii) reduced; (iii) partial; (iv) intensively . . . higher; (v) *SRAS*
p. 279: (i) Short . . . Long . . . shocks . . . shocks; (ii) recessionary . . . inflationary; (iii) demand-pull . . . cost-push; (iv) weaker . . . weaker

Consumption, Real GDP, and the Multiplier

I
n theory, higher interest rates should boost households' borrowing costs and give them an incentive to cut back on their consumption spending. Between 1945 and 1989, this is exactly what U.S. consumers did. During these years, a given 1-percentage-point increase in the interest rate would cause U.S. consumption expenditures to decline by 1 to 2 percent. In the years since 1989, however, the impact of interest rate changes on household consumption has decreased substantially. Why has this happened? What are the implications for U.S. aggregate demand and real GDP? To be able to answer these questions, you must learn more about the determinants of consumption spending and about consumption's role in influencing aggregate demand and equilibrium real GDP. These are key topics of this chapter.

LEARNING OBJECTIVES

MyEconLab helps you master each objective and study more efficiently. See end of chapter for details.

After reading this chapter, you should be able to:

➤ Distinguish between saving and savings and explain how saving and consumption are related

➤ Explain the key determinants of consumption and saving in the Keynesian model

➤ Identify the primary determinants of planned investment

➤ Describe how equilibrium real GDP is established in the Keynesian model

➤ Evaluate why autonomous changes in total planned expenditures have a multiplier effect on equilibrium real GDP

➤ Understand the relationship between total planned expenditures and the aggregate demand curve

? DID YOU KNOW THAT at the end of the 1990s, some businesspeople, numerous media pundits, and even a few economists were speculating that the adoption of new information technologies might have made recessions obsolete? Such speculation ended abruptly when a nearly 15 percent drop in investment in information technology (IT) helped bring about a mild recession in the latter half of 2001. A significant drop in IT investment also played a role in the Great Recession of the late 2000s. These downturns offered proof positive that recessions cannot be relegated to the dustbin of history.

Instead of putting an end to recessions, variations in investment in new information technologies arguably have had a lot to do with fluctuations in real GDP during the first decade of the twenty-first century. John Maynard Keynes focused much of his research on how unanticipated changes in investment spending affect a nation's aggregate spending and real GDP. The key to determining the broader economic effects of investment fluctuations, Keynes reasoned, was to understand the relationship between how much people earn and their willingness to engage in personal consumption spending. Thus, Keynes argued that a prerequisite to understanding how investment affects a nation's economy is to understand the determinants of household consumption. In this chapter, you will learn how an understanding of consumption expenditures can assist you in evaluating the effects of variations in business investment on real GDP.

Some Simplifying Assumptions in a Keynesian Model

Continuing in the Keynesian tradition, we will assume that the short-run aggregate supply curve within the current range of real GDP is horizontal. That is, we assume that it is similar to Figure 11-7 on page 269. Thus, the equilibrium level of real GDP is demand determined. This is why Keynes wished to examine the elements of desired aggregate expenditures. Because of the Keynesian assumption of inflexible prices, inflation is not a concern. Hence, real values are identical to nominal values.

To simplify the income determination model that follows, a number of assumptions are made:

1. Businesses pay no indirect taxes (for example, sales taxes).
2. Businesses distribute all of their profits to shareholders.
3. There is no depreciation (capital consumption allowance), so gross private domestic investment equals net investment.
4. The economy is closed—that is, there is no foreign trade.

Given all these simplifying assumptions, **real disposable income,** or after-tax real income, will be equal to real GDP minus net taxes—taxes paid less transfer payments received.

Another Look at Definitions and Relationships

You can do only two things with a dollar of disposable income: consume it or save it. If you consume it, it is gone forever. If you save the entire dollar, however, you will be able to consume it (and perhaps more if it earns interest) at some future time. That is the distinction between **consumption** and **saving.** Consumption is the act of using income for the purchase of consumption goods. **Consumption goods** are goods

Real disposable income
Real GDP minus net taxes, or after-tax real income.

Consumption
Spending on new goods and services to be used up out of a household's current income. Whatever is not consumed is saved. Consumption includes such things as buying food and going to a concert.

Saving
The act of not consuming all of one's current income. Whatever is not consumed out of spendable income is, by definition, saved. *Saving* is an action measured over time (a flow), whereas *savings* are a stock, an accumulation resulting from the act of saving in the past.

Consumption goods
Goods bought by households to use up, such as food and movies.

purchased by households for immediate satisfaction. (These also include services.) Consumption goods are such things as food and movies. By definition, whatever you do not consume you save and can consume at some time in the future.

STOCKS AND FLOWS: THE DIFFERENCE BETWEEN SAVING AND SAVINGS It is important to distinguish between *saving* and *savings*. *Saving* is an action that occurs at a particular rate—for example, $40 per week or $2,080 per year. This rate is a flow. It is expressed per unit of time, usually a year. Implicitly, then, when we talk about saving, we talk about a *flow*, or rate, of saving. *Savings*, by contrast, is a *stock* concept, measured at a certain point or instant in time. Your current *savings* are the result of past *saving*. You may currently have *savings* of $8,000 that are the result of four years' *saving* at a rate of $2,000 per year. Consumption is also a flow concept. You consume from after-tax income at a certain rate per week, per month, or per year.

When this person deposits his payroll check at the bank, what decision does he have to make next?

RELATING INCOME TO SAVING AND CONSUMPTION A dollar of take-home income can be allocated either to consumption or to saving. Realizing this, we can see the relationship among saving, consumption, and disposable income from the following expression:

$$\text{Consumption} + \text{saving} \equiv \text{disposable income}$$

This is called an *accounting identity*, meaning that it has to hold true at every moment in time. (To indicate that the relationship is always true, we use the $\equiv$ symbol.)

From this relationship, we can derive the following definition of saving:

$$\text{Saving} \equiv \text{disposable income} - \text{consumption}$$

Hence, saving is the amount of disposable income that is not spent to purchase consumption goods.

Investment

Investment is also a flow concept. As noted in Chapter 8, *investment* as used in economics differs from the common use of the term. In common speech, it is often used to describe putting funds into the stock market or real estate. In economic analysis, investment is defined to include expenditures on new machines and buildings—**capital goods**—that are expected to yield a future stream of income. This is called *fixed investment*. We also include changes in business inventories in our definition. This we call *inventory investment*.

Investment
Spending on items such as machines and buildings, which can be used to produce goods and services in the future. The investment part of real GDP is the portion that will be used in the process of producing goods in the future.

Capital goods
Producer durables; nonconsumable goods that firms use to make other goods.

QUICK QUIZ	*See page 316 for the answers. Review concepts from this section in MyEconLab.*

If we assume that we are operating on a _____ short-run aggregate supply curve, the equilibrium level of real GDP per year is completely demand determined.

_____ is a flow, something that occurs over time. It equals disposable income minus consumption.

_____ is a stock. It is the accumulation resulting from saving.

_____ is also a flow. It includes expenditures on new machines, buildings, and equipment and changes in business inventories.

Determinants of Planned Consumption and Planned Saving

In the classical model discussed in Chapter 11 on pages 262–268, the supply of saving was determined by the rate of interest. Specifically, the higher the rate of interest, the more people wanted to save and therefore the less people wanted to consume.

In contrast, according to Keynes, the interest rate is *not* the most important determinant of an individual's real saving and consumption decisions. In his view, income, not the interest rate, is the main determinant of saving. Thus:

> *Keynes argued that real saving and consumption decisions depend primarily on a household's present real disposable income.*

Consumption function

The relationship between amount consumed and disposable income. A consumption function tells us how much people plan to consume at various levels of disposable income.

The relationship between planned real consumption expenditures of households and their current level of real disposable income has been called the **consumption function.** It shows how much all households plan to consume per year at each level of real disposable income per year. Columns (1) and (2) of Table 12-1 illustrate a consumption function for a hypothetical household.

We see from Table 12-1 that as real disposable income rises, planned consumption also rises, but by a smaller amount, as Keynes suggested. Planned saving also increases with disposable income. Notice, however, that below an income of $60,000, the

TABLE 12-1

Real Consumption and Saving Schedules: A Hypothetical Case

Column 1 presents real disposable income from zero up to $120,000 per year; column 2 indicates planned consumption per year; column 3 presents planned saving per year. At levels of disposable income below $60,000, planned saving is negative. In column 4, we see the average propensity to consume, which is merely planned consumption divided by disposable income. Column 5 lists average propensity to save, which is planned saving divided by disposable income. Column 6 is the marginal propensity to consume, which shows the proportion of *additional* income that will be consumed. Finally, column 7 shows the proportion of *additional* income that will be saved, or the marginal propensity to save. (Δ represents "change in.")

Combination	(1) Real Disposable Income per Year (Y_d)	(2) Planned Real Consumption per Year (C)	(3) Planned Real Saving per Year ($S \equiv Y_d - C$) (1) − (2)	(4) Average Propensity to Consume ($APC \equiv C/Y_d$) (2) ÷ (1)	(5) Average Propensity to Save ($APS \equiv S/Y_d$) (3) ÷ (1)	(6) Marginal Propensity to Consume ($MPC \equiv \Delta C/\Delta Y_d$)	(7) Marginal Propensity to Save ($MPS \equiv \Delta S/\Delta Y_d$)
A	$ 0	$12,000	$−12,000	–	–	–	–
B	12,000	21,600	−9,600	1.8	−0.8	0.8	0.2
C	24,000	31,200	−7,200	1.3	−0.3	0.8	0.2
D	36,000	40,800	−4,800	1.133	−0.133	0.8	0.2
E	48,000	50,400	−2,400	1.05	−0.05	0.8	0.2
F	60,000	60,000	0	1.0	0.0	0.8	0.2
G	72,000	69,600	2,400	0.967	0.033	0.8	0.2
H	84,000	79,200	4,800	0.943	0.057	0.8	0.2
I	96,000	88,800	7,200	0.925	0.075	0.8	0.2
J	108,000	98,400	9,600	0.911	0.089	0.8	0.2
K	120,000	108,000	12,000	0.9	0.1	0.8	0.2

planned saving of this hypothetical household is actually negative. The farther that income drops below that level, the more the household engages in **dissaving,** either by going into debt or by using up some of its existing wealth.

Graphing the Numbers

We now graph the consumption and saving relationships presented in Table 12-1. In the upper part of Figure 12-1 on the following page, the vertical axis measures the level of planned real consumption per year, and the horizontal axis measures the level of real disposable income per year. In the lower part of the figure, the horizontal axis is again real disposable income per year, but now the vertical axis is planned real saving per year. All of these are on a dollars-per-year basis, which emphasizes the point that we are measuring flows, not stocks.

As you can see, we have taken income-consumption and income-saving combinations *A* through *K* and plotted them. In the upper part of Figure 12-1, the result is called the *consumption function.* In the lower part, the result is called the *saving function.* Mathematically, the saving function is the *complement* of the consumption function because consumption plus saving always equals disposable income. What is not consumed is, by definition, saved. The difference between actual disposable income and the planned rate of consumption per year *must* be the planned rate of saving per year.

How can we find the rate of saving or dissaving in the upper part of Figure 12-1? We begin by drawing a line that is equidistant from both the horizontal and the vertical axes. This line is 45 degrees from either axis and is often called the **45-degree reference line.** At every point on the 45-degree reference line, a vertical line drawn to the income axis is the same distance from the origin as a horizontal line drawn to the consumption axis. Thus, at point *F*, where the consumption function intersects the 45-degree line, real disposable income equals planned real consumption. Point *F* is sometimes called the *break-even income point* because there is neither positive nor negative real saving. This can be seen in the lower part of Figure 12-1 as well. The planned annual rate of real saving at a real disposable income level of $60,000 is indeed zero.

Dissaving and Autonomous Consumption

To the left of point *F* in either part of Figure 12-1, this hypothetical family engages in dissaving, either by going into debt or by consuming existing assets. The rate of real saving or dissaving in the upper part of the figure can be found by measuring the vertical distance between the 45-degree line and the consumption function. This simply tells us that if our hypothetical household sees its real disposable income fall to less than $60,000, it will not limit its consumption to this amount. It will instead go into debt or consume existing assets in some way to compensate for part of the lost income.

Now look at the point on the diagram where real disposable income is zero but planned consumption is $12,000. This amount of real planned consumption, which does not depend at all on actual real disposable income, is called **autonomous consumption.** The autonomous consumption of $12,000 is *independent* of disposable income. That means that no matter how low the level of real income of our hypothetical household falls, the household will always attempt to consume at least $12,000 per year. (We are, of course, assuming here that the household's real disposable income does not equal zero year in and year out. There is certainly a limit to how long our hypothetical household could finance autonomous consumption without any

Dissaving
Negative saving; a situation in which spending exceeds income. Dissaving can occur when a household is able to borrow or use up existing assets.

45-degree reference line
The line along which planned real expenditures equal real GDP per year.

Autonomous consumption
The part of consumption that is independent of (does not depend on) the level of disposable income. Changes in autonomous consumption shift the consumption function.

The Consumption and Saving Functions

If we plot the combinations of real disposable income and planned real consumption from columns 1 and 2 in Table 12-1 on page 290, we get the consumption function.

At every point on the 45-degree line, a vertical line drawn to the income axis is the same distance from the origin as a horizontal line drawn to the consumption axis. Where the consumption function crosses the 45-degree line at *F*, we know that planned real consumption equals real disposable income and there is zero saving. The vertical distance between the 45-degree line and the consumption function measures the rate of real saving or dissaving at any given income level. If we plot the relationship between column 1—real disposable income—and column 3—planned real saving—from Table 12-1 on page 290, we arrive at the saving function shown in the lower part of this diagram. It is the complement of the consumption function presented above it.

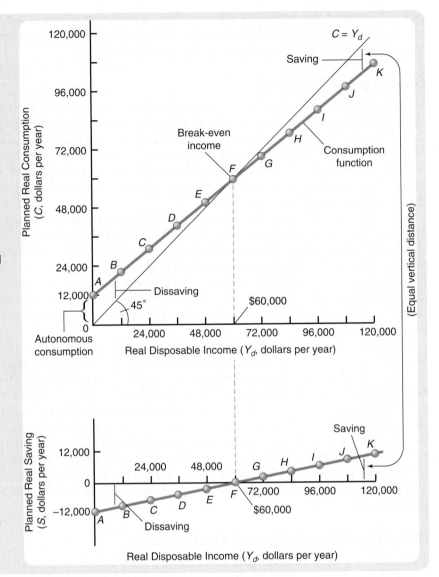

income.) That $12,000 of yearly consumption is determined by things other than the level of income. We don't need to specify what determines autonomous consumption; we merely state that it exists and that in our example it is $12,000 per year.

Just remember that the word *autonomous* means "existing independently." In our model, autonomous consumption exists independently of the hypothetical household's level of real disposable income. (Later we will review some of the determinants of consumption other than real disposable income.) There are many possible types of autonomous expenditures. Hypothetically, we can assume that investment is autonomous—independent of income. We can assume that government expenditures are autonomous. We will do just that at various times in our discussions to simplify our analysis of income determination.

Average Propensity to Consume and to Save

Let's now go back to Table 12-1 on page 290, and this time let's look at columns 4 and 5: **average propensity to consume (APC)** and **average propensity to save (APS).** They are defined as follows:

$$APC \equiv \frac{\text{real consumption}}{\text{real disposable income}}$$

$$APS \equiv \frac{\text{real saving}}{\text{real disposable income}}$$

Notice from column 4 in Table 12-1 that for this hypothetical household, the average propensity to consume decreases as real disposable income increases. This decrease simply means that the fraction of the household's real disposable income going to consumption falls as income rises. Column 5 shows that the average propensity to save, which at first is negative, finally hits zero at an income level of $60,000 and then becomes positive. In this example, the APS reaches a value of 0.1 at income level $120,000. This means that the household saves 10 percent of a $120,000 income.

It's quite easy for you to figure out your own average propensity to consume or to save. Just divide the value of what you consumed by your total real disposable income for the year, and the result will be your personal APC at your current level of income. Also, divide your real saving during the year by your real disposable income to calculate your own APS.

What is the value of the U.S. average propensity to save, and why has it recently increased?

Average propensity to consume (APC)
Real consumption divided by real disposable income; for any given level of real income, the proportion of total real disposable income that is consumed.

Average propensity to save (APS)
Real saving divided by real disposable income; for any given level of real income, the proportion of total real disposable income that is saved.

EXAMPLE
Explaining the Rising U.S. "Saving Rate"

The media do not refer to the ratio of real household saving to real disposable income as the "average propensity to save (APS)." Instead, they call this ratio, after it has been converted into a percentage, the nation's "saving rate." Between 1980 and 2007, the average U.S. saving rate declined from 9 percent to 1.8 percent, so the average value of the APS fell from 0.090 to 0.018. By the middle of 2009, however, the saving rate had risen to as high as 6.2 percent, meaning that the APS increased to 0.062.

Why did the saving rate and the APS decline from the 1980s until 2007? One reason may be that improved access to credit cards and other sources of credit induced many households to opt to borrow in order to expand their consumption and, hence, reduce their saving. In addition, the official measure of household saving understates actual saving because it fails to include capital gains on financial assets, which were higher in the early 2000s than previously. Finally, many households may have viewed increases in values of residential property as a form of saving. Consequently, as inflation-adjusted house values increased into the mid-2000s, real saving declined relative to disposable income.

Between 2007 and 2009, struggling banks cut back on lending, values of financial assets plummeted, and residential property values declined dramatically. These reversals of fortune generated the increase in the saving rate and the APS during this period.

FOR CRITICAL ANALYSIS
Why do you suppose that the government officially calculates saving as the residual difference between disposable income and consumption instead of computing consumption as the residual difference between disposable income and saving? (Hint: Which do you think is likely to be easier to measure—total household expenditures on goods and services or total household saving?)

Marginal propensity to consume (MPC)
The ratio of the change in consumption to the change in disposable income. A marginal propensity to consume of 0.8 tells us that an additional $100 in take-home pay will lead to an additional $80 consumed.

Marginal propensity to save (MPS)
The ratio of the change in saving to the change in disposable income. A marginal propensity to save of 0.2 indicates that out of an additional $100 in take-home pay, $20 will be saved. Whatever is not saved is consumed. The marginal propensity to save plus the marginal propensity to consume must always equal 1, by definition.

Marginal Propensity to Consume and to Save

Now we go to the last two columns in Table 12-1 on page 290: **marginal propensity to consume (MPC)** and **marginal propensity to save (MPS).** The term *marginal* refers to a small incremental or decremental change (represented by the Greek letter delta, Δ, in Table 12-1). The marginal propensity to consume, then, is defined as

$$\text{MPC} \equiv \frac{\text{change in real consumption}}{\text{change in real disposable income}}$$

The marginal propensity to save is defined similarly as

$$\text{MPS} \equiv \frac{\text{change in real saving}}{\text{change in real disposable income}}$$

MARGINAL VERSUS AVERAGE PROPENSITIES What do MPC and MPS tell you? They tell you what percentage of a given increase or decrease in real income will go toward consumption and saving, respectively. The emphasis here is on the word *change*. The marginal propensity to consume indicates how much you will change your planned real consumption if there is a change in your actual real disposable income. If your marginal propensity to consume is 0.8, that does *not* mean that you consume 80 percent of *all* disposable income. The percentage of your total real disposable income that you consume is given by the average propensity to consume, or APC. As Table 12-1 indicates, the APC is not equal to 0.8. Instead, an MPC of 0.8 means that you will consume 80 percent of any *increase* in your disposable income. Hence, the MPC cannot be less than zero or greater than one. It follows that households increase their planned real consumption by more than zero and less than 100 percent of any increase in real disposable income that they receive.

DISTINGUISHING THE MPC FROM THE APC Consider a simple example in which we show the difference between the average propensity to consume and the marginal propensity to consume. Assume that your consumption behavior is exactly the same as our hypothetical household's behavior depicted in Table 12-1. You have an annual real disposable income of $108,000. Your planned consumption rate, then, from column 2 of Table 12-1 is $98,400. So your average propensity to consume is $98,400/$108,000 = 0.911. Now suppose that at the end of the year, your boss gives you an after-tax bonus of $12,000. What would you do with that additional $12,000 in real disposable income? According to the table, you would consume $9,600 of it and save $2,400. In that case, your *marginal* propensity to consume would be $9,600/$12,000 = 0.8 and your marginal propensity to save would be $2,400/$12,000 = 0.2. What would happen to your *average* propensity to consume? To find out, we add $9,600 to $98,400 of planned consumption, which gives us a new consumption rate of $108,000. The average propensity to consume is then $108,000 divided by the new higher salary of $120,000. Your APC drops from 0.911 to 0.9.

In contrast, your MPC remains, in our simplified example, 0.8 all the time. Look at column 6 in Table 12-1 on page 290. The MPC is 0.8 at every level of income. (Therefore, the MPS is always equal to 0.2 at every level of income.) The constancy of MPC reflects the assumption that the amount that you are willing to consume out of additional income

If the market value of this couple's newly purchased house goes up significantly in the next ten years, do you think that the couple's measured saving rate will go up or down?

will remain the same in percentage terms no matter what level of real disposable income is your starting point.

Some Relationships

Consumption plus saving must equal income. Both your total real disposable income and the change in total real disposable income are either consumed or saved. The proportions of either measure must equal 1, or 100 percent. This allows us to make the following statements:

$$\text{APC} + \text{APS} \equiv 1\ (= 100\ \text{percent of total income})$$

$$\text{MPC} + \text{MPS} \equiv 1\ (= 100\ \text{percent of the } change \text{ in income})$$

The average propensities as well as the marginal propensities to consume and save must total 1, or 100 percent. Check the two statements by adding the figures in columns 4 and 5 for each level of real disposable income in Table 12-1. Do the same for columns 6 and 7.

Causes of Shifts in the Consumption Function

A change in any other relevant economic variable besides real disposable income will cause the consumption function to shift. The number of such nonincome determinants of the position of the consumption function is virtually unlimited. Real household **wealth** is one determinant of the position of the consumption function. An increase in the real wealth of the average household will cause the consumption function to shift upward. A decrease in real wealth will cause it to shift downward. So far we have been talking about the consumption function of an individual or a household. Now let's move on to the national economy.

Are some wealth effects on consumption larger than others?

You Are There

To think about why a government might try to convince its nation's residents to increase their autonomous consumption expenditures, read **Listen to the German Chancellor: It's Time to Go Shopping!** on page 310.

Wealth

The stock of assets owned by a person, household, firm, or nation. For a household, wealth can consist of a house, cars, personal belongings, stocks, bonds, bank accounts, and cash.

EXAMPLE

Consumption Effects of Changes in Housing versus Financial Wealth

In the United States, as much as 60 percent of household wealth is in the form of home ownership. Tax rates on this wealth are low compared with those on stocks, bonds, and other financial assets, and borrowing costs often are lower when home equity rather than financial assets is used as collateral. Thus, a change in the real value of housing wealth generates a larger effect on real consumption spending than a change in the real value of financial wealth. Most estimates indicate that a constant-dollar decrease in real housing wealth pushes down real consumption spending by 6 cents. In contrast, a constant-dollar fall in real financial wealth reduces real consumption by only about 2 cents. Thus, every $1 decrease in real housing wealth that occurred in the United States in the late 2000s likely shifted the consumption function downward by about three times as much as each $1 decrease in real financial wealth.

FOR CRITICAL ANALYSIS

In nations such as Finland and Italy, in which more than 80 percent of household wealth is in the form of housing, would you expect a change in real housing wealth to have a greater or smaller effect on consumption than in the United States?

QUICK QUIZ   *See page 316 for the answers. Review concepts from this section in MyEconLab.*

The **consumption function** shows the relationship between planned rates of real consumption and real _____ _____ per year. The saving function is the complement of the consumption function because real saving plus real _____ must equal real disposable income.

The _____ propensity to consume is equal to real consumption divided by real disposable income. The _____ propensity to save is equal to real saving divided by real disposable income.

The _____ propensity to consume is equal to the change in planned real consumption divided by the change in real disposable income. The _____ propensity to save is equal to the change in planned real saving divided by the change in real disposable income.

Any change in real disposable income will cause the planned rate of consumption to change; this is represented by a_____ _____ the consumption function. Any change in a nonincome determinant of consumption will cause a _____ _____ the consumption function.

Determinants of Investment

Investment, you will remember, consists of expenditures on new buildings and equipment and changes in business inventories. Historically, real gross private domestic investment in the United States has been extremely volatile over the years, relative to real consumption. If we were to look at net private domestic investment (investment after depreciation has been deducted), we would see that in the depths of the Great Depression and at the peak of the World War II effort, the figure was negative. In other words, we were eating away at our capital stock—we weren't even maintaining it by completely replacing depreciated equipment.

If we compare real investment expenditures historically with real consumption expenditures, we find that the latter are less variable over time than the former. Why is this so? One possible reason is that the real investment decisions of businesses are based on highly variable, subjective estimates of how the economic future looks.

The Planned Investment Function

Consider that at all times, businesses perceive an array of investment opportunities. These investment opportunities have rates of return ranging from zero to very high, with the number (or dollar value) of all such projects inversely related to the rate of return. Because a project is profitable only if its rate of return exceeds the opportunity cost of the investment—the rate of interest—it follows that as the interest rate falls, planned investment spending increases, and vice versa. Even if firms use retained earnings (internal financing) to fund an investment, the lower the market rate of interest, the smaller the *opportunity cost* of using those retained earnings.

Thus, it does not matter in our analysis whether the firm must seek financing from external sources or can obtain such financing by using retained earnings. Whatever the method of financing, as the interest rate falls, more investment opportunities will be profitable, and planned investment will be higher.

It should be no surprise, therefore, that the investment function is represented as an inverse relationship between the rate of interest and the value of planned real investment. A hypothetical investment schedule is given in panel (a) of Figure 12-2 and plotted in panel (b). We see from this schedule that if, for example, the rate of interest is 5 percent, the dollar value of planned investment will be $2 trillion per year. Notice that planned investment is also given on a per-year basis, showing that it represents

Does the spending on computers for this new high-tech company represent additions to net private domestic investment?

FIGURE 12-2

Planned Real Investment

As shown in the hypothetical planned investment schedule in panel (a), the rate of planned real investment is inversely related to the rate of interest. If we plot the data pairs from panel (a), we obtain the investment function, *I*, in panel (b). It is negatively sloped.

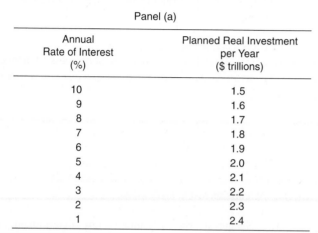

Panel (a)

Annual Rate of Interest (%)	Planned Real Investment per Year ($ trillions)
10	1.5
9	1.6
8	1.7
7	1.8
6	1.9
5	2.0
4	2.1
3	2.2
2	2.3
1	2.4

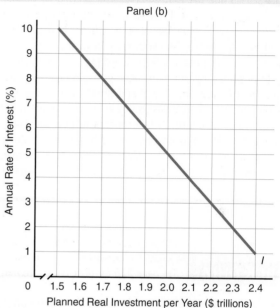

a flow, not a stock. (The stock counterpart of investment is the stock of capital in the economy measured in inflation-adjusted dollars at a point in time.)

What Causes the Investment Function to Shift?

Because planned real investment is assumed to be a function of the rate of interest, any non-interest-rate variable that changes can have the potential of shifting the investment function. One of those variables is the expectations of businesses. If higher profits are expected, more machines and bigger plants will be planned for the future. More investment will be undertaken because of the expectation of higher profits. In this case, the investment schedule, *I*, would shift outward to the right, meaning that more investment would be desired at all rates of interest. Any change in productive technology can potentially shift the investment function. A positive change in productive technology would stimulate demand for additional capital goods and shift *I* outward to the right. Changes in business taxes can also shift the investment schedule. If they increase, we predict a leftward shift in the planned investment function because higher taxes imply a lower (after-tax) rate of return.

Could a collapse in business confidence be the main explanation for the considerable drop in U.S. business investment spending during the Great Recession of the late 2000s?

Go to economic data provided by the Federal Reserve Bank of St. Louis via the link at **www.econtoday.com/chapter12** to see how U.S. real private investment has varied in recent years.

Since the end of 2007, the flow of U.S. business investment spending has decreased by more than 25 percent. George Akerlof of the University of California at Berkeley and Robert Shiller of Yale University suggest that a decline in business confidence explains this significant drop in business investment expenditures. Prior to the onset of the Great Recession, Akerlof and Shiller argue, businesspeople made decisions based on overconfident assessments of future rates of return on investments in new plants and equipment. This led to an upswing in business investment spending in the mid-2000s. After market values of many assets and of newly produced goods and services unexpectedly decreased in 2007 and 2008, businesspeople became much less confident. According to Akerlof and Shiller, the result was the substantial reduction in investment that the U.S. economy has experienced. As a consequence, the investment schedule has shifted leftward, so that businesspeople are now making fewer investment expenditures at any given rate of interest.

FOR CRITICAL ANALYSIS
What besides a return to a higher level of business confidence could generate a shift back to the right in the U.S. investment schedule?

QUICK QUIZ *See page 316 for the answers. Review concepts from this section in MyEconLab.*

The planned investment schedule shows the relationship between real investment and the _____ _____; it slopes _____.

The non-interest-rate determinants of planned investment are _____, innovation and technological changes, and _____ _____.

Any change in the non-interest-rate determinants of planned investment will cause a _____ _____ the planned investment function so that at each and every rate of interest a different amount of planned investment will be made.

Determining Equilibrium Real GDP

We are interested in determining the equilibrium level of real GDP per year. But when we examined the consumption function earlier in this chapter, it related planned real consumption expenditures to the level of real disposable income per year. We have already shown where adjustments must be made to GDP in order to get real disposable income (see Table 8-2 on page 199). Real disposable income turns out to be less than real GDP because real net taxes (real taxes minus real government transfer payments) are usually about 14 to 21 percent of GDP. A representative average is about 18 percent, so disposable income, on average, has in recent years been around 82 percent of GDP.

Consumption as a Function of Real GDP

To simplify our model, assume that real disposable income, Y_d, differs from real GDP by the same absolute amount every year. Therefore, we can relatively easily substitute real GDP for real disposable income in the consumption function.

FIGURE 12-3

Consumption as a Function of Real GDP

This consumption function shows the rate of planned expenditures for each level of real GDP per year. In this example, there is an autonomous component of consumption equal to $0.2 trillion. Along the 45-degree reference line, planned real consumption expenditures per year, C, are identical to real GDP per year, Y. The consumption curve intersects the 45-degree reference line at a value of $1 trillion per year in base-year dollars.

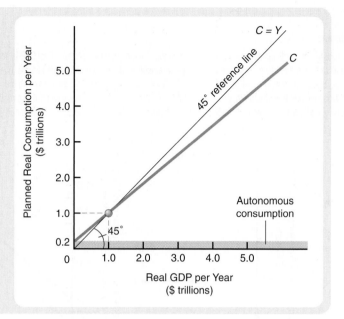

We can now plot any consumption function on a diagram in which the horizontal axis is no longer real disposable income but rather real GDP, as in Figure 12-3. Notice that there is an autonomous part of real consumption that is so labeled. The difference between this graph and the graphs presented earlier in this chapter is the change in the horizontal axis from real disposable income to real GDP per year. For the rest of this chapter, assume that the MPC out of real GDP equals 0.8, suggesting that 20 percent of changes in real disposable income is saved: In other words, of an additional after-tax $100 earned, an additional $80 will be consumed.

The 45-Degree Reference Line

As in the earlier graphs, Figure 12-3 shows a 45-degree reference line. The 45-degree line bisects the quadrant into two equal spaces. Thus, along the 45-degree reference line, planned real consumption expenditures, C, equal real GDP per year, Y. One can see, then, that at any point where the consumption function intersects the 45-degree reference line, planned real consumption expenditures will be exactly equal to real GDP per year, or $C = Y$. Note that in this graph, because we are looking only at planned real consumption on the vertical axis, the 45-degree reference line is where planned real consumption, C, is always equal to real GDP per year, Y. Later, when we add real investment, government spending, and net exports to the graph, *all* planned real expenditures will be labeled along the vertical axis. In any event, real consumption and real GDP are equal at $1 trillion per year. That is where the consumption curve, C, intersects the 45-degree reference line. At that GDP level, all real GDP is consumed.

Adding the Investment Function

Another component of private aggregate demand is, of course, real investment spending, I. We have already looked at the planned investment function, which related real investment, which includes changes in inventories of final products, to

Combining Consumption and Investment

In panel (a), we show determination of real investment in trillions of dollars per year, occurring where the investment schedule intersects the saving schedule at an interest rate of 5 percent and equal to $2 trillion per year. In panel (b), investment is a constant $2 trillion per year. When we add this amount to the consumption line, we obtain in panel (c) the $C + I$ line, which is vertically higher than the C line by exactly $2 trillion. Real GDP is equal to $C + I$ at $11 trillion per year where total planned real expenditures, $C + I$, are equal to actual real GDP, for this is where the $C + I$ line intersects the 45-degree reference line, on which $C + I$ is equal to Y at every point. (For simplicity, we ignore the fact that the dependence of saving on income can influence investment.)

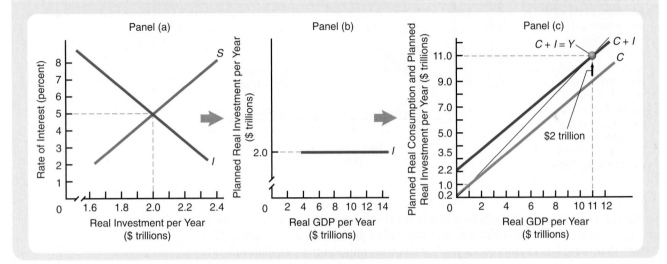

the rate of interest. You see that as the downward-sloping curve in panel (a) of Figure 12-4. Recall from Figure 11-2 (on page 264) that the equilibrium rate of interest is determined at the intersection of the desired saving schedule, which is labeled S and is upward sloping. The equilibrium rate of interest is 5 percent, and the equilibrium rate of real investment is $2 trillion per year. The $2 trillion of real investment per year is *autonomous* with respect to real GDP—that is, it is independent of real GDP. In other words, given that we have a determinant investment level of $2 trillion at a 5 percent rate of interest, we can treat this level of real investment as constant, regardless of the level of GDP. This is shown in panel (b) of Figure 12-4. The vertical distance of real investment spending is $2 trillion. Businesses plan on investing a particular amount—$2 trillion per year—and will do so no matter what the level of real GDP.

How do we add this amount of real investment spending to our consumption function? We simply add a line above the C line that we drew in Figure 12-3 that is higher by the vertical distance equal to $2 trillion of autonomous real investment spending. This is shown by the arrow in panel (c) of Figure 12-4. Our new line, now labeled $C + I$, is called the *consumption plus investment line*. In our simple economy without real government expenditures and net exports, the $C + I$ curve represents total planned real expenditures as they relate to different levels of real GDP per year. Because the 45-degree reference line shows all the points where planned real expenditures (now $C + I$) equal real GDP, we label it $C + I = Y$. Thus, in equilibrium, the sum of consumption spending (C) and investment spending (I) equals real GDP (Y), which is $11 trillion per year. Equilibrium occurs when total

---

FIGURE 12-5

Planned and Actual Rates of Saving and Investment

Only at the equilibrium level of real GDP of $11 trillion per year will planned saving equal actual saving, planned investment equal actual investment, and hence planned saving equal planned investment.

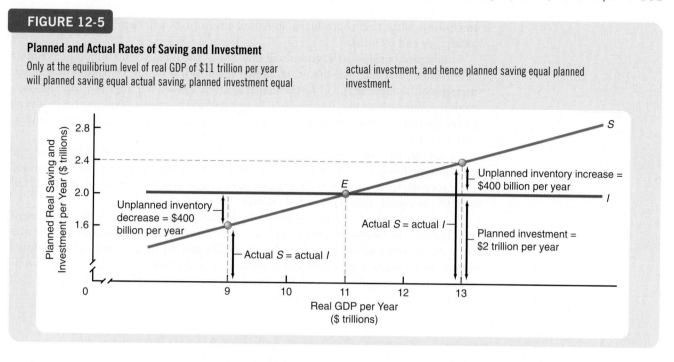

planned real expenditures equal real GDP (given that any amount of production of goods and services in this model in the short run can occur without a change in the price level).

Saving and Investment: Planned versus Actual

Figure 12-5 shows the planned investment curve as a horizontal line at $2 trillion per year in base-year dollars. Real investment is completely autonomous in this simplified model—it does not depend on real GDP.

The planned saving curve is represented by *S*. Because in our model whatever is not consumed is, by definition, saved, the planned saving schedule is the complement of the planned consumption schedule, represented by the *C* line in Figure 12-3 (on page 299). For better exposition, we look at only a part of the saving and investment schedules—annual levels of real GDP between $9 trillion and $13 trillion.

Why does equilibrium have to occur at the intersection of the planned saving and planned investment schedules? If we are at *E* in Figure 12-5, planned saving equals planned investment. All anticipations are validated by reality. There is no tendency for businesses to alter the rate of production or the level of employment because they are neither increasing nor decreasing their inventories in an unplanned way.

UNPLANNED CHANGES IN BUSINESS INVENTORIES If real GDP is $13 trillion instead of $11 trillion, planned investment, as usual, is $2 trillion per year. It is exceeded, however, by planned saving, which is $2.4 trillion per year. The additional $0.4 trillion ($400 billion) in saving by households over and above planned investment represents less consumption spending and will translate into unsold goods that accumulate as unplanned business inventory investment. Thus, consumers will *actually* purchase fewer goods and services than businesses had *anticipated*. This will leave firms with unsold products, and their inventories will begin to rise above the levels they had planned.

Unplanned business inventories will now rise at the rate of $400 billion per year, or $2.4 trillion in actual investment (including inventories) minus $2 trillion in planned investment by firms that had not anticipated an inventory buildup. But this situation cannot continue for long. Businesses will respond to the unplanned increase in inventories by cutting back production of goods and services and reducing employment, and we will move toward a lower level of real GDP.

Naturally, the adjustment process works in reverse if real GDP is less than the equilibrium level. For instance, if real GDP is $9 trillion per year, an unintended inventory decrease of $0.4 trillion ultimately brings about an increase in real GDP toward the equilibrium level of $11 trillion.

Every time the saving rate planned by households differs from the investment rate planned by businesses, there will be a shrinkage or an expansion in the circular flow of income and output (introduced in Chapter 8) in the form of unplanned inventory changes. Real GDP and employment will change until unplanned inventory changes are again zero—that is, until we have attained the equilibrium level of real GDP.

QUICK QUIZ   *See page 316 for the answers. Review concepts from this section in MyEconLab.*

We assume that the consumption function has an _____ part that is independent of the level of real GDP per year. It is labeled "_____ consumption."

For simplicity, we assume that real investment is _____ with respect to real GDP and therefore unaffected by the level of real GDP per year.

The _____ level of real GDP can be found where planned saving equals planned investment.

Whenever planned saving exceeds planned investment, there will be unplanned inventory _____, and real GDP will fall as producers cut production of goods and services. Whenever planned saving is less than planned investment, there will be unplanned inventory _____, and real GDP will rise as producers increase production of goods and services.

Keynesian Equilibrium with Government and the Foreign Sector Added

To this point, we have ignored the role of government in our model. We have also left out the foreign sector of the economy. Let's think about what happens when we also consider these as elements of the model.

Government

To add real government spending, *G*, to our macroeconomic model, we assume that the level of resource-using government purchases of goods and services (federal, state, and local), *not* including transfer payments, is determined by the political process. In other words, *G* will be considered autonomous, just like real investment (and a certain component of real consumption). In the United States, resource-using federal government expenditures account for about 20 percent of real GDP.

The other side of the coin, of course, is that there are real taxes, which are used to pay for much of government spending. We will simplify our model greatly by assuming that there is a constant **lump-sum tax** of $2.3 trillion a year to finance $2.3 trillion of government spending. This lump-sum tax will reduce disposable income by the same amount. We show this in Table 12-2 (column 2), where we give the numbers for a complete model.

Lump-sum tax
A tax that does not depend on income. An example is a $1,000 tax that every household must pay, irrespective of its economic situation.

The Foreign Sector

For years, the media have focused attention on the nation's foreign trade deficit. We have been buying merchandise and services from foreign residents—real imports—the value of which exceeds the value of the real exports we have been selling to them. The difference between real exports and real imports is *real net exports*, which we will label X in our graphs. The level of real exports depends on international economic conditions, especially in the countries that buy our products. Real imports depend on economic conditions here at home. For simplicity, assume that real imports exceed real exports (real net exports, X, is negative) and furthermore that the level of real net exports is autonomous—independent of real national income. Assume a level of X of −$0.8 trillion per year, as shown in column 8 of Table 12-2.

Determining the Equilibrium Level of GDP per Year

We are now in a position to determine the equilibrium level of real GDP per year under the continuing assumptions that the price level is unchanging; that investment, government, and the foreign sector are autonomous; and that planned consumption

TABLE 12-2

The Determination of Equilibrium Real GDP with Government and Net Exports Added
Figures are trillions of dollars.

(1) Real GDP	(2) Real Taxes	(3) Real Disposable Income	(4) Planned Real Consumption	(5) Planned Real Saving	(6) Planned Real Investment	(7) Real Government Spending	(8) Real Net Exports (exports minus imports)	(9) Total Planned Real Expenditures (4)+(6)+(7)+(8)	(10) Unplanned Inventory Changes	(11) Direction of Change in Real GDP
9.0	2.3	6.7	6.7	0.0	2.0	2.3	−0.8	10.2	−1.2	Increase
10.0	2.3	7.7	7.5	0.2	2.0	2.3	−0.8	11.0	−1.0	Increase
11.0	2.3	8.7	8.3	0.4	2.0	2.3	−0.8	11.8	−0.8	Increase
12.0	2.3	9.7	9.1	0.6	2.0	2.3	−0.8	12.6	−0.6	Increase
13.0	2.3	10.7	9.9	0.8	2.0	2.3	−0.8	13.4	−0.4	Increase
14.0	2.3	11.7	10.7	1.0	2.0	2.3	−0.8	14.2	−0.2	Increase
15.0	2.3	12.7	11.5	1.2	2.0	2.3	−0.8	15.0	0	Neither (equilibrium)
16.0	2.3	13.7	12.3	1.4	2.0	2.3	−0.8	15.8	+0.2	Decrease
17.0	2.3	14.7	13.1	1.6	2.0	2.3	−0.8	16.6	+0.4	Decrease

FIGURE 12-6

The Equilibrium Level of Real GDP

The consumption function, with no government and thus no taxes, is shown as C. When we add autonomous investment, government spending, and net exports, we obtain C + I + G + X. We move from E_1 to E_2. Equilibrium real GDP is $15 trillion per year.

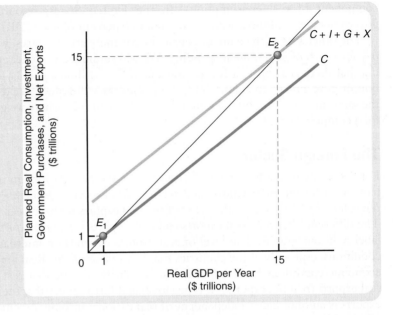

expenditures are determined by the level of real GDP. As can be seen in Table 12-2 on the preceding page, total planned real expenditures of $15 trillion per year equal real GDP of $15 trillion per year, and this is where we reach equilibrium.

Remember that equilibrium always occurs when total planned real expenditures equal real GDP. Now look at Figure 12-6, which shows the equilibrium level of real GDP. There are two curves, one showing the consumption function, which is the exact duplicate of the one shown in Figure 12-3 on page 299, and the other being the $C + I + G + X$ curve, which intersects the 45-degree reference line (representing equilibrium) at $15 trillion per year.

Whenever total planned real expenditures differ from real GDP, there are unplanned inventory changes. When total planned real expenditures are greater than real GDP, inventory levels drop in an unplanned manner. To get inventories back up, firms seek to expand their production of goods and services, which increases real GDP. Real GDP rises toward its equilibrium level. Whenever total planned real expenditures are less than real GDP, the opposite occurs. There are unplanned inventory increases, causing firms to cut back on their production of goods and services in an effort to push inventories back down to planned levels. The result is a drop in real GDP toward the equilibrium level.

QUICK QUIZ | *See page 316 for the answers. Review concepts from this section in MyEconLab.*

When we add autonomous investment, I, and autonomous government spending, G, to the consumption function, we obtain the $C + I + G$ curve, which represents total _____ _____ for a closed economy. In an open economy, we add the foreign sector, which consists of exports minus imports, or net exports, X. Total planned expenditures are thus represented by the $C + I + G + X$ curve.

Equilibrium real GDP can be found by locating the intersection of the total planned real expenditures curve with the _____-_____ reference line. At that level of real GDP per year, planned real consumption plus planned real investment plus real government expenditures plus real net exports will equal real GDP.

QUICK QUIZ *(continued)*

Whenever total planned real expenditures exceed real GDP, there will be unplanned _____ in inventories; production of goods and services will increase, and a higher level of equilibrium real GDP will prevail. Whenever total planned real expenditures are less than real GDP, there will be unplanned _____ in inventories; production of goods and services will decrease, and equilibrium real GDP will decrease.

The Multiplier

Look again at panel (c) of Figure 12-4 on page 300. Assume for the moment that the only real expenditures included in real GDP are real consumption expenditures. Where would the equilibrium level of real GDP be in this case? It would be where the consumption function (*C*) intersects the 45-degree reference line, which is at $1 trillion per year. Now we add the autonomous amount of planned real investment, $2 trillion, and then determine what the new equilibrium level of real GDP will be. It turns out to be $11 trillion per year. Adding $2 trillion per year of investment spending increased equilibrium real GDP by *five* times that amount, or by $10 trillion per year.

The Multiplier Effect

What is operating here is the multiplier effect of changes in autonomous spending. The **multiplier** is the number by which a permanent change in autonomous real investment or autonomous real consumption is multiplied to get the change in the equilibrium level of real GDP. Any permanent increases in autonomous real investment or in any autonomous component of consumption will cause an even larger increase in real GDP. Any permanent decreases in autonomous real spending will cause even larger decreases in real GDP per year. To understand why this multiple expansion (or contraction) in equilibrium real GDP occurs, let's look at a simple numerical example.

We'll use the same figures we used for the marginal propensity to consume and to save. MPC will equal 0.8, or $\frac{4}{5}$, and MPS will equal 0.2, or $\frac{1}{5}$. Now let's run an experiment and say that businesses decide to increase planned real investment permanently by $100 billion a year. We see in Table 12-3 on page 306 that during what we'll call the first round in column 1, investment is increased by $100 billion; this also means an increase in real GDP of $100 billion, because the spending by one group represents income for another, shown in column 2. Column 3 gives the resultant increase in consumption by households that received this additional $100 billion in income. This is found by multiplying the MPC by the increase in real GDP. Because the MPC equals 0.8, real consumption expenditures during the first round will increase by $80 billion.

But that's not the end of the story. This additional household consumption is also spending, and it will provide $80 billion of additional income for other individuals. Thus, during the second round, we see an increase in real GDP of $80 billion. Now, out of this increased real GDP, what will be the resultant increase in consumption expenditures? It will be 0.8 times $80 billion, or $64 billion. We continue these induced expenditure rounds and find that an initial increase in autonomous investment expenditures of $100 billion will eventually cause the equilibrium level of real GDP to increase by $500 billion. A permanent $100 billion increase in autonomous real investment spending has induced an additional $400 billion increase in real consumption spending, for a total increase in real GDP of $500 billion. In other words, equilibrium real GDP will change by an amount equal to five times the change in real investment.

Multiplier

The ratio of the change in the equilibrium level of real GDP to the change in autonomous real expenditures; the number by which a change in autonomous real investment or autonomous real consumption, for example, is multiplied to get the change in equilibrium real GDP.

The Multiplier Process

We trace the effects of a permanent $100 billion increase in autonomous real investment spending on real GDP per year. If we assume a marginal propensity to consume of 0.8, such an increase will eventually elicit a $500 billion increase in equilibrium real GDP per year.

	Assumption: MPC = 0.8, or $\frac{4}{5}$		
	(2)	(3)	(4)
(1)	Annual Increase in Real GDP ($ billions)	Annual Increase in Planned Real Consumption ($ billions)	Annual Increase in Planned Real Saving ($ billions)
Round			
1 ($100 billion per year increase in *I*)	100.00	80.000	20.000
2	80.00	64.000	16.000
3	64.00	51.200	12.800
4	51.20	40.960	10.240
5	40.96	32.768	8.192
.	.	.	.
.	.	.	.
.	.	.	.
All later rounds	163.84	131.072	32.768
Totals (*C + I + G*)	500.00	400.000	100.000

The Multiplier Formula

It turns out that the autonomous spending multiplier is equal to the reciprocal of the marginal propensity to save. In our example, the MPC was $\frac{4}{5}$; therefore, because MPC + MPS = 1, the MPS was equal to $\frac{1}{5}$. The reciprocal is 5. That was our multiplier. A $100 billion increase in real planned investment led to a $500 billion increase in the equilibrium level of real GDP. Our multiplier will always be the following:

$$\text{Multiplier} \equiv \frac{1}{1 - \text{MPC}} \equiv \frac{1}{\text{MPS}}$$

You can always figure out the multiplier if you know either the MPC or the MPS. Let's consider an example. If MPS = $\frac{1}{4}$,

$$\text{Multiplier} = \frac{1}{\frac{1}{4}} = 4$$

Because MPC + MPS = 1, it follows that MPS = 1 − MPC. Hence, we can always figure out the multiplier if we are given the marginal propensity to consume. In this example, if the marginal propensity to consume is given as $\frac{3}{4}$,

$$\text{Multiplier} = \frac{1}{1 - \frac{3}{4}} = \frac{1}{\frac{1}{4}} = 4$$

By taking a few numerical examples, you can demonstrate to yourself an important property of the multiplier:

The smaller the marginal propensity to save, the larger the multiplier.

Otherwise stated:

The larger the marginal propensity to consume, the larger the multiplier.

Demonstrate this to yourself by computing the multiplier when the marginal propensity to save equals $\frac{3}{4}$, $\frac{1}{2}$, and $\frac{1}{4}$. What happens to the multiplier as the MPS gets smaller?

When you have the multiplier, the following formula will then give you the change in equilibrium real GDP due to a permanent change in autonomous spending:

$$\text{Change in equilibrium real GDP} =$$
$$\text{multiplier} \times \text{change in autonomous spending}$$

The multiplier, as noted earlier, works for a permanent increase or a permanent decrease in autonomous spending per year. In our earlier example, if the autonomous component of real consumption had fallen permanently by $100 billion, the reduction in equilibrium real GDP would have been $500 billion per year.

Significance of the Multiplier

Depending on the size of the multiplier, it is possible that a relatively small change in planned investment or in autonomous consumption can trigger a much larger change in equilibrium real GDP per year. In essence, the multiplier magnifies the fluctuations in equilibrium real GDP initiated by changes in autonomous spending.

As was just noted, the larger the marginal propensity to consume, the larger the multiplier. If the marginal propensity to consume is $\frac{1}{2}$, the multiplier is 2. In that case, a $1 billion decrease in (autonomous) real investment will elicit a $2 billion decrease in equilibrium real GDP per year. Conversely, if the marginal propensity to consume is $\frac{9}{10}$, the multiplier will be 10. That same $1 billion decrease in planned real investment expenditures with a multiplier of 10 will lead to a $10 billion decrease in equilibrium real GDP per year.

How a Change in Real Autonomous Spending Affects Real GDP When the Price Level Can Change

So far, our examination of how changes in real autonomous spending affect equilibrium real GDP has considered a situation in which the price level remains unchanged. Thus, our analysis has only indicated how much the aggregate demand curve shifts in response to a change in investment, government spending, net exports, or lump-sum taxes.

Of course, when we take into account the aggregate supply curve, we must also consider responses of the equilibrium price level to a multiplier-induced change in aggregate demand. We do so in Figure 12-7 on the next page. The intersection of AD_1 and $SRAS$ is at a price level of 120 with equilibrium real GDP of $15 trillion per year. An increase in autonomous spending shifts the aggregate demand curve outward to the right to AD_2. If the price level remained at 120, the short-run equilibrium level of real GDP would increase to $15.5 trillion per year because, for the $100 billion increase in autonomous spending, the multiplier would be 5, as it was in Table 12-3.

The price level does not stay fixed, however, because ordinarily the $SRAS$ curve is positively sloped. In this diagram, the new short-run equilibrium level of real GDP is hypothetically $15.3 trillion. The ultimate effect on real GDP is smaller than the multiplier effect on nominal income because part of the additional income is used to

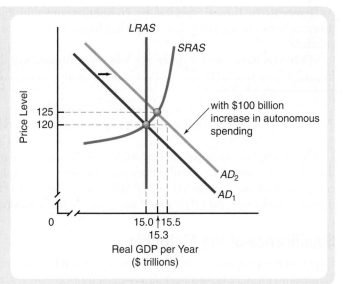

FIGURE 12-7

Effect of a Rise in Autonomous Spending on Equilibrium Real GDP

A $100 billion increase in autonomous spending (investment, government, or net exports) moves AD_1 to AD_2. If the price index increases from 120 to 125, equilibrium real GDP goes up only to, say, $15.3 trillion per year instead of $15.5 trillion per year.

pay higher prices. Not all is spent on additional goods and services, as is the case when the price level is fixed.

If the economy is at an equilibrium level of real GDP that is greater than *LRAS*, the implications for the eventual effect on real GDP are even more severe. Look again at Figure 12-7. The *SRAS* curve starts to slope upward more dramatically after $15 trillion of real GDP per year. Therefore, any increase in aggregate demand will lead to a proportionally greater increase in the price level and a smaller increase in equilibrium real GDP per year. The ultimate effect on real GDP of any increase in autonomous spending will be relatively small because most of the changes will be in the price level. Moreover, any increase in the short-run equilibrium level of real GDP will tend to be temporary because the economy is temporarily above *LRAS*—the strain on its productive capacity will raise the price level.

The Relationship Between Aggregate Demand and the $C + I + G + X$ Curve

There is clearly a relationship between the aggregate demand curves that you studied in Chapters 10 and 11 and the $C + I + G + X$ curve developed in this chapter. After all, aggregate demand consists of consumption, investment, and government purchases, plus the foreign sector of our economy. There is a major difference, however, between the aggregate demand curve, *AD*, and the $C + I + G + X$ curve: The latter is drawn with the price level held constant, whereas the former is drawn, by definition, with the price level changing. To derive the aggregate demand curve from the $C + I + G + X$ curve, we must now allow the price level to change. Look at the upper part of Figure 12-8. Here we see the $C + I + G + X$ curve at a price level equal to 100, and at $15 trillion of real GDP per year, planned real expenditures exactly equal real GDP. This gives us point *A* in the lower graph, for it shows what real GDP would be at a price level of 100.

FIGURE 12-8

The Relationship Between _AD_ and the _C_ + _I_ + _G_ + _X_ Curve

In the upper graph, the _C_ + _I_ + _G_ + _X_ curve at a price level equal to 100 intersects the 45-degree reference line at E_1, or $15 trillion of real GDP per year. That gives us point _A_ (price level = 100; real GDP = $15 trillion) in the lower graph. When the price level increases to 125, the _C_ + _I_ + _G_ + _X_ curve shifts downward, and the new level of real GDP at which planned real expenditures equal real GDP is at E_2 at $13 trillion per year. This gives us point _B_ in the lower graph. Connecting points _A_ and _B_, we obtain the aggregate demand curve.

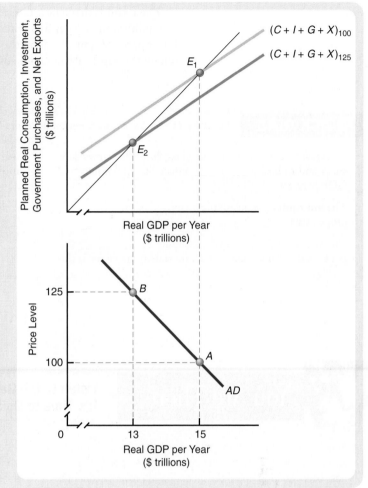

Now let's assume that in the upper graph, the price level increases to 125. What are the effects?

1. A higher price level can decrease the purchasing power of any cash that people hold (the real-balance effect). This is a decrease in real wealth, and it causes consumption expenditures, _C_, to fall, thereby putting downward pressure on the _C_ + _I_ + _G_ + _X_ curve.

2. Because individuals attempt to borrow more to replenish their real cash balances, interest rates will rise, which will make it more costly for people to buy houses and cars (the interest rate effect). Higher interest rates also make it less profitable to install new equipment and to erect new buildings. Therefore, the rise in the price level indirectly causes a reduction in total planned spending on goods and services.

3. In an open economy, our higher price level causes foreign spending on our goods to fall (the open economy effect). Simultaneously, it increases our demand for others' goods. If the foreign exchange price of the dollar stays constant for a while, there will be an increase in imports and a decrease in exports, thereby reducing the size of _X_, again putting downward pressure on the _C_ + _I_ + _G_ + _X_ curve.

The result is that a new $C + I + G + X$ curve at a price level equal to 125 generates an equilibrium at E_2 at \$13 trillion of real GDP per year. This gives us point B in the lower part of Figure 12-8 on the previous page. When we connect points A and B, we obtain the aggregate demand curve, AD.

QUICK QUIZ

See page 316 for the answers. Review concepts from this section in MyEconLab.

Any change in autonomous spending shifts the expenditure curve and causes a _____ effect on equilibrium real GDP per year.

The **multiplier** is equal to the reciprocal of the _____ propensity to _____.

The smaller is the marginal propensity to _____, the larger is the **multiplier.** Otherwise stated, the larger is the marginal propensity to _____, the larger is the **multiplier.**

The $C + I + G + X$ curve is drawn with the price level held constant, whereas the AD curve allows the price level to _____. Each different price level generates a new $C + I + G + X$ curve.

You Are There ➤ Listen to the German Chancellor: It's Time to Go Shopping!

Angela Merkel has been in office as chancellor of Germany for only a few weeks, and her government's approval rating has been soaring in anticipation of improved economic policies. Merkel recently directed her finance minister, Peer Steinbrück, to consider policies the government might adopt in an effort to boost real GDP growth above 2 percent and push the unemployment rate down from the current 11 percent. As Merkel reviews Steinbrück's response, her spirits drop. The finance ministry forecasts a real budget deficit equal to 3.3 percent of real GDP for the coming fiscal year. Under the terms of its membership in the European Monetary Union, the group of nations using the euro as a common currency, Germany's real budget deficit cannot exceed 3.0 percent of real GDP. Thus, the government must either reduce its real expenditures or find a way to collect more taxes.

After meeting with her cabinet ministers, Merkel reaches a conclusion. Her government must find a way to convince Germany's residents to increase their consumption spending. If household consumption increases, so will real GDP and taxable real incomes of the nation's residents, which in turn will boost the government's income tax revenues and

reduce its budget deficit. Merkel instructs Steinbrück and her other ministers to develop a public relations effort aimed at encouraging the nation's residents, whose average saving rate is among the world's highest, to spend a larger share of their disposable incomes. Essentially, her plan is that the German government will engage in a nationwide "marketing effort" aimed at generating a rise in household consumption spending. This path, Merkel has determined, is the best one to pursue in an effort to bring about higher real GDP, lower unemployment, and a smaller government budget deficit.

CRITICAL ANALYSIS QUESTIONS

1. Why would a decrease in government spending or an increase in taxes have been inconsistent with all of the German government's goals? (Hint: Could these actions have *simultaneously* boosted real GDP *and* reduced the budget deficit?)

2. If the German government's "marketing effort" turns out to be successful, through what economic process will it have brought about higher equilibrium real GDP per year?

The Diminishing Effect of Interest Rate Changes on U.S. Real Consumption Spending

I n the Keynesian theory of real income determination, the main determinant of real consumption spending is real disposable income. As noted in this chapter, there are also other determinants of real consumption expenditures. One important determinant is real household wealth. Another determinant is the interest rate. In recent years, however, the impact of interest rate changes on real consumption spending has been declining.

Interest Rate Changes and Consumption Spending

Recall from Chapter 10 that interest rate changes affect total planned expenditures and aggregate demand. For instance, when a rise in the price level pushes up the interest rate, businesses and households respond to higher borrowing costs by decreasing their desired spending. This is the interest rate effect that helps explain why the aggregate demand curve slopes downward. Furthermore, increases in real interest rates (nominal interest rates corrected for inflation) not due to price level changes also raise borrowing costs for businesses and households and induce them to decrease spending. The result is a decrease in aggregate demand.

Any decreases in real household spending induced by a higher real interest rate translate into lower consumption expenditures at any given level of real disposable income. Autonomous consumption falls in response to a rise in the real interest rate.

The Declining Impact of Interest Rate Changes on Consumption

Figure 12-9 depicts estimated effects, given a constant price level, of a 1-percentage-point increase in the interest rate on real U.S. consumption expenditures

FIGURE 12-9

Estimated Impacts of a 1-Percentage-Point Interest Rate Increase on Real U.S. Consumption Spending Since 1945

The estimated effects of a 1-percentage-point increase in the interest rate on real consumption spending have declined over time, indicating that consumption expenditures have become less sensitive to interest rate changes.

Source: Board of Governors of the Federal Reserve System.

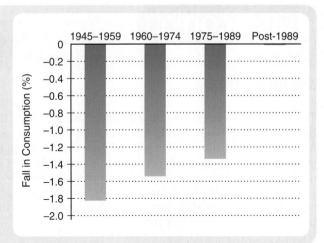

over four periods: 1945–1959, 1960–1974, 1975–1989, and post-1989. During the earliest period, a 1-percentage-point interest rate increase led on average to a decline of almost 2 percent in real consumption spending. Since the 1950s, however, the responsiveness of real consumption expenditures to a change in the interest rate has fallen. For the most recent period since 1990, the estimated impact of an interest rate increase on real consumption spending is negligible.

Federal Reserve economists suggest that one explanation for the reduced sensitivity of real consumption to interest rate changes is that more U.S. employers are able to cushion their responses to higher U.S. interest rates by borrowing internationally. As a consequence, employers are less likely than in years past to reduce workers' hours or engage in layoffs when U.S. interest rates increase. Thus, households' disposable incomes are less likely to decline in the face of a higher U.S. interest rate, and they are better able to maintain their consumption levels.

Test your understanding of this chapter by going online to **MyEconLab.**
In the Study Plan for this chapter, select Section N: News.

For Critical Analysis

1. Does an interest rate change cause a movement along or a shift in the consumption function?

2. How does reduced sensitivity of consumption spending to interest rate changes likely make real GDP less volatile in the face of variations in market interest rates? (Hint: If autonomous consumption is less responsive to interest rate changes, what must be true of variations in equilibrium real GDP in the face of those interest rate changes?)

Web Resources

1. To take a look at how assorted interest rates have changed over time, go to www.econtoday.com/chapter12.

2. Examine data on various measures of U.S. consumption expenditures at www.econtoday.com/chapter12.

Research Project

Figure 12-9 on the previous page indicates that the estimated effect of interest rate changes on autonomous consumption has become much smaller. Look back at the relationship between the AD curve and the $C + I + G + X$ curve displayed in Figure 12-8 on page 309, and suppose that it applies to a period before 1990. Explain how today's smaller interest rate impact on autonomous consumption affects the size of the shift in the $C + I + G + X$ curve depicted in Figure 12-8. What does your analysis imply about the size of the interest rate effect that helps to explain the downward slope of the AD curve?

Here is what you should know after reading this chapter. **MyEconLab** will help you identify what you know, and where to go when you need to practice.

WHAT YOU SHOULD KNOW		WHERE TO GO TO PRACTICE
The Difference Between Saving and Savings and the Relationship Between Saving and Consumption Saving is a flow over time, whereas savings is a stock of resources at a point in time. Thus, the portion of your disposable income that you do not consume during a week, a month, or a year is an addition to your stock of savings. By definition, saving during a year plus consumption during that year must equal total disposable (after-tax) income earned that year.	real disposable income, 288 consumption, 288 saving, 288 consumption goods, 288 investment, 289 capital goods, 289	• **MyEconLab** Study Plan 12.1 • Audio introduction to Chapter 12

(continued)

 *(continued)*

WHAT YOU SHOULD KNOW		WHERE TO GO TO PRACTICE

Key Determinants of Consumption and Saving in the Keynesian Model In the classical model, the interest rate is the main determinant of saving, but in the Keynesian model, the primary determinant is disposable income. The reason is that as real disposable income increases, so do real consumption expenditures. Consumption plus saving equal disposable income, so saving must also vary with changes in disposable income. Of course, factors other than disposable income can affect consumption and saving. The portion of consumption unrelated to disposable income is called autonomous consumption. The ratio of saving to disposable income is the average propensity to save (APS), and the ratio of consumption to disposable income is the average propensity to consume (APC). A change in saving divided by the corresponding change in disposable income is the marginal propensity to save (MPS), and a change in consumption divided by the corresponding change in disposable income is the marginal propensity to consume (MPC).

consumption function, 290
dissaving, 291
45-degree reference line, 291
autonomous consumption, 291
average propensity to consume (APC), 293
average propensity to save (APS), 293
marginal propensity to consume (MPC), 294
marginal propensity to save (MPS), 294
wealth, 295

KEY FIGURE
Figure 12-1, 292

- **MyEconLab** Study Plan 12.2
- Video: The Marginal Propensity to Consume
- Animated Figure 12-1

Key Determinants of Planned Investment A rise in the interest rate reduces the profitability of investment, so planned investment varies inversely with the interest rate. Hence, the investment schedule slopes downward. Changes in business expectations, productive technology, or business taxes cause the investment schedule to shift. In the basic Keynesian model, changes in real GDP do not affect planned investment, meaning that investment is autonomous with respect to real GDP.

- **MyEconLab** Study Plan 12.3
- Video: The Determinants of Investment

How Equilibrium Real GDP Is Established in the Keynesian Model In equilibrium, total planned real consumption, investment, government, and net export expenditures equal real GDP, so $C + I + G + X = Y$. This occurs at the point where the $C + I + G + X$ curve crosses the 45-degree reference line. In a world without government spending and taxes, equilibrium also occurs when planned saving is equal to planned investment. Furthermore, at equilibrium real GDP, there is no tendency for business inventories to expand or contract.

lump-sum tax, 303
KEY FIGURE
Figure 12-5, 301

- **MyEconLab** Study Plans 12.4, 12.5
- Animated Figure 12-5

Why Autonomous Changes in Total Planned Real Expenditures Have a Multiplier Effect on Equilibrium Real GDP Any increase in autonomous expenditures, such as an increase in autonomous investment, causes a direct rise in real GDP. The resulting increase in disposable income in turn stimulates

multiplier, 305
KEY TABLE
Table 12-3, 306

- **MyEconLab** Study Plans 12.6 and 12.7
- Animated Table 12-3
- Video: The Multiplier

(continued)

 *(continued)*

WHAT YOU SHOULD KNOW	WHERE TO GO TO PRACTICE

increased consumption by an amount equal to the marginal propensity to consume multiplied by the rise in disposable income that results. As consumption increases, so does real GDP, which induces a further increase in consumption spending. The ultimate expansion of real GDP is equal to the multiplier, $1/(1 - MPC)$, times the increase in autonomous expenditures. Because $MPS \equiv 1 - MPC$, the multiplier can also be written as $1/MPS$.

The Relationship Between Total Planned Expenditures and the Aggregate Demand Curve An increase in the price level decreases the purchasing power of cash holdings, which induces households and businesses to cut back on spending. As individuals and firms seek to borrow to replenish their cash balances, the interest rate tends to rise, which further discourages spending. A higher price level also reduces exports as foreign residents cut back on purchases of domestically produced goods. These combined effects shift the $C + I + G + X$ curve downward following a rise in the price level, so that equilibrium real GDP falls. This yields the downward-sloping aggregate demand curve.

KEY FIGURES
Figure 12-7, 308
Figure 12-8, 309

- **MyEconLab** Study Plan 12.8
- Animated Figures 12-7, 12-8

Log in to MyEconLab, take a chapter test, and get a personalized Study Plan that tells you which concepts you understand and which ones you need to review. From there, MyEconLab will give you further practice, tutorials, animations, videos, and guided solutions.
Log in to www.myeconlab.com

PROBLEMS

All problems are assignable in . *Answers to odd-numbered problems appear at the back of the book.*

12-1. Classify each of the following as either a stock or a flow.

a. Myung Park earns $850 per week.

b. Time Warner purchases $100 million in new computer equipment this month.

c. Sally Schmidt has $1,000 in a savings account at a credit union.

d. XYZ, Inc., produces 200 units of output per week.

e. Giorgio Giannelli owns three private jets.

f. General Motors' production declines by 750 autos per month.

g. Russia owes $25 billion to the International Monetary Fund.

12-2. Consider the table below when answering the following questions. For this hypothetical economy, the marginal propensity to save is constant at all levels of real GDP, and investment spending is autonomous. There is no government.

Real GDP	Consumption	Saving	Investment
$ 2,000	$2,200	$_____	$400
4,000	4,000	_____	_____
6,000	_____	_____	_____
8,000	_____	_____	_____
10,000	_____	_____	_____
12,000	_____	_____	_____

a. Complete the table. What is the marginal propensity to save? What is the marginal propensity to consume?

b. Draw a graph of the consumption function. Then add the investment function to obtain $C + I$.

c. Under the graph of $C + I$, draw another graph showing the saving and investment curves. Note that the $C + I$ curve crosses the 45-degree reference line in the upper graph at the same level of real GDP where the saving and investment curves cross in the lower graph. (If not, redraw your graphs.) What is this level of real GDP?

d. What is the numerical value of the multiplier?

e. What is equilibrium real GDP without investment? What is the multiplier effect from the inclusion of investment?

f. What is the average propensity to consume at equilibrium real GDP?

g. If autonomous investment declines from $400 to $200, what happens to equilibrium real GDP?

12-3. Consider the table below when answering the following questions. For this hypothetical economy, the marginal propensity to consume is constant at all levels of real GDP, and investment spending is autonomous. Equilibrium real GDP is equal to $8,000. There is no government.

Real GDP	Consumption	Saving	Investment
$ 2,000	$2,000	_____	_____
4,000	3,600	_____	_____
6,000	5,200	_____	_____
8,000	6,800	_____	_____
10,000	8,400	_____	_____
12,000	10,000	_____	_____

a. Complete the table. What is the marginal propensity to consume? What is the marginal propensity to save?

b. Draw a graph of the consumption function. Then add the investment function to obtain $C + I$.

c. Under the graph of $C + I$, draw another graph showing the saving and investment curves. Does the $C + I$ curve cross the 45-degree reference line in the upper graph at the same level of real GDP where the saving and investment curves cross in the lower graph, at the equilibrium real GDP of $8,000? (If not, redraw your graphs.)

d. What is the average propensity to save at equilibrium real GDP?

e. If autonomous consumption were to rise by $100, what would happen to equilibrium real GDP?

12-4. Calculate the multiplier for the following cases.

a. MPS = 0.25

b. MPC = $\frac{5}{6}$

c. MPS = 0.125

d. MPC = $\frac{6}{7}$

12-5. Assume that the multiplier in a country is equal to 4 and that autonomous real consumption spending is $1 trillion. If current real GDP is $15 trillion, what is the current value of real consumption spending?

12-6. The multiplier in a country is equal to 5, and households pay no taxes. At the current equilibrium real GDP of $14 trillion, total real consumption spending by households is $12 trillion. What is real autonomous consumption in this country?

12-7. At an initial point on the aggregate demand curve, the price level is 125, and real GDP is $15 trillion. When the price level falls to a value of 120, total autonomous expenditures increase by $250 billion. The marginal propensity to consume is 0.75. What is the level of real GDP at the new point on the aggregate demand curve?

12-8. At an initial point on the aggregate demand curve, the price level is 100, and real GDP is $15 trillion. After the price level rises to 110, however, there is an upward movement along the aggregate demand curve, and real GDP declines to $14 trillion. If total autonomous spending declined by $200 billion in response to the increase in the price level, what is the marginal propensity to consume in this economy?

12-9. In an economy in which the multiplier has a value of 3, the price level has decreased from 115 to 110. As a consequence, there has been a movement along the aggregate demand curve from $15 trillion in real GDP to $15.9 trillion in real GDP.

a. What is the marginal propensity to save?

b. What was the amount of the change in autonomous expenditures generated by the decline in the price level?

12-10. Consider the accompanying diagram, which applies to a nation with no government spending, taxes, and net exports. Use the information in the diagram to answer the following questions, and explain your answers.

a. What is the marginal propensity to save?

b. What is the present level of planned investment spending for the present period?

c. What is the equilibrium level of real GDP for the present period?

d. What is the equilibrium level of saving for the present period?

e. If planned investment spending for the present period increases by $25 billion, what will be the resulting *change* in equilibrium real GDP? What will be the new equilibrium level of real GDP if other things, including the price level, remain unchanged?

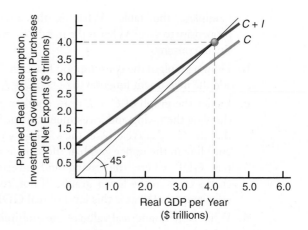

ECONOMICS ON THE NET

The Relationship Between Consumption and Real GDP According to the basic consumption function we considered in this chapter, consumption rises at a fixed rate when both disposable income and real GDP increase. Your task here is to evaluate how reasonable this assumption is and to determine the relative extent to which variations in consumption appear to be related to variations in real GDP.

Title: Gross Domestic Product and Components

Navigation: Use the link at **www.econtoday.com/ chapter12** to visit the Federal Reserve Bank of St. Louis's Web page on *Gross Domestic Product and Components.* Then click on *Personal Income and Outlays.*

Application

1. Scan down the alphabetical list, and click on *Personal Consumption Expenditure (Bil. of $; Q).* Then click on "Download Data." Write down consumption expenditures for the past eight quarters. Now back up to

Gross Domestic Product and Components, click on *Gross Domestic Product, 1 Decimal (Bil. $; Q),* click on "Download Data," and write down GDP for the past eight quarters. Use these data to calculate implied values for the marginal propensity to consume, assuming that taxes do not vary with income. Is there any problem with this assumption?

2. Back up to *Gross Domestic Product and Components.* Now click on *Gross Domestic Product: Implicit Price Deflator.* Scan through the data since the mid-1960s. In what years did the largest variations in GDP take place? What component or components of GDP appear to have accounted for these large movements?

For Group Study and Analysis Assign groups to use the FRED database to try to determine the best measure of aggregate U.S. disposable income for the past eight quarters. Reconvene as a class, and discuss each group's approach to this issue.

ANSWERS TO QUICK QUIZZES

p. 289: (i) horizontal; (ii) Saving . . . Savings; (iii) Investment

p. 296: (i) disposable income . . . consumption; (ii) average . . . average; (iii) marginal . . . marginal; (iv) movement along . . . shift in

p. 298: (i) interest rate . . . downward; (ii) expectations . . . business taxes; (iii) shift in

p. 302: (i) autonomous . . . autonomous; (ii) autonomous; (iii) equilibrium; (iv) increases . . . decreases

p. 304: (i) planned expenditures; (ii) 45-degree; (iii) decreases . . . increases

p. 310: (i) multiplier; (ii) marginal . . . save; (iii) save . . . consume; (iv) change

The Keynesian Model and the Multiplier

We can see the multiplier effect more clearly if we look at Figure B-1, in which we see only a small section of the graphs that we used in Chapter 12. We start with equilibrium real GDP of $14.5 trillion per year. This equilibrium occurs with total planned real expenditures represented by $C + I + G + X$. The $C + I + G + X$ curve intersects the 45-degree reference line at $14.5 trillion per year. Now we increase real investment, I, by $100 billion. This increase in investment shifts the entire $C + I + G + X$ curve vertically to $C + I' + G + X$. The vertical shift represents that $100 billion increase in autonomous investment. With the higher level of planned expenditures per year, we are no longer in equilibrium at E. Inventories are falling. Production of goods and services will increase as firms try to replenish their inventories. Eventually, real GDP will catch up with total planned expenditures. The new equilibrium level of real GDP is established at E' at the intersection of the new $C + I' + G + X$ curve and the 45-degree reference line, along which $C + I + G + X = Y$ (total planned expenditures equal real GDP). The new equilibrium level of real GDP is $15 trillion per year. Thus, the increase in equilibrium real GDP is equal to five times the permanent increase in planned investment spending.

FIGURE B-1

Graphing the Multiplier

We can translate Table 12-3 on page 306 into graphic form by looking at each successive round of additional spending induced by an autonomous increase in planned investment of $100 billion. The total planned expenditures curve shifts from $C + I + G + X$, with its associated equilibrium level of real GDP of $14.5 trillion, to a new curve labeled $C + I' + G + X$. The new equilibrium level of real GDP is $15 trillion. Equilibrium is again established.

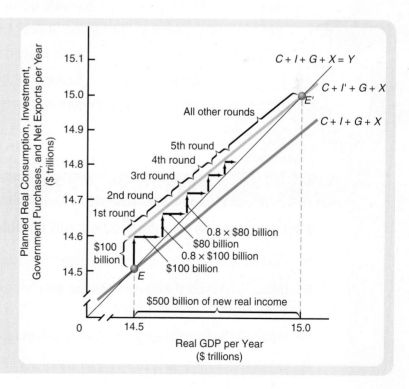

13

Fiscal Policy

Government expenditures on health care services have grown significantly since federal and state governments began paying for various types of health-related expenses in the mid-1960s. Today, government health care expenditures account for more than 30 percent of all federal and state government spending. This percentage will likely increase as Congress and separate state governments contemplate expanding their health care expenditures to as much as *half* of all government spending. Other things being equal, do ongoing increases in government health care spending generate dollar-for-dollar increases in total planned expenditures in the United States? Or do higher government health care expenditures displace a portion of private health care spending? Why do the answers to these questions matter? You will find out in this chapter.

LEARNING OBJECTIVES

myeconlab

MyEconLab helps you master each objective and study more efficiently. See end of chapter for details.

After reading this chapter, you should be able to:

➤ Use traditional Keynesian analysis to evaluate the effects of discretionary fiscal policies

➤ Discuss ways in which indirect crowding out and direct expenditure offsets can reduce the effectiveness of fiscal policy actions

➤ Explain why the Ricardian equivalence theorem calls into question the usefulness of tax changes

➤ List and define fiscal policy time lags and explain why they complicate efforts to engage in fiscal "fine-tuning"

➤ Describe how certain aspects of fiscal policy function as automatic stabilizers for the economy

Why do the income tax returns that U.S. residents file on April 15 not tell a complete story?

DID YOU KNOW THAT when President Woodrow Wilson signed the U.S. federal income tax into law in October 1913, only about 1 percent of the U.S. population owed any income taxes? Nevertheless, during a floor debate prior to passage of the law, one lawmaker predicted that if the law passed, eventually "a hand from Washington will stretch out to every man's house." Of course, not every income-earning household pays some kind of federal taxes today, but most do. How much taxpayers get back from the federal government in return, in the form of income transfers such as Social Security and Medicare or services such as police protection and education, depends on their incomes. The Tax Foundation estimates that for every dollar that households earning less than about $24,000 per year pay in taxes, they get back transfers and services valued at $8.21. Households earning between $42,000 and $62,000 per year receive transfers and services valued at an estimated $1.30 for each tax dollar they pay. Households earning more than about $100,000 per year get back an estimated $0.41 for each dollar of taxes.

Each year U.S. taxpayers transmit nearly $3 trillion in tax payments to the federal government, but in recent years, the federal government has spent in excess of $1.5 trillion per year more than this by borrowing the additional funds. Total annual federal government expenditures amount to about 30 percent of GDP. In this chapter, you will learn about how variations in federal taxes and government spending affect real GDP and the price level.

Discretionary Fiscal Policy

The making of deliberate, discretionary changes in federal government expenditures or taxes (or both) to achieve certain national economic goals is the realm of **fiscal policy.** Some national goals are high employment (low unemployment), price stability, and economic growth. Fiscal policy can be thought of as a deliberate attempt to cause the economy to move to full employment and price stability more quickly than it otherwise might.

Fiscal policy has typically been associated with the economic theories of John Maynard Keynes and what is now called *traditional* Keynesian analysis. Recall from Chapter 11 that Keynes's explanation of the Great Depression was that there was insufficient aggregate demand. Because he believed that wages and prices were "sticky downward," he argued that the classical economists' picture of an economy moving automatically and quickly toward full employment was inaccurate. To Keynes and his followers, government had to step in to increase aggregate demand. Expansionary fiscal policy initiated by the federal government was the way to ward off recessions and depressions.

Fiscal policy
The discretionary changing of government expenditures or taxes to achieve national economic goals, such as high employment with price stability.

Changes in Government Spending

In Chapter 11, we looked at the recessionary gap and the inflationary gap (see Figures 11-12 and 11-13 on pages 275 and 276). The recessionary gap was defined as the amount by which the current level of real GDP falls short of the economy's potential production if it were operating on its *LRAS* curve. The inflationary gap was defined as the amount by which the short-run equilibrium level of real GDP exceeds the long-run equilibrium level as given by *LRAS*. Let us examine fiscal policy first in the context of a recessionary gap.

WHEN THERE IS A RECESSIONARY GAP The government, along with firms, individuals, and foreign residents, is one of the spending agents in the economy. When the government decides to spend more, all other things held constant, the dollar value of total spending must rise. Look at panel (a) of Figure 13-1 on page 320. We begin by

---

FIGURE 13-1

**Expansionary and Contractionary Fiscal Policy:
Changes in Government Spending**

If there is a recessionary gap and short-run equilibrium is at E_1, in panel (a), fiscal policy can presumably increase aggregate demand to AD_2. The new equilibrium is at E_2 at higher real GDP per year and a higher price level. In panel (b), the economy is at short-run equilibrium at E_1, which is at a higher real GDP than the $LRAS$. To reduce this inflationary gap, fiscal policy can be used to decrease aggregate demand from AD_1 to AD_2. Eventually, equilibrium will fall to E_2, which is on the $LRAS$.

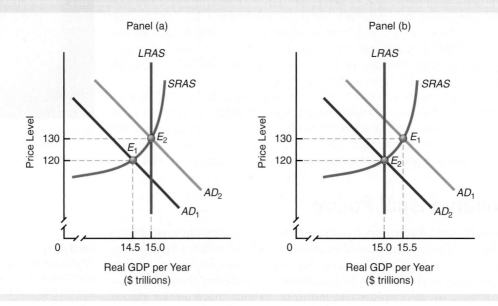

assuming that some negative shock in the near past has left the economy at point E_1, which is a short-run equilibrium in which AD_1 intersects $SRAS$ at $14.5 trillion of real GDP per year. There is a recessionary gap of $500 billion of real GDP per year—the difference between $LRAS$ (the economy's long-run potential) and the short-run equilibrium level of real GDP per year. When the government decides to spend more (expansionary fiscal policy), the aggregate demand curve shifts to the right to AD_2. Here we assume that the government knows exactly how much more to spend so that AD_2 intersects $SRAS$ at $15 trillion, or at $LRAS$. Because of the upward-sloping $SRAS$, the price level rises from 120 to 130 as real GDP goes to $15 trillion per year.

As the U.S. federal government engages in discretionary fiscal policy, is it facing difficulties similar to those that Peru's national government has experienced?

INTERNATIONAL POLICY EXAMPLE

Struggling to Boost Government Spending in Peru—and in the United States

In 2007, a new president of Peru proposed an immediate discretionary government spending "shock" to prevent a deep recession. The president received permission to spend $1 billion on roads, water resources, and improvements in schools and hospitals. Five months later, however, only about $160 million, or 16 percent of planned expenditures, had been dispersed. The main reason for the delay was Peru's complex system of laws requiring national government spending to be coordinated with regional governments. Abiding by these rules severely limited the Peruvian national government's spending discretion.

Shortly after Barack Obama assumed the U.S. presidency in January 2009, he convinced the U.S. Congress to authorize new spending aimed at heading off a worsening recession. Five months later, the federal government had managed to disperse only about $31 billion, or just over 10 percent, of $300 billion in planned expenditures on roads, waterways, and schools. As

in Peru, discretionary spending was slowed by delays in the transmission of funds to the state governments responsible for maintaining U.S. roads, water resources, and schools.

FOR CRITICAL ANALYSIS

Why might it be likely that the $160 million and the $31 billion spent by the Peruvian government and the U.S. government, respectively, ultimately shifted their nations' aggregate demand curves rightward by more than those amounts?

WHEN THERE IS AN INFLATIONARY GAP The entire process shown in panel (a) of Figure 13-1 can be reversed, as shown in panel (b). There, we assume that a recent shock has left the economy at point E_1, at which an inflationary gap exists at the intersection of *SRAS* and AD_1. Real GDP cannot be sustained at $15.5 trillion indefinitely, because this exceeds long-run aggregate supply, which in real terms is $15 trillion. If the government recognizes this and reduces its spending (pursues a contractionary fiscal policy), this action reduces aggregate demand from AD_1 to AD_2. Equilibrium will fall to E_2 on the *LRAS*, where real GDP per year is $15 trillion. The price level will fall from 130 to 120.

Changes in Taxes

The spending decisions of firms, individuals, and other countries' residents depend on the taxes levied on them. Individuals in their role as consumers look to their disposable (after-tax) income when determining their desired rates of consumption. Firms look at their after-tax profits when deciding on the levels of investment to undertake. Foreign residents look at the tax-inclusive cost of goods when deciding whether to buy in the United States or elsewhere. Therefore, holding all other things constant, a rise in taxes causes a reduction in aggregate demand because it reduces consumption, investment, or net exports.

WHEN THE CURRENT SHORT-RUN EQUILIBRIUM IS TO THE RIGHT OF *LRAS*
Assume that aggregate demand is AD_1 in panel (a) of Figure 13-2 on the following page. It intersects *SRAS* at E_1, which yields real GDP greater than *LRAS*. In this situation, an increase in taxes shifts the aggregate demand curve inward to the left. For argument's sake, assume that it intersects *SRAS* at E_2, or exactly where *LRAS* intersects AD_2. In this situation, the level of real GDP falls from $15.5 trillion per year to $15 trillion per year. The price level falls from 120 to 100.

WHEN THE CURRENT SHORT-RUN EQUILIBRIUM IS TO THE LEFT OF *LRAS*
Look at panel (b) in Figure 13-2. AD_1 intersects *SRAS* at E_1, with real GDP at $14.5 trillion, less than the *LRAS* of $15 trillion. In this situation, a decrease in taxes shifts the aggregate demand curve outward to the right. At AD_2, equilibrium is established at E_2, with the price level at 120 and equilibrium real GDP at $15 trillion per year.

> **You Are There**
>
> To contemplate whether temporary tax cuts have smaller effects on total planned spending than long-lasting tax reductions, take a look at **Assessing the Effects of a Temporary Tax Rebate,** on page 331.

FIGURE 13-2

Contractionary and Expansionary Fiscal Policy: Changes in Taxes

In panel (a), the economy is initially at E_1, where real GDP exceeds long-run equilibrium real GDP. Contractionary fiscal policy via a tax increase can move aggregate demand to AD_2 so that the new equilibrium is at E_2 at a lower price level. Real GDP is now consistent with *LRAS,* which eliminates the inflationary gap. In panel (b), with a recessionary gap (in this case of $500 billion), taxes are cut. AD_1 moves to AD_2. The economy moves from E_1 to E_2, and real GDP is now at $15 trillion per year, the long-run equilibrium level.

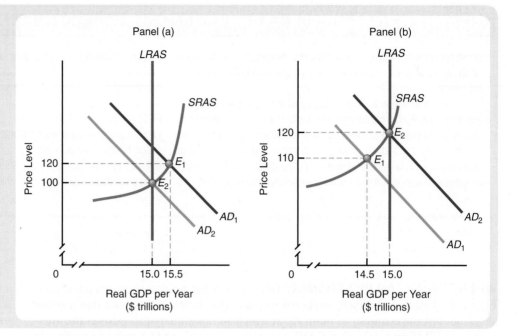

Fiscal policy is defined as making discretionary changes in government _____ or _____ to achieve such national goals as high employment or reduced inflation.

To address a situation in which there is a _____ gap and the economy is operating at less than long-run aggregate supply (*LRAS*), the government can _____ its spending and thereby shift the aggregate demand curve to the right, causing the equilibrium level of real GDP per year to increase.

To address a situation in which there is an _____ gap, the government can _____ its spending and cause the aggregate demand curve to shift to the left, which reduces the equilibrium level of real GDP per year.

Changes in taxes can have similar effects on the equilibrium rate of real GDP and the price level. A _____ in taxes can lead to an increase in the equilibrium level of real GDP per year. In contrast, if there is an inflationary gap, an _____ in taxes can decrease equilibrium real GDP.

Possible Offsets to Fiscal Policy

Fiscal policy does not operate in a vacuum. Important questions must be answered: If government spending rises by, say, $300 billion, how is the spending financed, and by whom? If taxes are increased, what does the government do with the taxes? What will happen if individuals anticipate higher *future* taxes because the government is spending more today without raising current taxes? These questions involve *offsets* to the effects of current fiscal policy. We will consider them in detail.

Indirect Crowding Out

Let's take the first example of fiscal policy in this chapter—an increase in government expenditures. If government expenditures rise and taxes are held constant, something has to give. Our government does not simply take goods and services when it wants them. It has to pay for them. When it pays for them and does not simultaneously collect the same amount in taxes, it must borrow. That means that an increase in government spending without raising taxes creates additional government borrowing from the private sector (or from other countries' residents).

INDUCED INTEREST RATE CHANGES If the government attempts to borrow $1.5 trillion more per year from the private sector, as it has since 2009, it will have to offer a higher interest rate to lure the additional funds from savers. This is the interest rate effect of expansionary fiscal policy financed by borrowing from the public. Consequently, when the federal government finances increased spending by additional borrowing, it will push interest rates up. When interest rates go up, it is less profitable for firms to finance new construction, equipment, and inventories. It is also more expensive for individuals to finance purchases of cars and homes.

Thus, a rise in government spending, holding taxes constant (that is, deficit spending), tends to crowd out private spending, dampening the positive effect of increased government spending on aggregate demand. This is called the **crowding-out effect.** In the extreme case, the crowding out may be complete, with the increased government spending having no net effect on aggregate demand. The final result is simply more government spending and less private investment and consumption. Figure 13-3 shows how the crowding-out effect occurs.

Crowding-out effect
The tendency of expansionary fiscal policy to cause a decrease in planned investment or planned consumption in the private sector; this decrease normally results from the rise in interest rates.

THE FIRM'S INVESTMENT DECISION To understand the crowding-out effect better, consider a firm that is contemplating borrowing $100,000 to expand its business. Suppose that the interest rate is 5 percent. The interest payments on the debt will be 5 percent times $100,000, or $5,000 per year ($417 per month). A rise in the interest rate to 8 percent will push the payments to 8 percent of $100,000, or $8,000 per year ($667 per month). The extra $250 per month in interest expenses will discourage some firms from making the investment. Consumers face similar decisions when they purchase houses and cars. An increase in the interest rate causes their monthly payments to go up, thereby discouraging some of them from purchasing cars and houses.

GRAPHICAL ANALYSIS You see in Figure 13-4 on the following page that the economy is in a situation in which, at point E_1, equilibrium real GDP is below the long-run level consistent with the position of the *LRAS* curve. But suppose that government

FIGURE 13-3

The Crowding-Out Effect, Step by Step

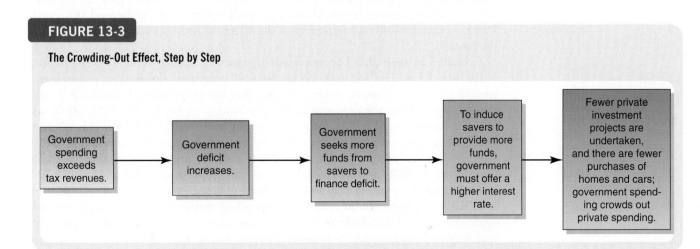

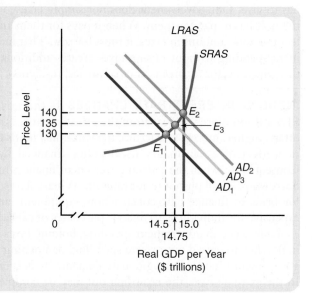

FIGURE 13-4

The Crowding-Out Effect

Expansionary fiscal policy that causes deficit financing initially shifts AD_1 to AD_2. Equilibrium initially moves toward E_2. But expansionary fiscal policy pushes up interest rates, thereby reducing interest-sensitive spending. This effect causes the aggregate demand curve to shift inward to AD_3, and the new short-run equilibrium is at E_3.

expansionary fiscal policy in the form of increased government spending (without increasing current taxes) attempts to shift aggregate demand from AD_1 to AD_2. In the absence of the crowding-out effect, real GDP would increase to $15 trillion per year, and the price level would rise to 140 (point E_2). With the (partial) crowding-out effect, however, as investment and consumption decline, partly offsetting the rise in government spending, the aggregate demand curve shifts inward to the left to AD_3. The new short-run equilibrium is now at E_3, with real GDP of $14.75 trillion per year at a price level of 135. In other words, crowding out dilutes the effect of expansionary fiscal policy, and a recessionary gap remains.

Planning for the Future: The Ricardian Equivalence Theorem

Economists have often implicitly assumed that people look at changes in taxes or changes in government spending only in the present. What if people actually think about the size of *future* tax payments? Does this have an effect on how they react to an increase in government spending with no current tax increases? Some economists believe that the answer is yes. What if people's horizons extend beyond this year? Don't we then have to take into account the effects of today's government policies on the future?

Consider an example. The government wants to reduce taxes by $150 billion today, as it did in 2008 and 2009 via tax "rebate" programs. Assume that government spending remains constant. Assume further that the government initially has a balanced budget. Thus, the only way for the government to pay for this $150 billion tax cut is to borrow $150 billion today. The public will owe $150 billion plus interest later. Realizing that a $150 billion tax cut today is mathematically equivalent to $150 billion plus interest later, people may wish to save the proceeds from the tax cut to meet future tax liabilities—payment of interest and repayment of debt.

Consequently, a tax cut may not affect total planned expenditures. A reduction in taxes without a reduction in government spending may therefore have no impact on aggregate demand. Similarly, an increase in taxes without an increase in government spending may not have a large (negative) impact on aggregate demand.

Suppose that a decrease in taxes shifts the aggregate demand curve from AD_1 to AD_2 in Figure 13-4. If consumers partly compensate for a higher future tax liability by saving more, the aggregate demand curve shifts leftward, to a position such as AD_3. In the extreme case in which individuals fully take into account their increased tax liabilities, the aggregate demand curve shifts all the way back to AD_1, so that there is no effect on the economy. This is known as the **Ricardian equivalence theorem,** after the nineteenth-century economist David Ricardo, who first developed the argument publicly.

According to the Ricardian equivalence theorem, it does not matter how government expenditures are financed—by taxes or by borrowing. Is the theorem correct? Research indicates that Ricardian equivalence effects likely exist but has not provided much compelling evidence about their magnitudes.

Ricardian equivalence theorem
The proposition that an increase in the government budget deficit has no effect on aggregate demand.

Direct Expenditure Offsets

Government has a distinct comparative advantage over the private sector in certain activities such as diplomacy and national defense. Otherwise stated, certain resource-using activities in which the government engages do not compete with the private sector. In contrast, some of what government does, such as public education, competes directly with the private sector. When government competes with the private sector, **direct expenditure offsets** to fiscal policy may occur. For example, if the government starts providing milk at no charge to students who are already purchasing milk, there is a direct expenditure offset. Direct household spending on milk decreases, but government spending on milk increases.

Normally, the impact of an increase in government spending on aggregate demand is analyzed by implicitly assuming that government spending is *not* a substitute for private spending. This is clearly the case for a cruise missile. Whenever government spending is a substitute for private spending, however, a rise in government spending causes a direct reduction in private spending to offset it.

How did actions by U.S. states receiving funds from the federal government in 2009 effectively create direct expenditure offsets analogous to private offsets?

Direct expenditure offsets
Actions on the part of the private sector in spending income that offset government fiscal policy actions. Any increase in government spending in an area that competes with the private sector will have some direct expenditure offset.

POLICY EXAMPLE
How U.S. States Created Direct Fiscal Offsets to Federal Spending

As part of a plan to boost discretionary government expenditures in an effort to ward off the deepening Great Recession, during the latter half of its 2009 fiscal year the federal government transmitted nearly $50 billion to state governments. Leaders in the executive branch and Congress suggested that states would target these funds to so-called shovel-ready programs—new road and construction projects that could be initiated as soon as the states received the funds.

In fact, most state governments that received federal funds had already committed to spending more during 2008 and the first half of fiscal 2009 than they could "afford," resulting in combined deficits of nearly $300 billion. Therefore, rather than

directing the federal funds to *additional* spending, the states used the bulk of the funds to pay off debts generated by spending projects already in progress or even completed. Consequently, state governments allocated most of the funds to projects that had already been "shoveled," resulting in little net addition to the nation's flow of total expenditures.

FOR CRITICAL ANALYSIS
Why do economists normally regard truly new spending on items such as roads, waterways and dams, or national security to be less subject to direct expenditure offsets than spending on items such as health care or education?

THE EXTREME CASE In the extreme case, the direct expenditure offset is dollar for dollar, so we merely end up with a relabeling of spending from private to public. Assume that you have decided to spend $100 on groceries. Upon your arrival at the checkout counter, you find a U.S. Department of Agriculture official. She announces that she will pay for your groceries—but only the ones in the cart. Here increased government spending is $100. You leave the store in bliss. But just as you are deciding how to spend the $100, an Internal Revenue Service agent appears. He announces that as a result of the current budgetary crisis, your taxes are going to rise by $100. You have to pay right now. Increases in taxes have now been $100. We have a balanced-budget increase in government spending. In this scenario, *total* spending does not change. We simply end up with higher government spending, which directly offsets exactly an equal reduction in consumption. Aggregate demand and GDP are unchanged. Otherwise stated, if there is a full direct expenditure offset, the government spending multiplier is zero.

THE LESS EXTREME CASE Much government spending has a private-sector substitute. When government expenditures increase, private spending tends to decline somewhat (but generally not dollar for dollar), thereby mitigating the upward impact on total aggregate demand. To the extent that there are some direct expenditure offsets to expansionary fiscal policy, predicted changes in aggregate demand will be lessened. Consequently, real GDP and the price level will be less affected.

The Supply-Side Effects of Changes in Taxes

We have talked about changing taxes and changing government spending, the traditional tools of fiscal policy. We have not really talked about the possibility of changing *marginal* tax rates. Recall from Chapter 6 that the marginal tax rate is the rate applied to the last, or highest, bracket of taxable income. In our federal tax system, higher marginal tax rates are applied as income rises. In that sense, the United States has a progressive federal individual income tax system. Expansionary fiscal policy could involve reducing marginal tax rates. Advocates of such changes argue that lower tax rates will lead to an increase in productivity because individuals will work harder and longer, save more, and invest more and that increased productivity will lead to more economic growth, which will lead to higher real GDP. The government, by applying lower marginal tax rates, will not necessarily lose tax revenues, for the lower marginal tax rates will be applied to a growing tax base because of economic growth—after all, tax revenues are the product of a tax rate times a tax base.

The relationship between tax rates and tax revenues, which you may recall from the discussion of sales taxes in Chapter 6, is sometimes called the *Laffer curve*, named after economist Arthur Laffer, who explained the relationship to some journalists and politicians in 1974. It is reproduced in Figure 13-5. On the vertical axis are tax revenues, and on the horizontal axis is the marginal tax rate. As you can see, total tax revenues initially rise but then eventually fall as the tax rate continues to increase after reaching some unspecified tax-revenue-maximizing rate at the top of the curve.

People who support the notion that reducing taxes does not necessarily lead to reduced tax revenues are called supply-side economists. **Supply-side economics** involves changing the tax structure to create incentives to increase productivity. Due to a shift in the aggregate supply curve to the right, there can be greater real GDP without upward pressure on the price level.

Consider the supply-side effects of changes in marginal tax rates on labor. An increase in tax rates reduces the opportunity cost of leisure, thereby inducing individuals to

Supply-side economics
The suggestion that creating incentives for individuals and firms to increase productivity will cause the aggregate supply curve to shift outward.

FIGURE 13-5

Laffer Curve

The Laffer curve indicates that tax revenues initially rise with a higher tax rate. Eventually, however, tax revenues decline as the tax rate increases.

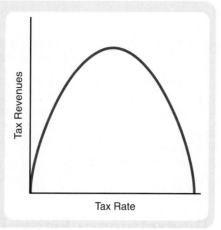

reduce their work effort and to consume more leisure. But an increase in tax rates will also reduce spendable income, thereby shifting the demand curve for leisure inward to the left, which tends to increase work effort. The outcome of these two effects on the choice of leisure (and thus work) depends on which of them is stronger. Supply-side economists argue that at various times, the first effect has dominated: Increases in marginal tax rates have caused workers to work less, and decreases in marginal tax rates have caused workers to work more.

Is it possible that the U.S. economy was operating at a tax rate higher than the revenue-maximizing tax rate before the tax rate cuts of 2003?

POLICY EXAMPLE
A Laffer Curve in the Mid-2000s?

In May 2003, at the urging of the administration of George W. Bush, Congress reduced the top tax rate on corporate dividends, from 39.6 percent to 15 percent, and the tax rate on capital gains, from 20 percent to 15 percent. In addition, Congress cut personal income tax rates slightly.

Many critics of the 2003 tax rate cuts predicted that the federal government's tax revenues would plummet after the rates were cut. Nevertheless, by the beginning of 2008, after four years of higher real GDP growth, total federal income tax receipts from corporations and individuals had increased by nearly 50 percent.

FOR CRITICAL ANALYSIS
In 2011, the Bush tax rate cuts will expire, so tax rates will return to their original, higher levels. Why do you suppose that some economists suggest that income tax revenues may not rise when the rates increase?

QUICK QUIZ   See page 338 for the answers. Review concepts from this section in MyEconLab.

Indirect crowding out occurs because of an interest rate effect in which the government's efforts to finance its

deficit spending cause interest rates to _____, thereby crowding out private investment and spending,

Discretionary Fiscal Policy in Practice: Coping with Time Lags

We can discuss fiscal policy in a relatively precise way. We draw graphs with aggregate demand and supply curves to show what we are doing. We could even in principle estimate the offsets that we just discussed. Even if we were able to measure all of these offsets exactly, however, would-be fiscal policymakers still face a problem: The conduct of fiscal policy involves a variety of time lags.

Policy Time Lags

Recognition time lag
The time required to gather information about the current state of the economy.

Action time lag
The time between recognizing an economic problem and implementing policy to solve it. The action time lag is quite long for fiscal policy, which requires congressional approval.

Effect time lag
The time that elapses between the implementation of a policy and the results of that policy.

Policymakers must be concerned with time lags. Quite apart from the fact that it is difficult to measure economic variables, it takes time to collect and assimilate such data. Thus, policymakers must contend with the **recognition time lag,** the months that may elapse before national economic problems can be identified.

After an economic problem is recognized, a solution must be formulated; thus, there will be an **action time lag** between the recognition of a problem and the implementation of policy to solve it. For fiscal policy, the action time lag is particularly long. Such policy must be approved by Congress and is subject to political wrangling and infighting. The action time lag can easily last a year or two. Then it takes time to actually implement the policy. After Congress enacts fiscal policy legislation, it takes time to decide such matters as who gets new federal construction contracts.

Finally, there is the **effect time lag:** After fiscal policy is enacted, it takes time for the policy to affect the economy. To demonstrate the effects, economists need only shift curves on a chalkboard, a whiteboard, or a piece of paper, but in real time, such effects take quite a while to work their way through the economy.

Problems Posed by Time Lags

Because the various fiscal policy time lags are long, a policy designed to combat a significant recession such as the Great Recession of the late 2000s might not produce results until the economy is already out of that recession and perhaps experiencing inflation, in which case the fiscal policy would worsen the situation. Or a fiscal policy designed to eliminate inflation might not produce effects until the economy is in a recession; in that case, too, fiscal policy would make the economic problem worse rather than better.

Furthermore, because fiscal policy time lags tend to be *variable* (each lasting anywhere from one to three years), policymakers have a difficult time fine-tuning the economy. Clearly, fiscal policy is more guesswork than science.

Automatic Stabilizers

Not all changes in taxes (or in tax rates) or in government spending (including government transfers) constitute discretionary fiscal policy. There are several types of automatic (or nondiscretionary) fiscal policies. Such policies do not require new legislation on the part of Congress. Specific automatic fiscal policies—called **automatic,** or **built-in, stabilizers**—include the tax system itself, unemployment compensation, and income transfer payments.

The Tax System as an Automatic Stabilizer

You know that if you work less, you are paid less, and therefore you pay fewer taxes. The amount of taxes that our government collects falls automatically during a recession. Basically, as observed in the U.S. economy during the severe recession of the late 2000s, incomes and profits fall when business activity slows down, and the government's tax revenues drop, too. Some economists consider this an automatic tax cut, which therefore stimulates aggregate demand. It reduces the extent of any negative economic fluctuation.

The progressive nature of the federal personal and corporate income tax systems magnifies any automatic stabilization effect that might exist. If your hours of work are reduced because of a recession, you still pay some federal personal income taxes. But because of our progressive system, you may drop into a lower tax bracket, thereby paying a lower marginal tax rate. As a result, your disposable income falls by a smaller percentage than your before-tax income falls.

Unemployment Compensation and Income Transfer Payments

Like our tax system, unemployment compensation payments stabilize aggregate demand. Throughout the course of business fluctuations, unemployment compensation reduces *changes* in people's disposable income. When business activity drops, most laid-off workers automatically become eligible for unemployment compensation from their state governments. Their disposable income therefore remains positive, although at a lower level than when they were employed. During boom periods, there is less unemployment, and consequently fewer unemployment payments are made to the labor force. Less purchasing power is being added to the economy because fewer unemployment checks are paid out. In contrast, during recessions the opposite is true.

Income transfer payments act similarly as an automatic stabilizer. When a recession occurs, more people become eligible for income transfer payments, such as Supplemental Security Income and temporary assistance to needy families. Therefore, those people do not experience so dramatic a drop in disposable income as they otherwise would have.

Stabilizing Impact

The key stabilizing impact of our tax system, unemployment compensation, and income transfer payments is their ability to mitigate changes in disposable income, consumption, and the equilibrium level of real GDP. If disposable income is prevented from falling as much as it otherwise would during a recession, the downturn will be moderated. In contrast, if disposable income is prevented from rising as rapidly as it otherwise would during a boom, the boom is less likely to get out of hand. The progressive income tax and unemployment compensation thus provide automatic stabilization to the economy. We present the argument graphically in Figure 13-6 on the following page.

Automatic, or **built-in, stabilizers**
Special provisions of certain federal programs that cause changes in desired aggregate expenditures without the action of Congress and the president. Examples are the federal progressive tax system and unemployment compensation.

Why do we consider that the unemployment compensation system in the United States is an automatic, rather than discretionary, stabilizer?

FIGURE 13-6

Automatic Stabilizers

Here we assume that as real GDP rises, tax revenues rise and government transfers fall, other things remaining constant. Thus, as the economy expands from Y_f to Y_1, a budget surplus automatically arises; as the economy contracts from Y_f to Y_2, a budget deficit automatically arises. Such automatic changes tend to drive the economy back toward its full-employment real GDP.

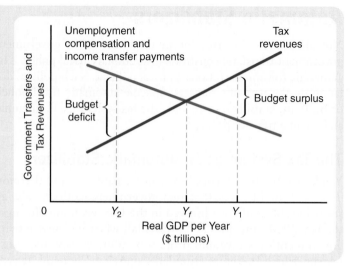

What Do We Really Know About Fiscal Policy?

There are two ways of looking at fiscal policy. One prevails during normal times and the other during abnormal times.

Fiscal Policy During Normal Times

Go to www.econtoday.com/chapter13 to learn about expanding spending and budget deficits of the U.S. government.

During normal times (without "excessive" unemployment, inflation, or unusual problems in the national economy), we know that due to the recognition time lag and the modest size of any fiscal policy action that Congress will actually take, discretionary fiscal policy is probably not very effective. Congress ends up doing too little too late to help in a minor recession. Moreover, fiscal policy that generates repeated tax changes (as has happened) creates uncertainty, which may do more harm than good. To the extent that fiscal policy has any effect during normal times, it probably achieves this by way of automatic stabilizers rather than by way of discretionary policy.

Fiscal Policy During Abnormal Times

During abnormal times, fiscal policy may be effective. Consider some classic examples: the Great Depression and war periods.

Why might discretionary fiscal policy work during another "Great Depression" whereas it probably works very little during normal times?

THE GREAT DEPRESSION When there is a catastrophic drop in real GDP, as there was during the Great Depression, fiscal policy may be able to stimulate aggregate demand. Because so many people have few assets left and thus are income-constrained during such periods, government spending is a way to get income into their hands—income that they are likely to spend immediately.

WARTIME Wars are in fact reserved for governments. War expenditures are not good substitutes for private expenditures—they have little or no direct expenditure offsets. Consequently, war spending as part of expansionary fiscal policy usually has noteworthy effects, such as occurred while we were waging World War II, when real

GDP increased dramatically (though much of the output of new goods and services was expended for military uses).

The "Soothing" Effect of Keynesian Fiscal Policy

One view of traditional Keynesian fiscal policy does not call for it to be used on a regular basis but nevertheless sees it as potentially useful. As you have learned in this chapter, many problems are associated with attempting to use fiscal policy. But if we should encounter a severe downturn, fiscal policy is available. Knowing this may reassure consumers and investors. Thus, the availability of fiscal policy may induce more buoyant and stable expectations of the future, thereby smoothing investment spending.

QUICK QUIZ   *See page 338 for the answers. Review concepts from this section in MyEconLab.*

Time lags of various sorts reduce the effectiveness of fiscal policy. These include the _____ time lag, the _____ time lag, and the _____ time lag.

Two _____, or built-in, stabilizers are the progressive income tax and unemployment compensation.

Built-in stabilizers automatically tend to _____ changes in disposable income resulting from changes in overall business activity.

Although discretionary fiscal policy may not necessarily be a useful policy tool in normal times because of time lags, it may work well during _____ times, such as depressions and wartimes. In addition, the existence of fiscal policy may have a soothing effect on consumers and investors.

 You Are There ▶ **Assessing the Effects of a Temporary Tax Rebate**

It is January 2009, and economists with the U.S. Treasury are considering a proposed income tax rebate program. Under the proposal, the U.S. government will provide a partial reimbursement of income taxes of as much as $300 for individuals who earned less than $75,000 and up to $600 for two-earner households that had incomes below $150,000. The rebate is to apply only to taxes paid in 2008.

The Treasury economists estimate that 130 million U.S. households will qualify for the tax rebates. Nevertheless, many of the economists are pessimistic about how much one-time tax rebates are likely to boost aggregate consumption. A similar rebate program the previous year contributed to a short-lived increase in aggregate disposable income of nearly $500 billion during the spring of 2008, but aggregate consumption did not rise. The one-time rebates did not have long-term effects on disposable incomes, so most people

receiving them either saved the funds or used them to pay off some of their debts. Thus, the previous year's tax rebates did not boost the circular flow of spending. A large majority of the economists at the meeting agree that a repeat of this outcome is likely if rebates are issued again this year.

CRITICAL ANALYSIS QUESTIONS

1. Congress did indeed authorize 2008 tax rebates to be issued in the spring of 2009, and personal saving jumped by as much as 6 percent while personal consumption barely changed. Does this outcome support the Treasury economists' prediction? Explain briefly.

2. Why do you suppose that people are less likely to increase their consumption spending in response to a one-time tax cut than to a permanent reduction?

Does Government Spending Crowd Out Private Health Care Expenditures?

CONCEPTS APPLIED

- Fiscal Policy
- Crowding-Out Effect
- Direct Expenditure Offsets

Since the mid-1960s, the federal government has directed an increasing share of tax dollars to expenditures on health care services for U.S. residents. Today, nearly one-third of all federal government expenditures are related to health care. Hence, health care spending cannot be ignored in any evaluation of U.S. fiscal policy.

A Continuing Expansion of Government Health Care Spending

The primary U.S. government health care program is Medicare, which covers many medical and pharmaceutical expenses incurred by elderly U.S. residents. The nearly $500 billion per year that the government spends on Medicare is about 20 percent of total—combined public and private—health care spending.

During the 1990s, Congress also broadened the existing Medicaid program to cover almost all health care spending for children and pregnant women in families with incomes below the official poverty line (about $22,000). As many elderly individuals are outliving their savings and falling below the income ceiling for Medicaid, the program now also covers expenses of more than 60 percent of all people in nursing homes. Annual Medicaid spending has expanded to nearly $400 billion per year. In addition, in 1997 Congress created the jointly federal- and state-subsidized State Children's Health Insurance Program (SCHIP), which in most states pays for the health care of children in families with incomes as high as 3.5 times the official poverty income.

Considering Adding New Items to Taxpayers' Health Care Bill

Recently, President Obama and congressional leaders have pressed for further expansions of the federal government's health care spending. They argue that increases are necessary to provide for U.S. residents who lack private insurance and cannot pay for health care from their own resources.

One proposal under consideration is for the federal government to provide "start-up funds" for nonprofit cooperatives charged with providing health care to millions of uninsured individuals. Another more ambitious proposal calls for the government to provide health care directly. Under these proposals, the government's new health care expenses could range from several billion dollars to hundreds of billions of dollars per year, depending on which plan is adopted.

The Crowding-Out Effect of Government Health Care Spending

Congress typically justifies increases in health care spending as necessary to provide for U.S. residents who cannot obtain private insurance and are unable to pay for health care from their own resources. Nevertheless, there is considerable evidence that government health care expenditures crowd out a significant amount of health care spending that otherwise would be undertaken from private funds.

For instance, Jonathan Gruber of the Massachusetts Institute of Technology and Kosali Simon of Cornell University have studied the crowding-out effect of various expansions of government health care spending between 1996 and 2002. They estimate that new government spending on health care during that period reduced private health care expenditures by about 60 percent. In other words, every $1.00 of government expenditures on health care in the 1996–2002 period offset $0.60 of private spending. Thus, a significant direct expenditure offset is associated with government spending on health care.

Test your understanding of this chapter by going online to **MyEconLab.**
In the Study Plan for this chapter, select Section N: News.

For Critical Analysis

1. Based on Gruber and Simon's estimate, has increased government health care spending succeeded in covering some people who otherwise might not have had insurance coverage of health care expenses? (Hint: How much of each $1.00 of government expenditures on health care did Gruber and Simon estimate did *not* offset private helath care spending?)

2. If we assume that 60 percent of *all* Medicare and Medicaid spending directly offsets private spending, about how many dollars of private health care spending are crowded out by combined Medicare and Medicaid expenditures by the federal government? (Hint: As noted above, the government currently spends about $500 billion per year on Medicare and about $400 billion per year on Medicaid.)

Web Resources

1. For information about Medicare spending, go to www .econtoday.com/chapter13.
2. For updates on Medicaid expenditures, go to www .econtoday.com/chapter13.

Research Project

Suppose that you have been appointed to help the Obama administration design a new government health care spending program. One of your goals is to limit the direct expenditure offset of the new program. How might you go about designing the program to attain this objective? (Hint: Think of incentives that might induce people without private insurance to utilize the government program and disincentives that would prevent people who now possess private insurance from switching to the government program.)

Here is what you should know after reading this chapter. **MyEconLab** will help you identify what you know, and where to go when you need to practice.

WHAT YOU SHOULD KNOW

The Effects of Discretionary Fiscal Policies Using Traditional Keynesian Analysis In short-run Keynesian analysis, a deliberate increase in government spending or a reduction in taxes shifts the aggregate demand curve outward and thereby closes a recessionary gap in which current real GDP is less than the long-run level of real GDP. Likewise, an intentional reduction in government spending or a tax increase shifts the aggregate demand curve inward and closes an inflationary gap in which current real GDP exceeds the long-run level of real GDP.

fiscal policy, 319

KEY FIGURES
Figure 13-1, 320
Figure 13-2, 322

WHERE TO GO TO PRACTICE

- **MyEconLab** Study Plan 13.1
- Audio introduction to Chapter 13
- Animated Figures 13-1, 13-2

(*continued*)

 *(continued)*

| WHAT YOU SHOULD KNOW | | WHERE TO GO TO PRACTICE |

How Indirect Crowding Out and Direct Expenditure Offsets Can Reduce the Effectiveness of Fiscal Policy Actions Indirect crowding out occurs when the government engages in expansionary fiscal policy by increasing government spending or reducing taxes. When government spending exceeds tax revenues, the government must borrow from the private sector. To obtain the necessary funds, the government must offer a higher interest rate, thereby driving up market interest rates. This reduces, or crowds out, interest-sensitive private spending, thereby reducing the net effect of the fiscal expansion on aggregate demand. As a result, the aggregate demand curve shifts by a smaller amount than it would have in the absence of the crowding-out effect, and fiscal policy has a somewhat lessened net effect on equilibrium real GDP. Increased government spending may also substitute directly for private expenditures, and the resulting decline in private spending directly offsets the increase in total planned expenditures that the government had intended to bring about. This also reduces the net change in aggregate demand brought about by a fiscal policy action.

crowding-out effect, 323
direct expenditure
  offsets, 325
supply-side economics,
  326

KEY FIGURES
Figure 13-3, 323
Figure 13-4, 324
Figure 13-5, 327

- **MyEconLab** Study Plan 13.2
- Video: The Crowding-Out Effect
- Animated Figures 13-3, 13-4, 13-5

The Ricardian Equivalence Theorem According to this proposition, when the government cuts taxes and borrows to finance the tax reduction, people realize that eventually the government will have to repay the loan. Thus, they anticipate that taxes will have to increase in the future. This induces them to save the proceeds of the tax cut to meet their future tax liabilities. Thus, a tax cut fails to induce an increase in aggregate consumption spending and consequently has no effect on total planned expenditures and aggregate demand.

Ricardian equivalence
  theorem, 325

KEY FIGURE
Figure 13-4, 324

- **MyEconLab** Study Plan 13.2
- Animated Figure 13-4

Fiscal Policy Time Lags and the Effectiveness of Fiscal "Fine-Tuning" Efforts to engage in fiscal policy actions intended to bring about changes in aggregate demand are complicated by policy time lags. One of these is the recognition time lag, which is the time required to collect information about the economy's current situation. Another is the action time lag, the period between recognition of a problem and implementation of a policy intended to address it. Finally, there is the effect time lag, which is the interval between the implementation of a policy and its having an effect on the economy. For fiscal policy, all of these lags can be lengthy and variable, often lasting one to three years. Hence, fiscal "fine-tuning" may be a poor choice of words.

recognition time lag, 328
action time lag, 328
effect time lag, 328

- **MyEconLab** Study Plan 13.3
- Video: Time Lags

(continued)

 (continued)

WHAT YOU SHOULD KNOW

Automatic Stabilizers In our tax system, income taxes diminish automatically when economic activity drops, and unemployment compensation and income transfer payments increase. Thus, when there is a decline in real GDP, the automatic reduction in income tax collections and increases in unemployment compensation and income transfer payments tend to minimize the reduction in total planned expenditures that would otherwise have resulted. The existence of these programs thereby helps to stabilize the economy automatically in the face of variations in autonomous expenditures that induce fluctuations in economic activity.

automatic, or built-in, stabilizers, 329

KEY FIGURE
Figure 13-6, 330

WHERE TO GO TO PRACTICE

- **MyEconLab** Study Plans 13.4, 13.5
- Animated Figure 13-6

Log in to MyEconLab, take a chapter test, and get a personalized Study Plan that tells you which concepts you understand and which ones you need to review. From there, MyEconLab will give you further practice, tutorials, animations, videos, and guided solutions.
Log in to www.myeconlab.com

PROBLEMS

All problems are assignable in . *Answers to odd-numbered problems appear at the back of the book.*

13-1. Suppose that Congress and the president decide that the nation's economic performance is weakening and that the government should "do something" about the situation. They make no tax changes but do enact new laws increasing government spending on a variety of programs.

   a. Prior to the congressional and presidential action, careful studies by government economists indicated that the direct multiplier effect of a rise in government expenditures on equilibrium real GDP is equal to 6. In the 12 months since the increase in government spending, however, it has become clear that the actual ultimate effect on real GDP will be less than half of that amount. What factors might account for this?

   b. Another year and a half elapses following passage of the government spending boost. The government has undertaken no additional policy actions, nor have there been any other events of significance. Nevertheless, by the end of the second year, real GDP has returned to its

original level, and the price level has increased sharply. Provide a possible explanation for this outcome.

13-2. Suppose that Congress enacts a significant tax cut with the expectation that this action will stimulate aggregate demand and push up real GDP in the short run. In fact, however, neither real GDP nor the price level changes significantly as a result of the tax cut. What might account for this outcome?

13-3. Explain how time lags in discretionary fiscal policymaking could thwart the efforts of Congress and the president to stabilize real GDP in the face of an economic downturn. Is it possible that these time lags could actually cause discretionary fiscal policy to *destabilize* real GDP?

13-4. Determine whether each of the following is an example of a direct expenditure offset to fiscal policy.

   a. In an effort to help rejuvenate the nation's railroad system, a new government agency buys unused track, locomotives, and passenger and freight cars, many of which private companies would otherwise have purchased and put into regular use.

b. The government increases its expenditures without raising taxes; to cover the resulting budget deficit, it borrows more funds from the private sector, thereby pushing up the market interest rate and discouraging private planned investment spending.

c. The government finances the construction of a classical music museum that otherwise would never have received private funding.

13-5. Determine whether each of the following is an example of indirect crowding out resulting from an expansionary fiscal policy action.

a. The government provides a subsidy to help keep an existing firm operating, even though a group of investors otherwise would have provided a cash infusion that would have kept the company in business.

b. The government reduces its taxes without decreasing its expenditures; to cover the resulting budget deficit, it borrows more funds from the private sector, thereby pushing up the market interest rate and discouraging private planned investment spending.

c. Government expenditures fund construction of a high-rise office building on a plot of land where a private company otherwise would have constructed an essentially identical building.

13-6. The U.S. government is in the midst of spending more than $1 billion on seven buildings containing more than 100,000 square feet of space to be used for study of infectious diseases. Prior to the government's decision to construct these buildings, a few universities had been planning to build essentially the same facilities using privately obtained funds. After construction on the government buildings began, however, the universities dropped their plans. Evaluate whether the government's $1 billion expenditure is actually likely to push U.S. real GDP above the level it would have reached in the absence of the government's construction spree.

13-7. Determine whether each of the following is an example of a discretionary fiscal policy action.

a. A recession occurs, and government-funded unemployment compensation is paid to laid-off workers.

b. Congress votes to fund a new jobs program designed to put unemployed workers to work.

c. The Federal Reserve decides to reduce the quantity of money in circulation in an effort to slow inflation.

d. Under powers authorized by an act of Congress, the president decides to authorize an emergency release of funds for spending programs intended to head off economic crises.

13-8. Determine whether each of the following is an example of an automatic fiscal stabilizer.

a. A government agency arranges to make loans to businesses whenever an economic downturn begins.

b. As the economy heats up, the resulting increase in equilibrium real GDP immediately results in higher income tax payments, which dampen consumption spending somewhat.

c. As the economy starts to recover from a recession and more people go back to work, government-funded unemployment compensation payments begin to decline.

d. To stem an overheated economy, the president, using special powers granted by Congress, authorizes emergency impoundment of funds that Congress had previously authorized for spending on government programs.

13-9. Consider the diagram below, in which the current short-run equilibrium is at point *A*, and answer the questions that follow.

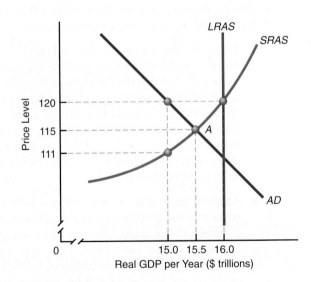

a. What type of gap exists at point *A*?

b. If the marginal propensity to save equals 0.20, what change in government spending could eliminate the gap identified in part (a)? Explain.

13-10. Consider the diagram below, in which the current short-run equilibrium is at point *A*, and answer the questions that follow.

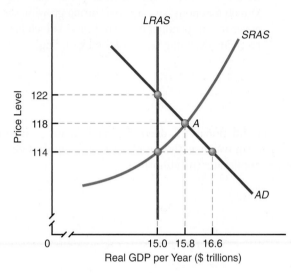

a. What type of gap exists at point *A*?

b. If the marginal propensity to consume equals 0.75, what change in government spending could eliminate the gap identified in part (a)? Explain.

13-11. Currently, a government's budget is balanced. The marginal propensity to consume is 0.80. The government has determined that each additional $10 billion it borrows to finance a budget deficit pushes up the market interest rate by 0.1 percentage point. It has also determined that every 0.1-percentage-point change in the market interest rate generates a change in planned investment expenditures equal to $2 billion. Finally, the government knows that to close a recessionary gap and take into account the resulting change in the price level, it must generate a net rightward shift in the aggregate demand curve equal to $200 billion. Assuming that there are no direct expenditure offsets to fiscal policy, how much should the government increase its expenditures? (Hint: How much private investment spending will each $10 billion increase in government spending crowd out?)

13-12. A government is currently operating with an annual budget deficit of $40 billion. The government has determined that every $10 billion reduction in the amount it borrows each year would reduce the market interest rate by 0.1 percentage point. Furthermore, it has determined that every 0.1-percentage-point change in the market interest rate generates a change in planned investment expenditures in the opposite direction equal to $5 billion. The marginal propensity to consume is 0.75. Finally, the government knows that to eliminate an inflationary gap and take into account the resulting change in the price level, it must generate a net leftward shift in the aggregate demand curve equal to $40 billion. Assuming that there are no direct expenditure offsets to fiscal policy, how much should the government increase taxes? (Hint: How much new private investment spending is induced by each $10 billion decrease in government spending?)

13-13. Assume that the Ricardian equivalence theorem is not relevant. Explain why an income-tax-rate cut should affect short-run equilibrium real GDP.

13-14. Suppose that Congress enacts a lump-sum tax cut of $750 billion. The marginal propensity to consume is equal to 0.75. Assuming that Ricardian equivalence holds true, what is the effect on equilibrium real GDP? On saving?

ECONOMICS ON THE NET

Federal Government Spending and Taxation A quick way to keep up with the federal government's spending and taxation is by examining federal budget data at the White House Internet address.

Title: Historical Tables: Budget of the United States Government

Navigation: Use the link at **www.econtoday.com/chapter13** to visit the Office of Management and Budget. Select the most recent budget. Then click on *Historical Tables*.

Application After the document downloads, perform the indicated operations and answer the questions.

1. Go to section 2, "Composition of Federal Government Receipts." Take a look at Table 2.2, "Percentage Composition of Receipts by Source." Before World War II, what was the key source of revenues of the federal government? What has been the key revenue source since World War II?

2. Now scan down the document to Table 2.3, "Receipts by Source as Percentages of GDP." Have any government revenue sources declined as a percentage of GDP? Which ones have noticeably risen in recent years?

For Group Study and Analysis Split into four groups, and have each group examine section 3, "Federal Government Outlays by Function," and in particular Table 3.1, "Outlays by Superfunction and Function." Assign groups to the following functions: national defense, health, income security, and Social Security. Have each group prepare a brief report concerning recent and long-term trends in government spending on each function. Which functions have been capturing growing shares of government spending in recent years? Which have been receiving declining shares of total spending?

ANSWERS TO QUICK QUIZZES

p. 322: (i) expenditures . . . taxes; (ii) recessionary . . . increase; (iii) inflationary . . . decrease; (iv) decrease . . . increase

p. 327: (i) increase; (ii) Direct expenditure offsets; (iii) Ricardian equivalence; (iv) supply-side . . . supply-side

p. 331: (i) recognition . . . action . . . effect; (ii) automatic; (iii) moderate; (iv) abnormal

Fiscal Policy: A Keynesian Perspective

The traditional Keynesian approach to fiscal policy differs in three ways from that presented in Chapter 13. First, it emphasizes the underpinnings of the components of aggregate demand. Second, it assumes that government expenditures are not substitutes for private expenditures and that current taxes are the only taxes taken into account by consumers and firms. Third, the traditional Keynesian approach focuses on the short run and so assumes that as a first approximation, the price level is constant.

Changes in Government Spending

Figure C-1 measures real GDP along the horizontal axis and total planned real expenditures (aggregate demand) along the vertical axis. The components of aggregate demand are real consumption (C), investment (I), government spending (G), and net exports (X). The height of the schedule labeled $C + I + G + X$ shows total planned real expenditures (aggregate demand) as a function of real GDP. This schedule slopes upward because consumption depends positively on real GDP. Everywhere along the 45-degree reference line, planned real spending equals real GDP. At the point Y^*, where the $C + I + G + X$ line intersects the 45-degree line, planned real spending is consistent with real GDP per year. At any income less than Y^*, spending exceeds real GDP, and so real GDP and thus real spending will tend to rise. At any level of real GDP greater than Y^*, planned spending is less than real GDP, and so real GDP and thus spending will tend to decline. Given the determinants of C, I, G, and X, total real spending (aggregate demand) will be Y^*.

The Keynesian approach assumes that changes in government spending cause no direct offsets in either consumption or investment spending because G is not a substitute

---

FIGURE C-1

The Impact of Higher Government Spending on Aggregate Demand

Government spending increases, causing $C + I + G + X$ to move to $C + I + G' + X$. Equilibrium real GDP per year increases to Y^{**}.

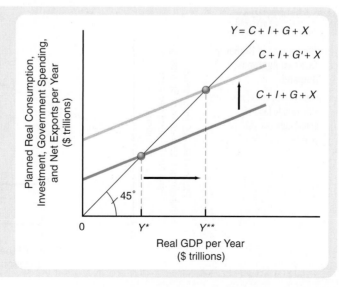

for C, I, or X. Hence, a rise in government spending from G to G' causes the $C + I + G + X$ line to shift upward by the full amount of the rise in government spending, yielding the line $C + I + G' + X$. The rise in real government spending causes real GDP to rise, which in turn causes consumption spending to rise, which further increases real GDP. Ultimately, aggregate demand rises to Y^{**}, where spending again equals real GDP. A key conclusion of the traditional Keynesian analysis is that total spending rises by *more* than the original rise in government spending because consumption spending depends positively on real GDP.

Changes in Taxes

According to the Keynesian approach, changes in current taxes affect aggregate demand by changing the amount of real disposable (after-tax) income available to consumers. A rise in taxes reduces disposable income and thus reduces real consumption; conversely, a tax cut raises disposable income and thus causes a rise in consumption spending. The effects of a tax increase are shown in Figure C-2. Higher taxes cause consumption spending to decline from C to C', causing total spending to shift downward to $C' + I + G + X$. In general, the decline in consumption will be less than the increase in taxes because people will also reduce their saving to help pay the higher taxes.

The Balanced-Budget Multiplier

One interesting implication of the Keynesian approach concerns the impact of a balanced-budget change in government real spending. Suppose that the government increases spending by $1 billion and pays for it by raising current taxes by $1 billion. Such a policy is called a *balanced-budget increase in real spending*. Because the higher spending tends to push aggregate demand *up* by *more* than $1 billion while the higher taxes tend to push aggregate demand *down* by *less* than $1 billion, a most remarkable thing happens: A balanced-budget increase in G causes total spending to rise by *exactly* the amount of the rise in G—in this case, $1 billion. We say that the *balanced-budget*

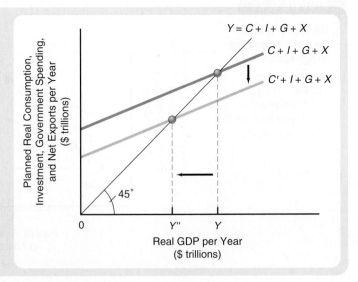

FIGURE C-2

The Impact of Higher Taxes on Aggregate Demand

Higher taxes cause consumption to fall to C'. Equilibrium real GDP per year decreases to Y''.

multiplier is equal to 1. Similarly, a balanced-budget reduction in government spending will cause total spending to fall by exactly the amount of the government spending cut.

The Fixed Price Level Assumption

The final key feature of the traditional Keynesian approach is that it typically assumes that as a first approximation, the price level is fixed. Recall that nominal GDP equals the price level multiplied by real GDP. If the price level is fixed, an increase in government spending that causes nominal GDP to rise will show up exclusively as a rise in *real* GDP. This will in turn be accompanied by a decline in the unemployment rate because the additional real GDP can be produced only if additional factors of production, such as labor, are utilized.

PROBLEMS

All problems are assignable in myeconlab. *Answers to odd-numbered problems appear at the back of the book.*

C-1. Assume that equilibrium real GDP is $15.2 trillion and full-employment equilibrium (*FE*) is $15.55 trillion. The marginal propensity to save is $\frac{1}{7}$. Answer the questions using the data in the following graph.

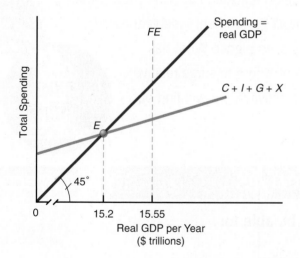

  a. What is the marginal propensity to consume?

  b. By how much must new investment or government spending increase to bring the economy up to full employment?

  c. By how much must government cut personal taxes to stimulate the economy to the full-employment equilibrium?

C-2. Assume that MPC = $\frac{4}{5}$ when answering the following questions.

  a. If government expenditures rise by $2 billion, by how much will the aggregate expenditure curve shift upward? By how much will equilibrium real GDP per year change?

  b. If taxes increase by $2 billion, by how much will the aggregate expenditure curve shift downward? By how much will equilibrium real GDP per year change?

C-3. Assume that MPC = $\frac{4}{5}$ when answering the following questions.

  a. If government expenditures rise by $1 billion, by how much will the aggregate expenditure curve shift upward?

  b. If taxes rise by $1 billion, by how much will the aggregate expenditure curve shift downward?

  c. If both taxes and government expenditures rise by $1 billion, by how much will the aggregate expenditure curve shift? What will happen to the equilibrium level of real GDP?

  d. How does your response to the second question in part (c) change if MPC = $\frac{3}{4}$? If MPC = $\frac{1}{2}$?

14

Deficit Spending and the Public Debt

rom the mid-1990s until 2001, the ratio of the inflation-adjusted *net public debt*—the amount that the U.S. government owes to U.S. residents and others around the world—to U.S. real GDP steadily declined, from about 50 percent to 34 percent. This ratio rose very slightly from 2002 through 2006. Since 2007, however, the ratio of the official real net public debt to real GDP has increased dramatically, from 36 percent to more than 67 percent. Nevertheless, critics of the government's debt accounting argue that the reported ratio is actually too low. They contend that the ratio of the *true* inflation-adjusted net public debt—the amount that taxpayers *actually* owe on *all* government indebtedness, official and unofficial—to real GDP is even higher. What has caused the government's indebtedness to surge relative to the amount of economic activity? You will find out in this chapter.

LEARNING OBJECTIVES

myeconlab

MyEconLab helps you master each objective and study more efficiently. See end of chapter for details.

After reading this chapter, you should be able to:

- Explain how federal government budget deficits occur
- Define the public debt and understand alternative measures of the public debt
- Evaluate circumstances under which the public debt could be a burden to future generations
- Discuss why the federal budget deficit might be measured incorrectly
- Analyze the macroeconomic effects of government budget deficits
- Describe possible ways to reduce the government budget deficit

HOW TODAY'S BUDGET DEFICITS MIGHT BURDEN FUTURE GENERATIONS If the federal government wishes to purchase goods and services valued at $300 billion, it can finance this expenditure either by raising taxes by $300 billion or by selling $300 billion in bonds. Many economists maintain that the second option, deficit spending, would lead to a higher level of national consumption and a lower level of national saving than the first option.

The reason, say these economists, is that if people are taxed, they will have to forgo private consumption now as society substitutes government goods for private goods. If the government does not raise taxes but instead sells bonds to finance the $300 billion in expenditures, the public's disposable income remains the same. Members of the public have merely shifted their allocations of assets to include $300 billion in additional government bonds. There are two possible circumstances that could cause people to treat government borrowing differently than they treat taxes. One is that people will fail to realize that their liabilities (in the form of higher future taxes due to increased interest payments on the public debt) have *also* increased by $300 billion. Another is that people will believe that they can consume the governmentally provided goods without forgoing any private consumption because the bill for the government goods will be paid by *future* taxpayers.

THE CROWDING-OUT EFFECT But if full employment exists, and society raises its present consumption by adding consumption of government-provided goods to the original quantity of privately provided goods, then something must be *crowded out*. In a closed economy, investment expenditures on capital goods must decline. As you learned in Chapter 13, the mechanism by which investment is crowded out is an increase in the interest rate. Deficit spending increases the total demand for credit but leaves the total supply of credit unaltered. The rise in interest rates causes a reduction in the growth of investment and capital formation, which in turn slows the growth of productivity and improvement in society's living standard.

If this government highway project increases the deficit, what might be the effect on private investment expenditures?

This perspective suggests that deficit spending can impose a burden on future generations in two ways. First, unless the deficit spending is allocated to purchases that lead to long-term increases in real GDP, future generations will have to be taxed at a higher rate. That is, only by imposing higher taxes on future generations will the government be able to retire the higher public debt resulting from the present generation's consumption of governmentally provided goods. Second, the increased level of consumption by the present generation crowds out investment and reduces the growth of capital goods, leaving future generations with a smaller capital stock and thereby reducing their wealth.

PAYING OFF THE PUBLIC DEBT IN THE FUTURE Suppose that after 50 years of running deficits financed by selling bonds to U.S. residents, the public debt becomes so large that each adult person's implicit share of the net public debt liability is $50,000. Suppose further that the government chooses (or is forced) to pay off the debt at that time. Will that generation be burdened with our government's overspending? Assume that a large portion of the debt is owed to ourselves. It is true that every adult will have to come up with $50,000 in taxes to pay off the debt, but then the government will use these funds to pay off the bondholders. Sometimes the bondholders and taxpayers will be the same people. Thus, *some* people will be burdened because they owe $50,000 and own less than $50,000 in government bonds. Others, however, will receive more than $50,000 for the bonds they own. Nevertheless, as a generation within society, they will pay and receive about the same amount of funds.

Of course, there could be a burden on some low-income adults who will find it difficult or impossible to obtain $50,000 to pay off the tax liability. Still, nothing says that taxes to pay off the debt must be assessed equally. Indeed, it seems likely that a special tax would be levied, based on the ability to pay.

OUR DEBT TO FOREIGN RESIDENTS So far we have been assuming that we owe all of the public debt to ourselves. But, as we saw earlier, that is not the case. What about the more than 50 percent owned by foreign residents?

It is true that if foreign residents buy U.S. government bonds, we do not owe that debt to ourselves. Thus, when debts held by foreign residents come due, future U.S. residents will be taxed to repay these debts plus accumulated interest. Portions of the incomes of future U.S. residents will then be transferred abroad. In this way, a potential burden on future generations may result.

But this transfer of income from U.S. residents to residents of other nations will not necessarily be a burden. It is important to realize that if the rate of return on projects that the government funds by operating with deficits exceeds the interest rate paid to foreign residents, both foreign residents and future U.S. residents will be better off. If funds obtained by selling bonds to foreign residents are expended on wasteful projects, however, a burden may well be placed on future generations.

We can apply the same reasoning to the problem of current investment and capital creation being crowded out by current deficits. If deficits lead to slower growth rates, future generations will be poorer. But if the government expenditures are really investments, and if the rate of return on such public investments exceeds the interest rate paid on the bonds, both present and future generations will be economically better off.

Do the U.S. government's contributions to the International Monetary Fund add to the net public debt if the government does not classify the contributions as "expenditures"?

POLICY EXAMPLE
How a Special "Contribution" Increased the U.S. Debt Burden Without Changing the Official Budget Deficit

Recently, President Obama sought to contribute an additional $108 billion to the International Monetary Fund (IMF), thereby providing the IMF with more funds to lend to governments of countries hit hard by the worldwide recession. When the president requested this extra $108 billion from Congress, however, the U.S. economy was in the midst of the Great Recession of the late 2000s. Because the incomes of individuals and companies had declined, the U.S. government's tax revenues had fallen well below its outlays. Consequently, counting the $108 billion as spending would add to the already rapidly increasing federal government budget deficit. To prevent the requested IMF contribution from adding to the official deficit, the president asked Congress not to classify the funds as expenditures. There was, he argued, a chance that the IMF might eventually repay at least a small portion of the amount. Congress agreed and classified the funds as a "loan" to the IMF.

Nevertheless, the U.S. Treasury Department had to borrow the $108 billion that it planned to transmit to the IMF. Thus, the U.S. government's total borrowing rose by an additional $108 billion even though Congress did not classify the funds as spending, thereby leaving the official government budget deficit unaffected. This extra borrowing added to the government's total indebtedness and the total burden of a higher net public debt for U.S. residents even though the amount was not included in the officially reported deficit when the government extended the "loan" to the IMF.

FOR CRITICAL ANALYSIS
Why do you suppose economists argue that the best measure of the U.S. government's actual indebtedness is equal to the total net amount that it has borrowed?

QUICK QUIZ *See page 364 for the answers. Review concepts from this section in MyEconLab.*

When we subtract the funds that government agencies borrow from each other from the _____ public debt, we obtain the _____ public debt.

The public debt may impose a burden on _____ generations if they have to be taxed at higher rates to pay for the _____ generation's increased consumption of governmentally provided goods. In addition, there may be a burden if the debt leads to crowding out of current investment, resulting in _____ capital formation and hence a _____ economic growth rate.

If foreign residents hold a significant part of our public debt, then we no longer "owe it to ourselves." If the rate of return on the borrowed funds is _____ than the interest to be paid to foreign residents, future generations can be made better off by government borrowing. Future generations will be worse off, however, if the opposite is true.

Federal Budget Deficits in an Open Economy

Many economists believe that it is no accident that foreign residents hold such a large portion of the U.S. public debt. Their reasoning suggests that a U.S. trade deficit—a situation in which the value of U.S. imports of goods and services exceeds the value of its exports—will often accompany a government budget deficit.

Trade Deficits and Government Budget Deficits

Figure 14-4 on the following page shows U.S. trade deficits and surpluses compared to federal budget deficits and surpluses. In 1983, imports of goods and services began to consistently exceed exports of those items on an annual basis in the United States. At the same time, the federal budget deficit rose dramatically. Both deficits increased once again in the early 2000s. Then, during the economic turmoil of the late 2000s, the budget deficit exploded while the trade deficit shrank somewhat.

Overall, however, it appears that larger trade deficits tend to accompany larger government budget deficits.

Why the Two Deficits Tend to Be Related

Intuitively, there is a reason why we would expect federal budget deficits to be associated with trade deficits. You might call this the unpleasant arithmetic of trade and budget deficits.

Suppose that, initially, the government's budget is balanced; government expenditures are matched by an equal amount of tax collections and other government revenues. Now assume that the federal government begins to operate with a budget deficit; it increases its spending, collects fewer taxes, or both. Assume further that domestic consumption and domestic investment do not decrease relative to GDP. Where, then, do the funds come from to finance the government's budget deficit? A portion of these funds must come from abroad. That is to say, dollar holders abroad will have to purchase newly created government bonds.

Of course, foreign dollar holders will choose to hold the new government bonds only if there is an economic inducement to do so, such as an increase in U.S. interest rates. Given that private domestic spending and other factors are unchanged, interest rates will indeed rise whenever there is an increase in deficits financed by increased borrowing.

FIGURE 14-4

The Related U.S. Deficits

The United States exported more than it imported until 1983. Then it started experiencing large trade deficits, as shown in this diagram. The federal budget has been in deficit most years since the 1960s.

The question is, has the federal budget deficit created the trade deficit?

Sources: Economic Report of the President; Economic Indicators, various issues; author's estimates.

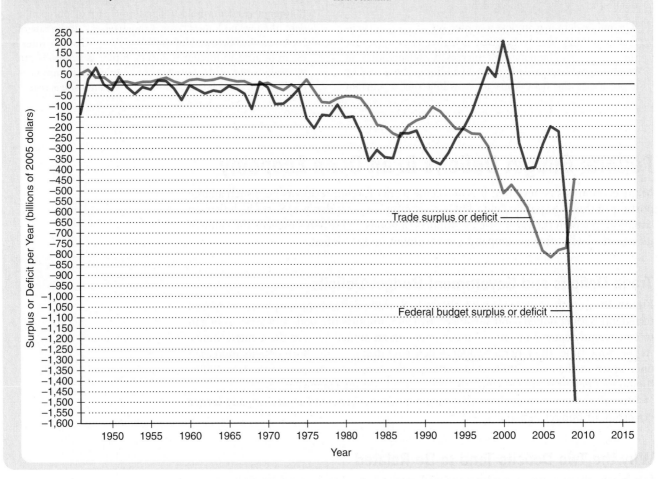

When foreign dollar holders purchase the new U.S. government bonds, they will have fewer dollars to spend on U.S. items, including U.S. export goods. Hence, when our nation's government operates with a budget deficit, we should expect to see foreign dollar holders spending more on U.S. government bonds and less on U.S.-produced goods and services. As a consequence of the U.S. government deficit, therefore, we should generally anticipate a decline in U.S. exports relative to U.S. imports, or a higher U.S. trade deficit.

Growing U.S. Government Deficits: Implications for U.S. Economic Performance

We have seen that one consequence of higher U.S. government budget deficits tends to be higher international trade deficits. Higher budget deficits are also likely to have broader consequences for the economy. Reaching a consensus about these broader consequences, however, requires agreement about exactly how to measure deficits within the government's overall budget.

Which Government Deficit Is the "True" Deficit?

Assessing the implications of higher government deficits is complicated by the fact that the government may report distorted measures of its own budget. One problem is that the U.S. government has never adopted a particularly business-like approach to tracking its expenditures and receipts. Another is that even within its own accounting system, the government persists in choosing "official" measures that yield the lowest reported deficits and highest reported surpluses.

CAPITAL BUDGETING THEORY The federal government has only one budget to guide its spending and taxing each fiscal year. It does not distinguish between current spending for upkeep of the grounds of the U.S. Capitol building, for example, and spending for a new aircraft carrier that will last for many years to come. In contrast, businesses, as well as state and local governments, have two budgets. One, called the *operating budget*, includes expenditures for current operations, such as salaries and interest payments. The other, called a *capital budget*, includes expenditures on investment items, such as machines, buildings, roads, and dams. Municipal governments, for example, may pay for items on the capital budget by long-term borrowing.

If the federal government used a capital budgeting system, we would see that some portion of the more than $1.4 trillion deficit estimated for fiscal year 2009 was being used to finance activities or assets yielding long-term returns. According to Office of Management and Budget (OMB) estimates for 2009, investment-type outlays such as payments for military equipment and subsidies for research and development exceeded $220 billion.

For years, many economists have recommended that Congress create a capital budget and remove investment outlays from its operating budget. Opponents of such a change point out that it would allow the government to grow even faster than currently. After all, many new expenditures could be placed in the capital budget, thereby cutting the size of the operating budget deficit and reducing pressure on Congress to curtail the growth of federal government spending.

PICK A DEFICIT, ANY DEFICIT Even using standard accounting techniques, the "official" U.S. government budget deficit can vary drastically, depending on what the government chooses to include or not include. Every year, the OMB makes predictions about the federal budget deficit. So does the Congressional Budget Office. The two budget agencies each produce several deficit estimates for each fiscal year. They give them names such as the "baseline deficit," the "policy deficit," or the "on-budget deficit."

There is also a deficit that is reduced by the amount of the Social Security surplus—for 2007 and 2008 combined a reduction on the order of $500 billion—even though Congress supposedly regards the Social Security surplus as a pool of funds set aside for future disbursement rather than a source of funds for current spending. We could go on, but the point is not to know the details of these various measures of "the government deficit," but rather to understand that no one number gives a complete picture of the total amount of the government budget deficit.

Public discourse might be simplified if everyone could agree on a single measure of the deficit, but the government's accounting system does not make it easy to determine which deficit figure is clearly "best." Thus, we should probably anticipate that

Why do some economists argue that expenditures on a new aircraft carrier should not be mixed up with federal expenditures on, say, welfare payments?

For more information about the role of the Office of Management and Budget in the government's budgeting process, go to www .econtoday.com/chapter14.

for years to come, politicians and government officials will continue to bandy about whatever deficit figures best advance their own particular causes.

The Macroeconomic Consequences of Budget Deficits

No matter how we choose to measure the federal government's deficit, everyone can agree that it has been rising in recent years. Let's consider, therefore, the broader effects of higher government budget deficits, such as the much higher deficits in recent years (especially during the Great Recession), on the U.S. economy. When evaluating additional macroeconomic effects of government deficits, two important points must be kept well in mind. First, given the level of government expenditures, the main alternative to the deficit is higher taxes. Therefore, the effects of a deficit should be compared to the effects of higher taxes, not to zero. Second, it is important to distinguish between the effects of deficits when full employment exists and the effects when substantial unemployment exists.

SHORT-RUN MACROECONOMIC EFFECTS OF HIGHER BUDGET DEFICITS How do increased government budget deficits affect the economy in the short run? The answer depends on the initial state of the economy. Recall from Chapter 13 that higher government spending and lower taxes that generate budget deficits typically add to total planned expenditures, even after taking into account direct and indirect expenditure offsets. When there is a recessionary gap, the increase in aggregate demand can eliminate the recessionary gap and push the economy toward its full-employment real GDP level. In the presence of a short-run recessionary gap, therefore, government deficit spending can influence both real GDP and employment.

If the economy is at the full-employment level of real GDP, however, increased total planned expenditures and higher aggregate demand generated by a larger government budget deficit create an inflationary gap. Although greater deficit spending temporarily raises equilibrium real GDP above the full-employment level, the price level also increases.

LONG-RUN MACROECONOMIC EFFECTS OF HIGHER BUDGET DEFICITS In a long-run macroeconomic equilibrium, the economy has fully adjusted to changes in all factors. These factors include changes in government spending and taxes and, consequently, the government budget deficit. Although increasing the government budget deficit raises aggregate demand, in the long run equilibrium real GDP remains at its full-employment level. Further increases in the government deficit via higher government expenditures or tax cuts can only be inflationary. They have no effect on equilibrium real GDP, which remains at the full-employment level in the long run.

The fact that long-run equilibrium real GDP is unaffected in the face of increased government deficits has an important implication:

> *In the long run, higher government budget deficits have no effect on equilibrium real GDP. Ultimately, therefore, government spending in excess of government receipts simply redistributes a larger share of real GDP to government-provided goods and services.*

Thus, if the government operates with higher deficits over an extended period, the ultimate result is a shrinkage in the share of privately provided goods and services. By continually spending more than it collects in taxes and other revenue sources, the government takes up a larger portion of economic activity.

According to U.S. government estimates, what is likely to happen to the federal government's share of GDP during the coming decade?

POLICY EXAMPLE
What Is the Outlook for the U.S. Government's Share of GDP?

Each year, the Office of Management and Budget (OMB), an agency housed within the executive branch of the U.S. government, makes a projection of federal government deficits for each of the next 10 years. At the beginning of 2009, the OMB projected that the average annual budget deficit from 2010 to 2019 would be nearly $712 billion, or an annual amount nearly $186 billion higher than the average annual deficit of $526 billion experienced during the previous 10 years. This projection implied that the U.S. government anticipated taking an extra $186-billion-per-year slice of GDP over the next decade.

Seven months later, the OMB redid its deficit projections. When it had completed its new calculations, the OMB announced that its earlier projections had been flawed. The OMB now anticipated that the annual budget deficit for the following 10-year period would be approximately $900 billion. This meant that over the coming decade, the federal government's share of annual GDP would be about $188 billion per year higher than the $712 billion previously announced. Compared with the average annual deficit during the prior decade, this projection indicated that the federal government's share of GDP would be an average of $374 billion per year higher, or about $1,225 per year for a typical U.S. resident.

FOR CRITICAL ANALYSIS
If the federal government raises marginal tax rates in an effort to fund higher budget deficits, will real GDP necessarily be unaffected in the long run? (Hint: How do higher marginal tax rates affect the long-run aggregate supply curve?)

QUICK QUIZ   See page 364 for the answers. Review concepts from this section in MyEconLab.

Given constant shares of domestic consumption and domestic investment relative to GDP, funds to finance higher government budget deficits must come from abroad. To obtain the dollars required to purchase newly issued government bonds, foreign residents must sell _____ goods and services in the United States than U.S. residents sell abroad; thus, U.S. imports must _____ U.S. exports. For this reason, the federal budget deficit and the international trade _____ tend to be related.

Some people argue that the federal budget deficit is measured incorrectly because it lumps together spending on capital and spending on consumption. Establishing separate _____ and _____ budgets might, according to this view, promote more accurate measurement of federal finances.

Higher government deficits arise from increased government spending or tax cuts, which raise aggregate demand. Thus, larger government budget deficits can raise real GDP in a _____ gap situation. If the economy is already at the full-employment level of real GDP, however, higher government deficits can only temporarily push equilibrium real GDP _____ the full-employment level.

In the long run, higher government budget deficits cause the equilibrium price level to rise but fail to raise equilibrium real GDP above the full-employment level. Thus, the long-run effect of increased government deficits is simply a redistribution of real GDP from _____ provided goods and services to_____-provided goods and services.

How Could the Government Reduce All Its Red Ink?

There have been many suggestions about how to reduce the government deficit. One way to reduce the deficit is to increase tax collections.

INCREASING TAXES FOR EVERYONE From an arithmetic point of view, a federal budget deficit can be wiped out by simply increasing the amount of taxes collected. Let's see what this would require. Projections for 2009 are instructive. The Office of Management and Budget estimated the 2009 federal budget deficit at about $1.5 trillion. To have prevented this deficit from occurring by raising taxes, in 2009 the government would have had to collect almost $9,000 more in taxes from *every worker* in the United States. Needless to say, reality is such that we will never see annual federal budget deficits wiped out by simple tax increases.

TAXING THE RICH Some people suggest that the way to eliminate the deficit is to raise taxes on the rich. What does it mean to tax the rich more? If you talk about taxing "millionaires," you are referring to those who pay taxes on more than $1 million in income per year. There are fewer than 100,000 of them. Even if you were to double the taxes they currently pay, the reduction in the deficit would be relatively trivial. Changing marginal tax rates at the upper end will produce similarly unimpressive results. The Internal Revenue Service (IRS) has determined that an increase in the top marginal tax rate from 35 percent to 45 percent would raise, at best, only about $35 billion in additional taxes. (This assumes that people do not figure out a way to avoid the higher tax rate.) Extra revenues of $35 billion per year represent less than 3 percent of the estimated 2009 federal budget deficit.

The reality is that the data do not support the notion that tax increases can completely *eliminate* deficits. Although eliminating a deficit in this way is possible arithmetically, politically just the opposite has occurred. When more tax revenues have been collected, Congress has usually responded by increasing government spending.

REDUCING EXPENDITURES Reducing expenditures is another way to decrease the federal budget deficit. Figure 14-5 shows various components of government spending as a percentage of total expenditures. There you see that military spending (national defense) as a share of total federal expenditures has risen slightly in recent years, though it remains much lower than in most previous years.

During the period from the conclusion of World War II until 1972, military spending was the most important aspect of the federal budget. Figure 14-5 shows that it no longer is, even taking into account the war on terrorism that began in late 2001. **Entitlements,** which are legislated federal government payments that anyone who qualifies is entitled to receive, are now the most important component of the federal budget. These include payments for Social Security and other income security programs and for Medicare and other health programs such as Medicaid. Entitlements are consequently often called **noncontrollable expenditures,** or nondiscretionary expenditures unrelated to national defense that automatically change without any direct action by Congress.

Entitlements
Guaranteed benefits under a government program such as Social Security, Medicare, or Medicaid.

Noncontrollable expenditures
Government spending that changes automatically without action by Congress.

IS IT TIME TO BEGIN WHITTLING AWAY AT ENTITLEMENTS? In 1960, spending on entitlements represented about 20 percent of the total federal budget. Today, entitlement expenditures make up about one-third of total federal spending. Consider Social Security, Medicare, and Medicaid. In constant 2005 dollars, in 2009 Social Security, Medicare, and Medicaid represented about $1,350 billion of estimated federal expenditures. (This excludes military and international payments and interest on the government debt.)

FIGURE 14-5

Components of Federal Expenditures as Percentages of Total Federal Spending

Although military spending as a percentage of total federal spending has risen and fallen with changing national defense concerns, national defense expenditures as a percentage of total spending have generally trended downward since the mid-1950s. Social Security and other income security programs and

Medicare and other health programs now account for larger shares of total federal spending than any other programs.

Source: Office of Management and Budget.

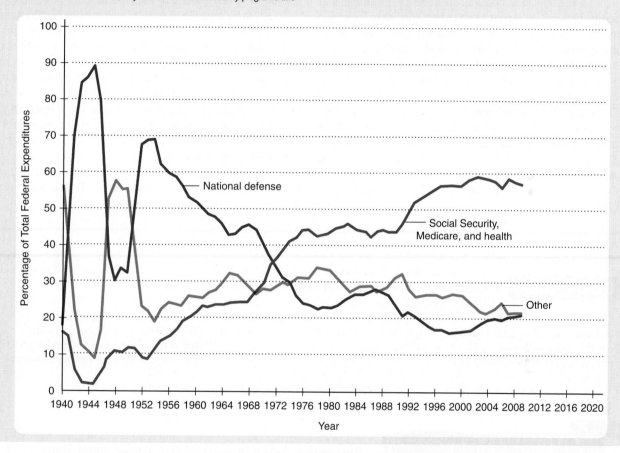

Entitlement payments for Social Security, Medicare, and Medicaid now exceed all other domestic spending. Entitlements are growing faster than any other part of the federal government budget. During the past two decades, real spending on entitlements (adjusted for inflation) grew between 7 and 8 percent per year, while the economy grew less than 3 percent per year. Social Security payments are growing in real terms at about 6 percent per year, but Medicare and Medicaid are growing at double-digit rates. The passage of Medicare prescription drug benefits in 2003 simply added to the already rapid growth of these health care entitlements.

Many people believe that entitlement programs are "necessary" federal expenditures. Interest on the public debt must be paid, but Congress can change just about every other federal expenditure labeled "necessary." The federal budget deficit is not expected to drop in the near future because entitlement programs are not likely to be eliminated. Governments have trouble cutting government benefit programs once they are established. This means that containing federal budget deficits is likely to prove to be a difficult task.

Does the Medicare program affect the federal budget deficit?

POLICY EXAMPLE
Medicare Is Contributing to a Higher Federal Budget Deficit

Since 2008, the Medicare entitlement program has officially operated at a deficit, meaning that health care benefits paid out to recipients have exceeded the funds generated by payroll taxes and other revenues formally budgeted to Medicare. Current projections suggest that the Medicare program will continue operating with an annual deficit and contribute to federal budget deficits indefinitely.

As part of a plan to prevent these Medicare deficits from occurring, Congress passed a law several years ago that cut allowed payments to Medicare providers by more than 20 percent. Each year since, however, Congress has passed one-year amendments canceling the payment reductions. In addition, Congress has boosted Medicare costs by expanding the scope of its coverage every year.

In light of the continuing escalation of Medicare's costs relative to payroll taxes and other sources of funding, trustees of the program recently reevaluated its long-term future. Congress establishes an annual trust fund for Medicare entitlement. Each year Congress borrows the entire trust fund to spend, and in the following year it uses Medicare revenues to return the trust fund to its previous level. Medicare's trustees have determined that by 2017, accumulated annual Medicare deficits will wipe out the trust fund unless Congress finds new sources of revenues to replenish it. At that point, Medicare officially will be insolvent.

FOR CRITICAL ANALYSIS
Why do you suppose that many economists call the Medicare trust fund an accounting fiction that Congress maintains for the sake of appearances?

QUICK QUIZ See page 364 for the answers. Review concepts from this section in MyEconLab.

One way to reduce federal budget _____ is to increase taxes. Proposals to reduce deficits by raising taxes on the highest-income individuals will not appreciably reduce budget deficits, however.

Another way to decrease federal budget _____ is to cut back on government spending, particularly on _____, defined as benefits guaranteed under government programs such as Social Security and Medicare.

You Are There ◀ Reassuring Asian Owners of U.S. Government Debt

Residents, businesses, and governments in Asia own more than $4 trillion of U.S. government debt. The single largest holder of government debt is the government of China. It is 2009, and the jump in U.S. government spending in the wake of the U.S. financial panic has led Chinese Vice Premier Wang Qishan to call on the U.S. government to "take all necessary measures to stabilize its economy and financial markets to ensure the security of China's assets and investments in the United States." He and other Chinese representatives have been quietly pressuring officials of the U.S. Treasury to begin providing

periodic briefings. Treasury officials have responded by setting up regular meetings with Chinese representatives.

The first of these briefings is now in progress. In attendance are both government finance ministry officials and representatives of a Chinese government investment fund called CIC. Before the Treasury official conducting the briefing has uttered two sentences, a CIC representative interrupts with a pointed question about a recent upswing in U.S. government bond sales. Halfway through the Treasury official's answer, two representatives of the Chinese finance ministry begin bombarding the Treasury official with their own related queries.

You Are There (cont.)

The Treasury official begins a PowerPoint presentation of the U.S. government's plan for funding its mounting debt obligations. Within minutes, however, it is clear that this meeting will not be short, as the Chinese officials are questioning and debating every single bullet point of the PowerPoint presentation.

Finally, one Chinese finance ministry official explains why all the Chinese officials are so upset. They were shocked, he says, that the Treasury Department actually agreed to provide them with special briefings. The Treasury officials' quick willingness to meet with them, he explains, has made the Chinese government even more concerned about the capability of the U.S. government to pay all of its debt holdings. The U.S. Treasury, he suggests, will have to offer a higher interest return to induce Chinese institutions to purchase even more of its bonds.

CRITICAL ANALYSIS QUESTIONS

1. Why do you suppose that Chinese holders of U.S. government debt are so concerned about the upswing in the U.S. Treasury's borrowing?

2. Why do you think that Chinese investors will require a higher interest return to buy more U.S. Treasury bonds?

Issues and Applications

How Much of U.S. GDP Would Be Required to Pay Off the Net Public Debt?

CONCEPTS APPLIED

➤ Net Public Debt

➤ Interest Payments on the Public Debt

➤ Burdens of the Public Debt

The inflation-adjusted value, in 2005 dollars, of the net public debt has more than doubled since 2007, from about $5 trillion to more than $10 trillion. As the net public debt has increased, so have interest payments owed on that debt, which you have learned are included in the accumulated amount of indebtedness.

As you have also learned, there are burdens associated with the net public debt. A measure of the magnitude of these burdens is the share of real GDP that would be required to pay off the inflation-adjusted net public debt. The purple bars in Figure 14-6 on page 360 show that this share—the inflation-adjusted official net public debt as a percentage of real GDP—has nearly doubled since 2007, to more than 67 percent. Yet some observers suggest that the true share would be much higher than this if government guarantees of housing-related debts were taken into account.

FIGURE 14-6

The Rapidly Expanding Ratio of the Inflation-Adjusted Net Public Debt to Real GDP

As a percentage of real GDP, the officially reported inflation-adjusted net public debt has nearly doubled since 2007, from 36 percent to close to 70 percent. The official ratio does not take into account debts of the housing-related government-sponsored enterprises—the Federal National Mortgage Association and the Federal Home Loan Mortgage Corporation. When these government-backed debts are included, the ratio rises to slightly above 90 percent.

Source: Office of Management and Budget.

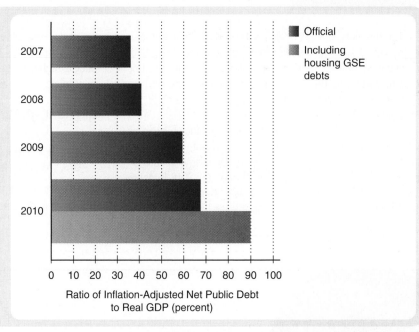

Ratio of Inflation-Adjusted Net Public Debt to Real GDP (percent)

Government IOUs Excluded from the Official Net Public Debt

Since the 1930s, the federal government has promoted home ownership. Toward this end, the federal government directly operates the Government National Mortgage Association and the Federal Housing Administration, which direct U.S. tax dollars to subsidies of mortgage loans to low-income households.

In addition, the federal government has long guaranteed the debts of two housing-related government-sponsored enterprises (GSEs), the Federal National Mortgage Association and the Federal Home Loan Mortgage Corporation. These housing GSEs raise funds from investors, which they use to purchase home mortgages from originating banks. In exchange for the investors' funds, the GSEs provide the investors with IOUs called *mortgage-backed securities*. The GSEs use funds from households' continuing payments on the home mortgages to pay interest to investors who hold the mortgage-backed securities, which are the GSEs' debts that the federal government guarantees.

Taking into Account Guaranteed Debts of the Housing GSEs

As average U.S. house prices dropped considerably between 2006 and 2010, many households found that they owed more on their mortgage loans than the houses purchased with the funds from those loans were worth. Many people stopped making payments on their mortgage loans, and as a consequence, the GSEs lacked funds to repay investors amounts owed on the GSEs' mortgage-backed securities.

Although the federal government assumed direct control of the GSEs in 2008, in the years since then the GSEs' debts have not been included as part of the official net public debt. The orange bar in Figure 14-6 shows the ratio of the inflation-adjusted net public debt to real GDP if the housing GSEs' debts guaranteed by government are taken into account. Doing so indicates that the government owes $3.5 trillion more than it officially reports, or almost another one-fourth of a year's total U.S. income from production of goods and services.

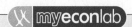

Test your understanding of this chapter by going online to **MyEconLab**.
In the Study Plan for this chapter, select Section N: News.

For Critical Analysis

1. What individuals are ultimately responsible for paying off any government-guaranteed housing debts that the government may find itself having to honor?

2. Who has actually paid for the homes funded by mortgages that GSEs purchased but on which households stopped making payments?

Web Resources

1. To learn more about the activities of the Federal National Mortgage Association and the Federal Home Loan Mortgage Corporation, go to www.econtoday.com/chapter14.

2. For historical background on the housing GSEs until just before their takeover by the federal government, go to www.econtoday.com/chapter14.

Research Project

In recent years, the federal government has taken in on average about $2.4 trillion annually in receipts from taxes and fees. If the government used its receipts *solely* to pay down today's official net public debt including indebtedness of GSEs, about how many years would be required to repay the entire amount (not including interest)? If the government pursued this strategy of paying off all of today's net public debt including GSE debts but continued to spend the current average of about $3.5 trillion per year, approximately how much more debt would accumulate in the meantime (not including interest)?

---

myeconlab

Here is what you should know after reading this chapter. **MyEconLab** will help you identify what you know, and where to go when you need to practice.

WHAT YOU SHOULD KNOW		WHERE TO GO TO PRACTICE
Federal Government Budget Deficits Whenever the flow of government expenditures exceeds the flow of government revenues during a period of time, a budget deficit occurs. If government expenditures are less than government revenues during a given interval, a budget surplus occurs. The government operates with a balanced budget during a specific period if its expenditures equal its revenues. The federal budget deficit expressed as a percentage of GDP reached about 6 percent in the early 1980s. The federal government operated with a surplus between 1998 and 2001. The government budget went into deficit once more in 2002. The deficit recently has risen to nearly 11 percent of GDP.	government budget deficit, 343 balanced budget, 343 government budget surplus, 343 public debt, 344 **KEY FIGURES** Figure 14-1, 345 Figure 14-2, 345	• **MyEconLab** Study Plans 14.1, 14.2 • Audio introduction to Chapter 14 • ABC News Video: Big Government: Who Is Going to Pay the Bill? • Animated Figures 14-1, 14-2
The Public Debt The federal budget deficit is a flow, whereas accumulated budget deficits are a stock, called the public debt. The gross public debt is the stock of total government bonds, and the net public debt is the difference between the gross public debt and the amount of government agencies' holdings of government bonds. In recent years, the net public debt as a share of GDP has exceeded 67 percent of GDP.	gross public debt, 346 net public debt, 346 **KEY FIGURE** Figure 14-3, 348	• **MyEconLab** Study Plan 14.3 • Animated Figure 14-3

(continued)

 *(continued)*

WHAT YOU SHOULD KNOW		WHERE TO GO TO PRACTICE
How the Public Debt Might Prove a Burden to Future Generations If people are taxed, they must forgo private consumption as society substitutes government goods for private goods. Thus, if future generations must be taxed at higher rates to pay for the current generation's increased consumption of governmentally provided goods, future generations may experience a burden from the public debt. Any current crowding out of investment as a consequence of additional debt accumulation can reduce capital formation and future economic growth. Furthermore, if capital invested by foreign residents who purchase some of the U.S. public debt has not been productively used, future generations will be worse off.	KEY FIGURE Figure 14-4, 352	• **MyEconLab** Study Plans 14.3, 14.4 • Animated Figure 14-4
Why the Federal Budget Deficit Might Be Incorrectly Measured Some people contend that the federal budget deficit is measured incorrectly because it combines government capital and consumption expenditures. They argue that the federal government should have an operating budget and a capital budget.		• **MyEconLab** Study Plan 14.5
The Macroeconomic Effects of Government Budget Deficits Because higher government deficits are caused by increased government spending or tax cuts, they contribute to a rise in total planned expenditures and aggregate demand. If there is a short-run recessionary gap, higher government deficits can thereby push equilibrium real GDP toward the full-employment level. If the economy is already at the full-employment level of real GDP, however, then a higher deficit creates a short-run inflationary gap.		• **MyEconLab** Study Plan 14.5
Possible Ways to Reduce the Government Budget Deficit Suggested ways to reduce the deficit are to increase taxes, particularly on the rich, and to reduce expenditures, particularly on entitlements, defined as guaranteed benefits under government programs such as Social Security and Medicare.	entitlements, 356 noncontrollable expenditures, 356 KEY FIGURE Figure 14-5, 357	• **MyEconLab** Study Plan 14.5 • Animated Figure 14-5

Log in to MyEconLab, take a chapter test, and get a personalized Study Plan that tells you which concepts you understand and which ones you need to review. From there, MyEconLab will give you further practice, tutorials, animations, videos, and guided solutions.
Log in to www.myeconlab.com

PROBLEMS

All problems are assignable in **myeconlab**. *Answers to odd-numbered problems appear at the back of the book.*

14-1. In 2011, government spending is $3.3 trillion, and taxes collected are $2.9 trillion. What is the federal government deficit in that year?

14-2. Suppose that the Office of Management and Budget provides the following estimates of federal budget receipts, federal budget spending, and GDP, all expressed in billions of dollars. Calculate the implied estimates of the federal budget deficit as a percentage of GDP for each year.

Year	Federal Budget Receipts	Federal Budget Spending	GDP
2011	2,829.8	3,382.6	15,573.2
2012	2,892.4	3,441.6	16,316.0
2013	2,964.2	3,529.3	16,852.1
2014	3,013.5	3,600.1	17,454.4

14-3. It may be argued that the effects of a higher public debt are the same as the effects of a higher deficit. Why?

14-4. What happens to the net public debt if the federal government operates next year with a:

    a. budget deficit?

    b. balanced budget?

    c. budget surplus?

14-5. What is the relationship between the gross public debt and the net public debt?

14-6. Explain how each of the following will affect the net public debt, other things being equal.

    a. Previously, the government operated with a balanced budget, but recently there has been a sudden increase in federal tax collections.

    b. The federal government had been operating with a very small annual budget deficit until three successive hurricanes hit the Atlantic Coast, and now government spending has risen substantially.

    c. The Government National Mortgage Association, a federal government agency that purchases certain types of home mortgages, buys U.S. Treasury bonds from another government agency.

14-7. Explain in your own words why there is likely to be a relationship between federal budget deficits and U.S. international trade deficits.

14-8. Suppose that the share of U.S. GDP going to domestic consumption remains constant. Initially, the federal government was operating with a balanced budget, but this year it has increased its spending well above its collections of taxes and other sources of revenues. To fund its deficit spending, the government has issued bonds. So far, very few foreign residents have shown any interest in purchasing the bonds.

    a. What must happen to induce foreign residents to buy the bonds?

    b. If foreign residents desire to purchase the bonds, what is the most important source of dollars to buy them?

14-9. Suppose that the economy is experiencing the short-run equilibrium position depicted at point *A* in the diagram below. Then the government raises its spending and thereby runs a budget deficit in an effort to boost equilibrium real GDP to its long-run equilibrium level of $15 trillion (in base-year dollars). Explain the effects of an increase in the government deficit on equilibrium real GDP and the equilibrium price level. In addition, given that many taxes and government benefits vary with real GDP, discuss what change we might

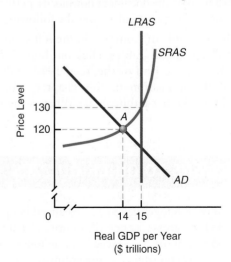

expect to see in the budget deficit as a result of the effects on equilibrium real GDP.

14-10. Suppose that the economy is experiencing the short-run equilibrium position depicted at point *B* in the diagram to the right. Explain the short-run effects of an increase in the government deficit on equilibrium real GDP and the equilibrium price level. What will be the long-run effects?

14-11. To reduce the size of the deficit (and reduce the growth of the net public debt), a politician suggests that "we should tax the rich." The politician makes a simple arithmetic calculation in which he applies the higher tax rate to the total income reported by "the rich" in a previous year. He says that this is how much the government could receive from increasing taxes on "the rich." What is the major fallacy in such calculations?

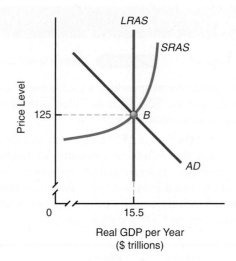

ECONOMICS ON THE NET

The Public Debt By examining the federal government's budget data, its current estimates of the public debt can be determined.

Title: Historical Tables: Budget of the United States Government

Navigation: Use the link at **www.econtoday.com/chapter14** to visit the Office of Management and Budget. Select the most recent budget. Then select *Historical Tables*.

Application After the document downloads, perform the indicated operations and answer the following questions.

1. In the Table of Contents in the left-hand margin of the Historical Tables, click on Table 7.1, "Federal Debt at the End of the Year, 1940–2009." In light of the discussion in this chapter, which column shows the net public debt? What is the conceptual difference between the gross public debt and the net public debt? Last year, what was the dollar difference between these two amounts?

2. Table 7.1 includes estimates of the gross and net public debt over the next several years. Suppose that these estimates turn out to be accurate. Calculate how much the net public debt would increase on average each year. What are possible ways that the government could prevent these predicted increases from occurring?

For Group Study and Analysis Divide into two groups, and have each group take one side in answering the question, "Is the public debt a burden or a blessing?" Have each group develop rationales for supporting its position. Then reconvene the entire class, and discuss the relative merits of the alternative positions and rationales.

ANSWERS TO QUICK QUIZZES

p. 346: (i) budget deficit . . . balanced budget . . . budget surplus; (ii) stock; (iii) surplus . . . deficit . . . deficit
p. 351: (i) gross . . . net; (ii) future . . . current . . . less . . . lower; (iii) higher
p. 355: (i) more . . . exceed . . . deficit; (ii) operating . . . capital; (iii) recessionary . . . above;
      (iv) privately . . . government
p. 358: (i) deficits; (ii) deficits . . . entitlements

Money, Banking, and Central Banking

On April 6, 2009, Federal Reserve Governor Kevin Warsh used the word that all other Federal Reserve officials had avoided using up to that point to describe the financial meltdown that had been in full swing since the middle of 2008: *panic*. The Panic of 2008 joins a long list of U.S. financial panics, including the panics of 1837, 1857, 1873, 1893, 1908, and 1929. In these and other panics throughout history, the market values of financial assets such as bonds and bank loans decrease, and banks and other financial institutions collapse. Since 1933, federal deposit insurance has helped protect the funds of those who hold deposits with banks and to limit the potential for panics to occur. Nevertheless, a panic undeniably occurred in 2008. What is the structure of the U.S. banking system, how are bank deposits insured, and what is the Federal Reserve's role? These are key questions addressed in this chapter.

LEARNING OBJECTIVES

MyEconLab helps you master each objective and study more efficiently. See end of chapter for details.

After reading this chapter, you should be able to:

➤ Define the fundamental functions of money

➤ Identify key properties that any good that functions as money must possess

➤ Explain official definitions of the quantity of money in circulation

➤ Understand why financial intermediaries such as banks exist

➤ Explain the essential features of federal deposit insurance

➤ Describe the basic structure and functions of the Federal Reserve System

DID YOU KNOW THAT many residents of the Solomon Islands, an island nation in the South Pacific, are pouring their savings into dolphin teeth? People in the Solomon Islands have used the teeth of spinner dolphins to facilitate exchanges for centuries, but in recent years the teeth have made a comeback as a type of *money* used to buy goods and services.

Solomon Islands residents are increasingly using dolphin teeth as money for three reasons. One is that in recent years tribal strife on the islands has been on the upswing, and a time-honored way to resolve personal disputes is to pay dolphin teeth as a form of compensation. A second reason is that there has been an upsurge in the population of marriageable young people, and each Solomon Islands groom traditionally provides his bride with a thousand dolphin teeth as a dowry. A third reason is that the value of the Solomon Islands' dollar, which is worth about 13 U.S. cents, is linked closely to the value of the U.S. dollar. In recent years, the value of the U.S. dollar in terms of goods and services that it can be used to purchase has declined. As a result, the amount of goods and services that a Solomon Islands dollar can buy also has decreased. In contrast, the amount of goods and services that residents can purchase with dolphin teeth has remained stable. Thus, an increasing number of residents are choosing to use dolphin teeth as a form of money alongside the Solomons Islands dollar.

Of course, nearly all U.S. residents make exchanges using coins, currency, and bank accounts from which they can transmit debit-card and check payments in order to purchase goods and services. Money has been important to society for thousands of years. In the fourth century B.C., Aristotle claimed that everything had to "be accessed in money, for this enables men always to exchange their services, and so makes society possible." Money is indeed a part of our everyday existence. Nevertheless, we have to be careful when we talk about money. Often we hear a person say, "I wish I had more money," instead of "I wish I had more wealth," thereby confusing the concepts of money and wealth. Economists use the term **money** to mean anything that people generally accept in exchange for goods and services. Table 15-1 provides a list of some items that various civilizations have used as money. The best way to understand how these items served this purpose is to examine the functions of money.

What is the main use that people have for coins such as these?

Money

Any medium that is universally accepted in an economy both by sellers of goods and services as payment for those goods and services and by creditors as payment for debts.

TABLE 15-1

Types of Money

This is a partial list of items that have been used as money. Native Americans used *wampum*, beads made from shells. Fijians used whale teeth. The early colonists in North America used tobacco. And cigarettes were used in post–World War II Germany and in Poland during the breakdown of Communist rule in the late 1980s.

Iron	Boar tusk	Playing cards
Copper	Red woodpecker scalps	Leather
Brass	Feathers	Gold
Wine	Glass	Silver
Corn	Polished beads (wampum)	Knives
Salt	Rum	Pots
Horses	Molasses	Boats
Sheep	Tobacco	Pitch
Goats	Agricultural implements	Rice
Tortoise shells	Round stones with centers removed	Cows
Porpoise teeth	Crystal salt bars	Paper
Whale teeth	Snail shells	Cigarettes

Source: Roger LeRoy Miller and David D. VanHoose, *Money, Banking, and Financial Markets,* 3rd ed. (Cincinnati: South-Western, 2007), p. 7.

The Functions of Money

Money traditionally has four functions. The one that most people are familiar with is money's function as a *medium of exchange*. Money also serves as a *unit of accounting*, a *store of value* or *purchasing power*, and a *standard of deferred payment*. Anything that serves these four functions is money. Anything that could serve these four functions could be considered money.

Money as a Medium of Exchange

When we say that money serves as a **medium of exchange,** we mean that sellers will accept it as payment in market transactions. Without some generally accepted medium of exchange, we would have to resort to *barter*. In fact, before money was used, transactions took place by means of barter. **Barter** is simply a direct exchange of goods for goods. In a barter economy, the shoemaker who wants to obtain a dozen water glasses must seek out a glassmaker who at exactly the same time is interested in obtaining a pair of shoes. For this to occur, there has to be a high likelihood of a *double coincidence of wants* for each specific item to be exchanged. If there isn't, the shoemaker must go through several trades in order to obtain the desired dozen glasses—perhaps first trading shoes for jewelry, then jewelry for some pots and pans, and then the pots and pans for the desired glasses.

Money facilitates exchange by reducing the transaction costs associated with means-of-payment uncertainty. That is, the existence of money means that individuals no longer have to hold a diverse collection of goods as an exchange inventory. As a medium of exchange, money allows individuals to specialize in producing those goods for which they have a comparative advantage and to receive money payments for their labor. Money payments can then be exchanged for the fruits of other people's labor. The use of money as a medium of exchange permits more specialization and the inherent economic efficiencies that come with it (and hence greater economic growth).

How did the recent economic downturn generate an increase in barter among small businesses?

Medium of exchange
Any item that sellers will accept as payment.

Barter
The direct exchange of goods and services for other goods and services without the use of money.

EXAMPLE
Cash-Squeezed Small Businesses Resort to Barter

In the midst of the Great Recession of the late 2000s, many small businesses found that customer payments were trickling in slowly. In addition, small businesses had difficulty obtaining loans from banks hit hard by financial troubles of their own. Consequently, a number of small firms found themselves strapped for cash.

Indeed, so many small businesses in the United States were low on cash that they resorted to bartering goods and services. For instance, a small accounting firm might provide its services to a small advertising agency in exchange for advertising services. In many cases, small businesses also allowed customers pinched for cash and behind on paying their bills to provide goods and services instead. A company with past-due bills from a sandwich shop, for example, might accept payment from the shop in the form of catered lunches. Estimates indicate that during 2008 and 2009, small U.S. companies conducted barter transactions worth nearly $25 billion.

FOR CRITICAL ANALYSIS
Why do you suppose that during the recession, many small businesses utilized the services of "barter companies" that specialize in matching parties interested in barter transactions—typically in exchange for fees paid in cash?

Money as a Unit of Accounting

Unit of accounting
A measure by which prices are expressed; the common denominator of the price system; a central property of money.

A **unit of accounting** is a way of placing a specific price on economic goods and services. It is the common denominator, the commonly recognized measure of value. The dollar is the unit of accounting in the United States. It is the yardstick that allows individuals easily to compare the relative value of goods and services. Accountants at the U.S. Department of Commerce use dollar prices to measure national income and domestic product, a business uses dollar prices to calculate profits and losses, and a typical household budgets regularly anticipated expenses using dollar prices as its unit of accounting.

Another way of describing money as a unit of accounting is to say that it serves as a *standard of value* that allows people to compare the relative worth of various goods and services. This allows for comparison shopping, for example?

Money as a Store of Value

Store of value
The ability to hold value over time; a necessary property of money.

One of the most important functions of money is that it serves as a **store of value** or purchasing power. The money you have today can be set aside to purchase things later on. In the meantime, money retains its nominal value, which you can apply to those future purchases. If you have $1,000 in your checking account, you can choose to spend it today on goods and services, spend it tomorrow, or spend it a month from now. In this way, money provides a way to transfer value (wealth) into the future.

What metallic stores of value do some people prefer over money?

INTERNATIONAL EXAMPLE
Spooked Savers Choose Precious Metals as Stores of Value over National Moneys

During the financial panic that swept the United States and Europe in 2008, many savers fretted that the U.S. dollar, the British pound, and the European euro might lose much of their future values in terms of goods and services. A number of these worried savers sought out precious metals such as gold and silver as standby stores of value. Some savers purchased precious metals indirectly by buying shares in exchange-traded funds (ETFs) that track the market value of a metal such as gold or silver. Thus, when the world price of the precious metal increases, the value of an ETF share rises in equal proportion.

Other savers opted to own a precious metal as a store of value that they could see with their own eyes and hold in their own hands, typically in the form of coins or bars offered for sale by national governments or private mints. A few savers were so eager to obtain alternative stores of value to government-issued moneys that they were willing to pay significant transportation, storage, and insurance costs to obtain these coins or bars. One resident of Idaho, for instance, paid $3,000 to have 100,000 ounces of silver transported from New York by armored truck. Thus, although some people may feel more secure holding precious metals as stores of value instead of national moneys, doing so can be a relatively costly endeavor.

FOR CRITICAL ANALYSIS
Are precious metals more or less easy to use as media of exchange than national moneys such as dollars, pounds, or euros? Explain briefly.

Money as a Standard of Deferred Payment

Standard of deferred payment
A property of an item that makes it desirable for use as a means of settling debts maturing in the future; an essential property of money.

The fourth function of the monetary unit is as a **standard of deferred payment.** This function involves the use of money both as a medium of exchange and as a unit of accounting. Debts are typically stated in terms of a unit of accounting; they are paid with a monetary medium of exchange. That is to say, a debt is specified in a dollar amount and paid in currency (or by debit card or check). A corporate bond, for example, has a face value—the dollar value stated on it, which is to be paid upon maturity. The periodic interest payments on that corporate bond are specified and paid in dollars, and when the bond comes due (at maturity), the corporation pays the face value in dollars to the holder of the bond.

Properties of Money

Money is an asset—something of value—that accounts for part of personal wealth. Wealth in the form of money can be exchanged later for other assets, goods, or services. Although money is not the only form of wealth that can be exchanged for goods and services, it is the most widely and readily accepted one.

Money—The Most Liquid Asset

Money's attribute as the most readily tradable asset is called **liquidity.** We say that an asset is *liquid* when it can easily be acquired or disposed of without high transaction costs and with relative certainty as to its value. Money is by definition the most liquid asset. People can easily convert money to other asset forms. Therefore, most individuals hold at least a part of their wealth in the form of the most liquid of assets, money. You can see how assets rank in liquidity relative to one another in Figure 15-1.

When we hold money, however, we incur a cost for this advantage of liquidity. Because cash in your pocket and many checking or debit account balances do not earn interest, that cost is the interest yield that could have been obtained had the asset been held in another form—for example, in the form of stocks and bonds.

> *The cost of holding money (its opportunity cost) is measured by the alternative interest yield obtainable by holding some other asset.*

Monetary Standards, or What Backs Money

In the past, many different monetary standards have existed. For example, commodity money, which is a physical good that may be valued for other uses it provides, has

Liquidity
The degree to which an asset can be acquired or disposed of without much danger of any intervening loss in *nominal* value and with small transaction costs. Money is the most liquid asset.

FIGURE 15-1

Degrees of Liquidity
The most liquid asset is cash. Liquidity decreases as you move from right to left.

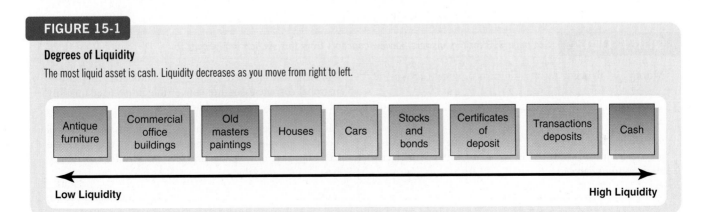

| Antique furniture | Commercial office buildings | Old masters paintings | Houses | Cars | Stocks and bonds | Certificates of deposit | Transactions deposits | Cash |

Low Liquidity ←——————————————————————————→ **High Liquidity**

Transactions deposits
Checkable and debitable account balances in commercial banks and other types of financial institutions, such as credit unions and savings banks; any accounts in financial institutions from which you can easily transmit debit-card and check payments without many restrictions.

Fiduciary monetary system
A system in which money is issued by the government and its value is based uniquely on the public's faith that the currency represents command over goods and services.

been used (see Table 15-1 on page 366). The main forms of commodity money were gold and silver. Today, though, most people throughout the world accept coins, paper currency, and balances held on deposit as **transactions deposits** (debitable and checkable accounts with banks and other financial institutions) in exchange for items sold, including labor services.

But these forms of money raise a question: Why are we willing to accept as payment something that has no intrinsic value? After all, you could not sell checks or debit cards to very many producers for use as a raw material in manufacturing. The reason is that payments in the modern world arise from a **fiduciary monetary system.** This means that the value of the payments rests on the public's confidence that such payments can be exchanged for goods and services. *Fiduciary* comes from the Latin *fiducia*, which means "trust" or "confidence." In our fiduciary monetary system, there is no legal requirement for money, in the form of currency or transactions deposits, to be convertible to a fixed quantity of gold, silver, or some other precious commodity. The bills are just pieces of paper. Usually, coins have a value stamped on them that today is greater than the market value of the metal in them. Nevertheless, currency and transactions deposits are money because of their acceptability and predictability of value.

ACCEPTABILITY Transactions deposits and currency are money because they are accepted in exchange for goods and services. They are accepted because people have confidence that these items can later be exchanged for other goods and services. This confidence is based on the knowledge that such exchanges have occurred in the past without problems.

PREDICTABILITY OF VALUE Money retains its usefulness even if its purchasing power is declining year in and year out, as in periods of inflation, if it still retains the characteristic of predictability of value. If you anticipate that the inflation rate is going to be around 3 percent during the next year, you know that any dollar you receive a year from now will have a purchasing power equal to 3 percent less than that same dollar today. Thus, you will not necessarily refuse to accept money in exchange simply because you know that its value will decline by the rate of inflation during the next year. You may, however, wish to be compensated for that *expected* decline in money's real value.

QUICK QUIZ | *See page 393 for the answers. Review concepts from this section in MyEconLab.*

Money is defined by its functions, which are as a _____ of _____, _____ of _____, _____ of _____, and _____ of _____ _____.

Money is a highly _____ asset because it can be disposed of with low transaction costs and with relative certainty as to its value.

Modern nations have _____ monetary systems—national currencies are not convertible into a fixed quantity of a commodity such as gold or silver.

Money is accepted in exchange for goods and services because people have confidence that it can later be exchanged for other goods and services. In addition, money has _____ value.

Defining Money

Money is important. Changes in the total **money supply**—the amount of money in circulation—and changes in the rate at which the money supply increases or decreases affect important economic variables, such as the rate of inflation, interest rates, and (at least in the short run) employment and the level of real GDP. Economists have struggled to reach agreement about how to define and measure money, however. There are two basic approaches: the **transactions approach,** which stresses the role of money as a medium of exchange, and the **liquidity approach,** which stresses the role of money as a temporary store of value.

The Transactions Approach to Measuring Money: M1

Using the transactions approach to measuring money, the money supply consists of currency, transactions deposits, and traveler's checks not issued by banks. One key designation of the money supply, including currency, transactions deposits, and traveler's checks not issued by banks, is **M1.** The various elements of M1 for a typical year are presented in panel (a) of Figure 15-2.

CURRENCY The largest component of U.S. currency is paper bills called Federal Reserve notes, which are designed and printed by the U.S. Bureau of Engraving and Printing. U.S. currency also consists of coins minted by the U.S. Treasury. Federal Reserve banks (to be discussed shortly) issue paper notes and coins throughout the U.S. banking system.

Money supply
The amount of money in circulation.

Transactions approach
A method of measuring the money supply by looking at money as a medium of exchange.

Liquidity approach
A method of measuring the money supply by looking at money as a temporary store of value.

M1
The money supply, measured as the total value of currency plus transactions deposits plus traveler's checks not issued by banks.

FIGURE 15-2

Composition of the U.S. M1 and M2 Money Supply, 2009

Panel (a) shows estimates of the M1 money supply, of which the largest component (over 51 percent) is currency. M2 consists of M1 plus three other components, the most important of which is savings deposits at all depository institutions.

Sources: Federal Reserve Bulletin; Economic Indicators, various issues; author's estimates.

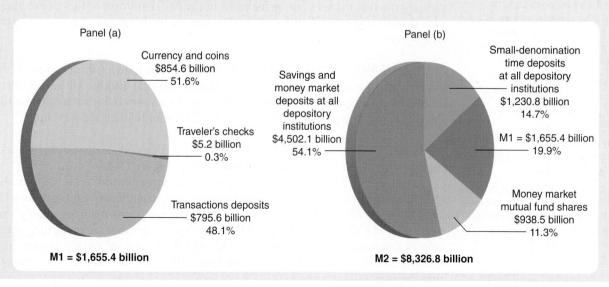

Panel (a)

Currency and coins
$854.6 billion
51.6%

Traveler's checks
$5.2 billion
0.3%

Transactions deposits
$795.6 billion
48.1%

M1 = $1,655.4 billion

Panel (b)

Savings and money market deposits at all depository institutions
$4,502.1 billion
54.1%

Small-denomination time deposits at all depository institutions
$1,230.8 billion
14.7%

M1 = $1,655.4 billion
19.9%

Money market mutual fund shares
$938.5 billion
11.3%

M2 = $8,326.8 billion

Thrift institutions

Financial institutions that receive most of their funds from the savings of the public; they include savings banks, savings and loan associations, and credit unions.

Traveler's checks

Financial instruments obtained from a bank or a nonbanking organization and signed during purchase that can be used as cash upon a second signature by the purchaser.

M2

M1 plus (1) savings and small-denomination time deposits at all depository institutions, (2) balances in retail money market mutual funds, and (3) money market deposit accounts (MMDAs).

Savings deposits

Interest-earning funds that can be withdrawn at any time without payment of a penalty.

Depository institutions

Financial institutions that accept deposits from savers and lend funds from those deposits out at interest.

Money market deposit accounts (MMDAs)

Accounts issued by banks yielding a market rate of interest with a minimum balance requirement and a limit on transactions. They have no minimum maturity.

Time deposit

A deposit in a financial institution that requires notice of intent to withdraw or must be left for an agreed period. Withdrawal of funds prior to the end of the agreed period may result in a penalty.

Certificate of deposit (CD)

A time deposit with a fixed maturity date offered by banks and other financial institutions.

Money market mutual funds

Funds that investment companies obtain from the public and are very liquid.

For Federal Reserve data concerning the latest trends in the monetary aggregates, go to **www.econtoday.com/chapter15** and click on "Money Stock Measures–H.6" under Money Stock and Reserve Balances.

TRANSACTIONS DEPOSITS Individuals transfer ownership of deposits in financial institutions by using debit cards and checks. Hence, debitable and checkable transactions deposits are normally acceptable as a medium of exchange. The financial institutions that offer transactions deposits are numerous and include commercial banks and virtually all **thrift institutions**—savings banks, savings and loan associations (S&Ls), and credit unions.

TRAVELER'S CHECKS **Traveler's checks** are paid for by the purchaser at the time of transfer. The total quantity of traveler's checks outstanding issued by institutions other than banks is part of the M1 money supply. American Express, Cook's, and other institutions issue traveler's checks.

The Liquidity Approach to Measuring Money: M2

The liquidity approach to defining and measuring the U.S. money supply views money as a temporary store of value and so includes all of M1 *plus* several other highly liquid assets. Panel (b) of Figure 15-2 above shows the components of **M2**—money as a temporary store of value.

SAVINGS DEPOSITS Total **savings deposits** in all **depository institutions** (such as commercial banks, savings banks, savings and loan associations, and credit unions) are part of the M2 money supply. A savings deposit has no set maturity.

Money market deposit accounts (MMDAs) are one popular form of savings deposit. These deposits usually require a minimum balance and set limits on the number of monthly transactions (deposits and withdrawals by check).

SMALL-DENOMINATION TIME DEPOSITS A **time deposit** requires funds to be left in a financial institution for a given period before they can be withdrawn without penalty. Time deposits include savings certificates and small **certificates of deposit (CDs).** The owner of a savings certificate is given a receipt indicating the amount deposited, the interest rate to be paid, and the maturity date. A CD is an actual certificate that indicates the date of issue, its maturity date, and other relevant contractual matters. To be included in the M2 definition of the money supply, time deposits must be less than $100,000—hence, the designation *small-denomination time deposits*.

MONEY MARKET MUTUAL FUND BALANCES Many individuals keep part of their assets in the form of shares in **money market mutual funds.** All money market mutual fund balances except those held by large institutions (which typically use them more like large time deposits) are included in M2, because they are very liquid.

M2 AND OTHER MONEY SUPPLY DEFINITIONS When all of these assets are added together, the result is M2, as shown in panel (b) of Figure 15-2.

Economists and other researchers have come up with additional definitions of money. Some businesspeople and policymakers prefer a monetary aggregate known as *MZM*. The MZM aggregate is the so-called money-at-zero-maturity money stock. Obtaining MZM entails adding to M1 those deposits without set maturities, such as savings deposits, that are included in M2. MZM includes *all* money market funds, however MZM excludes all deposits with fixed maturities, such as small-denomination time deposits.

Furthermore, President Obama and Congress have discussed adding to the Federal Reserve's functions by making it the nation's primary *systemic risk regulator*. A *systemic risk* is the potential for a financial breakdown at a large institution to spread throughout banks and other firms and thereby create a crisis such as the one experienced in recent years. Under this proposal, as the nation's systemic risk regulator, the Fed would possess authority to implement policies aimed at heading off sources of such risks before they could undermine the stability of the nation's financial system.

"MISSION CREEP" AT THE FED? A number of economists, legislators, and other policymakers have expressed reservations about both the expanded scale of the Fed's lender-of-last-resort activities and the proposal for it to regulate systemic risks. Those who question the magnitude of the Fed's last-resort lending worry that by providing so much credit to so many institutions, the Fed exerts too much control over the distribution of funds throughout the banking system and the broader economy. They contend that what Congress intended for the Fed to control is the overall money supply, not which firms are able to obtain Fed loans to keep their weakened businesses alive. By controlling flows of funds to firms that it handpicks, the critics argue, the Fed is preventing private markets from directing funds to the best managed, most creditworthy borrowers.

You Are There

To learn about a recent suggestion that the Fed should borrow to finance its operations, read **Is It Time for the Federal Reserve to Issue Its Own Bonds?** on pages 386 and 387.

Analogous concerns have caused some observers to question whether a systemic-regulator function should be added to the Fed's already long list of responsibilities. They worry that a further empowered Fed would engage in even more interventions in private markets. Systemic risks that might threaten the financial system could originate with any large companies, so ultimately the Fed could become involved in regulating parts of the economy far from the banking system. Another concern is the potential for the Fed to take on responsibilities that conflict with its primary responsibility of regulating the money supply. Indeed, a few years ago, as a professor, current Fed Chair Ben Bernanke wrote about the potential for such a conflict of interest. A Federal Reserve too heavily involved in trying to assure the success of banks and other institutions, Bernanke noted, might regulate the money supply with an aim to assist these firms and lose sight of broader economic effects. Alternatively, as a systemic regulator, the Fed might be tempted to require the institutions it regulates to engage in activities to further its monetary policy objectives even if those activities were not in those institutions' best interests.

A third concern is that the Fed might become so heavily involved in regulating so many companies that it would become ensnarled in political controversies relating to those firms. Greater exposure to associated pressures, some observers worry, could threaten the Fed's authority to conduct monetary policy independently of politics.

Why are some observers and members of Congress suggesting it may be time to restructure the Federal Reserve System?

POLICY EXAMPLE
Is the Fed Facing a Future Restructuring?

Since 2002, employment at the Washington offices of the Federal Reserve's Board of Governors has increased by 6 percent. During the same period, nonsupervisory employment at the Federal Reserve district banks has declined

POLICY EXAMPLE (cont.)

by 8 percent, as the nationwide switch from checks to debit cards has reduced their roles in clearing checks. The number of more highly paid supervisors at Federal Reserve banks has remained unchanged, however. As a consequence, annual expenses incurred by the Federal Reserve System as a whole have increased even as the volumes of services provided have declined.

This cost trend has induced critics to suggest that today the Fed must reduce its expenses in order to operate at the lowest cost to society. Perceived Fed failures during the financial melt-down of the late 2000s have also caused some to question whether the Fed is best structured for effective policymaking. Congress has taken note of these concerns. Recently, the U.S. Senate voted 96-2 in favor of a resolution calling for "an evaluation of the appropriate number and the associated costs of Federal Reserve banks."

FOR CRITICAL ANALYSIS

Why do you suppose that, in light of the structure of the Federal Open Market Committee noted in Figure 15-6 on page 382, some economists suggest that the appropriate number of Federal Reserve banks is 5 instead of 12?

QUICK QUIZ *See page 393 for the answers. Review concepts from this section in MyEconLab.*

A central bank is a banker's bank that typically acts as the _____ _____ for its nation's government as well. The central bank in the United States is the _____ _____ _____, which was established on December 13, 1913.

There are 12 Federal Reserve district banks, with 25 branches. The Federal Reserve System is managed by the _____ of _____ in Washington, D.C. The Fed interacts with virtually all depository institutions in the United States, most of which must keep a certain percentage of their transactions deposits on reserve with the Fed. The Fed serves as the chief regulatory agency for all depository institutions that have Federal Reserve System membership.

The functions of the Federal Reserve System are to supply fiduciary _____, provide payment-clearing services, hold depository institution _____, act as the government's fiscal agent, supervise depository institutions, regulate the supply of money, intervene in foreign currency markets, and act as the _____ of _____ _____.

You Are There ▶ Is It Time for the Federal Reserve to Issue Its Own Bonds?

It is March 2009. Since 2007, the Federal Reserve has embarked on a number of actions that previously fell outside its usual activities. First, in an effort to bail out banks indirectly when a number of them began to falter in 2007, the Fed began auctioning off credit to banks instead of lending to them directly. Second, as part of a plan to prevent the collapse of financial institutions deemed "too big to fail," the Fed started making special loans to these financial firms and buying some of their assets that had lost much of their market value. Third, the Fed commenced buying short-term debts of both financial and nonfinancial firms, including companies that helped finance auto loans and even firms that manufactured the autos, to help keep these firms from going bankrupt.

Now the Fed has made so many loans to faltering institutions and purchased so many assets with declining market values that it is in danger of technically going bankrupt itself. The new president of the Federal Reserve Bank of New York, William Dudley, is making his first speech. The centerpiece is a proposal aimed at allowing the Fed to continue and perhaps even expand its lending and asset-purchase activities. Dudley suggests that Congress should empower

You Are There **(cont.)**

the Fed to sell its own bonds. Allowing the Fed to issue such debts, he argues, will enable it to raise the funds required to continue its bailout activities. In addition, he contends, having the power to issue its own bonds will enable the Fed to maintain its independence from the U.S. government.

CRITICAL ANALYSIS QUESTIONS

1. In principle, the Fed could create new U.S. dollars to lend to banks and to be used to buy assets from other financial and nonfinancial firms. What would increase if the Fed were to do this?

2. If the Fed technically were to go bankrupt, it might be able to obtain funds from the U.S. Treasury to prevent the bankruptcy from actually taking place. If so, who would provide those funds?

Issues and Applications

The Federal Reserve's Role in the Panic of 2008

CONCEPTS APPLIED

- Liquidity
- Lender of Last Resort
- Federal Deposit Insurance

Like most financial panics, the 2008 financial meltdown and the troubles still haunting the U.S. banking system had their origins several years earlier. In 2006, average prices of U.S. houses began dropping. In some areas, such as large portions of California and Florida, house prices fell below the amounts people still owed to banks on mortgage loans that had financed their home purchases. Rather than continuing to make payments on the loans, many people began defaulting on their debts, leaving the houses to be seized by the banks that had originated the loans. As banks sought to sell these residences, they added to the supply of available housing, which depressed home prices further and raised pressures for people to abandon thier houses and default on mortgage loans.

Soon, a number of large banks in California and the southeastern United States that specialized in mortgage lending, such as IndyMac, Countrywide, Washington Mutual, and Wachovia, were failing. They began to experience difficulties obtaining short-term loans from other private financial institutions.

In late 2006 and early 2007, the Federal Reserve interpreted their troubles obtaining funds as what it called a "liquidity crunch." The Fed decided that in its capacity as lender of last resort, it should provide credit for some of the affected institutions. As more and more banks were unable to obtain loans in private credit markets, the Fed developed new programs for providing funds. One program that became particularly large in scope was a type of auction in which institutions could bid for funds by offering interest rates at which they were willing to borrow from the Fed. By early 2008, this auction program involved more funds than the banks previously had obtained through the private credit markets. Thus, the Fed's role in coordinating flows of funds in the banking system increased, and that of private markets declined. In effect, the Fed's funds auction program replaced private markets.

Panic Hits, and the Fed's Role Expands Even Further

By the spring of 2008, problems in the housing market had spread well beyond commercial banks, savings banks, and credit unions. So-called *investment banks* that specialized in assisting companies wishing to issue new stocks, bonds, and other securities became entangled as well. The top five U.S. investment banks—Bear Stearns, Goldman Sachs, Lehman Brothers, Merrill Lynch, and Morgan Stanley—held many securities related to real estate debts. Continuing sharp drops in housing prices caused the market values of these securities to plummet. Under powers granted by the original Federal Reserve Act, the Fed made an emergency guarantee to J.P. Morgan Chase to induce that commercial bank to buy Bear Stearns and prevent it from failing.

Then the Fed reconsidered its foray into supporting the investment banks. In September 2008, the Fed did nothing to prevent the failure of Lehman Brothers. In the wake of that failure, however, many financial institutions began refusing to lend to one another, fearing that the recipients of such loans might also fail. The Fed again interpreted this as a liquidity problem requiring it to assert its role as lender of last resort. It broadened its special funds auction program to include investment banks. It added more direct-lending mechanisms that commercial banks, savings banks, credit unions, and investment banks could utilize. By the end of the year, the Fed had expanded its lending even further. Using additional emergency powers available to it, the Fed

began buying debts of other kinds of firms, such as the auto credit provider GMAC and the insurance giant AIG. The Fed also arranged for the remaining three investment banks and other financial firms such as GMAC to be taken over by commercial banks or to become commercial banks.

Deposit Insurance Acts as the Ultimate Backstop

Admirers of the Fed's actions conclude that it staved off an even worse crisis. Critics of its actions argue that by bailing out weak banks back in 2007, the Fed signaled to other institutions that it would save them in a pinch, thereby reducing their incentives to cut back on their mortgage loans. Both admirers and critics agree on one thing, though: The Fed's actions failed to prevent the Panic of 2008, the first financial panic since 1929.

What ultimately kept the panic from wiping out many people's savings held at banking institutions was deposit insurance, not the Fed's actions. When IndyMac and Countrywide ultimately failed, long lines of depositors waited to withdraw their funds in scenes reminiscent of the bank runs of the 1930s. After seeing these long lines—and even brief episodes of violence—on TV, Congress quickly raised the minimum coverage of deposit insurance. Congress even guaranteed that the government would do anything required to support large banks, including having the U.S. Treasury oversee management of large banks such as Citibank and Bank of

America. Nevertheless, the nation continues to experience lingering banking troubles, with hundreds of banks still hovering on the edge of failure.

For Critical Analysis

1. Why do you suppose that economists have long recommended that the Fed lend only to banks facing liquidity problems rather than to those in danger of failing for other reasons?

2. Why do you think that most economists agree that deposit insurance guarantees ultimately prevented a collapse of the U.S. banking system in 2008?

Web Resources

1. To view timelines for the Panic of 2008 provided by the Federal Reserve Bank of New York, go to www.econtoday .com/chapter15.

2. To read about the actions by the Fed to assist struggling mortgage borrowers, go to www.econtoday.com/chapter15.

Research Project

Take a stand on whether the Federal Reserve's actions between 2006 and the end of 2008 helped to stabilize the banking system or instead contributed to the Panic of 2008. Support your position.

---

myeconlab   Here is what you should know after reading this chapter. **MyEconLab** will help you identify what you know, and where to go when you need to practice.

WHAT YOU SHOULD KNOW		WHERE TO GO TO PRACTICE
The Key Functions of Money Money is a medium of exchange that people use to make payments for goods, services, and financial assets. It is also a unit of accounting for quoting prices in terms of money values. In addition, money is a store of value, so people can hold money for future use in exchange. Finally, money is a standard of deferred payment, enabling lenders to make loans and buyers to repay those loans with money.	money, 366 medium of exchange, 367 barter, 367 unit of accounting, 368 store of value, 368 standard of deferred payment, 368	• **MyEconLab** Study Plan 15.1 • Audio introduction to Chapter 15 • Video: The Functions of Money
Important Properties of Goods That Serve as Money A good will successfully function as money only if people are widely willing to accept the good in exchange for other goods and services. People must have confidence that others will be willing to trade their goods and services for the good used as money. In addition, though people may continue to use money even if inflation erodes its real purchasing power, they will do so only if the value of money is relatively predictable.	liquidity, 369 transactions deposits, 370 fiduciary monetary system, 370 KEY FIGURE Figure 15-1, 369	• **MyEconLab** Study Plan 15.2 • Video: Monetary Standards, or What Backs Money • Animated Figure 15-1

(continued)

 *(continued)*

WHAT YOU SHOULD KNOW		WHERE TO GO TO PRACTICE
Official Definitions of the Quantity of Money in Circulation The narrow definition of the quantity of money in circulation, called M1, focuses on money's role as a medium of exchange. It includes only currency, transactions deposits, and traveler's checks. A broader definition, called M2, stresses money's role as a temporary store of value. M2 is equal to M1 plus other highly liquid assets such as savings deposits, small-denomination time deposits, money market deposit accounts, and noninstitutional holdings of money market mutual fund balances.	money supply, 371 transactions approach, 371 liquidity approach, 371 M1, 371 thrift institutions, 372 traveler's checks, 372 M2, 372 savings deposits, 372 depository institutions, 372 money market deposit accounts (MMDAs), 372 time deposit, 372 certificate of deposit (CD), 372 money market mutual funds, 372	• **MyEconLab** Study Plan 15.3
Why Financial Intermediaries Such as Banks Exist Financial intermediaries help reduce problems stemming from the existence of asymmetric information in financial transactions. Asymmetric information can lead to adverse selection, in which uncreditworthy individuals and firms seek loans, and moral hazard problems, in which an individual or business that has been granted credit begins to engage in riskier practices. Financial intermediaries may also permit savers to benefit from economies of scale, which is the ability to reduce the costs and risks of managing funds by pooling funds and spreading costs and risks across many savers.	central bank, 373 financial intermediation, 373 financial intermediaries, 373 asymmetric information, 373 adverse selection, 373 moral hazard, 374 liabilities, 375 assets, 375 payment intermediaries, 376 **KEY FIGURES** Figure 15-3, 374 Figure 15-4, 376	• **MyEconLab** Study Plan 15.4 • Animated Figures 15-3, 15-4
Features of Federal Deposit Insurance To help prevent runs on banks, the U.S. government in 1933 established the Federal Deposit Insurance Corporation (FDIC). This agency charges some depository institutions premiums, and it places these funds in accounts for use in reimbursing failed banks' depositors. Deposit insurance creates an adverse selection problem because its availability can attract risk-taking individuals into banking. A moral hazard problem also exists when deposit insurance premiums fail to reflect the full extent of the risks taken on by bank managers and when depositors have little incentive to monitor the performance of the institutions that hold their deposit funds.	Federal Deposit Insurance Corporation (FDIC), 378 bank runs, 378	• **MyEconLab** Study Plan 15.5 • Video: Deposit Insurance and Risk Taking

 *(continued)*

WHAT YOU SHOULD KNOW		WHERE TO GO TO PRACTICE

The Basic Structure and Functions of the Federal Reserve System The Federal Reserve System consists of 12 district banks. The governing body of the Fed is the Board of Governors. Decisions about the quantity of money in circulation are made by the Federal Open Market Committee, which is composed of the Board of Governors and five Federal Reserve bank presidents. The Fed's main functions are supplying fiduciary currency, clearing payments, holding banks' reserves, acting as the government's fiscal agent, supervising banks, acting as a lender of last resort, regulating the money supply, and intervening in foreign exchange markets.

The Fed, 381
lender of last resort, 385
KEY FIGURE
Figure 15-7, 384

- **MyEconLab** Study Plan 15.6
- Animated Figure 15-7
- Video: The Federal Reserve System

Log in to MyEconLab, take a chapter test, and get a personalized Study Plan that tells you which concepts you understand and which ones you need to review. From there, MyEconLab will give you further practice, tutorials, animations, videos, and guided solutions.
Log in to www.myeconlab.com

PROBLEMS

All problems are assignable in  *. Answers to odd-numbered problems appear at the back of the book.*

15-1. Until 1946, residents of the island of Yap used large doughnut-shaped stones as financial assets. Although prices of goods and services were not quoted in terms of the stones, the stones were often used in exchange for particularly large purchases, such as payments for livestock. To make the transaction, several individuals would insert a large stick through a stone's center and carry it to its new owner. A stone was difficult for any one person to steal, so an owner typically would lean it against the side of his or her home as a sign to others of accumulated purchasing power that would hold value for later use in exchange. Loans would often be repaid using the stones. In what ways did these stones function as money?

15-2. During the late 1970s, prices quoted in terms of the Israeli currency, the shekel, rose so fast that grocery stores listed their prices in terms of the U.S. dollar and provided customers with dollar-shekel conversion tables that they updated daily.

Although people continued to buy goods and services and make loans using shekels, many Israeli citizens converted shekels to dollars to avoid a reduction in their wealth due to inflation. In what way did the U.S. dollar function as money in Israel during this period?

15-3. During the 1945–1946 Hungarian hyperinflation, when the rate of inflation reached 41.9 *quadrillion* percent per month, the Hungarian government discovered that the real value of its tax receipts was falling dramatically. To keep real tax revenues more stable, it created a good called a "tax pengö," in which all bank deposits were denominated for purposes of taxation. Nevertheless, payments for goods and services were made only in terms of the regular Hungarian currency, whose value tended to fall rapidly even though the value of a tax pengö remained stable. Prices were also quoted only in terms of the regular currency. Lenders, however, began denominating loan payments in terms of tax pengös. In what ways did the tax pengö function as money in Hungary in 1945 and 1946?

15-4. Considering the following data (expressed in billions of U.S. dollars), calculate M1 and M2.

Currency	850
Savings deposits and money market deposit accounts	3,500
Small-denomination time deposits	2,000
Traveler's checks outside banks and thrifts	10
Total money market mutual funds	1,300
Institution-only money market mutual funds	200
Transactions deposits	940

15-5. Considering the following data (expressed in billions of U.S. dollars), calculate M1 and M2.

Transactions deposits	825
Savings deposits	2,300
Small-denomination time deposits	1,450
Money market deposit accounts	1,950
Noninstitution money market mutual funds	1,900
Traveler's checks outside banks and thrifts	25
Currency	850
Institution-only money market mutual funds	250

15-6. Identify whether each of the following items is counted in M1 only, M2 only, both M1 and M2, or neither:

a. A $1,000 balance in a transactions deposit at a mutual savings bank

b. A $100,000 certificate of deposit issued by a New York bank

c. A $10,000 time deposit an elderly widow holds at her credit union

d. A $50 traveler's check not issued by a bank

e. A $50,000 money market deposit account balance

15-7. Identify whether each of the following amounts is counted in M1 only, M2 only, both M1 and M2, or neither:

a. $50 billion in U.S. Treasury bills

b. $15 billion in small-denomination time deposits

c. $5 billion in traveler's checks not issued by a bank

d. $20 billion in money market deposit accounts

15-8. Indicate which of the following items are counted in M2 but not in M1.

a. A $20 Federal Reserve note

b. A $500 time deposit

c. A $50 traveler's check not issued by a bank

d. A $25,000 money market deposit account

15-8. Match each of the rationales for financial intermediation listed below with at least one of the following financial intermediaries: insurance company, pension fund, savings bank. Explain your choices.

a. Adverse selection

b. Moral hazard

c. Lower management costs generated by larger scale

15-10. Match each of the rationales for financial intermediation listed below with at least one of the following financial intermediaries: commercial bank, money market mutual fund, stockbroker. Explain your choices.

a. Adverse selection

b. Moral hazard

c. Lower management costs generated by larger scale

15-11. Identify whether each of the following events poses an adverse selection problem or a moral hazard problem in financial markets.

a. A manager of a savings and loan association responds to reports of a likely increase in federal deposit insurance coverage. She directs loan officers to extend mortgage loans to less creditworthy borrowers.

b. A loan applicant does not mention that a legal judgment in his divorce case will require him to make alimony payments to his ex-wife.

c. An individual who was recently approved for a loan to start a new business decides to use some of the funds to take a Hawaiian vacation.

15-12. Identify whether each of the following events poses an adverse selection problem or a moral hazard problem in financial markets.

a. An individual with several children who has just learned that she has lung cancer applies for life insurance but fails to report this recent medical diagnosis.

b. A corporation that recently obtained a loan from several banks to finance installation of a new computer network instead directs some of the funds to executive bonuses.

c. A state-chartered financial institution exempt from laws requiring it to have federal deposit insurance decides to apply for deposit insurance after experiencing severe financial problems that may bankrupt the institution.

15-13. In what sense is currency a liability of the Federal Reserve System?

15-14. In what respects is the Fed like a private banking institution? In what respects is it more like a government agency?

15-15. Take a look at the map of the locations of the Federal Reserve districts and their headquarters in Figure 15-7 on page 384. Today, the U.S. population is centered just west of the Mississippi River—that is, about half of the population is either to the west or the east of a line running roughly just west of this river. Can you reconcile the current locations of Fed districts and banks with this fact? Why do you suppose the Fed has its current geographic structure?

ECONOMICS ON THE NET

What's Happened to the Money Supply? Deposits at banks and other financial institutions make up a portion of the U.S. money supply. This exercise gives you the chance to see how changes in these deposits influence the Fed's measures of money.

Title: FRED (Federal Reserve Economic Data)

Navigation: Go to **www.econtoday.com/chapter15** to visit the Web page of the Federal Reserve Bank of St. Louis.

Application

1. Select the data series for Demand Deposits at Commercial Banks (Bil. of $; M), either seasonally adjusted or not. Scan through the data. Do you notice any recent trend? (Hint: Compare the growth in the figures before 1993 with their growth after 1993.) In addition, take a look at the data series for currency and for other transactions

deposits. Do you observe similar recent trends in these series?

2. Back up, and click on *M1 Money Stock (Bil. of $; M)*, again, either seasonally adjusted or not. Does it show any change in pattern beginning around 1993?

For Group Study and Analysis FRED contains considerable financial data series. Assign individual members or groups of the class the task of examining data on assets included in M1, M2, and MZM. Have each student or group look for big swings in the data. Then ask the groups to report to the class as a whole. When did clear changes occur in various categories of the monetary aggregates? Were there times when people appeared to shift funds from one aggregate to another? Are there any other noticeable patterns that may have had something to do with economic events during various periods?

ANSWERS TO QUICK QUIZZES

p. 370: (i) medium of exchange . . . unit of accounting . . . store of value . . . standard of deferred payment; (ii) liquid; (iii) fiduciary; (iv) predictable

p. 373: (i) transactions . . . M1; (ii) Transactions; (iii) M1 . . . M2

p. 377: (i) Financial . . . payment; (ii) asymmetric . . . adverse selection . . . moral hazard

p. 380: (i) Federal Deposit Insurance Corporation; (ii) less . . . riskier . . . higher; (iii) moral . . . premiums . . . moral

p. 386: (i) fiscal agent . . . Federal Reserve System; (ii) Board . . . Governors; (iii) currency . . . reserves . . . lender of last resort

16

Money Creation, the Demand for Money, and Monetary Policy

I n the weeks and months prior to October 2008, all U.S. banks together typically held about $2 billion in reserves over and above those that they were required to hold by the Federal Reserve System. Since October 2008, however, banks' holdings of reserves in excess of those they are required to hold have jumped to an average of more than $800 billion. How does the Federal Reserve implement its requirement for banks to hold reserves? Why have banks' holdings of excess reserves increased so much? What difference does it make whether banks hold $2 billion in additional reserves or in excess of $800 billion? In this chapter, you will learn the answers to these questions.

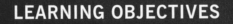

LEARNING OBJECTIVES

After reading this chapter, you should be able to:

- Describe how the Federal Reserve assesses reserve requirements on banks and other depository institutions
- Understand why the money supply is unaffected when someone deposits in a depository institution funds transferred from a transactions account at another depository institution
- Explain why the money supply changes when someone deposits in a depository institution funds transferred from the Federal Reserve System
- Determine the maximum potential extent to which the money supply will change following a Federal Reserve monetary policy action
- Identify the key factors that influence the quantity of money that people desire to hold
- Describe how Federal Reserve monetary policy actions influence market interest rates

? DID YOU KNOW THAT during the latter half of 2008, when banking institutions such as IndyMac and Washington Mutual were failing and several other banks appeared on the verge of collapse, many U.S. residents shifted deposits among banks? People with deposits in troubled banks moved their funds to banks that they regarded as safe. Thus, Wachovia, a bank that was near failure before being purchased by Wells Fargo, lost several billion dollars of deposits and responded by cutting back on its lending. In contrast, J.P. Morgan Chase, which may have weathered the financial crisis better than any other large U.S. bank, received more than $10 billion of new deposits and expanded its lending. After all of the deposit reshufflings, however, the quantity of money in circulation was almost unchanged.

Thus, new deposits funding new loans at some banks generated by funds shifted from deposits at other banks that contracted their loans left the money supply unaltered. As any banker will tell you, *by itself* no individual bank can create money. But through actions initiated by a central bank such as the Federal Reserve, depository institutions *together* do create money by adding to the quantity of checkable and debitable deposits. In this chapter, you will learn how policy actions such as Fed purchases of U.S. government bonds and lending to private banks influence the money supply. You will also learn about the money multiplier process, which explains how a Fed injection of funds into the banking system leads to an eventual multiple expansion of the total money supply. Finally, you will learn how the policy actions of central banks influence interest rates.

Banks and Money

As early as 1000 B.C., uncoined gold and silver were being used as money in Mesopotamia. Goldsmiths weighed and assessed the purity of those metals; later they started issuing paper notes indicating that the bearers held gold or silver of given weights and purity on deposit with the goldsmith. These notes could be transferred in exchange for goods and became the first paper currency. The gold and silver on deposit with the goldsmiths were the first bank deposits. Eventually, goldsmiths realized that inflows of gold and silver for deposit always exceeded the average amount of gold and silver withdrawn at any given time—often by a predictable ratio. These goldsmiths started making loans by issuing to borrowers paper notes that exceeded in value the amount of gold and silver the goldsmiths actually kept on hand. They charged interest on these loans. This constituted the earliest form of what is now called **fractional reserve banking.** We know that goldsmiths operated this way in Delphi, Didyma, and Olympia in Greece as early as the seventh century B.C. In Athens, fractional reserve banking was well developed by the sixth century B.C.

Fractional reserve banking
A system in which depository institutions hold reserves that are less than the amount of total deposits.

Why is fractional reserve banking in Germany increasingly connected to the auto industry?

INTERNATIONAL EXAMPLE
In Germany, Fractional Reserve Banking Moves to the Auto Showroom

Even as auto sales slumped in Germany in 2008 and 2009, savers began withdrawing funds from traditional depository institutions and placing them on deposit with the banking arms of auto manufacturers. Between November 2008 and March 2009, for instance, deposits at Volkswagen's banking subsidiary increased by more than 70 percent, and deposits at Mercedes-Benz Bank increased by more than 100 percent. The automakers promptly funneled the portion of deposits not held as reserves into financing the sale and leasing of new vehicles to consumers.

German savers had two incentives for shifting funds to the auto manufacturers' financial subsidiaries. One was that the German government had guaranteed deposits at all banks, thereby making deposits at the automakers' banks as safe as any others. The other was that the German government gave special subsidies to auto manufacturers, which used some of

these funds to offer higher rates of interest on deposits than the rates offered by traditional institutions.

FOR CRITICAL ANALYSIS
Is fractional reserve banking by the financial subsidiary of a German auto manufacturer conceptually any different from fractional reserve banking by a traditional depository institution? Explain your answer.

Depository Institution Reserves

In a fractional reserve banking system, banks do not keep sufficient reserves on hand to cover 100 percent of their depositors' accounts. And the reserves that are held by depository institutions in the United States are not kept in gold and silver, as they were with the early goldsmiths, but rather in the form of deposits on reserve with Federal Reserve district banks and in vault cash. Depository institutions are required by the Fed to maintain a specified percentage of certain customer deposits as **reserves** either in the form of deposits at Federal Reserve banks or as vault cash. There are two types of reserves: required reserves and excess reserves.

Required Reserves

Required reserves are the minimum amount of reserves that a depository institution (which, for simplicity, we shall assume to be a commercial bank) must have to "back" transactions deposits. They are calculated as a ratio of required reserves to total transactions deposits (banks need hold no reserves on nontransactions deposits such as savings accounts). The **required reserve ratio** for almost all transactions deposits is 10 percent (except for about the first $50 million in deposits at any depository institution, which is subject to only a 3 percent requirement). The general formula is

$$\text{Required reserves} = \text{transactions deposits} \times \text{required reserve ratio}$$

Take a hypothetical example. If the required reserve ratio is 10 percent and the bank has $1 billion in customer transactions deposits, it must hold at least $100 million as reserves. As we shall discuss later in this chapter, during the 1990s, banks discovered a novel way to reduce the amounts of reserves that they are required to hold.

Excess Reserves

Depository institutions often hold reserves in excess of what is required by the Fed. This difference between actual reserves and required reserves is called **excess reserves.** (Excess reserves can be negative, but they rarely are. Negative excess reserves indicate that depository institutions do not have sufficient reserves to meet their required reserves. When this happens, they borrow from other depository institutions or from a Federal Reserve district bank, sell assets such as securities including Treasury bills, or call in loans.) Excess reserves are an important potential determinant of the money supply, for as we shall see, it is only to the extent that depository institutions

---

Reserves
In the U.S. Federal Reserve System, deposits held by Federal Reserve district banks for depository institutions, plus depository institutions' vault cash.

Required reserves
The value of reserves that a depository institution must hold in the form of vault cash or deposits with the Fed.

Required reserve ratio
The percentage of total transactions deposits that the Fed requires depository institutions to hold in the form of vault cash or deposits with the Fed.

Excess reserves
The difference between actual reserves and required reserves.

Go to www.econtoday.com/chapter16 to see Federal Reserve reports on the current amounts of required and excess reserves at U.S. depository institutions.

have excess reserves that they can make new loans. Because reserves produce little income, profit-seeking financial institutions have an incentive to minimize excess reserves, disposing of them either to purchase income-producing securities or to make loans with which they earn income through interest payments received.

In the analysis that follows, we examine the relationship between the total level of reserves and the size of the money supply. This analysis implies that factors influencing the level of the reserves of the banking system as a whole will ultimately affect the size of the money supply, other things held constant. We show first that when someone deposits in one depository institution funds transmitted by debit card or check from an account at another depository institution, the two depository institutions involved are individually affected, but the overall money supply does not change. Then we show that when someone deposits in a depository institution funds transmitted from the Fed, a multiple expansion in the money supply results.

Ours is a **fractional reserve banking** system in which depository institutions must hold only a _____ of their deposits as reserves, either on deposit with a Federal Reserve district bank or as _____ cash.

Required reserves are usually expressed as a _____, in percentage terms, of required reserves to total transactions deposits.

The Relationship Between Total Reserves and Total Deposits

To show the relationship between reserves and bank deposits, we first analyze a single bank (existing alongside many others). A single bank is able to make new loans only to the extent that it has reserves above the level legally required to cover the new deposits. When an individual bank has no excess reserves, it cannot make loans.

How a Single Bank Reacts to an Increase in Reserves

To examine the **balance sheet** of a single bank after its reserves are increased, let's make the following assumptions:

1. The required reserve ratio is 10 percent for all transactions deposits.
2. Transactions deposits are the bank's only liabilities; reserves at a Federal Reserve district bank and loans are the bank's only assets. Loans are customer IOUs and, as such, are assets to the bank.
3. An individual bank can lend as much as it is legally allowed.
4. Every time a loan is made to a borrower, all the proceeds from the loan are put into a transactions deposit account; no cash (currency or coins) is withdrawn.

You Are There

To contemplate how changes in bank procedures for accepting deposits of checks are yielding significant benefits to small businesses, read **Scanning Checks Benefits a Bank's Small-Business Customer,** on page 415.

Balance sheet
A statement of the assets and liabilities of any business entity, including financial institutions and the Federal Reserve System. Assets are what is owned; liabilities are what is owed.

5. Profit-seeking depository institutions seek to keep zero excess reserves because reserves do not earn interest.

Net worth
The difference between assets and liabilities.

6. Depository institutions have zero **net worth.** (In reality, all depository institutions are required to have some positive owners' equity, or capital. It is usually a small percentage of the institutions' total assets.)

Look at the simplified initial position of Typical Bank in Balance Sheet 16-1. Liabilities consist of $1 million in transactions deposits. Assets consist of $100,000 in reserves and $900,000 in loans to customers. Total assets of $1 million equal total liabilities of $1 million. With a 10 percent reserve requirement and $1 million in transactions deposits, the bank has required reserves of $100,000 and therefore no excess reserves.

BALANCE SHEET 16-1

Typical Bank

Assets			Liabilities	
Total reserves		$100,000	Transactions deposits	$1,000,000
Required reserves	$100,000			
Excess reserves	0			
Loans		900,000		
Total		$1,000,000	Total	$1,000,000

Assume that a depositor deposits in Typical Bank a $100,000 debit-card payment drawn on a transactions account at another depository institution. Transactions deposits in Typical Bank immediately increase by $100,000, bringing the total to $1.1 million. After the debit-card transaction is finalized, total reserves of Typical Bank increase to $200,000. A $1.1 million total in transactions deposits means that required reserves will have to be 10 percent of $1.1 million, or $110,000. Typical Bank now has excess reserves equal to $200,000 minus $110,000, or $90,000. This is shown in Balance Sheet 16-2.

BALANCE SHEET 16-2

Typical Bank

Assets			Liabilities	
Total reserves		$200,000	Transactions deposits	$1,100,000
Required reserves	$110,000			
Excess reserves	90,000			
Loans		900,000		
Total		$1,100,000	Total	$1,100,000

Effect on Typical Bank's Balance Sheet

Look at excess reserves in Balance Sheet 16-2. Excess reserves were zero before the $100,000 deposit, and now they are $90,000—that's $90,000 worth of assets not earning any income. By assumption, Typical Bank will now lend out this entire $90,000 in excess reserves. Loans will increase to $990,000. The borrowers who receive the new loans will not leave them on deposit in Typical Bank. As they spend the funds by making debit-card and check transfers that are deposited in other banks, actual reserves will fall to $110,000 (as required), and excess reserves will again become zero, as indicated in Balance Sheet 16-3.

BALANCE SHEET 16-3	Assets		Liabilities	
Typical Bank				
	Total reserves	$110,000	Transactions deposits	$1,100,000
	Required reserves $110,000			
	Excess reserves 0			
	Loans	990,000		
	Total	$1,100,000	Total	$1,100,000

In this example, a person transmitted a $100,000 debit-card payment from an account at another bank. That $100,000 became part of Typical Bank's reserves. Because the deposit created excess reserves in Typical Bank, it could make new interest-earning loans. A bank will not lend more than its excess reserves because, by law, it must hold a certain amount of required reserves.

Effect on the Money Supply

A look at the balance sheets for Typical Bank might give the impression that the money supply increased because of the new customer's $100,000 deposit. Remember, though, that the deposit resulted from a debit-card transfer from *another* bank. Therefore, the other bank suffered a *decline* in its transactions deposits and its reserves. While total assets and liabilities in Typical Bank have increased by $100,000, they have *decreased* in the other bank by $100,000. The total amount of money and credit is unaffected by transfers from one depository institution to another.

The thing to remember is that new reserves for the banking system as a whole are not created when debit-card or check payments transferred from one bank are deposited in another bank. The Federal Reserve System can, however, create new reserves; that is the subject of the next section.

Why do some airplane pilots stand to lose from rapid decreases in the physical clearing of paper checks by the Federal Reserve and private banks?

EXAMPLE
Why the Decline in Clearing of Paper Checks Is Bad News for Airplane Pilots

The number of transactions deposit payments initiated via debit cards surpassed the number of check transfers a few years back. In a few years, checks likely will account for only one-third of all such transfers. Furthermore, the share of checks cleared physically has fallen as banks now transmit digital images of checks electronically rather than clearing physical checks.

The rapid reduction in the rate at which paper checks are physically cleared has affected everyone involved in this process, including airplane pilots. Until recently, the Federal Reserve used a fleet of 47 Lear jets and small cargo planes to transport checks cleared by Federal Reserve banks. In addition, clearinghouses operated by private banks used to contract with private air couriers to ship checks. Today, the

---

EXAMPLE (cont.)

Fed has sold off the bulk of its air fleet, and large banks have drastically cut back on contracted air freight services. Of course, pilots continue to fly planes transporting other forms of air freight. Nevertheless, there has been a decline in the demand for their services.

FOR CRITICAL ANALYSIS
What types of jobs do you suppose will experience increases in demand as a result of the expansion of electronic payment networks? (Hint: What types of jobs relate to electronic networks?)

QUICK QUIZ See page 421 for the answers. Review concepts from this section in MyEconLab.

If funds are transferred from a transactions deposit account at one depository institution and deposited in another, there is _____ _____ in total deposits or in the total money supply.

_____ additional reserves in the banking system are created following a transfer of funds between transactions deposit accounts at two depository institutions.

Money Expansion by the Banking System

Now let's shift our focus from a single bank and consider the entire banking system. For practical purposes, we can look at all depository institutions taken as a whole. To understand how money is created, we must understand how depository institutions respond to Fed actions that increase reserves in the entire system.

Federal Open Market Committee

The decisions that essentially determine the level of reserves in the monetary system are made by the Fed's Federal Open Market Committee (FOMC). The mechanism through which it works is open market operations. **Open market operations** are FOMC-directed Fed purchases and sales of existing U.S. government securities in the open market, which is the private secondary U.S. securities market in which people exchange government securities that have not yet matured. If the FOMC decides that the Fed should buy or sell bonds, it instructs the New York Federal Reserve Bank's Trading Desk to do so.

Open market operations
The purchase and sale of existing U.S. government securities (such as bonds) in the open private market by the Federal Reserve System.

Fed Purchases of U.S. Government Securities

Assume that the Fed's Trading Desk purchases a $100,000 U.S. government security from a bond dealer. The Trading Desk electronically transfers $100,000 to the bond dealer's transactions deposit account at Bank 1, which prior to this transaction is in the position depicted in Balance Sheet 16-4.

BALANCE SHEET 16-4

Bank 1

This shows Bank 1's original position before the Federal Reserve's purchase of a $100,000 U.S. government security.

Assets			Liabilities	
Total reserves		$100,000	Transactions deposits	$1,000,000
Required reserves	$100,000			
Excess reserves	0			
Loans		900,000		
Total		$1,000,000	Total	$1,000,000

Now look at the balance sheet for Bank 1 shown in Balance Sheet 16-5. Transactions deposits have been increased by $100,000, and total reserves have also increased by $100,000, to $200,000.

Thus, the Fed has created $100,000 of reserves. The Fed can create reserves because whenever it buys U.S. securities, it adds to the reserve accounts of depository institutions. When the Fed buys a U.S. government security in the open market, total reserves initially expand by the amount of the purchase.

BALANCE SHEET 16-5	Assets			Liabilities	
Bank 1	Total reserves		$200,000	Transactions deposits	$1,100,000
	Required reserves	$110,000			
	Excess reserves	90,000			
	Loans		900,000		
	Total		$1,100,000	Total	$1,100,000

EFFECT ON THE MONEY SUPPLY   The Fed's purchase of a $100,000 U.S. government security from a bond dealer increases the money supply immediately by $100,000 because transactions deposits held by the public—bond dealers are members of the public—are part of the money supply, and no other bank has lost deposits.

The process of money creation does not stop here. Look again at Balance Sheet 16-5. Because required reserves on $1.1 million of transactions deposits are only $110,000, Bank 1 has excess reserves of $90,000. No other depository institution (or combination of depository institutions) has negative excess reserves of $90,000 as a result of the Fed's bond purchase. (Remember, the Fed simply *created* the reserves to pay for the bond purchase.)

Bank 1 will not wish to hold non-interest-bearing excess reserves. Assume that it will expand its loans by $90,000. This is shown in Balance Sheet 16-6.

BALANCE SHEET 16-6	Assets			Liabilities	
Bank 1	Total reserves		$110,000	Transactions deposits	$1,100,000
	Required reserves	$110,000			
	Excess reserves	0			
	Loans		990,000		
	Total		$1,100,000	Total	$1,100,000

The borrower who receives the $90,000 loan will spend these funds, which will then be deposited in other banks. For simplicity, concentrate only on the balance sheet *changes* resulting from this new deposit, shown in Balance Sheet 16-7 (p. 402).

BALANCE SHEET 16-7	Assets		Liabilities	
Bank 2 (Changes Only)	Total reserves	+$90,000	New transactions deposits	+$90,000
	Required reserves +$9,000			
	Excess reserves +$81,000			
	Total	+$90,000	Total	+$90,000

For Bank 2, the $90,000 deposit becomes an increase in reserves as well as an increase in transactions deposits and hence the money supply. Because the reserve requirement is 10 percent, required reserves increase by $9,000, so Bank 2 will have excess reserves of $81,000. Bank 2 will reduce these excess reserves to zero by making a loan of $81,000 (which will earn interest income). This is shown in Balance Sheet 16-8.

BALANCE SHEET 16-8	Assets		Liabilities	
Bank 2 (Changes Only)	Total reserves	+$9,000	Transactions deposits	+$90,000
	Required reserves +$9,000			
	Excess reserves 0			
	Loans	+$81,000		
	Total	+$90,000	Total	+$90,000

Remember that in this example, the original $100,000 deposit was transmitted electronically by the Fed to the bond dealer's transactions deposit account. That $100,000 constituted an immediate increase in the money supply of $100,000. The deposit creation process (in addition to the original $100,000) occurs because of the fractional reserve banking system, coupled with depository institutions' desire to minimize excess reserves. Under fractional reserve banking, banks must hold only a portion of new deposits as required reserves, and in their quest to earn profits, they seek to transform excess reserves into holdings of loans and securities.

CONTINUATION OF THE DEPOSIT CREATION PROCESS Look at Bank 3's account in Balance Sheet 16-9, which again shows only *changes* in the assets and liabilities. Assume that the firm borrowing $81,000 from Bank 2 spends these funds, which are deposited in Bank 3. Transactions deposits and the money supply increase by $81,000. Total reserves of Bank 3 rise by that amount when the payment transfer occurs.

BALANCE SHEET 16-9	Assets		Liabilities	
Bank 3 (Changes Only)	Total reserves	+$81,000	New transactions deposits	+$81,000
	Required reserves +$8,100			
	Excess reserves +$72,900			
	Total	+$81,000	Total	+$81,000

Because the reserve requirement is 10 percent, required reserves rise by $8,100, and excess reserves therefore increase by $72,900. We assume that Bank 3 will want to lend all of those non-interest-earning assets (excess reserves). When it does, loans (and newly created transactions deposits) will increase by $72,900. This bank's total reserves will fall to $8,100, and excess reserves become zero as debit-card or check payments are transferred from the new deposit. This is shown in Balance Sheet 16-10.

BALANCE SHEET 16-10	Assets		Liabilities	
Bank 3 (Changes Only)	Total reserves	+$8,100	New transactions deposits	+$81,000
	Required reserves +$8,100			
	Excess reserves 0			
	Loans	+$72,900		
	Total	+$81,000	Total	+$81,000

PROGRESSION TO OTHER BANKS This process continues to Banks 4, 5, 6, and so forth. Each bank obtains smaller and smaller increases in deposits because 10 percent of each deposit must be held in required reserves. Thus, each succeeding depository institution makes correspondingly smaller loans. Table 16-1 shows new deposits, required reserves, and possible loans for the remaining depository institutions.

EFFECT ON TOTAL DEPOSITS In this example, deposits (and the money supply) increased initially by the $100,000 that the Fed paid the bond dealer in exchange for a bond. Deposits (and the money supply) were further increased by a $90,000 deposit in Bank 2, and they were again increased by an $81,000 deposit in Bank 3. Eventually, total deposits and the money supply will increase by $1 million, as shown in Table 16-1. The $1 million consists of the original $100,000 created by the Fed, plus an extra $900,000 generated by deposit-creating bank loans. The deposit creation process is portrayed graphically in Figure 16-1 on the next page.

TABLE 16-1

Maximum Money Creation with 10 Percent Required Reserves

This table shows the maximum new loans plus investments that banks can make, given the Fed's electronic transfer of $100,000 to a transactions deposit account at Bank 1. The required reserve ratio is 10 percent. We assume that all excess reserves in each bank are used for new loans or investments.

Bank	New Deposits	New Required Reserves	Maximum New Loans
1	$100,000 (from Fed)	$10,000	$90,000
2	90,000	9,000	81,000
3	81,000	8,100	72,900
4	72,900	7,290	65,610
.	.	.	.
.	.	.	.
.	.	.	.
All other banks	656,100	65,610	590,490
Totals	$1,000,000	$100,000	$900,000

FIGURE 16-1

The Multiple Expansion in the Money Supply Due to $100,000 in New Reserves When the Required Reserve Ratio Is 10 Percent

The banks are all aligned in decreasing order of new deposits created. Bank 1 receives the $100,000 in new reserves and lends out $90,000. Bank 2 receives the $90,000 and lends out $81,000. The process continues through Banks 3 to 19 and then the rest of the banking system. Ultimately, assuming no leakages into currency, the $100,000 of new reserves results in an increase in the money supply of $1 million, or 10 times the new reserves, because the required reserve ratio is 10 percent.

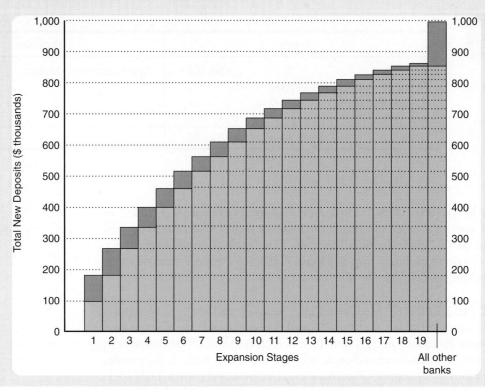

Increase in Total Banking System Reserves

Even with fractional reserve banking, if there are zero excess reserves, deposits cannot expand unless total banking system reserves are increased. In our example, the original new deposit in Bank 1 was created by an electronic transfer from the Fed. It therefore represented new reserves to the banking system. Had that transfer been from an existing account at Bank 3, in contrast, nothing would have happened to the total amount of transactions deposits or the total money supply. To repeat: Funds transferred electronically or by check from accounts at banks within the system, without any expansion of overall reserves within the banking system, represent transfers of reserves and deposits among depository institutions that do not affect the money supply. *The fundamental way in which the money supply can increase is when additional new reserves and deposits are created by the Federal Reserve System.*

You should be able to work through the foregoing example to show the reverse process when there is a *decrease* in reserves because the Fed sells a $100,000 U.S. government security. The result is a multiple contraction of deposits and, therefore, of the total money supply in circulation.

QUICK QUIZ *See page 421 for the answers. Review concepts from this section in MyEconLab.*

When the Fed _____ reserves through a purchase of U.S. government securities, the result is a multiple _____ of deposits and therefore of the supply of money.

When the Fed _____ the banking system's reserves by selling U.S. government securities, the result is a multiple _____ of deposits and therefore of the money supply.

The Money Multiplier

In the example just given, a $100,000 increase in excess reserves generated by the Fed's purchase of a security yielded a $1 million increase in total deposits; deposits increased by a multiple of 10 times the initial $100,000 increase in overall reserves. Conversely, a $100,000 decrease in excess reserves generated by the Fed's sale of a security will yield a $1 million decrease in total deposits; they will decrease by a multiple of 10 times the initial $100,000 decrease in overall reserves.

We can now make a generalization about the extent to which the total money supply will change when the banking system's reserves are increased or decreased. The **money multiplier** gives the change in the money supply due to a change in reserves.

If we assume that no excess reserves are kept and that all loan proceeds are deposited in depository institutions in the system, we obtain the **potential money multiplier**—the *maximum* possible value of the money multiplier when there is a reserve requirement. The following equation applies:

$$\text{Potential money multiplier} = \frac{1}{\text{required reserve ratio}}$$

That is, the maximum possible value of the money multiplier is equal to 1 divided by the required reserve ratio for transactions deposits. The *actual* change in the money supply—currency plus transactions account balances—will be equal to the following:

Actual change in money supply = actual money multiplier × change in total reserves

Now we examine why there is a difference between the potential money multiplier—1 divided by the required reserve ratio—and the actual money multiplier.

Money multiplier
A number that, when multiplied by a change in reserves in the banking system, yields the resulting change in the money supply.

Potential money multiplier
The reciprocal of the required reserve ratio, assuming no leakages into currency and no excess reserves. It is equal to 1 divided by the required reserve ratio.

Going from the Potential Money Multiplier to the Actual Money Multiplier

We made a number of simplifying assumptions to come up with the potential money multiplier. In the real world, the actual money multiplier is considerably smaller. Two key factors account for this.

LEAKAGES The entire loan from one bank is not always deposited in another bank. At least two leakages can occur:

- *Currency drains.* When deposits increase, the public will want to hold more currency. Currency that is kept in a person's wallet remains outside the banking system and cannot be held by banks as reserves from which to make loans. The greater the amount of cash leakage, the smaller the actual money multiplier.

- *Excess reserves*. Depository institutions may wish to maintain excess reserves greater than zero. For example, a bank may wish to keep excess reserves so that it can make speedy loans when creditworthy borrowers seek funds. To the extent that banks want to keep positive excess reserves, the money multiplier will be smaller. The greater the excess reserves that banks maintain, the smaller the actual money multiplier.

Empirically, the currency drain is more significant than the effect of desired positive excess reserves.

REAL-WORLD MONEY MULTIPLIERS   The potential money multiplier is the reciprocal of the required reserve ratio. This potential is never attained for the system as a whole because of currency drains and excess reserves.

Each definition of the money supply, M1 or M2, will yield a different actual money multiplier. In recent years, the actual M1 multiplier has been in a range between 1.5 and 2.0. The actual M2 multiplier, however, has shown an upward trend, rising from 6.5 in the 1960s to over 12 in the mid-2000s. It has since declined.

Other Ways That the Federal Reserve Can Change the Money Supply

As we have just seen, the Fed can change the money supply by directly changing reserves available to the banking system. It does this by engaging in open market operations. To repeat: The purchase of a U.S. government security by the Fed results in an increase in reserves and leads to a multiple expansion in the money supply. A sale of a U.S. government security by the Fed results in a decrease in reserves and leads to a multiple contraction in the money supply.

In principle, the Fed can change the money supply in three other ways, each of which will have multiplier effects similar to those outlined earlier.

BORROWED RESERVES, THE DISCOUNT RATE, AND THE FEDERAL FUNDS RATE   If a depository institution wants to increase its loans but has no excess reserves, it can borrow reserves. One place it can borrow reserves is from the Fed itself. The depository institution goes to the Federal Reserve and asks for a loan of a certain amount of reserves. The Fed charges these institutions for any reserves that it lends them. The interest rate that the Fed charges is the **discount rate,** and the borrowing is said to be done through the Fed's "discount window." Borrowing from the Fed increases reserves and thereby enhances the ability of the depository institution to engage in deposit creation, thus increasing the money supply.

Depository institutions rarely go to the Fed to borrow reserves. In years past, this was because the Fed would not lend them all they wanted to borrow. The Fed encouraged banks to tap an alternative source when they wanted to expand their reserves or when they needed reserves to meet a requirement. The primary source for banks to obtain funds is the **federal funds market.** The federal funds market is an interbank market in reserves, with one bank borrowing the excess reserves of another. The generic term *federal funds market* refers to the borrowing or lending of reserve funds that are usually repaid within the same 24-hour period.

Depository institutions that borrow in the federal funds market pay an interest rate called the **federal funds rate.** Because the federal funds rate is a ready measure of the cost that banks must incur to raise funds, the Federal Reserve often uses it as a yardstick by which to measure the effects of its policies. Consequently, the federal funds rate is a closely watched indicator of the Fed's anticipated intentions.

Discount rate
The interest rate that the Federal Reserve charges for reserves that it lends to depository institutions. It is sometimes referred to as the *rediscount rate* or, in Canada and England, as the *bank rate.*

Federal funds market
A private market (made up mostly of banks) in which banks can borrow reserves from other banks that want to lend them. Federal funds are usually lent for overnight use.

Federal funds rate
The interest rate that depository institutions pay to borrow reserves in the interbank federal funds market.

For almost 80 years, the Fed tended to keep the discount rate unchanged for weeks at a time. From the late 1960s through the early 2000s, the Fed typically set the discount rate slightly below the federal funds rate. Because this gave depository institutions an incentive to borrow from the Fed instead of from other banks in the federal funds market, the Fed established tougher lending conditions. Often, when the Fed changed the discount rate, its objective was not necessarily to encourage or discourage depository institutions from borrowing from the Fed. Instead, altering the discount rate would signal to the banking system and financial markets that there had been a change in the Fed's monetary policy.

TODAY'S DISCOUNT RATE POLICY In 2003, the Fed altered the way it lends to depository institutions. It now sets the discount rate *above* the federal funds rate. This discourages depository institutions from seeking loans unless they face significant liquidity problems. Currently, the Fed typically keeps the discount rate between 0.5 and 1.0 percentage point higher than the market-determined federal funds rate. Thus, if the market federal funds rate is 2 percent, the discount rate may be set 0.5 percentage point higher, at 2.5 percent. Then, if the federal funds rate increases to 2.5 percent, the Fed automatically raises the discount rate to 3 percent.

In principle, the Fed can continue to use the discount rate as an instrument of monetary policy by changing the amount by which the discount rate exceeds the federal funds rate. For instance, if the Fed reduced the differential from 0.5 percentage point to 0.25 percentage point, this would reduce depository institutions' disincentive from borrowing from the Fed. As Fed lending increased in response, borrowed reserves would rise, and total reserves in the banking system would increase. The Fed has indicated that it does not plan to conduct monetary policy in this way, however.

RESERVE REQUIREMENT CHANGES The Fed can also potentially alter the money supply by changing the reserve requirements it imposes on all depository institutions. Earlier we assumed that reserve requirements were fixed. Actually, these requirements are set by the Fed within limits established by Congress. The Fed can vary reserve requirements within these broad limits.

What would a change in reserve requirements from 10 to 20 percent do (if there were no excess reserves and if we ignore currency leakages)? We have already seen that the potential money multiplier is the reciprocal of the required reserve ratio. If the required reserve ratio is 10 percent, then the potential money multiplier is the reciprocal of $\frac{1}{10}$, or 10 (assuming no leakages). If, for some reason, the Fed decided to increase reserve requirements to 20 percent, the potential money multiplier would equal the reciprocal of $\frac{1}{5}$, or 5. The potential money multiplier is therefore inversely related to the required reserve ratio. So is the actual money multiplier. If the Fed decides to increase reserve requirements, the actual money multiplier will decrease. Therefore, with any given level of reserves already in existence, the money supply will contract.

In practice, open market operations allow the Federal Reserve to control the money supply much more precisely than changes in reserve requirements do, and they also allow the Fed to reverse itself quickly. In contrast, a small change in reserve requirements could, at least initially, result in a very large change in the money supply. Reserve requirement increases also impose costs on banks by restricting the portion of funds that they can lend, thereby inducing them to find legal ways to evade reserve requirements. That is why the Federal Reserve does not change reserve requirements very often.

CHANGES IN INTEREST RATES ON RESERVES In the 1970s and again in the 1980s, the Fed sought congressional permission to pay banks interest on required reserves held at Federal Reserve banks. Each time, Congress balked at the idea, because paying interest on these reserves would cut into the Fed's annual net income—which the Fed turns over to the U.S. Treasury—by at least $2 billion. Thus, Congress would have had fewer funds available to spend.

In 2008, however, Congress relented and authorized the Fed to start paying interest on *all* reserves—*both* required reserves and excess reserves—at Federal Reserve banks beginning in October of that year. Initially, the Fed set different interest payments on required reserves and excess reserves, but throughout most of the period since it received authorization to pay interest, the Fed has paid the same interest rate on both types of reserves.

What happens if the Fed raises the interest rate on reserves? Banks' required reserves do not change, but their desired holdings of excess reserves increase. This results in less lending at each stage of the money creation process. Thus, a higher interest rate paid on excess reserves reduces the value of the money multiplier, which other things being equal causes the money supply to contract.

Sweep Accounts and the Decreased Relevance of Reserve Requirements

To many economists, reserve requirements are an outdated relic. They argue that reserve requirements might prove useful as a stabilizing tool if central banks really sought to achieve targets for the quantity of money in circulation, but they note that most central banks today pay little attention to variations in money growth. Hence, they contend, reserve requirements around the world should be reduced or even eliminated. In the United States, banks have already taken matters into their own hands through a mechanism called *sweep accounts*.

THE GREAT RESERVE REQUIREMENT LOOPHOLE: SWEEP ACCOUNTS A key simplifying assumption in our example of the money creation process was that transactions deposits were the only bank liability that changes when total reserves change. Of course, banks also issue savings and time deposits. In addition, they offer *automatic transfer accounts*. In these accounts, which banks have offered since the 1970s, funds are automatically transferred from savings deposits to transactions deposits whenever the account holder makes a debit-card transaction or writes a check that would otherwise cause the balance of transactions deposits to become negative. Automatic transfer accounts thereby protect individuals and businesses from overdrawing their transactions deposit accounts.

Beginning in 1993, several U.S. banks discovered a way to use automatic transfer accounts to reduce their required reserves. The banks shift funds *out of* their customers' transactions deposit accounts, which are subject to reserve requirements, and *into* the customers' savings deposits—mainly money market deposit accounts—which are *not* subject to reserve requirements. Automatic transfer accounts with provisions permitting banks to shift funds from transactions deposits to savings deposits to avoid reserve requirements are called **sweep accounts.** Banks gave the accounts this name because they effectively use them to "sweep" funds from one deposit to another.

How are some banks profiting from directing the funds of customers of their brokerage subsidiaries to sweep accounts?

Sweep account
A depository institution account that entails regular shifts of funds from transactions deposits that are subject to reserve requirements to savings deposits that are exempt from reserve requirements.

EXAMPLE
Why Sweep Accounts Help Boost Profits at Banks' Brokerage Units

Bank of America and J.P. Morgan Chase now own two of the top stockbrokerage firms, Merrill Lynch and Bear Stearns. Citibank also operates its own brokerage arm, called Citibank Global Capital Markets. These brokerage subsidiaries, in turn, typically direct a portion of their customers' funds to sweep accounts at their own savings bank subsidiaries. Market interest rates on deposits in sweep accounts are about 0.75 to 1 percentage point lower than the rates that the brokerage firms pay to other customers holding mutual funds with these firms. Thus, steering brokerage funds held on deposit to sweep accounts widens banks' profit rates by 0.75 to 1 percentage point per dollar of customer funds.

FOR CRITICAL ANALYSIS
Why might the fact that sweep account deposits are federally insured but mutual fund balances are not help to explain why the market interest rate on sweep account deposits is lower than the rate on balances at mutual funds?

As panel (a) of Figure 16-2 shows, total funds in U.S. sweep accounts exempt from the 10 percent required reserve ratio increased dramatically after 1995. Panel (b) indicates that the immediate result was a decline in the reserves that U.S. banks hold at Federal Reserve banks. Reserves then generally leveled off.

FIGURE 16-2

Sweep Accounts and Reserves of U.S. Depository Institutions at Federal Reserve Banks

Panel (a) depicts the growth of sweep accounts, which shift funds from transactions deposits subject to reserve requirements to savings deposits with no legally required reserve ratios. Panel (b) shows that sweep accounts induced an abrupt decline in reserve balances that depository institutions hold at Federal Reserve banks. Reserves later rose slightly and then fell (with a brief jump when the Fed made an emergency reserve injection after the 2001 terrorist attacks).

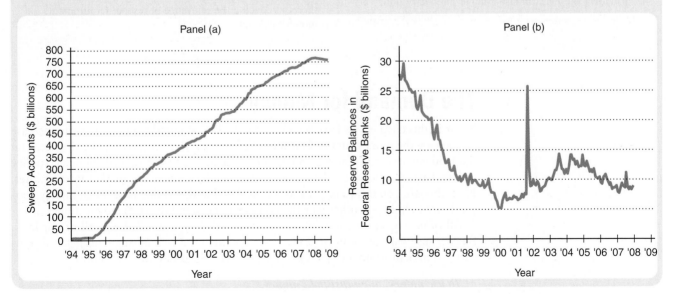

To learn more from the Federal Reserve Bank of St. Louis about the growth of sweep accounts, go to www.econtoday .com/chapter16, and scan down the page to "Retail and Deposit Sweep Program."

IMPLICATIONS OF SWEEP ACCOUNTS FOR MEASURES OF THE MONEY SUPPLY Recall from Chapter 15 that there are two key measures of the U.S. money supply. One is M1, which consists of currency, transactions deposits, and traveler's checks. The other is M2, which is composed of M1 plus various other liquid assets, such as savings accounts, money market deposit accounts, and small-denomination time deposits.

Between 1984 and 1993, M2 grew at an annual rate of just under 5 percent, and M1 grew at an annual rate of just over 8 percent. Since 1993, the annual rate of growth in M2 has varied considerably but on average has been close to 6 percent. The average annual rate of growth of M1 has been much lower because of the widespread use of sweep accounts since 1993. When depository institutions began using sweep accounts to shift funds from transactions deposits into savings accounts, the growth of the funds in transactions deposits abruptly halted. Since 1993, M1 has increased by only a few billion dollars. Growth in M2 has continued, however, because funds that depository institutions shift from transactions deposits to savings accounts are already included in M2.

Thus, sweep accounts have artificially changed the behavior of the M1 measure of the money supply. From the Fed's perspective, this has made M1 a less useful way to track total U.S. liquidity. It now relies on M2 as its key measure of the money supply.

QUICK QUIZ   *See page 421 for the answers. Review concepts from this section in MyEconLab.*

The _____ money multiplier is equal to the reciprocal of the required reserve ratio. The _____ money multiplier is smaller than the _____ money multiplier because of currency drains and excess reserves held by banks.

The Fed can change the money supply through _____ _____ _____, in which it buys and sells existing U.S. government securities. This is the key way in which the Fed conducts monetary policy.

In principle, the Fed can also conduct monetary policy by varying the _____ _____ to encourage changes

in depository institutions' borrowings of reserves from the Fed. Starting in 2003, the Fed has kept the _____ _____ above the federal funds rate.

The Fed can change the amount of deposits created from reserves by changing reserve requirements, but it has rarely done so. Furthermore, since the mid-1990s, U.S. depository institutions have used _____ _____ to shift funds from transactions deposits to savings deposits that are exempt from reserve requirements, thereby reducing the relevance of reserve requirements for monetary policy.

The Demand for Money

So far in this chapter, we have seen how the Fed's open market operations can increase or decrease the money supply. Our focus has been on the effects of the Fed's actions on the banking system. Now we widen our discussion to see how Fed monetary policy actions have an impact on the broader economy by influencing market interest rates. First, though, you must understand the factors that determine how much money people desire to hold—in other words, you must understand the demand for money.

All of us engage in a flow of transactions. We buy and sell things all of our lives. But because we use money—dollars—as our medium of exchange, all *flows* of non-barter transactions involve a *stock* of money. We can restate this as follows:

To use money, one must hold money.

Given that everybody must hold money, we can now talk about the *demand* to hold it. People do not demand to hold money just to look at pictures of past leaders. They hold it to be able to use it to buy goods and services.

The Demand for Money: What People Wish to Hold

People have a certain motivation that causes them to want to hold **money balances**. Individuals and firms could try to do without non-interest-bearing money balances. But life is inconvenient without a ready supply of money balances. There is a demand for money by the public, motivated by several factors.

Money balances
Synonymous with money, money stock, money holdings.

THE TRANSACTIONS DEMAND The main reason people hold money is that money can be used to purchase goods and services. People are paid at specific intervals (once a week, once a month, and so on), but they wish to make purchases more or less continuously. To free themselves from having to buy goods and services only on payday, people find it beneficial to hold money. The benefit they receive is convenience: They willingly forgo interest earnings in order to avoid the inconvenience of cashing in nonmoney assets such as bonds every time they wish to make a purchase. Thus, people hold money to make regular, *expected* expenditures under the **transactions demand.** As nominal GDP rises, people will want to hold more money because they will be making more transactions.

Transactions demand
Holding money as a medium of exchange to make payments. The level varies directly with nominal GDP.

THE PRECAUTIONARY DEMAND The transactions demand involves money held to make *expected* expenditures. People also hold money for the **precautionary demand** to make *unexpected* purchases or to meet emergencies. When people hold money for the precautionary demand, they incur a cost in forgone interest earnings that they balance against the benefit of having cash on hand. The higher the rate of interest, the lower the precautionary money balances people wish to hold.

Precautionary demand
Holding money to meet unplanned expenditures and emergencies.

THE ASSET DEMAND Remember that one of the functions of money is to serve as a store of value. People can hold money balances as a store of value, or they can hold bonds or stocks or other interest-earning assets. The desire to hold money as a store of value leads to the **asset demand** for money. People choose to hold money rather than other assets for two reasons: its liquidity and the lack of risk.

The disadvantage of holding money balances as an asset, of course, is the interest earnings forgone. Each individual or business decides how much money to hold as an asset by looking at the opportunity cost of holding money. The higher the interest rate—which is the opportunity cost of holding money—the lower the money balances people will want to hold as assets. Conversely, the lower the interest rate offered on alternative assets, the higher the money balances people will want to hold as assets.

Asset demand
Holding money as a store of value instead of other assets such as certificates of deposit, corporate bonds, and stocks.

The Demand for Money Curve

Assume for simplicity's sake that the amount of money demanded for transactions purposes is proportionate to income. That leaves the precautionary and asset demands for money, both determined by the opportunity cost of holding money. If we assume that the interest rate represents the cost of holding money balances, we can graph the relationship between the interest rate and the quantity of money demanded. In Figure 16-3 on page 412, the demand for money curve shows a familiar downward slope. The horizontal axis measures the quantity of money demanded, and the vertical axis is the interest rate. The rate of interest is the cost

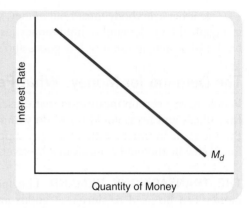

FIGURE 16-3

The Demand for Money Curve
If we use the interest rate as a proxy for the opportunity cost of holding money balances, the demand for money curve, M_d, is downward sloping, similar to other demand curves.

of holding money. At a higher interest rate, a lower quantity of money is demanded, and vice versa.

To see this, imagine two scenarios. In the first one, you can earn 20 percent a year if you put your cash into purchases of U.S. government securities. In the other scenario, you can earn 1 percent if you put your cash into purchases of U.S. government securities. If you have $1,000 average cash balances in a non-interest-bearing checking account, in the second scenario over a one-year period, your opportunity cost would be 1 percent of $1,000, or $10. In the first scenario, your opportunity cost would be 20 percent of $1,000, or $200. Under which scenario would you hold more cash instead of securities?

QUICK QUIZ *See page 421 for the answers. Review concepts from this section in MyEconLab.*

To use money, people must hold money. Therefore, they have a _____ for money balances.

The determinants of the demand for money balances are the _____ demand, the _____ demand, and the _____ demand.

Because holding money carries an _____ cost—the interest income forgone—the demand for money curve showing the relationship between the quantity of money balances demanded and the interest rate slopes _____.

How the Fed Influences Interest Rates

When the Fed takes actions that alter the rate of growth of the money supply, it is seeking to influence investment, consumption, and total aggregate expenditures. As we discussed earlier in the chapter, in taking these monetary policy actions, the Fed in principle has four tools at its disposal: open market operations, discount rate changes, changes in the required reserve ratio, and changes in the interest rates paid on reserves. Let's consider the effects of open market operations, the tool that the Fed regularly employs on a day-to-day basis.

Open Market Operations

As we saw earlier in this chapter, the Fed changes the amount of reserves in the banking system by its purchases and sales of government bonds issued by the U.S. Treasury. To understand how these actions by the Fed influence the market interest rate, you must first start out in an equilibrium in which all individuals, including the holders of bonds, are satisfied with the current situation. There is some equilibrium level of interest rate (and bond prices). Now, if the Fed wants to conduct open market operations, it must somehow induce individuals, businesses, and foreign residents to hold more or fewer U.S. Treasury bonds. The inducement must take the form of making people better off. So, if the Fed wants to buy bonds, it will have to offer to buy them at a higher price than exists in the marketplace. If the Fed wants to sell bonds, it will have to offer them at a lower price than exists in the marketplace. Thus, an open market operation must cause a change in the price of bonds.

GRAPHING THE SALE OF BONDS   The Fed sells some of the bonds in its portfolio. This is shown in panel (a) of Figure 16-4 on the following page. Notice that the supply of bonds is shown here as a vertical line with respect to price. The demand for bonds is downward sloping. If the Fed offers more bonds it owns for sale, the supply curve shifts from S_1 to S_2. People will not be willing to buy the extra bonds at the initial equilibrium bond price, P_1. They will be satisfied holding the additional bonds at the new equilibrium price, P_2.

THE FED'S PURCHASE OF BONDS   The opposite occurs when the Fed purchases bonds. You can view this purchase of bonds as a reduction in the stock of bonds available for private investors to hold. In panel (b) of Figure 16-4 on the next page, the original supply curve is S_1. The new supply curve of outstanding bonds will end up being S_3 because of the Fed's purchases of bonds. To get people to give up these bonds, the Fed must offer them a more attractive price. The price will rise from to P_1 to P_3.

Relationship Between the Price of Existing Bonds and the Rate of Interest

There is an inverse relationship between the price of existing bonds and the rate of interest. Assume that the average yield on bonds is 5 percent. You decide to purchase a bond. A local corporation agrees to sell you a bond that will pay you $50 a year forever. What is the price you are willing to pay for the bond? It is $1,000. Why? Because $50 divided by $1,000 equals 5 percent, which is as good as the best return you can earn elsewhere. You purchase the bond. The next year something happens in the economy, and you can now obtain bonds that have effective yields of 10 percent. (In other words, the prevailing interest rate in the economy is now 10 percent.) What will happen to the market price of the existing bond that you own, the one you purchased the year before? It will fall. If you try to sell the bond for $1,000, you will discover that no investors will buy it from you. Why should they when they can obtain the same $50-a-year yield from someone else by paying only $500? Indeed, unless you offer your bond for sale at a price of $500, no buyers will be forthcoming. Hence, an increase in the prevailing interest rate in the economy has caused the market value of your existing bond to fall.

Go to www.econtoday.com/chapter16 to learn about the Federal Reserve's current policy regarding open market operations. Scan down the page, and select the "Minutes" for the most recent date.

FIGURE 16-4

Determining the Price of Bonds

In panel (a), the Fed offers more bonds for sale. The price drops from P_1 to P_2. In panel (b), the Fed purchases bonds. This is the equivalent of a reduction in the supply of bonds available for private investors to hold. The price of bonds must rise from P_1 to P_3 to clear the market.

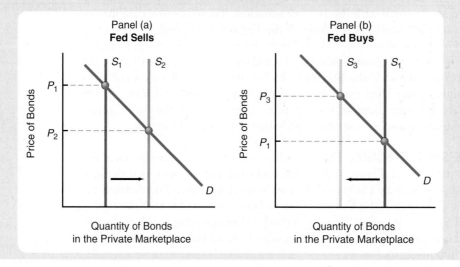

The important point to be understood is this:

The market price of existing bonds (and all fixed-income assets) is inversely related to the rate of interest prevailing in the economy.

As a consequence of the inverse relationship between the price of existing bonds and the interest rate, engaging in open market operations allows the Fed to influence the interest rate. A Fed open market sale that reduces the equilibrium price of bonds brings about an increase in the interest rate. A Fed open market purchase that boosts the equilibrium price of bonds generates a decrease in the interest rate.

QUICK QUIZ   *See page 421 for the answers. Review concepts from this section in MyEconLab.*

When the Fed sells bonds, it must offer them at a _____ price. When the Fed buys bonds, it must pay a _____ price.

There is an _____ relationship between the prevailing rate of interest in the economy and the market price of existing bonds (and all fixed-income assets).

A Federal Reserve open market sale generates a _____ in the price of existing bonds and an _____ in the market interest rate. An open market purchase brings about an _____ in the price of existing bonds and a _____ in the market rate of interest.

You Are There

 Scanning Checks Benefits a Bank's Small-Business Customer

Jack Longo, a co-owner of The Stone Age, a business that sells decorative stones, bricks, and statues to landscapers in Totowa, New Jersey, used to spend five hours per week driving from his office to the nearest bank branch of PNC Financial Services. At the end of every weekday, he had to transport check payments from customers to the bank and deposit them in the firm's deposit account.

Now Longo rarely makes the 10-mile trip more than a couple of times per month. Instead, his employees utilize a single-feed check-scanning device to make digital images of each check received in the regular course of business. After both sides of the check are scanned, the device reads the routing number and dollar value of the check and creates an electronic deposit slip. Accompanying software updates the company's income statement, transmits the virtual deposit slip to the firm's bank via the Internet, and credits the company's account balance with the bank.

Now The Stone Age no longer has to pay an outside bookkeeper to perform these accounting tasks. Of course,

cutting down on trips to the bank has reduced the firm's gasoline costs and expenses related to wear and tear on its vehicles. Additionally, there is an implicit cost reduction: Longo now can devote about five additional hours per week to other aspects of his business, which previously were the opportunity cost of the time allocated to those daily bank visits. In these ways, a small check-scanning device and an inexpensive software program have generated significant cost reductions for his small business.

CRITICAL ANALYSIS QUESTIONS

1. How do The Stone Age's check-scanning activities help to speed the clearing of the checks it electronically deposits with PNC Financial Services?

2. How do you suppose that digital scanning of checks has helped to hasten the deposit creation process?

Issues and Applications

Ballooning Excess Reserves and a Shrinking Money Multiplier

CONCEPTS APPLIED

- Money Multiplier
- Excess Reserves
- Interest on Reserves

As you have learned, the actual money multiplier typically is smaller than the potential money multiplier. Currency drains are one reason for this. When people keep funds instead of depositing them at banks, banks have fewer funds available to lend, and hence the actual money multiplier is smaller. Another reason is that banks hold excess reserves. By holding excess reserves, banks opt to lend fewer funds, which also reduces the actual money multiplier.

Panel (a) of Figure 16-5 below displays the excess reserve holdings of U.S. banks since June 2008. Between June 2008 and September 2008, banks' holdings of excess reserves averaged just over $2 billion. After October 2008, excess reserve holdings grew rapidly, and they have remained at an average exceeding $800 billion—a previously unheard-of level—since December 2008. Panel (b) shows that there was an associated reduction in the money multiplier.

FIGURE 16-5

Excess Reserves and the Money Multiplier in the United States

After the Federal Reserve began paying interest on reserves in October 2008, excess reserve holdings of U.S. banks jumped from an average of just over $2 billion to well over $800 billion. When banks' desired holdings of excess reserves increased, the M2 money multiplier declined.

Source: Board of Governors of the Federal Reserve System.

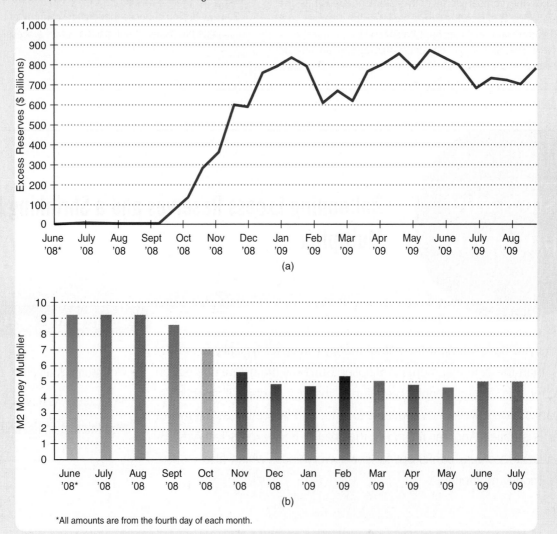

*All amounts are from the fourth day of each month.

Explaining the Explosion of Excess Reserves

There are two main explanations for the significant increase in excess reserves at U.S. banks. One is that in the wake of the crisis that swept U.S. financial markets in the summer of 2008, bank managers and owners have sought to contain risks, and one way to do so is to make fewer loans. Of course, banks could have held nearly riskless U.S. Treasury securities, but they chose not to do so.

Banks had another option. Beginning in October 2008, they could hold excess reserves with Federal Reserve banks, which paid them an interest rate of about 0.25 percent, which was higher than the 0.15 percent rate typically available on Treasury securities during this period. Given this choice, banks opted for the higher return on excess reserves. Therefore, their holdings of excess reserves with Federal Reserve banks rose considerably, and consequently the money multiplier declined.

What Has the Fed Done with All the Excess Reserves?

The Fed has used these funds for a number of purposes. First, it has used a portion of the funds to make loans to banks. The Fed has made many of these loans at the traditional discount window, and it has made others via "auctions" of reserves to banks. Second, the Fed has contributed some funds to programs operated in conjunction with other central banks aimed at providing liquidity in international financial markets. Third, the Fed has used most of the remainder of the funds to finance purchases of a number of debt securities issued by various firms. These include securities issued by government-sponsored financial institutions, such as the Federal National Mortgage Association, and private firms whose identities the Fed has not yet divulged.

Thus, the Fed has induced U.S. banks to hold more than $700 billion in excess reserves by paying them interest at a rate above Treasury security rates, but it has not allowed these funds to lie idle. Indeed, the Fed has directed these funds to a variety of its own lending programs. The Fed, therefore, has become the ultimate controller of a large volume of credit and, hence, resources in the U.S. economy.

Test your understanding of this chapter by going online to **MyEconLab.**
In the Study Plan for this chapter, select Section N: News.

For Critical Analysis

1. Why do you suppose that some economists have suggested that by paying interest on excess reserves, the Fed is discouraging banks from lending in private credit markets so that the Fed can instead make loans to companies it prefers to receive credit?

2. What do you think would happen to the money multiplier if the Fed were to reduce the interest rate it pays on excess reserves to a level below the interest rate on Treasury securities?

Web Resources

1. To find out what rates of interest the Fed is currently paying banks on their holdings of required and excess reserves, go to www.econtoday.com/chapter16.

2. For a more complete explanation of how paying interest on reserves affects banks' excess reserve holdings, go to www.econtoday.com/chapter16.

Research Project

Evaluate what likely would happen to banks' excess reserves holdings, the money multiplier, and the M2 measure of the quantity of money in circulation if market interest rates were to rise sharply relative to the Fed's interest rate on reserves. What could the Fed do if it wished to prevent your predicted outcomes from occurring?

Here is what you should know after reading this chapter. **MyEconLab** will help you identify what you know, and where to go when you need to practice.

WHAT YOU SHOULD KNOW		WHERE TO GO TO PRACTICE
How the Federal Reserve Assesses Reserve Requirements The Federal Reserve establishes a required reserve ratio, which is currently 10 percent of nearly all transactions deposits at depository institutions. Reserves that depository institutions may hold to satisfy their reserve requirements include deposits they hold at Federal Reserve district banks and as cash in their vaults. Any reserves that a depository institution holds over and above its required reserves are called excess reserves.	fractional reserve banking, 395 reserves, 396 required reserves, 396 required reserve ratio, 396 excess reserves, 396	• **MyEconLab** Study Plans 16.1, 16.2 • Audio introduction to Chapter 16 • Video: Depository Institution Reserves
Why the Money Supply Does Not Change When Someone Deposits in a Depository Institution Funds Transferred from Another Depository Institution When someone deposits funds transferred from another depository institution, two things occur. First, the depository institution from which the funds were transferred experiences a reduction in its total deposits. Second, the depository institution that receives the deposit experiences an equal-sized increase in its total deposits. For the banking system as a whole, therefore, total deposits remain unchanged. Thus, the money supply is unaffected by the transaction.	balance sheet, 397 net worth, 398	• **MyEconLab** Study Plan 16.3
Why the Money Supply Does Change When Someone Deposits in a Depository Institution Funds Transferred from the Federal Reserve System When someone (typically a bond dealer) deposits funds transferred from the Fed, the depository institution that receives the deposit experiences an equal-sized increase in its total deposits. There is an immediate increase in total deposits in the banking system as a whole, and the money supply increases by the amount of the initial deposit. The depository institution that receives this deposit can lend any reserves in excess of required reserves, which will generate a rise in deposits at another bank. This process continues as each bank receiving a deposit has additional funds over and above required reserves that it can lend.	open market operations, 400 **KEY TABLE** Table 16-1, 403 **KEY FIGURE** Figure 16-1, 404	• **MyEconLab** Study Plan 16.3 • Animated Table 16-1 • Animated Figure 16-1
The Maximum Potential Change in the Money Supply Following a Federal Reserve Monetary Policy Action When the Federal Reserve buys or sells securities, the maximum potential change in the money supply occurs when there are no leakages of currency or excess reserves during the process of money creation. The amount of the maximum potential change is equal to the amount of reserves that the Fed injects into or withdraws from the banking system times the reciprocal of the required reserve ratio. When the Fed engages in open market	money multiplier, 405 potential money multiplier, 405 discount rate, 406 federal funds market, 406 federal funds rate, 406 sweep account, 408 **KEY FIGURE** Figure 16-2, 409	• **MyEconLab** Study Plan 16.4 • Animated Figure 16-2

(continued)

? DID YOU KNOW THAT during the mid-2000s, the Bank of Japan, the Japanese central bank, sought to keep the interest rate on "overnight call-money loans" that private banks in Japan extend to bond dealers equal to 0 percent? By the end of 2008, the Federal Reserve was mimicking this policy stance by setting a target range of 0 percent to 0.25 percent for the *federal funds rate*—the interest rate at which U.S. banks lend to one another. Both central banks argued that these targets were consistent with broader objectives for their nations' economies.

What does varying the supply of money or the rate at which it grows have to do with interest rates such as the federal funds rate? Answering this question is one objective of this chapter. Let's begin, however, by considering how changes in the quantity of money in circulation affect real GDP and the price level.

Effects of an Increase in the Money Supply

How does monetary policy influence real GDP and the price level? To understand how monetary policy works in its simplest form, we are going to run an experiment in which you increase the money supply in a very direct way. Assume that the government has given you hundreds of millions of dollars in just-printed bills that you load into a helicopter. You then fly around the country, dropping the money out of the window. People pick it up and put it in their pockets. Some deposit the money in their transactions deposit accounts. The first thing that happens is that they have too much money—not in the sense that they want to throw it away but rather in relation to other assets that they own. There are a variety of ways to dispose of this "new" money.

What types of decisions do these directors of the Bank of Japan make?

Direct Effect

The simplest thing that people can do when they have excess money balances is to go out and spend them on goods and services. Here they have a direct impact on aggregate demand. Aggregate demand rises because with an increase in the money supply, at any given price level people now want to purchase more output of real goods and services.

Indirect Effect

Not everybody will necessarily spend the newfound money on goods and services. Some people may wish to deposit a portion or all of those excess money balances in banks. The recipient banks now discover that they have higher reserves than they wish to hold. As you learned in Chapter 16, one thing that banks can do to get higher-interest-earning assets is to lend out the excess reserves. But banks cannot induce people to borrow more funds than they were borrowing before unless the banks lower the interest rate that they charge on loans. This lower interest rate encourages people to take out those loans. Businesses will therefore engage in new investment with the funds loaned. Individuals will engage in more consumption of durable goods such as housing, autos, and home entertainment centers. Either way, the increased loans generate a rise in aggregate demand. More people will be involved in more spending—even those who did not pick up any of the money that was originally dropped out of your helicopter.

Graphing the Effects of an Expansionary Monetary Policy

Look at Figure 17-1 on the following page. We start out in a situation in which the economy is operating at less than full employment. You see a recessionary gap in the

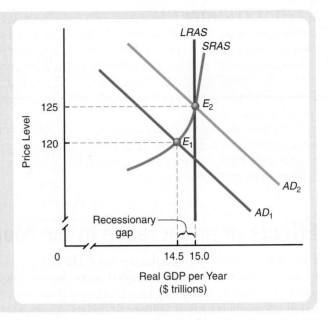

FIGURE 17-1

Expansionary Monetary Policy with Underutilized Resources

If we start out with equilibrium at E_1, expansionary monetary policy will shift AD_1 to AD_2. The new equilibrium will be at E_2.

figure, which is measured as the horizontal difference between the long-run aggregate supply curve, *LRAS*, and the current equilibrium. Short-run equilibrium is at E_1, with a price level of 120 and real GDP of $14.5 trillion. The *LRAS* curve is at $15 trillion. Assume now that the Fed increases the money supply. Because of the direct and indirect effects of this increase in the money supply, aggregate demand shifts outward to the right to AD_2. The new equilibrium is at an output rate of $15 trillion of real GDP per year and a price level of 125. Here expansionary monetary policy can move the economy toward its *LRAS* curve sooner than otherwise.

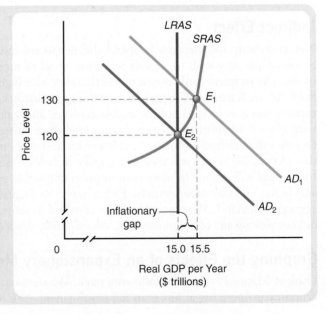

FIGURE 17-2

Contractionary Monetary Policy with Overutilized Resources

If we begin at short-run equilibrium at point E_1, contractionary monetary policy will shift the aggregate demand curve from AD_1 to AD_2. The new equilibrium will be at point E_2.

Graphing the Effects of Contractionary Monetary Policy

Assume that there is an inflationary gap as shown in Figure 17-2 on the facing page. There you see that the short-run aggregate supply curve, *SRAS*, intersects aggregate demand, AD_1, at E_1. This is to the right of the *LRAS* of real GDP per year of $15 trillion. Contractionary monetary policy can eliminate this inflationary gap. Because of both the direct and indirect effects of monetary policy, the aggregate demand curve shifts inward from AD_1 to AD_2. Equilibrium is now at E_2, which is at a lower price level, 120. Equilibrium real GDP has now fallen from $15.5 trillion to $15 trillion.

Note that contractionary monetary policy involves a reduction in the money supply, with a consequent decline in the price level (deflation). In the real world, contractionary monetary policy more commonly involves reducing the *rate of growth* of the money supply, thereby reducing the rate of increase in the price level (inflation). Similarly, real-world expansionary monetary policy typically involves increasing the rate of growth of the money supply.

QUICK QUIZ *See page 444 for the answers. Review concepts from this section in MyEconLab.*

The _____ effect of an increase in the money supply arises because people desire to spend more on real goods and services when they have excess money balances.

The _____ effect of an increase in the money supply works through a _____ in the interest rate, which encourages businesses to make new investments with the funds loaned to them. Individuals will also engage in more consumption (on consumer durables) because of _____ interest rates.

Open Economy Transmission of Monetary Policy

So far we have discussed monetary policy in a closed economy. When we move to an open economy, with international trade and the international purchase and sale of all assets including dollars and other currencies, monetary policy becomes more complex. Consider first the effect of monetary policy on exports.

Go to www.econtoday.com/chapter17 for links to central banks around the globe, provided by the Bank for International Settlements.

The Net Export Effect of Contractionary Monetary Policy

To see how a change in monetary policy can affect net exports, suppose that the Federal Reserve implements a contractionary policy that boosts the market interest rate. The higher U.S. interest rate, in turn, tends to attract foreign investment in U.S. financial assets, such as U.S. government securities.

If more residents of foreign countries decide that they want to purchase U.S. government securities or other U.S. assets, they first have to obtain U.S. dollars. As a consequence, the demand for dollars goes up in foreign exchange markets. The international price of the dollar therefore rises. This is called an *appreciation* of the dollar, and it tends to reduce net exports because it makes our exports more expensive in terms of foreign currency and imports cheaper in terms of dollars. Foreign residents demand fewer of our goods and services, and we demand more of theirs.

This reasoning implies that when contractionary monetary policy increases the after-tax U.S. interest rate at the current price level, there will be a negative net export effect because foreign residents will want more U.S. financial instruments. Hence, they will demand additional dollars, thereby causing the international price of the dollar to rise. This makes our exports more expensive for the rest of the world, which then demands a smaller quantity of our exports. It also means that foreign goods and services are less expensive in the United States, so we therefore demand more imports. We come up with this conclusion:

Contractionary monetary policy causes interest rates to rise. Such a rise will induce international inflows of financial capital, thereby raising the international value of the dollar and making U.S. goods less attractive abroad. The net export effect of contractionary monetary policy will be in the same direction as the monetary policy effect, thereby amplifying the effect of such policy.

The Net Export Effect of Expansionary Monetary Policy

Now assume that the economy is experiencing a recession and the Federal Reserve wants to pursue an expansionary monetary policy. In so doing, it will cause interest rates to fall in the short run, as discussed earlier. Declining interest rates will cause financial capital to flow out of the United States. The demand for dollars will decrease, and their international price will go down. Foreign goods will now look more expensive to U.S. residents, and imports will fall. Foreign residents will desire more of our exports, and exports will rise. The result will be an increase in net exports. Again, the international consequences reinforce the domestic consequences of monetary policy.

Globalization of International Money Markets

On a broader level, the Fed's ability to control the rate of growth of the money supply may be hampered as U.S. money markets become less isolated. With the push of a computer button, billions of dollars can change hands halfway around the world. If the Fed reduces the growth of the money supply, individuals and firms in the United States can obtain dollars from other sources. People in the United States who want more liquidity can obtain their dollars from foreign residents. Indeed, as world markets become increasingly integrated, U.S. residents, who can already hold U.S. bank accounts denominated in foreign currencies, more regularly conduct transactions using other nations' currencies.

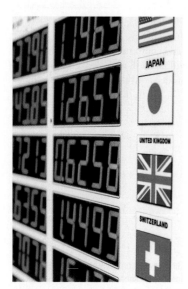

When the international price of the dollar goes up, how do residents of foreign nations react?

See page 444 for the answers. Review concepts from this section in MyEconLab.

Monetary policy in an open economy has repercussions for net _____.

If contractionary monetary policy raises U.S. interest rates, there is a _____ net export effect because foreign residents will demand _____ U.S. financial instruments, thereby demanding _____ dollars and hence causing the international price of the dollar to rise. This makes our exports more expensive for the rest of the world.

When expansionary monetary policy causes interest rates to fall, foreign residents will want _____ U.S. financial instruments. The resulting _____ in the demand for dollars will reduce the dollar's value in foreign exchange markets, leading to an _____ in net exports.

Monetary Policy and Inflation

Most media discussions of inflation focus on the short run. The price index can fluctuate in the short run because of events such as oil price shocks, labor union strikes, or discoveries of large amounts of new natural resources. In the long run, however, empirical studies show that excessive growth in the money supply results in inflation.

If the supply of money rises relative to the demand for money, people have more money balances than desired. They adjust their mix of assets to reduce money balances in favor of other items. This ultimately causes their spending on goods and services to increase. The result is a rise in the price level, or inflation.

The Equation of Exchange and the Quantity Theory

A simple way to show the relationship between changes in the quantity of money in circulation and the price level is through the **equation of exchange,** developed by Irving Fisher (note that $\equiv$ refers to an identity or truism):

$$M_s V \equiv PY$$

where M_s = actual money balances held by the nonbanking public
V = **income velocity of money,** which is the number of times, on average per year, each monetary unit is spent on final goods and services
P = price level or price index
Y = real GDP per year

Equation of exchange
The formula indicating that the number of monetary units (M_s) times the number of times each unit is spent on final goods and services (V) is identical to the price level (P) times real GDP (Y).

Income velocity of money (V)
The number of times per year a dollar is spent on final goods and services; identically equal to nominal GDP divided by the money supply.

Consider a numerical example involving a one-commodity economy. Assume that in this economy, the total money supply, M_s, is \$10 trillion; real GDP, Y, is \$15 trillion (in base-year dollars); and the price level, P, is 1.1134 (111.34 in index number terms). Using the equation of exchange,

$$M_s V \equiv PY$$

$$\$10 \text{ trillion} \times V \equiv 1.1134 \times \$15 \text{ trillion}$$

$$\$10 \text{ trillion} \times V \equiv \$16.7 \text{ trillion}$$

$$V \equiv 1.67$$

Thus, each dollar is spent an average of 1.67 times per year.

THE EQUATION OF EXCHANGE AS AN IDENTITY The equation of exchange must always be true—it is an *accounting identity*. The equation of exchange states that the total amount of funds spent on final output, $M_s V$, is equal to the total amount of funds *received* for final output, PY. Thus, a given flow of funds can be viewed from either the buyers' side or the producers' side. The value of goods purchased is equal to the value of goods sold.

If Y represents real GDP and P is the price level, PY equals the dollar value of national output of goods and services or *nominal* GDP. Thus,

$$M_s V \equiv PY \equiv \text{nominal GDP}$$

THE QUANTITY THEORY OF MONEY AND PRICES If we now make some assumptions about different variables in the equation of exchange, we come up with the simplified theory of why the price level changes, called the **quantity theory of money and prices.** If we assume that the velocity of money, V, is constant and that real GDP, Y, is also constant, the simple equation of exchange tells us that a change in the money supply can lead only to an equiproportional change in the price level. Continue with

Quantity theory of money and prices
The hypothesis that changes in the money supply lead to equiproportional changes in the price level.

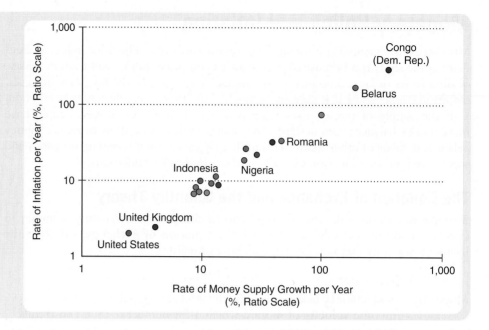

FIGURE 17-3

The Relationship Between Money Supply Growth Rates and Rates of Inflation

If we plot rates of inflation and rates of monetary growth for different countries, we come up with a scatter diagram that reveals an obvious direct relationship. If you were to draw a line through the "average" of the points in this figure, it would be upward sloping, showing that an increase in the rate of growth of the money supply leads to an increase in the rate of inflation.

Sources: International Monetary Fund and national central banks. Data are for latest available periods.

our numerical example. Y is $15 trillion. V equals 1.67. If the money supply increases by 20 percent, to $12 trillion, the only thing that can happen is that the price level, P, has to go up from 1.113 to 1.336. In other words, the price level must also increase by 20 percent. Otherwise the equation is no longer in balance. Money supply growth at a rate of 20 percent results in an inflation rate of 20 percent.

EMPIRICAL VERIFICATION There is considerable evidence of the empirical validity of the relationship between monetary growth and high rates of inflation. Figure 17-3 above tracks the correspondence between money supply growth and the rates of inflation in various countries around the world.

What do you suppose accounted for Zimbabwe's astronomically high inflation rate in the late 2000s?

INTERNATIONAL POLICY EXAMPLE
Zimbabwe Discovers What Happens When It Adds Zeros to Its Currency Notes

In 2004, Zimbabwe's inflation rate reached 600 percent per year before dropping. Then, in 2006, its central bank decided to pay off debts to the International Monetary Fund by printing more currency denominated in Zimbabwean dollars. Soon, its annual inflation rate rose above 1,000 percent. Nevertheless, the central bank continued printing money, and by 2007 the inflation rate exceeded 100,000 percent per year. In 2008, to avoid having to print so many currency notes, the central bank began adding zeros to the denominations. In December 2008, the central bank introduced notes denominated in 500 million Zimbabwean dollars, but within a month's time it was printing notes bearing 50 billion. A consequence of adding all these zeros was that Zimbabwe's price level increased ever faster. Ultimately, the annual inflation rate exceeded 200 million percent per year.

FOR CRITICAL ANALYSIS
Why do you suppose that by March 2009, most residents of Zimbabwe were using foreign currencies as media of exchange, units of accounting, stores of value, and standards of deferred payment?

The _____ of _____ states that the expenditures by some people will equal income receipts by others, or $M_sV \equiv PY$ (money supply times velocity equals nominal GDP).

Viewed as an accounting identity, the equation of exchange is always _____, because the amount of funds

_____ on final output of goods and services must equal the total amount of funds _____ for final output.

The quantity theory of money and prices states that a change in the _____ _____ will bring about an equiproportional change in the _____ _____.

Monetary Policy in Action: The Transmission Mechanism

At the start of this chapter, we talked about the direct and indirect effects of monetary policy. The direct effect is simply that an increase in the money supply causes people to have excess money balances. To get rid of these excess money balances, people increase their expenditures. The indirect effect, depicted in Figure 17-4 as the interest-rate-based money transmission mechanism, occurs because some people have decided to purchase interest-bearing assets with their excess money balances. This causes the price of such assets—bonds—to go up. Because of the inverse relationship between the price of existing bonds and the interest rate, the interest rate in the economy falls. This lower interest rate induces people and businesses to spend more than they otherwise would have spent.

An Interest-Rate-Based Transmission Mechanism

The indirect, interest-rate-based transmission mechanism can be seen explicitly in Figure 17-5 on the following page. In panel (a), you see that an increase in the money supply reduces the interest rate. The economywide demand curve for money is labeled M_d in panel (a). At first, the money supply is at M_s, a vertical line determined by our central bank, the Federal Reserve System. The equilibrium interest rate is r_1. This occurs where the money supply curve intersects the money demand curve. Now assume that the Fed increases the money supply, say, via open market operations. This will shift the money supply curve outward to the right to M_s'. People find themselves with too much cash (liquidity). They buy bonds. When they buy bonds, they bid up the prices of bonds, thereby lowering the interest rate. The interest rate falls to r_2, where the new money supply curve M_s' intersects the money demand curve M_d. This

---

FIGURE 17-4

The Interest-Rate-Based Money Transmission Mechanism

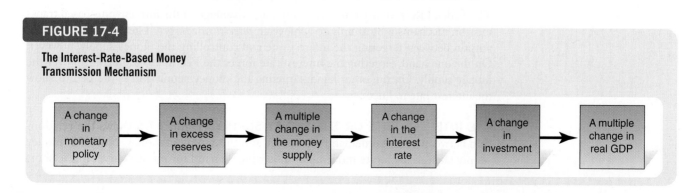

FIGURE 17-5

Adding Monetary Policy to the Aggregate Demand–Aggregate Supply Model

In panel (a), we show a demand for money function, M_d. It slopes downward to show that at lower rates of interest, a larger quantity of money will be demanded. The money supply is given initially as M_s, so the equilibrium rate of interest will be r_1. At this rate of interest, we see from the planned investment schedule given in panel (b) that the quantity of planned investment demanded

per year will be I_1. After the shift in the money supply to M'_s, the resulting increase in investment from I_1 to I_2 shifts the aggregate demand curve in panel (c) outward from AD_1 to AD_2. Equilibrium moves from E_1 to E_2, at real GDP of $15 trillion per year.

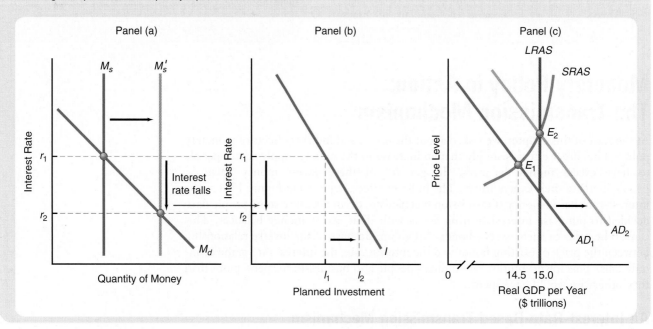

reduction in the interest rate from r_1 to r_2 has an effect on planned investment, as can be seen in panel (b). Planned investment per year increases from I_1 to I_2. An increase in investment will increase aggregate demand, as shown in panel (c). Aggregate demand increases from AD_1 to AD_2. Equilibrium in the economy increases from real GDP per year of $14.5 trillion, which is not on the *LRAS*, to equilibrium real GDP per year of $15 trillion, which is on the *LRAS*.

The Fed's Target Choice:
The Interest Rate or the Money Supply?

The Federal Reserve has often sought to take advantage of the interest-rate-based transmission mechanism by aiming to achieve an *interest rate target*. There is a fundamental tension between targeting the interest rate and controlling the money supply, however. On the one hand, targeting the interest rate forces the Fed to abandon control over the money supply. On the other hand, targeting the money supply forces the Fed to allow the interest rate to fluctuate.

THE INTEREST RATE OR THE MONEY SUPPLY? Figure 17-6 shows the relationship between the total demand for money and the supply of money. Note that money supply changes generate movements along the demand for money curve. In the short

FIGURE 17-6

Choosing a Monetary Policy Target

The Fed, in the short run, can select an interest rate or a money supply target, but not both. It cannot, for example, choose r_e and M_s'. If it selects r_e, it must accept M_s. If it selects M_s', it must allow the interest rate to fall to r_1. The Fed can obtain point A or B. It cannot get to point C or D. It must therefore choose one target or the other.

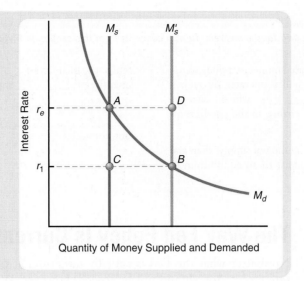

run, the Fed can choose either a particular interest rate (r_e or r_1) or a particular money supply (M_s or M_s').

If the Fed wants interest rate r_e, it must select money supply M_s. If it desires a lower interest rate in the short run, it must increase the money supply. Thus, by targeting an interest rate, the Fed must relinquish control of the money supply. Conversely, if the Fed wants to target the money supply at, say, M_s', it must allow the interest rate to fall to r_1.

CHOOSING A POLICY TARGET But which target should the Fed choose—the interest rate or the money supply? It is generally agreed that the answer depends on whether variations in autonomous spending on goods and services, such as changes in autonomous consumption, are larger or smaller than variations in the demand for money. If variations in autonomous spending are relatively large and commonplace, a money supply target should be set and pursued because if the interest rate were targeted, spending variations would cause maximum volatility of real GDP. To see this, suppose that changed profit expectations induce firms to decrease their flow of autonomous investment spending. The resulting decline in real GDP causes the demand for money curve to shift leftward and pushes down the equilibrium interest rate. To keep the interest rate from falling, the Fed would have to cut the money supply, which would reduce aggregate demand and cause real GDP to fall even farther, thereby destabilizing the economy. Thus, keeping the money supply unchanged at a target level would be preferable to targeting the interest rate.

If the demand for money is highly variable, however, an interest rate target automatically offsets the effect of changes in money demand. For example, suppose that people anticipate significant drops in stock and bond prices. They react to these altered expectations by shifting more of their wealth from holdings of stocks and bonds to holdings of money. This causes the demand for money curve to shift rightward. If the Fed were to keep the money supply unchanged at a target level, the equilibrium interest rate would rise, which would cause total planned expenditures to drop. Real GDP would decline. In this situation, when the demand for money increases, it would be better for the Fed to increase the money supply and keep the interest rate from changing, thereby preventing real GDP from falling.

Go to www.econtoday.com/chapter17 for Federal Reserve news events announcing its latest monetary policy actions.

According to the interest-rate-based monetary policy transmission mechanism, monetary policy operates through a change in _____ _____, which changes _____, causing a multiple change in the equilibrium level of real GDP per year.

If the Federal Reserve targets the money supply, then the _____ _____ must adjust to an equilibrium at which the quantity of _____ demanded is equal to the quantity of _____ supplied.

The Federal Reserve can attempt to stabilize the _____ _____ or the _____ _____, but not both.

The Way Fed Policy Is Currently Implemented

No matter what the Fed is actually targeting, at present it announces an interest rate target. You should not be fooled, however. When the chair of the Fed states that the Fed is raising "the" interest rate from, say, 2.25 percent to 2.50 percent, he is really referring to the federal funds rate, or the rate at which banks can borrow excess reserves from other banks. Furthermore, even if the Fed talks about changing interest rates, it can do so only by actively entering the market for federal government securities (usually Treasury bills). So, if the Fed wants to raise "the" interest rate, it essentially must engage in contractionary open market operations. That is to say, it must sell more Treasury securities than it buys, thereby reducing total reserves in the banking system and, hence, the money supply. This tends to boost the rate of interest. Conversely, when the Fed wants to decrease "the" rate of interest, it engages in expansionary open market operations, thereby increasing reserves and the money supply.

The Market for Bank Reserves and the Federal Funds Rate

To see how the Federal Reserve can use open market operations to influence the federal funds rate, consider Figure 17-7. This figure depicts the market for bank reserves. The Fed supplies these reserves. Banks demand reserves to hold on reserve as vault cash or reserve deposits at Federal Reserve district banks.

THE EQUILIBRIUM FEDERAL FUNDS RATE Panel (a) depicts the determination of the equilibrium federal funds rate in the market for bank reserves. The quantity of reserves supplied is equal to the accumulated amount of reserves that the Fed has created via past open market operations and loans to banks—$800 billion in panel (a). Fed actions determine this amount of reserves, so the quantity of reserves supplied is unrelated to the federal funds rate. Thus, the supply curve is vertical at $800 billion.

Because banks must satisfy their reserve requirements, the minimum quantity of reserves that they must hold is required reserves—the required reserve ratio times transactions deposits. This is $RR = \$60$ billion in panel (a) of Figure 17-7. In addition, many banks also desire to hold some excess reserves. By holding excess reserves, banks forgo the opportunity to lend the reserves to other banks in the federal funds market and thereby earn interest at the federal funds rate, which exceeds the interest rate paid on reserves held with the Fed. Thus, as the opportunity cost of excess reserves, the federal funds rate less the Fed's interest rate on reserves, declines, banks are more willing to hold additional excess reserves. At lower values of the federal funds

FIGURE 17-7

The Market for Bank Reserves and the Federal Funds Rate

In panel (a), the minimum quantity of reserves demanded by banks is their required reserves, which equal $60 billion. As the federal funds rate declines, the opportunity cost of holding excess reserves falls, and banks are willing to hold more excess reserves. Hence, the demand for reserves is a downward-sloping curve, D. At the equilibrium federal funds rate of 2 percent, the total

quantity of reserves demanded by banks equals the quantity of reserves supplied by the Fed, which is $800 billion. Panel (b) shows how the Fed can bring about a reduction in the equilibrium federal funds rate. A reserve supply increase of $20 billion increases the supply of reserves from S to S', which reduces the equilibrium federal funds rate to 1.9 percent.

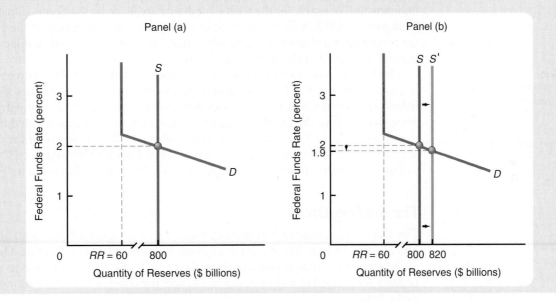

rate, banks hold more excess reserves. Thus, the demand for reserves is a downward-sloping curve, as shown in panel (a). At the equilibrium federal funds rate, which is 6 percent, the quantity of reserves demanded by banks is equal to the quantity of reserves supplied by the Fed.

CHANGING THE SUPPLY OF RESERVES TO INFLUENCE THE EQUILIBRIUM FEDERAL FUNDS RATE Panel (b) of Figure 17-7 shows how the Fed can influence the equilibrium federal funds rate by changing the supply of reserves. In panel (b), the initial equilibrium federal funds rate is 2 percent, as in panel (a). Suppose that the Fed desires for the federal funds rate to be 1.9 percent instead of 2 percent. By conducting an open market purchase or making loans in a total amount equal to $20 billion, the Fed can increase the supply of reserves. Consequently, the supply schedule in panal (b) shifts rightward by $20 billion.

Immediately following the Fed's action, at the initial federal funds rate of 2 percent, the quantity of reserves supplied increases to $820 billion in panel (b). The quantity of reserves demanded at the 2 percent rate, however, is still $800 billion. Hence, after the Fed's action, there is an excess quantity of reserves supplied equal to $20 billion, the amount of its purchase or loan. Banks desire to hold fewer reserves than the quantity supplied at the original 2 percent rate. They will offer to lend more reserves to other banks in the federal funds market, and as they do so, the federal funds rate declines to a new equilibrium value of 1.9 percent. At this new equilibrium federal funds rate, the quantity of reserves demanded by banks is again equal to the quantity of reserves supplied by the Fed. In this way, the increase in reserve supply enables the Fed to push the federal funds rate to the desired value, which in this example is the Fed's *target* for the federal funds rate.

Laying Out the Fed Policy Strategy

The policy decisions that determine open market operations by which the Fed pursues its announced objective for the federal funds rate are made by the Federal Open Market Committee (FOMC). Every six to eight weeks, the voting members of the FOMC—the seven Fed board governors and five regional bank presidents—determine the Fed's general strategy of open market operations.

FOMC Directive

A document that summarizes the Federal Open Market Committee's general policy strategy, establishes near-term objectives for the federal funds rate, and specifies target ranges for money supply growth.

The FOMC outlines its strategy in a document called the **FOMC Directive.** This document lays out the FOMC's general economic objectives, establishes short-term federal funds rate objectives, and specifies target ranges for money supply growth. After each meeting, the FOMC issues a brief statement to the media, which then publish stories about the Fed's action or inaction and what it is likely to mean for the economy. Typically, these stories have headlines such as "Fed Cuts Key Interest Rate," "Fed Acts to Push Up Interest Rates," or "Fed Decides to Leave Interest Rates Alone."

The Trading Desk

Trading Desk

An office at the Federal Reserve Bank of New York charged with implementing monetary policy strategies developed by the Federal Open Market Committee.

The FOMC leaves the task of implementing the Directive to officials who manage an office at the Federal Reserve Bank of New York known as the **Trading Desk.** The media spend little time considering how the Fed's Trading Desk conducts its activities, taking it for granted that the Fed can implement the policy action that it has announced to the public.

The Trading Desk's open market operations typically are confined within a one-hour interval each weekday morning. If the Trading Desk purchases government securities during this interval, it increases the quantity of reserves available to banks, thereby increasing the supply of reserves as depicted in panel (b) of Figure 17-7 on page 435.

How much variation has there been in recent forecasts of the Fed's future policy intentions?

POLICY EXAMPLE
The Wide Variation in Forecasts of Fed Policy in the Late 2000s

For much of 2009, the Federal Open Market Committee instructed the Trading Desk to aim for a federal funds rate target near 0 percent in an effort to boost aggregate spending and bring an end to the Great Recession. When signs of a possible upswing in economic activity emerged late in the summer of 2009, many people began to suspect that the time might be nearing for the Fed to boost its federal funds rate target in an effort to hold off inflationary pressures.

Economic forecasters reached differing conclusions, however, about when and by how much the Fed might raise its target for the federal funds rate. In July 2009, a survey of professional forecasters revealed that some anticipated that the Fed

would push its target up to 0.5 percent by late in the summer. A few even thought that the target value might reach 4 percent by the middle of 2010. Nevertheless, a number of forecasters believed that the Fed would leave its target rate near zero through the end of 2010. Thus, there was a 4-percentage-point range across the forecasts of Fed interest rate policymaking through the next year.

FOR CRITICAL ANALYSIS
Why might difficulties in predicting the strength of economic recovery in 2009 complicate forecasting Fed policy choices through the end of 2010?

Selecting the Federal Funds Rate Target

Now that you have seen how the Federal Reserve adjusts the supply of reserves to achieve the Federal Open Market Committee's target for the federal funds rate, we can address another question: How does the FOMC select the target value of this interest rate?

The Neutral Federal Funds Rate

The FOMC aims to set the target value of the federal funds rate equal to the **neutral federal funds rate.** At the neutral federal funds rate, the growth rate of real GDP tends neither to speed up nor to slow down in relation to the long-run, or potential, rate of real GDP growth, given the expected rate of inflation.

IDENTIFYING THE NEUTRAL FEDERAL FUNDS RATE Suppose, for instance, that the actual equilibrium federal funds rate is 2 percent, but the neutral federal funds rate is 1.9 percent. The higher actual federal funds rate of 2 percent would inhibit growth in interest-sensitive consumption and investment spending. The depressed short-run growth in aggregate demand would, in the short run, cause real GDP to grow at a slower pace than the potential real GDP growth rate.

To boost aggregate demand and increase real GDP growth to the long-run rate of real GDP growth, the Fed would seek to push the equilibrium federal funds rate down to the target level—the neutral federal funds rate of 1.9 percent. The Trading Desk would conduct open market purchases or make loans to raise the supply of reserves sufficiently to attain the 1.9 percent target, as depicted in Figure 17-7 on page 433.

TRYING TO TARGET THE NEUTRAL FEDERAL FUNDS RATE Policymakers on the FOMC face a fundamental problem: The value of the neutral federal funds rate varies over time. The potential rate of growth of real GDP is not constant. It depends on the speed at which the economy's long-run aggregate supply increases over time, which varies with factors such as productivity growth and the pace of technological improvements. Naturally, aggregate supply shocks can suddenly add to or subtract from the natural pace at which aggregate supply rises, thereby causing the potential real GDP growth rate to speed up or slow down unexpectedly.

Whenever the rate of growth of potential real GDP rises or falls, so does the value of the neutral federal funds rate. The FOMC, in turn, must respond by *changing* the target for the federal funds rate that it includes in the FOMC Directive transmitted to the Trading Desk. This explains why you so often see media reports speculating about whether the "Fed has decided to push interest rates up" or to "push interest rates down." The FOMC is always trying to aim at a moving interest rate target—a neutral federal funds rate that varies as economic conditions change.

The Taylor Rule

In light of the difficulties the Fed faces in determining the neutral federal funds rate at any given point in time, could an easier procedure exist for selecting a federal funds rate target? In 1990, John Taylor suggested a relatively simple equation that the Fed might use for this purpose. This equation would direct the Fed to set the federal funds rate target based on an estimated long-run real interest rate (see page 172 in Chapter 7), the current deviation of the actual inflation rate from the Fed's inflation objective, and the proportionate gap between actual real GDP and a measure of potential real GDP. Taylor and other economists have applied his equation, which has become known as the **Taylor rule,** to actual Fed policy choices. They have concluded

Neutral federal funds rate
A value of the interest rate on interbank loans at which the growth rate of real GDP tends neither to rise nor to fall relative to the rate of growth of potential, long-run, real GDP, given the expected rate of inflation.

You Are There

To contemplate difficulties the Fed has recently experienced in trying to push down interest rates on long-term Treasury bonds, read **The Harder the Fed Works to Push Down Treasury Bond Rates, the More They Rise,** on page 437.

Taylor rule
An equation that specifies a federal funds rate target based on an estimated long-run real interest rate, the current deviation of the actual inflation rate from the Federal Reserve's inflation objective, and the gap between actual real GDP and a measure of potential real GDP.

that the Taylor rule's recommendations for federal funds rate target values come close to the actual targets the Fed has selected over time.

PLOTTING THE TAYLOR RULE ON A GRAPH The Federal Reserve Bank of St. Louis now regularly tracks target levels for the federal funds rate predicted by a basic Taylor-rule equation. Figure 17-8 displays paths of both the actual federal funds rate (the orange line) and alternative Taylor-rule recommendations under different assumptions about the Fed's inflation objective (represented by green lines consistent with goals of 0, 1, 2, 3, or 4 percent inflation).

When the actual federal funds rate is at a level consistent with a particular inflation rate goal, then the Taylor rule indicates that Fed policymaking will tend to produce that inflation rate. For instance, at the middle of 2002 the actual federal funds rate was at a level that the Taylor rule specified to be consistent with a 3 percent inflation target.

ASSESSING THE STANCE OF FED POLICY WITH THE TAYLOR RULE Suppose that the actual federal funds rate is *below* the rate implied by a particular inflation goal. In this situation, the Taylor rule implies that the Fed's policymaking is expansionary. As a consequence, the actual inflation rate will rise above the Fed's goal for the inflation rate. Thus, during most of the 2003–2005 interval, the actual federal funds rate was below the level consistent with a 4 percent inflation rate. This implies that Fed policymaking was very expansionary during this period, sufficiently so as to be expected to yield a long-run inflation rate in excess of 4 percent per year. The Taylor-rule graph implies that in the first half of 2007, the Fed's policy stance became much more contractionary, with the actual federal funds rate above the level consistent with 0 percent inflation. Then, the graph suggests, Fed policymaking became expansionary once more beginning in late 2007.

Until the early 2000s, the actual federal funds rate remained relatively close to the Taylor-rule predictions over time. Since 2003, the Fed failed to set its federal funds rate target in a manner consistent with the Taylor rule.

FIGURE 17-8

Actual Federal Funds Rates and Values Predicted by a Taylor Rule

This figure displays both the actual path of the federal funds rate since 2000 and the target paths specified by a Taylor-rule equation for alternative annual inflation objectives of 0, 1, 2, 3, and 4 percent.

Source: Federal Reserve Bank of St. Louis; *Monetary Trends,* various issues.

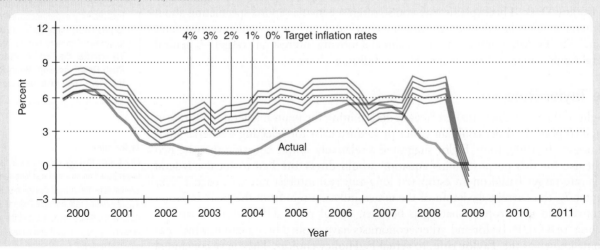

Why do some economists promote the "Taylor principle" as a supplement to the
Taylor rule?

POLICY EXAMPLE
Supplementing the Taylor Rule with the Taylor Principle

The Taylor rule yields a proposed target for the federal funds rate that is based on both the Fed's inflation goal and the gap between actual and potential real GDP. The rule's designer, John Taylor, has also suggested adding another element to the proposed rule, now known as the *Taylor principle*: The Fed should adjust its federal funds rate target more than one-for-one with movements in the rate of inflation. That is, if the inflation rate rises by 0.25 percentage point, the Taylor principle calls for the Fed to boost the federal funds rate by more than 0.25 percentage point.

A key presumption of the Taylor principle is that the public's expectations of inflation adjust rapidly to changes in actual inflation. Thus, the principle is based on the assumption that if the actual inflation rate rises by 0.25 percentage point, inflation expectations will reflect this change. Thus, if the Fed fails to

push the federal funds rate up by at least 0.25 percentage point, the *real* federal funds rate—the difference between the nominal federal funds rate that the Fed targets and the expected inflation rate—will actually decline. A fall in the real interest rate would give businesses an incentive to raise their planned investment spending, thereby causing aggregate demand to rise and pushing up the price level and actual inflation. In contrast, raising the federal funds rate more than one-for-one with an increase in the inflation rate ensures that the real federal funds rate will rise, which automatically tends to dampen inflation.

FOR CRITICAL ANALYSIS
Why is it impossible for the Fed to precisely target the real federal funds rate? (Hint: Can the Fed "control" inflation expectations?)

QUICK QUIZ
See page 444 for the answers. Review concepts from this section in MyEconLab.

At present, the policy strategy of the Federal Open Market Committee (FOMC) focuses on aiming for a target value of the _____ _____ rate, which the FOMC seeks to achieve via _____ _____ _____ that alter the supply of reserves to the banking system.

The FOMC outlines the Fed's general monetary policy strategy in the FOMC _____, which it transmits to the Trading Desk of the Federal Reserve Bank of _____ _____ for implementation.

In principle, the appropriate target for the federal funds rate is the _____ federal funds rate. Given the difficulties in determining this rate, some economists have promoted the _____ _____, which is based on an equation involving an estimated long-run real interest rate, the deviation of inflation from the Fed's inflation goal, and the gap between actual real GDP and potential real GDP.

You Are There ➤ The Harder the Fed Works to Push Down Treasury Bond Rates, the More They Rise

Fed Chair Ben Bernanke and other members of the Federal Open Market Committee are meeting during the depths of the Great Recession, in early 2009. Their goal is to develop a scheme for inducing a reduction in interest rates on long-term loans to help stimulate the economy. Bernanke and

others at the Fed have decided that decreases in interest rates on long-term loans, such as commercial loans, mortgage loans, and consumer loans, would generate greater total planned expenditures that would boost aggregate demand.

At the meeting, there is general agreement that the key to bringing down interest rates on long-term loans is to push down the interest rate on long-term Treasury bonds. Interest rates on financial assets with similar durations tend to move together, so depressing long-term Treasury bond rates should help reduce rates on other long-term assets such as bank loans. To push down interest rates on Treasury bonds, the officials conclude, the Fed must begin purchasing these bonds in large quantities. Careful study by Fed staff economists has determined that about $300 billion in Trading Desk purchases of Treasury bonds should be sufficient to generate the desired drop in rates on those bonds. Thus, after the meeting ends, the Fed announces a commitment to buy $300 billion in Treasury bonds by the end of 2009.

At a subsequent FOMC meeting, however, staff economists report that, instead of declining, interest rates on Treasury bonds have drifted very slightly *upward*. The problem is that the public has recognized that, other things being equal, the Fed's large-scale purchase of Treasury bonds promises eventually to boost the money supply. Even though

the Fed's injection of greater liquidity into the Treasury bond market has placed downward pressure on bond rates, people are beginning to anticipate higher future inflation. The increase in inflation expectations is causing all nominal interest rates, including interest rates on Treasury bonds, to rise. On net, the tendency for Treasury bond rates to rise to reflect the higher inflation expectations has exceeded the tendency for Treasury bond rates to fall as a consequence of the Fed's bond purchases. Thus, Treasury bond rates have moved in the opposite direction from what the Fed intended.

CRITICAL ANALYSIS QUESTIONS

1. Why is it impossible for the Fed to "control" *any* nominal interest rate but especially interest rates on bonds that come due many years from now?
2. Why do you suppose that the Fed decided not to purchase any more Treasury bonds beyond the $300 billion that it bought in 2009?

The Rise and Fall of the Income Velocity of Money

Issues and Applications

CONCEPTS APPLIED

- Income Velocity of Money
- Equation of Exchange
- Quantity Theory of Money and Prices

Figure 17-9 shows considerable variation in the value of the income velocity of money. After increasing by about 25 percent between the mid-1980s and the late 1990s, it dropped, recovered somewhat, and recently has declined once again.

Explaining Movements in Velocity

The equation of exchange is a truism. It provides no explanation of the determinants of the income velocity of money. The early-twentieth-century Yale economist Irving Fisher, who did much to develop the quantity theory of money and prices, argued that there are two key determinants. One is the available payments technology. The other, he contended, is people's payments "habits"—their desired holdings of money in relation to the amounts of goods and services that they buy.

When the sawtooth pattern of the income velocity of money between 1970 and the mid-1990s exhibited a generally upward trend, many economists regarded this as a reflection of improved payments technology. Phone banking, automated teller machines, and electronic funds transfers, they suggested, were allowing people to use each unit of money more efficiently, thereby pushing up velocity.

A Change in Payments Habits?

In light of further developments, including the ability to transmit digital payments via the Internet and other technologies, what caused the sudden decreases in velocity that occurred between 1998 and 2003 and again after 2006? Based on Fisher's reasoning, the answer appears to be a change in people's desired holdings of money relative to their purchases of goods and services. Apparently in recent years, people have opted to hold relatively more cash than they did in preceding years, in spite of new payments technologies.

Of course, since 2006 the U.S. economy has been mired in a significant housing-price downturn that degenerated into the worst financial catastrophe since the Great Depression. Many households have responded to these events by increasing their desired holdings of money and by cutting back on their purchases of goods and services. Both of these responses have contributed to the decline in the income velocity of money observed in recent years.

FIGURE 17-9

The Income Velocity of Money in the United States

The income velocity of money generally trended upward until the mid-1990s. Since then it has, except for a slight upturn in the mid-2000s, trended downward.

Source: Board of Governors of the Federal Reserve System.

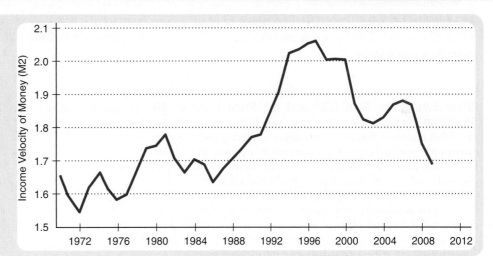

Test your understanding of this chapter by going online to **MyEconLab.**
In the Study Plan for this chapter, select Section N: News.

For Critical Analysis

1. How do you think that a sudden increase in the demand for money affects the income velocity of money?

2. According to the quantity theory of money and prices, if the income velocity of money suddenly declines and real GDP remains nearly unchanged, what should the Fed do to prevent deflation from occurring?

Web Resources

1. To read a short discussion of how the income velocity of money typically behaves during periods of high inflation versus depression periods, go to www.econtoday.com/chapter17.

2. For a summary of different views on the equation of exchange, go to www.econtoday.com/chapter17.

Research Project

Take a look back at Figure 17-9 on the previous page. Suppose that real GDP had been growing at a constant rate throughout the entire period. If so, to maintain price stability, should the growth rate of the quantity of money in circulation generally have been positive or negative between the mid-1980s and the late 1990s? What about between the late 1990s and late 2000s?

---

myeconlab

Here is what you should know after reading this chapter. **MyEconLab** will help you identify what you know, and where to go when you need to practice.

WHAT YOU SHOULD KNOW		WHERE TO GO TO PRACTICE
How Expansionary and Contractionary Monetary Policies Affect Equilibrium Real GDP and the Price Level in the Short Run By pushing up the money supply and inducing a fall in market interest rates, an expansionary monetary policy action causes total planned expenditures to rise at any given price level. Hence, the aggregate demand curve shifts rightward, which can eliminate a short-run recessionary gap in real GDP. In contrast, a contractionary monetary policy action reduces the money supply and causes an increase in market interest rates, thereby generating a fall in total planned expenditures at any given price level. This results in a leftward shift in the aggregate demand curve, which can eliminate a short-run inflationary gap.	KEY FIGURES Figure 17-1, 424 Figure 17-2, 424	• **MyEconLab** Study Plans 17.1, 17.2 • Audio introduction to Chapter 17 • Animated Figures 17-1, 17-2
The Equation of Exchange and the Quantity Theory of Money and Prices The equation of exchange is a truism that states that the quantity of money in circulation times the average number of times a unit of money is used in exchange—the income velocity of money—must equal nominal GDP, or the price level times real GDP. The quantity theory of money and prices assumes that the income velocity of money is constant and real GDP is relatively stable. Thus, a rise in the quantity of money leads to an equiproportional increase in the price level.	equation of exchange, 427 income velocity of money (V), 427 quantity theory of money and prices, 427	• **MyEconLab** Study Plan 17.3 • Video: The Quantity Theory of Money

(continued)

 *(continued)*

WHAT YOU SHOULD KNOW

WHERE TO GO TO PRACTICE

The Interest-Rate-Based Transmission Mechanism of Monetary Policy The interest-rate-based approach to the monetary policy transmission mechanism operates through effects of monetary policy actions on market interest rates, which bring about changes in desired investment and thereby affect equilibrium real GDP via the multiplier effect.

KEY FIGURES
Figure 17-4, 429
Figure 17-5, 430

- **MyEconLab** Study Plan 17.4
- Animated Figures 17-4, 17-5
- Video: The Monetary Rule

Why the Federal Reserve Cannot Stabilize the Money Supply and the Interest Rate Simultaneously To target the money supply, the Fed must let the market interest rate vary whenever the demand for money rises or falls. Thus, stabilizing the money supply entails some interest rate volatility. To target the interest rate, however, the Federal Reserve must be willing to adjust the money supply when there are variations in the demand for money. Hence, stabilizing the interest rate requires variations in the money supply.

KEY FIGURE
Figure 17-6, 431

- **MyEconLab** Study Plans 17.5, 17.6
- Animated Figure 17-6

How the Federal Reserve Achieves a Target Value of the Federal Funds Rate At present, the Fed uses an interest rate target, which is the federal funds rate, or the interest rate at which banks can borrow excess reserves from other banks. This interest rate is at an equilibrium level when the quantity of reserves demanded by banks—the sum of required reserves and excess reserves—equals the quantity of reserves supplied by the Fed. The Trading Desk at the Federal Reserve Bank of New York is responsible for achieving the target for the federal funds rate specified by the policy Directive of the Federal Open Market Committee (FOMC). The Trading Desk conducts open market purchases or sales to alter the supply of reserves as necessary to keep the equilibrium federal funds rate at the FOMC's target.

FOMC Directive, 434
Trading Desk, 434

- **MyEconLab** Study Plans 17.5, 17.6

Issues the Federal Reserve Confronts in Selecting Its Target for the Federal Funds Rate In principle, the Federal Open Market Committee's target is the neutral federal funds rate, at which the growth rate of real GDP tends neither to rise above nor fall below the rate of growth of long-run potential real GDP. It is difficult, however, for Fed policymakers to identify the neutral federal funds rate, particularly because it varies over time with changes in factors such as productivity growth and technological change. For this reason, some economists favor using a Taylor rule to determine the federal funds rate target. A Taylor rule specifies an equation for the federal funds rate target based on an estimated long-run real interest rate, the current deviation of actual inflation from the Fed's inflation goal, and the gap between actual real GDP and a measure of potential real GDP.

neutral federal funds rate, 435
Taylor rule, 435

- **MyEconLab** Study Plans 17.5, 17.6

Log in to MyEconLab, take a chapter test, and get a personalized Study Plan that tells you which concepts you understand and which ones you need to review. From there, MyEconLab will give you further practice, tutorials, animations, videos, and guided solutions.
Log in to www.myeconlab.com

PROBLEMS

All problems are assignable in ⓧ **myeconlab**. *Answers to odd-numbered problems appear at the back of the book.*

17-1. You learned in Chapter 11 that if there is an inflationary gap in the short run, then in the long run a new equilibrium arises when input prices and expectations adjust upward, causing the aggregate supply curve to shift upward and to the left and pushing equilibrium real GDP back to its long-run potential value. In this chapter, however, you learned that the Federal Reserve can eliminate an inflationary gap in the short run by undertaking a policy action that reduces aggregate demand.

    a. Propose one monetary policy action that could eliminate an inflationary gap in the short run.

    b. In what way might society gain if the Fed implements the policy you have proposed instead of simply permitting long-run adjustments to take place?

17-2. In addition, you learned in Chapter 11 that if there is a recessionary gap in the short run, then in the long run a new equilibrium arises when input prices and expectations adjust downward, causing the aggregate supply curve to shift downward and to the right and pushing equilibrium real GDP back to its long-run potential value. In this chapter, however, you learned that the Federal Reserve can eliminate a recessionary gap in the short run by undertaking a policy action that raises aggregate demand.

    a. Propose a monetary policy action that could eliminate a recessionary gap in the short run but uses a different tool of monetary policy than the one you considered in Problem 17-1.

    b. In what way might society gain if the Fed implements the policy you have proposed instead of simply permitting long-run adjustments to take place?

17-3. Explain why the net export effect of a contractionary monetary policy reinforces the usual impact that monetary policy has on equilibrium real GDP in the short run.

17-4. Suppose that, initially, the U.S. economy was in an aggregate demand–aggregate supply equilibrium at point *A* along the aggregate demand curve *AD* in the diagram in the next column. Now, however, the value of the U.S. dollar has suddenly appreciated relative to foreign currencies. This appreciation

happens to have no measurable effects on either the short-run or the long-run aggregate supply curve in the United States. It does, however, influence U.S. aggregate demand.

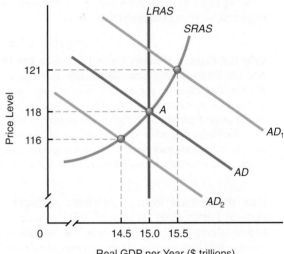

    a. Explain in your own words how the dollar appreciation will affect U.S. net export expenditures.

    b. Of the alternative aggregate demand curves depicted in the figure—AD_1 versus AD_2—which could represent the aggregate demand effect of the U.S. dollar's appreciation? What effects does the appreciation have on real GDP and the price level?

    c. What policy action might the Federal Reserve take to prevent the dollar's appreciation from affecting equilibrium real GDP in the short run?

17-5. Use a diagram to illustrate how the Fed can reduce inflationary pressures by conducting open market sales of U.S. government securities.

17-6. Suppose that the quantity of money in circulation is fixed but the income velocity of money doubles. If real GDP remains at its long-run potential level, what happens to the equilibrium price level?

17-7. Suppose that following the events in Problem 17-6, the Fed cuts the money supply in half. How does the price level now compare with its value before the income velocity and the money supply changed?

17-8. Consider the following data: The money supply is $1 trillion, the price level equals 2, and real GDP is $5 trillion in base-year dollars. What is the income velocity of money?

17-9. Consider the data in Problem 17-8. Suppose that the money supply increases by $100 billion and real GDP and the income velocity remain unchanged.

  a. According to the quantity theory of money and prices, what is the new price level after the increase in the money supply?

  b. What is the percentage increase in the money supply?

  c. What is the percentage change in the price level?

  d. How do the percentage changes in the money supply and price level compare?

17-10. Assuming that the Fed judges inflation to be the most significant problem in the economy and that it wishes to employ all of its policy instruments except interest on reserves, what should the Fed do with its three policy tools?

17-11. Suppose that the Fed implements each of the policy changes you discussed in Problem 17-10. Now explain how the net export effect resulting from these monetary policy actions will reinforce their effects that operate through interest rate changes.

17-12. Suppose that the Federal Reserve wishes to keep the nominal interest rate at a target level of 4 percent. Draw a money supply and demand diagram in which the current equilibrium interest rate is 4 percent. Explain a specific policy action, except for a change in the interest rate on reserves, that the Fed could take to keep the interest rate at its target level if the demand for money suddenly declines.

17-13. Imagine working at the Trading Desk at the New York Fed. Explain whether you would conduct open market purchases or sales in response to each of the following events. Justify your recommendation.

  a. The latest FOMC Directive calls for an increase in the target value of the federal funds rate.

  b. For a reason unrelated to monetary policy, the Fed's Board of Governors has decided to raise the differential between the discount rate and the federal funds rate. Nevertheless, the FOMC

Directive calls for maintaining the present federal funds rate target.

17-14. Consider the following diagram of the market for bank reserves, in which the current equilibrium value of the federal funds rate, 5.50 percent, also corresponds to the Federal Open Market Committee's target for this interest rate.

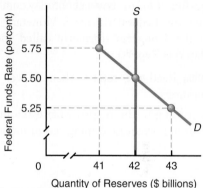

  a. Suppose that the FOMC issues a new Directive to the Trading Desk at the Federal Reserve Bank of New York specifying a new federal funds rate target of 5.25 percent. What policy action should the Trading Desk implement to comply with the new FOMC Directive?

  b. Explain the adjustments that will take place in the above diagram following the policy action you identified in part (a).

17-15. Explain the concept of the neutral federal funds rate in your own words, and then answer the following questions.

  a. Suppose that the Federal Open Market Committee's current target for the federal funds rate is lower than the neutral federal funds rate that Fed staff economists are confident they have correctly identified. If the FOMC is convinced that the Fed staff economists are correct, what new policy strategy should the FOMC implement with its next Directive to the Trading Desk?

  b. What action should the Trading Desk undertake to carry out the new FOMC policy strategy you identified in part (a)?

ECONOMICS ON THE NET

The Fed's Policy Report to Congress Congress requires the Fed to make periodic reports on its recent activities. In this application, you will study recent reports to learn about what factors affect Fed decisions.

Title: Monetary Policy Report to the Congress

Navigation: Go to **www.econtoday.com/chapter17** to view the Federal Reserve's Monetary Policy Report to the Congress (formerly called the Humphrey-Hawkins Report).

Application Read the report; then answer the following questions.

1. According to the report, what economic events were most important in shaping recent monetary policy?

2. Based on the report, what are the Fed's current monetary policy goals?

For Group Study and Analysis Divide the class into "domestic" and "foreign" groups. Have each group read the past four monetary policy reports and then explain to the class how domestic and foreign factors, respectively, appear to have influenced recent Fed monetary policy decisions. Which of the two types of factors seems to have mattered most during the past year?

ANSWERS TO QUICK QUIZZES

p. 425: (i) direct; (ii) indirect . . . reduction . . . lower
p. 426: (i) exports; (ii) negative . . . more . . . more; (iii) fewer . . . decrease . . . increase
p. 429: (i) equation . . . exchange; (ii) true . . . spent . . . received; (iii) money supply . . . price level
p. 432: (i) interest rates . . . investment; (ii) interest rate . . . money . . . money; (iii) interest rate . . . money supply
p. 437: (i) federal funds . . . open market operations; (ii) Directive . . . New York; (iii) neutral . . . Taylor rule

Monetary Policy: A Keynesian Perspective

According to the traditional Keynesian approach to monetary policy, changes in the money supply can affect the level of aggregate demand only through their effect on interest rates. Moreover, interest rate changes act on aggregate demand solely by changing the level of real planned investment spending. Finally, the traditional Keynesian approach argues that there are plausible circumstances under which monetary policy may have little or no effect on interest rates and thus on aggregate demand.

Figure D-1 measures real GDP along the horizontal axis and total planned expenditures (aggregate demand) along the vertical axis. The components of aggregate demand are real consumption (C), investment (I), government spending (G), and net exports (X). The height of the schedule labeled $C + I + G + X$ shows total real planned expenditures (aggregate demand) as a function of real GDP. This schedule slopes upward because consumption depends positively on real GDP. All along the line labeled $Y = C + I + G + X$, real planned spending equals real GDP. At point Y^*, where the $C + I + G + X$ line intersects this 45-degree reference line, real planned spending is consistent with real GDP. At any real GDP level less than Y^*, spending exceeds real GDP, so real GDP and thus spending will tend to rise. At any level of real GDP greater than Y^*, real planned spending is less than real GDP, so real GDP and thus spending will tend to decline. Given the determinants of C, I, G, and X, total spending (aggregate demand) will be Y^*.

Increasing the Money Supply

According to the Keynesian approach, an increase in the money supply pushes interest rates down. This induces firms to increase the level of investment spending from I to I'. As a result, the $C + I + G + X$ line shifts upward in Figure D-1 by the full

---

FIGURE D-1

An Increase in the Money Supply

An increase in the money supply increases real GDP by lowering interest rates and thus increasing investment from I to I'.

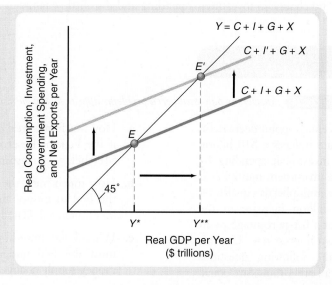

amount of the rise in investment spending, thus yielding the line $C + I' + G + X$. The rise in investment spending causes real GDP to rise, which in turn causes real consumption spending to rise, which further increases real GDP. Ultimately, aggregate demand rises to Y^{**}, where spending again equals real GDP. A key conclusion of the Keynesian analysis is that total spending rises by *more* than the original rise in investment spending because consumption spending depends positively on real GDP.

Decreasing the Money Supply

Not surprisingly, contractionary monetary policy works in exactly the reverse manner. A reduction in the money supply pushes interest rates up. Firms respond by reducing their investment spending, and this pushes real GDP downward. Consumers react to the lower real GDP by scaling back on their real consumption spending, which further depresses real GDP. Thus, the ultimate decline in real GDP is larger than the initial drop in investment spending. Indeed, because the change in real GDP is a multiple of the change in investment, Keynesians note that changes in investment spending (similar to changes in government spending) have a *multiplier* effect on the economy.

Arguments Against Monetary Policy

It might be thought that this multiplier effect would make monetary policy a potent tool in the Keynesian arsenal, particularly when it comes to getting the economy out of a recession. In fact, however, many traditional Keynesians argue that monetary policy is likely to be relatively ineffective as a recession fighter. According to their line of reasoning, although monetary policy has the potential to reduce interest rates, changes in the money supply have little *actual* impact on interest rates. Instead, during recessions, people try to build up as much as they can in liquid assets to protect themselves from risks of unemployment and other losses of income. When the monetary authorities increase the money supply, individuals are willing to allow most of it to accumulate in their bank accounts. This desire for increased liquidity thus prevents interest rates from falling very much, which in turn means that there will be virtually no change in investment spending and thus little change in aggregate demand.

PROBLEMS

All problems are assignable in myeconlab. *Answers to odd-numbered problems appear at the back of the book.*

D-1. Suppose that each 0.1-percentage-point decrease in the equilibrium interest rate induces a $10 billion increase in real planned investment spending by businesses. In addition, the investment multiplier is equal to 5, and the money multiplier is equal to 4. Furthermore, every $20 billion increase in the money supply brings about a 0.1-percentage-point reduction in the equilibrium interest rate. Use this information to answer the following questions under the assumption that all other things are equal.

    a. How much must real planned investment increase if the Federal Reserve desires to bring about a $100 billion increase in equilibrium real GDP?

    b. How much must the money supply change for the Fed to induce the change in real planned investment calculated in part (a)?

    c. What dollar amount of open market operations must the Fed undertake to bring about the money supply change calculated in part (b)?

D-2. Suppose that each 0.1-percentage-point increase in the equilibrium interest rate induces a $5 billion decrease in real planned investment spending by businesses. In addition, the investment multiplier is equal to 4, and the money multiplier is equal to 3. Furthermore, every $9 billion decrease in the money supply brings about a 0.1-percentage-point increase in the equilibrium interest rate. Use this information to answer the following questions under the assumption that all other things are equal.

  a. How much must real planned investment decrease if the Federal Reserve desires to bring about an $80 billion decrease in equilibrium real GDP?

  b. How much must the money supply change for the Fed to induce the change in real planned investment calculated in part (a)?

  c. What dollar amount of open market operations must the Fed undertake to bring about the money supply change calculated in part (b)?

D-3. Assume that the following conditions exist:

  a. All banks are fully loaned up—there are no excess reserves, and desired excess reserves are always zero.

  b. The money multiplier is 3.

  c. The planned investment schedule is such that at a 6 percent rate of interest, investment is $1,200 billion; at 5 percent, investment is $1,225 billion.

  d. The investment multiplier is 3.

  e. The initial equilibrium level of real GDP is $12 trillion.

  f. The equilibrium rate of interest is 6 percent.

Now the Fed engages in expansionary monetary policy. It buys $1 billion worth of bonds, which increases the money supply, which in turn lowers the market rate of interest by 1 percentage point. Determine how much the money supply must have increased, and then trace out the numerical consequences of the associated reduction in interest rates on all the other variables mentioned.

D-4. Assume that the following conditions exist:

  a. All banks are fully loaned up—there are no excess reserves, and desired excess reserves are always zero.

  b. The money multiplier is 4.

  c. The planned investment schedule is such that at a 4 percent rate of interest, investment is $1,400 billion. At 5 percent, investment is $1,380 billion.

  d. The investment multiplier is 5.

  e. The initial equilibrium level of real GDP is $13 trillion.

  f. The equilibrium rate of interest is 4 percent.

Now the Fed engages in contractionary monetary policy. It sells $2 billion worth of bonds, which reduces the money supply, which in turn raises the market rate of interest by 1 percentage point. Determine how much the money supply must have decreased, and then trace out the numerical consequences of the associated increase in interest rates on all the other variables mentioned.

18

Stabilization in an Integrated World Economy

etween the mid-1990s and the mid-2000s, the nations of the European Monetary Union (EMU), which use the euro as a common currency, and the United States generally experienced lower inflation rates than in previous years. During the same period, the unemployment rate among EMU nations ranged from 7 to 9 percent, and the U.S. unemployment rate ranged from 4 to 6 percent. During the Great Recession of the late 2000s, however, the EMU unemployment rate rose above 12 percent, and the U.S. unemployment rate jumped to above 10 percent. By the end of 2009, many economists concluded that policymakers could not reduce these unemployment rates to their previous ranges without generating significantly higher inflation than in prior years. In this chapter, you will learn why these economists reached this conclusion.

LEARNING OBJECTIVES

After reading this chapter, you should be able to:

➤ Explain why the actual unemployment rate might depart from the natural rate of unemployment

➤ Describe why there may be an inverse relationship between the inflation rate and the unemployment rate, reflected by the Phillips curve

➤ Evaluate how expectations affect the actual relationship between the inflation rate and the unemployment rate

➤ Understand the rational expectations hypothesis and its implications for economic policymaking

➤ Distinguish among alternative modern approaches to strengthening the case for active policymaking

? **DID YOU KNOW THAT** prior to the onset of the Great Recession of the late 2000s, the average length of the 21 recessions since the beginning of the twentieth century was about 15 months? In recent decades, the average recession has shortened. Between 1900 and 1945, a recession lasted approximately 19 months on average. Between 1945 and 2007, the average duration of a recession fell to about 9 months.

In contrast, business expansions have lengthened. The 21 business expansions since the start of the twentieth century have lasted 40 months on average. Splitting the twentieth century into two periods, the average expansion between 1900 and 1945 lasted about 31 months. Since 1945, the average duration of an expansion has been 58 months.

To some observers, shorter recessions and longer expansions have obviously resulted from improved monetary and fiscal policymaking. Others, however, are not so sure that policymakers really deserve much of the credit.

Active versus Passive Policymaking

Central to determining if policymakers deserve a collective pat on the back is whether the credit for a generally more stable U.S. economy should be given to **active (discretionary) policymaking.** This is the term for actions that monetary and fiscal policymakers undertake in reaction to or in anticipation of a change in economic performance. On the other side of the debate is the view that the best way to achieve economic stability is through **passive (nondiscretionary) policymaking,** in which there is no deliberate stabilization policy at all. Policymakers follow a rule and do not attempt to respond in a discretionary manner to actual or potential changes in economic activity. Recall from Chapter 13 that there are lags between the time when the national economy enters a recession or a boom and the time when that fact becomes known and acted on by policymakers. Proponents of passive policy argue that such time lags often render short-term stabilization policy ineffective or, worse, procyclical.

To take a stand on this debate concerning active versus passive policymaking, you first need to know the potential trade-offs that policymakers believe they face. Then you need to see what the data actually show. The most important policy trade-off appears to be between price stability and unemployment. Before exploring that, however, we need to look at the economy's natural, or long-run, rate of unemployment.

Active (discretionary) policymaking
All actions on the part of monetary and fiscal policymakers that are undertaken in response to or in anticipation of some change in the overall economy.

Passive (nondiscretionary) policymaking
Policymaking that is carried out in response to a rule. It is therefore not in response to an actual or potential change in overall economic activity.

> **You Are There**
>
> To consider how the Fed might passively target the inflation rate, read **Inflation Targeting Catches on even at the Fed— Sort Of,** on page 470.

The Natural Rate of Unemployment

Recall from Chapter 7 that there are different types of unemployment: frictional, cyclical, structural, and seasonal. *Frictional unemployment* arises because individuals take the time to search for the best job opportunities. Much unemployment is of this type, except when the economy is in a recession or a depression, when cyclical unemployment rises.

Note that we did not say that frictional unemployment was the *sole* form of unemployment during normal times. *Structural unemployment* is caused by a variety of "rigidities" throughout the economy. Structural unemployment results from factors such as these:

1. Government-imposed minimum wage laws, laws restricting entry into occupations, and welfare and unemployment insurance benefits that reduce incentives to work

2. Union activity that sets wages above the equilibrium level and also restricts the mobility of labor

All of these factors reduce individuals' abilities or incentives to choose employment rather than unemployment.

Consider the effect of unemployment insurance benefits on the probability of an unemployed person's finding a job. When unemployment benefits run out, according to economists Lawrence Katz and Bruce Meyer, the probability of an unemployed person's finding a job doubles. The conclusion is that unemployed workers are more serious about finding a job when they are no longer receiving such benefits.

Frictional unemployment and structural unemployment both exist even when the economy is in long-run equilibrium—they are a natural consequence of costly information (the need to conduct a job search) and the existence of rigidities such as those noted above. Because these two types of unemployment are a natural consequence of imperfect and costly information and rigidities, they are components of what economists call the **natural rate of unemployment.** As we discussed in Chapter 7, this is defined as the rate of unemployment that would exist in the long run after everyone in the economy fully adjusted to any changes that have occurred. Recall that real GDP tends to return to the level implied by the long-run aggregate supply curve (*LRAS*). Thus, whatever rate of unemployment the economy tends to return to in long-run equilibrium can be called the natural rate of unemployment.

How has the natural rate of unemployment changed over the years?

Natural rate of unemployment

The rate of unemployment that is estimated to prevail in long-run macroeconomic equilibrium, when all workers and employers have fully adjusted to any changes in the economy.

EXAMPLE
The U.S. Natural Rate of Unemployment

In 1982, the unemployment rate was nearly 10 percent. By the late 2000s, it was at this level once again. These two nearly matching unemployment rates prove nothing by themselves. But look at Figure 18-1. There you see not only what has happened to the unemployment rate since 1950 but an estimate of the natural rate of unemployment. The line labeled "Natural rate of unemployment" is produced by averaging unemployment rates from five years earlier to five years later at each point in time (except for the end period, which is estimated). This computation reveals that until the late 1980s, the natural rate of unemployment was rising. Then it trended downward until the late 2000s, when it began to rise once more, to above 10 percent in late 2009.

FOR CRITICAL ANALYSIS
Why does the natural rate of unemployment differ from the actual rate of unemployment?

EXAMPLE (cont.)

FIGURE 18-1

Estimated Natural Rate of Unemployment in the United States

As you can see, the actual rate of unemployment has varied widely in the United States in recent decades. If we generate the natural rate of unemployment by averaging unemployment rates from five years earlier to five years later at each point in time, we get the line so labeled. It rose from the 1950s until the late 1980s and then gradually declined until the late 2000s.

Sources: Economic Report of the President; Economic Indicators, various issues; author's estimates.

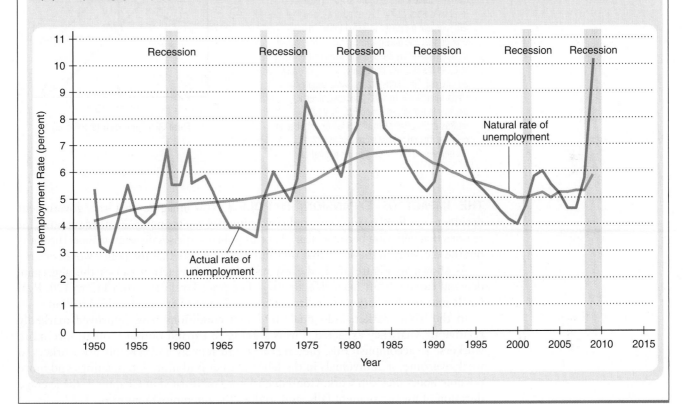

Departures from the Natural Rate of Unemployment

Even though the unemployment rate has a strong tendency to stay at and return to the natural rate, it is possible for other factors, such as changes in private spending or fiscal and monetary policy actions, to move the actual unemployment rate away from the natural rate, at least in the short run. Deviations of the actual unemployment rate from the natural rate are called *cyclical unemployment* because they are observed over the course of nationwide business fluctuations. During recessions, the overall unemployment rate exceeds the natural rate; cyclical unemployment is positive. During periods of economic booms, the overall unemployment rate can go below the natural rate; at such times, cyclical unemployment is negative.

To see how departures from the natural rate of unemployment can occur, let's consider two examples. In Figure 18-2 on the next page, we begin in equilibrium at point E_1 with the associated price level 117 and real GDP per year of $15 trillion.

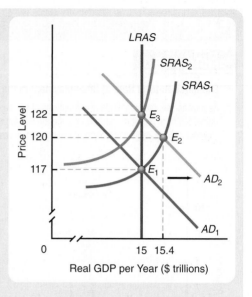

FIGURE 18-2

Impact of an Increase in Aggregate Demand on Real GDP and Unemployment

If the economy is operating at E_1, it is in both short-run and long-run equilibrium. Here the actual rate of unemployment is equal to the natural rate of unemployment. Subsequent to expansionary monetary or fiscal policy, the aggregate demand curve shifts outward to AD_2. The price level rises from 117 to 120 at point E_2, and real GDP per year increases to $15.4 trillion in base-year dollars. The unemployment rate is now below its natural rate. We are at a short-run equilibrium at E_2. In the long run, expectations of input owners are revised. The short-run aggregate supply curve shifts from $SRAS_1$ to $SRAS_2$ because of higher prices and higher resource costs. Real GDP returns to the $LRAS$ level of $15 trillion per year, at point E_3. The price level increases to 122. The unemployment rate returns to the natural rate.

THE IMPACT OF EXPANSIONARY POLICY Now imagine that the government decides to use fiscal or monetary policy to stimulate the economy. Further suppose, for reasons that will soon become clear, that this policy surprises decision makers throughout the economy in the sense that they did not anticipate that the policy would occur.

As shown in Figure 18-2, the expansionary policy action causes the aggregate demand curve to shift from AD_1 to AD_2. The price level rises from 117 to 120. Real GDP, measured in base-year dollars, increases from $15 trillion to $15.4 trillion.

In the labor market, individuals find that conditions have improved markedly relative to what they expected. Firms seeking to expand output want to hire more workers. To accomplish this, they recruit more actively and possibly ask workers to work overtime, so individuals in the labor market find more job openings and more possible hours they can work. Consequently, as you learned in Chapter 7, the average duration of unemployment falls, and so does the unemployment rate.

The $SRAS$ curve does not stay at $SRAS_1$ indefinitely, however. Input owners, such as workers and owners of capital and raw materials, revise their expectations. The short-run aggregate supply curve shifts to $SRAS_2$ as input prices rise. We find ourselves at a new equilibrium at E_3, which is on the $LRAS$. Long-run real GDP per year is $15 trillion again, but at a higher price level, 122. The unemployment rate returns to its original, natural level.

THE CONSEQUENCES OF CONTRACTIONARY POLICY Instead of expansionary policy, the government could have decided to engage in contractionary (or deflationary) policy. As shown in Figure 18-3, the sequence of events would have been in the opposite direction of those in Figure 18-2.

Beginning from an initial equilibrium E_1, an unanticipated reduction in aggregate demand puts downward pressure on both prices and real GDP; the price level falls from 120 to 118, and real GDP declines from $15 trillion to $14.7 trillion. Fewer firms are hiring, and those that are hiring offer fewer overtime possibilities. Individuals looking for jobs find that it takes longer than predicted. As a result, unemployed individuals remain unemployed longer. The average duration of unemployment rises, and so does the rate of unemployment.

FIGURE 18-3

Impact of a Decline in Aggregate Demand on Real GDP and Unemployment

Starting from equilibrium at E_1, a decline in aggregate demand to AD_2 leads to a lower price level, 118, and real GDP declines to $14.7 trillion. The unemployment rate will rise above the natural rate of unemployment. Equilibrium at E_2 is temporary, however. At the lower price level, the expectations of input owners are revised. $SRAS_1$ shifts to $SRAS_2$. The new long-run equilibrium is at E_3, with real GDP equal to $15 trillion and a price level of 116. The actual unemployment rate is once again equal to the natural rate of unemployment.

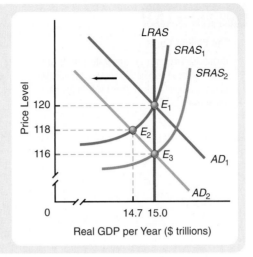

The equilibrium at E_2 is only a short-run situation, however. As input owners change their expectations about future prices, $SRAS_1$ shifts to $SRAS_2$, and input prices fall. The new long-run equilibrium is at E_3, which is on the long-run aggregate supply curve, *LRAS*. In the long run, the price level declines farther, to 116, as real GDP returns to $15 trillion. Thus, in the long run the unemployment rate returns to its natural level.

The Phillips Curve: A Rationale for Active Policymaking?

Let's recap what we have just observed. In the short run, an *unexpected increase* in aggregate demand causes the price level to rise and the unemployment rate to fall. Conversely, in the short run, an *unexpected decrease* in aggregate demand causes the price level to fall and the unemployment rate to rise. Moreover, although not shown explicitly in either diagram, two additional points are true:

1. The greater the unexpected increase in aggregate demand, the greater the amount of inflation that results in the short run, and the lower the unemployment rate.

2. The greater the unexpected decrease in aggregate demand, the greater the deflation that results in the short run, and the higher the unemployment rate.

THE NEGATIVE SHORT-RUN RELATIONSHIP BETWEEN INFLATION AND UNEMPLOYMENT Figure 18-4 on the following page summarizes these findings. The inflation rate (*not* the price level) is measured along the vertical axis, and the unemployment rate is measured along the horizontal axis. Point *A* shows an initial starting point, with the unemployment rate at the natural rate, U^*.

Note that as a matter of convenience, we are starting from an equilibrium in which the price level is stable (the inflation rate is zero). In the short run, unexpected increases in aggregate demand cause the price level to rise—the inflation rate becomes positive—and cause the unemployment rate to fall. Thus, the economy moves upward to the left from *A* to *B*.

Conversely, in the short run, unexpected decreases in aggregate demand cause the price level to fall and the unemployment rate to rise above the natural rate—the economy moves from point *A* to point *C*. If we look at both increases and decreases in aggregate demand, we see that high inflation rates tend to be associated with low unemployment rates (as at *B*) and that low (or negative) inflation rates tend to be accompanied by high unemployment rates (as at *C*).

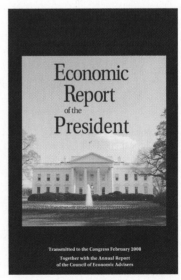

Do you think the economists who work for the president and who write the Economic Report of the President *are in favor of active or passive policymaking?*

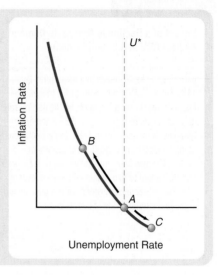

FIGURE 18-4

The Phillips Curve

Unanticipated changes in aggregate demand produce a negative relationship between the inflation rate and unemployment. U^* is the natural rate of unemployment.

IS THERE A TRADE-OFF? The apparent negative relationship between the inflation rate and the unemployment rate shown in Figure 18-4 has come to be called the **Phillips curve,** after A. W. Phillips, who discovered that a similar relationship existed historically in Great Britain. Although Phillips presented his findings only as an empirical regularity, economists quickly came to view the relationship as representing a *trade-off* between inflation and unemployment. In particular, policymakers who favored active policymaking believed that they could *choose* alternative combinations of unemployment and inflation. Thus, it seemed that a government that disliked unemployment could select a point like B in Figure 18-4, with a positive inflation rate but a relatively low unemployment rate. Conversely, a government that feared inflation could choose a stable price level at A, but only at the expense of a higher associated unemployment rate. Indeed, the Phillips curve seemed to suggest that it was possible for discretionary policymakers to fine-tune the economy by selecting the policies that would produce the exact mix of unemployment and inflation that suited current government objectives. As it turned out, matters are not so simple.

THE NAIRU If one accepts that a trade-off exists between the rate of inflation and the rate of unemployment, then the notion of "noninflationary" rates of unemployment seems appropriate. In fact, some economists have proposed what they call the **nonaccelerating inflation rate of unemployment (NAIRU).** The NAIRU is the rate of unemployment that corresponds to a stable rate of inflation. When the unemployment rate is less than the NAIRU, the rate of inflation tends to increase. When the unemployment rate is more than the NAIRU, the rate of inflation tends to decrease. When the rate of unemployment is equal to the NAIRU, inflation continues at an unchanged rate. If the Phillips curve trade-off exists and if the NAIRU can be estimated, that estimate will define the potential short-run trade-off between the rate of unemployment and the rate of inflation.

DISTINGUISHING BETWEEN THE NATURAL UNEMPLOYMENT RATE AND THE NAIRU The NAIRU is not always the same as the natural rate of unemployment. Recall that the natural rate of unemployment is the unemployment rate that is observed whenever all cyclical factors have played themselves out. Thus, the natural

Phillips curve
A curve showing the relationship between unemployment and changes in wages or prices. It was long thought to reflect a trade-off between unemployment and inflation.

Nonaccelerating inflation rate of unemployment (NAIRU)
The rate of unemployment below which the rate of inflation tends to rise and above which the rate of inflation tends to fall.

unemployment rate applies to a long-run equilibrium in which any short-run adjustments have concluded. It depends on structural factors in the labor market and typically changes gradually over relatively lengthy intervals.

In contrast, the NAIRU is simply the rate of unemployment that is consistent at present with a steady rate of inflation. The unemployment rate consistent with a steady inflation rate can potentially change during the course of cyclical adjustments in the economy. Thus, the NAIRU typically varies by a relatively greater amount and relatively more frequently than the natural rate of unemployment.

How have increases in legislated minimum wages throughout the United States contributed to a higher natural rate of unemployment and a larger NAIRU?

POLICY EXAMPLE
Will a Higher Minimum Wage Boost the Natural Unemployment Rate and the NAIRU?

Although a nation's nonaccelerating inflation rate of unemployment (NAIRU) varies with cyclical factors, it also depends on the same structural factors that influence the natural rate of unemployment. These include the extent of government regulation of product and labor markets and potentially persistent mismatches between labor skills desired by firms and those possessed by workers. In recent years, a key structural change in U.S. labor markets has been an upswing in legally specified minimum wage rates.

During the 2000s, a number of cities established their own minimum wage rules, called "living wage laws," which set wage floors above equilibrium wage levels in some labor markets. Basic economics, of course, suggests that the result of such laws must be a surplus of labor, or unemployment, in the affected labor markets. Nevertheless, as one New York politician recently observed, city governments are not interested in "theoretical recommendations of economists." Apparently, neither is the U.S. Congress, which in a series of steps raised the U.S. minimum wage from $5.15 per hour in 2006 to $7.25 per hour in 2009.

Of course, $7.25 per hour is lower than equilibrium wage rates in many U.S. labor markets, and in those markets the higher minimum wage has no effect on employment. In a number of industries, such as certain manufacturing and service industries, however, the $7.25 minimum wage is above the equilibrium wage rate and hence contributes to structural unemployment irrespective of any cyclical causes. Thus, during the late 2000s, minimum wage laws implemented by both cities and Congress pushed up both the natural rate of unemployment and the NAIRU even as cyclical unemployment was already rising during the Great Recession.

FOR CRITICAL ANALYSIS
Why has the more than 25 percent U.S. teen unemployment rate since mid-2009 likely resulted from both structural and cyclical causes?

The Importance of Expectations

The reduction in unemployment that takes place as the economy moves from *A* to *B* in Figure 18-4 on the previous page occurs because the wage offers encountered by unemployed workers are unexpectedly high. As far as the workers are concerned, these higher *nominal* wages appear, at least initially, to be increases in *real* wages; it is this perception that induces them to reduce the duration of their job search. This is a sensible way for the workers to view the world if aggregate demand fluctuates up and down at random, with no systematic or predictable variation one way or another. But if activist policymakers attempt to exploit the apparent trade-off in the Phillips curve, according to economists who support passive policymaking, aggregate demand will no longer move up and down in an *unpredictable* way.

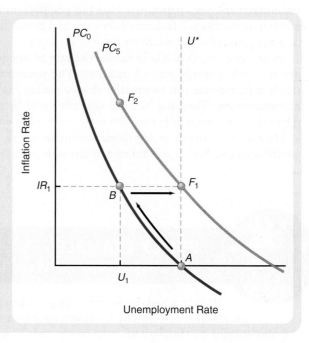

FIGURE 18-5

A Shift in the Phillips Curve

When there is a change in the expected inflation rate, the Phillips curve (PC) shifts to incorporate the new expectations. PC_0 shows expectations of zero inflation. PC_5 reflects a higher expected inflation rate, such as 5 percent.

THE EFFECTS OF AN UNANTICIPATED POLICY Consider Figure 18-5, for example. If the Federal Reserve attempts to reduce the unemployment rate to U_1, it must increase the rate of growth of the money supply enough to produce an inflation rate (IR) of IR_1. If this is an unexpected one-shot action in which the rate of growth of the money supply is first increased and then returned to its previous level, the inflation rate will temporarily rise to IR_1, and the unemployment rate will temporarily fall to U_1. Proponents of passive policymaking contend that past experience with active policies indicates that after the money supply stops growing, the inflation rate will soon return to zero and unemployment will return to U^*, its natural rate. Thus, an unexpected temporary increase in money supply growth will cause a movement from point A to point B, and the economy will move on its own back to A.

ADJUSTING EXPECTATIONS AND A SHIFTING PHILLIPS CURVE Why do those advocating passive policymaking argue that variations in the unemployment rate from its natural rate typically are temporary? If activist authorities wish to prevent the unemployment rate from returning to U^* in Figure 18-5, they will conclude that the money supply must grow fast enough to keep the inflation rate up at IR_1. But if the Fed does this, argue those who favor passive policymaking, all of the economic participants in the economy—workers and job seekers included—will come to *expect* that inflation rate to continue. This, in turn, will change their expectations about wages. For example, suppose that IR_1 equals 5 percent per year. When the expected inflation rate was zero, a 5 percent rise in nominal wages meant a 5 percent expected rise in real wages, and this was sufficient to induce some individuals to take jobs rather than remain unemployed. It was this expectation of a rise in real wages that reduced search duration and caused the unemployment rate to drop from U^* to U_1. But if the expected inflation rate becomes 5 percent, a 5 percent rise in nominal wages means *no* rise in *real* wages. Once workers come to expect the higher inflation rate, rising nom-

To try out the "biz/ed" Web site's virtual economy and use the Phillips curve as a guide for policymaking in the United Kingdom, go to **www.econtoday.com/chapter18**.

inal wages will no longer be sufficient to entice them out of unemployment. As a result, as the *expected* inflation rate moves up from 0 percent to 5 percent, the unemployment rate will move up also.

In terms of Figure 18-5, as authorities initially increase aggregate demand, the economy moves from point A to point B. If the authorities continue the stimulus in an effort to keep the unemployment rate down, workers' expectations will adjust, causing the unemployment rate to rise. In this second stage, the economy moves from B to point F_1. The unemployment rate returns to the natural rate, U^*, but the inflation rate is now IR_1 instead of zero. Once the adjustment of expectations has taken place, any further changes in policy will have to take place along a curve such as PC_5, say, a movement from F_1 to F_2. This new schedule is also a Phillips curve, differing from the first, PC_0, in that the actual inflation rate consistent with any given unemployment rate is higher because the expected inflation rate is higher.

QUICK QUIZ   *See page 476 for the answers. Review concepts from this section in MyEconLab.*

The **natural rate of unemployment** is the rate that exists in _____-run equilibrium, when workers' _____ are consistent with actual conditions.

Departures from the natural rate of unemployment can occur when individuals encounter unanticipated changes in fiscal or monetary policy. An unexpected _____ in aggregate demand will reduce unemployment below the natural rate, whereas an unanticipated _____ in aggregate demand will push unemployment above the natural rate.

The _____ curve exhibits a negative short-run relationship between the inflation rate and the unemployment rate that can be observed when there are *unanticipated* changes in aggregate _____.

_____ policymakers seek to take advantage of a proposed Phillips curve trade-off between inflation and unemployment.

Rational Expectations, the Policy Irrelevance Proposition, and Real Business Cycles

You already know that economists assume that economic participants act *as though* they were rational and calculating. We assume that firms rationally maximize profits when they choose today's rate of output and that consumers rationally maximize satisfaction when they choose how much of what goods to consume today. One of the pivotal features of current macro policy research is the assumption that economic participants think rationally about the future as well as the present. This relationship was developed by Robert Lucas, who won the Nobel Prize in 1995 for his work. In particular, there is widespread agreement among many macroeconomics researchers that the **rational expectations hypothesis** extends our understanding of the behavior of the macroeconomy. This hypothesis has two key elements:

1. Individuals base their forecasts (expectations) about the future values of economic variables on all readily available past and current information.

2. These expectations incorporate individuals' understanding about how the economy operates, including the operation of monetary and fiscal policy.

Rational expectations hypothesis
A theory stating that people combine the effects of past policy changes on important economic variables with their own judgment about the future effects of current and future policy changes.

In essence, the rational expectations hypothesis holds that Abraham Lincoln was correct when he said, "You can fool all the people some of the time; you can even fool some of the people all of the time; but you can't fool *all* of the people *all* the time."

If we further assume that there is pure competition in all markets and that all prices and wages are flexible, we obtain what many call the *new classical* approach to evaluating the effects of macroeconomic policies. To see how rational expectations operate in the new classical perspective, let's take a simple example of the economy's response to a change in monetary policy.

Flexible Wages and Prices, Rational Expectations, and Policy Irrelevance

Consider Figure 18-6, which shows the long-run aggregate supply curve (*LRAS*) for the economy, as well as the initial aggregate demand curve (*AD_1*) and the short-run aggregate supply curve (*$SRAS_1$*). The money supply is initially given by $M = M_1$, and the price level and real GDP are shown by P_1 and Y_1, respectively. Thus, point *A* represents the initial long-run equilibrium.

Suppose now that the money supply is unexpectedly increased to M_2, thereby causing the aggregate demand curve to shift outward to AD_2. Given the location of the short-run aggregate supply curve, this increase in aggregate demand will cause real GDP and the price level to rise to Y_2 and P_2, respectively. The new short-run equilibrium is at *B*. Because real GDP is *above* the long-run equilibrium level of Y_1, unemployment must be below long-run levels (the natural rate), and so workers will soon respond to the higher price level by demanding higher nominal wages. This will cause the short-run aggregate supply curve to shift upward vertically. As indicated by the black arrow, the economy moves from point *B* to a new long-run equilibrium at *C*. The price level thus continues its rise to P_3, even as real GDP declines back down to Y_1 (and unemployment returns to the natural rate). So, as we have seen before, even though an increase in the money supply can raise real GDP and lower unemployment in the short run, it has no effect on either variable in the long run.

FIGURE 18-6

Responses to Anticipated and Unanticipated Increases in Aggregate Demand

An increase in the money supply, from M_1 to M_2, causes the aggregate demand curve to shift rightward. If people anticipate the increase in the money supply, then workers will insist on higher nominal wages, which causes the short-run aggregate supply curve to shift leftward immediately, from $SRAS_1$ to $SRAS_2$. Hence, there is a direct movement, indicated by the green arrow, from point *A* to point *C*. In contrast, an unanticipated increase in the money supply causes an initial upward movement along $SRAS_1$ from point *A* to point *B*, indicated by the black arrow. Thus, in the short run, real GDP rises from Y_1 to Y_2. In the long run, workers then recognize that the price level has increased and demand higher wages, causing the $SRAS$ curve to shift leftward, resulting in a movement from point *B* to point *C*.

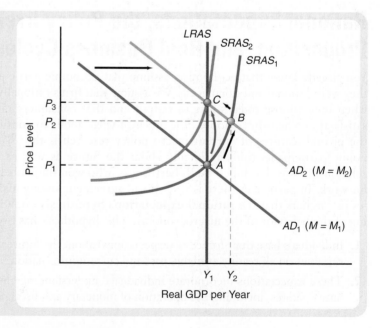

THE RESPONSE TO ANTICIPATED POLICY Now let's look at this disturbance with the perspective given by the rational expectations hypothesis when wages and prices are flexible in a purely competitive environment. Suppose that workers (and other input owners) know ahead of time that this increase in the money supply is about to take place. Assume also that they know when it is going to occur and understand that its ultimate effect will be to push the price level from P_1 to P_3. Will workers wait until after the price level has increased to insist that their nominal wages go up? The rational expectations hypothesis says that they will not. Instead, they will go to employers and insist that their nominal wages move upward in step with the higher prices. From the workers' perspective, this is the only way to protect their real wages from declining due to the anticipated increase in the money supply.

THE POLICY IRRELEVANCE PROPOSITION As long as economic participants behave in this manner, we must take their expectations into account when we consider the *SRAS* curve. Let's look again at Figure 18-6 to do this. In the initial equilibrium at point *A* of the figure, the short-run aggregate supply curve $SRAS_1$ corresponds to a situation in which the expected money supply and the actual money supply are equal. When the money supply changes in a way that is anticipated by economic participants, the aggregate supply curve will shift to reflect this expected change in the money supply. The new short-run aggregate supply curve $SRAS_2$ reflects this. According to the rational expectations hypothesis, the short-run aggregate supply curve will shift upward *simultaneously* with the rise in aggregate demand. As a result, the economy will move directly from point *A* to point *C*, without passing through *B*, as depicted by the green arrow in Figure 18-6. The *only* response to the rise in the money supply is a rise in the price level from P_1 to P_3. Neither output nor unemployment changes at all. This conclusion—that fully anticipated monetary policy is irrelevant in determining the levels of real variables—is called the **policy irrelevance proposition**:

> *Under the assumption of rational expectations on the part of decision makers in the economy,* anticipated *monetary policy cannot alter either the rate of unemployment or the level of real GDP. Regardless of the nature of the anticipated policy, the unemployment rate will equal the natural rate, and real GDP will be determined solely by the economy's long-run aggregate supply curve.*

Policy irrelevance proposition
The conclusion that policy actions have no real effects in the short run if the policy actions are anticipated and none in the long run even if the policy actions are unanticipated.

WHAT MUST PEOPLE KNOW? There are two important matters to keep in mind when considering this proposition. First, our discussion has assumed that economic participants know in advance exactly what the change in monetary policy is going to be and precisely when it is going to occur. In fact, the Federal Reserve does not announce exactly what the future course of monetary policy is going to be. Instead, the Fed tries to keep most of its plans secret, announcing only in general terms what policy actions are intended for the future.

It is tempting to conclude that because the Fed's intended policies are not fully known, they are not available at all. But such a conclusion would be wrong. Economic participants have great incentives to learn how to predict the future behavior of the monetary authorities, just as businesses try to forecast consumer behavior and college students do their best to forecast what their next economics exam will look like. Even if the economic participants are not perfect at forecasting the course of policy, they are likely to come a lot closer than they would in total ignorance. The policy irrelevance proposition really assumes only that *people don't persistently make the same mistakes in forecasting the future.*

If you believe that the Federal Reserve's monetary policy cannot alter the level of real GDP or the rate of unemployment, then you subscribe to what proposition?

WHAT HAPPENS IF PEOPLE DON'T KNOW EVERYTHING? This brings us to our second point. Once we accept the fact that people's ability to predict the future is not perfect, the possibility emerges that some policy actions will have systematic effects that look much like the movements, depicted by black arrows, from A to B to C in Figure 18-6 on page 458. For example, just as other economic participants sometimes make mistakes, it is likely that the Federal Reserve sometimes makes mistakes—meaning that the money supply may change in ways that even the Fed does not predict. And even if the Fed always accomplished every policy action it intended, there is no guarantee that other economic participants would fully forecast those actions.

What happens if the Fed makes a mistake or if firms and workers misjudge the future course of policy? Matters will look much as they do in panel (a) of Figure 18-7, which shows the effects of an *unanticipated* increase in the money supply. Economic participants' expectation of the money supply, M_e, is equal to a quantity of money M_1, but the actual money supply turns out to be M_2. Because $M_2 > M_1$, aggregate demand shifts relative to aggregate supply. The result is a rise in real GDP in the short run from Y_1 to Y_2. Corresponding to this rise in real GDP will be an increase in employment and hence a fall in the unemployment rate. So, even under the rational expectations hypothesis, monetary policy *can* have an effect on real variables in the short run, but only if the policy is unsystematic and therefore unanticipated.

FIGURE 18-7

Effects of an Unanticipated Rise in Aggregate Demand

In panel (a), an unanticipated increase in the money supply shifts the *AD* curve rightward, generating an upward movement along the *SRAS* curve, which remains in position because the rise in the money supply is unexpected. Thus, there is a movement from point E_1 to point E_2. The equilibrium price level increases, from P_1 to P_2, and equilibrium real GDP increases, from Y_1 to Y_2.

In contrast, in panel (b), a rise in the money supply, which again shifts the *AD* curve rightward, is fully anticipated, and as a result the *SRAS* curve shifts leftward. The final equilibrium is at point E_3. The equilibrium price level increases, from P_1 to P_3, and equilibrium real GDP remains at its initial level.

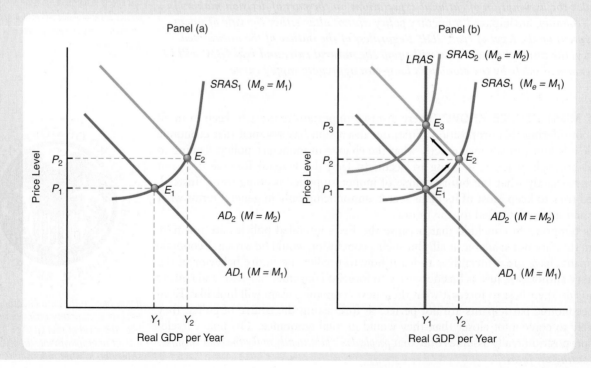

In the long run, this effect on real variables will disappear because people will figure out that the Fed either accidentally increased the money supply or intentionally increased it in a way that somehow fooled individuals. Either way, people will soon revise their money supply expectation to match the actual money supply ($M_e = M_2$), and as a result the short-run aggregate supply curve will shift upward. As shown in panel (b) of Figure 18-7 on the previous page, real GDP will return to long-run levels, meaning that so will the employment and unemployment rates.

Another Challenge to Policy Activism: Real Business Cycles

When confronted with the policy irrelevance proposition, many economists began to reexamine the first principles of macroeconomics with fully flexible wages and prices.

THE DISTINCTION BETWEEN REAL AND MONETARY SHOCKS Some economists argue that real, as opposed to purely monetary, forces might help explain aggregate economic fluctuations. Consider Figure 18-8, which illustrates the concept of *real business cycles*. We begin at point E_1 with the economy in both short- and long-run equilibrium, with the associated supply curves, $SRAS_1$ and $LRAS_1$. Initially, the level of real GDP is $15 trillion, and the price level is 108. Because the economy is in long-run equilibrium, the unemployment rate must be at the natural rate.

A reduction in the supply of a key productive resource, such as oil, causes the $SRAS$ curve to shift to the left to $SRAS_2$ because fewer goods will be available for sale due to the reduced supplies. If the reduction in, for example, oil supplies is (or is believed to be) permanent, the $LRAS$ shifts to the left also. This assumption is reflected in Figure 18-8, where $LRAS_2$ shows the new long-run aggregate supply curve associated with the lowered output of oil.

FIGURE 18-8

Effects of a Reduction in the Supply of Resources

The position of the *LRAS* depends on our endowments of all types of resources. Hence, a permanent reduction in the supply of one of those resources, such as oil, causes a reduction—an inward shift—in the aggregate supply curve from $LRAS_1$ to $LRAS_2$. In addition, there is a rise in the equilibrium price level and a fall in the equilibrium rate of real GDP per year.

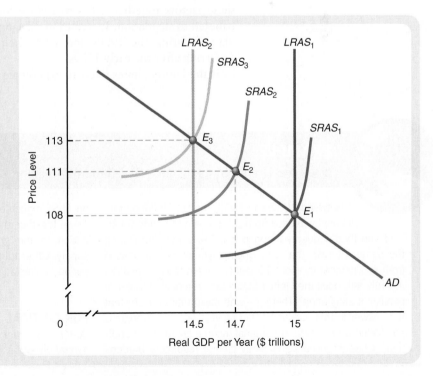

In the short run, two adjustments begin to occur simultaneously. First, the prices of oil and petroleum-based products begin to rise, so the overall price level rises to 111. Second, the higher costs of production occasioned by the rise in oil prices induce firms to cut back production, so real GDP falls to $14.7 trillion in the short run. The new temporary short-run equilibrium occurs at E_2, with a higher price level (111) and a lower level of real GDP ($14.7 trillion).

This is not the full story, however. Owners of nonoil inputs, such as labor, are also affected by the reduction in oil supplies. For instance, individuals who are employed experience real wage reductions as the price level increases following the movement from point E_1 to point E_2. Even though most individuals may be willing to put up with reduced real payments in the short run, not every worker will tolerate them in the long run. Thus, some workers who were willing to continue on the job at lower real wages in the short run will eventually decide to switch from full-time to part-time employment or to drop out of the labor force altogether. In effect, there will be a fall in the supply of nonoil inputs, reflected in an upward shift in the $SRAS$ curve from $SRAS_2$ to $SRAS_3$. This puts additional upward pressure on the price level and exerts a downward force on real GDP. Thus, the final long-run equilibrium occurs at point E_3, with the price level at 113 and real GDP at $14.5 trillion.

Stagflation

A situation characterized by lower real GDP, lower employment, and a higher unemployment rate during the same period that the rate of inflation increases.

STAGFLATION Notice that in the example depicted in Figure 18-8 on the previous page, real GDP declines over the same interval that the price level increases. Hence, there is real economic stagnation, which is associated with lower employment and a higher unemployment rate, combined with higher inflation, often called **stagflation.**

The most recent prolonged periods of stagflation in the United States occurred during the 1970s and early 1980s. One factor contributing to stagflation episodes during those years was sharp reductions in the supply of oil, as in the example illustrated in Figure 18-8. In addition, Congress enacted steep increases in marginal tax rates and implemented a host of new federal regulations on firms in the early 1970s. All these factors together acted to reduce long-run aggregate supply and hence contributed to stagflation. Increases in oil supplies, cuts in marginal tax rates, and deregulation during the 1980s and 1990s helped to prevent stagflation episodes from occurring after the early 1980s.

Is the United States likely to experience a new stagflation episode?

EXAMPLE
Does the United States Face a Stagflation Threat?

Between 2006 and 2009, the U.S. inflation rate steadily increased from 2.5 percent to nearly 5 percent and then suddenly dropped to below 1 percent. During the same interval, the U.S. unemployment rate increased from 4.6 percent to about 10 percent. Even though inflation recently fell, does the United States face a renewed threat of persistent stagflation? There is some reason for concern that the answer to this question could be yes. The U.S. Congress has slated an increase in marginal income tax rates. In addition, it has imposed significantly greater regulatory burdens on U.S. industries and is contemplating further increases. Taken together, these developments have contributed to stagnation in the growth of the nation's long-run aggregate supply. Other things being equal, the result could be a new period of stagflation for the U.S. economy.

FOR CRITICAL ANALYSIS
Could U.S. stagflation be averted if labor productivity and capital investment were to increase independently?

The _____ _____ hypothesis assumes that individuals' forecasts incorporate all readily available information, including an understanding of government policy and its effects on the economy.

If the **rational expectations hypothesis** is valid, there is pure competition, and all prices and wages are flexible, then the _____ _____ proposition follows: Fully anticipated monetary policy actions cannot alter either the rate of unemployment or the level of real GDP.

Even if all prices and wages are perfectly flexible, aggregate _____ shocks such as sudden changes in technology or in the supplies of factors of production can cause national economic fluctuations. To the extent that these _____ _____ cycles predominate as sources of economic fluctuations, the case for active policymaking is weakened.

Modern Approaches to Justifying Active Policymaking

The policy irrelevance proposition and the idea that real shocks are important causes of business cycles are major attacks on the desirability of trying to stabilize economic activity with activist policies. Both anti-activism suggestions arise from combining the rational expectations hypothesis with the assumptions of pure competition and flexible wages and prices. It should not be surprising, therefore, to learn that economists who see a role for activist policymaking do not believe that market clearing models of the economy can explain business cycles. They contend that the "sticky" wages and prices assumed by Keynes in his major work (see Chapter 11) remain important in today's economy. To explain how aggregate demand shocks and policies can influence a nation's real GDP and unemployment rate, these economists, who are sometimes called *new Keynesians*, have tried to refine the theory of aggregate supply.

Small Menu Costs and Sticky Prices

If prices do not respond to demand changes, two conditions must be true: someone must be consciously deciding not to change prices, and that decision must be in the decision maker's self-interest. One approach to explaining why many prices might be sticky in the short run supposes that much of the economy is characterized by imperfect competition and that it is costly for firms to change their prices in response to changes in demand. The costs associated with changing prices are called *menu costs*, and they include the costs of renegotiating contracts, printing price lists (such as menus), and informing customers of price changes.

Many such costs may not be very large, so economists call them **small menu costs.** Some of the costs of changing prices, however, such as those incurred in bringing together business managers from points around the nation or the world for meetings on price changes or renegotiating deals with customers, may be significant.

Firms in different industries have different cost structures. Such differences explain diverse small menu costs. Therefore, the extent to which firms hold their prices constant in the face of changes in demand for their products will vary across industries. Not all prices will be rigid. Nonetheless, some economists who promote policy activism argue that many—even most—firms' prices are sticky for relatively long time intervals. As a result, in the short run the aggregate level of prices could be very nearly rigid because of small menu costs. In recent years, these economists have produced a

Small menu costs

Costs that deter firms from changing prices in response to demand changes—for example, the costs of renegotiating contracts or printing new price lists.

theory in which temporary rigidities in firms' price adjustments cause the short-run aggregate supply curve to be horizontal, as in the traditional Keynesian model.

Real GDP and the Price Level in a Sticky-Price Economy

According to the new Keynesians, sticky prices strengthen the argument favoring active policymaking as a means of preventing substantial short-run swings in real GDP and, as a consequence, employment.

NEW KEYNESIAN INFLATION DYNAMICS To see why the idea of price stickiness strengthens the case for active policymaking, consider panel (a) of Figure 18-9. If a significant portion of all prices do not adjust rapidly, then in the short run the aggregate supply curve effectively is horizontal, as assumed in the traditional Keynesian theory discussed in Chapter 11. This means that a decline in aggregate demand, such as the shift from AD_1 to AD_2 shown in panel (a), will induce the largest possible decline in equilibrium real GDP, from $15 trillion to $14.7 trillion. When prices are sticky, economic contractions induced by aggregate demand shocks are as severe as they can be.

As panel (a) shows, in contrast to the traditional Keynesian theory, the new Keynesian sticky-price theory indicates that the economy will find its own way back to a long-run equilibrium. The theory presumes that small menu costs induce firms not to

FIGURE 18-9

Short- and Long-Run Adjustments in the New Keynesian Sticky-Price Theory

Panel (a) shows that when prices are sticky, the short-run aggregate supply curve is horizontal, here at a price level of 118. As a consequence, the short-run effect of a fall in aggregate demand from AD_1 to AD_2 generates the largest possible decline in real GDP, from $15 trillion at point E_1 to $14.7 trillion at point E_2. In the long run, producers perceive that they can increase their profits sufficiently by cutting prices and incurring the menu costs of doing so. The resulting decline in the price level implies a downward shift of the *SRAS* curve, so that the price level falls to 116 and real GDP returns to $15 trillion at point E_3. Panel (b) illustrates the argument for active policymaking based on the new Keynesian theory. Instead of waiting for long-run adjustments to occur, policymakers can engage in expansionary policies that shift the aggregate demand curve back to its original position, thereby shortening or even eliminating a recession.

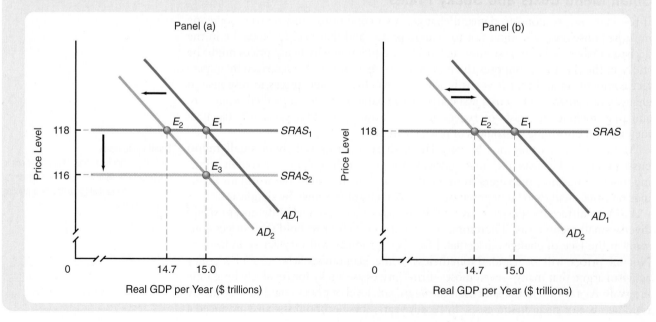

change their prices in the short run. In the long run, however, the profit gains to firms from reducing their prices to induce purchases of more goods and services cause them to cut their prices. Thus, in the long run, the price level declines in response to the decrease in aggregate demand. As firms reduce their prices, the horizontal aggregate supply curve shifts downward, from $SRAS_1$ to $SRAS_2$, and equilibrium real GDP returns to its former level, other things being equal.

Of course, an increase in aggregate demand would have effects opposite to those depicted in panel (a) of Figure 18-9. A rise in aggregate demand would cause real GDP to rise in the short run. In the long run, firms would gain sufficient profits from raising their prices to compensate for incurring menu costs, and the short-run aggregate supply curve would shift upward. Consequently, an economy with growing aggregate demand should exhibit so-called **new Keynesian inflation dynamics:** initial sluggish adjustment of the price level in response to aggregate demand increases followed by higher inflation later on.

New Keynesian inflation dynamics
In new Keynesian theory, the pattern of inflation exhibited by an economy with growing aggregate demand—initial sluggish adjustment of the price level in response to increased aggregate demand followed by higher inflation later.

WHY ACTIVE POLICYMAKING CAN PAY OFF WHEN PRICES ARE STICKY To think about why the new Keynesian sticky-price theory supports the argument for active policymaking, let's return to the case of a decline in aggregate demand illustrated in panel (a) of Figure 18-9. Panel (b) shows the same decline in aggregate demand as in panel (a) and the resulting maximum contractionary effect on real GDP.

Monetary and fiscal policy actions that influence aggregate demand are as potent as possible when prices are sticky and short-run aggregate supply is horizontal. In principle, therefore, all that a policymaker confronted by the leftward shift in aggregate demand depicted in panel (b) must do is to conduct the appropriate policy to induce a rightward shift in the *AD* curve back to its previous position. Indeed, if the policymaker acts rapidly enough, the period of contraction experienced by the economy may be very brief. Active policymaking can thereby moderate or even eliminate recessions.

Is There a New Keynesian Phillips Curve?

A fundamental thrust of the new Keynesian theory is that activist policymaking can promote economic stability. Assessing this implication requires evaluating whether policymakers face an *exploitable* relationship between the inflation rate and the unemployment rate and between inflation and real GDP. By "exploitable," economists mean a relationship that is sufficiently predictable and long-lived to allow enough time for policymakers to reduce unemployment or to push up real GDP when economic activity falls below its long-run level.

The U.S. Experience with the Phillips Curve

For more than 40 years, economists have debated the existence of a policy-exploitable Phillips curve relationship between the inflation rate and the rate of unemployment. In separate articles in 1968, the late Milton Friedman and Edmond Phelps published pioneering studies suggesting that the apparent trade-off suggested by the Phillips curve could *not* be exploited by activist policymakers. Friedman and Phelps both argued that any attempt to reduce unemployment by boosting inflation would soon be thwarted by the incorporation of the new higher inflation rate into the public's expectations. The Friedman-Phelps research thus implies that for any given unemployment rate, *any* inflation rate is possible, depending on the actions of policymakers.

Figure 18-10 appears to provide support for the propositions of Friedman and Phelps. It clearly shows that in the past, a number of inflation rates have proved feasible at the same rates of unemployment.

The New Keynesian Phillips Curve

Today's new Keynesian theorists are not concerned about the lack of an apparent long-lived relationship between inflation and unemployment revealed by Figure 18-10. From their point of view, the issue is not whether a relationship between inflation and unemployment or between inflation and real GDP breaks down over a period of years. All that matters for policymakers, the new Keynesians suggest, is whether such a relationship is exploitable in the near term. If so, policymakers can intervene in the economy as soon as actual unemployment and real GDP vary from their long-run levels. Appropriate activist policies, new Keynesians conclude, can dampen cyclical fluctuations and make them shorter-lived.

EVALUATING NEW KEYNESIAN INFLATION DYNAMICS To assess the predictions of new Keynesian inflation dynamics, economists seek to evaluate whether inflation is closely related to two key factors that theory indicates should determine the inflation rate. The first of these factors is anticipated future inflation. The new Keynesian theory implies that menu costs reduce firms' incentive to adjust their prices. When some

FIGURE 18-10

The Phillips Curve: Theory versus Data

If we plot points representing the rate of inflation and the rate of unemployment for the United States from 1953 to the present, there does not appear to be any trade-off between the two variables.

Sources: Economic Report of the President; Economic Indicators, various issues.

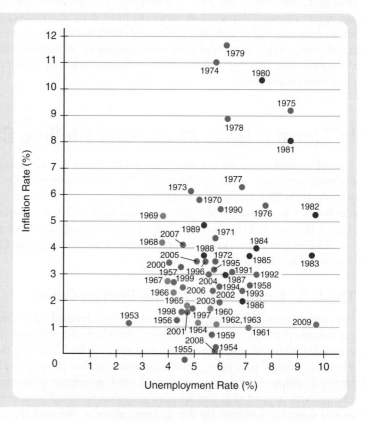

firms *do* adjust their prices, however, they will seek to set prices at levels based on expected future positions of demand curves for their products. The expected future inflation rate signals to firms how much equilibrium prices are likely to increase during future months, so firms will take into account the expected future inflation rate when setting prices at the present time.

The second key factor that new Keynesian theory indicates should affect current inflation is the average inflation-adjusted (real) per-unit costs that firms incur in producing goods and services. Thus, new Keynesians propose a positive relationship between inflation and an aggregate measure of real per-unit costs faced by firms throughout the economy. If firms' average inflation-adjusted per-unit costs increase, the prediction is that there will be higher prices charged by that portion of firms that do adjust their prices in the current period and, hence, greater current inflation.

Empirical evidence does indicate that increases in expected future inflation and greater real per-unit production costs are indeed associated with higher observed rates of inflation. In light of this support for these key predictions of the new Keynesian theory, the theory is exerting increasing influence on U.S. policymakers. For instance, media reports commonly refer to Fed officials' careful attention to changes in inflation expectations and firms' production costs that they interpret as signals of altered inflationary pressures.

JUST HOW EXPLOITABLE IS THE NEW KEYNESIAN PHILLIPS CURVE? Not all economists are persuaded that the new Keynesian theory is correct. They point out that new classical theory already indicates that when prices are *flexible*, higher inflation expectations should reduce short-run aggregate supply and contribute to increased inflation. In addition, all macroeconomic theories suggest that various factors that push up firms' production costs should have the same effect on short-run aggregate supply and inflation in a flexible-price economy.

Even if one were convinced that new Keynesian theory is correct, a fundamental issue is whether the new Keynesian theory has truly identified *exploitable* relationships. At the heart of this issue is just how often firms adjust their prices. If the average interval between firms' price adjustments is relatively long, then the horizontal new Keynesian aggregate supply curve will remain in position for a longer interval. As a result, a decline in aggregate demand will have a longer-lasting negative effect on real GDP. Then there will be a greater potential scope for activist policymaking to be able to boost aggregate demand and stabilize real GDP and unemployment. In contrast, if the average interval between changes in prices is short, then prices will adjust relatively quickly to a change in aggregate demand. There will be less scope for activist policies to stabilize the economy, because speedier adjustments of prices will automatically tend to dampen movements in real GDP and the unemployment rate.

Naturally, economists are hard at work trying to determine the average interval between price changes in national economies. So far, conclusions are mixed. Initially, studies of new Keynesian inflation dynamics yielded estimates of average price-adjustment intervals for the United States as long as two years. More recent studies, however, have produced estimated price-adjustment intervals no longer than one year. Some suggest that average periods between price adjustments are even shorter. At present, therefore, little agreement exists about just how much scope activist policymakers might have to stabilize real GDP and the unemployment rate under the new Keynesian theory.

Why are there such wide differences in estimated average periods between price changes by U.S. firms?

EXAMPLE
Measurement Issues Complicate Assessing the Speed of U.S. Price Adjustment

A by-product of the methods that new Keynesian economists use to assess how expectations of future inflation and per-unit real production costs influence actual inflation is an estimate of the average interval between price changes. Most studies measure the inflation rate as the percentage change in the GDP deflator. They also measure changes in average per-unit real production costs as deviations of aggregate real labor costs from their average level, and they assume no cyclical variation in real labor costs. Evaluating U.S. data from the mid-1960s through the mid-2000s using the percentage change in the GDP deflator yields an estimated average interval between price changes at U.S. firms of almost 19 months, or just over 1.5 years.

New Keynesian sticky-price theories focus on how menu costs affect the prices firms charge to consumers. The Producer Price Index (PPI) measures the actual prices charged by firms, so it is arguable that the percentage change in the PPI is a better inflation measure for evaluating the new Keynesian theory. Carl Gwin of Pepperdine University and David VanHoose of Baylor University have found that using this measure of inflation cuts the estimated average price-adjustment interval by about 50 percent, to just over 9 months.

There is another complication. Even though most studies of new Keynesian inflation dynamics assume that real labor costs are constant, these costs vary considerably over time. Gwin and VanHoose find that taking into account variations in real labor costs over time slashes the estimate of the average price-adjustment interval to just over 5 months. Clearly, how economists decide to measure inflation and real per-unit production costs influences their estimates of how often firms change prices.

FOR CRITICAL ANALYSIS
Why do you suppose that some economists worry that measuring inflation as the percentage change in the GDP deflator, which varies more smoothly over time than other price indexes, biases the estimate toward the conclusion that prices are "sticky"?

Summing Up: Economic Factors Favoring Active versus Passive Policymaking

To many people who have never taken a principles of economics course, it seems apparent that the world's governments should engage in active policymaking aimed at achieving high and stable real GDP growth and a low and stable unemployment rate. As you have learned in this chapter, the advisability of policy activism is not so obvious.

Several factors are involved in assessing whether policy activism is really preferable to passive policymaking. Table 18-1 summarizes the issues involved in evaluating the case for active policymaking versus the case for passive policymaking.

The current state of thinking on the relative desirability of active or passive policymaking may leave you somewhat frustrated. On the one hand, most economists agree that active policymaking is unlikely to exert sizable long-run effects on any nation's economy. Most also agree that aggregate supply shocks contribute to business cycles. Consequently, there is general agreement that there are limits on the effectiveness of monetary and fiscal policies. On the other hand, a number of economists continue to argue that there is evidence indicating stickiness of prices and wages. They argue, therefore, that monetary and fiscal policy actions can offset, at least in the short run and perhaps even in the long run, the effects that aggregate demand shocks would otherwise have on real GDP and unemployment.

What might be some of the topics for discussion at this meeting of leaders from the eight largest industrialized nations?

TABLE 18-1

Issues That Must Be Assessed in Determining the Desirability of Active versus Passive Policymaking

Economists who contend that active policymaking is justified argue that for each issue listed in the first column, there is evidence supporting the conclusions listed in the second column. In contrast, economists who suggest that passive policymaking is appropriate argue that for each issue in the first column, there is evidence leading to the conclusions in the third column.

Issue	Support for Active Policymaking	Support for Passive Policymaking
Phillips curve inflation–unemployment trade-off	Stable in the short run; perhaps predictable in the long run	Varies with inflation expectations; at best fleeting in the short run and nonexistent in the long run
Aggregate demand shocks	Induce short-run and perhaps long-run effects on real GDP and unemployment	Have little or no short-run effects and certainly no long-run effects on real GDP and unemployment
Aggregate supply shocks	Can, along with aggregate demand shocks, influence real GDP and unemployment	Cause movements in real GDP and unemployment and hence explain most business cycles
Pure competition	Is not typical in most markets, where imperfect competition predominates	Is widespread in markets throughout the economy
Price flexibility	Is uncommon because factors such as small menu costs induce firms to change prices infrequently	Is common because firms adjust prices immediately when demand changes
Wage flexibility	Is uncommon because labor market adjustments occur relatively slowly	Is common because nominal wages adjust speedily to price changes, making real wages flexible

These diverging perspectives help explain why economists reach differing conclusions about the advisability of pursuing active or passive approaches to macroeconomic policymaking. Different interpretations of evidence on the issues summarized in Table 18-1 will likely continue to divide economists for years to come.

QUICK QUIZ   *See page 476 for the answers. Review concepts from this section in MyEconLab.*

Some new Keynesian economists suggest that _____ _____ costs inhibit many firms from making speedy changes in their prices and that this price stickiness can make the short-run aggregate supply curve _____. Variations in aggregate demand have the largest possible effects on real GDP in the short run, so policies that influence aggregate demand also have the greatest capability to stabilize real GDP in the face of aggregate demand shocks.

Even though there is little evidence supporting a long-run trade-off between inflation and unemployment, new Keynesian theory suggests that activist policymaking may be able to stabilize real GDP and employment in the _____ run. This is possible, according to the theory, if stickiness of _____ adjustment is sufficiently great that policymakers can exploit a _____-run trade-off between inflation and real GDP.

You Are There Inflation Targeting Catches on even at the Fed—Sort Of

It is 2006, early in Ben Bernanke's first term as Fed chair. A special Fed conference is examining *inflation targeting,* a policy of trying to achieve a target rate of inflation that is already being used by the central banks of Canada, New Zealand, and the United Kingdom. To understand how central banks try to target inflation, recall from Chapter 17 that the equation of exchange is $M_s V \equiv PY$. If the income velocity of money (V) and real GDP (Y) are predictable, then a central bank can seek to attain a specific percentage change in the price level (P)—that is, an inflation target—by ensuring appropriate growth of the money supply (M_s).

As soon as Congress confirmed Bernanke as Fed chair, many observers had anticipated that the Fed might consider inflation targeting because Bernanke was known to be a proponent of the policy. Indeed, before the 2006 conference, some observers had anticipated that Bernanke might actively push for the Fed to join the growing list of inflation-targeting central banks. By the conclusion of the conference, however, reporters adept at vote counting in the political arena concluded that fewer than half of the members of the Federal Open Market Committee expressed even lukewarm support for the idea of adopting an explicit inflation target. Several FOMC members echoed Fed Vice Chair Don Kohn's view that inflation targeting would inhibit the Fed's ability to respond actively to short-term real GDP downturns or inflation

upswings. Others expressed doubts that the Fed could settle on a single inflation measure appropriate for such a targeting policy. The idea of Fed inflation targeting appeared dead.

Now fast-forward to an FOMC meeting on February 18, 2009. Following the meeting, the Fed makes a surprise announcement: From this meeting forward, the FOMC will issue inflation forecasts. Of course, everyone realizes what this announcement means. Because the Fed's actions largely determine the inflation rate, any Fed forecasts of inflation signal the inflation rate that the Fed intends, through its actions, to achieve. Thus, the Fed's inflation forecast will constitute a "de facto inflation target." Unlike the inflation targets of other central banks, however, the Fed's target will not be fixed over time. The target will vary with the membership of the FOMC and hence the members' relative preferences about inflation versus real GDP stability.

CRITICAL ANALYSIS QUESTIONS

1. Does inflation targeting represent active or passive policy-making?

2. Why do you suppose that some new Keynesian theorists have suggested that the Fed should try to target a measure of the expected rate of inflation, which is essentially what the Fed has chosen to do?

Are Actual Unemployment Rates or NAIRUs Rising Faster in the United States and Europe?

Issues and Applications

CONCEPTS APPLIED

- Nonaccelerating Inflation Rate of Unemployment
- Natural Rate of Unemployment
- Active Policymaking

Figure 18-11 displays actual unemployment rates experienced in the United States since 1970 and in European Monetary Union (EMU) nations (which use the euro as a common currency) since 1990. In addition, the figure provides the Organization for Economic Cooperation and Development's estimates of the nonaccelerating inflation rate of unemployment (NAIRU) over the same period. The figure shows that in both the United States and the EMU nations, the actual unemployment rates have risen significantly since the Great Recession began in December 2007. The figure also indicates that the NAIRUs in both areas are still increasing even as actual unemployment rates are showing signs of leveling off. Why are the U.S. and European NAIRUs increasing? What are the implications of higher NAIRUs for macroeconomic policymaking? Let's consider each of these questions in turn.

Alternative Explanations for the Rising NAIRUs

Recall that the NAIRU is the rate of unemployment at which the rate of inflation remains steady. In contrast to the natural rate of unemployment, which reflects only the influence of structural factors after all long-run adjustments have occurred, the NAIRU depends on cyclical factors as well. When there is a significant economic downturn such as the recent Great Recession, part of a nation's capital stock falls into disuse—such as idled U.S. and European auto factories—and remains unutilized until people figure out a new way to apply it to producing different goods and services. Likewise, some people who lose their jobs—such as autoworkers—must undergo a period of retraining to develop skills desired by employers in other industries. During these periods, the NAIRU exhibits cyclical variations. A

number of economists suggest that this is why the U.S. and European NAIRUs have risen during the recent sharp economic downturn. If this view is correct, then the NAIRUs should eventually begin to decline again when economic expansions take place.

Other economists suggest a less optimistic scenario. Although they agree that part of the rise in the NAIRUs is related to cyclical factors, they argue that longer-term structural changes are taking place as well. An upsurge in government regulations, they contend, is boosting natural rates of unemployment and consequently must also push up the NAIRUs. They point out that the main reason that the European NAIRU is persistently so much higher than the U.S. NAIRU is that European nations impose heavier regulations on their product

---

FIGURE 18-11

Actual Unemployment Rates and Estimated Nonaccelerating Inflation Rates of Unemployment in the United States and the EMU

The actual unemployment rates and the NAIRUs in the United States and the European Monetary Union trended downward from the mid-1990s through the mid-2000s. Both have increased in recent years, however.

Source: Organization for Economic Cooperation and Development.

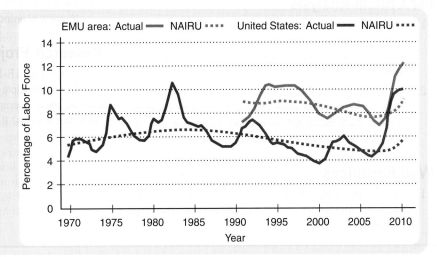

 *(continued)*

WHAT YOU SHOULD KNOW		WHERE TO GO TO PRACTICE

immediately, so real GDP remains unaffected. A key implication is the policy irrelevance proposition, which states that the unemployment rate is unaffected by fully anticipated policy actions. Technological changes and labor market shocks such as variations in the composition of the labor force can induce business fluctuations, called real business cycles, which weaken the case for active policymaking.

Modern Approaches to Bolstering the Case for Active Policymaking New Keynesian approaches suggest that firms facing costs of adjusting their prices may be slow to change prices in the face of variations in demand. Thus, the short-run aggregate supply curve is horizontal, and changes in aggregate demand have the largest possible effects on real GDP in the short run, which gives discretionary policies scope to offset aggregate demand shocks. Hence, prices and wages are sufficiently inflexible in the short run that there is an exploitable trade-off between inflation and real GDP. According to new Keynesian theory, therefore, discretionary policy actions can stabilize real GDP.

small menu costs, 463
new Keynesian inflation
    dynamics, 465

- **MyEconLab** Study
  Plans 18.4, 18.5, 18.6
- Video: The New
  Keynesian Economics

Log in to MyEconLab, take a chapter test, and get a personalized Study Plan that tells you which concepts you understand and which ones you need to review. From there, MyEconLab will give you further practice, tutorials, animations, videos, and guided solutions.
Log in to www.myeconlab.com

PROBLEMS

All problems are assignable in  myeconlab *. Answers to odd-numbered problems appear at the back of the book.*

18-1. Suppose that the government altered the computation of the unemployment rate by including people in the military as part of the labor force.

   a. How would this affect the actual unemployment rate?

   b. How would such a change affect estimates of the natural rate of unemployment?

   c. If this computational change were made, would it in any way affect the logic of the short-run and long-run Phillips curve analysis and its implications for policymaking? Why might the government wish to make such a change?

18-2. When Alan Greenspan was nominated for his third term as chair of the Federal Reserve's Board of Governors, a few senators held up his confirmation. One of them explained their joint action to hinder his confirmation by saying, "Every time growth starts to go up, they [the Federal Reserve] push on the brakes, robbing working families and businesses of the benefits of faster growth." Evaluate this statement in the context of short-run and long-run perspectives on the Phillips curve.

18-3. Economists have not reached agreement on how lengthy the time horizon for "the long run" is in the context of Phillips curve analysis. Would you anticipate that this period is likely to have been shortened or extended by the advent of more sophisticated computer and communications technology? Explain your reasoning.

18-4. The natural rate of unemployment depends on factors that affect the behavior of both workers and firms. Make lists of possible factors affecting workers and firms that you believe are likely to influence the natural rate of unemployment.

18-5. What distinguishes the nonaccelerating inflation rate of unemployment (NAIRU) from the natural rate of unemployment? (Hint: Which is easier to quantify?)

18-6. When will the natural rate of unemployment and the NAIRU differ? When will they be the same?

18-7. Suppose that more unemployed people who are classified as part of frictional unemployment decide to stop looking for work and start their own businesses instead. What is likely to happen to each of the following, other things being equal?

a. The natural unemployment rate

b. The NAIRU

c. The economy's Phillips curve

18-8. People called "Fed watchers" earn their living by trying to forecast what policies the Federal Reserve will implement within the next few weeks and months. Suppose that Fed watchers discover that the current group of Fed officials is following very systematic and predictable policies intended to reduce the unemployment rate. The Fed watchers then sell this information to firms, unions, and others in the private sector. If pure competition prevails, prices and wages are flexible, and people form rational expectations, are the Fed's policies enacted after the information sale likely to have their intended effects on the unemployment rate?

18-9. Suppose that economists were able to use U.S. economic data to demonstrate that the rational expectations hypothesis is true. Would this be sufficient to demonstrate the validity of the policy irrelevance proposition?

18-10. Evaluate the following statement: "In an important sense, the term *policy irrelevance proposition* is misleading because even if the rational expectations hypothesis is valid, economic policy actions can have significant effects on real GDP and the unemployment rate."

18-11. Consider the diagram below, which is drawn under the assumption that the new Keynesian sticky-price theory of aggregate supply applies. Assume that at present, the economy is in long-run equilibrium at point *A*. Answer the following questions.

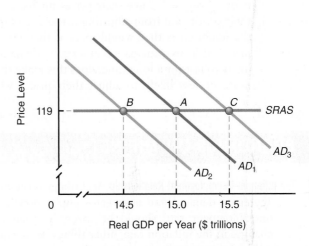

a. Suppose that there is a sudden increase in desired investment expenditures. Which of the alternative aggregate demand curves—AD_2 or AD_3—will apply after this event occurs? Other things being equal, what will happen to the equilibrium price level and to equilibrium real GDP in the *short run*? Explain.

b. Other things being equal, after the event and adjustments discussed in part (a) have taken place, what will happen to the equilibrium price level and to equilibrium real GDP in the *long run*? Explain.

18-12. Both the traditional Keynesian theory discussed in Chapter 11 and the new Keynesian theory considered in this chapter indicate that the short-run aggregate supply curve is horizontal.

a. In terms of their *short-run* implications for the price level and real GDP, is there any difference between the two approaches?

b. In terms of their *long-run* implications for the price level and real GDP, is there any difference between the two approaches?

18-13. The real-business-cycle approach attributes even short-run increases in real GDP largely to aggregate supply shocks. Rightward shifts in aggregate supply tend to push down the equilibrium price level. How could the real-business-cycle perspective explain the low but persistent inflation that the United States experienced until 2007?

18-14. Normally, when aggregate demand increases, firms find it more profitable to raise prices than to leave prices unchanged. The idea behind the small-menu-cost explanation for price stickiness is that firms will leave their prices unchanged if their profit gain from adjusting prices is less than the menu costs they would incur if they change prices. If firms anticipate that a rise in demand is likely to last for a long time, does this make them more or less likely to adjust their prices when they face small menu costs? (Hint: Profits are a flow that firms earn from week to week and month to month, but small menu costs are a one-time expense.)

18-15. The policy relevance of new Keynesian inflation dynamics based on the theory of small menu costs and sticky prices depends on the exploitability of the implied relationship between inflation and real GDP. Explain in your own words why the average time between price adjustments by firms is a crucial determinant of whether policymakers can actively exploit this relationship to try to stabilize real GDP.

ECONOMICS ON THE NET

The Inflation–Unemployment Relationship According to the basic aggregate demand and aggregate supply model, the unemployment rate should be inversely related to changes in the inflation rate, other things being equal. This application allows you to take a direct look at unemployment and inflation data to judge for yourself whether the two variables appear to be related.

Title: Bureau of Labor Statistics: Economy at a Glance

Navigation: Go to www.econtoday.com/chapter18 to visit the Bureau of Labor Statistics Economy at a Glance home page.

Application Perform the indicated operations, and then answer the following questions.

1. Click on the graph box next to *Consumer Price Index*. Take a look at the solid line showing inflation. How much has inflation varied in recent years? Compare this with previous years, especially the mid-1970s to mid-1980s.

2. Back up to *Economy at a Glance*, and now click on the graph box next to *Unemployment Rate*. During what recent years was the unemployment rate approaching and at its peak value? Do you note any appearance of an inverse relationship between the unemployment rate and the inflation rate?

For Group Study and Analysis Divide the class into groups, and have each group search through the *Economy at a Glance* site to develop an explanation for the key factors accounting for the recent behavior of the unemployment rate. Have each group report on its explanation. Is there any one factor that best explains the recent behavior of the unemployment rate?

ANSWERS TO QUICK QUIZZES

p. 457: (i) long . . . expectations; (ii) increase . . . decrease; (iii) Phillips . . . demand; (iv) Activist
p. 463: (i) rational expectations; (ii) policy irrelevance; (iii) supply . . . real business
p. 469: (i) small menu . . . horizontal; (ii) short . . . price . . . short

Policies and Prospects for Global Economic Growth

Since the mid-2000s, the volume of commercial *microlending*—loans in amounts ranging from $100 to around $1,500—has increased substantially. Most of the nearly $20 billion in internationally funded microlending has been provided by multinational banks, mutual funds, and hedge funds located in the United States and Europe. The loans have helped a portion of the world's poor to escape from their day-to-day poverty by enabling them to acquire capital goods that they utilize to produce more goods and services in the future—and thereby remain relieved from poverty. How does internationally funded microlending contribute to the economic growth of developing nations? Why are some observers worried that the volume of commercial microlending may have risen "too much" in recent years? In this chapter, you will learn the answers to these questions.

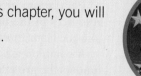

LEARNING OBJECTIVES

After reading this chapter, you should be able to:

▶ Explain why population growth can have uncertain effects on economic growth

▶ Understand why the existence of dead capital retards investment and economic growth in much of the developing world

▶ Describe how government inefficiencies have contributed to the creation of relatively large quantities of dead capital in the world's developing nations

▶ Discuss the sources of international investment funds for developing nations and identify obstacles to international investment in these nations

▶ Identify the key functions of the World Bank and the International Monetary Fund

▶ Explain the basis for recent criticisms of policymaking at the World Bank and the International Monetary Fund

myeconlab

MyEconLab helps you master each objective and study more efficiently. See end of chapter for details.

? DID YOU KNOW THAT in April 2007, the World Bank reported that for the first time since data had been recorded, the number of people around the globe living in extreme poverty had dropped below 1 billion—to 986 million? Recently, however, the World Bank announced that its 2007 estimate was too low. Based on a tabulation of those living on less than $1.25 per day in 2005 base-year U.S. dollars, the World Bank had recalculated and decided that 1.4 billion live in extreme poverty. Of these people, the World Bank estimated, nearly 880 million make do with even lower incomes—less than $1 per day in 2005 base-year U.S. dollars. More than 33 percent of those living on less than $1 per day reside in sub-Saharan Africa. Another 40 percent live in China and India. The rest reside in other locales scattered around the globe.

The World Bank is a multinational institution that, along with the International Monetary Fund, is charged with providing financial assistance aimed at improving the lot of the world's poorest residents. Examining the activities of these multinational institutions is one focus of this chapter. First, however, we look at factors that play key roles in speeding up or slowing down the pace of economic growth, as measured by rates of growth in per capita real GDP.

Labor Resources and Economic Growth

You learned in Chapter 9 that the main determinants of economic growth are the growth of labor and capital resources and the rate of increase of labor and capital productivity. Human resources are abundant around the globe. Currently, the world's population increases by more than 75 million people each year. This population growth is not spread evenly over the earth's surface. Among the relatively wealthy nations of Europe, women bear an average of just over one child during their lifetimes. In the United States, a typical woman bears about 1.5 children. But in the generally poorer nations of Africa, women bear an average of six children.

Population growth does not necessarily translate into an increase in labor resources in the poorest regions of the world. Many people in poor nations do not join the labor force. Many who do so have trouble obtaining employment.

A common assumption is that high population growth in a less developed nation hinders the growth of its per capita GDP. Certainly, this is the presumption in China, where the government has imposed an absolute limit of one child per female resident. In fact, however, the relationship between population growth and economic growth is not really so clear-cut.

Basic Arithmetic of Population Growth and Economic Growth

Does a larger population raise or lower per capita real GDP? If a country has fixed borders and an unchanged level of aggregate real GDP, a higher population directly reduces per capita real GDP. After all, if there are more people, then dividing a constant amount of real GDP by a larger number of people reduces real GDP per capita.

This basic arithmetic works for growth rates too. We can express the growth rate of per capita real GDP in a nation as

$$\text{Rate of growth of per capita real GDP} = \text{rate of growth in real GDP} - \text{rate of growth of population}$$

Hence, if real GDP grows at a constant rate of 4 percent per year and the annual rate of population growth increases from 2 percent to 3 percent, the annual rate of growth of per capita real GDP will decline, from 2 percent to 1 percent.

Why has the Chinese government imposed a limit of one child per female resident?

HOW POPULATION GROWTH CAN CONTRIBUTE TO ECONOMIC GROWTH The arithmetic of the relationship between economic growth and population growth can be misleading. Certainly, it is a mathematical fact that the rate of growth of per capita real GDP equals the difference between the rate of growth in real GDP and the rate of growth of the population. Economic analysis, however, indicates that population growth can affect the rate of growth of real GDP. Thus, these two growth rates generally are not independent.

Recall from Chapter 9 that a higher rate of labor force participation by a nation's population contributes to increased growth of real GDP. If population growth is also accompanied by growth in the rate of labor force participation, then population growth can contribute to *per capita* real GDP growth. Even though population growth by itself tends to reduce the growth of per capita real GDP, greater labor force participation by an enlarged population can boost real GDP growth sufficiently to more than compensate for the increase in population. On balance, the rate of growth of per capita real GDP can thereby increase.

WHETHER POPULATION GROWTH HINDERS OR CONTRIBUTES TO ECONOMIC GROWTH DEPENDS ON WHERE YOU LIVE On net, does an increased rate of population growth detract from or add to the rate of economic growth? Table 19-1 indicates that the answer depends on which nation one considers. In some nations that have experienced relatively high average rates of population growth, such as Egypt, Indonesia, and Malaysia, and, to a lesser extent, Chile and China, economic growth has accompanied population growth. In contrast, in nations such as Congo Democratic Republic, Liberia, and Togo, there has been a negative relationship between population growth and per capita real GDP growth. Other factors apparently must affect how population growth and economic growth ultimately interrelate.

The Role of Economic Freedom

A crucial factor influencing economic growth is the relative freedom of a nation's residents. Particularly important is the degree of **economic freedom**—the rights to own private property and to exchange goods, services, and financial assets with minimal government interference—available to the residents of a nation.

Economic freedom
The rights to own private property and to exchange goods, services, and financial assets with minimal government interference.

TABLE 19-1

Population Growth and Growth in Per Capita Real GDP in Selected Nations Since 1970

Country	Average Annual Population Growth Rate (%)	Average Annual Rate of Growth of Per Capita Real GDP (%)
Central African Republic	2.4	−1.1
Chile	1.5	2.7
China	1.3	7.2
Congo Democratic Republic	3.0	−3.3
Egypt	2.4	3.4
Haiti	1.8	0.0
Indonesia	1.8	4.1
Liberia	2.4	−1.3
Madagascar	2.9	−0.4
Malaysia	2.3	4.7
Togo	2.9	−1.0
United States	1.0	1.9

Source: Penn World Tables, International Monetary Fund.

Go to www.econtoday.com/chapter19 to review the Heritage Foundation's evaluations of the degree of economic freedom in different nations.

Approximately two-thirds of the world's people reside in about three dozen nations with governments unwilling to grant residents significant economic freedom. The economies of these nations, even though they have the majority of the world's population, produce only 13 percent of the world's total output. Several of these countries have experienced rates of economic growth at or above the 1.2 percent annual average for the world's nations during the past 30 years, but many are growing much more slowly. More than 30 of these countries have experienced negative rates of per capita income growth.

Only 17 nations, with 17 percent of the world's people, grant their residents high degrees of economic freedom. These nations, some of which have very high population densities, together account for 81 percent of total world output. All of the countries that grant considerable economic freedom have experienced positive rates of economic growth, and most are close to or above the world's average rate of economic growth.

How did millions of residents of Argentina suddenly discover that they were no longer free to manage their own pension savings?

INTERNATIONAL EXAMPLE
Savings Freedom Disappears in Argentina

In the midst of the financial crisis that gripped the world in the late 2000s, Argentina's president, Cristina Kirchner, made a startling announcement. The government would seize more than $24 billion in pension funds from private firms. Within two weeks, the nation's senate approved her plan, which transferred the funds to Anses, Argentina's social security agency.

The government's move, the president said, was aimed at protecting savers from losses caused by the global financial turmoil. Private firms, she claimed, were mismanaging pension savings and generating substantial losses, and only the government could ensure that pension funds would be protected.

The move also came as Argentina's government was struggling to raise sufficient taxes to finance growing deficits. Critics noted that once savers' funds had been shifted to Anses, the government would be able to raid the pension savings to cover short-term debts that would be coming due within the next few years. Whatever the government's true intentions may have been, it was certain that residents of Argentina were no longer free to manage their own pensions.

FOR CRITICAL ANALYSIS
Why do you suppose that the market values of stocks and bonds in Argentina dropped dramatically following the president's announcement?

The Role of Political Freedom

Interestingly, *political freedom*—the right to openly support and democratically select national leaders—appears to be less important than economic freedom in determining economic growth. Some countries that grant considerable economic freedom to their citizens have relatively strong restrictions on their residents' freedoms of speech and the press.

When nondemocratic countries have achieved high standards of living through consistent economic growth, they tend to become more democratic over time. This suggests that economic freedom tends to stimulate economic growth, which then leads to more political freedom.

QUICK QUIZ   *See page 499 for the answers. Review concepts from this section in MyEconLab.*

For a given rate of growth of aggregate real GDP, higher population growth tends to _____ the growth of per capita real GDP.

To the extent that increased population growth leads to greater _____ _____ participation that raises the growth of total real GDP, a higher population growth rate can potentially _____ the rate of growth in per capita real GDP.

In general, the extent of _____ freedom does not necessarily increase the rate of economic growth. A greater degree of _____ freedom, however, does have a positive effect on a nation's growth prospects.

Capital Goods and Economic Growth

A fundamental problem developing countries face is that a significant portion of their capital goods, or manufactured resources that may be used to produce other items in the future, is what economists call **dead capital**, a term coined by economist Hernando de Soto. This term describes a capital resource lacking clear title of ownership. Dead capital may actually be put to some productive purpose, but individuals and firms face difficulties in exchanging, insuring, and legally protecting their rights to this resource. Thus, dead capital is a resource that people cannot readily allocate to its *most efficient* use. As economists have dug deeper into the difficulties confronting residents of the world's poorest nations, they have found that dead capital is among the most significant impediments to growth of per capita incomes in these countries.

Dead capital
Any capital resource that lacks clear title of ownership.

Dead Capital and Inefficient Production

Physical structures used to house both business operations and labor resources are forms of capital goods. Current estimates indicate that unofficial, nontransferrable physical structures valued at more than $9 trillion are found in developing nations around the world. Because people in developing countries do not officially own this huge volume of capital goods, they cannot easily trade these resources. Thus, it is hard for many of the world's people to use capital goods in ways that will yield the largest feasible output of goods and services.

Consider, for instance, a hypothetical situation faced by an individual in Cairo, Egypt, a city in which an estimated 90 percent of all physical structures are unofficially owned. Suppose this person unofficially owns a run-down apartment building but has no official title of ownership for this structure. Also suppose that the building is better suited for use as a distribution center for a new import-export firm. The individual would like to sell or lease the structure to the new firm, but because he does not formally own the building, he is unable to do so. If the costs of obtaining formal title to the property are sufficiently high relative to the potential benefit—as they apparently are at present for about 9 out of every 10 Cairo businesses and households—this individual's capital resource will likely not be allocated to its highest-valued use.

This example illustrates a basic problem of dead capital. People who unofficially own capital goods are commonly constrained in their ability to use them efficiently. As a result, large quantities of capital goods throughout the developing world are inefficiently employed.

Dead Capital and Economic Growth

Recall from Chapter 2 that when we take into account production choices over time, any society faces a trade-off between consumption goods and capital goods. Whenever we make a choice to produce more consumption goods today, we incur an opportunity cost of fewer goods in the future. This means that when we make a choice to aim for more future economic growth to permit consumption of more goods in the future, we must allocate more resources to producing capital goods today. This entails incurring an opportunity cost today because society must allocate fewer resources to the current production of consumption goods.

This growth trade-off applies to any society, whether in a highly industrialized nation or a developing country. In a developing country, however, the inefficiencies of dead capital greatly reduce the rate of return on investment by individuals and firms. The resulting disincentives to invest in new capital goods can greatly hinder economic growth.

GOVERNMENT INEFFICIENCIES, INVESTMENT, AND GROWTH A major factor contributing to the problem of dead capital in many developing nations is significant and often highly inefficient government regulation. Governments in many of the world's poorest nations place tremendous obstacles in the way of entrepreneurs interested in owning capital goods and directing them to profitable opportunities.

In addition to creating a problem with dead capital, overzealously administered government regulations that impede private resource allocation tend to reduce investment in new capital goods. If newly produced capital goods cannot be easily devoted to their most efficient uses, there is less incentive to invest. In a nation with a stifling government bureaucracy regulating the uses of capital goods, newly created capital will all too likely become dead capital.

Thus, government inefficiency can be a major barrier to economic growth. Figure 19-1 depicts the relationship between average growth of per capita incomes and index measures of governmental inefficiency for various nations. As you can see, the

FIGURE 19-1

Bureaucratic Inefficiency and Economic Growth

Inefficiencies in government bureaucracies reduce the incentive to invest and thereby detract from economic growth.

Sources: International Monetary Fund; World Bank.

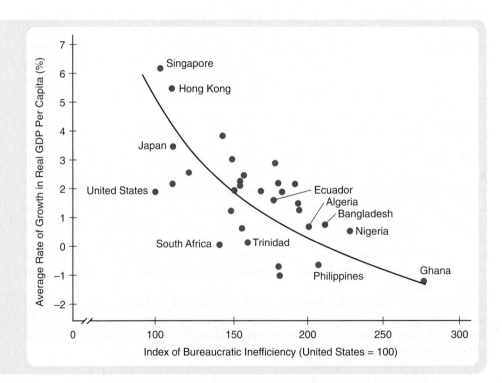

economies of countries with less efficient governments tend to grow at relatively slower rates. The reason is that bureaucratic inefficiencies in these nations complicate efforts to direct capital goods to their most efficient uses.

ACCESS TO CREDIT MATTERS The 2006 Nobel Peace Prize went to Muhammad Yunus of Bangladesh. Yunus contends that access to private credit is vital for promoting economic growth in poverty-stricken countries, where, in his view, present credit arrangements are inadequate.

Private lenders, Yunus suggests, are more likely to grant loans if borrowers can provide marketable collateral in the form of capital assets that lenders can obtain if a borrower defaults. Loan applicants cannot offer as collateral capital assets that they do not officially own, however. Even if an applicant has legal title to capital assets, a lender is unlikely to accept them as collateral if government rules and inefficiencies inhibit the marketability of those assets in the event that the borrower defaults.

Figure 19-2 on the following page displays both the top five and the bottom five nations of the world ranked by their ratios of private credit to GDP. Common features of the bottom five nations are significant stocks of informally used but officially unowned capital goods and very inefficient government bureaucracies. Access to credit in these nations is very limited, so ratios of private credit to GDP are low.

Yunus received his Nobel Peace Prize for his efforts to operate a *microlender*, a banking institution that specializes in making very small loans to entrepreneurs seeking to lift themselves up from the lowest rungs of poverty. In some of the poorest nations in which microlending activities are beginning to flourish, tens of millions of people are obtaining access to credit for the first time in their lives. As a consequence, ratios of private credit to GDP are climbing.

Why is access to financial markets of fundamental importance even to the world's poorest people?

You Are There

To learn about the real-world experience of a company that specializes in offering small amounts of private credit in rural India, read **A Microlender Succeeds in India—In Part by Avoiding Overexposure to Water Buffalo,** on pages 491 and 492.

INTERNATIONAL EXAMPLE
Sophisticated Finance on Less Than $2 per Day

Recently, a group of economists spent time tracking the financial dealings of some of the world's poorest people. The economists observed the operations of informal financial markets in India and Africa, where they discovered that even people who get by on less than $2 per day engage in relatively sophisticated financial arrangements. Indeed, financial transactions are often crucial to the survival of the poorest individuals.

In an Indian slum, for instance, the economists found a woman who operated a type of microinsurance operation, which pooled the meager savings of several individuals and families. These people trusted her to use the funds to extend emergency loans to people who on some days found themselves lacking even a crust of bread to eat. On net, everyone in the group earned *negative* rates of return from placing some of their savings with the woman's microinsurance operation. In effect, they paid insurance premiums to be assured of assistance when they were in dire straits.

In a relatively isolated South African village, several women operated cooperative microlending businesses. They pooled their savings and authorized an elected oversight board to extend loans to those among them who experienced unexpected events such as the loss of a job or the death of a family member. The oversight board was also charged with collecting the loans as well as interest—which the economists found was consistent with the market interest rate in more sophisticated credit markets in South African cities.

FOR CRITICAL ANALYSIS
Why do you suppose that even rudimentary financial markets are necessary to support the process of economic growth? (Hint: Think about how the ability to engage in investment in capital goods depends on the ability of investors to borrow from savers.)

FIGURE 19-2

The Ratio of Private Credit to GDP in Selected Nations

This figure displays the top five and bottom five nations of the world ranked according to ratios of private credit to GDP.

Source: Federal Reserve Bank of St. Louis.

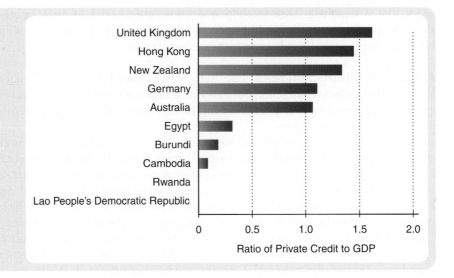

Dead capital is a capital resource without clear title of _____. It is difficult for a buyer to trade, insure, or maintain a right to use dead capital.

The inability to put dead capital to its most efficient use contributes to _____ economic growth, particularly

in _____ nations, where dead capital can be a relatively large portion of total capital goods.

Inefficient government _____ contribute to the dead capital problem, which reduces the incentive to invest in additional capital goods.

Private International Financial Flows as a Source of Global Growth

Given the large volume of inefficiently employed capital goods in developing nations, what can be done to promote greater global growth? One approach is to rely on private markets to find ways to direct capital goods toward their best uses in most nations. Another is to entrust the world's governments with the task of developing and implementing policies that enhance economic growth in developing nations. Let's begin by considering the market-based approach to promoting global growth.

Private Investment in Developing Nations

Between 1995 and 2007, at least $150 billion per year in private funds flowed to developing nations in the form of loans or purchases of bonds or stock. Of course, in some years, as during the Panic of 2008, international investors stop lending to developing countries or sell off government-issued bonds and private-company stocks of those countries. When these international outflows of funds are taken into account, the *net* flows of funds to developing countries have averaged just over $80 billion per year since 1995. This is nearly 5 percent of the annual net investment within the United States.

Nearly all the funds that flow into developing countries do so to finance investment projects in those nations. Economists group these international flows of investment funds into three categories. One is loans from banks and other sources. The second is **portfolio investment,** or purchases of less than 10 percent of the shares of ownership in a company. The third is **foreign direct investment,** or the acquisition of sufficient stocks to obtain more than a 10 percent share of a firm's ownership.

Figure 19-3 displays percentages of each type of international investment financing provided to developing nations since 1980. As you can see, three decades ago, bank loans accounted for the bulk of international funding of investment in the world's less developed nations. Today, direct ownership shares in the form of portfolio investment and foreign direct investment together account for most international investment financing.

Portfolio investment
The purchase of less than 10 percent of the shares of ownership in a company in another nation.

Foreign direct investment
The acquisition of more than 10 percent of the shares of ownership in a company in another nation.

Obstacles to International Investment

There is an important difficulty with depending on international flows of funds to finance capital investment in developing nations. The markets for loans, bonds, and stocks in developing countries are particularly susceptible to problems relating to *asymmetric information* (see Chapter 15). International investors are well aware of the informational problems to which they are exposed in developing nations, so many stand ready to withdraw their financial support at a moment's notice.

For a link to an Asian Development Bank analysis of the effects of foreign direct investment on developing nations, go to www.econtoday.com/chapter19.

ASYMMETRIC INFORMATION AS A BARRIER TO FINANCING GLOBAL GROWTH
Recall from Chapter 15 that asymmetric information in financial markets exists when institutions that make loans or investors who hold bonds or stocks have less information than those who seek to use the funds. *Adverse selection* problems arise when those who wish to obtain funds for the least worthy projects are among those who attempt to borrow or issue bonds or stocks. If banks and investors have trouble identifying these higher-risk individuals and firms, they may be less willing to channel funds to even creditworthy borrowers. Another asymmetric information problem is *moral hazard*. This is the potential for recipients of funds to engage in riskier behavior after receiving financing.

FIGURE 19-3

Sources of International Investment Funds

Since 1980, international funding of capital investment in developing nations has shifted from lending by banks to ownership shares via portfolio investment and foreign direct investment.

Source: International Monetary Fund (including estimates).

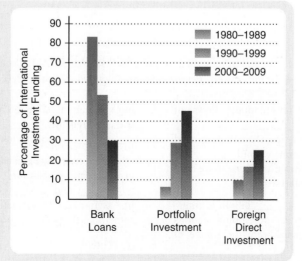

In light of the adverse selection problem, anyone thinking about funding a business endeavor in any locale must study the firm carefully before extending financial support. The potential for moral hazard requires a lender to a firm or someone who has purchased the firm's bonds or stock to continue to monitor the company's performance after providing financial support.

By definition, financial intermediation is still relatively undeveloped in less advanced regions of the world. Consequently, individuals interested in financing potentially profitable investments in developing nations typically cannot rely on financial intermediaries based in these countries. Asymmetric information problems may be so great in some developing nations that very few private lenders or investors will wish to direct their funds to worthy capital investment projects. In some countries, therefore, concerns about adverse selection and moral hazard can be a significant obstacle to economic growth.

INCOMPLETE INFORMATION AND INTERNATIONAL FINANCIAL CRISES Those who are willing to contemplate making loans or buying bonds or stocks issued in developing nations must either do their own careful homework or follow the example of other lenders or investors whom they regard as better informed. Many relatively unsophisticated lenders and investors, such as relatively small banks and individual savers, rely on larger lenders and investors to evaluate risks in developing nations.

International financial crisis
The rapid withdrawal of foreign investments and loans from a nation.

This has led some economists to suggest that a follow-the-leader mentality can influence international flows of funds. In extreme cases, they contend, the result can be an **international financial crisis.** This is a situation in which lenders rapidly withdraw loans made to residents of developing nations and investors sell off bonds and stocks issued by firms and governments in those countries. Of course, an international financial crisis has been under way since 2008. Unlike the crisis during the early 2000s that radiated outward from Southeast Asia, Central Asia, and Latin America, the current crisis began in the United States. It then spread to Europe before adversely affecting most developing nations. Although economies of several Asian nations have weathered the crisis relatively well so far, the world economy shrank for the first time in decades. Undoubtedly, this has contributed to a decline in flows of private funds to developing nations.

QUICK QUIZ *See page 499 for the answers. Review concepts from this section in MyEconLab.*

The three main categories of international flows of investment funds are loans by _____, _____ investment that involves purchasing less than 10 percent of the shares of ownership in a company, and _____ _____ investment that involves purchasing more than 10 percent of a company's ownership shares.

On net, an average of about $_____ billion in international investment funds flows to developing nations each year. In years past, bank loans were the source of most foreign funding of investment in developing countries, but recently _____ investment and _____ _____ investment have increased.

Obstacles to private financing of capital accumulation and growth in developing nations include _____ _____ and _____ _____ problems caused by asymmetric information, which can restrain and sometimes destabilize private flows of funds.

International Institutions and Policies for Global Growth

There has long been a recognition that adverse selection and moral hazard problems can both reduce international flows of private funds to developing nations and make these flows relatively variable. Since 1945, the world's governments have taken an active role in supplementing private markets. Two international institutions, the World Bank and the International Monetary Fund, have been at the center of government-directed efforts to attain higher rates of global economic growth.

The World Bank

The **World Bank** specializes in extending relatively long-term loans for capital investment projects that otherwise might not receive private financial support. When the World Bank was first formed in 1945, it provided assistance in the post–World War II rebuilding period. In the 1960s, the World Bank broadened its mission by widening its scope to encompass global antipoverty efforts.

Today, the World Bank makes loans solely to about 100 developing nations containing roughly half the world's population. Governments and firms in these countries typically seek loans from the World Bank to finance specific projects, such as improved irrigation systems, road improvements, and better hospitals.

The World Bank is actually composed of five separate institutions: the International Development Association, the International Bank for Reconstruction and Development, the International Finance Corporation, the Multinational Investment Guarantee Agency, and the International Center for Settlement of Investment Disputes. These World Bank organizations each have between 144 and 186 member nations, and on their behalf, the approximately 10,000 people employed by World Bank institutions coordinate the funding of investment activities undertaken by various governments and private firms in developing nations. Figure 19-4 displays the current regional distribution of about $20 billion in World Bank lending. Governments of the world's wealthiest countries provide most of the funds that the World Bank lends each year, although the World Bank also raises some of its funds in private financial markets.

World Bank

A multinational agency that specializes in making loans to about 100 developing nations in an effort to promote their long-term development and growth.

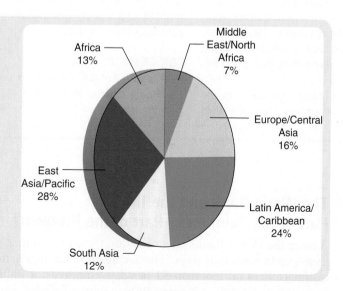

FIGURE 19-4

Distribution of World Bank Lending Since 1990

Currently, about 40 percent of the World Bank's loans go to developing nations in the East Asia/Pacific and South Asia regions.

Source: World Bank.

Africa 13%

Middle East/North Africa 7%

Europe/Central Asia 16%

Latin America/ Caribbean 24%

South Asia 12%

East Asia/Pacific 28%

The International Monetary Fund

International Monetary Fund (IMF)
A multinational organization that aims to promote world economic growth through more financial stability.

Quota subscription
A nation's account with the International Monetary Fund, denominated in special drawing rights.

The **International Monetary Fund (IMF)** is an international organization that aims to promote global economic growth by fostering financial stability. At present, the IMF has more than 180 member nations.

When a country joins the IMF, it deposits funds to an account called its **quota subscription.** These funds are measured in terms of an international unit of accounting called *special drawing rights* (*SDRs*), which have a value based on a weighted average of a basket of four key currencies: the euro, the pound sterling, the yen, and the dollar. At present, one SDR is equivalent to just over $1.50.

The IMF assists developing nations primarily by making loans to their governments. Originally, the IMF's primary function was to provide short-term loans, and it continues to offer these forms of assistance.

After the 1970s, however, nations' demands for short-term credit declined, and the IMF adapted by expanding its other lending programs. It now provides certain types of credit directly to poor and heavily indebted countries, either as long-term loans intended to support growth-promoting projects or as short- or long-term assistance aimed at helping countries experiencing problems in repaying existing debts. Under these funding programs, the IMF seeks to assist any qualifying member experiencing an unusual fluctuation in exports or imports, a loss of confidence in its own financial system, or spillover effects from financial problems originating elsewhere.

Why, in the midst of a financial panic, did the governments of the world's richest nations provide extra funding to the IMF?

INTERNATIONAL EXAMPLE
The IMF Gets an Emergency Cash Infusion—But Why?

Recently, governments of many the world's wealthiest countries provided emergency support to the IMF. This decision seemed curious to many observers. After all, the wealthiest nations were in the midst of a serious financial crisis. Furthermore, the IMF had only about $20 billion in loans outstanding and almost $150 billion in cash reserves available to lend to countries requiring assistance. Nevertheless, 20 nations, including the United States, several European nations, Japan, and even China, agreed to provide $500 billion in additional IMF funding.

What motivated these wealthy nations to build up the IMF's cash reserves was the recognition that their own residents were in the process of conducting one of the largest "cash withdrawals" in global history. To try to replenish their own depleted stocks of liquid assets, residents of wealthy nations were cashing in investments in developing countries. Thus, many developing nations were experiencing their own financial crises and were preparing to apply for financial assistance from the IMF.

FOR CRITICAL ANALYSIS
Why would the IMF be a more appropriate institution for developing nations to turn to for speedy short-term loans than the World Bank?

The World Bank and the IMF: Part of the Solution or Part of the Problem?

Among the World Bank's client nations, meager economic growth in recent decades shows up in numerous ways. The average resident in a nation receiving World Bank assistance lives on less than $2 per day. Hundreds of millions of people in nations receiving its financial support will never attend school, and about 40,000 people in these countries die of preventable diseases every day. Thus, there is an enormous range of areas where World Bank funds might be put to use.

The International Monetary Fund also continues to deal with an ongoing string of major international financial crisis situations. Countries most notably involved in such crises have included Mexico in 1995; Thailand, Indonesia, Malaysia, and South Korea in 1997; Russia in 1998; Brazil in 1999 and 2000; Turkey in 2001; Argentina in 2001 and 2002; and Mexico (again) and other nations since 2008.

Naturally, officials of both organizations conclude that world economic growth would have been even lower and financial instability even greater if the institutions did not exist. In recent years, however, economists have increasingly questioned World Bank and IMF policymaking.

DOES THE WORLD BANK REALLY HAVE A MISSION ANYMORE? In some nations, particularly in Africa, attracting private investment has proved difficult. Consequently, the World Bank has been a key source of credit for these nations. Nevertheless, as Figure 19-4 on page 487 indicates, only about 13 percent of lending by the World Bank since 1990 has been directed to African countries.

The World Bank's official mission is to make loans to developing nations that fund projects incapable of attracting private financing from investors at home or abroad. Nevertheless, the World Bank makes many of its loans to nations that have little trouble attracting private funds, such as rapidly growing Asian countries. Critics of such loans argue that they often interfere with the private market for financing capital goods and encourage the kind of inefficient investment that contributed to Asia's economic woes in the late 1990s and to Argentina's financial collapse in the early 2000s.

Some observers also contend that a number of countries that receive World Bank funds are inappropriate recipients of development assistance. For instance, China has reserves of currencies of other nations exceeding $1 trillion, and its residents are net *lenders* of funds to other nations of the world. Nevertheless, the Chinese government and Chinese companies annually borrow between $2 billion and $3 billion from the World Bank.

ASYMMETRIC INFORMATION AND THE WORLD BANK AND IMF Like any other lenders, the World Bank and IMF encounter adverse selection and moral hazard problems. In an effort to address these problems, both institutions impose conditions that borrowers must meet to receive funds.

Officials of these organizations do not publicly announce all terms of lending agreements, however, so it is largely up to the organizations to monitor whether borrower nations are wisely using funds donated by other countries. In addition, the World Bank and IMF tend to place very imprecise initial conditions on the loans they extend. They typically toughen conditions only after a borrowing nation has violated the original arrangement. By giving nations that are most likely to try to take advantage of vague conditions a greater incentive to seek funding, this policy worsens the adverse selection problem the World Bank and IMF face.

Some policymakers, economists, and other observers contend that the policies of the World Bank and the IMF have contributed to international financial crises. They argue that when the World Bank and the IMF provide subsidized credit for industries and governments, private lenders and investors anticipate that these two institutions will back up nations' debts. Thus, private lenders and investors may lower their standards and make loans to, and buy bonds and stocks from, less creditworthy borrowers. Furthermore, if governments know that they can apply for World Bank and IMF assistance in the event of widespread financial failures, they have little incentive to rein in risky business practices.

RETHINKING LONG-TERM DEVELOPMENT LENDING   Since the early 1990s, one of the main themes of development economics has been the reform of market processes in developing nations. Markets work better at promoting growth when a developing nation has more effective institutions, such as basic property rights, well-run legal systems, and uncorrupt government agencies.

Hence, there is considerable agreement that a top priority of the World Bank and the IMF should be to identify ways to put basic market foundations into place by guaranteeing property and contract rights. This requires constructing legal systems that can credibly enforce laws protecting these rights. Another key requirement is simplifying the processes for putting capital goods to work in developing countries.

A fundamental issue is what, if anything, international organizations such as the World Bank and the IMF can do to promote pro-growth institutional improvements in developing nations. From one standpoint, there may be little that the World Bank and the IMF can accomplish. After all, the forms of national legal institutions are largely political matters for the nations' leaders to decide. Nevertheless, a number of economists have suggested that the World Bank and the IMF should adopt strict policies against countries with institutional structures that fail to promote individual property rights, law enforcement, and anticorruption efforts. This would, they argue, give countries an incentive to shape up their institutional structures.

Other economists, in contrast, advocate direct financial assistance to governments attempting to implement such institutional reforms. Funds put to such use, they argue, could compensate those who lose power as a result of reform efforts, when shifting to a more capitalist system takes away a ruling group's dictatorial powers to control national resources. Such financial assistance could also help fund investments required to make reforms work. Those proposing this more active role for international lenders contend that the result could be much larger long-term returns for borrowing and lending nations alike. They argue that the overall return would be much greater than the sum of piecemeal payoffs from such projects as dams, power plants, and bridges.

ALTERNATIVE INSTITUTIONAL STRUCTURES FOR LIMITING FINANCIAL CRISES
There are also different views on the appropriate role for the International Monetary Fund in anticipating and reacting to international financial crises. In recent years, economists have advanced a wide variety of proposals. Many of these proposals share common features, such as more frequent and in-depth releases of information both by the IMF and by countries that borrow from this institution. Nearly all economists also recommend improved financial and accounting standards for those receiving funds from multinational lenders, as well as other changes that might help reduce moral hazard problems in IMF lending.

Nevertheless, many of the proposals for change diverge sharply. The IMF and its supporters have proposed maintaining its current structure but working harder to develop so-called early warning systems of financial crises so that aid can be provided to head off crises before they develop. Some economists have proposed establishing an international system of rules restricting capital outflows that might threaten international financial stability.

Other economists call for more dramatic changes. For instance, one proposal suggests creating a board composed of finance ministers of member nations to be directly in charge of day-to-day management of the IMF. Another suggests providing government incentives, in the form of tax breaks and subsidies, for increased private-sector lending that would supplement or even replace loans now made by the IMF.

To learn about the International Monetary Fund's view on its role in international financial crises, go to www.econtoday.com/chapter19.

TIME TO REPLACE THE WORLD BANK AND THE IMF? A few economists have called for completely eliminating both the World Bank and the IMF. Even economists who think these institutions should disappear, however, disagree on what should replace them. On the one hand, a proposal calls for reducing the current scope of government involvement in multinational lending by replacing the World Bank and the IMF with a single institution that would make only short-term loans to countries experiencing temporary financial difficulties. On the other hand, another proposal suggests broadening the roles of governments by developing a "global central bank" that would engage in open market operations using funds raised from new international taxes and other government funds.

So far, few proposals for altering the international financial architecture have led to actual change. The IMF has adopted some minor changes in its procedures for collecting and releasing information, and it has stiffened some of the financial and accounting standards that borrowers must follow to obtain credit. Naturally, the member nations of the IMF would have to agree to the adoption of more dramatic proposals for change. To date there has been little movement in this direction. Undoubtedly, consideration of proposals for an altered international financial structure will continue to generate global debate in the years to come.

QUICK QUIZ   See page 499 for the answers. Review concepts from this section in MyEconLab.

The **World Bank** is an umbrella institution for _____ international organizations, each of which has more than 140 member nations, which coordinate _____-term loans to governments and private firms in developing nations.

The **International Monetary Fund** is an organization with more than 180 member nations. It coordinates mainly _____-term and some longer-term financial assistance to developing nations in an effort to _____ international flows of funds.

In principle, the World Bank's role is to provide loans to developing countries where _____ _____ prob-

lems deter private investment. But in recent years, the World Bank has provided funds to countries and companies that could have obtained financing from private investors.

Like other lenders, the World Bank and the IMF confront _____ _____ and _____ _____ problems. Some observers worry that failure to deal with these problems has actually contributed to a string of international financial crises. Recently, there have been suggestions that both institutions should impose tougher preconditions on borrowers, such as requiring internal reforms that promote domestic investment.

You Are There   ▶   A Microlender Succeeds in India—In Part by Avoiding Overexposure to Water Buffalo

In the poorest regions of India, access to credit traditionally has been almost nonexistent. Now, however, it is possible to obtain loans of $350 or less to purchase items such as water buffalo or bicycles. Residents are acquiring the loans from microlenders, which are spreading throughout the countryside.

Vikram Akula operates a typical Indian microlender, SKS Microfinance, which he founded about four years ago. After waiting six months for government approval to start SKS Microfinance, Akula and his company's first employee extended their first loans. Initially, to collect the loan payments, they had to traipse through muddy fields to find individual borrowers. To make their microlending operation more efficient, Akula began requiring groups of borrowers to meet at designated times. When the profits from the company's microlending operations increased, Akula obtained loan-management software that helps his firm avoid overexposing itself to certain risks. For instance, at one point Akula realized that customers were using 80 percent of his loans to buy water buffalo. This meant that SKS Microfinance could have faced huge defaults if an epidemic killed off water buffalo or if the price of buffalo milk dropped. The company adjusted by gradually redirecting more of its loans to brick makers, owners of tea shops, tire re-treaders, and tractor mechanics.

To date, SKS Microfinance has extended in excess of $60 million in loans to more than 200,000 people, many of whom are repeat borrowers. The company is expanding its operations following investments by several foreign banks, which now see that there are profits to be earned by making small loans to some of the world's poorest people. Now that these people have access to credit, they likely will not be so poor in the future.

CRITICAL ANALYSIS QUESTIONS

1. Why is microlending in developing nations likely to be both a labor-intensive business and a risky business?

2. In light of your answer to Question 1, why do you suppose that annual interest rates on Indian microloans typically range between 24 percent and 36 percent?

Is Microlending Headed for a Crash?

Issues and Applications

CONCEPTS APPLIED

- Microlending
- Foreign Direct Investment
- Portfolio Investment

Economists estimate that 3 billion poor individuals around the world constitute the eventual clientele of commercial microlenders—financial firms that specialize in loans that may be as small as $100 in India or as large as $1,500 in Bolivia. Today, there are at least 1,000 commercial microlenders. Most are stand-alone institutions, but some are owned by multinational banks that regard microlenders as a foreign direct investment. A few even offer ownership shares that are purchased by mutual funds and hedge funds as a form of international portfolio investment. All told, the volume of loans extended globally by commercial microlenders is estimated at more than $20 billion.

Are Microlenders Doing Too Much Business for Their Own Good?

In spite of the potential benefits of microlending for millions of the world's poor, some economists have become concerned that commercial microlenders may be extending too many loans. They point, for instance, to the substantial increase in microlending in India, shown in Figure 19-5. The total amount of credit extended as microloans in that nation is now more than 26 times greater than in 2004!

Some observers suggest that there is a parallel between the growth of microlending and the increase in U.S. banks' loans to so-called subprime borrowers during the mid-2000s. Like U.S. subprime borrowers, most recipients of microloans barely meet the minimum creditworthiness standards for loans. Thus, the risk of default on microloans is substantial. These observers note that the values of assets used as collateral in obtaining microloans could fall below the values of the loans, as did the values of U.S. houses financed with subprime loans in the late 2000s. If so, then many borrowers of microloans might simultaneously stop paying on the loans, as did substantial numbers of subprime borrowers in the United States in 2007 and 2008. The result could be a microlending meltdown in the 2010s that would be an eerie reflection of the U.S. subprime meltdown.

How Would Curtailed Microlending Affect the Developing World?

If the global buildup of microlending were to collapse, what would be the impacts? The "good news" is that even a global microlending meltdown would involve less than $20 billion and thus would be only a pale reflection of the U.S. subprime meltdown, in which trillions of dollars of credit ultimately was adversely affected by the U.S. financial crisis. Nevertheless, a microlending collapse would negatively affect multinational banks, mutual funds, and hedge funds that have invested funds with microlenders. The annual flow of billions of dollars of foreign direct investment and portfolio investment would cease, at least temporarily, which would remove a source of credit that has helped many people escape abject poverty.

Undoubtedly, many of the world's poor would adjust to a halt in microlending from abroad by returning to informal sources of credit located in their villages, towns, and cities. Of course, the loan volumes provided by traditional, informal microlenders would be much smaller than those provided by commercial firms. Consequently, aggregate credit in developing nations necessarily would shrink, resulting in cutbacks in capital investment. Thus, economic growth in the developing world would decline.

FIGURE 19-5

Growth of Microlending in India

Since 2005, the volume of microlending in India has increased from less than $100 million to about $2.5 billion.

Source: World Bank.

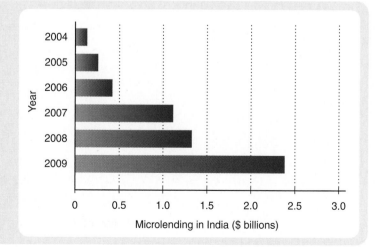

Test your understanding of this chapter by going online to **MyEconLab**.
In the Study Plan for this chapter, select Section N: News.

For Critical Analysis

1. Why do you suppose that some economists suggest that one advantage of internationally financed commercial microlending is that it helps the world's poor obtain ownership of their own capital goods?

2. What do you think motivates multinational banks to engage in foreign direct investment by purchasing commercial microlenders in developing nations?

Web Resources

1. For a good review of the pros and cons of foreign direct investment for economic growth of developing nations, go to www.econtoday.com/chapter19.

2. For access to detailed World Bank data on foreign direct investment, go to www.econtoday.com/chapter19.

Research Project

Read the first of the Web resources. Why does the author conclude that from the perspective of developing nations, foreign direct investment "should be the preferred form of foreign investment"? Why does the author suggest that the risks associated with foreign direct investment are more likely to fall on the investors themselves, rather than on the residents of developing countries?

 Here is what you should know after reading this chapter. **MyEconLab** will help you identify what you know, and where to go when you need to practice.

WHAT YOU SHOULD KNOW		WHERE TO GO TO PRACTICE
Effects of Population Growth on Economic Growth Increased population growth has contradictory effects on economic growth. On the one hand, for a given growth rate of real GDP, increased population growth tends to reduce growth of per capita real GDP. On the other hand, if increased population growth is accompanied by higher labor productivity, the growth rate of real GDP can increase. The net effect can be an increase in the growth rate of per capita GDP.	economic freedom, 479	• **MyEconLab** Study Plan 19.1 • Audio introduction to Chapter 19
Why Dead Capital Deters Investment and Slows Economic Growth Relatively few people in less developed countries establish legal ownership of capital goods. These unofficially owned resources are known as dead capital. Inability to trade, insure, and enforce rights to dead capital make it difficult for unofficial owners to use these resources most efficiently. As a result, in many developing nations, there is a disincentive to accumulate capital, which tends to limit economic growth.	dead capital, 481	• **MyEconLab** Study Plan 19.2
Government Inefficiencies and Dead Capital in Developing Nations In many developing nations, government regulations and red tape impose very high costs on those who officially register capital ownership. The dead capital problem that these government inefficiencies create reduces investment and growth. Thus, there is a negative relationship between measures of government inefficiency and economic growth.	KEY FIGURE Figure 19-1, 482	• **MyEconLab** Study Plan 19.2 • Animated Figure 19-1
Sources of International Investment Funds and Obstacles to Investing in Developing Nations International flows of funds to developing nations can potentially do much to promote global economic growth. There are three basic categories of these flows of funds: (1) bank loans; (2) portfolio investment, or purchases of less than 10 percent of the shares of ownership in a company; and (3) foreign direct investment, or purchases of more than 10 percent of the shares of ownership in a company. Problems relating to asymmetric information, such as adverse selection and moral hazard problems, are likely to be particularly acute in developing nations. Thus, asymmetric information problems present obstacles to international flows of funds.	portfolio investment, 485 foreign direct investment, 485 international financial crisis, 486 KEY FIGURE Figure 19-3, 485	• **MyEconLab** Study Plan 19.3 • Animated Figure 19-3

(continued)

 *(continued)*

WHAT YOU SHOULD KNOW

		WHERE TO GO TO PRACTICE

The Functions of the World Bank and the International Monetary Fund Adverse selection and moral hazard problems faced by private investors can both limit and destabilize international flows of funds to developing countries. The World Bank's function is to finance capital investment in countries that have trouble attracting funds from private individuals and firms. A fundamental duty of the International Monetary Fund is to stabilize international financial flows by extending loans to countries caught up in international financial crises.

World Bank, 487
International Monetary
  Fund (IMF), 488
quota subscription, 488

- **MyEconLab** Study Plan 19.4

The Basis for Recent Criticisms of World Bank and IMF Policymaking Critics of the World Bank contend that it has recently extended credit to companies and governments that could have obtained funds in private loan markets. Critics also contend that the World Bank and the IMF have failed to deal effectively with the adverse selection and moral hazard problems they face. These critics suggest that the World Bank and the IMF should place more stringent conditions on access to credit, including requiring government borrowers to implement reforms that give domestic residents more incentive to invest.

- **MyEconLab** Study Plan 19.4

Log in to MyEconLab, take a chapter test, and get a personalized Study Plan that tells you which concepts you understand and which ones you need to review. From there, MyEconLab will give you further practice, tutorials, animations, videos, and guided solutions.
Log in to www.myeconlab.com

PROBLEMS

All problems are assignable in *. Answers to odd-numbered problems appear at the back of the book.*

19-1. A country's real GDP is growing at an annual rate of 3.1 percent, and the current rate of growth of per capita real GDP is 0.3 percent. What is the population growth rate in this nation?

19-2. The annual rate of growth of real GDP in a developing nation is 0.3 percent. Initially, the country's population was stable from year to year. Recently, however, a significant increase in the nation's birthrate has raised the annual rate of population growth to 0.5 percent.

   a. What was the rate of growth of per capita real GDP before the increase in population growth?

   b. If the rate of growth of real GDP remains unchanged, what is the new rate of growth of per capita real GDP following the increase in the birthrate?

19-3. A developing country has determined that each additional $1 billion of investment in capital goods adds 0.01 percentage point to its long-run average annual rate of growth of per capita real GDP.

   a. Domestic entrepreneurs recently began to seek official approval to open a range of businesses employing capital resources valued at $20 billion. If the entrepreneurs undertake these investments, by what fraction of a percentage point will the nation's long-run average annual rate of growth of per capita real GDP increase, other things being equal?

2. The longer the time allowed for adjustment, the entry (or exit) of firms increases (or decreases) production in an industry. Consider what happens if the price of gasoline remains higher than before as a result of a sustained rise in gasoline demand. Even as existing refiners add to their capability to produce gasoline by retooling old equipment, purchasing new equipment, and adding new refining facilities, additional businesses may seek to earn profits at the now-higher gasoline prices. Over time, the entry of new gasoline-refining companies adds to the productive capabilities of the entire refining industry, and the quantity of gasoline supplied increases.

We therefore talk about short-run and long-run price elasticities of supply. The short run is defined as the time period during which full adjustment has not yet taken place. The long run is the time period during which firms have been able to adjust fully to the change in price.

Why is there a significant difference between the values of the short-run and long-run elasticities of housing supply?

EXAMPLE
Short-Run versus Long-Run Price Elasticities of Housing Supply

Constructing apartment buildings, condominium complexes, and houses typically requires time to coordinate various activities related to building construction, stretching from initial design to finished housing units. It is not particularly surprising, therefore, that estimated values of the short-run U.S. price elasticity of housing supply—with the short run defined to be one year—rarely exceed 0.1. Thus, within a one-year interval, a 10 percent increase in the price of housing generates a less than 1 percent increase in the quantity of housing supplied. When given a period of several years to adjust to a price change, however, builders' quantity responses are much greater. Recent estimates of the long-run U.S. price elasticity of housing supply—with the long run defined in this example to be 10 years—exceed 3.0. Consequently, if builders have 10 years to adjust to a 10 percent increase in the price of housing, the quantity of new housing supplied over the 10-year period rises by at least 30 percent.

FOR CRITICAL ANALYSIS
How would a technological development enabling builders to construct frames and walls more rapidly likely affect the short-run price elasticity of supply?

A GRAPHIC PRESENTATION We can show a whole set of supply curves similar to the ones we generated for demand. As Figure 20-6 on the following page shows, when nothing can be done in the immediate run, the supply curve is vertical, S_1. As more time is allowed for adjustment, the supply curve rotates to S_2 and then to S_3, becoming more elastic as it rotates.

QUICK QUIZ   *See page 524 for the answers. Review concepts from this section in MyEconLab.*

Price elasticity of supply is calculated by dividing the percentage change in _____ _____ by the percentage change in _____.

Usually, price elasticities of supply are_____ —higher prices yield _____ quantities supplied.

Long-run supply curves are _____ elastic than short-run supply curves because the _____ the time allowed, the more resources can flow into or out of an industry when price changes.

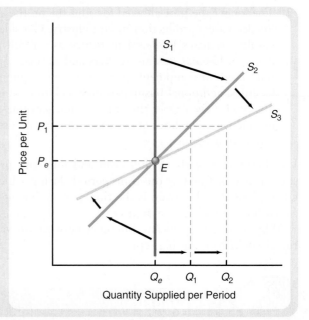

FIGURE 20-6

Short-Run and Long-Run Price Elasticity of Supply

Consider a situation in which the price is P_e and the quantity supplied is Q_e. In the immediate run, we hypothesize a vertical supply curve, S_1. With the price increase to P_1, therefore, there will be no change in the short run in quantity supplied; it will remain at Q_e. Given some time for adjustment, the supply curve will rotate to S_2. The new amount supplied will increase to Q_1. The long-run supply curve is shown by S_3. The amount supplied again increases to Q_2.

You Are There ▶ Using Cross Price Elasticities to Assess Brand and Supermarket "Loyalty"

Benaissa Chidmi of Texas Tech University and Rigoberto Lopez of the University of Connecticut recently sought to understand the distinction between "brand loyalty" and "supermarket loyalty." To do so, they tried to determine if consumers tend to purchase the same brands of breakfast cereals at the same Boston supermarkets even in the face of price increases.

Chidmi and Lopez first examined the price elasticities of demand for 37 brands of breakfast cereal. The absolute price elasticities ranged from 2.7 to just over 3.6. Thus, the demands for breakfast cereal brands were elastic: A 1 percent increase in the price of a particular brand of breakfast cereal caused the quantity of that breakfast cereal demanded to decline by more than 1 percent.

Chidmi and Lopez found that *within* a typical individual supermarket, the cross price elasticities for different pairings of breakfast cereals ranged from +0.02 to just over +0.04. Hence, a 10 percent increase in the price of a breakfast cereal brand would cause the amount of an alternative brand of breakfast cereal demanded to rise by 0.2 to 0.4 percent. The somewhat small values of the cross price elasticities within stores indicated that consumers were relatively loyal to cereal brands but nonetheless were sometimes willing to substitute to other brands when one brand's price increased.

To assess "supermarket loyalty," Chidmi and Lopez examined the cross price elasticities of demand for identical brands at different supermarkets. For instance, they estimated the cross price elasticity of Kellogg's Corn Flakes at Stop & Shop versus Shaw's Supermarket. They did the same for the other 36 cereals and obtained estimates of cross price elasticities for the same product at different stores ranging from as low as +0.005 to as high as almost +0.05. Thus, consumers sometimes responded to a higher price of, say, Corn Flakes at Stop & Shop by purchasing Corn Flakes at Shaw's instead. Nevertheless, the small values of these cross price elasticities of demand for the same cereal brands at different supermarkets imply relatively high loyalty to individual supermarkets. Apparently, not many Boston consumers go to the trouble to drive to another supermarket to buy Corn Flakes when the price of Corn Flakes at Stop & Shop rises by 10 percent.

CRITICAL ANALYSIS QUESTIONS

1. How would the price elasticity of demand for brands of breakfast cereals likely change if the number of substitute "quick breakfasts" available to consumers increased?

2. What do you think would happen to the cross price elasticities of demand for the same brands at Stop & Shop versus Shaw's if Shaw's were to locate all of its supermarkets immediately adjacent to Stop & Shop supermarkets?

Price Elasticity of Demand and the Upswing in Marijuana Use

CONCEPTS APPLIED

- Price Elasticity of Demand
- Elastic Demand
- Elasticity and Total Revenues

In the early 1990s, studies of marijuana use indicated that the percentage of people buying marijuana declined by more than 50 percent between 1981 and 1992. Private groups and government agencies that provide education about the ill effects of using the illicit drug hailed this decline as evidence of success in fighting marijuana use. Today, however, more than 40 percent of high school seniors are reporting marijuana purchases, and marijuana use among adults has jumped. Indeed, the percentage of drug-using adults indicating that marijuana is the "primary problem drug" in their lives has more than doubled since the mid-1990s.

What happened between the early 1990s and today? The answer comes in two parts, both of which have to do with a change in the price of marijuana.

A Big Price Drop

When antidrug agencies first tried to determine why the upsurge in marijuana use has occurred, they distributed surveys to teens and adults who had tried marijuana or were using the drug regularly. They learned from answers to the survey questions that people had heard the agencies' messages about the drug's unhealthful effects. They also learned, however, that the market price of marijuana was dropping considerably and that people were responding by consuming more of the drug.

Since 1992, the estimated price of marijuana has fallen by more than 30 percent. At the same time, the potency of a typical ounce of marijuana sold on the street has increased by more than 50 percent. Combined, these two factors have translated into a decline in the constant-quality price per ounce of marijuana of more than 60 percent. Of course, a result of this significant fall in price has been a movement down along the marijuana demand curve and a corresponding increase in the quantity of marijuana demanded.

The Role of Price Elasticities in Marijuana Usage

When evaluating the sensitivity of illicit drug use to changes in drug prices, economists typically examine two different types of price elasticities. Naturally, one of these is the price elasticity of demand. Most estimates indicate that the absolute price elasticity of demand for regular users of marijuana is about 2.8. Thus, the demand for marijuana is elastic. A 1 percent decrease in price generates roughly a 2.8 percent increase in marijuana consumption. This means that the more than 60 percent decrease in the constant-quality price of marijuana may have boosted consumption by regular marijuana users by as much as 140 percent.

Another elasticity that economists look at when examining the usage of illicit drugs is the *price elasticity of participation*, which is the responsiveness of people's first experiments with drugs to observed price changes. For most drugs, this elasticity is typically higher than the price elasticity of demand. Estimates of the price elasticity of participation for marijuana range between about 3.1 and 4.5. This range of estimates implies that a 1 percent decrease in marijuana's price leads to a 3.1 percent to 4.5 percent increase in first tries of the drug. Thus, the nearly 60 percent drop in the price of marijuana since 1992 has likely increased first uses of the drug by somewhere between 155 percent and 225 percent.

Medical studies indicate that between 2 and 3 percent of those who try and continue to use marijuana become habitual users of the drug within two years. About 10 percent of all who try the drug eventually become regular users. Lower marijuana prices and high price elasticities of marijuana demand and of participation in use of the drug explain why so many more people now report that marijuana is their "primary problem drug." Because the price of marijuana has declined considerably and the price elasticity of participation is high, more people than ever are responding to the price drop by trying marijuana. The price elasticity of demand by regular users is high, so once people become regular users, they are responding to the price decrease by consuming much larger amounts of the drug.

Test your understanding of this chapter by going online to **MyEconLab**.
In the Study Plan for this chapter, select Section N: News.

For Critical Analysis

1. Why do you suppose that people who propose stiffer penalties for violations of laws prohibiting the sale and use of marijuana argue that toughened enforcement would push up the market price of marijuana and significantly reduce its use? (Hint: Tougher penalties push up suppliers' costs and reduce users' quantity demanded.)

2. Why do you think that economists interpret the high price elasticity of demand for marijuana by regular users to be consistent with the fact that 90 percent of users do not become habitual users of the drug?

Web Resources

1. For information about estimates of price elasticities of demand for marijuana and other illicit drugs, go to www.econtoday.com/chapter20.

2. To see a recent study of short-run and longer-term effects of changes in enforcement efforts against marijuana, go to www.econtoday.com/chapter20.

Research Project

In light of the information provided above, evaluate whether the total revenues of marijuana sellers have likely increased or decreased. Explain your reasoning.

 Here is what you should know after reading this chapter. **MyEconLab** will help you identify what you know, and where to go when you need to practice.

WHAT YOU SHOULD KNOW

WHERE TO GO TO PRACTICE

Expressing and Calculating the Price Elasticity of Demand The price elasticity of demand is the responsiveness of the quantity demanded of a good to a change in the price of the good. It is the percentage change in quantity demanded divided by the percentage change in price. To calculate the price elasticity of demand for relatively small changes in price, the percentage change in quantity demanded is equal to the change in the quantity resulting from a price change divided by the average of the initial and final quantities, and the percentage change in price is equal to the price change divided by the average of the initial and final prices.

price elasticity of demand (E_p), 501

- **MyEconLab** Study Plan 20.1
- Audio introduction to Chapter 20

The Relationship Between the Price Elasticity of Demand and Total Revenues Demand is elastic when the price elasticity of demand exceeds 1, and over the elastic range of a demand curve, an increase in price reduces total revenues. Demand is inelastic when the price elasticity of demand is less than 1, and over this range of a demand curve, an increase in price raises total revenues. Finally, demand is unit-elastic when the price elasticity of demand equals 1, and over this range of a demand curve, an increase in price does not affect total revenues.

elastic demand, 503
unit elasticity of demand, 504
inelastic demand, 504
perfectly inelastic demand, 504
perfectly elastic demand, 504

KEY FIGURES
Figure 20-1, 504
Figure 20-2, 505
Figure 20-3, 507
Figure 20-4, 511

- **MyEconLab** Study Plans 20.2, 20.3
- Animated Figures 20-1, 20-2, 20-3, 20-4

Factors That Determine the Price Elasticity of Demand Three factors affect the price elasticity of demand. If there are more close substitutes for a good, the price elasticity of demand increases. The price elasticity of demand for a good also tends to be higher when a larger portion of a person's budget is spent on the good. In addition, if people have a longer period of time to adjust to a price change and change their consumption patterns, the price elasticity of demand tends to be higher.

- **MyEconLab** Study Plan 20.4
- Video: The Determinants of the Price Elasticity of Demand

The Cross Price Elasticity of Demand and Using It to Determine Whether Two Goods Are Substitutes or Complements The cross price elasticity of demand for a good is the percentage change in the demand for that good divided by the percentage change in the price of a related good. If two goods are substitutes in consumption, an increase in the price of one of the goods induces an increase in the demand for the other good, so that the cross price elasticity of demand is positive. In contrast, if two goods are complements in consumption, an increase in the price of one of the goods brings about a decrease in the demand for the other good, so that the cross price elasticity of demand is negative.

cross price elasticity of demand (E_{xy}), 513

- **MyEconLab** Study Plan 20.5
- Video: Cross Price Elasticity of Demand

(continued)

 (continued)

WHAT YOU SHOULD KNOW		WHERE TO GO TO PRACTICE
The Income Elasticity of Demand The income elasticity of demand for any good is the responsiveness of the demand for the good to a change in income, holding the good's relative price unchanged. It is equal to the percentage change in demand for the good divided by the percentage change in income.	income elasticity of demand (E_i), 514	• **MyEconLab** Study Plan 20.6 • Video: Income Elasticity of Demand
Classifying Supply Elasticities and How the Length of Time for Adjustment Affects the Price Elasticity of Supply The price elasticity of supply is equal to the percentage change in quantity supplied divided by the percentage change in price. If the price elasticity of supply is greater than 1, supply is elastic, and if the price elasticity of supply is less than 1, supply is inelastic. Supply is unit-elastic if the price elasticity of supply equals 1. Supply is more likely to be elastic when sellers have more time to adjust to price changes.	price elasticity of supply (E_s), 515 perfectly elastic supply, 516 perfectly inelastic supply, 516 **KEY FIGURE** Figure 20-6, 518	• **MyEconLab** Study Plan 20.7 • Animated Figure 20-6

Log in to MyEconLab, take a chapter test, and get a personalized Study Plan that tells you which concepts you understand and which ones you need to review. From there, MyEconLab will give you further practice, tutorials, animations, videos, and guided solutions.
Log in to www.myeconlab.com

PROBLEMS

All problems are assignable in **myeconlab** *. Answers to odd-numbered problems appear at the back of the book.*

20-1. When the price of shirts emblazoned with a college logo is $10, consumers buy 150 per week. When the price declines to $9, consumers purchase 200 per week. Based on this information, calculate the price elasticity of demand for logo-emblazoned shirts.

20-2. Table 20-2 on page 512 indicates that the short-run price elasticity of demand for tires is 0.9. If an increase in the price of petroleum (used in producing tires) causes the market prices of tires to rise from $50 to $60, by what percentage would you expect the quantity of tires demanded to change?

20-3. The diagram alongside depicts the demand curve for "miniburgers" in a local fast-food market. Use the information in this diagram to answer the questions that follow.

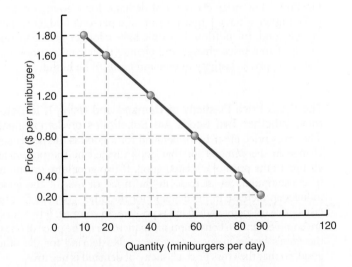

a. What is the price elasticity of demand along the range of the demand curve between a price of $0.20 per miniburger and a price of $0.40 per miniburger? Is demand elastic or inelastic over this range?

b. What is the price elasticity of demand along the range of the demand curve between a price of $0.80 per miniburger and a price of $1.20 per miniburger? Is demand elastic or inelastic over this range?

c. What is the price elasticity of demand along the range of the demand curve between a price of $1.60 per miniburger and a price of $1.80 per miniburger? Is demand elastic or inelastic over this range?

20-4. In a local market, the monthly price of Internet access service decreases from $20 to $10, and the total quantity of monthly accounts across all Internet access providers increases from 100,000 to 200,000. What is the price elasticity of demand? Is demand elastic, unit-elastic, or inelastic?

20-5. At a price of $30.00 to play 18 holes on local golf courses, 1,200 consumers pay to play a game of golf each day. A rise in the price to $32.50 causes the number of consumers to decline to 800. What is the price elasticity of demand? Is demand elastic, unit-elastic, or inelastic?

20-6. It is very difficult to find goods with perfectly elastic or perfectly inelastic demand. We can, however, find goods that lie near these extremes. Characterize demands for the following goods as being near perfectly elastic or near perfectly inelastic.

a. Corn grown and harvested by a small farmer in Iowa

b. Heroin for a drug addict

c. Water for a desert hiker

d. One of several optional textbooks in a pass-fail course

20-7. In the market for hand-made guitars, when the price of guitars is $800, annual revenues are $640,000. When the price falls to $700, annual revenues decline to $630,000. Over this range of guitar prices, is the demand for hand-made guitars elastic, unit-elastic, or inelastic?

20-8. Suppose that over a range of prices, the price elasticity of demand varies from 15.0 to 2.5. Over another range of prices, the price elasticity of demand varies from 1.5 to 0.75. What can you say

about total revenues and the total revenues curve over these two ranges of the demand curve as price falls?

20-9. Based on the information provided alone, characterize the demands for the following goods as being more elastic or more inelastic.

a. A 45-cent box of salt that you buy once a year

b. A type of high-powered ski boat that you can rent from any one of a number of rental agencies

c. A specific brand of bottled water

d. Automobile insurance in a state that requires autos to be insured but has few insurance companies

e. A 75-cent guitar pick for the lead guitarist of a major rock band

20-10. The value of cross price elasticity of demand between goods X and Y is 1.25, while the cross price elasticity of demand between goods X and Z is −2.0. Characterize X and Y and X and Z as substitutes or complements.

20-11. Suppose that the cross price elasticity of demand between eggs and bacon is −0.5. What would you expect to happen to sales of bacon if the price of eggs rises by 10 percent?

20-12. Assume that the income elasticity of demand for hot dogs is −1.25 and that the income elasticity of demand for lobster is 1.25. Based on the fact that the measure for hot dogs is negative while that for lobster is positive, are these normal or inferior goods? (Hint: You may want to refer to the discussion of normal and inferior goods in Chapter 3.)

20-13. At a price of $25,000, producers of midsized automobiles are willing to manufacture and sell 75,000 cars per month. At a price of $35,000, they are willing to produce and sell 125,000 a month. Using the same type of calculation method used to compute the price elasticity of demand, what is the price elasticity of supply? Is supply elastic, unit-elastic, or inelastic?

20-14. The price elasticity of supply of a basic commodity that a nation imports from producers in other countries is 2. What would you expect to happen to the volume of imports if the price of this commodity rises by 10 percent?

20-15. A 20 percent increase in the price of skis induces ski manufacturers to increase production of skis by 10 percent in the short run. In the long run, other things being equal, the 20 percent price increase generates a production increase of 40 percent. What is the short-run price elasticity of supply? What is the long-run price elasticity of supply?

20-16. An increase in the market price of men's haircuts, from $15 per haircut to $25 per haircut, initially causes a local barbershop to have its employees work overtime to increase the number of daily haircuts provided from 35 to 45. When the $25 market price remains unchanged for several weeks and all other things remain equal as well, the barbershop hires additional employees and provides 65 haircuts per day. What is the short-run price elasticity of supply? What is the long-run price elasticity of supply?

ECONOMICS ON THE NET

Price Elasticity and Consumption of Illegal Drugs Making the use of certain drugs illegal drives up their market prices, so the price elasticity of demand is a key factor affecting the use of illegal drugs. This application applies concepts from this chapter to analyze how price elasticity of demand affects drug consumption.

Title: The Demand for Illicit Drugs

Navigation: Go to www.econtoday.com/chapter20, and follow the link to the summary of this paper published by the National Bureau of Economic Research.

Application Read the summary of the results of this study of price elasticities of participation in use of illegal drugs, and answer the following questions.

1. Based on the results of the study, is the demand for cocaine more or less price elastic than the demand for heroin? For which drug, therefore, will quantity demanded fall by a greater percentage in response to a proportionate increase in price?

2. The study finds that decriminalizing currently illegal drugs would bring about sizable increases both in overall consumption of heroin and cocaine and in the price elasticity of demand for both drugs. Why do you suppose that the price elasticity of demand would rise? (Hint: At present, users of cocaine and heroin are restricted to only a few illegal sources of the drugs, but if the drugs could legally be produced and sold, there would be many more suppliers providing a variety of different types of both drugs.)

For Group Study and Analysis Discuss ways that government officials might use information about the price elasticities of demand for illicit drugs to assist in developing policies intended to reduce the use of these drugs. Which of these proposed policies might prove most effective? Why?

ANSWERS TO QUICK QUIZZES

p. 502: (i) responsiveness; (ii) quantity demanded . . . price; (iii) percentage . . . independent; (iv) inversely . . . negative

p. 505: (i) zero . . . inelastic; (ii) elastic . . . infinite

p. 509: (i) revenues; (ii) opposite; (iii) zero; (iv) same

p. 515: (i) substitutes . . . share . . . adjustment; (ii) Cross . . . positive . . . negative; (iii) demand . . . income

p. 517: (i) quantity supplied . . . price; (ii) positive . . . greater; (iii) more . . . longer

Consumer Choice

"Taken all together, how would you say things are these days—would you say that you are very happy, pretty happy, or not too happy?" A social science research center at the University of Chicago has been posing this question to a sample of several thousand U.S. residents each year since 1972. Researchers now commonly address similar questions to people around the world. Then they compare expressed levels of satisfaction both within countries and across countries. For more than two centuries, economists have been contemplating how people seek to maximize their happiness levels when making choices. Nevertheless, until recently most economists doubted that answers to survey questions could yield measures of happiness that can be compared across individuals. In this chapter, you will learn about economists' traditional measure of happiness, called *utility*, which economists apply to developing an understanding of how people make choices.

LEARNING OBJECTIVES

After reading this chapter, you should be able to:

- Distinguish between total utility and marginal utility

- Discuss why marginal utility first rises but ultimately tends to decline as a person consumes more of a good or service

- Explain why an individual's optimal choice of how much to consume of each good or service entails equalizing the marginal utility per dollar spent across all goods and services

- Describe the substitution effect of a price change on the quantity demanded of a good or service

- Understand how the real-income effect of a price change affects the quantity demanded of a good or service

- Evaluate why the price of diamonds is so much higher than the price of water even though people cannot survive long without water

? DID YOU KNOW THAT the human brain does its intelligent computing with 10^{11} (100,000,000,000) neurons? These neurons are interconnected in a complex network of about 10^{16} (10,000,000,000,000,000) electrochemical connections called synapses, each of which performs about 1,000 operations per second. Evidence indicates that all this computing power makes the human brain at least 10,000 times more intelligent than most artificially constructed supercomputers. Thus, there is general agreement that the human brain is thousands of times better at making choices among desirable alternatives than the computing machines available today. Human beings have considerable capability to evaluate choices and determine the quantities of different goods and services they wish to consume.

In Chapter 3, you learned that a determinant of the quantity demanded of any particular item is the price of that item. The law of demand implies that at a lower overall price, there will be a higher quantity demanded. Understanding the derivation of the law of demand is useful because it allows us to examine the relevant variables, such as price, income, and tastes, in such a way as to make better sense of the world and even perhaps generate predictions about it. One way of deriving the law of demand involves an analysis of the logic of consumer choice in a world of limited resources. In this chapter, therefore, we discuss what is called *utility analysis*.

What are some of the determinants of this consumer's decision to buy a new cell phone?

Utility
The want-satisfying power of a good or service.

Utility analysis
The analysis of consumer decision making based on utility maximization.

Utility Theory

When you buy something, you do so because of the satisfaction you expect to receive from having and using that good. For everything that you like to have, the more you have of it, the higher the level of total satisfaction you receive. Another term that can be used for satisfaction is **utility,** or want-satisfying power. This property is common to all goods that are desired. The concept of utility is purely subjective, however. There is no way that you or I can measure the amount of utility that a consumer might be able to obtain from a particular good, for utility does not imply "useful" or "utilitarian" or "practical." Thus, there can be no accurate scientific assessment of the utility that someone might receive by consuming a fast-food dinner or a movie relative to the utility that another person might receive from that same good or service.

The utility that individuals receive from consuming a good depends on their tastes and preferences. These tastes and preferences are normally assumed to be given and stable for a particular individual. An individual's tastes determine how much utility that individual derives from consuming a good, and this in turn determines how that individual allocates his or her income to purchases of that good. But we cannot explain why tastes are different between individuals. For example, we cannot explain why some people like yogurt but others do not.

We can analyze in terms of utility the way consumers decide what to buy, just as physicists have analyzed some of their problems in terms of what they call force. No physicist has ever seen a unit of force, and no economist has ever seen a unit of utility. In both cases, however, these concepts have proved useful for analysis.

Throughout this chapter, we will be discussing **utility analysis,** which is the analysis of consumer decision making based on utility maximization—that is, making choices with the aim of attaining the highest feasible satisfaction.

Utility and Utils

Economists once believed that utility could be measured. In fact, there is a philosophical school of thought based on utility theory called *utilitarianism*, developed by the English philosopher Jeremy Bentham (1748–1832). Bentham held that society should seek the greatest happiness for the greatest number. He sought to apply an arithmetic formula for measuring happiness. He and his followers developed the notion of measurable utility and invented the **util** to measure it. For the moment, we will also assume that we can measure satisfaction using this representative unit. Our assumption will allow us to quantify the way we examine consumer behavior. Thus, the first chocolate bar that you eat might yield you 4 utils of satisfaction; the first peanut cluster, 6 utils; and so on. Today, no one really believes that we can actually measure utils, but the ideas forthcoming from such analysis will prove useful in understanding how consumers choose among alternatives.

Util
A representative unit by which utility is measured.

Total and Marginal Utility

Consider the satisfaction, or utility, that you receive each time that you download and listen to digital music albums. To make the example straightforward, let's say that there are hundreds of downloadable music albums to choose from each year and that each of them is of the same quality. Let's say that you normally download and listen to one music album per week. You could, of course, download two, or three, or four per week. Presumably, each time you download and listen to another music album per week, you will get additional satisfaction, or utility. The question that we must ask though, is, given that you are already downloading and listening to one album per week, will the next one downloaded and listened to during that week give you the same amount of additional utility?

That additional, or incremental, utility is called **marginal utility**, where *marginal* means "incremental" or "additional." (Marginal changes also refer to decreases, in which cases we talk about *decremental* changes.) The concept of marginality is important in economics because we can think of people comparing additional (marginal) benefits with additional (marginal) costs.

Marginal utility
The change in total utility due to a one-unit change in the quantity of a good or service consumed.

Applying Marginal Analysis to Utility

The example in Figure 21-1 on the following page will clarify the distinction between total utility and marginal utility. The table in panel (a) shows the total utility and the marginal utility of downloading and listening to digital music albums each week. Marginal utility is the difference between total utility derived from one level of consumption and total utility derived from another level of consumption within a given time interval. A simple formula for marginal utility is this:

$$\text{Marginal utility} = \frac{\text{change in total utility}}{\text{change in number of units consumed}}$$

In our example, when a person has already downloaded and listened to two music albums in one week and then downloads and listens to another, total utility increases from 16 utils to 19 utils. Therefore, the marginal utility (of downloading and listening to one more album of Internet music after already having downloaded and listened to two in one week) is equal to 3 utils.

Graphical Analysis

We can transfer the information in panel (a) onto a graph, as we do in panels (b) and (c) of Figure 21-1 on the next page. Total utility, which is represented in column 2 of panel (a), is transferred to panel (b).

Total and Marginal Utility of Downloading and Listening to Digital Music Albums

If we were able to assign specific values to the utility derived from downloading and listening to digital music albums each week, we could obtain a marginal utility schedule similar in pattern to the one shown in panel (a). In column 1 is the number of music albums downloaded and listened to per week; in column 2, the total utility derived from each quantity; and in column 3, the marginal utility derived from each additional quantity, which is defined as the change in total utility due to a change of one unit of listening to downloaded albums per week. Total utility from panel (a) is plotted in panel (b). Marginal utility is plotted in panel (c), where you see that it reaches zero where total utility hits its maximum at between 4 and 5 units.

Panel (a)

(1) Number of Music Albums Downloaded and Listened to per Week	(2) Total Utility (utils per week)	(3) Marginal Utility (utils per week)
0	0	
		10 (10 − 0)
1	10	
		6 (16 − 10)
2	16	
		3 (19 − 16)
3	19	
		1 (20 − 19)
4	20	
		0 (20 − 20)
5	20	
		−2 (18 − 20)
6	18	

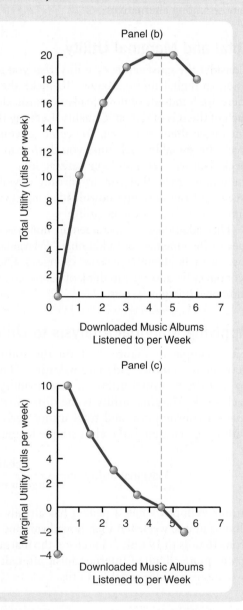

Total utility continues to rise until four digital music albums are downloaded and listened to per week. This measure of utility remains at 20 utils through the fifth album, and at the sixth album per week it falls to 18 utils; we assume that at some quantity consumed per unit time period, boredom with consuming more digital music albums begins to set in. Thus, at some quantity consumed, the additional utility from consuming an additional album begins to fall, so total utility first rises and then declines in panel (b).

Marginal Utility

If you look carefully at panels (b) and (c) of Figure 21-1, the notion of marginal utility becomes clear. In economics, the term *marginal* always refers to a *change* in the total. The marginal utility of listening to three downloaded digital music albums per week instead of two albums per week is the increment in total utility and is equal to 3 utils per week. All of the points in panel (c) are taken from column 3 of the table in panel (a). Notice that marginal utility falls throughout the graph. A special point occurs after four albums are downloaded and listened to per week because the total utility curve in panel (b) is unchanged after the consumption of the fourth album. That means that the consumer receives no additional (marginal) utility from downloading and listening to the fifth album. This is shown in panel (c) as *zero* marginal utility. After that point, marginal utility becomes negative.

In our example, when marginal utility becomes negative, it means that the consumer is tired of downloading and listening to digital music albums and would require some form of compensation to listen to any more. When marginal utility is negative, an additional unit consumed actually lowers total utility by becoming a nuisance. Rarely does a consumer face a situation of negative marginal utility. Whenever this point is reached, goods in effect become "bads." Consuming more units actually causes total utility to *fall* so that marginal utility is negative. A rational consumer will stop consuming at the point at which marginal utility becomes negative, even if the good is available at a price of zero.

Why is Hollywood concerned about the possibility that some viewers of motion pictures may soon begin to experience rapidly falling marginal utility?

E-COMMERCE EXAMPLE
Moviemakers Try to Avoid Projecting Negative Marginal Utility

In an average week during 1948, when the U.S. population was less than half its present level, 90 million people paid to view a motion picture at a movie theater. Today, the average weekly number of moviegoers is only 30 million. Since the late 1940s, a steady wave of close substitutes—television, videocassettes, DVDs, digital movie downloads—has reduced the number of movies that people choose to see at theaters. One way that moviemakers hope to lure people back to theaters is by producing more movies in digital three-dimensional (3D) formats. More than 2,000 U.S. theaters are now equipped with 3D digital projection systems, and some directors have indicated that they plan to make only digital 3D movies.

Hollywood's newfound fascination with digital 3D has one drawback, however: viewing digital 3D movies for much longer than 90 minutes causes some viewers to experience headaches, dizziness, or even nausea. Thus, a key objective of today's designers of digital 3D projection systems is to minimize the potential for some moviegoers to derive negative marginal utility from viewing 3D motion pictures.

FOR CRITICAL ANALYSIS
Why do you suppose that some in Hollywood are predicting that initially most digital 3D movies will be action packed and relatively short?

QUICK QUIZ *See page 545 for the answers. Review concepts from this section in MyEconLab.*

_____ is defined as want-satisfying power; it is a power common to all desired goods and services.

We arbitrarily measure **utility** in units called _____.

It is important to distinguish between **total utility** and **marginal utility**. _____ utility is the total satisfaction derived from the consumption of a given quantity of a good or service. _____ utility is the *change* in total utility due to a one-unit change in the consumption of the good or service.

Diminishing Marginal Utility

Diminishing marginal utility

The principle that as more of any good or service is consumed, its extra benefit declines. Otherwise stated, increases in total utility from the consumption of a good or service become smaller and smaller as more is consumed during a given time period.

Notice that in panel (c) of Figure 21-1 on page 528, marginal utility is continuously declining. This property has been named the principle of **diminishing marginal utility.** There is no way that we can prove diminishing marginal utility. Nevertheless, diminishing marginal utility has even been called a law. This supposed law concerns a psychological, or subjective, utility that you receive as you consume more and more of a particular good. Stated formally, the law is as follows:

As an individual consumes more of a particular commodity, the total level of utility, or satisfaction, derived from that consumption usually increases. Eventually, however, the rate at which it increases diminishes as more is consumed.

Take a hungry individual at a dinner table. The first serving is greatly appreciated, and the individual derives a substantial amount of utility from it. The second serving does not have quite as much pleasurable impact as the first one, and the third serving is likely to be even less satisfying. This individual experiences diminishing marginal utility of food until he or she stops eating, and this is true for most people. All-you-can-eat restaurants count on this fact; a second helping of ribs may provide some marginal utility, but the third helping would have only a little or even negative marginal utility.

Consider for a moment the opposite possibility—increasing marginal utility. Under such a situation, the marginal utility after consuming, say, one hamburger would increase. The second hamburger would be more valuable to you, and the third would be even more valuable yet. If increasing marginal utility existed, each of us would consume only one good or service! Rather than observing that "variety is the spice of life," we would see that monotony in consumption was preferred. We do not observe this, and therefore we have great confidence in the concept of diminishing marginal utility.

Can diminishing marginal utility explain why newspaper vending machines rarely prevent people from taking more than the one current issue they have paid to purchase?

EXAMPLE
Newspaper Vending Machines versus Candy Vending Machines

Have you ever noticed that newspaper vending machines nearly everywhere in the United States allow you to put in the correct change, lift up the door, and—if you were willing to violate the law—take as many newspapers as you want? Contrast this type of vending machine with candy machines. They are securely locked at all times. You must designate the candy that you wish, normally by using some type of keypad. The candy then drops down so that you can retrieve it but cannot grab any other candy.

The difference between these two types of vending machines is explained by diminishing marginal utility. Newspaper companies dispense newspapers from coin-operated boxes that allow dishonest people to take more copies than they pay for. What would a dishonest person do with more than one copy of a newspaper, however? The marginal utility of a second newspaper is normally zero. The benefit of storing excessive newspapers is usually nil because yesterday's news has no value. But the same analysis does not hold for candy. The marginal utility of a second candy bar is certainly less than the first, but it is normally not zero. Moreover, one can store candy for relatively long periods of time at relatively low cost. Consequently, food vending machine companies have to worry about dishonest users of their equipment and must make that equipment more theftproof than newspaper vending machines.

FOR CRITICAL ANALYSIS
Can you think of a circumstance under which a substantial number of newspaper purchasers might be inclined to take more than one newspaper out of a vending machine?

Optimizing Consumption Choices

Every consumer has a limited income, so choices must be made. When a consumer has made all of his or her choices about what to buy and in what quantities, and when the total level of satisfaction, or utility, from that set of choices is as great as it can be, we say that the consumer has *optimized*. When the consumer has attained an optimum consumption set of goods and services, we say that he or she has reached **consumer optimum.**

Consumer optimum
A choice of a set of goods and services that maximizes the level of satisfaction for each consumer, subject to limited income.

A Two-Good Example

Consider a simple two-good example. The consumer has to choose between spending income on downloads of digital music albums at $5 per download and on purchasing cappuccinos at $3 each. Let's say that when the consumer has spent all income on music album downloads and cappuccinos, the last dollar spent on a cappuccino yields 3 utils of utility but the last dollar spent on downloading music albums yields 10 utils. Wouldn't this consumer increase total utility if some dollars were taken away from consumption of cappuccinos and allocated to music album downloads? The answer is yes. More dollars spent downloading music albums will reduce marginal utility per last dollar spent, whereas fewer dollars spent on consumption of cappuccinos will increase marginal utility per last dollar spent. The loss in utility from spending fewer dollars purchasing fewer cappuccinos is more than made up by spending additional dollars on more album downloads. As a consequence, total utility increases. The consumer optimum—where total utility is maximized—occurs when the satisfaction per last dollar spent on both cappuccinos and music album downloads per week is equal for the two goods. Thus, the amount of goods consumed depends on the prices of the goods, the income of the consumer, and the marginal utility derived from the amounts of each good consumed.

Table 21-1 on the next page presents information on utility derived from consuming various quantities of music album downloads and cappuccinos. Columns 4 and 8 show the marginal utility per dollar spent on music downloads and cappuccinos, respectively. If the prices of both goods are zero, individuals will consume each as long as their respective marginal utility is positive (at least five units of each and probably much more). It is also true that a consumer with unlimited income will

How does marginal utility derived from a music download influence the quantity of music downloads consumed?

continue consuming goods until the marginal utility of each is equal to zero. When the price is zero or the consumer's income is unlimited, there is no effective constraint on consumption.

What happens when people are confronted with "too many" choices, or with too few?

EXAMPLE
Which Is Worse—Too Many Choices or No Choice?

Consider the following experiment, which is intended to illustrate that consumers can sometimes confront "too many choices." The experimenter asks groups of students to look inside boxes containing a variety of chocolates and to discuss which type of chocolate they might choose to buy based on its name and shape. Then the experimenter allows half of the people in each group to eat the chocolate they selected. Some students are shown a box containing 6 types of chocolates, but others view a box with 30 different selections. The students choosing from boxes containing 6 chocolates usually report higher levels of satisfaction from eating their selected chocolates than students who must choose from boxes with 30. Typically, students choosing from the boxes with 30 chocolates report that the larger array of choices caused them to worry that they might

not have selected the best chocolate. Hence, confronting too much choice appears to reduce overall satisfaction.

What about the students in the other half of each group, who are *not* allowed to eat the chocolate they selected? For these students, the *experimenter* selects the chocolate they receive. Consistently, students who are not allowed to make their own choices report less satisfaction than the students who are permitted to choose from boxes containing either 6 or 30 chocolates. Being denied the opportunity to choose yields the least satisfaction.

FOR CRITICAL ANALYSIS
Why is it that a choice that yields greatest utility to one person does not necessarily maximize the satisfaction of someone else?

TABLE 21-1

Total and Marginal Utility from Consuming Music Album Downloads and Cappuccinos on an Income of $26

(1) Music Album Downloads per Period	(2) Total Utility of Music Album Downloads per Period (utils)	(3) Marginal Utility (utils) MU_d	(4) Marginal Utility per Dollar Spent (MU_d/P_d) (price = $5)	(5) Cappuccinos per Period	(6) Total Utility of Cappuccinos per Period (utils)	(7) Marginal Utility (utils) MU_c	(8) Marginal Utility per Dollar Spent (MU_c/P_c) (price = $3)
0	0	–	–	0	0	–	–
1	50.0	50.0	10.0	1	25	25	8.3
2	95.0	45.0	9.0	2	47	22	7.3
3	135.0	40.0	8.0	3	65	18	6.0
4	171.5	36.5	7.3	4	80	15	5.0
5	200.0	28.5	5.7	5	89	9	3.0

A Two-Good Consumer Optimum

Consumer optimum is attained when the marginal utility of the last dollar spent on each good yields the same utility and income is completely exhausted. In the situation in Table 21-1, the individual's income is $26. From columns 4 and 8 of Table 21-1, equal marginal utilities per dollar spent occur at the consumption level of four music album downloads and two cappuccinos (the marginal utility per dollar spent equals 7.3). Notice that the marginal utility per dollar spent for both goods is also (approximately) equal at the consumption level of three music album downloads and one cappuccino, but here total income is not completely exhausted. Likewise, the marginal utility per dollar spent is (approximately) equal at five music album downloads and three cappuccinos, but the expenditures necessary for that level of consumption ($34) exceed the individual's income.

Table 21-2 shows the steps taken to arrive at consumer optimum. The first download of a music album from the Internet would yield a marginal utility per dollar of 10 (50 units of utility divided by $5 per music album download), while the first cappuccino would yield a marginal utility of only 8.3 per dollar (25 units of utility divided by $3 per cappuccino). Because it yields the higher marginal utility per dollar, the music album is downloaded. This leaves $21 of income. The second download of a music album yields a higher marginal utility per dollar (9, versus 8.3 for a cappuccino), so it is also purchased, leaving an unspent income of $16. At the third purchase, the first cappuccino now yields a higher marginal utility per dollar than the next download of a music album (8.3 versus 8), so the first cappuccino is purchased. This leaves income of $13 to spend. The process continues until all income is exhausted and the marginal utility per dollar spent is equal for both goods.

To restate, consumer optimum requires the following:

A consumer's money income should be allocated so that the last dollar spent on each good purchased yields the same amount of marginal utility (when all income is spent), because this rule yields the largest possible total utility.

TABLE 21-2

Steps to Consumer Optimum

In each purchase situation described here, the consumer always purchases the good with the higher marginal utility per dollar spent (MU/P). For example, at the time of the third purchase, the marginal utility per last dollar spent on downloads of music albums is 8, but it is 8.3 for cappuccinos, and $16 of income remains, so the next purchase will be a cappuccino. Here $P_d = \$5$, $P_c = \$3$, MU_d is the marginal utility of consumption of music album downloads, and MU_c is the marginal utility of consumption of cappuccinos.

	Choices					
	Music Album Downloads		Cappuccinos			
Purchase	Unit	MU_d/P_d	Unit	MU_c/P_c	Buying Decision	Remaining Income
1	First	10.0	First	8.3	First music album download	$26 − $5 = $21
2	Second	9.0	First	8.3	Second music album download	$21 − $5 = $16
3	Third	8.0	First	8.3	First cappuccino	$16 − $3 = $13
4	Third	8.0	Second	7.3	Third music album download	$13 − $5 = $8
5	Fourth	7.3	Second	7.3	Fourth music album download and second cappuccino	$8 − $5 = $3 $3 − $3 = $0

A Little Math

We can state the rule of consumer optimum in algebraic terms by examining the ratio of marginal utilities and prices of individual products. The rule simply states that a consumer maximizes personal satisfaction when allocating money income in such a way that the last dollars spent on good A, good B, good C, and so on, yield equal amounts of marginal utility. Marginal utility (*MU*) from good A is indicated by "*MU* of good A." For good B, it is "*MU* of good B." Our algebraic formulation of this rule, therefore, becomes

$$\frac{MU \text{ of good A}}{\text{Price of good A}} = \frac{MU \text{ of good B}}{\text{Price of good B}} = \cdots = \frac{MU \text{ of good Z}}{\text{price of good Z}}$$

The letters A, B, . . . , Z indicate the various goods and services that the consumer might purchase.

We know, then, that in order for the consumer to maximize utility, the marginal utility of good A divided by the price of good A must equal the marginal utility of any other good divided by its price. Note, though, that the application of the rule of equal marginal utility per dollar spent does not necessarily describe an explicit or conscious act on the part of consumers. Rather, this is a *model* of consumer optimum.

Does this model of a consumer optimum apply even to the poorest of the poor?

You Are There

To think about how consideration of the consumer optimum can influence an individual's decision about health insurance coverage, read **Opting Out of Company Health Plans**, on page 540.

INTERNATIONAL EXAMPLE
A Consumer Optimum with One Inflation-Adjusted Dollar a Day

In 2000, the governments of 189 nations agreed to a so-called Millennium Development Goal of reducing by one-half the percentage of people who live on less than $1 per day. At the time, these nations were basing their estimates of the number of people living on less than $1 per day on global prices prevailing in the early 1990s. In today's dollars this translates into living on less than about $1.50 per day.

How do people get by on less than the equivalent of $1.50 per day? Studies of some of the world's poorest people in rural India reveal that half of them are anemic. About 14 percent have poor eyesight. Most are underweight. Nevertheless, nearly all of those in rural India who have less than $1.50 per day available for consumption manage to buy more than food. They also

allocate these meager resources to expenditures on items such as alcohol, tobacco, weddings, funerals, and religious events. Thus, even the world's poorest people choose to consume a variety of goods and services. Instead of equating the marginal utility of the last *dollar* of purchasing power spent on each item, however, these people consume to the point at which the marginal utility per last *penny* spent is the same for all items.

FOR CRITICAL ANALYSIS

Why does the model of consumer optimum imply that the highest-price goods are unlikely to be consumed by the world's poorest people? (Hint: The last dollar, or penny, spent must be taken from funds actually available to a consumer.)

How a Price Change Affects Consumer Optimum

Consumption decisions are summarized in the law of demand, which states that the amount purchased is inversely related to price. We can now see why by using utility analysis.

and twentieth centuries generally concluded that utility—expressed as satisfaction, pleasure, happiness, and related concepts—could not be objectively measured.

Now, in the twenty-first century, behavioral economists have rejuvenated the idea of measuring utility. They aim to do so through the use of "happiness studies," which utilize surveys of people's subjective reporting of their level of happiness. Using these surveys, behavioral economists seek to gauge levels of satisfaction for society as a whole and across individual members of society. Eventually, they suggest, measuring changes in happiness ratings resulting from additional consumption of a good or service could provide information about marginal utility. Policymakers could use such information to assess the effects of policy-induced income changes on utility, and firms could apply happiness measures to assess consumers' satisfaction with their products.

Assessing the Happiness of Individual Workers and Consumers

Today, efforts to measure happiness include more than just surveys of samples taken from national populations. David's Bridal, the largest U.S. bridal-store chain, has employed happiness measures to assess approaches to keeping sales associates more cheery in the face of pressures of dealing with anxious brides. Sensory Logic, a Minnesota-based company, conducts studies for firms such as Whirlpool and Sherwin Williams, in which it examines videos of people's facial reactions to products. Based on incremental changes of expression that may last no longer than 0.03 second, Sensory Logic claims to be able to assess a customer's initial satisfaction with a new product.

Of course, implicit in the use of happiness surveys or careful studies of individuals' responses are two assumptions. One is that numerical ratings from surveys and information gleaned from facial expressions *truly* measure subjectively unobservable satisfaction levels so reliably that they can be treated as objective measures of happiness. The other is that it is reasonable to compare survey ratings or other measures of happiness *across* individuals. If one person, say, scores a "10" for happiness on a survey while another scores only a "7," does this unambiguously mean that the person with the higher score is the more satisfied of the two?

Where Happiness Research Is Headed

Not all economists are convinced that proposed happiness measures actually tell us anything about how to rate a *single* individual's satisfaction levels. In fact, most are uncomfortable with the idea that *any* objective happiness measure could be developed that would enable comparisons of satisfaction levels *across* individuals.

Nevertheless, considerable research is under way to evaluate whether satisfaction measures, such as numerical ratings derived from surveys, are consistent for individuals and among groups of people. One approach to evaluating life satisfaction surveys has been to utilize psychiatric measures of people's moods to check for the reliability of happiness measures. For instance, researchers have asked the same basic questions each year on a regular basis, such as every couple of weeks, over an extended period of time. At the time the questions are asked, researchers interview respondents in an effort to determine their *affect*, or mood as defined by psychiatric classification techniques. A tentative conclusion from such studies is that life satisfaction surveys may provide a measure of happiness that is at least as reliable as affect measures utilized by psychiatrists.

An alternative approach has been to look at hypertension (blood pressure) levels of people who participate in happiness surveys. Physicians have found that psychological well-being and blood pressure are inversely related. Examining the hypertension levels of people who provide happiness ratings in surveys indicates that people with higher happiness ratings tend to

have lower blood pressure than people with lower happiness ratings. To proponents of happiness measures, this fact provides additional evidence that happiness studies can provide useful measures of satisfaction.

Test your understanding of this chapter by going online to **MyEconLab**.
In the Study Plan for this chapter, select Section N: News.

For Critical Analysis

1. Why would evidence of inconsistency of measured happiness levels for a single individual cast considerable doubt on the appropriateness of comparing happiness levels across individuals?

2. Why is the utility theory applied to consumer choice theory silent about comparing people's utility levels? (Hint: Does a consumer optimum for an individual typically depend on the utility levels of other consumers?)

Web Resources

1. To learn more details about the General Social Surveys, use the link at www.econtoday.com/chapter21.

2. To read a recent study by David Blanchflower and Andrew Oswald applying happiness measures derived from surveys to the United States and the United Kingdom, go to www.econtoday.com/chapter21.

Research Project

Discuss the pros and cons of attempting to use happiness survey questions to measure one individual's levels of happiness at different points in time, such as the beginning of every month, throughout the individual's life. Next, evaluate the pros and cons of trying to compare "happiness scores" based on posing the same questions to two people at the same points in time. What can you deduce about the pros and cons of applying results from such survey questions to compare measured happiness levels of thousands of people?

 Here is what you should know after reading this chapter. **MyEconLab** will help you identify what you know, and where to go when you need to practice.

WHAT YOU SHOULD KNOW		WHERE TO GO TO PRACTICE
Total Utility versus Marginal Utility Total utility is the total satisfaction that an individual derives from consuming a given amount of a good or service during a given period. Marginal utility is the additional satisfaction that a person gains by consuming an additional unit of the good or service.	utility, 526 utility analysis, 526 util, 527 marginal utility, 527 **KEY FIGURE** Figure 21-1, 528	• **MyEconLab** Study Plans 21.1, 21.2 • Audio introduction to Chapter 21 • Animated Figure 21-1
The Law of Diminishing Marginal Utility For at least the first unit of consumption of a good or service, a person's total utility increases with increased consumption. Eventually, however, the rate at which an individual's utility rises with greater consumption tends to fall. Thus, marginal utility ultimately declines as the person consumes more and more of the good or service.	diminishing marginal utility, 530	• **MyEconLab** Study Plan 21.3

(continued)

WHAT YOU SHOULD KNOW

The Consumer Optimum An individual optimally allocates available income to consumption of all goods and services when the marginal utility per dollar spent on the last unit consumed of each good is equalized. Thus, a consumer optimum occurs when (1) the ratio of the marginal utility derived from an item to the price of that item is equal across all items that the person consumes and (2) when the person spends all available income.

consumer optimum, 531

- **MyEconLab** Study Plan 21.4
- Video: Optimizing Consumption Choices

The Substitution Effect of a Price Change One effect of a change in the price of a good or service is that the price change induces people to substitute among goods. For example, if the price of a good rises, the individual will tend to consume some other good that has become relatively less expensive as a result. In addition, the individual will tend to reduce consumption of the good whose price increased.

substitution effect, 536
principle of substitution, 536

KEY FIGURE
Figure 21-2, 535

- **MyEconLab** Study Plan 21.5
- Animated Figure 21-2

The Real-Income Effect of a Price Change If the price of a good increases, a person responds to the loss of purchasing power of available income by reducing purchases of either the now higher-priced good or other goods (or a combination of both of these responses). Normally, we anticipate that the real-income effect is smaller than the substitution effect, so that when the price of a good or service increases, people will purchase more of goods or services that have lower relative prices as a result.

purchasing power, 536
real-income effect, 536

KEY FIGURE
Figure 21-2, 535

- **MyEconLab** Study Plan 21.5
- Animated Figure 21-2

The Price of Diamonds versus the Price of Water and Behavioral Economics versus Consumer Choice Theory The typical consumer purchases a small number of diamonds, so the marginal utility derived from consuming a diamond is relatively high. People consume relatively large volumes of water, so the marginal utility of the last unit of water consumed is relatively low. Thus, at a consumer optimum, in which the marginal utility per dollar spent is equalized for diamonds and water, people are willing to pay a much higher price for diamonds. Proponents of behavioral economics suggest that people sometimes depart from adherence to a consumer optimum when emotions come into play or insufficient time or information is available. A difficulty with this perspective is that outside of a consumer optimum, many behaviors could be possible, yielding few testable predictions. Predictions of consumer choice theory, such as the price of diamonds will be higher than the price of a unit of water, are, in contrast, testable.

KEY FIGURE
Figure 21-3, 537

- **MyEconLab** Study Plans 21.6, 21.7
- Animated Figure 21-3

Log in to MyEconLab, take a chapter test, and get a personalized Study Plan that tells you which concepts you understand and which ones you need to review. From there, MyEconLab will give you further practice, tutorials, animations, videos, and guided solutions.
Log in to www.myeconlab.com

PROBLEMS

All problems are assignable in ✕ myeconlab. *Answers to odd-numbered problems appear at the back of the book.*

21-1. The campus pizzeria sells a single pizza for $12. If you order a second pizza, however, the pizzeria charges a price of only $5 for the additional pizza. Explain how an understanding of marginal utility helps to explain the pizzeria's pricing strategy.

21-2. As an individual consumes more units of an item, the person eventually experiences diminishing marginal utility. This means that to increase marginal utility, the person must consume less of an item. Explain the logic of this behavior using the example in Problem 21-1.

21-3. Where possible, complete the missing cells in the table.

Number of Cheese-burgers	Total Utility of Cheese-burgers	Marginal Utility of Cheese-burgers	Bags of French Fries	Total Utility of French Fries	Marginal Utility of French Fries
0	0	—	0	0	—
1	20	—	1	—	10
2	36	—	2	—	8
3	—	12	3	—	2
4	—	8	4	21	—
5	—	4	5	21	—

21-4. From the data in Problem 21-3, if the price of a cheeseburger is $2, the price of a bag of french fries is $1, and you have $6 to spend (and you spend all of it), what is the utility-maximizing combination of cheeseburgers and french fries?

21-5. Return to Problem 21-4. Suppose that the price of cheeseburgers falls to $1. Determine the new utility-maximizing combination of cheeseburgers and french fries.

21-6. Suppose that you observe that total utility rises as more of an item is consumed. What can you say for certain about marginal utility? Can you say for sure that it is rising or falling or that it is positive or negative?

21-7. After monitoring your daily consumption patterns, you determine that your daily consumption of soft drinks is 3 and your daily consumption of tacos is 4 when the prices per unit are 50 cents and $1, respectively. Explain what happens to your consumption bundle, the marginal utility of soft

drinks, and the marginal utility of tacos when the price of soft drinks rises to 75 cents.

21-8. At a consumer optimum, for all goods purchased, marginal utility per dollar spent is equalized. A high school student is deciding between attending Western State University and Eastern State University. The student cannot attend both universities simultaneously. Both are fine universities, but the reputation of Western is slightly higher, as is the tuition. Use the rule of consumer optimum to explain how the student will go about deciding which university to attend.

21-9. Consider the movements that take place from one point to the next (*A* to *B* to *C* and so on) along the total utility curve below as the individual successively increases consumption by one more unit, and answer the questions that follow.

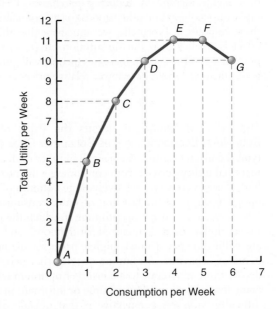

a. Which one-unit increase in consumption from one point to the next along the total utility curve generates the highest marginal utility?

b. Which one-unit increase in consumption from one point to the next along the total utility curve generates zero marginal utility?

c. Which one-unit increase in consumption from one point to the next along the total utility curve generates negative marginal utility?

Income-Consumption Curve

We start off with income sufficient to yield budget constraint bb'. The highest attainable indifference curve is I_1, which is just tangent to bb' at E. Next we increase income. The budget line moves outward to cc', which is parallel to bb'. The new highest indifference curve is I_2, which is just tangent to cc' at E'. We increase income again, which is represented by a shift in the budget line to dd'. The new tangency point of the highest indifference curve, I_3, with dd' is at point E''. When we connect these three points, we obtain the income-consumption curve.

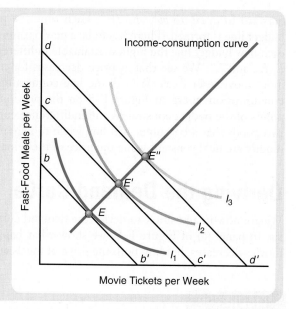

The **income-consumption curve** shows the optimum consumption points that would occur if income for that consumer were increased continuously, holding the prices of fast-food meals and movie tickets constant.

Income-consumption curve
The set of optimal consumption points that would occur if income were increased, relative prices remaining constant.

The Price-Consumption Curve

In Figure E-8, we hold money income and the price of fast-food meals constant while we lower the price of tickets to movies. As we keep lowering the price of movie tickets, the quantity of tickets that could be purchased if all income were spent on viewing movies increases; thus, the extreme points for the budget constraint keep moving outward to the right as the price of movie tickets falls. In other words, the budget line rotates

Price-Consumption Curve

As we lower the price of movie tickets, income measured in terms of movie tickets per week increases. We show this by rotating the budget constraint from bb' to bb'' and finally to bb'''. We then find the highest indifference curve that is attainable for each successive budget constraint. For budget constraint bb', the highest indifference curve is I_1, which is tangent to bb' at point E. We do this for the next two budget constraints. When we connect the optimum points, E, E', and E'', we derive the price-consumption curve, which shows the combinations of the two commodities that a consumer will purchase when money income and the price of one commodity remain constant while the other commodity's price changes.

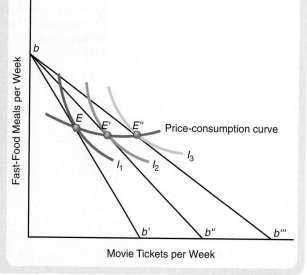

outward from bb' to bb'' and bb'''. Each time the price of movie tickets falls, a new budget line is formed. There has to be a new optimum point. We find it by locating on each new budget line the highest attainable indifference curve. This is shown at points E, E', and E''. We see that as price decreases for movie tickets, the consumer views more movies per week. We call the line connecting points E, E', and E'' the **price-consumption curve** in Figure E-8 on the previous page. It connects the tangency points of the budget constraints and indifference curves, thus showing the amounts of two goods that a consumer will buy when money income and the price of one commodity are held constant while the price of the remaining good changes.

Price-consumption curve
The set of consumer-optimum combinations of two goods that the consumer would choose as the price of one good changes while money income and the price of the other good remain constant.

Deriving the Demand Curve

We are now in a position to derive the demand curve using indifference curve analysis. In panel (a) of Figure E-9, we show what happens when the price of tickets to movies decreases, holding both the price of meals at fast-food restaurants and income

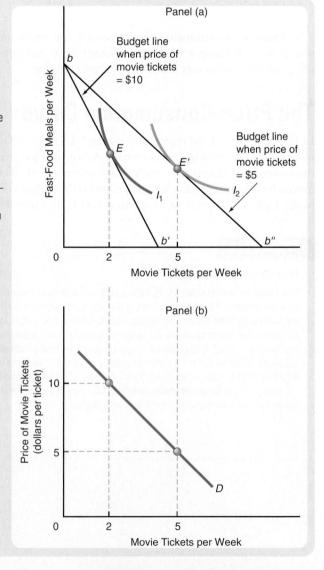

FIGURE E-9

Deriving the Demand Curve

In panel (a), we show the effects of a decrease in the price of movie tickets from $10 to $5. At $10, the highest indifference curve touches the budget line bb' at point E. The number of movies viewed is two. We transfer this combination—price, $10; quantity demanded, 2—down to panel (b). Next we decrease the price of movie tickets to $5. This generates a new budget line, or constraint, which is bb''. Consumer optimum is now at E'. The optimum quantity of movie tickets demanded at a price of $5 is five. We transfer this point—price, $5; quantity demanded, 5—down to panel (b). When we connect these two points, we have a demand curve, D, for tickets to movies.

? DID YOU KNOW THAT since 1897, nearly all the increase in the values of ownership shares of companies traded in U.S. stock markets has occurred when Congress has been in recess? Indeed, returns earned on shares of stock have been almost eight times higher on days when Congress has not been in session. The reason, most financial economists agree, is that when Congress is in session, representatives and senators propose numerous bills that might reduce firms' profits. The possibility that some of these bills may pass creates uncertainty about future profitability that tends to depress stock prices. How do firms measure their profits, and what factors determine profits? Why do anticipations of future profits of companies affect the prices of their ownership shares today? In this chapter, you will learn the answers to these questions. First, however, you must learn about the important function of *economic rent*.

Economic Rent

When you hear the term *rent*, you are accustomed to having it mean the payment made to property owners for the use of land or dwellings. The term *rent* has a different meaning in economics. **Economic rent** is payment to the owner of a resource in excess of its *opportunity cost*—that is, the minimum payment that would be necessary to call forth production of that amount of the resource.

Economic rent
A payment for the use of any resource over and above its opportunity cost.

Determining Land Rent

Economists originally used the term *rent* to designate payment for the use of land. What was thought to be important about land was that its supply was completely inelastic. That is, the supply curve for land was thought to be a vertical line, so that no matter what the prevailing market price for land, the quantity supplied would remain the same.

The concept of economic rent is associated with the British economist David Ricardo (1772–1823). Here is how Ricardo analyzed economic rent for land. He first simplified his model by assuming that all land is equally productive. Then Ricardo assumed that the quantity of land in a country is *fixed* so that land's opportunity cost is equal to zero. Graphically, then, in terms of supply and demand, we draw the supply curve for land vertically (zero price elasticity). In Figure 22-1 on the following page, the supply curve of land is represented by S. If the demand curve is D_1, it intersects the supply curve, S, at price P_1. The entire amount of revenues obtained, $P_1 \times Q_1$, is labeled "Economic rent." If the demand for land increases to D_2, the equilibrium price will rise to P_2. Additions to economic rent are labeled "More economic rent." Notice that the quantity of land remains insensitive to the change in price. Another way of stating this is that the supply curve is perfectly inelastic.

Economic Rent to Labor

Land and natural resources are not the only factors of production to which the analysis of economic rent can be applied. In fact, the analysis is probably more often applicable to labor. Here is a list of people who provide different labor services, some of whom probably receive large amounts of economic rent:

- Professional sports superstars
- Rock stars

- Movie stars
- World-class models
- Successful inventors and innovators
- World-famous opera stars

Just apply the definition of economic rent to the phenomenal earnings that these people make. They would undoubtedly work for considerably less than they earn. Therefore, much of their earnings constitutes economic rent (but not all, as we shall see). Economic rent occurs because specific resources cannot be replicated exactly. No one can duplicate today's most highly paid entertainment figures, and therefore they receive economic rent.

Economic Rent and the Allocation of Resources

Suppose that a highly paid movie star would make the same number of movies at half his or her current annual earnings. Why, then, does the superstar receive a higher income? Look again at Figure 22-1, but substitute *entertainment activities of the super-stars* for the word *land*. The high "price" received by the superstar is due to the demand for his or her services. If Reese Witherspoon announces that she will work for a million dollars per movie and do two movies a year, how is she going to know which production company values her services the most highly? Witherspoon and other movie stars let the market decide where their resources should be used. In this sense, we can say the following:

Economic rent allocates resources to their highest-valued use.

Otherwise stated, economic rent directs resources to the people who can use them most efficiently.

How much do top performers earn?

Do you think that actor George Clooney earns economic rent? Why or why not?

FIGURE 22-1

Economic Rent

If indeed the supply curve of land were completely price-inelastic in the long run, it would be depicted by S. The opportunity cost of land is zero, so the same quantity of land is forthcoming at any constant-quality price. Thus, at the quantity in existence, Q_1, any and all revenues are economic rent. If demand is D_1, the price will be P_1; if demand is D_2, price will rise to P_2. Economic rent would be $P_1 \times Q_1$ and $P_2 \times Q_1$, respectively.

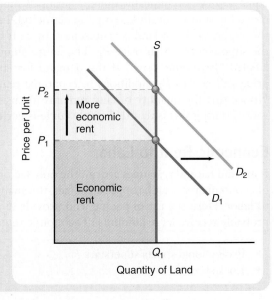

EXAMPLE

Do Entertainment Superstars Make Super Economic Rents?

Superstars certainly do well financially. Table 22–1 shows the earnings of selected individuals in the entertainment industry as estimated by *Forbes* magazine. Earnings are totaled for a two-year period. How much of these earnings can be called economic rent? The question is not easy to answer, because an entertainment newcomer would almost certainly work for much less than he or she earns, implying that the newcomer is making high economic rent. The same cannot necessarily be said for entertainers who have been raking in millions for years. They probably have very high accumulated wealth and also a more jaded outlook about their work. It is therefore not clear how much they would work if they were not offered those huge sums of money.

FOR CRITICAL ANALYSIS

Even if some superstar entertainers would work for less, what forces cause them to make so much income anyway?

TABLE 22-1

Superstar Earnings

Name	Occupation	Two-Year Earnings
Oprah Winfrey	Talk show host and owner, author	$275,000,000
50 Cent	Hip-hop artist	150,000,000
Jerry Bruckheimer	Director, producer	145,000,000
Steven Spielberg	Director, producer	130,000,000
Tyler Perry	Director, producer	125,000,000
The Police	Rock group	115,000,000
Jerry Seinfeld	Actor, Comedian	85,000,000
Jay-Z	Hip-hop artist	82,000,000
Beyonce Knowles	Musician	80,000,000
Will Smith	Actor	80,000,000

Source: *Forbes*, 2008.

QUICK QUIZ   *See page 582 for the answers. Review concepts from this section in MyEconLab.*

Economic rent is defined as payment for a factor of production that is completely _____ in supply.

Economic rent _____ resources to their _____-valued use.

Firms and Profits

Firms or businesses, like individuals, seek to earn the highest possible returns. We define a **firm** as follows:

A firm is an organization that brings together factors of production—labor, land, physical capital, human capital, and entrepreneurial skill—to produce a product or service that it hopes can be sold at a profit.

Firm

A business organization that employs resources to produce goods or services for profit. A firm normally owns and operates at least one "plant" or facility in order to produce.

A typical firm will have an organizational structure consisting of an entrepreneur, managers, and workers. The entrepreneur is the person who takes the risks, mainly of losing his or her personal wealth. In compensation, the entrepreneur will get any profits that are made. Recall from Chapter 2 that entrepreneurs take the initiative in combining land, labor, and capital to produce a good or a service. Entrepreneurs are the ones who innovate in the form of new production and new products. The entrepreneur also decides whom to hire to manage the firm. Some economists maintain that the true quality of an entrepreneur becomes evident with his or her selection of managers.

Managers, in turn, decide who should be hired and fired and how the business should be operated on a day-to-day basis. The workers ultimately use the other inputs to produce the products or services that are being sold by the firm. Workers and managers are paid contractual wages. They receive a specified amount of income for a specified time period. Entrepreneurs are not paid contractual wages. They receive no reward specified in advance. The entrepreneurs make profits if there are any, for profits accrue to those who are willing to take risks. (Because the entrepreneur gets only what is left over after all expenses are paid, he or she is often referred to as a *residual claimant*. The entrepreneur lays claim to the residual—whatever is left.)

The Legal Organization of Firms

We all know that firms differ from one another. Some sell frozen yogurt, others make automobiles; some advertise, some do not; some have annual sales of a few thousand dollars, others have sales in the billions of dollars. The list of differences is probably endless. Yet for all this diversity, the basic organization of *all* firms can be thought of in terms of a few simple structures, the most important of which are the proprietorship, the partnership, and the corporation.

PROPRIETORSHIP The most common form of business organization is the **proprietorship.** As shown in Table 22-2, close to 72 percent of all firms in the United States are proprietorships. Each is owned by a single individual who makes the business decisions, receives all the profits, and is legally responsible for all the debts of the firm. Although proprietorships are numerous, they are generally rather small businesses, with annual sales averaging not much more than $56,000. For this reason, even though there are nearly 21 million proprietorships in the United States, they account for less than 5 percent of all business revenues.

Advantages of Proprietorships. Proprietorships offer several advantages as a form of business organization. First, they are *easy to form and to dissolve*. In the simplest case, all one must do to start a business is to start working; to dissolve the firm, one simply stops

Proprietorship

A business owned by one individual who makes the business decisions, receives all the profits, and is legally responsible for the debts of the firm.

<table>
<tr><td colspan="5">TABLE 22-2</td></tr>
<tr><td>Forms of Business Organization</td><td>Type of Firm</td><td>Percentage of U.S. Firms</td><td>Average Size (annual sales in dollars)</td><td>Percentage of Total Business Revenues</td></tr>
<tr><td></td><td>Proprietorship</td><td>71.7</td><td>56,000</td><td>4.4</td></tr>
<tr><td></td><td>Partnership</td><td>8.9</td><td>1,234,000</td><td>12.1</td></tr>
<tr><td></td><td>Corporation</td><td>19.4</td><td>3,907,000</td><td>83.5</td></tr>
</table>

Sources: U.S. Bureau of the Census; *2008 Statistical Abstract.*

working. Second, *all decision-making power resides with the sole proprietor*. No partners, shareholders, or board of directors need be consulted. The third advantage is that its *profit is taxed only once*. All profit is treated by law as the net income of the proprietor and as such is subject only to personal income taxation.

Disadvantages of Proprietorships. The most important disadvantage of a proprietorship is that the proprietor faces **unlimited liability** *for the debts of the firm*. This means that the owner is personally responsible for all of the firm's debts. The second disadvantage is that many lenders are reluctant to lend large sums to a proprietorship. Consequently, a proprietorship may have a *limited ability to raise funds*, to expand the business or even simply to help it survive bad times. The third disadvantage of proprietorships is that they normally *end with the death of the proprietor*, which creates added uncertainty for prospective lenders or employees.

PARTNERSHIP The second important form of business organization is the **partnership.** As shown in Table 22-2, partnerships are far less numerous than proprietorships but tend to be larger businesses—about 22 times greater on average. A partnership differs from a proprietorship chiefly in that there are two or more co-owners, called partners. They share the responsibilities of operating the firm and its profits, and they are *each* legally responsible for *all* of the debts incurred by the firm. In this sense, a partnership may be viewed as a proprietorship with more than one owner.

Advantages of Partnerships. The first advantage of a partnership is that it is *easy to form*. In fact, it is almost as easy to form as a proprietorship. Second, partnerships, like proprietorships, often help *reduce the costs of monitoring job performance*. This is particularly true when interpersonal skills are important for successful performance and in lines of business in which, even after the fact, it is difficult to measure performance objectively. Thus, attorneys and physicians often organize themselves as partnerships. A third advantage of the partnership is that it *permits more effective specialization* in occupations in which, for legal or other reasons, the multiple talents required for success are unlikely to be uniform across individuals. Finally, the income of the partnership is treated as personal income and thus is *subject only to personal taxation*.

Disadvantages of Partnerships. Partnerships also have their disadvantages. First, the *partners each have unlimited liability*. Thus, the personal assets of *each* partner are at risk due to debts incurred on behalf of the partnership by *any* of the partners. Second, *decision making is generally more costly* in a partnership than in a proprietorship; more people are involved in making decisions, and they may have differences of opinion that must be resolved before action is possible. Finally, *dissolution of the partnership* often occurs when a partner dies or voluntarily withdraws or when one or more partners wish to remove someone from the partnership. This creates potential uncertainty for creditors and employees.

CORPORATION A **corporation** is a legal entity that may conduct business in its own name just as an individual does. The owners of a corporation are called *shareholders* because they own shares of the profits earned by the firm. By law, shareholders enjoy **limited liability,** meaning that if the corporation incurs debts that it cannot pay, the shareholders' personal property is shielded from claims by the firm's creditors. As shown in Table 22-2, corporations are far less numerous than proprietorships, but because of their large size, they are responsible for more than 83 percent of all business revenues in the United States.

Unlimited liability
A legal concept whereby the personal assets of the owner of a firm can be seized to pay off the firm's debts.

Partnership
A business owned by two or more joint owners, or partners, who share the responsibilities and the profits of the firm and are individually liable for all the debts of the partnership.

Corporation
A legal entity that may conduct business in its own name just as an individual does; the owners of a corporation, called shareholders, own shares of the firm's profits and enjoy the protection of limited liability.

Limited liability
A legal concept in which the responsibility, or liability, of the owners of a corporation is limited to the value of the shares in the firm that they own.

Advantages of Corporations. Perhaps the greatest advantage of corporations is that their owners (the shareholders) enjoy *limited liability*. The liability of shareholders is limited to the value of their shares. The second advantage is that, legally, the corporation *continues to exist* even if one or more owners cease to be owners. A third advantage of the corporation stems from the first two: Corporations are well positioned to *raise large sums of financial capital*. People are able to buy ownership shares or lend funds to the corporation knowing that their liability is limited to the amount of funds they invest and confident that the corporation's existence does not depend on the life of any one of the firm's owners.

Dividends

Portion of a corporation's profits paid to its owners (shareholders).

Disadvantages of Corporations. The chief disadvantage of the corporation is that corporate income is subject to *double taxation*. The profits of the corporation are subject first to corporate taxation. Then, if any of the after-tax profits are distributed to shareholders as **dividends,** such payments are treated as personal income to the shareholders and subject to personal taxation, although the dividends may be taxed at lower rates than other personal income. Despite the lower tax rates on dividends, owners of corporations generally pay higher taxes on corporate income than on other forms of income because the corporate income is also taxed at the corporate level.

A second disadvantage of the corporation is that corporations are potentially subject to problems associated with the *separation of ownership and control*. The owners and managers of a corporation are typically different persons and may have different incentives. The problems that can result are discussed later in the chapter.

Have recently enacted U.S. government regulations created a new disadvantage of the corporate form of business organization?

POLICY EXAMPLE
Why It Can Pay to Form a Partnership Instead of a Corporation

Each year between 1992 and 2002, an average of more than 135 new companies, called corporate *start-ups*, began issuing new ownership shares in U.S. stock markets. Since 2002, only about 40 start-ups have occurred on average per year. Most observers agree that a key reason for this big decline in corporate start-ups was the enactment of the Sarbanes-Oxley Act in 2002. This law imposes tougher internal auditing requirements on publicly traded companies and requires executives to certify a firm's financial statements. Corporate officers who fail to fully abide by these provisions can face significant fines. The costs of complying with the Sarbanes-Oxley Act can be particularly burdensome for small companies. Thus, many more start-ups than in past years are opting for alternative business structures, such as limited liability companies and partnerships, instead of becoming publicly traded corporations.

FOR CRITICAL ANALYSIS
Why might the Sarbanes-Oxley Act help to explain why nearly 50 major corporations have opted to become private since 2002?

The Profits of a Firm

Most people think of a firm's profit as the difference between the amount of revenues the firm takes in and the amount it spends for wages, materials, and so on. In a bookkeeping sense, the following formula could be used:

$$\text{Accounting profit} = \text{total revenues} - \text{explicit costs}$$

Explicit costs

Costs that business managers must take account of because they must be paid; examples are wages, taxes, and rent.

Accounting profit

Total revenues minus total explicit costs.

where **explicit costs** are expenses that must actually be paid out by the firm. This definition of profit is known as **accounting profit.** It is appropriate when used by accountants to determine a firm's taxable income. Economists are more interested in how firm managers react not just to changes in explicit costs but also to changes in **implicit costs**, defined as expenses that business managers do not have to pay out of pocket but are costs to the firm nonetheless because they represent an opportunity cost. They do not involve any direct cash outlay by the firm and must therefore be measured by the *opportunity cost principle*. That is to say, they are measured by what the resources (land, capital) currently used in producing a particular good or service could earn in other uses. Therefore, a better definition of implicit cost is the opportunity cost of using factors that a producer does not buy or hire but already owns. Economists use the full opportunity cost of all resources (including both explicit and implicit costs) as the figure to subtract from revenues to obtain a definition of profit.

Opportunity Cost of Capital

Firms enter or remain in an industry if they earn, at minimum, a **normal rate of return.** People will not invest their wealth in a business unless they obtain a positive normal (competitive) rate of return—that is, unless their invested wealth pays off. Any business wishing to attract capital must expect to pay at least the same rate of return on that capital as all other businesses (of similar risk) are willing to pay. Put another way, when a firm requires the use of a resource in producing a particular product, it must bid against alternative users of that resource. Thus, the firm must offer a price that is at least as much as other potential users are offering to pay. For example, if individuals can invest their wealth in almost any publishing firm and get a rate of return of 10 percent per year, each firm in the publishing industry must *expect* to pay 10 percent as the normal rate of return to present and future investors. This 10 percent is a *cost to the firm*, the **opportunity cost of capital.** The opportunity cost of capital is the amount of income, or yield, that could have been earned by investing in the next-best alternative. Capital will not stay in firms or industries in which the expected rate of return falls below its opportunity cost—that is, what could be earned elsewhere. If a firm owns some capital equipment, it can either use it or lease it and earn a return. If the firm uses the equipment for production, part of the cost of using that equipment is the forgone revenue that the firm could have earned had it leased out that equipment.

Opportunity Cost of Owner-Provided Labor and Capital

Single-owner proprietorships often grossly exaggerate their profit rates because they understate the opportunity cost of the labor that the proprietor provides to the business. Here we are referring to the opportunity cost of labor. For example, you may know people who run a small grocery store. These people will sit down at the end of the year and figure out what their "profits" are. They will add up all their sales and subtract what they had to pay to other workers, what they had to pay to their suppliers, what they had to pay in taxes, and so on. The end result they will call "profit." They normally will not, however, have figured into their costs the salary that they could have made if they had worked for somebody else in a similar type of job. By working for themselves, they become residual claimants—they receive what is left after all explicit costs have been accounted for. Part of the costs, however, should include the salary the owner-operator could have received working for someone else.

Consider a simple example of a skilled auto mechanic working 14 hours a day at his own service station, six days a week. Compare this situation to how much he could earn working 84 hours a week as a trucking company mechanic. This self-employed auto mechanic might have an opportunity cost of about $35 an hour. For his 84-hour week in his own service station, he is forfeiting $2,940. Unless his service station shows accounting profits of more than that per week, he is incurring losses in an economic sense.

Go to **www.econtoday.com/chapter22** for a link to Internal Revenue Service reports on U.S. annual revenues and expenses of proprietorships, partnerships, and corporations based on tax returns. Click on recent quarters and choose relevant reports.

Another way of looking at the opportunity cost of running a business is that opportunity cost consists of all explicit and implicit costs. Accountants only take account of explicit costs. Therefore, accounting profit ends up being the residual after only explicit costs are subtracted from total revenues.

This same analysis can apply to owner-provided capital, such as land or buildings. The fact that the owner owns the building or the land with which he or she operates a business does not mean that it is "free." Rather, use of the building and land still has an opportunity cost—the value of the next-best alternative use for those assets.

Accounting Profits versus Economic Profits

The term *profits* in economics means the income that entrepreneurs earn, over and above all costs including their own opportunity cost of time, plus the opportunity cost of the capital they have invested in their business. Profits can be regarded as total revenues minus total costs—which is how accountants think of them—but we must now include *all* costs. Our definition of **economic profits** will be the following:

Economic profits
Total revenues minus total opportunity costs of all inputs used, or the total of all implicit and explicit costs.

Economic profits = total revenues − total opportunity cost of all input used

or

Economic profits = total revenues − (explicit + implicit costs)

Remember that implicit costs include a normal rate of return on invested capital. We show this relationship in Figure 22-2.

The Goal of the Firm: Profit Maximization

When we examined the theory of consumer demand, utility (or satisfaction) maximization by the individual provided the basis for the analysis. In the theory of the firm and

FIGURE 22-2

Simplified View of Economic and Accounting Profit

We see on the right column that accounting profit is the difference between total revenues and total explicit accounting costs. Conversely, we see on the left column that economic profit is equal to total revenues minus economic costs. Economic costs equal explicit accounting costs plus all implicit costs, including a normal rate of return on invested capital.

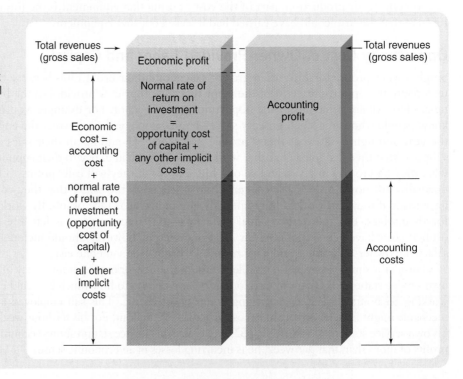

production, *profit maximization* is the underlying hypothesis of our predictive theory. The goal of the firm is to maximize economic profits, and the firm is expected to try to make the positive difference between total revenues and total costs as large as it can.

Our justification for assuming profit maximization by firms is similar to our assumption concerning utility maximization by individuals (see Chapter 21). To obtain labor, capital, and other resources required to produce commodities, firms must first obtain financing from investors. Although investors typically monitor managers' performances to ensure that the funds they provide are not misused, they are most interested in the earnings on these funds and the risk of obtaining lower returns or losing the funds they have invested. Firms that can provide relatively higher risk-corrected returns will therefore have an advantage in obtaining the financing needed to continue or expand production. Over time, we would expect a policy of profit maximization to become the dominant mode of behavior for firms that survive.

Why is it that in college sports, posting losses can be a profitable activity?

EXAMPLE
How Chalking Up Sports Losses Raises Schools' Profits

What do these pairings of college basketball opponents have in common: Texas Southern versus Illinois; Prairie View versus Texas; Chicago State versus Louisville; and State University of New York at Stony Brook versus Villanova? The answer is that in each of these matchups, the first opponent listed goes into the game almost certain of chalking up a mark in the season's loss column. Nevertheless, the teams' schools earn tens of thousands of dollars in revenues, paid by their opponents from ticket receipts, which more than cover the opportunity costs of playing top-rated opponents. Indeed, administrators at the colleges fielding underdog teams in such pairings sometimes worry that their teams might actually win stunning upsets. If so, the powerhouse schools looking for a few easy wins on their schedules may not want to play them in the future. Then the underdogs' revenues and profits would disappear.

FOR CRITICAL ANALYSIS
Why might colleges with top basketball programs determine that scheduling opponents that they anticipate their teams will defeat handily is a profit-maximizing strategy? (Hint: Why might colleges with powerhouse teams have a profit-maximizing motive to win a significant percentage of their games?)

QUICK QUIZ   See page 582 for the answers. Review concepts from this section in MyEconLab.

_____ are the most common form of business organization, comprising close to 72 percent of all firms. Each is owned by a single individual who makes all business decisions, receives all the profits, and has _____ liability for the firm's debts.

_____ are much like proprietorships, except that two or more individuals, or partners, share the decisions and the profits of the firm. In addition, each partner has _____ liability for the debts of the firm.

Corporations are responsible for the largest share of business revenues. The owners, called _____, share in the firm's profits but normally have little responsibility for the firm's day-to-day operations. They enjoy _____ liability for the debts of the firm.

Accounting profits differ from **economic profits**, which are defined as total revenues minus total costs, where costs include the full _____ cost of all of the factors of production plus all other implicit costs.

The full opportunity cost of capital invested in a business is generally not included as a cost when accounting profits are calculated. Thus, accounting profits often are _____ than economic profits. We assume throughout that the goal of the firm is to _____ economic profits.

Interest

Interest is the price paid by debtors to creditors for the use of loanable funds. Often businesses go to credit markets to obtain so-called **financial capital** in order to invest in physical capital and rights to patents and trademarks from which they hope to make a satisfactory return. In other words, in our complicated society, the production of capital goods is often facilitated by the existence of credit markets. These are markets in which borrowing and lending take place.

Financial capital
Funds used to purchase physical capital goods, such as buildings and equipment, and patents and trademarks.

Interest and Credit

When you obtain credit, you actually obtain funds to have command over resources today. We can say, then, that **interest** is the payment for current rather than future command over resources. Thus, interest is the payment for obtaining credit. If you borrow $100 from me, you have command over $100 worth of goods and services today. I no longer have that command. You promise to pay me back $100 plus interest at some future date. The interest that you pay is usually expressed as a percentage of the total loan, calculated on an annual basis. If at the end of one year you pay me back $105, the annual interest rate is $5 ÷ $100, or 5 percent. When you go out into the marketplace to obtain credit, you will find that the interest rate charged differs greatly. A loan to buy a house (a mortgage) may cost you 6 to 8 percent in annual interest. An installment loan to buy an automobile may cost you 7 to 9 percent in annual interest. The federal government, when it wishes to obtain credit (issue U.S. Treasury securities), may have to pay only 2 to 6 percent in annual interest. Variations in the rate of annual interest that must be paid for credit depend on the following factors.

Interest
The payment for current rather than future command over resources; the cost of obtaining credit.

When you borrow to finance your college or university studies, what do the interest payments represent?

1. *Length of loan.* In many (but not all) cases, the longer the loan will be outstanding, other things being equal, the greater will be the interest rate charged.

2. *Risk.* The greater the risk of nonrepayment of the loan, other things being equal, the greater the interest rate charged. Risk is assessed on the basis of the creditworthiness of the borrower and whether the borrower provides collateral for the loan. Collateral consists of any asset that will automatically become the property of the lender should the borrower fail to comply with the loan agreement.

3. *Handling charges.* It takes resources to set up a loan. Papers have to be filled out and filed, credit references have to be checked, collateral has to be examined, and so on. The larger the amount of the loan, the smaller the handling (or administrative) charges as a percentage of the total loan. Therefore, we would predict that, other things being equal, the larger the loan, the lower the interest rate.

Go to www.econtoday.com/chapter22 for Federal Reserve data on U.S. interest rates.

Real versus Nominal Interest Rates

We have been assuming that there is no inflation. In a world of inflation—a persistent rise in an average of all prices—the **nominal rate of interest** will be higher than it would be in a world with no inflation. Nominal, or market, rates of interest rise to take account of the anticipated rate of inflation. If, for example, no inflation is expected, the nominal rate of interest might be 5 percent for home mortgages. If the rate of inflation goes to 4 percent a year and stays there, everybody will anticipate that inflation rate. The nominal rate of interest will rise to about 9 percent to take account of the anticipated rate of inflation. If the interest rate did not rise to 9 percent, the principal plus interest earned at 5 percent would have lower purchasing power in the future because inflation would have eroded its real value. We can therefore say that

Nominal rate of interest
The market rate of interest expressed in today's dollars.

the nominal, or market, rate of interest is approximately equal to the real rate of interest plus the anticipated rate of inflation, or

$$i_n = i_r + \text{anticipated rate of inflation}$$

where i_n equals the nominal rate of interest and i_r equals the real rate of interest. In short, you can expect to see high nominal rates of interest in periods of high inflation rates. The **real rate of interest** may not necessarily be high, though. We must first correct the nominal rate of interest for the anticipated rate of inflation before determining whether the real interest rate is in fact higher than normal.

Real rate of interest
The nominal rate of interest minus the anticipated rate of inflation.

The Allocative Role of Interest

In Chapter 4, we talked about the price system and the role that prices play in the allocation of resources. Interest is a price that allocates loanable funds (credit) to consumers and to businesses. Within the business sector, interest allocates funds to different firms and therefore to different investment projects. An investment, or capital, project with a rate of return—an annual payoff as a percentage of the investment—higher than the market rate of interest in the credit market will be undertaken, given an unrestricted market for loanable funds. For example, if the expected rate of return on the purchase of a new factory or of intellectual property—patents or copyrights—in some industry is 10 percent and funds can be acquired for 6 percent, the investment project will proceed. If, however, that same project had an expected rate of return of only 4 percent, it would not be undertaken. In sum, the interest rate allocates funds to industries whose investments yield the highest (risk-adjusted) returns—where resources will be the most productive.

It is important to realize that the interest rate performs the function of allocating financial capital and that this ultimately allocates real physical capital to various firms for investment projects.

How has the Iranian government's policy regarding bank loan rates brought about a reallocation of financial capital in that nation?

INTERNATIONAL POLICY EXAMPLE
An Interest Rate Policy Reallocates Iranian Financial Capital

In Iran, the government sets limits on the interest rates that banks can charge on loans. Recently, it reduced the ceiling on bank loan rates to 12 percent per year. This rate is about 8 percentage points below the prevailing annual rate of inflation and hence less than the nominal loan rate banks otherwise would have charged. Owners of shares in Iranian banks have responded to the government's action by selling off their shares and using their financial capital to purchase gold and real estate instead.

FOR CRITICAL ANALYSIS
Why is the market loan rate that banks otherwise would charge borrowers in the absence of the Iranian government's legal limit likely to be higher than 20 percent?

Interest Rates and Present Value

Businesses make investments in which they often incur large costs today but don't make any profits until some time in the future. Somehow they have to be able to compare their investment cost today with a stream of future profits. How can they relate present cost to future benefits?

Interest rates are used to link the present with the future. After all, if you have to pay $105 at the end of the year when you borrow $100, that 5 percent interest rate gives you a measure of the premium on the earlier availability of goods and services. If you want to have things today, you have to pay the 5 percent interest rate in order to have current purchasing power.

The question could be put this way: What is the present value (the value today) of $105 that you could receive one year from now? That depends on the market rate of interest, or the rate of interest that you could earn in some appropriate savings institution, such as in a savings account. To make the arithmetic simple, let's assume that the rate of interest is 5 percent. Now you can figure out the **present value** of $105 to be received one year from now. You figure it out by asking, What sum must I put aside today at the market interest rate of 5 percent to receive $105 one year from now? Mathematically, we represent this equation as

$$(1 + 0.05)PV_1 = \$105$$

where PV_1 is the sum that you must set aside now.

Let's solve this simple equation to obtain PV_1:

$$PV_1 = \frac{\$105}{1.05} = \$100$$

That is, $100 will accumulate to $105 at the end of one year with a market rate of interest of 5 percent. Thus, the present value of $105 one year from now, using a rate of interest of 5 percent, is $100. The formula for present value of any sums to be received one year from now thus becomes

$$PV_1 = \frac{FV_1}{1 + i}$$

where

$$PV_1 = \text{present value of a sum one year hence}$$
$$FV_1 = \text{future sum paid or received one year hence}$$
$$i = \text{market rate of interest}$$

PRESENT VALUES FOR MORE DISTANT PERIODS The present-value formula for figuring out today's worth of dollars to be received at a future date can now be determined. How much would have to be put in the same savings account today to have $105 *two years* from now if the account pays a rate of 5 percent per year compounded annually?

After one year, the sum that would have to be set aside, which we will call PV_2, would have grown to $PV_2 \times 1.05$. This amount during the second year would increase to $PV_2 \times 1.05 \times 1.05$, or $PV_2 \times (1.05)^2$. To find the PV_2 that would grow to $105 over two years, let

$$PV_2 \times (1.05)^2 = \$105$$

and solve for PV_2:

$$PV_2 = \frac{\$105}{(1.05)^2} = \$95.24$$

Thus, the present value of $105 to be paid or received two years hence, discounted at an interest rate of 5 percent per year compounded annually, is equal to $95.24. In other words, $95.24 put into a savings account yielding 5 percent per year compounded interest would accumulate to $105 in two years.

Present value

The value of a future amount expressed in today's dollars; the most that someone would pay today to receive a certain sum at some point in the future.

Go to www.econtoday.com/chapter22 to utilize an MFM Communication Software, Inc., manual providing additional review of present value.

You Are There

To consider what a difference the rate of interest makes in present-value calculations involving sums to be received far into the future, contemplate **In a Cold Twist, a Millionaire Bequeaths His Wealth to Himself,** on pages 575 and 576.

TABLE 22-3

Present Value of a Future Dollar

This table shows how much a dollar received at the end of a certain number of years in the future is worth today. For example, at 5 percent a year, a dollar to be received 20 years in the future is worth 37.7 cents; if received in 50 years, it isn't even worth a dime today. To find out how much $10,000 would be worth a certain number of years from now, just multiply the figures in the table by 10,000. For example, $10,000 received at the end of 10 years discounted at a 5 percent rate of interest would have a present value of $6,140.

Discounted Present Values of $1					
Year	3%	5%	8%	10%	20%
1	.971	.952	.926	.909	.833
2	.943	.907	.857	.826	.694
3	.915	.864	.794	.751	.578
4	.889	.823	.735	.683	.482
5	.863	.784	.681	.620	.402
6	.838	.746	.630	.564	.335
7	.813	.711	.583	.513	.279
8	.789	.677	.540	.466	.233
9	.766	.645	.500	.424	.194
10	.744	.614	.463	.385	.162
15	.642	.481	.315	.239	.0649
20	.554	.377	.215	.148	.0261
25	.478	.295	.146	.0923	.0105
30	.412	.231	.0994	.0573	.00421
40	.307	.142	.0460	.0221	.000680
50	.228	.087	.0213	.00852	.000109

Discounting
The method by which the present value of a future sum or a future stream of sums is obtained.

THE GENERAL FORMULA FOR DISCOUNTING The general formula for **discounting** becomes

$$PV_t = \frac{FV_t}{(1 + i)^t}$$

where t refers to the number of periods in the future the money is to be paid or received.

Table 22-3 gives the present value of $1 to be received in future years at various interest rates. The interest rate used to derive the present value is called the **rate of discount.**

Rate of discount
The rate of interest used to discount future sums back to present value.

Why is General Motors Corporation installing virtual diagnostic components in many of its vehicles?

E-COMMERCE EXAMPLE
At GM, a Wireless Mechanic Helps Cut the Present Value of Future Warranty Costs

OnStar, a wireless satellite service, is a subsidiary of General Motors. The service appeals to owners of GM vehicles because it can open a car door when the owner is locked out and notify an ambulance when a vehicle's air bag deploys. Initially, OnStar charged about $17 per month for providing these and other services. Recently, GM has reduced this fee to induce more vehicle owners to utilize another feature: more than 1,600 diagnostic checks of a vehicle's operations that OnStar can process remotely. When OnStar identifies a problem in a vehicle, such as a minor malfunction in an electronic ventilation system, it automatically transmits an e-mail notification to the vehicle's owner. If the owner responds by taking the vehicle to a dealer for service, GM often benefits by incurring lower expenses for providing warranty services. Repairing such a small problem at an early stage is typically much less costly to GM than addressing it after it becomes a major malfunction. GM managers hope that a slight cut in OnStar's monthly fee today will induce more owners to utilize the service, thereby enabling the company to realize a significant present-value reduction in future warranty service costs.

FOR CRITICAL ANALYSIS
If the interest rate decreases, does GM have a larger or smaller incentive to cut the monthly fee for its OnStar service?

Corporate Financing Methods

When the Dutch East India Company was founded in 1602, it raised financial capital by selling shares of its expected future profits to investors. The investors thus became the owners of the company, and their ownership shares eventually became known as "shares of stock," or simply *stocks*. The company also issued notes of indebtedness, which involved borrowing funds in return for interest paid on the funds, plus eventual repayment of the principal amount borrowed. In modern parlance, these notes of indebtedness are called *bonds*. As the company prospered over time, some of its revenues were used to pay lenders the interest and principal owed them; of the profits that remained, some were paid to shareholders in the form of dividends, and some were retained by the company for reinvestment in further enterprises. The methods of financing used by the Dutch East India Company four centuries ago—stocks, bonds, and reinvestment—remain the principal methods of financing for today's corporations.

Stocks

Share of stock
A legal claim to a share of a corporation's future profits. If it is *common stock*, it incorporates certain voting rights regarding major policy decisions of the corporation. If it is *preferred stock*, its owners are accorded preferential treatment in the payment of dividends but do not have any voting rights.

A **share of stock** in a corporation is simply a legal claim to a share of the corporation's future profits. If there are 100,000 shares of stock in a company and you own 1,000 of them, you own the right to 1 percent of that company's future profits. If the stock you own is *common stock*, you also have the right to vote on major policy decisions affecting the company, such as the selection of the corporation's board of directors. Your 1,000 shares would entitle you to cast 1 percent of the votes on such issues.

If the stock you own is *preferred stock*, you own a share of the future profits of the corporation but do *not* have regular voting rights. You do, however, get something in return for giving up your voting rights: preferential treatment in the payment of dividends. Specifically, the owners of preferred stock generally must receive at least a certain amount of dividends in each period before the owners of common stock can receive *any* dividends.

Bonds

Bond
A legal claim against a firm, usually entitling the owner of the bond to receive a fixed annual coupon payment, plus a lump-sum payment at the bond's maturity date. Bonds are issued in return for funds lent to the firm.

A **bond** is a legal claim against a firm, entitling the owner of the bond to receive a fixed annual *coupon* payment, plus a lump-sum payment at the maturity date of the bond. Bonds are issued in return for funds lent to the firm; the coupon payments represent interest on the amount borrowed by the firm, and the lump-sum payment at maturity of the bond generally equals the amount originally borrowed by the firm.

Bonds are *not* claims on the future profits of the firm; legally, bondholders must be paid whether the firm prospers or not. To help ensure this, bondholders generally receive their coupon payments each year, along with any principal that is due, before *any* shareholders can receive dividend payments.

Reinvestment

Reinvestment takes place when the firm uses some of its profits to purchase new capital equipment rather than paying the profits out as dividends to shareholders. Although sales of stock are an important source of financing for new firms, reinvestment and borrowing are the primary means of financing for existing firms. Indeed, reinvestment by established firms is such an important source of financing that it dominates the other two sources of corporate finance, amounting to roughly 75 percent of new financial capital for corporations in recent years. Also, small businesses, which are the source of much current growth, often cannot rely on the stock market to raise investment funds.

Reinvestment
Profits (or depreciation reserves) used to purchase new capital equipment.

The Markets for Stocks and Bonds

Economists often refer to the "market for wheat" or the "market for labor," but these are concepts rather than actual places. For **securities** (stocks and bonds), however, there really are markets—centralized, physical locations where exchange takes place. The most prestigious of these markets are the New York Stock Exchange (NYSE) and the New York Bond Exchange, both located in New York City. More than 2,500 stocks are traded on the NYSE, which is sometimes called the "Big Board." Numerous other stock and bond markets, or exchanges, exist throughout the United States and in various financial capitals of the world, such as London and Tokyo.

Securities
Stocks and bonds.

Although the exact process by which exchanges are conducted in these markets varies slightly from one to another, the process used on the NYSE is representative of the principles involved. Essentially, brokers attempt to earn commissions from volumes of shares traded, while dealers attempt to profit from "buying low and selling high."

Even though the NYSE is traditionally the most prestigious of U.S. stock exchanges, it is no longer the largest. Since the mid-2000s, this title has belonged to the National Association of Securities Dealers Automated Quotations (Nasdaq), which began in 1971 as a tiny electronic network linking about 100 securities firms. Today, the Nasdaq market links about 500 dealers, and Nasdaq is home to nearly 4,000 stocks, including those of such companies as Microsoft, Intel, and Cisco.

What function does the New York Stock Exchange serve?

The Theory of Efficient Markets

At any point in time, there are tens of thousands, even millions, of persons looking for any bit of information that will enable them to forecast correctly the future prices of stocks. Responding to any information that seems useful, these people try to buy low and sell high. The result is that all publicly available information that might be used to forecast stock prices gets taken into account by those with access to the information and the knowledge and ability to learn from it, leaving no predictable profit opportunities. And because so many people are involved in this process, it occurs quite swiftly. Indeed, there is some evidence that *all* information entering the market is fully incorporated into stock prices within less than a minute of its arrival. One view is that any information about specific stocks will prove to have little value by the time it reaches you.

Consequently, stock prices tend to drift upward following a *random walk*, which is to say that the best forecast of tomorrow's price is today's price plus the effect of any upward drift. This is called the **random walk theory.** Although large values of the random component of stock price changes are less likely than small values, nothing else about the magnitude or direction of a stock price change can be predicted. Indeed,

Random walk theory
The theory that there are no predictable trends in securities prices that can be used to "get rich quick."

the random component of stock prices exhibits behavior much like what would occur if you rolled two dice and subtracted 7 from the resulting total. On average, the dice will show a total of 7, so after you subtract 7, the average result will be zero. It is true that rolling a 12 or a 2 (resulting in a total of + 5 or −5) is less likely than rolling an 8 or a 6 (yielding a total of +1 or −1). Nevertheless, positive and negative totals are equally likely, and the expected total is zero.

Why are doubts about whether markets utilize information as the efficient markets hypothesis implies important to a number of people currently serving prison terms?

EXAMPLE
Efficient Markets or Adaptive Markets?

In 1988, the U.S. Supreme Court endorsed a legal theory known as "fraud on the market," which in turn is based on the efficient markets hypothesis. The Supreme Court ruled that because the efficient markets hypothesis indicates that market prices reflect all available information, misleading statements affect the share price that investors use to assess a company's value. Thus, the Supreme Court decided, misleading statements about a firm's condition defraud those who buy the firm's stock even if they do not rely directly on such statements—indeed, even if they are not even aware of them. Under this reasoning, a number of corporate officers have been sentenced to prison terms ranging from several months to more than 20 years.

According to some behavioral economists, the Supreme Court may have relied on faulty economics. In place of the efficient markets hypothesis, they propose an *adaptive markets hypothesis*. They note that there is evidence that

traders are guided by emotion and thus use trial and error to develop rules of thumb to guide their purchases and sales. If correct, the adaptive markets hypothesis implies that markets do not efficiently process information. Thus, movements in stock prices following the release of misleading statements may not actually reflect the information in such statements. Naturally, some convicted corporate managers are basing their legal appeals on this alternative theory of how stock prices are determined.

FOR CRITICAL ANALYSIS
Why might proponents of the efficient markets hypothesis contend that even traders influenced by emotion still respond fully to all available market information? (Hint: The efficient markets hypothesis relies on the assumption that traders behave as if they are rational, not a claim that they behave like emotionless robots.)

Inside Information

Isn't there any way to "beat the market"? The answer is yes—but normally only if you have **inside information** that is not available to the public. Suppose that your best friend is in charge of new product development at the world's largest software firm, Microsoft Corporation. Your friend tells you that the company's smartest programmer has just come up with major new software that millions of computer users will want to buy. No one but your friend and the programmer—and now you—is aware of this. You could indeed make a killing using this information by purchasing shares of Microsoft and then selling them (at a higher price) as soon as the new product is publicly announced. There is one problem: Stock trading based on inside information such as this is illegal, punishable by substantial fines and even imprisonment. So, unless you happen to have a stronger-than-average desire for a long vacation in a federal prison, you might be better off investing in Microsoft after the new program is publicly announced.

It is, of course, possible for people to influence stock or bond prices through the accidental release of inside information. For instance, when the U.S. Treasury

Inside information
Information that is not available to the general public about what is happening in a corporation.

Go to www.econtoday.com/chapter22 to explore how the U.S. Securities and Exchange Commission seeks to prevent the use of inside information.

decided it would discontinue issuing 30-year bonds, it chose to announce its decision on October 31, 2001. Treasury officials told the media that the information of the bond's demise would be public as of 10 AM. Nevertheless, as a courtesy officials informed reporters in advance in an impromptu 9 AM meeting so that the reporters would have time to write stories to release at the later hour. Officials failed to check the credentials of everyone who attended the meeting, however, and one of those individuals was a financial consultant who did not understand that this early news of the bond's end was "embargoed" until 10 AM. After the news conference ended just before 9:30 AM, the consultant called some of his clients and told them of the media announcement. Within a very few minutes, word of the Treasury's plans had spread widely. Ten minutes before the Treasury's formal announcement, 30-year bond prices rose in response to higher demand for existing bonds.

QUICK QUIZ

See page 582 for the answers. Review concepts from this section in MyEconLab.

The three primary sources of corporate funds are _____, _____, and _____ of profits.

A **share of stock** is a share of _____ providing a legal claim to a corporation's future profits. A _____ is a legal claim entitling the owner to a fixed annual coupon payment and to a lump-sum payment on the date it matures.

Many economists believe that asset markets, especially the stock market, are _____, meaning that one cannot make a higher-than-normal rate of return without having inside information (information that the general public does not possess). Stock prices normally drift upward following a _____ _____, meaning that you cannot predict changes in future stock prices based on information about stock price behavior in the past.

You Are There

In a Cold Twist, a Millionaire Bequeaths His Wealth to Himself

David Pizer, the operator of a resort in Arizona, plans to hold onto his wealth following his death—literally. When the end of his life arrives, his body will be added to the more than 150 bodies (or, in some cases, heads only) held in cold storage at two U.S. cryonics facilities.

Pizer anticipates that future technological developments will enable medical scientists to remove his body from cold storage and reanimate it hundreds or perhaps even thousands of years from now. Thus, he has taken advantage of a legal arrangement known as a *dynasty trust*. Normally, such trusts shield assets from estate taxes by making payments to children, grandchildren, and subsequent generations. Instead, Pizer has structured a dynasty trust that will make payments to him whenever the time might arrive that medical scientists are able to bring him back to life.

Pizer's dynasty trust will manage roughly $10 million in wealth that he anticipates he will have accumulated by the time of his death. He speculates that with these funds earning interest while he is frozen, he could wake up in 100 years the "richest man in the world." Of course, even if his optimism about future advances in medical science turns out to be well placed, much depends on the average rate of interest earned by his dynasty trust. At an annual interest rate of 5 percent, $10 million is the present value of about $1,315 million to be received 100 years from now. Hence, at a 5 percent annual interest rate, Pizer could anticipate reawakening with more than $1.3 billion in wealth. In contrast, at an annual interest rate of 8 percent, $10 million is the present value of about $21,998 million to be received in 100 years. Thus, if this higher interest rate were to prevail for a century, Pizer would have about $22 billion in wealth when he awakened. This is still less than half of Bill Gates's current wealth, however.

You Are There (cont.)

CRITICAL ANALYSIS QUESTIONS

1. Why does Pizer's present value of $10 million translate into such widely varying future sums a century hence depending on the assumed annual interest rate?

2. Based on Table 22-3 on page 571, if Pizer is "reanimated" 50 years after his death and finds that his dynasty trust is worth "only" $43.86 million, what rate of interest must have prevailed over the 50-year interval?

How Musicians Increasingly Rely on Stocks and Bonds

Issues and Applications

CONCEPTS APPLIED

- Markets for Stocks and Bonds
- Securities
- Discounted Present Value

Some musicians take courses in economics. A few, such as Mick Jagger of the Rolling Stones, even allocate time to serious study of the subject. Nevertheless, many musicians choose to concentrate almost exclusively on becoming more proficient at playing or singing. Perhaps these musicians should change their tune, however, because professional musicians increasingly are issuing stocks and bonds to finance their activities.

Raising Funds for the Instrument

What if you are a classical music performer and desire one of the best string instruments—say, a 1712 Guarneri *filius Andreae* cello or a Stradivarius violin in mint condition—for the sound that will propel you into the best concert halls? If so, you face a fundamental complication: such instruments fetch auction prices that can exceed $3 million.

One possible solution is to follow the path of a growing number of classical performers by selling shares in one of these string instruments. Since 1970, such instruments have seen price increases more than 200 percent higher than the average increase in the prices of shares trading in U.S. stock markets. Indeed, prices of the very best instruments have more than tripled during the past 15 years. Thus, it is usually not difficult to line up investors willing to purchase shares in instruments—though some contracts also require the artist using the instrument to present private performances for the investors.

Selling Shares in the Band

Challenges in financing musical endeavors are not limited to classical musicians. Rock bands trying to get a start in the recording industry often struggle to raise sufficient funds to pay a producer and marketing representative and to cover the cost of manufacturing their first few thousand CDs.

The German company SellaBand coordinates start-up funding efforts for more than 250 fledgling rock bands. Fans—or simply interested investors—can buy shares in promising bands online for $10 apiece. After a band raises $50,000, SellaBand arranges production, marketing, and CD manufacturing. Revenues from CD sales and advertising on SellaBand are then shared by the company, members of the band, and the investors.

Issuing Bonds Backed by Music Royalties

What about the artist who has already had a big career touring the world's top concert halls and stadiums and a stream of top 40 hits but who now wishes to obtain extra funds to settle down into a calmer lifestyle? One approach might be to follow the example of rock musician David Bowie, who in 1997 raised $55 million by issuing securities with returns derived from the stream of revenues generated by continuing sales of his albums. Other artists, such as Ashford & Simpson, (the late) James Brown, and the Isley Brothers, issued similar bonds, which are called "Bowie bonds" in honor of the first issuer of music-revenue-backed securities.

In the early 2000s, market clearing prices of Bowie bonds dropped considerably when the recording industry experienced an extended downturn. Prices have recovered in recent years with the growth of iTunes and other online digital-download platforms, which promise to boost earnings of royalties on recorded music. The growing use of recorded music for cellphone "rings" has also helped boost Bowie bond prices. Every song downloaded for this purpose generates more than 8 cents in royalties for the song's owner—and hence boosts the stream of revenues for owners of the bonds.

Test your understanding of this chapter by going online to **MyEconLab**.
In the Study Plan for this chapter, select Section N: News.

For Critical Analysis

1. Why might shares in a cello or a violin be less liquid than shares of stock in a major U.S. corporation?

2. How would the market value of the first Bowie bonds likely respond if David Bowie were to experience a comeback as a performer for a new generation of rock fans?

Web Resources

1. For a description of Bowie bonds, use the link available at www.econtoday.com/chapter22.

2. To learn more about SellaBand, go to www.econtoday.com/chapter22.

Research Project

Evaluate whether the theory of efficient markets would likely apply to shares of stock in cellos, violins, or rock bands, just as it is hypothesized to apply to ownership shares in companies. If so, how should stock prices vary over time? If not, why not?

Here is what you should know after reading this chapter. **MyEconLab** will help you identify what you know, and where to go when you need to practice.

WHAT YOU SHOULD KNOW		WHERE TO GO TO PRACTICE
Economic Rent and Resource Allocation Owners of a resource in fixed supply, meaning that the resource supply curve is perfectly inelastic, are paid economic rent. Originally, this term was used to refer to payment for the use of land or any other natural resource that is considered to be in fixed supply. More generally, however, economic rent is a payment for the use of any resource that exceeds the opportunity cost of the resource. The economic rents received by the owners of such a resource reflect the maximum market valuation of the resource's value. Thus, economic rent allocates resources to their highest-valued use.	economic rent, 559 **KEY FIGURE** Figure 22-1, 560	• **MyEconLab** Study Plan 22.1 • Audio introduction to Chapter 22 • Animated Figure 22-1 • Video: Economic Rent and the Allocation of Resources
The Main Organizational Forms of Business and the Chief Advantages and Disadvantages of Each The primary organizational forms businesses take are the proprietorship, the partnership, and the corporation. The proprietorship is owned by a single person, who makes the business decisions, is entitled to all the profits, and is subject to unlimited liability. The partnership has two or more owners, who share the responsibility for decision making, share the firm's profits, and individually bear unlimited liability for the firm's debts. The corporation differs from proprietorships and partnerships in three important dimensions. Owners of corporations enjoy limited liability, so their responsibility for the debts of the corporation is limited to the value of their ownership shares. In addition, the income from corporations is subject to double taxation—corporate taxation when income is earned by the corporation and personal taxation when after-tax profits are paid as dividends to the owners. Finally, corporations do not legally cease to exist due to a change of ownership or the death of an owner.	firm, 561 proprietorship, 562 unlimited liability, 563 partnership, 563 corporation, 563 limited liability, 563 dividends, 564	• **MyEconLab** Study Plan 22.2 • Video: The Goal of the Firm Is Profit Maximization
Accounting Profits versus Economic Profits A firm's accounting profits equal its total revenues minus its total explicit costs, which are expenses directly paid out by the firm. Economic profits equal accounting profits minus implicit costs, which are expenses that managers do not have to pay out of pocket, such as the opportunity cost of factors of production dedicated to the firm's production process. Owners of a firm seek to maximize the firm's economic profits to ensure that they earn at least a normal rate of return, meaning that the firm's total revenues at least cover explicit costs and implicit opportunity costs.	explicit costs, 564 accounting profit, 564 implicit costs, 565 normal rate of return, 565 opportunity cost of capital, 565 economic profits, 566 **KEY FIGURE** Figure 22-2, 566	• **MyEconLab** Study Plan 22.2 • Animated Figure 22-2 • Video: The Goal of the Firm Is Profit Maximization

(continued)

 *(continued)*

WHAT YOU SHOULD KNOW

WHERE TO GO TO PRACTICE

Interest Rates Interest is a payment for the ability to use resources today instead of in the future. Factors that influence interest rates are the length of the term of a loan, the loan's risk, and handling charges. The nominal interest rate includes a factor that takes into account the anticipated inflation rate, so during periods of high anticipated inflation, current market (nominal) interest rates are high. Comparing the market interest rate with the rate of return on prospective capital investment projects enables owners of funds to determine the highest-valued uses of the funds. Thus, the interest rate allocates funds to industries whose investments yield the highest (risk-adjusted) returns, and available resources are put to their most productive uses.

financial capital, 568
interest, 568
nominal rate of interest, 568
real rate of interest, 569

- **MyEconLab** Study Plan 22.3
- Video: Interest Rates and Present Value

Calculating the Present Discounted Value of a Payment to Be Received at a Future Date The present value of a future payment is the value of the future amount expressed in today's dollars, and it is equal to the most that someone would pay today to receive that amount in the future. The method by which the present value of a future sum is calculated is called *discounting*. This method implies that the present value of a sum to be received a year from now is equal to the future amount divided by 1 plus the appropriate rate of interest, which is called the *rate of discount*.

present value, 570
discounting, 571
rate of discount, 571

- **MyEconLab** Study Plan 22.3
- Video: Interest Rates and Present Value

The Three Main Sources of Corporate Funds The main sources of financial capital for corporations are stocks, bonds, and reinvestment of profits. Stocks are ownership shares, promising a share of profits, sold to investors. Common stocks also embody voting rights regarding the major decisions of the firm; preferred stocks typically have no voting rights but enjoy priority status in the payment of dividends. Bonds are notes of indebtedness, issued in return for the loan of funds. They typically promise to pay interest in the form of annual coupon payments, plus repayment of the original principal amount upon maturity. Bondholders are generally promised payment before any payment of dividends to shareholders, and for this reason bonds are less risky than stocks. Reinvestment involves the purchase of assets by the firm, using retained profits or depreciation reserves it has set aside for this purpose. No new stocks or bonds are issued in the course of reinvestment, although the firm's value is fully reflected in the price of existing shares of stock.

share of stock, 572
bond, 572
reinvestment, 573
securities, 573
random walk theory, 573
inside information, 574

- **MyEconLab** Study Plans 22.4, 22.5
- Video: The Theory of Efficient Markets and Inside Information

Log in to MyEconLab, take a chapter test, and get a personalized Study Plan that tells you which concepts you understand and which ones you need to review. From there, MyEconLab will give you further practice, tutorials, animations, videos, and guided solutions.
Log in to www.myeconlab.com

PROBLEMS

All problems are assignable in **myeconlab** *. Answers to odd-numbered problems appear at the back of the book.*

22-1. Which of the following individuals would you expect to have a high level of economic rent, and which would you expect to have a low level of economic rent? Explain why for each.

  a. Bob has a highly specialized medical skill shared by very few individuals.

  b. Sally has never attended school. She is 25 years old and is an internationally known supermodel.

  c. Tim is a high school teacher and sells insurance part time.

22-2. Though he has retired as a professional football receiver, Jerry Rice still earns a sizable annual income from endorsements that advertisers view as closely tied to his "persona." Explain why, in economic terms, Rice's level of economic rent is so high.

22-3. Former professional basketball star Michael Jordan once left basketball to play baseball. As a result, his annual dollar income dropped from the millions to the thousands. Eventually, Jordan quit baseball and returned to basketball. What role did economic rents likely play in influencing his decision?

22-4. A British pharmaceutical company spent several years and considerable funds on the development of a treatment for HIV patients. Now, with the protection afforded by patent rights, the company has the potential to reap enormous gains. The government, in response, has threatened to tax away any rents the company may earn. Is this an advisable policy? Why or why not? (Hint: Contrast the short-run and long-run effects of taxing away the economic rents.)

22-5. Write a brief explanation of the differences among a sole proprietorship, a partnership, and a corporation. In addition, list one advantage and one disadvantage of a proprietorship, a partnership, and a corporation.

22-6. After graduation, you face a choice. One option is to work for a multinational consulting firm and earn a starting salary (benefits included) of $40,000. The other option is to use $5,000 in savings to start your own consulting firm. You could earn an interest return of 5 percent on your savings. You choose to start your own consulting firm. At the end of the first year, you add up all of your expenses and revenues. Your total includes $12,000 in rent, $1,000 in office supplies, $20,000 for office staff, and $4,000 in telephone expenses. What are your total explicit costs and total implicit costs?

22-7. Suppose, as in Problem 22-6, that you have now operated your consulting firm for a year. At the end of the first year, your total revenues are $77,250. Based on the information in Problem 22-6, what is the accounting profit, and what is your economic profit?

22-8. An individual leaves a college faculty, where she was earning $40,000 a year, to begin a new venture. She invests her savings of $10,000, which were earning 10 percent annually. She then spends $20,000 renting office equipment, hires two students at $30,000 a year each, rents office space for $12,000, and has other variable expenses of $40,000. At the end of the year, her revenues are $200,000. What are her accounting profit and her economic profit for the year?

22-9. Classify the following items as either financial capital or physical capital.

  a. A computer server owned by an information-processing company

  b. $100,000 set aside in an account to purchase a computer server

  c. Funds raised through a bond offer to expand plant and equipment

  d. A warehouse owned by a shipping company

22-10. Explain the difference between the dividends of a corporation and the profits of a proprietorship or partnership, particularly in their tax treatment.

22-11. The owner of WebCity is trying to decide whether to remain a proprietorship or to incorporate. Suppose that the corporate tax rate on profits is 20 percent and the personal income tax rate is 30 percent. For simplicity, assume that all corporate profits (after corporate taxes are paid) are distributed as dividends in the year they are earned and that such dividends are subject to tax at the personal income tax rate.

a. If the owner of WebCity expects to earn $100,000 in before-tax profits this year, regardless of whether the firm is a proprietorship or a corporation, which method of organization should be chosen?

b. What is the dollar value of the after-tax advantage of the form of organization determined in part (a)?

c. Suppose that the corporate form of organization has cost advantages that will raise before-tax profits by $50,000. Should the owner of WebCity incorporate?

d. By how much will after-tax profits change due to incorporation?

e. Suppose that tax policy is changed to completely exempt from personal taxation the first $40,000 per year in dividends. Would this change in policy affect the decision made in part (a)?

f. How can you explain the fact that even though corporate profits are subject to double taxation, most business in the United States is conducted by corporations rather than by proprietorships or partnerships?

22-12. Explain how the following events would likely affect the relevant interest rate.

a. A major bond-rating agency has improved the risk rating of a developing nation.

b. To regulate and to protect the public, the government has passed legislation that requires a considerable increase in the reporting paperwork when a bank makes a loan.

22-13. Suppose that the interest rate in Japan is only 2 percent, while the comparable rate in the United States is 4 percent. Japan's rate of inflation is 0.5 percent, while the U.S. inflation rate is 3 percent. Which economy has the higher real interest rate?

22-14. You expect to receive a payment of $104 one year from now.

a. Your discount rate is 4 percent. What is the present value of the payment to be received?

b. Suppose that your discount rate rises to 5 percent. What is the present value of the payment to be received?

22-15. Outline the differences between common stock and preferred stock.

22-16. Explain the basic differences between a share of stock and a bond.

22-17. Suppose that one of your classmates informs you that he has developed a method of forecasting stock market returns based on past trends. With a monetary investment by you, he claims that the two of you could profit handsomely from this forecasting method. How should you respond to your classmate?

22-18. Suppose that you are trying to decide whether to spend $1,000 on stocks issued by WildWeb or on bonds issued by the same company. There is a 50 percent chance that the value of the stock will rise to $2,200 at the end of the year and a 50 percent chance that the stock will be worthless at the end of the year. The bonds promise an interest rate of 20 percent per year, and it is certain that the bonds and interest will be repaid at the end of the year.

a. Assuming that your time horizon is exactly one year, will you choose the stocks or the bonds?

b. By how much is your expected end-of-year wealth reduced if you make the wrong choice?

c. Suppose the odds of success improve for WildWeb: Now there is a 60 percent chance that the value of the stock will be $2,200 at year's end and only a 40 percent chance that it will be worthless. Should you now choose the stocks or the bonds?

d. By how much did your expected end-of-year wealth rise as a result of the improved outlook for WildWeb?

ECONOMICS ON THE NET

How the New York Stock Exchange Operates This application gives you the chance to learn about how the New York Stock Exchange functions.

Title: The New York Stock Exchange: How a Stock Is Bought and Sold

Navigation: Follow the link at **www.econtoday.com/chapter22** to visit the New York Stock Exchange. Click "About us" in the left margin for a pop-up menu, and then click on *Education*. Select the tab named *Educational Materials*. Under "Publications for Investors," click on *How a Stock Is Bought and Sold*. Read the article.

Application Answer the following questions.

1. Why might companies contemplating issuing stock value the relatively low costs of trading shares on the New York Stock Exchange?

2. Why might people who buy and sell stocks value the relatively faster speeds of trade execution that the NYSE has achieved in recent years?

For Group Study and Analysis Go back up to "Publications for Investors," click on *NYSE Indexes*, and read the article. Divide the class into groups, and assign each group to examine one of the six NYSE indexes discussed in the article. Ask each group to evaluate how stock traders might use the specific index as a "benchmark" when evaluating whether to buy or sell stocks.

ANSWERS TO QUICK QUIZZES

p. 561: (i) inelastic; (ii) allocates . . . highest
p. 567: (i) Proprietorships . . . unlimited; (ii) Partnerships . . . unlimited; (iii) shareholders . . . limited; (iv) opportunity; (v) greater . . . maximize
p. 572: (i) length . . . risk; (ii) anticipated . . . anticipated; (iii) present value
p. 575: (i) stocks . . . bonds . . . reinvestment; (ii) ownership . . . bond; (iii) efficient . . . random walk

The Firm: Cost and Output Determination

23

Y ou report to your first appointment with a new family physician whom a friend has recommended highly. On the way, you remember that when you called to make the appointment, the physician herself answered and set the appointment time. Now that you have arrived, you are surprised to find no waiting room, no receptionist or nurses, and no large suite of offices. Instead, the physician herself greets you and asks you to enter her small but comfortable office. What you are encountering is the latest trend in family medicine, called the "micropractice." This scenario is increasingly relevant in light of an altered cost structure in the provision of family medical services. In this chapter, you will learn why, for family physicians at least, it now pays to think small when it comes to operating a medical practice.

LEARNING OBJECTIVES

After reading this chapter, you should be able to:

➤ Discuss the difference between the short run and the long run from the perspective of a firm

➤ Understand why the marginal physical product of labor eventually declines as more units of labor are employed

➤ Explain the short-run cost curves a typical firm faces

➤ Describe the long-run cost curves a typical firm faces

➤ Identify situations of economies and diseconomies of scale and define a firm's minimum efficient scale

? **DID YOU KNOW THAT** since 1997, openings of new U.S. manufacturing facilities as a percentage of existing factories have declined from more than 3.5 percent per year to about 2.5 percent per year? During the same period, U.S. companies have closed about 3.5 percent of existing factories each year. On net, therefore, the number of U.S. manufacturing facilities has shrunk by about 1 percent per year since 1997. Some politicians have worried that this negative growth rate in the number of factories suggests a decline in U.S. manufacturing capabilities. Many economists, however, point out that another trend since the late 1990s has been toward *larger* U.S. manufacturing facilities. Thus, even as the overall number of factories has declined, the scale of production of the average plant has increased.

How does a company determine the scale of its production? To find the answer to this question, we must consider how firms employ inputs in the production of goods and services. We must also consider the nature of the costs that firms incur in their productive endeavors. First, however, we must think about alternative time horizons over which firms make decisions regarding their costly productive activities.

Short Run versus Long Run

In Chapter 20, we discussed short-run and long-run price elasticities of supply and demand. As you will recall, for consumers, the long run means the time period during which all adjustments to a change in price can be made, and anything shorter than that is considered the short run. For suppliers, the long run is the time in which all adjustments can be made, and anything shorter than that is the short run.

Now that we are discussing firms only, we will maintain a similar distinction between the short and the long run, but we will be more specific. In the theory of the firm, the **short run** is defined as any time period that is so short that there is at least one input, such as current **plant size,** that the firm cannot alter. In other words, during the short run, a firm makes do with whatever big machines and factory size it already has, no matter how much more it wants to produce because of increased demand for its product. We consider the plant and heavy equipment, the size or amount of which cannot be varied in the short run, as fixed resources. In agriculture and in some other businesses, land may be a fixed resource.

There are, of course, variable resources that the firm can alter when it wants to change its rate of production. These are called *variable inputs* or *variable factors of production*. Typically, the variable inputs of a firm are its labor and its purchases of raw materials. In the short run, in response to changes in demand, the firm can, by definition, change only the amounts of its variable inputs.

The **long run** can now be considered the period of time in which *all* inputs can be varied. Specifically, in the long run, the firm can alter its plant size. How long is the long run? That depends on each individual industry. For Wendy's or McDonald's, the long run may be four or five months, because that is the time it takes to add new franchises. For a steel company, the long run may be several years, because that's how long it takes to plan and build a new plant. An electric utility might need more than a decade to build a new plant, as another example.

Short run and *long run* in our discussion are terms that apply to planning decisions made by managers. Managers routinely take account of both the short-run and the long-run consequences of their behavior. While always making decisions about what to do today, tomorrow, and next week—the short run as it were—they keep an eye on the long-run net benefits of all short-run actions. As an individual, you have long-run plans, such as going to graduate school or on vacation, and you make a series of short-run decisions with these long-run plans in mind.

Short run
The time period during which at least one input, such as plant size, cannot be changed.

Plant size
The physical size of the factories that a firm owns and operates to produce its output. Plant size can be defined by square footage, maximum physical capacity, and other physical measures.

Long run
The time period during which all factors of production can be varied.

The Relationship Between Output and Inputs

A firm takes numerous inputs, combines them using a technological production process, and ends up with an output. There are, of course, a great many factors of production, or inputs. Keeping the quantity of land fixed, we classify production inputs into two broad categories—capital and labor. The relationship between output and these two inputs is as follows:

Output per time period = some function of capital and labor inputs

We have used the word *production* but have not defined it. **Production** is any process by which resources are transformed into goods or services. Production includes not only making things but also transporting them, retailing, repackaging them, and so on. Notice that the production relationship tells nothing about the worth or value of the inputs or the output.

Production
Any activity that results in the conversion of resources into products that can be used in consumption.

The Production Function: A Numerical Example

The relationship between maximum physical output and the quantity of capital and labor used in the production process is sometimes called the **production function**. The production function is a technological relationship between inputs and output.

Production function
The relationship between inputs and maximum physical output. A production function is a technological, not an economic, relationship.

PROPERTIES OF THE PRODUCTION FUNCTION The production function specifies the maximum possible output that can be produced with a given amount of inputs. It also specifies the minimum amount of inputs necessary to produce a given level of output. Firms that are inefficient or wasteful in their use of capital and labor will obtain less output than the production function in theory will show. No firm can obtain more output than the production function allows, however. The production function also depends on the technology available to the firm. It follows that an improvement in technology that allows the firm to produce more output with the same amount of inputs (or the same output with fewer inputs) results in a new production function.

How has software that creates three-dimensional images allowed escalator manufacturers to produce the same output with fewer inputs?

E-COMMERCE EXAMPLE
Riding an Escalator to the Outer Edge of a Production Function

Since escalators were first invented back in 1891, figuring out how to put one together has been a highly labor-intensive process. Designers must determine how to mesh more than 4,500 different components. Essentially, developing a production process for an escalator is like assembling an incredibly complex three-dimensional jigsaw puzzle. Until very recently, working through the intricacies of a lower-cost process for escalator design and production took engineers more than one year. Today, the use of three-dimensional software, such as a widely used program called AutoCAD, enables engineers to devise production processes for producing escalators in less than 12 weeks.

FOR CRITICAL ANALYSIS
Why do you suppose that business managers regard the process of developing the best production procedures as a fundamental requirement of operating at a point on a firm's production function?

Panel (a) of Figure 23-1 shows a production function relating maximum output in column 2 to the quantity of labor in column 1. Zero workers per week produce no output. Five workers per week of input produce a total output of 50 computer printers per week. (Ignore for the moment the rest of that panel.) Panel (b) of Figure 23-1 displays this production function. It relates to the short run, because plant size is fixed, and it applies to a single firm.

TOTAL PHYSICAL PRODUCT Panel (b) shows a total physical product curve, or the maximum feasible output when we add successive equal-sized units of labor while holding all other inputs constant. The graph of the production function in panel (b) is not a straight line. It peaks at seven workers per week and then starts to go down.

Average and Marginal Physical Product

Average physical product
Total product divided by the variable input.

To understand the shape of the total physical product curve, let's examine columns 3 and 4 of panel (a) of Figure 23-1—that is, average and marginal physical products. **Average physical product** is the total product divided by the number of worker-weeks. You can see in column 3 of panel (a) of Figure 23-1 that the average physical product of labor first rises and then steadily falls after two workers are hired.

Marginal physical product
The physical output that is due to the addition of one more unit of a variable factor of production; the change in total product occurring when a variable input is increased and all other inputs are held constant; also called *marginal product*.

Marginal means "additional," so the **marginal physical product** of labor is the *change* in total product that occurs when a worker is added to a production process. (The term *physical* here emphasizes the fact that we are measuring in terms of material quantities of goods or tangible amounts of services, not in dollar terms.) The marginal physical product of labor therefore refers to the *change in output caused by a one-unit change in the labor input* as shown in column 4 of panel (a) of Figure 23-1. (Marginal physical product is also referred to as *marginal product*.)

Diminishing Marginal Product

Note that in Figure 23-1, after the second worker is employed, marginal product declines. The concept of diminishing marginal product applies to many situations. If you put a seat belt across your lap, a certain amount of safety is obtained. If you add another seat belt over your shoulder, some additional safety is obtained, but less than when the first belt was secured. When you add a third seat belt over the other shoulder, the amount of *additional* safety obtained is even smaller.

Measuring Diminishing Marginal Product

How do we measure diminishing marginal product? First, we limit the analysis to only one variable factor of production (or input)—let's say the factor is labor. Every other factor of production, such as machines, must be held constant. Only in this way can we calculate the marginal product from using more workers and know when we reach the point of diminishing marginal product.

SPECIALIZATION AND MARGINAL PRODUCT The marginal productivity of labor may increase rapidly at the very beginning. A firm starts with no workers, only machines. The firm then hires one worker, who finds it difficult to get the work

FIGURE 23-1

The Production Function and Marginal Product: A Hypothetical Case

Marginal product is the addition to the total product that results when one additional worker is hired. Thus, in panel (a), the marginal product of the fourth worker is eight computer printers. With four workers, 44 printers are produced, but with three workers, only 36 are produced; the difference is 8. In panel (b), we plot the numbers from columns 1 and 2 of panel (a). In panel (c), we plot the numbers from columns 1 and 4 of panel (a). When

we go from 0 to 1, marginal product is 10. When we go from one worker to two workers, marginal product increases to 16. After two workers, marginal product declines, but it is still positive. Total product (output) reaches its peak at seven workers, so after seven workers, marginal product is negative. When we move from seven to eight workers, marginal product becomes −1 printer.

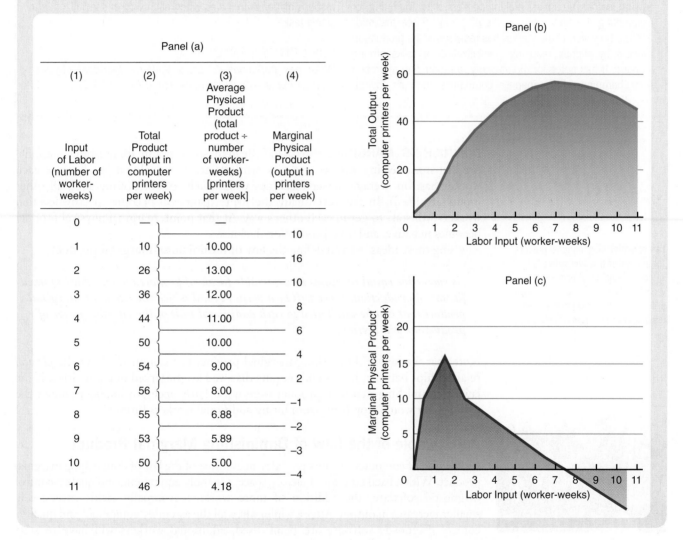

starting. But when the firm hires more workers, each is able to *specialize* in performing different tasks, and the marginal product of those additional workers may actually be greater than the marginal product of the previous few workers.

Can firms sometimes discover that avoiding *overspecialization* can raise marginal product?

INTERNATIONAL EXAMPLE
A French Handbag Manufacturer Opts for Multitasking

Louis Vuitton, a firm that specializes in producing high-fashion handbags, has long built specialization into its production process. For years, every factory has had about 250 employees, each of whom has specialized in a specific task: cutting leather or canvas; preparing, gluing, or sewing leather or canvas; making pockets; stitching lining; or assembling the final components of a bag. Since the mid-2000s, however, Louis Vuitton has reorganized its production process by slightly reducing specialization of tasks among workers. It has opted for *multitasking*, a production approach first championed by Japanese companies such as Toyota.

With this approach, a worker typically performs two or more tasks. Thus, individual workers at Louis Vuitton now perform multiple tasks, such as gluing, stitching, *and* finishing a pocket flap. The company has found that each worker's marginal product is higher with this system of slightly expanded responsibilities than it was when each worker specialized in a *single* task.

FOR CRITICAL ANALYSIS
What has happened to Louis Vuitton's marginal physical product curve—similar to panel (b) in Figure 23-1?

DIMINISHING MARGINAL PRODUCT Beyond some point, diminishing marginal product must set in—*not* because new workers are less qualified but because each worker has, on average, fewer machines with which to work (remember, all other inputs are fixed). In fact, eventually the firm's plant will become so crowded that workers will start to get in each other's way. At that point, marginal physical product becomes negative, and total production declines.

Using these ideas, we can define the **law of diminishing marginal product**:

Law of diminishing marginal product
The observation that after some point, successive equal-sized increases in a variable factor of production, such as labor, added to fixed factors of production will result in smaller increases in output.

> *As successive equal increases in a variable factor of production are added to fixed factors of production, there will be a point beyond which the extra, or marginal, product that can be attributed to each additional unit of the variable factor of production will decline.*

Note that the law of diminishing marginal product is a statement about the *physical* relationships between inputs and outputs that we have observed in many firms. If the law of diminishing marginal product were not a fairly accurate statement about the world, what would stop firms from hiring additional workers forever?

An Example of the Law of Diminishing Marginal Product

Production of computer printers provides an example of the law of diminishing marginal product. With a fixed amount of factory space, assembly equipment, and quality-control diagnostic software, the addition of more workers eventually yields successively smaller increases in output. After a while, when all the assembly equipment and quality-control diagnostic software are being used, additional workers will have to start assembling and troubleshooting quality problems manually. They obviously won't be as productive as the first workers, who had access to other productive inputs. The marginal physical product of an additional worker, given a specified amount of capital, must eventually be less than that for the previous workers.

GRAPHING THE MARGINAL PRODUCT OF LABOR A hypothetical set of numbers illustrating the law of diminishing marginal product is presented in panel (a) of Figure 23-1 on the previous page. The numbers are presented graphically in panel (c). Marginal

How has Louis Vuitton benefited from less specialization in the production process?

productivity (returns from adding more workers) first increases, then decreases, and finally becomes negative.

When one worker is hired, total output goes from 0 to 10. Thus, marginal physical product is 10 computer printers per week. When the second worker is hired, total product goes from 10 to 26 printers per week. Marginal physical product therefore increases to 16 printers per week. When a third worker is hired, total product again increases, from 26 to 36 printers per week. This represents a marginal physical product of only 10 printers per week. Therefore, the point of diminishing marginal product occurs after two workers are hired.

THE POINT OF SATURATION Notice that after seven workers per week, marginal physical product becomes negative. That means that the hiring of an eighth worker would reduce total product. Sometimes this is called the *point of saturation*, indicating that given the amount of fixed inputs, there is no further positive use for more of the variable input. We have entered the region of negative marginal product.

QUICK QUIZ   *See page 609 for the answers. Review concepts from this section in MyEconLab.*

The technological relationship between output and inputs is called the _____ function. It relates _____ per time period to several inputs, such as capital and labor.

After some rate of output, the firm generally experiences diminishing marginal _____.

The law of diminishing marginal product states that if all factors of production are held constant except one, equal increments in that one variable factor will eventually yield _____ increments in _____.

Short-Run Costs to the Firm

You will see that costs are the extension of the production ideas just presented. Let's consider the costs the firm faces in the short run. To make this example simple, assume that there are only two factors of production, capital and labor. Our definition of the short run will be the time during which capital is fixed but labor is variable.

In the short run, a firm incurs certain types of costs. We label all costs incurred **total costs.** Then we break total costs down into total fixed costs and total variable costs, which we will explain shortly. Therefore,

Total costs
The sum of total fixed costs and total variable costs.

Total costs (TC) = total fixed costs (TFC) + total variable costs (TVC)

Remember that these total costs include both explicit and implicit costs, including the normal rate of return on investment.

After we have looked at the elements of total costs, we will find out how to compute average and marginal costs.

Total Fixed Costs

Let's look at an ongoing business such as Hewlett-Packard (HP). The decision makers in that corporate giant can look around and see big machines, thousands of parts, huge buildings, and a multitude of other components of plant and equipment that have already been bought and are in place. HP has to take into account expenses to replace some worn-out equipment, no matter how many computers it produces. The payments on the loans taken out to buy the equipment will all be exactly the same regardless of the rate of output. The opportunity costs of any land that HP owns will all be exactly the same. In the short run, these costs are more or less the same for HP no matter how many computers it produces.

We also have to point out that the opportunity cost (or normal rate of return) of capital must be included along with other costs. Remember that we are dealing in the short run, during which capital is fixed. If investors in HP have already put $100 million into a factory addition, the opportunity cost of that capital invested is now, in essence, a *fixed cost*. Why? Because in the short run, nothing can be done about that cost; the investment has already been made. This leads us to a very straightforward definition of fixed costs: All costs that do not vary—that is, all costs that do not depend on the rate of production—are called **fixed costs.**

Let's now take as an example the fixed costs incurred by a producer of secure digital (SD) cards, digital storage cards used with digital cameras, laptop computers, and other devices. This firm's total fixed costs will usually include the cost of the rent for its plant and equipment and the insurance it has to pay. We see in panel (a) of Figure 23-2 that total fixed costs per hour are $10. In panel (b), these total fixed costs are represented by the horizontal line at $10 per hour. They are invariant to changes in the daily output of these SD cards—no matter how many are produced, fixed costs will remain at $10 per hour.

Fixed costs
Costs that do not vary with output. Fixed costs typically include such expenses as rent on a building. These costs are fixed for a certain period of time (in the long run, though, they are variable).

Total Variable Costs

Total **variable costs** are costs whose magnitude varies with the rate of production. Wages are an obvious variable cost. The more the firm produces, the more labor it has to hire; therefore, the more wages it has to pay. Parts are another variable cost. To manufacture secure digital cards, for example, microchips must be bought. The more SD cards that are made, the greater the number of chips that must be bought. A portion of the rate of depreciation (wear and tear) on machines that are used in the assembly process can also be considered a variable cost if depreciation depends partly on how long and how intensively the machines are used. Total variable costs are given in column 3 in panel (a) of Figure 23-2. These are translated into the total variable cost curve in panel (b). Notice that the total variable cost curve lies below the total cost curve by the vertical distance of $10. This vertical distance represents, of course, total fixed costs.

Variable costs
Costs that vary with the rate of production. They include wages paid to workers and purchases of materials.

Short-Run Average Cost Curves

In panel (b) of Figure 23-2, we see total costs, total variable costs, and total fixed costs. Now we want to look at average cost. With the average cost concept, we are measuring cost per unit of output. It is a matter of simple arithmetic to figure the averages of these three cost concepts. We can define them as follows:

$$\text{Average total costs (ATC)} = \frac{\text{total costs (TC)}}{\text{output } (Q)}$$

$$\text{Average variable costs (AVC)} = \frac{\text{total variable costs (TVC)}}{\text{output } (Q)}$$

$$\text{Average fixed costs (AFC)} = \frac{\text{total fixed costs (TFC)}}{\text{output } (Q)}$$

FIGURE 23-2

Cost of Production: An Example

In panel (a), the derivations of columns 4 through 9 are given in parentheses in each column heading. For example, column 6, average variable costs, is derived by dividing column 3, total variable costs, by column 1, total output per hour. Note that marginal cost (MC) in panel (c) intersects average variable costs (AVC) at the latter's minimum point. Also, MC intersects average total costs (ATC) at that latter's minimum point. It is a little more difficult to see that MC equals AVC and ATC at their respective minimum points in panel (a) because we are using discrete one-unit changes. You can see, though, that the marginal cost of going from 4 units per hour to 5 units per hour is $2 and increases to $3 when we move to 6 units per hour. Somewhere in between it equals AVC of $2.60, which is in fact the minimum average variable cost. The same analysis holds for ATC, which hits minimum at 7 units per day at $4.28 per unit. MC goes from $4 to $5 and just equals ATC somewhere in between.

Panel (a)

(1)	(2)	(3)	(4)	(5)	(6)	(7)	(8)	(9)
Total Output (Q/hour)	Total Fixed Costs (TFC)	Total Variable Costs (TVC)	Total Costs (TC) (4) = (2) + (3)	Average Fixed Costs (AFC) (5) = (2) ÷ (1)	Average Variable Costs (AVC) (6) = (3) ÷ (1)	Average Total Costs (ATC) (7) = (4) ÷ (1)	Total Costs (TC) (4)	Marginal Cost (MC) (9) = $\frac{\text{Change in (8)}}{\text{Change in (1)}}$
0	$10	$ 0	$10	—	—	—	$10	
1	10	5	15	$10.00	$5.00	$15.00	15	$5
2	10	8	18	5.00	4.00	9.00	18	3
3	10	10	20	3.33	3.33	6.67	20	2
4	10	11	21	2.50	2.75	5.25	21	1
5	10	13	23	2.00	2.60	4.60	23	2
6	10	16	26	1.67	2.67	4.33	26	3
7	10	20	30	1.43	2.86	4.28	30	4
8	10	25	35	1.25	3.12	4.38	35	5
9	10	31	41	1.11	3.44	4.56	41	6
10	10	38	48	1.00	3.80	4.80	48	7
11	10	46	56	.91	4.18	5.09	56	8

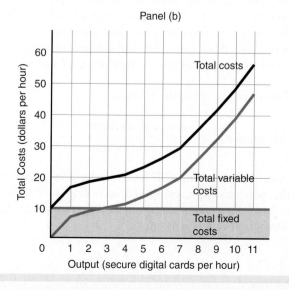

Panel (b)

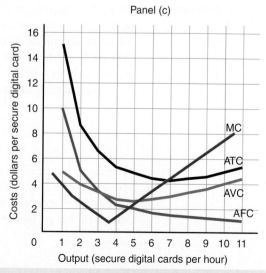

Panel (c)

The arithmetic is done in columns 5, 6, and 7 in panel (a) of Figure 23-2 on the preceding page. The numerical results are translated into a graphical format in panel (c). Because total costs (TC) equal variable costs (TVC) plus fixed costs (TFC), the difference between average total costs (ATC) and average variable costs (AVC) will always be identical to average fixed costs (AFC). That means that average total costs and average variable costs move together as output expands.

Now let's see what we can observe about the three average cost curves in Figure 23-2.

Average fixed costs
Total fixed costs divided by the number of units produced.

AVERAGE FIXED COSTS (AFC) **Average fixed costs** continue to fall throughout the output range. In fact, if we were to continue panel (c) of Figure 23-2 farther to the right, we would find that average fixed costs would get closer and closer to the horizontal axis. That is because total fixed costs remain constant. As we divide this fixed number by a larger and larger number of units of output, the resulting AFC becomes smaller and smaller. In business, this is called "spreading the overhead."

Average variable costs
Total variable costs divided by the number of units produced.

AVERAGE VARIABLE COSTS (AVC) We assume a particular form of the curve for **average variable costs.** The form that it takes is U-shaped: First it falls; then it starts to rise. It is possible for the AVC curve to take other shapes in the long run.

Average total costs
Total costs divided by the number of units produced; sometimes called *average per-unit total costs.*

AVERAGE TOTAL COSTS (ATC) This curve has a shape similar to that of the AVC curve. Nevertheless, it falls even more dramatically in the beginning and rises more slowly after it has reached a minimum point. It falls and then rises because **average total costs** are the vertical summation of the AFC curve and the AVC curve. Thus, when AFC and AVC are both falling, ATC must fall too. At some point, however, AVC starts to increase while AFC continues to fall. Once the increase in the AVC curve outweighs the decrease in the AFC curve, the ATC curve will start to increase and will develop a U shape, just like the AVC curve.

Marginal Cost

We have stated repeatedly that the basis of decisions is always on the margin—movement in economics is always determined at the margin. This dictum also holds true within the firm. Firms, according to the analysis we use to predict their behavior, are very concerned with their **marginal costs.** Because the term *marginal* means "additional" or "incremental" (or "decremental," too) here, *marginal costs* refer to costs that result from a one-unit change in the production rate. For example, if the production of 10 secure digital cards per hour costs a firm $48 and the production of 11 of these SD cards costs $56 per hour, the marginal cost of producing 11 rather than 10 SD cards per hour is $8.

Marginal costs
The change in total costs due to a one-unit change in production rate.

Marginal costs can be measured by using the formula

$$\text{Marginal cost} = \frac{\text{change in total cost}}{\text{change in output}}$$

We show the marginal costs of production of SD cards per hour in column 9 of panel (a) in Figure 23-2 on the previous page, computed according to the formula just given. In our example, we have changed output by one unit every time, so the denominator in that particular formula always equals one.

This marginal cost schedule is shown graphically in panel (c) of Figure 23-2 on page 591. Just like average variable costs and average total costs, marginal costs first fall and then rise. The U shape of the marginal cost curve is a result of increasing and then diminishing marginal product. At lower levels of output, the marginal cost curve declines. The reasoning is that as marginal physical product increases with each addition of output, the marginal cost of this last unit of output must fall. Conversely, when diminishing marginal product sets in, marginal physical product decreases (and eventually becomes negative); it follows that the marginal cost must rise when the marginal product begins its decline. These relationships are clearly reflected in the geometry of panels (b) and (c) of Figure 23-2.

In summary:

As long as marginal physical product rises, marginal cost will fall, and when marginal physical product starts to fall (after reaching the point of diminishing marginal product), marginal cost will begin to rise.

The Relationship Between Average and Marginal Costs

Let us now examine the relationship between average costs and marginal costs. There is always a definite relationship between averages and marginals. Consider the example of 10 football players with an average weight of 250 pounds. An eleventh player is added. His weight is 300 pounds. That represents the marginal weight. What happens now to the average weight of the team? It must increase. That is, when the marginal player weighs more than the average, the average must increase. Likewise, if the marginal player weighs less than 250 pounds, the average weight will decrease.

AVERAGE VARIABLE COSTS AND MARGINAL COSTS There is a similar relationship between average variable costs and marginal costs. When marginal costs are less than average costs, the latter must fall. Conversely, when marginal costs are greater than average costs, the latter must rise. When you think about it, the relationship makes sense. The only way average variable costs can fall is if the extra cost of the marginal unit produced is less than the average variable cost of all the preceding units. For example, if the average variable cost for two units of production is $4.00 a unit, the only way for the average variable cost of three units to be less than that of two units is for the variable costs attributable to the last unit—the marginal cost—to be less than the average of the past units. In this particular case, if average variable cost falls to $3.33 a unit, total variable cost for the three units would be three times $3.33, or almost exactly $10.00. Total variable cost for two units is two times $4.00 (average variable cost), or $8.00. The marginal cost is therefore $10.00 minus $8.00, or $2.00, which is less than the average variable cost of $3.33.

A similar type of computation can be carried out for rising average variable costs. The only way average variable costs can rise is if the average variable cost of additional units is more than that for units already produced. But the incremental cost is the marginal cost. In this particular case, the marginal costs have to be higher than the average variable costs.

AVERAGE TOTAL COSTS AND MARGINAL COSTS There is also a relationship between marginal costs and average total costs. Remember that average total cost is equal to total costs divided by the number of units produced. Also remember that marginal cost does not include any fixed costs. Fixed costs are, by definition, fixed and cannot influence marginal costs. Our example can therefore be repeated substituting *average total costs* for *average variable costs.*

These rising and falling relationships can be seen in panel (c) of Figure 23-2 on page 591, where MC intersects AVC and ATC at their respective minimum points.

Minimum Cost Points

At what rate of output of secure digital cards per hour does our representative firm experience the minimum average total costs? Column 7 in panel (a) of Figure 23-2 shows that the minimum average total cost is $4.28, which occurs at an output rate of seven of these SD cards per hour. We can also find this minimum cost by finding the point in panel (c) of Figure 23-2 where the marginal cost curve intersects the average total cost curve. This should not be surprising. When marginal cost is below average total cost, average total cost falls. When marginal cost is above average total cost, average total cost rises. At the point where average total cost is neither falling nor rising, marginal cost must then be equal to average total cost. When we represent this graphically, the marginal cost curve will intersect the average total cost curve at the latter's minimum.

The same analysis applies to the intersection of the marginal cost curve and the average variable cost curve. When are average variable costs at a minimum? According to panel (a) of Figure 23-2, average variable costs are at a minimum of $2.60 at an output rate of five SD cards per hour. This is where the marginal cost curve intersects the average variable cost curve in panel (c) of Figure 23-2.

Why has Wal-Mart recently experienced problems with minimizing its distribution costs?

E-COMMERCE EXAMPLE
Wal-Mart Encounters Interference in Inventory Radio-Tracking

In 2005, Wal-Mart launched "Remix," a plan to reduce the costs of distributing goods to its huge network of stores. A key part of the cost-cutting program was the use of radio-frequency identification (RFID) tags that provide more detailed information about shipments than traditional bar codes. In addition to pricing information, RFID tags store information about a product's serial number, the location of the facility that manufactured the product, and when the product was made and sold. All this logistical information, the company anticipated, would reduce costs by enabling employees to avoid time-wasting distributional inefficiencies.

So far, however, Wal-Mart's costs have been drifting *higher*, not lower. Whereas traditional bar codes are printed on boxes and cases at factories, Wal-Mart suppliers must attach RFID tags in warehouses, which pushes up labor costs and slows shipments. Furthermore, installing RFID-reading equipment in Wal-Mart facilities has proceeded more slowly than planned. When RFID-tagged merchandise arrives from suppliers, Wal-Mart warehouses and stores are not always prepared to use the technology and end up relying on the old bar codes. Thus, instead of declining as anticipated, Wal-Mart's total expenses as a percentage of sales have risen from 16.2 percent in the early 2000s to nearly 18.5 percent today.

FOR CRITICAL ANALYSIS
Do you think that the distribution costs Wal-Mart incurs are fixed costs or variable costs? Explain your reasoning.

QUICK QUIZ   *See page 609 for the answers. Review concepts from this section in MyEconLab.*

Total costs equal total _____ costs plus total _____ costs. Fixed costs are those that do not vary with the rate of production; variable costs are those that do vary with the rate of production.

_____ total costs equal total costs divided by output (_____ = TC/Q).

Average _____ costs equal total variable costs divided by output (_____ = TVC/Q).

Average _____ costs equal total fixed costs divided by output (_____ = TFC/Q).

_____ cost equals the change in _____ cost divided by the change in output (_____ = Δ _____/ΔQ, where the Greek letter Δ, delta, means "change in").

The marginal cost curve intersects the _____ point of the average total cost curve and the _____ point of the average variable cost curve.

The Relationship Between Diminishing Marginal Product and Cost Curves

There is a unique relationship between output and the shape of the various cost curves we have drawn. Let's consider Internet service calls and the relationship between marginal cost and diminishing marginal physical product shown in panel (a) of Figure 23-3 on the next page. It turns out that if wage rates are constant, the shape of the marginal cost curve in panel (d) of Figure 23-3 is both a reflection of and a consequence of the law of diminishing marginal product.

Marginal Cost and Marginal Physical Product

Let's assume that each unit of labor can be purchased at a constant price. Further assume that labor is the only variable input. We see that as more workers are hired, marginal physical product first rises and then falls. Thus, the marginal cost of each extra unit of output will first fall as long as marginal physical product is rising, and then it will rise as long as marginal physical product is falling. Recall that marginal cost is defined as

$$\text{MC} = \frac{\text{change in total cost}}{\text{change in output}}$$

Because the price of labor is assumed to be constant, the change in total cost depends solely on the unchanged price of labor, W. The change in output is simply the marginal physical product (MPP) of the one-unit increase in labor. Therefore, we see that

$$\text{Marginal cost} = \frac{W}{\text{MPP}}$$

This means that initially, when marginal physical product is increasing, marginal cost falls (we are dividing W by increasingly larger numbers), and later, when marginal product is falling, marginal cost must increase (we are dividing W by smaller numbers). So, as marginal physical product increases, marginal cost decreases, and as marginal

Panel (a)

(1) Labor Input	(2) Total Product (number of Internet access accounts serviced)	(3) Average Physical Product (accounts per technician) (3) = (2) ÷ (1)	(4) Marginal Physical Product	(5) Average Variable Cost (5) = W ($1,000) ÷ (3)	(6) Marginal Cost (6) = W ($1,000) ÷ (4)
0	0	—	—	—	—
1	50	50	50	$20.00	$20.00
2	110	55	60	18.18	16.67
3	180	60	70	16.67	14.29
4	240	60	60	16.67	16.67
5	290	58	50	17.24	20.00
6	330	55	40	18.18	25.00
7	360	51	30	19.61	33.33

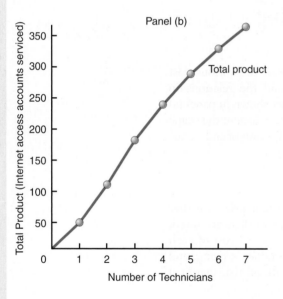

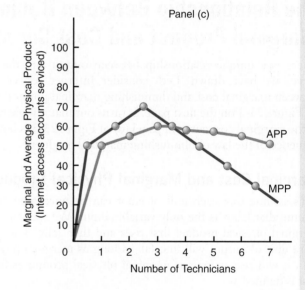

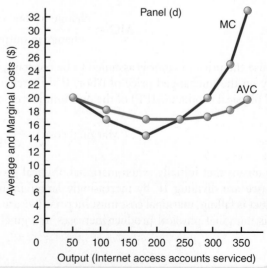

FIGURE 23-3

The Relationship Between Output and Costs

As the number of skilled technicians increases, the total number of Internet access accounts serviced each month rises, as shown in panels (a) and (b). In panel (c), marginal physical product (MPP) first rises and then falls. Average physical product (APP) follows. The near mirror image of panel (c) is shown in panel (d), in which MC and AVC first fall and then rise.

physical product decreases, marginal cost must increase. Thus, when marginal physical product reaches its maximum, marginal cost necessarily reaches its minimum.

An Illustration

To illustrate this, let's return to Figure 23-1 on page 587 and consider specifically panel (a). Assume that a skilled printer-assembly worker is paid $1,000 a week. When we go from zero labor input to one unit, output increases by 10 computer printers. Each of those 10 printers has a marginal cost of $100. Now the second unit of labor is hired, and this individual costs $1,000 per week. Output increases by 16. Thus, the marginal cost is $1,000 ÷ 16 = $62.50. We continue the experiment. We see that the next unit of labor yields only 10 additional computer printers, so marginal cost starts to rise again back to $100. The following unit of labor yields a marginal physical product of only 8, so marginal cost becomes $1,000 ÷ 8 = $125.

All of the foregoing can be restated in relatively straightforward terms:

> *Firms' short-run cost curves are a reflection of the law of diminishing marginal product. Given any constant price of the variable input, marginal costs decline as long as the marginal physical product of the variable resource is rising. At the point at which marginal product begins to diminish, marginal costs begin to rise as the marginal physical product of the variable input begins to decline.*

The result is a marginal cost curve that slopes down, hits a minimum, and then slopes up.

Average Costs and Average Physical Product

Of course, the average total cost curve and average variable cost curve are affected. They will have their familiar U shape in the short run. Again, to see this, recall that

Can the marginal cost of computer printers decline forever? Why or why not?

$$AVC = \frac{\text{total variable costs}}{\text{total output}}$$

As we move from zero labor input to one unit in panel (a) of Figure 23-1 on page 587, output increases from zero to 10 computer printers. The total variable costs are the price per worker, W ($1,000), times the number of workers (1). Because the average product of one worker (column 3) is 10, we can write the total product, 10, as the average product, 10, times the number of workers, 1. Thus, we see that

$$AVC = \frac{\$1,000 \times 1}{10 \times 1} = \frac{\$1,000}{10} = \frac{W}{AP}$$

From column 3 in panel (a) of Figure 23-1, we see that the average product increases, reaches a maximum, and then declines. Because AVC = W/AP, average variable cost decreases as average product increases and increases as average product decreases. AVC reaches its minimum when average product reaches its maximum. Furthermore, because ATC = AVC + AFC, the average total cost curve inherits the relationship between the average variable cost and diminishing returns.

To illustrate, consider an Internet service provider that employs skilled technicians to provide access services within a given geographic area. Panel (a) of Figure 23-3 on the previous page presents in column 2 the total number of Internet access accounts serviced as the number of technicians increases. Notice that the total product first increases at an increasing rate and later increases at a decreasing rate. This is reflected in column 4, which shows that the marginal physical product increases at first and then falls. The average physical product too first rises and then falls. The marginal and average physical products are graphed in panel (c) of Figure 23-3 on page 596.

Our immediate interest here is the average variable and marginal costs. Because we can define average variable cost as $1,000/AP (assuming that the wage paid is constant at $1,000), as the average product rises from 50 to 55 to 60 Internet access accounts, the average variable cost falls from $20.00 to $18.18 to $16.67. Conversely, as average product falls from 60 to 51, average variable cost rises from $16.67 to $19.61. Likewise, because marginal cost can also be defined as W/MPP, we see that as marginal physical product rises from 50 to 70, marginal cost falls from $20.00 to $14.29. As marginal physical product falls to 30, marginal cost rises to $33.33. These relationships are also expressed in panels (b), (c), and (d) of Figure 23-3 on page 596.

Long-Run Cost Curves

The long run is defined as a time period during which full adjustment can be made to any change in the economic environment. Thus, in the long run, *all* factors of production are variable. Long-run curves are sometimes called *planning curves*, and the long run is sometimes called the **planning horizon.** We start our analysis of long-run cost curves by considering a single firm contemplating the construction of a single plant. The firm has three alternative plant sizes from which to choose on the planning horizon. Each particular plant size generates its own short-run average total cost curve. Now that we are talking about the difference between long-run and short-run cost curves, we will label all short-run curves with an S and long-run curves with an L; short-run average (total) costs will be labeled SAC; and long-run average cost curves will be labeled LAC.

Panel (a) of Figure 23-4 shows short-run average cost curves for three successively larger plants. Which is the optimal size to build, if we can only choose among these three? That depends on the anticipated normal, sustained rate of output per time period. Assume for a moment that the anticipated normal, sustained rate is approximately Q_1. If a plant of size 1 is built, average cost will be C_1. If a plant of size 2 is built, we see on SAC_2 that average cost will be C_2, which is greater than C_1. Thus, if the anticipated rate of output is Q_1, the appropriate plant size is the one from which SAC_1 was derived.

However, if the anticipated sustained rate of output per time period increases from approximately Q_1 to a higher level such as Q_2 and a plant of size 1 is selected, average cost will be C_4. If a plant of size 2 is chosen, average cost will be C_3, which is clearly less than C_4.

In choosing the appropriate plant size for a single-plant firm during the planning horizon, the firm will pick the size whose short-run average cost curve generates an average cost that is lowest for the expected rate of output.

Long-Run Average Cost Curve

If we now assume that the entrepreneur faces an infinite number of choices of plant sizes in the long run, we can conceive of an infinite number of SAC curves similar to the three in panel (a) of Figure 23-4. We are not able, of course, to draw an infinite number, but we have drawn quite a few in panel (b) of Figure 23-4. We then draw the "envelope" to all these various short-run average cost curves. The resulting envelope is the **long-run average cost curve.** This long-run average cost curve is sometimes

Planning horizon
The long run, during which all inputs are variable.

Long-run average cost curve
The locus of points representing the minimum unit cost of producing any given rate of output, given current technology and resource prices.

FIGURE 23-4

Preferable Plant Size and the Long-Run Average Cost Curve

If the anticipated sustained rate of output per unit time period is approximately Q_1, the optimal plant to build is the one corresponding to SAC_1 in panel (a) because average cost is lower. However, if the sustained rate of output increases toward the higher level Q_2, it will be more profitable to have a plant size corresponding to SAC_2. If we draw all the possible short-run average cost curves that correspond to different plant sizes and then draw the envelope (a curve tangent to each member of a set of curves) to these various curves, $SAC_1 - SAC_8$, we obtain the long-run average cost (LAC) curve as shown in panel (b).

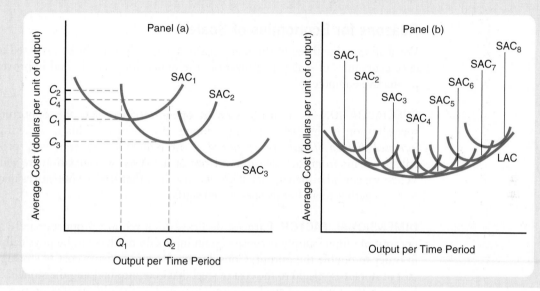

called the **planning curve,** for it represents the various average costs attainable at the planning stage of the firm's decision making. It represents the locus (path) of points giving the least unit cost of producing any given rate of output. Note that the LAC curve is *not* tangent to each individual SAC curve at the latter's minimum points, except at the minimum point of the LAC curve. Then and only then are minimum long-run average costs equal to minimum short-run average costs.

Planning curve
The long-run average cost curve.

Why the Long-Run Average Cost Curve Is U-Shaped

Notice that the long-run average cost curve, LAC, in panel (b) of Figure 23-4 is U-shaped, similar to the U shape of the short-run average cost curve developed earlier in this chapter. The reason behind the U shape of the two curves is not the same, however. The short-run average cost curve is U-shaped because of the law of diminishing marginal product. But the law cannot apply to the long run, because in the long run, all factors of production are variable; there is no point of diminishing marginal product because there is no fixed factor of production.

Why, then, do we see the U shape in the long-run average cost curve? The reasoning has to do with economies of scale, constant returns to scale, and diseconomies of scale. When the firm is experiencing **economies of scale,** the long-run average cost

Economies of scale
Decreases in long-run average costs resulting from increases in output.

Constant returns to scale
No change in long-run average costs when output increases.

Diseconomies of scale
Increases in long-run average costs that occur as output increases.

curve slopes downward—an increase in scale and production leads to a fall in unit costs. When the firm is experiencing **constant returns to scale,** the long-run average cost curve is at its minimum point, such that an increase in scale and production does not change unit costs. When the firm is experiencing **diseconomies of scale,** the long-run average cost curve slopes upward—an increase in scale and production increases unit costs. These three sections of the long-run average cost curve are broken up into panels (a), (b), and (c) in Figure 23-5.

Reasons for Economies of Scale

We shall examine three of the many reasons why a firm might be expected to experience economies of scale: specialization, the dimensional factor, and improvements in productive equipment.

SPECIALIZATION As a firm's scale of operation increases, the opportunities for specialization in the use of resource inputs also increase. This is sometimes called *increased division of tasks* or *operations*. Cost reductions generated by productivity enhancements from such division of labor or increased specialization are well known. When we consider managerial staffs, we also find that larger enterprises may be able to put together more highly specialized staffs.

DIMENSIONAL FACTOR Large-scale firms often require proportionately less input per unit of output simply because certain inputs do not have to be physically doubled in order to double the output. Consider an oil-storage firm's cost of storing oil. The cost of storage is related to the cost of steel that goes into building the storage container; however, the amount of steel required goes up less than in proportion to the volume (storage capacity) of the container (because the volume of a container increases more than proportionately with its surface area).

FIGURE 23-5

Economies of Scale, Constant Returns to Scale, and Diseconomies of Scale Shown with the Long-Run Average Cost Curve

The long-run average cost curve will fall when there are economies of scale, as shown in panel (a). It will be constant (flat) when the firm is experiencing constant returns to scale, as shown in panel (b). It will rise when the firm is experiencing diseconomies of scale, as shown in panel (c).

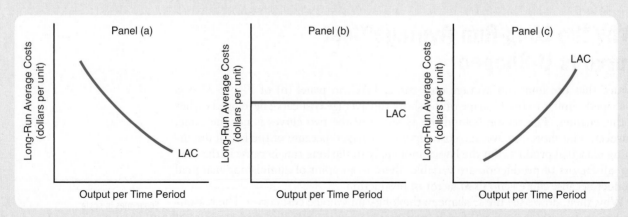

IMPROVEMENTS IN PRODUCTIVE EQUIPMENT The larger the scale of the enterprise, the more the firm is able to take advantage of larger-volume (output capacity) types of machinery. Small-scale operations may not be able to profitably use large-volume machines that can be more efficient per unit of output. Also, smaller firms often cannot use technologically more advanced machinery because they are unable to spread out the high cost of such sophisticated equipment over a large output.

For any of these reasons, the firm may experience economies of scale, which means that equal percentage increases in output result in a decrease in average cost. Thus, output can double, but total costs will less than double; hence, average cost falls. Note that the factors listed for causing economies of scale are all *internal* to the firm; they do not depend on what other firms are doing or what is happening in the economy.

Why are global cargo-shipping firms rushing to build dozens of massive new container ships?

INTERNATIONAL EXAMPLE
Global Cargo Shippers Pursue Scale Economies

For an international shipping firm, a "plant" is a cargo ship. In recent years, shippers have reduced their long-run average costs both by expanding the number of ships afloat and by increasing the absolute size of those ships. Worldwide, work is under way on more than 150 massive new cargo ships, several of which have recently put to sea. These ships are longer than three football fields and wider than the Panama Canal. Each ship has sufficient storage space for at least 8,000 20-foot-long cargo containers. Because the huge ships carry such large loads, the average transportation cost per ton of cargo is much lower than shippers incur by using traditional cargo ships. Thus, expanding scale through the use of additional larger ships has allowed global cargo shippers to experience economies of scale.

FOR CRITICAL ANALYSIS
What could you conclude if several years from now you noticed that shipping firms had stopped putting any additional massive container ships out to sea?

Why a Firm Might Experience Diseconomies of Scale

One of the basic reasons that a firm can expect to run into diseconomies of scale is that there are limits to the efficient functioning of management. This is so because larger levels of output imply successively larger *plant* size, which in turn implies successively larger *firm* size. Thus, as the level of output increases, more people must be hired, and the firm gets bigger. As this happens, however, the support, supervisory, and administrative staff and the general paperwork of the firm all increase. As the layers of supervision grow, the costs of information and communication grow more than proportionately; hence, the average unit cost will start to increase.

Some observers of corporate giants claim that many of them have been experiencing some diseconomies of scale. Witness the difficulties that firms such as Dell and General Motors have experienced in the 2000s. Some analysts say that the profitability declines they have encountered are at least partly a function of their size relative to their smaller, more flexible competitors, which can make decisions more quickly and then take advantage of changing market conditions more rapidly.

You Are There

To contemplate why airlines' efforts to achieve economies of scale might contribute to diseconomies of scale at the airports handling their flights, read **More Flights of Smaller Jets Translate into Higher Long-Run Average Costs at Airports,** on page 603.

Minimum Efficient Scale

Economists and statisticians have obtained actual data on the relationship between changes in all inputs and changes in average cost. It turns out that for many industries, the long-run average cost curve does not resemble the curve shown in panel (b) of Figure 23-4 on page 599. Rather, it more closely resembles Figure 23-6. What you observe there is a small portion of declining long-run average costs (economies of scale) and then a wide range of outputs over which the firm experiences relatively constant economies of scale. At the output rate when economies of scale end and constant economies of scale start, the **minimum efficient scale (MES)** for the firm is encountered. It occurs at point *A*. The minimum efficient scale is defined as the lowest rate of output at which long-run average costs are minimized. In any industry with a long-run average cost curve similar to the one in Figure 23-6, larger firms will have no cost-saving advantage over smaller firms as long as the smaller firms have at least obtained the minimum efficient scale at point *A*.

Why has Toyota decided to stop building new U.S. auto plants?

Minimum efficient scale (MES)
The lowest rate of output per unit time at which long-run average costs for a particular firm are at a minimum.

EXAMPLE
Toyota Finds Itself Just Beyond Its Minimum Efficient Scale

Since 2002, Japanese automaker Toyota has increased by more than 50 percent the number of vehicles it sells in the United States. This explains why the company has sharply increased the number of auto plants it operates in the United States. Recently, however, Toyota decided that it will build no more plants in the foreseeable future. The reason is that the company's long-run average cost of producing autos began to increase in the late 2000s. To avoid experiencing any further diseconomies and get back

to its minimum efficient scale, Toyota has cut back slightly on production of vehicles in portions of U.S. facilities built just a few years ago.

FOR CRITICAL ANALYSIS
In the long run, why might Toyota choose not to expand its production capabilities further even if it could sell more vehicles than it is currently producing? (Hint: Remember that the fundamental goal of a firm is to maximize profits.)

FIGURE 23-6

Minimum Efficient Scale

This long-run average cost curve reaches a minimum point at *A*. After that point, long-run average costs remain horizontal, or constant, and then rise at some later rate of output. Point *A* is called the minimum efficient scale for the firm because that is the point at which it reaches minimum costs. It is the lowest rate of output at which average long-run costs are minimized. At point *B*, diseconomies of scale arise, so long-run average cost begins to increase with further increases in output.

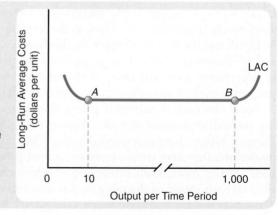

The _____ run is often called the **planning horizon.** The _____-run average cost curve is the planning curve. It is found by drawing a curve tangent to one point on a series of _____-run average cost curves, each corresponding to a different plant size.

The firm can experience **economies of scale**, **diseconomies of scale**, or **constant returns** to scale, all according to whether the long-run average cost curve slopes _____, slopes _____, or is _____. Economies of scale refer to what happens to average cost when all factors of production are increased.

We observe economies of scale for a number of reasons, including specialization, improved productive equipment, and the _____ factor, because large-scale firms require proportionately less input per unit of output. The firm may experience _____ of scale primarily because of limits to the efficient functioning of management.

The **minimum efficient scale** occurs at the _____ rate of output at which long-run average costs are _____.

You Are There

More Flights of Smaller Jets Translate into Higher Long-Run Average Costs at Airports

Why has Marion Blakely, an administrator with the Federal Aviation Administration (FAA), unveiled a plan aimed at forcing airlines to increase the average size of the planes they land at New York's La Guardia Airport? The answer is that she and other FAA officials have concluded that too many flights by small planes are driving up average operating costs at this and other U.S. airports.

From the airlines' perspective, the use of smaller planes has permitted an expansion of scale that has pushed down the long-run average costs of transporting passengers among both major-city airports and smaller regional airports. Consequently, scheduling more flights by smaller planes has created economies of scale for the airlines. Transporting more passengers using a larger number of smaller planes, however, translates into many more flights that the nation's airports must handle. This has pushed up airports' labor costs as they have increased runway crews, air traffic control and security staffs, and ground transportation services. In addition, airports have incurred higher costs by adding more aeronautical capital in the form of runways, radar facilities, and sophisticated computer equipment, as well as software for tracking all the additional flights.

Thus, as airlines have sought to attain economies of scale through more flights by smaller planes, airports have experienced diseconomies of scale. This is why airlines have responded to Blakely's plan with howls of protest. Nevertheless, a number of airport operators are already arguing that her plan to limit flights into La Guardia by smaller planes should also be extended to their airports.

CRITICAL ANALYSIS QUESTIONS

1. Why do you suppose that the operators of some of the nation's busiest airports have argued that airlines should pay some of the costs of expanding the airports' scales of operation?

2. Why do you think that some economists have argued that the economies-of-scale benefits attained with smaller planes and more flights might still be obtainable if more airports were built instead of expanding operating scale at existing airports? (Hint: Is it possible that increasing overall production by expanding the number of "plants" could result in lower long-run average costs even if expanding the sizes of existing "plants" fails to reduce long-run average costs?)

Family Physicians Downsize to Reduce Long-Run Average Costs

CONCEPTS APPLIED

→ Diseconomies of Scale

→ Long-Run Average Cost Curve

→ Minimum Efficient Scale

Today, fewer medical school students are becoming family practitioners than in years past. As Figure 23-7 indicates, the number of medical school graduates opting for medical school residency positions in the area of family medicine has dropped by about one-half since 1997. The reason is simple: For most new physicians, a family medicine practice simply is not as lucrative as it once was. Even though revenues earned by family practitioners have held steady, the average costs of operating family practices have risen.

FIGURE 23-7

The Number of Medical Students Opting for Family Practice Residencies

Since 1997, there has been a steady decline in the number of students in medical schools who have chosen to specialize in providing family medical services.

Source: U.S. Department of Health and Human Services.

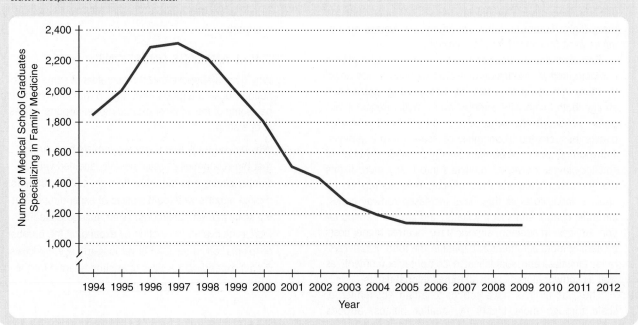

A More Skewed Long-Run Average Cost Curve

Many family physicians have discovered that trying to operate a family practice at the average scale that was typical in the 1990s now entails experiencing significant diseconomies of scale. Higher labor costs and increased capital expenses have boosted the long-run costs associated with operating family practices organized around large-scale operations.

In light of these changes, the long-run average cost curve faced by family physicians is bending upward at ever-smaller scales of operation. The minimum efficient scale in the provision of family medicine services has declined.

The New Trend in Family Medicine: Micropractices

The decline in the minimum efficient scale in family medicine explains why more of today's family physicians are opting to downsize their operations considerably.

For many family practitioners, the latest buzzword is "micropractice." Increasingly, family practice graduates from medical schools are not scouting out buildings with large amounts of office space and interviewing people for receptionist or nursing positions. Instead, these new physicians are leasing small offices and using their cellphones to take calls directly from patients. In addition, they are buying computer software. They use software programs to track patients' appointments, illnesses, and medications; to submit prescriptions and process insurance claims electronically; and to communicate with patients via e-mail.

Operating these high-tech micropractices allows family physicians to avoid the higher overhead expenses that they would incur if they attempted to operate a family practice at a yesteryear scale. Reducing the scale of operations to a micropractice level is enabling the new generation of family practitioners to attain the inflation-adjusted profit levels of years past. Ultimately, this should alter the incentives faced by coming generations of medical students. If so, the trend plotted in Figure 23-7 eventually should reverse.

Test your understanding of this chapter by going online to **MyEconLab**.
In the Study Plan for this chapter, select Section N: News.

For Critical Analysis

1. If a micropractice is the minimum efficient scale for a family practice, during the adjustment to this new minimum efficient scale, will there be a rightward or leftward movement along the long-run average cost curve?

2. Why do you suppose that most family practitioners who do *not* set up micropractices increasingly are opting to partner with numerous physicians in offices that previously would have been occupied by only one physician?

Web Resources

1. For a short summary of why some physicians might determine that they could benefit from a micropractice, go to www.econtoday.com/chapter23.

2. To learn about how physicians put micropractices into operation, go to www.econtoday.com/chapter23.

Research Project

Evaluate whether it is likely that the minimum efficient scale for physicians in other medical specialties is as small as the micropractices of many of today's family physicians. For instance, are practitioners of inpatient and outpatient surgery or radiology as likely to confront a long-run average cost curve that begins sloping upward at a micropractice scale of operations? (Hint: Could surgeons and radiologists function as efficiently without nurses, equipment that requires significant space, and other inputs requiring a larger overhead than is consistent with a micropractice?)

 Here is what you should know after reading this chapter. **MyEconLab** will help you identify what you know, and where to go when you need to practice.

WHAT YOU SHOULD KNOW		WHERE TO GO TO PRACTICE
The Short Run versus the Long Run from a Firm's Perspective The short run for a firm is a period during which at least one input, such as plant size, cannot be altered. Inputs that cannot be changed in the short run are fixed inputs, whereas factors of production that may be adjusted in the short run are variable inputs. The long run is a period in which a firm may vary all factors of production.	short run, 584 plant size, 584 long run, 584	• **MyEconLab** Study Plan 23.1 • Audio introduction to Chapter 23 • ABC News Videos: The Space Shuttle: Cost vs. Benefit and Incentives for Perfect Attendance
The Law of Diminishing Marginal Product The production function is the relationship between inputs and the maximum physical output, or total product, that a firm can produce. Typically, a firm's marginal physical product—the physical output resulting from the addition of one more unit of a variable factor of production—increases with the first few units of the variable factor of production that it employs. Eventually, however, as the firm adds more and more units of the variable input, the marginal physical product begins to decline. This is the law of diminishing marginal product.	production, 585 production function, 585 average physical product, 586 marginal physical product, 586 law of diminishing marginal product, 588 **KEY FIGURE** Figure 23-1, 587	• **MyEconLab** Study Plans 23.2, 23.3 • Animated Figure 23-1
A Firm's Short-Run Cost Curves The expenses for a firm's fixed inputs are its fixed costs, and the expenses for its variable inputs are variable costs. The total costs of a firm are the sum of its fixed costs and variable costs. Dividing fixed costs by various possible output levels traces out the firm's average fixed cost curve, which slopes downward because dividing fixed costs by a larger total product yields a lower average fixed cost. Average variable cost equals total variable cost divided by total product, and average total cost equals total cost divided by total product. For the latter two, doing these computations at various possible output levels yields U-shaped curves. Finally, marginal cost is the change in total cost resulting from a one-unit change in production. A firm's marginal costs typically decline as the firm produces the first few units of output, but at the point where marginal product begins to diminish, the marginal cost curve begins to slope upward. The marginal cost curve also intersects the minimum points of the average variable cost curve and average total cost curve.	total costs, 589 fixed costs, 590 variable costs, 590 average fixed costs, 592 average variable costs, 592 average total costs, 592 marginal costs, 592 **KEY FIGURE** Figure 23-2, 591	• **MyEconLab** Study Plans 23.4, 23.5 • Animated Figure 23-2 • Video: Short-Run Costs to the Firm
A Firm's Long-Run Cost Curves Over a firm's long-run, or planning, horizon, it can choose all factors of production, including plant size. Thus, it can choose a long-run scale of production along a long-run average cost curve. The long-run average cost curve, which for most firms is U-shaped, is traced out by the short-run average cost curves corresponding to various plant sizes.	planning horizon, 598 long-run average cost curve, 598 planning curve, 599 **KEY FIGURES** Figure 23-3, 596 Figure 23-4, 599	• **MyEconLab** Study Plans 23.6, 23.7 • Animated Figures 23-3, 23-4

(continued)

 (continued)

WHAT YOU SHOULD KNOW		WHERE TO GO TO PRACTICE

Economies and Diseconomies of Scale and a Firm's Minimum Efficient Scale Along the downward-sloping range of a firm's long-run average cost curve, the firm experiences economies of scale, meaning that its long-run production costs decline as it increases its plant size and thereby raises its output scale. In contrast, along the upward-sloping portion of the long-run average cost curve, the firm encounters diseconomies of scale, so that its long-run costs of production rise as it increases its output scale. The minimum point of the long-run average cost curve occurs at the firm's minimum efficient scale, which is the lowest rate of output at which the firm can achieve minimum long-run average cost.

economies of scale, 599
constant returns to scale, 600
diseconomies of scale, 600
minimum efficient scale (MES), 602

KEY FIGURES
Figure 23-5, 600
Figure 23-6, 602

- **MyEconLab** Study Plans 23.7, 23.8
- Animated Figures 23-5, 23-6
- Video: Reasons for Economies of Scale

Log in to MyEconLab, take a chapter test, and get a personalized Study Plan that tells you which concepts you understand and which ones you need to review. From there, MyEconLab will give you further practice, tutorials, animations, videos, and guided solutions.
Log in to www.myeconlab.com

PROBLEMS

All problems are assignable in myeconlab. *Answers to odd-numbered problems appear at the back of the book.*

23-1. The academic calendar for a university is August 15 through May 15. A professor commits to a contract that binds her to a teaching position at this university for this period. Based on this information, explain the short run and long run that the professor faces.

23-2. The short-run production function for a manufacturer of flash memory drives is shown in the table below. Based on this information, answer the following questions.

Input of Labor (workers per week)	Total Output of Flash Memory Drives
0	0
1	25
2	60
3	85
4	105
5	115
6	120

a. Calculate the average physical product at each quantity of labor.

b. Calculate the marginal physical product of labor at each quantity of labor.

c. At what point does marginal product begin to diminish?

23-3. At the end of the year, a firm produced 10,000 laptop computers. Its total costs were $5 million, and its fixed costs were $2 million. What are the average variable costs of this firm?

23-4. The cost structure of a manufacturer of microchips is described in the following table. The firm's fixed

Output (microchips per day)	Total Cost of Output ($ thousands)
0	10
25	60
50	95
75	150
100	220
125	325
150	465

costs equal $10 per day. Calculate the average variable cost, average fixed cost, and average total cost at each output level.

23-5. The diagram below displays short-run cost curves for a facility that produces liquid crystal display (LCD) screens for cellphones:

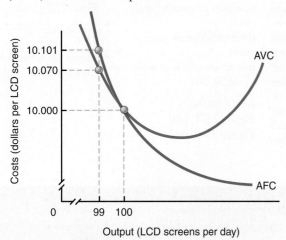

a. What are the daily total fixed costs of producing LCD screens?

b. What are the total variable costs of producing 100 LCD screens per day?

c. What are the total costs of producing 100 LCD screens per day?

d. What is the marginal cost of producing the hundredth LCD screen? (Hint: To answer this question, you must first determine the total costs—or, alternatively, the total variable costs—of producing 99 LCD screens.)

23-6. A watch manufacturer finds that at 1,000 units of output, its marginal costs are below average total costs. If it produces an additional watch, will its average total costs rise, fall, or stay the same?

23-7. At its current short-run level of production, a firm's average variable costs equal $20 per unit, and its average fixed costs equal $30 per unit. Its total costs at this production level equal $2,500.

a. What is the firm's current output level?

b. What are its total variable costs at this output level?

c. What are its total fixed costs?

23-8. In an effort to reduce their total costs, many companies are now replacing paychecks with payroll cards, which are stored-value cards onto which the companies can download employees' wages and salaries electronically. If the only factor of production that a company varies in the short run is the number of hours worked by people already on its payroll, would shifting from paychecks to payroll cards reduce the firm's total fixed costs or its total variable costs? Explain your answer.

23-9. During autumn months, passenger railroads across the globe deal with a condition called slippery rail. It results from a combination of water, leaf oil, and pressure from the train's weight, which creates a slippery black ooze that prevents trains from gaining traction.

a. One solution for slippery rail is to cut back trees from all of a rail firm's rail network on a regular basis, thereby helping prevent the problem from developing. If incurred, would this railroad expense be a better example of a fixed cost or a variable cost? Why?

b. Another way of addressing slippery rail is to wait until it begins to develop. Then the company purchases sand and dumps it on the slippery tracks so that trains already en route within the rail network can proceed. If incurred, would this railroad expense be a better example of a fixed cost or a variable cost? Why?

23-10. In the short run, a firm's total costs of producing 100 units of output equal $10,000. If it produces one more unit, its total costs will increase to $10,150.

a. What is the marginal cost of the 101st unit of output?

b. What is the firm's average total cost of producing 100 units?

c. What is the firm's average total cost of producing 101 units?

23-11. Suppose that a firm's only variable input is labor, and the constant hourly wage rate is $20 per hour. The last unit of labor hired enabled the firm to increase its hourly production from 250 units to 251 units. What was the marginal cost of the 251st unit of output?

23-12. Suppose that a firm's only variable input is labor. The firm increases the number of employees from four to five, thereby causing weekly output to rise by two units and total costs to increase from $3,000 per week to $3,300 per week.

a. What is the marginal physical product of the fifth worker?

b. What is the weekly wage rate earned by the fifth worker?

23-13. Suppose that a company currently employs 1,000 workers and produces 1 million units of output per month. Labor is its only variable input, and the company pays each worker the same monthly wage. The company's current total variable costs equal $2 million.

a. What are average variable costs at this firm's current output level?

b. What is the average physical product of labor?

c. What monthly wage does the firm pay each worker?

23-14. A manufacturing firm with a single plant is contemplating changing its plant size. It must choose from among seven alternative plant sizes. In the table, plant size A is the smallest it might build, and size G is the largest. Currently, the firm's plant size is B.

Plant Size	Average Total Cost ($)
A (smallest)	4,250
B	3,600
C	3,100
D	3,100
E	3,100
F	3,250
G (largest)	4,100

a. At plant site B, is this firm currently experiencing economies of scale or diseconomies of scale?

b. What is the firm's minimum efficient scale?

23-15. An electricity-generating company confronts the following long-run average total costs associated with alternative plant sizes. It is currently operating at plant size G.

Plant Size	Average Total Cost ($)
A (smallest)	2,000
B	1,800
C	1,600
D	1,550
E	1,500
F	1,500
G (largest)	1,500

a. What is this firm's minimum efficient scale?

b. If damage caused by a powerful hurricane generates a reduction in the firm's plant size from its current size to B, would there be a leftward or rightward movement along the firm's long-run average total cost curve?

ECONOMICS ON THE NET

Industry-Level Capital Expenditures In this chapter, you learned about the explicit and implicit costs that firms incur in the process of producing goods and services. This Internet application gives you an opportunity to consider one type of cost—expenditures on capital goods.

Title: U.S. Census Bureau's Annual Capital Expenditures Survey

Navigation: Follow the link at **www.econtoday.com/chapter23**, and select the most recent *Annual Capital Spending Report*.

Application Read the introductory summary of the report, and then answer the following questions.

1. What types of business expenditures does the Census Bureau include in this report?

2. Are the inputs that generate these business expenditures more likely to be inputs that firms can vary in the short run or in the long run?

3. Which inputs account for the largest portion of firms' capital expenditures? Why do you suppose this is so?

For Group Discussion and Analysis Review reports for the past several years. Do capital expenditures vary from year to year? What factors might account for such variations? Are there noticeable differences in capital expenditures from industry to industry?

ANSWERS TO QUICK QUIZZES

p. 589: (i) production . . . output; (ii) product; (iii) decreasing . . . output
p. 595: (i) fixed . . . variable; (ii) Average . . . ATC; (iii) variable . . . AVC; (iv) fixed . . . AFC; (v) Marginal . . . total . . . MC . . . TC; (vi) minimum . . . minimum
p. 603: (i) long . . . long . . . short; (ii) downward . . . upward . . . horizontal; (iii) dimensional . . . diseconomies; (iv) lowest . . . minimized

24

Perfect Competition

Since 2003, the total amount of stored digital data on planet Earth has increased from an estimated 5 exabytes (5,000,000,000,000,000,000 bytes of data) to more than 200 exabytes—enough data to fill the hard drives of about 200 billion personal computers. Naturally, this massive expansion of digital data has been accompanied by the development of a data-storage industry, with numerous companies providing essentially identical data-storage services. In spite of the considerable growth in demand for the services of such firms, the average price per byte of data stored has decreased over time. To understand how this has occurred, you must learn about the theory of perfect competition, the topic of this chapter.

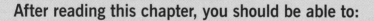

LEARNING OBJECTIVES

MyEconLab helps you master each objective and study more efficiently. See end of chapter for details.

After reading this chapter, you should be able to:

- ➤ Identify the characteristics of a perfectly competitive market structure

- ➤ Discuss the process by which a perfectly competitive firm decides how much output to produce

- ➤ Understand how the short-run supply curve for a perfectly competitive firm is determined

- ➤ Explain how the equilibrium price is determined in a perfectly competitive market

- ➤ Describe what factors induce firms to enter or exit a perfectly competitive industry

- ➤ Distinguish among constant-, increasing-, and decreasing-cost industries based on the shape of the long-run industry supply curve

? DID YOU KNOW THAT on average 6,000 farms have ceased independent operations in the United States during each of the past 30 years? Ease of exit from the industry is a fundamental characteristic of the theory of *perfect competition*, the topic of this chapter. In common speech, *competition* simply means "rivalry." In an extreme perfectly competitive situation, individual buyers and sellers cannot affect the market price—it is determined by the market forces of demand and supply. In addition, firms in a perfectly competitive industry that have been earning economic losses for a time begin to return to profitability as other firms respond to these losses by leaving the industry. In this chapter, we examine these and other implications of the theory of perfect competition.

Characteristics of a Perfectly Competitive Market Structure

We are interested in studying how a firm acting within a perfectly competitive market structure makes decisions about how much to produce. In a situation of **perfect competition,** each firm is such a small part of the total industry that it cannot affect the price of the product in question. That means that each **perfectly competitive firm** in the industry is a **price taker**—the firm takes price as a given, something determined *outside* the individual firm.

This definition of a competitive firm is obviously idealized, for in one sense the individual firm *has* to set prices. How can we ever have a situation in which firms regard prices as set by forces outside their control? The answer is that even though every firm sets its own prices, a firm in a perfectly competitive situation will find that it will eventually have no customers at all if it sets its price above the competitive price. The best example is in agriculture. Although the individual farmer can set any price for a bushel of wheat, if that price doesn't coincide with the market price of a bushel of similar-quality wheat, no one will purchase the wheat at a higher price; nor would the farmer be inclined to reduce revenues by selling below the market price.

Let's examine why a firm in a perfectly competitive industry is a price taker.

1. *There are large numbers of buyers and sellers.* When this is the case, the quantity demanded by one buyer or the quantity supplied by one seller is negligible relative to the market quantity. No one buyer or seller has any influence on price.

2. *The product sold by the firms in the industry is homogeneous.* The product sold by each firm in the industry is a perfect substitute for the product sold by every other firm. Buyers are able to choose from a large number of sellers of a product that the buyers regard as being the same.

3. *Both buyers and sellers have access to all relevant information.* Consumers are able to find out about lower prices charged by competing firms. Firms are able to find out about cost-saving innovations that can lower production costs and prices, and they are able to learn about profitable opportunities in other industries.

4. *Any firm can enter or leave the industry without serious impediments.* Firms in a competitive industry are not hampered in their ability to get resources or reallocate resources. In pursuit of profit-making opportunities, they move labor and capital to whatever business venture gives them their highest expected rate of return on their investment.

How is the art of blogging becoming a highly competitive, profit-generating line of business?

Perfect competition
A market structure in which the decisions of *individual* buyers and sellers have no effect on market price.

Perfectly competitive firm
A firm that is such a small part of the total *industry* that it cannot affect the price of the product it sells.

Price taker
A perfectly competitive firm that must take the price of its product as given because the firm cannot influence its price.

E-COMMERCE EXAMPLE
Blogging Becomes a Business

There are an estimated 60 million Web blogs in existence. Most of them are personal diaries that happen to be online, have tiny audiences, and earn not a single penny in revenues. Nevertheless, a few blogs have emerged as essentially niche magazines run as businesses and published in an online format by companies such as Gawker Media, Weblogs, Inc., and Engadget. Increasingly, others are also entering the blogging business. With today's low-cost computers and software in hand, the main impediment to entering the blogging market that bloggers face is the opportunity cost of the time they devote to their blogs. Once bloggers attract a sufficient readership, they sell online ad space and begin generating revenues. Many, such as Heather Armstrong, author of a blog called Dooce, are now earning sufficient profits to account for the bulk of their family incomes. Effectively, Armstrong and other bloggers who have entered this market operate small proprietorships.

Surveys indicate that about 7 percent of bloggers post their blogs in hopes of earning revenues. With some 60 million bloggers on the Web, this implies that more than 4 million people are competing to operate blogs as profitable businesses.

FOR CRITICAL ANALYSIS
Why is entry into the blogging market not entirely "free"?

Why does the blog perezhilton.com, run by Mario Lavanderia, satisfy the criteria necessary for a highly competitive firm?

The Demand Curve of the Perfect Competitor

When we discussed substitutes in Chapter 20, we pointed out that the more substitutes there are and the more similar they are to the commodity in question, the greater is the price elasticity of demand. Here we assume that the perfectly competitive firm is producing a homogeneous commodity that has perfect substitutes. That means that if the individual firm raises its price one penny, it will lose all of its business. This, then, is how we characterize the demand schedule for a perfectly competitive firm: It is the going market price as determined by the forces of market supply and market demand—that is, where the market demand curve intersects the market supply curve. The demand curve for the product of an individual firm in a perfectly competitive industry is perfectly elastic at the going market price. Remember that with a perfectly elastic demand curve, any increase in price leads to zero quantity demanded.

We show the market demand and supply curves in panel (a) of Figure 24-1. Their intersection occurs at the price of $5. The commodity in question is secure digital (SD) cards used with digital cameras, laptop computers, and other digital devices. Assume for the purposes of this exposition that all of these SD cards are perfect substitutes for all others. At the going market price of $5 apiece, a hypothetical individual demand curve for a producer of SD cards who sells a very, very small part of total industry production is shown in panel (b). At the market price, this firm can sell all the output it wants. At the market price of $5 each, which is where the demand curve for the individual producer lies, consumer demand for the SD cards of that one producer is perfectly elastic. This can be seen by noting that if the firm raises its price, consumers, who are assumed to know that this supplier is charging more than other producers, will buy elsewhere, and the producer in question will have no sales at all. Thus, the demand curve for that producer is perfectly elastic. We label the individual producer's demand curve *d*, whereas the *market* demand curve is always labeled *D*.

FIGURE 24-1

The Demand Curve for a Producer of Secure Digital Cards

At $5—where market demand, *D*, and market supply, *S*, intersect—the individual firm faces a perfectly elastic demand curve, *d*. If the firm raises its price even one penny, it will sell no secure digital cards, measured from its point of view in hourly production, at all. Notice the difference in the quantities of SD cards represented on the horizontal axes of panels (a) and (b).

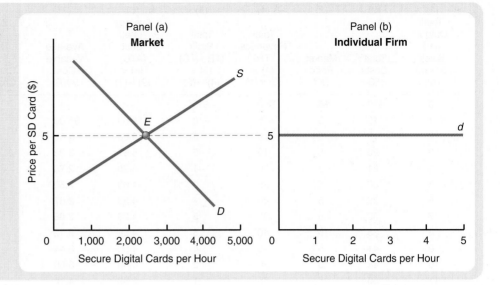

How Much Should the Perfect Competitor Produce?

As we have shown, a perfect competitor has to accept the price of the product as a given. If the firm raises its price, it sells nothing; if it lowers its price, it earns lower revenues per unit sold than it otherwise could. The firm has one decision left: How much should it produce? We will apply our model of the firm to this question to come up with an answer. We'll use the *profit-maximization model*, which assumes that firms attempt to maximize their total profits—the positive difference between total revenues and total costs. This also means that firms seek to minimize any losses that arise in times when total revenues may be less than total costs.

Total Revenues

Every firm has to consider its *total revenues*. **Total revenues** are defined as the quantity sold multiplied by the price per unit. (They are the same as total receipts from the sale of output.) The perfect competitor must take the price as a given.

Look at Figure 24-2 on the following page. The information in panel (a) comes from panel (a) of Figure 23-2 on page 591, but we have added some essential columns for our analysis. Column 3 is the market price, *P*, of $5 per SD card. Column 4 shows the total revenues, or TR, as equal to the market price, *P*, times the total output per hour, or *Q*. Thus, TR = *PQ*.

For the perfect competitor, price is also equal to average revenue (AR) because

Total revenues
The price per unit times the total quantity sold.

$$AR = \frac{TR}{Q} = \frac{PQ}{Q} = P$$

where *Q* stands for quantity. If we assume that all units sell for the same price, it becomes apparent that another name for the demand curve is the *average revenue curve* (this is true regardless of the type of market structure under consideration).

Panel (a)

(1) Total Output and Sales per Hour (Q)	(2) Total Costs (TC)	(3) Market Price (P)	(4) Total Revenues (TR) (4) = (3) x (1)	(5) Total Profit (TR – TC) (5) = (4) – (2)	(6) Average Total Cost (ATC) (6) = (2) ÷ (1)	(7) Average Variable Cost (AVC)	(8) Marginal Cost (MC) (8) = Change in (2) / Change in (1)	(9) Marginal Revenue (MR) (9) = Change in (4) / Change in (1)
0	$10	$5	$ 0	–$10	—	—		
1	15	5	5	–10	$15.00	$5.00	$5	$5
2	18	5	10	–8	9.00	4.00	3	5
3	20	5	15	–5	6.67	3.33	2	5
4	21	5	20	–1	5.25	2.75	1	5
5	23	5	25	2	4.60	2.60	2	5
6	26	5	30	4	4.33	2.67	3	5
7	30	5	35	5	4.28	2.86	4	5
8	35	5	40	5	4.38	3.12	5	5
9	41	5	45	4	4.56	3.44	6	5
10	48	5	50	2	4.80	3.80	7	5
11	56	5	55	–1	5.09	4.18	8	5

FIGURE 24-2

Profit Maximization

Profit maximization occurs where marginal revenue equals marginal cost. Panel (a) indicates that this point occurs at a rate of sales of between seven and eight secure digital cards per hour. In panel (b), we find maximum profits where total revenues exceed total costs by the largest amount. This occurs at a rate of production and sales per hour of seven or eight SD cards. In panel (c), the marginal cost curve, MC, intersects the marginal revenue curve at a rate of output and sales of somewhere between seven and eight SD cards per hour.

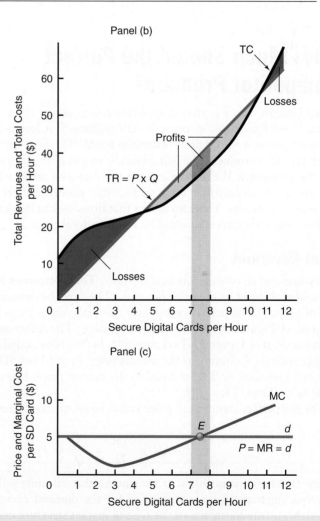

Panel (b)

Panel (c)

We are assuming that the market supply and demand schedules intersect at a price of $5 and that this price holds for all the firm's production. We are also assuming that because our maker of secure digital cards is a small part of the market, it can sell all that it produces at that price. Thus, panel (b) of Figure 24-2 shows the total revenue curve as a straight green line. For every additional SD card sold, total revenue increases by $5.

Comparing Total Costs with Total Revenues

Total costs are given in column 2 of panel (a) of Figure 24-2 and plotted in panel (b). Remember, the firm's costs always include a normal rate of return on investment. So, whenever we refer to total costs, we are talking not about accounting costs but about economic costs. When the total cost curve is above the total revenue curve, the firm is experiencing losses. When total costs are less than total revenues, the firm is making profits.

By comparing total costs with total revenues, we can figure out the number of SD cards the individual competitive firm should produce per hour. Our analysis rests on the assumption that the firm will attempt to maximize total profits. In panel (a) of Figure 24-2, we see that total profits reach a maximum at a production rate of between seven and eight SD cards per hour. We can see this graphically in panel (b) of the figure. The firm will maximize profits where the total revenue curve lies above the total cost curve by the greatest amount. That occurs at a rate of output and sales of between seven and eight SD cards per hour. This rate is called the **profit-maximizing rate of production.** (If output were continuously divisible or we were dealing with extremely large numbers of SD cards, we would get a unique profit-maximizing output.)

We can also find the profit-maximizing rate of production for the individual competitive firm by looking at marginal revenues and marginal costs.

Profit-maximizing rate of production
The rate of production that maximizes total profits, or the difference between total revenues and total costs; also, the rate of production at which marginal revenue equals marginal cost.

Using Marginal Analysis to Determine the Profit-Maximizing Rate of Production

It is possible—indeed, preferable—to use marginal analysis to determine the profit-maximizing rate of production. We end up with the same results derived in a different manner, one that focuses more on where decisions are really made—on the margin. Managers examine changes in costs and relate them to changes in revenues. In fact, whether the question is how much more or less to produce, how many more workers to hire or fire, or how much more to study or not study, we compare changes in costs with changes in benefits, where change is occurring at the margin.

Marginal Revenue

Marginal revenue represents the change in total revenues attributable to changing production of an item by one unit. Hence, a more formal definition of marginal revenue is

Marginal revenue
The change in total revenues resulting from a one-unit change in output (and sale) of the product in question.

$$\text{Marginal revenue} = \frac{\text{change in total revenues}}{\text{change in output}}$$

In a perfectly competitive market, the marginal revenue curve is exactly equivalent to the price line, which is the individual firm's demand curve. Each time the firm produces and sells one more unit, total revenues rise by an amount equal to the (constant) market price of the good. Thus, in Figure 24-1 on page 613, the demand curve, *d*, for the individual producer is at a price of $5—the price line is coincident with the demand curve. But so is the marginal revenue curve, for marginal revenue in this case also equals $5.

The marginal revenue curve for our competitive producer of secure digital cards is shown as a line at $5 in panel (c) of Figure 24-2 on page 614. Notice again that the marginal revenue curve is the price line, which is the firm's demand, or average revenue, curve, *d*. This equality of MR, *P*, AR, and *d* for an individual firm is a general feature of a perfectly competitive industry. The price line shows the quantity that consumers desire to purchase from this firm at each price—which is *any* quantity that the firm provides at the market price—and hence is the demand curve, *d*, faced by the firm. The market clearing price per unit does not change as the firm varies its output, so the average revenue and marginal revenue also are equal to this price. Thus, MR and AR are identically equal to *P* along the firm's demand curve.

When Are Profits Maximized?

Now we add the marginal cost curve, MC, taken from column 8 in panel (a) of Figure 24-2 on page 614. As shown in panel (c) of that figure, because of the law of diminishing marginal product, the marginal cost curve first falls and then starts to rise, eventually intersecting the marginal revenue curve and then rising above it. Notice that the numbers for both the marginal cost schedule, column 8 in panel (a), and the marginal revenue schedule, column 9 in panel (a), are printed *between* the rows on which the quantities appear. This indicates that we are looking at a *change* between one rate of output and the next rate of output.

EQUALIZING MARGINAL REVENUE AND MARGINAL COST In panel (c) of Figure 24-2 on page 614, the marginal cost curve intersects the marginal revenue curve somewhere between seven and eight SD cards per hour. The firm has an incentive to produce and sell until the amount of the additional revenue received from selling one more SD card just equals the additional costs incurred for producing and selling that SD card. This is how the firm maximizes profit. Whenever marginal cost is less than marginal revenue, the firm will always make more profit by increasing production.

Now consider the possibility of producing at an output rate of 10 SD cards per hour. The marginal cost at that output rate is higher than the marginal revenue. The firm would be spending more to produce that additional output than it would be receiving in revenues; it would be foolish to continue producing at this rate.

THE PROFIT-MAXIMIZING OUTPUT RATE But how much should the firm produce? It should produce at point *E* in panel (c) of Figure 24-2, where the marginal cost curve intersects the marginal revenue curve from below. The firm should continue production until the cost of increasing output by one more unit is just equal to the revenues obtainable from that extra unit. This is a fundamental rule in economics:

> *Profit maximization occurs at the rate of output at which marginal revenue equals marginal cost.*

For a perfectly competitive firm, this rate of output is at the intersection of the demand schedule, *d*, which is identical to the MR curve, and the marginal cost curve, MC. When MR exceeds MC, each additional unit of output adds more to total revenues than to total costs, so the additional unit should be produced. When MC is greater than MR, each unit produced adds more to total cost than to total revenues, so this unit should not be produced. Therefore, profit maximization occurs when MC equals MR. In our particular example, our profit-maximizing, perfectly competitive producer of secure digital cards will produce at a rate of between seven and eight SD cards per hour.

QUICK QUIZ *See page 638 for the answers. Review concepts from this section in MyEconLab.*

Four fundamental characteristics of the market in **perfect competition** are (1) _____ numbers of buyers and sellers, (2) a _____ product, (3) good information in the hands of both buyers and sellers, and (4) _____ exit from and entry into the industry by other firms.

A perfectly competitive firm is a **price taker.** It has _____ control over price and consequently has to take price as a given, but it can sell _____ that it wants at the going market price.

The demand curve for a perfect competitor is perfectly elastic at the going market price. The demand curve is also

the perfect competitor's _____ revenue curve because _____ revenue is defined as the change in total revenue due to a one-unit change in output.

Profit is maximized at the rate of output at which the positive difference between total revenues and total costs is the greatest. This is the same level of output at which marginal _____ equals marginal _____. The perfectly competitive firm produces at an output rate at which marginal cost equals the _____ per unit of output, because MR is always equal to *P*.

Short-Run Profits

To find what our competitive individual producer of secure digital cards is making in terms of profits in the short run, we have to add the average total cost curve to panel (c) of Figure 24-2 on page 614. We take the information from column 6 in panel (a) and add it to panel (c) to get Figure 24-3 on the following page. Again the profit-maximizing rate of output is between seven and eight SD cards per hour. If we have production and sales of seven SD cards per hour, total revenues will be $35 per hour. Total costs will be $30 a day, leaving a profit of $5 per hour. If the rate of output and sales is eight SD cards per hour, total revenues will be $40 and total costs will be $35, again leaving a profit of $5 per hour.

A Graphical Depiction of Maximum Profits

In Figure 24-3, the lower boundary of the rectangle labeled "Profits" is determined by the intersection of the profit-maximizing quantity line represented by vertical dashes and the average total cost curve. Why? Because the ATC curve gives us the cost per unit, whereas the price ($5), represented by *d*, gives us the revenue per unit, or average revenue. The difference is profit per unit.

Thus, the height of the rectangular box representing profits equals profit per unit, and the length equals the amount of units produced. When we multiply these two quantities, we get total profits. Note, as pointed out earlier, that we are talking about *economic profits* because a normal rate of return on investment plus all opportunity costs is included in the average total cost curve, ATC.

FIGURE 24-3

FIGURE 24-3

Measuring Total Profits

Profits are represented by the blue-shaded area. The height of the profit rectangle is given by the difference between average total costs and price ($5), where price is also equal to average revenue. This is found by the vertical difference between the ATC curve and the price, or average revenue, line *d*, at the profit-maximizing rate of output of between seven and eight SD cards per hour.

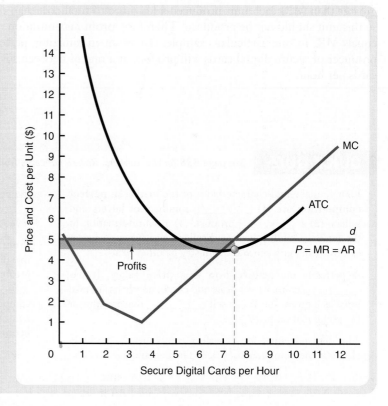

A Graphical Depiction of Minimum Profits

It is also certainly possible for the competitive firm to make short-run losses. We give an example in Figure 24-4, where we show the firm's demand curve shifting from d_1 to d_2. The going market price has fallen from $5 to $3 per secure digital card because of changes in market demand conditions. The firm will do the best it can by producing where marginal revenue equals marginal cost.

We see in Figure 24-4 that the marginal revenue (d_2) curve is intersected (from below) by the marginal cost curve at an output rate of about $5\frac{1}{2}$ SD cards per hour. The firm is clearly not making profits because average total costs at that output rate are greater than the price of $3 per SD card. The losses are shown in the shaded area. By producing where marginal revenue equals marginal cost, however, the firm is minimizing its losses; that is, losses would be greater at any other output.

The Short-Run Break-Even Price and the Short-Run Shutdown Price

In Figure 24-4, the firm is sustaining economic losses. Will it go out of business? In the long run it will, but in the short run the firm will not necessarily go out of business. In the short run, as long as the loss from staying in business is less than the loss from shutting down, the firm will remain in business and continue to produce. A firm *goes out of business* when the owners sell its assets to someone else. A firm temporarily *shuts down* when it stops producing, but it still is in business.

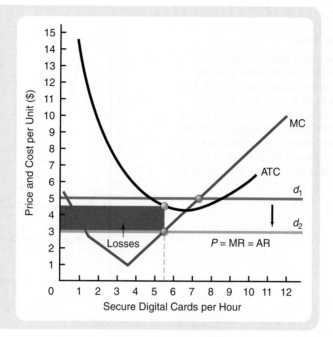

FIGURE 24-4

Minimization of Short-Run Losses

In situations in which average total costs exceed price, which in turn is greater than or equal to average variable cost, profit maximization is equivalent to loss minimization. This again occurs where marginal cost equals marginal revenue. Losses are shown in the red-shaded area.

Now how can a firm that is sustaining economic losses in the short run tell whether it is still worthwhile *not* to shut down? The firm must compare the loss incurred if it continues producing with the loss it incurs if it ceases production. Looking at the problem on a per-unit basis, as long as average variable cost (AVC) is covered by average revenues (price), the firm is better off continuing to produce. If average variable costs are exceeded even a little bit by the price of the product, staying in production produces some revenues in excess of variable costs. The logic is fairly straightforward:

> *As long as the price per unit sold exceeds the average variable cost per unit produced, the earnings of the firm's owners will be higher if it continues to produce in the short run than if it shuts down.*

Calculating the Short-Run Break-Even Price

Look at demand curve d_1 in Figure 24-5 on the next page. It just touches the minimum point of the average total cost curve, which is exactly where the marginal cost curve intersects the average total cost curve. At that price, which is about $4.30, the firm will be making exactly zero short-run *economic* profits. That price is called the **short-run break-even price,** and point E_1 therefore occurs at the short-run break-even price for a competitive firm. It is the point at which marginal revenue, marginal cost, and average total cost are all equal (that is, at which $P = MC$ and $P = ATC$). The break-even price is the one that yields zero short-run *economic* profits or losses.

Calculating the Short-Run Shutdown Price

To calculate the firm's shutdown price, we must introduce the average variable cost (AVC) to our graph. In Figure 24-5, we have plotted the AVC values from column 7 in panel (a) of Figure 24-2 on page 614. For the moment, consider two possible demand

Short-run break-even price
The price at which a firm's total revenues equal its total costs. At the break-even price, the firm is just making a normal rate of return on its capital investment. (It is covering its explicit and implicit costs.)

FIGURE 24-5

Short-Run Break-Even and Shutdown Prices

We can find the short-run break-even price and the short-run shutdown price by comparing price with average total costs and average variable costs. If the demand curve is d_1, profit maximization occurs at output E_1, where MC equals marginal revenue (the d_1 curve). Because the ATC curve includes all relevant opportunity costs, point E_1 is the break-even point, and zero economic profits are being made. The firm is earning a normal rate of return. If the demand curve falls to d_2, profit maximization (loss minimization) occurs at the intersection of MC and MR (the d_2 curve), or E_2. Below this price, it does not pay for the firm to continue in operation because its average variable costs are not covered by the price of the product.

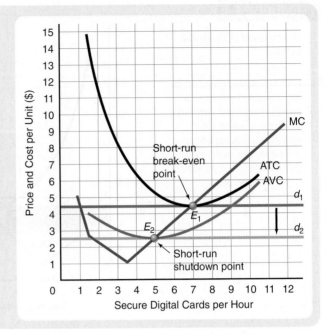

curves, d_1 and d_2, which are also the firm's respective marginal revenue curves. If demand is d_1, the firm will produce at E_1, where that curve intersects the marginal cost curve. If demand falls to d_2, the firm will produce at E_2. The special feature of the hypothetical demand curve, d_2, is that it just touches the average variable cost curve at the latter's minimum point, which is also where the marginal cost curve intersects it. This price is the **short-run shutdown price.** Why? Below this price, the firm would be paying out more in variable costs than it is receiving in revenues from the sale of its product. Each unit it sold would generate losses that could be avoided if it shut down operations.

The intersection of the price line, the marginal cost curve, and the average variable cost curve is labeled E_2. The resulting short-run shutdown price is valid only for the short run because, of course, in the long run the firm will not stay in business if it is earning less than a normal rate of return (zero economic profits).

Short-run shutdown price

The price that covers average variable costs. It occurs just below the intersection of the marginal cost curve and the average variable cost curve.

The Meaning of Zero Economic Profits

The fact that we labeled point E_1 in Figure 24-5 the break-even point may have disturbed you. At point E_1, price is just equal to average total cost. If this is the case, why would a firm continue to produce if it were making no profits whatsoever? If we again make the distinction between accounting profits and economic profits, you will realize that at that price, the firm has zero economic profits but positive accounting profits. Recall that accounting profits are total revenues minus total explicit costs. But such accounting ignores the reward offered to investors—the opportunity cost of capital—plus all other implicit costs.

In economic analysis, the average total cost curve includes the full opportunity cost of capital. Indeed, the average total cost curve includes the opportunity cost of *all* factors of production used in the production process. At the short-run break-even price, economic profits are, by definition, zero. Accounting profits at that price are not, however, equal to zero; they are positive. Consider an example. A baseball bat manufacturer sells bats at some price. The owners of the firm have supplied all the funds in the business. They have not borrowed from anyone else, and they explicitly pay the full opportunity cost to all factors of production, including any managerial labor that they themselves contribute to the business. Their salaries show up as a cost in the books and are equal to what they could have earned in the next-best alternative occupation. At the end of the year, the owners find that after they subtract all explicit costs from total revenues, accounting profits are $100,000. If their investment was $1 million, the rate of return on that investment is 10 percent per year. We will assume that this turns out to be equal to the market rate of return.

This $100,000, or 10 percent rate of return, is actually, then, a competitive, or normal, rate of return on invested capital in all industries with similar risks. If the owners had made only $50,000, or 5 percent on their investment, they would have been able to make higher profits by leaving the industry. The 10 percent rate of return is the opportunity cost of capital. Accountants show it as a profit; economists call it a cost. We include that cost in the average total cost curve, similar to the one shown in Figure 24-5. At the short-run break-even price, average total cost, including this opportunity cost of capital, will just equal that price. The firm will be making zero economic profits but a 10 percent *accounting profit*.

The Supply Curve for a Perfectly Competitive Industry

As you learned in Chapter 3, the relationship between a product's price and the quantity produced and offered for sale is a supply curve. Let's now examine the supply curve for a perfectly competitive industry.

The Perfect Competitor's Short-Run Supply Curve

What does the supply curve for the individual firm look like? Actually, we have been looking at it all along. We know that when the price of secure digital cards is $5, the firm will supply seven or eight of them per hour. If the price falls to $3, the firm will supply five or six SD cards per hour. And if the price falls below $3, the firm will shut down. Hence, in Figure 24-6, the firm's supply curve is the marginal cost curve above the short-run shutdown point. This is shown as the solid part of the marginal cost curve.

FIGURE 24-6

The Individual Firm's Short-Run Supply Curve

The individual firm's short-run supply curve is the portion of its marginal cost curve at and above the minimum point on the average variable cost curve.

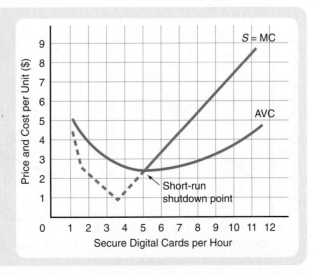

By definition, then, a firm's short-run supply curve in a competitive industry is its marginal cost curve at and above the point of intersection with the average variable cost curve.

The Short-Run Industry Supply Curve

In Chapter 3, we indicated that the market supply curve was the summation of individual supply curves. At the beginning of this chapter, we drew a market supply curve in Figure 24-1 on page 613. Now we want to derive more precisely a market, or industry, supply curve to reflect individual producer behavior in that industry. First we must ask, What is an industry? It is merely a collection of firms producing a particular product. Therefore, we have a way to figure out the total supply curve of any industry: As discussed in Chapter 3, we add the quantities that each firm will supply at every possible price. In other words, we sum the individual supply curves of all the competitive firms *horizontally*. The individual supply curves, as we just saw, are simply the marginal cost curves of each firm.

Consider doing this for a hypothetical world in which there are only two producers of SD cards in the industry, firm A and firm B. These two firms' marginal cost curves are given in panels (a) and (b) of Figure 24-7. The marginal cost curves for the two separate firms are presented as MC_A in panel (a) and MC_B in panel (b). Those two marginal cost curves are drawn only for prices above the minimum average variable cost for each respective firm. In panel (a), for firm A, at a price of $6 per unit, the quantity supplied would be 7 units. At a price of $10 per unit, the quantity supplied would be 12 units. In panel (b), we see the two different quantities that would be supplied by firm B corresponding to those two prices. Now, at a price of $6, we add horizontally the quantities 7 and 10 to obtain 17 units. This gives us one point, *F*, for our short-run **industry supply curve,** *S*. We obtain the other point, *G*, by doing the same

Industry supply curve
The locus of points showing the minimum prices at which given quantities will be forthcoming; also called the *market supply curve.*

FIGURE 24-7

Deriving the Industry Supply Curve

Marginal cost curves at and above minimum average variable cost are presented in panels (a) and (b) for firms A and B. We horizontally sum the two quantities supplied, 7 units by firm A and 10 units by firm B, at a price of $6. This gives us point *F* in panel (c). We do the same thing for the quantities supplied at a price of $10. This gives us point *G*. When we connect those points, we have the industry supply curve, *S*, which is the horizontal summation—represented by the Greek letter sigma (Σ)—of the firms' marginal cost curves above their respective minimum average variable costs.

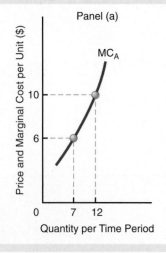

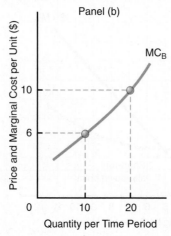

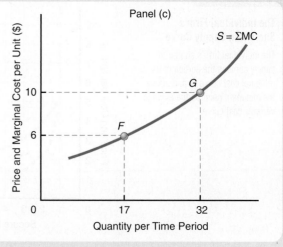

horizontal adding of quantities at a price of $10 per unit. When we connect all points such as F and G, we obtain the industry supply curve S, which is also marked ΣMC (where the capital Greek sigma, Σ, is the symbol for summation), indicating that it is the horizontal summation of the marginal cost curves (at and above the respective minimum average variable cost of each firm). Because the law of diminishing marginal product makes marginal cost curves rise, the short-run supply curve of a perfectly competitive industry must be upward sloping.

Factors That Influence the Industry Supply Curve

As you have just seen, the industry supply curve is the horizontal summation of all of the individual firms' marginal cost curves at and above their respective minimum average variable cost points. This means that anything that affects the marginal cost curves of the firm will influence the industry supply curve. Therefore, the individual factors that will influence the supply schedule in a competitive industry can be summarized as the factors that cause the variable costs of production to change. These are factors that affect the individual marginal cost curves, such as changes in the individual firm's productivity, in factor costs (such as wages paid to labor and prices of raw materials), in per-unit taxes, and in anything else that would influence the individual firm's marginal cost curve.

All of these are *ceteris paribus* conditions of supply (see page 66 in Chapter 3). Because they affect the position of the marginal cost curve for the individual firm, they affect the position of the industry supply curve. A change in any of these will shift the firms' marginal cost curves and thus shift the industry supply curve.

QUICK QUIZ   See page 638 for the answers. Review concepts from this section in MyEconLab.

Short-run average profits or losses are determined by comparing _____ total costs with _____ (average revenue) at the **profit-maximizing rate of output.** In the short run, the perfectly competitive firm can make economic profits or economic losses.

The perfectly competitive firm's short-run _____-_____ price equals the firm's minimum average total cost, which is at the point at which the _____ cost curve intersects the average total cost curve.

The perfectly competitive firm's short-run _____ price equals the firm's minimum average variable cost, which is at the point at which the _____ cost curve intersects the average variable cost curve. Shutdown will occur if price falls below average variable cost.

The firm will continue production at a price that exceeds average variable costs because revenues exceed total _____ costs of producing.

At the short-run break-even price, the firm is making _____ economic profits, which means that it is just making a _____ rate of return for industries with similar risks.

The firm's short-run supply curve is the portion of its marginal cost curve at and above its minimum average _____ cost. The industry short-run supply curve is a horizontal _____ of the individual firms' marginal cost curves at and above their respective minimum average _____ costs.

Price Determination Under Perfect Competition

How is the market, or "going," price established in a competitive market? This price is established by the interaction of all the suppliers (firms) and all the demanders (consumers).

The Market Clearing Price

The market demand schedule, D, in panel (a) of Figure 24-8 represents the demand schedule for the entire industry, and the supply schedule, S, represents the supply schedule for the entire industry. The market clearing price, P_e, is established by the forces of supply and demand at the intersection of D and the short-run industry supply curve, S. Even though each individual firm has no control or effect on the price of its product in a competitive industry, the interaction of *all* the producers and buyers determines the price at which the product will be sold.

We say that the price P_e and the quantity Q_e in panel (a) of Figure 24-8 constitute the competitive solution to the resource allocation problem in that particular industry. It is the equilibrium at which quantity demanded equals quantity supplied, and both suppliers and demanders are doing as well as they can. The resulting individual firm demand curve, d, is shown in panel (b) of Figure 24-8 at the price P_e.

Market Equilibrium and the Individual Firm

In a purely competitive industry, the individual producer takes price as a given and chooses the output level that maximizes profits. (This is also the equilibrium level of output from the producer's standpoint.) We see in panel (b) of Figure 24-8 that this is at q_e. If the producer's average costs are given by AC_1, the short-run break-even price arises at q_e (see Figure 24-5 on page 620). If its average costs are given by AC_2, then at q_e, AC exceeds price (average revenue), and the firm is incurring losses. Alternatively, if average costs are given by AC_3, the firm will be making economic profits at q_e. In the

---

FIGURE 24-8

Industry Demand and Supply Curves and the Individual Firm Demand Curve

The industry demand curve is represented by D in panel (a). The short-run industry supply curve is S and is equal to ΣMC. The intersection of the demand and supply curves at E determines the equilibrium or market clearing price at P_e. The demand curve faced by the individual firm in panel (b) is perfectly elastic at the market clearing price determined in panel (a). If the producer has a marginal cost curve MC, its profit-maximizing output level is at q_e. For AC_1, economic profits are zero; for AC_2, profits are negative; and for AC_3, profits are positive.

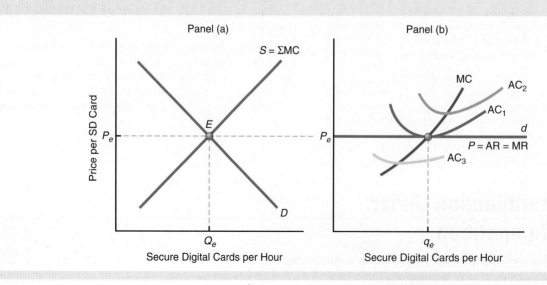

former case, we would expect, over time, that some firms will cease production (exit the industry), causing supply to shift inward, whereas in the latter case, we would expect new firms to enter the industry to take advantage of the economic profits, thereby causing supply to shift outward. We now turn to these long-run considerations.

The Long-Run Industry Situation: Exit and Entry

In the long run in a competitive situation, firms will be making zero economic profits. (Actually, this is true only for identical firms. Throughout the remainder of the discussion, we assume firms have the same cost structures.) We surmise, therefore, that in the long run a perfectly competitive firm's price (marginal and average revenue) curve will just touch its average total cost curve. How does this occur? It is through an adjustment process that depends on economic profits and losses.

Exit and Entry of Firms

Look back at Figure 24-3 on page 618 and Figure 24-4 on page 619. The existence of either profits or losses is a signal to owners of capital both inside and outside the industry. If the industry is characterized by firms showing economic profits as represented in Figure 24-3, this will signal owners of capital elsewhere in the economy that they, too, should enter this industry. If, by contrast, there are firms in the industry suffering economic losses as represented in Figure 24-4, this signals resource owners outside the industry to stay out. It also signals resource owners within the industry not to reinvest and if possible to leave the industry. It is in this sense that we say that profits direct resources to their highest-valued use. In the long run, capital will flow into industries in which profitability is highest and will flow out of industries in which profitability is lowest.

ALLOCATION OF CAPITAL AND MARKET SIGNALS The price system therefore allocates capital according to the relative expected rates of return on alternative investments. Hence, entry restrictions (such as limits on the numbers of taxicabs and banks permitted to enter the taxi service and banking industries) will hinder economic efficiency by not allowing resources to flow to their highest-valued use. Similarly, exit restrictions (such as laws that require firms to give advance notice of closings) will act to trap resources (temporarily) in sectors in which their value is below that in alternative uses. Such laws will also inhibit the ability of firms to respond to changes in both the domestic and international marketplaces.

Not every industry presents an immediate source of opportunity for every firm. In a brief period of time, it may be impossible for a firm that produces tractors to switch to the production of computers, even if there are very large profits to be made. Over the long run, however, we would expect to see owners of some other resources switch to producing computers. In a market economy, investors supply firms in the more profitable industry with more investment funds, which they take from firms in less profitable industries. (Also, positive economic profits induce existing firms to use internal investment funds for expansion.) Consequently, resources useful in the production of more profitable goods, such as labor, will be bid away from lower-valued opportunities. Investors and other suppliers of resources respond to market **signals** about their highest-valued opportunities.

Signals
Compact ways of conveying to economic decision makers information needed to make decisions. An effective signal not only conveys information but also provides the incentive to react appropriately. Economic profits and economic losses are such signals.

Why are farmers in the U.S. plains states selling off their farm implements and cattle and lodging thousands of human guests on their properties instead?

EXAMPLE
Sell the Livestock and Open the Farm to Pheasant Hunters!

Throughout the Great Plains, farmers who once grew wheat and raised cattle have opted for a new crop: pheasants. Hundreds of families whose lands have been farms for more than a century have sold off their tractors and livestock and converted barns and outbuildings into lodges for use by pheasant hunters. These ex-farming families have then given their farms new names, such as Medicine Creek Pheasant Ranch or Rooster Ridge Pheasant Lodge, and begun booking visits by hunters who roam their lands in search of game. Hunting lodge operators have found that reallocating their lands from crops and livestock to pheasant hunting has yielded profits several times higher than they had earned as farmers. Naturally, this has sent a clear signal to other farmers to consider shifting resources to the booming pheasant-hunting industry.

FOR CRITICAL ANALYSIS
At what point would you anticipate that farmers in the Great Plains will no longer have an incentive to enter the pheasant-hunting market?

TENDENCY TOWARD EQUILIBRIUM Market adjustment to changes in demand will occur regardless of the wishes of the managers of firms in less profitable markets. They can either attempt to adjust their product line to respond to the new demands, be replaced by managers who are more responsive to new conditions, or see their firms go bankrupt as they find themselves unable to replace worn-out plant and equipment.

In addition, when we say that in a competitive long-run equilibrium situation firms will be making zero economic profits, we must realize that at a particular point in time it would be pure coincidence for a firm to be making *exactly* zero economic profits. Real-world information is not as precise as the curves we use to simplify our analysis. Things change all the time in a dynamic world, and firms, even in a very competitive situation, may for many reasons not be making exactly zero economic profits. We say that there is a *tendency* toward that equilibrium position, but firms are adjusting all the time to changes in their cost curves and in the market demand curves.

Long-Run Industry Supply Curves

In panel (a) of Figure 24-8 on page 624, we drew the summation of all of the portions of the individual firms' marginal cost curves at and above each firm's respective minimum average variable costs as the upward-sloping supply curve of the entire industry. We should be aware, however, that a relatively inelastic supply curve may be appropriate only in the short run. After all, one of the prerequisites of a competitive industry is freedom of entry.

Remember that our definition of the long run is a period of time in which all adjustments can be made. The **long-run industry supply curve** is a supply curve showing the relationship between quantities supplied by the entire industry at different prices after firms have been allowed to either enter or leave the industry, depending on whether there have been positive or negative economic profits. Also, the long-run industry supply curve is drawn under the assumption that firms are identical and that

You Are There

For practice thinking about how a perfect competitor responds to market signals in the form of market prices and economic profits, take a look at **Conflicting Signals in the Crocodile Market,** on page 631.

Long-run industry supply curve
A market supply curve showing the relationship between prices and quantities after firms have been allowed the time to enter into or exit from an industry, depending on whether there have been positive or negative economic profits.

entry and exit have been completed. This means that along the long-run industry supply curve, firms in the industry earn zero economic profits.

The long-run industry supply curve can take one of three shapes, depending on whether input prices stay constant, increase, or decrease as the number of firms in the industry changes. In Chapter 23, we assumed that input prices remained constant to the *firm* regardless of the firm's rate of output. When we look at the entire *industry*, however, when all firms are expanding and new firms are entering, they may simultaneously bid up input prices.

CONSTANT-COST INDUSTRIES In principle, there are industries that use such a small percentage of the total supply of inputs required for industrywide production that firms can enter the industry without bidding up input prices. In such a situation, we are dealing with a **constant-cost industry.** Its long-run industry supply curve is therefore horizontal and is represented by S_L in panel (a) of Figure 24-9.

We can work through the case in which constant costs prevail. We start out in panel (a) with demand curve D_1 and supply curve S_1. The equilibrium price is P_1. Market demand shifts rightward to D_2. In the short run, the equilibrium price rises to P_2. This generates positive economic profits for existing firms in the industry. Such economic profits induce capital to flow into the industry. The existing firms expand or new firms enter (or both). The short-run supply curve shifts outward to S_2. The new intersection with the new demand curve is at E_3. The new equilibrium price is again P_1. The long-run supply curve, labeled S_L, is obtained by connecting the intersections of the corresponding pairs of demand and supply curves, E_1 and E_3. In a constant-cost industry, long-run supply is perfectly elastic. Any shift in demand is eventually met by just enough entry or exit of suppliers that the long-run price is constant at P_1.

Retail trade is often given as an example of such an industry because output can be expanded or contracted without affecting input prices. Banking is another example.

Why have some farmers sold their farm equipment and transformed their farmlands into pheasant-hunting estates?

Constant-cost industry
An industry whose total output can be increased without an increase in long-run per-unit costs; its long-run supply curve is horizontal.

FIGURE 24-9

Constant-Cost, Increasing-Cost, and Decreasing-Cost Industries

In panel (a), we show a situation in which the demand curve shifts from D_1 to D_2. Price increases from P_1 to P_2. In time, the short-run supply curve shifts outward because positive profits are being earned, and the equilibrium shifts from E_2 to E_3. The market clearing price is again P_1. If we connect points such as E_1 and E_3, we come up with the long-run supply curve S_L. This is a constant-cost industry. In panel (b), costs are increasing for the industry, and therefore the long-run supply curve, S_L', slopes upward and long-run prices rise from P_1 to P_2. In panel (c), costs are decreasing for the industry as it expands, and therefore the long-run supply curve, S_L'', slopes downward such that long-run prices decline from P_1 to P_2.

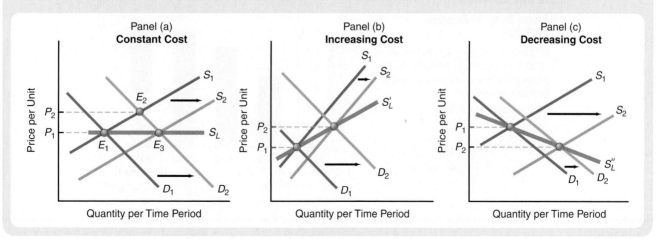

Increasing-cost industry

An industry in which an increase in industry output is accompanied by an increase in long-run per-unit costs, such that the long-run industry supply curve slopes upward.

INCREASING-COST INDUSTRIES In an **increasing-cost industry,** expansion by existing firms and the addition of new firms cause the price of inputs specialized to that industry to be bid up. As costs of production rise, the ATC curve and the firms' MC curves shift upward, causing short-run supply curves (each firm's marginal cost curve) to shift upward. Hence, industry supply shifts out by less than in a constant-cost industry. The result is a long-run industry supply curve that slopes upward, as represented by S_L' in panel (b) of Figure 24-9 on the previous page. Examples are residential construction and coal mining—both use specialized inputs that cannot be obtained in ever-increasing quantities without causing their prices to rise.

What are the implications of this discussion for the future of the oil industry?

INTERNATIONAL EXAMPLE
Increasing Costs and Future Prices in the Oil Industry

During the 1950s, there were predictions that the world would run out of a fixed stock of available oil reserves by the 1980s. In the late 1970s, the predicted oil depletion date was pushed back to the 2000s. As Figure 24-10 indicates, however, the world's known reserves of oil actually continued to increase. Today, once again there are dire predictions that the world's stock of nonrenewable oil reserves will be consumed by the end of the 2030s.

The problem with recurring pessimistic forecasts that current *stocks* of known oil reserves may be depleted at future dates at current rates of oil production and consumption is that they ignore long-run *flow* adjustments. Many times in the past, producers faced short-run situations in which the stocks of oil reserves they were tapping began to dwindle. Each time, the price of oil increased, which encouraged oil producers to find novel ways to search for and extract oil located at ever-increasing depths beneath the planet's surface.

As the world demand for oil has increased, so have the prices of inputs required to find new reserves of oil and to tap these reserves. These input price increases, in turn, have boosted oil prices. Since 1998, the inflation-adjusted price of oil has increased by more than 800 percent, and the quantity of oil supplied by petroleum firms has also risen. Many energy economists suggest that this increase in price is an indication that the oil industry may be an increasing-cost industry. In the long run, as predicted, prices have increased, and so has production.

FOR CRITICAL ANALYSIS
Why are industries that specialize in extracting minerals such as coal and oil increasing-cost industries?

FIGURE 24-10

Proven Global Oil Reserves, 1983–2013

In spite of periodic predictions that known stocks of oil reserves will eventually shrink, proven global oil reserves have continued to increase over time.

Source: U.S. Department of Energy.

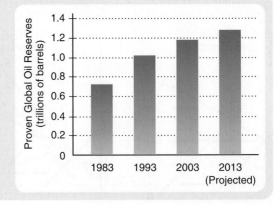

DECREASING-COST INDUSTRIES An expansion in the number of firms in an industry can lead to a reduction in input costs and a downward shift in the ATC and MC curves. When this occurs, the long-run industry supply curve will slope downward. An example, S_L'', is given in panel (c) of Figure 24-9. This is a **decreasing-cost industry**.

Decreasing-cost industry
An industry in which an increase in output leads to a reduction in long-run per-unit costs, such that the long-run industry supply curve slopes downward.

Long-Run Equilibrium

In the long run, the firm can change the scale of its plant, adjusting its plant size in such a way that it has no further incentive to change. It will do so until profits are maximized.

The Firm's Long-Run Situation

Figure 24-11 shows the long-run equilibrium of the perfectly competitive firm. Given a price of P and a marginal cost curve, MC, the firm produces at output q_e. Because profits must be zero in the long run, the firm's short-run average costs (SAC) must equal P at q_e, which occurs at minimum SAC. In addition, because we are in long-run equilibrium, any economies of scale must be exhausted, so we are on the minimum point of the long-run average cost curve (LAC). In other words, the long-run equilibrium position is where "everything is equal," which is at point E in Figure 24-11. There, *price* equals *marginal revenue* equals *marginal cost* equals *average cost* (minimum, short-run, and long-run).

Perfect Competition and Minimum Average Total Cost

Look again at Figure 24-11. In long-run equilibrium, the perfectly competitive firm finds itself producing at output rate q_e. At that rate of output, the price is just equal to the minimum long-run average cost as well as the minimum short-run average cost. In this sense, perfect competition results in the production of goods and services using the least costly combination of resources. This is an important attribute of a perfectly

---

FIGURE 24-11

Long-Run Firm Competitive Equilibrium

In the long run, the firm operates where price, marginal revenue, marginal cost, short-run minimum average cost, and long-run minimum average cost are all equal. This occurs at point E.

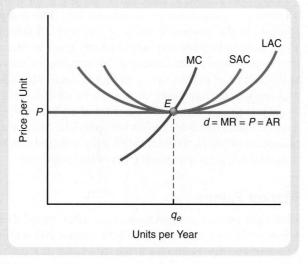

competitive long-run equilibrium, particularly when we wish to compare the market structure of perfect competition with other market structures that are less than perfectly competitive. We will examine these other market structures in later chapters.

Competitive Pricing: Marginal Cost Pricing

In a perfectly competitive industry, each firm produces where its marginal cost curve intersects its marginal revenue curve from below. Thus, perfectly competitive firms always sell their goods at a price that just equals marginal cost. This is said to be the optimal price of this good because the price that consumers pay reflects the opportunity cost to society of producing the good. Recall that marginal cost is the amount that a firm must spend to purchase the additional resources needed to expand output by one unit. Given competitive markets, the amount paid for a resource will be the same in all of its alternative uses. Thus, MC reflects relative resource input use; that is, if the MC of good 1 is twice the MC of good 2, one more unit of good 1 requires twice the resource input of one more unit of good 2.

Marginal Cost Pricing

Marginal cost pricing
A system of pricing in which the price charged is equal to the opportunity cost to society of producing one more unit of the good or service in question. The opportunity cost is the marginal cost to society.

The competitive firm produces up to the point at which the market price just equals the marginal cost. Herein lies the element of the optimal nature of a competitive solution. It is called **marginal cost pricing**. The competitive firm sells its product at a price that just equals the cost to society—the opportunity cost—for that is what the marginal cost curve represents. (But note here that it is the self-interest of firm owners that causes price to equal the marginal cost to society.) In other words, the marginal benefit to consumers, given by the price that they are willing to pay for the last unit of the good purchased, just equals the marginal cost to society of producing the last unit. (If the marginal benefit exceeds the marginal cost, that is, if $P > MC$, too little is being produced in that people value additional units more than the cost to society of producing them; if $P < MC$, the opposite is true.)

When an individual pays a price equal to the marginal cost of production, the cost to the user of that product is equal to the sacrifice or cost to society of producing that quantity of that good as opposed to more of some other good. (We are assuming that all marginal social costs are accounted for.) The competitive solution, then, is called *efficient*, in the economic sense of the word. Economic efficiency means that it is impossible to increase the output of any good without lowering the *value* of the total output produced in the economy. No juggling of resources, such as labor and capital, will result in an output that is higher in total value than the value of all of the goods and services already being produced. In an efficient equilibrium, it is impossible to make one person better off without making someone else worse off. All resources are used in the most advantageous way possible, and society therefore enjoys an efficient allocation of productive resources. All goods and services are sold at their opportunity cost, and marginal cost pricing prevails throughout.

Market Failure

Although perfect competition does offer many desirable results, situations arise when perfectly competitive markets cannot efficiently allocate resources. Either too many or too few resources are used in the production of a good or service. These situations are instances of **market failure.** Externalities arising from failures to fully assign property rights and public goods are examples. For reasons discussed in later chapters, perfectly competitive markets cannot efficiently allocate resources in these situations, and alternative allocation mechanisms are called for. In some cases, alternative market structures or government intervention *may* improve the economic outcome.

Market failure
A situation in which an unrestrained market operation leads to either too few or too many resources going to a specific economic activity.

QUICK QUIZ   *See page 638 for the answers. Review concepts from this section in MyEconLab.*

The perfectly competitive price is determined by the _____ of the market demand curve and the market supply curve; the market supply curve is equal to the horizontal summation of the portions of the individual marginal cost curves above their respective minimum average _____ costs.

In the long run, perfectly competitive firms make _____ economic profits because of entry and exit whenever there are industrywide economic profits or losses.

A constant-cost industry has a _____ long-run supply curve. An increasing-cost industry has an _____ -

sloping long-run supply curve. A decreasing-cost industry has a _____-sloping long-run supply curve.

In the long run, a perfectly competitive firm produces to the point at which price, marginal revenue, marginal cost, short-run minimum average cost, and long-run minimum average cost are all _____.

Perfectly competitive pricing is essentially _____ _____ pricing. Therefore, the perfectly competitive solution is called efficient because _____ _____ represents the social opportunity cost of producing one more unit of the good.

You Are There   Conflicting Signals in the Crocodile Market

In many parts of the world, the latest fashion in clothing and accessories is items made from the skins of exotic creatures, such as stingrays, anacondas and other snakes, and, especially, crocodiles. Crocodile shoes sell for around $300 a pair, and crocodile purses are priced at about $450. For Yingos Ratanakorn of the Suphan Buri province of Thailand, a big run-up in crocodile prices in the early 2000s was a signal that it was time to transform his farm into a crocodile ranch.

Today, however, Ratanakorn is contemplating going back to old-fashioned farming. The problem he faces is that too many others made the same decision he did. As a consequence, since the early 2000s, Thailand's population of captive crocodiles has nearly doubled, to more than 400,000 of the beasts. Thus, the market supply of crocodile hides has surged, and prices have declined. Indeed, the equilibrium price of crocodile hides started to fall as soon as

Ratanakorn opened his crocodile ranch in 2002. Initially, the market clearing price was sufficiently high that Ratanakorn was earning more than he did as a crop-raising farmer. Now, however, in most years the difference between his revenues and his costs is lower than he could be earning by planting, tending, and harvesting crops and raising less dangerous livestock.

CRITICAL ANALYSIS QUESTIONS

1. Are Ratanakorn's accounting profits currently positive or negative? What about his economic profits?

2. In 2002, did Ratanakorn's marginal revenue curve lie above or below his break-even point? What is the position of the marginal revenue curve today in relation to his break-even point?

The Data-Storage Industry Booms, and Price Declines

Long a dull backwater of the computer industry, the data-storage business is now growing by leaps and bounds. It is also a highly competitive industry with characteristics consistent with the theory of perfect competition.

The Data-Storage Industry's Roots

Firms offering to store commercial data—records of financial firms such as banks and insurance companies and other corporations with large amounts of accounting information stored on mainframe computers—have been around since the 1960s. Originally, data-storage companies did little more than place huge reels of magnetic tape in nondescript warehouse storage boxes. At the end of every business week, an employee of a data-storage firm would pick up a new reel of tape from a client's headquarters. If the client suffered a computer crash or damage from a fire or flood, the latest reel of tape would be available, so the client would lose no more than a few days' worth of data.

As data-storage firms' clients became more reliant on up-to-the minute, digitized data, and as computers became more sophisticated, data-storage firms gradually became more "high tech." Today's data-storage machines, known as "plain vanilla boxes"—a term coined by IBM salespeople back in the early 1980s—have capacities of a few terabytes. (A terabyte is about 2,500 gigabytes, or the hard-drive space of about 25 personal computers, but only 2.5 millionths of an exabyte.) The data-storage business remains "plain vanilla." Each data-storage company provides essentially the same type of service: backing up data in storage boxes. Thus, the numerous firms in the data-storage industry offer to sell a homogeneous product to many customers, and entering the business requires only obtaining the latest data-storage and networking equipment.

A Downward-Sloping Long-Run Supply Curve for Data-Storage Services

Over time, an increasing number of businesses have determined that they possess more precious digital data that they wish to store. Oil companies, for instance, now consume 50 times more data-storage space for surveys of oil fields than they did just a decade ago. Professional sports teams possess game videos taken by cameras at multiple angles that require considerable storage space. Scientists store massive amounts of data. Even college students have computer hard drives filled with supplementary course materials assigned by professors, drafts of course research papers, and music and video downloads that they may be willing to pay to place in backup storage. Thus, since the mid-1990s the demand for data-storage services has increased dramatically.

Figure 24-12 examines the adjustments that have taken place in the data-storage industry as demand has risen over time. Panel (a) displays the short-run adjustments that have occurred as the demand for the services of data-storage firms has increased, from D_1 to D_2. A few years ago, the equilibrium amount of data flowing to data-storage firms was about 500 million gigabytes, and the price of storing data was about $3.50 per gigabyte per year. When the demand for data-storage services increased during the late 1990s and early 2000s, the equilibrium flow of data stored rose to about 1 billion gigabytes per year. The market clearing price of these services rose to about $4 per gigabyte per year. In addition, existing providers of data-storage services began to earn positive economic profits. Panel (b) displays the

FIGURE 24-12

Short-Run and Long-Run Adjustments in the Data-Storage Industry

Panel (a) shows that when the demand for data-storage services increased in the late 1990s and early 2000s, the market clearing price rose from about $3.50 per gigabyte of data per year at point E_1 to about $4 per gigabyte per year at point E_2. The equilibrium quantity of data-storage services also increased. Panel (b) displays the long-run adjustments that took place during the rest of the 2000s as numerous firms entered the industry, causing market supply to increase. The equilibrium quantity of data-storage services continued to rise, but the market clearing price declined, to about $3.20 per gigabyte per year at point E_3. Hence, the long-run supply curve in this industry sloped downward, indicating that this is a decreasing-cost industry.

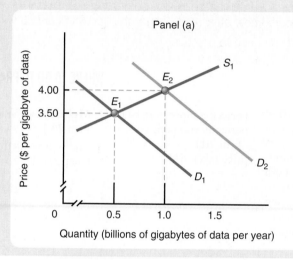

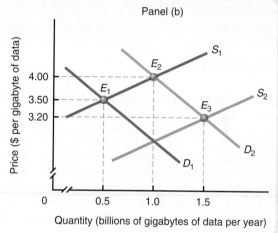

long-run effects of entry of new firms into the data-storage industry during the 2000s, which caused short-run market supply to increase. The equilibrium flow of data to data-storage firms rose to about 1.5 billion gigabytes per year. Accompanying the expansion of data-storage firms was a decrease in the prices of key inputs—data-storage and networking equipment. Consequently, the market price of data-storage services declined to about $3.20 per gigabyte per year. Thus, the data-storage industry is a decreasing-cost industry.

Test your understanding of this chapter by going online to **MyEconLab**.
In the Study Plan for this chapter, select Section N: News.

For Critical Analysis

1. What role might software improvements have played in helping reduce costs of employing other inputs in the provision of data-storage services, such as storage and networking equipment?

2. In the long run, what appears to have happened to the ATC and MC curves of firms that provide data-storage services?

Web Resources

1. To learn about the latest developments in the data-storage industry, go to www.econtoday.com/chapter24.

2. For links to information provided by data-storage trade associations, go to www.econtoday.com/chapter24.

Research Project

Suppose that a technological advance enables data-storage firms to squeeze even more data into their "plain vanilla box" storage machines. What short-run and long-run adjustments would then take place in the data-storage industry?

Here is what you should know after reading this chapter. **MyEconLab** will help you identify what you know, and where to go when you need to practice.

WHAT YOU SHOULD KNOW		WHERE TO GO TO PRACTICE
The Characteristics of a Perfectly Competitive Market Structure A perfectly competitive industry has four fundamental characteristics: (1) there are large numbers of buyers and sellers, (2) firms in the industry produce and sell a homogeneous product, (3) information is equally accessible to both buyers and sellers, and (4) there are insignificant barriers to industry entry or exit. These characteristics imply that each firm in a perfectly competitive industry is a price taker, meaning that the firm takes the market price as given and outside its control.	perfect competition, 611 perfectly competitive firm, 611 price taker, 611	• **MyEconLab** Study Plan 24.1 • Audio introduction to Chapter 24
How a Perfectly Competitive Firm Decides How Much to Produce Because a perfectly competitive firm sells the amount that it wishes at the market price, the additional revenue it earns from selling an additional unit of output is the market price. Thus, the firm's marginal revenue equals the market price, and its marginal revenue curve is the firm's own perfectly elastic demand curve. The firm maximizes economic profits when marginal cost equals marginal revenue, as long as the market price is not below the short-run shutdown price, where the marginal cost curve crosses the average variable cost curve.	total revenues, 613 profit-maximizing rate of production, 615 marginal revenue, 615 KEY FIGURES Figure 24-1, 613 Figure 24-2, 614	• **MyEconLab** Study Plans 24.2, 24.3 • Animated Figures 24-1, 24-2
The Short-Run Supply Curve of a Perfectly Competitive Firm If the market price is below the short-run shutdown price, the firm's total revenues fail to cover its variable costs. Then the firm would be better off halting production, thereby minimizing its economic loss in the short run. If the market price is above the short-run shutdown price, however, the firm produces the rate of output where marginal revenue, the market price, equals marginal cost. Thus, the range of the firm's marginal cost curve above the short-run shutdown price gives combinations of market prices and production choices of the perfectly competitive firm. This range of the firm's marginal cost curve is therefore the firm's short-run supply curve.	short-run break-even price, 619 short-run shutdown price, 620 industry supply curve, 622 KEY FIGURES Figure 24-3, 618 Figure 24-4, 619 Figure 24-5, 620 Figure 24-6, 621 Figure 24-7, 622	• **MyEconLab** Study Plans 24.4, 24.5, 24.6, 24.7 • Animated Figures 24-3, 24-4, 24-5, 24-6, 24-7 • Video: The Short-Run Shutdown Price • Video: The Meaning of Zero Economic Profits

(continued)

 *(continued)*

WHAT YOU SHOULD KNOW

WHERE TO GO TO PRACTICE

The Equilibrium Price in a Perfectly Competitive Market The short-run supply curve for a perfectly competitive industry is obtained by summing the quantities supplied at each price by all firms in the industry. At the equilibrium market price, the total amount of output supplied by all firms is equal to the total amount of output demanded by all buyers.

KEY FIGURE
Figure 24-8, 624

- **MyEconLab** Study Plan 24.8
- Animated Figure 24-8

Incentives to Enter or Exit a Perfectly Competitive Industry In the short run, a perfectly competitive firm will continue to produce output as long as the market price exceeds the short-run shutdown price. This is so even if the market price is below the short-run break-even point where the marginal cost curve crosses the firm's average total cost curve. Even though the firm earns an economic loss, it minimizes the amount of the loss by continuing to produce in the short run. In the long run, however, an economic loss is a signal that the firm is not engaged in the highest-value activity available to its owners, and continued economic losses in the long run will induce exit from the industry.

signals, 625

- **MyEconLab** Study Plan 24.9

The Long-Run Industry Supply Curve and Constant-, Increasing-, and Decreasing-Cost Industries The long-run industry supply curve in a perfectly competitive industry shows the relationship between prices and quantities after firms have the opportunity to enter or leave the industry in response to economic profits or losses. In a constant-cost industry, total output can increase without a rise in long-run per-unit production costs, so the long-run industry supply curve is horizontal. In an increasing-cost industry, however, per-unit costs increase with a rise in industry output, so the long-run industry supply curve slopes upward. In contrast, in a decreasing-cost industry per-unit costs decline as industry output increases, and the long-run industry supply curve slopes downward.

long-run industry supply curve, 626
constant-cost industry, 627
increasing-cost industry, 628
decreasing-cost industry, 629
marginal cost pricing, 630
market failure, 631

KEY FIGURE
Figure 24-11, 629

- **MyEconLab** Study Plans 24.10, 24.11
- Animated Figure 24-11

Log in to MyEconLab, take a chapter test, and get a personalized Study Plan that tells you which concepts you understand and which ones you need to review. From there, MyEconLab will give you further practice, tutorials, animations, videos, and guided solutions.
Log in to www.myeconlab.com

PROBLEMS

All problems are assignable in myeconlab. *Answers to odd-numbered problems appear at the back of the book.*

24-1. Explain why each of the following examples is *not* a perfectly competitive industry.

a. One firm produces a large portion of the industry's total output, but there are many firms in the industry, and their products are indistinguishable. Firms can easily exit and enter the industry.

b. There are many buyers and sellers in the industry. Consumers have equal information about the prices of firms' products, which differ slightly in quality from firm to firm.

c. Many taxicabs compete in a city. The city's government requires all taxicabs to provide identical service. Taxicabs are virtually identical, and all drivers must wear a designated uniform. The government also limits the number of taxicab companies that can operate within the city's boundaries.

24-2. Consider the market for DVD movie rentals, which is perfectly competitive. The market supply curve slopes upward, the market demand curve slopes downward, and the equilibrium rental price equals $3.50. Consider each of the following events, and discuss the effects they will have on the market clearing price and on the demand curve faced by the individual rental store.

a. People's tastes change in favor of going to see more movies at cinemas with their friends and family members.

b. National DVD-rental chains open a number of new stores in this market.

c. There is a significant increase in the price of downloading movies on the Internet.

24-3. Consider the diagram in the next column, which applies to a perfectly competitive firm, which at present faces a market clearing price of $20 per unit and produces 10,000 units of output per week.

a. What is the firm's current average revenue per unit?

b. What are the present economic profits of this firm? Is the firm maximizing economic profits? Explain.

c. If the market clearing price drops to $12.50 per unit, should this firm continue to produce in the short run if it wishes to maximize its economic profits (or minimize its economic losses)? Explain.

d. If the market clearing price drops to $7.50 per unit, should this firm continue to produce in the short run if it wishes to maximize its economic profits (or minimize its economic losses)? Explain.

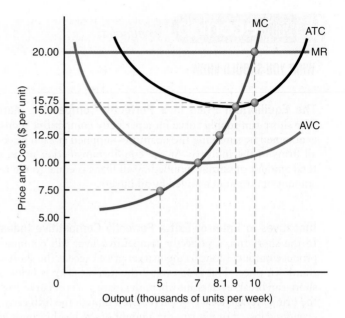

24-4. The following table represents the hourly output and cost structure for a local pizza shop. The market is perfectly competitive, and the market price of a pizza in the area is $10. Total costs include all opportunity costs.

Total Hourly Output and Sales of Pizzas	Total Hourly Cost ($)
0	5
1	9
2	11
3	12
4	14
5	18
6	24
7	32
8	42
9	54
10	68

a. Calculate the total revenue and total economic profit for this pizza shop at each rate of output.

b. Assuming that the pizza shop always produces and sells at least one pizza per hour, does this appear to be a situation of short-run or long-run equilibrium?

c. Calculate the pizza shop's marginal cost and marginal revenue at each rate of output. Based on marginal analysis, what is the profit-maximizing rate of output for the pizza shop?

d. Draw a diagram depicting the short-run marginal revenue and marginal cost curves for this pizza shop, and illustrate the determination of its profit-maximizing output rate.

24-5. Consider the information provided in Problem 24-4. Suppose the market price drops to only $5 per pizza. In the short run, should this pizza shop continue to make pizzas, or will it maximize its economic profits (that is, minimize its economic loss) by shutting down?

24-6. Yesterday, a perfectly competitive producer of construction bricks manufactured and sold 10,000 bricks per week at a market price that was just equal to the minimum average variable cost of producing each brick. Today, all the firm's costs are the same, but the market price of bricks has declined.

a. Assuming that this firm has positive fixed costs, did the firm earn economic profits, economic losses, or zero economic profits yesterday?

b. To maximize economic profits today, how many bricks should this firm produce today?

24-7. Suppose that a perfectly competitive firm faces a market price of $5 per unit, and at this price the upward-sloping portion of the firm's marginal cost curve crosses its marginal revenue curve at an output level of 1,500 units. If the firm produces 1,500 units, its average variable costs equal $5.50 per unit, and its average fixed costs equal 50 cents per unit. What is the firm's profit-maximizing (or loss-minimizing) output level? What is the amount of its economic profits (or losses) at this output level?

24-8. Suppose that the price of a service sold in a perfectly competitive market is $25 per unit. For a firm in this market, the output level corresponding to a marginal cost of $25 per unit is 2,000 units. Average variable costs at this output level equal $15 per unit, and average fixed costs equal $5 per unit. What is the firm's profit-maximizing (or loss-minimizing) output level? What is the amount of its economic profits (or losses) at this output level?

24-9. Suppose that a firm in a perfectly competitive industry finds that at its current output rate, marginal revenue exceeds the minimum average total cost of producing any feasible rate of output. Furthermore, the firm is producing an output rate at which marginal cost is less than the average total cost at that rate of output. Is the firm maximizing its economic profits? Why or why not?

24-10. A perfectly competitive industry is initially in a short-run equilibrium in which all firms are earning zero economic profits but in which firms are operating below their minimum efficient scale. Explain the long-run adjustments that will take place for the industry to attain long-run equilibrium with firms operating at their minimum efficient scale.

24-11. Two years ago, a large number of firms entered a market in which existing firms had been earning positive economic profits. By the end of last year, the typical firm in this industry had begun earning negative economic profits. No other events occurred in this market during the past two years.

a. Explain the adjustment process that occurred last year.

b. Predict what adjustments will take place in this market beginning this year, other things being equal.

24-12. Numerous "hookah bars," at which patrons can pay to utilize water pipes to smoke regular and flavored tobaccos, have popped up around the nation. Hookah bars are particularly popular with college students.

a. Suppose that the market for the services of hookah bars is in long-run equilibrium. Then two events occur: (1) more cities end regulations that had generated fixed costs for hookah bars, and (2) many nonstudent adults discover previously unknown preferences for the services of hookah bars. Use diagrams to trace through the short-run effects on the market price of hookah-bar services, the marginal revenue and marginal cost of these services at a typical hookah bar, and the equilibrium quantity of services provided both by a typical hookah bar and by the hookah-bar industry.

b. Redraw your diagrams showing the situation at the conclusion of your answer to part (a). Use these new diagrams to explain the long-run adjustments that will take place in this industry.

ECONOMICS ON THE NET

The Cost Structure of the Movie Theater Business A key idea in this chapter is that competition among firms in an industry can influence the long-run cost structure within the industry. Here you get a chance to apply this concept to a multinational company that owns movie theaters.

Title: AMC International

Navigation: Follow the link at **www.econtoday.com/ chapter24** to visit American Multi-Cinema's home page.

Application Answer the following questions.

1. Click on *Investor Resources.* What is the average number of screens in an AMC theater? How many theaters does AMC own and manage?

2. Click on *Locations Worldwide,* and use the map to select the theater in Hong Kong. This is the largest megaplex theater in Hong Kong. How many screens does the megaplex have?

3. Based on the average number of screens at an AMC theater and the number of screens at the Hong Kong facility, what can you conclude about the cost structure of this industry? Illustrate the long-run average cost curve for this industry.

For Group Discussion and Analysis Is the Hong Kong facility the largest multiplex? What do you think constrains the size of a multiplex in Hong Kong? How does the location of AMC's headquarters affect the cost structure of the firm? Is it easier for AMC to have fewer facilities that are larger in size than to have many smaller facilities?

ANSWERS TO QUICK QUIZZES

p. 617: (i) large . . . homogeneous . . . unrestrained; (ii) no . . . all; (iii) marginal . . . marginal; (iv) revenue . . . cost . . . price

p. 623: (i) average . . . price; (ii) break-even . . . marginal; (iii) shutdown . . . marginal; (iv) variable; (v) zero . . . normal; (vi) variable . . . summation . . . variable

p. 631: (i) intersection . . . variable; (ii) zero; (iii) horizontal . . . upward . . . downward; (iv) equal; (v) marginal cost . . . marginal cost

Monopoly

Economists have found that when a nation's government proclaims that a single church denomination represents the "official" state religion, the church loses attendance equal to an average of about 15 percent of the nation's population. At first glance, it might appear that economics probably can tell us little about why attendance falls when a denomination is declared to be the official state religion. In fact, lower attendance at such churches is a prediction of the theory of *monopoly* applied to religious institutions. Granting monopoly status to a single religious denomination is likely to reduce "religious output," thereby giving people less reason to attend church. In this chapter, you will learn why a monopoly produces less output of a good or service than we would observe in a perfectly competitive market.

LEARNING OBJECTIVES

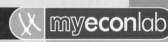

MyEconLab helps you master each objective and study more efficiently. See end of chapter for details.

After reading this chapter, you should be able to:

- Identify situations that can give rise to monopoly

- Describe the demand and marginal revenue conditions a monopolist faces

- Discuss how a monopolist determines how much output to produce and what price to charge

- Evaluate the profits earned by a monopolist

- Understand price discrimination

- Explain the social cost of monopolies

? DID YOU KNOW THAT many chefs are now patenting specific dishes? As the culinary world has become more interconnected with increased mobility of people and access to restaurant menus on the Internet, chefs have sought to protect their food-preparation inventions from duplication. Some chefs now have dozens of patents, all aimed at preventing other chefs from competing against them with copies of their own products.

In this chapter, you will learn about the consequences of allowing producers to patent their inventions, thereby giving only them authorization to sell all of the output of a particular patented good or service. These consequences stem from the fact that the holder of a patent faces the entire demand curve for its product. This creates a situation called *monopoly*.

Definition of a Monopolist

The word *monopoly* probably brings to mind notions of a business that gouges the consumer, sells faulty products, and gets unconscionably rich in the process. But if we are to succeed in analyzing and predicting the behavior of imperfectly competitive firms, we will have to be more objective in our definition. Although most monopolies in the United States are relatively large, our definition will be equally applicable to small businesses: A **monopolist** is the *single supplier* of a good or service for which there is no close substitute.

In a monopoly market structure, the firm (the monopolist) and the industry are one and the same. Occasionally, there may be a problem in identifying an industry and therefore determining if a monopoly exists. For example, should we think of aluminum and steel as separate industries, or should we define the industry in terms of basic metals? Our answer depends on the extent to which aluminum and steel can be substituted in the production of a wide range of products.

As we shall see in this chapter, a seller prefers to have a monopoly than to face competitors. In general, we think of monopoly prices as being higher than prices under perfect competition and of monopoly profits as being higher than profits under perfect competition (which are, in the long run, merely equivalent to a normal rate of return). How does a firm obtain a monopoly in an industry? Basically, there must be *barriers to entry* that enable firms to receive monopoly profits in the long run. Barriers to entry are restrictions on who can start a business or who can stay in a business.

Does it surprise you that the U.S. Department of Commerce oversees a global monopoly on the granting of names for Web addresses?

Monopolist
The single supplier of a good or service for which there is no close substitute. The monopolist therefore constitutes its entire industry.

INTERNATIONAL POLICY EXAMPLE
A Monopoly in the Assignment of Internet Addresses

In 1998, the U.S. Department of Commerce established the Internet Corporation for Assigned Names and Numbers (ICANN), which oversees names for Internet domains. Although ICANN has an international advisory board, the U.S. government, through the Commerce Department, exercises power over all decisions, including assignment of new Web domains and, in principle, specific Web addresses.

In the (perhaps mistaken) view of residents of many other nations, the U.S. government's effective control over Web addresses allows it to enforce restrictions on who can start a

Web-based business or stay in business on the Internet. Thus, these nations' residents worry that the U.S. government might use its control over ICANN to establish barriers to entry to Internet business on the part of non-U.S. firms. In this way, it could protect U.S. firms from foreign competition on the Web.

FOR CRITICAL ANALYSIS
How could U.S. restrictions on Web addresses protect U.S. firms from foreign competition?

Barriers to Entry

For any amount of monopoly power to continue to exist in the long run, the market must be closed to entry in some way. Either legal means or certain aspects of the industry's technical or cost structure may prevent entry. We will discuss several of the barriers to entry that have allowed firms to reap monopoly profits in the long run (even if they are not pure monopolists in the technical sense).

Ownership of Resources Without Close Substitutes

Preventing a newcomer from entering an industry is often difficult. Indeed, some economists contend that no monopoly acting without government support has been able to prevent entry into the industry unless that monopoly has had the control of some essential natural resource. Consider the possibility of one firm's owning the entire supply of a raw material input that is essential to the production of a particular commodity. The exclusive ownership of such a vital resource serves as a barrier to entry until an alternative source of the raw material input is found or an alternative technology not requiring the raw material in question is developed. A good example of control over a vital input is the Aluminum Company of America (Alcoa), a firm that prior to World War II owned most world stocks of bauxite, the essential raw material in the production of aluminum. Such a situation is rare, though, and is ordinarily temporary.

How do auto manufacturers use their control over production of diagnostic equipment to help their dealer networks try to maintain repair-service monopolies?

EXAMPLE
Keeping Customers Flowing to Mr. Goodwrench Instead of Independent Auto Mechanics

In 1996, under a federal mandate to reduce emissions from every vehicle sold, all auto manufacturers began installing small computers that closely monitor emission systems of autos and light-body trucks. When they designed these computers, the companies developed their own technologies for also monitoring nonemission systems. Today, such computers control virtually all information flows relating to a vehicle's internal functioning. Access to this information, which is required for a mechanic to diagnose most problems with a vehicle's operation, is only available through special equipment. This equipment is produced solely by vehicle manufacturers.

Hence, auto manufacturers have monopolies in the provision of diagnostic equipment for the vehicles they manufacture. Typically, they make such equipment available to independent mechanics at prices well above those charged to their own dealers. In a few cases, auto manufacturers have refused to sell the equipment to independent mechanics, thereby aiding their dealers in establishing monopolies in the provision of mechanical repair and maintenance services on the vehicles their companies produce.

FOR CRITICAL ANALYSIS
What incentives do independent auto mechanics have to try to join dealer repair-service networks?

Economies of Scale

Sometimes it is not profitable for more than one firm to exist in an industry. This is so if one firm would have to produce such a large quantity in order to realize lower unit costs that there would not be sufficient demand to warrant a second producer of the same product. Such a situation may arise because of a phenomenon we discussed in Chapter 23, economies of scale. When economies of scale exist, total costs increase less than proportionately to the increase in output. That is, proportional increases in output yield proportionately smaller increases in total costs, and per-unit costs drop. When economies of scale exist, larger firms (with larger output) have an advantage in that they have lower costs that enable them to charge lower prices and thereby drive smaller firms out of business.

When economies of scale occur over a wide range of outputs, a **natural monopoly** may develop. A natural monopoly is the first firm to take advantage of persistent declining long-run average costs as scale increases. The natural monopolist is able to underprice its competitors and eventually force all of them out of the market.

Figure 25-1 shows a downward-sloping long-run average cost curve (LAC). Recall that when average costs are falling, marginal costs are less than average costs. Thus, when the long-run average cost curve slopes downward, the long-run marginal cost curve (LMC) will be below the LAC.

In our example, long-run average costs are falling over such a large range of production rates that we would expect only one firm to survive in such an industry. That firm would be the natural monopolist. It would be the first one to take advantage of the decreasing average costs. That is, it would construct the large-scale facilities first. As its average costs fell, it would lower prices and get an ever-larger share of the market. Once that firm had driven all other firms out of the industry, it would set its price to maximize profits.

Natural monopoly

A monopoly that arises from the peculiar production characteristics in an industry. It usually arises when there are large economies of scale relative to the industry's demand such that one firm can produce at a lower average cost than can be achieved by multiple firms.

Legal or Governmental Restrictions

Governments and legislatures can also erect barriers to entry. These include licenses, franchises, patents, tariffs, and specific regulations that tend to limit entry.

In what nation does a law require that the government allocate about 8,000 geographic markets to monopolists?

INTERNATIONAL POLICY EXAMPLE
German Chimney-Sweep Competition Goes Up in Smoke

In 1937, the acting interior minister of Germany, the infamous Nazi leader Heinrich Himmler, decreed that chimney sweeps—people who specialize in cleaning chimneys—had to be German and would be assigned to "districts." The 8,000 districts were geographic regions in which only a single chimney sweep was allowed to practice the trade. In 1937, Himmler's rule was amended to permit non-Germans to qualify as chimney sweeps, but the requirement of only one chimney sweep per district remains in force today. Thus, within each district, a chimney sweep has a monopoly strictly enforced by German law.

FOR CRITICAL ANALYSIS
What is the basic shape of each of the demand curves faced by the 8,000 German chimney sweeps?

You Are There

For an example of how a government can go about enforcing restrictions on market competition, see **Why Pouring Vegetable Oil into a Car Is Illegal in Illinois,** on page 657.

LICENSES, FRANCHISES, AND CERTIFICATES OF CONVENIENCE It is illegal to enter many industries without a government license, or a "certificate of convenience and public necessity." For example, in some states you cannot form an electrical utility to compete with the electrical utility already operating in your area. You would first have to obtain a certificate of convenience and public necessity from the appropriate authority, which is usually the state's public utility commission. Yet public utility commissions in these states rarely, if ever, issue a certificate to a group of investors

FIGURE 25-1

The Cost Curves That Might Lead to a Natural Monopoly

Whenever long-run marginal costs (LMC) are less than long-run average costs (LAC), then long-run average costs will be falling. A natural monopoly might arise when this situation exists over most output rates. The first firm to establish low-unit-cost capacity would be able to take advantage of declining average total costs. This firm would drive out all rivals by charging a lower price than the others could sustain at their higher average costs.

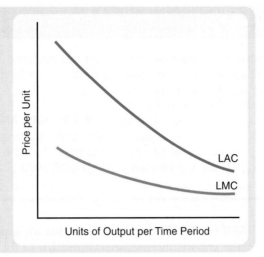

who want to compete directly in the same geographic area as an existing electrical utility. Hence, entry into the industry in a particular geographic area is prohibited, and long-run monopoly profits could conceivably be earned by the electrical utility already serving the area.

To enter interstate (and also many intrastate) markets for pipelines, television and radio broadcasting, and transmission of natural gas, to cite a few such industries, it is often necessary to obtain similar permits. Because these franchises or licenses are restricted, long-run monopoly profits might be earned by the firms already in the industry.

PATENTS A patent is issued to an inventor to provide protection from having the invention copied or stolen for a period of 20 years. Suppose that engineers working for Ford Motor Company discover a way to build an engine that requires half the parts of a regular engine and weighs only half as much. If Ford is successful in obtaining a patent on this discovery, it can (in principle) prevent others from copying it. The patent holder has a monopoly. It is the patent holder's responsibility to defend the patent, however. That means that Ford—like other patent owners—must expend resources to prevent others from imitating its invention. If the costs of enforcing a particular patent are greater than the benefits, though, the patent may not bestow any monopoly profits on its owner. The policing costs would be just too high.

Why does Hewlett-Packard incur the costs of policing its ink patents?

Go to www.econtoday.com/chapter25 to learn more about patents and trademarks from the U.S. Patent and Trademark Office and to learn all about copyrights from the U.S. Copyright Office.

EXAMPLE

For Hewlett-Packard, Ink Patents Generate the Color of Money

Hewlett-Packard Company, the giant manufacturer of computers, peripherals, and accessories, owns more than 33,000 different patents. Of these, 4,000 patents cover the company's formulations of inks and cartridges used in printers, copiers, and fax machines.

In a typical year, Hewlett-Packard earns nearly $3 billion in profits from sales of ink and toner supplies—or more than half of its operating profits. To protect its patents from infringement by competitors, Hewlett-Packard maintains a team of scientists to analyze the inks produced by other companies.

EXAMPLE (cont.)

This group analyzes 20 to 25 different inks every week. They use machines that heat the ink into a gaseous form, and then they test the gases for the chemical solvents utilized to create the ink. If they find scientific evidence that a competitor has combined solvents in ways specified by one or more of Hewlett-Packard's patents, then the company files a lawsuit against the alleged patent violator. In most case, an admitted violator settles out of court by paying Hewlett-Packard a lump sum and promising to stop infringing on Hewlett-Packard's patented ink formulations.

FOR CRITICAL ANALYSIS
Why do you suppose that Hewlett-Packard also regularly has engineers check the design of competitors' toner cartridges for possible violations of company patents?

Tariffs
Taxes on imported goods.

What are some of the costs associated with Hewlett-Packard's continuing attempts to maintain its monopoly in ink cartridges for its printers?

TARIFFS **Tariffs** are special taxes that are imposed on certain imported goods. Tariffs make imports more expensive relative to their domestic counterparts, encouraging consumers to switch to the relatively cheaper domestically made products. If the tariffs are high enough, domestic producers may be able to act together like a single firm and gain monopoly advantage as the sole suppliers. Many countries have tried this protectionist strategy by using high tariffs to shut out foreign competitors.

REGULATIONS Throughout the twentieth century and to the present, government regulation of the U.S. economy has increased, especially along the dimensions of safety and quality. U.S. firms incur hundreds of billions of dollars in expenses each year to comply with federal, state, and local government regulations of business conduct relating to workplace conditions, environmental protection, product safety, and various other activities. Presumably, these large fixed costs of complying with regulations can be spread over a greater number of units of output by larger firms than by smaller firms, thereby putting the smaller firms at a competitive disadvantage. Entry will also be deterred to the extent that the scale of operation of a potential entrant must be sufficiently large to cover the average fixed costs of compliance. We examine regulation in more detail in Chapter 28.

QUICK QUIZ See page 663 for the answers. Review concepts from this section in MyEconLab.

A **monopolist** is the single seller of a product or good for which there is no _____ substitute.

To maintain a monopoly, there must be barriers to entry. Barriers to entry include _____ of resources without close substitutes; economies of _____; legally required licenses, franchises, and certificates of convenience; patents; tariffs; and safety and quality regulations.

The Demand Curve a Monopolist Faces

A *pure monopolist* is the sole supplier of *one* product, good, or service. A pure monopolist faces a demand curve that is the demand curve for the entire market for that good.

The monopolist faces the industry demand curve because the monopolist is the entire industry.

Because the monopolist faces the industry demand curve, which is by definition downward sloping, its choice regarding how much to produce is not the same as for a perfect competitor. When a monopolist changes output, it does not automatically receive the same price per unit that it did before the change.

Profits to Be Made from Increasing Production

How do firms benefit from changing production rates? What happens to price in each case? Let's first review the situation among perfect competitors.

MARGINAL REVENUE FOR THE PERFECT COMPETITOR Recall that a firm in a perfectly competitive industry faces a perfectly elastic demand curve. That is because the perfectly competitive firm is such a small part of the market that it cannot influence the price of its product. It is a *price taker*. If the forces of supply and demand establish that the price per constant-quality pair of shoes is $50, the individual firm can sell all the pairs of shoes it wants to produce at $50 per pair. The average revenue is $50, the price is $50, and the marginal revenue is also $50.

Let us again define marginal revenue:

Marginal revenue equals the change in total revenue due to a one-unit change in the quantity produced and sold.

In the case of a perfectly competitive industry, each time a single firm changes production by one unit, total revenue changes by the going price, and price is unchanged. Marginal revenue always equals price, or average revenue. Average revenue was defined as total revenue divided by quantity demanded, or

$$\text{Average revenue} = \frac{\text{TR}}{Q} = \frac{PQ}{Q} = P$$

Hence, marginal revenue, average revenue, and price are all the same for the price-taking firm.

MARGINAL REVENUE FOR THE MONOPOLIST What about a monopoly firm? We begin by considering a situation in which a monopolist charges every buyer the same price for each unit of its product. Because a monopoly is the entire industry, the monopoly firm's demand curve is the market demand curve. The market demand curve slopes downward, just like the other demand curves that we have seen. Therefore, to induce consumers to buy more of a particular product, given the industry demand curve, the monopoly firm must lower the price. Thus, the monopoly firm moves *down* the demand curve. If all buyers are to be charged the same price, the monopoly must lower the price on *all* units sold in order to sell more. It cannot lower the price on just the *last* unit sold in any given time period in order to sell a larger quantity.

Put yourself in the shoes of a monopoly ferryboat owner. You have a government-bestowed franchise, and no one can compete with you. Your ferryboat goes between two islands. If you are charging $1 per crossing, a certain quantity of your services will be demanded. Let's say that you are ferrying 100 people a day each way at that price. If you decide that you would like to ferry more individuals, you must lower your price to all individuals—you must move *down* the existing demand curve for ferrying services. To calculate the marginal revenue of your change in price, you must first calculate the total revenues you received at $1 per passenger per crossing and then calculate the total revenues you would receive at, say, 90 cents per passenger per crossing.

Demand Curves for the Perfect Competitor and the Monopolist

The perfect competitor in panel (a) faces a perfectly elastic demand curve, *d*. The monopolist in panel (b) faces the entire industry demand curve, which slopes downward.

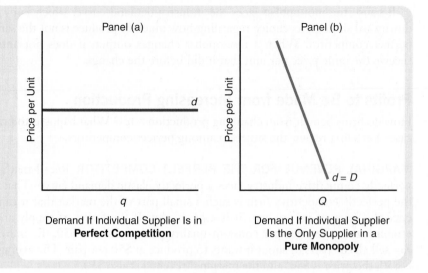

PERFECT COMPETITION VERSUS MONOPOLY It is sometimes useful to compare monopoly markets with perfectly competitive markets. The monopolist is constrained by the demand curve for its product, just as a perfectly competitive firm is constrained by its demand. The key difference is the nature of the demand curve each type of firm faces. We see this in Figure 25-2, which compares the demand curves of the perfect competitor and the monopolist.

Here we see the fundamental difference between the monopolist and the perfect competitor. The perfect competitor doesn't have to worry about lowering price to sell more. In a perfectly competitive situation, the perfectly competitive firm accounts for such a small part of the market that it can sell its entire output, whatever that may be, at the same price. The monopolist cannot. The more the monopolist wants to sell, the lower the price it has to charge on the last unit (and on *all* units put on the market for sale). To sell the last unit, the monopolist has to lower the price because it is facing a downward-sloping demand curve, and the only way to move down the demand curve is to lower the price. As long as this price must be the same for all units, the extra revenues the monopolist receives from selling one more unit are going to be smaller than the extra revenues received from selling the next-to-last unit.

The Monopolist's Marginal Revenue: Less Than Price

An essential point is that for the monopolist, marginal revenue is always less than price. To understand why, look at Figure 25-3, which shows a unit increase in output sold due to a reduction in the price of a commodity from P_1 to P_2. Price P_2 is the price received for the last unit, so selling this unit contributes P_2 to revenues. That is equal to the vertical column (area A). Area A is one unit wide by P_2 high.

But price times the last unit sold is *not* the net addition to *total* revenues received from selling that last unit. Why? Because price had to be reduced on all previous units sold (Q) in order to sell the larger quantity $Q + 1$. The reduction in price is represented by the vertical distance from P_1 to P_2 on the vertical axis. We must therefore subtract area B from area A to come up with the *change* in total revenues due to a one-unit increase in sales. Clearly, the change in total revenues—that is, marginal revenue—must be less than price because marginal revenue is always the

FIGURE 25-3

Marginal Revenue: Always Less Than Price

The price received for the last unit sold is equal to P_2. The revenues received from selling this last unit are equal to P_2 times one unit, or the orange-shaded area of the vertical column. However, if a single price is being charged for all units, total revenues do not go up by the amount of the area represented by that column. The price had to be reduced on all the previous Q units that were being sold at price P_1. Thus, we must subtract the green-shaded area B—the rectangle between P_1 and P_2 from the vertical axis to Q—from area A in order to derive marginal revenue. Marginal revenue is therefore always less than price.

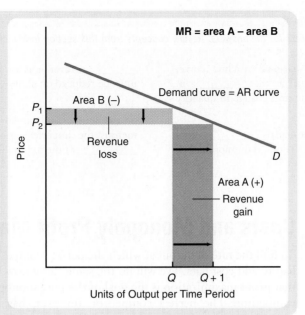

difference between areas A and B in Figure 25-3. For example, if the initial price is $8 and quantity demanded is 3, to increase quantity to 4 units, it is necessary to decrease price to $7, not just for the fourth unit, but on all three previous units as well. Thus, at a price of $7, marginal revenue is $7 − $3 = $4 because there is a $1 per unit price reduction on three previous units. Hence, marginal revenue, $4, is less than price, $7.

Elasticity and Monopoly

The monopolist faces a downward-sloping demand curve (its average revenue curve). That means that it cannot charge just *any* price with no changes in quantity (a common misconception) because, depending on the price charged, a different quantity will be demanded.

Earlier we defined a monopolist as the single seller of a well-defined good or service with no *close* substitute. This does not mean, however, that the demand curve for a monopoly is vertical or exhibits zero price elasticity of demand. After all, consumers have limited incomes and unlimited wants. The market demand curve, which the monopolist alone faces in this situation, slopes downward because individuals compare the marginal satisfaction they will receive to the cost of the commodity to be purchased. Take the example of telephone service. Even if miraculously there were absolutely no substitutes whatsoever for telephone service, the market demand curve would still slope downward. At lower prices, people will add more phones and separate lines for different family members.

Furthermore, the demand curve for telephone service slopes downward because there are at least several *imperfect* substitutes, such as letters, e-mail, in-person conversations, and Internet telephony. The more such substitutes there are, and the better these substitutes are, the more elastic will be the monopolist's demand curve, all other things held constant.

Costs and Monopoly Profit Maximization

Price searcher
A firm that must determine the price-output combination that maximizes profit because it faces a downward-sloping demand curve.

To find the rate of output at which the perfect competitor would maximize profits, we had to add cost data. We will do the same thing now for the monopolist. We assume that profit maximization is the goal of the pure monopolist, just as it is for the perfect competitor. The perfect competitor, however, has only to decide on the profit-maximizing rate of output because price is given. The perfect competitor is a price taker. For the pure monopolist, we must seek a profit-maximizing *price-output combination* because the monopolist is a **price searcher.** We can determine this profit-maximizing price-output combination with either of two equivalent approaches—by looking at total revenues and total costs or by looking at marginal revenues and marginal costs. We shall examine both approaches.

The Total Revenues–Total Costs Approach

Suppose that the government of a small town located in a remote desert area grants a single satellite television company the right to offer services within its jurisdiction. It enforces rules that prevent other firms from offering television services. We show demand (weekly rate of output and price per unit), revenues, costs, and other data in panel (a) of Figure 25-4. In column 3, we see total revenues for this TV service monopolist, and in column 4, we see total costs. We can transfer these two columns to panel (b). The fundamental difference between the total revenue and total cost diagram in panel (b) and the one we showed for a perfect competitor in Chapter 24 is that the total revenue line is no longer straight. Rather, it curves. For any given demand curve, in order to sell more, the monopolist must lower the price. This reflects the fact that the basic difference between a monopolist and a perfect competitor has to do with the demand curve for the two types of firms. The monopolist faces a downward-sloping demand curve.

Profit maximization involves maximizing the positive difference between total revenues and total costs. This occurs at an output rate of between 9 and 10 units per week.

The Marginal Revenue–Marginal Cost Approach

Profit maximization will also occur where marginal revenue equals marginal cost. This is as true for a monopolist as it is for a perfect competitor (but the monopolist will charge a price in excess of marginal revenue). When we transfer marginal cost and marginal revenue information from columns 6 and 7 in panel (a) of Figure 25-4 to panel (c), we see that marginal revenue equals marginal cost at a weekly quantity of satellite TV services of between 9 and 10 units. Profit maximization must occur at the same output as in panel (b).

FIGURE 25-4

Monopoly Costs, Revenues, and Profits

In panel (a), we give demand (weekly satellite television services and price), revenues, costs, and other relevant data. As shown in panel (b), the satellite TV monopolist maximizes profits where the positive difference between TR and TC is greatest. This is at an output rate of between 9 and 10 units per week. Put another way, profit maximization occurs where marginal revenue equals marginal cost, as shown in panel (c). This is at the same weekly service rate of between 9 and 10 units. (The MC curve must cut the MR curve from below.)

Panel (a)

(1) Output (units)	(2) Price per Unit	(3) Total Revenues (TR) (3) = (2) x (1)	(4) Total Costs (TC)	(5) Total Profit (5) = (3) − (4)	(6) Marginal Cost (MC)	(7) Marginal Revenue (MR)
0	$8.00	$ .00	$10.00	−$10.00		
					$4.00	$7.80
1	7.80	7.80	14.00	−6.20		
					3.50	7.40
2	7.60	15.20	17.50	−2.30		
					3.25	7.00
3	7.40	22.20	20.75	1.45		
					3.05	6.60
4	7.20	28.80	23.80	5.00		
					2.90	6.20
5	7.00	35.00	26.70	8.30		
					2.80	5.80
6	6.80	40.80	29.50	11.30		
					2.75	5.40
7	6.60	46.20	32.25	13.95		
					2.85	5.00
8	6.40	51.20	35.10	16.10		
					3.20	4.60
9	6.20	55.80	38.30	17.50		
					4.40	4.20
10	6.00	60.00	42.70	17.30		
					6.00	3.80
11	5.80	63.80	48.70	15.10		
					9.00	3.40
12	5.60	67.20	57.70	9.50		

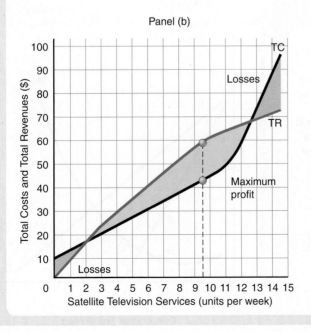

Panel (b)

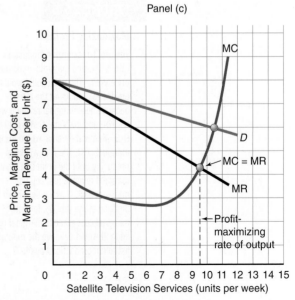

Panel (c)

WHY PRODUCE WHERE MARGINAL REVENUE EQUALS MARGINAL COST? If the monopolist produces past the point where marginal revenue equals marginal cost, marginal cost will exceed marginal revenue. That is, the incremental cost of producing any more units will exceed the incremental revenue. It just would not be worthwhile, as was true also in perfect competition. Furthermore, just as in the case of perfect competition, if the monopolist produces less than that, it is not making maximum profits. Look at output rate Q_1 in Figure 25-5. Here the monopolist's marginal revenue is at A, but marginal cost is at B. Marginal revenue exceeds marginal cost on the last unit sold; the profit for that *particular* unit, Q_1, is equal to the vertical difference between A and B, or the difference between marginal revenue and marginal cost. The monopolist would be foolish to stop at output rate Q_1 because if output is expanded, marginal revenue will still exceed marginal cost, and therefore total profits will be increased by selling more. In fact, the profit-maximizing monopolist will continue to expand output and sales until marginal revenue equals marginal cost, which is at output rate Q_m. The monopolist won't produce at rate Q_2 because here, as we see, marginal costs are C and marginal revenues are F. The difference between C and F represents the *reduction* in total profits from producing that additional unit. Total profits will rise as the monopolist reduces its rate of output back toward Q_m.

What Price to Charge for Output?

How does the monopolist set prices? We know the quantity is set at the point at which marginal revenue equals marginal cost. The monopolist then finds out how much can be charged—how much the market will bear—for that particular quantity, Q_m, in Figure 25-5.

THE MONOPOLY PRICE We know that the demand curve is defined as showing the *maximum* price for which a given quantity can be sold. That means that our monopolist knows that to sell Q_m, it can charge only P_m because that is the price at which that

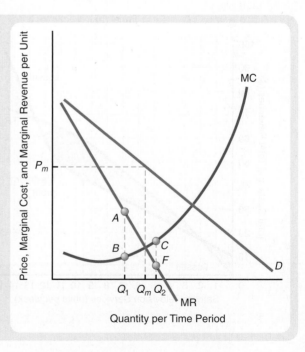

FIGURE 25-5

Maximizing Profits

The profit-maximizing production rate is Q_m, and the profit-maximizing price is P_m. The monopolist would be unwise to produce at the rate Q_1 because here marginal revenue would be Q_1A, and marginal cost would be Q_1B. Marginal revenue would exceed marginal cost. The firm will keep producing until the point Q_m, where marginal revenue just equals marginal cost. It would be foolish to produce at the rate Q_2, for here marginal cost exceeds marginal revenue. It would behoove the monopolist to cut production back to Q_m.

specific quantity, Q_m, is demanded. This price is found by drawing a vertical line from the quantity, Q_m, to the market demand curve. Where that line hits the market demand curve, the price is determined. We find that price by drawing a horizontal line from the demand curve over to the price axis; that gives us the profit-maximizing price, P_m.

In our numerical example, at a profit-maximizing quantity of satellite TV services of between 9 and 10 units in Figure 25-4 on page 649, the firm can charge a maximum price of about $6 and still sell all the services it provides, all at the same price.

The basic procedure for finding the profit-maximizing short-run price-quantity combination for the monopolist is first to determine the profit-maximizing rate of output, by either the total revenue–total cost method or the marginal revenue–marginal cost method, and then to determine by use of the demand curve, D, the maximum price that can be charged to sell that output.

REAL-WORLD INFORMATIONAL LIMITATIONS Don't get the impression that just because we are able to draw an exact demand curve in Figures 25-4 and 25-5, real-world monopolists have such perfect information. The process of price searching by a less-than-perfect competitor is just that—a process. A monopolist can only estimate the actual demand curve and therefore can make only an educated guess when it sets its profit-maximizing price. This is not a problem for the perfect competitor because price is given already by the intersection of market demand and market supply. The monopolist, in contrast, reaches the profit-maximizing output-price combination by trial and error.

Calculating Monopoly Profit

We have talked about the monopolist's profit. We have yet to indicate how much profit the monopolist makes, which we do in Figure 25-6.

FIGURE 25-6

Monopoly Profit

We find monopoly profit by subtracting total costs from total revenues at a quantity of satellite TV services of between 9 and 10 units per week, labeled Q_m, which is the profit-maximizing rate of output for the satellite TV monopolist. The profit-maximizing price is therefore about $6 per week and is labeled P_m. Monopoly profit is given by the green-shaded area, which is equal to total revenues ($P \times Q$) minus total costs (ATC $\times Q$). This diagram is similar to panel (c) of Figure 25-4 on page 649, with the short-run average total cost curve (ATC) added.

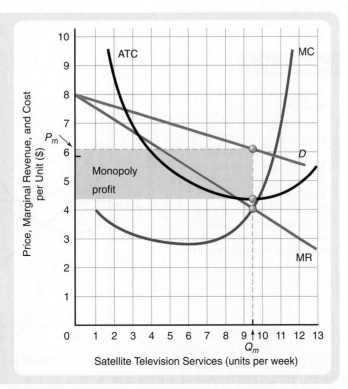

The Graphical Depiction of Monopoly Profits

We have actually shown total profits in column 5 of panel (a) in Figure 25-4 on page 649. We can also find total profits by adding an average total cost curve to panel (c) of that figure, as shown in Figure 25-6 on the preceding page. When we add the average total cost curve, we find that the profit that a monopolist makes is equal to the green-shaded area—or total revenues $(P \times Q)$ minus total costs $(ATC \times Q)$. Given the demand curve and a uniform pricing system (that is, all units sold at the same price), there is no way for a monopolist to make greater profits than those shown by the green-shaded area. The monopolist is maximizing profits where marginal cost equals marginal revenue. If the monopolist produces less than that, it will be forfeiting some profits. If the monopolist produces more than that, it will also be forfeiting some profits.

No Guarantee of Profits

The term *monopoly* conjures up the notion of a greedy firm ripping off the public and making exorbitant profits. The mere existence of a monopoly, however, does not guarantee high profits. Numerous monopolies have gone bankrupt. Figure 25-7 shows the monopolist's demand curve as D and the resultant marginal revenue curve as MR. It does not matter at what rate of output this particular monopolist operates; total costs cannot be covered. Look at the position of the average total cost curve. It lies everywhere above D (the average revenue curve). Thus, there is no price-output combination that will allow the monopolist even to cover costs, much less earn profits. This monopolist will, in the short run, suffer economic losses as shown by the red-shaded area. The graph in Figure 25-7, which applies to many inventions, depicts a situation of resulting monopoly. The owner of a patented invention or discovery has a pure legal monopoly, but the demand and cost curves are such that production is not profitable. Every year at inventors' conventions, one can see many inventions that have never been put into production because they were deemed "uneconomic" by potential producers and users.

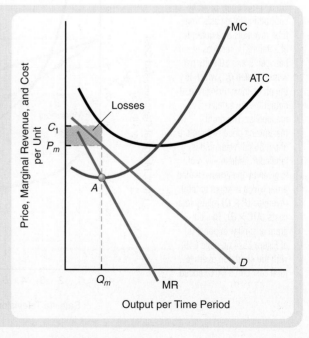

FIGURE 25-7

Monopolies: Not Always Profitable

Some monopolists face the situation shown here. The average total cost curve, ATC, is everywhere above the average revenue, or demand, curve, D. In the short run, the monopolist will produce where MC = MR at point A. Output Q_m will be sold at price P_m, but average total cost per unit is C_1. Losses are the red-shaded rectangle. Eventually, the monopolist will go out of business.

The basic difference between a monopolist and a perfect competitor is that a monopolist faces a _____ - sloping demand curve, and therefore marginal revenue is _____ than price.

The monopolist must choose the profit-maximizing price-output combination—the output at which _____ revenue equals _____ cost and the highest price possible as given by the _____ curve for that particular output rate.

Monopoly profits are found by looking at average _____ costs compared to price per unit. This difference multiplied by the _____ sold at that price determines monopoly profit.

A monopolist does not necessarily earn a profit. If the average _____ cost curve lies entirely _____ the demand curve for a monopoly, no production rate will be profitable.

On Making Higher Profits: Price Discrimination

In a perfectly competitive market, each buyer is charged the same price for every constant-quality unit of the particular commodity (corrected for differential transportation charges). Because the product is homogeneous and we also assume full knowledge on the part of the buyers, a difference in price cannot exist. Any seller of the product who tried to charge a price higher than the going market price would find that no one would purchase it from that seller.

In this chapter, we have assumed until now that the monopolist charged all consumers the same price for all units. A monopolist, however, may be able to charge different people different prices or different unit prices for successive units sought by a given buyer. When there is no cost difference, such strategies are called **price discrimination.** A firm will engage in price discrimination whenever feasible to increase profits. A price-discriminating firm is able to charge some customers more than other customers.

How do online retailers engage in price discrimination?

Price discrimination
Selling a given product at more than one price, with the price difference being unrelated to differences in marginal cost.

E-COMMERCE EXAMPLE
Online Retailers Are Watching

A Web site's price for an item that you express an interest in buying online may depend on your gender. Where you live may also influence the price, as may the time of day that you shop. Even the speed of your Internet connection may affect how much you have to pay.

Whenever you surf a seller's Web site, your computer's Internet connection automatically leaves a limited trail of information, including the location of your Internet service provider and the speed of your connection to the Internet. *Price-optimization software* utilized by the seller can directly access this information. It can also transmit small programs called "cookies" to your own computer, and these can gather additional information about how you search among the firm's products. If you have already provided the seller with other information about yourself, such as your gender, a cookie will recognize your computer and relay that information to the software. Naturally, the software also logs the time of day that you are shopping. Using complex algorithms, price-optimization software estimates your price elasticity of demand for the item. Based on this estimate, the software then quotes you a price. This is the price that the software determines you are most likely to be willing to pay. If the software estimates that your price elasticity of demand is lower than that of another Web shopper, you will be quoted a higher price than that other individual. Hence, price-optimization software might more aptly be named "price-discrimination software."

E-COMMERCE EXAMPLE (cont.)

FOR CRITICAL ANALYSIS

Why might information about your location and the speed of your Internet connection provide information about your price elasticity of demand? (Hint: On average, someone in Beverly Hills, California, using an ultra-high-speed Internet connection *is likely to have a higher income than someone in South Central Los Angeles using a phone dial-up connection. Price elasticity of demand depends, in part, on expenditures on an item as a share of total income.)*

Price differentiation

Establishing different prices for similar products to reflect differences in marginal cost in providing those commodities to different groups of buyers.

It must be made clear at the outset that charging different prices to different people or for different units to reflect differences in the cost of service does not amount to price discrimination. This is **price differentiation:** differences in price that reflect differences in marginal cost.

We can also say that a uniform price does not necessarily indicate an absence of price discrimination. Charging all customers the same price when production costs vary by customer is actually a situation of price discrimination.

Necessary Conditions for Price Discrimination

Three conditions are necessary for price discrimination to exist:

1. The firm must face a downward-sloping demand curve.
2. The firm must be able to readily (and cheaply) identify buyers or groups of buyers with predictably different elasticities of demand.
3. The firm must be able to prevent resale of the product or service.

Has it ever occurred to you that most of the other students seated in your college classroom pay different overall tuition rates than you do because your college and others use financial aid packages to engage in price discrimination?

EXAMPLE
Why Students Pay Different Prices to Attend College

Out-of-pocket tuition rates for any two college students can differ by considerable amounts, even if the students happen to major in the same subjects and enroll in many of the same courses. The reason is that colleges offer students diverse financial aid packages depending on their "financial need."

To document their "need" for financial aid, students must provide detailed information about family income and wealth. This information, of course, helps the college determine the prices that different families are most likely to be willing and able to pay, so that it can engage in price discrimination. Figure 25-8 shows how this collegiate price-discrimination process works. The college charges the price P_7, which is the college's official posted "tuition rate," to students with families judged to be most willing and able to pay the highest price.

Students whose families have the lowest levels of income and wealth are judged to be willing and able to pay a much lower price, such as P_1. To charge these students this lower tuition rate, the college provides them with a financial aid package that reduces the price they pay by the difference between P_7, the full tuition price, and P_1. In this way, the actual price paid by these "neediest" students is only P_1.

Likewise, the college groups other, somewhat less "needy" students into a slightly higher income-and-wealth category and determines that they are likely to be willing to pay a somewhat higher price, P_2. Hence, it grants them a smaller financial aid package, equal to $P_7 - P_2$, so that the students actually pay the price P_2. The college continues this process for other groups, thereby engaging in price discrimination in its tuition charges.

FIGURE 25-8

Toward Perfect Price Discrimination in College Tuition Rates

Students that a college determines to be "neediest" and least able to pay the full tuition price, P_7, receive a financial aid package equal to $P_7 - P_1$. These students effectively pay only the price P_1. The college groups the remaining students into categories on the basis of their willingness and ability to pay a higher price, and each group receives a progressively smaller financial aid package. Those students who are willing and able to pay the full price, P_7, receive no financial aid from the college.

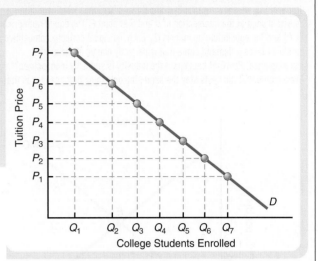

FOR CRITICAL ANALYSIS

Does the educational product supplied by colleges satisfy all three conditions necessary for price discrimination?

The Social Cost of Monopolies

Let's run a little experiment. We will start with a purely competitive industry with numerous firms, each one unable to affect the price of its product. The supply curve of the industry is equal to the horizontal sum of the marginal cost curves of the individual producers above their respective minimum average variable costs. In panel (a) of Figure 25-9 on the following page, we show the market demand curve and the market supply curve in a perfectly competitive situation. The perfectly competitive price in equilibrium is equal to P_e, and the equilibrium quantity at that price is equal to Q_e. Each individual perfect competitor faces a demand curve (not shown) that is coincident with the price line P_e. No individual supplier faces the market demand curve, D.

Comparing Monopoly with Perfect Competition

Now let's assume that a monopolist comes in and buys up every single perfect competitor in the industry. In so doing, we'll assume that monopolization does not affect any of the marginal cost curves or demand. We can therefore redraw D and S in panel (b) of Figure 25-9, exactly the same as in panel (a).

How does this monopolist decide how much to charge and how much to produce? If the monopolist is profit maximizing, it is going to look at the marginal revenue curve and produce at the output where marginal revenue equals marginal cost. But what is the marginal cost curve in panel (b) of Figure 25-9 on the next page? It is merely S, because we said that S was equal to the horizontal summation of the portions of the individual marginal cost curves above each firm's respective minimum average variable cost. The monopolist therefore produces quantity Q_m, and sells it at price P_m. Notice that Q_m is less than Q_e and that P_m is greater than P_e. A monopolist therefore produces a smaller quantity and sells it at a higher price. This is the reason usually given when economists criticize monopolists. Monopolists raise the

FIGURE 25-9

The Effects of Monopolizing an Industry

In panel (a), we show a perfectly competitive situation in which equilibrium is established at the intersection of D and S at point E. The equilibrium price is P_e and the equilibrium quantity is Q_e. Each individual perfectly competitive producer faces a demand curve that is perfectly elastic at the market clearing price, P_e. What happens if the industry is suddenly monopolized? We assume that the costs stay the same; the only thing that changes is that the monopolist now faces the entire downward-sloping demand curve. In panel (b), we draw the marginal revenue curve. Marginal cost is S because that is the horizontal summation of all the individual marginal cost curves. The monopolist therefore produces at Q_m and charges price P_m. This price P_m in panel (b) is higher than P_e in panel (a), and Q_m is less than Q_e.

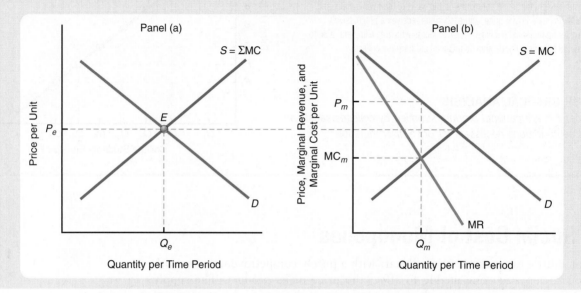

price and restrict production, compared to a perfectly competitive situation. For a monopolist's product, consumers pay a price that exceeds the marginal cost of production. Resources are misallocated in such a situation—too few resources are being used in the monopolist's industry, and too many are used elsewhere. (See Appendix F at the end of this chapter.)

Implications of Higher Monopoly Prices

Notice from Figure 25-9 that by setting MR = MC, the monopolist produces at a rate of output where $P > $ MC (compare P_m to MC_m). The marginal cost of a commodity (MC) represents what society had to give up in order to obtain the last unit produced. Price, by contrast, represents what buyers are willing to pay to acquire that last unit. Thus, the price of a good represents society's valuation of the last unit produced. The monopoly outcome of $P > $ MC means that the value to society of the last unit produced is greater than its cost (MC); hence, not enough of the good is being produced. As we have pointed out before, these differences between monopoly and perfect competition arise not because of differences in costs but rather because of differences in the demand curves the individual firms face. The monopolist faces a downward-sloping demand curve. The individual perfect competitor faces a perfectly elastic demand curve.

Before we leave the topic of the cost to society of monopolies, we must repeat that our analysis is based on a heroic assumption. That assumption is that the monopolization of the perfectly competitive industry does not change the cost structure. If monopolization results in higher marginal cost, the net cost of monopoly to society is even greater.

Conversely, if monopolization results in cost savings, the net cost of monopoly to society is less than we infer from our analysis. Indeed, we could have presented a hypothetical example in which monopolization led to such a dramatic reduction in cost that society actually benefited. Such a situation is a possibility in industries in which economies of scale exist for a very great range of outputs.

QUICK QUIZ   *See page 663 for the answers. Review concepts from this section in MyEconLab.*

Three conditions are necessary for price discrimination: (1) The firm must face a _____-sloping demand curve, (2) the firm must be able to identify buyers with predictably different price _____ of demand, and (3) _____ of the product or service must be preventable.

Price _____ should not be confused with price _____, which occurs when differences in price reflect differences in marginal cost.

Monopoly tends to result in a _____ quantity being sold, because the price is _____ than it would be in an ideal perfectly competitive industry in which the cost curves were essentially the same as the monopolist's.

You Are There   Why Pouring Vegetable Oil into a Car Is Illegal in Illinois

David and Eileen Wetzel were surprised when two well-dressed men who had knocked on the door of their home in Decatur, Illinois, pulled out badges indicating that they were from the Illinois Department of Revenue. The Wetzels were even more surprised when the state revenue agents threatened them with felony charges and asked them to post a $2,500 bond to avoid arrest.

What was the elderly couple's crime? They were driving a 1986 Volkswagen Golf that Mr. Wetzel, a retired chemist and food plant manager, had converted to operate on a mixture of diesel fuel and vegetable oil. Illinois law prohibits acting as either a "special fuel supplier" or a "special fuel receiver" without a license. After getting information about the Wetzels' car, the Illinois Department of Revenue had deter-

mined that the Wetzels had both illegally supplied themselves with fuel and illegally received it. Thus, the couple had illegally entered the vehicle fuel industry.

CRITICAL ANALYSIS QUESTIONS

1. Why do producers of a government-licensed product, such as fuel for motor vehicles, have an incentive to report all others who try to produce similar products without a license?

2. Why do you suppose that many economists worry that government restraints on competition can impede innovation in markets?

The Predictable Consequences of European State Religion Monopolies

CONCEPTS APPLIED

- Monopolist
- Social Cost of Monopoly
- Comparing Monopoly with Perfect Competition

For years, the Church of Sweden, a Christian religious denomination affiliated with the Lutheran Church, was an official institution of the Swedish state. Today, about 75 percent of all Swedes, or nearly 7 million people, remain official members. Nevertheless, a recent Sunday service at Stockholm's Hedvig Eleonara Church is typical of the scene in most individual parishes of the Church of Sweden. About 40 people, nearly all of them elderly, gathered beneath a huge, beautifully decorated dome in pews designed to hold more than 1,000 churchgoers. As this scene plays out at Church of Sweden parishes throughout the nation, one might be tempted to conclude that the bulk of Swedes are atheists. To an economist, however, the key to understanding low attendance by members of the Church of Sweden is its traditional status as a state monopoly.

The Usual Monopoly Outcome: Lower Output

Even though the Church of Sweden's state monopoly status formally ended in 2000, its 1,800 congregations continue to receive substantial subsidies from the state. For instance, the Hedvig Eleonara Church receives more than $2 million each year in funds raised from special taxes. Although most other European nations officially dethroned formal "state churches" many years ago, a number of governments continue to favor specific churches. In Italy, for instance, the government offers taxpayers a slate of churches to which they can direct the proceeds of a special "religious tax," of which the Catholic Church typically receives about 87 percent, or approximately $1 billion per year. Yet attendance rates in Italy's Catholic Church are nearly as low as those experienced by the Church of Sweden.

Economists who study the economics of religion have found that the Swedish and Italian pattern of low attendance holds true in all nations in which a single church predominates through state favors. The reason, they suggest, is that granting a religion a monopoly has a very predictable effect: restriction of religious output and higher-priced services. Consider the implied price of religious services at Stockholm's Hedvig Eleonara Church. Its $2 million in state subsidies translates into more than $38,000 per week. Yet the church has only three priests to provide spiritual support and guidance and other religious services to a membership of more than 1,000. Many members are offered low levels of religious output and hence do not attend church services regularly. Most do not attend at all. Indeed, the Hedvig Eleonara Church recently scrapped Sunday school because only five children were regularly attending.

The Effects of Increasing Religious Competition in Europe

On the Sundays when only about 40 members attend services at the Hedvig Eleonara Church, more than 100 young Swedes typically crowd into a small hall rented from Stockholm's Casino Theatre. These members of the nondenominational "Passion Church" attend evangelical religious services that include rock music blared out by a high-decibel band. Together, this church and a number of other small evangelical churches that operate outside the Church of Sweden have only about 31,000 members. Yet their facilities are packed every Sunday. Their per-member religious output is much higher than the output produced by the Church of Sweden.

Religious competition gradually is developing across Europe. Much of this competition is in the form of independent "market entrants," such as the nondenominational evangelical churches spreading through Sweden. But some of it comes from traditionally U.S.-based Christian denominations, the Islamic faith, and other world religions. Although Europe is hardly experiencing a competitive free-for-all in the "religious marketplace," competition does now exist and is growing. For this reason, a number of economists predict that religious output is likely to increase in Europe in the coming years.

Test your understanding of this chapter by going online to **MyEconLab**. In the Study Plan for this chapter, select Section N: News.

For Critical Analysis

1. Why might economists disagree about the appropriateness of using rates of church attendance as a proxy measure of "religious output"?

2. What is the shape of the demand curve for religious services faced by a monopoly church?

Web Resources

1. For a discussion of how economics can be applied to religious institutions, go to www.econtoday.com/chapter25.

2. To download a study indicating lower levels of social spending by U.S. churches that are more nearly monopolies in their local areas, go to www.econtoday.com/chapter25.

Research Project

Based on this discussion, is there any evidence that the price of religious output is higher under a religious monopoly than it would be in a perfectly competitive religious marketplace? (Hint: Compare the price paid in member taxes to support the limited activities of Stockholm's Hedvig Eleonara Church with the likely price paid, undoubtedly in the form of private donations, by members of the Stockholm Passion Church.)

Here is what you should know after reading this chapter. **MyEconLab** will help you identify what you know, and where to go when you need to practice.

WHAT YOU SHOULD KNOW		WHERE TO GO TO PRACTICE

Why Monopoly Can Occur Monopoly, a situation in which a single firm produces and sells a good or service that has no close substitute, can occur when there are significant barriers to market entry by other firms. Examples of barriers to entry include (1) ownership of important resources for which there are no close substitutes; (2) economies of scale for ever-larger ranges of output, or natural monopoly conditions; and (3) legal or governmental restrictions.

monopolist, 640
natural monopoly, 642
tariffs, 644

- **MyEconLab** Study Plans 25.1, 25.2
- Audio introduction to Chapter 25
- Video: Barriers to Entry
- ABC News Video: Optometrists as Monopolists?
- ABC News Video: Tradeoffs to Higher-Priced Cancer Drugs

Demand and Marginal Revenue Conditions a Monopolist Faces Because a monopolist constitutes the entire industry, it faces the entire market demand curve. When it reduces the price of its product, it is able to sell more units at the new price, which pushes up its revenues, but it also sells other units at this lower price, which pushes its revenues down somewhat. Thus, the monopolist's marginal revenue at any given quantity is less than the price at which it sells that quantity. Its marginal revenue curve slopes downward and lies below the demand curve it faces.

KEY FIGURES
Figure 25-2, 646
Figure 25-3, 647

- **MyEconLab** Study Plans 25.3, 25.4
- Video: The Demand Curve Facing a Monopoly Is Not Vertical
- Animated Figures 25-2, 25-3

How a Monopolist Determines How Much Output to Produce and What Price to Charge A monopolist is a price searcher, meaning that it seeks to charge the price consistent with the production level that maximizes its economic profits. It maximizes its profits by producing to the point at which marginal revenue equals marginal cost. The monopolist then charges the maximum price for this amount of output, which is the price that consumers are willing to pay for that quantity of output.

price searcher, 648
KEY FIGURES
Figure 25-4, 649
Figure 25-5, 650

- **MyEconLab** Study Plan 25.5
- Animated Figures 25-4, 25-5

A Monopolist's Profits The profits earned by a monopolist equal the difference between the price it charges and its average production cost times the quantity it sells. The monopolist's price is at the point on the demand curve corresponding to the profit-maximizing output rate, and its average total cost of producing this output rate is at the corresponding point on the average total cost curve. A monopolist commonly earns positive economic profits, but situations can arise in which average total cost exceeds the profit-maximizing price, yielding negative profits.

KEY FIGURES
Figure 25-6, 651
Figure 25-7, 652

- **MyEconLab** Study Plan 25.6
- Animated Figures 25-6, 25-7

(continued)

 (continued)

WHAT YOU SHOULD KNOW

WHERE TO GO TO PRACTICE

Price Discrimination If a monopolist engages in price discrimination, it sells its product at more than one price, with the price difference being unrelated to differences in production costs. To be able to engage successfully in price discrimination, a monopolist must be able to identify and separate buyers with different price elasticities of demand. If the monopolist can prevent those with more elastic demand from reselling its product to those with less elastic demand, it can sell some of its output at higher prices to consumers with less elastic demand.

price discrimination, 653
price differentiation, 654

• **MyEconLab** Study
  Plan 25.7
• Video: Price
  Discrimination

Social Cost of Monopolies Because a monopoly is a price searcher, it is able to charge the highest price that people are willing to pay for the amount of output it produces. This price exceeds the marginal cost of producing the output. In addition, if the monopolist's marginal cost curve corresponds to the sum of the marginal cost curves for the number of firms that would exist if the industry were perfectly competitive instead, then the monopolist produces and sells less output than perfectly competitive firms would have produced and sold.

KEY FIGURE
Figure 25-9, 656

• **MyEconLab** Study
  Plan 25.8
• Animated Figure 25-9

Log in to MyEconLab, take a chapter test, and get a personalized Study Plan that tells you which concepts you understand and which ones you need to review. From there, MyEconLab will give you further practice, tutorials, animations, videos, and guided solutions.
Log in to www.myeconlab.com

PROBLEMS

All problems are assignable in ⟨X⟩ myeconlab . *Answers to odd-numbered problems appear at the back of the book.*

25-1. Under federal law, only the U.S. Postal Service has the right to deliver first-class mail. Thus, a consumer can either send a letter via the U.S. Postal Service for just over 40 cents or pay FedEx, UPS, or DHL $10 or more to deliver it. What is the shape of the demand curve faced by the U.S. Postal Service in the market for first-class mail?

25-2. Recently, a top constitutional law expert who had been licensed to practice law in Massachusetts and was under consideration for nomination to the California Supreme Court failed the California bar examination. In doing so, she joined a long list of accomplished lawyers who have failed

to pass the notoriously difficult examination, including a former governor who required four attempts to pass and a Los Angeles mayor who gave up after four tries. In the legal industry, what is a key economic function of the California bar examination?

25-3. Suppose that it is the year 2038. Exclusive ownership of a resource found to be required for the production of fusion power has given a firm monopoly power in the provision of this good. What is true of the relationship between the price of this resource and the marginal revenue the firm receives?

25-4. Consider the resource owner and seller discussed in Problem 25-3. Discuss what would have been true of the price elasticity of demand facing this firm if the firm had been a perfectly competitive seller of this resource. Contrast this with the price elasticity of demand for this firm in its actual role as monopoly provider. Explain why the price elasticities in the two situations are different.

25-5. The following table depicts the daily output, price, and costs of a monopoly dry cleaner located near the campus of a remote college town.

Output (suits cleaned)	Price per Suit ($)	Total Costs ($)
0	8.00	3.00
1	7.50	6.00
2	7.00	8.50
3	6.50	10.50
4	6.00	11.50
5	5.50	13.50
6	5.00	16.00
7	4.50	19.00
8	4.00	24.00

  a. Compute revenues and profits at each output rate.

  b. What is the profit-maximizing rate of output?

  c. Calculate the dry cleaner's marginal revenue and marginal cost at each output level. What is the profit-maximizing level of output?

25-6. A manager of a monopoly firm notices that the firm is producing output at a rate at which average total cost is falling but is not at its minimum feasible point. The manager argues that surely the firm must not be maximizing its economic profits. Is this argument correct?

25-7. Use the graph at the top of the next column to answer the following questions.

  a. What is the monopolist's profit-maximizing output?

  b. At the profit-maximizing output rate, what are average total cost and average revenue?

  c. At the profit-maximizing output rate, what are the monopolist's total cost and total revenue?

  d. What is the maximum profit?

  e. Suppose that the marginal cost and average total cost curves in the diagram also illustrate the horizontal summation of the firms in a perfectly com-

petitive industry in the long run. What would the equilibrium price and output be if the market were perfectly competitive? Explain the economic cost to society of allowing a monopoly to exist.

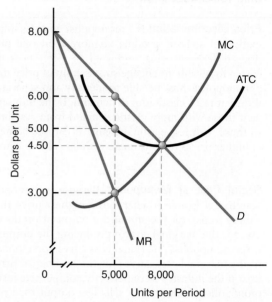

25-8. The marginal revenue curve of a monopoly crosses its marginal cost curve at $30 per unit and an output of 2 million units. The price that consumers are willing to pay for this output is $40 per unit. If it produces this output, the firm's average total cost is $43 per unit, and its average fixed cost is $8 per unit. What is the profit-maximizing (loss-minimizing) output? What are the firm's economic profits (or economic losses)?

25-9. Consider the revenue and cost conditions for a monopolist that are depicted in the figure below.

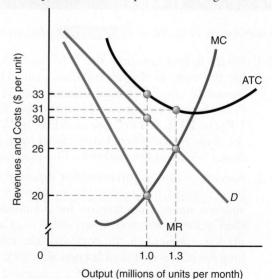

a. What is this producer's profit-maximizing (or loss-minimizing) output?

b. What are the firm's economic profits (or losses)?

25-10. For each of the following examples, explain how and why a monopoly would try to price discriminate.

a. Air transport for businesspeople and tourists

b. Serving food on weekdays to businesspeople and retired people. (Hint: Which group has more flexibility during a weekday to adjust to a price change and, hence, a higher price elasticity of demand?)

c. A theater that shows the same movie to large families and to individuals and couples. (Hint: For which set of people will the overall expense of a movie be a larger part of their budget, so that demand is more elastic?)

25-11. A monopolist's revenues vary directly with price. Is it maximizing its economic profits? Why or

why not? (Hint: Recall that the relationship between revenues and price depends on price elasticity of demand.)

25-12. A new competitor enters the industry and competes with a second firm, which had been a monopolist. The second firm finds that although demand is not perfectly elastic, it is now relatively more elastic. What will happen to the second firm's marginal revenue curve and to its profit-maximizing price?

25-13. A monopolist's marginal cost curve has shifted upward. What is likely to happen to the monopolist's price, output rate, and economic profits?

25-14. Demand has fallen. What is likely to happen to the monopolist's price, output rate, and economic profits?

ECONOMICS ON THE NET

Patents, Trademarks, and Intellectual Property This Internet application explores a firm's view on legal protections.

Title: Intellectual Property

Navigation: Follow the link at **www.econtoday.com/chapter25** to the GlaxoSmithKline Web site. Select *Investors*, then *Annual Reports and Reviews*. View the PDF of Annual Report 2007. Scroll down to Intellectual Property (page 28).

Application Read the statement and table; then answer the following questions.

1. How do patents, trademarks, and registered designs and copyrights differ?

2. What are GlaxoSmithKline's intellectual property goals? Do patents or trademarks seem to be more important?

For Group Discussion and Analysis In 1969, GlaxoSmith Kline developed Ventolin, a treatment for asthma symptoms. Though the patent and trademark have long expired, the company still retains over a third of the annual market sales of this treatment. Explain, in economic terms, the source of GlaxoSmithKline's strength in this area. Discuss whether patents and trademarks are beneficial for the development and discovery of new treatments.

ANSWERS TO QUICK QUIZZES

p. 644: (i) close; (ii) ownership . . . scale
p. 648: (i) change . . . total; (ii) marginal . . . marginal; (iii) elasticity . . . elasticity
p. 653: (i) downward . . . less; (ii) marginal . . . marginal . . . demand; (iii) total . . . quantity; (iv) total . . . above
p. 657: (i) downward . . . elasticities . . . resale; (ii) discrimination . . . differentiation; (iii) lower . . . higher

Consumer Surplus and the Losses Resulting from Monopoly

You have learned that a monopolist produces fewer units than would otherwise be produced in a perfectly competitive market and that it sells these units at a higher price. It seems that consumers surely must be worse off under monopoly than they would be under perfect competition. This appendix shows that, in fact, consumers are harmed by the existence of a monopoly in a market that otherwise could be perfectly competitive.

Consumer Surplus

Let's first examine how economists measure the benefits that consumers gain from engaging in market transactions. Consider Figure F-1, which displays a market demand curve, D. We assume that at the present time consumers face a per-unit price of this item given by P_A. Thus, the quantity demanded of this particular product is equal to Q_A at point A on the demand curve.

Typically, we visualize the market demand curve indicating the quantities that all consumers are willing to purchase at each possible price. In addition, however, the demand curve tells us the price that consumers are willing to pay for a unit of output at various possible quantities. For instance, if consumers were to buy Q_1 units of this good, they would be willing to pay a price equal to P_1 for the last unit purchased. If they only have to pay the price P_A for each unit they buy, however, consumers gain an amount equal to $P_1 - P_A$ for the last of the Q_1 units purchased. This benefit to consumers equals the vertical distance between the demand curve and the level of the market clearing price. Economists call this vertical distance a *surplus* value to consumers from being able to consume the last of the Q_1 units at the lower, market clearing price.

FIGURE F-1

Consumer Surplus

If the per-unit price is P_A, then at point A on the demand curve D, consumers desire to purchase Q_A units. To purchase Q_1 units of this item, consumers would have been willing to pay the price P_1 for the last unit purchased but only have to pay the per-unit price P_A, so they gain a surplus equal to $P_1 - P_A$ for the last of the Q_1 units purchased. Likewise, to buy Q_2 units, consumers would have been willing to pay P_2 for the last unit purchased but only have to pay P_A, so they gain the surplus $P_2 - P_A$ for the last of the Q_2 units purchased. Summing these and all other surpluses consumers receive from purchasing all Q_A units at the price P_A yields the total consumer surplus at this price, shown by the blue-shaded area.

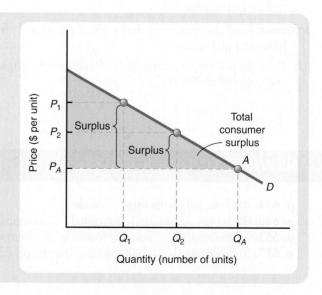

Likewise, if consumers were to purchase Q_2 units of this good, they would be willing to pay a price equal to P_2 for the last unit. Nevertheless, because they only have to pay the price P_A for each unit purchased, consumers gain an amount equal to $P_2 - P_A$. Hence, this is the surplus value associated with the last of the Q_2 units that consumers buy.

Of course, when they pay the same per-unit price P_A for every unit of this product that they purchase at point A, consumers obtain Q_A units. Thus, consumers gain surplus values—vertical distances between the demand curve and the level of the market clearing price—for each unit consumed, up to the total of Q_A units. Graphically, this is equivalent to the *entire blue-shaded area under the demand curve* but above the market clearing price. This entire area equals the total **consumer surplus,** which is the difference between the total amount that consumers *would have been willing to pay* for an item and the total amount that they *actually pay*.

Consumer surplus
The difference between the total amount that consumers would have been willing to pay for a good or service and the total amount that they actually pay.

Consumer Surplus in a Perfectly Competitive Market

Now let's consider the determination of consumer surplus in a perfectly competitive market. Take a look at the market diagram depicted in Figure F-2. In the figure, we assume that all firms producing in this market incur no fixed costs. We also assume that each firm faces the same marginal cost that does not vary with its output. These assumptions imply that the marginal cost curve is horizontal and that marginal cost is the same as average total cost at any level of output. Thus, if many perfectly competitive firms operate in this market, the horizontal summation of all firms' marginal cost curves, which is the market supply curve, is this same horizontal curve, labeled MC = ATC.

Under perfect competition, the point at which this market supply curve crosses the market demand curve, D, determines the equilibrium quantity, Q_{pc}, and the market clearing price, P_{pc}. Thus, in a perfectly competitive market, consumers obtain Q_{pc} units at the same per-unit price of P_{pc}. Consumers gain surplus values—vertical

---

FIGURE F-2

Consumer Surplus in a Perfectly Competitive Market

If all firms in this market incur no fixed costs and face the same, constant marginal costs, then the marginal cost curve, MC, and the average total cost curve, ATC, are equivalent and horizontal. Under perfect competition, the horizontal summation of all firms' marginal cost curves is this same horizontal curve, which is the market supply curve, so the market clearing price is P_{pc}, and the equilibrium quantity is Q_{pc}. The total consumer surplus in a perfectly competitive market is the striped area.

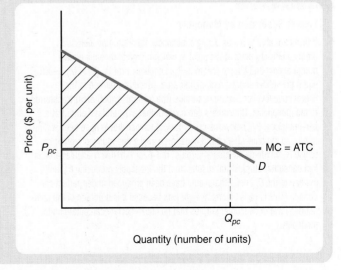

distances between the demand curve and the level of the market clearing price—for each unit consumed, up to the total of Q_{pc} units. This totals to the entire striped area under the demand curve above the market clearing price. Consumer surplus is the difference between the total amount that consumers would have been willing to pay and the total amount that they actually pay, given the market clearing price that prevails in the perfectly competitive market.

How Society Loses from Monopoly

Now let's think about what happens if a monopoly situation arises in this market, perhaps because a government licenses the firms to conduct joint operations as a single producer. These producers respond by acting as a single monopoly firm, which searches for the profit-maximizing quantity and price.

In this altered situation, which is depicted in Figure F-3, the new monopolist (which we assume is unable to engage in price discrimination—see pages 653 to 655) will produce to the point at which marginal revenue equals marginal cost. This rate of output is Q_m units. The demand curve indicates that consumers are willing to pay a price equal to P_m for this quantity of output. Consequently, as you learned in this chapter, the monopolist will produce fewer units of output than the quantity, Q_{pc}, that firms would have produced in a perfectly competitive market. The monopolist also charges a higher price than the market clearing price, P_{pc}, that would have prevailed under perfect competition.

Recall that the monopolist's maximized economic profits equal its output times the difference between price and average total cost, or the yellow-shaded rectangular area equal to $Q_m \times (P_m - ATC)$. By setting its price at P_m, therefore, the monopolist is able to transfer this portion of the competitive level of consumer surplus to itself in the form of monopoly profits. Consumers are still able to purchase Q_m units of output at a per-unit price, P_m, below the prices they would otherwise have been willing to pay. Hence, the blue-shaded triangular area above this monopoly-profit rectangle is consumer surplus that remains in the new monopoly situation.

FIGURE F-3

Losses Generated by Monopoly

If firms are able to act as a single monopoly, then the monopolist will produce only Q_m units at the point at which marginal revenue equals marginal cost and charge the price P_m. Economic profits, $Q_m \times (P_m - ATC)$, equal the yellow-shaded rectangular area, which is a portion of the competitive level of consumer surplus (the original striped area) transferred to the monopolist. Consumers can now purchase Q_m units of output at a per-unit price, P_m, below the prices they otherwise would have been willing to pay, so the blue-shaded triangular area above this monopoly-profit rectangle is remaining consumer surplus. The green-shaded triangular area is lost consumer surplus that results from the monopoly producing Q_m units instead of the Q_{pc} units that would have been produced under perfect competition. This is called a *deadweight loss* because it is a portion of the competitive level of consumer surplus that no one in society can obtain under monopoly.

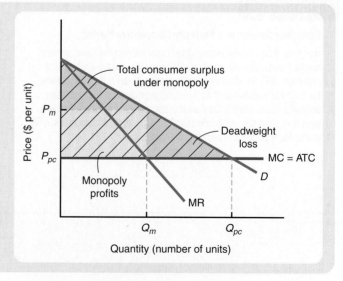

Once the monopoly is formed, what happens to the green-shaded portion of the competitive consumer surplus? The answer is that this portion of consumer surplus is lost to society. The monopolist's failure to produce the additional $Q_{pc} - Q_m$ units of output that would have been forthcoming in a perfectly competitive market eliminates this portion of the original consumer surplus. This lost consumer surplus resulting from monopoly production and pricing is called a **deadweight loss** because it is a portion of the competitive level of consumer surplus that no one in society can obtain in a monopoly situation.

Thus, as a result of monopoly, consumers are worse off in two ways. First, the monopoly profits that result constitute a transfer of a portion of consumer surplus away from consumers to the monopolist. Second, the failure of the monopoly to produce as many units as would have been produced under perfect competition eliminates consumer surplus that otherwise would have been a benefit to consumers. No one in society, not even the monopoly, can obtain this deadweight loss.

Deadweight loss
The portion of consumer surplus that no one in society is able to obtain in a situation of monopoly.

26

Monopolistic Competition

After spending an afternoon on the lots of auto dealers, you still can't decide among the available vehicle models. Should you go with one firm's MDX, or should you contemplate a competitor's MKX? One company's RSX has a nice look, but what about the RX brand offered elsewhere? The Q7 on one dealer's lot has a nice feel, but the Q45 at the dealer of a competing firm also has a number of desirable features. One company's M3 may be worth another look, but the M35 sold by another company is also attractive. Plus there are two different firms' LS models to consider. How do automakers selling similarly named yet slightly different brands determine how many vehicles to produce and what prices to charge? To find out the answer to this question, you must learn about the market structure in which today's auto producers interact, known as *monopolistic competition*.

LEARNING OBJECTIVES

After reading this chapter, you should be able to:

- Discuss the key characteristics of a monopolistically competitive industry

- Contrast the output and pricing decisions of monopolistically competitive firms with those of perfectly competitive firms

- Explain why brand names and advertising are important features of monopolistically competitive industries

- Describe the fundamental properties of information products and evaluate how the prices of these products are determined under monopolistic competition

? **DID YOU KNOW THAT** only one out of every three new soft drinks that sellers introduce ultimately remains in production longer than a few years? Every new product entry into the soft-drink market is introduced with advertising aimed at helping consumers find that they have a taste for an innovative flavor that is slightly different from every other. Nevertheless, two-thirds of soft drinks that sellers introduce into the market ultimately are withdrawn from production.

Product heterogeneity and advertising did not show up in our analysis of perfect competition. They play large roles, however, in industries that cannot be described as perfectly competitive but cannot be described as pure monopolies, either. A combination of consumers' preferences for variety and competition among producers has led to similar but *differentiated* products in the marketplace. This situation has been described as *monopolistic competition*, the subject of this chapter.

Monopolistic Competition

In the 1920s and 1930s, economists became increasingly aware that there were many industries for which both the perfectly competitive model and the pure monopoly model did not apply and did not seem to yield very accurate predictions. Theoretical and empirical research was instituted to develop some sort of middle ground. Two separately developed models of **monopolistic competition** resulted. At Harvard, Edward Chamberlin published *Theory of Monopolistic Competition* in 1933. The same year, Britain's Joan Robinson published *The Economics of Imperfect Competition*. In this chapter, we will outline the theory as presented by Chamberlin.

Monopolistic competition
A market situation in which a large number of firms produce similar but not identical products. Entry into the industry is relatively easy.

Chamberlin defined monopolistic competition as a market structure in which a relatively large number of producers offer similar but differentiated products. Monopolistic competition therefore has the following features:

1. Significant numbers of sellers in a highly competitive market
2. Differentiated products
3. Sales promotion and advertising
4. Easy entry of new firms in the long run

Even a cursory look at the U.S. economy leads to the conclusion that monopolistic competition is an important form of market structure in the United States. Indeed, that is true of all developed economies.

Number of Firms

In a perfectly competitive industry, there is an extremely large number of firms; in pure monopoly, there is only one. In monopolistic competition, there is a large number of firms, but not as many as in perfect competition. This fact has several important implications for a monopolistically competitive industry.

1. *Small share of market*. With so many firms, each firm has a relatively small share of the total market.
2. *Lack of collusion*. With so many firms, it is very difficult for all of them to get together to collude—to cooperate in setting a pure monopoly price (and output). Collusive pricing in a monopolistically competitive industry is virtually impossible. Also, barriers to entry are minor, and the flow of new firms into the industry makes collusive agreements less likely. The large number of firms makes the monitoring

and detection of cheating very costly and extremely difficult. This difficulty is compounded by differentiated products and high rates of innovation; collusive agreements are easier for a homogeneous product than for heterogeneous ones.

3. *Independence*. Because there are so many firms, each one acts independently of the others. No firm attempts to take into account the reaction of all of its rival firms—that would be impossible with so many rivals. Thus, an individual producer does not try to take into account possible reactions of rivals to its own output and price changes.

Follow the link at **www.econtoday.com/chapter26** to *Wall Street Journal* articles about real-world examples of monopolistic competition.

Product Differentiation

Product differentiation

The distinguishing of products by brand name, color, and other minor attributes. Product differentiation occurs in other than perfectly competitive markets in which products are, in theory, homogeneous, such as wheat or corn.

Perhaps the most important feature of the monopolistically competitive market is **product differentiation.** We can say that each individual manufacturer of a product has an absolute monopoly over its own product, which is slightly differentiated from other similar products. This means that the firm has some control over the price it charges. Unlike the perfectly competitive firm, it faces a downward-sloping demand curve.

Consider the abundance of brand names for toothpaste, soap, gasoline, vitamins, shampoo, and most other consumer goods and a great many services. We are not obliged to buy just one type of television set, just one type of jeans, or just one type of footwear. We can usually choose from a number of similar but differentiated products. The greater a firm's success at product differentiation, the greater the firm's pricing options.

How is a tombstone producer using a high-tech approach to product differentiation?

EXAMPLE
Differentiation at the Graveyard—High-Definition RIP

For centuries, graveyard operators have explored the limits of product differentiation. In most graveyards, tombstones come in all manner of shapes, sizes, and colors. In the latest twist on tombstone differentiation, one producer, Vidstone, offers tombstones that come equipped with solar-powered speaker systems and flat-panel screens. At a mourner's touch, a tombstone will display a photo slideshow of the deceased individual and play back audio commentaries, including recordings of the individual's voice. For situations when quiet visitations are desired, the tombstones are equipped with headphone jacks.

FOR CRITICAL ANALYSIS
What does a seller of grave markers gain from product differentiation?

Each separate differentiated product has numerous similar substitutes. This clearly has an impact on the price elasticity of demand for the individual firm. Recall that one determinant of price elasticity of demand is the availability of substitutes: The greater the number and closeness of substitutes available, other things being equal, the greater the price elasticity of demand. If the consumer has a vast array of alternatives that are just about as good as the product under study, a relatively small increase in the price of that product will lead many consumers to switch to one of the many close substitutes. Thus, the ability of a firm to raise the price above the price of *close* substitutes is very small. At a given price, the demand curve is highly elastic compared to a monopolist's demand curve. In the extreme case, with perfect competition, the substitutes are perfect because we are dealing with only one particular undifferentiated product. In that case, the individual firm has a perfectly elastic demand curve.

Sales Promotion and Advertising

Monopolistic competition differs from perfect competition in that no individual firm in a perfectly competitive market will advertise. A perfectly competitive firm, by definition, can sell all that it wants to sell at the going market price anyway. Why, then, would it spend even one penny on advertising? Furthermore, by definition, the perfect competitor is selling a product that is identical to the product that all other firms in the industry are selling. Any advertisement that induces consumers to buy more of that product will, in effect, be helping all the competitors too. A perfect competitor therefore cannot be expected to incur any advertising costs (except when all firms in an industry collectively agree to advertise to urge the public to buy more beef or drink more milk, for example).

The monopolistic competitor, however, has at least *some* monopoly power. Because consumers regard the monopolistic competitor's product as distinguishable from the products of the other firms, the firm can search for the price consumers are willing to pay for its differentiated product. Advertising, therefore, may result in increased profits. Advertising is used to increase demand and to differentiate one's product. How much advertising should be undertaken? It should be carried to the point at which the additional revenue from one more dollar of advertising just equals that one dollar of additional cost.

How are companies increasingly using odors to advertise their products?

EXAMPLE
Firms Sell with Smell

A booming new approach to advertising is to sell with smell. Increasingly, companies are developing new ways to advertise products on the basis of odor differentiation. A chain of gasoline stations in California now wafts coffee aroma at the pumps to inform consumers about the quality of the brand of coffee sold inside the stations. Similarly, Westin Hotels & Resorts now pumps the fragrance of a white tea it sells at its gift shops into the lobbies of more than 100 of its hotels. Procter & Gamble, the manufacturer of numerous household products, is experimenting with fragrance-enhanced product displays at retail outlets. Thus, firms are using product odors to try to induce consumers to discover a preference for their fragrance-differentiated products.

FOR CRITICAL ANALYSIS
How will successful advertising affect the demand for a monopolistically competitive firm's differentiated product?

Ease of Entry

For any current monopolistic competitor, potential competition is always lurking in the background. The easier—that is, the less costly—entry is, the more a current monopolistic competitor must worry about losing business.

A good example of a monopolistic competitive industry is the computer software industry. Many small firms provide different programs for many applications. The fixed capital costs required to enter this industry are small; all you need are skilled programmers. In addition, there are few legal restrictions. The firms in this industry also engage in extensive advertising in more than 150 computer publications.

Price and Output for the Monopolistic Competitor

Now that we are aware of the assumptions underlying the monopolistic competition model, we can analyze the price and output behavior of each firm in a monopolistically competitive industry. We assume in the analysis that follows that the desired product type and quality have been chosen. We further assume that the budget and the type of promotional activity have already been chosen and do not change.

The Individual Firm's Demand and Cost Curves

Because the individual firm is not a perfect competitor, its demand curve slopes downward, as in all three panels of Figure 26-1. Hence, it faces a marginal revenue curve that is also downward sloping and below the demand curve. To find the profit-maximizing rate of output and the profit-maximizing price, we go to the output where the marginal cost (MC) curve intersects the marginal revenue (MR) curve from below. That gives us the profit-maximizing output rate. Then we draw a vertical line up to the demand curve. That gives us the price that can be charged to sell exactly that quantity produced. This is what we have done in Figure 26-1. In each panel, a marginal cost curve intersects the marginal revenue curve at A. The profit-maximizing rate of output is q, and the profit-maximizing price is P.

Short-Run Equilibrium

In the short run, it is possible for a monopolistic competitor to make economic profits—profits over and above the normal rate of return or beyond what is necessary to keep that firm in that industry. We show such a situation in panel (a) of Figure 26-1. The average total cost (ATC) curve is drawn below the demand curve, d, at the profit-maximizing rate of output, q. Economic profits are shown by the blue-shaded rectangle in that panel.

Losses in the short run are clearly also possible. They are presented in panel (b) of Figure 26-1. Here the average total cost curve lies everywhere above the individual firm's demand curve, d. The losses are indicated by the red-shaded rectangle.

Just as with any market structure or any firm, in the short run it is possible to observe either economic profits or economic losses. In either case, the price does not equal marginal cost but rather is above it.

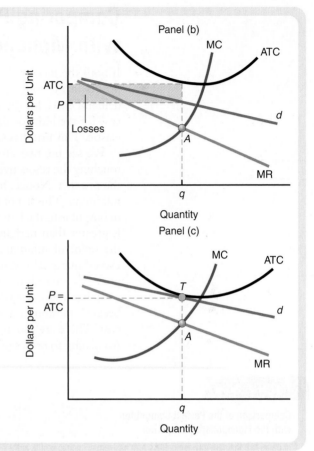

FIGURE 26-1

Short-Run and Long-Run Equilibrium with Monopolistic Competition

In panel (a), the typical monopolistic competitor is shown making economic profits. In this situation, there would be entry into the industry, forcing the demand curve for the individual monopolistic competitor leftward. Eventually, firms would find themselves in the situation depicted in panel (c), where zero *economic* profits are being made. In panel (b), the typical firm is in a monopolistically competitive industry making economic losses. In this situation, firms would leave the industry. Each remaining firm's demand curve would shift outward to the right. Eventually, the typical firm would find itself in the situation depicted in panel (c).

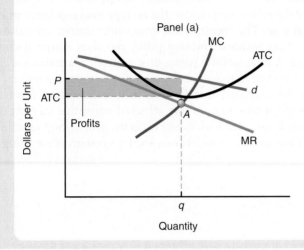

The Long Run: Zero Economic Profits

The long run is where the similarity between perfect competition and monopolistic competition becomes more obvious. In the long run, because so many firms produce substitutes for the product in question, any economic profits will disappear with competition. They will be reduced to zero either through entry by new firms seeing a chance to make a higher rate of return than elsewhere or by changes in product quality and advertising outlays by existing firms in the industry. (Profitable products will be imitated by other firms.) As for economic losses in the short run, they will disappear in the long run because the firms that suffer them will leave the industry. They will go into another business where the expected rate of return is at least normal. Panels (a) and (b) of Figure 26-1 therefore represent only short-run situations for a monopolistically competitive firm. In the long run, the individual firm's demand curve *d* will just touch the average total cost curve at the particular price that is profit maximizing for that particular firm. This is shown in panel (c) of Figure 26-1.

A word of warning: This is an idealized, long-run equilibrium situation for each firm in the industry. It does not mean that even in the long run we will observe every single firm in a monopolistically competitive industry making *exactly* zero economic profits or *just* a normal rate of return. We live in a dynamic world. All we are saying is that if this model is correct, the rate of return will *tend toward* normal—economic profits will *tend toward* zero.

Comparing Perfect Competition with Monopolistic Competition

If both the monopolistic competitor and the perfect competitor make zero economic profits in the long run, how are they different? The answer lies in the fact that the demand curve for the individual perfect competitor is perfectly elastic. Such is not the case for the individual monopolistic competitor; its demand curve is less than perfectly elastic. This firm has some control over price. Price elasticity of demand is not infinite.

We see the two situations in Figure 26-2. Both panels show average total costs just touching the respective demand curves at the particular price at which the firm is selling the product. Notice, however, that the perfect competitor's average total costs are at a minimum. This is not the case with the monopolistic competitor. The equilibrium rate of output is to the left of the minimum point on the average total cost curve where price is greater than marginal cost. The monopolistic competitor cannot expand output to the point of minimum costs without lowering price, and then marginal cost would exceed marginal revenue. A monopolistic competitor at profit maximization charges a price that exceeds marginal cost. In this respect it is similar to the monopolist.

It has consequently been argued that monopolistic competition involves *waste* because minimum average total costs are not achieved and price exceeds marginal cost. There are too many firms, each with excess capacity, producing too little output. According to critics of monopolistic competition, society's resources are being wasted.

FIGURE 26-2

Comparison of the Perfect Competitor with the Monopolistic Competitor

In panel (a), the perfectly competitive firm has zero economic profits in the long run. The price is set equal to marginal cost, and the price is P_1. The firm's demand curve is just tangent to the minimum point on its average total cost curve. With the monopolistically competitive firm in panel (b), there are also zero economic profits in the long run. The price is greater than marginal cost. The monopolistically competitive firm does not find itself at the minimum point on its average total cost curve. It is operating at a rate of output to the left of the minimum point on the ATC curve.

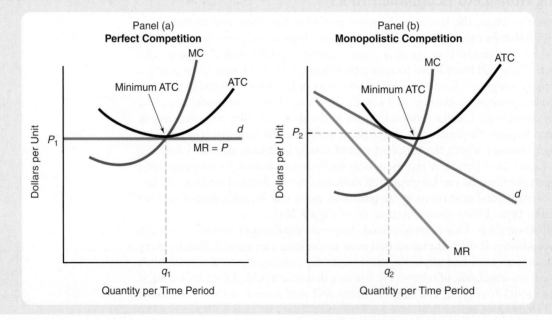

Chamberlin had an answer to this criticism. He contended that the difference between the average cost of production for a monopolistically competitive firm in an open market and the minimum average total cost represented what he called the cost of producing "differentness." Chamberlin did not consider this difference in cost between perfect competition and monopolistic competition a waste. In fact, he argued that it is rational for consumers to have a taste for differentiation; consumers willingly accept the resultant increased production costs in return for more choice and variety of output.

QUICK QUIZ   *See page 688 for the answers. Review concepts from this section in MyEconLab.*

In the _____ run, it is possible for monopolistically competitive firms to make economic profits or economic losses.

In the _____ run, monopolistically competitive firms will make _____ economic profits—that is, they will make a _____ rate of return.

Because the monopolistic competitor faces a downward-sloping demand curve, it does not produce at the minimum point on its average _____ cost curve. Hence, we say that a monopolistic competitor has higher average _____ costs per unit than a perfect competitor would have.

Chamberlin argued that the difference between the _____ _____ cost of production for a monopolistically competitive firm and the _____ average total cost at which a perfectly competitive firm would produce is the cost of producing "differentness."

Brand Names and Advertising

Because "differentness" has value to consumers, monopolistically competitive firms regard their brand names as valuable. Firms use trademarks—words, symbols, and logos—to distinguish their product brands from goods or services sold by other firms. Consumers associate these trademarks with the firms' products. Thus, companies regard their brands as valuable private (intellectual) property, and they engage in advertising to maintain the differentiation of their products from those of other firms.

Why do firms consider their brand names to be valuable?

Brand Names and Trademarks

A firm's ongoing sales generate current profits and, as long as the firm is viable, the prospect of future profits. A company's value in the marketplace, or its purchase value, depends largely on its current profitability and perceptions of its future profitability.

Table 26-1 on the following page gives the market values of the world's most valuable product brands. Each valuation depends on the market prices of shares of stock in a company times the number of shares traded. Brand names, symbols, and logos relate to consumers' perceptions of product differentiation and hence to the market values of firms. Companies protect their trademarks from misuse by registering them with the U.S. Patent and Trademark Office. Once its trademark application is approved, a company has the right to seek legal damages if someone makes unauthorized use of its brand name, spreads false rumors about the company, or engages in other underhanded activities that can reduce the value of its brand.

Advertising

To help ensure that consumers differentiate their product brands from those of other firms, monopolistically competitive firms commonly engage in advertising. Advertising

---

You Are There

Contemplate how a company seeks economic profits by creating a variety of trademarked brands of clothing and accessories in **Trademarked Differentiation at Polo Ralph Lauren Corporation,** on pages 682 and 683.

TABLE 26-1

Values of the Top Ten Brands

The market value of a company is equal to the number of shares of stock ownership issued by the company times the market price of each share. To a large extent, the company's value reflects the value of its brand.

Brand	Market Value ($ billions)
Coca-Cola	65.3
Microsoft	58.7
International Business Machines (IBM)	57.1
General Electric (GE)	51.6
Nokia	33.7
Toyota	32.1
Intel	31.0
McDonald's	29.4
Disney	29.2
Mercedes-Benz	23.6

Source: Interbrand Annual Survey, 2008.

comes in various forms, and the nature of advertising can depend considerably on the types of products that firms wish to distinguish from competing brands.

METHODS OF ADVERTISING Figure 26-3 shows the current distribution of advertising expenses among the various advertising media. Today, as in the past, firms primarily rely on two approaches to advertising their products. One is **direct marketing,** in which firms engage in personalized advertising using postal mailings, phone calls, and e-mail messages (excluding so-called banner and pop-up ads on Web sites). The other is **mass marketing,** in which firms aim advertising messages at as many consumers as possible via media such as television, newspapers, radio, and magazines.

A third advertising method is called **interactive marketing.** This advertising approach allows a consumer to respond directly to an advertising message; often the consumer is able to search for more detailed information and place an order as part of the response. Sales booths and some types of Internet advertising, such as banner ads with links to sellers' Web pages, are forms of interactive marketing.

How has the Internet search engine company Google found a way to use interactive marketing to create real-time connections between potential buyers and product sellers?

Direct marketing

Advertising targeted at specific consumers, typically in the form of postal mailings, telephone calls, or e-mail messages.

Mass marketing

Advertising intended to reach as many consumers as possible, typically through television, newspaper, radio, or magazine ads.

Interactive marketing

Advertising that permits a consumer to follow up directly by searching for more information and placing direct product orders.

E-COMMERCE EXAMPLE
Clicking a Phone Connection

Google, Inc., the operator of the Internet search engine, has developed a way to make interactive marketing nearly instantaneous. Called "click to call," the new feature is a small telephone-handset icon that appears with some merchant ads on search pages. For an immediate connection to the seller of a product, a Web surfer can type in his or her phone number and click on the icon. Then both the individual's phone and the seller's phone ring simultaneously after Google establishes a connection.

FOR CRITICAL ANALYSIS

Why do you suppose that Internet sellers often agree to pay search engines an extra commission when interactive marketing generates a sale to a Web surfer?

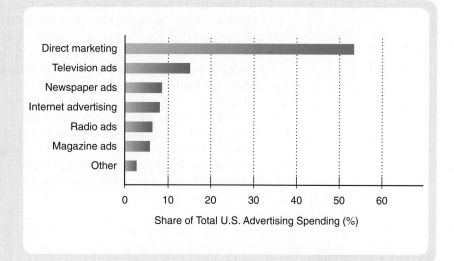

FIGURE 26-3

Distribution of U.S. Advertising Expenses
Direct marketing accounts for more than half of
advertising expenses in the United States.

*Sources: Advertising Today; Direct Marketing Today;
and Internet Advertising Bureau.*

INFORMATIONAL VERSUS PERSUASIVE ADVERTISING Some ads provide considerable information about products, while others seem designed mainly to attract a consumer's attention. The qualities and characteristics of a product determine how the firm should advertise that product. Some types of products, known as **search goods,** possess qualities that are relatively easy for consumers to assess in advance of their purchase. Clothing and music are common examples of items that have features that a consumer may assess, or perhaps even sample, before purchasing. Other products, known as **experience goods,** are products that people must actually consume before they can determine their qualities. Soft drinks, restaurant meals, and haircutting services are examples of experience goods. A third category of products, called **credence goods,** includes goods and services with qualities that might be difficult for consumers lacking expertise to assess without assistance. Products such as pharmaceuticals and services such as health care and legal advice are examples of credence goods.

The forms of advertising that firms use to market a search good are likely to be considerably different from those employed in marketing an experience good. If the item is a search good, a firm is more likely to use **informational advertising** that emphasizes the features of its product. An audio or video ad for the latest CD by a pop star is likely to include snippets of songs that are featured on the CD, which helps potential buyers assess the quality of the music. In contrast, if the product is an experience good, a firm is more likely to engage in **persuasive advertising** intended to induce a consumer to try the product and, as a consequence, discover a previously unknown taste for it. For example, a soft-drink ad is likely to depict happy people drinking the clearly identified product during breaks from enjoyable outdoor activities on a hot day. If a product is a credence good, producers commonly use a mix of informational and persuasive advertising. For instance, an ad for a pharmaceutical product commonly provides both detailed information about the product's curative properties and side effects and suggestions to consumers to ask physicians to help them assess the drug.

Search good
A product with characteristics that enable an individual to evaluate the product's quality in advance of a purchase.

Experience good
A product that an individual must consume before the product's quality can be established.

Credence good
A product with qualities that consumers lack the expertise to assess without assistance.

Informational advertising
Advertising that emphasizes transmitting knowledge about the features of a product.

Persuasive advertising
Advertising that is intended to induce a consumer to purchase a particular product and discover a previously unknown taste for the item.

ADVERTISING AS SIGNALING BEHAVIOR Recall from Chapter 24 that *signals* are compact gestures or actions that convey information. For example, high profits in an industry are signals that resources should flow to that industry. Individual companies can explicitly engage in signaling behavior. A firm can do so by establishing brand names or trademarks and then promoting them heavily. This is a signal to prospective consumers that this is a company that plans to stay in business. Before the modern age of advertising, U.S. banks needed a way to signal their soundness. To do this, they constructed large, imposing bank buildings using marble and granite. Stone structures communicated permanence. The effect was to give bank customers confidence that they were not doing business with fly-by-night operations.

When Toyota advertises its brand name heavily, it incurs substantial costs. The only way it can recoup those costs is by selling many Toyota vehicles over a long period of time. Heavy advertising in the company's brand name thereby signals to car buyers that Toyota intends to stay in business a long time and wants to develop a loyal customer base—because loyal customers are repeat customers.

QUICK QUIZ   *See page 688 for the answers. Review concepts from this section in MyEconLab.*

_____ such as words, symbols, and logos distinguish firms' products from those of other firms. Firms seek to differentiate their brands through advertising, via _____ marketing, _____ marketing, or _____ marketing.

A firm is more likely to use _____ advertising that emphasizes the features of its product if the item is a **search good** with features that consumers can assess in advance.

A firm is more likely to use _____ advertising to affect consumers' tastes and preferences if it sells an **experience good.** This is an item that people must actually consume before they can determine its qualities.

A firm that sells a _____ good, which is an item possessing qualities that consumers lack the expertise to fully assess, typically uses a combination of informational and persuasive advertising.

Information Products and Monopolistic Competition

Information product
An item that is produced using information-intensive inputs at a relatively high fixed cost but distributed for sale at a relatively low marginal cost.

A number of industries sell **information products,** which entail relatively high fixed costs associated with the use of knowledge and other information-intensive inputs as key factors of production. Once the first unit has been produced, however, it is possible to produce additional units at a relatively low per-unit cost. Most information products can be put into digital form. Good examples are computer games, computer operating systems, digital music and videos, educational and training software, electronic books and encyclopedias, and office productivity software.

Special Cost Characteristics of Information Products

Creating the first copy of an information product often entails incurring a relatively sizable up-front cost. Once the first copy is created, however, making additional copies can be very inexpensive. For instance, a firm that sells a computer game can simply make properly formatted copies of the original digital file of the game on a CD-ROM or DVD. Alternatively, the firm might make the game available for consumers to download, at a price, via the Internet.

COSTS OF PRODUCING INFORMATION PRODUCTS To think about the cost conditions faced by the seller of an information product, consider the production and sale of a computer game. The company that creates a computer game must devote many hours of labor to developing and editing its content. Each hour of labor and each unit of other resources devoted to performing this task entail an opportunity cost. The sum of all these up-front costs constitutes a relatively sizable *fixed cost* that the company must incur to generate the first copy of the computer game.

Once the company has developed the computer game in a form that is readable by personal computers, the marginal cost of making and distributing additional copies is very low. In the case of a computer game, it is simply a matter of incurring a minuscule cost to place the required files on a CD, on a DVD, or on the company's Web site.

COST CURVES FOR AN INFORMATION PRODUCT Suppose that a manufacturer decides to produce and sell a computer game. Creating the first copy of the game requires incurring a total fixed cost equal to $250,000. The marginal cost that the company incurs to place the computer game on a CD, on a DVD, or in downloadable format is a constant amount equal to $2.50 per computer game.

Figure 26-4 displays the firm's cost curves for this information product. By definition, average fixed cost is total fixed cost divided by the quantity produced and sold. Hence, the average fixed cost of the first computer game is $250,000. But if the company sells 5,000 copies, the average fixed cost drops to $50 per game. If the total quantity sold is 50,000, average fixed cost declines to $5 per game. The average fixed cost (AFC) curve slopes downward over the entire range of possible quantities of computer games.

Average variable cost equals total variable cost divided by the number of units of a product that a firm sells. If this company sells only one copy, then the total variable cost it incurs is the per-unit cost of $2.50, and this is also the average variable cost of producing one unit. Because the per-unit cost of producing the computer game is a

FIGURE 26-4

Cost Curves for a Producer of an Information Product

The total fixed cost of producing a computer game is $250,000. If the producer sells 5,000 copies, average fixed cost falls to $50 per copy. If quantity sold rises to 50,000, average fixed cost decreases to $5 per copy. Thus, the producer's average fixed cost (AFC) curve slopes downward. If the per-unit cost of producing each copy of the game is $2.50, then both the marginal cost (MC) and average variable cost (AVC) curves are horizontal at $2.50 per copy. Adding the AFC and AVC curves yields the ATC curve. Because the ATC curve slopes downward, the producer of this information product experiences short-run economies of operation.

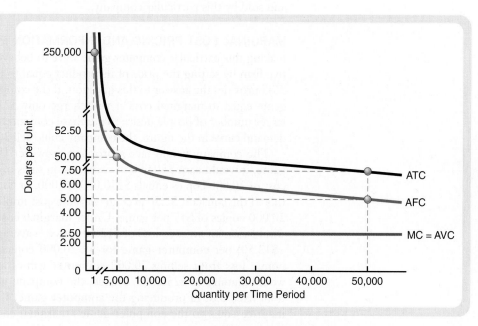

constant $2.50, producing two games entails a total variable cost of $5.00, and the average variable cost of producing two games is $5.00 ÷ 2 = $2.50. Thus, as shown in Figure 26-4, the average variable cost of producing and selling this computer game is always equal to the constant marginal cost of $2.50 per game that the company incurs. The average variable cost (AVC) curve is the same as the marginal cost (MC) curve, which for this company is the horizontal line depicted in Figure 26-4.

SHORT-RUN ECONOMIES OF OPERATION By definition, average total cost equals the sum of average fixed cost and average variable cost. The average total cost (ATC) curve for this computer game company slopes downward over its entire range.

Recall from Chapter 23 that along the downward-sloping range of an individual firm's *long-run* average cost curve, the firm experiences *economies of scale*. For the producer of an information product such as a computer game, the *short-run* average total cost curve slopes downward. Consequently, sellers of information products typically experience **short-run economies of operation.** The average total cost of producing and selling an information product declines as more units of the product are sold. Short-run economies of operation are a distinguishing characteristic of information products that sets them apart from most other goods and services.

Short-run economies of operation
A distinguishing characteristic of an information product arising from declining short-run average total cost as more units of the product are sold.

Monopolistic Competition and Information Products

In the example depicted in Figure 26-4 on the preceding page, the information product is a computer game. There are numerous computer games among which consumers can choose. Hence, there are many products that are close substitutes in the market for computer games. Yet no two computer games are exactly the same. This means that the particular computer game product sold by the company in our example is distinguishable from other competing products.

For the sake of argument, therefore, let's suppose that this company participates in a monopolistically competitive market for this computer game. Panels (a) and (b) of Figure 26-5 display a possible demand curve for the computer game manufactured and sold by this particular company.

MARGINAL COST PRICING AND INFORMATION PRODUCTS What if the company making this particular computer game were to behave *as if* it were a perfectly competitive firm by setting the price of its product equal to marginal cost? Panel (a) of Figure 26-5 provides the answer to this question. If the company sets the price of the computer game equal to marginal cost, it will charge only $2.50 per game it sells. Naturally, a larger number of people desire to purchase computer games at this price, and given the demand curve in the figure, the company could sell 20,000 copies of this game.

The company would face a problem, however. At a price of $2.50 per computer game, it would earn $50,000 in revenues on sales of 20,000 copies. The average fixed cost of 20,000 copies equals $250,000/20,000, or $12.50 per computer game. Adding this to the constant $2.50 average variable cost implies an average total cost of selling 20,000 copies of $15 per game. Under marginal cost pricing, therefore, the company would earn an average loss of $12.50 (price − average total cost = $2.50 − $15.00 = −$12.50) per computer game for all 20,000 copies sold. The company's total economic loss from selling 20,000 computer games at a price equal to marginal cost would amount to $250,000. Hence, the company would fail to recoup the $250,000 total fixed cost of producing the computer game. If the company had planned to set its price equal to the computer game's marginal cost, it would never have sought to produce the computer game in the first place!

FIGURE 26-5

The Infeasibility of Marginal Cost Pricing of an Information Product

In panel (a), if the firm with the average total cost and marginal cost curves shown in Figure 26-4 on page 679 sets the price of the computer game equal to its constant marginal cost of $2.50 per copy, then consumers will purchase 20,000 copies. This yields $50,000 in revenues. The firm's average total cost of 20,000 games is $15 per copy, so its total cost of selling that number of copies is $15 × 20,000 = $300,000. Marginal cost pricing thereby entails a $250,000 loss, which is the total fixed cost of producing the computer game.

Panel (b) illustrates how the price of the game is ultimately determined under monopolistic competition. Setting a price of $27.50 per game induces consumers to buy 10,000 copies, and the average total cost of producing this number of copies is also $27.50. Consequently, total revenues equal $275,000, which just covers the sum of the $250,000 in total fixed costs and $25,000 (the 10,000 copies times the constant $2.50 average variable cost) in total variable costs. The firm earns zero economic profits.

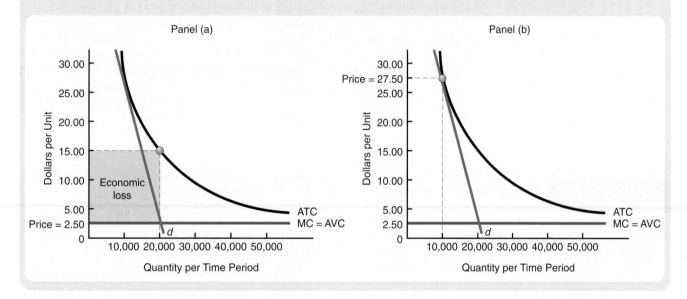

The failure of marginal cost pricing to allow firms selling information products to cover the fixed costs of producing those products is intrinsic to the nature of such products. In the presence of short-run economies of operation in producing information products, marginal cost pricing is simply not feasible in the marketplace.

Recall that marginal cost pricing is associated with perfect competition. An important implication of this example is that markets for information products cannot function as perfectly competitive markets. Imperfect competition is the rule, not the exception, in the market for information products.

THE CASE IN WHICH PRICE EQUALS AVERAGE TOTAL COST Panel (b) of Figure 26-5 illustrates how the *price* of the computer game is ultimately determined in a monopolistically competitive market. After all entry or exit from the market has occurred, the price of the computer game will equal the producer's average cost of production, including all implicit opportunity costs. The price charged for the game generates total revenues sufficient to cover all explicit and implicit costs and therefore is consistent with earning a normal return on invested capital.

Given the demand curve depicted in Figure 26-5, at a price of $27.50 per computer game, consumers are willing to purchase 10,000 copies. The company's average total cost of offering 10,000 copies for sale is also equal to $27.50 per computer game. Consequently, the price of each copy equals the average total cost of producing the game.

At a price of $27.50 per computer game, the company's revenues from selling 10,000 copies equal $275,000. This amount of revenues is just sufficient to cover the company's total fixed cost (including the opportunity cost of capital) of $250,000 and the $25,000 total variable cost it incurs in producing 10,000 copies at an average variable cost of $2.50 per game. Thus, the company earns zero economic profits.

LONG-RUN EQUILIBRIUM FOR AN INFORMATION PRODUCT INDUSTRY When the price of an information product equals average total cost, sellers charge the minimum price required to cover their production costs, including the relatively high initial costs they must incur to develop their products in the first place. Consumers thereby pay the lowest price necessary to induce sellers to provide the item.

The situation illustrated in panel (b) of Figure 26-5 on the previous page corresponds to a long-run equilibrium for this particular firm in a monopolistically competitive market for computer games. If this and other companies face a situation such as the diagram depicts, there is no incentive for additional companies to enter or leave the computer game industry. Consequently, the product price naturally tends to adjust to equality with average total cost as a monopolistically competitive industry composed of sellers of information products moves toward long-run equilibrium.

QUICK QUIZ   See page 688 for the answers. Review concepts from this section in MyEconLab.

Firms that sell **information products** experience relatively _____ fixed costs, but once they have produced the first unit, they can sell additional units at a relatively _____ per-unit cost. Consequently, the manufacturer of an information product experiences short-run _____ of _____.

If a firm sets the price of an information product equal to marginal cost, it earns only sufficient revenues to cover its

_____ costs. Engaging in marginal cost pricing, therefore, fails to cover the relatively high fixed costs of making an information product.

In a long-run equilibrium outcome under monopolistic competition, the price of an information product equals _____ _____ cost. The seller's total revenues exactly cover _____ costs, including the opportunity cost of capital.

You Are There   ▶ Trademarked Differentiation at Polo Ralph Lauren Corporation

Some call him a master of product differentiation. Ralph Lauren, chair and chief executive of Polo Ralph Lauren Corporation, offers a brand of clothing and accessories to fit every possible product niche. At one end are his Black Label collections, which are shown on New York fashion runways twice each year and feature $250 shirts and $3,000 suede jackets. His Polo brand offers accessories that include $14,000 alligator handbags.

At the other end are Lauren's Chaps clothing brands. The Chaps brands feature men's dress shirts at less than $50 and linen trousers at less than $80. They commonly are

sold at outlets of discount retailers such as Kohl and Belk. Recently, Lauren began offering moderately priced apparel and accessories at J.C. Penney under the American Label brand name. Lauren's company also operates nearly 150 Polo Ralph Lauren Factory Stores that generate about $750 million in annual sales of discounted clothing.

Between these extremes are a host of other differentiated brands: Lauren by Ralph Lauren, RRL, RLX, Polo Sport, and Rugby. The total market value of Lauren's fashion empire of brand trademarks amounts to more than $4 billion.

You Are There (cont.)

CRITICAL ANALYSIS QUESTIONS

1. How is it possible that Polo Ralph Lauren Corporation can earn short-run economic profits each time it creates a slightly differentiated brand?

2. Why do you suppose that Polo Ralph Lauren uses mass marketing that draws consumers' attention to high-priced brands when promoting the company's discount brands but primarily uses direct marketing to advertise the high-priced brands?

Issues and Applications

What's in a Name? The Auto Name Game Heats Up

CONCEPTS APPLIED

- Product Differentiation
- Monopolistic Competition
- Trademarks

The world's auto companies now offer more than 80 different groups of automobile brands. In addition, within each group, there typically are several different models from which consumers can choose. All of this product differentiation is creating a problem for automakers, however. They are running out of names to differentiate their vehicles from the pack.

The Monopolistically Competitive Auto Industry

In the auto industry, brand name groups now range across nearly the entire alphabet, from Honda's Acura model and Alfa Romeo Automobiles to Ford Motor Company's Volvo and Zimmer Motor Cars. In between, of course, are well-known brand groups such as Audi, BMW, Chevrolet, Dodge, Fiat, Isuzu, Jaguar, Land Rover, Mitsubishi, Saab, and Volkswagen. Others, such as Aston Martin Lagonda Limited, Bugatti, Holden, Morgan Motor Company, and Škoda, offer their own particularly differentiated brands.

Today's auto industry possesses all of the classic features of monopolistic competition: numerous producers, differentiated products, and considerable use of advertising. Furthermore, technological improvements in recent decades have reduced the costs of industry entry and exit. Thus, manufacturers now come and go with regularity. So do product names, as automakers continually seek to differentiate their vehicles from the similar but slightly different brands marketed by their competitors.

The Naming of Names

For decades, automakers have struggled to come up with vehicle names that differentiate their products in the minds of consumers. Henry Ford began with plain vanilla names such as "Model 1" and "Model A," but his company soon switched to more comprehensible names such as "Edsel," after a Ford family member, and the prestigious sounding "Lincoln Town Car." More recently, scientists have offered a helping hand in vehicle naming. Physicists have contributed vehicle names such as "Ion" and "Proton." Auto-naming consultants lately have been looking beyond earth to the planetary moons in our solar system for names, such as "Io," after Jupiter's volcanic moon, and "Hyperion," from Saturn's heavily crater-pockmarked moon.

In recent years, however, car companies have especially favored combinations of letters and numbers, such as the BMW X5 or the Lexus LS 450, which they have found resonate with consumers of their brands. The difficulty is that as more manufacturers have jumped on the letter-number combination bandwagon, effective product differentiation has become increasingly problematic. Currently, at least 22 of the 26 letters of the alphabet are used in the names of luxury cars. The letters L, M, S, and Z are particularly popular, although no letter tops X, which automakers now use to designate about two dozen different vehicles. Least popular is the letter O, which looks "empty" and, of course, is easily confused with zero.

A Trademark War Begins

The limited set of letters creates an additional problem when manufacturers begin combining letters and numbers. Consider, for instance, the following pairings of vehicle groups: Acura MDX and Lincoln MKX, Acura RSX and Lexus RX, Audi Q7/Q5 and Infiniti Q45, BMW M3/M5 and Infiniti M35/M45, and Lexus LS and Lincoln LS. In addition, among broad groups of vehicles, there are the Audi S Series, the Jaguar S Type, and the Mercedes S-Class.

Of course, every manufacturer seeks to build brand images in the minds of consumers and hence obtains a trademark for names of vehicle groups and models. Growing similarities among letter-number name combinations have set off a trademark free-for-all. When Infiniti ran ads in Canada announcing the arrival of a "new M," BMW charged that a trademark violation had occurred. The decision by Volkswagen's Audi to name its sport utility vehicle the Q7, taking the letter from its "quattro" all-wheel drive technology, prompted Nissan to allege that the act was a trademark violation. And when Ford's Lincoln division decided to use the MKX name, Acura's management suggested that the name infringed on its MDX trademark. Thus, as the naming wars heat up, so does the pace at which new quibbles over trademarks are erupting throughout the auto industry.

Test your understanding of this chapter by going online to **MyEconLab**.
In the Study Plan for this chapter, select Section N: News.

For Critical Analysis

1. What is the economic objective behind automakers' efforts to come up with new vehicle names on a regular basis?

2. Why do you suppose names of products such as vehicles sometimes become similar but not quite the same, just as the actual products share analogous but not quite identical features?

Web Resources

1. For links to information about the various vehicle brands marketed by the world's many auto companies, go to www.econtoday.com/chapter26.

2. Learn about how a branding consulting firm called Gravity Branding goes about helping automakers and other firms select brand names at www.econtoday.com/chapter26.

Research Project

Consider a monopolistically competitive auto company that is in an initial long-run equilibrium. What are two ways that identifying a new name for a slightly altered version of a vehicle might succeed in boosting the firm's economic profits? (Hint: What two changes in a product demand curve can enable the producer to boost the product's price?) Why are these economic profits likely to disappear in the long run?

Here is what you should know after reading this chapter. **MyEconLab** will help you identify what you know, and where to go when you need to practice.

WHAT YOU SHOULD KNOW		WHERE TO GO TO PRACTICE
The Key Characteristics of a Monopolistically Competitive Industry A monopolistically competitive industry consists of a large number of firms that sell differentiated products that are close substitutes. Firms can easily enter or exit a monopolistically competitive industry. Because monopolistically competitive firms can increase their profits if they can successfully distinguish their products from those of their rivals, they have an incentive to engage in sales promotions and advertising.	monopolistic competition, 669 product differentiation, 670	• **MyEconLab** Study Plan 26.1 • Audio introduction to Chapter 26 • Video: Characteristics of Monopolistic Competition
Contrasting the Output and Pricing Decisions of Monopolistically Competitive Firms with Those of Perfectly Competitive Firms In the short run, a monopolistically competitive firm produces output to the point at which marginal revenue equals marginal cost. The price it charges for this output can exceed both marginal cost and average total cost in the short run. The resulting economic profits induce new firms to enter the industry. In the long run, therefore, monopolistically competitive firms, like perfectly competitive firms, earn zero economic profits. In contrast to perfectly competitive firms, however, price exceeds marginal cost in the long-run equilibrium.	KEY FIGURES Figure 26-1, 673 Figure 26-2, 674	• **MyEconLab** Study Plans 26.2, 26.3 • Animated Figures 26-1, 26-2
Why Brand Names and Advertising Are Important Features of Monopolistically Competitive Industries Monopolistically competitive firms use product differentiation to boost the demand for their products. They engage in advertising, in the form of direct marketing, mass marketing, or interactive marketing. If the product is a search good with features that consumers can evaluate prior to purchase, the seller is more likely to use advertising to transmit information about product features. If the firm sells an experience good, with features that are apparent only when consumed, it is more likely to use persuasive advertising to induce consumers to discover unknown tastes. If the product is a credence good with characteristics that consumers cannot readily assess unaided, then the firm often uses a mix of informational and persuasive advertising.	direct marketing, 676 mass marketing, 676 interactive marketing, 676 search good, 677 experience good, 677 credence good, 677 informational advertising, 677 persuasive advertising, 677	• **MyEconLab** Study Plan 26.4

(continued)

 (continued)

WHAT YOU SHOULD KNOW

Properties of Information Products and Determining Their Prices Providing an information product entails incurring relatively high fixed costs but a relatively low per-unit cost for additional units of output. Hence, the average total cost curve for a firm that sells an information product slopes downward, meaning that the firm experiences economies of operation in the short run. In a long-run equilibrium, price adjusts to equality with average total cost.

information product, 678
short-run economies of operation, 680

KEY FIGURES
Figure 26-4, 679
Figure 26-5, 681

WHERE TO GO TO PRACTICE

- **MyEconLab** Study Plan 26.5
- Animated Figures 26-4, 26-5

PROBLEMS

All problems are assignable in myeconlab *. Answers to odd-numbered problems appear at the back of the book.*

26-1. Explain why the following are examples of monopolistic competition.

  a. There are a number of fast-food restaurants in town, and they compete fiercely. Some restaurants cook their hamburgers over open flames. Others fry their hamburgers. In addition, some serve broiled fish sandwiches, while others serve fried fish sandwiches. A few serve ice cream cones for dessert, while others offer frozen ice cream pies.

  b. There is a vast number of colleges and universities across the country. Each competes for top students. All offer similar courses and programs, but some have better programs in business, while others have stronger programs in the arts and humanities. Still others are academically stronger in the sciences.

26-2. Consider the diagram at the right depicting the revenue and cost conditions faced by a monopolistically competitive firm.

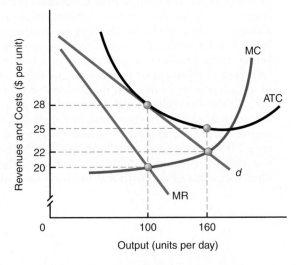

  a. What are the total revenues, total costs, and economic profits experienced by this firm?

  b. Is this firm more likely in short- or long-run equilibrium? Explain.

26-3. The following table depicts the prices and total costs a local used-book store faces. The bookstore competes with a number of similar stores, but it capitalizes on its location and the word-of-mouth reputation of the coffee it serves to its customers. Calculate the store's total revenue, total profit, marginal revenue, and marginal cost at each level of output, beginning with the first unit. Based on marginal analysis, what is the approximate profit-maximizing level of output for this business?

Output	Price per Book ($)	Total Costs ($)
0	6.00	2.00
1	5.75	5.25
2	5.50	7.50
3	5.25	9.60
4	5.00	12.10
5	4.75	15.80
6	4.50	20.00
7	4.00	24.75

26-4. Calculate total average costs for the bookstore in Problem 26-3. Illustrate the store's short-run equilibrium by plotting demand, marginal revenue, average total costs, and marginal costs. What is its total profit?

26-5. Suppose that after long-run adjustments take place in the used-book market, the business in Problem 26-3 ends up producing 4 units of output. What are the market price and economic profits of this monopolistic competitor in the long run?

26-6. It is a typical Christmas electronics shopping season, and makers of flat-panel TVs are marketing the latest available models through their own Web sites as well as via retailers such as Best Buy, Wal-Mart, and Circuit City. Each manufacturer offers its own unique versions of flat-panel TVs in differing arrays of shapes and sizes. As usual, each is hoping to maintain a stream of economic profits earned since it first introduced these most recent models late last year or perhaps just a few months before Christmas. Nevertheless, as sales figures arrive at the headquarters of companies such as Dell, Samsung, Sharp, and Sony, it is clear that most of the companies will end up earning only a normal rate of return this year.

  a. How can makers of flat-panel TVs earn economic profits during the first few months after the introduction of new models?

  b. What economic forces result in the dissipation of economic profits earned by manufacturers of flat-panel TVs?

26-7. Classify each of the following as an example of direct, interactive, and/or mass marketing.

  a. The sales force of a pharmaceutical company visits physicians' offices to promote new medications and to answer physicians' questions about treatment options and possible side effects.

  b. A mortgage company targets a list of specific low-risk borrowers for a barrage of e-mail messages touting its low interest rates and fees.

  c. An online bookseller pays fees to an Internet search engine to post banner ads relating to each search topic chosen by someone conducting a search; in part, this helps promote the bookseller's brand, but clicking on the banner ad also directs the person to a Web page displaying books on the topic that are available for purchase.

  d. A national rental car chain runs advertisements on all of the nation's major television networks.

26-8. Classify each of the following as an example of direct, interactive, and/or mass marketing.

  a. A cosmetics firm pays for full-page display ads in a number of top women's magazines.

  b. A magazine distributor mails a fold-out flyer advertising its products to the addresses of all individuals it has identified as possibly interested in magazine subscriptions.

  c. An online gambling operation arranges for pop-up ads to appear on the computer screen every time a person uses a media player to listen to digital music or play video files, and clicking on the ads directs an individual to its Web gambling site.

  d. A car dealership places advertisements in newspapers throughout the region where potential customers reside.

26-9. Categorize each of the following as an experience good, a search good, or a credence good or service, and justify your answer.

  a. A heavy-duty filing cabinet

  b. A restaurant meal

  c. A wool overcoat

  d. Psychotherapy

26-10. Categorize each of the following as an experience good, a search good, or a credence good or service, and justify your answer.

 a. Services of a carpet cleaning company

 b. A new cancer treatment

 c. Athletic socks

 d. A silk necktie

26-11. In what ways do credence goods share certain characteristics of both experience goods and search goods? How do credence goods differ from both experience goods and search goods? Why does advertising of credence goods commonly contain both informational and persuasive elements? Explain your answers.

26-12. Is each of the following items more likely to be the subject of an informational or a persuasive advertisement? Why?

 a. An office copying machine

 b. An automobile loan

 c. A deodorant

 d. A soft drink

26-13. Discuss the special characteristics of an information product, and explain the implications for a producer's short-run average and marginal cost curves. In addition, explain why having a price equal to marginal cost is not feasible for the producer of an information product.

26-14. A firm that sells e-books—books in digital form downloadable from the Internet—sells all e-books relating to do-it-yourself topics (home plumbing, gardening, and the like) at the same price. At present, the company can earn a maximum annual profit of $25,000 when it sells 10,000 copies within a year's time. The firm incurs a 50-cent expense each time a consumer downloads a copy, but the company must spend $100,000 per year developing new editions of the e-books. The company has determined that it would earn zero economic profits if price were equal to average total cost, and in this case it could sell 20,000 copies. Under marginal cost pricing, it could sell 100,000 copies.

 a. In the short run, what is the profit-maximizing price of e-books relating to do-it-yourself topics?

 b. At the profit-maximizing quantity, what is the average total cost of producing e-books?

ECONOMICS ON THE NET

Legal Services on the Internet A number of legal firms now offer services on the Internet, and in this application you contemplate features of the market for Web-based legal services.

Title: Nolo.com—Law for All

Navigation: Link to the Nolo.com site via **www.econtoday.com/chapter26.**

Application Answer the following questions.

 1. In what respects does the market for legal services, such as those provided online by Nolo.com, have the characteristics of a monopolistically competitive industry?

 2. How can providers of legal services differentiate their products? How does Nolo.com attempt to do this?

For Group Discussion and Analysis Assign groups to search the Web for at least three additional online legal firms and compare the services these firms offer. Reconvene the entire class and discuss whether it is reasonable to classify the market for online legal services as monopolistically competitive.

ANSWERS TO QUICK QUIZZES

p. 672: (i) large . . . highly; (ii) differentiated; (iii) easy
p. 675: (i) short; (ii) long . . . zero . . . normal; (iii) total . . . total; (iv) average total . . . minimum
p. 678: (i) Trademarks . . . direct . . . mass . . . interactive; (ii) informational; (iii) persuasive; (iv) credence
p. 682: (i) high . . . low . . . economies . . . operation; (ii) variable; (iii) average total . . . total

Oligopoly and Strategic Behavior

A s your jet taxis its way around the airport, you begin to notice a pattern. One company's wide-bodied airliners were manufactured by Boeing. Another company's were built by Airbus, while a third airline's jets were built by Boeing. The jet in which you happen to be seated was made by Airbus. In fact, during the past several years, these two firms—Airbus and Boeing—have been the only manufacturers of large commercial passenger jets. You might ask yourself, "How do quantities and prices get determined in a market with so few firms competing with each other?" In this chapter, you will learn the answer to this question.

LEARNING OBJECTIVES

After reading this chapter, you should be able to:

- ➤ Outline the fundamental characteristics of oligopoly

- ➤ Understand how to apply game theory to evaluate the pricing strategies of oligopolistic firms

- ➤ Identify features of an industry that help or hinder efforts to form a cartel that seeks to restrain output and earn economic profits

- ➤ Illustrate how network effects and market feedback can explain why some industries are oligopolies

- ➤ Explain why multiproduct firms selling complementary sets of products may or may not want their products to be compatible with those of their competitors

only 5 years instead of 10. Conversely, if Sam confesses, Carol's best strategy is also to confess—she'll get 5 years instead of 10. Now let's say that Sam is being interrogated and Carol doesn't confess. Sam's best strategy is still to confess, because then he goes free instead of serving two years. Conversely, if Carol is being interrogated, her best strategy is still to confess even if Sam hasn't. She'll go free instead of serving 10 years. To confess is a dominant strategy for Sam. To confess is also a dominant strategy for Carol. The situation is exactly symmetrical. So this is the prisoners' dilemma. The prisoners know that both of them will be better off if neither confesses. Yet it is in each individual prisoner's interest to confess, even though the *collective* outcome of each prisoner's pursuit of his or her own interest is inferior for both.

FOR CRITICAL ANALYSIS

Can you apply the prisoners' dilemma to the firms in a two-firm industry that agree to share market sales equally? (Hint: Think about the payoff to cheating on the market-sharing agreement.)

Applying Game Theory to Pricing Strategies

We can apply game strategy to two firms—oligopolists—that have to decide on their pricing strategy. Each can choose either a high or a low price. Their payoff matrix is shown in Figure 27-2. If they both choose a high price, each will make $6 million, but if they both choose a low price, each will make only $4 million. If one sets a high price and the other a low one, the low-priced firm will make $8 million, but the high-priced firm will make only $2 million. As in the prisoners' dilemma, in the absence of collusion, they will end up choosing low prices.

Opportunistic Behavior

In the prisoners' dilemma, it is clear that cooperative behavior—both parties standing firm without admitting to anything—leads to the best outcome for both players. But each prisoner (player) stands to gain by cheating. Such action is called **opportunistic behavior.** Our daily economic activities involve the potential for the prisoners' dilemma all the time. We could engage in opportunistic behavior. You could write a check for a purchase knowing that it is going to bounce because you have just closed

Opportunistic behavior
Actions that focus solely on short-run gains because long-run benefits of cooperation are perceived to be smaller.

FIGURE 27-2

Game Theory and Pricing Strategies

This payoff matrix shows that if both oligopolists choose a high price, each makes $6 million. If they both choose a low price, each makes $4 million. If one chooses a low price and the other doesn't, the low-priced firm will make $8 million. Unless they collude, they will end up at the low-priced solution, because charging a low price is the dominant strategy.

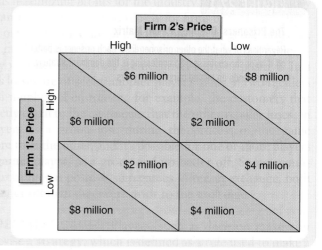

that bank account. When you agree to perform a specific task for pay, you could perform your work in a substandard way. When you go to buy an item, the seller might be able to cheat you by selling you a defective item.

In short, if all of us—sellers and buyers—engaged in opportunistic behavior all of the time, we would constantly be acting in a world of noncooperative behavior. That is not the world in which most of us live, however. Why not? Because most of us engage in *repeat transactions*. Manufacturers would like us to keep purchasing their products. Sellers would like us to keep coming back to their stores. As sellers of labor services, we all would like to keep our jobs, get promotions, or be hired away by another firm at a higher wage rate. Therefore, we engage in **tit-for-tat strategic behavior.** A consumer using a tit-for-tat strategy may, for instance, continue to purchase items from a firm each period as long as the firm provides products of the same quality and abides by any guarantees. If the firm fails in any period to provide high-quality products and honor its product guarantees, the consumer purchases items elsewhere.

Tit-for-tat strategic behavior
In game theory, cooperation that continues as long as the other players continue to cooperate.

QUICK QUIZ   *See page 713 for the answers. Review concepts from this section in MyEconLab.*

Each oligopolist has a _____ function because oligopolistic competitors are interdependent. They must therefore engage in _____ behavior. One way to model this behavior is to use **game theory.**

Games can be either **cooperative** or **noncooperative.** In a _____-sum game, one player's losses are exactly offset by

another player's gains. In a _____-sum game, all players collectively lose, perhaps one player more than the others. In a _____-sum game, the players as a group end up better off.

Decision makers in oligopolistic firms must devise a strategy. A _____ strategy is one that is generally successful no matter what actions competitors take.

The Cooperative Game: A Collusive Cartel

According to Adam Smith (1723–1790), "People of the same trade seldom meet together, even for merriment and diversion, but the conversation ends in a conspiracy against the public, or in some contrivance to raise prices." Why can firms profit from engaging in a "conspiracy against the public"? How can firms work together to create a "contrivance to raise prices"? Why does accomplishing this task turn out to be a feat only occasionally achieved by certain industries? Let's consider each of these questions in turn.

The Rationale for a Cartel and the Seeds of Its Undoing

If all the firms in an industry can find a way to cooperatively determine how much to produce to maximize their combined profits, then they can form a **cartel** and jointly act as a single producer. This means that they must *collude*. They must act together to attain the same outcome that a monopoly firm would aim to achieve: producing to the point at which marginal revenue derived from the *market* demand curve is equal to marginal cost. To do so, they must set common prices and output quotas for their members. If the firms are able to accomplish this task, they can all charge the same profit-maximizing price that a monopoly would have charged. Then they can share in the maximized monopoly profits.

Cartel
An association of producers in an industry that agree to set common prices and output quotas to prevent competition.

CUTTING BACK ON PRODUCTION Although the prospect of monopoly profits provides a strong incentive to collude, a fledgling cartel faces two fundamental problems. First, recall that a monopoly producer maximizes economic profits by restraining its production to a rate below the competitive output rate. Thus, the first problem for the members of the cartel is to determine how much each producer will restrain its output.

Once the first problem is solved, another immediately appears. As soon as all producers in the cartel begin restraining production and charging a higher price, each individual member could increase its revenues and profits by charging a slightly lower price, raising production, and selling more units. Hence, if all other cartel members honor their agreement to reduce production, one member could boost its economic profits by reneging on its promise to the rest of the cartel and increasing its production.

Enforcing a Cartel Agreement

There are four conditions that make it more likely that firms will be able to coordinate their efforts to restrain output and detect cheating, thereby reducing the temptation for participating firms to cheat:

1. *A small number of firms in the industry.* If an industry consists of only a few firms, it is easier to assess how much each firm should restrain production to yield the monopoly output and hence maximum industry profits. In addition, it is easier for each cartel member to monitor other firms' output rates for signs of cheating. For instance, when a cartel has only a few members, they might agree to keep their sales a certain percentage below pre-cartel levels. Failure to do so could be regarded as evidence of cheating.

2. *Relatively undifferentiated products.* If cartel members sell nearly homogeneous products, it is easier for them to agree on how much each firm should reduce its production. In contrast, if each firm sells a highly differentiated product, then some members can reasonably claim that the prices of their products should differ from the prices of other firms' products to reflect differences in costs of production. Thus, a firm with a differentiated product can reasonably claim that it is selling at a lower price for its differentiated good because its good is less valued by consumers—when in fact the firm may simply be using this as an excuse to cheat on the cartel agreement.

3. *Easily observable prices.* Naturally, one way to make sure that a producer is abiding by a cartel agreement is to look at the prices at which it actually sells its output. If the terms of industry transactions are publicly available, cartel members can more readily spot a firm's efforts to cheat.

4. *Little variation in prices.* If the industry's market is susceptible to frequent shifts in demand for firms' products or in prices of key inputs, the firms' prices will tend to fluctuate. Establishing a cartel agreement and monitoring cheating consequently will be more difficult. Hence, stable demand and cost conditions help a cartel form and continue to operate effectively.

Sometimes cartels use mechanisms for preventing cheating on prices that masquerade as contracts that are favorable to buyers. For example, all members of a cartel might agree to offer buyers contracts that permit a buyer to switch to another seller if that seller offers the product at a lower price. Naturally, if a customer can

Go to www.econtoday.com/chapter27 to find out from WTRG Economics how effective the Organization of Petroleum Exporting Countries has been in acting as an oil market cartel.

You Are There

To consider how cartel enforcement can affect even a small realty company, read **A Real Estate Cartel Corrals a "Cheater,"** on page 707.

Why has the Organization of Petroleum Exporting Countries (OPEC) been a successful long-term cartel?

provide evidence that a lower price is available from another firm claiming to participate in the cartel, this would constitute evidence that the other firm is cheating. In this way, cartel members use their customers to police other cartel participants!

Why Cartel Agreements Usually Break Down

Studies have shown that most cartel agreements do not last for more than 10 years. In many cases, cartel agreements break down more quickly than that. Even industries that usually satisfy the four conditions listed above have difficulty keeping cartels together over time.

One reason that cartels tend to break down is that the economic profits that existing firms obtain from holding prices above competitive levels provide an incentive for new firms to enter the market. Effectively, market entrants can earn profits by acting as a cheating cartel firm would behave. Their entry then provides incentives to cartel members to reduce their own prices and boost their production, and ultimately the cartel unravels.

Variations in overall economic activity also tend to make cartels unsustainable. During general business downturns, market demands tend to decline across all industries as consumers' incomes fall. So do profits of firms participating in a cartel. This increases the incentive for individual firms to cheat on a cartel agreement.

How are thousands of potato farmers attempting to organize a cartel?

EXAMPLE
Trying to Coordinate a Potato Cartel

Under the Capper-Volstead Act of 1922, U.S. farmers are permitted to form cooperative organizations aimed at influencing aggregate production and market prices of their crops. Today, many of the nation's 10,000 potato farmers are aiming to expand the United Potato Growers of America (UPGA), an organization dedicated to restricting potato production, pushing up potato prices, and boosting profits. The UPGA includes farmers from California, Colorado, Idaho, Oregon, Texas, Washington, and Wisconsin. Members sign an agreement to restrict their production of potatoes. The UPGA uses satellite photography and global-positioning-system technology to enforce the agreement and fines members who are caught cheating.

FOR CRITICAL ANALYSIS
Based on the discussion of the factors favoring the organization and enforcement of a cartel, what aspects of U.S. potato farming make the ultimate success of the UPGA's potato cartel more or less likely?

QUICK QUIZ   *See page 713 for the answers. Review concepts from this section in MyEconLab.*

A _____ is a group of firms in an industry that agree to set common prices and output quotas to restrict competition.

Characteristics of an industry that make it more likely that firms can coordinate efforts to restrain output and earn economic profits are a _____ number of firms, relatively _____ products, easily _____ prices, and little _____ in prices.

Factors that contribute to the breakdown of a cartel are the _____ of firms seeking the economic profits earned by the cartel members and _____ in economic activity.

Network Effects

Network effect

A situation in which a consumer's willingness to purchase a good or service is influenced by how many others also buy or have bought the item.

A feature sometimes present in oligopolistic industries is **network effects,** or situations in which a consumer's willingness to use an item depends on how many others use it. Commonplace examples are telephones and fax machines. Ownership of a phone or fax machine is not particularly useful if no one else has one, but once a number of people own a phone or fax machine, the benefits that others gain from consuming these devices increases.

In like manner, people who commonly work on joint projects within a network of fellow employees, consultants, or clients naturally find it useful to share computer files. Trading digital files is an easier process if all use common word processing and office productivity software. The benefit that each person receives from using word processing and office productivity software increases when others also use the same software.

Network Effects and Market Feedback

Industries in which firms produce goods or services subject to network effects can experience sudden surges in growth, but the fortunes of such industries can also undergo significant and sometimes sudden reversals.

Positive market feedback

A tendency for a good or service to come into favor with additional consumers because other consumers have chosen to buy the item.

POSITIVE MARKET FEEDBACK When network effects are an important characteristic of an industry's product, an industry can experience **positive market feedback.** This is the potential for a network effect to arise when an industry's product catches on with consumers. Increased use of the product by some consumers then induces other consumers to purchase the product.

Positive market feedback can affect the prospects of an entire industry. The market for Internet service provider (ISP) servers is an example. The growth of this industry has roughly paralleled the rapid growth of Internet servers worldwide. Undoubtedly, positive market feedback resulting from network effects associated with Internet communications and interactions resulted in additional people desiring to obtain access to the Internet.

Negative market feedback

A tendency for a good or service to fall out of favor with more consumers because other consumers have stopped purchasing the item.

NEGATIVE MARKET FEEDBACK Network effects can also result in **negative market feedback,** in which a speedy downward spiral of product sales occurs for a product subject to network effects. If a sufficient number of consumers cut back on their use of the product, others are induced to reduce their consumption as well, and the product can rapidly become a "has-been."

An example of an industry that has experienced negative market feedback of late is the telecommunications industry. Traditional telecommunications firms such as AT&T, WorldCom, and Sprint experienced positive market feedback during the late 1980s and early 1990s as cellphones and fax machines proliferated and individuals and firms began making long-distance phone calls from cellphones or via fax machines. Since the mid-1990s, as more people have acquired Internet access via cable and satellite Internet service providers, e-mail communications and e-mail document attachments have supplanted large volumes of phone and fax communications. For the telecommunications industry, the greater use of e-mail and e-mail attachments by some individuals induced others to follow suit. This resulted in negative market feedback that reduced the overall demand for traditional long-distance phone services.

Network Effects and Industry Concentration

In some industries, a few firms can potentially reap most of the benefits of positive market feedback. Suppose that firms in an industry sell differentiated products that are subject to network effects. If the products of two or three firms catch on, these firms will capture the bulk of the sales due to industry network effects.

A good example is the market for online auction services. An individual is more likely to use the services of an auction site if there is a significant likelihood that many other potential buyers or sellers also trade items at that site. Hence, there is a network effect present in the online auction industry, in which eBay, Amazon, and Overstock account for more than 80 percent of total sales. eBay in particular has experienced positive market feedback, and its share of sales of online auction services has increased to more than 50 percent.

Consequently, in an industry that produces and sells products subject to network effects, a small number of firms may be able to secure the bulk of the payoffs resulting from positive market feedback. In such an industry, oligopoly is likely to emerge as the prevailing market structure.

QUICK QUIZ   *See page 713 for the answers. Review concepts from this section in MyEconLab.*

_____ effects exist when a consumer's demand for an item depends in part on how many other consumers also use the product.

_____ market feedback arises if consumption of a product by a sufficient number of individuals induces others to purchase it. _____ market feedback can take place if

a falloff in usage of a product by some consumers causes others to stop purchasing the item.

In an industry with differentiated products subject to **network effects,** an oligopoly may arise if a few firms can reap most of the sales _____ resulting from _____ market feedback.

Product Compatibility in Multiproduct Oligopolies Facing Network Effects

In addition to helping make industries more concentrated, network effects influence decisions that firms make regarding **product compatibility.** That is, firms must take into account the longer-term implications of network effects when deciding whether to offer products that function when used together with complementary products of competitors.

Product compatibility
The capability of a product sold by one firm to function together with another firm's complementary product.

Why Firms Face Product Compatibility Issues

Should a company share the computer code for its new office productivity software program with another software producer so that consumers will be able to use either firm's program, separately or together? Is the answer to this question altered if both companies sell hardware products that consumers regard as complements to their software products? How does the potential existence of network effects further complicate the issue? In today's information-technology-intensive economy, a growing number of firms must address these kinds of questions regularly.

THE BETA-VHS BATTLE Questions about product compatibility are not new. More than two decades ago, when the possibility of recording television shows and renting and selling movies for home viewing was a new idea, firms battled over two video-cassette formats known as Beta and VHS. The Beta format was the brainchild of Sony, which also offered a line of videocassette recorders and players compatible only with the Beta videocassette format. In the meantime, another firm, JVC, developed the rival VHS format, a bulkier videocassette that could hold more videotape. VHS videocassettes had room for longer movies and more recorded programming than Beta videocassettes.

Soon people were sharing lengthy VHS videotapes of children at play, complete sporting events, and the like with friends and relatives—as long as they had access to VHS players, which other consumer electronics firms were willing to produce. Within a few years, Sony realized that it had erred by opting to make its products compatible only with Beta videocassettes. Sony's decision had harmed its sales of video recorders and players and, ultimately, its sales of videocassettes. Eventually, Sony discontinued the production of all Beta-format products and switched to the VHS format.

WHY PRODUCT COMPATIBILITY MATTERS The Beta-VHS format battle involved three key economic features. First, the products involved—lines of videocassettes, recorders, players, and related accessories—were items that consumers regarded as *complementary*. Second, these complementary goods were manufactured and sold by **multiproduct firms,** or firms that produce more than one product. Third, network effects were present. Because people shared their videotapes, the fact that most people preferred the VHS longer-play format led others to prefer VHS over Beta as well.

Multiproduct firm
A firm that produces and sells two or more different items.

These features figure in many interactions in oligopolistic industries today, as new information technologies have led to the development of many complementary products sold by multiproduct firms and subject to network effects. In such situations, firms face a crucial product compatibility issue. Should a firm that produces two or more products that consumers regard as complements sell each one in a form that allows consumers to use the products only as a set? Or should the firm sell the items in a form that permits consumers to utilize each product individually, perhaps in conjunction with a complementary product offered by a competing firm?

DIFFERENT COMPATIBILITY DECISIONS, DIFFERENT PAYOFFS In the battle between Beta and VHS formats, Sony opted for incompatibility with an intent to earn higher economic profits. What actually happened was that the demand for its VHS-incompatible products eventually disappeared as consumers substituted away from Beta videocassettes into VHS videocassettes. Consequently, Sony's profits from its video-related businesses plummeted, and the firm ultimately had to completely abandon its Beta-format video product line.

Does this mean that multiproduct firms should always make complementary products compatible with those of other firms? The answer is no. Sometimes firms lose, as Sony did, from making complementary products incompatible with those offered by other firms. Other times, however, firms reap exactly the same types of gains that Sony sought. Consider, for instance, Apple's experience with its iPod products during the 2000s. Apple offered a number of complementary products, such as iTunes downloadable music products, downloadable videos, and various accessories, in forms that were incompatible with products sold by other firms. In contrast to Sony, Apple boosted its profits by making its complementary products incompatible with those of its competitors.

While VHS videocassettes won the format war over Beta cassettes and machines, what happened with respect to a similar "war" between HD-DVDs and Blu-ray formats?

Product Compatibility and Network Effects

The fact that Sony and Apple experienced such different outcomes indicates that multiproduct firms could experience either losses or gains by offering their products in forms that are incompatible with those sold by competing firms. Before we consider how firms' product compatibility choices affect oligopoly outcomes, let's consider why network effects matter to individual firms.

HOW A FIRM CAN GAIN FROM OPTING FOR INCOMPATIBILITY To see how a multiproduct firm might gain from making the complementary products it sells incompatible with those of competitors, again consider Apple's strategy of intentionally making its iPod-related product line incompatible with many other items sold by competitors. Alongside the iPod, Apple—or firms that paid Apple licensing royalties—offered a variety of complementary speaker systems, memory storage devices, and accessories.

For Apple, the main objective of opting for incompatibility was to sharply differentiate its own line of products. This tended to reduce price elasticities of demand for Apple's complementary product set. In addition, when its iPod-related products experienced positive market feedback, demand for these products increased. Consequently, Apple was able to charge higher prices for its entire line of complementary iPod products, and the firm's profits soared.

HOW A FIRM CAN LOSE FROM MAKING INCOMPATIBLE PRODUCTS Given how well product incompatibility turned out for Apple, why did things go wrong for Sony back in the days of videocassettes? After all, Sony also sought to differentiate its complementary Beta video products by making them incompatible with the products offered by competing firms.

The answer is that whereas Apple experienced positive market feedback in the downloadable-media industry, Sony's Beta-format video products suffered *negative* market feedback in the videocassette industry. Sony certainly succeeded in differentiating its products by making them incompatible with those offered by competitors. As more consumers opted for the larger-capacity VHS videocassettes, however, a bandwagon effect led other consumers to choose VHS as well, which led to a wave of substitutions away from Sony's Beta-format video products.

Why is Comcast developing what amounts to its own separate Internet?

E-COMMERCE EXAMPLE
Comcast Builds a Mini Internet for Its Online Programming

During the past two decades, the cable TV industry has been the predominant format for transmitting TV programming into homes and offices. Today, however, new formats for TV transmission have emerged. Telephone companies have begun offering TV transmissions on high-speed DSL lines, and TV networks such as CBS have begun experimenting with online services that transmit programming via the Internet.

One cable TV operator, Comcast, has responded by seeking to make its TV programming format incompatible with those of competitors. It has employed 400 software engineers to construct what amounts to a walled-off, TV version of the Internet. Within this exclusive "mini Internet" of TV programming, Comcast is placing movies, archived TV programs, and various interactive features including a search engine. Thus, Comcast is hoping that if there are network effects in the provision of TV programming, it will be able to internalize those effects with its own customers via positive market feedback within its own "mini Internet."

FOR CRITICAL ANALYSIS
Why do you suppose that some Comcast stockholders have expressed concern that the company's strategy might ultimately expose it to negative market feedback?

Product Compatibility, Oligopolies, and Prices

Of course, oligopolistic multiproduct firms cannot make choices about product compatibility in isolation from the decisions of their competitors. In light of their strategic dependence, they must also take into account the reactions of other firms.

HOW INDUSTRY PRODUCT INCOMPATIBILITY CAN EMERGE To see how *industry* outcomes with regard to product compatibility can differ, begin by taking a look at Figure 27-3. This figure displays a payoff matrix for an industry composed of two multiproduct firms, "Firm 1" and "Firm 2," which are contemplating offering sets of complementary products in one of two incompatible formats, "Format A" or "Format B." We also assume that, at the outset, neither firm believes that network effects are likely to prove to be important to the industry in which they operate.

If both firms offer their products in Format A, each firm anticipates that the resulting homogeneity of their product lines will yield only $1 million in profits during the relevant period. If both firms offer their products in Format B, each expects to earn only $2 million in profits. If Firm 1 differentiates its product set by offering it in Format B while Firm 2 selects Format A, then each firm anticipates earning $3 million in profits. If Firm 1 uses Format A while Firm 2 selects Format B, then each firm expects to earn $4 million in profits. Firm 1, therefore, will opt for Format A, and Firm 2 will opt for Format B. Thus, the firms favor mutual incompatibility that differentiates their product sets and yields the highest anticipated profits. Each firm opts to go its separate way with its own different format, which is why in game theory the configuration of payoffs depicted in Figure 27-3 is often known as the *Tweedle Dee–Tweedle Dum game*.

THE COMPLICATING IMPACTS OF NETWORK EFFECTS If both of the firms with the payoffs depicted in Figure 27-3 are correct in assuming that network effects are minuscule in their industry, then they can achieve anticipated profit levels. What happens if their shared supposition about network effects is incorrect? Once the presence of network effects is discovered, Firm 1 will fight for Format A to be the industry standard, and Firm 2 will battle for Format B. That is, *after* opting for an incompatible format, each firm actually is likely to expend more resources than previously anticipated to promote its format and achieve positive market feedback.

For instance, suppose that Firms 1 and 2 manufacture videogame systems and various complementary accessories. After the firms have opted for incompatible formats,

FIGURE 27-3

Payoffs Yielding a Product Format Conflict

If two firms face the depicted payoff matrix, known as a *Tweedle Dee–Tweedle Dum game* situation, Firm 1 expects to earn the highest profits if it adopts Format A, and Firm 2 anticipates earning the highest profits if it opts for Format B. Hence, the firms choose these incompatible product formats.

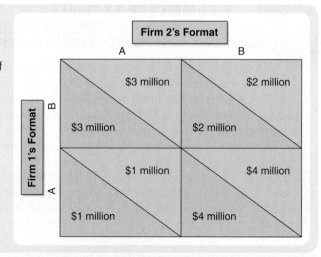

consumers unexpectedly develop an interest in remote multiplayer gaming via the Internet. Each firm may respond by offering inducements to creators of multiplayer games to produce games compatible only with its selected format. Each may also "pre-announce" forthcoming complementary products in its selected format that allow multi-player gaming in an effort to discourage consumers from purchasing items in the other firm's product line. Either of these actions would push up each firm's operating costs. In addition, the firms may try to induce consumers to opt for their product formats by cut-ting prices, which would reduce the competitors' revenues. Thus, during the current period, both firms likely will earn lower profits than they anticipated when they selected their formats. If one firm ultimately loses the battle to become the industry standard, its profits likely will plummet, much as Sony's did when it lost the Beta-VHS battle. The profits of its competitor will then rise, much as Apple's profits soared when its iPod product line became a predominant downloadable-media system during the 2000s.

WHY PRODUCT COMPATIBILITY MIGHT BE AN INDUSTRY OUTCOME Now consider a different industry situation, depicted by the payoff matrices in Figure 27-4, in which Firm 1 and Firm 2 recognize in advance that network effects will result in one of the two formats winning out over the other with consumers. Panel (a) dis-plays the simplest possible outcome, in which Firm 1 and Firm 2 each anticipate earning the most profits if both choose the same format. In this example, both firms earn the highest profits, $4 million during the relevant period, by mutually adopt-ing the compatible Format A.

Panel (b) of Figure 27-4 depicts a more complicated situation. It is still true that both firms earn the most profits if they each choose the same format. Nevertheless, Firm 1 earns the highest profits if the firms mutually adopt the compatible Format A, but Firm 2 earns the most profits if the firms agree to choose Format B. The fact that

---

FIGURE 27-4

Payoffs Inducing Firms to Seek to Coordinate Product Formats

If two firms face the payoff matrix in panel (a), then both firms earn the highest profits by utilizing Format A, and they will gain by coordinating their choice of this compatible product format. In panel (b), both firms earn greater profits if their products have the same formats. Nevertheless, Firm 1 earns the highest profits if both firms opt for Format A, while Firm 2 earns the highest profits if both agree to use Format B. Hence, both parties wish to coordinate but may not agree on how to do so, which is why this game situation is called the *Battle of the Sexes*.

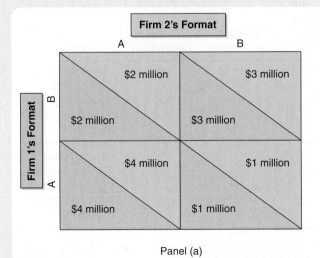

Panel (a)

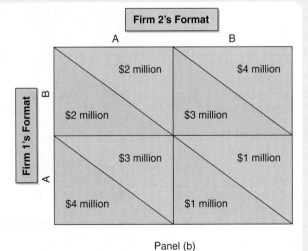

Panel (b)

each party desires to coordinate with the other but agreement is not immediately forthcoming is why in game theory this payoff configuration is often referred to as the *Battle of the Sexes*.

As with the payoff matrix in Figure 27-3 on page 704, one result could be a battle between the firms over which format to adopt. Another possible result, given that both firms recognize the role of network effects, is that the firms might work together to develop one common format and arrange to share the profits.

QUICK QUIZ *See page 713 for the answers. Review concepts from this section in MyEconLab.*

Product compatibility is the capability of an item sold by one firm to function with another firm's _____ product.

Product compatibility is an industrywide issue for _____ firms selling two or more complementary products subject to _____ effects.

An industry battle between incompatible product formats can occur if competing firms selling sets of _____ products fail to take into account _____ effects.

Comparing Market Structures

Now that we have looked at perfect competition, pure monopoly, monopolistic competition, and oligopoly, we are in a position to compare the attributes of these four different market structures. We do this in summary form in Table 27-3, in which we compare the number of sellers, their ability to set price, and the degree of product differentiation and also give some examples of each of the four market structures.

TABLE 27-3

Comparing Market Structures

Market Structure	Number of Sellers	Unrestricted Entry and Exit	Ability to Set Price	Long-Run Economic Profits Possible	Product Differentiation	Nonprice Competition	Examples
Perfect competition	Numerous	Yes	None	No	None	None	Agriculture, roofing nails
Monopolistic competition	Many	Yes	Some	No	Considerable	Yes	Toothpaste, toilet paper, soap, retail trade
Oligopoly	Few	Partial	Some	Yes	Frequent	Yes	Recorded music, college textbooks
Pure monopoly	One	No (for entry)	Considerable	Yes	None (product is unique)	Yes	Some electric companies, some local telephone companies

You Are There **A Real Estate Cartel Corrals a "Cheater"**

Sharon Jebavy, owner of HomeWise Real Estate Services in Columbus, Ohio, recently offered to include listings of homes for sale on the main Ohio real estate database. Customers had to pay a flat fee of $500 to be listed.

Although the number of Jebavy's customers nearly tripled, she soon found herself in hot water with the group of Ohio real estate brokers that operates the database. According to this group, Jebavy and other "discount real estate agents" fail to provide the "minimum services" required of real estate agents, who typically receive commission rates of 2 to 3 percent. Jebavy's offense, according to the brokers' group, was that she charged her customers a flat $500 fee to list their homes on the database even though these home sellers were not utilizing any additional services from Jebavy. Thus, Jebavy was charging a price for a key service that was "too low"—and profiting from the increase in customers that her low price attracted. In short, the brokers' group felt that Jebavy had cheated on the agreement under which she obtained access to the database—which in classic cartel

fashion required her to charge a predetermined price and restrict her service output. In the end, to maintain access to the database, Jebavy had to pay $6,250 in fines to the brokers' group and restrict the range of services she offered to home sellers.

CRITICAL ANALYSIS QUESTIONS

1. Why do you suppose that the Ohio real estate brokers' group was unhappy when Jebavy set her price to a flat fee of $500 and nearly tripled the volume of customers she served as a result?

2. Demand for real estate brokers' services in Ohio had declined sharply in the months preceding Jebavy's price cut and increase in customer volume. Why does this help explain why she had an increased incentive to "cheat" on the real estate cartel agreement governing use of the Ohio real estate database?

Issues and Applications

Oligopoly in the Global Commercial Aircraft Industry

CONCEPTS APPLIED

- ▶ Oligopoly
- ▶ Strategic Dependence
- ▶ Reaction Function

There are a large number of aircraft manufacturers around the globe. Nevertheless, only two firms—the European firm Airbus and the U.S. company Boeing—produce large commercial aircraft used by airline companies to transport more than 140 people at a time. Thus, the industry specializing in production of this type of aircraft is only one firm short of being a monopoly and hence is unambiguously oligopolistic.

The "Duopoly" in the Market for Large Commercial Aircraft

When only two firms comprise an industry, economists call the industry a *duopoly*. Figure 27-5 displays the market shares of Airbus and Boeing since 1996. As the figure indicates, because these two firms constitute the entire industry, a rise in the market share of one firm comes directly at the expense of the other firm.

Strategic dependence is as pronounced as it can possibly be in a duopoly setting. One firm's decisions unmistakably affect the outcomes experienced by the other firm. Thus, in the market for large commercial aircraft, Boeing's reaction function depends solely on the decisions made by managers at Airbus. Likewise, the reaction function for Airbus reflects managerial choices made only at Boeing.

Dimensions of Strategic Dependence: Airbus versus Boeing

In light of the one-on-one nature of the strategic dependence between Airbus and Boeing, the reaction functions of the two firms involve more than just the prices of their products. Considerable nonprice competition occurs as well. Key choices for both firms involve features of the jet aircraft that they produce, which each company adjusts to distinguish its planes from those of the other firm.

In recent years, Airbus and Boeing have even competed to top one another in the efficiency with which their planes can be recycled when they become obsolete. In light of increased global efforts to deplete fewer nonrenewable resources, each company is striving to convince customers that it is more adept at transforming aged aircraft into reusable materials. In 2007, Boeing claimed that more than 90 percent of the components in its old jets could be reclaimed for reuse. Airbus scoffed at that figure, arguing that available technology permitted only 60 percent of any large commercial aircraft to be recycled. Nevertheless, Airbus has launched its own effort to be able to recycle 95 percent of its obsolete jetliners by 2015. Thus, recycling capabilities have become one of a long list of nonprice elements of competition as each firm constantly vies to boost its market share at the other firm's expense.

FIGURE 27-5

Market Shares in Global Sales of Large Commercial Airliners

For more than a decade, Airbus and Boeing have been the only producers of large commercial aircraft for use by airline companies, so each year the sum of the two companies' market shares equals 100 percent.

Source: U.S. Department of Transportation.

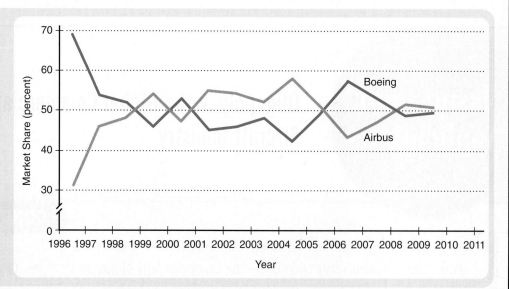

Test your understanding of this chapter by going online to **MyEconLab**.
In the Study Plan for this chapter, select Section N: News.

For Critical Analysis

1. In the most recent year for which data are plotted in Figure 27-5, what was the approximate one-firm concentration ratio in the large-commercial-aircraft industry, and what was this industry's two-firm concentration ratio?

2. Why are oligopolists more likely to engage in nonprice competition when their products are differentiated?

Web Resources

1. For a discussion of recent ways in which Airbus and Boeing have sought to differentiate their products, go to www.econtoday.com/chapter27.

2. To learn about the potential entry of new competitors that might end the duopoly situation in the market for large commercial aircraft, go to www.econtoday.com/chapter27.

Research Project

Suppose that Airbus and Boeing were to enter into secret discussions to form a cartel in the market for large commercial aircraft. Assuming that the two companies could find a way to hide their collusion, evaluate whether the features of their industry make formation and enforcement of a cartel agreement relatively easy or relatively difficult.

Here is what you should know after reading this chapter. MyEconLab will help you identify what you know, and where to go when you need to practice.

WHAT YOU SHOULD KNOW

WHERE TO GO TO PRACTICE

The Fundamental Characteristics of Oligopoly Economies of scale, certain barriers to entry, and horizontal mergers among firms that sell similar products can result in an oligopoly, a situation in which a few firms produce the bulk of an industry's total output. To measure the extent to which a few firms account for an industry's production and sales, economists calculate concentration ratios, which are the percentages of total sales or total production by the top handful of firms in an industry. Strategic dependence is an important characteristic of oligopoly. One firm's decisions concerning price, product quality, or advertising can bring about responses by other firms. Thus, one firm's choices can affect the prices charged by other firms in the industry.

oligopoly, 690
strategic dependence, 690
vertical merger, 691
horizontal merger, 691
concentration ratio, 692

- **MyEconLab** Study Plan 27.1
- Audio introduction to Chapter 27

Applying Game Theory to Evaluate the Pricing Strategies of Oligopolistic Firms Game theory is the analytical framework that economists apply to evaluate how two or more individuals, companies, or nations compete for payoffs that depend on the strategies that others employ. When firms work together for a common objective such as maximizing industry profits, they participate in cooperative games, but when they cannot work together, they engage in noncooperative games. One important type of game often applied to oligopoly situations is the prisoners' dilemma, in which the inability to cooperate in determining prices of their products can cause firms to choose lower prices than they otherwise would prefer.

reaction function, 693
game theory, 694
cooperative game, 694
noncooperative game, 694
zero-sum game, 694
negative-sum game, 694
positive-sum game, 695
strategy, 695
dominant strategies, 695
prisoners' dilemma, 695
payoff matrix, 695

- **MyEconLab** Study Plan 27.2
- Video: Opportunistic Behavior
- Animated Figures 27-1, 27-2

(*continued*)

 *(continued)*

WHAT YOU SHOULD KNOW		WHERE TO GO TO PRACTICE
	opportunistic behavior, 696 tit-for-tat strategic behavior, 697 **KEY FIGURES** Figure 27-1, 695 Figure 27-2, 696	
Industry Features That Contribute to or Detract from Efforts to Form a Cartel A cartel is an organization of firms in an industry that collude to earn economic profits by producing a combined output consistent with monopoly profit maximization. Four conditions make a collusive cartel agreement easier to create and enforce: (1) a small number of firms in the industry, (2) relatively undifferentiated products, (3) easily observable prices, and (4) little variation in prices. Even when these conditions are satisfied, economic profits earned by a cartel attract entry by competing firms, which tends to undermine the cartel. In addition, downturns in general economic conditions can place pressure on cartel members to expand output beyond agreed levels. This also tends to destabilize a cartel agreement.	cartel, 697	• **MyEconLab** Study Plan 27.3
Why Network Effects and Market Feedback Encourage Oligopoly Network effects arise when a consumer's demand for a good or service is affected by how many other consumers also use the item. There is positive market feedback when enough people consume a product to induce others to purchase it as well. Negative market feedback occurs when decreased purchases of a good or service by some consumers give others an incentive to stop buying the item. Oligopoly can develop in an industry with differentiated products subject to network effects because a few firms may be able to capture most of the growth in demand induced by positive market feedback.	network effect, 700 positive market feedback, 700 negative market feedback, 700	• **MyEconLab** Study Plans 27.4 • Video: Price Leadership and Price Wars
Why Multiproduct Firms Selling Complementary Sets of Products May or May Not Wish for Their Products to Be Compatible with Those of Competitors Product compatibility refers to the capability of an item sold by one firm to function with another firm's complementary product. A multiproduct firm selling two or more complementary products may opt for incompatibility with competing firms' products if it anticipates that lack of compatibility will differentiate its product set and maximize its profits. If network effects are important in the	product compatibility, 701 multiproduct firm, 702 **KEY TABLE** Table 27-3, 706	• **MyEconLab** Study Plans 27.5, 27.6 • Animated Table 27-3

(continued)

PROBLEMS

All problems are assignable in ✗ **myecon**lab . *Answers to odd-numbered problems appear at the back of the book.*

27-1. Suppose that the distribution of sales within an industry is as shown in the table.

Firm	Share of Total Market Sales
A	15%
B	14
C	12
D	11
E	10
F	10
G	8
H	7
All others	13
Total	100%

   a. What is the four-firm concentration ratio for this industry?

   b. What is the eight-firm concentration ratio for this industry?

27-2. The table at the right shows recent worldwide market shares of producers of inkjet printers.

   a. In this year, what was the four-firm concentration ratio in the inkjet-printer industry?

   b. In this year, what was the seven-firm concentration ratio in the inkjet-printer industry?

Firm	Share of Worldwide Market Sales
Brother	3%
Canon	17
Dell	6
Epson	18
Hewlett-Packard	41
Lexmark	13
Samsung	1
Other	1

27-3. Characterize each of the following as a positive-sum game, a zero-sum game, or a negative-sum game.

   a. Office workers contribute $10 each to a pool of funds, and whoever best predicts the winners in a professional sports playoff wins the entire sum.

   b. After three years of fighting with large losses of human lives and materiél, neither nation involved in a war is any closer to its objective than it was before the war began.

   c. Two collectors who previously owned incomplete and nearly worthless sets of trading cards exchange several cards, and as a result both end up with completed sets with significant market value.

27-4. Characterize each of the following as a positive-sum game, a zero-sum game, or a negative-sum game.

  a. You play a card game in your dorm room with three other students. Each player brings $5 to the game to bet on the outcome, winner take all.

  b. Two nations exchange goods in a mutually beneficial transaction.

  c. A thousand people buy $1 lottery tickets with a single payoff of $800.

27-5. Last weekend, Bob attended the university football game. At the opening kickoff, the crowd stood up. Bob therefore realized that he would have to stand up as well to see the game. For the crowd (not the football team), explain the outcomes of a cooperative game and a noncooperative game. Explain what Bob's "tit-for-tat strategic behavior" would be if he wished to see the game.

27-6. Consider two strategically dependent firms in an oligopolistic industry, Firm A and Firm B. Firm A knows that if it offers extended warranties on its products but Firm B does not, it will earn $6 million in profits, and Firm B will earn $2 million. Likewise, Firm B knows that if it offers extended warranties but Firm A does not, it will earn $6 million in profits, and Firm A will earn $2 million. The two firms know that if they both offer extended warranties on their products, each will earn $3 million in profits. Finally, the two firms know that if neither offers extended warranties, each will earn $5 million in profits.

  a. Set up a payoff matrix that fits the situation faced by these two firms.

  b. What is the dominant strategy for each firm in this situation? Explain.

27-7. Take a look back at the data regarding the inkjet-printer industry in Problem 27-2, and answer the following questions.

  a. Suppose that consumer demands for inkjet printers, the prices of which are readily observable in office supply outlets and at Internet sites, are growing at a stable pace. Discuss whether circumstances are favorable to an effort by firms in this industry to form a cartel.

  b. If the firms successfully establish a cartel, why will there naturally be pressures for the cartel to break down, either from within or from outside?

27-8. Consider the following payoff matrix. Firm 1 and Firm 2 are seeking to choose between Format A

and Format B for their products, under the assumption that there are *not* any network effects. Will they desire to produce and sell compatible product formats?

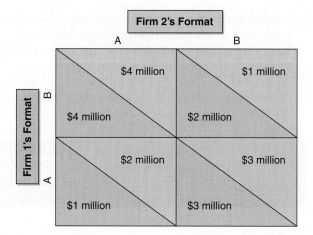

27-9. Consider the payoff matrix below, in which Firm 1 and Firm 2 seek to choose between product Format A and product Format B, under the assumption that there *are* network effects. Will they desire to produce and sell compatible product formats?

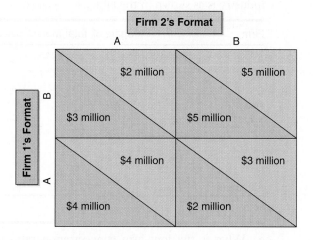

27-10. Explain why network effects can cause the demand for a product *either* to expand *or* to contract relative to what it would be if there were no network effects.

27-11. List three products that you think are subject to network effects. For each product, indicate whether, in your view, all or just a few firms within the industry that produces each product experience market feedback effects. In your view, are any market feedback effects in these industries currently positive or negative?

ECONOMICS ON THE NET

Current Concentration Ratios in U.S. Manufacturing Industries As you learned in this chapter, economists sometimes use concentration ratios to evaluate whether industries are oligopolies. In this application, you will make your own determination using the most recent data available.

Title: Concentration Ratios in Manufacturing

Navigation: Follow the link at **www.econtoday.com/chapter27** to get to the U.S. Census Bureau's report on Concentration Ratios in Manufacturing.

Application Answer the following questions.

1. Select the report for the most recent year. Find the four-firm concentration ratios for the following industries: fluid milk (311511), women's and girls' cut & sew dresses (315233), envelopes (322232), electronic computers (334111).

2. Which industries are characterized by a high level of competition? Which industries are characterized by a low level of competition? Which industries qualify as oligopolies?

3. Name some of the firms that operate in the industries that qualify as oligopolies.

For Group Study and Analysis Discuss whether the four-firm concentration ratio is a good measure of competition. Consider some of the firms you named in item 3. Do you consider these firms to be "competitive" in their pricing and output decisions? Consider the four-firm concentration ratio for ready-mix concrete (327320). Do you think that on a local basis, this industry is competitive? Why or why not?

ANSWERS TO QUICK QUIZZES

p. 693: (i) small . . . interdependent; (ii) economies . . . mergers; (iii) Vertical; (iv) Horizontal; (v) percentage . . . sales

p. 697: (i) reaction . . . strategic; (ii) zero . . . negative . . . positive; (iii) dominant

p. 699: (i) cartel; (ii) small . . . undifferentiated . . . observable . . . variation; (iii) entry . . . variations

p. 701: (i) Network; (ii) Positive . . . Negative; (iii) gains . . . positive

p. 706: (i) complementary; (ii) multiproduct . . . network; (iii) complementary . . . network

28

Regulation and Antitrust Policy in a Globalized Economy

The term *sticker shock* has come into widespread use to describe consumers' surprise and dismay about higher-than-anticipated prices for an item. Of course, the term originally referred to consumers' surprise when confronted with prices listed on stickers attached to the windows of new and used vehicles on the lots of auto dealers. Today, after consumers have agreed on a final purchase price for a vehicle, they often experience another surprise: document-fee shock. In Nevada, auto dealers regularly charge $400 or more to process the documents required to finalize the sale of a vehicle. In Florida and Georgia, document fees range upward from $600. Why are document fees so high? As you will learn in this chapter, auto dealers' document fees are just one example of a cost of government regulation. In the auto market, an increased regulatory burden on sellers has boosted this cost of purchasing a vehicle.

LEARNING OBJECTIVES

After reading this chapter, you should be able to:

➤ Distinguish between economic regulation and social regulation

➤ Recognize the practical difficulties in regulating the prices charged by natural monopolies

➤ Explain the main rationales for regulation of industries that are not inherently monopolistic

➤ Identify alternative theories aimed at explaining the behavior of regulators

➤ Understand the foundations of antitrust laws and regulations

➤ Discuss basic issues in enforcing antitrust laws

?**DID YOU KNOW THAT** a recent estimate indicates that the gross costs of complying with government rules regulating U.S. health care are about $339 billion per year? The estimated dollar value of the benefits from these regulations is $170 billion. If correct, these estimates indicate that health care regulations generate a net cost to society of $169 billion, or about $1,500 per U.S. household.

Certainly, firms in the U.S. health care industry are highly regulated. So are firms in many other industries in the United States and throughout the world. Consequently, how regulations and other forms of government oversight *should act* to promote greater economic efficiency and how they *actually act* are important topics for understanding how every economy works. Nevertheless, before you can begin your study of the economic effects of regulation, it is important to understand the various ways in which the government oversees the activities of U.S. businesses.

Forms of Industry Regulation

The U.S. government began regulating social and economic activity early in the nation's history. The amount of government regulation began increasing in the twentieth century and has grown considerably since 1970. Figure 28-1 displays two common measures of regulation in the United States. Panel (a) shows that regulatory spending

---

FIGURE 28-1

Regulation on the Rise

Panel (a) shows that federal government regulatory spending is now more than $40 billion per year. State and local spending is not shown. As panel (b) shows, the number of pages in the *Federal Register* per year rose sharply in the 1970s, dropped off somewhat in the 1980s, and then began to rise once more.

Sources: Institute for University Studies; *Federal Register,* various issues.

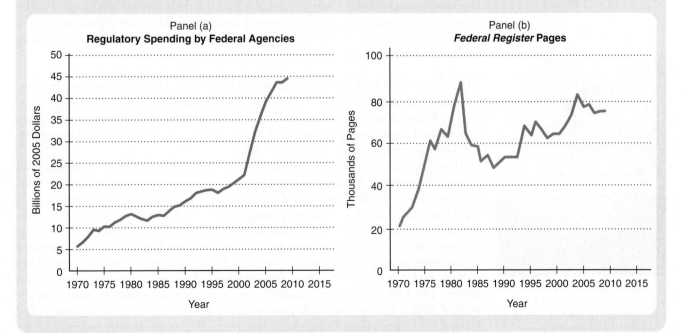

by federal agencies (in 2005 dollars) has generally trended upward since 1970 and has risen considerably during the 2000s. New national security regulations following the 2001 terrorist attacks in New York City and Washington, D.C., have fueled a significant portion of this growth. The remainder of the increase in spending is related to a general upswing in regulatory enforcement by the federal government during this period. Panel (b) on Figure 28-1 on the previous page depicts the number of pages in the *Federal Register*, a government publication that lists all new regulatory rules. According to this measure, the scope of new federal regulations increased sharply during the 1970s, dropped off in the 1980s, and has generally increased since then.

There are two basic types of government regulation. One is *economic regulation* of natural monopolies and of specific nonmonopolistic industries. For instance, some state commissions regulate the prices and quality of services provided by electric power companies, which are considered natural monopolies that experience lower long-run average costs as their output increases. Financial services industries and interstate transportation industries are examples of nonmonopolistic industries that are subjected to considerable government regulation. The other form of government regulation is *social regulation*, which covers all industries. Examples include various occupational, health, and safety rules that federal and state governments impose on most businesses.

Economic Regulation

Initially, most economic regulation in the United States was aimed at controlling prices in industries considered to be natural monopolies. Over time, federal and state governments have also sought to influence the characteristics of products or processes of firms in a variety of industries without inherently monopolistic features.

REGULATION OF NATURAL MONOPOLIES The regulation of natural monopolies has tended to emphasize restrictions on product prices. Various public utility commissions throughout the United States regulate the rates (prices) of electrical utility companies and some telephone operating companies. This *rate regulation*, as it is usually called, officially has been aimed at preventing such industries from earning monopoly profits.

REGULATION OF NONMONOPOLISTIC INDUSTRIES The prices charged by firms in many other industries that do not have steadily declining long-run average costs, such as financial services industries, have also been subjected to regulations. Every state in the United States, for instance, has a government agency devoted to regulating the prices that insurance companies charge.

More broadly, government regulations establish rules pertaining to production, product (or service) features, and entry and exit within a number of specific nonmonopolistic industries. The federal government is heavily involved, for instance, in regulating the securities, banking, transportation, and communications industries. The Securities and Exchange Commission regulates securities markets. The Federal Reserve, Office of the Comptroller of the Currency, and Federal Deposit Insurance Corporation regulate commercial banks. The Office of Thrift Supervision regulates savings banks, and the National Credit Union Administration supervises credit unions. The Federal Aviation Administration supervises the airline industry, and the Federal Motor Carrier Safety Administration regulates the trucking industry. The Federal Communications Commission has oversight powers relating to broadcasting and telephone and communications services.

What is the reason given for the regulation by state commissions of the prices and qualities of services provided by some electric power companies?

TABLE 28-1

Federal Agencies Engaged in Social Regulation

Agency	Jurisdiction	Date Formed	Major Regulatory Functions
Federal Trade Commission (FTC)	Product markets	1914	Responsible for preventing businesses from engaging in misleading advertising, unfair trade practices, and monopolistic actions, as well as for protecting consumer rights.
Food and Drug Administration (FDA)	Food and pharmaceuticals	1938	Regulates the quality and safety of foods, health and medical products, pharmaceuticals, cosmetics, and animal feed.
Equal Employment Opportunity Commission (EEOC)	Labor markets	1964	Investigates complaints of discrimination based on race, religion, gender, or age in hiring, promotion, firing, wages, testing, and all other conditions of employment.
Environmental Protection Agency (EPA)	Environment	1970	Develops and enforces environmental standards for air, water, waste, and noise.
Occupational Safety and Health Administration (OSHA)	Health and safety	1970	Regulates workplace safety and health conditions.
Consumer Product Safety Commission (CPSC)	Consumer product safety	1972	Responsible for protecting consumers from products posing fire, electrical, chemical, or mechanical hazards or dangers to children.

Social Regulation

In contrast to economic regulation, which covers only particular industries, social regulation applies to all firms in the economy. In principle, the aim of social regulation is a better quality of life through improved products, a less polluted environment, and better working conditions. Since the 1970s, an increasing array of government resources has been directed toward regulating product safety, advertising, and environmental effects. Table 28-1 lists some major federal agencies involved in these broad regulatory activities.

The *possible* benefits of social regulations are many. For example, the water supply in some cities is known to be contaminated with potentially hazardous chemicals, and air pollution contributes to many illnesses. Society might well benefit from cleaning up these pollutants. As we shall discuss, however, broad social regulations also entail costs that we all pay, and not just as taxpayers who fund the regulatory activities of agencies such as those listed in Table 28-1.

QUICK QUIZ   *See page 740 for the answers. Review concepts from this section in MyEconLab.*

_____ regulation applies to specific industries, whereas _____ regulation applies to businesses throughout the economy.

Governments commonly regulate the prices and quality of services provided by electric, gas, and other utilities, which traditionally have been considered _____ monopolies.

Governments also single out various nonmonopolistic industries, such as the financial and transportation industries, for special forms of _____ regulation.

Among the common forms of _____ regulation covering all industries are the occupational, health, and safety rules that federal and state governments impose on producers.

Regulating Natural Monopolies

At one time, much government regulation of business purportedly aimed to solve the so-called monopoly problem. Of particular concern was implementing appropriate regulations for natural monopolies.

The Theory of Natural Monopoly Regulation

Recall from Chapter 25 that a natural monopoly arises whenever a single firm can produce all of an industry's output at a lower per-unit cost than other firms attempting to produce less than total industry output. In a natural monopoly, therefore, economies of large-scale production exist, leading to a single-firm industry.

THE UNREGULATED NATURAL MONOPOLY Like any other firm, an unregulated natural monopolist will produce to the point at which marginal revenue equals marginal cost. Panel (a) of Figure 28-2 depicts a situation in which a monopolist faces the market demand curve, D, and the marginal revenue curve, MR. The monopolist searches along the demand curve for the profit-maximizing price and quantity. The

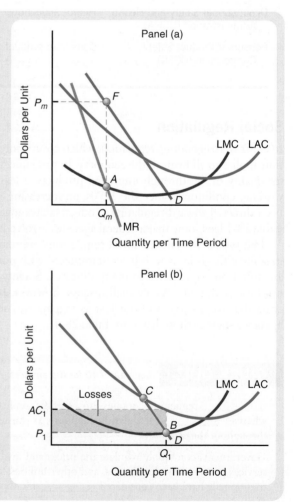

FIGURE 28-2

Profit Maximization and Regulation Through Marginal Cost Pricing

The profit-maximizing natural monopolist here would produce at the point in panel (a) at which marginal costs equal marginal revenue—that is, at point A, which gives the quantity of production Q_m. The per-unit price charged would be P_m at point F, which is the price consumers would be willing to pay for the quantity produced. If a regulatory commission attempted to regulate natural monopolies so that price equaled long-run marginal cost, the commission would make the monopolist set production at the point where the long-run marginal cost (LMC) curve intersects the demand schedule. This is shown in panel (b). The quantity produced would be Q_1, and the per-unit price would be P_1. Average costs at output rate Q_1 are equal to AC_1, however. Losses would ensue, equal to the red-shaded area. It would be self-defeating for a regulatory commission to force a natural monopolist to produce at an output rate at which MC $= P$ without subsidizing some of its costs because losses would eventually drive the natural monopolist out of business.

profit-maximizing quantity is at point A, at which the marginal revenue curve crosses the long-run marginal cost curve, LMC, and the unregulated monopolist maximizes profits by producing the quantity Q_m. Consumers are willing and able to pay the price per unit P_m for this quantity at point F. This price is above marginal cost, so it leads to a socially inefficient allocation of resources by restricting production to a rate below that at which price equals marginal cost.

THE IMPRACTICALITY OF MARGINAL COST PRICING What would happen if the government were to require the monopolist in Figure 28-2 to produce to the point at which price equals marginal cost, which is point B in panel (b)? Then it would produce a larger output rate, Q_1. Consumers, however, would pay only the price per unit P_1 for this quantity, which would be less than the average cost of producing this output rate, AC_1. Consequently, requiring the monopolist to engage in marginal cost pricing would yield a loss for the firm equal to the shaded rectangular area in panel (b). The profit-maximizing monopolist would go out of business rather than face such regulation.

AVERAGE COST PRICING Regulators cannot practically force a natural monopolist to engage in marginal cost pricing. Thus, regulation of natural monopolies has often taken the form of allowing the firm to set price at the point at which the long-run average cost (LAC) curve intersects the demand curve. In panel (b) of Figure 28-2, this is point C. In this situation, the regulator forces the firm to engage in *average cost pricing*, with average cost including what the regulators deem a "fair" rate of return on investment. For instance, a regulator might impose **cost-of-service regulation,** which requires a natural monopoly to charge only prices that reflect the actual average cost of providing products to consumers. Alternatively, although in a similar vein, a regulator might use **rate-of-return regulation,** which allows firms to set prices that ensure a normal return on investment.

Could the way in which cost-of-service and rate-of-return regulations are implemented be contributing to electrical power failures and fires?

Cost-of-service regulation
Regulation that allows prices to reflect only the actual average cost of production and no monopoly profits.

Rate-of-return regulation
Regulation that seeks to keep the rate of return in an industry at a competitive level by not allowing prices that would produce economic profits.

POLICY EXAMPLE
How Keeping Costs Low to Maintain Low Electricity Rates Creates Social Spillovers

In 2003, an old high-power line comes into contact with overgrown trees in Ohio. Then a computer software error in an aging computer system fails to alert technicians to a resulting power surge. The result: Power failures cascade across several eastern U.S. states. Now fast-forward to 2007. A power line falls from a tower into some dry brush in a remote location in Southern California. The result: Sparks fly, and soon a huge fire fanned by high winds engulfs thousands of acres.

These are only two of the more dramatic examples of costly accidents resulting from the use of worn-out equipment by electric utilities. Although U.S. electric utilities spend more than $18 billion every year on their power networks, most of this spending pays for stringing wire to *new* housing developments and commercial structures. To deal with obsolete and corroded *old* equipment,

utilities would have to spend roughly $10 billion more every year, which estimates indicate would boost electricity rates for the average U.S. consumer by about 5 percent. The problem that utilities face is that it is easier to convince regulators that expenditures on network *expansions* fueled by new consumer demand justify rate increases. Convincing regulators to authorize rate increases to cover replacing worn-out equipment is a harder sell, and many utilities do not even try. Thus, the nation's electrical networks continue to age, resulting in recurring power failures and fires.

FOR CRITICAL ANALYSIS
How could utility regulators adjust their practices to allow for replacement of obsolete power-generating equipment while ensuring average cost pricing?

Natural Monopolies No More?

For years, the electricity, natural gas, and telecommunications industries have been subjected to regulations intended to induce firms in these industries to engage in average cost pricing. Traditionally, a feature common to all three industries has been that they utilize large networks of wires or pipelines to transmit their products to consumers. Federal, state, and local governments concluded that the average costs of providing electricity, natural gas, and telecommunications declined as the output rates of firms in these industries increased. Consequently, governments treated these industries as natural monopolies and established regulatory commissions to subject the industries to forms of cost-of-service and rate-of-return regulation.

ELECTRICITY AND NATURAL GAS: SEPARATING PRODUCTION FROM DELIVERY

Today, 15 different companies provide electricity to homes, office buildings, and factories in Houston. Eight different firms compete to sell electricity in New York City, and six companies provide electricity in Philadelphia. Similarly, various producers of natural gas vie to market their product in a number of cities across the country. In nearly half of the U.S. states, there is active competition in the production of electricity and natural gas.

What circumstances led to this transformation? The answer is that regulators of electricity and natural gas companies figured out that the function of *producing* electricity or natural gas did not necessarily have to be combined with the *delivery* of the product. Until the mid-1980s, producers of natural gas and electricity had exclusive ownership of the pipeline and wire networks that provided energy for homes, office buildings, and factories. Since then, various regulators have gradually implemented policies that have separated production of electricity and natural gas from the distribution of these items to consumers.

Thus, in a growing number of U.S. locales, multiple producers now pay to use wire and pipeline networks to get their products to buyers. Economies of scale still exist in these distribution networks, and regulatory commissions impose cost-of-service or rate-of-return regulations on the network owners. Individual producers of electricity and natural gas openly compete, nonetheless, in the markets for the products that consumers actually utilize in their homes and businesses. The market clearing rates that consumers pay to consume electricity and natural gas reflect both the costs of producing these items and the transportation costs that producers pay to deliver them via regulated distribution networks.

TELECOMMUNICATIONS SERVICES MEET THE INTERNET

As the production and sale of electricity and natural gas began to become more competitive undertakings, regulators started to apply the same principles to telecommunications services. In the 1980s, the Federal Communications Commission (FCC) required AT&T to open its existing phone networks to competing providers of long-distance phone services. Gradually, during the 1990s and 2000s, federal, state, and local regulators applied the same principles to local telecommunications services. Today, many U.S. cities and towns are served by two or more competing producers of wired phone services.

At the same time, other forces reshaped the cost structure of the telecommunications industry. First, during the 1990s, significant technological advances drastically reduced the costs of providing wireless telecommunications. Most individuals and businesses regarded cellphone services as imperfect substitutes for wire-based telecommunications. Nevertheless, the growing use of cellphones slowed growth in the demand for services delivered over traditional wire networks.

Second, during the 2000s, Internet phone service became more widely available. Most cable television companies that provide Internet access now offer Web-based telephone services as well. Many other companies also offer Web phone services for purchase by anyone who already has access to the Internet.

ARE NATURAL MONOPOLIES RELICS OF THE PAST? Clearly, the scope of the government's role as regulator of natural monopolies has decreased with the unraveling of conditions that previously created this market structure. In many U.S. electricity and natural gas markets, government agencies now apply traditional cost-of-service or rate-of-return regulations primarily to wire and pipeline owners. Otherwise, the government's main role in many regional markets is to serve as a "traffic cop," enforcing property rights and rules governing the regulated networks that serve competing electricity and natural gas producers.

How has the increased use of cellular phone services and Internet phone services affected the demand for traditional land-line telecommunication services?

In telecommunications, any natural monopoly rationale for a governmental regulator role is rapidly dissipating as more and more households and businesses substitute cellular and Web-based phone services for wired phone services. Since 2000, consumers have stopped using more than 30 million land phone lines. At present, phone signals stop flowing on an additional 3 percent of existing lines each year. Telecommunications has become a technology-driven, competitive free-for-all. This industry is now far from being a natural monopoly.

QUICK QUIZ   *See page 740 for the answers. Review concepts from this section in MyEconLab.*

A **natural monopoly** arises when one firm can produce all of an industry's output at a _____ per-unit cost than other firms. A profit-maximizing natural monopolist produces to the point at which marginal _____ equals long-run marginal _____ and charges the price that people are willing to pay for the quantity produced.

Because a natural monopolist that is required to set price equal to long-run marginal cost will sustain long-run losses and shut down, regulators typically allow natural monopolists to charge prices that just cover _____

costs. Traditionally, regulators have done this through **cost-of-service regulation**, in which prices are based on actual production costs, or **rate-of-return regulation**, in which prices are set to yield a rate of return consistent with _____ economic profits.

Technological and regulatory innovations have made the concept of natural monopoly less relevant. In the electricity, natural gas, and telecommunications industries, production increasingly is accomplished by numerous competing firms that _____ their products through regulated _____.

Regulating Nonmonopolistic Industries

Traditionally, one of the fundamental purposes of governments has been to provide a coordinated system of safeguarding the interests of their citizens. Not surprisingly, protecting consumer interests is the main rationale offered for governmental regulatory functions.

Rationales for Consumer Protection in Nonmonopolistic Industries

The Latin phrase *caveat emptor*, or "let the buyer beware," was once the operative principle in most consumer dealings with businesses. The phrase embodies the idea that the buyer alone is ultimately responsible for assessing a producer and the quality of the items it sells before agreeing to purchase the firm's product. Today, various federal agencies require companies to meet specific minimal standards in their dealings with consumers. For instance, a few years ago, the U.S. Federal Trade Commission assessed monetary penalties on Toys "Я" Us and KB Toys because they failed to ship goods sold on their Web sites in time for a pre-Christmas delivery. Such a government action would have been unheard of a few decades ago.

In some industries, federal agencies dictate the rules of the game for firms' interactions with consumers. The Federal Aviation Administration (FAA), for example, oversees virtually every aspect of the delivery of services by airline companies. The FAA regulates the process by which tickets for flights are sold and distributed, oversees all flight operations, and even establishes rules governing the procedures for returning luggage after flights are concluded.

REASONS FOR GOVERNMENT-ORCHESTRATED CONSUMER PROTECTION Two rationales are commonly advanced for heavy government involvement in overseeing and supervising nonmonopolistic industries. One, which you encountered in Chapter 5, is the possibility of *market failures*. For example, the presence of negative externalities such as pollution may induce governments to regulate industries that create such externalities.

The second common rationale is *asymmetric information*. In the context of many producer-consumer interactions, this term refers to situations in which a producer has information about a product that the consumer lacks. For instance, administrators of your college or university may know that another school in your vicinity offers better-quality degree programs in certain fields. If so, it would not be in your college or university's interest to transmit this information to applicants who are interested in pursuing degrees in those fields.

For certain products, asymmetric information problems can pose special difficulties for consumers trying to assess product quality in advance of purchase. In unregulated financial markets, for example, individuals contemplating buying a company's stock, a municipality's bond, or a bank's certificate of deposit might struggle to assess the associated risks of financial loss. If the air transportation industry were unregulated, a person might have trouble determining if one airline's planes were less safe than those of competing airlines. In an unregulated market for pharmaceuticals, parents might worry about whether one company's childhood-asthma medication could have more dangerous side effects than medications sold by other firms.

ASYMMETRIC INFORMATION AND PRODUCT QUALITY In extreme cases, asymmetric information can create situations in which most of the available products are of low quality. A commonly cited example is the market for used automobiles. Current owners of cars that *appear* to be in good condition know the autos' service records. Some owners know that their cars have been well maintained and really do run great. Others, however, have not kept their autos in good repair and thus are aware that they will be susceptible to greater-than-normal mechanical or electrical problems.

Suppose that in your local used-car market, half of all used cars offered for sale are high-quality autos. The other half are low-quality cars, commonly called "lemons," that are likely to break down within a few months or perhaps even weeks. In addition, suppose that a consumer is willing to pay $20,000 for a particular car model if it is in excellent condition but is willing to pay only $10,000 if it is a lemon. Finally, suppose that people who own truly high-quality used cars are only willing to sell at a price of at least $20,000, but people who own lemons are willing to sell at any price at or above $10,000.

Because there is a 50–50 chance that a given car up for sale is of either quality, the average amount that a prospective buyer is willing to pay equals $(\frac{1}{2} \times \$20,000) + (\frac{1}{2} \times \$10,000) = \$15,000$. Owners of low-quality used cars are willing to sell them at this price, but owners of high-quality used cars are not. In this example, only lemons will be traded, at a price of $10,000, because owners of cars in excellent condition will not sell their cars at a price that prospective buyers are willing to pay.

THE LEMONS PROBLEM Economists refer to the possibility that asymmetric information can lead to a general reduction in product quality in an industry as the **lemons problem.** This problem does not apply only to the used-car industry. In principle, any product with qualities that are difficult for consumers to fully assess is susceptible to the same problem. *Credence goods*, which you learned in Chapter 26 are items such as pharmaceuticals, health care, and professional services, also may be particularly vulnerable to the lemons problem.

Lemons problem
The potential for asymmetric information to bring about a general decline in product quality in an industry.

MARKET SOLUTIONS TO THE LEMONS PROBLEM Firms offering truly high-quality products for sale can address the lemons problem in a variety of ways. They can offer product guarantees and warranties. In addition, to help consumers separate high-quality producers from incompetent or unscrupulous competitors, the high-quality producers may work together to establish industry standards.

In some cases, firms in an industry may even seek external product certification. They may, for example, solicit scientific reports supporting proposed industry standards and bearing witness that products of certain firms in the industry meet those standards. To legitimize a product-certification process, firms may hire outside companies or groups to issue such reports.

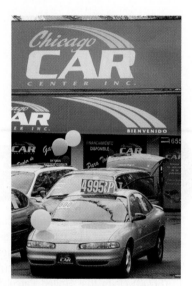

Why might it be difficult to be sure that you are purchasing a high-quality used car?

Implementing Consumer Protection Regulation

Governments offering asymmetric information and lemons problems as rationales for regulation presumably have concluded that private market solutions such as warranties, industry standards, and product certification are insufficient. To address asymmetric information problems, governments may offer legal remedies to consumers or enforce licensing requirements in an effort to provide minimum product standards. In some cases, governments go well beyond simple licensing requirements by establishing a regulatory apparatus for overseeing all aspects of an industry's operations.

Go to **www.econtoday.com/chapter28** to see how the Federal Trade Commission imposes regulations intended to protect consumers.

LIABILITY LAWS AND GOVERNMENT LICENSING Sometimes liability laws, which specify penalties for product failures, provide consumers with protections similar to guarantees and warranties. When the Federal Trade Commission (FTC) charged Toys "Я" Us and KB Toys with failing to meet pre-Christmas delivery dates for Internet toy orders, it operated under a mail-order statute Congress passed in the early 1970s. The mail-order law effectively made the toy companies' delivery guarantees legally enforceable. Although the FTC applied the law in this particular case, any consumer could have filed suit for damages under the terms of the statute.

Federal and state governments also get involved in consumer protection by issuing licenses granting only qualifying firms the legal right to produce and sell certain products. For instance, governments of nearly half of the states give the right to sell caskets only to people who have a mortuary or funeral director's license, allegedly to ensure that bodies of deceased individuals are handled with care and dignity.

Although government licensing may successfully limit the sale of low-quality goods, licensing requirements also often limit the number of providers. As you learned in Chapter 25, this can ease efforts by established firms to act as monopolists. In addition, if governments rely on the expertise of established firms for assistance in drafting licensing requirements, these firms may have strong incentives to recommend low standards for themselves but high standards for prospective entrants.

DIRECT ECONOMIC AND SOCIAL REGULATION In some instances, governments determine that liability laws and licensing requirements are insufficient to protect the interests of consumers. A government may decide that lemons problems in banking are so severe that without an extensive banking regulatory apparatus, consumers will lose confidence in banks, and bank runs may ensue. It may rely on similar rationales to establish economic regulation of other financial services industries. Eventually, it may apply consumer protection rationales to justify the economic regulation of additional industries such as trucking or air transportation.

The government may establish an oversight authority to make certain that consumers are protected from incompetent producers of foods and pharmaceuticals. Eventually, the government may determine that a host of other products should meet government consumer protection standards. It may also decide that the people who produce the products also require government agencies to ensure workplace safety. In this way, widespread social regulation emerges, as it has in the United States and most other developed nations.

Can two government regulations sometimes come into apparent conflict?

POLICY EXAMPLE
Trying to Satisfy One Regulation Can Violate Another Regulation

Under federal transportation laws, drivers of trucks with weights exceeding 10,000 pounds must be able to hear. Nevertheless, a federal appeals court recently supported an Equal Employment Opportunity Commission (EEOC) claim that United Parcel Service's refusal to allow a deaf individual to drive a 20,000-pound truck violated the 1990 Americans with Disabilities Act. Separately, the EEOC is also citing age discrimination regulations in trying to force some firms to permit people over the age of 60 to fly airplanes. The EEOC is pursuing this claim even though a federal law prohibits people over 60 from piloting commercial passenger planes. Clearly, regulations can come into conflict.

FOR CRITICAL ANALYSIS
Are rules governing the characteristics of truck drivers and airplane pilots examples of economic or social regulations?

QUICK QUIZ
See page 740 for the answers. Review concepts from this section in MyEconLab.

Governments tend to regulate industries in which they think market _____ and _____ information problems are most severe.

A common justification for government regulation is to protect consumers from adverse effects of _____ information.

To address the _____ problem, or the potential for _____-quality products to predominate when asymmetric information is widespread, governments often supplement private firms' guarantees, warranties, and certification standards with liability laws and licensing requirements.

Incentives and Costs of Regulation

Abiding by government regulations is a costly undertaking for firms. Consequently, businesses engage in a number of activities intended to avoid the true intent of regulations or to bring about changes in the regulations that government agencies establish.

Creative Response and Feedback Effects: Results of Regulation

Sometimes individuals and firms respond to a regulation in a way that conforms to the letter of the law but undermines its spirit. When they do so, they engage in **creative response** to regulations.

One type of creative response has been labeled a *feedback effect*. Individuals' behaviors may change after a regulation has been put into effect. If a regulation requires fluoridated water, then parents know that their children's teeth have significant protection against tooth decay. Consequently, the feedback effect is that parents become less concerned about how many sweets their children eat.

What feedback effect sometimes occurs when products are almost covered with warning labels?

Creative response
Behavior on the part of a firm that allows it to comply with the letter of the law but violate the spirit, significantly lessening the law's effects.

POLICY EXAMPLE
The Feedback Effect of Warning-Label Overkill

At the behest of the Consumer Product Safety Commission, warning labels appear on many common products. For instance, stamped onto a standard ladder purchased at a hardware store are warnings that typically contain about 600 words, including a warning not to place the ladder in front of a swinging door. The labels that many toy makers attach to every toy include the blanket warning, "Small parts may cause a choking risk," even though a hammer would be required to break some toys into parts small enough to cause choking.

Studies indicate that consumers typically read a single, short warning that offers guidance about the key safety risks associated with using a product. When confronted with numerous and lengthy warning labels, however, consumers do not take the time to read *any* of the warnings, including the label most relevant to the main risks of using an item. Thus, a feedback effect of requiring labels warning of every conceivable risk is that consumers fail to read warnings about those risks most likely to matter for their safety.

FOR CRITICAL ANALYSIS
Why do you suppose that consumers are more likely to read a single safety label than to read multiple safety labels?

Explaining Regulators' Behavior

Those charged with enforcing government regulations operate outside the market, so their decisions are determined by nonmarket processes. A number of theories have emerged to describe the behavior of regulators. These theories explain how regulation can harm consumers by generating higher prices and fewer product choices while benefiting producers by reducing competitive forces and allowing higher profits. Two of the best-known theories of regulatory behavior are the *capture hypothesis* and the *share-the-gains, share-the-pains theory*.

THE CAPTURE HYPOTHESIS Regulators often end up becoming champions of the firms they are charged with regulating. According to the **capture hypothesis,** regardless of why a regulatory agency was originally established, eventually special interests of the

Capture hypothesis
A theory of regulatory behavior that predicts that regulators will eventually be captured by special interests of the industry being regulated.

industry it regulates will capture it. After all, the people who know the most about a regulated industry are the people already in the industry. Thus, people who have been in the industry and have allegiances and friendships with others in the industry will most likely be asked to regulate the industry.

According to the capture hypothesis, individual consumers of a regulated industry's products and individual taxpayers who finance a regulatory agency have interests too diverse to be greatly concerned with the industry's actions. In contrast, special interests of the industry are well organized and well defined. These interests also have more to offer political entrepreneurs within a regulatory agency, such as future employment with one of the regulated firms. Therefore, regulators have a strong incentive to support the position of a well-organized special-interest group within the regulated industry.

Share-the-gains, share-the-pains theory
A theory of regulatory behavior that holds that regulators must take account of the demands of three groups: legislators, who established and oversee the regulatory agency; firms in the regulated industry; and consumers of the regulated industry's products.

"SHARE THE GAINS, SHARE THE PAINS" The **share-the-gains, share-the-pains theory** offers a somewhat different view of regulators' behavior. This theory focuses on the specific aims of regulators. It proposes that a regulator's main objective is simply to keep his or her job as a regulator. To do so, the regulator must obtain the approval of both the legislators who originally established and continue to oversee the regulatory agency and the regulated industry. The regulator must also take into account the views of the industry's customers.

In contrast to the capture hypothesis, which holds that regulators must take into account only industry special interests, the share-the-gains, share-the-pains theory contends that regulators must worry about legislators and consumers as well. After all, if industry customers who are hurt by improper regulation complain to legislators, the regulators might lose their jobs. Whereas the capture theory predicts that regulators will quickly allow electric utilities to raise their rates in the face of higher fuel costs, the share-the-gains, share-the-pains theory predicts a slower, more measured regulatory response. Ultimately, regulators will permit an increase in utility rates, but the allowed adjustment will not be as speedy or complete as predicted by the capture hypothesis. The regulatory agency is not completely captured by the industry. It also has to consider the views of consumers and legislators.

The Benefits and Costs of Regulation

As noted earlier, regulation offers many *potential* benefits. *Actual* benefits, however, are difficult to measure. Putting a dollar value on safer products, a cleaner environment, and better working conditions is a difficult proposition. Furthermore, the benefits of most regulations accrue to society over a long time.

You Are There

To contemplate why the benefits of enforcing regulations might be hard to measure in relation to known regulatory costs, take a look at **Regulation of U.S. Currency Moves into the Court System,** on pages 733 and 734.

THE DIRECT COSTS OF REGULATION TO TAXPAYERS Measuring the costs of regulation is also a challenging undertaking. After all, about 5,000 new federal regulations are issued each year. One cost, though, is certain: U.S. taxpayers pay more than $40 billion per year to staff regulatory agencies with more than 250,000 employees and to fund their various activities. Figure 28-3 displays the distribution of total federal government outlays for economic and social regulation of various areas of the economy.

The *total* cost of regulation is much higher than just the explicit government outlays to fund the administration of various regulations, however. After all, businesses must expend resources complying with regulations, developing creative responses to regulations, and funding special-interest lobbying efforts directed at legislators and regulatory officials. Sometimes companies find that it is impossible to comply with one regulation without violating another, and determining how to avoid the resulting legal entanglements can entail significant expenditures.

How have lawmakers in the European Union (EU) exempted—at least temporarily—EU firms from costly regulations that have already been imposed on U.S. competitors?

INTERNATIONAL POLICY EXAMPLE
The Long Arm of Europe's REACH Slaps U.S. Firms

The European Union (EU) recently put into place a regulatory system for products containing chemicals. The system is called REACH, which is an acronym for "registration, evaluation, and authorization of chemicals." The nearly 2,000-page body of rules applies to more than 30,000 chemicals. Before a firm can sell any chemical-containing product in any of the 27 EU nations, the product must satisfy numerous testing requirements. The REACH regulations went into effect on June 1, 2008—but only for non-EU firms, including U.S. manufacturers. EU lawmakers gave firms based in EU nations until 2010 to satisfy the regulations. Hence, U.S. firms were saddled immediately with REACH-related costs, but EU firms were granted additional time to comply.

FOR CRITICAL ANALYSIS
Why do you suppose that U.S. critics suggest that by implementing the REACH rules in this manner, the EU intended, at least in part, to protect EU firms from competition?

FIGURE 28-3

The Distribution of Federal Regulatory Spending

This figure shows the areas of the economy to which more than $40 billion of taxpayer-provided funds are distributed to finance economic and social regulation.

Source: Office of Management and Budget.

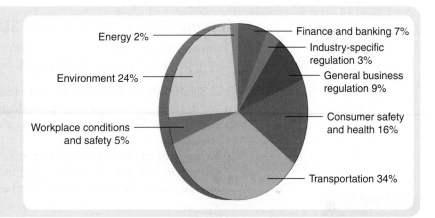

Energy 2%
Environment 24%
Workplace conditions and safety 5%
Finance and banking 7%
Industry-specific regulation 3%
General business regulation 9%
Consumer safety and health 16%
Transportation 34%

THE TOTAL SOCIAL COST OF REGULATION According to the Office of Management and Budget, annual expenditures that U.S. businesses must make solely to comply with regulations issued by various federal agencies amount to between $500 billion and $600 billion per year. Nevertheless, this estimate encompasses only explicit costs of satisfying regulatory demands placed on businesses. It ignores relevant opportunity costs. After all, owners, managers, and employees of companies could be doing other things with their time and resources than complying with regulations. Economists estimate that the opportunity costs of complying with federal regulations may be as high as $270 billion per year.

All told, therefore, the total social cost associated with satisfying federal regulations in the United States is probably between $800 billion and $900 billion per year. This figure, of course, applies only to federal regulations. It does not include the explicit and implicit opportunity costs associated with regulations issued by 50 different state governments and thousands of municipalities. Undoubtedly, the annual cost of regulation throughout the United States exceeds $1 trillion per year.

QUICK QUIZ
See page 740 for the answers. Review concepts from this section in MyEconLab.

The **capture hypothesis** holds that regulatory agencies will eventually be captured by industry special interests because

_____ individually are not greatly influenced by regulation, whereas regulated _____ are directly affected.

Antitrust Policy

An expressed aim of the U.S. government is to foster competition. To this end, Congress has made numerous attempts to legislate against business practices it has perceived to be anticompetitive. This is the general idea behind antitrust legislation. If the courts can prevent collusion among sellers of a product, there will be no restriction of output, and monopoly prices will not result. Instead, prices of goods and services will be close to their marginal social opportunity costs.

Antitrust Policy in the United States

Congress has enacted four key antitrust laws, which Table 28-2 summarizes. The most important of these is the original U.S. antitrust law, called the Sherman Act.

THE SHERMAN ANTITRUST ACT OF 1890 The Sherman Antitrust Act, which was passed in 1890, was the first attempt by the federal government to control the growth of monopoly in the United States. The most important provisions of that act are as follows:

> *Section 1*: Every contract, combination in the form of a trust or otherwise, or conspiracy, in restraint of trade or commerce among the several states, or with foreign nations, is hereby declared to be illegal.

TABLE 28-2

Key U.S. Antitrust Laws

Sherman Antitrust Act of 1890	Forbids any contract, combination, or conspiracy to restrain trade or commerce within the United States or across U.S. borders. Holds any person who attempts to monopolize trade or commerce criminally liable.
Clayton Act of 1914	Prohibits specific business practices deemed to restrain trade or commerce. Bans discrimination in prices charged to various purchasers when price differences are not due to actual differences in selling or transportation costs. Also forbids a company from selling goods on the condition that the purchaser must deal exclusively with that company. Finally, it prevents corporations from holding stock in other companies when this may lessen competition.
Federal Trade Commission Act of 1914 (and 1938 Amendment)	Outlaws business practices that reduce the extent of competition, such as alleged cutthroat pricing intended to drive rivals from the marketplace. Also established the Federal Trade Commission and empowered it to issue cease and desist orders in situations in which it determines "unfair methods of competition in commerce" exist. The 1938 amendment added deceptive business practices to the list of illegal acts.
Robinson-Patman Act of 1936	Bans selected discriminatory price cuts by chain stores that allegedly drive smaller competitors from the marketplace. In addition, forbids price discrimination through special concessions in the form of price or quantity discounts, free advertising, or promotional allowances granted to one buyer but not to others, if these actions substantially reduce competition.

Section 2: Every person who shall monopolize, or attempt to monopolize, or combine or conspire with any other person or persons to monopolize any part of the trade or commerce . . . shall be guilty of a misdemeanor [now a felony].

Notice how vague this act really is. No definition is given for the terms *restraint of trade* or *monopolize*. Despite this vagueness, however, the act was used to prosecute the infamous Standard Oil Trust of New Jersey. This company was charged with and convicted of violations of Sections 1 and 2 of the Sherman Antitrust Act in 1906. At the time it controlled more than 80 percent of the nation's oil-refining capacity. In addressing the company's legal appeal, the U.S. Supreme Court ruled that Standard Oil's predominance in the oil market created "a *prima facie* presumption of intent and purpose to control and maintain dominancy . . . not as a result from normal methods of industrial development, but by means of combinations." Here the word *combination* meant entering into associations and preferential arrangements with the intent of restraining competition. The Supreme Court forced Standard Oil of New Jersey to break up into many smaller companies that would have no choice but to compete.

The Sherman Act applies today just as it did more than a century ago. In June 2001, the federal Court of Appeals for the District of Columbia determined that Microsoft Corporation had violated the Sherman Act. The court ruled that Microsoft had engaged in anticompetitive conduct in an effort to monopolize the market for operating systems for personal computers. Initially, the U.S. Justice Department proposed a Standard Oil–style remedy: splitting Microsoft into several companies. Ultimately, however, Microsoft reached a settlement that kept the company intact but required it to alter many of its business practices.

Do admitted violations of the 1890 Sherman Act ever occur in our modern, high-tech world?

E-COMMERCE EXAMPLE
The Justice Department Focuses on Flash Memory Price Fixing

In the early 2000s, officials representing four companies—Elpida Memory, Hunix Semiconductor, Infineon Technologies, and Samsung—colluded in setting prices of dynamic random-access memory (DRAM) microchips. In 2006, the U.S. Justice Department secured convictions under the Sherman Antitrust Act. All four companies admitted that officials representing their firms conspired to restrain trade in the market for DRAM microchips.

DRAM microchips are inputs in devices such as personal computers, digital cameras, music players, and cellphones. So are static random-access memory (SRAM) microchips and flash memory chips. After the Justice Department first unearthed evidence of price fixing in DRAM microchips in the early 2000s, it began an investigation of potential Sherman Act violations by firms producing SRAM microchips. In addi-

tion, when prices of flash memory chips rose in the late 2000s, the Justice Department opened a preliminary investigation into possible price fixing of those newer-technology chips. Most market observers suggested that the prices of flash memory chips rose for a less sinister reason—an increased demand for the newer, faster chips by makers of all kinds of digital gadgets. Nevertheless, the Justice Department continues to investigate possible price fixing of computer chips.

FOR CRITICAL ANALYSIS
How does the fact that higher prices could result from either higher market demand or collusive efforts to monopolize a market complicate efforts to determine whether a Sherman Act violation may have occurred?

OTHER IMPORTANT ANTITRUST LEGISLATION Table 28-2 lists three other important antitrust laws. In 1914, Congress passed the Clayton Act to clarify some of the vague provisions of the Sherman Act by identifying specific business practices that were to be legally prohibited.

Congress also passed the Federal Trade Commission Act in 1914. In addition to establishing the Federal Trade Commission to investigate unfair trade practices, this law enumerated certain business practices that, according to Congress, involved overly aggressive competition. A 1938 amendment to this law expressly prohibited "unfair or deceptive acts or practices in commerce" and empowered the FTC to regulate advertising and marketing practices by U.S. firms.

The Robinson-Patman Act of 1936 amended the Clayton Act by singling out specific business practices, such as selected price cuts, aimed at driving smaller competitors out of business. The act is often referred to as the "Chain Store Act" because it was intended to protect *independent* retailers and wholesalers from "unfair competition" by chain stores.

EXEMPTIONS FROM ANTITRUST LAWS Numerous laws exempt the following industries and business practices from antitrust legislation:

- Labor unions
- Public utilities—electric, gas, and telephone companies
- Professional baseball
- Cooperative activities among U.S. exporters
- Hospitals
- Public transit and water systems
- Suppliers of military equipment
- Joint publishing arrangements in a single city by two or more newspapers

Thus, not all U.S. businesses are subject to antitrust laws.

International Discord in Antitrust Policy

What, if anything, should U.S. antitrust authorities do if AT&T decides that it wishes to merge with British Telecommunications or if Germany's Deutsche Telecom wants to acquire Sprint Nextel? What, if anything, should they do if Time Warner, the largest U.S. entertainment company, attempts to merge with London-based EMI, one of the world's largest recorded-music companies? These are not just rhetorical questions, as U.S. and European antitrust authorities learned in the 2000s when these issues actually surfaced. Growing international linkages among markets for many goods and services have increasingly made antitrust policy a global undertaking.

The international dimensions of antitrust pose a problem for U.S. antitrust authorities in the Department of Justice and the Federal Trade Commission. In the United States, the overriding goal of antitrust policies has traditionally been protecting the interests of consumers. This is also a formal objective of antitrust efforts of European Union (EU) antitrust authorities. In the EU, however, policymakers are also required to reject any business combination that "creates or strengthens a dominant position as a result of which effective competition would be significantly impeded."

This additional clause is creating tension between U.S. and EU policymaking. In the United States, increasing dominance of a market by a single firm arouses the concern of antitrust authorities. Nevertheless, U.S. authorities typically will remain passive if they determine that the larger market dominance arises from factors such as exceptional management and greater cost efficiencies that ultimately benefit consumers by reducing prices. In contrast, under EU rules antitrust authorities are obliged to block *any* business combination that increases the dominance of any producer. They must do so regardless of what factors might have caused the business's preeminence in the marketplace or whether the antitrust action might have adverse implications for consumers.

QUICK QUIZ   *See page 740 for the answers. Review concepts from this section in MyEconLab.*

The first national antitrust law was the _____ Antitrust Act of 1890, which made illegal every contract and combination in restraint of trade; it remains the single most important antitrust law in the United States.

The _____ Act of 1914 made illegal various specific business practices, such as price discrimination.

The _____ _____ _____ Act of 1914 and its 1938 amendment established the Federal Trade Commission and prohibited "unfair or deceptive acts or practices in commerce."

The _____-_____ Act of 1936 aimed to prevent large producers from driving out small competitors by means of selective discriminatory price cuts.

Antitrust Enforcement

How are antitrust laws enforced? In the United States, most enforcement continues to be based on the Sherman Act. The Supreme Court has defined the offense of **monopolization** as involving the following elements: "(1) the possession of monopoly power in the relevant market and (2) the willful acquisition or maintenance of that power, as distinguished from growth or development as a consequence of a superior product, business acumen, or historical accident."

Monopoly Power and the Relevant Market

The Sherman Act does not define monopoly. Monopoly need not be a single entity. Also, monopoly is not a function of size alone. For example a "mom and pop" grocery store located in an isolated town can function as a monopolist.

It is difficult to define and measure market power precisely. As a workable proxy, courts often look to the firm's percentage share of the "relevant market." This is the so-called **market share test.** A firm is generally considered to have monopoly power if its share of the relevant market is 70 percent or more. This is only a rule of thumb, however, not an absolute dictum. In some cases, a smaller share may be held to constitute monopoly power.

The relevant market consists of two elements: a relevant *product* market and a relevant *geographic* market. What should the relevant product market include? It must include all items produced by different firms that have identical attributes, such as sugar. Yet products that are not identical may sometimes be substituted for one another. Coffee may be substituted for tea, for example. In defining the relevant product market, the key issue is the degree to which products are interchangeable. If one product is sufficiently substitutable for another, then the two products are considered to be part of the same product market.

The second component of the relevant market is the geographic boundaries of the market. For items that are sold nationwide, the geographic boundaries of the market encompass the entire United States. If a producer and its competitors sell in only a limited area (one in which customers have no access to other sources of the product), the geographic market is limited to that area. A national firm may thus compete in several distinct areas and have monopoly power in one area but not in another.

Monopolization
The possession of monopoly power in the relevant market and the willful acquisition or maintenance of that power, as distinguished from growth or development as a consequence of a superior product, business acumen, or historical accident.

Market share test
The percentage of a market that a particular firm supplies; used as the primary measure of monopoly power.

Product Packaging and Antitrust Enforcement

A particular problem in U.S. antitrust enforcement is determining whether a firm has engaged in "willful acquisition or maintenance" of market power. Unfortunately, actions that appear to some observers to be good business look like antitrust violations to others. To illustrate why quandaries can arise in antitrust enforcement, let's consider two examples: *versioning* and *bundling*.

Versioning
Selling a product in slightly altered forms to different groups of consumers.

PRODUCT VERSIONING A firm engages in product **versioning** when it sells an item in slightly altered forms to different groups of consumers. A typical method of versioning is to remove certain features from an item and offer what remains as a somewhat stripped-down version of the product at a different price.

Consider an office-productivity software program, such as Adobe Acrobat or Microsoft Word. Firms selling such programs typically offer both a "professional" version containing a full range of features and a "standard" version providing only basic functions. One perspective on this practice regards it as a form of price discrimination, or selling essentially the same product at different prices to different consumers. People who desire to use the full range of features in Adobe Acrobat or Microsoft Word are likely to be computing professionals. Compared to most other consumers, their demand for the full-featured version of an office-productivity software program is likely to be less elastic. In principle, therefore, Adobe and Microsoft can earn higher profits by offering "professional" versions at higher prices and selling a "standard" version at a lower price.

Price discrimination—charging varying prices to different consumers when the price differences are not a result of different production or transportation costs—is illegal under the Clayton Act of 1914. Are Adobe, Microsoft, and other companies engaging in illegal price discrimination? Another perspective on versioning indicates that they are not. According to this point of view, consumers regard "professional" and "standard" versions of software packages as imperfect substitutes. Consequently, each version is a distinctive product sold in a unique market. If so, versioning increases overall consumer satisfaction because consumers who are not computing professionals are able to utilize certain features of software products at a lower price. So far, antitrust authorities in the United States and elsewhere have been inclined toward this view of the economic effects of versioning, rather than perceiving it as a form of price discrimination.

Bundling
Offering two or more products for sale as a set.

Tie-in sales
Purchases of one product that are permitted by the seller only if the consumer buys another good or service from the same firm.

PRODUCT BUNDLING Antitrust authorities have been less tolerant of another form of product packaging, known as **bundling,** which involves the joint sale of two or more products as a set. Antitrust authorities usually are not concerned if a firm allows consumers to purchase the products either individually or as a set. They are more likely to investigate a firm's business practices, however, when it allows consumers to purchase one product only when it is bundled with another. Antitrust officials often view this form of bundling as a method of price discrimination known as **tie-in sales,** in which a firm requires consumers who wish to buy one of its products to purchase another item the firm sells as well.

To understand their reasoning, consider a situation in which one group of consumers is willing to pay $200 for a computer operating system but only $100 for an Internet-browsing program. A second group of consumers is willing to pay only $100 for the same computer operating system but is willing to pay $200 for the same Internet-browsing program. If the same company that sells both types of software offers the operating system at a price above $100, then only consumers in the first group will buy this software. Likewise, if it sells the Internet-browsing program at a price above $100, then only the second group of consumers will purchase that program.

But if the firm sells both products as a bundled set, it can charge $300 and generate sales of both software products to both groups. One interpretation is that the first group pays $200 for the operating system, but for the second group, the operating system's price is $100. At the same time, the first group has paid $100 for the Internet-browsing program, while the second group perceives the price of the program to be $200. Effectively, bundling enables the software company to engage in price discrimination by charging different prices to different groups.

Antitrust enforcers in the Justice Department applied this interpretation in their prosecution of Microsoft, which for years had bundled its Internet-browsing program, Internet Explorer, together with its Windows operating system. Enforcement officials added another twist by contending that Microsoft also had monopoly power in the market for computer operating systems. By bundling the two products, they argued, Microsoft had sought both to price-discriminate and to extend its monopoly power to the market for Internet-browsing software. The remedy that the courts imposed was for Microsoft to alter some of its business practices. As part of this legal remedy, Microsoft was required to unbundle its Windows and Internet Explorer products.

QUICK QUIZ   *See page 740 for the answers. Review concepts from this section in MyEconLab.*

As part of the enforcement of antitrust laws, officials at the U.S. Department of Justice and the Federal Trade Commission often apply _____ _____ tests to determine if a few firms account for most of industry _____.

Antitrust enforcers must decide whether producers seek to monopolize the relevant market, which involves determining both the relevant _____ market and the relevant _____ market.

Antitrust authorities generally have not considered product _____, or offering different versions of essentially the same product for sale at different prices, to be illegal price discrimination. U.S. authorities have, however, raised antitrust concerns about product _____, which they view as a method of engaging in **tie-in sales** that require consumers to purchase one product in order to obtain another.

 You Are There Regulation of U.S. Currency Moves into the Court System

Under the Federal Reserve Act of 1913, the Federal Reserve System (the "Fed") is responsible for determining the amount of currency to be distributed through the nation's banking system. The U.S. Treasury's Bureau of Engraving and Printing designs and prints this currency. For years, the Bureau's main goal has been to produce recognizable, sturdy bills that are hard to counterfeit. The Bureau's efforts have yielded a national currency that has long consisted of

uniform bills distinguished mainly by portraits of famous patriots and different numerical denominations printed in corners of the bills.

In 2006, U.S. District Court Judge James Robertson was asked to rule on whether the uniformity of the nation's currency violates antidiscrimination regulations established by the Rehabilitation Act of 1973. According to the American Council of the Blind (ACB), these regulations require the

You Are There (cont.)

U.S. government to avoid actions that discriminate against people suffering from disabilities. The ACB argued that the Bureau of Engraving and Printing designed the nation's currency without taking into account the difficulties that blind individuals might have in distinguishing currency denominations. Thus, it failed to abide by the Rehabilitation Act's regulations.

After studying the currencies of about 180 other nations, Judge Robertson found that the U.S. government is the only one that has not taken steps to make its currency denominations readily identifiable by blind individuals. Thus, he ruled that the U.S. government is consciously discriminating against the blind by illegally denying them "meaningful access" to the currency in violation of the Rehabilitation Act's regulations. In May 2008, a federal appeals court upheld Judge Robertson's decision. Even though redesigning the nation's currency and its production process could cost millions of dollars, a majority of the appeals court judges agreed with Judge Robertson that the costs would

not be an "undue burden" on the U.S. Treasury. A third judge disagreed with the majority's decision and pointed out that retooling vending machines so that they would accept the new currency would cost *billions* of dollars.

CRITICAL ANALYSIS QUESTIONS

1. The president of another group, the National Federation of the Blind, noted that "blind people transact business with paper money every day" and attacked Judge Robertson's decision as a "feel-good gimmick that misinforms the public." Given that two different organizations claiming to represent the interests of the blind disagree on the benefits of a currency redesign, why might it be hard to put a monetary value on the actual benefits?

2. If the U.S. Treasury decides not to pursue any further appeals, who will ultimately pay for the costs of a redesign of U.S. currency?

The Latest in Spiraling Regulation Costs: "Doc Fees"

Issues and Applications

CONCEPTS APPLIED

- ➤ Economic Regulation
- ➤ Lemons Problem
- ➤ Social Regulation

The costs of finalizing vehicle purchases have increased considerably in recent years. The reason is that fees for processing documents associated with these transactions, or, as auto dealers commonly refer to them, "doc fees," have ballooned as a variety of regulations have expanded the range of legally required documents.

Doc Fees Related to Economic Regulation of Vehicle Sales

The transferal of ownership of a vehicle has long required a number of legal documents. Vehicle sellers, such as auto dealers, must be certain that documents such as formal title of ownership and state vehicle registration for tax purposes meet requirements established by law. To comply with these requirements, they must pay attorneys, specially trained employees, and others.

Beginning in the 1980s, a number of auto sellers started to charge separate fees for the service they provided in documenting the transferal of vehicle ownership. Until the 1990s, document-processing fees associated with vehicle purchases rarely exceeded $50 per transaction. Then state governments became more concerned about asymmetric information and lemons problems in auto sales. Since the early 1990s, many state legislatures have established regulations requiring auto sellers to provide detailed documents to purchasers verifying features that are present or absent in their vehicles. In addition, newly enacted or amended federal laws mandate that dealers provide buyers with documents detailing the monthly costs they will face if they borrow to finance vehicle purchases. Finally, many states now require sellers to provide buyers with documents attesting to vehicle inspections and repairs.

As a consequence of these forms of economic regulation, more documents must be processed when a transfer of vehicle ownership takes place. In addition to charging title processing fees and vehicle registration fees, auto sellers began adding fees for reports on financing costs, inspection documents, and used-vehicle

certifications. Thus, within a few years, vehicle doc fees more than doubled in most states.

The Latest in Doc Fees: Social Regulation of Vehicle Sales

During the 2000s, a new wave of document requirements swept across auto dealers' lots, as state and federal governments began subjecting vehicle sales transactions to various mandates related to social regulation. For instance, in an effort to protect the safety of future vehicle occupants, occupants of other vehicles, and pedestrians, state governments began requiring more detailed evidence of carefully conducted safety inspections. Additionally, the federal Gramm-Leach-Bliley Act included privacy rules requiring documents attesting that an auto seller will safeguard a buyer's private information. Furthermore, among the many antiterrorism measures passed by Congress in recent years is a requirement that auto sellers check customers against federal lists of people suspected of terrorist activities. The auto dealer must provide a document attesting that this task has been completed.

These and other laws specifying new forms of social regulation have pushed up doc fees markedly in many states. According to the American Automobile Association, in 2001 the average doc fees for a U.S. vehicle transaction were less than $200. Today, at least in states without legal ceilings on doc fees, average doc fees are close to $500. In some states, doc fees can exceed $1,000. Hence, expanded economic and social regulations have generated significant costs associated with transferring vehicle ownership. As usual, the benefits of many of the regulations that have pushed up doc fees are harder to pin down.

Test your understanding of this chapter by going online to **MyEconLab.**
In the Study Plan for this chapter, select Section N: News.

For Critical Analysis

1. How does requiring an auto seller to prepare additional documents affect the marginal cost that the seller faces in completing a vehicle transaction?

2. Why does a requirement to document that a customer has been checked against terrorist watch lists constitute social regulation instead of economic regulation?

Web Resources

1. To read a review of vehicle doc fees, go to www. econtoday.com/chapter28.

2. For a list of various fees associated with transferal of ownership of a vehicle, go to www.econtoday.com/ chapter28.

Research Project

Under the Gramm-Leach-Bliley Act, in addition to documenting that a customer's private information has been protected, an auto seller must also develop and implement privacy-protection train- ing programs for all employees. Are the costs generated by this requirement more likely to be borne largely by auto sellers or by buyers of vehicles? Explain your reasoning.

myeconlab

Here is what you should know after reading this chapter. **MyEconLab** will help you identify what you know, and where to go when you need to practice.

WHAT YOU SHOULD KNOW		WHERE TO GO TO PRACTICE
Government Regulation of Business There are two basic forms of government regulation of business: economic regula- tion and social regulation. Economic regulation applies to spe- cific industries; it includes the regulation of prices charged by natural monopolies and the regulation of certain activities of specific nonmonopolistic industries. Social regulations affect nearly all businesses and encompass a broad range of objectives concerning such issues as product safety, environmental quality, and working conditions.	**KEY FIGURE** Figure 28-1, 715	• **MyEconLab** Study Plan 28.1 • Audio introduction to Chapter 28 • Animated Figure 28-1
Practical Difficulties in Regulating the Prices Charged by Natural Monopolies To try to ensure that a monopolist charges a price consistent with marginal cost, a government regulator might contemplate requiring the firm to set price equal to marginal cost at the point where the demand curve crosses the marginal cost curve. For a natural monopoly, how- ever, long-run marginal cost is typically less than long-run aver- age total cost, so requiring marginal cost pricing forces the firm to incur an economic loss. Hence, regulators normally aim for a natural monopoly to charge a price equal to average total cost so that the firm earns zero economic profits. In recent years, uncoupling production of electricity, natural gas, and telecom- munications from their distribution has enabled regulators to promote competition in these industries.	cost-of-service regulation, 719 rate-of-return regulation, 719 **KEY FIGURE** Figure 28-2, 718	• **MyEconLab** Study Plan 28.2 • Animated Figure 28-2
Rationales for Regulating Nonmonopolistic Industries The two most common rationales for regulation of nonmonopolistic industries relate to addressing market failures and protecting consumers from problems arising from information asymmetries they face in some markets. Asymmetric information can also cre- ate a lemons problem, which occurs when uncertainty about product quality leads to markets containing mostly low-quality	lemons problem, 723	• **MyEconLab** Study Plan 28.3

(continued)

 (continued)

WHAT YOU SHOULD KNOW		WHERE TO GO TO PRACTICE

items. Governments may seek to reduce the lemons problem by establishing liability laws and business licensing requirements.

Regulators' Incentives and the Costs of Regulation The capture theory of regulator behavior predicts that regulators will eventually find themselves supporting the positions of the firms that they regulate. An alternative view, called the share-the-gains, share-the-pains theory, predicts that a regulator will try to satisfy all constituencies, at least in part. The costs of regulation are easier to quantify in dollar terms than the benefits. These costs include both the direct costs to taxpayers of funding regulatory agencies and the explicit and implicit opportunity costs that businesses must incur to comply with regulations.

creative response, 725
capture hypothesis, 725
share-the-gains, share-the-pains theory, 726

KEY FIGURE
Figure 28-3, 727

- **MyEconLab** Study Plan 28.4
- Animated Figure 28-3
- Video: Creative Response and Feedback Effects: Results of Regulation

---

Foundations of Antitrust There are four key antitrust laws. The Sherman Act of 1890 forbids attempts to monopolize an industry. The Clayton Act of 1914 clarified antitrust law by prohibiting specific types of business practices that Congress determined were aimed at restraining trade. In addition, the Federal Trade Commission Act of 1914, as amended in 1938, seeks to prohibit deceptive business practices and to prevent "cutthroat pricing," which Congress felt could unfairly eliminate too many competitors. Finally, the Robinson-Patman Act of 1936 outlawed price cuts that Congress had determined to be discriminatory and predatory.

- **MyEconLab** Study Plan 28.5
- Video: Antitrust Laws

Issues in Enforcing Antitrust Laws Antitrust laws are vague, so enforcement of the laws is based on court interpretations of their meaning. The Supreme Court has defined monopolization as possessing or seeking monopoly pricing power in the "relevant market." Authorities charged with enforcing antitrust laws use a market share test, which involves determining the percentage of market production or sales supplied by a firm. A key issue in applying the market share test is defining the relevant market. In recent years, antitrust officials have raised questions about whether product packaging, either in the form of different versions or as bundled sets, is a type of price discrimination. Versioning generally is not considered to constitute price discrimination, so it has not attracted much antitrust attention. In contrast, U.S. antitrust authorities have charged that product bundling is a means of engaging in tie-in sales, in

monopolization, 731
market share test, 731
versioning, 732
bundling, 732
tie-in sales, 732

- **MyEconLab** Study Plan 28.6
- Video: Theory of Contestable Markets

(continued)

 (continued)

PROBLEMS

All problems are assignable in myeconlab. *Answers to odd-numbered problems appear at the back of the book.*

28-1. Local cable television companies are sometimes granted monopoly rights to service a particular territory of a metropolitan area. The companies typically pay special taxes and licensing fees to local municipalities. Why might a municipality give monopoly rights to a cable company?

28-2. A local cable company, the sole provider of cable television service, is regulated by the municipal government. The owner of the company claims that she is normally opposed to regulation by government, but asserts that regulation is necessary because local residents would not want a large number of different cables crisscrossing the city. Why do you think the owner is defending regulation by the city?

28-3. The table below depicts the cost and demand structure a natural monopoly faces.

Quantity	Price ($)	Long-Run Total Cost ($)
0	100	0
1	95	92
2	90	177
3	85	255
4	80	331
5	75	406
6	70	480

a. Calculate total revenues, marginal revenue, and marginal cost at each output level. If this firm is allowed to operate as a monopolist, what will be the quantity produced and the price charged by the firm? What will be the amount of monopoly profit?

b. If regulators require the firm to practice marginal cost pricing, what quantity will it produce, and what price will it charge? What is the firm's profit under this regulatory framework?

c. If regulators require the firm to practice average cost pricing, what quantity will it produce, and what price will it charge? What is the firm's profit under this regulatory framework?

28-4. As noted in the chapter, separating the *production* of electricity from its *delivery* has led to considerable deregulation of producers.

a. Briefly explain which of these two aspects of the sale of electricity remains susceptible to natural monopoly problems.

b. Suppose that the potential natural monopoly problem you identified in part (a) actually arises. Why is marginal cost pricing not a feasible solution? What makes average cost pricing a feasible solution?

c. Discuss two approaches that a regulator could use to try to implement an average-cost-pricing solution to the problem identified in part (a).

28-5. Are lemons problems likely to be more common in some industries and less common in others? Based on your answer to this question, should government regulatory activities designed to reduce the scope of lemons problems take the form of economic regulation or social regulation? Take a stand, and support your reasoning.

28-6. Research into genetically modified crops has led to significant productivity gains for countries such as the United States that employ these techniques. Countries such as the European Union's member nations, however, have imposed controls on the import of these products, citing concern for public health. Is the European Union's regulation of genetically modified crops social regulation or economic regulation?

28-7. Do you think that the regulation described in Problem 28-6 is more likely an example of the capture hypothesis or the share-the-gains, share-the-pains theory? Why?

28-8. Prices of tickets for seats on commercial passenger planes are typically in the hundreds of dollars, whereas trips can be made by automobile at much lower cost. Accident rates per person per trip in the airline industry are considerably lower than auto accident rates per person per trip. Based on these facts, discuss how regulatory costs and benefits may help to explain why government regulations require children to be placed in safety seats in automobiles but not on commercial passenger planes.

28-9. In 2003, the U.S. government created a "Do Not Call Registry" and forbade marketing firms from calling people who placed their names on this list. Today, an increasing number of companies are sending mail solicitations to individuals inviting them to send back an enclosed postcard for more information about the firms' products. What these solicitations fail to mention is that they are worded in such a way that someone who returns the postcard gives up protection from telephone solicitations, even if they are on the government's "Do Not Call Registry." In what type of behavior are these companies engaging? Explain your answer. (Hint: Are these firms meeting the letter of the law but violating its spirit?)

28-10. Suppose that a business has developed a very high-quality product and operates more efficiently in producing that product than any other potential competitor. As a consequence, at present it is the only seller of this product, for which there are few close substitutes. Is this firm in violation of U.S. antitrust laws? Explain.

28-11. Consider the following fictitious sales data (in thousands of dollars) for books sold both over the Internet and in physical retail establishments. Firms have numbers instead of names, and Firm 1 generates book sales only over the Internet. Antitrust authorities judge that a single firm possesses "monopoly power" if its share of sales in the relevant market exceeds 70 percent.

Internet Book Sales		Book Sales in Physical Stores		Combined Book Sales	
Firm	Sales	Firm	Sales	Firm	Sales
1	$ 750	2	$4,200	2	$ 4,250
2	50	3	2,000	3	2,050
3	50	4	1,950	4	2,000
4	50	5	450	1	750
5	50	6	400	5	500
6	50			6	450
Total	$1,000		$9,000		$10,000

a. Suppose that the antitrust authorities determine that bookselling in physical retail stores and Internet bookselling are individually separate relevant markets. Does any single firm have monopoly power, as defined by the antitrust authorities?

b. Suppose that in fact there is really only a single book industry, in which firms compete both in physical retail stores and via the Internet. According to the antitrust authorities' measure of monopoly power, is there actually cause for concern?

28-12. In recent years, the Internet auction firm eBay has sought to make its auction technology the favorite of software programmers, and it has begun licensing its technology to other Web sites. The company's managers have publicly stated that their goal is for eBay's auction system to become the dominant "operating system" of all auction applications on the Internet. Are there any potential antitrust issues related to the company's efforts?

28-13. Recently, the U.S. Justice Department initiated an antitrust investigation of Homestore.com, a Web site containing the property listings of thousands of real estate agents in the United States. In cities and in local communities, there is considerable rivalry among real estate agents. Nevertheless, nearly all belong to the National Association of Realtors (NAR), which is the majority owner of Homestore.com. In 2000, Homestore.com purchased a rival site, Move.com, and took its name. This left Homeadvisor.com as its only remaining key rival. Why do you suppose the Justice Department became concerned about the activities of the NAR? What factors are likely to affect its decision about whether the NAR violated any antitrust laws?

28-14. A package delivery company provides both overnight and second-day delivery services. It charges almost twice as much to deliver an overnight package to any world location as it does to deliver the same package to the same location in two days. Often, second-day packages arrive at company warehouses in destination cities by the next day, but drivers intentionally do not deliver these packages until the following day. What is this business practice called? Briefly summarize alternative perspectives concerning whether this activity should or should not be viewed as a form of price discrimination.

28-15. A firm that sells both Internet-security software and computer antivirus software will sell the antivirus software as a stand-alone product. It will only sell the Internet-security software to consumers in a combined package that also includes the antivirus software. What is this business practice called? Briefly explain why an antitrust authority might view this practice as a form of price discrimination.

28-16. Recently, a food retailer called Whole Foods sought to purchase Wild Oats, a competitor in the market for organic foods. When the Federal Trade Commission (FTC) sought to block this merger on antitrust grounds, FTC officials argued that such a merger would dramatically increase concentration in the market for "premium organic foods." Whole Foods' counterargument was that it considered itself to be part of the broadly defined supermarket industry that includes retailers such as Albertson's, Kroger, and Safeway. What key issue of antitrust regulation was involved in this dispute? Explain.

ECONOMICS ON THE NET

Guidelines for U.S. Antitrust Merger Enforcement How does the U.S. government apply antitrust laws to mergers? This application gives you the opportunity to learn about the standards applied by the Antitrust Division of the U.S. Department of Justice when it evaluates a proposed merger.

Title: U.S. Department of Justice Antitrust Merger Enforcement Guidelines

Navigation: Go to **www.econtoday.com/chapter28** to access the home page of the Antitrust Division of the U.S. Department of Justice.

Application Answer the following questions.

1. Click on *Horizontal Merger Guidelines*. In section 1, click on *Overview*, and read this section. What factors do U.S. antitrust authorities consider when evaluating the potential for a horizontal merger to "enhance

market power"—that is, to place the combination in a monopoly situation?

2. Back up to the page titled *Merger Enforcement Guidelines*, and click on *Non-Horizontal Merger Guidelines*. Read the guidelines. In what situations will the antitrust authorities most likely question a nonhorizontal merger?

For Group Study and Analysis Have three groups of students from the class examine sections 1, 2, and 3 of the *Horizontal Merger Guidelines* discussed in item 1. After each group reports on all the factors that the antitrust authorities consider when evaluating a horizontal merger, discuss why large teams of lawyers and many economic consultants are typically involved when the Antitrust Division of the Department of Justice alleges that a proposed merger would be "anticompetitive."

ANSWERS TO QUICK QUIZZES

p. 717: (i) Economic . . . social; (ii) natural . . . economic; (iii) social
p. 721: (i) lower . . . revenue . . . cost; (ii) average . . . zero; (iii) deliver . . . networks
p. 724: (i) failures . . . asymmetric; (ii) asymmetric; (iii) lemons . . . low
p. 727: (i) consumers . . . firms; (ii) industry . . . legislators . . . consumers; (iii) government . . . firms'
p. 731: (i) Sherman; (ii) Clayton; (iii) Federal Trade Commission; (iv) Robinson-Patman
p. 733: (i) market share . . . sales; (ii) product . . . geographic; (iii) versioning . . . bundling

The Labor Market: Demand, Supply, and Outsourcing

29

Ever since economists first began collecting data on wages to try to determine key factors influencing variations in earnings across different individuals, they have found that, on average, women consistently earn less than men. This differential between the average earnings of men and women, which is often called the "male-female wage gap," has narrowed in recent years. Nevertheless, the gap remains substantial. What factors account for the average pay gap between men and women? To be able to consider potential answers to this question, you must first learn about the determinants of labor demand and supply, which together determine the market clearing wages earned by both men and women.

LEARNING OBJECTIVES

MyEconLab helps you master each objective and study more efficiently. See end of chapter for details.

After reading this chapter, you should be able to:

➤ Understand why a firm's marginal revenue product curve is its labor demand curve

➤ Explain in what sense the demand for labor is a "derived" demand

➤ Identify the key factors influencing the elasticity of demand for inputs

➤ Describe how equilibrium wage rates are determined for perfectly competitive firms

➤ Explain what labor outsourcing is and how it is ultimately likely to affect U.S. workers' earnings and employment prospects

➤ Contrast the demand for labor and wage determination by a product market monopolist with outcomes that would arise under perfect competition

DID YOU KNOW THAT when European advocacy groups wish to hold a protest march but find themselves short on protesters, some of them turn to a German firm called Erento that specializes in renting demonstrators? The firm's Web site features about 300 demonstrators-for-hire and lists personal characteristics such as height, skin color, and ethnicity. The company charges a fee of nearly $190 per demonstrator for a six-hour day of protesting.

The demand for demonstrators-for-hire by advocacy groups or for any other inputs on the part of businesses can be studied in much the same manner as we studied the demand for output. Our analysis will always end with the same conclusion: A firm will hire employees up to the point beyond which it isn't profitable to hire any more. It will hire employees to the point at which the marginal benefit of hiring a worker will just equal the marginal cost. Indeed, in every profit-maximizing situation, it is most profitable to carry out an activity up to the point at which the marginal benefit equals the marginal cost. Remembering that guideline will help you in analyzing decision making at the firm level, which is where we will begin our discussion of the demand for labor.

Labor Demand for a Perfectly Competitive Firm

We will start our analysis under the assumption that the market for input factors is perfectly competitive. We will further assume that the output market is perfectly competitive. This provides a benchmark against which to compare other situations in which labor markets or product markets are not perfectly competitive.

Competition in the Product Market

Let's take as our example a firm that sells flash memory drives and is in competition with many companies selling the same kind of product. Assume that the laborers hired by this manufacturing firm do not need any special skills. This firm sells flash memory drives in a perfectly competitive market. It also buys labor (its variable input) in a perfectly competitive market. A firm that hires labor under perfectly competitive conditions hires only a minuscule proportion of all the workers who are potentially available to the firm. By "potentially available," we mean all the workers in a given geographic area who possess the skills demanded by our perfect competitor. In such a market, it is always possible for the individual firm to hire extra workers without having to offer a higher wage. Thus, the supply of labor to the firm is perfectly elastic at the going wage rate established by the forces of supply and demand in the entire labor market. The firm is a *price taker* in the labor market.

Marginal Physical Product

Look at panel (a) of Figure 29-1. In column 1, we show the number of workers per week that the firm can employ. In column 2, we show total physical product (TPP) per week, the total *physical* production of flash memory drives that different quantities of the labor input (in combination with a fixed amount of other inputs) will generate in a week's time. In column 3, we show the additional output gained when the company adds workers to its existing manufacturing facility. This column, the **marginal physical product (MPP) of labor,** represents the extra (additional) output attributed to employing additional units of the variable input factor. If this firm employs seven workers rather than six, the MPP is 118. The law of diminishing marginal product predicts that additional units of a variable factor will, after some point, cause the MPP to decline, other things held constant.

Marginal physical product (MPP) of labor
The change in output resulting from the addition of one more worker. The MPP of the worker equals the change in total output accounted for by hiring the worker, holding all other factors of production constant.

FIGURE 29-1

Marginal Revenue Product

In panel (a), column 4 shows marginal revenue product (MRP), which is the additional revenue the firm receives for the sale of that additional output. Marginal revenue product is simply the revenue the additional worker brings in—the combination of that worker's contribution to production and the revenue that that production will bring to the firm. For this perfectly competitive firm, marginal revenue is equal to the price of the product, or $10 per unit. At a weekly wage of $830, the profit-maximizing employer will pay for only 12 workers because then the marginal revenue product is just equal to the wage rate or weekly salary.

Panel (a)

(1) Labor Input (workers per week)	(2) Total Physical Product (TPP) (flash drives per week)	(3) Marginal Physical Product (MPP) (flash drives per week)	(4) Marginal Revenue (MR = P = $10) x MPP = Marginal Revenue Product (MRP) ($ per additional worker)	(5) Wage Rate ($ per week) = Marginal Factor Cost (MFC) = Change in Total Costs ÷ Change in Labor
6	882			
		118	$1,180	$830
7	1,000			
		111	1,110	830
8	1,111			
		104	1,040	830
9	1,215			
		97	970	830
10	1,312			
		90	900	830
11	1,402			
		83	830	830
12	1,485			
		76	760	830
13	1,561			

In panel (b), we find the number of workers the firm will want to hire by observing the wage rate that is established by the forces of supply and demand in the entire labor market. We show that this employer is hiring labor in a perfectly competitive labor market and therefore faces a perfectly elastic supply curve represented by s at a constant marginal factor cost (MFC) of $830 per week. As in other situations, we have a supply and demand model; in this example, the demand curve is represented by MRP, and the supply curve is s. Profit maximization occurs at their intersection, which is the point at which MRP = MFC.

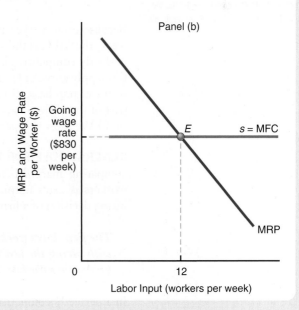

We are assuming that all other nonlabor factors of production are held constant. So, if our manufacturing firm wants to add one more worker to its production line, it has to crowd all the existing workers a little closer together because it does not increase its capital stock (the production equipment). Therefore, as we add more workers, each one has a smaller and smaller fraction of the available capital stock with which to work. If one worker uses one machine, adding another worker usually won't double the output because the machine can run only so fast and for so many hours per day. In other words, MPP declines because of the law of diminishing marginal product (see Chapter 23).

Marginal Revenue Product

We now need to translate into a dollar value the physical product that results from hiring an additional worker. This is done by multiplying the marginal physical product by the marginal revenue of the firm. Because this firm sells flash memory drives in a perfectly competitive market, marginal revenue is equal to the price of the product. If employing seven workers rather than six yields an MPP of 118 and the marginal revenue is $10 per flash memory drive, the **marginal revenue product (MRP)** is $1,180 (118 × $10). The MRP is shown in column 4 of panel (a) of Figure 29-1 on the preceding page. *The marginal revenue product represents the incremental worker's contribution to the firm's total revenues.*

When a firm operates in a perfectly competitive product market, the marginal physical product times the product price is also referred to as the *value of marginal product (VMP)*. Because price and marginal revenue are the same for a perfectly competitive firm, the VMP is also the MRP for such a firm.

In column 5 of panel (a) of Figure 29-1, we show the wage rate, or *marginal factor cost*, of each worker. The marginal cost of workers is the extra cost incurred in employing an additional unit of that factor of production. We call that cost the **marginal factor cost (MFC).** Otherwise stated,

$$\text{Marginal factor cost} = \frac{\text{change in total cost}}{\text{change in amount of resource used}}$$

Because each worker is paid the same competitively determined wage of $830 per week, the MFC is the same for all workers. And because the firm is buying labor in a perfectly competitive labor market, the wage rate of $830 per week really represents the supply curve of labor to the firm. That supply curve is perfectly elastic because the firm can purchase all labor at the same wage rate, considering that it is a minuscule part of the entire labor-purchasing market. (Recall the definition of perfect competition.) We show this perfectly elastic supply curve as *s* in panel (b) of Figure 29-1.

GENERAL RULE FOR HIRING Virtually every optimizing rule in economics involves comparing marginal benefits with marginal cost. Because the benefit from added workers is extra output and consequently more revenues, the general rule for the hiring decision of a firm is this:

> *The firm hires workers up to the point at which the additional cost associated with hiring the last worker is equal to the additional revenue generated by hiring that worker.*

In a perfectly competitive market, this is the point at which the wage rate just equals the marginal revenue product. If the firm were to hire more workers, the additional wages would not be covered by additional increases in total revenue. If the firm were

---

Marginal revenue product (MRP)
The marginal physical product (MPP) times marginal revenue (MR). The MRP gives the additional revenue obtained from a one-unit change in labor input.

Marginal factor cost (MFC)
The cost of using an additional unit of an input. For example, if a firm can hire all the workers it wants at the going wage rate, the marginal factor cost of labor is the wage rate.

to hire fewer workers, it would be forfeiting the contributions that those workers otherwise could make to total profits.

Therefore, referring to columns 4 and 5 in panel (a) of Figure 29-1 on page 743, we see that this firm would certainly employ at least seven workers because the MRP is $1,180 while the MFC is only $830. The firm would continue to add workers up to the point at which MFC = MRP because as workers are added, those additional workers contribute more to revenue than to cost.

THE MRP CURVE: DEMAND FOR LABOR We can also use panel (b) of Figure 29-1 to find how many workers our firm should hire. First, we draw a line at the going wage rate, which is determined by demand and supply in the labor market. The line is labeled *s* to indicate that it is the supply curve of labor for the *individual* firm purchasing labor in a perfectly competitive labor market. That firm can purchase all the labor it wants of equal quality at $830 per worker. This perfectly elastic supply curve, *s*, intersects the marginal revenue product curve at 12 workers per week. At the intersection, *E*, the wage rate is equal to the marginal revenue product. The firm maximizes profits where its demand curve for labor, which turns out to be its MRP curve, intersects the firm's supply curve for labor, shown as *s*. The firm in our example would not hire the thirteenth worker, who would add only $760 to revenue but $830 to cost. If the price of labor should fall to, say, $760 per worker per week, the firm would hire an additional worker. Thus, the quantity of labor demanded increases as the wage decreases.

Derived Demand for Labor

We have identified an individual firm's demand for labor curve, which shows the quantity of labor that the firm will wish to hire at each wage rate, as its MRP curve. Under conditions of perfect competition in both product and labor markets, MRP is determined by multiplying MPP times the product's price. This suggests that the demand for labor is a **derived demand.** Factors of production are rented or purchased not because they give any intrinsic satisfaction to the firms' owners but because they can be used to manufacture output that is expected to be sold at a profit.

We know that an increase in the market demand for a given product raises the product's price (all other things held constant), which in turn increases the marginal revenue product, or demand for the resource. Figure 29-2 on the following page illustrates the effective role played by changes in product demand in a perfectly competitive product market. The MRP curve shifts whenever there is a change in the price of the final product that the workers are producing. Suppose, for example, that the market price of flash memory drives declines. In that case, the MRP curve will shift to the left from MRP_0 to MRP_1. We know that $MRP \equiv MPP \times MR$. If marginal revenue (here the output price) falls, so does the demand for labor. At the same going wage rate, the firm will hire fewer workers. This is because at various levels of labor use, the marginal revenue product of labor is now lower. At the initial equilibrium, therefore, the price of labor (here the MFC) becomes greater than MRP. Thus, the firm would reduce the number of workers hired. Conversely, if marginal revenue (the output price) rises, the demand for labor will also rise, and the firm will want to hire more workers at each and every possible wage rate.

We just pointed out that $MRP \equiv MPP \times MR$. Clearly, then, a change in marginal productivity, or in the marginal physical product of labor, will shift the MRP curve. If the marginal productivity of labor decreases, the MRP curve, or demand curve, for

Derived demand
Input factor demand derived from demand for the final product being produced.

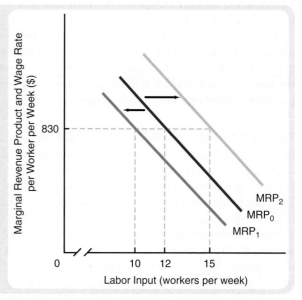

FIGURE 29-2

Demand for Labor, a Derived Demand

The demand for labor is derived from the demand for the final product being produced. Therefore, the marginal revenue product curve will shift whenever the price of the product changes. If we start with the marginal revenue product curve MRP_0 at the going wage rate of $830 per week, 12 workers will be hired. If the price of flash memory drives goes down, the marginal product curve will shift to MRP_1, and the number of workers hired will fall, in this case to 10. If the price of flash memory drives goes up, the marginal revenue product curve will shift to MRP_2, and the number of workers hired will increase, in this case to 15.

labor will shift inward to the left. Again, this is because at every quantity of labor used, the MRP will be lower. A lower quantity of labor will be demanded at every possible wage rate.

QUICK QUIZ   See page 767 for the answers. Review concepts from this section in MyEconLab.

The change in total _____ due to a one-unit change in one variable _____, holding all other _____ constant, is called the **marginal physical product (MPP).** When we multiply marginal physical product times _____ _____, we obtain the **marginal revenue product (MRP).**

A firm will hire workers up to the point at which the additional cost of hiring one more worker is equal to the

additional revenue generated. For the individual firm, therefore, its MRP of labor curve is also its _____ _____ labor curve.

The demand for labor is a _____ demand, _____ from the demand for final output. Therefore, a change in the price of the final output will cause a _____ in the MRP curve (which is also the firm's demand for labor curve).

The Market Demand for Labor

The downward-sloping portion of each individual firm's marginal revenue product curve is also its demand curve for the one variable factor of production—in our example, labor. When we go to the entire market for a particular type of labor in a particular industry, we will also find that the quantity of labor demanded will vary inversely as the wage rate changes.

Constructing the Market Labor Demand Curve

Given that the market demand curve for labor is made up of the individual firms' downward-sloping demand curves for labor, we can safely infer that the market demand curve for labor will look like D in panel (b) of Figure 29-3: It will slope

3. *Change in the price of related factors.* Labor is not the only resource that firms use. Some resources are substitutes and some are complements in the production process. If we hold output constant, we have the following general rule:

> **A change in the price of a substitute input will cause the demand for labor (or any other input) to change in the same direction.**

Thus, if the price of an input for which labor can substitute as a factor of production decreases, the demand for labor falls. For instance, if the price of mechanized ditch-digging equipment decreases, the demand for workers who, in contrast, can use shovels to dig ditches decreases.

In general, a fall in the price of an input generates a decline in demand for any substitute input. How are computer programs contributing to a reduction in the demand for the skills of performing musicians?

E-COMMERCE EXAMPLE
Why Hire an Orchestra When a Computer Program Will Do?

Today, when a composer wishes to record a six-minute musical composition written for an ensemble of 18 string instruments, one option is to pay about $50,000 for 18 musicians to produce a professional recording. Another option is to pay $800 to firms such as Fauxharmonic Orchestra to create a recording using a computer program that re-creates the tones of the required 18 instruments. For most composers, this is an easy decision to make. As the price of computer-generated musical recordings has decreased, the demand for human musicians has declined.

FOR CRITICAL ANALYSIS
What do you suppose has happened to the demand for string instruments used by performing musicians as a result of the decrease in the demand for musicians' services?

Suppose that a particular type of capital equipment and labor are complementary. In general, we predict the following:

> **A change in the price of a complementary input will cause the demand for labor to change in the opposite direction.**

If the price of machines goes up but they must be used with labor, fewer machines will be purchased and therefore fewer workers will be used.

DETERMINANTS OF THE SUPPLY OF LABOR Labor supply curves may shift in a particular industry for a number of reasons. For example, if wage rates for factory workers in the digital camera industry remain constant while wages for factory workers in the computer industry go up dramatically, the supply curve of factory workers in the digital camera industry will shift inward to the left as these workers move to the computer industry.

Why are highly trained divers supplying their labor to the nuclear power industry?

EXAMPLE
Why Divers Are Supplying Labor to Nuclear Reactors

Many professional divers work for oil companies. They inspect oil rigs and sometimes engage in underwater repair work. Municipal governments also employ divers to repair aging bridges and water tanks and to perform lifesaving rescue missions.

Another line of work for trained divers is nuclear diving. Nuclear reactors range in size from 35 feet to 70 feet tall and 14 feet to 20 feet wide. During normal operations, reactors are partially filled with about 60,000 gallons of water to cool the nuclear fuel and to be transformed into steam to power turbines. When reactors are shut down for refueling and maintenance, primary and secondary pools are filled with more than 500,000 gallons of water to cool them down. During these periods, divers are lowered into the pools to replace cylinders of fuel and to perform routine maintenance. Divers are attracted to nuclear diving because a diver who is certified for this specialized work earns as much as $100,000 per year, an annual salary that is higher than the salaries available in most other diving-related occupations.

FOR CRITICAL ANALYSIS
What happened to the labor supply curve in the market for nuclear divers when wages earned by divers in other industries fell relative to those available in the nuclear power industry?

Changes in working conditions in an industry can also affect its labor supply curve. If employers in the digital camera industry discover a new production technique that makes working conditions much more pleasant, the supply curve of labor to the digital camera industry will shift outward to the right.

Job flexibility also determines the position of the labor supply curve. For example, when an industry allows workers more flexibility, such as the ability to work at home via computer, the workers are likely to provide more hours of labor. That is to say, their supply curve will shift outward to the right. Some industries in which firms offer *job sharing*, particularly to people raising families, have found that the supply curve of labor has shifted outward to the right.

QUICK QUIZ   See page 767 for the answers. Review concepts from this section in MyEconLab.

The individual perfectly competitive firm faces a perfectly _____ labor supply curve—it can hire all the labor it wants at the going market wage rate. The industry supply curve of labor slopes _____.

By plotting an industrywide supply curve for labor and an industrywide demand curve for labor on the same graph, we obtain the _____ wage rate in the industry.

The labor demand curve can shift because the _____ for the final product shifts, labor _____ changes, or the price of a related (_____ or _____) factor of production changes.

Labor Outsourcing, Wages, and Employment

In addition to making it easier for people to work at home, computer technology has made it possible for them to provide labor services to companies located in another country. Some companies based in Canada regularly transmit financial records—often via the Internet—to U.S. accountants so that they can process payrolls and compile income statements. Meanwhile, some U.S. manufacturers of personal computers and peripheral devices arrange for customers' calls for assistance to be directed to call centers in India, where English-speaking technical-support specialists help the customers with their problems.

A firm that employs labor located outside the country in which it is based engages in labor **outsourcing.** Canadian companies that hire U.S. accountants outsource accounting services to the United States. U.S. computer manufacturers that employ Indian call-center staff outsource technical-support services to India. How does outsourcing affect employment and wages in the United States? Who loses and who gains from outsourcing? Let's consider each of these questions in turn.

Outsourcing
A firm's employment of labor outside the country in which the firm is located.

Wage and Employment Effects of Outsourcing

Equilibrium wages and levels of employment in U.S. labor markets are determined by the demands for and supplies of labor in those markets. As you have learned, one of the determinants of the market demand for labor is the price of a substitute input. Availability of a lower-priced substitute, you also learned, causes the demand for labor to fall. Thus, the *immediate* economic effects of labor outsourcing are straightforward. When a home industry's firms can obtain *foreign* labor services that are a close substitute for *home* labor services, the demand for labor services provided by home workers will decrease. What this economic reasoning ultimately implies for U.S. labor markets, however, depends on whether we view the United States as the "home" country or the "foreign" country.

U.S. LABOR MARKET EFFECTS OF OUTSOURCING BY U.S. FIRMS To begin, let's view the United States as the home country. Suppose that initially all U.S. firms employ only U.S. workers. Then developments in computer, communications, and transportation technologies enable an increasing number of U.S. firms to regard the labor of foreign workers as a close substitute for labor provided by U.S. workers. Take a look at Figure 29-5 on the following page. Panel (a) depicts demand and supply curves in the U.S. market for workers who handle calls for technical support for U.S. manufacturers of personal computers. Suppose that before technological change makes foreign labor substitutable for U.S. labor, point E_1 is the initial equilibrium. At this point, the market wage rate in this U.S. labor market is $19 per hour.

Now suppose that improvements in communications technologies enable U.S. personal computer manufacturers to consider foreign labor as a substitute input for U.S. labor. Panel (b) displays demand and supply curves in a market for substitutable labor services in India. At the initial equilibrium point E_1, the wage rate denominated in U.S. dollars is $8 per hour. Firms in this U.S. industry will respond to the lower price of substitute labor in India by increasing their demand for labor services in that country and reducing their demand for U.S. labor. Thus, in panel (b), the market demand for the substitute labor services available in India rises. The market wage in India rises to $13 per hour, at point E_2, and Indian employment increases. In panel (a), the market demand for U.S. labor services decreases. At the new equilibrium point E_2, the U.S. market wage has fallen to $16 per hour, and equilibrium employment has decreased.

Consequently, when U.S. firms are the home firms engaging in labor outsourcing, the effects are lower wages and decreased employment in the relevant U.S. labor markets. In those nations where workers providing the outsourced labor reside, the effects are higher wages and increased employment.

How are U.S. educational tutoring services being outsourced? (See the next page.)

When U.S. firms employ the services of Indian call centers, what happens to the demand curve for suitable Indian labor and what happens to wage rates for this type of labor in India?

FIGURE 29-5

Outsourcing of U.S. Computer Technical-Support Services

Initially, the market wage for U.S. workers providing technical support for customers of U.S. computer manufacturers is $19 per hour at point E_1 in panel (a), while the market wage for Indian workers who provide the same service is $8 per hour in panel (b). Then, improvements in communications technologies enable U.S. firms to substitute away from U.S. workers in favor of Indian workers. The market demand for U.S. labor decreases in panel (a), generating a new equilibrium at point E_2 at a lower U.S. market wage and employment level. The market demand for Indian labor increases in panel (b), bringing about higher wages and employment at point E_2.

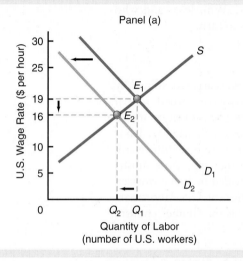

Panel (a)

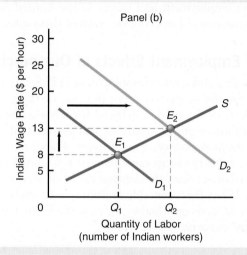

Panel (b)

INTERNATIONAL EXAMPLE
Real-Time Tutoring from the Far Side of the World

To U.S. residents with access to a personal computer, a webcam, and the appropriate software, tutoring services are available from anyone willing to provide them via the Internet. Online tutoring firms based in India, such as Educomp, TutorVista, and Career Launcher, offer real-time, interactive video tutoring for students at levels ranging from elementary school through junior college. These firms charge as little as $150 per month, whereas a single session with a U.S. tutor might run as high as $100. Not surprisingly, an increasing number of U.S. parents are opting to outsource tutoring to these Indian tutoring companies.

FOR CRITICAL ANALYSIS
How does U.S. labor outsourcing help to fuel the demand for U.S. export products? (Hint: How does outsourcing by U.S. firms affect foreign workers' wage incomes, which they can use to buy items from other nations, including the United States?)

U.S. LABOR MARKET EFFECTS OF OUTSOURCING BY FOREIGN FIRMS U.S. firms are not the only companies that engage in outsourcing. Consider the Canadian companies that hire U.S. accountants to calculate their payrolls and maintain their financial records. Figure 29-6 shows the effects in the Canadian and U.S. markets for labor services provided by accountants before and after *Canadian* outsourcing of accountants' labor. At point E_1 in panel (a), before any outsourcing takes place, the initial market wage for qualified accountants in Canada is $29 per hour. In panel (b), the market wage for similarly qualified U.S. accountants is $21 per hour.

FIGURE 29-6

Outsourcing of Accounting Services by Canadian Firms

Suppose that the market wage for accounting services in Canada is initially $29 per hour, at point E_1 in panel (a), but in the United States accountants earn just $21 per hour at point E_1 in panel (b). Then, Internet access enables Canadian firms to substitute labor services provided by U.S. accountants for the services of Canadian accountants. The market demand for the services of

Canadian accountants decreases in panel (a), and at point E_2 fewer Canadian accountants are employed at a lower market wage. The market demand for U.S. accounting services increases in panel (b). This generates higher wages and employment for U.S. accountants at point E_2.

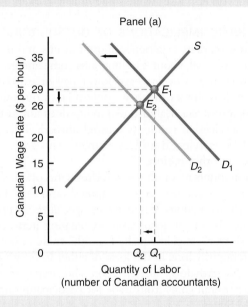

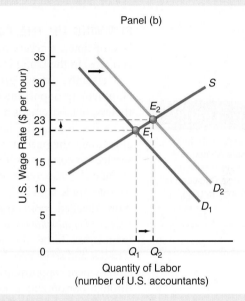

After Internet access allows companies in Canada to transfer financial data electronically, the services of U.S. accountants become available as a less expensive substitute for those provided by Canadian accountants. When Canadian firms respond by seeking to outsource to U.S. accountants, the demand for U.S. accountants' labor services rises in panel (b). This causes the market wage earned by U.S. accountants to increase to $23 per hour. Canadian firms substitute away from the services of Canadian accountants, so in panel (a) the demand for the labor of accountants in Canada declines. Canadian accountants' wages decline to $26 per hour.

In contrast to the situation in which U.S. firms are the home firms engaging in labor outsourcing, when foreign firms outsource by hiring workers in the United States, wages and employment levels rise in the affected U.S. markets. In the nations where the firms engaging in outsourcing are located, the effects are lower wages and decreased employment.

Gauging the Net Effects of Outsourcing on the U.S. Economy

In the example depicted in Figure 29-5, the market wage and employment level for U.S. technical-support workers declined as a result of outsourcing by U.S. firms. In contrast, in the example shown in Figure 29-6, U.S. accountants earned higher wages and experienced increased employment as a result of outsourcing by Canadian firms. Together, these examples illustrate a fundamental conclusion concerning the short-run effects of global labor outsourcing in U.S. labor markets:

To read a Heritage Foundation lecture about the net effects of outsourcing on U.S. jobs, use the link at **www.econtoday.com/chapter29**.

Labor outsourcing by U.S. firms tends to reduce U.S. wages and employment. Whenever foreign firms engage in labor outsourcing in the United States, however, U.S. wages and employment increase.

Consequently, the immediate effects of increased worldwide labor outsourcing are lower wages and employment in some U.S. labor markets and higher wages and employment in others. In this narrow sense, some U.S. workers "lose" from outsourcing while others "gain," just as some Canadian workers "lose" while some Indian workers "gain."

SUMMING UP THE ECONOMIC IMPLICATIONS OF OUTSOURCING Even in the best of times, workers in labor markets experience short-run ups and downs in wages and jobs. In the United States, after all, about 4 million jobs come and go every month.

Certainly, various groups of U.S. workers earn lower pay or experience reduced employment opportunities, at least for a time, as a result of labor outsourcing. Nevertheless, outsourcing is a two-way street. Labor outsourcing does not just involve U.S. firms purchasing the labor services of residents located abroad. This phenomenon also entails the purchase of labor services from U.S. workers who provide outsourcing services to companies located in other nations.

Indeed, outsourcing really amounts to another way for residents of different nations to conduct trade with one another. As you learned in Chapter 2 (also see Chapter 33 for a more detailed look), trade allows nations' residents to specialize according to their *comparative advantages* and thereby obtain gains from exchanging items across country boundaries. To be sure, not all workers gain equally from the trade of outsourced labor services, and some people temporarily lose, in the form of either lower wages or reduced employment opportunities. Nevertheless, specialization and trade of labor services through outsourcing generate overall gains from trade for participating nations, such as India, Canada, and the United States.

You Are There

To learn about how U.S. jobs are already being created as a by-product of foreign outsourcing, read **"Reverse Outsourcing" Provides New Jobs in Ohio,** on page 761.

QUICK QUIZ *See page 767 for the answers. Review concepts from this section in MyEconLab.*

Advances in telecommunications and computer networking are making foreign labor more easily _____ for home labor, and home firms' _____ of foreign labor for home labor is known as labor **outsourcing.**

In the short run, outsourcing by U.S. firms _____ the demand for labor, market wages, and equilibrium employment in U.S. labor markets. Outsourcing by foreign firms

that hire U.S. labor _____ the demand for labor, market wages, and equilibrium employment in U.S. labor markets. The net short-run effects on U.S. wages and employment are mixed.

In the long run, outsourcing enables U.S. firms to operate more efficiently and this activity generates overall _____ _____ _____ for U.S. residents.

Monopoly in the Product Market

So far we've considered only perfectly competitive markets, both in selling the final product and in buying factors of production. We will continue our assumption that the firm purchases its factors of production in a perfectly competitive factor market. Now, however, we will assume that the firm sells its product in an *imperfectly* competitive output market. In other words, we are considering the output market structures of monopoly, oligopoly, and monopolistic competition. In all such cases, the firm, be it a monopolist, an oligopolist, or a monopolistic competitor, faces a downward-sloping demand curve for its product.

Throughout the rest of this chapter, we will simply refer to a monopoly situation for ease of analysis. The analysis holds for all industry structures that are less than perfectly competitive. In any event, the fact that our firm now faces a downward-sloping demand curve for its product means that if it wants to sell more of its product (at a uniform price), it has to lower the price, *not just on the last unit, but on all preceding units*. The *marginal revenue* received from selling an additional unit is continuously falling (and is less than price) as the firm attempts to sell more and more. This is certainly different from our earlier discussions in this chapter in which the firm could sell all it wanted at a constant price. Why? Because the firm we discussed until now was a perfect competitor.

Constructing the Monopolist's Input Demand Curve

In reconstructing our demand schedule for an input, we must account for the facts that (1) the marginal *physical* product falls because of the law of diminishing marginal product as more workers are added and (2) the price (and marginal revenue) received for the product sold also falls as more is produced and sold. That is, for the monopolist, we have to account for both the diminishing marginal physical product and the diminishing marginal revenue. Marginal revenue is always less than price for the monopolist. The marginal revenue curve always lies below the downward-sloping product demand curve.

MARGINAL REVENUE PRODUCT FOR A PERFECTLY COMPETITIVE FIRM Marginal revenue for the perfect competitor is equal to the price of the product because all units can be sold at the going market price. In our example involving the production of flash memory drives, we assumed that the perfect competitor could sell all it wanted at $10 per unit. A one-unit change in sales always led to a $10 change in total revenues. Hence, marginal revenue was always equal to $10 for that perfect competitor. Multiplying this unchanging marginal revenue by the marginal physical product of labor then yielded the perfectly competitive firm's marginal revenue product.

MARGINAL REVENUE PRODUCT FOR A MONOPOLY FIRM The monopolist, however, cannot simply calculate marginal revenue by looking at the price of the product. To sell the additional output from an additional unit of input, the monopolist has to cut prices on all previous units of output. As output is increasing, then, marginal revenue is falling. The underlying concept is, of course, the same for both the perfect competitor and the monopolist. We are asking exactly the same question in both cases: When an additional worker is hired, what is the benefit? In either case, the benefit is obviously the change in total revenues due to the one-unit change in the variable input, labor. In our discussion of the perfect competitor, we were able simply to look at the marginal physical product and multiply it by the *constant* per-unit price of the product because the price of the product never changed (for the perfect competitor, $P \equiv MR$).

A single monopolist ends up hiring fewer workers than would all of the perfectly competitive firms added together. To see this, we must consider the marginal revenue product for the monopolist, which varies with each one-unit change in the monopolist's labor input. This is what we do in panel (a) of Figure 29-7 on the next page, where

FIGURE 29-7

A Monopolist's Marginal Revenue Product

The monopolist hires just enough workers to make marginal revenue product equal to the going wage rate. If the going wage rate is $830 per week, as shown by the labor supply curve, *s*, in panel (b), the monopolist would want to hire approximately 10 workers per week. That is the profit-maximizing amount of labor. The labor demand curve for a perfectly competitive industry from Figure 29-4 on page 749 is also plotted (*D*). The monopolist's MRP curve will always be less elastic around the going wage rate than it would be if marginal revenue were constant.

Panel (a)

(1) Labor Input (workers per week)	(2) Marginal Physical Product (MPP) (flash drives per week)	(3) Price of Product (*P*)	(4) Marginal Revenue (MR)	(5) Marginal Revenue Product (MRP$_m$) = (2) x (4)
8	111	$11.60	$9.40	$1,043.40
9	104	11.40	9.00	936.00
10	97	11.20	8.60	834.20
11	90	11.00	8.20	738.00
12	83	10.80	7.80	647.40
13	76	10.60	7.40	562.40

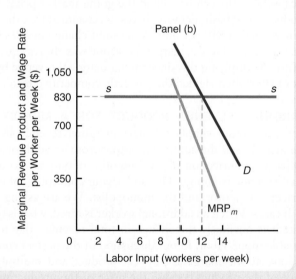

column 5, "Marginal Revenue Product," gives the monopolist a quantitative notion of how additional workers and additional production generate additional revenues. The marginal revenue product curve for this monopolist has been plotted in panel (b) of the figure. To emphasize the lower elasticity of the monopolist's MRP curve (MRP$_m$) around the wage rate $830, the labor demand curve for a perfectly competitive industry (labeled *D*) has been plotted on the same graph in Figure 29-7. Recall that this curve is not simply the sum of the marginal revenue product curves of all perfectly competitive firms, because when competitive firms together increase employment, their output expands and the product price declines. Nevertheless, at any given wage rate, the quantity of labor demanded by the monopoly is still less than the quantity of labor demanded by a perfectly competitive industry.

Why does MRP$_m$ represent the monopolist's input demand curve? As always, our profit-maximizing monopolist will continue to hire labor as long as additional profits result. Profits are made as long as the additional cost of more workers is outweighed by the additional revenues made from selling the output of those workers. When the wage rate equals these additional revenues, the monopolist stops hiring. That is, the firm stops hiring when the wage rate is equal to the marginal revenue product because additional workers would add more to cost than to revenue.

Why the Monopolist Hires Fewer Workers

Because we have used the same numbers as in Figure 29-1 on page 743, we can see that the monopolist hires fewer workers per week than firms in a perfect competitive market would. That is to say, if we could magically change the flash memory drive industry in our example from one in which there is perfect competition in the output market to one in which there is monopoly in the output market, the amount of employment would fall. Why? Because the monopolist must take account of the declining product price that must be charged in order to sell a larger number of flash memory drives. Remember that every firm hires up to the point at which marginal benefit equals marginal cost. The marginal benefit to the monopolist of hiring an additional worker is not simply the additional output times the price of the product. Rather, the monopolist faces a reduction in the price charged on *all* units sold in order to be able to sell more.

So the monopolist ends up hiring fewer workers than all of the perfect competitors taken together, assuming that all other factors remain the same for the two hypothetical examples. But this should not come as a surprise. In considering product markets, by implication we saw that a monopolized flash memory drive industry would produce less output than a competitive one. Therefore, the monopolized industry would hire fewer workers.

The Utilization of Other Factors of Production

The analysis in this chapter has been given in terms of the demand for the variable input labor. The same analysis holds for any other variable factor input. We could have talked about the demand for fertilizer or the demand for the services of tractors by a farmer instead of the demand for labor and reached the same conclusions. The entrepreneur will hire or buy any variable input up to the point at which its price equals the marginal revenue product.

A further question remains: How much of each variable factor should the firm utilize when all the variable factors are combined to produce the product? We can answer this question by looking at either the cost-minimizing side of the question or the profit-maximizing side.

Cost Minimization and Factor Utilization

From the cost minimization point of view, how can the firm minimize its total costs for a given output? Assume that you are an entrepreneur attempting to minimize costs. Consider a hypothetical situation in which if you spend $1 more on labor, you would get 20 more units of output, but if you spend $1 more on machines, you would get only 10 more units of output. What would you want to do in such a situation? You would wish to hire more workers or sell off some of your machines, for you are not getting as much output per *last* dollar spent on machines as you are per *last* dollar spent on labor. You would want to employ factors of production so that the marginal products per last dollar spent on each are equal. Thus, the least-cost, or cost minimization, rule will be as follows:

> *To minimize total costs for a particular rate of production, the firm will hire factors of production up to the point at which the marginal physical product per last dollar spent on each factor of production is equalized.*

That is,

$$\frac{\text{MPP of labor}}{\text{price of labor (wage rate)}} = \frac{\text{MPP of capital}}{\text{price of capital (cost per unit of service)}} = \frac{\text{MPP of land}}{\text{price of land (rental rate per unit)}}$$

All we are saying here is that the cost-minimizing firm will always utilize *all* resources in such combinations that cost will be minimized for any given output rate. This is commonly called the *least-cost combination of resources*.

What new variable resource is finding employment at hospitals?

EXAMPLE
Employing a New Nurse's Aide

Each year, the average 300-bed hospital spends about $3 million to pay employees for time they spend transporting medical instruments, medications, meals, and other items on carts along hallways and corridors. This is why hospitals are considering utilizing robots, such as the "Tug" produced by robotics firm Aethon, to perform some of these tasks. These robots wheel across floors; attach themselves to carts holding pumps, prescriptions, linen hampers, or other items; and transport the carts from one room to another according to preprogrammed sequences of steps. Currently, such robots can be leased for about $1,500 per month, so a hospital effectively pays just over $2 per hour for a robot's services. Not surprisingly, a number of hospitals are experimenting with investing in these capital resources as a way of attaining a new least-cost combination of resources.

FOR CRITICAL ANALYSIS
At the least-cost combination of hospital resources, what will be true of the marginal physical product of robot utilization divided by the hourly price of robots in relation to the marginal physical product of labor divided by the price of labor?

Profit Maximization Revisited

If a firm wants to maximize profits, how much of each factor should be hired (or bought)? As you have learned, the firm will never utilize a factor of production unless the marginal benefit from hiring that factor is at least equal to the marginal cost. What is the marginal benefit? As we have pointed out several times, the marginal benefit is the change in total revenues due to a one-unit change in utilization of the variable input. What is the marginal cost? In the case of a firm buying in a perfectly competitive market, it is the price of the variable factor—the wage rate if we are referring to labor.

The profit-maximizing combination of resources for the firm will be where, in a perfectly competitive market structure,

MRP of labor = price of labor (wage rates)

MRP of capital = price of capital (cost per unit of service)

MRP of land = price of land (rental rate per unit)

To attain maximum profits, the marginal revenue product of each of a firm's resources must be exactly equal to its price. If the MRP of labor is $20 and its price is only $15, the firm will expand its employment of labor.

There is an exact match between the profit-maximizing combination of resources and the least-cost combination of resources discussed above. In other words, either rule can be used to yield the same cost-minimizing rate of utilization of each variable resource.

QUICK QUIZ   *See page 767 for the answers. Review concepts from this section in MyEconLab.*

When a firm sells its output in a monopoly market, marginal revenue is _____ than price.

Just as the MRP is the perfectly competitive firm's input demand curve, the MRP is also the _____ input demand curve.

The profit-maximizing combination of factors will occur when each factor is used up to the point at which its MRP is equal to its unit _____.

To minimize total costs for a given output, the profit-maximizing firm will hire each factor of production up to the point at which the marginal _____ product per last dollar spent on each factor is equal to the marginal _____ product per last dollar spent on each of the other factors of production.

You Are There ▶ "Reverse Outsourcing" Provides New Jobs in Ohio

Christy Rice has been designated senior team leader at a call center in Reno, Ohio. The call center, which employs 250 individuals to answer phones for clients such as the online travel agency Expedia, is owned by an outsourcing company called Tata Group, which is based in Mumbai, India. Although most of Tata Group's employees are based in India, it recently decided to outsource some of its operations to the United States. The company has found that many U.S. callers feel more comfortable talking to a fellow U.S. resident over the telephone. Furthermore, the outsourcing services that Tata Group provides for some U.S. firms such as Expedia require that employees have a firm grasp of U.S. geography. There is also one additional incentive. Market clearing wages for English-speaking Indian workers with skills that Tata Group and other outsourcing firms require have been increasing. Wages in Ohio, in contrast, have declined in recent years.

Rice and her co-workers are benefiting from a phenomenon called "reverse outsourcing." As wages of workers in other nations have risen, the demand for U.S. labor by outsourcing firms in those countries has increased. This is perhaps the most important reason why Tata Group and other outsourcing firms based in India have begun hiring workers located in the United States.

CRITICAL ANALYSIS QUESTIONS

1. If Indian and U.S. call center workers were equally skilled, what would you predict would gradually happen over time to the differential between the market clearing wages of call center workers in the two countries?

2. Can you think of any types of jobs that would be difficult to outsource to India?

The Narrowing Male-Female Wage Gap

CONCEPTS APPLIED

- Marginal Revenue Product (MRP)
- Derived Demand
- Labor Demand

Women have consistently earned lower average wages than men, even after taking into account differences in education and age, as shown in Figure 29-8. What accounts for the existence of this male-female wage gap? Even though it persists, why has it declined over time?

Explaining Why the Male-Female Pay Gap Exists

Economists have offered several rationales for the existence of a gap between the earnings of men and women. One possible reason is gender-based discrimination. Some employers may consciously choose to pay men more than women, despite laws prohibiting differential treatment of a man and a woman when both are equally qualified for a position. Another rationale is differences in skills. Suppose that men obtain more skills that generate higher marginal revenue product than women obtain. Then the derived demand for skills possessed by men will be higher, and so will men's wages, other things being equal. Furthermore, in years past, women have tended to be more likely than men to seek employment in traditionally lower-paying occupations. Indeed, to the extent that women have supplied more labor in lower-wage markets, the resulting increases in labor supply have tended to push those wages down even farther.

FIGURE 29-8

The Male-Female Wage Gap

Even after taking into account differences in education and age, there has been a persistent, albeit declining, differential between the average wages of men and women holding full-time positions.

Sources: U.S. Department of Labor; author's estimates.

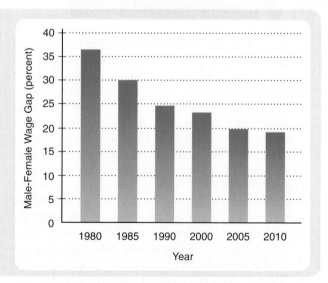

Economists have verified that an important factor accounting for the male-female wage gap is observed differences in men's and women's attachment to the labor force. On average, men are more likely than women to remain in the labor force and to be employed from year to year. As a consequence, men tend to obtain more on-the-job training and accumulate more human capital. If the growth in demand for labor in markets for high-skilled labor is greater than the growth in demand for labor in markets for lower-skilled positions, men will benefit from their more persistent involvement in the labor market by earning higher wages.

Why the Male-Female Wage Gap Has Narrowed

Although some discrimination against women undoubtedly exists in labor markets, economists argue that it should gradually dissipate over time. If firms hire men who are less qualified for positions than women, then those firms experience lower marginal revenue product and hence lower profits than firms that do not discriminate. In the long run, firms that discriminate against more highly qualified women will fail to survive in the marketplace. Hence, one possible explanation for the declining male-female wage gap is a reduction in discriminatory behavior by employers.

In all likelihood, a much more important factor, however, has been a steady increase in the skills obtained by women. Today, there are more young women than men graduating from colleges and universities. Furthermore, more young women are supplying labor in markets for traditionally higher-paying occupations, such as law and medicine. Finally, the average amount of time that women remain in the labor force has increased. Taken together, these factors explain why the male-female wage gap has continued to decline over time.

Test your understanding of this chapter by going online to **MyEconLab.**
In the Study Plan for this chapter, select Section N: News.

For Critical Analysis

1. How would a gradual increase in the percentage of fathers who stay home to care for young children while their wives continue working ultimately alter the male-female wage gap?

2. What is likely to eventually happen to the male-female wage gap if a higher percentage of college graduates continue to be women in future years?

Web Resources

1. For a detailed discussion of factors contributing to the male-female wage gap and its gradual decline, go to www.econtoday.com/chapter29.

2. To learn about the first major piece of legislation making it illegal to pay men and women differently for performing the same tasks on the job, go to www.econtoday.com/chapter29.

Research Project

Recently, officials at The Championships, Wimbledon, the annual tennis tournament, decided that their profit-maximizing strategy was to offer equal prizes to women and men. Evaluate what this decision implies about the marginal revenue products of male and female tennis players at Wimbledon. In light of your conclusion, what does this imply about tennis fans' demands for viewing tennis matches played by male and female players? (Hint: Keep in mind that the demand for the services of tennis players is derived from the fans' demand for tournament tickets.)

Here is what you should know after reading this chapter. **MyEconLab** will help you identify what you know, and where to go when you need to practice.

WHAT YOU SHOULD KNOW

| | | WHERE TO GO TO PRACTICE |

Why a Firm's Marginal Revenue Product Curve Is Its Labor Demand Curve The marginal revenue product of labor equals marginal revenue times the marginal physical product of labor. Because of the law of diminishing marginal product, for a perfectly competitive producer the marginal revenue product curve slopes downward. To maximize profits, a firm hires labor to the point where the marginal factor cost of labor—the addition to total input costs resulting from employing an additional unit of labor—equals the marginal revenue product. In a competitive labor market, the market wage rate is the marginal factor cost of labor, so profit maximization requires hiring labor to the point where the wage rate equals marginal revenue product.

marginal physical product (MPP) of labor, 742
marginal revenue product (MRP), 744
marginal factor cost (MFC), 744

KEY FIGURES
Figure 29-1, 743
Figure 29-2, 746

- **MyEconLab** Study Plan 29.1
- Audio introduction to Chapter 29
- Animated Figures 29-1, 29-2
- ABC News Video: How Outsourcing Affects Our Lives

The Demand for Labor as a Derived Demand For firms that are perfect competitors in their product markets, marginal revenue equals the market price of their output, so the marginal revenue product of labor equals the product price times the marginal physical product of labor. As product-market conditions vary and cause the market price at which firms sell their output to change, their marginal revenue product curves shift. Hence, the demand for labor by perfectly competitive firms is derived from the demand for the final products these firms produce.

derived demand, 745

- **MyEconLab** Study Plan 29.2

Key Factors Affecting the Elasticity of Demand for Inputs The price elasticity of demand for an input, such as labor, is equal to the percentage change in the quantity of the input demanded divided by the percentage change in the price of the input, such as the wage rate. The price elasticity of demand for an input is relatively high when any one of the following is true: (1) the price elasticity of demand for the final product is relatively high; (2) it is relatively easy to substitute other inputs in production; (3) the proportion of total costs accounted for by the input is relatively large; or (4) the firm has a longer time period to adjust to the change in the input's price.

KEY FIGURE
Figure 29-3, 747

- **MyEconLab** Study Plan 29.2
- Animated Figure 29-3
- Video: Determinants of Demand Elasticity for Inputs

(continued)

 (continued)

WHAT YOU SHOULD KNOW		WHERE TO GO TO PRACTICE
How Equilibrium Wage Rates at Perfectly Competitive Firms Are Determined In a perfectly competitive labor market, at the equilibrium wage rate, the quantity of labor demanded by all firms is equal to the quantity of labor supplied by all workers in the marketplace. At this wage rate, each firm looks to its own labor demand curve to determine how much labor to employ.	**KEY FIGURE** Figure 29-4, 749	• **MyEconLab** Study Plan 29.3 • Animated Figure 29-4 • Video: Shifts in the Market Demand for Labor
U.S. Wage and Employment Effects of Labor Outsourcing Technological changes have made foreign labor more readily available as a cheaper substitute for home labor for firms that engage in labor outsourcing. The immediate, short-run effects on wages and employment in U.S. labor markets are mixed. Outsourcing by U.S. firms reduces the demand for labor in affected U.S. labor markets and thereby pushes down wages and employment. Outsourcing by foreign firms that hire U.S. labor, however, raises the demand for labor in related U.S. labor markets, which boosts U.S. wages and employment.	outsourcing, 753 **KEY FIGURES** Figure 29-5, 754 Figure 29-6, 755	• **MyEconLab** Study Plan 29.4 • Animated Figures 29-5, 29-6
Contrasting the Demand for Labor and Wage Determination Under Monopoly with Outcomes Under Perfect Competition If a firm that is a monopolist in its product market competes for labor in a competitive labor market, it takes the market wage rate as given. Its labor demand curve, however, lies to the left of the labor demand curve for the industry that would have arisen in a perfectly competitive industry. The reason is that marginal revenue is less than price for a monopolist, so the marginal revenue product of the monopolist is lower than under competition. Thus, at the competitively determined wage rate, a monopolized industry employs fewer workers than the industry otherwise would if it were perfectly competitive.	**KEY FIGURE** Figure 29-7, 758	• **MyEconLab** Study Plans 29.5, 29.6 • Animated Figure 29-7

Log in to MyEconLab, take a chapter test, and get a personalized Study Plan that tells you which concepts you understand and which ones you need to review. From there, MyEconLab will give you further practice, tutorials, animations, videos, and guided solutions.
Log in to www.myeconlab.com

PROBLEMS

All problems are assignable in mmyeconlab. *Answers to the odd-numbered problems appear at the back of the book.*

29-1. The following table depicts the output of a firm that manufactures computer printers. The printers sell for $100 each.

Labor Input (workers per week)	Total Physical Output (printers per week)
10	200
11	218
12	234
13	248
14	260
15	270
16	278

Calculate the marginal physical product and marginal revenue product at each input level above 10 units.

29-2. Refer back to your answers to Problem 29-1 in answering the following questions.

   a. What is the maximum wage the firm will be willing to pay if it hires 15 workers?

   b. The weekly wage paid by computer printer manufacturers in a perfectly competitive market is $1,200. How many workers will the profit-maximizing employer hire?

   c. Suppose that there is an increase in the demand for personal computer systems. Explain the likely effects on marginal revenue product, marginal factor cost, and the number of workers hired by the firm.

29-3. Explain what happens to the elasticity of demand for labor in a given industry after each of the following events.

   a. A new manufacturing technique makes capital easier to substitute for labor.

   b. There is an increase in the number of substitutes for the final product that labor produces.

   c. After a drop in the prices of capital inputs, labor accounts for a larger portion of a firm's factor costs.

29-4. Explain how the following events would affect the demand for labor.

   a. A new education program administered by the company increases labor's marginal product.

   b. The firm completes a new plant with a larger workspace and new machinery.

29-5. The following table depicts the product market and labor market an MP3 player manufacturer faces.

Labor Input (workers per day)	Total Physical Product	Product Price ($)
10	100	50
11	109	49
12	116	48
13	121	47
14	124	46
15	125	45

   a. Calculate the firm's marginal physical product, total revenue, and marginal revenue product at each input level above 10 units.

   b. The firm competes in a perfectly competitive labor market, and the market wage it faces is $100 per worker per day. How many workers will the profit-maximizing employer hire?

29-6. Recently, there has been an increase in the market demand for products of firms in manufacturing industries. The production of many of these products requires the skills of welders. Because welding is a dirty and dangerous job compared with other occupations, in recent years fewer people have sought employment as welders. Draw a diagram of the market for the labor of welders. Use this diagram to explain the likely implications of these recent trends for the market clearing wage earned by welders and the equilibrium quantity of welding services hired.

29-7. During most of the 2000s, there was a significant increase in the price of corn-based ethanol.

   a. A key input in the production of corn-based ethanol is corn. Use an appropriate diagram to explain what likely occurred in the market for corn.

   b. In light of your answer to part (a), explain why many hog farmers, who in the past used corn as the main feed input in hog production, switched to cookies, licorice, cheese curls, candy bars, and other human snack foods instead of corn as food for their hogs.

29-8. A firm hires labor in a perfectly competitive labor market. Its current profit-maximizing hourly output is 100 units, which the firm sells at a price of $5 per unit. The marginal physical product of the last unit of labor employed is 5 units per hour. The firm pays each worker an hourly wage of $15.

    a. What marginal revenue does the firm earn from sale of the output produced by the last worker employed?

    b. Does this firm sell its output in a perfectly competitive market?

29-9. Explain why the short-term effects of outsourcing on U.S. wages and employment tend to be more ambiguous than the long-term effects.

29-10. A profit-maximizing monopolist hires workers in a perfectly competitive labor market. Employing the last worker increased the firm's total weekly output from 110 units to 111 units and caused the firm's weekly revenues to rise from $25,000 to $25,750. What is the current prevailing weekly wage rate in the labor market?

29-11. A monopoly firm hires workers in a perfectly competitive labor market in which the market wage rate is $20 per day. If the firm maximizes profit, and if the marginal revenue from the last unit of output produced by the last worker hired equals $10, what is the marginal physical product of that worker?

29-12. The current market wage rate is $10, the rental rate of land is $1,000 per unit, and the rental rate of capital is $500. Production managers at a firm find that under their current allocation of factors of production, the marginal physical product of labor is 100, the marginal physical product of land is 10,000, and the marginal physical product of capital is 4,000. Is the firm minimizing costs? Why or why not?

29-13. The current wage rate is $10, and the rental rate of capital is $500. A firm's marginal physical product of labor is 200, and its marginal physical product of capital is 20,000. Is the firm maximizing profits for the given cost outlay? Why or why not?

ECONOMICS ON THE NET

Current Trends in U.S. Labor Markets The Federal Reserve's "Beige Book," which summarizes regional economic conditions around the United States, provides a wealth of information about the current status of U.S. labor markets. This Internet application helps you assess developments in employment and wages in the United States.

Title: The Beige Book—Summary

Navigation: Go to **www.econtoday.com/chapter29** to access the home page of the Federal Reserve's Board of Governors. Click on *Monetary Policy,* and then click on *Beige Book.* Then select the report for the most recent period.

Application Read the section entitled "Prices and Wages," and answer the following questions.

1. Has overall employment been rising or falling during the most recent year? Based on what you learned in this chapter, what factors might account for this pattern? Does the Beige Book summary bear our any of these explanations for changes in U.S. employment?

2. Have U.S. workers' wages been rising or falling during the most recent year?

For Group Study and Analysis The left-hand margin of the Beige Book site lists the reports of the 12 Federal Reserve districts. Divide the class into two groups, and have each group develop brief summaries of the main conclusions of one district's report concerning employment and wages within that district. Reconvene and compare the reports. Are there pronounced regional differences?

ANSWERS TO QUICK QUIZZES

p. 746: (i) output . . . input . . . inputs . . . marginal revenue; (ii) demand for; (iii) derived . . . derived . . . shift
p. 748: (i) wage . . . price . . . downward; (ii) elasticity . . . inputs . . . costs . . . adjustment
p. 752: (i) elastic . . . upward; (ii) equilibrium; (iii) demand . . . productivity . . . substitute . . . complementary
p. 756: (i) substitutable . . . substitution; (ii) reduces . . . increases; (iii) gains from trade
p. 761: (i) less; (ii) monopolist's; (iii) price; (iv) physical . . . physical

30

Unions and Labor Market Monopoly Power

F rom the 1930s, Chrysler employed thousands of workers at its plant in New Castle, Indiana, and the union wages it paid them fueled the town's economy—until 2003 when Chrysler closed the plant, putting hundreds out of work. Since then, Chrysler retirees residing in the town have been worrying about whether their pension and health benefits will continue. The town's school board has even dropped "Chrysler" from the high school's name, to which it had been added in 1958 in honor of the company's founder. The experience of this town is indicative of the sea change taking place in relations between U.S. auto companies and their unionized workers. U.S. automakers have been unprofitable, and the United Auto Workers union has been struggling to maintain workers' wages and retirees' benefits. To understand the transformation under way in the U.S. auto industry, you must first learn about the economic role of unions, which is a key topic of this chapter.

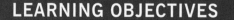

LEARNING OBJECTIVES

MyEconLab helps you master each objective and study more efficiently. See end of chapter for details.

After reading this chapter, you should be able to:

- Outline the essential history of the labor union movement

- Discuss the current status of labor unions

- Describe the basic economic goals and strategies of labor unions

- Evaluate the potential effects of labor unions on wages and productivity

- Explain how a monopsonist determines how much labor to employ and what wage rate to pay

- Compare wage and employment decisions by a monopsonistic firm with the choices made by firms in industries with alternative market structures

? DID YOU KNOW THAT the average civilian employee of the federal government receives two times the annual earnings and benefits earned by the average private worker? In 1950, the average federal government worker earned 19 percent more than a private worker, and by 1990 the differential was 50 percent. Now, the differential is 100 percent. One factor helping to boost wages earned by employees of the federal government is that an increasing percentage of them belong to **labor unions**—organizations that seek to secure economic improvements for their members. In the early 1960s, only about 10 percent of all government employees in the United States belonged to unions. Now nearly 40 percent of government workers are union members, and 46 percent of *all* U.S. union members work in the public sector.

Clearly, the labor landscape is shifting in the United States. Traditionally, one rationale for forming a union was that members might be able to earn more than they would in a competitive labor market by obtaining a type of monopoly power. Because the entire supply of a particular group of workers is controlled by a single source when a union bargains as a single entity with management, a certain monopoly element enters into the determination of employment. We can no longer talk about a perfectly competitive supply of labor. Later in the chapter, we will examine the converse—a single employer who is the sole employer of a particular group of workers.

Labor unions
Worker organizations that seek to secure economic improvements for their members; they also seek to improve the safety, health, and other benefits (such as job security) of their members.

Industrialization and Labor Unions

In most parts of the world, labor movements began with local **craft unions.** These were groups of workers in individual trades, such as shoemaking, printing, or baking. Beginning around the middle of the eighteenth century, new technologies permitted reductions in unit production costs through the formation of larger-scale enterprises that hired dozens or more workers. By the late 1790s, workers in some British craft unions began trying to convince employers to engage in **collective bargaining,** in which business management negotiates with representatives of all union members about wages and hours of work.

In 1799 and 1800, the British Parliament passed laws called the Combination Acts aimed at prohibiting the formation of unions. In 1825, Parliament enacted a replacement Combination Act allowing unions to exist and to engage in limited collective bargaining. Unions on the European continent managed to convince most governments throughout Europe to enact similar laws during the first half of the nineteenth century.

Craft unions
Labor unions composed of workers who engage in a particular trade or skill, such as baking, carpentry, or plumbing.

Collective bargaining
Negotiation between the management of a company or of a group of companies and the management of a union or a group of unions for the purpose of reaching a mutually agreeable contract that sets wages, fringe benefits, and working conditions for all employees in all the unions involved.

Unions in the United States

The development of unions in the United States lagged several decades behind events in Europe. In the years between the Civil War and World War I (1861–1914), the Knights of Labor, an organized group of both skilled and unskilled workers, pushed for an eight-hour workday and equal pay for women and men. In 1886, a dissident group split from the Knights of Labor to form the American Federation of Labor (AFL) under the leadership of Samuel Gompers. During World War I, union membership increased to more than 5 million. But after the war, the government decided to stop protecting labor's right to organize. Membership began to fall.

THE FORMATION OF INDUSTRIAL UNIONS The Great Depression was a landmark event in U.S. labor history. Franklin Roosevelt's National Industrial Recovery Act of 1933 gave labor the federal right to bargain collectively, but that act was declared unconstitutional. The 1935 National Labor Relations Act (NLRA), otherwise known as the Wagner Act, took its place. The NLRA guaranteed workers the right to form unions, to engage in collective bargaining, and to be members of any union.

In 1938, the Congress of Industrial Organizations (CIO) was formed by John L. Lewis, the president of the United Mine Workers. Prior to the formation of the CIO, most labor organizations were craft unions. The CIO was composed of **industrial unions,** which drew their membership from an entire industry such as steel or automobiles. In 1955, the CIO and the AFL merged because the leaders of both associations thought a merger would help organized labor grow faster.

CONGRESSIONAL CONTROL OVER LABOR UNIONS Since the Great Depression, Congress has occasionally altered the relationship between labor and management through significant legislation. One of the most important pieces of legislation was the Taft-Hartley Act of 1947 (the Labor Management Relations Act). In general, the Taft-Hartley Act outlawed certain labor practices of unions, such as imposing make-work rules and forcing unwilling workers to join a particular union. Among other things, it allowed individual states to pass their own **right-to-work laws.** A right-to-work law makes it illegal for union membership to be a requirement for continued employment in any establishment.

The Taft-Hartley Act also made a **closed shop** illegal; a closed shop requires union membership before employment can be obtained. A **union shop,** however, is legal. A union shop does not require membership as a prerequisite for employment, but it can, and usually does, require that workers join the union after a specified amount of time on the job. (Even a union shop is illegal in states with right-to-work laws.)

Jurisdictional disputes, sympathy strikes, and secondary boycotts were also made illegal by the Taft-Hartley Act. A **jurisdictional dispute** involves two or more unions fighting (and striking) over which should have control in a particular jurisdiction. For example, should carpenters working for a steel manufacturer be members of the steelworkers' union or the carpenters' union? A **sympathy strike** occurs when one union strikes in sympathy with another union's cause or strike. For example, if the retail clerks' union in an area is striking grocery stores, Teamsters union members may refuse to deliver products to those stores in sympathy with the retail clerks' demands for higher wages or better working conditions. A **secondary boycott** is a boycott of a company that deals with a struck company. For example, if union workers strike a baking company, the boycotting of grocery stores that continue to sell that company's products is a secondary boycott. A secondary boycott brings pressure on third parties to force them to stop dealing with an employer who is being struck.

Perhaps the most famous aspect of the Taft-Hartley Act is its provision allowing the president to obtain a court injunction that will stop a strike for an 80-day cooling-off period if the strike is expected to imperil the nation's safety or health.

The Current Status of U.S. Labor Unions

As Figure 30-1 shows, union membership has been declining in the United States since the 1960s. At present, only about 12 percent of U.S. workers are union members. Only about 9 percent of workers in the private sector belong to unions.

A DECLINE IN MANUFACTURING EMPLOYMENT A large part of the explanation for the decline in union membership has to do with the shift away from manufacturing. In 1948, workers in manufacturing industries, transportation, and utilities, which traditionally have been among the most heavily unionized industries, constituted

---

Industrial unions
Labor unions that consist of workers from a particular industry, such as automobile manufacturing or steel manufacturing.

Right-to-work laws
Laws that make it illegal to require union membership as a condition of continuing employment in a particular firm.

Closed shop
A business enterprise in which employees must belong to the union before they can be hired and must remain in the union after they are hired.

Union shop
A business enterprise that may hire nonunion members, conditional on their joining the union by some specified date after employment begins.

Jurisdictional dispute
A disagreement involving two or more unions over which should have control of a particular jurisdiction, such as a particular craft or skill or a particular firm or industry.

Sympathy strike
A work stoppage by a union in sympathy with another union's strike or cause.

Secondary boycott
A refusal to deal with companies or purchase products sold by companies that are dealing with a company being struck.

Go to www.econtoday.com/chapter30 to link to the Legal Information Institute's review of all the key U.S. labor laws.

FIGURE 30-1

Decline in Union Membership

Numerically, union membership in the United States has increased dramatically since the 1930s, but as a percentage of the labor force, union membership peaked around 1960 and has been falling ever since. Most

recently, the absolute number of union members has also diminished.

Sources: L. Davis et al., *American Economic Growth* (New York: HarperCollins, 1972), p. 220; U.S. Department of Labor, Bureau of Labor Statistics.

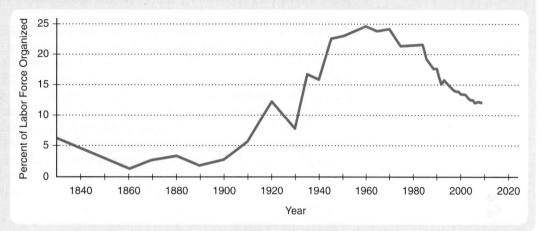

more than half of private nonagricultural employment. Today, that fraction is less than one-fifth.

The relative decline in manufacturing employment helps explain why most of the largest U.S. unions now draw their members primarily from workers in service industries and governments. As you can see in Table 30-1, five of the ten largest unions now represent workers in these areas. The remaining five largest unions represent the manufacturing industries, transportation, and utilities that once dominated the U.S. union movement.

TABLE 30-1

The Ten Largest Unions in the United States

Half of the top ten U.S. unions have members who work in service and government occupations.

Union	Industry	Members
National Education Association	Education	2,731,000
Service Employees International Union	Health care, public, and janitorial services	1,505,000
American Federation of State, County, and Municipal Employees	Government services	1,405,000
International Brotherhood of Teamsters	Trucking, delivery	1,396,000
United Food and Commercial Workers International Union	Food and grocery services	1,312,000
American Federation of Teachers	Education	829,000
United Steelworkers of America	Steel	755,000
International Brotherhood of Electrical Workers	Electrical	705,000
Laborers' International Union of North America	Construction, utilities	670,000
International Association of Machinists and Aerospace Workers	Machine and aerospace	654,000

Source: U.S. Department of Labor.

DEREGULATION AND IMMIGRATION Although the trend away from manufacturing is the main reason for the decline in unionism, the deregulation of certain industries, such as airlines and trucking, has also contributed, as has increased global competition. In addition, immigration has weakened the power of unions. Much of the unskilled and typically nonunionized work in the United States is done by foreign-born workers, and immigrant workers who are undocumented cannot legally join a union.

CHANGES IN THE STRUCTURE OF THE U.S. UNION MOVEMENT After its founding in 1955, the AFL-CIO remained the predominant labor union organization for 50 years. In 2005, however, seven unions with more than 45 percent of total AFL-CIO membership broke off to form a separate union organization called Change to Win. More recently, two construction industry unions also left the AFL-CIO and joined with ironworkers and bricklayers unions to form the National Construction Alliance.

Unions in these new umbrella groups, which represent mainly workers in growing service industries, had become frustrated because they felt that the AFL-CIO was not working hard enough to expand union membership. In addition, some of these unions were more interested than the AFL-CIO in pursuing boycotts against companies viewed as anti-union, such as Wal-Mart, and strikes against industries trying to slow the growth of union membership, such as the hotel industry.

QUICK QUIZ See page 790 for the answers. Review concepts from this section in MyEconLab.

The _____ _____ of _____, composed of **craft unions**, was formed in 1886 under the leadership of Samuel Gompers. Membership increased until after World War I, when the government temporarily stopped protecting labor's right to organize.

During the Great Depression, legislation was passed that allowed for **collective bargaining.** The _____ _____ _____ Act of 1935 guaranteed workers

the right to form unions. The Congress of Industrial Organizations (CIO), composed of _____ unions, was formed during the Great Depression. The AFL and the CIO merged in 1955.

In the United States, union membership as a percentage of the labor force peaked at nearly _____ percent in 1960 and has declined since then to only about _____ percent.

Union Goals and Strategies

Through collective bargaining, unions establish the wages below which no individual worker may legally offer his or her services. Each year, union representatives and management negotiate collective bargaining contracts covering wages as well as working conditions and fringe benefits for about 6 million workers. If approved by the members, a union labor contract sets wage rates, maximum workdays, working conditions, fringe benefits, and other matters, usually for the next two or three years.

Strike: The Ultimate Bargaining Tool

Whenever union-management negotiations break down, union negotiators may turn to their ultimate bargaining tool, the threat or the reality of a strike. Strikes make headlines, but a strike occurs in less than 2 percent of all labor-management disputes before the contract is signed. In the other 98 percent, contracts are signed without much public fanfare.

The purpose of a strike is to impose costs on recalcitrant management to force it to accept the union's proposed contract terms. Strikes disrupt production and interfere with a company's or an industry's ability to sell goods and services. The strike works both ways, though, because workers receive no wages while on strike (though they may be partly compensated out of union strike funds). Striking union workers may also be eligible to draw state unemployment benefits.

The impact of a strike is closely related to the ability of striking unions to prevent nonstriking (and perhaps nonunion) employees from continuing to work for the targeted company or industry. Therefore, steps are usually taken to prevent others from working for the employer. **Strikebreakers** can effectively destroy whatever bargaining power rests behind a strike. Numerous methods have been used to prevent strikebreakers from breaking strikes. Violence has been known to erupt, almost always in connection with union attempts to prevent strikebreaking.

In recent years, companies have had less incentive to hire strikebreakers, because work stoppages have become much less common. From 1945 until 1990, on average more than 200 union strikes took place in the United States each year. Since 1990, however, the average has been closer to 25 strikes per year.

Can strikes occur in any organization whose workers are unionized? As the Brazilian central bank has learned, the answer to this question is yes.

Strikebreakers
Temporary or permanent workers hired by a company to replace union members who are striking.

Why would these Hollywood screenwriters choose to strike?

INTERNATIONAL EXAMPLE
No Pay Raise, No Data!

A recent strike by workers at the Brazilian central bank shut down many of the institution's operations for more than a month. Although a skeleton staff of nonunionized supervisors continued to perform the central bank's day-to-day monetary policy responsibilities, its regulatory and data-processing departments experienced significant slowdowns. Production of weekly and monthly statistical reports halted, leaving those seeking the latest information about the state of Brazil's financial system and economy in the dark. When workers settled for a 10 percent pay increase spread over two years instead of the 15 percent raise they had been demanding, financial and economic data began to flow once more.

FOR CRITICAL ANALYSIS
Why do you suppose that Brazil's central bank and most other unionized organizations always make sure that their nonunionized personnel are trained to operate their organizations' core functions?

Union Goals with Direct Wage Setting

We have already pointed out that one of the goals of unions is to set minimum wages. The effects of setting a wage rate higher than a competitive market clearing wage rate can be seen in Figure 30-2 on the next page. The market for labor is perfectly competitive. The market demand curve is D, and the market supply curve is S. The market clearing wage rate is W_e. The equilibrium quantity of labor is Q_e. If the union establishes by collective bargaining a minimum wage rate that exceeds W_e, an excess quantity of labor will be supplied (assuming no change in the labor demand schedule). If the minimum wage established by union collective bargaining is W_U, the quantity supplied will be Q_S. The quantity demanded will be Q_D. The difference is the excess quantity supplied, or surplus. Hence, the following point becomes clear:

One of the major roles of a union that establishes a wage rate above the market clearing wage rate is to ration available jobs among the excess number of workers who wish to work in the unionized industry.

FIGURE 30-2

Unions Must Ration Jobs

The market clearing wage rate is W_e, at point E, at which the equilibrium quantity of labor is Q_e. If the union succeeds in obtaining wage rate W_U, the quantity of labor demanded will be Q_D, at point A on the labor demand curve, but the quantity of labor supplied will be Q_S, at point B on the labor supply curve. The union must ration a limited number of jobs among a greater number of workers; the surplus of labor is equivalent to a shortage of jobs at that wage rate.

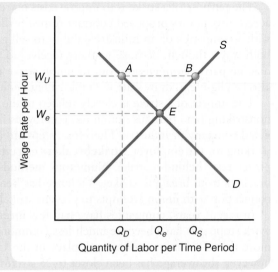

Note also that the surplus of labor is equivalent to a shortage of jobs at wage rates above equilibrium.

To ration jobs, the union may use a seniority system, lengthen the apprenticeship period to discourage potential members from joining, or institute other rationing methods. This has the effect of shifting the supply of labor curve to the left in order to support the higher wage, W_U.

There is a trade-off here that any union's leadership must face: Higher wages inevitably mean a reduction in total union employment—fewer union positions. When facing higher wages, management may replace part of the workforce with machinery or may even seek to hire nonunion workers.

If we view unions as monopoly sellers of a service, we can identify three different types of goals that they may pursue: ensuring employment for all members of the union, maximizing aggregate income of workers, and maximizing wage rates for some workers.

EMPLOYING ALL MEMBERS IN THE UNION Assume that the union has Q_1 workers. If it faces a labor demand curve such as D in Figure 30-3, the only way it can "sell" all of those workers' services is to accept a wage rate of W_1. This is similar to any other market. The demand curve tells the maximum price that can be charged to sell any particular quantity of a good or service. Here the service happens to be labor.

MAXIMIZING MEMBER INCOME If the union is interested in maximizing the gross income of its members, it will normally want a smaller membership than Q_1—namely, Q_2 workers, all employed and paid a wage rate of W_2. The aggregate income to all members of the union is represented by the wages of only the ones who work. Total income earned by union members is maximized where the price elasticity of demand is numerically equal to 1. That occurs where marginal revenue equals zero. In Figure 30-3, marginal revenue equals zero at a quantity of labor Q_2. So we know that if the union obtains a wage rate equal to W_2, and therefore Q_2 workers are demanded, the total income to the union membership will be maximized. In other words, $Q_2 \times W_2$ (the blue-shaded area) will be greater than any other combination of

FIGURE 30-3

What Do Unions Maximize?

Assume that the union wants to employ all its Q_1 members. It will attempt to get wage rate W_1. If the union wants to maximize total wage receipts (income) of members who have jobs in this industry, it will do so at wage rate W_2, where the elasticity of the demand for labor is equal to 1. (The blue-shaded area represents the maximum total income that the union membership would earn at W_2.) If the union wants to maximize the wage rate for a given number of workers, say, Q_3, it will set the wage rate at W_3.

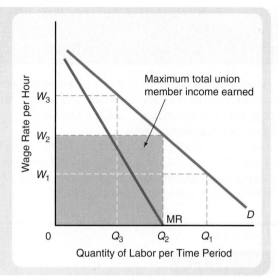

wage rates and quantities of union workers demanded. It is, for example, greater than $Q_1 \times W_1$. Note that in this situation, if the union started out with Q_1 members, there would be $Q_1 - Q_2$ members out of *union* work at the wage rate W_2. (Those out of union work either remain unemployed or go to other industries. Such actions have a depressing effect on wages in nonunion industries due to the increase in supply of workers there.)

MAXIMIZING WAGE RATES FOR CERTAIN WORKERS Assume that the union wants to maximize the wage rates for some of its workers—perhaps those with the most seniority. If it wants to maximize the wage rate for a given quantity of workers, Q_3, it will seek to obtain a wage rate of W_3. This will require deciding which workers should be unemployed and which workers should work and for how long each week or each year they should be employed.

Union Strategies to Raise Wages Indirectly

One way or another, unions seek above-market wages for some or all of their members. Sometimes unions try to achieve this goal without making wage increases direct features of contract negotiations.

LIMITING ENTRY OVER TIME One way to raise wage rates without specifically setting wages is for a union to limit the size of its membership to the size of its employed workforce at the time the union was first organized. No workers are put out of work when the union is formed. Over time, as the demand for labor in the industry increases, the union prevents any net increase in membership, so larger wage increases are obtained than would otherwise be the case. We see this in Figure 30-4 on the following page. In this example, union members freeze entry into their union, thereby obtaining a wage rate of $21 per hour instead of allowing a wage rate of $20 per hour with no restriction on labor supply.

How have longshoremen's unions used their control over key technologies to restrict the supply of labor at U.S. ports?

EXAMPLE
Longshoremen's Unions Win Control over Key Technologies

Recently, two longshoremen's unions, the International Longshoremen's Association on the U.S. East Coast and the International Longshore and Warehouse Union on the West Coast, won an important negotiation victory. The unions received authorization to develop and implement software that governs the filling of shipping containers and the use of global positioning systems for tracking cargoes. Through their control over this technology, they can determine who receives training in its use and thereby effectively control entry into workforces at most U.S. port facilities.

FOR CRITICAL ANALYSIS
Why does the ability to restrict the supply of labor tend to push up the wages of employed members of longshoremen's unions?

FIGURE 30-4

Restricting Supply over Time

When the union was formed, it didn't affect wage rates or employment, which remained at $19 and Q_1 (the equilibrium wage rate and quantity at point E_1). However, as demand increased—that is, as the demand schedule shifted outward from D_1 to D_2 —the union restricted membership to its original level of Q_1. The new supply curve is S_1S_2, which intersects D_2 at E_2, or at a wage rate of $21. Without the union, equilibrium would be at E_3, with a wage rate of $20 and employment of Q_2.

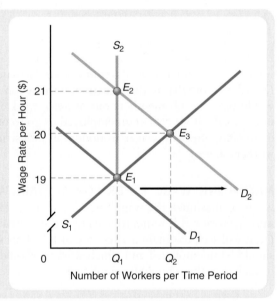

ALTERING THE DEMAND FOR UNION LABOR Another way that unions can increase wages is to shift the demand curve for labor outward to the right. This approach has the advantage of increasing both wage rates and the employment level. The demand for union labor can be increased by increasing worker productivity, increasing the demand for union-made goods, and decreasing the demand for non-union-made goods.

1. *Increasing worker productivity.* Supporters of unions have argued that unions provide a good system of industrial jurisprudence. The presence of unions may induce workers to feel that they are working in fair and just circumstances. If so, they work harder, increasing labor productivity. Productivity is also increased when unions resolve differences and reduce conflicts between workers and management, thereby providing a more peaceful administrative environment.

2. *Increasing demand for union-made goods.* Because the demand for labor is a derived demand, a rise in the demand for products produced by union labor will increase the demand for union labor itself. One way that unions attempt to increase the

demand for goods produced by union labor is by advertising "Look for the union label."

3. *Decreasing the demand for non-union-made goods.* When the demand for goods that are competing with (or are substitutes for) union-made goods is reduced, consumers shift to union-made goods, increasing the demand. The campaigns of various unions against buying foreign imports are a good example. The result is greater demand for goods "made in the USA," which in turn presumably increases the demand for U.S. union (and nonunion) labor.

How is a union trying to reduce the demand for products sold by nonunionized Wal-Mart?

EXAMPLE
Advertising Against Wal-Mart

The United Food and Commercial Workers union operates a Web site called WakeUpWal-Mart.com, through which it seeks to dissuade consumers from shopping at Wal-Mart, which hires nonunion labor. Recently, the union took its anti-Wal-Mart efforts a step farther by financing television ads criticizing the retailer's more than $35 billion in annual purchases of goods from China as "just not American." The union hoped that identifying Wal-Mart as a company that buys non-U.S.-made goods would discourage people from shopping at the retailer's nonunion stores.

FOR CRITICAL ANALYSIS
What does the United Food and Commercial Workers union seek to gain from trying to convince people to stop shopping at Wal-Mart?

Economic Effects of Labor Unions

Today, the most heavily unionized occupations are government service, transportation and material moving, and construction. Do union members in these and other occupations earn higher wages? Are they more or less productive than nonunionized workers in their industries? What are the broader economic effects of unionization? Let's consider each of these questions in turn.

Unions and Wages

You have learned that unions are able to raise the wages of their members if they can successfully limit the supply of labor in a particular industry. Unions are also able to raise wages if they can induce increases in the demand for union labor.

Economists have extensively studied the differences between union wages and nonunion wages. They have found that the average *hourly* wage earned by a typical private-sector union worker is about $2.25 higher than the hourly wage earned by a typical worker who is not a union member. Adjusted for inflation, this union-nonunion hourly wage differential is only about half as large as it was two decades ago, however.

Comparisons of the *annual* earnings of union and nonunion workers indicate that in recent years, unions have not succeeded in raising the annual incomes of their members. In 1985, workers who belonged to unions earned nearly 7 percent more per year than nonunion workers, even though union workers worked fewer hours per week. Today, a typical nonunion employee still works slightly longer each week, but the average nonunion worker also has a higher annual income than the average union worker.

Even the $2.25 hourly wage differential already mentioned is somewhat misleading because it is an average across *all* U.S. workers. In the private sector, union workers earn only about 4 percent more than nonunion workers, or a little less than 60 cents per hour. The hourly wage gain for government workers is more than six times higher at about $3.55 per hour. A state government employee who belongs to a union currently earns an hourly wage more than 20 percent higher than a state government worker who is not a union member.

Unions and Labor Productivity

Featherbedding

Any practice that forces employers to use more labor than they would otherwise or to use existing labor in an inefficient manner.

A traditional view of union behavior is that unions decrease productivity by artificially shifting the demand curve for union labor outward through excessive staffing and make-work requirements. For example, some economists have traditionally argued that unions tend to bargain for excessive use of workers, as when an airline union requires an engineer on all flights. This is called **featherbedding.** Many painters' unions, for example, resisted the use of paint sprayers and required that their members use only brushes. They even specified the maximum width of the brush. Moreover, whenever a union strikes, productivity drops, and this reduction in productivity in one sector of the economy can spill over into other sectors.

Economic Benefits and Costs of Labor Unions

As should be clear by now, there are two opposing views of unions. One sees them as monopolies whose main effect is to raise the wage rate of high-seniority members at the expense of low-seniority members (and nonunion workers). The other contends that unions can increase labor productivity by promoting safer working conditions and generally better work environments and that they contribute to workforce stability by providing arbitration and grievance procedures.

Critics point out that the positive view of unionism overlooks the fact that many of the benefits that unions provide do not require that unions engage in restrictive labor practices, such as the closed shop. Unions could still provide benefits for their members without restricting the labor market.

Consequently, a key issue that economists seek to assess when judging the social costs of unions is the extent to which their existence has a negative effect on employment growth. Most evidence indicates that while unions do significantly reduce employment in some of the most heavily unionized occupations, the overall effects on U.S. employment are modest. On the whole, therefore, the social costs of unions in the U.S. private sector are probably relatively low.

QUICK QUIZ *See page 790 for the answers. Review concepts from this section in MyEconLab.*

When unions set wage rates _____ market clearing prices, they face the problem of _____ a restricted number of jobs to workers who desire to earn the higher wages.

Unions may pursue any one of three goals: (1) to employ _____ union members, (2) to maximize total _____ of the union's members, or (3) to _____ wages for certain, usually high-seniority, workers.

Unions can increase the wage rate of members by engaging in practices that shift the union labor supply curve _____ or shift the demand curve for union labor _____ (or both).

Some economists believe that unions can increase _____ by promoting safer working conditions and generally better work environments.

Monopsony: A Buyer's Monopoly

Let's assume that a firm is a perfect competitor in the product market. The firm cannot alter the price of the product it sells, and it faces a perfectly elastic demand curve for its product. We also assume that the firm is the only buyer of a particular input. Although this situation may not occur often, it is useful to consider. Let's think in terms of a factory town, like those dominated by textile mills or those in the mining industry. One company not only hires the workers but also owns the businesses in the community, owns the apartments that workers live in, and hires the clerks, waiters, and all other personnel. This buyer of labor is called a **monopsonist,** the only buyer in the market.

What does this situation mean to a monopsonist in terms of the costs of hiring extra workers? It means that if the monopsonist wants to hire more workers, it has to offer higher wages. Our monopsonist firm cannot hire all the labor it wants at the going wage rate. Instead, it faces an upward-sloping supply curve. If it wants to hire more workers, it has to raise wage rates, including the wages of all its current workers (assuming a non-wage-discriminating monopsonist). It therefore has to take account of these increased costs when deciding how many more workers to hire.

Monopsonist
The only buyer in a market.

You Are There

To learn about how Chinese consumers regularly band together in an effort to act as a single monopsony buyer, read **In China, Consumers Seek to Act Together as a Monopsonist,** on page 784.

Marginal Factor Cost

The monopsonist faces an upward-sloping supply curve of the input in question because as the only buyer, it faces the entire market supply curve. Each time the monopsonist buyer of labor, for example, wishes to hire more workers, it must raise wage rates. Thus, the marginal cost of another unit of labor is rising. In fact, the marginal cost of increasing its workforce will always be greater than the wage rate. This is because the monopsonist must pay the same wage rate to everyone in order to obtain another unit of labor; thus, the higher wage rate has to be offered not only to the last worker but also to *all* its other workers. We call the additional cost to the monopsonist of hiring one more worker the marginal factor cost (MFC).

The marginal factor cost of hiring the last worker is therefore that worker's wages plus the increase in the wages of all other existing workers. As we pointed out in Chapter 29, marginal factor cost is equal to the change in total variable costs due to a one-unit change in the one variable factor of production—in this case, labor. In Chapter 29, marginal factor cost was simply the competitive wage rate because the employer could hire all workers at the same wage rate.

Derivation of a Marginal Factor Cost Curve

Panel (a) of Figure 30-5 on the following page shows the quantity of labor purchased, the wage rate per hour, the total cost of the quantity of labor supplied per hour, and the marginal factor cost per hour for the additional labor bought.

We translate the columns from panel (a) to the graph in panel (b) of the figure. We show the supply curve as *S*, which is taken from columns 1 and 2. (Note that this is the same as the *average* factor cost curve. Hence, you can view Figure 30-5 as showing the relationship between average factor cost and marginal factor cost.) The marginal factor cost curve (MFC) is taken from columns 1 and 4. The MFC curve must be above the supply curve whenever the supply curve is upward sloping. If the supply curve is upward sloping, the firm must pay a higher wage rate in order to attract a larger amount of labor. This higher wage rate must be paid to all workers; thus, the increase in total costs due to an increase in the labor input will exceed the wage rate.

FIGURE 30-5

Derivation of a Marginal Factor Cost Curve

The supply curve, *S*, in panel (b) is taken from columns 1 and 2 of panel (a). The marginal factor cost curve (MFC) is taken from columns 1 and 4. It is the increase in the total wage bill resulting from a one-unit increase in labor input.

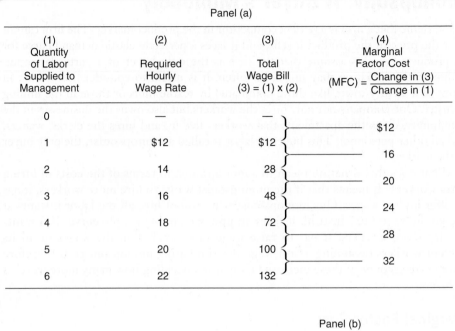

Panel (a)

(1) Quantity of Labor Supplied to Management	(2) Required Hourly Wage Rate	(3) Total Wage Bill (3) = (1) x (2)	(4) Marginal Factor Cost $(MFC) = \dfrac{\text{Change in (3)}}{\text{Change in (1)}}$
0	—	—	
			$12
1	$12	$12	
			16
2	14	28	
			20
3	16	48	
			24
4	18	72	
			28
5	20	100	
			32
6	22	132	

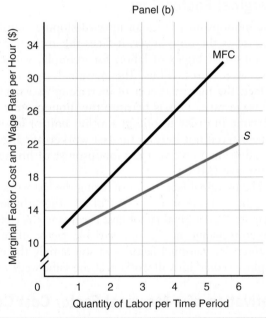

Panel (b)

(Recall from Chapter 29 that in a perfectly competitive input market, the supply curve facing the firm is perfectly elastic and the marginal factor cost curve is identical to the supply curve.)

Employment and Wages Under Monopsony

To determine the number of workers that a monopsonist desires to hire, we compare the marginal benefit to the marginal cost of each hiring decision. The marginal cost

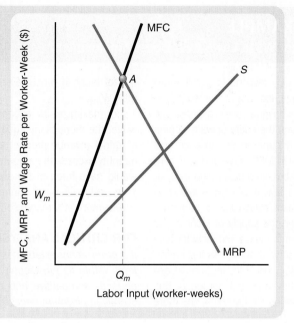

FIGURE 30-6

Wage and Employment Determination for a Monopsonist

The monopsonist firm looks at a marginal cost curve, MFC, that slopes upward and lies above its labor supply curve, S. The marginal benefit of hiring additional workers is given by the firm's MRP curve (its demand-for-labor curve). The intersection of MFC with MRP, at point A, determines the number of workers hired. The firm hires Q_m workers but has to pay them only W_m in order to attract them.

is the marginal factor cost (MFC) curve, and the marginal benefit is the marginal revenue product (MRP) curve. In Figure 30-6, we assume competition in the output market and monopsony in the input market. A monopsonist finds its profit-maximizing quantity of labor demanded at A, where the marginal revenue product is just equal to the marginal factor cost. The monopsonist will therefore desire to hire exactly Q_m workers.

THE INPUT PRICE PAID BY A MONOPSONY How much is the firm going to pay these workers? The monopsonist sets the wage rate so that it will get exactly the quantity, Q_m, supplied to it by its "captive" labor force. We find that wage rate is W_m. There is no reason to pay the workers any more than W_m because at that wage rate, the firm can get exactly the quantity it wants. The actual quantity used is determined by the intersection of the marginal factor cost curve and the marginal revenue product curve for labor—that is, at the point at which the marginal revenue from expanding employment just equals the marginal cost of doing so (point A in Figure 30-6).

Notice that the profit-maximizing wage rate paid to workers (W_m) is lower than the marginal revenue product. That is to say, workers are paid a wage that is less than their contribution to the monopsonist's revenues. This is sometimes referred to as **monopsonistic exploitation** of labor.

You learned in Chapter 4 that in a perfectly competitive labor market, establishing a minimum wage rate above the market clearing wage rate causes employers to reduce the quantity of labor demanded, resulting in a decline in employment. What happens if a minimum wage rate is established above the wage rate that a *monopsony* would otherwise pay its workers?

Monopsonistic exploitation
Paying a price for the variable input that is less than its marginal revenue product; the difference between marginal revenue product and the wage rate.

POLICY EXAMPLE
Can Minimum Wage Laws Ever Boost Employment?

How does a monopsony respond to a minimum wage law that sets a wage floor above the wage rate it otherwise would pay its workers? Figure 30-7 provides the answer to this question. In the figure, the entire upward-sloping curve labeled S is the labor supply curve in the absence of a minimum wage. Given the associated MFC curve and the firm's MRP curve, Q_m is the quantity of labor hired by a monopsony in the absence of a minimum wage law. The profit-maximizing wage rate is W_m. If the government establishes a minimum wage equal to W_{min}, however, then the supply of labor to the firm becomes horizontal at the minimum wage and includes only the upward-sloping portion of the curve S above this legal minimum. In addition, the wage rate W_{min} becomes the monopsonist's marginal factor cost along the horizontal portion of this new labor supply curve, because when the firm hires one more unit of labor, it must pay each unit of labor the same wage rate, W_{min}.

To maximize its economic profits under the minimum wage, the monopsony equalizes the minimum wage rate with marginal revenue product and hires Q_{min} units of labor. This quantity exceeds the amount of labor, Q_m, that the monopsony would have hired in the absence of the minimum wage law. Thus, establishing a minimum wage can generate a rise in employment at a monopsony firm.

FOR CRITICAL ANALYSIS
If a government establishes a minimum wage law covering all firms within its jurisdiction, including firms operating in both perfectly competitive and monopsonistic labor markets, will overall employment necessarily increase?

FIGURE 30-7

A Monopsony's Response to a Minimum Wage

In the absence of a minimum wage law, a monopsony faces the upward-sloping labor supply curve, S, and the marginal factor cost curve, MFC. To maximize its profits, the monopsony hires Q_m units of labor, at which MFC is equal to MRP, and it pays the wage rate W_m. Once the minimum wage rate, W_{min}, is established, the supply of labor becomes horizontal at the minimum wage and includes only the upward-sloping portion of the labor supply curve above this legal minimum. Because the monopsony must pay the same wage rate W_{min} for each unit of labor along this horizontal portion of the new labor supply curve, its marginal factor cost is also equal to the minimum wage rate, W_{min}. Thus, the monopsony hires Q_{min} units of labor. Employment at the monopsony firm increases.

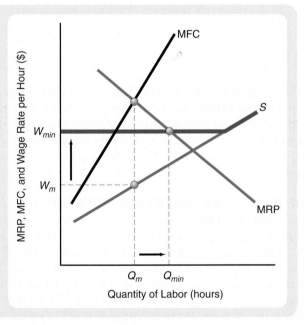

BILATERAL MONOPOLY We have studied the pricing of labor in various situations, including perfect competition in both the output and input markets and monopoly in both the output and input markets. Figure 30-8 shows four possible situations graphically.

The organization of workers into a union normally creates a monopoly supplier of labor, which gives the union some power to bargain for higher wages. What happens when a monopsonist meets a monopolist? This situation is called **bilateral monopoly,** defined as a market structure in which a single buyer faces a single seller. An example of bilateral monopoly is a county education employer facing a single teachers' union

Bilateral monopoly
A market structure consisting of a monopolist and a monopsonist.

FIGURE 30-8

Pricing and Employment Under Various Market Conditions

In panel (a), the firm operates in perfect competition in both the input and output markets. It purchases labor up to the point where the going rate W_e is equal to MRP_c. It hires quantity Q_e of labor. In panel (b), the firm is a perfect competitor in the input market but has a monopoly in the output market. It purchases labor up to the point where W_e is equal to MRP_m. In panel (c), the firm is a monopsonist in the input market and a perfect competitor in the output market. It hires labor up to the point where $MFC = MRP_c$. It will hire quantity Q_1 and pay wage rate W_c. Panel (d) shows a situation in which the firm is both a monopolist in the market for its output and a monopsonist in its labor market. It hires the quantity of labor Q_2 at which $MFC = MRP_m$ and pays the wage rate W_m.

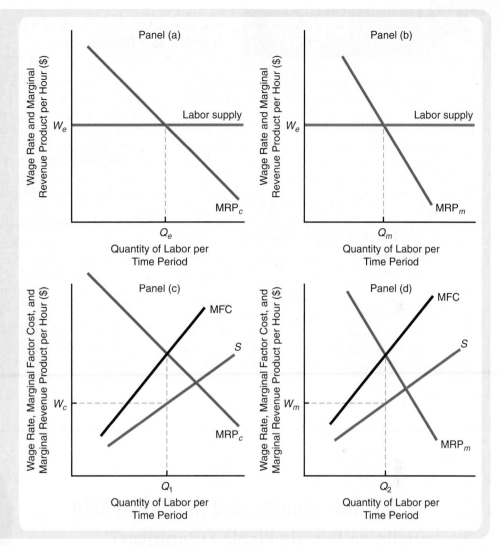

in that labor market. Another example is a players' union facing an organized group of team owners, as has occurred in professional baseball and football. To analyze bilateral monopoly, we would have to look at the interaction of both sides, buyer and seller. The price outcome turns out to be indeterminate.

QUICK QUIZ

See page 790 for the answers. Review concepts from this section in MyEconLab.

A **monopsonist** is the _____ _____ in a market. The monopsonist faces an _____-sloping supply curve of labor.

Because the monopsonist faces an _____-sloping supply curve of labor, the marginal factor cost of increasing the labor input by one unit is _____ than the wage

rate. Thus, the marginal factor cost curve always lies _____ the supply curve.

A monopsonist will hire workers up to the point at which marginal _____ cost equals marginal _____ product. Then the monopsonist will find the lowest necessary wage to attract that number of workers, as indicated by the supply curve.

You Are There

In China, Consumers Seek to Act Together as a Monopsonist

Zhang Qinyong, the owner of a kitchen-cabinetry shop in Suzhou, China, a city not far from Shanghai, finds himself cornered against his display cabinets by an organized team of about 20 shoppers. For more than an hour, he tries to convince the group that the products in his store are worth the tagged prices. "Forget quality. Let's talk about price," one member of the team snaps, and others join in, demanding 35 percent off the ticketed prices.

Haggling over prices is a tradition in China. Now, many Chinese consumers have taken the practice to a new level by engaging in *tuangou*, or "team buying." Via Internet chat rooms or organized Web sites such as 51tuangou.com and Teambuy.com, they organize mobs of people to descend, sometimes unannounced, on retail establishments that sell items such as kitchen appliances. These large groups often spend hours in retailers' stores. Sometimes the presence of a mob of *tuangou* members scares away other shoppers, but at other times the regular shoppers join forces with the buying team. Either outcome makes the buying team the

retailer's only shoppers for an extended period, and the team members join together in calling for group price cuts on items on display. In this way, the buying team members seek to act as a single buyer and obtain a lower price for items sold by the retailer. The buying teams often secure discounts ranging from 10 percent to 30 percent on kitchen gadgets, ovens, and other goods that the teams regard as inputs in household production.

CRITICAL ANALYSIS QUESTIONS

1. During the period of time that the only shoppers in a retail store are the members of a buying team, what is true of the marginal factor cost curve in relation to the supply curve for an item offered for sale by the retailer?

2. In what respects is the behavior of a monopsonistic buying team in China analogous to the behavior of a cartel, as discussed in Chapter 27?

Can the U.S. Auto Industry and the United Auto Workers Union Remain Viable Enterprises?

Issues and Applications

CONCEPTS APPLIED

- Industrial Unions
- Collective Bargaining
- Union Goals and Strategies

For the past several years, U.S. automakers have struggled to remain profitable. Beginning in the late 1990s, General Motors, Ford, and Chrysler have all experienced prolonged intervals of U.S. losses punctuated by a few promising but short-lived bursts of profitability. By the mid-2000s, it was clear to all in the auto industry, including its industrial union, the United Auto Workers (UAW), that significant changes would be necessary if U.S. automakers were to survive.

The Good Old Days for the UAW

From the 1950s through the 1970s, collective bargaining between the three major U.S. automakers and the UAW produced negotiated agreements that were the envy of most other U.S. unions. Before health and dental insurance became commonplace in numerous U.S. industries, the auto industry led the way in offering such benefits. U.S. auto companies and the UAW also negotiated generous pension plans for employees.

By the mid-1970s, UAW members received pay and benefits packages that ranked among the best available to U.S. unskilled and semiskilled workers. Very few U.S. workers who were members of other unions had negotiated packages that came close to those of UAW members.

Foreign Competition Becomes Domestic Competition

Starting in the 1980s, however, competitive pressures on automakers began to build. Quality improvements by foreign automakers induced U.S. consumers to substitute away from U.S.-manufactured vehicles in favor of imported vehicles manufactured by foreign firms such as Toyota, Honda, and BMW.

Then, in the 1990s, these and other foreign automakers, such as Mercedes and Subaru, began opening production facilities in the United States. In contrast to their U.S. competitors, foreign firms hired mostly nonunion labor to produce their vehicles.

Mounting "Legacy Costs" Associated with Union Workforces

Soon, the wage and benefits packages received by UAW workers translated into a competitive disadvantage for U.S. automakers. For instance, the higher average wages paid to UAW workers caused per-vehicle production costs to be nearly $300 higher for U.S. automakers than for Toyota. In addition, the average UAW worker received at least 10 more days of vacation than a worker in a U.S. Toyota plant, adding another $140 to U.S. firms' per-vehicle costs relative to those incurred by Toyota. A UAW worker even had about 16 minutes more break time per vehicle produced, pushing U.S. automakers' costs an additional $20 per vehicle above Toyota's.

Expenses related to all those UAW health and pension benefits, however, accounted for U.S. automakers' primary cost disadvantage relative to foreign firms. These benefits, which automakers call "legacy costs," were so generous that they increased the per-vehicle cost differential between U.S. automakers and Toyota by about $600. When other factors, such as inefficient production techniques, were taken into account, U.S. firms spent about $1,700 more to produce a vehicle than Toyota did.

A Period of Readjustment Commences

By the mid-2000s, following several years of meager or negative profitability in the United States, General Motors, Ford, and Chrysler were all experiencing severe financial difficulties. All three companies had responded by slashing slow-selling vehicle brands, closing plants, and terminating the employment of thousands of workers. When the time came for the UAW to renegotiate new four-year contracts with these U.S. firms, the issue was not how much more the UAW could achieve. It was which wage and benefit advantages the UAW could successfully retain for remaining autoworkers and for retirees who outnumbered active workers by nearly three to one. Faced with a dwindling demand for its membership, the UAW had to plot new strategies in light of its two-part goal to retain current working members while protecting the benefits of retired members.

In the end, the UAW showed that it valued job retention more highly than wages. It agreed to nearly 50 percent wage reductions for newly hired workers in exchange for maintaining the wage levels of senior employees. The most significant aspect of the new UAW contracts, however, was an agreement by U.S. automakers to transmit lump sums amounting to tens of billions of dollars to health care trusts. These trusts, managed by the UAW, will use interest earnings from all the funds set aside by automakers to provide health care benefits to retired workers. Thus, the UAW saved jobs for current workers—albeit at lower wages in the future—and protected the benefits of its retired members. At the same time, U.S. automakers accepted higher costs in the present in exchange for lower costs in the future that they hope will enable them to better compete with foreign firms.

Test your understanding of this chapter by going online to **MyEconLab**.
In the Study Plan for this chapter, select Section N: News.

For Critical Analysis

1. To U.S. automakers, are costs of retiree benefits variable costs or fixed costs?

2. How will the lower negotiated wages of newly employed autoworkers likely affect future employment at U.S. automakers, other things being equal?

Web Resources

1. To find out more about the United Auto Workers, go to www.econtoday.com/chapter30.

2. To learn more about the specifics of the current UAW agreement with Ford Motor Company, go to www.econtoday.com/chapter30.

Research Project

Do the UAW's objectives appear to correspond to any single goal discussed in this chapter? Or has the union sought to satisfy more than one goal as well as it could under the circumstances? Take a stand, and support your answer.

Here is what you should know after reading this chapter. **MyEconLab** will help you identify what you know, and where to go when you need to practice.

WHAT YOU SHOULD KNOW

WHERE TO GO TO PRACTICE

Labor Unions The first labor unions were craft unions, representing workers in specific trades. In the United States, the American Federation of Labor (AFL) emerged in the late nineteenth century. In 1935, the National Labor Relations Act (or Wagner Act) granted workers the right to form unions and bargain collectively. Industrial unions, which represent workers of specific industries, formed the Congress of Industrial Organizations (CIO) in 1938, and in 1955 a merger formed the AFL-CIO. The Taft-Hartley Act of 1947 placed limitations on unions' rights to organize, strike, and boycott.

labor unions, 769
craft unions, 769
collective bargaining, 769
industrial unions, 770
right-to-work laws, 770
closed shop, 770
union shop, 770
jurisdictional dispute, 770
sympathy strike, 770
secondary boycott, 770

- **MyEconLab** Study Plan 30.1
- Audio introduction to Chapter 30

The Current Status of Labor Unions In recent years, overall U.S. union membership has decreased. A key reason for the decline in U.S. union membership rates is undoubtedly the relative decline in manufacturing jobs as a share of total employment. In addition, in less skilled occupations that would otherwise be attractive to union organizers, many workers are undocumented and foreign-born (i.e., illegal immigrants). Greater domestic and global competition has probably also had a part in bringing about a decline in unions in the United States.

- **MyEconLab** Study Plan 30.1

(continued)

 *(continued)*

WHAT YOU SHOULD KNOW		WHERE TO GO TO PRACTICE
Basic Goals and Strategies of Labor Unions A key goal of most unions is to achieve higher wages. Often this entails bargaining for wages above competitive levels, which produces surplus labor. Thus, a major task of many unions is to ration available jobs among the excess number of individuals who desire to work at the wages established by collective bargaining agreements. One strategy that unions often use to address this trade-off between wages and the number of jobs is to maximize the total income of members. If the focus of union objectives is the well-being of current members only, the union may bargain for limits on entry of new workers and seek to maximize the wages of current union members only. Another way for unions to try to push up wages is to try to increase worker productivity and lobby consumers to increase their demands for union-produced goods and reduce their demands for goods produced by nonunionized industries.	strikebreakers, 773 **KEY FIGURES** Figure 30-2, 774 Figure 30-3, 775 Figure 30-4, 776	• **MyEconLab** Study Plan 30.2 • Video: Union Goals • Animated Figures 30-2, 30-3, 30-4
Effects of Labor Unions on Wages and Productivity Economists have found that hourly wages of unionized workers are typically higher than those of workers who are not union members. On average, union hourly wages are about $2.25 higher than wages of nonunionized workers. Because unionized employees typically work fewer hours per year, however, their average annual earnings are lower than those of nonunionized employees. It is less clear how unions affect worker productivity. On the one hand, some collective bargaining rules specifying how jobs are performed appear to reduce productivity. On the other hand, unionization promotes generally better work environments, which may enhance productivity.	featherbedding, 778	• **MyEconLab** Study Plan 30.3 • Video: The Benefits of Labor Unions
How a Monopsonist Determines How Much Labor to Employ and What Wage Rate to Pay A monopsony is the only firm that buys a particular input, such as labor, in a specific market. For a monopsonist in a labor market, paying a higher wage to attract an additional unit of labor increases its total factor costs for all other labor employed. For this reason, the marginal factor cost of labor is always higher than the wage rate, so the marginal factor cost schedule lies above the labor supply schedule. The labor market monopsonist employs labor to the point at which the marginal factor cost of labor equals the marginal revenue product of labor. It then pays the workers it hires the wage at which they are willing to work, as determined by the labor supply curve, which lies below the marginal factor cost curve. As a result, the monopsonist pays workers a wage that is less than their marginal revenue product.	monopsonist, 779 monopsonistic exploitation, 781 bilateral monopoly, 782 **KEY FIGURES** Figure 30-5, 780 Figure 30-6, 781 Figure 30-7, 782	• **MyEconLab** Study Plan 30.4 • Video: The Buyer's Monopoly—Monopsony • Animated Figures 30-5, 30-6, 30-7

(continued)

 *(continued)*

| **WHAT YOU SHOULD KNOW** | | **WHERE TO GO TO PRACTICE** |

Comparing a Monopsonist's Wage and Employment Decisions with Choices by Firms in Industries with Other Market Structures Firms that are perfect competitors or monopolies in their product markets but hire workers in perfectly competitive labor markets take the wage rate as market determined, meaning that their individual actions are unable to influence the market wage rate. A product market monopolist tends to employ fewer workers than would be employed if the monopolist's industry were perfectly competitive, but the product market monopolist nonetheless cannot affect the market wage rate. In contrast, a monopsonist is the only employer of labor, so it searches for the wage rate that maximizes its profit. This wage rate is less than the marginal revenue product of labor. In a situation in which a firm is both a product market monopolist and a labor market monopsonist, the firm's demand for labor is also lower than it would be if the firm's product market were competitive, and hence the firm hires fewer workers as well.

KEY FIGURE
Figure 30-8, 783

- **MyEconLab** Study Plan 30.4
- Animated Figure 30-8

Log in to MyEconLab, take a chapter test, and get a personalized Study Plan that tells you which concepts you understand and which ones you need to review. From there, MyEconLab will give you further practice, tutorials, animations, videos, and guided solutions.
Log in to www.myeconlab.com

PROBLEMS

All problems are assignable in myeconlab. *Answers to the odd-numbered problems appear at the back of the book.*

30-1. Discuss three aspects of collective bargaining that society might deem desirable.

30-2. Give three reasons why a government might seek to limit the power of a union.

30-3. Recently, the Writers Guild of America (WGA), which represents TV and film screenwriters, called for a strike, and most screenwriters stopped working. Nevertheless, writers for certain TV soap operas, such as *The Young and Restless*—which have had shrinking audiences for years, draw small numbers of viewers for repeat shows, and rarely sell on DVDs—opted to drop their WGA memberships and tried to continue working during the strike. Why do you suppose that the WGA posted on its Web site a phone number for union members to report "strike-breaking activities and 'scab writing'" to the union's 12-person Strike Rules

Compliance Committee? What effect do strike-breakers have on the collective bargaining power of a union?

30-4. Suppose that the objective of a union is to maximize the total dues paid to the union by its membership. Explain the union's strategy, in terms of the wage level and employment level, under the following two scenarios.

a. Union dues are a percentage of total earnings of the union membership.

b. Union dues are paid as a flat amount per union member employed.

30-5. Explain why, in economic terms, the total income of union membership is maximized when marginal revenue is zero. (Hint: How much more revenue is forthcoming when marginal revenue is equal to zero?)

30-6. Explain the impact of each of the following events on the market for union labor.

   a. Union-produced TV and radio commercials convince consumers to buy domestically manufactured clothing instead of imported clothing.

   b. The union sponsors periodic training programs that instruct union laborers about the most efficient use of machinery and tools.

30-7. Why are unions in industries in which inputs such as machines are poor substitutes for labor more likely to be able to bargain for wages higher than market levels?

30-8. How is it possible for the average annual earnings of nonunionized workers to exceed those of unionized workers even though unionized workers' hourly wages are more than $2 higher?

30-9. In the short run, a tool manufacturer has a fixed amount of capital. Labor is a variable input. The cost and output structure that the firm faces is depicted in the following table:

Labor Supplied	Total Physical Product	Hourly Wage Rate ($)
10	100	5
11	109	6
12	116	7
13	121	8
14	124	9
15	125	10

Derive, at each level of labor supplied, the firm's total wage costs and marginal factor cost.

30-10. Suppose that for the firm in Problem 30-9, the goods market is perfectly competitive. The market price of the product the firm produces is $4 at each quantity supplied by the firm. What is the amount of labor that this profit-maximizing firm will hire, and what wage rate will it pay?

30-11. The price and wage structure that a firm faces is depicted in the following table.

Labor Supplied	Total Physical Product	Hourly Wage Rate ($)	Product Price ($)
10	100	5	3.11
11	109	6	3.00
12	116	7	2.95
13	121	8	2.92
14	124	9	2.90
15	125	10	2.89

The firm finds that the price of its product changes with the rate of output. In addition, the wage it pays its workers varies with the amount of labor it employs. This firm maximizes profits. How many units of labor will it hire? What wage will it pay?

30-12. What is the amount of monopsonistic exploitation that takes place at the firm examined in Problem 30-11?

30-13. A profit-maximizing clothing producer in a remote area is the only employer of people in that area. It sells its clothing in a perfectly competitive market. The firm pays each worker the same weekly wage rate. The last worker hired raised the firm's total weekly wage expenses from $105,600 to $106,480. What is the marginal revenue product of the last worker hired by this firm if it is maximizing profits?

30-14. A single firm is the only employer in a labor market. The marginal revenue product, labor supply, and marginal factor cost curves that it faces are displayed in the diagram below. Use this information to answer the following questions.

   a. How many units of labor will this firm employ in order to maximize its economic profits?

   b. What hourly wage rate will this firm pay its workers?

   c. What is the total amount of wage payments that this firm will make to its workers each hour?

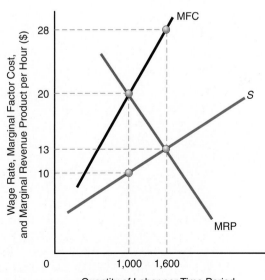

ECONOMICS ON THE NET

Evaluating Union Goals As discussed in this chapter, unions can pursue any of a number of goals. The AFL-CIO's home page provides links to the Web sites of several unions, and reviewing these sites can help you determine the objectives these unions have selected.

Title: American Federation of Labor–Congress of Industrial Organizations

Navigation: Go to **www.econtoday.com/chapter30** to visit the AFL-CIO's home page.

Application Perform the indicated operations, and answer the following questions.

1. Click on *About Us*, then click on *This Is the AFL-CIO*, and finally click on *Mission Statement*. Does the AFL-CIO claim to represent the interests of all workers or just workers in specific firms or industries? Can you discern what broad wage and employment strategy the AFL-CIO pursues?

2. Click on *Unions of the AFL-CIO*. Explore two or three of these Web sites. Do these unions appear to represent the interests of all workers or just workers in specific firms or industries? What general wage and employment strategies do these unions appear to pursue?

For Group Study and Analysis Divide up all the unions affiliated with the AFL-CIO among groups, and have each group explore the Web sites listed under *Unions of the AFL-CIO* at the AFL-CIO Web site. Have each group report on the wage and employment strategies that appear to prevail for the unions it examined.

ANSWERS TO QUICK QUIZZES

p. 772: (i) American Federation . . . Labor; (ii) National Labor Relations . . . industrial; (iii) 25 . . . 12
p. 778: (i) above . . . rationing; (ii) all . . . income . . . maximize; (iii) inward . . . outward; (iv) productivity
p. 783: (i) only buyer . . . upward; (ii) upward . . . greater . . . above; (iii) factor . . . revenue

Income, Poverty, and Health Care

31

Like many studies with provocative implications, a recent study by economists at the Brookings Institution and the Federal Reserve has been the topic of a number of media reports. The study found that a measure of the variability of household incomes had generally increased since the early 1970s, from an index value of 18 to a value of more than 22, or by about 23 percent. The authors' conclusion was that today's households tend to experience more sudden increases in income than households did more than three decades ago. Households also face more risk of unexpected income declines. What factors determine households' income levels and their stability over time? How much do incomes vary *across* households? These are key questions considered in this chapter.

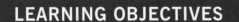

LEARNING OBJECTIVES

 myeconlab

After reading this chapter, you should be able to:

- Describe how to use a Lorenz curve to represent a nation's income distribution
- Identify the key determinants of income differences across individuals
- Discuss theories of desired income distribution
- Distinguish among alternative approaches to measuring and addressing poverty
- Recognize the major reasons for rising health care costs
- Describe alternative approaches to paying for health care

? **DID YOU KNOW THAT** additional education that culminates with a bachelor's degree is worth an average of about $24,000 per year in additional income? The average income of a college graduate is now more than $55,000 per year, whereas the average high school graduate earns just under $31,000 per year. Furthermore, not only does more education push up average earnings even farther, but less education yields even lower earnings. The average annual income of someone who obtains a graduate degree exceeds $80,000, but those who fail to graduate from high school earn average annual incomes of only a little more than $20,000.

Clearly, education must play an important role in determining the **distribution of income,** which is the way that income is allocated among the population. What other factors influence the distribution of income? Economists have devised various theories to explain income distribution. We will present some of these theories in this chapter. We will also present some of the more obvious institutional reasons why income is not distributed equally in the United States. In addition, we will examine what might be done about health care problems confronting individuals in all income groups.

Distribution of income
The way income is allocated among the population.

Why is this couple on an island vacation likely to be college or graduate-school graduates?

Lorenz curve
A geometric representation of the distribution of income. A Lorenz curve that is perfectly straight represents complete income equality. The more bowed a Lorenz curve, the more unequally income is distributed.

Income

Income provides each of us with the means of consuming and saving. Income can be the result of a payment for labor services or a payment for ownership of one of the other factors of production besides labor—land, physical capital, or entrepreneurship. In addition, individuals obtain spendable income from gifts and government transfers. (Some individuals also obtain income by stealing, but we will not treat this matter here.) Right now, let us examine how money income is distributed across classes of income earners within the United States.

Measuring Income Distribution: The Lorenz Curve

We can represent the distribution of money income graphically with what is known as the **Lorenz curve,** named after a U.S.-born statistician, Max Otto Lorenz, who proposed it in 1905. The Lorenz curve shows what share of total money income is accounted for by different proportions of the nation's households. Look at Figure 31-1. On the horizontal axis, we measure the *cumulative* percentage of households, lowest-income households first. Starting at the left corner, there are zero households; at the right corner, we have 100 percent of households; and in the middle, we have 50 percent of households. The vertical axis represents the cumulative percentage of money income. The 45-degree line represents complete equality: 50 percent of the households obtain 50 percent of total income, 60 percent of the households obtain 60 percent of total income, and so on. Of course, in no real-world situation is there such complete equality of income; no actual Lorenz curve would be a straight line. Rather, it would be some curved line, like the one labeled "Actual money income distribution" in Figure 31-1. For example, the bottom 50 percent of households in the United States receive about 28 percent of total money income.

In Figure 31-2, we again show the actual money income distribution Lorenz curve for the United States, and we also compare it to the distribution of money income in 1929. Since that year, the Lorenz curve has generally become less bowed; that is, it has moved closer to the line of complete equality.

CRITICISMS OF THE LORENZ CURVE In recent years, economists have placed less and less emphasis on the shape of the Lorenz curve as an indication of the degree of

FIGURE 31-1

The Lorenz Curve

The horizontal axis measures the cumulative percentage of households, with lowest-income households first, from 0 to 100 percent. The vertical axis measures the cumulative percentage of money income from 0 to 100. A straight line at a 45-degree angle cuts the box in half and represents a line of complete income equality, along which 25 percent of the families get 25 percent of the money income, 50 percent get 50 percent, and so on. The observed Lorenz curve, showing the actual U.S. money income distribution, is not a straight line but rather a curved line as shown. The difference between complete money income equality and the Lorenz curve is the inequality gap.

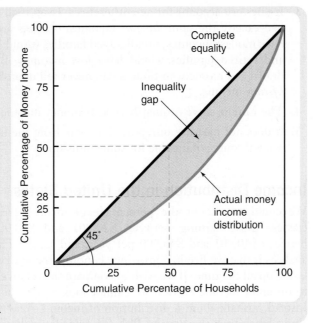

income inequality in a country. There are five basic reasons why the Lorenz curve has been criticized:

1. The Lorenz curve is typically presented in terms of the distribution of *money* income only. It does not include **income in kind,** such as government-provided food stamps, education, medical care, or housing aid, and goods or services produced and consumed in the home or on the farm.

2. The Lorenz curve does not account for differences in the size of households or the number of wage earners they contain.

Income in kind

Income received in the form of goods and services, such as housing or medical care; to be contrasted with money income, which is simply income in dollars, or general purchasing power, that can be used to buy *any* goods and services.

FIGURE 31-2

Lorenz Curves of Income Distribution, 1929 and 2009

Since 1929, the Lorenz curve has moved inward toward the straight line of perfect income equality.

Source: U.S. Department of Commerce.

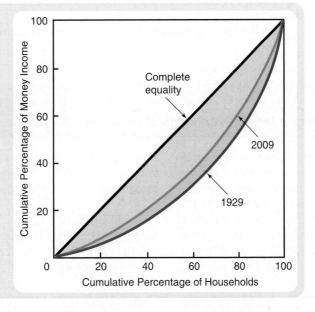

3. It does not account for age differences. Even if all families in the United States had exactly the same *lifetime* incomes, chances are that young families would have modest incomes, middle-aged families would have relatively high incomes, and retired families would have low incomes. Because the Lorenz curve is drawn at a moment in time, it can never tell us anything about the inequality of *lifetime* income.

4. The Lorenz curve ordinarily reflects money income *before* taxes.

5. It does not measure unreported income from the underground economy, a substantial source of income for some individuals.

Income Distribution in the United States

Go to www.econtoday/chapter31 to view the U.S. Census Bureau's most recent data on the U.S. income distribution. Click on the most recent year next to "Money Income in the United States."

We could talk about the percentage of income earners within specific income classes—those earning between $20,001 and $30,000 per year, those earning between $30,001 and $40,000 per year, and so on. The problem with this type of analysis is that we live in a growing economy. Income, with infrequent exceptions, is going up all the time. If we wish to compare the relative shares of total income going to different income classes, we cannot look at specific amounts of money income. Instead, we talk about a distribution of income over five groups. Then we can talk about how much the bottom fifth (or quintile) makes compared with the top fifth, and so on.

In Table 31-1, we see the percentage share of income for households before direct taxes. The table groups households according to whether they are in the lowest 20 percent of the income distribution, the second lowest 20 percent, and so on. We see that in 2009, the lowest 20 percent had an estimated combined money income of 3.4 percent of the total money income of the entire population. This is less than the lowest 20 percent had at the end of World War II. Accordingly, some have concluded that the distribution of money income has become slightly more unequal. *Money* income, however, understates *total* income for individuals who receive in-kind transfers from the government in the form of food stamps, public housing, education, and the like. In particular, since World War II, the share of *total* income—money income plus in-kind benefits—going to the bottom 20 percent of households has more than doubled.

How has the distribution of income in China changed in recent decades?

INTERNATIONAL EXAMPLE
Evidence of a More Unequal Distribution of Income in China

In addition to using Lorenz curves to measure the degree of income inequality, economists sometimes calculate an index measure of inequality known as the *Gini coefficient*, which has a value varying between 0 and 1. A Gini-coefficient value of 0 represents complete equality of income, and a value of 1 represents complete income inequality in which one person receives all income. In the late 1970s, the value of the Gini coefficient for China was 0.15, indicating considerable income equality. Today, it is estimated to be closer to 0.60, indicating that income in China has become much more unequal during the past three decades.

FOR CRITICAL ANALYSIS
Based on the change in value of the Gini coefficient since the late 1970s, has the Lorenz curve for China likely become more or less outward bowed?

TABLE 31-1

Percentage Share of Money Income for Households Before Direct Taxes

Income Group	2009	1975	1960	1947
Lowest fifth	3.4	4.4	4.8	5.1
Second fifth	8.6	10.5	12.2	11.8
Third fifth	14.6	17.1	17.8	16.7
Fourth fifth	23.0	24.8	24.0	23.2
Highest fifth	50.4	43.2	41.3	43.3

Note: Figures may not sum to 100 percent due to rounding.
Sources: U.S. Bureau of the Census; author's estimates.

The Distribution of Wealth

When referring to the distribution of income, we must realize that income—a flow—can be viewed as a return on wealth (both human and nonhuman)—a stock. A discussion of the distribution of income is not necessarily the same thing as a discussion of the distribution of wealth, however. A complete concept of wealth would include not only tangible objects, such as buildings, machinery, land, cars, and houses—nonhuman wealth—but also people who have skills, knowledge, initiative, talents, and the like—human wealth. The total of human and nonhuman wealth in the United States makes up our nation's capital stock.

Figure 31-3 shows that the richest 10 percent of U.S. households hold more than two-thirds of all measured wealth. The problem with those data, gathered by the Federal Reserve System, however, is that they do not include many important assets. One of these is workers' claims on private pension plans, which equal at least $6 trillion. If you add the value of these pensions, household wealth increases by almost 25 percent and reveals that many more U.S. households are middle-wealth households (popularly known as the *middle class*). Another asset excluded from the data is anticipated claims on the Social Security system, which tend to comprise a larger share of the wealth of lower-income individuals.

FIGURE 31-3

Measured Total Wealth Distribution

The top 10 percent of households have 71 percent of all *measured* wealth. This distribution changes dramatically if other nonmeasured components of wealth, such as claims on private pension plans and on government-guaranteed Social Security commitments, are taken into account.

Source: Board of Governors of the Federal Reserve.

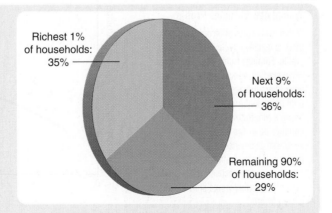

Richest 1% of households: 35%

Next 9% of households: 36%

Remaining 90% of households: 29%

Determinants of Income Differences

We know that there are income differences—that is not in dispute. A more important question is why these differences in income occur. We will look at four determinants of income differences: age, marginal productivity, inheritance, and discrimination.

Age

Age turns out to be a determinant of income because with age come, usually, more education, more training, and more experience. It is not surprising that within every class of income earners, there seem to be regular cycles of earning behavior. Most individuals earn more when they are middle-aged than when they are younger or older. We call this the **age-earnings cycle.**

Age-earnings cycle

The regular earnings profile of an individual throughout his or her lifetime. The age-earnings cycle usually starts with a low income, builds gradually to a peak at around age 50, and then gradually curves down until it approaches zero at retirement.

THE AGE-EARNINGS CYCLE Every occupation has its own age-earnings cycle, and every individual will probably experience some variation from the average. Nonetheless, we can characterize the typical age-earnings cycle graphically in Figure 31-4. Here we see that at age 18, earnings from wages are relatively low. As a person's productivity increases through more training and experience, earnings gradually rise until they peak at about age 50. Then they fall until retirement, when they become zero (that is, currently earned wages become zero, although retirement payments may then commence).

FIGURE 31-4

Typical Age-Earnings Profile

Within every class of income earners there is usually a typical age-earnings profile. Earnings from wages are lowest when starting work at age 18, reach their peak at around age 50, and then taper off until retirement around age 65, when they become zero for most people. The rise in earnings up to age 50 is usually due to increased experience, longer working hours, and better training and schooling. (We abstract from economywide productivity changes that would shift the entire curve upward.)

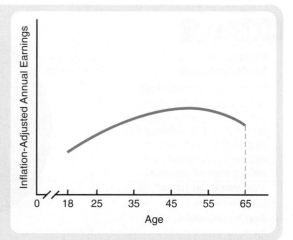

Note that general increases in overall productivity for the entire workforce will result in an upward shift in the typical age-earnings profile depicted in Figure 31-4. Thus, even at the end of the age-earnings cycle, when just about to retire, the worker would receive a relatively high wage compared with the starting wage 45 years earlier. The wage would be higher due to factors that contribute to rising real wages for everyone, regardless of the stage in the age-earnings cycle.

In light of the shape of the age-earnings profile, how do you suppose that U.S. households' assets are distributed by age group?

EXAMPLE
Higher Incomes Imply More Assets for the Older Set

Because people's incomes typically rise as they reach their fifties, so does their saving and hence their accumulation of assets. People over the age of 60 currently comprise 30 percent of U.S. individuals aged 18 and older, but they own more than 41 percent of all assets held by adult individuals. Roughly another 30 percent of adults are between the ages of 18 and 41, but they own less than 20 percent of assets.

FOR CRITICAL ANALYSIS
What is likely to happen to the share of assets of those currently aged 18 to 41 as they grow older?

Now we have some idea why specific individuals earn different incomes at different times in their lives, but we have yet to explain why different people are paid different amounts for their labor. One way to explain this is to recall the marginal productivity theory developed in Chapter 29.

Marginal Productivity

When trying to determine how many workers a firm would hire, we had to construct a marginal revenue product curve. We found that as more workers were hired, the marginal revenue product fell due to diminishing marginal product. If the forces of demand and supply established a certain wage rate, workers would be hired until their marginal physical product times marginal revenue (which equals the market price under perfect competition) was equal to the going wage rate. Then the hiring would stop. This analysis suggests what workers can expect to be paid in the labor market: As long as there are low-cost information flows and the labor and product markets are competitive, each worker can expect to be paid his or her marginal revenue product.

DETERMINANTS OF MARGINAL PRODUCTIVITY According to marginal revenue product theory, if people can increase their marginal physical product, they can expect to earn higher incomes. Key determinants of marginal physical product are talent, experience, and training.

Talent. Talent is the easiest factor to explain, but it is difficult to acquire if you don't have it. Innate abilities and attributes can be very strong, if not overwhelming, determinants of a person's potential productivity. Strength, coordination, and mental alertness are facets of nonacquired human capital and thus have some bearing on the ability to earn income. Someone who is tall and agile has a better chance of being a basketball player than someone who is short and unathletic. A person born with a superior talent for abstract thinking has a better chance of earning a relatively high income as a mathematician or a physicist than someone who is not born with that capability.

Experience. Additional experience at particular tasks is another way to increase productivity. Experience can be linked to the well-known *learning curve* that applies when the same task is done over and over. The worker repeating a task becomes more efficient: The worker can do the same task in less time or in the same amount of time but better. Take an example of a person going to work on an automobile assembly line. At first she is able to fasten only three bolts every two minutes. Then the worker becomes more adept and can fasten four bolts in the same time plus insert a rubber guard on the bumper. After a few more weeks, another task can be added. Experience allows this individual to improve her productivity. The more effectively people learn to do something, the more productive they are.

Training. Training is similar to experience but is more formal. Much of a person's increased productivity is due to on-the-job training. Many companies have training programs for new workers.

INVESTMENT IN HUMAN CAPITAL Investment in human capital is just like investment in anything else. If you invest in yourself by going to college, rather than going to work after high school and earning more current income, you will presumably be rewarded in the future with a higher income or a more interesting job (or both). This is exactly the motivation that underlies the decision of many college-bound students to obtain a formal higher education.

As with other investments, we can determine the rate of return on an investment in a college education. To do so, we first have to figure out the marginal cost of going to school. A major cost is not simply what you have to pay for books, fees, and tuition but rather the income you forgo. *A key cost of education is the income forgone—the opportunity cost of not working.* In addition, the direct expenses of college must be paid for. Certainly, not all students forgo all income during their college years. Many work part time. Taking account of those who work part time and those who are supported by tuition grants and other scholarships, the average rate of return on going to college ranges between 6 and 8 percent per year.

Inheritance

It is not unusual to inherit cash, jewelry, stocks, bonds, homes, or other real estate. Yet only about 10 percent of income inequality in the United States can be traced to differences in inherited wealth. If for some reason the government confiscated all property that had been inherited, the immediate result would be only a modest change in the distribution of income in the United States. In any event, at both federal and state levels substantial inheritance taxes are levied on the estates of relatively wealthy deceased Americans (although there are some legally valid ways to avoid certain estate taxes).

Discrimination

Economic discrimination occurs whenever workers with the same marginal revenue product receive unequal pay due to some noneconomic factor such as their race, gender, or age. It is possible—and indeed quite obvious—that discrimination affects the distribution of income. Certain groups in our society are not paid wages at rates comparable to those received by other groups, even when we correct for productivity.

Differences in income remain between whites and nonwhites and between men and women. For example, the median income of black families is about 65 percent that of white families. The median wage rate of women is about 80 percent that of men. Some people argue that all of these differences are due to discrimination against non-whites and against women.

We cannot simply accept *any* differences in income as due to discrimination, though. What we need to do is discover why differences in income between groups exist and then determine if factors other than discrimination in the labor market can explain them. The unexplained part of income differences can rightfully be considered the result of discrimination.

ACCESS TO EDUCATION African Americans and other minorities have faced discrimination in the acquisition of human capital. The amount and quality of schooling offered black U.S. residents has generally been inferior to that offered whites. As a result, among other things, African Americans and certain other minority groups, such as Hispanics, suffer from reduced investment in human capital. Even when this difference in human capital is taken into account, however, there still appears to be an income differential that cannot be explained.

The unexplained income differential between whites and blacks is often attributed to discrimination in the labor market. Because no better explanation is offered, we will infer that discrimination in the labor market does indeed still exist.

Theories of Desired Income Distribution

We have talked about the factors affecting the distribution of income, but we have not yet mentioned the normative issue of how income *ought* to be distributed. This, of course, requires a value judgment. We are talking about the problem of economic justice. We can never completely resolve this problem because there are always going to be conflicting values. It is impossible to give all people what each thinks is just. Nonetheless, two particular normative standards for the distribution of income have been popular with economists. These are income distribution based on productivity and income distribution based on equality.

Productivity

The *productivity standard* for the distribution of income can be stated simply as "To each according to what he or she produces." This is also called the *contributive standard* because it is based on the principle of rewarding according to the contribution to society's total output. It is also sometimes referred to as the *merit standard* and is one of the oldest concepts of justice. People are rewarded according to merit, and merit is judged by one's ability to produce what is considered useful by society.

We measure a person's productive contribution in a capitalist system by the market value of that person's output. We have already referred to this as the marginal revenue product theory of wage determination.

Equality

The *egalitarian principle* of income distribution is simply "To each exactly the same." Everyone would have exactly the same amount of income. This criterion of income distribution has been debated as far back as biblical times. This system of income distribution has been considered equitable, meaning that presumably everybody is dealt with fairly and equally. There are problems, however, with an income distribution that is completely equal.

Some jobs are more unpleasant or more dangerous than others. Should the people undertaking these jobs be paid exactly the same as everyone else? Indeed, under an equal distribution of income, what incentive would there be for individuals to take risky, hazardous, or unpleasant jobs at all? What about overtime? Who would be willing to work overtime without additional pay? There is another problem: If everyone earned the same income, what incentive would there be for individuals to invest in their own human capital—a costly and time-consuming process?

Just consider the incentive structure within a corporation. Within corporations, much of the differential between, say, the pay of the CEO and the pay of all of the vice presidents is meant to create competition among the vice presidents for the CEO's job. The result is higher productivity. If all incomes were the same, much of this competition would disappear, and productivity would fall.

There is some evidence that differences in income lead to higher rates of economic growth. Future generations are therefore made better off. Elimination of income differences may reduce the rate of economic growth and cause future generations to be poorer than they otherwise might have been.

QUICK QUIZ *See page 817 for the answers. Review concepts from this section in MyEconLab.*

Most people follow an _____-_____ cycle in which they earn relatively small incomes when they first start working, increase their incomes until about age 50, and then slowly experience a decrease in their real incomes as they approach retirement.

According to the marginal _____ theory of wages, workers can expect to be paid their marginal _____ product.

Marginal physical productivity depends on _____, _____, _____, and _____.

Going to school and receiving on-the-job training can be considered an investment in _____ capital. A key cost of education is the _____ cost of not working.

Two normative standards for income distribution are income distribution based on _____ and income distribution based on _____.

Poverty and Attempts to Eliminate It

Throughout the history of the world, mass poverty has been accepted as inevitable. This nation and others, particularly in the Western world, however, have sustained enough economic growth in the past several hundred years so that *mass* poverty can no longer be said to be a problem for these fortunate countries. As a matter of fact, the residual of poverty in the United States strikes us as bizarre, an anomaly. How can there still be so much poverty in a nation of such abundance? Having talked about the determinants of the distribution of income, we now have at least some ideas of why some people are destined to remain low-income earners throughout their lives.

Income can be transferred from the relatively well-to-do to the relatively poor by various methods, and as a nation we have been using them for a long time. Today, we have a vast array of welfare programs set up for the purpose of redistributing income.

As we know, however, these programs have not been entirely successful. Are there alternatives to our current welfare system? Is there a better method of helping the poor? Before we answer these questions, take a look at Figure 31-5, which displays the percentage of the U.S. population determined to be in a state of poverty by the U.S. government. This percentage, called the *poverty rate*, has varied between roughly 11 percent and 16 percent since 1965.

Defining Poverty

The threshold income level, which is used to determine who falls into the poverty category, was originally based on the cost of a nutritionally adequate food plan designed by the U.S. Department of Agriculture. The threshold was determined by multiplying the food plan cost by 3 on the assumption that food expenses comprise approximately one-third of a poor family's income. Annual revisions of the threshold level were based only on price changes in the food budget. In 1969, a federal interagency committee looked at the calculations of the threshold and decided to set new standards, with adjustments made on the basis of changes in the Consumer Price Index. For example, in 2009, the official poverty level for an urban family of four was around $22,000. It goes up each year to reflect whatever inflation has occurred.

Absolute Poverty

Because the low-income threshold is an absolute measure, we know that if it never changes in real terms, we will reduce poverty even if we do nothing. How can that be? The reasoning is straightforward. Real incomes in the United States have been growing at a compounded annual rate of almost 2 percent per capita for at least the past century and at about 2.5 percent since World War II. If we define the poverty line at a specific real income level, more and more individuals will make incomes that exceed that poverty line. Thus, in absolute terms, we will eliminate poverty (assuming continued per capita growth and no change in income distribution).

Go to **www.econtoday.com/chapter31** to learn about the World Bank's programs intended to combat global poverty.

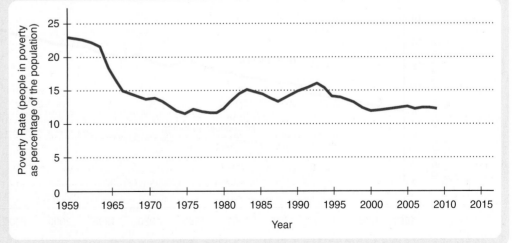

FIGURE 31-5

The Official Poverty Rate in the United States

The official poverty rate, or the number of people in poverty as a percentage of the U.S. population, has remained in a range of roughly 11 to 16 percent since 1965.

Source: U.S. Department of Labor.

Relative Poverty

Be careful with this analysis, however. Poverty can also be defined in relative terms, that is, in terms of the income levels of individuals or families relative to the rest of the population. As long as the distribution of income is not perfectly equal, there will always be some people who make less income than others, even if their relatively low income is high by historical standards. Thus, in a relative sense, the problem of poverty will always exist.

Transfer Payments as Income

The official poverty level is based on pretax income, including cash but not in-kind subsidies—food stamps, housing vouchers, and the like. If we correct poverty levels for such benefits, the percentage of the population that is below the poverty line drops dramatically. Some economists argue that the way the official poverty level is calculated makes no sense in a nation that redistributed more than $1.4 trillion in cash and noncash transfers in 2008.

Furthermore, some of the nation's official poor partake in the informal, or underground, sectors of the economy without reporting their income from these sources. And some of the officially defined poor obtain benefits from owning their own home (40 percent of all poor households do own their own homes). Look at Figure 31-6 for two different views of what has happened to the relative position of this nation's poor. The graph shows the ratio of the top fifth of the nation's households to the bottom fifth of the nation's households. If we look only at measured income, it appears that the poor are getting relatively poorer compared to the rich (the top line). If we compare household spending (consumption), however, a different picture emerges. The nation's poorest households are in fact holding their own in relative terms.

FIGURE 31-6

Relative Poverty: Comparing Household Income and Household Spending

This graph shows on the vertical axis the ratio of the top 20 percent of income-earning households to the bottom 20 percent. If measured household income is used, there appears to be increasing income inequality. If we look at household *spending*, though, inequality is more nearly constant.

Sources: U.S. Bureau of Labor Statistics; U.S. Bureau of the Census.

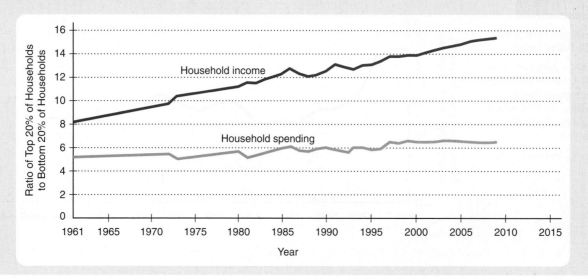

Attacks on Poverty: Major Income Maintenance Programs

There are a variety of income maintenance programs designed to help the poor. We examine a few of them here.

SOCIAL SECURITY For the retired, the unemployed, and the disabled, social insurance programs provide income payments in prescribed situations. The best known is Social Security, which includes what has been called old-age, survivors', and disability insurance (OASDI). As discussed in Chapter 6, this was originally supposed to be a program of compulsory saving financed from payroll taxes levied on both employers and employees. Workers pay for Social Security while working and receive the benefits after retirement. The benefit payments are usually made to people who have reached retirement age. When the insured worker dies, benefits accrue to the survivors, including widows and children. Special benefits provide for disabled workers. Over 90 percent of all employed persons in the United States are covered by OASDI. Today, Social Security is an intergenerational income transfer that is only vaguely related to past earnings. It transfers income from U.S. residents who work—the young through the middle-aged—to those who do not work—older retired persons.

In 2009, more than 50 million people were receiving OASDI checks averaging about $1,000 a month. Benefit payments from OASDI redistribute income to some degree. Benefit payments, however, are not based on recipient need. Participants' contributions give them the right to benefits even if they would be financially secure without them. Social Security is not really an insurance program because people are not guaranteed that the benefits they receive will be in line with the "contributions" they have made. It is not a personal savings account. The benefits are legislated by Congress. In the future, Congress may not be as sympathetic toward older people as it is today. It could (and probably will have to) legislate for lower real levels of benefits instead of higher ones.

SUPPLEMENTAL SECURITY INCOME AND TEMPORARY ASSISTANCE TO NEEDY FAMILIES Many people who are poor but do not qualify for Social Security benefits are assisted through other programs. The federally financed and administered Supplemental Security Income (SSI) program was instituted in 1974. The purpose of SSI is to establish a nationwide minimum income for the aged, the blind, and the disabled. SSI has become one of the fastest-growing transfer programs in the United States. Whereas in 1974 less than $8 billion was spent, the prediction for 2010 is $47 billion. U.S. residents currently eligible for SSI include children and individuals with mental disabilities, including drug addicts and alcoholics.

Temporary Assistance to Needy Families (TANF) is a state-administered program, financed in part by federal grants. The program provides aid to families in need. TANF replaced Aid to Families with Dependent Children (AFDC) in 1996. TANF payments are intended to be temporary. Projected expenditures for TANF are $20 billion in 2009.

FOOD STAMPS Food stamps are government-issued coupons (or, increasingly, electronic debit cards) that can be used to purchase food. In 1964, some 367,000 Americans were receiving food stamps. In 2009, the estimate is over 29 million recipients. The annual cost has jumped from $860,000 to more than $36 billion. In 2009, almost one in every nine citizens (including children) was using food stamps.

THE EARNED INCOME TAX CREDIT PROGRAM In 1975, the Earned Income Tax Credit (EITC) Program was created to provide rebates of Social Security taxes to low-income workers. Over one-fifth of all tax returns claim an earned income tax credit; each year the federal government grants more than $43 billion in these credits. In some states, such as Mississippi, nearly half of all families are eligible for an EITC. The program works as follows: Single-income households with two children that report income of about $39,000 (exclusive of welfare payments) receive EITC benefits up to about $5,000. There is a catch, though. Those with earnings up to a threshold of about $13,000 receive higher benefits as their incomes rise. But families earning more than this threshold income are penalized about 18 cents for every dollar they earn above the income threshold. Thus, on net the EITC discourages work by low- or moderate-income earners more than it rewards work. In particular, it discourages low-income earners from taking on second jobs. The Government Accounting Office estimates that hours worked by working wives in EITC-beneficiary households have consequently decreased by 15 percent. The average EITC recipient works 1,700 hours a year compared to a normal work year of about 2,000 hours.

No Apparent Reduction in Poverty Rates

In spite of the numerous programs in existence and the trillions of dollars transferred to the poor, the officially defined rate of poverty in the United States has shown no long-run tendency to decline. From 1945 until the early 1970s, the percentage of U.S. residents in poverty fell steadily every year. As Figure 31-5 on page 801 shows, it reached a low of around 11 percent in 1974, shot back up beyond 15 percent in 1983, fell to 13.1 percent in 1990, and has since fallen to near 12 percent. Why this pattern has emerged is a real puzzle. Since the War on Poverty was launched under President Lyndon B. Johnson in 1965, more than $13 trillion has been transferred to the poor, and yet more U.S. residents are poor today than ever before. This fact created the political will to pass the Welfare Reform Act of 1996, putting limits on people's use of welfare. The law's goal has been to get people off welfare and into jobs.

QUICK QUIZ   *See page 817 for the answers. Review concepts from this section in MyEconLab.*

If poverty is defined in _____ terms, economic growth eventually decreases the number of officially defined poor. If poverty is defined in _____ terms, however, we will never eliminate it.

Although the relative position of the _____ measured by household _____ seems to have worsened, household spending by the bottom 20 percent of households compared to that of the top 20 percent has shown little change since the 1960s.

Major attacks on poverty have been made through social insurance programs, including _____ Security, _____ Security Income (SSI), Temporary Assistance to Needy Families, the _____ _____ tax credit, and _____ stamps.

Health Care

It may seem strange to be reading about health care in a chapter on the distribution of income and poverty. Yet health care is intimately related to those two topics. For example, sometimes people become poor because they do not have adequate health insurance (or have none at all), fall ill, and deplete all of their wealth in obtaining medical care. Moreover, some individuals remain in certain jobs simply because their employer's health care package seems so good that they are afraid to change jobs and risk not being covered by health insurance in the process. Finally, as you will see, much of the cause of the increased health care spending in the United States can be attributed to a change in the incentives that U.S. residents face.

The U.S. Health Care Situation

Spending for health care is estimated to account for about 16 percent of U.S. real GDP. You can see from Figure 31-7 that in 1965, about 6 percent of annual income was spent on health care, but that percentage has been increasing ever since.

WHY HAVE HEALTH CARE COSTS RISEN SO MUCH? There are numerous explanations for why health care costs have risen so much. At least one has to do with changing demographics: The U.S. population is getting older.

The Age–Health Care Expenditure Equation. The top 5 percent of health care users incur over 50 percent of all health costs. The bottom 70 percent of health care users account for only 10 percent of health care expenditures. Not surprisingly, the elderly make up most of the top users of health care services. Nursing home expenditures are made primarily by people older than 70. The use of hospitals is also dominated by the aged.

The U.S. population is aging steadily. More than 13 percent of the 300 million U.S. residents are over 65. It is estimated that by the year 2035, senior citizens will comprise about 22 percent of our population. This aging population stimulates the demand for health care. The elderly consume more than four times as much per capita health care services as the rest of the population. In short, whatever the demand for health care services is today, it is likely to be considerably higher in the future as the U.S. population ages.

New Technologies. Another reason that health care costs have risen so dramatically is advancing technology. Each CT (computerized tomography) scanner costs at least $100,000. An MRI (magnetic resonance imaging) scanner can cost over $2 million.

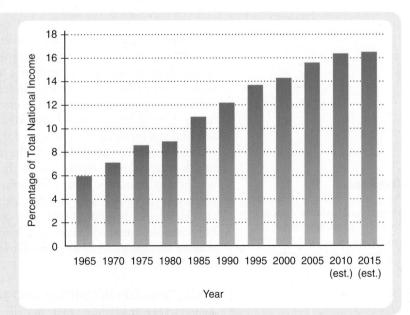

FIGURE 31-7

Percentage of Total National Income Spent on Health Care in the United States

The portion of total national income spent on health care has risen steadily since 1965.

Sources: U.S. Department of Commerce; U.S. Department of Health and Human Services; Deloitte and Touche LLP; VHA, Inc.

A PET (positron emission tomography) scanner costs around $4 million. All of these machines have become increasingly available in recent decades and are desired throughout the country. Typical fees for procedures using them range from $300 to $400 for a CT scan to as high as $2,000 for a PET scan. The development of new technologies that help physicians and hospitals prolong human life is an ongoing process in an ever-advancing industry. New procedures at even higher prices can be expected in the future.

What new pill technologies promise to boost health care costs?

E-COMMERCE EXAMPLE
High-Priced Pills and Future Health Care Costs

Several new pill technologies have emerged in the past few years. For instance, one new pill, called the accordion pill, releases medication slowly, thereby reducing the side effects of medications that currently must be taken several times per day. The accordion pill unfolds inside the stomach and remains anchored there for up to 20 hours. Each pill costs a little less than $10.

Other pills are much more high tech. One, called Smart-Pill, transmits data wirelessly via a radio frequency identification system to a receiver worn around the patient's neck or waist. The pill transmits information about acidity, pressure, temperature, and digestive activity. Each pill costs $500. A complete SmartPill monitoring system marketed to hospitals—including laptop, software, docking station, data receiver, activation device, and a set of 10 pills—is priced at $20,000.

Clearly, average pill prices will be on the upswing in the short run if physicians begin prescribing many of these and other high-tech pills. In the long run, however, new pill technologies could succeed in reducing costs of other forms of health care. Thus, medical technologies that appear to raise costs in the short run may well offer hope for lower costs in the future.

FOR CRITICAL ANALYSIS
Are high-priced health care technologies necessarily inefficient simply because they currently have high relative prices? Why or why not?

Third-Party Financing. Currently, government spending on health care constitutes over 40 percent of total health care spending (of which the *federal* government pays about 70 percent). Private insurance accounts for a little over 35 percent of payments for health care. The remainder—less than 20 percent—is paid directly by individuals. Figure 31-8 shows the change in the payment scheme for medical care in the United States since 1930. Medicare and Medicaid are the main sources of hospital and other medical benefits for more than 40 million U.S. residents, most of whom are over 65. Medicaid—the joint state-federal program—provides long-term health care, particularly for people living in nursing homes. Medicare, Medicaid, and private insurance companies are considered **third parties** in the medical care equation. Caregivers and patients are the two primary parties. When third parties step in to pay for medical care, the quantity demanded of those services increases. For example, when Medicare and Medicaid went into effect in the 1960s, the volume of federal government–reimbursed medical services increased by more than 65 percent.

Third parties
Parties who are not directly involved in a given activity or transaction. For example, in the relationship between caregivers and patients, fees may be paid by third parties (insurance companies, government).

PRICE, QUANTITY DEMANDED, AND THE QUESTION OF MORAL HAZARD Although some people may think that the demand for health care is insensitive to price

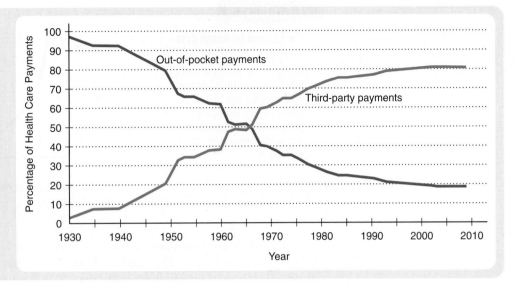

FIGURE 31-8

Third-Party versus Out-of-Pocket Health Care Payments

Out-of-pocket payments for health care services have been falling steadily since the 1930s. In contrast, third-party payments for health care have risen to the point that they account for over 80 percent of all such outlays today.

Sources: Health Care Financing Administration; U.S. Department of Health and Human Services.

changes, theory clearly indicates otherwise. Look at Figure 31-9 on the following page. There you see a hypothetical demand curve for health care services. To the extent that third parties—whether government or private insurance—pay for health care, the out-of-pocket cost, or net price, to the individual decreases. If all medical expenses were paid for by third parties, dropping the price to zero in Figure 31-9, the quantity demanded would increase.

One of the issues here has to do with the problem of *moral hazard*. Consider two individuals with two different health insurance policies. The first policy pays for all medical expenses, but under the second, the individual has to pay the first $1,000 a year (this amount is known as the *deductible*). Will the behavior of the two individuals be different? Generally, the answer is yes. The individual with no deductible is more likely to seek treatment for health problems after they develop rather than try to avoid them and will generally seek medical attention on a more regular basis. In contrast, the individual who faces the first $1,000 of medical expenses each year will tend to engage in more wellness activities and will be less inclined to seek medical care for minor problems. The moral hazard here is that the individual with the zero deductible for medical care expenses will tend to engage in a less healthful lifestyle than will the individual with the $1,000 deductible.

MORAL HAZARD AS IT AFFECTS PHYSICIANS AND HOSPITALS The issue of moral hazard also has a direct effect on the behavior of physicians and hospital administrators. Due to third-party payments, patients rarely have to worry about the expense of operations and other medical procedures. As a consequence, both physicians and hospitals order more procedures. Physicians are typically reimbursed on the basis of medical procedures. Thus, they have no financial interest in trying to keep hospital costs down. Indeed, many have an incentive to raise costs.

Such actions are most evident with terminally ill patients. A physician may order a CT scan and other costly procedures for a terminally ill patient. The physician knows that Medicare or some other type of insurance will pay. Then the physician can charge a fee for analyzing the CT scan. Fully 30 percent of Medicare expenditures are for U.S. residents who are in the last six months of their lives.

You Are There

To read about why moral hazard concerns associated with health insurance posed a practical problem for a West Virginia clinic, consider **The New Experimental Therapy: Prepaid Clinics,** on pages 810 and 811.

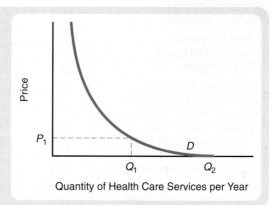

FIGURE 31-9

The Demand for Health Care Services

At price P_1, the quantity of health care services demanded per year would hypothetically be Q_1. If the price fell to zero (third-party payment with zero deductible), the quantity demanded would expand to Q_2.

Rising Medicare expenditures are one of the most serious problems facing the federal government today. The number of beneficiaries has increased from 19.1 million in 1966 (first year of operation) to more than 40 million in 2009. Figure 31-10 shows that federal spending on Medicare has been growing at an average of about 10 percent per year, adjusted for inflation. The rate of growth in Medicare spending will be even higher in the future as a result of the Medicare prescription drug benefit that was implemented in 2006.

Is National Health Insurance the Answer?

Proponents of a national health care system believe that the current system relies too heavily on private insurers. They argue in favor of a Canadian-style system. In Canada, the government sets the fees that are paid to each physician for seeing a patient and prohibits most private practice. The Canadian government also imposes a cap on the income that any physician can receive in a given year. The Canadian federal

FIGURE 31-10

Federal Medicare Spending

Federal spending on Medicare has increased about 10 percent per year, *after adjusting for inflation*, since its inception in 1966. (All figures expressed in constant 2005 dollars per year.)

Sources: Economic Report of the President; U.S. Bureau of Labor Statistics.

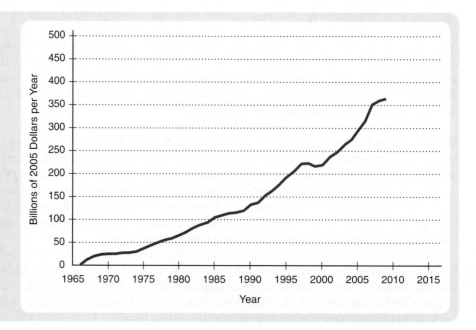

government provides a specified amount of funding to hospitals, leaving it to them to decide how to allocate the funds. If we were to follow the Canadian model, the average U.S. resident would receive considerably fewer health services than at present. Hospital stays would be longer, but there would be fewer tests and procedures.

Alternatives to a national health care policy involve some type of national health insurance, perhaps offered only to people who qualify on the basis of low annual income. A number of politicians have offered variations on such a program. The more than 40 million U.S. residents who have no health insurance at some time during each year might benefit. The share of annual national income that goes to health care expenditures would rise, however. Also, federal government spending might increase by another $60 billion to $100 billion (or more) per year to pay for the program.

How is care rationed under most national health insurance programs?

INTERNATIONAL EXAMPLE
A Symptom of National Health Plans—Long Queues

Most national health plans fix prices for a long period. Thus, when the market clearing price of a health care service rises above the government price, alternative rationing mechanisms arise to address the resulting shortage. In most nations, rationing by queues—that is, waiting in line—is the primary rationing mechanism. For instance, in Canada, the average wait time to see a specialist upon the recommendation of a general physician is nearly 18 weeks. In the United Kingdom (UK), long wait times prevail even to see general practitioners. Wait times

are so lengthy to see UK National Health Center dentists that some British residents have resorted to pulling their own teeth or to repairing broken teeth or replacing crowns with Super Glue.

FOR CRITICAL ANALYSIS
Why do you suppose that when the state of Massachusetts implemented a universal-coverage health plan for state residents, the average wait time to see a physician jumped by nearly 60 percent, to more than seven weeks?

Countering the Moral Hazard Problem: A Health Savings Account

As an alternative to completely changing the U.S. health care industry, in 2003 Congress authorized **health savings accounts (HSAs).** These accounts replaced experimental *medical savings accounts* that Congress had previously permitted in only a limited number nationwide. Anyone with a relatively high health insurance deductible—a minimum level of out-of-pocket expenses of slightly more than $1,000 for an individual or just over $2,000 for a family—can open an HSA at a financial institution offering such accounts. Individuals younger than 55 can make annual deposits of up to about $3,000 per person per year, and families can deposit as much as about $6,000 per year. Once a person reaches the age of 55, allowable deposits can be even higher, but contributions must end once the person reaches 65 and becomes eligible for Medicare.

People with HSAs may use deposited funds and tax-free interest earnings to cover any out-of-pocket health care expenses. In addition, they can draw on HSAs to pay health insurance premiums if they become unemployed or to cover medical expenses they incur after they have retired. There is a 10 percent penalty for most withdrawals

Health savings account (HSA)
A tax-exempt health care account into which individuals can pay on a regular basis and out of which medical expenses can be paid.

used for nonmedical purposes before retirement, but when a person retires, funds in an HSA may be used to supplement other sources of income. A single person depositing the maximum amount each year with no withdrawals will have hundreds of thousands of dollars in the account after 40 years.

COMBATING MORAL HAZARD A major benefit of an HSA is that the moral hazard problem is reduced. Individuals ultimately pay for their own *minor* medical expenses. They do not have the incentive to seek medical care as frequently for minor problems. In addition, they have an incentive to engage in wellness activities. Finally, for those using an HSA, the physician-patient relationship remains intact because third parties (insurance companies or the government) do not intervene in paying or monitoring medical expenses. Patients with HSAs usually will not allow physicians to routinely order expensive tests for every minor ache or pain because they get to keep any funds saved in the HSA.

CRITICS' RESPONSES Some critics argue that because individuals get to keep whatever they don't spend from their HSAs, they will forgo necessary visits to medical care facilities and may develop more serious medical problems as a consequence. Other critics argue that HSAs will sabotage managed care plans. Under managed care plans, deductibles are either reduced or eliminated completely. In exchange, managed health care plan participants are extremely limited in physician choice. Just the opposite is true with HSAs—high deductibles and unlimited choice of physicians.

QUICK QUIZ   See page 817 for the answers. Review concepts from this section in MyEconLab.

Health care costs have risen because (1) our population has been getting older and the elderly use _____ health care services, (2) new technologies and medicines cost more, and (3) _____-_____ financing (private and government-sponsored health insurance) _____ the incentive for individuals to decrease their spending on health care services.

_____ health insurance has been proposed as an answer to our current problems, but it does little

to alter the reasons why health care costs continue to rise.

In 2003, Congress authorized _____ _____ accounts, which allow individuals to set aside funds that are tax-exempt and can be used only for medical care. Whatever is left over becomes a type of _____ account.

You Are There ▶ The New Experimental Therapy: Prepaid Clinics

Vic Wood's clinic in Wheeling, West Virginia, is open 11 hours per day, six days per week. At the clinic, Wood, another physician, and four physician assistants treat people seeking care for problems ranging from cold symptoms to severe chest pains. Many of them do so under a prepaid-care plan offered by the clinic, in which individuals pay less

than $90 per month and families pay about $125 per month for unlimited primary health care. More than one in five of the clinic's patients have no health insurance, and many of them have opted for the clinic's prepaid plan. Others who had employer-provided health insurance plans with high deductibles—spending levels that must be met out of

You Are There (cont.)

pocket before insurance payments begin—have dropped those plans in favor of Wood's prepaid plan.

Not too long ago, Wood hit a major roadblock to his prepaid-care arrangement. When he began advertising the plan, West Virginia's state insurance commissioner argued that his clinic was operating as an unlicensed insurer and would have to obtain approval of the prices it was charging. In the commissioner's view, the clinic's prices were "too low" and gave people an incentive to switch from regular health insurance plans to Wood's lower-priced plan. The commissioner worried that Wood's plan might be under-funded in light of the moral hazard problem associated with health insurance.

At a chance meeting with the state's governor, Wood was able to argue successfully for a law authorizing an experi-ment in prepaid health plans in West Virginia. Now Wood is

signing up about a dozen additional patients to the clinic's prepaid plan every month. He estimates that about 1,200 enrollees will provide sufficient monthly funding to keep the clinic in operation.

CRITICAL ANALYSIS QUESTIONS

1. How might it be possible for a health insurance plan to set its prices too low to remain viable for a long period? (Hint: Insurers always keep reserves of cash to handle claims by policyholders, but how do they build up those reserves?)

2. Why do you suppose that some small employers in Wheeling have opted to offer their employees prepaid plans at Wood's clinic instead of traditional health insurance plans?

Issues and Applications

The Volatility of U.S. Households' Incomes

CONCEPTS APPLIED

- Income
- Distribution of Income
- Age-Earnings Cycle

A recent study by Douglas Elmendorf of the Brookings Institution and Federal Reserve economists Karen Dynan and Daniel Sichel found that a measure of U.S. household income volatility has risen by almost one-fourth since the early 1970s. The study attracted considerable media attention. Even though the authors cautioned against interpreting their findings as evidence that U.S. households face more risk of hardship than before, that conclusion is exactly the one that the media reported. Were the media reports justified? Do households today face a much greater potential for sudden drops in their incomes than in years past?

The Two-Sided Implication of Greater Income Variability

By emphasizing only downside income risks faced by households, media reports on the study by Dynan, Elmendorf, and Sichel overlooked an important fact. Any measure of income variability applies to the potential for both downward *and* upward movements in income.

Certainly, the media reports were correct that a general increase in the variability of household incomes implies a greater risk of income declines. Indeed, based on the rise in income variability found in their study, the authors calculated that the probability that a family will experience a decline in income of 50 percent or more in one year, in relation to their income three years earlier, nearly tripled between the early 1970s and the late 2000s. Nevertheless, a rise in income variability also implies an increased probability of unexpected *increases* in incomes of similar magnitude. When income is more volatile, households can receive sudden bursts of income as well as experience abrupt income declines. The media, however, chose not to emphasize this positive aspect of the rise in income volatility.

Has the Share of Households with Large Income Drops Risen?

A 50 percent decline in household income is not as rare as you might think. Figure 31-11 indicates that in the years since 1981, between 12 percent and just over 20 percent of households have experienced an earnings decline of at least 50 percent during the previous year. Thus, in a given year, many households in the United States experience sharp drops in their incomes.

Note, however, that the *actual* share of households experiencing annual income declines of at least 50 percent generally decreased between 1982 and 2000. Although the actual percentage of households with income drops of 50 percent or more has increased slightly during the 2000s, this percentage remains lower than during the 1980s, a fact that the media ignored.

Gender-Based Income Distribution Aspects of Income Volatility

Figure 31-11 also displays percentages for males and females. In every year, more men than women experienced a drop in their incomes of 50 percent or more in relation to the preceding year. This is consistent with

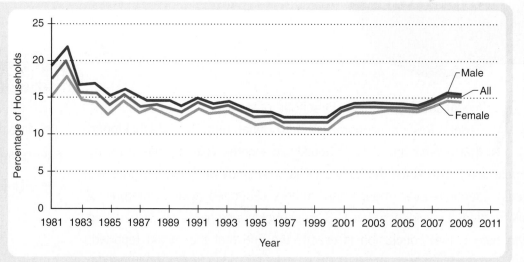

FIGURE 31-11

Percentage of U.S. Households Experiencing at Least a 50 Percent Decline in Earnings

In recent years, nearly 15 percent of households in the United States have experienced earnings reductions of at least 50 percent. Men are more likely than women to experience significant decreases in earnings.

Sources: U.S. Department of Labor; author's estimates.

conclusions that Dynan, Elmendorf, and Sichel reported in their study. Thus, men face a greater risk of sudden drops in income than do women. Because men typically earn more than women, in married households this implies greater income volatility overall. Consequently, couples and families more dependant on a male's income face a higher risk of income reductions.

Nevertheless, there is potentially good news as well as bad news in the greater income variability experienced by men. Sudden *increases* in men's incomes can also occur. The higher male income risks are on the upside as well as on the downside. Once again, however, this is an implication of the study that the media chose not to emphasize.

Test your understanding of this chapter by going online to **MyEconLab**.
In the Study Plan for this chapter, select Section N: News.

For Critical Analysis

1. If the variability of men's incomes were to decline, why might this change be regarded as either "good news" or "bad news" for males?

2. If the variability of men's incomes were to decline without any change taking place in the volatility of women's incomes, what would be the net effect on the income variability of all households?

Web Resources

1. To read the study of household income volatility by Dynan, Elmendorf, and Sichel, go to www.econtoday.com/chapter31.

2. To learn about why increased male income volatility might increase the probability of divorce, go to www.econtoday.com/chapter31.

Research Project

Could differences in the variability of incomes for high-, middle-, and low-income households affect the distribution of income? If not, why not? If so, would the distribution of income necessarily become more or less equal? Explain.

   Here is what you should know after reading this chapter. **MyEconLab** will help you identify what you know, and where to go when you need to practice.

WHAT YOU SHOULD KNOW		WHERE TO GO TO PRACTICE
Using a Lorenz Curve to Represent a Nation's Income Distribution A Lorenz curve is a diagram that illustrates the distribution of income geometrically by measuring the percentage of households in relation to the cumulative percentage of income earnings. A perfectly straight Lorenz curve depicts perfect income equality because at each percentage of households measured along a straight-line Lorenz curve, those households earn exactly the same percentage of income. The more bowed a Lorenz curve is, the more unequally income is distributed.	distribution of income, 792 Lorenz curve, 792 income in kind, 793 **KEY FIGURES** Figure 31-1, 793 Figure 31-2, 793	• **MyEconLab** Study Plan 31.1 • Audio introduction to Chapter 31 • Animated Figures 31-1, 31-2 • ABC News Video: Tradeoffs to High-Priced Cancer Drugs

(continued)

 *(continued)*

WHAT YOU SHOULD KNOW		WHERE TO GO TO PRACTICE
Key Determinants of Income Differences Across Individuals Because of the age-earnings cycle, in which people typically begin working at relatively low incomes when young, age is an important factor influencing income differences. So are marginal productivity differences, which arise from differences in talent, experience, and training due to different investments in human capital. Discrimination likely plays a role as well, and economists attribute some of the unexplained portions of income differences across people to factors related to discrimination.	age-earnings cycle, 796 KEY FIGURE Figure 31-4, 796	• **MyEconLab** Study Plan 31.2 • Video: The Determinants of Income Differences • Animated Figure 31-4
Theories of Desired Income Distribution Economists agree that determining how income ought to be distributed is a normative issue influenced by alternative notions of economic justice. Nevertheless, two theories of desired income distribution receive considerable attention. One is the productivity standard (also called the contributive or merit standard), according to which each person receives income according to the value of what the person produces. The other is the egalitarian principle of income distribution, which proposes that each person should receive exactly the same income.		• **MyEconLab** Study Plan 31.3
Alternative Approaches to Measuring and Addressing Poverty One approach to measuring poverty is to define an absolute poverty standard, such as a specific and unchanging income level. If an absolute measure of poverty is used and the economy experiences persistent real growth, poverty will eventually disappear. Another approach defines poverty in terms of income levels relative to the rest of the population. Under this definition, poverty exists as long as the distribution of incomes is unequal. Official poverty measures are often based on pretax income and fail to take transfer payments into account. Currently, the U.S. government seeks to address poverty via income maintenance programs such as Social Security, Supplemental Security Income, Temporary Assistance to Needy Families, food stamps, and the Earned Income Tax Credit Program.	KEY FIGURES Figure 31-5, 801 Figure 31-6, 802	• **MyEconLab** Study Plan 31.4 • Video: Defining Poverty • Animated Figure 31-5, 31-6
Major Reasons for Rising Health Care Costs Spending on health care as a percentage of total U.S. national income has increased during recent decades. One reason is that the U.S. population is aging, and older people typically experience more health problems. Another contributing factor is the adoption of higher-quality but also higher-priced technologies for diagnosing and treating health problems. In addition, third-party financing of health care expenditures by private and government	third parties, 806 KEY FIGURES Figure 31-7, 805 Figure 31-8, 807 Figure 31-9, 808	• **MyEconLab** Study Plan 31.5 • Animated Figures 31-7, 31-8, 31-9

(continued)

myeconlab (continued)

WHAT YOU SHOULD KNOW	WHERE TO GO TO PRACTICE
insurance programs gives covered individuals an incentive to purchase more health care than they would if they paid all expenses out of pocket. Moral hazard problems can also arise because consumers may be more likely to seek treatment for insured health problems after they develop instead of trying to avoid them, and physicians and hospitals may order more procedures than they otherwise would require.	
Alternative Approaches to Paying for Health Care An alternative approach to funding health care would be to rely less on private insurers and more on governmental funding of care for all citizens. Under such a system, the government typically sets fees and establishes limits on access to care. Another approach would be to establish an income-based national health insurance program, in which only lower-income people would qualify for government assistance in meeting their health care expenses. Another option, which Congress authorized in 2003, is to provide incentives for people to save some of their income in health savings accounts, from which they can draw funds to pay for health care expenses in the future.	health savings account (HSA), 809	• **MyEconLab** Study Plan 31.5

Log in to MyEconLab, take a chapter test, and get a personalized Study Plan that tells you which concepts you understand and which ones you need to review. From there, MyEconLab will give you further practice, tutorials, animations, videos, and guided solutions.
Log in to www.myeconlab.com

PROBLEMS

All problems are assignable in myeconlab. *Answers to the odd-numbered problems appear at the back of the book.*

31-1. Consider the graph at the right, which depicts Lorenz curves for countries X, Y, and Z.

 a. Which country has the least income inequality?

 b. Which country has the most income inequality?

 c. Countries Y and Z are identical in all but one respect: population distribution. The share of the population made up of children below working age is much higher in country Z. Recently, however, birthrates have declined in country Z and risen in country Y. Assuming that the countries remain identical in all other respects, would you expect that in 20 years the Lorenz curves for the two countries will be

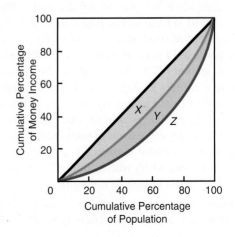

closer together or farther apart? (Hint: According to the age-earnings cycle, what typically happens to income as an individual begins working and ages?)

31-2. Consider the following estimates from the mid-2000s of shares of income to each group. Use graph paper or a hand-drawn diagram to draw rough Lorenz curves for each country. Which has the most nearly equal distribution, based on your diagram?

Country	Poorest 40%	Next 30%	Next 20%	Richest 10%
Bolivia	13	21	26	40
Chile	13	20	26	41
Uruguay	22	26	26	26

31-3. Suppose that the 20 percent of people with the highest incomes decide to increase their annual giving to charities, which pass nearly all the funds on to the 20 percent of people with the lowest incomes. What is the effect on the shape of the Lorenz curve?

31-4. Suppose that a nation has implemented a system for applying a tax rate of 2 percent to the incomes earned by the 10 percent of its residents with the highest incomes. All funds collected are then transferred directly to the 10 percent of the nation's residents with the lowest incomes.

a. What is the general effect on the shape of a Lorenz curve based on incomes prior to collection and redistribution of the tax?

b. What is the general effect on the shape of a Lorenz curve based on after-tax, post-redistribution incomes?

31-5. Estimates indicate that during the mid-2000s, the poorest 40 percent of the population earned about 15 percent of total income in Argentina. In Brazil, the poorest 40 percent earned about 10 percent of total income. The next-highest 30 percent of income earners in Argentina received roughly 25 percent of total income. By contrast, in Brazil, the next-highest 30 percent of income earners received approximately 20 percent of total income. Can you determine, without drawing a diagram (though you can if you wish), which country's Lorenz curve was bowed out farther to the right?

31-6. Explain why the productivity standard for the distribution of income entails rewarding people based on their contribution to society's total output. Why does the productivity standard typically fail to yield an equal distribution of income?

31-7. Identify whether each of the following proposed poverty measures is an absolute or relative measure of poverty, and discuss whether poverty could ever be eliminated if that measure were utilized.

a. An inflation-adjusted annual income of $25,000 for an urban family of four

b. Individuals with annual incomes among the lowest 15 percent

c. An inflation-adjusted annual income of $10,000 per person

31-8. Some economists have argued that if the government wishes to subsidize health care, it should instead provide predetermined sums of payments (based on the type of health care problems experienced) directly to patients, who then would be free to choose their health care providers. Whether or not you agree, can you give an economic rationale for this approach to governmental health care funding?

31-9. Suppose that a government agency guarantees to pay all of an individual's future health care expenses after the end of this year, so that the effective price of health care for the individual will be zero from that date onward. In what ways might this well-intended policy induce the individual to consume "excessive" health care services in future years?

31-10. Suppose that a group of physicians establishes a joint practice in a remote area. This group provides the only health care available to people in the local community, and its objective is to maximize total economic profits for the group's members. Draw a diagram illustrating how the price and quantity of health care will be determined in this community. (Hint: How does a single producer of any service determine its output and price?)

31-11. A government agency determines that the entire community discussed in Problem 31-10 qualifies for a special program in which the government will pay for a number of health care services that most residents previously had not consumed. Many residents immediately make appointments with the community physicians' group. Given the information in Problem 31-10, what is the likely effect on the profit-maximizing price and the equilibrium quantity of health care services provided by the physicians' group in this community?

31-12. A government agency notifies the physicians' group in Problem 31-10 that to continue providing services in the community, the group must document its activities. The resulting paperwork expenses raise the cost of each unit of health care services that the group provides. What is the likely effect on the profit-maximizing price and the equilibrium quantity of health care services provided by the physicians' group in this community?

31-13. As discussed in this chapter, interest-bearing health savings accounts (HSAs) allow individuals with qualifying health insurance plans to use deposited funds to pay out-of-pocket medical expenses. Subject to penalties and taxation, holders of HSAs can use funds in the accounts and tax-free interest earnings to pay non-health-related expenses if they wish. Many people, however, participate in optional *health reimbursement accounts (HRAs)* offered alongside employer-provided health insurance plans. HRAs, into which people typically make payments via tax-free deductions from their weekly or monthly earnings, are non-interest-bearing and can be used only to pay medical expenses. In most plans, any funds in HRAs that individuals fail to use for medical expenses within a calendar year revert to the employer at the end of the year. Is an HSA or an HRA more likely to create moral hazard problems? Explain your reasoning.

ECONOMICS ON THE NET

Measuring Poverty In this application, you will learn why poverty can be difficult to measure.

Title: World Bank PovertyNet: Understanding Poverty

Navigation: Go to **www.econtoday.com/chapter31** to visit the World Bank's home page. Click on *Topics* and then *Poverty Analysis*. Then click on *Measuring Poverty*.

Application Perform the indicated operations, and answer the following questions.

1. Click on "Defining welfare measures." Why does this discussion suggest that measures of consumption are more useful to use in measuring poverty than income measures? Does the U.S. government's use of income thresholds for its official definition of poverty accord with this discussion?

2. Click on "Choose and estimate a poverty line." What alternative absolute poverty definitions are discussed? If the U.S. government were to adopt any of these absolute measures for its official poverty definition, what would happen to the U.S. poverty rate as real incomes and living standards rise over time?

For Group Study and Analysis Click on "Choose and estimate poverty indicators." What are the advantages and disadvantages of the poverty indicators that are discussed? Which indicator does the U.S. government utilize?

ANSWERS TO QUICK QUIZZES

p. 796: (i) income . . . equality . . . unequally; (ii) assets . . . more
p. 800: (i) age-earnings; (ii) productivity . . . revenue; (iii) talent . . . education . . . experience . . . training; (iv) human . . . opportunity; (v) productivity . . . equality
p. 804: (i) absolute . . . relative; (ii) poor . . . income; (iii) Social . . . Supplemental . . . earned income . . . food
p. 810: (i) more . . . third-party . . . reduces; (ii) National; (iii) health savings . . . retirement

32

Environmental Economics

Market activities in China currently generate about 200 million tons of solid waste annually. Estimates indicate that this flow of trash is rising by about 12 million additional tons with each passing year. Yet only about 30 percent of China's solid waste is incinerated or buried in sequestered landfills, as compared with 90 percent in the United States. Much of China's solid waste contains harmful chemicals, which have contaminated the water supplies of an estimated 90 percent of the nation's cities. Why are residents of China apparently willing to tolerate so much pollution? Will ongoing economic growth contribute to even more pollution in China, or can we anticipate efforts to engage in more pollution abatement in the future? After reading this chapter, you will be prepared to contemplate these questions.

LEARNING OBJECTIVES

MyEconLab helps you master each objective and study more efficiently. See end of chapter for details.

After reading this chapter, you should be able to:

- Distinguish between private costs and social costs

- Understand market externalities and possible ways to correct externalities

- Explain how economists can conceptually determine the optimal quantity of pollution

- Contrast the roles of private and common property rights in alternative approaches to addressing the problem of pollution

- Describe how many of the world's governments are seeking to reduce pollution by capping and controlling the use of pollution-generating resources

- Discuss how the assignment of property rights may influence the fates of endangered species

? DID YOU KNOW THAT the Portland, Oregon–based Bonneville Power Administration, an agency of the U.S. Department of Energy, has spent more than $9 billion over the past three decades trying to increase the U.S. salmon population? These fish travel from the mountain streams of their birth to the Pacific Ocean and then back again to lay eggs in their home streams. As part of their trek, they must navigate several human-made dams administered by the Bonneville Power Administration. To help the salmon along, the agency has created artificial waterways to enable the salmon to traverse its dams. It has even used barges to give the salmon rides around the dams. To try to learn why salmon populations remain low despite these efforts, agency employees attached tracking equipment to fish. They discovered that salmon are succumbing to several dangers in addition to the dams. Key threats include predatory birds and sea lions, whose numbers have increased in recent years—in part because other government agencies have spent millions of dollars to boost populations of these salmon predators.

The economic way of thinking about potentially endangered species, including certain fish species such as salmon, requires considering the costs of protecting endangered species. Likewise, the economic way of thinking about nonrenewable resources or the environment requires taking into account the costs of resource conservation and environmental protection. What additional portion of your weekly wages are you willing to give up to take measures to protect declining populations of species such as salmon? To some people, framing questions in terms of the dollars-and-cents costs of environmental improvement sounds anti-ecological. But this is not so. Economists want to help citizens and policymakers opt for informed policies that have the maximum possible *net* benefits (benefits minus costs). As you will see, every decision made in favor of "the environment" involves a trade-off.

Private versus Social Costs

Human actions often give rise to unwanted side effects—the destruction of our environment is one. Human actions generate pollutants that go into the air and the water. The question that is often asked is, Why do individuals and businesses continue to create pollution without necessarily paying directly for the negative consequences?

Until now, we've been dealing with settings in which the costs of an individual's actions are borne directly by the individual. When a business has to pay wages to workers, it knows exactly what its labor costs are. When it has to buy materials or build a plant, it knows quite well what these will cost. An individual who has to pay for car repairs or a theater ticket knows exactly what the cost will be. These costs are what we term *private costs*. **Private costs** are borne solely by the individuals who incur them. They are *internal* in the sense that the firm or household must explicitly take account of them.

What about a situation in which a business dumps the waste products from its production process into a nearby river or an individual litters a public park or beach? Obviously, a cost is involved in these actions. When the firm pollutes the water, people downstream suffer the consequences. They may not want to swim in or drink the polluted water. They may also be unable to catch as many fish as before because of the pollution. In the case of littering, the people who come along after the litterer has cluttered the park or the beach are the ones who bear the costs. The cost of these actions is borne by people other than those who commit the actions. The creator of the cost is not the sole bearer. The costs are not internalized by the individual or firm; they are external. When we add *external* costs to *internal*, or private, costs, we get **social costs.** Pollution problems—indeed, all problems pertaining to the environment—may be

Private costs
Costs borne solely by the individuals who incur them. Also called *internal costs*.

Social costs
The full costs borne by society whenever a resource use occurs. Social costs can be measured by adding external costs to private, or internal, costs.

viewed as situations in which social costs exceed private costs. Because some economic participants pay only the smaller private costs of their actions, not the full social costs, their actions ultimately contribute to higher external costs on the rest of society. In such situations in which social and private costs diverge, we therefore see "too much" steel production, automobile driving, and beach littering, to pick only a few of the many possible examples.

The Costs of Polluted Air

Why is the air in cities so polluted from automobile exhaust fumes? When automobile drivers step into their cars, they bear only the private costs of driving. That is, they must pay for the gas, maintenance, depreciation, and insurance on their automobiles. But they cause an additional cost, that of air pollution, which they are not forced to take into account when they make the decision to drive. Air pollution is a cost because it causes harm to individuals—burning eyes, respiratory ailments, and dirtier clothes, cars, and buildings—and adds to accumulations of various gases that may contribute to global warming. The air pollution created by automobile exhaust is a cost that individual operators of automobiles do not yet bear directly. The social cost of driving includes all the private costs plus at least the cost of air pollution, which society bears. Decisions made only on the basis of private costs lead to too much automobile driving. Clean air is a scarce resource used by automobile drivers free of charge. They will use more of it than they would if they had to pay the full social costs.

Externalities

Externality
A situation in which a private cost (or benefit) diverges from a social cost (or benefit); a situation in which the costs (or benefits) of an action are not fully borne (or gained) by the decision makers engaging in a scarce-resource-using activity.

When a private cost differs from a social cost, we say that there is an **externality** because individual decision makers are not paying (internalizing) all the costs. (We briefly covered this topic in Chapter 5.) Some of these costs remain external to the decision-making process. Remember that the full cost of using a scarce resource is borne one way or another by all who live in the society. That is, members of society must pay the full opportunity cost of any activity that uses scarce resources. The individual decision maker is the firm or the customer, and external costs and benefits will not enter into that individual's or firm's decision-making processes.

We might want to view the problem as it is presented in Figure 32-1. Here we have the market demand curve, D, for product X and the supply curve, S_1, for product X. The supply curve, S_1, includes only internal, or private, costs, which for simplicity are assumed to be identical for each producer. The intersection of the demand and supply curves as drawn will be at price P_1 and quantity Q_1 (at E_1). We now assume that the production of good X involves externalities that the private firms did not take into account. Those externalities could be air pollution, water pollution, scenery destruction, or anything of that nature.

We know that the social costs of producing product X exceed the private costs. We show this by drawing curve S_2. It is above the original supply curve S_1 because it includes the full social costs of producing the product. If firms could be made to bear these costs, their willingness to supply the good would be reduced, so the price would be P_2 and the quantity Q_2 (at E_2). The inclusion of external costs in the decision-making process would lead to a higher-priced product and a decline in quantity produced. Thus, we see that when social costs are not being fully borne by the creators of those costs, the quantity produced is "excessive" because the price to consumers is too low.

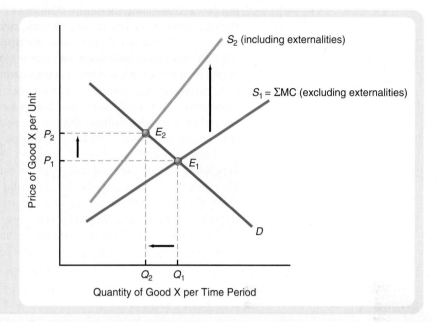

FIGURE 32-1

Reckoning with Full Social Costs

The supply curve, S_1, is equal to the horizontal summation (represented by the capital Greek letter Σ) of the individual marginal cost curves above the respective minimum average variable costs of all the firms producing good X. These individual marginal cost curves include only internal, or private, costs, assumed to be identical for all producers. If the external costs were included and added to the private costs, we would have social costs. The supply curve would shift upward to S_2. In the uncorrected situation, the equilibrium price is P_1, and the equilibrium quantity is Q_1. In the corrected situation, the equilibrium price would rise to P_2, and the equilibrium quantity would fall to Q_2.

Correcting for Externalities

We can see here a method for reducing pollution and environmental degradation. Somehow the signals in the economy must be changed so that decision makers will take into account *all* the costs of their actions. In the case of automobile pollution, we might want to devise some method of taxing motorists according to the amount of pollution they cause. In the case of a firm, we might want to devise a system of taxing businesses according to the amount of pollution for which they are responsible. They might then have an incentive to install pollution abatement equipment.

The Polluters' Choice

Facing an additional private cost for polluting, firms will be induced to (1) install pollution abatement equipment or otherwise change production techniques so as to reduce the amount of pollution, (2) reduce pollution-causing activity, or (3) simply pay the price and reduce its pollution-generating activities. The relative costs and benefits of each option for each polluter will determine which one or combination will be chosen. Allowing the choice is the efficient way to decide who pollutes and who doesn't. In principle, just as with the use of all other scarce resources, each polluter faces the full social cost of its actions and makes a production decision accordingly.

Is a Uniform Tax Appropriate?

It may not be appropriate to levy a *uniform* tax according to physical quantities of pollution. After all, we're talking about external costs. Such costs are not necessarily the same everywhere in the United States for the same action.

Essentially, we must establish the amount of the *economic damages* rather than the amount of the physical pollution. A polluting electrical plant in New York City will cause much more damage than the same plant in Montana. There are already innumerable demands on the air in New York City, so the pollution from smokestacks will not be cleansed away naturally. Millions of people will breathe the polluted air and thereby incur the costs of sore throats, sickness, emphysema, and even early death. Buildings will become dirtier faster because of the pollution, as will cars and clothes. A given quantity of pollution will cause more harm in concentrated urban environments than it will in less dense rural environments. If we were to establish some form of taxation to align private costs with social costs and to force people to internalize externalities, we would somehow have to come up with a measure of *economic* costs instead of *physical* quantities. But the tax, in any event, would fall on the private sector and modify individuals' and firms' behavior. Therefore, because the economic cost for the same physical quantity of pollution would be different in different locations depending on population density, natural formations of mountains and rivers, and the like, so-called optimal taxes on pollution would vary from location to location. (Nonetheless, a uniform tax might make sense when administrative costs, particularly the cost of ascertaining the actual economic costs, are relatively high.)

Could raising uniform taxes on cigarettes be more effective than outright bans on public smoking in protecting nonsmokers from harmful effects of cigarette smoke?

POLICY EXAMPLE
Passive Smoking Effects of Smoking Bans versus Cigarette Taxes

By studying data on concentrations of *cotinine*, a by-product of nicotine that shows up in people's blood samples, economists have found that bans on public cigarette smoking have mixed effects. On the one hand, such bans certainly cut down on the amount of cigarette smoke inhaled by nonsmokers in public places. On the other hand, the bans encourage more cigarette smoking at home, thereby exposing nonsmokers who live with smokers, such as children and other relatives, to even more smoke. Economists have found that nonsmoking family members' exposure to cigarette smoke increases significantly, particularly in lower-income households, in cities where smoking bans are in effect.

In contrast, economists have found evidence that higher cigarette taxes reduce exposure to smoke among *all* nonsmokers,

including family members of smokers. Every 10 percent increase in the excise tax on cigarettes is associated with a 3 to 4 percent reduction in nonsmokers' exposure to cigarette smoke. One possible explanation is that when smokers cut back on cigarette consumption in response to higher excise taxes, they smoke the smaller number of cigarettes alone, rather than in the presence of nonsmokers. Thus, imposing higher uniform taxes on cigarettes may be more effective at shielding nonsmokers from cigarette smoke than bans on public smoking.

FOR CRITICAL ANALYSIS
Where does the post-tax cigarette supply curve lie in relation to the pre-tax cigarette supply curve?

QUICK QUIZ
See page 837 for the answers. Review concepts from this section in MyEconLab.

_____ costs are costs that are borne directly by consumers and producers when they engage in any resource-using activity.

Social costs are _____ costs plus any other costs that are external to the decision maker. For example, the social

costs of driving include all the _____ costs plus, at a minimum, any pollution caused.

When _____ costs differ from social costs, _____ exist because individual decision makers are not internalizing all the costs that society is bearing.

Pollution

The term *pollution* is used quite loosely and can refer to a variety of by-products of any activity. Industrial pollution involves mainly air and water but can also include noise and even aesthetic pollution, as when a landscape is altered in a negative way. For the most part, we will be analyzing the most common forms—air and water pollution.

Assessing the Appropriate Amount of Pollution

When asked how much pollution there should be in the economy, many people will respond, "None." But if we ask those same people how much starvation or deprivation of consumer products should exist in the economy, many will again say, "None." Growing and distributing food or producing consumer products creates pollution, however. There is no correct answer to how much pollution should be in an economy because when we ask how much pollution there *should* be, we are entering the realm of normative economics. We are asking people to express values. There is no way to disprove somebody's value system scientifically.

One way we can approach a discussion of the "correct" amount of pollution is to set up the same type of marginal analysis we used in our discussion of a firm's employment and output decisions. That is to say, we can consider pursuing measures to reduce pollution only up to the point at which the marginal benefit from pollution reduction equals the marginal cost of pollution reduction.

Go to **www.econtoday.com/chapter32** to see a review by the ACCF Center for Policy Research of possible economic effects of efforts to reduce pollution.

THE MARGINAL BENEFIT OF A LESS POLLUTED ENVIRONMENT Look at Figure 32-2. On the horizontal axis, we show the degree of air cleanliness. A vertical line is drawn at 100 percent cleanliness—the air cannot become any cleaner. Consider the benefits of obtaining a greater degree of air cleanliness. The benefits of obtaining cleaner air are represented by the marginal benefit curve, which slopes downward.

FIGURE 32-2

The Optimal Quantity of Air Pollution

As we attempt to get a greater degree of air cleanliness, the marginal cost rises until trying to increase air cleanliness even slightly leads to a very high marginal cost, as can be seen at the upper right of the graph. Conversely, the marginal benefit curve slopes downward: The more pure air we have, the less we value an additional unit of pure air. Marginal cost and marginal benefit intersect at point E. The optimal degree of air cleanliness is something less than 100 percent at Q_0. The price that we should pay for the last unit of air cleanup is no greater than P_0, for that is where marginal cost equals marginal benefit.

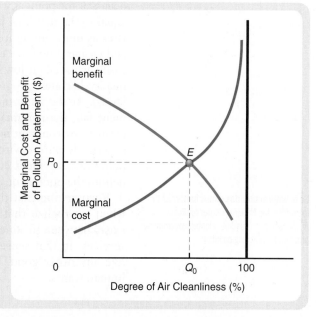

When the air is very dirty, the marginal benefit from air that is a little cleaner appears to be relatively high, as shown on the vertical axis. As the air becomes cleaner, however, the marginal benefit of a little bit more air cleanliness falls.

THE MARGINAL COST OF POLLUTION ABATEMENT Consider the marginal cost of pollution abatement—that is, the marginal cost of obtaining cleaner air. In the 1960s, automobiles had no pollution abatement devices. Eliminating only 20 percent of the pollutants emitted by internal-combustion engines entailed a relatively small cost per unit of pollution removed. The per-unit cost of eliminating the next 20 percent increased, though. Finally, as we now get to the upper limits of removal of pollutants from the emissions of internal-combustion engines, we find that the elimination of one more percentage point of the amount of pollutants becomes astronomically expensive. In the short run, moving from 97 percent cleanliness to 98 percent cleanliness involves a marginal cost that is many times greater than the marginal cost of going from 10 percent cleanliness to 11 percent cleanliness.

It is realistic, therefore, to draw the marginal cost of pollution abatement as an upward-sloping curve, as shown in Figure 32-2 on the preceding page. (The marginal cost curve slopes up because of the law of diminishing marginal product.)

The Optimal Quantity of Pollution

Optimal quantity of pollution
The level of pollution for which the marginal benefit of one additional unit of pollution abatement just equals the marginal cost of that additional unit of pollution abatement.

The **optimal quantity of pollution** is defined as the level of pollution at which the marginal benefit equals the marginal cost of pollution abatement. This occurs at the intersection of the marginal benefit curve and the marginal cost curve in Figure 32-2, at point E. This solution is analytically exactly the same as for every other economic activity. If we increased pollution control by one unit beyond Q_0, the marginal cost of that small increase in the degree of air cleanliness would be greater than the marginal benefit to society.

As is usually the case in economic analysis, the optimal quantity occurs when marginal cost equals marginal benefit. That is, the optimal quantity of pollution occurs at the point at which the marginal cost of reducing (or abating) pollution is just equal to the marginal benefit of doing so. The marginal cost of pollution abatement rises as more and more abatement is achieved (as the environment becomes cleaner and cleaner, the *extra* cost of cleansing rises). Early units of pollution abatement are easily achieved (at low cost), but attaining higher and higher levels of environmental quality becomes progressively more difficult (as the extra cost rises to prohibitive levels). At the same time, the marginal benefits of an increasingly cleaner environment fall; the marginal benefit of pollution abatement declines as our notion of a cleaner environment moves from sustenance of human life to recreation to beauty to a perfectly pure environment. The point at which the increasing marginal cost of pollution abatement equals the decreasing marginal benefit of pollution abatement defines the optimal quantity of pollution.

Recognizing that the optimal quantity of pollution is not zero becomes easier when we realize that it takes scarce resources to reduce pollution. A trade-off exists between producing a cleaner environment and producing other goods and services. In that sense, environmental cleanliness is a good that can be analyzed like any other good, and a cleaner environment must take its place with other human wants.

Go to www.econtoday.com/chapter32 to learn from the National Center for Policy Analysis about a market-oriented government program for reducing pollution.

QUICK QUIZ   *See page 837 for the answers. Review concepts from this section in MyEconLab.*

The marginal cost of cleaning up the environment _____ as we get closer to 100 percent cleanliness. Indeed, it _____ at an _____ rate.

The marginal benefit of environmental cleanliness _____ as we have more of it.

The **optimal quantity of pollution** is the quantity at which the _____ _____ of cleanup equals the _____ _____ of cleanup.

Pollution abatement is a trade-off. We trade off _____ and _____ for cleaner air and water, and vice versa.

Common Property

In most cases, you do not have **private property rights**, or exclusive ownership rights, to the air surrounding you, nor does anyone else. Air is a **common property**, or a nonexclusive resource. Therein lies the crux of the problem. When no one owns a particular resource, no one has any incentive (conscience aside) to consider externality spillovers associated with that resource. If one person decides not to add to externality spillovers and avoids polluting the air, normally there will not be any significant effect on the total level of pollution. If one person decides not to pollute the ocean, there will still be approximately the same amount of ocean pollution—provided, of course, that the individual was previously responsible for only a small part of the total amount of ocean pollution.

Basically, pollution and other activities that create spillovers occur when we have poorly defined private property rights, as in air and common bodies of water. We do not, for example, have a visual pollution problem in people's attics. That is their own property, which they choose to keep as clean as they want, depending on their preferences for cleanliness weighed against the costs of keeping the attic neat and tidy.

When private property rights exist, individuals have legal recourse for any damages sustained through the use of their property. When private property rights are well defined, the use of property—that is, the use of resources—will generally involve contracting between the owners of those resources. If you own land, you might contract with another person who wants to use your land for raising cattle. The contract would most likely take the form of a written lease agreement.

Voluntary Agreements and Transaction Costs

Is it possible for externalities to be internalized via voluntary agreement? Take a simple example. You live in a house with a nice view of a lake. The family living below you plants a tree. The tree grows so tall that it eventually starts to cut off your view. In most cities, no one has property rights to views; therefore, you usually cannot go to court to obtain relief. You do have the option of contracting with your neighbors, however.

VOLUNTARY AGREEMENTS: CONTRACTING You have the option of paying your neighbors (contracting) to cut back the tree. You could start out by offering a small amount and keep going up until your neighbors agree or until you reach your limit. Your limit will equal the value you place on having an unobstructed view of the lake. Your neighbors will be willing if the payment is at least equal to the reduction in

Private property rights
Exclusive rights of ownership that allow the use, transfer, and exchange of property.

Common property
Property that is owned by everyone and therefore by no one. Air and water are examples of common property resources.

You Are There

For practice thinking about why private versus common property matters when considering how to limit pollution spillovers, contemplate **A U.S. Senator Finds the Largest U.S. Carbon Footprint**, on page 831.

The issues are not straightforward. Today, the earth has only 0.02 percent of all of the species that have ever lived, and nearly all the 99.98 percent of extinct species became extinct before humans appeared. Every year, 1,000 to 3,000 new species are discovered and classified. Estimates of how many species are actually dying out range from a high of 50,000 a year (based on the assumption that undiscovered insect species are dying off before being discovered) to a low of one every four years.

Why does determining whether one species differs from another become a dollars-and-cents issue when it comes to enforcing laws protecting endangered species?

POLICY EXAMPLE
Determining Whether Species Are Distinct Can Have a Dollar Value

Every once in a while, scientists cannot agree on whether one species is different from another. For instance, in the mid-2000s, biologists studying jungle life in Southeast Asia announced that they had found a new species of "rock rat." When some paleontologists who study long-extinct creatures such as dinosaurs took a look at the animal, which has a face like a rat and a body like a skinny squirrel, they realized that it was already known to scientists. Until the biologists came across living specimens in Southeast Asia, however, paleontologists had recorded the animal as having been extinct for more than 11 million years. Now the biologists are attempting to determine if this rare, multi-million-years-old species qualifies for taxpayer-funded protection by Southeast Asian governments.

In Colorado, a slightly different issue has arisen regarding the status of a rodent called the Preble's meadow jumping mouse. Studies have shown that this mouse is 99.5 percent genetically identical to other mice. Thus, some biologists have concluded that it is basically a run-of-the-mill field mouse, untold millions of which populate planet Earth. Nevertheless, the U.S. government has classified the Colorado mouse as an endangered species. The U.S. Fish and Wildlife Service estimates that the opportunity cost to those forced to quarantine lands they own from development in an effort to protect the mouse from human encroachment is probably at least $180 million.

FOR CRITICAL ANALYSIS

Why do you suppose that there is a growing demand for the skills of biologists who can help prove or disprove whether a group of distinguishable animals is a subset of a broad species or constitutes its own narrow, endangered species?

QUICK QUIZ   See page 837 for the answers. Review concepts from this section in MyEconLab.

The more than three dozen countries that participated in the 1997 Kyoto Protocol of the Framework Convention on Climate Change agreed to reduce their emissions of greenhouse gases by the year _____ to at least _____ percent below the levels that prevailed in the year _____.

Under a program called the Emissions Trading Scheme, the governments of European Union member nations establish overall targets for greenhouse gas emissions and issue _____, or permits, authorizing companies to emit certain amounts. In theory, an increase in the market clearing price of _____ should induce firms to develop methods of _____ their emissions of greenhouse gases.

In contrast to domesticated animals that are _____ property, most endangered species are _____ property. Consequently, there is a problem in perpetuating these species that the federal government has sought to address through legislation governing use of lands where such species reside.

You Are There A U.S. Senator Finds the Largest U.S. Carbon Footprint

Senator Barbara Boxer of California, head of the Senate Environment and Public Works Committee, has been searching for ways to cut electricity consumption in an effort to reduce sources of atmospheric carbon pollutants, such as coal burning. After considerable study, her staff has discovered the consumer of the most energy in the United States.

The single largest U.S. energy consumer, it turns out, is neither a large corporation such as General Motors nor a huge concentration of households in a city such as Los Angeles. The entity consuming the most energy in the United States, and hence contributing the largest carbon footprint, is the U.S. government. All told, the federal government consumes an average of 32 percent more energy per square foot of space than the total building stock of the private sector. Estimated explicit costs to taxpayers generated by inefficiencies in government energy consumption are at least $1 billion per year. According to the staff of

Boxer's committee, the spillover effect of the government's energy waste to the nation's pollution levels is more difficult to estimate. Nevertheless, staff members agree that it probably accounts for a substantial fraction of the spillovers. Boxer suggests to her committee that it would be a good idea for heads of government departments to ask employees to use more efficient light bulbs and to turn off their computers at night.

CRITICAL ANALYSIS QUESTIONS

1. Are pollution-generating activities of governments included among private costs in markets in which governments operate?

2. How might efforts to reduce the U.S. government's contribution to the nation's pollution levels encounter a common property problem?

Issues and Applications

The Economics of Pollution in China—Present and Future

CONCEPTS APPLIED

➤ Common Property
➤ Social Costs
➤ Private Property Rights

According to estimates, arsenic taints groundwater that serves as the source of drinking water for more than 2 million people in China. There is excess fluorine in the water supplies of 63 million Chinese residents. All told, about 300 million people in China drink contaminated water.

China's air is also experiencing pollution problems. Air quality is unhealthful in more than 350 of the nation's cities. Winds carry pollution to Hong Kong, where levels of particulate matter—tiny flakes of soot, dust, and ash considered to be the most harmful form of air pollution—average more than *250 percent* higher than recommended safe levels. Some of China's air pollution makes its way to Korea and Japan, and even as far as the United States.

What accounts for the high pollution levels experienced by residents of China? Does economic theory offer any hope that pollution spillovers will eventually level off or even decline in this rapidly growing nation?

The Obvious and Less Visible Contributors to China's Pollution

The most apparent factor contributing to China's growing pollution problem is the nation's striking rate of economic growth, which has exceeded 8 percent annually for most of the past 30 years. Accompanying this growth have been spillover effects onto the environment. Since 2000, annual emissions of sulfur dioxide into the air have risen by about 30 percent. Total wastewater discharges from industries now exceed 55 billion tons, up almost one-third since 2000. The nation currently experiences more than 100 major water-pollution incidents every year as firms, in their haste to rush chemical-laden products to customers, inadvertently spill portions of them into rivers and lakes.

Another, less obvious factor has also contributed to China's pollution problems. This is a common property problem. China's government owns, either in part or in full, many of the nation's businesses. The government also owns large shares of its land and other resources. Because so many businesses and resources are owned by everyone, no readily identifiable parties must shoulder responsibility for internalizing the social costs of economic activities that create pollution. Thus, China's pollution problem continues to grow, seemingly unabated.

Hope for Pollution Containment and Abatement in China

Is China's environmental future likely to be literally darkened by escalating pollution? There is good economic reason to suspect that the answer ultimately must be no. The reason is that in recent years, China's government has adopted new guarantees of property rights for its residents. Although the government remains Communist from a political point of view, private ownership of resources is becoming much more commonplace. The government is also actively trying to disengage itself from its ownership of many of the nation's industries.

As more individuals become property owners, it will be easier to assign responsibility for activities that create spillover costs for others. Hence, the potential for voluntary agreements to help reduce pollution will broaden over time. As more and more of China's pollution-generating activities are covered by agreements that internalize pollution externalities, the scope of the nation's pollution problem should level off. Eventually, it may even begin to shrink as the private owners of resources seek to bring the marginal benefit of pollution abatement into alignment with its marginal cost.

Test your understanding of this chapter by going online to **MyEconLab**.
In the Study Plan for this chapter, select Section N: News.

For Critical Analysis

1. In your own words, explain in a sentence how the Chinese government's ownership of so many of the nation's resources contributes to the nation's pollution problem.

2. Recently, an increasing number of people who had done business in the most heavily polluted cities of China have decided to move their operations to Korea, Japan, and Australia in order to avoid the health risks caused by

China's air pollution. How might this trend influence the interplay between marginal costs and benefits of pollution abatement and alter the optimal quantity of pollution in China?

Web Resources

1. For a detailed discussion of the scope of China's pollution difficulties, go to www.econtoday.com/chapter32.
2. To read a World Bank assessment of the social costs of pollution in China, go to www.econtoday.com/chapter32.

Research Project

Recently, some government leaders in China have expressed the view that the nation's pollution problem is not the government's fault. In their view, the fault lies with consumers in other nations who import Chinese products manufactured using pollution-generating processes. Thus, they conclude,

the costs of abating at least part of the air and water pollution in China should be borne by other countries' governments—that is, foreign taxpayers who are also the consumers of Chinese products. Based on this argument, these Chinese government officials suggest that Chinese firms (many of which are at least partly government owned) should not be expected to bear the costs of pollution abatement. Evaluate this argument from an economic standpoint. If China's firms were to incur the costs of cutting back on pollution-generating activities, would their owners (including the Chinese government) really bear *all* of the abatement costs? In light of your answer, are the government officials necessarily seeking to insulate private residents of China from bearing pollution abatement costs, or are they mainly promoting the government's own interest? Explain your reasoning. (Hint: Recall the effects that *any* costly pollution abatement efforts in China will have on market supply curves and prices, and consider will who pay these prices both inside and outside China.)

---

myeconlab   Here is what you should know after reading this chapter. **MyEconLab** will help you identify what you know, and where to go when you need to practice.

WHAT YOU SHOULD KNOW		WHERE TO GO TO PRACTICE
Private Costs versus Social Costs Private, or internal, costs are borne solely by individuals who use resources. Social costs are the full costs that society bears whenever resources are used. Problems related to the environment arise when individuals take into account only private costs instead of the broader social costs arising from their use of resources.	private costs, 819 social costs, 819	• **MyEconLab** Study Plan 32.1 • Audio introduction to Chapter 32 • ABC News Video: Coca-Cola in India
Market Externalities and Ways to Correct Them A market externality is a situation in which a private cost (or benefit) differs from the social cost (or benefit) associated with a market transaction between two parties or from the use of a scarce resource. Correcting an externality arising from differences between private and social costs, such as pollution, requires forcing individuals to take all the social costs of their actions into account. This might be accomplished by taxing those who create externalities, such as polluters.	externality, 820 **KEY FIGURE** Figure 32-1, 821	• **MyEconLab** Study Plan 32.2 • Video: Correcting for Externalities • Animated Figure 32-1

(continued)

 *(continued)*

WHAT YOU SHOULD KNOW

WHERE TO GO TO PRACTICE

Determining the Optimal Amount of Pollution The marginal benefit of pollution abatement, or the additional benefit to society from reducing pollution, declines as the quality of the environment improves. At the same time, however, the marginal cost of pollution abatement, or the additional cost to society from reducing pollution, increases as more and more resources are devoted to bringing about an improved environment. The optimal quantity of pollution is the amount of pollution for which the marginal benefit of pollution abatement just equals the marginal cost of pollution abatement. Beyond this level of pollution, the additional cost of cleaning the environment exceeds the additional benefit.

optimal quantity of pollution, 824

KEY FIGURE
Figure 32-2, 823

- **MyEconLab** Study Plan 32.3
- Animated Figure 32-2

Private and Common Property Rights and the Pollution Problem Private property rights are exclusive individual rights of ownership that permit the use and exchange of a resource. Common property is owned by everyone and therefore by no single individual. A pollution problem often arises because air and many water resources are common property, and private property rights relating to them are not well defined. Therefore, no one has an individual incentive to take the long-run pernicious effects of excessive pollution into account. This is a common rationale for using taxes, subsidies, or regulations to address the pollution problem.

private property rights, 825
common property, 825
transaction costs, 826

- **MyEconLab** Study Plan 32.4

Restraining Pollution-Causing Activities Through Caps and Allowances Under the terms of the Kyoto Protocol, a number of countries have agreed to reduce their emissions of greenhouse gases, such as carbon dioxide and sulfur dioxide, which some scientists suggest could harm the planet's climate. Toward this end, the European Union (EU) has established a program called the Emissions Trading Scheme. Each EU nation's government establishes an overall target level of greenhouse gas emissions and distributes allowances, or permits, granting companies the right to emit a certain amount of gases. If a firm's greenhouse gas emissions exceed its allowances, it must purchase a sufficient number of allowances from firms emitting less than the allowances they possess. In theory, the market clearing price of allowances will increase, giving EU companies incentives to develop methods of restraining their emissions of greenhouse gases.

- **MyEconLab** Study Plan 32.5

Endangered Species and the Assignment of Property Rights Many members of such species as dogs, pigs, and horses are the private property of human beings. Thus, people have economic

- **MyEconLab** Study Plan 32.6

(continued)

WHAT YOU SHOULD KNOW

WHERE TO GO TO PRACTICE

incentives—satisfaction derived from pet ownership, the desire for pork as a food product, a preference for animal-borne transport—to protect members of these species. In contrast, most members of species such as spotted owls, condors, or tigers are common property, so no specific individuals have incentives to keep these species in good health. A possible way to address the endangered species problem is government involvement via regulations.

PROBLEMS

All problems are assignable in **myeconlab**. *Answers to the odd-numbered problems appear at the back of the book.*

32-1. The market price of insecticide is initially $10 per unit. To address a negative externality in this market, the government decides to charge producers of insecticide for the privilege of polluting during the production process. A fee that fully takes into account the social costs of pollution is determined, and once it is put into effect, the market supply curve for insecticide shifts upward by $4 per unit. The market price of insecticide also increases, to $12 per unit. What fee is the government charging insecticide manufacturers?

32-2. One possible method for reducing emissions of greenhouse gases such as carbon dioxide is to inject the gases into deep saltwater-laden rock formations where they would be trapped for thousands of years. Suppose that the federal government provides a fixed per-unit subsidy to firms that utilize this technology in West Virginia and other locales where such rock formations are known to exist.

    a. Use an appropriate diagram to examine the effects of the government subsidy on the production and sale of equipment that injects greenhouse gases into underground rock formations. What happens to the market clearing price of such pollution abatement equipment?

    b. Who pays to achieve the results discussed in part (a)?

32-3. Examine the following marginal costs and marginal benefits associated with water cleanliness in a given locale:

Quantity of Clean Water (%)	Marginal Cost ($)	Marginal Benefit ($)
0	3,000	200,000
20	15,000	120,000
40	50,000	90,000
60	85,000	85,000
80	100,000	40,000
100	Infinite	0

    a. What is the optimal degree of water cleanliness?

    b. What is the optimal degree of water pollution?

    c. Suppose that a company creates a food additive that offsets most of the harmful effects of drinking polluted water. As a result, the marginal benefit of water cleanliness declines by $40,000 at each degree of water cleanliness at or less than 80 percent. What is the optimal degree of water cleanliness after this change?

32-4. Consider the diagram below, which displays the marginal cost and marginal benefit of water pollution abatement in a particular city, and answer the following questions.

   a. What is the optimal percentage degree of water cleanliness?

   b. When the optimal percentage degree of water cleanliness has been attained, what price will be paid for the last unit of water cleanup?

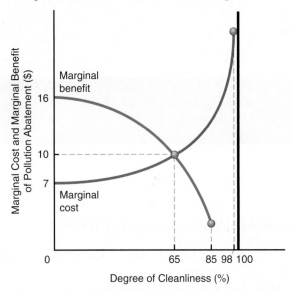

32-5. Consider the diagram in Problem 32-4, and answer the following questions.

   a. Suppose that a new technology for reducing water pollution generates a reduction in the marginal cost of pollution abatement at every degree of water cleanliness. After this event occurs, will the optimal percentage degree of water cleanliness rise or fall? Will the cost incurred for the last unit of water cleanup increase or decrease? Provide a diagram to assist in your explanation.

   b. Suppose that the event discussed in part (a) occurs and that, in addition, medical studies determine that the marginal benefit from water pollution abatement is higher at every degree of water cleanliness. Following *both* events, will the optimal percentage degree of water cleanliness increase or decrease? In comparison with the *initial* optimum, can you determine whether the price paid for the last unit of water cleanup will increase or decrease? Use a new diagram to assist in explaining your answers.

32-6. Under an agreement with U.S. regulators, American Electric Power Company of Columbus, Ohio, has agreed to offset part of its 145 million metric tons of carbon dioxide emissions by paying another company to lay plastic tarps. These tarps cover farm lagoons holding rotting livestock wastes that emit methane gas 21 times more damaging to the atmosphere than carbon dioxide. The annual methane produced by a typical 1,330-pound cow translates into about 5 metric tons of carbon dioxide emissions per year.

   a. How many cows' worth of manure would have to be covered to offset the carbon dioxide emissions of this single electric utility?

   b. Given that there are about 9 million cows in the United States in a typical year, what percentage of its carbon dioxide emissions could this firm offset if it paid for all cow manure in the entire nation to be covered with tarps?

32-7. The following table displays hypothetical annual total costs and total benefits of conserving wild tigers at several possible worldwide tiger population levels.

Population of Wild Tigers	Total Cost ($ millions)	Total Benefit ($ millions)
0	0	40
2,000	25	90
4,000	35	130
6,000	50	160
8,000	75	185
10,000	110	205
12,000	165	215

   a. Calculate the marginal costs and benefits.

   b. Given the data, what is the socially optimal world population of wild tigers?

   c. Suppose that tiger farming is legalized and that this has the effect of reducing the marginal cost of tiger conservation by $15 million for each 2,000-tiger population increment in the table. What is the new socially optimal population of wild tigers?

32-8. The following table gives hypothetical annual total costs and total benefits of maintaining alternative populations of Asian elephants.

Population of Asian Elephants	Total Cost ($ millions)	Total Benefit ($ millions)
0	0	0
7,500	20	100
15,000	45	185
22,500	90	260
30,000	155	325
37,500	235	375
45,000	330	410

a. Calculate the marginal costs and benefits, and draw marginal benefit and cost schedules.

b. Given the data, what is the socially optimal world population of Asian elephants?

c. Suppose that two events occur simultaneously. Technological development allows machines to do more efficiently much of the work that elephants once did, which reduces by $10 million the marginal benefit of maintaining the elephant population for each 7,500 increment in the elephant population. In addition, new techniques for breeding, feeding, and protecting elephants reduce the marginal cost by $40 million for each 7,500 increment in the elephant population. What is the new socially optimal population of Asian elephants?

ECONOMICS ON THE NET

Economic Analysis at the Environmental Protection Agency In this chapter, you learned how to use economic analysis to think about environmental problems. Does the U.S. government use economic analysis? This application helps you learn the extent to which the government uses economics in its environmental policymaking.

Title: National Center for Environmental Economics (NCEE)

Navigation: Go to **www.econtoday.com/chapter32** to visit the NCEE's home page. Click on *Publications*. Under *related publications*, select *Plain English*. Click on "Environmental Protection: Is It Bad for the Economy? A Non-Technical Summary of the Literature," and view the table of contents. Read "What Do We Spend on Environmental Protection?"

Application Read this section of the article; then answer the following questions.

1. According to the article, what are the key objectives of the EPA? What role does cost-benefit analysis appear to play in the EPA's efforts? Does the EPA appear to take other issues into account in its policymaking?

2. Back up to Table of Contents, and click on "Regardless of the Cost of Environmental Protection, Is It Still Money Well Spent?" In what ways does this discussion help clarify your answers in Question 1?

For Group Study and Analysis Have a class discussion of the following question: Should the EPA apply economic analysis in all aspects of its policymaking? If not, why not? If so, in what manner should economic analysis be applied?

ANSWERS TO QUICK QUIZZES

p. 822: (i) Private; (ii) private . . . private; (iii) private . . . externalities

p. 825: (i) rises . . . rises . . . increasing; (ii) falls; (iii) marginal cost . . . marginal benefit; (iv) goods . . . services

p. 827: (i) no one . . . everyone; (ii) private property; (iii) social . . . contract

p. 830: (i) 2020 . . . 20 . . . 1990; (ii) allowances . . . allowances . . . reducing; (iii) private . . . common

33

Comparative Advantage and the Open Economy

I n the midst of the Great Recession of the late 2000s, the governments of the Group of Twenty (G20) nations—an informal association that includes the most industrialized countries—promised to keep their economies open to international trade. Nevertheless, within a few months nearly every G20 nation had enacted measures that limited or even prohibited inflows of foreign goods across their borders. Although their exact nature varied from country to country, the common objective of such measures was to protect domestic firms from foreign competition. Who gains and who loses from international trade? Why does international trade occur at all? This chapter addresses these questions.

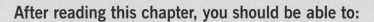

 **LEARNING OBJECTIVES**

After reading this chapter, you should be able to:

➤ Discuss the worldwide importance of international trade

➤ Explain why nations can gain from specializing in production and engaging in international trade

➤ Understand common arguments against free trade

➤ Describe ways that nations restrict foreign trade

➤ Identify key international agreements and organizations that adjudicate trade disputes among nations

? **DID YOU KNOW THAT** the 2009 stimulus law requires U.S. construction projects receiving federal funding to use only U.S. materials? The consequences reverberated across the United States and its trading partners, such as Canada. For instance, the U.S. Navy had to rip Canadian pipe fittings out of the ground in California and replace them with U.S.-made pipes. The Canadian government retaliated by prohibiting U.S. companies from providing materials for Canadian municipal projects. Canada's retaliation and similar acts by other nations had measurable negative consequences in the United States. For instance, steel companies in Pennsylvania furloughed workers because of canceled foreign orders.

What effects do restrictions on imports have on quantities and prices of domestically produced goods and services? You will learn the answer to this question in this chapter. First, however, you must learn more about international trade.

The Worldwide Importance of International Trade

Look at panel (a) of Figure 33-1 on the following page. Since the end of World War II, world output of goods and services (world real gross domestic product, or world real GDP) has increased almost every year; it is now almost nine times what it was then. Look at the top line in panel (a). Even taking into account its recent dip, world trade has increased to more than 25 times its level in 1950.

The United States has figured prominently in this expansion of world trade. In panel (b) of Figure 33-1, you see imports and exports expressed as a percentage of total annual yearly income (GDP). Whereas imports added up to barely 4 percent of annual U.S. GDP in 1950, today they account for more than 12 percent. Despite the recent drop, international trade has become more important to the U.S. economy, and it may become even more so as other countries loosen their trade restrictions.

How has the recent worldwide decrease in international trade affected the shipping industry?

> ### You Are There
>
> To contemplate how the Great Recession of the late 2000s affected the flow of imports into the United States, read **In Retrospect, a "Good Idea" Has Become an Empty Space,** on page 857.

Go to **www.econtoday.com/chapter33** for the World Trade Organization's most recent data on world trade.

INTERNATIONAL EXAMPLE
Bad Timing for a Global Shipping Fleet Expansion

During the early and mid-2000s, when world trade was growing rapidly, shippers expanded both the number of freight-hauling ships afloat and the average sizes of the ships. Not only were hundreds of standard ships launched, but more than 150 massive new cargo ships were under construction.

Today, in the midst of a global slump in international trade, shippers have discovered that their fleets are too large. About 750 ships lie idle in Asian bays, and nearly 300 are docked in Europe. All told, more than 10 percent of the world's entire merchant marine fleet is swaying at anchor instead of carrying cargoes between ports. After all of the ships under construction, including the 150 new super-sized ships, are launched, the available global shipping capacity will exceed the market's current requirements by an estimated 70 percent.

FOR CRITICAL ANALYSIS
Why do you suppose the slump in international trade followed on the heels of the global economic downturn?

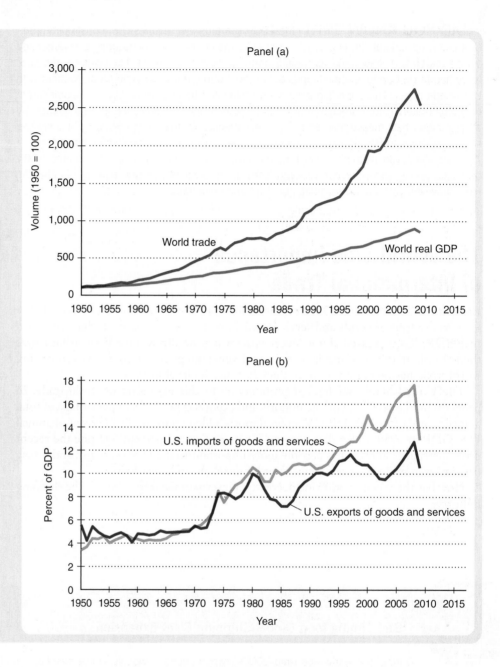

FIGURE 33-1

The Growth of World Trade

In panel (a), you can see the growth in world trade in relative terms because we use an index of 100 to represent real world trade in 1950. By the late 2000s, that index had increased to over 2,800 before dropping during the recent economic downturn. At the same time, the index of world real GDP (annual world real income) had gone up to only around 900 before turning downward. Thus, until recently, world trade has been on the rise: In the United States, both imports and exports, expressed as a percentage of annual national income (GDP) in panel (b), generally rose after 1950 until the Great Recession.

Sources: Steven Husted and Michael Melvin, *International Economics*, 3d ed. (New York: HarperCollins, 1995), p. 11, used with permission; World Trade Organization; Federal Reserve System; U.S. Department of Commerce.

Why We Trade: Comparative Advantage and Mutual Gains from Exchange

You have already been introduced to the concept of specialization and mutual gains from trade in Chapter 2. These concepts are worth repeating because they are essential to understanding why the world is better off because of more international trade. The best way to understand the gains from trade among nations is first to understand the output gains from specialization between individuals.

The Output Gains from Specialization

Suppose that a creative advertising specialist can come up with two pages of ad copy (written words) an hour or generate one computerized art rendering per hour. At the same time, a computer artist can write one page of ad copy per hour or complete one computerized art rendering per hour. Here the ad specialist can come up with more pages of ad copy per hour than the computer specialist and seemingly is just as good as the computer specialist at doing computerized art renderings. Is there any reason for the creative specialist and the computer specialist to "trade"? The answer is yes because such trading will lead to higher output.

Consider the scenario of no trading. Assume that during each eight-hour day, the ad specialist and the computer whiz devote half of their day to writing ad copy and half to computerized art rendering. The ad specialist would create eight pages of ad copy (4 hours × 2) and four computerized art renderings (4 × 1). During that same period, the computer specialist would create four pages of ad copy (4 hours × 1) and four computerized art renderings (4 × 1). Each day, the combined output for the ad specialist and the computer specialist would be 12 pages of ad copy and eight computerized art renderings.

Go to **www.econtoday.com/chapter33** for data on U.S. trade with all other nations of the world.

If the ad specialist specialized only in writing ad copy and the computer whiz specialized only in creating computerized art renderings, their combined output would rise to 16 pages of ad copy (8 × 2) and eight computerized art renderings (8 × 1). Overall, production would increase by four pages of ad copy per day with no decline in art renderings.

Note that this example implies that to create one additional computerized art rendering during a day, the ad specialist has to sacrifice creating two pages of ad copy. The computer specialist, however, only has to give up creating one page of ad copy to create one more computerized art rendering. Thus, the creative advertising employee has a comparative advantage in writing ad copy, and the computer specialist has a comparative advantage in doing computerized art renderings. **Comparative advantage** is simply the ability to produce something at a lower opportunity cost than other producers, as we pointed out in Chapter 2.

Comparative advantage
The ability to produce a good or service at a lower opportunity cost than other producers.

Why does Europe have a comparative advantage in constructing high-speed rail networks?

INTERNATIONAL EXAMPLE
A European Comparative Advantage in Bullet Trains

The U.S. federal government's 2009 stimulus package included $13 billion allocated to upgrading existing rail lines and building new lines capable of carrying high-speed "bullet" trains such as those utilized for a number of years in Europe. Not surprisingly, European companies are expecting to export their materials, equipment, and engineering knowledge for construction of high-speed train lines to the United States. These firms have already developed the technological and engineering know-how to construct rail lines capable of handling bullet trains. Thus, European producers can produce high-speed rail lines at a lower opportunity cost than potential U.S. competitors, meaning that they possess a comparative advantage in putting bullet trains in place.

FOR CRITICAL ANALYSIS
Why do you suppose that many observers have suggested that European bullet-train companies may also have a comparative advantage in operating high-speed trains on a day-to-day basis?

Specialization Among Nations

To demonstrate the concept of comparative advantage for nations, let's consider a simple two-country, two-good world. As a hypothetical example, let's suppose that the nations in this world are India and the United States.

PRODUCTION AND CONSUMPTION CAPABILITIES IN A TWO-COUNTRY, TWO-GOOD WORLD In Table 33-1, we show maximum feasible quantities of computer software and personal computers (PCs) that may be produced during an hour using all resources—labor, capital, land, and entrepreneurship—available in the United States and in India. As you can see from the table, U.S. residents can utilize all their resources to produce either 90 units of software per hour or 225 PCs per hour. Residents of India are able to utilize all their resources to produce either 100 units of software per hour or 50 PCs per hour.

COMPARATIVE ADVANTAGE Suppose that in each country, there are constant opportunity costs of producing software and PCs. Table 33-1 implies that allocating all available resources to production of 50 PCs would require residents of India to sacrifice the production of 100 units of software. Thus, the opportunity cost in India of producing 1 PC is equal to 2 units of software. At the same time, the opportunity cost of producing 1 unit of software in India is 0.5 PC.

In the United States, allocating all available resources to production of 225 PCs would require U.S. residents to give up producing 90 units of software. This means that the opportunity cost in the United States of producing 1 PC is equal to 0.4 unit of software. Alternatively, we can say that the opportunity cost to U.S. residents of producing 1 unit of software is 2.5 PCs.

The opportunity cost of producing a PC is lower in the United States than in India. At the same time, the opportunity cost of producing software is lower in India than in the United States. Thus, the United States has a comparative advantage in manufacturing PCs, and India has a comparative advantage in producing software.

PRODUCTION WITHOUT TRADE Table 33-2 tabulates two possible production choices in a situation in which U.S. and Indian residents choose not to engage in international trade. Let's suppose that in the United States, residents choose to produce and

---

TABLE 33-1

Maximum Feasible Hourly Production Rates of Either Commercial Software or Personal Computers Using All Available Resources

This table indicates maximum feasible rates of production of software and personal computers if all available resources are allocated to producing either one item or the other. If U.S. residents allocate all resources to producing a single good, they can produce either 90 units of software per hour or 225 PCs per hour. If residents of India allocate all resources to manufacturing one good, they can produce either 100 units of software per hour or 50 PCs per hour.

Product	United States	India
Units of software	90	100
Personal computers	225	50

TABLE 33-2

U.S. and Indian Production and Consumption Without Trade

This table indicates two possible hourly combinations of production and consumption of software and personal computers in the absence of trade in a "world" encompassing the United States and India. U.S. residents produce 30 units of software, and residents of India produce 25 units of software, so the total amount of software that can be consumed worldwide is 55 units. In addition, U.S. residents produce 150 PCs, and Indian residents produce 37.5 PCs, so worldwide production and consumption of PCs amount to 187.5 PCs per hour.

Product	United States	India	Actual World Output
Units of software (per hour)	30	25	55
Personal computers (per hour)	150	37.5	187.5

consume 30 units of software. To produce this amount of software requires producing 75 fewer PCs (30 units of software times 2.5 PCs per unit of software) than the maximum feasible PC production of 225 PCs, or 150 PCs. Thus, in the absence of trade, 30 units of software and 150 PCs are produced and consumed in the United States.

Table 33-2 indicates that during an hour's time in India, residents choose to produce and consume 37.5 PCs. Obtaining this amount of PCs entails producing 75 fewer units of software (37.5 PCs times 2 units of software per PC) than the maximum of 100 units, or 25 units of software. Thus, in the absence of trade, 37.5 PCs and 25 units of software are produced and consumed in India.

Finally, Table 33-2 displays production of software and PCs for this two-country world given the nations' production (and, implicitly, consumption) choices in the absence of trade. In an hour's time, U.S. software production is 30 units, and Indian software production is 25 units, so total world software production is 55 units. Thus, the total amount of software available for world consumption is also 55 units. Hourly U.S. PC production is 150 PCs, and Indian PC production is 37.5 PCs, so total world production is 187.5 PCs per hour. Consequently, the total number of PCs available for consumption in this two-country world is 187.5 PCs per hour.

SPECIALIZATION IN PRODUCTION More realistically, residents of the United States will choose to specialize in the activity for which they experience a lower opportunity cost. In other words, U.S. residents will specialize in the activity in which they have a comparative advantage, which is the production of personal computers, which they can offer in trade to residents of India. Likewise, residents of India will specialize in the area of manufacturing in which they have a comparative advantage, which is the production of commercial software, which they can offer in trade to residents of the United States.

By specializing, the two countries can gain from engaging in international trade. To see why, suppose that U.S. residents allocate all available resources to producing 225 PCs, the good in which they have a comparative advantage. In addition, residents of India utilize all resources they have on hand to produce 100 units of commercial software, the good in which they have a comparative advantage.

CONSUMPTION WITH SPECIALIZATION AND TRADE U.S. residents will be willing to buy a unit of Indian commercial software as long as they must provide in exchange no more than 2.5 PCs, which is the opportunity cost of producing 1 unit of software at home. At the same time, residents of India will be willing to buy a U.S. PC as long as they must provide in exchange no more than 2 units of software, which is their opportunity cost of producing a PC.

For instance, suppose that residents of both countries agree to trade at a rate of exchange of 1 PC for 1 unit of software and that U.S. residents agree with Indian residents to trade 75 PCs for 75 units of software. Table 33-3 displays the outcomes that result in both countries. By specializing in PC production and engaging in trade, U.S. residents can continue consuming 150 PCs. In addition, U.S. residents are also able to import and consume 75 units of software produced in India. At the same time, specialization and exchange allow residents of India to continue to consume 25 units of software. Producing 75 more units of software for export to the United States allows India to import 75 PCs.

GAINS FROM TRADE Table 33-4 summarizes the rates of consumption of U.S. and Indian residents with and without trade. Column 1 displays U.S. and Indian software and PC consumption rates with specialization and trade from Table 33-3, and it sums these to determine total consumption rates in this two-country world. Column 2 shows U.S., Indian, and worldwide consumption rates without international trade from Table 33-2. Column 3 gives the differences between the two columns.

Table 33-4 indicates that by producing 75 additional PCs for export to India in exchange for 75 units of software, U.S. residents are able to expand their software consumption from 30 units to 75 units. Thus, the U.S. gain from specialization and trade is 45 units of software. This is a net gain in software consumption for the two-country world as a whole, because neither country had to give up consuming any PCs for U.S. residents to realize this gain from trade.

TABLE 33-3

U.S. and Indian Production and Consumption with Specialization and Trade

In this table, U.S. residents produce 225 personal computers and no software, and Indian residents produce 100 units of software and no PCs. Residents of the two nations then agree to a rate of exchange of 1 PC for 1 unit of software and proceed to trade 75 U.S. PCs for 75 units of Indian software. Specialization and trade allow U.S. residents to consume 75 units of software imported from India and to consume 150 PCs produced at home. By specializing and engaging in trade, Indian residents consume 25 units of software produced at home and import 75 PCs from the United States.

Product	U.S. Production and Consumption with Trade		Indian Production and Consumption with Trade	
Units of software (per hour)	U.S. production	0	Indian production	100
	+Imports from India	75	−Exports to U.S.	75
	Total U.S. consumption	75	Total Indian consumption	25
Personal computers (per hour)	U.S. production	225	Indian production	0
	−Exports to India	75	+Imports from U.S.	75
	Total U.S. consumption	150	Total Indian consumption	75

TABLE 33-4

National and Worldwide Gains from Specialization and Trade

This table summarizes the consumption gains experienced by the United States, India, and the two-country world. U.S. and Indian software and PC consumption rates with specialization and trade from Table 33-3 are listed in column 1, which sums the national consumption rates to determine total worldwide consumption with trade. Column 2 shows U.S., Indian, and worldwide consumption rates without international trade, as reported in Table 33-2. Column 3 gives the differences between the two columns, which are the resulting national and worldwide gains from international trade.

Product	(1) National and World Consumption with Trade	(2) National and World Consumption without Trade	(3) Worldwide Consumption Gains from Trade
Units of software (per hour)	U.S. consumption 75 +Indian consumption 25 World consumption 100	U.S. consumption 30 +Indian consumption 25 World consumption 55	Change in U.S. consumption +45 Change in Indian consumption +0 **Change in world consumption +45**
Personal computers (per hour)	U.S. consumption 150 +Indian consumption 75 World consumption 225	U.S. consumption 150 +Indian consumption 37.5 World consumption 187.5	Change in U.S. consumption +0 Change in Indian consumption +37.5 **Change in world consumption +37.5**

In addition, without trade residents of India could have used all resources to produce and consume only 37.5 PCs and 25 units of software. By using all resources to specialize in producing 100 units of software and engaging in trade, residents of India can consume 37.5 *more* PCs than they could have produced and consumed alone without reducing their software consumption. Thus, the Indian gain from trade is 37.5 PCs. This represents a worldwide gain in PC consumption, because neither country had to give up consuming any PCs for Indian residents to realize this gain from trade.

SPECIALIZATION IS THE KEY This example shows that when nations specialize in producing goods for which they have a comparative advantage and engage in international trade, considerable consumption gains are possible for those nations and hence for the world. Why is this so? The answer is that specialization and trade enable Indian residents to obtain each PC at an opportunity cost of 1 unit of software instead of 2 units of software and permit U.S. residents to obtain each unit of software at an opportunity cost of 1 PC instead of 2.5 PCs. Indian residents effectively experience a gain from trade of 1 unit of software for each PC purchased from the United States, and U.S. residents experience a gain from trade of 1.5 PCs for each unit of software purchased from India. Thus, specializing in producing goods for which the two nations have a comparative advantage allows both nations to produce more efficiently. As a consequence, worldwide production capabilities increase. This makes greater worldwide consumption possible through international trade.

Of course, not everybody in our example is better off when free trade occurs. In our example, the U.S. software industry and Indian computer industry have disappeared. Thus, U.S. software makers and Indian computer manufacturers are worse off.

Some people are worried that the United States (or any country, for that matter) might someday "run out of exports" because of overaggressive foreign competition. The analysis of comparative advantage tells us the contrary. No matter how much

FIGURE 33-2

World Trade Flows

International merchandise trade amounts to more than $14.4 trillion worldwide. The percentage figures show the proportion of trade flowing in the various directions throughout the globe.

Sources: World Trade Organization and author's estimates (data are for 2009).

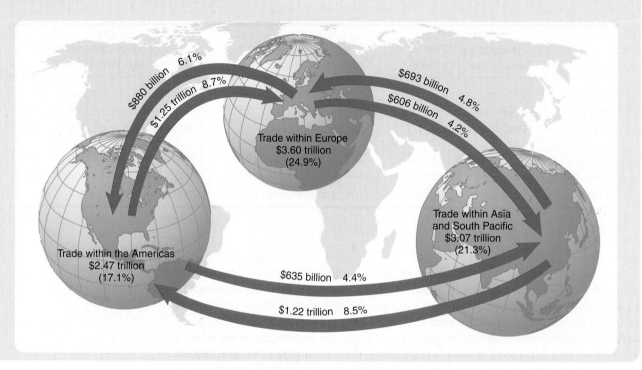

other countries compete for our business, the United States (or any other country) will always have a comparative advantage in something that it can export. In 10 or 20 years, that something may not be what we export today, but it will be exportable nonetheless because we will have a comparative advantage in producing it. Consequently, the significant flows of world trade shown in Figure 33-2 will continue because the United States and other nations will retain comparative advantages in producing various goods and services.

During the Great Recession of the late 2000s, why did global trade in services remain stable even as merchandise trade dropped sharply?

INTERNATIONAL EXAMPLE
During a Recession, Are Comparative Advantages in Services More Stable Sources of Trade?

During the recent economic downturn, annual trade of physical goods dropped by more than 20 percent worldwide, but global trade in services did not perceptibly change. Many internationally traded services are financial services that firms buy even as their production and sales decline. In addition, during recessions, companies work harder to speed the receipt of revenues and thus purchase more services of collection agencies, including those based in other countries. Firms also seek to cut expenses by buying lower-cost foreign services. Hence, international trade in services potentially can increase during a recession. Indeed, even as annual U.S. trade in merchandise fell by more than 25 percent, annual U.S. exports and imports of services actually increased by more than 7 percent.

FOR CRITICAL ANALYSIS
Can you think of any reasons why the United States might have a comparative advantage in producing various types of bookkeeping and financial services?

Other Benefits from International Trade: The Transmission of Ideas

Beyond the fact that comparative advantage results in an overall increase in the output of goods produced and consumed, there is another benefit to international trade. International trade bestows benefits on countries through the international transmission of ideas. According to economic historians, international trade has been the principal means by which new goods, services, and processes have spread around the world. For example, coffee was initially grown in Arabia near the Red Sea. Around AD 675, it began to be roasted and consumed as a beverage. Eventually, it was exported to other parts of the world, and the Dutch started cultivating it in their colonies during the seventeenth century and the French in the eighteenth century. The lowly potato is native to the Peruvian Andes. In the sixteenth century, it was brought to Europe by Spanish explorers. Thereafter, its cultivation and consumption spread rapidly. It became part of the North American agricultural scene in the early eighteenth century.

New processes have also been transmitted through international trade. An example is the Japanese manufacturing innovation that emphasized redesigning the system rather than running the existing system in the best possible way. Inventories were reduced to just-in-time levels by reengineering machine setup methods.

In addition, international trade has enabled *intellectual property* to spread throughout the world. New music, such as rock and roll in the 1950s and 1960s and hip-hop in the 1990s and 2000s, has been transmitted in this way, as have the software applications and computer communications tools that are common for computer users everywhere.

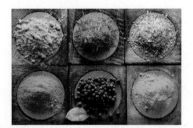

To what extent has international trade been responsible for the world-wide spread of spices and coffee?

The Relationship Between Imports and Exports

The basic proposition in understanding all of international trade is this:

> *In the long run, imports are paid for by exports.*

The reason that imports are ultimately paid for by exports is that foreign residents want something in exchange for the goods that are shipped to the United States. For the most part, they want U.S.-made goods. From this truism comes a remarkable corollary:

> *Any restriction of imports ultimately reduces exports.*

How has international trade benefited the music industry?

This is a shocking revelation to many people who want to restrict foreign competition to protect domestic jobs. Although it is possible to "protect" certain U.S. jobs by restricting foreign competition, it is impossible to make *everyone* better off by imposing import restrictions. Why? The reason is that ultimately such restrictions lead to a reduction in employment and output—and hence incomes—in the export industries of the nation.

International Competitiveness

"The United States is falling behind." "We need to stay competitive internationally." Statements such as these are often heard in government circles when the subject of international trade comes up. There are two problems with such talk. The first has to do with a simple definition. What does "global competitiveness" really mean? When one company competes against another, it is in competition. Is the United States like one big corporation, in competition with other countries? Certainly not. The standard of living in each country is almost solely a function of how well the economy functions *within that country*, not relative to other countries.

Another point relates to real-world observations. According to the Institute for Management Development in Lausanne, Switzerland, the United States continues to lead the pack in overall productive efficiency, ahead of Japan, Germany, and the rest of the European Union. According to the report, the top ranking of the United States over the years has been due to widespread entrepreneurship, more than a decade of economic restructuring, and information-technology investments. Other factors include the open U.S. financial system and large investments in scientific research.

How did the introduction of shipping containers make some world ports more competitive while causing other ports' competitiveness to decline?

INTERNATIONAL EXAMPLE
How Shipping Containers Made Some Nations More Competitive

Until the 1970s, ships that arrived in ports around the globe had to be unloaded by dozens of workers who lifted out boxes and other items, one by one. Then many of the same workers would reload the ships by hand. Naturally, labor costs were a significant portion of the expenses incurred by shipping firms using these ports.

Then firms began using shipping containers, which could be stuffed with boxes and items by manufacturers, transported by truck, and then loaded onto departing ships by only a few workers using specially designed cranes. When those ships arrived in ports with their cargoes, a few workers could use cranes to load the containers onto trucks for transport to final destinations. The dramatic reduction in labor

costs made possible by utilizing shipping containers significantly increased the competitiveness of ports in locales such as Hong Kong; Singapore; Newark, New Jersey; and Charleston, South Carolina. In contrast, ports that failed to adapt to the use of shipping containers, in locales such as London, Boston, and New York City, became uncompetitive and fell into disuse.

FOR CRITICAL ANALYSIS
Why did choices about whether to adapt to the use of shipping containers alter nations' comparative advantages in providing port facility services to shippers? (Hint: Recall the definition of comparative advantage.)

A nation has a **comparative advantage** when its residents are able to produce a good or service at a _____ opportunity cost than residents of another nation.

Specializing in production of goods and services for which residents of a nation have a _____ _____ allows the nation's residents to _____ more of all goods and services.

_____ from trade arise for all nations in the world that engage in international trade because specialization and trade allow countries' residents to _____ more goods and services without necessarily giving up consumption of other goods and services.

Arguments Against Free Trade

Numerous arguments are raised against free trade. They mainly focus on the costs of trade; they do not consider the benefits or the possible alternatives for reducing the costs of free trade while still reaping benefits.

The Infant Industry Argument

A nation may feel that if a particular industry is allowed to develop domestically, it will eventually become efficient enough to compete effectively in the world market. Therefore, the nation may impose some restrictions on imports in order to give domestic producers the time they need to develop their efficiency to the point where they can compete in the domestic market without any restrictions on imports. In graphic terminology, we would expect that if the protected industry truly does experience improvements in production techniques or technological breakthroughs toward greater efficiency in the future, the supply curve will shift outward to the right so that the domestic industry can produce larger quantities at each and every price. National policymakers often assert that this **infant industry argument** has some merit in the short run. They have used it to protect a number of industries in their infancy around the world.

Infant industry argument
The contention that tariffs should be imposed to protect from import competition an industry that is trying to get started. Presumably, after the industry becomes technologically efficient, the tariff can be lifted.

Such a policy can be abused, however. Often the protective import-restricting arrangements remain even after the infant has matured. If other countries can still produce more cheaply, the people who benefit from this type of situation are obviously the stockholders (and specialized factors of production that will earn economic rents) in the industry that is still being protected from world competition. The people who lose out are the consumers, who must pay a price higher than the world price for the product in question. In any event, it is very difficult to know beforehand which industries will eventually survive making it possible, perhaps even likely, that policymakers will choose to protect industries that have no reasonable chance of competing on their own in world markets. Note that when we speculate about which industries "should" be protected, we are in the realm of *normative economics*. We are making a value judgment, a subjective statement of what *ought to be*.

Why do Japan's residents have to pay such a high price for energy to operate computers, netbooks, and other electronic gadgets?

E-COMMERCE EXAMPLE
Protectionism Boosts Japan's Electricity Bill

Japan's islands are nearly devoid of oil, natural gas, uranium, and most other energy resources, so the nation imports a significant portion of its energy sources. Nevertheless, the Organization for Economic Cooperation and Development, a multinational association whose members include the world's most industrialized nations, rates Japan as the least open to international trade in electricity sales.

Only a handful of firms produce electricity for sale to Japanese consumers, and each of the companies is based in Japan. No foreign electricity producers have been permitted to compete. As a consequence, even though inflation-adjusted electricity prices have fallen around the globe since the 1980s, the decline in prices paid by Japanese consumers has been much smaller. Today, thanks to protectionist policies that restrain competition, Japanese electricity prices remain among the highest in the world.

FOR CRITICAL ANALYSIS
Who gains from restrictions on the production and sale of electricity in Japan?

Countering Foreign Subsidies and Dumping

Go to www.econtoday.com/chapter33 for a Congressional Budget Office review of antidumping actions in the United States and around the world.

Another common argument against unrestricted foreign trade has to do with countering other nations' subsidies to their own producers. When a foreign government subsidizes its producers, our producers claim that they cannot compete fairly with these subsidized foreign producers. To the extent that such subsidies fluctuate, it can be argued that unrestricted free trade will seriously disrupt domestic producers. They will not know when foreign governments are going to subsidize their producers and when they are not. Our competing industries will be expanding and contracting too frequently.

The phenomenon called *dumping* is also used as an argument against unrestricted trade. **Dumping** is said to occur when a producer sells its products abroad below the price that is charged in the home market or at a price below its cost of production. Often, when a foreign producer is accused of dumping, further investigation reveals that the foreign nation is in the throes of a recession. The foreign producer does not want to slow down its production at home. Because it anticipates an end to the recession and doesn't want to hold large inventories, it dumps its products abroad at prices below home prices. U.S. competitors may also allege that it sells its output at prices below its full costs in an effort to cover variable costs of production.

Dumping
Selling a good or a service abroad below the price charged in the home market or at a price below its cost of production.

Protecting Domestic Jobs

Perhaps the argument used most often against free trade is that unrestrained competition from other countries will eliminate jobs in the United States because other countries have lower-cost labor than we do. (Less restrictive environmental standards in other countries might also lower their private costs relative to ours.) This is a compelling argument, particularly for politicians from areas that might be threatened by foreign competition. For example, a representative from an area with shoe factories would certainly be upset about the possibility of constituents' losing their jobs because of competition from lower-priced shoe manufacturers in Brazil and Italy. But, of course, this argument against free trade is equally applicable to trade between the states within the United States.

Economists David Gould, G. L. Woodbridge, and Roy Ruffin examined the data on the relationship between increases in imports and the rate of unemployment. Their conclusion was that there is no causal link between the two. Indeed, in half the cases they studied, when imports increased, the unemployment rate fell.

Another issue has to do with the cost of protecting U.S. jobs by restricting international trade. The Institute for International Economics examined just the restrictions on foreign textiles and apparel goods. U.S. consumers pay $9 billion a year more than they would otherwise pay for those goods to protect jobs in those industries. That comes out to $50,000 *a year* for each job saved in an industry in which the average job pays only $20,000 a year. Similar studies have yielded similar results: Restrictions on imports of Japanese cars have cost $160,000 *per year* for every job saved in the auto industry. Every job preserved in the glass industry has cost $200,000 each and every year. Every job preserved in the U.S. steel industry has cost an astounding $750,000 per year.

Emerging Arguments Against Free Trade

In recent years, two new antitrade arguments have been advanced. One of these focuses on environmental and safety concerns. For instance, many critics of free trade have suggested that genetic engineering of plants and animals could lead to accidental production of new diseases and that people, livestock, and pets could be harmed by tainted foods imported for human and animal consumption. These worries have induced the European Union to restrain trade in such products.

Why do some environmental groups support protecting the U.S. steel industry from competition from firms in countries such as China?

POLICY EXAMPLE
Does the U.S. Steel Industry Deserve Environmental Protection?

Since 1995, complaints from the U.S. steel industry about alleged dumping of steel and related products ultimately generated more than half of the hundreds of dumping claims brought by the U.S. government against companies in other nations. If U.S. environmental groups have their way, an even larger share of antidumping claims will involve the U.S. steel industry. These groups claim that the production of steel in China leaves a "carbon footprint" three times as large as the "footprint" left by U.S. steelmakers and that Chinese prices fail to reflect the global social costs of pollution generated by Chinese steel production. Thus, these environmentalists maintain that Chinese steel prices are "too low" and that almost all of the U.S. steelmakers' allegations of dumping by Chinese producers are justified.

FOR CRITICAL ANALYSIS
What do you suppose explains support by U.S. environmental groups for a "carbon equalization tariff" on U.S. steel imports from China?

Another argument against free trade arises from national defense concerns. Major espionage successes by China in the late 1990s and 2000s led some U.S. strategic experts to propose sweeping restrictions on exports of new technology.

Free trade proponents counter that at best these are arguments for the judicious regulation of trade. They continue to argue that, by and large, broad trade restrictions mainly harm the interests of the nations that impose them.

Ways to Restrict Foreign Trade

International trade can be stopped or at least stifled in many ways. These include quotas and taxes (the latter are usually called *tariffs* when applied to internationally traded items). Let's talk first about quotas.

Quotas

Quota system
A government-imposed restriction on the quantity of a specific good that another country is allowed to sell in the United States. In other words, quotas are restrictions on imports. These restrictions are usually applied to one or several specific countries.

Under a **quota system,** individual countries or groups of foreign producers are restricted to a certain amount of trade. An import quota specifies the maximum amount of a commodity that may be imported during a specified period of time. For example, the government might allow no more than 200 million barrels of foreign crude oil to enter the United States in a particular month.

Consider the example of quotas on textiles. Figure 33-3 presents the demand and supply curves for imported textiles. In an unrestricted import market, the equilibrium quantity imported is 900 million yards at a price of $1 per yard (expressed in

FIGURE 33-3

The Effect of Quotas on Textile Imports

Without restrictions, at point E_1, 900 million yards of textiles would be imported each year into the United States at the world price of $1.00 per yard. If the federal government imposes a quota of only 800 million yards, the effective supply curve becomes vertical at that quantity. It intersects the demand curve at point E_2, so the new equilibrium price is $1.50 per yard.

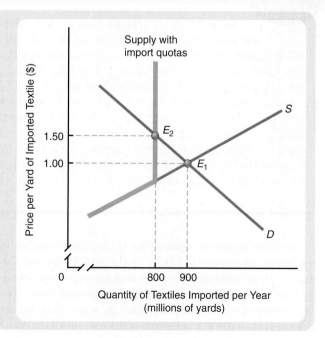

constant-quality units). When an import quota is imposed, the supply curve is no longer *S*. Instead, the supply curve becomes vertical at some amount less than the equilibrium quantity—here, 800 million yards per year. The price to the U.S. consumer increases from $1.00 to $1.50.

Clearly, the output restriction generated by a quota on foreign imports of a particular item has the effect of raising the domestic price of the imported item. Two groups benefit. One group is importers that are able to obtain the rights to sell imported items domestically at the higher price, which raises their revenues and boosts their profits. The other group is domestic producers. Naturally, a rise in the price of an imported item induces an increase in the demand for domestic substitutes. Thus, the domestic prices of close substitutes for the item subject to the import restriction also increase, which generates higher revenues and profits for domestic producers.

VOLUNTARY QUOTAS Quotas do not have to be explicit and defined by law. They can be "voluntary." Such a quota is called a **voluntary restraint agreement (VRA)**. In the early 1980s, Japanese automakers voluntarily restrained exports to the United States. These restraints stayed in place into the 1990s. Today, there are VRAs on machine tools and textiles.

The opposite of a VRA is a **voluntary import expansion (VIE)**. Under a VIE, a foreign government agrees to have its companies import more foreign goods from another country. The United States almost started a major international trade war with Japan in 1995 over just such an issue. The U.S. government wanted Japanese automobile manufacturers to voluntarily increase their imports of U.S.-made automobile parts. Ultimately, Japanese companies did make a token increase in their imports of U.S. auto parts.

Voluntary restraint agreement (VRA)
An official agreement with another country that "voluntarily" restricts the quantity of its exports to the United States.

Voluntary import expansion (VIE)
An official agreement with another country in which it agrees to import more from the United States.

Tariffs

We can analyze tariffs by using standard supply and demand diagrams. Let's use as our commodity laptop computers, some of which are made in Japan and some of which are made domestically. In panel (a) of Figure 33-4 on the following page, you see the demand for and supply of Japanese laptops. The equilibrium price is $1,000 per constant-quality unit, and the equilibrium quantity is 10 million per year. In panel (b), you see the same equilibrium price of $1,000, and the *domestic* equilibrium quantity is 5 million units per year.

Now a tariff of $500 is imposed on all imported Japanese laptops. The supply curve shifts upward by $500 to S_2. For purchasers of Japanese laptops, the price increases to $1,250. The quantity demanded falls to 8 million per year. In panel (b), you see that at the higher price of imported Japanese laptops, the demand curve for U.S.-made laptops shifts outward to the right to D_2. The equilibrium price increases to $1,250, and the equilibrium quantity increases to 6.5 million units per year. So the tariff benefits domestic laptop producers because it increases the demand for their products due to the higher price of a close substitute, Japanese laptops. This causes a redistribution of income from Japanese producers and U.S. consumers of laptops to U.S. producers of laptops.

Go to **www.econtoday.com/chapter33** to take a look at the U.S. State Department's reports on economic policy and trade practices.

TARIFFS IN THE UNITED STATES In Figure 33-5 on page 855, we see that tariffs on all imported goods have varied widely. The highest rates in the twentieth century occurred with the passage of the Smoot-Hawley Tariff in 1930.

CURRENT TARIFF LAWS The Trade Expansion Act of 1962 gave the president the authority to reduce tariffs by up to 50 percent. Subsequently, tariffs were reduced by

FIGURE 33-4

The Effect of a Tariff on Japanese-Made Laptop Computers

Without a tariff, the United States buys 10 million Japanese laptops per year at an average price of $1,000, at point E_1 in panel (a). U.S. producers sell 5 million domestically made laptops, also at $1,000 each, at point E_1 in panel (b). A $500-per-laptop tariff will shift the Japanese import supply curve to S_2 in panel (a), so that the new equilibrium is at E_2 with price increased to $1,250 and quantity sold reduced to 8 million per year. The demand curve for U.S.-made laptops (for which there is no tariff) shifts to D_2, in panel (b). Domestic sales increase to 6.5 million per year, at point E_2.

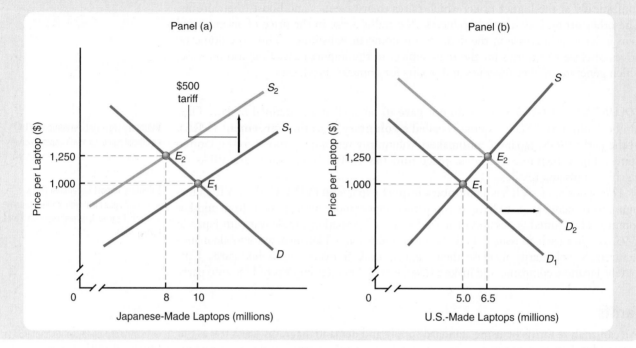

about 35 percent. In 1974, the Trade Reform Act allowed the president to reduce tariffs further. In 1984, the Trade and Tariff Act resulted in the lowest tariff rates ever. All such trade agreement obligations of the United States were carried out under the auspices of the **General Agreement on Tariffs and Trade (GATT),** which was signed in 1947. Member nations of the GATT account for more than 85 percent of world trade. As you can see in Figure 33-5, U.S. tariff rates have declined since the early 1960s, when several rounds of negotiations under the GATT were initiated. In 2002, the U.S. government proposed eliminating all tariffs on manufactured goods by 2015.

General Agreement on Tariffs and Trade (GATT)

An international agreement established in 1947 to further world trade by reducing barriers and tariffs. The GATT was replaced by the World Trade Organization in 1995.

International Trade Organizations

The widespread effort to reduce tariffs around the world has generated interest among nations in joining various international trade organizations. These organizations promote trade by granting preferences in the form of reduced or eliminated tariffs, duties, or quotas.

The World Trade Organization (WTO)

World Trade Organization (WTO)

The successor organization to the GATT that handles trade disputes among its member nations.

The most important international trade organization with the largest membership is the **World Trade Organization (WTO),** which was ratified by the final round of negotiations of the General Agreement on Tariffs and Trade at the end of 1993. The

FIGURE 33-5

Tariff Rates in the United States Since 1820

Tariff rates in the United States have bounced around like a football; indeed, in Congress, tariffs are a political football. Import-competing industries prefer high tariffs. In the twentieth century, the highest tariff was the Smoot-Hawley Tariff of 1930, which was about as high as the "tariff of abominations" in 1828.

Source: U.S. Department of Commerce.

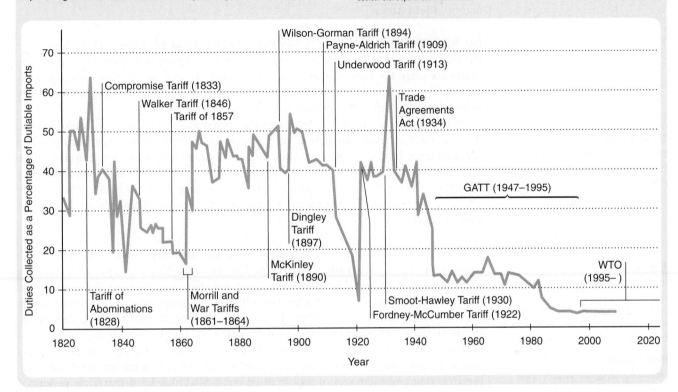

WTO, which as of 2009 had 153 member nations and included 30 observer governments, began operations on January 1, 1995. WTO decisions have concerned such topics as special U.S. steel tariffs imposed in the early 2000s, which the U.S. government removed after the WTO determined that they violated its rules. The WTO also adjudicated the European Union's "banana wars" and determined that the EU's policies unfairly favored many former European colonies in Africa, the Caribbean, and the Pacific at the expense of banana-exporting countries in Latin America. Now those former colonies no longer have a privileged position in European markets.

On a larger scale, the WTO fostered the most important and far-reaching global trade agreement ever covering financial institutions, including banks, insurers, and investment companies. The more than 100 signatories to this new treaty have legally committed themselves to giving foreign residents more freedom to own and operate companies in virtually all segments of the financial services industry.

Regional Trade Agreements

Numerous other international trade organizations exist alongside the WTO. Sometimes known as **regional trade blocs,** these organizations are created by special deals among groups of countries that grant trade preferences only to countries within their groups. Currently, more than 230 bilateral or regional trade agreements are in effect

Regional trade bloc

A group of nations that grants members special trade privileges.

around the globe. Examples include groups of industrial powerhouses, such as the European Union, the North American Free Trade Agreement, and the Association of Southeast Asian Nations. Nations in South America with per capita real GDP nearer the world average have also formed regional trade blocs called Mercosur and the Andean Community. Less developed nations have also formed regional trade blocs, such as the Economic Community of West African States and the Community of East and Southern Africa.

DO REGIONAL TRADE BLOCS SIMPLY DIVERT TRADE? Figure 33-6 shows that the formation of regional trade blocs, in which the European Union and the United States are often key participants, is on an upswing. An average African nation participates in four separate regional trading agreements. A typical Latin American country belongs to eight different regional trade blocs.

In the past, economists worried that the formation of regional trade blocs could mainly result in **trade diversion,** or the shifting of trade from countries outside a regional trade bloc to nations within a bloc. Indeed, a study by Jeffrey Frankel of the University of California at Berkeley found evidence that some trade diversion does take place. Nevertheless, Frankel and other economists have concluded that the net effect of regional trade agreements has been to boost overall international trade, in some cases considerably.

THE TRADE DEFLECTION ISSUE Today, the primary issue associated with regional trade blocs is **trade deflection.** This occurs when a company located in a nation outside a regional trade bloc moves goods that are not quite fully assembled into a member country, completes assembly of the goods there, and then exports them to other nations in the bloc. To try to reduce incentives for trade deflection, regional trade agreements often include **rules of origin,** which are regulations carefully defining categories of products that are eligible for trading preferences under the agreements. Some rules of origin, for instance, require any products trading freely among members of a bloc to be composed mainly of materials produced within a member nation.

Trade diversion

Shifting existing international trade from countries outside a regional trade bloc to nations within the bloc.

Trade deflection

Moving partially assembled products into a member nation of a regional trade bloc, completing assembly, and then exporting them to other nations within the bloc, so as to benefit from preferences granted by the trade bloc.

Rules of origin

Regulations that nations in regional trade blocs establish to delineate product categories eligible for trading preferences.

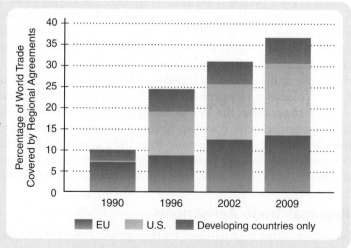

FIGURE 33-6

The Percentage of World Trade Within Regional Trade Blocs

As the number of regional trade agreements has increased since 1990, the share of world trade undertaken among nations that are members of regional trade blocs—involving the European Union (EU), United States, and developing nations—has also increased.

Source: World Bank.

Proponents of free trade worry, however, about the potential for parties to regional trade agreements to use rules of origin to create barriers to trade. Sufficiently complex rules of origin, they suggest, can provide disincentives for countries to utilize the trade-promoting preferences that regional trade agreements ought to provide. Indeed, some free trade proponents applaud successful trade deflection. They contend that it helps to circumvent trade restrictions and thus allows nations within regional trade blocs to experience additional gains from trade.

QUICK QUIZ   *See page 862 for the answers. Review concepts from this section in MyEconLab.*

One means of restricting foreign trade is an import quota, which specifies a _____ amount of a good that may be imported during a certain period. The resulting increase in import prices benefits those who gain the right to sell the imported item and domestic _____ that receive higher prices resulting from substitution to domestic goods.

Another means of restricting imports is a **tariff,** which is a _____ on imports only. An import tariff _____ import-competing industries and harms consumers by raising prices.

The main international institution created to improve trade among nations was the General Agreement on Tariffs and Trade (GATT). The last round of trade talks under the GATT led to the creation of the _____ _____ _____.

_____ _____ agreements among numerous nations of the world have established more than 230 _____ _____ blocs, which grant special trade privileges such as reduced tariff barriers and quota exemptions to member nations.

You Are There ▶ In Retrospect, a "Good Idea" Has Become an Empty Space

It is the early 2000s, and property developers in Phoenix, Arizona, have what they regard as a good idea for a profitable venture in distributing imported merchandise. During the preceding years, imported goods have become increasingly snarled in the distribution network originating at Los Angeles ports. To speed the distribution of these goods, reason the developers, a massive import-distribution hub could be constructed in Phoenix, 370 miles inland from Los Angeles.

Now fast-forward to the present. Thirteen massive warehouses covering a combined 8.2 million square feet of space are finished. The largest one has 1.2 million square feet of interior space—enough room to store 193 full-size copies of the Statue of Liberty—and its exterior parking space can hold 292 tractor trailers. Nevertheless, almost 90 percent of the new storage complex lies vacant. The Phoenix developers failed to anticipate the global economic slowdown and its negative impact on U.S. imports. The good news, of course, is that whenever U.S. imports return to their former levels, the distribution of merchandise eastward from Los Angeles is likely to proceed much more smoothly and efficiently.

CRITICAL ANALYSIS QUESTIONS

1. Why do U.S. imports of goods and services from abroad decline when U.S. national income falls? (Hint: Recall that income is one of the *ceteris paribus* determinants of the demand for any good or service.)

2. How might income generated from storing and distributing internationally traded merchandise constitute a potential gain from trade?

Is Protectionist History Destined to Be Repeated?

CONCEPTS APPLIED

- Comparative Advantage
- Gains from Trade
- Tariffs and Quotas

Comparative advantage enables the world's nations to gain from international trade. Because industries in countries not possessing comparative advantages lose out, however, there are always some who favor tariffs, quotas, and other measures aimed at protecting domestic firms from competition from international trade.

Tariffs, Quotas, and Trade in the Great Depression

In 1930, when the major economic downturn that we know as the Great Depression had just begun and world trade had declined by 7.5 percent from the prior year, Congress passed the Tariff Act of 1930, also known as the Smoot-Hawley Act. Congress approved this measure in spite of considerable opposition. Scores of newspaper editorials had called for Congress to reject the tariffs, as had former U.S. presidents. Furthermore, more than a thousand economists had signed a petition opposing the legislation. Nevertheless, the U.S. House of Representatives passed the act by a large margin, and it narrowly cleared the U.S. Senate on a 44-42 vote. Finally, in contrast to recent predecessors who had vetoed tariff bills, President Herbert Hoover signed the legislation into law.

During the following months, other nations around the world retaliated by raising their own tariffs and imposing various trade quotas. Soon all the tariffs and quotas began to accomplish what they had been designed to do: reducing imports around the globe and thereby slashing international trade flows. A year later, the global flow of international trade was 38 percent lower than in 1929. The aggregate flow of international trade continued to plummet during the next two years. By 1933, the worldwide flow of international trade was 66 percent below the 1929 level.

Rerunning a Protectionist Newsreel in the 2010s?

Since the onset of the Great Recession in December 2007, leaders of nations around the world have issued statements proclaiming the importance of international trade to the global economy. Nevertheless, the World Bank has noted that since the Great Recession began, more than 70 countries, including the United States, have enacted significant laws or rules to protect their domestic industries from competition. These measures have been implemented even as the global flow of international trade has declined more than 10 percent from its 2007 level. To many observers, these recent events are an eerie repeat of the early 1930s.

Can the lost gains from global trade caused by a modern upsurge in protectionism be quantified? Economists at the European Central Bank have estimated that a 5-percentage-point increase in import tariffs by a major entity such as the United States or the European Union would reduce annual world real GDP growth by 1 percentage point. If all countries were to adopt such increases simultaneously, the economists conclude, the adverse effect would be a drop in world GDP growth of several percentage points—implying zero or even negative growth.

Test your understanding of this chapter by going online to **MyEconLab**.
In the Study Plan for this chapter, select Section N: News.

For Critical Analysis

1. What other key element besides higher tariffs and quotas do you suppose contributed to the drop in international trade in the early 1930s?

2. How can a failure to achieve gains from international trade potentially lead to lower real GDP growth?

Web Resources

1. To read a description of the effects of the Smoot-Hawley tariffs on international trade in the 1930s, go to www.econtoday.com/chapter33.

2. To view a summary of the European Central Bank's conclusions about the adverse effects of protectionist policies, go to www.econtoday.com/chapter33.

Research Project

Discuss possible channels by which import tariffs and quotas bring about decreases in international trade. What channel do you view as likely to be most significant in generating a reduction in trade in response to a tariff or a quota? Does your answer depend on whether the policy action is a higher tariff or a lower quota? Support your position.

---

myeconlab

Here is what you should know after reading this chapter. **MyEconLab** will help you identify what you know, and where to go when you need to practice.

WHAT YOU SHOULD KNOW		WHERE TO GO TO PRACTICE
The Worldwide Importance of International Trade Total trade among nations has been growing faster than total world GDP. The growth of U.S. exports and imports relative to U.S. GDP parallels this global trend. Today, exports constitute more than 10 percent of total national production. In some countries, trade accounts for a much higher share of total economic activity.	KEY FIGURE Figure 33-1, 840	• **MyEconLab** Study Plan 33.1 • Audio introduction to Chapter 33 • Animated Figure 33-1 • ABC News Video: How Outsourcing Affects Our Lives
Why Nations Can Gain from Specializing in Production and Engaging in Trade A country has a comparative advantage in producing a good if it can produce that good at a lower opportunity cost, in terms of forgone production of a second good, than another nation. Because the other nation has a comparative	comparative advantage, 841 KEY FIGURE Figure 33-2, 846	• **MyEconLab** Study Plan 33.2 • Animated Figure 33-2 • Video: The Gains from Trade

(continued)

 *(continued)*

WHAT YOU SHOULD KNOW		WHERE TO GO TO PRACTICE

advantage in producing the second good, both nations can gain by specializing in producing the goods in which they have a comparative advantage and engaging in international trade. Together, they can then produce and consume more than they would have produced and consumed in the absence of specialization and trade.

Arguments Against Free Trade One argument against free trade is that temporary import restrictions might permit an "infant industry" to develop to the point at which it could compete without such restrictions. Another argument concerns dumping, in which foreign companies allegedly sell some of their output in domestic markets at prices below the prices in the companies' home markets or even below the companies' costs of production. In addition, some environmentalists contend that nations should restrain foreign trade to prevent exposing their countries to environmental hazards to plants, animals, or even humans. Finally, some contend that countries should limit exports of technologies that could pose a threat to their national defense.

infant industry argument, 849
dumping, 850

- **MyEconLab** Study Plans 33.3, 33.4, 33.5
- Video: Arguments Against Free Trade

Ways That Nations Restrict Foreign Trade One way to restrain trade is to impose a quota, or a limit on imports of a good. This action restricts the supply of the good in the domestic market, thereby pushing up the equilibrium price of the good. Another way to reduce trade is to place a tariff on imported goods. This reduces the supply of foreign-made goods and increases the demand for domestically produced goods, thereby bringing about a rise in the price of the good.

quota system, 852
voluntary restraint agreement (VRA), 853
voluntary import expansion (VIE), 853
General Agreement on Tariffs and Trade (GATT), 854

KEY FIGURES
Figure 33-3, 852
Figure 33-4, 854

- **MyEconLab** Study Plan 33.6
- Animated Figures 33-3, 33-4

Key International Trade Agreements and Organizations From 1947 to 1995, nations agreed to abide by the General Agreement on Tariffs and Trade (GATT), which laid an international legal foundation for relaxing quotas and reducing tariffs. Since 1995, the World Trade Organization (WTO) has adjudicated trade disputes that arise between or among nations. Now there are also more than 230 regional trade blocs, including the North American Free Trade Agreement and the European Union, that provide special trade preferences to member nations.

World Trade Organization, 854
regional trade bloc, 855
trade diversion, 856
trade deflection, 856
rules of origin, 856

KEY FIGURE
Figure 33-5, 855

- **MyEconLab** Study Plan 33.7
- Animated Figure 33-5

PROBLEMS

All problems are assignable in (X) **myeconlab** . *Answers to the odd-numbered problems appear at the back of the book.*

33-1. To answer the questions that follow, consider the following table for the neighboring nations of Northland and West Coast. The table lists maximum feasible hourly rates of production of pastries if no sandwiches are produced and maximum feasible hourly rates of production of sandwiches if no pastries are produced. Assume that the opportunity costs of producing these goods are constant in both nations.

Product	Northland	West Coast
Pastries (per hour)	50,000	100,000
Sandwiches (per hour)	25,000	200,000

   a. What is the opportunity cost of producing pastries in Northland? Of producing sandwiches in Northland?

   b. What is the opportunity cost of producing pastries in West Coast? Of producing sandwiches in West Coast?

33-2. Based on your answers to Problem 33-1, which nation has a comparative advantage in producing pastries? Which nation has a comparative advantage in producing sandwiches?

33-3. Suppose that the two nations in Problems 33-1 and 33-2 choose to specialize in producing the goods for which they have a comparative advantage. They agree to trade at a rate of exchange of 1 pastry for 1 sandwich. At this rate of exchange, what are the maximum possible numbers of pastries and sandwiches that they could agree to trade?

33-4. Residents of the nation of Border Kingdom can forgo production of digital televisions and utilize all available resources to produce 300 bottles of high-quality wine per hour. Alternatively, they can forgo producing wine and instead produce 60 digital TVs per hour. In the neighboring country of Coastal Realm, residents can forgo production of digital TVs and use all resources to produce 150 bottles of high-quality wine per hour, or they can forgo wine production and produce 50 digital TVs per hour. In both nations, the opportunity costs of producing the two goods are constant.

   a. What is the opportunity cost of producing digital TVs in Border Kingdom? Of producing bottles of wine in Border Kingdom?

   b. What is the opportunity cost of producing digital TVs in Coastal Realm? Of producing bottles of wine in Coastal Realm?

33-5. Based on your answers to Problem 33-4, which nation has a comparative advantage in producing digital TVs? Which nation has a comparative advantage in producing bottles of wine?

33-6. Suppose that the two nations in Problem 33-4 decide to specialize in producing the good for which they have a comparative advantage and to engage in trade. Will residents of both nations agree to trade wine for digital TVs at a rate of exchange of 4 bottles of wine for 1 digital TV? Why or why not?

To answer Problems 33-7 and 33-8, refer to the following table, which shows possible combinations of hourly outputs of modems and flash memory drives in South Shore and neighboring East Isle, in which opportunity costs of producing both products are constant.

South Shore		East Isle	
Modems	Flash Drives	Modems	Flash Drives
75	0	100	0
60	30	80	10
45	60	60	20
30	90	40	30
15	120	20	40
0	150	0	50

33-7. Consider the above table and answer the questions that follow.

   a. What is the opportunity cost of producing modems in South Shore? Of producing flash memory drives in South Shore?

   b. What is the opportunity cost of producing modems in East Isle? Of producing flash memory drives in East Isle?

   c. Which nation has a comparative advantage in producing modems? Which nation has a comparative advantage in producing flash memory drives?

33-8. Refer to your answers to Problem 33-7 when answering the following questions.

    a. Which *one* of the following rates of exchange of modems for flash memory drives will be acceptable to *both* nations: (i) 3 modems for 1 flash drive; (ii) 1 modem for 1 flash drive; or (iii) 1 flash drive for 2.5 modems? Explain.

    b. Suppose that each nation decides to use all available resources to produce only the good for which it has a comparative advantage and to engage in trade at the single feasible rate of exchange you identified in part (a). Prior to specialization and trade, residents of South Shore chose to produce and consume 30 modems per hour and 90 flash drives per hour, and residents of East Isle chose to produce and consume 40 modems per hour and 30 flash drives per hour. Now, residents of South Shore agree to export to East Isle the same quantity of South Shore's specialty good that East Isle residents were consuming prior to engaging in international trade.

How many units of East Isle's specialty good does South Shore import from East Isle?

    c. What is South Shore's hourly consumption of modems and flash drives after the nation specializes and trades with East Isle? What is East Isle's hourly consumption of modems and flash drives after the nation specializes and trades with South Shore?

    d. What consumption gains from trade are experienced by South Shore and East Isle?

33-9. Critics of the North American Free Trade Agreement (NAFTA) suggest that much of the increase in exports from Mexico to the United States now involves goods that Mexico otherwise would have exported to other nations. Mexican firms choose to export the goods to the United States, the critics argue, solely because the items receive preferential treatment under NAFTA tariff rules. What term describes what these critics are claiming is occurring with regard to U.S.-Mexican trade as a result of NAFTA? Explain your reasoning.

ECONOMICS ON THE NET

How the World Trade Organization Settles Trade Disputes A key function of the WTO is to adjudicate trade disagreements that arise among nations. This application helps you learn about the process that the WTO follows when considering international trade disputes.

Title: The World Trade Organization: Settling Trade Disputes

Navigation: Go to **www.econtoday.com/chapter33** to access the WTO's Web page titled *Dispute Settlement*. Under "Introduction to dispute settlement in the WTO," click on *How does the WTO settle disputes?*

Application Read the article; then answer the following questions.

1. As the article discusses, settling trade disputes often takes at least a year. What aspects of the WTO's dispute settlement process take the longest time?

2. Does the WTO actually "punish" a country it finds has broken international trading agreements? If not, who does impose sanctions?

For Group Study and Analysis Go to the WTO's main site at **www.econtoday.com/chapter33**, and click on *About the WTO*. Divide the class into groups, and have the groups explore this information on areas of WTO involvement. Have a class discussion of the pros and cons of WTO involvement in these areas. Which are most important for promoting world trade? Which are least important?

ANSWERS TO QUICK QUIZZES

p. 849: (i) lower; (ii) comparative advantage . . . consume; (iii) Gains . . . consume

p. 852: (i) infant . . . protected; (ii) dumping . . . dumping

p. 857: (i) maximum . . . producers; (ii) tax . . . benefits; (iii) World Trade Organization; (iv) Regional trade . . . regional trade

Exchange Rates and the Balance of Payments

34

I n the mid-1990s, the world's developed nations together exported more goods and services to other countries than they imported. Since then, however, they have become net importers of goods and services. During the same period, previously less developed nations experiencing rapid rates of economic growth observed the opposite trend. These nations—now called *emerging countries*—began as net importers of goods and services in the mid-1990s, but today they export significantly more than they import. In this chapter, you will learn how economists keep track of nations' exports and imports of goods and services. By the time you have finished reading the chapter, you will also understand why emerging countries have become net exporters at the same time that developed nations have switched to being net importers.

LEARNING OBJECTIVES

 myeconlab

MyEconLab helps you master each objective and study more efficiently. See end of chapter for details.

After reading this chapter, you should be able to:

➤ Distinguish between the balance of trade and the balance of payments

➤ Identify the key accounts within the balance of payments

➤ Outline how exchange rates are determined in the markets for foreign exchange

➤ Discuss factors that can induce changes in equilibrium exchange rates

➤ Understand how policymakers can go about attempting to fix exchange rates

➤ Explain alternative approaches to limiting exchange rate variability

? DID YOU KNOW THAT firms such as FX Solutions, Gain Capital, and Interbank FX offer an array of Internet-based systems that individuals can use to trade the currencies of various nations? Gain Capital, for instance, has account holders from 140 countries who engage in currency exchanges valued at more than $3 billion per day. Online currency-trading firms typically allow prospective clients to practice before they actually put funds at risk. There is good reason for people to engage in considerable practice before trading currencies. Online currency firms usually permit traders to provide only $1 up front for every *$400* of currency orders they complete. Thus, a trader who ends up losing $400 on a currency exchange must then come up with $399. Of course, a net profit of $399 on a trade that gains $400 is also possible, which is why many people are attracted to online currency trading.

In this chapter, you will learn about how the price of one currency in terms of another, called the *exchange rate*, is determined. First, however, you must learn about how the U.S. trade deficit is measured. You will also learn that this deficit is just part of an international accounting system called the *balance of payments*.

The Balance of Payments and International Capital Movements

Governments typically keep track of each year's economic activities by calculating the gross domestic product—the total of expenditures on all newly produced final domestic goods and services—and its components. A summary information system has also been developed for international trade. It covers the balance of trade and the balance of payments. The **balance of trade** refers specifically to exports and imports of physical goods, or merchandise, as discussed in Chapter 33. When international trade is in balance, the value of exports equals the value of imports. When the value of imports exceeds the value of exports, we are running a deficit in the balance of trade. When the value of exports exceeds the value of imports, we are running a surplus.

The **balance of payments** is a more general concept that expresses the total of all economic transactions between a nation and the rest of the world, usually for a period of one year. Each country's balance of payments summarizes information about that country's exports and imports of services as well as physical goods, earnings by domestic residents on assets located abroad, earnings on domestic assets owned by foreign residents, international capital movements, and official transactions by central banks and governments. In essence, then, the balance of payments is a record of all the transactions between households, firms, and the government of one country and the rest of the world. Any transaction that leads to a *payment* by a country's residents (or government) is a deficit item, identified by a negative sign (−) when the actual numbers are given for the items listed in the second column of Table 34-1. Any transaction that leads to a *receipt* by a country's residents (or government) is a surplus item and is identified by a plus sign (+) when actual numbers are considered. Table 34-1 gives a listing of the surplus and deficit items on international accounts.

Accounting Identities

Accounting identities—definitions of equivalent values—exist for financial institutions and other businesses. We begin with simple accounting identities that must hold for families and then go on to describe international accounting identities.

Balance of trade
The difference between exports and imports of physical goods.

Balance of payments
A system of accounts that measures transactions of goods, services, income, and financial assets between domestic households, businesses, and governments and residents of the rest of the world during a specific time period.

Accounting identities
Values that are equivalent by definition.

TABLE 34-1

Surplus (+) and Deficit (−) Items on the International Accounts

Surplus Items (+)	Deficit Items (−)
Exports of merchandise	Imports of merchandise
Private and governmental gifts from foreign residents	Private and governmental gifts to foreign residents
Foreign use of domestically operated travel and transportation services	Use of foreign-operated travel and transportation services
Foreign tourists' expenditures in this country	U.S. tourists' expenditures abroad
Foreign military spending in this country	Military spending abroad
Interest and dividend receipts from foreign entities	Interest and dividends paid to foreign residents
Sales of domestic assets to foreign residents	Purchases of foreign assets
Funds deposited in this country by foreign residents	Funds placed in foreign depository institutions
Sales of gold to foreign residents	Purchases of gold from foreign residents
Sales of domestic currency to foreign residents	Purchases of foreign currency

If a family unit is spending more than its current income, such a situation necessarily implies that the family unit must be doing one of the following:

1. Reducing its money holdings or selling stocks, bonds, or other assets
2. Borrowing
3. Receiving gifts from friends or relatives
4. Receiving public transfers from a government, which obtained the funds by taxing others (a transfer is a payment, in money or in goods or services, made without receiving goods or services in return)

We can use this information to derive an identity: If a family unit is currently spending more than it is earning, it must draw on previously acquired wealth, borrow, or receive either private or public aid. Similarly, an identity exists for a family unit that is currently spending less than it is earning: It must be increasing its money holdings or be lending and acquiring other financial assets, or it must pay taxes or bestow gifts on others. When we consider businesses and governments, each unit in each group faces its own identities or constraints. Ultimately, net lending by households must equal net borrowing by businesses and governments.

DISEQUILIBRIUM Even though our individual family unit's accounts must balance, in the sense that the identity discussed previously must hold, sometimes the item that brings about the balance cannot continue indefinitely. *If family expenditures exceed family income and this situation is financed by borrowing, the household may be considered to be in disequilibrium because such a situation cannot continue indefinitely.* If such a deficit is financed by drawing on previously accumulated assets, the family may also be in disequilibrium because it cannot continue indefinitely to draw on its wealth. Eventually, it will become impossible for that family to continue such a lifestyle. (Of course, if the family members are retired, they may well be in equilibrium by drawing on previously acquired assets to finance current deficits. This example illustrates that it is necessary to understand circumstances fully before pronouncing an economic unit in disequilibrium.)

EQUILIBRIUM Individual households, businesses, and governments, as well as the entire group of households, businesses, and governments, must eventually reach equilibrium. Certain economic adjustment mechanisms have evolved to ensure equilibrium. Deficit households must eventually increase their income or decrease their expenditures. They will find that they have to pay higher interest rates if they wish to borrow to finance their deficits. Eventually, their credit sources will dry up, and they will be forced into equilibrium. Businesses, on occasion, must lower costs or prices—or go bankrupt—to reach equilibrium.

AN ACCOUNTING IDENTITY AMONG NATIONS When people from different nations trade or interact, certain identities or constraints must also hold. People buy goods from people in other nations; they also lend to and present gifts to people in other nations. If residents of a nation interact with residents of other nations, an accounting identity ensures a balance (but not necessarily an equilibrium, as will soon become clear). Let's look at the three categories of balance of payments transactions: current account transactions, capital account transactions, and official reserve account transactions.

Current Account Transactions

During any designated period, all payments and gifts that are related to the purchase or sale of both goods and services constitute the **current account** in international trade. Major types of current account transactions include the exchange of merchandise, the exchange of services, and unilateral transfers.

Current account

A category of balance of payments transactions that measures the exchange of merchandise, the exchange of services, and unilateral transfers.

MERCHANDISE TRADE EXPORTS AND IMPORTS The largest portion of any nation's balance of payments current account is typically the importing and exporting of merchandise. During 2009, for example, as can be seen in lines 1 and 2 of Table 34-2, the United States exported an estimated $997.6 billion of merchandise and imported $1,493.6 billion. The balance of merchandise trade is defined as the difference between the value of merchandise exports and the value of merchandise imports. For 2009, the United States had a balance of merchandise trade deficit because the value of its merchandise imports exceeded the value of its merchandise exports. This deficit was about $496 billion (line 3).

SERVICE EXPORTS AND IMPORTS The balance of (merchandise) trade has to do with tangible items—things you can feel, touch, and see. Service exports and imports have to do with invisible or intangible items that are bought and sold, such as shipping, insurance, tourist expenditures, and banking services. Also, income earned by foreign residents on U.S. investments and income earned by U.S. residents on foreign investments are part of service imports and exports. As can be seen in lines 4 and 5 of Table 34-2, in 2009, estimated service exports were $476.7 billion, and service imports were $332.2 billion. Thus, the balance of services was about $144.5 billion in 2009 (line 6). Exports constitute receipts or inflows into the United States and are positive; imports constitute payments abroad or outflows of money and are negative.

When we combine the balance of merchandise trade with the balance of services, we obtain a balance on goods and services equal to –$351.5 billion in 2009 (line 7).

UNILATERAL TRANSFERS U.S. residents give gifts to relatives and others abroad, the federal government makes grants to foreign nations, foreign residents give gifts to U.S. residents, and in the past some foreign governments have granted funds to the U.S. government. In the current account, we see that net unilateral transfers—the total amount of gifts given by U.S. residents and the government minus the total

TABLE 34-2

U.S. Balance of Payments Account, 2009 (in billions of dollars)

Current Account		
(1) Exports of merchandise goods	+997.6	
(2) Imports of merchandise goods	−1,493.6	
(3) Balance of merchandise trade		−496.0
(4) Exports of services	+476.7	
(5) Imports of services	−332.2	
(6) Balance of services		+144.5
(7) Balance on goods and services [(3) + (6)]		−351.5
(8) Net unilateral transfers	−132.1	
(9) Balance on current account		−483.6
Capital Account		
(10) U.S. private capital going abroad	−471.6	
(11) Foreign private capital coming into the United States	+1,095.0*	
(12) Balance on capital account [(10) + (11)]		+623.4
(13) Balance on current account plus balance on capital account [(9) + (12)]		−139.8
Official Reserve Transactions Account		
(14) Official transactions balance		+139.8
(15) Total (balance)		0

Sources: U.S. Department of Commerce, Bureau of Economic Analysis; author's estimates.
*Includes an approximately $28 billion statistical discrepancy, probably uncounted capital inflows, many of which relate to the illegal drug trade.

amount received from abroad by U.S. residents and the government—came to an estimated −$132.1 billion in 2009 (line 8). The fact that there is a minus sign before the number for unilateral transfers means that U.S. residents gave more to foreign residents than foreign residents gave to U.S. residents.

BALANCING THE CURRENT ACCOUNT The balance on current account tracks the value of a country's exports of goods and services (including military receipts plus income on investments abroad) and transfer payments (private and government) relative to the value of that country's imports of goods and services and transfer payments (private and government). In 2009, it was estimated to be −$483.6 billion (line 9).

If the sum of net exports of goods and services plus net unilateral transfers plus net investment income exceeds zero, a **current account surplus** *is said to exist; if this sum is negative, a* **current account deficit** *is said to exist. A* **current account deficit** *means that we are importing more goods and services than we are exporting. Such a deficit must be paid for by the export of financial assets.*

Go to www.econtoday.com/chapter34 for the latest U.S. balance of payments data from the Bureau of Economic Analysis.

Capital Account Transactions

In world markets, it is possible to buy and sell not only goods and services but also real (e.g., real estate) and financial assets. These are the international transactions measured in the **capital account.** Capital account transactions occur because of foreign investments—either by foreign residents investing in the United States or by

Capital account
A category of balance of payments transactions that measures flows of real and financial assets.

U.S. residents investing in other countries. The purchase of shares of stock in British firms on the London stock market by a U.S. resident causes an outflow of funds from the United States to Britain. The construction of a Japanese automobile factory in the United States causes an inflow of funds from Japan to the United States. Any time foreign residents buy U.S. government securities, there is an inflow of funds from other countries to the United States. Any time U.S. residents buy foreign government securities, there is an outflow of funds from the United States to other countries. Loans to and from foreign residents cause outflows and inflows.

Line 10 of Table 34-2 on the preceding page indicates that in 2009, the value of private capital going out of the United States was an estimated −$471.6 billion, and line 11 shows that the value of private capital coming into the United States (including a statistical discrepancy) was $1,095 billion. U.S. capital going abroad constitutes payments or outflows and is therefore negative. Foreign capital coming into the United States constitutes receipts or inflows and is therefore positive. Thus, there was a positive net capital movement of $623.4 billion into the United States (line 12). This net private flow of capital is also called the balance on capital account.

There is a relationship between the current account balance and the capital account balance, assuming no interventions by the finance ministries or central banks of nations.

> *In the absence of interventions by finance ministries or central banks, the current account balance and the capital account balance must sum to zero. Stated differently, the current account deficit must equal the capital account surplus when governments or central banks do not engage in foreign exchange interventions. In this situation, any nation experiencing a current account deficit, such as the United States, must also be running a capital account surplus.*

This basic relationship is apparent in the United States, as you can see in Figure 34-1. As the figure shows, U.S. current account deficits experienced since the early 1980s have largely been balanced by private capital inflows, but there are exceptions, for reasons that we explain in the next section.

Official Reserve Account Transactions

The third type of balance of payments transaction concerns official reserve assets, which consist of the following:

1. Foreign currencies
2. Gold
3. **Special drawing rights (SDRs),** which are reserve assets that the **International Monetary Fund** created to be used by countries to settle international payment obligations
4. The reserve position in the International Monetary Fund
5. Financial assets held by an official agency, such as the U.S. Treasury Department

To consider how official reserve account transactions occur, look again at Table 34-2 on the previous page. The surplus in the U.S. capital account was $623.4 billion. But the deficit in the U.S. current account was −$483.6 billion, so the United States had a net deficit on the combined accounts (line 13) of −$139.8 billion. In other words, the United States obtained less in foreign funds in all its international transactions than it used. How is this deficiency made up? By foreign central banks and governments adding to their U.S. funds, shown by the +$139.8 billion in official transactions on line 14 in Table 34-2. There is a plus sign on line 14 because this represents an *inflow* of foreign exchange in our international transactions.

Special drawing rights (SDRs)
Reserve assets created by the International Monetary Fund for countries to use in settling international payment obligations.

International Monetary Fund
An agency founded to administer an international foreign exchange system and to lend to member countries that had balance of payments problems. The IMF now functions as a lender of last resort for national governments.

FIGURE 34-1

The Relationship Between the Current Account and the Capital Account

To a large extent, the capital account is the mirror image of the current account. We can see this in most years since 1970. Typically, when the current account was in surplus, the capital account was in deficit. When the current account was in deficit, the capital account was in surplus. There are exceptions, such as the 1996–1998 and 2005–2010 intervals, during

which the current account balance and capital account balance moved together. During these periods, the official reserve transactions balance increased significantly as a result of particularly large purchases of financial assets by governments and central banks.

Sources: International Monetary Fund; *Economic Indicators.*

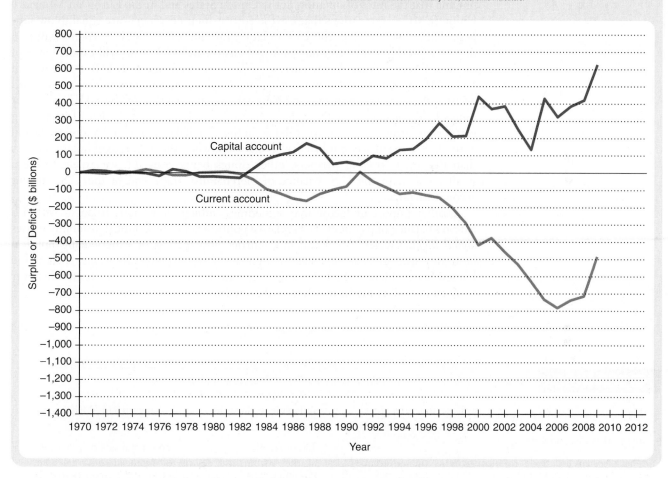

The balance (line 15) in Table 34-2 is zero, as it must be with double-entry book-keeping. The U.S. balance of payments deficit is measured by the official transactions figure on line 14.

The official reserve account transactions also explain why the movements in the current account balance and the capital account balance in Figure 34-1 are not exact mirror images. This is because the official reserve transactions balance has also varied over time. In recent years, there have been significant surpluses in the official reserve transactions balance. Foreign governments and central banks have purchased large volumes of U.S. financial assets, and these official capital inflows have also offset U.S. current account deficits within the overall balance of payments account.

For instance, between 1996 and 1998 and again between 2005 and 2010, the current account balance and the capital account balance moved together. During these periods, governments and central banks purchased particularly large quantities of financial assets. Thus, the official reserve transactions balance increased significantly during these intervals.

What Affects the Distribution of Account Balances Within the Balance of Payments?

A major factor affecting the distribution of account balances within any nation's balance of payments is its rate of inflation relative to that of its trading partners. Assume that the rates of inflation in the United States and in the European Monetary Union (EMU)—the nations that use the euro as their currency—are equal. Now suppose that all of a sudden, the U.S. inflation rate increases. EMU residents will find that U.S. products are becoming more expensive, and U.S. firms will export fewer of them to EMU nations. At the current dollar-euro exchange rate, U.S. residents will find EMU products relatively cheaper, and they will import more. The reverse will occur if the U.S. inflation rate suddenly falls relative to that of the EMU. All other things held constant, whenever the U.S. rate of inflation exceeds that of its trading partners, we expect to see a larger deficit in the U.S. balance of merchandise trade and in the U.S. current account balance. Conversely, when the U.S. rate of inflation is less than that of its trading partners, other things being constant, we expect to see a smaller deficit in the U.S. balance of merchandise trade and in the U.S. current account balance.

Another important factor that sometimes influences account balances within a nation's balance of payments is its relative political stability. Political instability causes *capital flight*. Owners of capital in countries anticipating or experiencing political instability will often move assets to countries that are politically stable, such as the United States. Hence, the U.S. capital account balance is likely to increase whenever political instability looms in other nations in the world.

QUICK QUIZ *See page 890 for the answers. Review concepts from this section in MyEconLab.*

The _____ of _____ reflects the value of all transactions in international trade, including goods, services, financial assets, and gifts.

The merchandise trade balance gives us the difference between exports and imports of _____ items.

Included in the _____ account along with merchandise trade are service exports and imports relating to commerce in intangible items, such as shipping, insurance, and tourist expenditures. The _____ account also includes income earned by foreign residents on U.S. investments and income earned by U.S. residents on foreign investments.

_____ _____ involve international private gifts and federal government grants or gifts to foreign nations.

When we add the balance of merchandise trade and the balance of services and take account of net unilateral transfers

and net investment income, we come up with the balance on the _____ account, a summary statistic.

There are also _____ account transactions that relate to the buying and selling of financial and real assets. Foreign capital is always entering the United States, and U.S. capital is always flowing abroad. The difference is called the balance on the _____ account.

Another type of balance of payments transaction concerns the _____ _____ assets of individual countries, or what is often simply called official transactions. By standard accounting convention, official transactions are exactly equal to but opposite in sign from the sum of the current account balance and the capital account balance.

Account balances within a nation's balance of payments can be affected by its relative rate of _____ and by its _____ stability relative to other nations.

Determining Foreign Exchange Rates

When you buy foreign products, such as European pharmaceuticals, you have dollars with which to pay the European manufacturer. The European manufacturer, however, cannot pay workers in dollars. The workers are European, they live in Europe, and they must have euros to buy goods and services in nations that are members of the European Monetary Union (EMU) and use the euro as their currency. There must therefore be some way of exchanging dollars for euros that the pharmaceuticals manufacturer will accept. That exchange occurs in a **foreign exchange market,** which in this case involves the exchange of euros and dollars.

The particular **exchange rate** between euros and dollars that prevails—the dollar price of the euro—depends on the current demand for and supply of euros and dollars. In a sense, then, our analysis of the exchange rate between dollars and euros will be familiar, for we have used supply and demand throughout this book. If it costs you $1.50 to buy 1 euro, that is the foreign exchange rate determined by the current demand for and supply of euros in the foreign exchange market. The European person going to the foreign exchange market would need 0.67 euro to buy 1 dollar.

Now let's consider what determines the demand for and supply of foreign currency in the foreign exchange market. We will continue to assume that the only two regions in the world are the EMU and the United States.

Foreign exchange market
A market in which households, firms, and governments buy and sell national currencies.

Exchange rate
The price of one nation's currency in terms of the currency of another country.

Demand for and Supply of Foreign Currency

You wish to purchase European-produced pharmaceuticals directly from a manufacturer located in an EMU nation. To do so, you must have euros. You go to the foreign exchange market (or your U.S. bank). Your desire to buy the pharmaceuticals therefore causes you to offer (supply) dollars to the foreign exchange market. Your demand for EMU euros is equivalent to your supply of U.S. dollars to the foreign exchange market.

> *Every U.S. transaction involving the importation of foreign goods constitutes a supply of dollars and a demand for some foreign currency, and the opposite is true for export transactions.*

In this case, the import transaction constitutes a demand for EMU euros.

In our example, we will assume that only two goods are being traded, European pharmaceuticals and U.S. computer printers. The U.S. demand for European pharmaceuticals creates a supply of dollars and a demand for euros in the foreign exchange market. Similarly, the European demand for U.S. computer printers creates a supply of euros and a demand for dollars in the foreign exchange market. Under a system of **flexible exchange rates,** the supply of and demand for dollars and euros in the foreign exchange market will determine the equilibrium foreign exchange rate. The equilibrium exchange rate will tell us how many euros a dollar can be exchanged for—that is, the euro price of dollars—or how many dollars a euro can be exchanged for—the dollar price of euros.

Flexible exchange rates
Exchange rates that are allowed to fluctuate in the open market in response to changes in supply and demand. Sometimes called *floating exchange rates*.

The Equilibrium Foreign Exchange Rate

To determine the equilibrium foreign exchange rate, we have to find out what determines the demand for and supply of foreign exchange. We will ignore for the moment any speculative aspect of buying foreign exchange. That is, we assume that there are no individuals who wish to buy euros simply because they think that their price will go up in the future.

The idea of an exchange rate is no different from the idea of paying a certain price for something you want to buy. If you like coffee, you know you have to pay about $1.50 a cup. If the price went up to $2.50, you would probably buy fewer cups. If the price went

Go to www.econtoday.com/chapter34 for recent data from the Federal Reserve Bank of St. Louis on the exchange value of the U.S. dollar relative to the major currencies of the world.

down to 50 cents, you would likely buy more. In other words, the demand curve for cups of coffee, expressed in terms of dollars, slopes downward following the law of demand. The demand curve for euros slopes downward also, and we will see why.

Let's think more closely about the demand schedule for euros. Let's say that it costs you $1.35 to purchase 1 euro; that is the exchange rate between dollars and euros. If tomorrow you had to pay $1.50 for the same euro, the exchange rate would have changed. Looking at such a change, we would say that there has been an **appreciation** in the value of the euro in the foreign exchange market. But another way to view this increase in the value of the euro is to say that there has been a **depreciation** in the value of the dollar in the foreign exchange market. The dollar used to buy 0.74 euro; tomorrow, the dollar will be able to buy only 0.67 euro at a price of $1.50 per euro. If the dollar price of euros rises, you will probably demand fewer euros. Why? The answer lies in the reason you and others demand euros in the first place.

Why has a generally persistent depreciation of the U.S. dollar relative to the European euro had an impact on study abroad programs offered by U.S. colleges and universities?

Appreciation
An increase in the exchange value of one nation's currency in terms of the currency of another nation.

Depreciation
A decrease in the exchange value of one nation's currency in terms of the currency of another nation.

INTERNATIONAL EXAMPLE
How a Depreciating Dollar Affects Study Abroad Programs

Since the 1990s, U.S. colleges and universities have developed thousands of study abroad programs. These programs enable students to apply their tuition payments to taking courses for academic credit in other nations. European nations have long been popular destinations for U.S. students participating in study abroad programs.

During the late 2000s, however, the U.S. dollar's value began to depreciate steadily relative to the euro. As a consequence, academic institutions experienced increases in the dollar costs of operating study abroad programs on the European continent. As the dollar generally continued to depreciate, many colleges and universities began establishing higher tuition rates for European study abroad programs. Academic institutions also began expanding programs in the United Kingdom, because in the late 2000s the British pound was the only European currency that depreciated persistently in relation to the dollar.

FOR CRITICAL ANALYSIS
Given that the pound was depreciating relative to the dollar as the dollar was simultaneously depreciating in relation to the euro, was the pound appreciating or depreciating relative to the euro?

APPRECIATION AND DEPRECIATION OF EUROS Recall that in our example, you and others demand euros to buy European pharmaceuticals. The demand curve for European pharmaceuticals follows the law of demand and therefore slopes downward. If it costs more U.S. dollars to buy the same quantity of European pharmaceuticals, presumably you and other U.S. residents will not buy the same quantity; your quantity demanded will be less. We say that your demand for euros is *derived from* your demand for European pharmaceuticals. In panel (a) of Figure 34-2 we present the hypothetical demand schedule for packages of European pharmaceuticals by a representative set of U.S. consumers during a typical week. In panel (b), we show graphically the U.S. demand curve for European pharmaceuticals in terms of U.S. dollars taken from panel (a).

AN EXAMPLE OF DERIVED DEMAND Let us assume that the price of a package of European pharmaceuticals in Europe is 100 euros. Given that price, we can find the

Panel (a)
Demand Schedule for Packages of European Pharmaceuticals in the United States per Week

Price per Package	Quantity Demanded
$155	100
150	300
145	500
140	700

Panel (b)
U.S. Demand Curve for European Pharmaceuticals

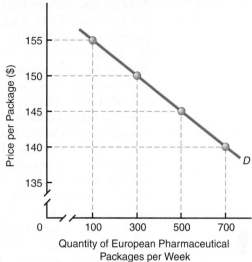

Panel (c)
Euros Required to Purchase Quantity Demanded (at P = 100 euros per package of pharmaceuticals)

Quantity Demanded	Euros Required
100	10,000
300	30,000
500	50,000
700	70,000

Panel (d)
Derived Demand Schedule for Euros in the United States with Which to Pay for Imports of Pharmaceuticals

Dollar Price of One Euro	Dollar Price of Pharmaceuticals	Quantity of Pharmaceuticals Demanded	Quantity of Euros Demanded per Week
$1.55	$155	100	10,000
1.50	150	300	30,000
1.45	145	500	50,000
1.40	140	700	70,000

FIGURE 34-2

Deriving the Demand for Euros

In panel (a), we show the demand schedule for European pharmaceuticals in the United States, expressed in terms of dollars per package of pharmaceuticals. In panel (b), we show the demand curve, D, which slopes downward. In panel (c), we show the number of euros required to purchase up to 700 packages of pharmaceuticals. If the price per package of pharmaceuticals is 100 euros, we can now find the quantity of euros needed to pay for the various quantities demanded. In panel (d), we see the derived demand for euros in the United States in order to purchase the various quantities of pharmaceuticals given in panel (a). The resultant demand curve, D_1, is shown in panel (e). This is the U.S. derived demand for euros.

Panel (e)
U.S. Derived Demand for Euros

number of euros required to purchase 500 packages of European pharmaceuticals. That information is given in panel (c) of Figure 34-2. If purchasing one package of European pharmaceuticals requires 100 euros, 500 packages require 50,000 euros. Now we have enough information to determine the derived demand curve for euros. If 1 euro costs $1.45, a package of pharmaceuticals would cost $145 (100 euros per package × $1.45 per euro = $145 per package). At $145 per package, the representative group of U.S. consumers would, we see from panel (a) of Figure 34-2, demand 500 packages of pharmaceuticals.

From panel (c), we see that 50,000 euros would be demanded to buy the 500 packages of pharmaceuticals. We show this quantity demanded in panel (d). In panel (e), we draw the derived demand curve for euros. Now consider what happens if the price of euros goes up to $1.50. A package of European pharmaceuticals priced at 100 euros in Europe would now cost $150. From panel (a), we see that at $150 per package, 300 packages of pharmaceuticals will be imported from Europe into the United States by our representative group of U.S. consumers. From panel (c), we see that 300 packages of pharmaceuticals would require 30,000 euros to be purchased; thus, in panels (d) and (e), we see that at a price of $1.50 per euro, the quantity demanded will be 30,000 euros.

We continue similar calculations all the way up to a price of $1.55 per euro. At that price, a package of European pharmaceuticals costing 100 euros in Europe would cost $155, and our representative U.S. consumers would import only 100 packages of pharmaceuticals.

DOWNWARD-SLOPING DERIVED DEMAND As can be expected, as the price of the euro rises, the quantity demanded will fall. The only difference here from the standard demand analysis developed in Chapter 3 and used throughout this text is that the demand for euros is derived from the demand for a final product—European pharmaceuticals in our example.

You Are There

To think about how U.S. entertainers respond to a change in the dollar-euro exchange rate when determining their concert schedules, consider **Why U.S. Entertainers Have Moved Their Acts Overseas,** on page 884.

SUPPLY OF EUROS Assume that European pharmaceutical manufacturers buy U.S. computer printers. The supply of euros is a derived supply in that it is derived from the European demand for U.S. computer printers. We could go through an example similar to the one for pharmaceuticals to come up with a supply schedule of euros in Europe. It slopes upward. Obviously, Europeans want dollars to purchase U.S. goods. European residents will be willing to supply more euros when the dollar price of euros goes up, because they can then buy more U.S. goods with the same quantity of euros. That is, the euro would be worth more in exchange for U.S. goods than when the dollar price for euros was lower.

AN EXAMPLE Let's take an example. Suppose a U.S.-produced computer printer costs $200. If the exchange rate is $1.45 per euro, a European resident will have to come up with 137.93 euros (= $200 at $1.45 per euro) to buy one computer printer. If, however, the exchange rate goes up to $1.50 per euro, a European resident must come up with only 133.33 euros (= $200 at $1.50 per euro) to buy a U.S. computer printer. At this lower price (in euros) of U.S. computer printers, Europeans will demand a larger quantity. In other words, as the price of euros goes up in terms of dollars, the quantity of U.S. computer printers demanded will go up, and hence the quantity of euros supplied will go up. Therefore, the supply schedule of euros, which is derived from the European demand for U.S. goods, will slope upward, as seen in Figure 34-3 on the following page.

TOTAL DEMAND FOR AND SUPPLY OF EUROS Let us now look at the total demand for and supply of euros. We take all U.S. consumers of European pharma-

FIGURE 34-3

The Supply of Euros

If the market price of a U.S.-produced computer printer is $200, then at an exchange rate of $1.45 per euro, the price of the printer to a European consumer is 137.93 euros. If the exchange rate rises to $1.50 per euro, the European price of the printer falls to 133.33 euros. This induces an increase in the quantity of printers demanded by European consumers and consequently an increase in the quantity of euros supplied in exchange for dollars in the foreign exchange market. In contrast, if the exchange rate falls to $1.40 per euro, the European price of the printer rises to 142.86 euros. This causes a decrease in the quantity of printers demanded by European consumers. As a result, there is a decline in the quantity of euros supplied in exchange for dollars in the foreign exchange market.

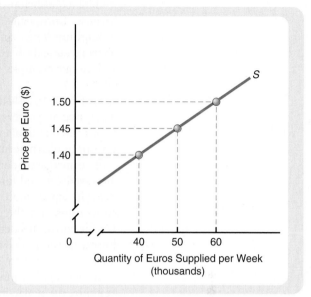

ceuticals and all European consumers of U.S. computer printers and put their demands for and supplies of euros together into one diagram. Thus, we are showing the total demand for and total supply of euros. The horizontal axis in Figure 34-4 represents the quantity of foreign exchange—the number of euros per year. The vertical axis represents the exchange rate—the price of foreign currency (euros) expressed in dollars (per euro). The foreign currency price of $1.50 per euro means it will cost you $1.50 to buy 1 euro. At the foreign currency price of $1.45 per euro, you know that it will cost you $1.45 to buy 1 euro. The equilibrium, E, is again established at $1.45 for 1 euro.

In our hypothetical example, assuming that there are only representative groups of pharmaceutical consumers in the United States and computer printer consumers in Europe, the equilibrium exchange rate will be set at $1.45 per euro.

FIGURE 34-4

Total Demand for and Supply of Euros

The market supply curve for euros results from the total European demand for U.S. computer printers. The demand curve, D, slopes downward like most demand curves, and the supply curve, S, slopes upward. The foreign exchange price, or the U.S. dollar price of euros, is given on the vertical axis. The number of euros is represented on the horizontal axis. If the foreign exchange rate is $1.50—that is, if it takes $1.50 to buy 1 euro—U.S. residents will demand 20 billion euros. The equilibrium exchange rate is at the intersection of D and S, or point E. The equilibrium exchange rate is $1.45 per euro. At this point, 30 billion euros are both demanded and supplied each year.

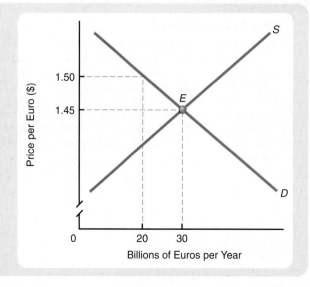

This equilibrium is not established because U.S. residents like to buy euros or because Europeans like to buy dollars. Rather, the equilibrium exchange rate depends on how many computer printers Europeans want and how many European pharmaceuticals U.S. residents want (given their respective incomes, their tastes, and, in our example, the relative prices of pharmaceuticals and computer printers).

A SHIFT IN DEMAND Assume that a successful advertising campaign by U.S. pharmaceutical importers has caused U.S. demand for European pharmaceuticals to rise. U.S. residents demand more pharmaceuticals at all prices. Their demand curve for European pharmaceuticals has shifted outward to the right.

The increased demand for European pharmaceuticals can be translated into an increased demand for euros. All U.S. residents clamoring for European pharmaceuticals will supply more dollars to the foreign exchange market while demanding more euros to pay for the pharmaceuticals. Figure 34-5 presents a new demand schedule, D_2, for euros; this demand schedule is to the right of the original demand schedule. If Europeans do not change their desire for U.S. computer printers, the supply schedule for euros will remain stable.

A new equilibrium will be established at a higher exchange rate. In our particular example, the new equilibrium is established at an exchange rate of $1.50 per euro. It now takes $1.50 to buy 1 euro, whereas formerly it took $1.45. This will be translated into an increase in the price of European pharmaceuticals to U.S. residents and into a decrease in the price of U.S. computer printers to Europeans. For example, a package of European pharmaceuticals priced at 100 euros that sold for $145 in the United States will now be priced at $150. Conversely, a U.S. printer priced at $200 that previously sold for 137.93 euros will now sell for 133.33 euros.

A SHIFT IN SUPPLY We just assumed that the U.S. demand for European pharmaceuticals had shifted due to a successful ad campaign. Because the demand for euros is derived from the demand by U.S. residents for pharmaceuticals, this is translated into a shift in the demand curve for euros. As an alternative exercise, we might assume that the supply curve of euros shifts outward to the right. Such a supply shift could occur

---

FIGURE 34-5

A Shift in the Demand Schedule

The demand schedule for European pharmaceuticals shifts to the right, causing the derived demand schedule for euros to shift to the right also. We have shown this as a shift from D_1 to D_2. We have assumed that the supply schedule for euros has remained stable—that is, European demand for U.S. computer printers has remained constant. The old equilibrium foreign exchange rate was $1.45 per euro. The new equilibrium exchange rate will be E_2. It will now cost $1.50 to buy 1 euro. The higher price of euros will be translated into a higher U.S. dollar price for European pharmaceuticals and a lower euro price for U.S. computer printers.

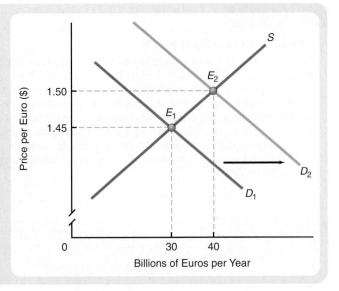

FIGURE 34-6

A Shift in the Supply of Euros

There has been a shift in the supply curve for euros. The new equilibrium will occur at E_1, meaning that $1.40, rather than $1.45, will now buy 1 euro. After the exchange rate adjustment, the annual amount of euros demanded and supplied will increase from 30 billion to 60 billion.

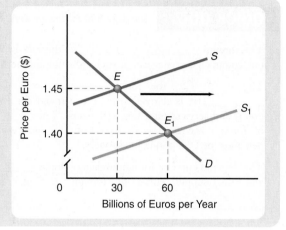

for many reasons, one of which is a relative rise in the European price level. For example, if the prices of all European-manufactured computer peripherals went up 20 percent in euros, U.S. computer printers would become relatively cheaper. That would mean that European residents would want to buy more U.S. computer printers. But remember that when they want to buy more U.S. printers, they supply more euros to the foreign exchange market.

Thus, we see in Figure 34-6 that the supply curve of euros moves from S to S_1. In the absence of restrictions—that is, in a system of flexible exchange rates—the new equilibrium exchange rate will be $1.40 equals 1 euro. The quantity of euros demanded and supplied will increase from 30 billion per year to 60 billion per year. We say, then, that in a flexible international exchange rate system, shifts in the demand for and supply of foreign currencies will cause changes in the equilibrium foreign exchange rates. Those rates will remain in effect until world supply or demand shifts.

Market Determinants of Exchange Rates

The foreign exchange market is affected by many other variables in addition to changes in relative price levels, including the following:

- *Changes in real interest rates.* Suppose that the U.S. interest rate, corrected for people's expectations of inflation, increases relative to the rest of the world. Then international investors elsewhere seeking the higher returns now available in the United States will increase their demand for dollar-denominated assets, thereby increasing the demand for dollars in foreign exchange markets. An increased demand for dollars in foreign exchange markets, other things held constant, will cause the dollar to appreciate and other currencies to depreciate.

- *Changes in consumer preferences.* If Germany's citizens suddenly develop a taste for U.S.-made automobiles, this will increase the derived demand for U.S. dollars in foreign exchange markets.

- *Perceptions of economic stability.* As already mentioned, if the United States looks economically and politically more stable relative to other countries, more foreign residents will want to put their savings into U.S. assets than in their own domestic assets. This will increase the demand for dollars.

The foreign _____ _____ is the rate at which one country's currency can be exchanged for another's.

The _____ for foreign exchange is a derived _____; it is derived from the demand for foreign goods and services (and financial assets). The _____ of foreign exchange is derived from foreign residents' demands for U.S. goods and services.

The demand curve of foreign exchange slopes _____, and the supply curve of foreign exchange slopes

_____. The equilibrium foreign exchange rate occurs at the intersection of the demand and supply curves for a currency.

A _____ in the demand for foreign goods will result in a shift in the _____ for foreign exchange, thereby changing the equilibrium foreign exchange rate. A shift in the supply of foreign currency will also cause a change in the equilibrium exchange rate.

The Gold Standard and the International Monetary Fund

The current system of more or less freely floating exchange rates is a relatively recent development. In the past, we have had periods of a gold standard, fixed exchange rates under the International Monetary Fund, and variants of the two.

The Gold Standard

Until the 1930s, many nations were on a gold standard. The value of their domestic currency was fixed, or *pegged*, in units of gold. Nations operating under this gold standard agreed to redeem their currencies for a fixed amount of gold at the request of any holder of that currency. Although gold was not necessarily the means of exchange for world trade, it was the unit to which all currencies under the gold standard were pegged. And because all currencies in the system were pegged to gold, exchange rates between those currencies were fixed. Indeed, the gold standard has been offered as the prototype of a fixed exchange rate system. The heyday of the gold standard was from about 1870 to 1914.

There was (and always is) a relationship between the balance of payments and changes in domestic money supplies throughout the world. Under a gold standard, the international financial market reached equilibrium through the effect of gold flows on each country's money supply. When the sum of a nation's current account balance and its capital account balance was negative, more gold would flow out than in. Because the domestic money supply was based on gold, an outflow of gold to foreign residents caused an automatic reduction in the domestic money supply. This caused several things to happen. Interest rates rose, thereby attracting foreign capital and pushing the sum of the current account balance and the capital account balance back toward zero. At the same time, the reduction in the money supply was equivalent to a restrictive monetary policy, which caused national output and prices to fall. Imports were discouraged and exports were encouraged, thereby again increasing net exports.

Two problems plagued the gold standard. One was that by fixing the value of its currency in relation to the amount of gold, a nation gave up control of its domestic monetary policy. Another was that the world's commerce was at the mercy of gold discoveries. Throughout history, each time new veins of gold were found, desired domestic expenditures on goods and services increased. If production of goods and services failed to increase proportionately, inflation resulted.

Bretton Woods and the International Monetary Fund

In 1944, as World War II was ending, representatives from the world's capitalist countries met in Bretton Woods, New Hampshire, to create a new international payment system to replace the gold standard, which had collapsed during the 1930s. The Bretton Woods Agreement Act was signed on July 31, 1945, by President Harry Truman. It created a new permanent institution, the International Monetary Fund (IMF). The IMF's task was to administer the agreement and to lend to member countries for which the sum of the current account balance and the capital account balance was negative, thereby helping them maintain an offsetting surplus in their official reserve transactions accounts. The arrangements thus provided are now called the old IMF system or the Bretton Woods system.

Member governments agreed to maintain the value of their currencies within 1 percent of the declared **par value**—the officially determined value. The United States, which owned most of the world's gold stock, was similarly obligated to maintain gold prices within a 1 percent margin of the official rate of $35 an ounce. Except for a transitional arrangement permitting a onetime adjustment of up to 10 percent in par value, members could alter exchange rates thereafter only with the approval of the IMF.

On August 15, 1971, President Richard Nixon suspended the convertibility of the dollar into gold. On December 18, 1971, the United States officially devalued the dollar—that is, lowered its official value—relative to the currencies of 14 major industrial nations. Finally, on March 16, 1973, the finance ministers of the European Economic Community (now the European Union) announced that they would let their currencies float against the dollar, something Japan had already begun doing with its yen. Since 1973, the United States and most other trading countries have had either freely floating exchange rates or managed ("dirty") floating exchange rates, in which their governments or central banks intervene from time to time to try to influence world market exchange rates.

Par value
The officially determined value of a currency.

Fixed versus Floating Exchange Rates

The United States went off the Bretton Woods system of fixed exchange rates in 1973. As Figure 34-7 indicates, many other nations of the world have been less willing to permit the values of their currencies to vary in the foreign exchange markets.

FIGURE 34-7

Current Foreign Exchange Rate Arrangements

Today, 19 percent of the member nations of the International Monetary Fund have an independent float, and 26 percent have a managed float exchange rate arrangement. Another 12 percent of all nations use the currencies of other nations instead of issuing their own currencies.

Source: International Monetary Fund.

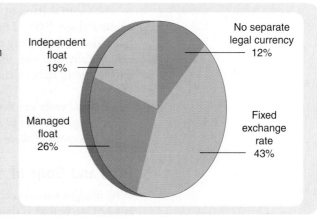

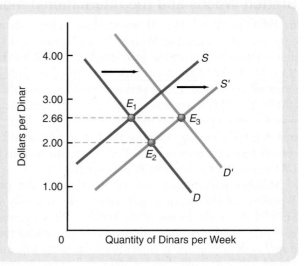

FIGURE 34-8

A Fixed Exchange Rate

This figure illustrates how the Central Bank of Bahrain could fix the dollar-dinar exchange rate in the face of an increase in the supply of dinars caused by a rise in the demand for U.S. goods by Bahraini residents. In the absence of any action by the Central Bank of Bahrain, the result would be a movement from point E_1 to point E_2. The dollar value of the dinar would fall from \$2.66 to \$2.00. The Central Bank of Bahrain can prevent this exchange rate change by purchasing dinars with dollars in the foreign exchange market, thereby raising the demand for dinars. At the new equilibrium point, E_3, the dinar's value remains at \$2.66.

Fixing the Exchange Rate

How did nations fix their exchange rates in years past? How do many countries accomplish this today? Figure 34-8 shows the market for dinars, the currency of Bahrain. At the initial equilibrium point E_1, U.S. residents had to give up \$2.66 to obtain 1 dinar. Suppose now that there is an increase in the supply of dinars for dollars, perhaps because Bahraini residents wish to buy more U.S. goods. Other things being equal, the result would be a movement to point E_2 in Figure 34-8. The dollar value of the dinar would fall to \$2.00.

To prevent a dinar depreciation from occurring, however, the Central Bank of Bahrain could increase the demand for dinars in the foreign exchange market by purchasing dinars with dollars. The Central Bank of Bahrain can do this using dollars that it has on hand as part of its *foreign exchange reserves*. All central banks hold reserves of foreign currencies. Because the U.S. dollar is a key international currency, the Central Bank of Bahrain and other central banks typically hold billions of dollars in reserve so that they can make transactions such as the one in this example. Note that a sufficiently large purchase of dinars could, as shown in Figure 34-8, cause the demand curve to shift rightward to achieve the new equilibrium point E_3, at which the dinar's value remains at \$2.66. Provided that it has enough dollar reserves on hand, the Central Bank of Bahrain could maintain—effectively fix—the exchange rate in the face of the rise in the supply of dinars.

The Central Bank of Bahrain has maintained the dollar-dinar exchange rate in this manner since 2001. This basic approach—varying the amount of the national currency demanded at any given exchange rate in foreign exchange markets when necessary—is also the way that *any* central bank seeks to keep its nation's currency value unchanged in light of changing market forces.

> *Central banks can keep exchange rates fixed as long as they have enough foreign exchange reserves to deal with potentially long-lasting changes in the demand for or supply of their nation's currency.*

Pros and Cons of a Fixed Exchange Rate

Why might a nation such as Bahrain wish to keep the value of its currency from fluctuating? One reason is that changes in the exchange rate can affect the market values of assets that are denominated in foreign currencies. This can increase the financial risks that a nation's residents face, thereby forcing them to incur costs to avoid these risks.

FOREIGN EXCHANGE RISK The possibility that variations in the market value of assets can take place due to changes in the value of a nation's currency is the **foreign exchange risk** that residents of a country face because their nation's currency value can vary. For instance, if companies in Bahrain had many loans denominated in dollars but earned nearly all their revenues in dinars from sales within Bahrain, a decline in the dollar value of the dinar would mean that Bahraini companies would have to allocate a larger portion of their earnings to make the same *dollar* loan payments as before. Thus, a fall in the dinar's value would increase the operating costs of these companies, thereby reducing their profitability and raising the likelihood of eventual bankruptcy.

Limiting foreign exchange risk is a classic rationale for adopting a fixed exchange rate. Nevertheless, a country's residents are not defenseless against foreign exchange risk. In what is known as a **hedge,** they can adopt strategies intended to offset the risk arising from exchange rate variations. For example, a company in Bahrain that has significant euro earnings from sales in Germany but sizable loans from U.S. investors could arrange to convert its euro earnings into dollars via special types of foreign exchange contracts called *currency swaps*. The Bahraini company could likewise avoid holdings of dinars and shield itself—*hedge*—against variations in the dinar's value.

Why might Bahrain and other oil-producing countries be rethinking their willingness to fix the values of their currencies relative to the U.S. dollar?

Foreign exchange risk
The possibility that changes in the value of a nation's currency will result in variations in the market value of assets.

Hedge
A financial strategy that reduces the chance of suffering losses arising from foreign exchange risk.

INTERNATIONAL EXAMPLE
Oil-Rich Middle Eastern Nations Rethink Their Dollar Ties

As the U.S. inflation rate approached 6 percent in early 2007, oil-producing Middle Eastern nations that had long fixed their currency values to the dollar began to reconsider. Tying the values of their currencies to a dollar that was losing its purchasing power was resulting in lower purchasing power for their own currencies. By the end of 2007, this problem had induced Syria and Kuwait to stop tying the values of their currencies to the dollar.

Then the U.S. inflation rate plunged. The U.S. economy experienced a brief spell of deflation before settling at an inflation rate below 1 percent. Nevertheless, many investors around the world worried that the Federal Reserve might eventually resort to more inflationary policies. The dramatic

increase in uncertainty about the U.S. dollar's future purchasing power resulting from swings in the actual and anticipated U.S. rates of inflation began to take their toll on Qatar and the United Arab Emirates. In 2009 the governments of these nations announced that they, too, were contemplating ending their practice of fixing their currency values in relation to the U.S. dollar.

FOR CRITICAL ANALYSIS
Why might the fact that the United States is the world's largest importer of oil help to explain why Middle Eastern nations have—at least until recently—tied the values of their currencies to the U.S. dollar?

THE EXCHANGE RATE AS A SHOCK ABSORBER If fixing the exchange rate limits foreign exchange risk, why do so many nations allow the exchange rates to float? The answer must be that there are potential drawbacks associated with fixing exchange rates. One is that exchange rate variations can actually perform a valuable service for a nation's economy. Consider a situation in which residents of a nation speak only their own nation's language. As a result, the country's residents are very *immobile*: They cannot trade their labor skills outside their own nation's borders.

Now think about what happens if this nation chooses to fix its exchange rate. Imagine a situation in which other countries begin to sell products that are close substitutes for the products its people specialize in producing, causing a sizable drop in worldwide demand for the nation's goods. If wages and prices do not instantly and completely adjust downward, the result will be a sharp decline in production of goods and services, a falloff in national income, and higher unemployment. Contrast this situation with one in which the exchange rate floats. In this case, a sizable decline in outside demand for the nation's products will cause it to experience a trade deficit, which will lead to a significant drop in the demand for that nation's currency. As a result, the nation's currency will experience a sizable depreciation, making the goods that the nation offers to sell abroad much less expensive in other countries. People abroad who continue to consume the nation's products will increase their purchases, and the nation's exports will increase. Its production will begin to recover somewhat, as will its residents' incomes. Unemployment will begin to fall.

This example illustrates how exchange rate variations can be beneficial, especially if a nation's residents are relatively immobile. It can be difficult, for example, for a Polish resident who has never studied Portuguese to move to Lisbon, even if she is highly qualified for available jobs there. If many residents of Poland face similar linguistic or cultural barriers, Poland could be better off with a floating exchange rate even if its residents must incur significant costs hedging against foreign exchange risk as a result.

Splitting the Difference: Dirty Floats and Target Zones

In recent years, national policymakers have tried to soften the choice between adopting a fixed exchange rate and allowing exchange rates full flexibility in the foreign exchange markets by "splitting the difference" between the two extremes.

Dirty float
Active management of a floating exchange rate on the part of a country's government, often in cooperation with other nations.

A DIRTY FLOAT One way to split the difference is to let exchange rates float most of the time but "manage" exchange rate movements part of the time. U.S. policymakers have occasionally engaged in what is called a **dirty float,** the active management of flexible exchange rates. The management of flexible exchange rates has usually come about through international policy cooperation.

Is it possible for nations to "manage" foreign exchange rates? Some economists do not think so. For example, economists Michael Bordo and Anna Schwartz studied the foreign exchange intervention actions coordinated by the Federal Reserve and the U.S. Treasury during the second half of the 1980s. Besides showing that such interventions were sporadic and variable, Bordo and Schwartz came to an even more compelling conclusion: Exchange rate interventions were trivial relative to the total trading of foreign exchange on a daily basis. For example, in April 1989, total foreign exchange trading amounted to $129 billion per day, yet the U.S. central bank purchased only $100 million in deutsche marks and yen during that entire month (and did so on a single day). For all of 1989, Fed purchases of marks and yen were only $17.7 billion, or the equivalent of less than 13 percent of the amount of an average *day's* trading in April of that year. Their conclusion is that foreign exchange market interventions by the U.S. central bank or the central banks of other nations do not influence exchange rates in the long run.

CRAWLING PEGS Another approach to splitting the difference between fixed and floating exchange rates is called a **crawling peg.** This is an automatically adjusting target for the value of a nation's currency. For instance, a central bank might announce that it wants the value of its currency relative to the U.S. dollar to decline at an annual rate of 5 percent, a rate of depreciation that it feels is consistent with long-run market forces. The central bank would then try to buy or sell foreign exchange reserves in sufficient quantities to be sure that the currency depreciation takes place gradually, thereby reducing the foreign exchange risk faced by the nation's residents. In this way, a crawling peg functions like a floating exchange rate in the sense that the exchange rate can change over time. But it is like a fixed exchange rate in the sense that the central bank always tries to keep the exchange rate close to a target value. In this way, a crawling peg has elements of both kinds of exchange rate systems.

Crawling peg
An exchange rate arrangement in which a country pegs the value of its currency to the exchange value of another nation's currency but allows the par value to change at regular intervals.

TARGET ZONES A third way to try to split the difference between fixed and floating exchange rates is to adopt an exchange rate **target zone.** Under this policy, a central bank announces that there are specific upper and lower *bands*, or limits, for permissible values for the exchange rate. Within those limits, which define the exchange rate target zone, the central bank permits the exchange rate to move flexibly. The central bank commits itself, however, to intervene in the foreign exchange markets to ensure that its nation's currency value will not rise above the upper band or fall below the lower band. For instance, if the exchange rate measured in units of foreign currency per unit of domestic currency approaches the upper band, the central bank must sell foreign exchange reserves in sufficient quantities to prevent additional depreciation of its nation's currency. If the exchange rate approaches the lower band, the central bank must purchase sufficient amounts of foreign exchange reserves to halt any further currency appreciation.

Target zone
A range of permitted exchange rate variations between upper and lower exchange rate bands that a central bank defends by selling or buying foreign exchange reserves.

In 1999, officials from the European Union attempted to get the U.S. and Japanese governments to agree to target zones for the exchange rate between the newly created euro, the dollar, and the yen. So far, however, no target zones have been created, and the euro has floated freely.

QUICK QUIZ   *See page 890 for the answers. Review concepts from this section in MyEconLab.*

The International Monetary Fund was developed after World War II as an institution to maintain _____ exchange rates in the world. Since 1973, however, _____ exchange rates have disappeared in most major trading countries. For these nations, exchange rates are largely determined by the forces of demand and supply in foreign exchange markets.

Many other nations, however, have tried to fix their exchange rates, with varying degrees of success. Although fixing the exchange rate helps protect a nation's residents from foreign exchange _____, this policy makes less mobile residents susceptible to greater volatility in income and employment.

Countries have experimented with exchange rate systems between the extremes of fixed and floating exchange rates. Under a _____ float, a central bank permits the value of its nation's currency to float in foreign exchange markets but intervenes from time to time to influence the exchange rate. Under a _____ peg, a central bank tries to push the value of its nation's currency in a desired direction. Pursuing a _____ _____ policy, a central bank aims to keep the exchange rate between upper and lower bands, intervening only when the exchange rate approaches either limit.

You Are There Why U.S. Entertainers Have Moved Their Acts Overseas

In recent years, Marc Geiger, senior vice president of the contemporary music division of the William Morris Agency, says that he has a single message for all of his U.S. clients. "I tell every one of our artists who is American to get out of here," Geiger says. Exchange rates, he says, "have caught up with the live music industry."

For instance, U.S. soft-pop crooner Lionel Richie discovered in May 2008 that a three-night concert stint in a typical European venue provided him with a net inflation-adjusted dollar profit $400,000 higher than a couple of years earlier. Inflation-adjusted ticket prices in euros had not changed, however, nor had the number of tickets sold at an average European venue. What had changed was the exchange rate. As a result of the dollar's depreciation in relation to the euro, the euros that Richie earned from each ticket sold for a European performance translated into dollar revenues at least 20 percent higher than two years before. Thus, Richie's profits from European concerts began to outpace his profits from performances in the United States, even after taking into account the higher costs he incurred for international concert tours. Not surprisingly, Richie responded by altering his schedules for 2009 and 2010,

adding dozens more European concerts but cutting dozens from his U.S. schedule.

Richie was not alone. Other U.S. entertainers, from hard rock and rap musicians to magicians and stand-up comics, have shifted their tour schedules in favor of European venues and away from the United States. Geiger and other agents suggest that the reallocation of concert tour slots from the United States to Europe will continue for the foreseeable future. U.S. entertainers will shift back toward more U.S. concerts, Geiger suggests, only when the dollar has recovered its value relative to the euro in the foreign exchange market.

CRITICAL ANALYSIS QUESTIONS

1. Would an increase or a decrease in the *supply* of euros in the foreign exchange market give U.S. entertainers an incentive to perform more U.S. concerts? Explain briefly.

2. Would an increase or a decrease in the *demand* for euros in the foreign exchange market give U.S. entertainers an incentive to perform more U.S. concerts? Explain briefly.

The Current Account Deficit for One Group of Nations Is the Current Account Surplus for Another

Issues and Applications

CONCEPTS APPLIED

- Current Account
- Balance of Payments
- Capital Account

As you have learned in this chapter, the United States has been experiencing a significant current account deficit in recent years. It is not the only developed nation with a deficit in the current account of its balance of payments. All told, the United States and other highly developed nations are experiencing a combined current account deficit of close to $1 trillion per year. Who is financing these current account deficits? The answer must be the so-called *emerging countries*—nations with previously less developed economies, such as China and India, that are now experiencing significant growth. Let's see why this is so and contemplate the implications.

Mirror Image Current Account Balances for Developed and Developing Countries

Figure 34-9 displays the combined current account balances of the world's most developed nations since 1996. Until 1997, developed nations were operating with a combined current account surplus, but then they fell into a deficit position that widened until the recent global economic downturn.

The figure also shows the combined current account balances of emerging countries. Until 1997, emerging countries experienced a combined current account deficit. Since then, they have operated with current account surpluses that have steadily increased in magnitude. The fact that emerging countries' combined current account surpluses have been nearly the mirror image of the deficits of developed nations is no accident. After all, in the long run, net imports of goods, services, and gifts from abroad by developed nations must correspond to net exports of goods, services, and gifts by the rest of the world—which means primarily emerging countries.

Implications for Capital Account Balances

Recall that because surplus and deficit items cancel out in the balance of payments, any nation's current account deficit will be associated with a capital account surplus. Hence, the recent combined current account deficit experienced by the world's developed nations closely

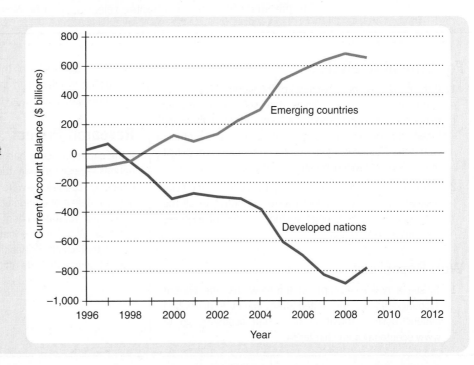

FIGURE 34-9

Combined Current Account Balances of Developed Nations and of Emerging Countries

Since 1997, developed nations have experienced higher combined current account deficits. During the same time, emerging nations have had increasing combined current account surpluses that have been nearly a mirror image of the developed nations' current account deficits.

Sources: International Monetary Fund; author's estimates.

corresponds to a combined capital account surplus. Conversely, the combined current account surpluses recently experienced by emerging countries imply a combined capital account deficit for these countries.

This means that residents of developed nations have been financing their imports and thus their current account deficits by obtaining funds from emerging countries. As funds have flowed out of emerging countries, their capital accounts have experienced deficits. As the funds have flowed into developed nations, their capital accounts have experienced surpluses. Effectively, emerging countries have provided developed nations with the funds required to buy the emerging countries' exports.

Two Contrasting Scenarios for the Future

Some observers look at Figure 34-9 on the previous page and see the potential for major balance of payments readjustments in the future. In their view, residents of emerging countries are likely to tire of financing the current account deficits of developed nations by purchasing the latter's stocks and bonds. Once this occurs, according to this view, residents of developed nations will no longer be able to finance their spending on goods and services imported from emerging countries. If this happens all at once, these observers worry, the world may experience significant difficulties: Residents of emerging countries will be unable to find buyers for their exports, and residents of developed nations will be unable to pay their debts.

Others examine Figure 34-9 and see only evidence of the gains from trade discussed in Chapter 33. In their view, emerging countries are willing to invest in developed nations because the latter offer high rates of return on investments. The emerging countries gain because residents of developed nations buy their exports. Residents of developed nations, in turn, expand their consumption of items imported from emerging countries and thereby gain from trade. From this perspective, the relationship shown in Figure 34-9 is a "win-win situation" for both sets of nations—and hence is likely to continue for years to come.

Test your understanding of this chapter by going online to **MyEconLab**.
In the Study Plan for this chapter, select Section N: News.

For Critical Analysis

1. If the current account balances of the world's least developed nations—those outside the sets of developed nations and emerging countries—were added to the combined current account surplus of emerging countries, would the result exactly mirror the current account deficit of the world's developed nations? Why or why not?

2. If combined capital account, current account, and official reserve transactions balances were computed for all the nations of the world, what should the sum of all three turn out to be? Explain.

Web Resources

1. To see a typical example of the view that the current account deficits of the United States and other developed nations pose a threat to the world economy, go to www.econtoday.com/chapter34.

2. For a discussion of the size of the U.S. current account deficit in relation to the current account deficits of other developed nations, go to www.econtoday.com/chapter34.

Research Project

If the capital account balances of the world's least developed nations—those outside the sets of developed nations and emerging countries—were added to the combined capital account deficit of emerging countries, would the result exactly mirror the capital account surplus of the world's developed nations? Why or why not? Explain your reasoning. (Hint: Recall that another financial account in every country's balance of payments is its official reserve transactions account.)

Here is what you should know after reading this chapter. **MyEconLab** will help you identify what you know, and where to go when you need to practice.

WHAT YOU SHOULD KNOW

WHERE TO GO TO PRACTICE

The Balance of Trade versus the Balance of Payments
The balance of trade is the difference between exports and imports of physical goods, or merchandise, during a given period. The balance of payments is a system of accounts for all transactions between a nation's residents and the residents of other countries of the world. In addition to exports and imports, therefore, the balance of payments includes cross-border exchanges of services and financial assets within a given time interval.

balance of trade, 864
balance of payments, 864
accounting identities, 864

- **MyEconLab** Study Plan 34.1
- Audio introduction to Chapter 34

The Key Accounts Within the Balance of Payments
There are three important accounts within the balance of payments. The current account measures net exchanges of goods and services, transfers, and income flows across a nation's borders. The capital account measures net flows of financial assets. The official reserve transactions account tabulates cross-border exchanges of financial assets involving the home nation's government and central bank as well as foreign governments and central banks. Because each international exchange generates both an inflow and an outflow, the sum of the balances on all three accounts must equal zero.

current account, 866
capital account, 867
special drawing rights (SDRs), 868
International Monetary Fund, 868

KEY FIGURE
Figure 34-1, 869

- **MyEconLab** Study Plan 34.1
- Animated Figure 34-1

Exchange Rate Determination in the Market for Foreign Exchange From the perspective of the United States, the demand for a nation's currency by U.S. residents is derived largely from the demand for imports from that nation. Likewise, the supply of a nation's currency is derived mainly from the supply of U.S. exports to that country. The equilibrium exchange rate is the rate of exchange between the dollar and the other nation's currency at which the quantity of the currency demanded is equal to the quantity supplied.

foreign exchange market, 871
exchange rate, 871
flexible exchange rates, 871
appreciation, 872
depreciation, 872

KEY FIGURES
Figure 34-2, 873
Figure 34-3, 875
Figure 34-4, 875
Figure 34-5, 876

- **MyEconLab** Study Plan 34.2
- Animated Figures 34-2, 34-3, 34-4, 34-5
- Video: Market Determinants of Foreign Exchange Rates

Factors That Can Induce Changes in Equilibrium Exchange Rates The equilibrium exchange rate changes in response to changes in the demand for or supply of another nation's currency. Changes in desired flows of exports or imports, real interest rates, tastes and preferences of consumers, and perceptions of economic stability are key factors that can affect the positions of the demand and supply curves in foreign exchange markets. Thus, changes in these factors can induce variations in equilibrium exchange rates.

KEY FIGURE
Figure 34-6, 877

- **MyEconLab** Study Plan 34.2
- Animated Figure 34-6
- Video: Market Determinants of Foreign Exchange Rates

(continued)

 *(continued)*

WHAT YOU SHOULD KNOW		WHERE TO GO TO PRACTICE
How Policymakers Can Attempt to Keep Exchange Rates Fixed If the current price of the home currency in terms of another nation's currency starts to fall below the level where the home country wants it to remain, the home country's central bank can use reserves of the other nation's currency to purchase the home currency in foreign exchange markets. This raises the demand for the home currency and thereby pushes up the currency's value in terms of the other nation's currency. In this way, the home country can keep the exchange rate fixed at a desired value, as long as it has sufficient reserves of the other currency to use for this purpose.	par value, 879 foreign exchange risk, 881 hedge, 881 **KEY FIGURE** Figure 34-8, 880	• **MyEconLab** Study Plans 34.3, 34.4 • Animated Figure 34-8 • Video: Pros and Cons of a Fixed Exchange Rate
Alternative Approaches to Limiting Exchange Rate Variability Today, many nations permit their exchange rates to vary in foreign exchange markets. Others pursue policies that limit the variability of exchange rates. Some engage in a dirty float, in which they manage exchange rates, often in cooperation with other nations. Some establish crawling pegs, in which the target value of the exchange rate is adjusted automatically over time. And some establish target zones, with upper and lower limits on the extent to which exchange rates are allowed to vary.	dirty float, 882 crawling peg, 883 target zone, 883	• **MyEconLab** Study Plan 34.4

Log in to MyEconLab, take a chapter test, and get a personalized Study Plan that tells you which concepts you understand and which ones you need to review. From there, MyEconLab will give you further practice, tutorials, animations, videos, and guided solutions.
Log in to www.myeconlab.com

PROBLEMS

All problems are assignable in myeconlab *. Answers to the odd-numbered problems appear at the back of the book.*

34-1. Over the course of a year, a nation tracked its foreign transactions and arrived at the following amounts:

Merchandise exports	500
Service exports	75
Net unilateral transfers	10
Domestic assets abroad (capital outflows)	−200
Foreign assets at home (capital inflows)	300
Changes in official reserves	−35
Merchandise imports	600
Service imports	50

What are this nation's balance of trade, current account balance, and capital account balance?

34-2. Identify whether each of the following items creates a surplus item or a deficit item in the current account of the U.S. balance of payments.

   a. A Central European company sells products to a U.S. hobby-store chain.

   b. Japanese residents pay a U.S. travel company to arrange hotel stays, ground transportation, and tours of various U.S. cities, including New York, Chicago, and Orlando.

    c. A Mexican company pays a U.S. accounting firm to audit its income statements.

    d. U.S. churches and mosques send relief aid to Pakistan following a major earthquake in that nation.

    e. A U.S. microprocessor manufacturer purchases raw materials from a Canadian firm.

34-3. Explain how the following events would affect the market for the Mexican peso, assuming a floating exchange rate.

    a. Improvements in Mexican production technology yield superior guitars, and many musicians around the world buy these guitars.

    b. Perceptions of political instability surrounding regular elections in Mexico make international investors nervous about future business prospects in Mexico.

34-4. Explain how the following events would affect the market for South Africa's currency, the rand, assuming a floating exchange rate.

    a. A rise in U.S. inflation causes many U.S. residents to seek to buy gold, which is a major South African export good, as a hedge against inflation.

    b. Major discoveries of the highest-quality diamonds ever found occur in Russia and Central Asia, causing a significant decline in purchases of South African diamonds.

34-5. Suppose that the following two events take place in the market for China's currency, the yuan: U.S. parents are more willing than before to buy action figures and other Chinese toy exports, and China's government tightens restrictions on the amount of U.S. dollar–denominated financial assets that Chinese residents may legally purchase. What happens to the dollar price of the yuan? Does the yuan appreciate or depreciate relative to the dollar?

34-6. On Wednesday, the exchange rate between the Japanese yen and the U.S. dollar was $0.0125 per yen. On Thursday, it was $0.0110. Did the dollar appreciate or depreciate against the yen? By how much, expressed as a percentage change?

34-7. On Wednesday, the exchange rate between the euro and the U.S. dollar was $1.45 per euro, and the exchange rate between the Canadian dollar and the U.S. dollar was U.S. $0.94 per Canadian dollar. What is the exchange rate between the Canadian dollar and the euro?

34-8. Suppose that signs of an improvement in the Japanese economy lead international investors to resume lending to the Japanese government and businesses. Policymakers, however, are worried about how this will influence the yen. How would this event affect the market for the yen? How should the central bank, the Bank of Japan, respond to this event if it wants to keep the value of the yen unchanged?

34-9. Briefly explain the differences between a flexible exchange rate system, a fixed exchange rate system, a dirty float, and the use of target zones.

34-10. Suppose that under a gold standard, the U.S. dollar is pegged to gold at a rate of $35 per ounce and the pound sterling is pegged to gold at a rate of £17.50 per ounce. Explain how the gold standard constitutes an exchange rate arrangement between the dollar and the pound. What is the exchange rate between the U.S. dollar and the pound sterling?

34-11. Suppose that under the Bretton Woods system, the dollar is pegged to gold at a rate of $35 per ounce and the pound sterling is pegged to the dollar at a rate of $2 = £1. If the dollar is devalued against gold and the pegged rate is changed to $40 per ounce, what does this imply for the exchange value of the pound in terms of dollars?

34-12. Suppose that the People's Bank of China wishes to peg the rate of exchange of its currency, the yuan, in terms of the U.S. dollar. In each of the following situations, should it add to or subtract from its dollar foreign exchange reserves? Why?

    a. U.S. parents worrying about safety begin buying fewer Chinese-made toys for their children.

    b. U.S. interest rates rise relative to interest rates in China, so Chinese residents seek to purchase additional U.S. financial assets.

    c. Chinese furniture manufacturers produce high-quality early American furniture and successfully export large quantities of the furniture to the United States.

ECONOMICS ON THE NET

Daily Exchange Rates It is an easy matter to keep up with changes in exchange rates every day using the Web site of the Federal Reserve Bank of New York. In this application, you will learn how hard it is to predict exchange rate movements, and you will get some practice thinking about what factors can cause exchange rates to change.

Title: The Federal Reserve Bank of New York: Foreign Exchange 12 PM Rates

Navigation: Go to **www.econtoday.com/chapter34** to visit the Federal Reserve Bank of New York's Statistics home page. Click on *Foreign Exchange 12 PM Rates*.

Application Answer the following questions.

1. For each currency listed, how many dollars does it take to purchase a unit of the currency in the spot foreign exchange market?

2. For each day during a given week (or month), choose a currency from those listed and keep track of its value relative to the dollar. Based on your tabulations, try to predict the value of the currency at the end of the week *following* your data collections. Use any information you may have, or just do your best without any additional information. How far off did your prediction turn out to be?

For Group Study and Analysis Each day, you can also click on a report titled "Foreign Exchange 10 AM Rates," which shows exchange rates for a subset of countries listed in the noon report. Assign each country in the 10 AM report to a group. Ask the group to determine whether the currency's value appreciated or depreciated relative to the dollar between 10 AM and noon. In addition, ask each group to discuss what kinds of demand or supply shifts could have caused the change that occurred during this interval.

ANSWERS TO QUICK QUIZZES

p. 870: (i) balance . . . payments; (ii) physical; (iii) current . . . current; (iv) Unilateral transfers; (v) current; (vi) capital . . . capital; (vii) official reserve; (viii) inflation . . . political

p. 878: (i) exchange rate; (ii) demand . . . demand . . . supply; (iii) downward . . . upward; (iv) shift . . . demand

p. 883: (i) fixed . . . fixed; (ii) risk; (iii) dirty . . . crawling . . . target zone

Answers to Odd-Numbered Problems

Chapter 1

1-1. Economics is the study of how individuals allocate limited resources to satisfy unlimited wants.

    a. Among the factors that a rational, self-interested student will take into account are her income, the price of the textbook, her anticipation of how much she is likely to study the textbook, and how much studying the book is likely to affect her grade.

    b. A rational, self-interested government official will, for example, recognize that higher taxes will raise more funds for mass transit while making more voters, who have limited resources, willing to elect other officials.

    c. A municipality's rational, self-interested government will, for instance, take into account that higher hotel taxes will produce more funds if as many visitors continue staying at hotels, but that the higher taxes will also discourage some visitors from spending nights at hotels.

1-3. Because wants are unlimited, the phrase applies to very high-income households as well as low- and middle-income households. Consider, for instance, a household with a low income and unlimited wants at the beginning of the year. The household's wants will still remain unlimited if it becomes a high-income household later in the year.

1-5. Sally is displaying rational behavior if all of these activities are in her self-interest. For example, Sally likely derives intrinsic benefit from volunteer and extracurricular activities and may believe that these activities, along with good grades, improve her prospects of finding a job after she completes her studies. Hence, these activities are in her self-interest even though they reduce some available study time.

1-7. The rationality assumption states that people do not intentionally make choices that leave them worse off. The bounded rationality hypothesis suggests that people are *almost*, but not completely, rational.

1-9. Suppose that there is a change in the environment that a person faces, and the person adjusts to this change as predicted by the rationality assumption. If the new environment becomes predictable, then the individual who actually behaves as predicted by the traditional rationality assumption may settle into behavior that *appears* to involve repetitive applications of a rule of thumb.

1-11. a. The model using prices from the Iowa Electronic Market is more firmly based on the rationality assumption, because people who trade assets on this exchange based on poor forecasts actually experience losses. This gives them a strong incentive to make the best possible forecasts. Unpaid respondents to opinion polls have less incentive to give truthful answers about whether and how they will vote.

    b. An economist would develop a means of evaluating whether prices in the Iowa Electronic Market or results of opinion polls did a better job of matching actual electoral outcomes.

1-13. a. Positive
    b. Normative
    c. Normative
    d. Positive

APPENDIX A

A-1. a. Independent: price of a notebook; Dependent: quantity of notebooks
    b. Independent: work-study hours; Dependent: credit hours
    c. Independent: hours of study; Dependent: economics grade

A-3. a. above x axis; left of y axis
    b. below x axis, right of y axis
    c. on x axis; to right of y axis

A-5.

y	x
−20	−4
−10	−2
0	0
10	2
20	4

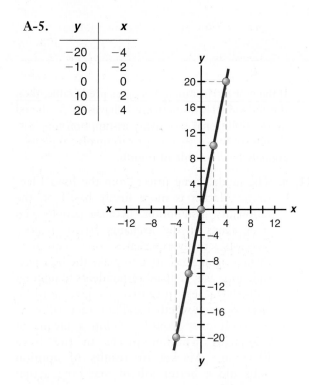

A-7. Each one-unit increase in x yields a 5-unit increase in y, so the slope given by the change in y corresponding to the change in x is equal to 5.

Chapter 2

2-1. The opportunity cost of attending a class at 11:00 A.M. is the next-best use of that hour of the day. Likewise, the opportunity cost of attending an 8:00 A.M. class is the next-best use of that particular hour of the day. If you are an early riser, it is arguable that the opportunity cost of the 8:00 A.M. hour is lower, because you will already be up at that time but have fewer choices compared with the 11:00 A.M. hour when shops, recreation centers, and the like are open. If you are a late riser, it may be that the opportunity cost of the 8:00 A.M. hour is higher, because you place a relatively high value on an additional hour of sleep in the morning.

2-3. The bank apparently determined that the net gain that it anticipated receiving from trying to sell the house to someone else, taking into account the opportunity cost of resources that the bank would have had to devote to renovating the house, was less than $10.

2-5. If the student allocates additional study time to economics in order to increase her score from 90

to 100, her biology score declines from 50 to 40, so the opportunity cost of earning 10 additional points in economics is 10 fewer points in biology.

2-7.

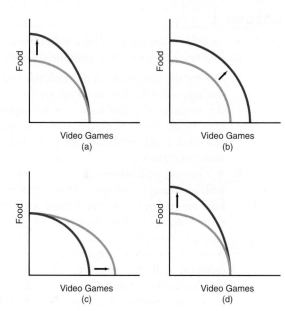

2-9. D

2-11. a. If the nation's residents increase production of consumption goods from 0 units to 10 units, the opportunity cost is 3 units of human capital forgone. If the nation's residents increase production of consumption goods from 0 units to 60 units, the opportunity cost is 100 units of human capital.

b. Yes, because successive 10-unit increases in production of consumption goods generate larger sacrifices of human capital, equal to 3, 7, 15, 20, 25, and 30.

2-13. Because it takes you less time to do laundry, you have an absolute advantage in laundry. Neither you nor your roommate has an absolute advantage in meal preparation. You require 2 hours to fold a basket of laundry, so your opportunity cost of folding a basket of laundry is 2 meals. Your roommate's opportunity cost of folding a basket of laundry is 3 meals. Hence, you have a comparative advantage in laundry, and your roommate has a comparative advantage in meal preparation.

2-15. It may be that the professor is very proficient at doing yard work relative to teaching and research activities, so in fact the professor may have a comparative advantage in doing yard work.

Chapter 3

3-1. The equilibrium price is $21 per DVD, and the equilibrium quantity is 80 million DVDs. At a price of $20 per DVD, the quantity of DVDs demanded is 90 million, and the quantity of DVDs supplied is 60 million. Hence, there is a shortage of 30 million DVDs at a price of $20 per DVD.

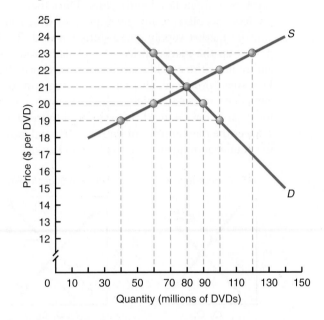

3-3. a. DSL and cable Internet access services are substitutes, so a reduction in the price of cable Internet access services causes a decrease in the demand for DSL high-speed Internet access services.

b. A decrease in the price of DSL Internet access services generates an increase in the quantity of these services demanded.

c. DSL high-speed Internet access services are a normal good, so a fall in the incomes of consumers reduces the demand for these services.

d. If consumers expect that the price of DSL high-speed Internet services will fall in the future, then the demand for these services will tend to decrease today.

3-5. a. Complement: eggs; Substitute: sausage

b. Complement: tennis balls; Substitute: racquet-ball racquets

c. Complement: cream; Substitute: tea

d. Complement: gasoline; Substitute: city bus

3-7. a. At the $1,000 rental rate, the quantity of one-bedroom apartments supplied is 8,500 per month, but the quantity demanded is only 7,000 per month. Thus, there is an excess quantity of one-bedroom apartments supplied equal to 1,500 apartments per month.

b. To induce consumers to lease unrented one-bedroom apartments, some landlords will reduce their rental rates. As they do so, the quantity demanded will increase. In addition, some landlords will choose not to offer apartments for rent at lower rates, and the quantity supplied will decrease. At the equilibrium rental rate of $800 per month, there will be no excess quantity supplied.

c. At the $600 rental rate, the quantity of one-bedroom apartments demanded is 8,000 per month, but the quantity supplied is only 6,500 per month. Thus, there is an excess quantity of one-bedroom apartments demanded equal to 1,500 apartments per month.

d. To induce landlords to make more one-bedroom apartments available for rent, some consumers will offer to pay higher rental rates. As they do so, the quantity supplied will increase. In addition, some consumers will choose not to try to rent apartments at higher rates, and the quantity demanded will decrease. At the equilibrium rental rate of $800 per month, there will be no excess quantity demanded.

3-9. a. Because memory chips are an input in the production of laptop computers, a decrease in the price of memory chips causes an increase in the supply of laptop computers. The market supply curve shifts to the right, which causes the market price of laptop computers to fall and the equilibrium quantity of laptop computers to increase.

b. Machinery used to produce laptop computers is an input in the production of these devices, so an increase in the price of machinery generates a decrease in the supply of laptop computers. The market supply curve shifts to the left, which causes the market price of laptop computers to rise and the equilibrium quantity of laptop computers to decrease.

c. An increase in the number of manufacturers of laptop computers causes an increase in the supply of laptop computers. The market supply curve shifts rightward. The market price of laptop computers declines, and the equilibrium quantity of laptop computers increases.

d. The demand curve for laptop computers shifts to the left along the supply curve, so there is a decrease in the quantity supplied. The market price falls, and the equilibrium quantity declines.

3-11. The decline in the price of palladium, a substitute for platinum, will cause a decrease in the demand for platinum, so the platinum demand curve will shift leftward. Both the market clearing price and the equilibrium quantity of platinum will decrease.

3-13. Because processor chips are an input in the production of personal computers, a decrease in the price of processor chips generates an increase in the supply of personal computers. The market price of personal computers will decrease, and the equilibrium quantity will increase.

Chapter 4

4-1. The ability to produce music CDs at lower cost and the entry of additional producers shift the supply curve rightward, from S_1 to S_2. At the same time, reduced prices of substitute goods result in a leftward shift in the demand for music CDs, from D_1 to D_2. Consequently, the equilibrium price of music CDs declines, from P_1 to P_2. The equilibrium quantity may rise, fall, or, as shown in the diagram, remain unchanged.

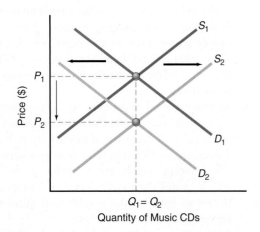

Quantity of Music CDs

4-3. The market rental rate is $700 per apartment, and the equilibrium quantity of apartments rented to tenants is 2,000. At a ceiling price of $650 per month, the number of apartments students desire to rent increases to 2,500. At the ceiling price, the number of apartments that owners are willing to supply decreases to 1,800 apartments. Thus, there is a shortage of 700 apartments at the ceiling price, and only 1,800 are rented at the ceiling price.

4-5. At the above-market price of sugar in the U.S. sugar market, U.S. chocolate manufacturers that use sugar as an input face higher costs. Thus, they supply less chocolate at any given price of chocolate, and the market supply curve shifts leftward. This pushes up the market price of chocolate products and reduces the equilibrium quantity of chocolate. U.S. sugar producers also sell surplus sugar in foreign sugar markets, which causes the supply curve for sugar in foreign markets to shift rightward. This reduces the market price of foreign sugar and raises the equilibrium quantity in the foreign market.

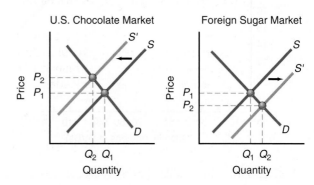

4-7. The market price is $400, and the equilibrium quantity of seats is 1,600. If airlines cannot sell tickets to more than 1,200 passengers, then passengers are willing to pay $600 per seat. Normally, airlines would be willing to sell each ticket for $200, but they will be able to charge a price as high as $600 for each of the 1,200 tickets they sell. Hence, the quantity of tickets sold declines from 1,600, and the price of a ticket rises from $400 to as high as $600.

4-9. a. Consumers buy 10 billion kilograms at the support price of $0.20 per kilogram and hence spend $2 billion on wheat.

b. The amount of surplus wheat at the support price is 8 billion kilograms, so at the $0.20-per-kilogram support price, the government must spend $1.6 billion to purchase this surplus wheat.

c. Pakistani wheat farmers receive a total of $3.6 billion for the wheat they produce at the support price.

4-11. a. At the present minimum wage of $9 per hour, the quantity of labor supplied is 102,000 workers, and the quantity of labor demanded by firms is 98,000. There is an excess quantity supplied of 4,000 workers, which is the number of people who are unemployed.

b. At a minimum wage of $6 per hour, there would be nothing to prevent market forces from pushing the wage rate to the market clearing level of $8 per hour. This $8-per-hour wage rate would exceed the legal minimum and hence would prevail. There would be no unemployed workers.

c. At a $10-per-hour minimum wage, the quantity of labor supplied would increase to 106,000 workers, and the quantity of labor demanded would decline to 96,000. There would be an excess quantity of labor supplied equal to 10,000 workers, which would then be the number of people unemployed.

4-13. a. The rise in the number of wheat producers causes the market supply curve to shift rightward, so more wheat is supplied at the support price.

b. The quantity of wheat demanded at the same support price is unchanged.

c. Because quantity demanded is unchanged while quantity supplied has increased, the amount of surplus wheat that the government must purchase has risen.

Chapter 5

5-1. In the absence of laws forbidding cigar smoking in public places, people who are bothered by the odor of cigar smoke will experience costs not borne by cigar producers. Because the supply of cigars will not reflect these costs, from society's perspective the market cigar supply curve will be in a position too far to the right. The market price of cigars will be too low, and too many cigars will be produced and consumed.

5-3. Imposing the tax on pesticides causes an increase in the price of pesticides, which are an input in the production of oranges. Hence, the supply curve in the orange market shifts leftward. The market price of oranges increases, and the equilibrium quantity of oranges declines. Hence, orange consumers indirectly help to pay for dealing with the spillover costs of pesticide production by paying more for oranges.

5-5. a. As shown in the figure below, if the social benefits associated with bus ridership were taken into account, the demand schedule would be D' instead of D, and the market price would be higher. The equilibrium quantity of bus rides would be higher.

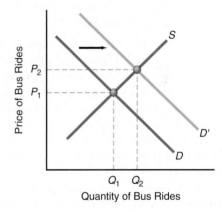

b. The government could pay commuters a subsidy to ride the bus, thereby shifting the demand curve outward and to the right. This would increase the market price and equilibrium number of bus rides.

5-7. At present, the equilibrium quantity of residences with Internet access is 2 million. To take into account the external benefit of Internet access and boost the quantity of residences with access to 3 million, the demand curve would have to shift upward by $20 per month at any given quantity, to D_2 from the current position D_1. Thus, the government would have to offer a $20-per-month subsidy to raise the quantity of residences with Internet access to 3 million.

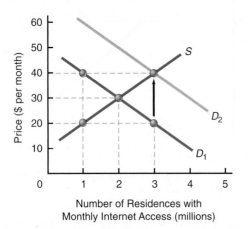

Number of Residences with Monthly Internet Access (millions)

5-9. The problem is that although most people around the lighthouse will benefit from its presence, there is no incentive for people to voluntarily contribute if they believe that others ultimately will pay for it. That is, the city is likely to face a free-rider problem in its efforts to raise its share of the funds required for the lighthouse.

5-11. No, the outcome will be different. If the government had simply provided grants to attend private schools at the current market tuition rate, parents and students receiving the grants would have paid a price equal to the market valuation of the last unit of educational services provided. Granting a subsidy to private schools allows the private schools to charge parents and students a price less than the market price. Private schools thereby will receive a higher-than-market price for the last unit of educational services they provide. Consequently, they will provide a quantity of educational services in excess of the market equilibrium quantity. At this quantity, parents and students place a lower value on the services than the price received by the private schools.

5-13. **a.** $40 million
b. The effective price of a DVD drive to consumers will be lower after the government pays the subsidy, so people will purchase a larger quantity.
c. $60 million
d. $90 million

5-15. **a.** $60 − $50 = $10
b. Expenditures after the program expansion are $2.4 million. Before the program expansion, expenditures were $1 million. Hence, the increase in expenditures is $1.4 million.
c. At a per-unit subsidy of $50, the share of the per-unit $60 price paid by the government is 5/6, or 83.3 percent. Hence, this is the government's share of total expenditures on the 40,000 devices that consumers purchase.

Chapter 6

6-1. **a.** The average tax rate is the total tax of $40 divided by the $200 in income: $40/$200 = 0.2, or 20 percent.
b. The marginal tax rate for the last hour of work is the change in taxes, $3, divided by the change in income, $8: $3/$8 = 0.375, or 37.5 percent.

6-3. 2001: $300 million; 2003: $350 million; 2005: $400 million; 2007: $400 million; 2009: $420 million

6-5. During 2008, the income tax base was an amount of income equal to $20 million/0.05 = $400 million. During 2009, the income tax base was equal to $19.2 million/0.06 = $320 million. Although various factors could have contributed to the fall in taxable income, dynamic tax analysis suggests that the higher income tax rate induced people to reduce their reported income. For instance, some people might have earned less income subject to city income taxes, and others might have even moved outside the city to avoid paying the higher income tax rate.

6-7. **a.** The supply of tickets for flights into and out of London shifts upward by $154. The equilibrium quantity of flights in and out of London declines. The market clearing price of London airline tickets rises by an amount less than the tax.

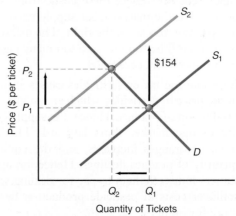

Quantity of Tickets

b. Tickets for flights into and out of London are substitutes for tickets for flights into and out of nearby cities. Thus, the demand for tickets for flights into and out of these cities will increase. This will cause an increase in the equilibrium quantities of these tickets and an increase in the market clearing prices.

6-9. As shown in the diagram, if the supply and demand curves have their normal shapes, then the $2-per-month tax on DSL Internet access services shifts the market supply curve upward by $2. The equilibrium quantity of DSL access services produced and consumed declines. In addition, the monthly market price of DSL access increases by an amount less than $2 per month. Consequently, consumers and producers share in paying the tax on each unit.

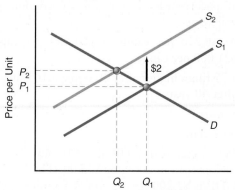

Quantity of DSL Access Services

6-11. If the market price of DSL access for businesses does not change, then as shown in the diagram, over the relevant range the demand for Internet access services by businesses is horizontal. The quantity of services demanded by businesses is very highly responsive to the tax, so DSL access providers must bear the tax in the form of higher costs. Providers of DSL access services pay all of the tax.

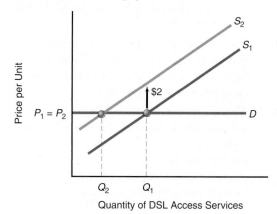

Quantity of DSL Access Services

6-13. a. 50 percent
b. −20 percent

Chapter 7

7-1. a. Multiplying the fraction of people who participate in the labor force, 0.7, times the adult, noninstitutionalized, nonmilitary population of 200.0 million yields a labor force of 140.0 million.
b. Subtracting the 7.5 million unemployed from the labor force of 140.0 million yields 132.5 million people who are employed.
c. Dividing the 7.5 million unemployed by the 140.0 million in the labor force and multiplying by 100 yields an unemployment rate of about 5.36 percent.

7-3. a. The labor force equals the number employed plus the number unemployed, or 156 million + 8 million = 164 million. In percentage terms, therefore, the unemployment rate is 100 times 8 million/164 million, or 4.9 percent.
b. These 60 million people are not in the labor force. The labor force participation rate is, in percentage terms, 100 times 164 million/224 million, or 73.2 percent.

7-5. a. Four of the 100 people are always continuously unemployed because they are between jobs, so the frictional unemployment rate is $(4/100) \times 100 = 4$ percent.
b. Three of the 100 people are always unemployed as a result of government regulations, so the structural unemployment rate is $(3/100) \times 100 = 3$ percent.
c. The unemployment rate is the sum of the frictional and structural rates of unemployment, or 7 percent.

7-7. The overall unemployment rate is 8 percent, and the natural rate of unemployment is 5 percent.

7-9. a. 2010
b. 10 percent
c. 10 percent
d. $1,800 in 2009; $3,000 in 2013

7-11. The expected rate of inflation is equal to $100 \times [(99 - 90)/90] = 10$ percent. Hence, the real interest rate equals the difference between the 12 percent nominal interest rate and the 10 percent anticipated inflation rate, or 2 percent.

7-13. a. The homeowner gains; the savings bank loses.
  b. The tenants gain; the landlord loses.
  c. The auto buyer gains; the bank loses.
  d. The employer gains; the pensioner loses.

Chapter 8

8-1. a. When Juanita does all the work herself, only purchases of the materials in markets (magazines, texturing materials, paint brushes, and paints), which total to $280 per year, count in GDP.
  b. She must pay the market price of $200 for the texturing, so her contribution to annual GDP from this project, including the materials, is $480.
  c. Because Juanita now pays for the entire project via market transactions, her total contribution to GDP equals the sum of the $280 for material purchases from part (a), $200 for the texturing from part (b), and $350 for the painting, or $830 per year.

8-3. a. GDP = $16.6 trillion; NDP = $15.3 trillion; NI = $14.5 trillion.
  b. GDP in 2013 will equal $15.5 trillion.

8-5. a. Gross domestic income = $14.6 trillion; GDP = $14.6 trillion.
  b. Gross private domestic investment = $2.0 trillion.
  c. Personal income = $12.0 trillion; personal disposable income = $10.3 trillion.

8-7. a. Measured GDP declines.
  b. Measured GDP increases.
  c. Measured GDP does not change (the firearms are not newly produced).

8-9. a. The chip is an intermediate good, so its purchase in June is not included in GDP; only the final sale in November is included.
  b. This is a final sale of a good that is included in GDP for the year.
  c. This is a final sale of a service that is included in GDP for the year.

8-11. a. Nominal GDP for 2009 is $2,300; for 2013, nominal GDP is $2,832.
  b. Real GDP for 2009 is $2,300; for 2013, real GDP is $2,229.

8-13. The price index is (2012 nominal GDP/2012 real GDP) × 100 = ($88,000/$136,000) × 100 = 64.7.

8-15. The $1 billion expended to pay for employees and equipment and the additional $1 billion paid to clean up the oil spill would be included in GDP, for a total of $2 billion added to GDP in 2013. The rise in oil reserves increases the stock of wealth but is not included in the current flow of newly produced goods and services. In addition, the welfare loss relating to the deaths of wildlife is also not measured in the marketplace and therefore is not included in GDP.

Chapter 9

9-1. a. Y
  b. X

9-3. The nation will maintain its stock of capital goods at its current level, so its rate of economic growth will be zero.

9-5. A: $8,250 per capita; B: $4,500 per capita; C: $21,000 per capita

9-7. 1.77 times higher after 20 years; 3.16 times higher after 40 years

9-9. 5 years

9-11. 4 percent

9-13. Per capita real GDP in 2010 was 10 percent higher than in 2009, or $2,200. The level of real GDP is $2,200 per person × 5 million people = $11 billion.

Chapter 10

10-1. The amount of unemployment would be the sum of frictional, structural, and seasonal unemployment.

10-3. The real value of the new full-employment level of nominal GDP is ($17.7 trillion/1.15) = $15.39 trillion, so the long-run aggregate supply curve has shifted rightward by $2.35 trillion, in base-year dollars.

10-5. This change implies a rightward shift of the long-run aggregate supply curve along the unchanged aggregate demand curve, so the long-run equilibrium price level will decline.

10-7. There are three effects. First, there is a real-balance effect, because the rise in the price level reduces real money balances, inducing people to cut back on their spending. In addition, there is an interest rate effect as a higher price level pushes up interest rates, thereby reducing the attractiveness of purchases of autos, houses, and plants and equipment. Finally, there is an open-economy effect as home residents respond to the higher price level by reducing purchases of domestically produced goods in favor of foreign-produced goods, while foreign residents cut back on their purchases of home-produced goods. All three effects entail a reduction in purchases of goods and services, so the aggregate demand curve slopes downward.

10-9. **a.** At the price level P_2 above the equilibrium price level P_1, the total quantity of real goods and services that people plan to consume is less than the total quantity that is consistent with firms' production plans. One reason is that at the higher-than-equilibrium price level, real money balances are lower, which reduces real wealth and induces lower planned consumption. Another is that interest rates are higher at the higher-than-equilibrium price level, which generates a cutback in consumption spending. Finally, at the higher-than-equilibrium price level P_2, people tend to cut back on purchasing domestic goods in favor of foreign-produced goods, and foreign residents reduce purchases of domestic goods. As unsold inventories of output accumulate, the price level drops toward the equilibrium price level P_1, which ultimately causes planned consumption to rise toward equality with total production.

b. At the price level P_3 below the equilibrium price level P_1, the total quantity of real goods and services that people plan to consume exceeds the total quantity that is consistent with firms' production plans. One reason is that at the lower-than-equilibrium price level, real money balances are higher, which raises real wealth and induces higher planned consumption. Another is that interest rates are lower at the lower-than-equilibrium price level, which generates an increase in consumption spending. Finally, at the lower-than-equilibrium price level P_3, people tend to raise their purchases of domestic goods and cut back on buying foreign-produced goods, and foreign residents increase purchases of domestic goods. As inventories of output are depleted, the price level begins to rise toward the equilibrium price level P_1, which ultimately causes planned consumption to fall toward equality with total production.

10-11. **a.** When the price level falls with deflation, there is a movement downward along the *AD* curve.

b. The decline in foreign real GDP levels reduces incomes of foreign residents, who cut back on their spending on domestic exports. Thus, the domestic *AD* curve shifts leftward.

c. The fall in the foreign exchange value of the nation's currency makes domestic-produced goods and services less expensive to foreign residents, who increase their spending on domestic exports. Thus, the domestic *AD* curve shifts rightward.

d. An increase in the price level causes a movement upward along the *AD* curve.

10-13. **a.** The aggregate demand curve shifts leftward along the long-run aggregate supply curve; the equilibrium price level falls, and equilibrium real GDP remains unchanged.

b. The aggregate demand curve shifts rightward along the long-run aggregate supply curve; the equilibrium price level rises, and equilibrium real GDP remains unchanged.

c. The long-run aggregate supply curve shifts rightward along the aggregate demand curve; the equilibrium price level falls, and equilibrium real GDP increases.

d. The aggregate demand curve shifts rightward along the long-run aggregate supply curve; the equilibrium price level rises, and equilibrium real GDP remains unchanged.

10-15. **a.** The income flows are mainly influencing relatives' consumption, so the main effect is on the aggregate demand curve.

b. A rise in aggregate demand will lead to an increase in the equilibrium price level.

Chapter 11

11-1. **a.** Because saving increases at any given interest rate, the desired saving curve shifts rightward. This causes the equilibrium interest rate to decline.

b. There is no effect on current equilibrium real GDP, because in the classical model the vertical long-run aggregate supply curve always applies.

c. A change in the saving rate does not directly affect the demand for labor or the supply of labor in the classical model, so equilibrium employment does not change.

d. The decrease in the equilibrium interest rate generates a rightward and downward movement along the demand curve for investment. Consequently, desired investment increases.

e. The rise in current investment implies greater capital accumulation. Other things being equal, this will imply increased future production and higher equilibrium real GDP in the future.

11-3. False. In fact, there is an important distinction. The classical model of short-run real GDP determination applies to an interval short enough that some factors of production, such as capital, are fixed. Nevertheless, the classical model implies that even in the short run the economy's aggregate supply curve is the same as its long-run aggregate supply curve.

11-5. a. The labor supply curve shifts rightward, and equilibrium employment increases.

b. The rise in employment causes the aggregate supply curve to shift rightward, and real GDP rises.

c. Because the immigrants have higher saving rates, the nation's saving supply curve shifts to the right along its investment curve, and the equilibrium interest rate declines.

d. The fall in the equilibrium interest rate induces a rise in investment, and equilibrium saving also rises.

e. Capital accumulation rises, and more real GDP will be forthcoming in future years.

11-7. In the long run, the aggregate supply curve is vertical because all input prices adjust fully and people are fully informed in the long run. Thus, the short-run aggregate supply curve is more steeply sloped if input prices adjust more rapidly and people become more fully informed within a short-run interval.

11-9. This event would cause the aggregate demand curve to shift leftward. In the short run, the equilibrium price level would decline, and equilibrium real GDP would fall.

11-11. To prevent a short-run decrease in real GDP from taking place after the temporary rise in oil prices shifts the SRAS curve leftward, policymakers should increase the quantity of money in circulation. This will shift the AD curve rightward and prevent equilibrium real GDP from declining in the short run.

11-13. a. *E:* The union wage boost causes the SRAS curve to shift leftward, from $SRAS_1$ to $SRAS_3$. The reduction in incomes abroad causes import spending in this nation to fall, which induces a leftward shift in the AD curve, from AD_1 to AD_3.

b. *B:* The short-term reduction in production capabilities causes the SRAS curve to shift leftward, from $SRAS_1$ to $SRAS_3$, and the increase in money supply growth generates a rightward shift in the AD curve, from AD_1 to AD_2.

c. *C:* The strengthening of the value of this nation's currency reduces the prices of imported inputs that domestic firms utilize to produce goods and services, which causes the SRAS curve to shift rightward, from $SRAS_1$ to $SRAS_2$. At the same time, the currency's strengthening raises the prices of exports and reduces the prices of imports, so net export spending declines, thereby inducing a leftward shift in the AD curve, from AD_1 to AD_3.

Chapter 12

12-1. a. Flow
b. Flow
c. Stock
d. Flow
e. Stock
f. Flow
g. Stock

12-3. a. The completed table follows (all amounts in dollars):

Real GDP	Consumption	Saving	Investment
2,000	2,000	0	1,200
4,000	3,600	400	1,200
6,000	5,200	800	1,200
8,000	6,800	1,200	1,200
10,000	8,400	1,600	1,200
12,000	10,000	2,000	1,200

MPC = 1,600/2000 = 0.8; MPS = 400/2,000 = 0.2.

b. The graph appears below.

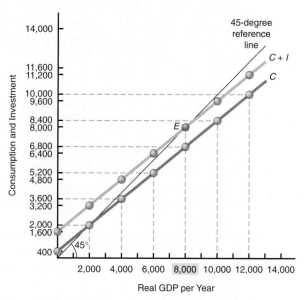

c. The graph appears below. Equilibrium real GDP on both graphs equals $8,000.

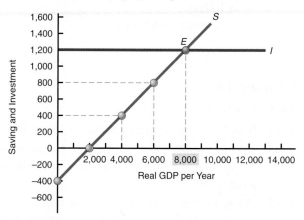

d. APS = $1,200/$8,000 = 0.15.

e. The multiplier is $1/(1 - MPC) = 1/(1 - 0.8) = 1/0.2 = 5$. Thus, if autonomous consumption were to rise by $100, then equilibrium real GDP would increase by $100 times 5, or $500.

12-5. The multiplier is $1/(1 - MPC) = 4$, so $1 - MPC = 0.25$, which implies that MPC = 0.75. Thus, when real GDP equals $15 trillion, consumption is $1 trillion + (0.75 × $15 trillion) = $12.25 trillion.

12-7. The multiplier is $1/(1 - MPC) = 1/(1 - 0.75) = 4$, so the increase in equilibrium real GDP is $250 billion × 4 = $1 trillion, and the level of real GDP at the new point on the aggregate demand curve is $16 trillion.

12-9. a. The MPS is equal to 1/3.
  b. $0.1 trillion

Chapter 13

13-1. a. A key factor that could help explain why the actual effect may have turned out to be lower is the crowding-out effect. Some government spending may have entailed direct expenditure offsets that reduced private expenditures on a dollar-for-dollar basis. In addition, indirect crowding out may have occurred. Because the government did not change taxes, it probably sold bonds to finance its increased expenditures, and this action likely pushed up interest rates, thereby discouraging private investment. Furthermore, the increase in government spending likely pushed up aggregate demand, which may have caused a short-run increase in the price level. This, in turn, may have induced foreign residents to reduce their expenditures on U.S. goods. It also could have reduced real money holdings sufficiently to discourage consumers from spending as much as before. On net, therefore, real GDP rose in the short run but not by the full amount predicted by the basic multiplier effect.

  b. In the long run, as the increased spending raised aggregate demand, wages and other input prices likely increased in proportion to the resulting increase in the price level. Thus, in the long run the aggregate supply schedule was vertical, and the increase in government spending induced only a rise in the price level.

13-3. Because of the recognition time lag entailed in gathering information about the economy, policymakers may be slow to respond to a downturn in real GDP. Congressional approval of policy actions to address the downturn may be delayed; hence, an action time lag may also arise. Finally, there is an effect time lag, because policy actions take time to exert their full effects on the economy. If these lags are sufficiently long, it is possible that by the time a policy to address a downturn has begun to have its effects, real GDP may already be rising. If so, the policy action may push real GDP up faster than intended, thereby making real GDP less stable.

13-5. Situation *b* is an example of indirect crowding out because the reduction in private expenditures takes place indirectly in response to a change in the interest rate. In contrast, situations *a* and *c* are examples of direct expenditure offsets.

13-7. Situation *b* is an example of a discretionary fiscal policy action because this is a discretionary action by Congress. So is situation *d* because the president uses discretionary authority. Situation *c* is an example of monetary policy, not fiscal policy, and situation *a* is an example of an automatic stabilizer.

13-9. There is a recessionary gap, because at point *A* equilibrium real GDP of $15.5 trillion is below the long-run level of $16.0 trillion. To eliminate the recessionary gap of $0.5 trillion, government spending must increase sufficiently to shift the *AD* curve rightward to a long-run equilibrium, which will entail a price level increase from 115 to 120. Hence, the spending increase must shift the *AD* curve rightward by $1 trillion, or by the multiplier, which is $1/0.20 = 5$, times the increase in spending. Government spending must rise by $200 billion, or $0.2 trillion.

13-11. Because the MPC is 0.80, the multiplier equals $1/(1 - MPC) = 1/0.2 = 5$. Net of indirect crowding out, therefore, total autonomous expenditures must rise by $40 billion in order to shift the aggregate demand curve rightward by $200 billion. If the government raises its spending by $50 billion, the market interest rate rises by 0.5 percentage point and thereby causes planned investment spending to fall by $10 billion, which results in a net rise in total autonomous expenditures equal to $40 billion. Consequently, to accomplish its objective the government should increase its spending by $50 billion.

13-13. A cut in the tax rate should induce a rise in consumption and, consequently, a multiple short-run increase in equilibrium real GDP. In addition, however, a tax-rate reduction reduces the automatic-stabilizer properties of the tax system, so equilibrium real GDP would be less stable in the face of changes in autonomous spending.

APPENDIX C

C-1. a. The marginal propensity to consume is equal to 1 − MPS, or 6/7.

b. The required increase in equilibrium real GDP is $0.35 trillion, or $350 billion. The multiplier equals $1/(1 - MPC) = 1/MPS = 1/(1/7) = 7$. Hence, investment or government spending must increase by $50 billion to bring about a $350 billion increase in equilibrium real GDP.

c. The multiplier relevant for a tax change equals $-MPC/(1-MPC) = -MPC/MPS = -(6/7)/(1/7) = -6$. Thus, the government would have to cut taxes by $58.33 billion to induce a rise in equilibrium real GDP equal to $350 billion.

C-3. a. The aggregate expenditures curve shifts up by $1 billion; equilibrium real GDP increases by $5 billion.

b. The aggregate expenditures curve shifts down by the MPC times the tax increase, or by $0.8 \times$ $1 billion = 0.8 billion; equilibrium real income falls by $4 billion.

c. The aggregate expenditures curve shifts upward by $(1 - MPC)$ times $1 billion = $0.2 billion. Equilibrium real income rises by $1 billion.

d. No change; no change.

Chapter 14

14-1. $0.4 trillion

14-3. A higher deficit creates a higher public debt.

14-5. The net public debt is obtained by subtracting government interagency borrowing from the gross public debt.

14-7. When foreign dollar holders hold more domestic government bonds issued to finance higher domestic government budget deficits, they purchase fewer domestic exports, so the domestic trade deficit rises, other things being equal.

14-9. In the diagram on the next page, the increase in government spending and/or tax reduction that creates the budget deficit also causes the aggregate demand curve to shift rightward, from *AD* to AD_2. Real GDP rises to its long-run equilibrium level of $15 trillion at point *B*. The equilibrium price level increases to a value of 130 at this point. As real GDP rises, the government's tax collections increase and benefit payouts fall, both of which will help ultimately reduce the deficit.

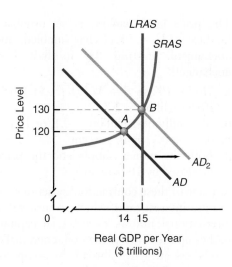

Real GDP per Year
($ trillions)

14-11. "The rich" are likely to respond to higher tax rates by reducing their activities that generate taxable income, so actual tax collections from "the rich" will not turn out to be as high as the politician suggests.

Chapter 15

15-1. medium of exchange; store of value; standard of deferred payment

15-3. store of value; standard of deferred payment

15-5. M1 equals transactions deposits plus currency plus traveler's checks, or $825 billion + $850 billion + $25 billion = $1,700 billion; M2 equals M1 + savings deposits plus small-denomination time deposits plus money market deposit accounts plus retail (noninstitution) money market mutual funds, or $1,700 billion + $2,300 billion + $1,450 billion + $1,950 billion + $1,900 billion = $9,300 billion.

15-7. **a.** neither
b. M2 only
c. M1 and M2
d. M2 only

15-9. In principle, each institution can match with each rationale; your explanations are the most important aspects of your answers.
a. Insurance companies limit adverse selection by screening applicants for policies.
b. Savings banks limit moral hazard by monitoring borrowers after loans have been made.
c. Pension funds reduce management costs by pooling the funds of many future pensioners.

15-11. **a.** moral hazard problem
b. adverse selection problem
c. moral hazard problem

15-13. In an extreme case in which the U.S. government were to close down the Federal Reserve System, it would have to compensate holders of Federal Reserve notes for the market value of those notes.

15-15. Back in 1913, the population was centered farther to the east. Thus, congressional representation was centered farther to the east, so political concerns together with a view that the Fed districts should be designed to best serve the existing population helped determine the geographic boundaries. These have not been redrawn since.

Chapter 16

16-1. **a.** asset
b. liability
c. liability
d. asset

16-3. The bank's reserves are its required reserves, which equal 0.10 × $15 million = $1.5 million. Total assets equal total liabilities, or $15 million. Hence, its remaining loans and securities must amount to its total assets of $15 million minus its reserves of $1.5 million, or $13.5 million.

16-5. Yes, the bank holds $50 million in excess reserves. The bank's current total assets equal its $2 billion in total liabilities. It must hold 15 percent of its $2 billion in transactions deposits, or $0.30 billion, as required reserves. Its total reserves equal $2 billion in total assets minus $1.65 billion in loans and securities, or $0.35 billion. Hence, the bank has $0.05 billion, or $50 million, in excess reserves.

16-7. The dealer's bank must hold 15 percent of the $1 million, or $150,000, as required reserves. Thus, the bank can lend out the excess reserves of $850,000.

16-9. **a.** Total liabilities and net worth = total assets = $0.26 billion in total reserves + $3.6 billion in loans + $1 billion in securities + $0.14 billion in other assets = $5 billion.

b. The bank could lend its $10 million in excess reserves.

c. Transactions deposits equal required reserves of $0.25 billion/0.1 = $2.5 billion.

16-11. When you purchase a U.S. government security, you draw on existing funds in a deposit account and thereby redistribute funds already within the banking system; in contrast, the Federal Reserve creates funds that had not previously existed in the banking system.

16-13. The maximum potential money multiplier is $1/0.01 = 100$, so total deposits in the banking system will increase by $5 million $\times$ 100 = $500 million.

16-15. **a.** You expect that the value of your bond holdings will decline by one-half.

b. You would reduce your bond holdings, which implies a reallocation of wealth to money holdings. Consequently, the quantity of money that you desire to hold would increase.

Chapter 17

17-1. **a.** One possible policy action would be an open market sale of securities, which would reduce the money supply and shift the aggregate demand curve leftward. Others would be to increase the discount rate relative to the federal funds rate or to raise the required reserve ratio.

b. In principle, the Fed's action would reduce inflation more quickly.

17-3. Because a contractionary monetary policy causes interest rates to increase, financial capital begins to flow into the United States. This causes the demand for dollars to rise, which pushes up the international value of the dollar and makes U.S. exports more expensive to foreign residents. They cut back on their purchases of U.S. products, which tends to reduce U.S. real GDP.

17-5.

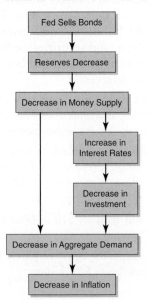

Fed Sells Bonds → Reserves Decrease → Decrease in Money Supply → Increase in Interest Rates → Decrease in Investment → Decrease in Aggregate Demand → Decrease in Inflation

17-7. The price level remains at its original value. Because $M_sV = PY$, V has doubled, and Y is unchanged, cutting M_s in half leaves P unchanged.

17-9. **a.** $M_sV = PY$, so $P = M_sV/Y = (\$1.1$ trillion $\times$ 10)/$5 trillion = 2.2.

b. $100 billion/$1 trillion = 0.1, or 10 percent

c. 0.2/2 = 0.1, or 10 percent

d. Both the money supply and the price level increased by 10 percent.

17-11. Any one of these contractionary actions will tend to raise interest rates, which in turn will induce international inflows of financial capital. This pushes up the value of the dollar and makes U.S. goods less attractive abroad. As a consequence, real planned total expenditures on U.S. goods decline even further.

17-13. **a.** To push the equilibrium federal funds rate up to the new target value, the Trading Desk will have to reduce the money supply by selling U.S. government securities.

b. The increase in the differential between the discount rate and the federal funds rate will induce more depository institutions to borrow reserves from Federal Reserve banks. In the absence of a Trading Desk action, this would cause the equilibrium interest rate to increase. To prevent this from occurring, the Trading Desk will have to boost the money supply by purchasing U.S. government securities.

17-15. The neutral federal funds rate is the level of the interest rate on interbank loans at which, given current inflation expectations, the growth rate of real GDP tends neither to rise nor to fall relative to the rate of growth of potential, long-run, real GDP.

a. The FOMC should instruct the Trading Desk to aim to achieve a higher target for the federal funds rate.

b. The Trading Desk should engage in open market sales and thereby reduce the quantity of reserves supplied, which will bring about an increase in the equilibrium federal funds rate.

APPENDIX D

D-1. **a.** $20 billion increase

b. $40 billion increase

c. $10 billion open market purchase

D-3. Through its purchase of $1 billion in bonds, the Fed increased reserves by $1 billion. This ultimately caused a $3 billion increase in the money supply after full multiple expansion. The 1 percentage-point drop in the interest rate, from 6 percent to 5 percent, caused investment to rise by $25 billion, from $1,200 billion to $1,225 billion. An investment multiplier of 3 indicates that equilibrium real GDP rose by $75 billion, to $12,075 billion, or $12.075 trillion.

Chapter 18

18-1. a. The actual unemployment rate, which equals the number of people unemployed divided by the labor force, would decline, because the labor force would rise while the number of people unemployed would remain unchanged.
   b. Natural unemployment rate estimates also would be lower.
   c. The logic of the short- and long-run Phillips curves would not be altered. The government might wish to make this change if it feels that those in the military "hold jobs" and therefore should be counted as employed within the U.S. economy.

18-3. The "long run" is an interval sufficiently long that input prices fully adjust and people have full information. Adoption of more sophisticated computer and communications technology provides people with more immediate access to information, which can reduce this interval.

18-5. The natural rate of unemployment is the rate of unemployment that would exist after full adjustment has taken place in response to any changes that have occurred. In contrast, the nonaccelerating inflation rate of unemployment is the rate of unemployment that corresponds to a stable rate of inflation, which is easier to quantify.

18-7. a. The measured unemployment rate when all adjustments have occurred will now always be lower than before, so the natural unemployment rate will be smaller.
   b. The unemployment rate consistent with stable inflation will now be reduced, so the NAIRU will be smaller.
   c. The Phillips curve will shift inward.

18-9. No. It could still be true that wages and other prices of factors of production adjust sluggishly to changes in the price level. Then a rise in aggregate demand that boosts the price level brings about an upward movement along the short-run aggregate supply curve, causing equilibrium real GDP to rise.

18-11. a. An increase in desired investment spending induces an increase in aggregate demand, so AD_3 applies. The price level is unchanged in the short run, and equilibrium real GDP rises from $15 trillion at point A to $15.5 trillion at point C.
   b. Over time, firms perceive that they can increase their profits by adjusting prices upward in response to the increase in aggregate demand. Thus, firms eventually will incur the menu costs required to make these price adjustments. As they do so, the aggregate supply curve will shift upward, from $SRAS_1$ to $SRAS_2$, as shown in the diagram below. Real GDP will return to its original level of $15 trillion, in base-year dollars. The price level will increase to a level above 119, such as 124.

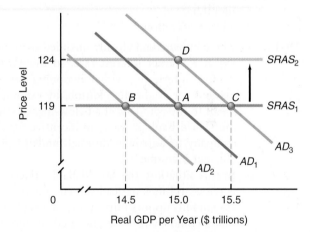

18-13. The explanation would be that aggregate demand increased at a faster pace than the rise in aggregate supply caused by economic growth. On net, therefore, the price level rose during those years.

18-15. If the average time between price adjustments by firms is significant, then the short-run aggregate supply curve could be regarded as horizontal, as hypothesized by the New Keynesian theorists. As a consequence, there would be a short-run trade-off between inflation and real GDP that policymakers potentially could exploit.

Chapter 19

19-1. Population growth rate = real GDP growth rate − rate of growth of per capita real GDP = 3.1 percent − 0.3 percent = 2.8 percent.

19-3. **a.** 20×0.01 percent = 0.2 percent.
b. 10×0.01 percent = 0.1 percent.

19-5. \$10 trillion/\$0.5 trillion $\times 0.1 = 2$ percentage points.

19-7. **a.** Portfolio investment is equal to \$150 million in bonds plus \$100 million in stocks representing ownership of less than 10 percent, or \$250 million. (Bank loans are neither portfolio investment nor foreign direct investment.)
b. Foreign direct investment is equal to \$250 million in stocks representing an ownership share of at least 10 percent. (Bank loans are neither portfolio investment nor foreign direct investment.)

19-9. **a.** adverse selection
b. adverse selection
c. moral hazard
d. adverse selection

19-11. **a.** The company had already qualified for funding at a market interest rate, so the World Bank is interfering with functioning private markets for credit. In addition, by extending credit to the company at a below-market rate, the World Bank provides an incentive for the company to borrow additional funds for less efficient investment.
b. In this situation, the World Bank effectively is tying up funds in dead capital. There is an associated opportunity cost, because the funds could instead be allocated to another investment that would yield more immediate returns.
c. In this case, the IMF contributes to a moral hazard problem, because the government has every incentive not to make reforms that will enable it to repay this and future loans it may receive.

19-13. **a.** There is an incentive for at least some governments to fail to follow through with reforms, even if those governments might have had good intentions when they applied for World Bank loans.
b. National governments most interested in obtaining funds to "buy" votes will be among those most interested in obtaining IMF loans. The proposed IMF rule could help reduce the number of nations whose governments seek to obtain funds to try to "buy" votes.

Chapter 20

20-1. $-[(200 - 150)/(350/2)]/[(9 - 10)/(19/2)]$, which is approximately equal to −2.7. Thus, the absolute price elasticity of demand equals 2.7.

20-3. **a.** $-[(90 - 80)/(85)]/[(0.20 - 0.40)/(0.30)]$, which is approximately equal to −0.18. Consequently, the absolute price elasticity of demand is 0.18, so demand is inelastic over this range.
b. $-[(60 - 40)/(50)]/[(0.80 - 1.20)/(1.00)] = -1.00$. The absolute price elasticity of demand, therefore, equals 1.00, which implies that demand is unit-elastic over this range.
c. $-[(20 - 10)/(15)]/[(1.60 - 1.80)/(1.70)]$, which is approximately equal to −5.67. Thus, the absolute price elasticity of demand is 5.67, so demand is elastic over this range.

20-5. $-[(80 - 120)/(200/2)]/[(\$22.50 - \$17.50)/(\$40/2)] = -1.6$. Hence, the absolute price elasticity of demand equals 1.6. Demand is elastic over this range.

20-7. Because price and total revenue move in the same direction, then over this range of demand, the demand for handmade guitars is inelastic.

20-9. **a.** More inelastic, because it represents a smaller portion of the budget
b. More elastic, because there are many close substitutes
c. More elastic, because there are a number of substitutes
d. More inelastic, because there are few close substitutes
e. More inelastic, because it represents a small portion of the budget

20-11. Let X denote the percentage change in the quantity of bacon. Then $X/10$ percent = −0.5. X, therefore, is −5 percent.

20-13. $[(125,000 - 75,000)/(200,000/2)]/[(\$35,000 - \$25,000)/(\$60,000/2)] = 1.5$. Supply is elastic.

20-15. The short-run price elasticity of supply is 10 percent/20 percent = 0.5, and the long-run price elasticity of supply is 40 percent/20 percent = 2.0.

Chapter 21

21-1. The campus pizzeria indicates by its pricing policy that it recognizes the principle of diminishing marginal utility. As shown in Figure 21-1 on page 528, a customer's marginal utility for the second pizza is typically lower than for the first. Thus, the customer is likely to value the second pizza less and, therefore, only be willing to pay less for it.

21-3. The total utility of the third, fourth, and fifth cheeseburgers is 48, 56, and 60, respectively. The marginal utility of the first and second cheeseburgers is 20 and 16, respectively. The total utility of the first, second, and third bags of french fries is 10, 18, and 20, respectively. The marginal utility of the fourth and fifth bags of french fries is 1 and 0, respectively.

21-5. The new utility-maximizing combination is four cheeseburgers and two orders of french fries, at which the marginal utility per dollar spent is 2 units per dollar and the entire $6 is spent.

21-7. Other things being equal, when the price of soft drinks rises, the substitution effect comes into play, and the individual tends to consume less of the more expensive item, soft drinks, and more of the item with the unchanged price, tacos. Hence, the marginal utility of soft drinks rises, and the marginal utility of tacos falls.

21-9. **a.** Of all the possible one-unit increases in consumption displayed, the movement from point A to point B generates the highest marginal utility. Total utility rises by 5 units between these points, so the marginal utility of the first unit consumed is 5 units.

b. Between points E and F, a one-unit increase in the quantity consumed leaves total utility unchanged at 11 units, so marginal utility is equal to zero.

c. Between points F and G, a one-unit increase in the quantity consumed causes total utility to decline from 11 units to 10 units, so marginal utility is negative and equal to -1 unit.

21-11. For this consumer, at these prices the marginal utility per dollar spent on 2 fudge bars is 500 units of utility per dollar, and the marginal utility per dollar spent on 5 popsicles is also 500 units of utility per dollar. In addition, the entire budget of $9 is spent at this combination, which is the consumer optimum.

21-13. The marginal utility per dollar spent is equalized at 2.50 if 5 hot dogs and 3 baseball games are consumed, and this consumption combination just exhausts the now-available $190 in income.

21-15. The marginal utility of good Y is three times the marginal utility of good X, or 3×3 utils = 9 utils.

APPENDIX E

E-1. The indifference curve is convex to the origin because of a diminishing marginal rate of substitution. As an individual consumes more and more of an item, the less the individual is willing to forgo of the other item. The diminishing marginal rate of substitution is due to diminishing marginal utility.

E-3. Sue's marginal rate of substitution is calculated below:

Combination of Bottled Water and Soft Drinks	Bottled Water per Month	Soft Drinks per Month	MRS
A	5	11	
B	10	7	5:4
C	15	4	5:3
D	20	2	5:2
E	25	1	5:1

The diminishing marginal rate of substitution of soft drinks for water shows Sue's diminishing marginal utility of bottled water. She is willing to forgo fewer and fewer soft drinks to get an additional five bottles of water.

E-5. Given that water is measured along the horizontal axis and soft drinks are measured along the vertical axis, the slope of Sue's budget constraint is the price of water divided by the price of soft drinks, or $P_W/P_S = \frac{1}{2}$. The only combination of bottled water and soft drinks that is on Sue's indifference curve and budget constraint is combination C. For this combination, total expenditures on water and soft drinks equal $(15 \times \$1) + (4 \times \$2) = \$15 + \$8 = \$23$.

E-7. With the quantity of bottled water measured along the horizontal axis and the quantity of soft drinks measured along the vertical axis, the slope of Sue's budget constraint is the price of water divided by the price of soft drinks. This ratio equals $\frac{1}{2}$. The only combination of bottled water and soft drinks that is on Sue's indifference curve and budget constraint is combination C, where expenditures on water and soft drinks total $23.

E-9. Yes, Sue's revealed preferences indicate that her demand for soft drinks obeys the law of demand. When the price of soft drinks declines from $2 to $1, her quantity demanded rises from 4 to 8.

Chapter 22

22-1. **a.** Bob earns a high economic rent. Because he has a specialized skill that is in great demand, his income is likely to be high, and his opportunity cost relatively low.

b. Sally earns a high economic rent. Because she is a supermodel, her income is likely to be relatively high, and, without any education, her opportunity cost is likely to be relatively low.

c. If Tim were to leave teaching, not a relatively high-paying occupation, he could sell insurance full time. Hence, his opportunity cost is high relative to his income, and his economic rent is low.

22-3. The economic rents that Michael Jordan was able to earn as a basketball player relative to those he could earn as a baseball player surely played a large role in his decision to return to basketball. Hence, they helped direct his resources (athletic talents) to their most efficient uses.

22-5. A sole proprietorship is a business entity owned by a single individual, whereas a partnership is a business entity jointly owned by more than one individual. A corporation, in contrast, is a legal entity that is owned by shareholders, who own shares of the profits of the entity. Sole proprietorships and partnerships do not face double taxation, but corporations do. The owners of corporations, however, enjoy limited liability, whereas the sole proprietor or partner does not.

22-7. Accounting profit is total revenue, $77,250, minus explicit costs, $37,000, for a total of $40,250. Economic profit is total revenue, $77,250, less explicit costs, $37,000, and implicit costs, $40,250, for a total equal to zero.

22-9. **a.** Physical capital
b. Financial capital
c. Financial capital
d. Physical capital

22-11. **a.** The owner of WebCity faces both tax rates if the firm is a corporation, but if it is a proprietorship, the owner faces only the 30 percent personal income tax rate. Thus, it should choose to be a proprietorship.

b. If WebCity is a corporation, the $100,000 in corporate earnings is taxed at a 20 percent rate, so after-tax dividends are $80,000, and these are taxed at the personal income tax rate of 30 percent, leaving $56,000 in after-tax income for the owner. Hence, the firm should be organized as a proprietorship, with after-tax earnings $70,000, or a value advantage of $14,000.

c. Yes. In this case, incorporation raises earnings to $150,000, which are taxed at a rate of 20 percent, yielding after-tax dividends of $120,000 that are taxed at the personal rate of 30 percent. This leaves an after-tax income for the owner of $84,000, which is higher than the after-tax earnings of $70,000 if WebCity is a proprietorship that earns lower pre-tax income taxed at the personal rate.

d. After-tax profits rise from $56,000 to $84,000, or by $28,000.

e. This policy change would only increase the incentive to incorporate.

f. A corporate structure provides limited liability for owners, which can be a major advantage. Furthermore, owners may believe that the corporate structure will yield higher pre-tax earnings, as in the above example.

22-13. The real rate of interest in Japan is 2% − 0.5% = 1.5%. The real rate of interest in the United States is 4% − 3% = 1%. Japan, therefore, has the higher *real* rate of interest.

22-15. Ownership of common stock provides voting rights within the firm but also entails immediate loss if assets fall below the value of the firm's liabilities. Preferred stockholders are repaid prior to owners of common stock, but preferred stockholders do not have voting rights.

22-17. You should point out to your classmate that stock prices tend to drift upward following a random walk. That is, yesterday's price plus any upward drift is the best guide to today's price. Therefore, there are no predictable trends that can be used to "beat" the market.

Chapter 23

23-1. The short run is a time period during which the professor cannot enter the job market and find employment elsewhere. This is the nine-month period from August 15 through May 15. The professor can find employment elsewhere after the contract has been fulfilled, so the short run is nine months and the long run is greater than nine months.

23-3. Total variable costs are equal to total costs, $5 million, less total fixed costs, $2 million, which equals $3 million. Average variable costs are equal to total variable costs divided by the number of units produced. Average variable costs, therefore, equal $3 million divided by 10,000, or $300.

23-5. **a.** Total fixed costs equal average fixed costs, $10 per LCD screen, times the quantity produced per day, 100 LCD screens, which equals $1,000 per day.

b. The total variable costs of producing 100 LCD screens equal average variable costs, $10 per unit, times the quantity produced per day, 100 LCD screens, which equals $1,000 per day.

c. The total costs of producing 100 LCD screens equal total fixed costs plus the total variable costs of producing 100 LCD screens, or $1,000 per day plus $1,000 per day, which equals $2,000 per day.

d. The average total costs of producing 99 LCD screens equal the average fixed costs of $10.101 plus the average variable costs of $10.070, or $20.171 per LCD screen. Thus, the total cost of producing 99 LCD screens equals $20.171 times 99, or $1,996.929. The marginal cost of producing the hundredth LCD screen equals the change in total costs from increasing production from 99 to 100, or $2,000 − $1,996.929, or $3.071 per LCD screen.

23-7. **a.** Average total costs are $20 per unit plus $30 per unit, or $50 per unit, and total costs divided by average total costs equal output, which therefore is $2,500/$50 per unit, or 50 units.

b. TVC = AVC × Q = $20 per unit × 50 units = $1,000.

c. TFC = AFC × Q = $30 per unit × 50 units = $1,500; or TFC = TC − TVC = $2,500 − $1,000 = $1,500.

23-9. **a.** The expense incurred in cutting back trees on a regular basis would be unrelated to the quantity of rail services provided on the tracks and hence would represent a fixed cost.

b. The expense of dumping sand on the slippery tracks in advance of trains would vary with the number of trains that run on the tracks and hence would constitute a variable cost.

23-11. Hiring 1 more unit of labor at a wage rate of $20 to increase output by 1 unit causes total costs to rise by $20, so the marginal cost of the 251st unit is $20.

23-13. **a.** AVC = $2 million/1 million units = $2 per unit.

b. APP = 1 million units/1,000 units of labor = 1,000 units of output per unit of labor.

c. Wage rate = $2 million/1,000 units of labor = $2,000 per unit of labor.

23-15. **a.** plant size E, because this is the minimum output scale at which LRATC is at a minimum level

b. leftward movement, because the functioning plant size for the firm would decrease

Chapter 24

24-1. **a.** The single firm producing much of the industry's output can affect price. Therefore, this is currently not a perfectly competitive industry.

b. The output of each firm is not homogeneous, so this is not a perfectly competitive industry.

c. Firms must obtain government permission to enter the industry and hence cannot easily enter, so this is not a perfectly competitive industry.

24-3. **a.** For a perfectly competitive firm, marginal revenue and average revenue are equal to the market clearing price. Hence, average revenue equals $20 per unit at each possible output rate.

b. At the present output of 10,000 units per week, the firm's total revenues equal price times output, or $20 per unit times 10,000 units per week, which equals $200,000 per week. The firm's total costs equal ATC times output, or $15.75 per unit times 10,000 units per week, which equals $157,500 per week. Weekly economic profits equal total revenues minus total costs, or $200,000 − $157,500 = $42,500. The firm is maximizing economic profits, because it is producing the output rate at which marginal revenue equals marginal cost.

c. If the market clearing price were to fall to $12.50 per unit, the marginal revenue curve would shift down to this level. Average total costs would exceed the price at this output rate, but in the short run the firm would minimize its short-run economic losses by producing 8,100 units per week.

d. If the market clearing price were to fall to $7.50 per unit, the marginal revenue curve would shift down to this level. Average variable costs at an output rate of 5,000 units per week would exceed the market clearing price, so total variable costs of producing 5,000 units per week would exceed total revenues. The firm should cease production if this event takes place.

24-5. Even though the price of pizzas, and hence marginal revenue, falls to only $5, this covers average variable costs. Thus, the shop should stay open.

24-7. Because price is less than average variable cost at this rate of output, the firm's total revenues ($5 per unit × 1,500 units = $7,500) fail to cover its total variable costs ($5.50 per unit × 1,500 units = $8,250). Thus, in the short run the firm should shut down and incur only its fixed costs, which equal AVC × Q, or $0.50 per unit × 1,500 units = $750.

24-9. In the described situation, the firm is producing an output rate at a point on the marginal cost curve below the average total cost curve. Marginal revenue is above the minimum point of the average total cost curve, however. Hence, marginal cost at the current rate of production is less than marginal revenue. The firm is not maximizing profit, and it should increase its rate of production.

24-11. a. There was a significant increase in market supply as more firms entered the industry. A consequence for the typical firm was that the market price fell below the minimum average total cost, resulting in negative economic profits.

b. Firms will consider leaving the industry, and some firms probably will leave the industry.

Chapter 25

25-1. The alternatives are not close substitutes for first-class mail, so the U.S. Postal Service faces a downward-sloping demand curve for first-class mail.

25-3. The demand curve faced by the firm is the downward-sloping market demand curve, so price exceeds marginal revenue at all quantities beyond the first unit produced.

25-5. a. The total revenue and total profits of the dry cleaner are as follows.

Output (suits cleaned)	Price ($ per unit)	Total Costs ($)	Total Revenue ($)	Total Profit ($)
0	8.00	3.00	0	−3.00
1	7.50	6.00	7.50	1.50
2	7.00	8.50	14.00	5.50
3	6.50	10.50	19.50	9.00
4	6.00	11.50	24.00	12.50
5	5.50	13.50	27.50	14.00
6	5.00	16.00	30.00	14.00
7	4.50	19.00	31.50	12.50
8	4.00	24.00	32.00	8.00

b. The profit-maximizing rate of output is between 5 and 6 units.

c. The marginal cost and marginal revenue of the dry cleaner are as follows. The profit-maximizing rate of output is 6 units.

Output (suits cleaned)	Price ($ per unit)	Total Costs ($)	Total Revenue ($)	Total Profit ($)	Marginal Cost ($ per unit)	Marginal Revenue ($ per unit)
0	8.00	3.00	0	−3.00	—	—
1	7.50	6.00	7.50	1.50	3.00	7.50
2	7.00	8.50	14.00	5.50	2.50	6.50
3	6.50	10.50	19.50	9.00	2.00	5.50
4	6.00	11.50	24.00	12.50	1.00	4.50
5	5.50	13.50	27.50	14.00	2.00	3.50
6	5.00	16.00	30.00	14.00	2.50	2.50
7	4.50	19.00	31.50	12.50	3.00	1.50
8	4.00	24.00	32.00	8.00	4.00	0.50

25-7. a. The profit-maximizing output rate is 5,000 units.

b. Average total cost is $5 per unit. Average revenue is $6 per unit.

c. Total costs equal $5 per unit × 5,000 units = $25,000. Total revenue equals $6 per unit × 5,000 units = $30,000.

d. ($6 per unit − $5 per unit) × 5,000 units = $5,000.

e. In a perfectly competitive market, price would equal marginal cost at $4.50 unit, at which the quantity is 8,000 units. Because the monopolist produces less and charges a higher price than under perfect competition, price exceeds marginal cost at the profit-maximizing level of output. The difference between the price and marginal cost is the per-unit cost to society of a monopolized industry.

25-9. **a.** The monopoly maximizes economic profits or minimizes economic losses by producing to the point at which marginal revenue is equal to marginal cost, which is 1 million units of output per month.

b. The profit-maximizing or loss-minimizing price of 1 million units per month is $30 per unit, so total revenues equal $30 million per month. The average total cost of producing 1 million units per month is $33 per unit, so total costs equal $33 million per month. Hence, in the short run, producing 1 million units minimizes the monopoly's loss at $3 million per month.

25-11. If price varies positively with total revenue, then the monopolist is operating on the inelastic portion of the demand curve. This corresponds to the range where marginal revenue is negative. The monopolist cannot, therefore, be at the point where its profits are maximized. In other words, the monopolist is not producing where marginal cost equals marginal revenue.

25-13. Because marginal cost has risen, the monopolist will be operating at a lower rate of output and charging a higher price. Economic profits are likely to decline because even though the price is higher, its output will be more than proportionately lower.

Chapter 26

26-1. **a.** There are many fast-food restaurants producing and selling differentiated products. Both of these features of this industry are consistent with the theory of monopolistic competition.

b. There are numerous colleges and universities, but each specializes in different academic areas and hence produces heterogeneous products, as in the theory of monopolistic competition.

26-3. The values for marginal cost and marginal revenue appear below. Marginal revenue equals marginal

cost at approximately the fifth unit of output, so marginal analysis indicates that 5 units is the profit-maximizing production level.

Output	Price ($ per unit)	Total Costs ($)	Total Revenue ($)	Marginal Cost ($ per unit)	Marginal Revenue ($ per unit)	Total Profit ($)
0	6.00	2.00	0	—	—	−2.00
1	5.75	5.25	5.75	3.25	5.75	0.00
2	5.50	7.50	11.00	2.25	5.25	3.50
3	5.25	9.60	15.75	2.10	4.75	6.15
4	5.00	12.10	20.00	2.50	4.25	7.90
5	4.75	15.80	23.75	3.70	3.75	7.95
6	4.50	20.00	27.00	4.20	3.25	7.00
7	4.00	24.75	28.00	4.75	1.00	3.25

26-5. After these long-run adjustments have occurred, the demand curve will have shifted to tangency with the average total cost curve at 4 units of output. At this production level, average total cost is $3.03, so this will be the long-run equilibrium price. Because price and average total cost will be equal, the firm will earn zero economic profits.

26-7. **a.** interactive
b. direct
c. mass and interactive
d. mass

26-9. **a.** search good. Given the knowledge that it is a heavy-duty filing cabinet, a photo and description providing features such as dimensions are sufficient to evaluate the characteristics of a filing cabinet.

b. experience good. A meal must be eaten for its characteristics to be determined.

c. search good. Given the knowledge that the coat is made of wool, a photo and description providing size information are sufficient to evaluate the characteristics of the coat.

d. credence good. Psychotherapy services have characteristics that are likely to be difficult for consumers lacking expertise to assess without assistance from another health care provider, such as a general practitioner who guides someone experiencing depression in seeking psychotherapy treatment from a psychiatrist.

26-11. Consumers may be able to assess certain features of a credence good in advance of purchase, so in this sense a credence good is similar to a search good. Consumers lack expertise to evaluate the full qualities of a credence good until after they have purchased it, which is somewhat analogous to the characteristics of an experience good. Nevertheless, the fact that consumers cannot fully evaluate a credence good's qualities in advance of purchase makes it different from a search good. Likewise, the inability to be certain, without assistance, of the qualities of a credence good following purchase of the good also distinguishes a credence good from an experience good. The fact that consumers can evaluate certain aspects of a credence good in advance of purchase, as in the case of a search good, explains why ads for credence goods, such as pharmaceuticals, often have informational elements. At the same time, however, the fact that consumers cannot truly evaluate credence goods until after purchase, and even then only with assistance, explains why ads for credence goods also commonly include persuasive elements.

26-13. Typically, the fixed costs of producing an information product are relatively high, while average variable cost is equal to a very small per-unit amount. As a consequence, the average total cost curve slopes downward with increased output, and average variable cost equals marginal cost at a low, constant amount irrespective of the quantity produced. For an information product, marginal cost is always below average total cost. Consequently, if price were equal to marginal cost, it would always be less than average total cost, so the producer would always earn short-run economic losses.

Chapter 27

27-1. **a.** 15 percent + 14 percent + 12 percent + 11 percent = 52 percent.
b. 52 percent + 10 percent + 10 percent + 8 percent + 7 percent = 87 percent; or 100 percent − 13 percent = 87 percent.

27-3. **a.** zero-sum game
b. negative-sum game
c. positive-sum game

27-5. Bob is currently a participant in a noncooperative game, in which some people stand and block his view of the football game. His tit-for-tat strategy is to stand up as well. If he stands, however, he will block the view of another spectator. In a cooperative game, all would sit or stand up simultaneously, so that no individual's view is blocked.

27-7. **a.** The fact that prices are growing at a stable rate and readily observable favor enforcing a cartel agreement So does the fact that there are only seven firms of significant size in the inkjet-printer industry, which is a relatively small number. Therefore, much depends on degree of heterogeneity of inkjet printers; if these products are relatively homogeneous, then taken together these characteristics of the industry would generally support an effort to form a cartel.
b. Once the cartel is formed, any one of the firms that produce inkjet printers could enlarge its profits by expanding production at the higher cartel price, so there is always an incentive to cheat. In addition, the presence of positive economic profits in the industry could induce firms outside the industry cartel to begin manufacturing and selling inkjet printers.

27-9. If Firm 2 opts for Format A, Firm 1 also prefers Format A, and if Firm 2 opts for Format B, Firm 1 prefers Format A. At the same time, if Firm 1 opts for Format A, Firm 2 prefers Format B, and if Firm 1 opts for Format B, Firm 2 prefers Format A. Thus, both firms will wish to produce compatible formats, although they will have to find a mechanism for settling on a format.

27-11. Possible examples include office productivity software, online auction services, telecommunications services, and Internet payment services. In each case, more people are likely to choose to consume the item when others do, because the inherent usefulness of consuming the item for each person increases as the number of consumers rises.

Chapter 28

28-1. If cable service is an industry that experiences diminishing long-run average total costs, then the city may determine that it is more efficient to have a single, large firm that produces at a lower long-run average cost. The city could then regulate the activity of the firm.

28-3. **a.** As the table indicates, long-run average cost and long-run marginal cost decline with greater output. If the firm were allowed to operate as a monopolist, it would produce to the point at which marginal cost equals marginal revenue, which is 2 units of output. The

Quantity	Price ($ per unit)	Long-Run Total Cost ($)	LRAC ($ per unit)	LRMC ($ per unit)	MR ($ per unit)
0	$100	$ 0	—	—	
1	95	92	$92.00	$92	$95
2	90	177	88.50	85	85
3	85	255	85.00	78	75
4	80	331	82.75	76	65
5	75	406	81.20	75	55
6	70	480	80.00	74	45

price that consumers are willing to pay for this quantity is $90 per unit, and maximum economic profits are $180 − $175 = $5.

b. Long-run marginal cost and price both equal $75 per unit at 5 units of output. At a price of $75 per unit, the firm experiences economic losses equal to $375 − $407 = −$32.

c. Long-run average cost and price both equal $85 per unit at 3 units of output. At a price of $80 per unit, the firm's economic profits equal $255 − $255 = $0.

28-5. Lemons problems are likely to be more common in industries in which evaluating the characteristics of goods or services by simple inspection is difficult, as is true of the credence goods discussed in Chapter 26. Unaddressed lemons problems tend to depress the prices that sellers of high-quality items can obtain, which induces them to refrain from selling their high-quality items, resulting in sales of only lower-quality items. The main concern of economic regulation is to balance the trade-off between service and price, with economic regulation aiming to keep price lower than the price a profit-maximizing monopolist would charge. Social regulation seeks to improve working conditions and minimize adverse spillovers of production. The adverse incentives resulting from lemons problems are a form of market spillover, so it is arguable that social regulation is most appropriate for addressing lemons problems.

28-7. If European regulation is designed to protect domestic industries, then this is an example of the capture hypothesis. If, on the other hand, there are legitimate health concerns, then this is an example of the share-the-pain, share-the-gain hypothesis.

28-9. This is a creative response to the do-not-call legislation, in which firms are legally satisfying the

terms of the regulation but evading the regulation's intent.

28-11. a. In this case, Firm 1 makes 75.0 percent of the sales in the Internet book market, and Firm 2 makes 46.7 percent of the sales in physical retail stores. By the antitrust authority's definition, there is a monopoly situation in the Internet book market.

b. In the combined market, Firm 2 accounts for 42.5 percent of all sales, and Firm 1's share drops to 7.5 percent, so under this alternative definition there is no cause for concern about monopoly.

28-13. If the Justice Department viewed Internet Realtor listing services as a "relevant market" for antitrust policy, then the growing concentration of ownership within this single retailing association might be a concern. Control over Internet listings by this group could help promote cartel-type behavior. A key issue is whether the Internet marketplace for Realtor listings is separate from the physical market.

28-15. This is an example of bundling. Because consumers who purchase the bundled product perceive that they have effectively paid different prices for the bundled products based on their willingness to pay, an antitrust authority might view this practice as charging consumers different prices for the same products, or price discrimination.

Chapter 29

29-1.

Labor Input (workers per week)	Total Physical Output (printers per day)	Marginal Physical Product	Marginal Revenue Product ($)
10	200	—	—
11	218	18	1,800
12	234	16	1,600
13	248	14	1,400
14	260	12	1,200
15	270	10	1,000
16	278	8	800

29-3. a. The greater the substitutability of capital, the more elastic is the demand for labor.

b. Because the demand for labor is a derived demand, the greater the elasticity of demand for the final product, the greater is the elasticity of demand for labor.

c. The larger the portion of factor costs accounted for by labor, the larger is the price elasticity of demand for labor.

29-5. a.

Labor Input (workers per week)	Total Physical Product	Product Price ($ per unit)	Marginal Physical Product	Total Revenue ($)	Marginal Revenue Product ($)
10	100	50	—	5,000	—
11	109	49	9	5,341	341
12	116	48	7	5,568	227
13	121	47	5	5,687	119
14	124	46	3	5,704	17
15	125	45	1	5,625	−79

b. The profit-maximizing firm would hire 13 workers, which is the quantity of labor beyond which the marginal revenue product of labor falls below the marginal factor cost.

29-7. a. The rise in the price of ethanol results in an increase in the marginal revenue product of corn, the key input in the production of ethanol. Thus, each ethanol producer's marginal revenue product curve shifts rightward, which ultimately translates into an increase in the demand for corn, from D_1 to D_2. The market clearing price of corn increases, from P_1 to P_2, and the equilibrium quantity of corn rises, from Q_1 to Q_2.

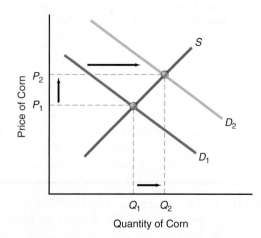

b. Human snack foods are a substitute input in the production of hogs, so the increase in the price of corn induced farmers to substitute in favor of snack foods.

29-9. Labor outsourcing by U.S. firms tends to push down market wages and employment in affected U.S. labor markets, but labor outsourcing by foreign firms that hire U.S. workers tends to push up market wages and employment in affected U.S. labor markets. Consequently, the overall wage and employment effects are ambiguous in the short run. In the long run, however, outsourcing enables U.S. and foreign firms to specialize in producing and trading the goods and services that they can produce most efficiently. The resulting resource saving ultimately expands the ability of U.S. residents to consume more goods and services than they could have otherwise.

29-11. The wage rate, $20 per unit of labor, equals marginal revenue product, so the marginal physical product of labor is $20 per unit of labor divided by the marginal revenue, $10 per unit of output, or 2 units of output per unit of labor.

29-13. In order to maximize profits, the firm should hire inputs up to the point at which the marginal physical product per dollar spent on the input is equalized across all inputs. This is not the case in this example. The marginal physical product of labor per dollar spent on wages is 200/$10 = 20 units of output per dollar spent on labor, which is less than the marginal physical product of capital per dollar spent on capital, which is 20,000/$500 or 40 units of output per dollar spent on capital. Thus, the firm should increase the additional output per dollar spent on labor by reducing the number of labor units it hires, and it should reduce the additional output per dollar spent on capital by increasing its use of capital, to the point where these amounts are equalized.

Chapter 30

30-1. Individual workers can air grievances to the collective voice who then takes the issue to the employer. The individual does not run the risk of being singled out by an employer. The individual employee does not waste work time trying to convince the employer that changes are needed in the workplace.

30-3. The reporting system probably was intended to provide information to union officials charged with seeking to impede strikebreaking activities by nonunion workers such as the soap opera writers. Strikebreakers can replace union employees, so they diminish the collective bargaining power of a union.

30-5. When marginal revenue is zero, demand for labor is unit-elastic, and total revenue is neither rising nor falling. No additional revenues can be earned by altering the quantity of labor, so the union's total wage revenues are maximized.

30-7. When unions in these industries attempt to bargain for higher-than-market levels of wages, the firms that employ members of these unions will not be able to readily substitute to alternative inputs. Hence, these unions are more likely to be able to achieve their wage objectives.

30-9.

Quantity of Labor Supplied	Total Physical Product	Required Hourly Wage Rate ($ per unit of labor)	Total Wage Bill ($)	Marginal Factor Cost ($ per unit of labor)
10	100	5	50	—
11	109	6	66	16
12	116	7	84	18
13	121	8	104	20
14	124	9	126	22
15	125	10	150	24

30-11. At 11 units of labor, the marginal revenue product of labor equals $16. This is equal to the marginal factor cost at this level of employment. The firm, therefore, will hire 11 units of labor and pay a wage of $6 an hour.

Quantity of Labor Supplied	Required Hourly Wage Rate ($ per unit of labor)	Total Factor Cost ($)	Marginal Factor Cost ($ per unit of labor)	Total Physical Product	Product Price ($ per unit)	Total Revenue ($)	Marginal Revenue Product ($ per unit of labor)
10	5	50	—	100	3.11	311.00	—
11	6	66	16.00	109	3.00	327.00	16.00
12	7	84	18.00	116	2.95	342.20	15.20
13	8	104	20.00	121	2.92	353.32	11.12
14	9	126	22.00	124	2.90	359.60	6.28
15	10	150	24.00	125	2.89	361.25	1.65

30-13. The marginal factor cost of the last worker hired was $106,480 − $105,600 = $880, so this is the marginal product of this worker if the firm is maximizing its profits.

Chapter 31

31-1. **a.** X, because for this country the Lorenz curve implies complete income equality.

b. Z, because this country's Lorenz curve is bowed farthest away from the case of complete income equality.

c. Closer, because if all other things including aggregate income remain unchanged, when more people in country Y are children below working age the share of income to people this age will decline, while the reverse will occur in country Z as more of its people reach working age and begin to earn incomes.

31-3. If the Lorenz curve is based on incomes net of transfer payments, then the Lorenz curve will become less bowed. But if the Lorenz curve does not account for transfer payments, its shape will remain unaffected.

31-5. Brazil

31-7. **a.** Absolute. If economic growth ultimately led to inflation-adjusted annual incomes for all urban families of four rising above $25,000 per year, then by this definition poverty would be ended.

b. Relative. By this definition, the lowest 15 percent of income earners will always be classified as being in a state of poverty.

c. Absolute. If economic growth eventually raised inflation-adjusted annual incomes of all individuals above $10,000, then by this definition poverty would cease to exist.

31-9. First, a moral hazard problem will exist, because government action would reduce the individual's incentive to continue a healthful lifestyle, thereby increasing the likelihood of greater health problems that will require future treatment. Second, an individual who currently has health problems will have an incentive to substitute future care that will be available at a zero price for current care that the individual must purchase at a positive price. Finally, in future years the patient will no longer have an incentive to contain health care expenses, and health care providers will have no incentive to minimize their costs.

31-11. The demand for health care will increase, and the marginal revenue curve will shift rightward. Hence, the profit-maximizing price and equilibrium quantity of health care services will increase.

31-13. Because funds in HRAs earn no interest, can be used to pay only medical expenses, and revert back to the employer at the end of the year if unused, an individual faces incentives to spend all these funds on every possible health care expense. In contrast, because funds in HSAs earn interest and can be used (subject to penalties and taxation) for other types of expenses, an individual has at least some incentive to try not to spend all the funds on health care expenses. Consequently, moral hazard problems are greater with HRAs than with HSAs.

Chapter 32

32-1. $4 per unit, which exactly accounts for the per-unit social cost of pollution.

32-3. a. 60 percent
b. 40 percent
c. 40 percent

32-5. a. There is a downward shift in the position of the marginal cost curve. The optimal degree of water cleanliness will rise above 65 percent, to a level such as 70 percent, and the cost incurred for the last unit of water clean-up will decrease to less than $10, such as a per-unit cost of $7.

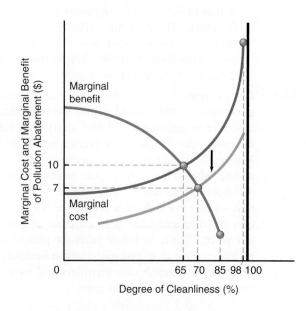

b. The second event induces an upward shift in the marginal benefit curve. Taken together, as shown in the diagram below, the two events unambiguously indicate that the optimal degree of water cleanliness increases above 65 percent, such as a level of 85 percent. The cost incurred for the last unit of water clean-up may rise or fall, however, and could end up at the initial level, which is the situation illustrated in the diagram.

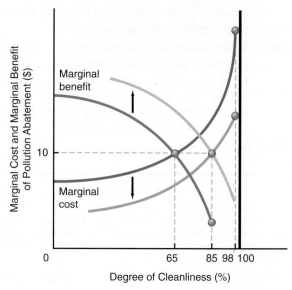

32-7. a. The marginal costs and benefits are tabulated below:

Population of Wild Tigers	Marginal Cost ($)	Marginal Benefit ($)
0	—	—
2,000	25	50
4,000	10	40
6,000	15	30
8,000	25	25
10,000	35	20
12,000	50	10

b. 8,000
c. 10,000

Chapter 33

33-1. a. The opportunity cost of pastries in Northland is 0.5 sandwich per pastry. The opportunity cost of sandwiches in Northland is 2 pastries per sandwich.

b. The opportunity cost of pastries in West Coast is 2 sandwiches per pastry. The opportunity cost of sandwiches in West Coast is 0.5 pastries per sandwich.

33-3. If Northland specializes in producing pastries, the maximum number of pastries it can produce and trade to West Coast is 50,000 pastries. Hence, the maximum number of units of each good that the two countries can trade at a rate of exchange of 1 pastry for 1 sandwich is 50,000.

33-5. Coastal Realm has a comparative advantage in producing digital TVs, and Border Kingdom has a comparative advantage in wine production.

33-7. a. The opportunity cost of modems in South Shore is 2 flash drives per modem. The opportunity cost of flash drives in South Shore is 0.5 modem per flash drive.

b. The opportunity cost of modems in East Isle is 0.5 flash drive per modem. The opportunity cost of flash drives in East Isle is 2 modems per flash drive.

c. Residents of South Shore have a comparative advantage in producing flash drives, and residents of East Isle have a comparative advantage in producing modems.

33-9. The critics are suggesting that Mexican exporters are shifting exports that would have gone to other nations to the United States, a nation within NAFTA, which would constitute trade diversion.

Chapter 34

34-1. The trade balance is merchandise exports minus merchandise imports, which equals 500 – 600 = −100, or a deficit of 100. Adding service exports of 75 and subtracting net unilateral transfers of 10 and service imports of 50 yields −100 + 75 − 10 − 50 = −85, or a current account balance of −85. The capital account balance equals the difference between capital inflows and capital outflows, or 300 − 200 = +100, or a capital account surplus of 100.

34-3. a. The increase in demand for Mexican-made guitars increases the demand for Mexican pesos, and the peso appreciates.

b. International investors will remove some of their financial capital from Mexico. The increase in the supply of pesos in the foreign exchange market will cause the peso to depreciate.

34-5. The demand for Chinese yuan increases, and the supply of yuan decreases. The dollar-yuan exchange rate rises, so the yuan appreciates.

34-7. The Canadian dollar–euro exchange rate is found by dividing the U.S. dollar–euro exchange rate by the U.S. dollar–Canadian dollar exchange rate, or (1.45 \$US/euro)/(0.94 \$US/\$C) = 1.54 \$C/euro, or 1.54 Canadian dollars per euro.

34-9. A flexible exchange rate system allows the exchange value of a currency to be determined freely in the foreign exchange market with no intervention by the government. A fixed exchange rate pegs the value of the currency, and the authorities responsible for the value of the currency intervene in foreign exchange markets to maintain this value. A dirty float involves occasional intervention by the exchange authorities. A target zone allows the exchange rate to fluctuate, but only within a given range of values.

34-11. When the dollar is pegged to gold at a rate of \$35 and the pound is pegged to the dollar at \$2 = £1, an implicit value between gold and the pound is established at £17.50 = 1 ounce of gold. If the dollar falls in value relative to gold, yet the pound is still valued to the dollar at \$2 = £1, the pound become undervalued relative to gold. The exchange rate between the dollar and the pound will have to be adjusted to 2.29 \$/£.

Photo Credits

Glossary

A

Absolute advantage The ability to produce more units of a good or service using a given quantity of labor or resource inputs. Equivalently, the ability to produce the same quantity of a good or service using fewer units of labor or resource inputs.

Accounting identities Values that are equivalent by definition.

Accounting profit Total revenues minus total explicit costs.

Action time lag The time between recognizing an economic problem and implementing policy to solve it. The action time lag is quite long for fiscal policy, which requires congressional approval.

Active (discretionary) policymaking All actions on the part of monetary and fiscal policymakers that are undertaken in response to or in anticipation of some change in the overall economy.

Ad valorem taxation Assessing taxes by charging a tax rate equal to a fraction of the market price of each unit purchased.

Adverse selection The likelihood that individuals who seek to borrow may use the funds that they receive for high-risk projects.

Age-earnings cycle The regular earnings profile of an individual throughout his or her lifetime. The age-earnings cycle usually starts with a low income, builds gradually to a peak at around age 50, and then gradually curves down until it approaches zero at retirement.

Aggregate demand The total of all planned expenditures in the entire economy.

Aggregate demand curve A curve showing planned purchase rates for all final goods and services in the economy at various price levels, all other things held constant.

Aggregate demand shock Any event that causes the aggregate demand curve to shift inward or outward.

Aggregate supply The total of all planned production for the economy.

Aggregate supply shock Any event that causes the aggregate supply curve to shift inward or outward.

Aggregates Total amounts or quantities; aggregate demand, for example, is total planned expenditures throughout a nation.

Anticipated inflation The inflation rate that we believe will occur; when it does, we are in a situation of fully anticipated inflation.

Antitrust legislation Laws that restrict the formation of monopolies and regulate certain anticompetitive business practices.

Appreciation An increase in the exchange value of one nation's currency in terms of the currency of another nation.

Asset demand Holding money as a store of value instead of other assets such as certificates of deposit, corporate bonds, and stocks.

Assets Amounts owned; all items to which a business or household holds legal claim.

Asymmetric information Information possessed by one party in a financial transaction but not by the other party.

Automatic, or built-in, stabilizers Special provisions of certain federal programs that cause changes in desired aggregate expenditures without the action of Congress and the president. Examples are the federal progressive tax system and unemployment compensation.

Autonomous consumption The part of consumption that is independent of (does not depend on) the level of disposable income. Changes in autonomous consumption shift the consumption function.

Average fixed costs Total fixed costs divided by the number of units produced.

Average physical product Total product divided by the variable input.

Average propensity to consume (APC) Real consumption divided by real disposable income; for any given level of real income, the proportion of total real disposable income that is consumed.

Average propensity to save (APS) Real saving divided by real disposable income; for any given level of real income, the proportion of total real disposable income that is saved.

Average tax rate The total tax payment divided by total income. It is the proportion of total income paid in taxes.

Average total costs Total costs divided by the number of units produced; sometimes called *average per-unit total costs*.

Average variable costs Total variable costs divided by the number of units produced.

B

Balance of payments A system of accounts that measures transactions of goods, services, income, and financial assets between domestic households, businesses, and governments and residents of the rest of the world during a specific time period.

Balance of trade The difference between exports and imports of physical goods.

Balance sheet A statement of the assets and liabilities of any business entity, including financial institutions and the Federal Reserve System. Assets are what is owned; liabilities are what is owed.

Balanced budget A situation in which the government's spending is exactly equal to the total taxes and other revenues it collects during a given period of time.

Bank runs Attempts by many of a bank's depositors to convert transactions and time deposits into currency out of fear that the bank's liabilities may exceed its assets.

Barter The direct exchange of goods and services for other goods and services without the use of money.

Base year The year that is chosen as the point of reference for comparison of prices in other years.

Base-year dollars The value of a current sum expressed in terms of prices in a base year.

Behavioral economics An approach to the study of consumer behavior that emphasizes psychological limitations and complications that potentially interfere with rational decision making.

Bilateral monopoly A market structure consisting of a monopolist and a monopsonist.

Black market A market in which goods are traded at prices above their legal maximum prices or in which illegal goods are sold.

Bond A legal claim against a firm, usually entitling the owner of the bond to receive a fixed annual coupon payment, plus a lump-sum payment at the bond's maturity date. Bonds are issued in return for funds lent to the firm.

Bounded rationality The hypothesis that people are *nearly*, but not fully, rational, so that they cannot examine every possible choice available to them but instead use simple rules of thumb to sort among the alternatives that happen to occur to them.

Budget constraint All of the possible combinations of goods that can be purchased (at fixed prices) with a specific budget.

Bundling Offering two or more products for sale as a set.

Business fluctuations The ups and downs in business activity throughout the economy.

C

Capital account A category of balance of payments transactions that measures flows of real and financial assets.

Capital consumption allowance Another name for depreciation, the amount that businesses would have to save in order to take care of deteriorating machines and other equipment.

Capital gain A positive difference between the purchase price and the sale price of an asset. If a share of stock is bought for $5 and then sold for $15, the capital gain is $10.

Capital goods Producer durables; nonconsumable goods that firms use to make other goods.

Capital loss A negative difference between the purchase price and the sale price of an asset.

Capture hypothesis A theory of regulatory behavior that predicts that regulators will eventually be captured by

special interests of the industry being regulated.

Cartel An association of producers in an industry that agree to set common prices and output quotas to prevent competition.

Central bank A banker's bank, usually an official institution that also serves as a country's treasury's bank. Central banks normally regulate commercial banks.

Certificate of deposit (CD) A time deposit with a fixed maturity date offered by banks and other financial institutions.

Ceteris paribus **[KAY-ter-us PEAR-uh-bus] assumption** The assumption that nothing changes except the factor or factors being studied.

Ceteris paribus **conditions** Determinants of the relationship between price and quantity that are unchanged along a curve; changes in these factors cause the curve to shift.

Closed shop A business enterprise in which employees must belong to the union before they can be hired and must remain in the union after they are hired.

Collective bargaining Negotiation between the management of a company or of a group of companies and the management of a union or a group of unions for the purpose of reaching a mutually agreeable contract that sets wages, fringe benefits, and working conditions for all employees in all the unions involved.

Collective decision making How voters, politicians, and other interested parties act and how these actions influence nonmarket decisions.

Common property Property that is owned by everyone and therefore by no one. Air and water are examples of common property resources.

Comparative advantage The ability to produce a good or service at a lower opportunity cost than other producers.

Complements Two goods are complements when a change in the price of one causes an opposite shift in the demand for the other.

Concentration ratio The percentage of all sales contributed by the leading four or leading eight firms in an industry; sometimes called the *industry concentration ratio*.

Constant dollars Dollars expressed in terms of real purchasing power using a particular year as the base or standard of comparison, in contrast to current dollars.

Constant returns to scale No change in long-run average costs when output increases.

Constant-cost industry An industry whose total output can be increased without an increase in long-run per-unit costs; its long-run supply curve is horizontal.

Consumer optimum A choice of a set of goods and services that maximizes the level of satisfaction for each consumer, subject to limited income.

Consumer Price Index (CPI) A statistical measure of a weighted average of prices of a specified set of goods and services purchased by typical consumers in urban areas.

Consumer surplus The total difference between the total amount that consumers would have been willing to pay for a good or service and the total amount that they actually pay.

Consumption Spending on new goods and services to be used up out of a household's current income. Whatever is not consumed is saved. Consumption includes such things as buying food and going to a concert.

Consumption function The relationship between amount consumed and disposable income. A consumption function tells us how much people plan to consume at various levels of disposable income.

Consumption goods Goods bought by households to use up, such as food and movies.

Contraction A business fluctuation during which the pace of national economic activity is slowing down.

Cooperative game A game in which the players explicitly cooperate to make themselves better off. As applied to firms, it involves companies colluding in order to make higher than perfectly competitive rates of return.

Corporation A legal entity that may conduct business in its own name just as an individual does; the owners of a corporation, called shareholders, own shares of the firm's profits and enjoy the protection of limited liability.

Cost-of-living adjustments (COLAs) Clauses in contracts that allow for increases in specified nominal values to take account of changes in the cost of living.

Cost-of-service regulation Regulation that allows prices to reflect only the actual average cost of production and no monopoly profits.

Cost-push inflation Inflation caused by decreases in short-run aggregate supply.

Craft unions Labor unions composed of workers who engage in a particular trade or skill, such as baking, carpentry, or plumbing.

Crawling peg An exchange rate arrangement in which a country pegs the value of its currency to the exchange value of another nation's currency but allows the par value to change at regular intervals.

Creative response Behavior on the part of a firm that allows it to comply with the letter of the law but violate the spirit, significantly lessening the law's effects.

Credence good A product with qualities that consumers lack the expertise to assess without assistance.

Cross price elasticity of demand (E_{xy}) The percentage change in the demand for one good (holding its price constant) divided by the percentage change in the price of a related good.

Crowding-out effect The tendency of expansionary fiscal policy to cause a decrease in planned investment or planned consumption in the private sector; this decrease normally results from the rise in interest rates.

Current account A category of balance of payments transactions that measures the exchange of merchandise, the exchange of services, and unilateral transfers.

Cyclical unemployment Unemployment resulting from business recessions that occur when aggregate (total) demand is insufficient to create full employment.

D

Dead capital Any capital resource that lacks clear title of ownership.

Deadweight loss The portion of consumer surplus that no one in society is able to obtain in a situation of monopoly.

Decreasing-cost industry An industry in which an increase in output leads to a reduction in long-run per-unit costs, such that the long-run industry supply curve slopes downward.

Deflation A sustained decrease in the average of all prices of goods and services in an economy.

Demand A schedule showing how much of a good or service people will purchase at any price during a specified time period, other things being constant.

Demand curve A graphical representation of the demand schedule; a negatively sloped line showing the inverse relationship between the price and the quantity demanded (other things being equal).

Demand-pull inflation Inflation caused by increases in aggregate demand not matched by increases in aggregate supply.

Dependent variable A variable whose value changes according to changes in the value of one or more independent variables.

Depository institutions Financial institutions that accept deposits from savers and lend funds from those deposits out at interest.

Depreciation A decrease in the exchange value of one nation's currency in terms of the currency of another nation.

Depression An extremely severe recession.

Derived demand Input factor demand derived from demand for the final product being produced.

Development economics The study of factors that contribute to the economic growth of a country.

Diminishing marginal utility The principle that as more of any good or service is consumed, its extra benefit declines. Otherwise stated, increases in total utility from the consumption of a good or service become smaller and

smaller as more is consumed during a given time period.

Direct expenditure offsets Actions on the part of the private sector in spending income that offset government fiscal policy actions. Any increase in government spending in an area that competes with the private sector will have some direct expenditure offset.

Direct marketing Advertising targeted at specific consumers, typically in the form of postal mailings, telephone calls, or e-mail messages.

Direct relationship A relationship between two variables that is positive, meaning that an increase in one variable is associated with an increase in the other and a decrease in one variable is associated with a decrease in the other.

Dirty float Active management of a floating exchange rate on the part of a country's government, often in cooperation with other nations.

Discount rate The interest rate that the Federal Reserve charges for reserves that it lends to depository institutions. It is sometimes referred to as the *rediscount rate* or, in Canada and England, as the *bank rate*.

Discounting The method by which the present value of a future sum or a future stream of sums is obtained.

Discouraged workers Individuals who have stopped looking for a job because they are convinced that they will not find a suitable one.

Diseconomies of scale Increases in long-run average costs that occur as output increases.

Disposable personal income (DPI) Personal income after personal income taxes have been paid.

Dissaving Negative saving; a situation in which spending exceeds income. Dissaving can occur when a household is able to borrow or use up existing assets.

Distribution of income The way income is allocated among the population.

Dividends Portion of a corporation's profits paid to its owners (shareholders).

Division of labor The segregation of resources into different specific tasks; for example, one automobile worker puts on bumpers, another doors, and so on.

Dominant strategies Strategies that always yield the highest benefit. Regardless of what other players do, a dominant strategy will yield the most benefit for the player using it.

Dumping Selling a good or a service abroad below the price charged in the home market or at a price below its cost of production.

Durable consumer goods Consumer goods that have a life span of more than three years.

Dynamic tax analysis Economic evaluation of tax rate changes that recognizes that the tax base eventually declines with ever-higher tax rates, so that tax revenues may eventually decline if the tax rate is raised sufficiently.

E

Economic freedom The rights to own private property and to exchange goods, services, and financial assets with minimal government interference.

Economic goods Goods that are scarce, for which the quantity demanded exceeds the quantity supplied at a zero price.

Economic growth Increases in per capita real GDP measured by its rate of change per year.

Economic profits Total revenues minus total opportunity costs of all inputs used, or the total of all implicit and explicit costs.

Economic rent A payment for the use of any resource over and above its opportunity cost.

Economics The study of how people allocate their limited resources to satisfy their unlimited wants.

Economies of scale Decreases in long-run average costs resulting from increases in output.

Effect time lag The time that elapses between the implementation of a policy and the results of that policy.

Efficiency The case in which a given level of inputs is used to produce the maximum output possible. Alternatively, the situation in which a given output is produced at minimum cost.

Effluent fee A charge to a polluter that gives the right to discharge into the air or water a certain amount of pollution; also called a *pollution tax*

Elastic demand A demand relationship in which a given percentage change in price will result in a larger percentage change in quantity demanded.

Empirical Relying on real-world data in evaluating the usefulness of a model.

Endowments The various resources in an economy, including both physical resources and such human resources as ingenuity and management skills.

Entitlements Guaranteed benefits under a government program such as Social Security, Medicare, or Medicaid.

Entrepreneurship The component of human resources that performs the functions of raising capital, organizing, managing, and assembling other factors of production, making basic business policy decisions, and taking risks.

Equation of exchange The formula indicating that the number of monetary units (M_s) times the number of times each unit is spent on final goods and services (V) is identical to the price level (P) times real GDP (Y).

Equilibrium The situation when quantity supplied equals quantity demanded at a particular price.

Excess reserves The difference between actual reserves and required reserves.

Exchange rate The price of one nation's currency in terms of the currency of another country.

Excise tax A tax levied on purchases of a particular good or service.

Expansion A business fluctuation in which the pace of national economic activity is speeding up.

Expenditure approach Computing GDP by adding up the dollar value at current market prices of all final goods and services.

Experience good A product that an individual must consume before the product's quality can be established.

Explicit costs Costs that business managers must take account of because they must be paid; examples are wages, taxes, and rent.

Externality A consequence of an economic activity that spills over to affect third parties. Pollution is an externality.

F

Featherbedding Any practice that forces employers to use more labor than they would otherwise or to use existing labor in an inefficient manner.

Federal Deposit Insurance Corporation (FDIC) A government agency that insures the deposits held in banks and most other depository institutions; all U.S. banks are insured this way.

Federal funds market A private market (made up mostly of banks) in which banks can borrow reserves from other banks that want to lend them. Federal funds are usually lent for overnight use.

Federal funds rate The interest rate that depository institutions pay to borrow reserves in the interbank federal funds market.

Fiduciary monetary system A system in which money is issued by the government and its value is based uniquely on the public's faith that the currency represents command over goods and services.

Final goods and services Goods and services that are at their final stage of production and will not be transformed into yet other goods or services. For example, wheat ordinarily is not considered a final good because it is usually used to make a final good, bread.

Financial capital Funds used to purchase physical capital goods, such as buildings and equipment, and patents and trademarks.

Financial intermediaries Institutions that transfer funds between ultimate lenders (savers) and ultimate borrowers.

Financial intermediation The process by which financial institutions accept savings from businesses, households, and governments and lend the savings to other businesses, households, and governments.

Firm A business organization that employs resources to produce goods or services for profit. A firm normally owns and operates at least one "plant" or facility in order to produce.

Fiscal policy The discretionary changing of government expenditures or taxes to achieve national economic goals, such as high employment with price stability.

Fixed costs Costs that do not vary with output. Fixed costs typically include such expenses as rent on a building. These costs are fixed for a certain period of time (in the long run, though, they are variable).

Fixed investment Purchases by businesses of newly produced producer durables, or capital goods, such as production machinery and office equipment.

Flexible exchange rates Exchange rates that are allowed to fluctuate in the open market in response to changes in supply and demand. Sometimes called *floating exchange rates*.

Flow A quantity measured per unit of time; something that occurs over time, such as the income you make per week or per year or the number of individuals who are fired every month.

FOMC Directive A document that summarizes the Federal Open Market Committee's general policy strategy, establishes near-term objectives for the federal funds rate, and specifies target ranges for money supply growth.

Foreign direct investment The acquisition of more than 10 percent of the shares of ownership in a company in another nation.

Foreign exchange market A market in which households, firms, and governments buy and sell national currencies.

Foreign exchange rate The price of one currency in terms of another.

Foreign exchange risk The possibility that changes in the value of a nation's currency will result in variations in the market value of assets.

45-degree reference line The line along which planned real expenditures equal real GDP per year.

Fractional reserve banking A system in which depository institutions hold reserves that are less than the amount of total deposits.

Free-rider problem A problem that arises when individuals presume that others will pay for public goods so that, individually, they can escape paying for their portion without causing a reduction in production.

Frictional unemployment Unemployment due to the fact that workers must search for appropriate job offers. This

takes time, and so they remain temporarily unemployed.

Full employment An arbitrary level of unemployment that corresponds to "normal" friction in the labor market. In 1986, a 6.5 percent rate of unemployment was considered full employment. Today, it is assumed to be around 5 percent.

G

Game theory A way of describing the various possible outcomes in any situation involving two or more interacting individuals when those individuals are aware of the interactive nature of their situation and plan accordingly. The plans made by these individuals are known as *game strategies*.

GDP deflator A price index measuring the changes in prices of all new goods and services produced in the economy.

General Agreement on Tariffs and Trade (GATT) An international agreement established in 1947 to further world trade by reducing barriers and tariffs. The GATT was replaced by the World Trade Organization in 1995.

Goods All things from which individuals derive satisfaction or happiness.

Government budget constraint The limit on government spending and transfers imposed by the fact that every dollar the government spends, transfers, or uses to repay borrowed funds must ultimately be provided by the user charges and taxes it collects.

Government budget deficit An excess of government spending over government revenues during a given period of time.

Government budget surplus An excess of government revenues over government spending during a given period of time.

Government, or political, goods Goods (and services) provided by the public sector; they can be either private or public goods.

Government-inhibited good A good that has been deemed socially undesirable through the political process. Heroin is an example.

Government-sponsored good A good that has been deemed socially desirable through the political process. Museums are an example.

Gross domestic income (GDI) The sum of all income—wages, interest, rent, and profits—paid to the four factors of production.

Gross domestic product (GDP) The total market value of all final goods and services produced during a year by factors of production located within a nation's borders.

Gross private domestic investment The creation of capital goods, such as factories and machines, that can yield production and hence consumption in the future. Also included in this definition are changes in business inventories and repairs made to machines or buildings.

Gross public debt All federal government debt irrespective of who owns it.

H

Health savings account (HSA) A tax-exempt health care account into which individuals can pay on a regular basis and out of which medical expenses can be paid.

Hedge A financial strategy that reduces the chance of suffering losses arising from foreign exchange risk.

Horizontal merger The joining of firms that are producing or selling a similar product.

Human capital The accumulated training and education of workers.

I

Implicit costs Expenses that managers do not have to pay out of pocket and hence normally do not explicitly calculate, such as the opportunity cost of factors of production that are owned; examples are owner-provided capital and owner-provided labor.

Import quota A physical supply restriction on imports of a particular good, such as sugar. Foreign exporters are unable to sell in the United States more than the quantity specified in the import quota.

Incentive structure The system of rewards and punishments individuals face with respect to their own actions.

Incentives Rewards for engaging in a particular activity.

Income approach Measuring GDP by adding up all components of national income, including wages, interest, rent, and profits.

Income elasticity of demand (E_i) The percentage change in demand for any good, holding its price constant, divided by the percentage change in income; the responsiveness of demand to changes in income, holding the good's relative price constant.

Income in kind Income received in the form of goods and services, such as housing or medical care; to be contrasted with money income, which is simply income in dollars, or general purchasing power, that can be used to buy any goods and services.

Income velocity of money (V) The number of times per year a dollar is spent on final goods and services; identically equal to nominal GDP divided by the money supply.

Income-consumption curve The set of optimal consumption points that would occur if income were increased, relative prices remaining constant.

Increasing-cost industry An industry in which an increase in industry output is accompanied by an increase in long-run per-unit costs, such that the long-run industry supply curve slopes upward.

Independent variable A variable whose value is determined independently of, or outside, the equation under study.

Indifference curve A curve composed of a set of consumption alternatives, each of which yields the same total amount of satisfaction.

Indirect business taxes All business taxes except the tax on corporate profits. Indirect business taxes include sales and business property taxes.

Industrial unions Labor unions that consist of workers from a particular industry, such as automobile manufacturing or steel manufacturing.

Industry supply curve The locus of points showing the minimum prices at which given quantities will be forthcoming; also called the *market supply curve*.

Inefficient point Any point below the production possibilities curve, at which the use of resources is not generating the maximum possible output.

Inelastic demand A demand relationship in which a given percentage change in price will result in a less than propor-

tionate percentage change in the quantity demanded.

Infant industry argument The contention that tariffs should be imposed to protect from import competition an industry that is trying to get started. Presumably, after the industry becomes technologically efficient, the tariff can be lifted.

Inferior goods Goods for which demand falls as income rises.

Inflation A sustained increase in the average of all prices of goods and services in an economy.

Inflation-adjusted return A rate of return that is measured in terms of real goods and services; that is, after the effects of inflation have been factored out.

Inflationary gap The gap that exists whenever equilibrium real GDP per year is greater than full-employment real GDP as shown by the position of the long-run aggregate supply curve.

Information product An item that is produced using information-intensive inputs at a relatively high fixed cost but distributed for sale at a relatively low marginal cost.

Informational advertising Advertising that emphasizes transmitting knowledge about the features of a product.

Innovation Transforming an invention into something that is useful to humans.

Inside information Information that is not available to the general public about what is happening in a corporation.

Interactive marketing Advertising that permits a consumer to follow up directly by searching for more information and placing direct product orders.

Interest The payment for current rather than future command over resources; the cost of obtaining credit.

Interest rate effect One of the reasons that the aggregate demand curve slopes downward: Higher price levels increase the interest rate, which in turn causes businesses and consumers to reduce desired spending due to the higher cost of borrowing.

Intermediate goods Goods used up entirely in the production of final goods.

International financial crisis The rapid withdrawal of foreign investments and loans from a nation.

International Monetary Fund An agency founded to administer an international foreign exchange system and to lend to member countries that had balance of payments problems. The IMF now functions as a lender of last resort for national governments.

Inventory investment Changes in the stocks of finished goods and goods in process, as well as changes in the raw materials that businesses keep on hand. Whenever inventories are decreasing, inventory investment is negative; whenever they are increasing, inventory investment is positive.

Inverse relationship A relationship between two variables that is negative, meaning that an increase in one variable is associated with a decrease in the other and a decrease in one variable is associated with an increase in the other.

Investment Any use of today's resources to expand tomorrow's production or consumption.

J

Job leaver An individual in the labor force who quits voluntarily.

Job loser An individual in the labor force whose employment was involuntarily terminated.

Jurisdictional dispute A disagreement involving two or more unions over which should have control of a particular jurisdiction, such as a particular craft or skill or a particular firm or industry.

K

Keynesian short-run aggregate supply curve The horizontal portion of the aggregate supply curve in which there is excessive unemployment and unused capacity in the economy.

L

Labor Productive contributions of humans who work.

Labor force Individuals aged 16 years or older who either have jobs or who are looking and available for jobs; the number of employed plus the number of unemployed.

Labor force participation rate The percentage of noninstitutionalized working-age individuals who are employed or seeking employment.

Labor productivity Total real domestic output (real GDP) divided by the number of workers (output per worker).

Labor unions Worker organizations that seek to secure economic improvements for their members; they also seek to improve the safety, health, and other benefits (such as job security) of their members.

Land The natural resources that are available from nature. Land as a resource includes location, original fertility and mineral deposits, topography, climate, water, and vegetation.

Law of demand The observation that there is a negative, or inverse, relationship between the price of any good or service and the quantity demanded, holding other factors constant.

Law of diminishing marginal product The observation that after some point, successive equal-sized increases in a variable factor of production, such as labor, added to fixed factors of production, will result in smaller increases in output.

Law of increasing relative cost The fact that the opportunity cost of additional units of a good generally increases as society attempts to produce more of that good. This accounts for the bowed-out shape of the production possibilities curve.

Law of supply The observation that the higher the price of a good, the more of that good sellers will make available over a specified time period, other things being equal.

Leading indicators Events that have been found to occur before changes in business activity.

Lemons problem The potential for asymmetric information to bring about a general decline in product quality in an industry.

Lender of last resort The Federal Reserve's role as an institution that is willing and able to lend to a temporarily illiquid bank that is otherwise in good financial condition to prevent the bank's illiquid position from leading to a general loss of confidence in that bank or in others.

Liabilities Amounts owed; the legal claims against a business or household by nonowners.

Limited liability A legal concept in which the responsibility, or liability, of the owners of a corporation is limited to the value of the shares in the firm that they own.

Liquidity The degree to which an asset can be acquired or disposed of without much danger of any intervening loss in *nominal* value and with small transaction costs. Money is the most liquid asset.

Liquidity approach A method of measuring the money supply by looking at money as a temporary store of value.

Long run The time period during which all factors of production can be varied.

Long-run aggregate supply curve A vertical line representing the real output of goods and services after full adjustment has occurred. It can also be viewed as representing the real GDP of the economy under conditions of full employment—the full-employment level of real GDP.

Long-run average cost curve The locus of points representing the minimum unit cost of producing any given rate of output, given current technology and resource prices.

Long-run industry supply curve A market supply curve showing the relationship between prices and quantities after firms have been allowed the time to enter into or exit from an industry, depending on whether there have been positive or negative economic profits.

Lorenz curve A geometric representation of the distribution of income. A Lorenz curve that is perfectly straight represents complete income equality. The more bowed a Lorenz curve, the more unequally income is distributed.

Lump-sum tax A tax that does not depend on income. An example is a $1,000 tax that every household must pay, irrespective of its economic situation.

M

M1 The money supply, measured as the total value of currency plus transactions deposits plus traveler's checks not issued by banks.

M2 M1 plus (1) savings and small-denomination time deposits at all depository institutions, (2) balances in retail money market mutual funds, and (3) money market deposit accounts (MMDAs).

Macroeconomics The study of the behavior of the economy as a whole, including such economywide phenomena as changes in unemployment, the general price level, and national income.

Majority rule A collective decision-making system in which group decisions are made on the basis of more than 50 percent of the vote. In other words, whatever more than half of the electorate votes for, the entire electorate has to accept.

Marginal cost pricing A system of pricing in which the price charged is equal to the opportunity cost to society of producing one more unit of the good or service in question. The opportunity cost is the marginal cost to society.

Marginal costs The change in total costs due to a one-unit change in production rate.

Marginal factor cost (MFC) The cost of using an additional unit of an input. For example, if a firm can hire all the workers it wants at the going wage rate, the marginal factor cost of labor is the wage rate.

Marginal physical product The physical output that is due to the addition of one more unit of a variable factor of production; the change in total product occurring when a variable input is increased and all other inputs are held constant; also called *marginal product*.

Marginal physical product (MPP) of labor The change in output resulting from the addition of one more worker. The MPP of the worker equals the change in total output accounted for by hiring the worker, holding all other factors of production constant.

Marginal propensity to consume (MPC) The ratio of the change in consumption to the change in disposable income. A marginal propensity to consume of 0.8 tells us that an additional $100 in take-home pay will lead to an additional $80 consumed.

Marginal propensity to save (MPS) The ratio of the change in saving to the change in disposable income. A marginal propensity to save of 0.2 indicates that out of an additional $100 in take-home pay, $20 will be saved. Whatever is not saved is consumed. The marginal propensity to save plus the marginal propensity to consume must always equal 1, by definition.

Marginal revenue The change in total revenues resulting from a one-unit change in output (and sale) of the product in question.

Marginal revenue product (MRP) The marginal physical product (MPP) times marginal revenue (MR). The MRP gives the additional revenue obtained from a one-unit change in labor input.

Marginal tax rate The change in the tax payment divided by the change in income, or the percentage of additional dollars that must be paid in taxes. The marginal tax rate is applied to the highest tax bracket of taxable income reached.

Marginal utility The change in total utility due to a one-unit change in the quantity of a good or service consumed.

Market All of the arrangements that individuals have for exchanging with one another. Thus, for example, we can speak of the labor market, the automobile market, and the credit market.

Market clearing, or equilibrium, price The price that clears the market, at which quantity demanded equals quantity supplied; the price where the demand curve intersects the supply curve.

Market demand The demand of all consumers in the marketplace for a particular good or service. The summation at each price of the quantity demanded by each individual.

Market failure A situation in which an unrestrained market operation leads to either too few or too many resources going to a specific economic activity.

Market share test The percentage of a market that a particular firm supplies; used as the primary measure of monopoly power.

Mass marketing Advertising intended to reach as many consumers as possible, typically through television, newspaper, radio, or magazine ads.

Medium of exchange Any item that sellers will accept as payment.

Microeconomics The study of decision making undertaken by individuals (or households) and by firms.

Minimum efficient scale (MES) The lowest rate of output per unit time at which long-run average costs for a particular firm are at a minimum.

Minimum wage A wage floor, legislated by government, setting the lowest hourly rate that firms may legally pay workers.

Models, or theories Simplified representations of the real world used as the basis for predictions or explanations.

Money Any medium that is universally accepted in an economy both by sellers of goods and services as payment for those goods and services and by creditors as payment for debts.

Money balances Synonymous with money, money stock, money holdings.

Money illusion Reacting to changes in money prices rather than relative prices. If a worker whose wages double when the price level also doubles thinks he or she is better off, that worker is suffering from money illusion.

Money market deposit accounts (MMDAs) Accounts issued by banks yielding a market rate of interest with a minimum balance requirement and a limit on transactions. They have no minimum maturity.

Money market mutual funds Funds obtained from the public that investment companies hold in common and use to acquire short-maturity credit instruments, such as certificates of deposit and securities sold by the U.S. government.

Money multiplier A number that, when multiplied by a change in reserves in the banking system, yields the resulting change in the money supply.

Money price The price that we observe today, expressed in today's dollars; also called the *absolute* or *nominal price*.

Money supply The amount of money in circulation.

Monopolist The single supplier of a good or service for which there is no close substitute. The monopolist therefore constitutes its entire industry.

Monopolistic competition A market situation in which a large number of firms produce similar but not identical products. Entry into the industry is relatively easy.

Monopolization The possession of monopoly power in the relevant market and the willful acquisition or maintenance of that power, as distinguished from growth or development as a consequence of a superior product, business acumen, or historical accident.

Monopoly A firm that can determine the market price of a good. In the extreme case, a monopoly is the only seller of a good or service.

Monopsonist The only buyer in a market.

Monopsonistic exploitation Paying a price for the variable input that is less than its marginal revenue product; the difference between marginal revenue product and the wage rate.

Moral hazard The possibility that a borrower might engage in riskier behavior after a loan has been obtained.

Multiplier The ratio of the change in the equilibrium level of real GDP to the change in autonomous real expenditures; the number by which a change in autonomous real investment or autonomous real consumption, for example, is multiplied to get the change in equilibrium real GDP.

Multiproduct firm A firm that produces and sells two or more different items.

N

National income (NI) The total of all factor payments to resource owners. It can be obtained from net domestic product (NDP) by subtracting indirect business taxes and transfers and adding net U.S. income earned abroad and other business income adjustments.

National income accounting A measurement system used to estimate national income and its components; one approach to measuring an economy's aggregate performance.

Natural monopoly A monopoly that arises from the peculiar production characteristics in an industry. It usually arises when there are large economies of scale relative to the industry's demand such that one firm can produce at a lower average cost than can be achieved by multiple firms.

Natural rate of unemployment The rate of unemployment that is estimated to prevail in long-run macroeconomic equilibrium, when all workers and employers have fully adjusted to any changes in the economy.

Negative market feedback A tendency for a good or service to fall out of favor with more consumers because other consumers have stopped purchasing the item.

Negative-sum game A game in which players as a group lose during the process of the game.

Net domestic product (NDP) GDP minus depreciation.

Net investment Gross private domestic investment minus an estimate of the wear and tear on the existing capital stock. Net investment therefore measures the change in the capital stock over a one-year period.

Net public debt Gross public debt minus all government interagency borrowing.

Net worth The difference between assets and liabilities.

Network effect A situation in which a consumer's willingness to purchase a good or service is influenced by how many others also buy or have bought the item.

Neutral federal funds rate A value of the interest rate on interbank loans at which the growth rate of real GDP tends neither to rise nor to fall relative to the rate of growth of potential, long-run, real GDP, given the expected rate of inflation.

New entrant An individual who has never held a full-time job lasting two weeks or longer but is now seeking employment.

New growth theory A theory of economic growth that examines the factors that determine why technology, research, innovation, and the like are undertaken and how they interact.

New Keynesian inflation dynamics In new Keynesian theory, the pattern of inflation exhibited by an economy with growing aggregate demand—initial sluggish adjustment of the price level in response to increased aggregate demand followed by higher inflation later.

Nominal rate of interest The market rate of interest expressed in today's dollars.

Nominal values The values of variables such as GDP and investment expressed in current dollars, also called *money values*; measurement in terms of the actual market prices at which goods and services are sold.

Nonaccelerating inflation rate of unemployment (NAIRU) The rate of unemployment below which the rate of inflation tends to rise and above which the rate of inflation tends to fall.

Noncontrollable expenditures Government spending that changes automatically without action by Congress.

Noncooperative game A game in which the players neither negotiate nor cooperate in any way. As applied to firms in an industry, this is the common situation in which there are relatively few firms and each has some ability to change price.

Nondurable consumer goods Consumer goods that are used up within three years.

Nonincome expense items The total of indirect business taxes and depreciation.

Nonprice rationing devices All methods used to ration scarce goods that are price-controlled. Whenever the price system is not allowed to work, nonprice rationing devices will evolve to ration the affected goods and services.

Normal goods Goods for which demand rises as income rises. Most goods are normal goods.

Normal rate of return The amount that must be paid to an investor to induce investment in a business; also known as the *opportunity cost of capital*.

Normative economics Analysis involving value judgments about economic policies; relates to whether things are good or bad. A statement of *what ought to be*.

Number line A line that can be divided into segments of equal length, each associated with a number.

O

Oligopoly A market structure in which there are very few sellers. Each seller knows that the other sellers will react to its changes in prices, quantities, and qualities.

Open economy effect One of the reasons that the aggregate demand curve slopes downward: Higher price levels result in foreign residents desiring to buy fewer U.S.-made goods, while U.S. residents now desire more foreign-made goods, thereby reducing net exports. This is equivalent to a reduction in the amount of real goods and services purchased in the United States.

Open market operations The purchase and sale of existing U.S. government securities (such as bonds) in the open private market by the Federal Reserve System.

Opportunistic behavior Actions that focus solely on short-run gains because long-run benefits of cooperation are perceived to be smaller.

Opportunity cost The highest-valued, next-best alternative that must be sacrificed to obtain something or to satisfy a want.

Opportunity cost of capital The normal rate of return, or the available return on the next-best alternative investment. Economists consider this a cost of production, and it is included in our cost examples.

Optimal quantity of pollution The level of pollution for which the marginal benefit of one additional unit of pollution abatement just equals the marginal cost of that additional unit of pollution abatement.

Origin The intersection of the *y* axis and the *x* axis in a graph.

Outsourcing A firm's employment of labor outside the country in which the firm is located.

P

Par value The officially determined value of a currency.

Partnership A business owned by two or more joint owners, or partners, who share the responsibilities and the profits of the firm and are individually liable for all the debts of the partnership.

Passive (nondiscretionary) policymaking Policymaking that is carried out in response to a rule. It is therefore not in response to an actual or potential change in overall economic activity.

Patent A government protection that gives an inventor the exclusive right to make, use, or sell an invention for a limited period of time (currently, 20 years).

Payment intermediaries Institutions that facilitate transfers of funds between depositors who hold transactions deposits with those institutions.

Payoff matrix A matrix of outcomes, or consequences, of the strategies available to the players in a game.

Perfect competition A market structure in which the decisions of *individual* buyers and sellers have no effect on market price.

Perfectly competitive firm A firm that is such a small part of the total *industry* that it cannot affect the price of the product it sells.

Perfectly elastic demand A demand that has the characteristic that even the slightest increase in price will lead to zero quantity demanded.

Perfectly elastic supply A supply characterized by a reduction in quantity supplied to zero when there is the slightest decrease in price.

Perfectly inelastic demand A demand that exhibits zero responsiveness to price changes; no matter what the price is, the quantity demanded remains the same.

Perfectly inelastic supply A supply for which quantity supplied remains constant, no matter what happens to price.

Personal Consumption Expenditure (PCE) Index A statistical measure of average prices that uses annually updated weights based on surveys of consumer spending.

Personal income (PI) The amount of income that households actually receive before they pay personal income taxes.

Persuasive advertising Advertising that is intended to induce a consumer to purchase a particular product and discover a previously unknown taste for the item.

Phillips curve A curve showing the relationship between unemployment and changes in wages or prices. It was long thought to reflect a trade-off between unemployment and inflation.

Physical capital All manufactured resources, including buildings, equipment, machines, and improvements to land that are used for production.

Planning curve The long-run average cost curve.

Planning horizon The long run, during which all inputs are variable.

Plant size The physical size of the factories that a firm owns and operates to produce its output. Plant size can be defined by square footage, maximum physical capacity, and other physical measures.

Policy irrelevance proposition The conclusion that policy actions have no real effects in the short run if the policy actions are anticipated and none in the long run even if the policy actions are unanticipated.

Portfolio investment The purchase of less than 10 percent of the shares of ownership in a company in another nation.

Positive economics Analysis that is *strictly* limited to making either purely descriptive statements or scientific predictions; for example, "If A, then B." A statement of *what is*.

Positive market feedback A tendency for a good or service to come into favor with additional consumers because other consumers have chosen to buy the item.

Positive-sum game A game in which players as a group are better off at the end of the game.

Potential money multiplier The reciprocal of the required reserve ratio, assuming no leakages into currency and no excess reserves. It is equal to 1 divided by the required reserve ratio.

Precautionary demand Holding money to meet unplanned expenditures and emergencies.

Present value The value of a future amount expressed in today's dollars; the most that someone would pay today to receive a certain sum at some point in the future.

Price ceiling A legal maximum price that may be charged for a particular good or service.

Price controls Government-mandated minimum or maximum prices that may be charged for goods and services.

Price differentiation Establishing different prices for similar products to reflect differences in marginal cost in providing those commodities to different groups of buyers.

Price discrimination Selling a given product at more than one price, with the price difference being unrelated to differences in marginal cost.

Price elasticity of demand (E_p) The responsiveness of the quantity demanded of a commodity to changes in its price; defined as the percentage change in quantity demanded divided by the percentage change in price.

Price elasticity of supply (E_s) The responsiveness of the quantity supplied of a commodity to a change in its price; the percentage change in quantity supplied divided by the percentage change in price.

Price floor A legal minimum price below which a good or service may not be sold. Legal minimum wages are an example.

Price index The cost of today's market basket of goods expressed as a percentage of the cost of the same market basket during a base year.

Price searcher A firm that must determine the price-output combination that maximizes profit because it faces a downward-sloping demand curve.

Price system An economic system in which relative prices are constantly changing to reflect changes in supply and demand for different commodities. The prices of those commodities are signals to everyone within the system as to what is relatively scarce and what is relatively abundant.

Price taker A perfectly competitive firm that must take the price of its product as given because the firm cannot influence its price.

Price-consumption curve The set of consumer-optimum combinations of two goods that the consumer would choose as the price of one good changes, while money income and the price of the other good remain constant.

Principle of rival consumption The recognition that individuals are rivals in consuming private goods because one person's consumption reduces the amount available for others to consume.

Principle of substitution The principle that consumers shift away from goods and services that become priced relatively higher in favor of goods and services that are now priced relatively lower.

Prisoners' dilemma A famous strategic game in which two prisoners have a choice between confessing and not confessing to a crime. If neither confesses, they serve a minimum sentence. If both confess, they serve a longer sentence. If one confesses and the other doesn't, the one who confesses goes free. The dominant strategy is always to confess.

Private costs Costs borne solely by the individuals who incur them. Also called *internal costs*.

Private goods Goods that can be consumed by only one individual at a time.

Private goods are subject to the principle of rival consumption.

Private property rights Exclusive rights of ownership that allow the use, transfer, and exchange of property.

Producer durables, or capital goods Durable goods having an expected service life of more than three years that are used by businesses to produce other goods and services.

Producer Price Index (PPI) A statistical measure of a weighted average of prices of goods and services that firms produce and sell.

Product compatibility The capability of a product sold by one firm to function together with another firm's complementary product.

Product differentiation The distinguishing of products by brand name, color, and other minor attributes. Product differentiation occurs in other than perfectly competitive markets in which products are, in theory, homogeneous, such as wheat or corn.

Production function The relationship between inputs and maximum physical output. A production function is a technological, not an economic, relationship.

Production possibilities curve (PPC) A curve representing all possible combinations of maximum outputs that could be produced assuming a fixed amount of productive resources of a given quality.

Production Any activity that results in the conversion of resources into products that can be used in consumption.

Profit-maximizing rate of production The rate of production that maximizes total profits, or the difference between total revenues and total costs; also, the rate of production at which marginal revenue equals marginal cost.

Progressive taxation A tax system in which, as income increases, a higher percentage of the additional income is paid as taxes. The marginal tax rate exceeds the average tax rate as income rises.

Property rights The rights of an owner to use and to exchange property.

Proportional rule A decision-making system in which actions are based on the proportion of the "votes" cast and are in proportion to them. In a market system, if 10 percent of the "dollar votes" are cast for blue cars, 10 percent of automobile output will be blue

Proportional taxation A tax system in which, regardless of an individual's income, the tax bill comprises exactly the same proportion.

Proprietorship A business owned by one individual who makes the business decisions, receives all the profits, and is legally responsible for the debts of the firm.

Public debt The total value of all outstanding federal government securities.

Public goods Goods for which the principle of rival consumption does not apply; they can be jointly consumed by many individuals simultaneously at no additional cost and with no reduction in quality or quantity. Also no one who fails to help pay for the good can be denied the benefit of the good.

Purchasing power The value of money for buying goods and services. If your money income stays the same but the price of one good that you are buying goes up, your effective purchasing power falls, and vice versa.

Purchasing power parity Adjustment in exchange rate conversions that takes into account differences in the true cost of living across countries.

Q

Quantity theory of money and prices The hypothesis that changes in the money supply lead to equiproportional changes in the price level.

Quota subscription A nation's account with the International Monetary Fund, denominated in special drawing rights.

Quota system A government-imposed restriction on the quantity of a specific good that another country is allowed to sell in the United States. In other words, quotas are restrictions on imports. These restrictions are usually applied to one or several specific countries.

R

Random walk theory The theory that there are no predictable trends in securities prices that can be used to "get rich quick."

Rate of discount The rate of interest used to discount future sums back to present value.

Rate of return The proportional annual benefit that results from making an investment.

Rate-of-return regulation Regulation that seeks to keep the rate of return in an industry at a competitive level by not allowing prices that would produce economic profits.

Rational expectations hypothesis A theory stating that people combine the effects of past policy changes on important economic variables with their own judgment about the future effects of current and future policy changes.

Rationality assumption The assumption that people do not intentionally make decisions that would leave them worse off.

Reaction function The manner in which one oligopolist reacts to a change in price, output, or quality made by another oligopolist in the industry.

Real disposable income Real GDP minus net taxes, or after-tax real income.

Real rate of interest The nominal rate of interest minus the anticipated rate of inflation.

Real values Measurement of economic values after adjustments have been made for changes in the average of prices between years.

Real-balance effect The change in expenditures resulting from a change in the real value of money balances when the price level changes, all other things held constant; also called the wealth effect.

Real-income effect The change in people's purchasing power that occurs when, other things being constant, the price of one good that they purchase changes. When that price goes up, real income, or purchasing power, falls, and when that price goes down, real income increases.

Recession A period of time during which the rate of growth of business activity is consistently less than its long-term trend or is negative.

Recessionary gap The gap that exists whenever equilibrium real GDP per year is less than full-employment real GDP as shown by the position of the long-run aggregate supply curve.

Recognition time lag The time required to gather information about the current state of the economy.

Reentrant An individual who used to work full-time but left the labor force and has now reentered it looking for a job.

Regional trade bloc A group of nations that grants members special trade privileges.

Regressive taxation A tax system in which as more dollars are earned, the percentage of tax paid on them falls. The marginal tax rate is less than the average tax rate as income rises.

Reinvestment Profits (or depreciation reserves) used to purchase new capital equipment.

Relative price The money price of one commodity divided by the money price of another commodity; the number of units of one commodity that must be sacrificed to purchase one unit of another commodity.

Rent control Price ceilings on rents.

Repricing, or menu, cost of inflation The cost associated with recalculating prices and printing new price lists when there is inflation.

Required reserve ratio The percentage of total transactions deposits that the Fed requires depository institutions to hold in the form of vault cash or deposits with the Fed.

Required reserves The value of reserves that a depository institution must hold in the form of vault cash or deposits with the Fed.

Reserves In the U.S. Federal Reserve System, deposits held by Federal Reserve district banks for depository institutions, plus depository institutions' vault cash.

Resources Things used to produce goods and services to satisfy people's wants.

Retained earnings Earnings that a corporation saves, or retains, for investment in other productive activities; earnings that are not distributed to stockholders.

Ricardian equivalence theorem The proposition that an increase in the government budget deficit has no effect on aggregate demand.

Right-to-work laws Laws that make it illegal to require union membership as a condition of continuing employment in a particular firm.

Rule of 70 A rule stating that the approximate number of years required for per capita real GDP to double is equal to 70 divided by the average rate of economic growth.

Rules of origin Regulations that nations in regional trade blocs establish to delineate product categories eligible for trading preferences.

S

Sales taxes Taxes assessed on the prices paid on most goods and services.

Saving The act of not consuming all of one's current income. Whatever is not consumed out of spendable income is, by definition, saved. *Saving* is an action measured over time (a flow), whereas *savings* are a stock, an accumulation resulting from the act of saving in the past.

Savings deposits Interest-earning funds that can be withdrawn at any time without payment of a penalty.

Say's law A dictum of economist J. B. Say that supply creates its own demand; producing goods and services generates the means and the willingness to purchase other goods and services.

Scarcity A situation in which the ingredients for producing the things that people desire are insufficient to satisfy all wants at a zero price.

Search good A product with characteristics that enable an individual to evaluate the product's quality in advance of a purchase.

Seasonal unemployment Unemployment resulting from the seasonal pattern of work in specific industries. It is usually due to seasonal fluctuations in demand or to changing weather conditions that render work difficult, if not impossible, as in the agriculture, construction, and tourist industries.

Secondary boycott A refusal to deal with companies or purchase products sold by companies that are dealing with a company being struck.

Secular deflation A persistent decline in prices resulting from economic growth in the presence of stable aggregate demand.

Securities Stocks and bonds.

Services Mental or physical labor or help purchased by consumers. Examples are the assistance of physicians, lawyers, dentists, repair personnel, housecleaners, educators, retailers, and wholesalers; items purchased or used by consumers that do not have physical characteristics.

Share of stock A legal claim to a share of a corporation's future profits. If it is *common stock*, it incorporates certain voting rights regarding major policy decisions of the corporation. If it is *preferred stock*, its owners are accorded preferential treatment in the payment of dividends but do not have any voting rights.

Share-the-gains, share-the-pains theory A theory of regulatory behavior that holds that regulators must take account of the demands of three groups: legislators, who established and oversee the regulatory agency; firms in the regulated industry; and consumers of the regulated industry's products.

Short run The time period during which at least one input, such as plant size, cannot be changed.

Shortage A situation in which quantity demanded is greater than quantity supplied at a price below the market clearing price.

Short-run aggregate supply curve The relationship between total planned economywide production and the price level in the short run, all other things held constant. If prices adjust incompletely in the short run, the curve is positively sloped.

Short-run break-even price The price at which a firm's total revenues equal its total costs. At the break-even price, the firm is just making a normal rate of return on its capital investment. (It is covering its explicit and implicit costs.)

Short-run economies of operation A distinguishing characteristic of an information product arising from declining short-run average total cost as more units of the product are sold.

Short-run shutdown price The price that covers average variable costs. It occurs just below the intersection of the marginal cost curve and the average variable cost curve.

Signals Compact ways of conveying to economic decision makers information needed to make decisions. An effective signal not only conveys information but also provides the incentive to react appropriately. Economic profits and economic losses are such signals.

Slope The change in the *y* value divided by the corresponding change in the *x* value of a curve; the "incline" of the curve.

Small menu costs Costs that deter firms from changing prices in response to demand changes—for example, the costs of renegotiating contracts or printing new price lists.

Social costs The full costs borne by society whenever a resource use occurs. Social costs can be measured by adding external costs to private, or internal, costs.

Social Security contributions The mandatory taxes paid out of workers' wages and salaries.

Special drawing rights (SDRs) Reserve assets created by the International Monetary Fund for countries to use in settling international payment obligations.

Specialization The organization of economic activity so that what each person (or region) consumes is not identical to what that person (or region) produces. An individual may specialize, for example, in law or medicine. A nation may specialize in the production of coffee, computers, or digital cameras.

Stagflation A situation characterized by lower real GDP, lower employment, and a higher unemployment rate during the same period that the rate of inflation increases.

Standard of deferred payment A property of an item that makes it desirable for use as a means of settling debts maturing in the future; an essential property of money.

Static tax analysis Economic evaluation of the effects of tax rate changes under the assumption that there is no effect on the tax base, meaning that there is an unambiguous positive relationship between tax rates and tax revenues.

Stock The quantity of something, measured at a given point in time—for example, an inventory of goods or a bank account. Stocks are defined

independently of time, although they are assessed at a point in time.

Store of value The ability to hold value over time; a necessary property of money.

Strategic dependence A situation in which one firm's actions with respect to price, quality, advertising, and related changes may be strategically countered by the reactions of one or more other firms in the industry. Such dependence can exist only when there are a limited number of major firms in an industry.

Strategy Any rule that is used to make a choice, such as "Always pick heads."

Strikebreakers Temporary or permanent workers hired by a company to replace union members who are striking.

Structural unemployment Unemployment resulting from a poor match of workers' abilities and skills with current requirements of employers.

Subsidy A negative tax; a payment to a producer from the government, usually in the form of a cash grant per unit.

Substitutes Two goods are substitutes when a change in the price of one causes a shift in demand for the other in the same direction as the price change.

Substitution effects The tendency of people to substitute cheaper commodities for more expensive commodities.

Supply A schedule showing the relationship between price and quantity supplied for a specified period of time, other things being equal.

Supply curve The graphical representation of the supply schedule; a line (curve) showing the supply schedule, which generally slopes upward (has a positive slope), other things being equal.

Supply-side economics The suggestion that creating incentives for individuals and firms to increase productivity will cause the aggregate supply curve to shift outward.

Surplus A situation in which quantity supplied is greater than quantity demanded at a price above the market clearing price.

Sweep account A depository institution account that entails regular shifts of funds from transactions deposits that are subject to reserve requirements to savings deposits that are exempt from reserve requirements.

Sympathy strike A work stoppage by a union in sympathy with another union's strike or cause.

T

Target zone A range of permitted exchange rate variations between upper and lower exchange rate bands that a central bank defends by selling or buying foreign exchange reserves.

Tariffs Taxes on imported goods.

Tax base The value of goods, services, wealth, or incomes subject to taxation.

Tax bracket A specified interval of income to which a specific and unique marginal tax rate is applied.

Tax incidence The distribution of tax burdens among various groups in society.

Tax rate The proportion of a tax base that must be paid to a government as taxes.

Taylor rule An equation that specifies a federal funds rate target based on an estimated long-run real interest rate, the current deviation of the actual inflation rate from the Federal Reserve's inflation objective, and the gap between actual real GDP and a measure of potential real GDP.

Technology Society's pool of applied knowledge concerning how goods and services can be produced.

Terms of exchange The conditions under which trading takes place. Usually, the terms of exchange are equal to the price at which a good is traded.

The Fed The Federal Reserve System; the central bank of the United States.

Theory of public choice The study of collective decision making.

Third parties Parties who are not directly involved in a given activity or transaction. For example, in the relationship between caregivers and patients, fees may be paid by third parties (insurance companies, government).

Thrift institutions Financial institutions that receive most of their funds from the savings of the public; they include savings banks, savings and loan associations, and credit unions.

Tie-in sales Purchases of one product that are permitted by the seller only if the consumer buys another good or service from the same firm.

Time deposit A deposit in a financial institution that requires notice of intent to withdraw or must be left for an agreed period. Withdrawal of funds prior to the end of the agreed period may result in a penalty.

Tit-for-tat strategic behavior In game theory, cooperation that continues as long as the other players continue to cooperate.

Total costs The sum of total fixed costs and total variable costs.

Total income The yearly amount earned by the nation's resources (factors of production). Total income therefore includes wages, rent, interest payments, and profits that are received by workers, landowners, capital owners, and entrepreneurs, respectively.

Total revenues The price per unit times the total quantity sold.

Trade deflection Moving partially assembled products into a member nation of a regional trade bloc, completing assembly, and then exporting them to other nations within the bloc, so as to benefit from preferences granted by the trade bloc.

Trade diversion Shifting existing international trade from countries outside a regional trade bloc to nations within the bloc.

Trading Desk An office at the Federal Reserve Bank of New York charged with implementing monetary policy strategies developed by the Federal Open Market Committee.

Transaction costs All costs associated with making, reaching, and enforcing agreements.

Transactions approach A method of measuring the money supply by looking at money as a medium of exchange.

Transactions demand Holding money as a medium of exchange to make payments. The level varies directly with nominal GDP.

Transactions deposits Checkable and debitable account balances in commercial banks and other types of financial institutions, such as credit unions and savings banks; any accounts in financial institutions from which you can easily transmit debit-card and check payments.

Transfer payments Money payments made by governments to individuals for which no services or goods are rendered in return. Examples are Social Security old-age and disability benefits and unemployment insurance benefits.

Transfers in kind Payments that are in the form of actual goods and services, such as food stamps, subsidized public housing, and medical care, and for which no goods or services are rendered in return.

Traveler's checks Financial instruments obtained from a bank or a nonbanking organization and signed during purchase that can be used as cash upon a second signature by the purchaser.

U

Unanticipated inflation Inflation at a rate that comes as a surprise, either higher or lower than the rate anticipated.

Unemployment The total number of adults (aged 16 years or older) who are willing and able to work and who are actively looking for work but have not found a job.

Union shop A business enterprise that may hire nonunion members, conditional on their joining the union by some specified date after employment begins.

Unit elasticity of demand A demand relationship in which the quantity demanded changes exactly in proportion to the change in price.

Unit of accounting A measure by which prices are expressed; the common denominator of the price system; a central property of money.

Unit tax A constant tax assessed on each unit of a good that consumers purchase.

Unlimited liability A legal concept whereby the personal assets of the owner of a firm can be seized to pay off the firm's debts.

Util A representative unit by which utility is measured.

Utility The want-satisfying power of a good or service.

Utility analysis The analysis of consumer decision making based on utility maximization.

V

Value added The dollar value of an industry's sales minus the value of intermediate goods (for example, raw materials and parts) used in production.

Variable costs Costs that vary with the rate of production. They include wages paid to workers and purchases of materials.

Versioning Selling a product in slightly altered forms to different groups of consumers.

Vertical merger The joining of a firm with another to which it sells an output or from which it buys an input.

Voluntary exchange An act of trading, done on an elective basis, in which both parties to the trade expect to be better off after the exchange.

Voluntary import expansion (VIE) An official agreement with another country in which it agrees to import more from the United States.

Voluntary restraint agreement (VRA) An official agreement with another country that "voluntarily" restricts the quantity of its exports to the United States.

W

Wants What people would buy if their incomes were unlimited.

Wealth The stock of assets owned by a person, household, firm, or nation. For a household, wealth can consist of a house, cars, personal belongings, stocks, bonds, bank accounts, and cash.

World Bank A multinational agency that specializes in making loans to about 100 developing nations in an effort to promote their long-term development and growth.

World Trade Organization (WTO) The successor organization to the GATT that handles trade disputes among its member nations.

X

x axis The horizontal axis in a graph.

Y

y axis The vertical axis in a graph.

Z

Zero-sum game A game in which any gains within the group are exactly offset by equal losses by the end of the game.

Index

Cost of Holding Money

The cost of holding money (its opportunity cost) is measured by the alternative interest yield obtainable by holding some other asset.

Policy Irrelevance Proposition

Under the assumption of rational expectations on the part of decision makers in the economy, anticipated monetary policy cannot alter either the rate of unemployment or the level of real GDP. Regardless of the nature of the anticipated policy, the unemployment rate will equal the natural rate, and real GDP will be determined solely by the economy's long-run aggregate supply curve.

Natural Rate of Unemployment

The natural rate of unemployment is the rate of unemployment that exists when workers and employers correctly anticipate the rate of inflation.

Equation of Exchange

$$M_s V = PY$$

where M_s = actual money balances held by the nonbanking public
V = income velocity of money, or the number of times, on average, each monetary unit is spent on final goods and services
P = price level or price index
Y = real GDP

Potential Money Multiplier

The reciprocal of the required reserve ratio, assuming no leakages into currency and no excess reserves, is the potential money multiplier.

$$\text{Potential money multiplier} = \frac{1}{\text{required reserve ratio}}$$

Definition of Money Supply

M1 = currency + transactions deposits + traveler's checks

M2 = M1 +
1. Savings and small-denomination time deposits at all depository institutions
2. Balances in retail money market mutual funds
3. Money market deposit accounts (MMDAs)

Relationship Between Imports and Exports

In the long run, imports are paid for by exports.

Therefore, any restriction of imports ultimately reduces exports.

MICROECONOMIC PRINCIPLES

Opportunity Cost

In economics, cost is always a forgone opportunity.

Law of Demand

When the price of a good goes up, people buy less of it, *other things being equal*.

Movement Along, versus Shift in, a Curve

If the relative price changes, we *move along* a curve—there is a change in quantity demanded and/or supplied. If something else changes, we *shift* a curve—there is a change in demand and/or supply.

Income Elasticity of Demand

$$\text{Income elasticity of demand} = \frac{\text{percentage change in demand for a good}}{\text{percentage change in income}}$$

Law of Diminishing Marginal Product

As successive equal increases in a variable factor of production, such as labor, are added to other fixed factors of production, such as capital, there will be a point beyond which the extra, or marginal, product that can be attributed to each additional unit of the variable factor of production will decline.

Supply

At higher prices, a larger quantity will generally be supplied than at lower prices, *all other things held constant*.

Or stated otherwise:

At lower prices, a smaller quantity will generally be supplied than at higher prices, *all other things held constant*.

Profits

$$\text{Accounting profits} = \text{total revenues} - \text{total costs}$$

$$\text{Economic profits} = \text{total revenues} - \text{total opportunity cost of all inputs used}$$

Elasticity of Demand

$$E_p = \frac{\text{percentage change in quantity demanded}}{\text{percentage change in price}}$$

Elasticity of Supply

$$E_s = \frac{\text{percentage change in quantity supplied}}{\text{percentage change in price}}$$

Monopsony and Monopoly

		Output Market Structure	
		Perfect Competition	**Monopoly**
Input Market Structure	**Perfect Competition**	$MC = MR = P$ $W = MFC = MRP_c$	$MC = MR(< P)$ $W = MFC = MRP_m (< MRP_c)$
	Monopsony	$MC = MR = P$ $W < MFC = MRP_c$	$MC = MR(< P)$ $W < MFC = MRP_m (< MRP_c)$